LA 411®

PRODUCTION RESOURCE • VOL. 34 2013 EDITION

WWW.LA411.COM

THE PROFESSIONAL REFERENCE GUIDE FOR FILM, TELEVISION, COMMERCIAL AND MUSIC VIDEO PRODUCTION

Cover Photo by John Saade

The Hollywood Walk of Fame is a trademark and the intellectual property of Hollywood Chamber of Commerce.
All Rights Reserved.

Publisher: **Sean Killebrew**
Publishing Director: **Linda Buckley-Bruno**

Associate Publisher: **Steve Atinsky**
Assistant Editor: **Bryan Cuprill**
Marketing Manager/Reporter: **Marjorie Galas**
Media Manager/Assistant Editor: **Tom Wilson**

Advertising Director, New York: **Jeffry Gitter**
Account Executive: **Aaron Biberstein**
Account Executive: **Ira Liss**
Sales Coordinator: **Maria Salcedo-Puerto**

Sr. Production Director: **Natalie Longman**
Art Director: **Frank Nudge**

Senior Manager of Operations: **Joni Ballinger**
Business Manager: **Juliette Nichols**
Client Service Manager: **James Dennis**
Manager of Online Services: **Apul Bhalani**

Penske Business Media

Jay Penske
Chief Executive Officer

Address all con
411 Publishing Company, 5900 Wilshire Bouleva ...geles, California 90036 USA
411 Publishing
(800) 357-4745
FAX (678) 680-0671
www.la411.com

A *VARIETY* Group Publication

Dear Customer,

What's new for 2013?

For starters: a redesign of the LA 411 website. The new design will make it easier for users to access many features on our site, including:

Tech Tip Videos, highlighting the industry's top designers, producers, and technical innovators; red-carpet interviews with nominees and winners at the Creative Emmys and Visual Effects Society Award ceremonies and award events honoring members of the ASC (cinematographers), ACE (Eddie), Art Directors, and Costume Designers Guilds.

Feature Articles, spotlighting the creators, designers, and producers of the latest movies and most popular television shows.

411 Film Finance and Tax Incentive Webinar Series, produced in partnership with the Producers Guild of America and Entertainment Parters and sponsored by The Association of Film Commissioners International (AFCI), featuring producers and executives from both studio and independently produced movies.

LA 411 Stage Charts, the most comprehensive information you will find in searching out a stage for your film, television or commercial project in Southern California.

All this, while giving the site a new, clean look and increasing the ease with which you can search our sections and categories.

For production managers and producers shooting out of town, 411 Publishing is introducing smartphone apps for Connecticut, Florida, Georgia, Louisiana, Massachusetts, Michigan, New Mexico, North Carolina, Pennsylvania, and Texas. Every listing in these state apps has been vetted by the 411 editorial staff to help you find qualified crew, vendors, and services while working out of town.

Finally, LA 411 as part of the Variety Group is under new ownership: Penske Media Corporation. We look forward to working with our new owner as we move ahead with these innovations that will help us sustain the status we have held since first introduced in 1980 as "the production bible for the entertainment industry."

Thank you,

Sean Killebrew
Publisher

Steve Atinsky
Asscoiate Publisher

The listings are organized into 10 general tabbed sections and divided within the sections by category. The section Advertising Agencies and Production Companies, for example, contains categories relating to pre-production, such as Commercial Directors and Storyboard Artists, while the Post Production tab contains categories such as Post Houses and Digital Intermediates. Descriptions have been included in those categories and listings where the editors felt that additional information was needed. These descriptions are included solely at the discretion of the editors of LA 411.

Some of the categories in LA 411 are 'built' from other categories. For example, the listings in Composers & Sound Designers are drawn from the composer and sound designer rosters of the Music Production & Sound Design category. This makes it easier to find a composer, editor, commercial or music video director, because they are built into their own index of sorts. The 'built' categories are: Commercial Directors, Music Video Directors, Composers & Sound Designers and Editors; these categories also contain freelancers.

You will find three indices bound at the front of the book. The General Index uses keywords and cross-referencing to help you find whatever service or item you require. The Company/Crew index has the companies and crew who are listed in the book. And, of course, an Advertiser's Index is included. LA 411 has several charts, digests and miscellaneous resources that may come in handy during your production. Look to the back of the Crew Section to find employment guidelines for child and adult players, as well as your trusty crew. In Sets & Stages, you'll find our extensive stage chart and a handy standing sets chart. In the front matter, you'll find sunrise and sunset times, holidays, festival and awards dates and a list of charitable organizations, some of which will accept your production's excess food.

Information about listing, advertising and ordering LA 411 can be found in the front of the book. You can always call our editorial department at (323) 617-9402 for guidance or assistance with your listing.

411 Publishing offers a variety of ad packages in our print and online directories.

Because we strive to maintain a balance of editorial content and advertising in our print directories, ad space is limited. Additionally, since key spots, including tabs, go quickly, we recommend that you reserve space early for the 2014 edition.

Among the options that will increase your company's prominence in our online directory are:

iPhone and Android Apps: Run a banner in your category or sponsor your entire section on the dedicated LA 411 iPhone or Android App.

Impact Listing: Puts you in the blue section at the top of all searches. Also includes 12 search terms.

Premium Impact Listing: Includes all of the features of an Impact Listing and also allows full customization of your listing page, complete with a text description, photos and downloads.

411 Features: Have you produced a video showcasing your products and/or services? 411 Features will give you the opportunity to display that video exclusively in your category, on your listing page and on the Home Page (in rotation with other videos).

To become an online advertiser or to learn more about our print and online advertising programs please call us at (323) 617-9204.

To Update Your Current Listing

LA 411 sends out an e-mail in the summer to every company listed in the book prompting you to make changes to your existing listing. If at any time you wish to update your current listing, please send us an e-mail at 411update@reedbusiness.com.

You can also go to **www.la411.com** and click the "Edit Your Listing" tab in the upper right corner where you will be prompted to enter your User Name and password for verification. Your User Name is the e-mail address that you have provided us for contacting you. If you are unsure what your User Name is, or if you need to be issued one, please e-mail us at 411update@reedbusiness.com. If you are unsure what your password is, use the "Forgot Password" link and we'll send this information to you. Please note: the e-mail you enter to request your password must match your User Name e-mail.

Unless you are applying for a NEW CATEGORY please do not fill out a new application, as you will be charged for something you already have. There is no charge for changes to existing listings. You may also download an application or apply online at **www.la411.com.**

Since our first edition in 1980, 411's editorial staff has meticulously researched and verified that every listing is qualified to be included in our directories and on our Web sites. We reserve the right to remove and/or requalify listings at any time.

Listing Requirements:

1. For LA 411: Applicants must be located in Southern California (Los Angeles, Orange, Riverside, Santa Barbara, San Bernardino, San Diego or Ventura counties). For the majority of our categories, work must be performed in the aforementioned areas.

For New York 411: Applicants must be located in the Tri State (New York, New Jersey and Connecticut) or Philadelphia areas. For the majority of our categories, work must be performed in the aforementioned areas.

2. You are allowed to apply for up to five (5) categories.

3. All applicants must include a current resume or letter on company letterhead OR you may create a text version in our online application process.

4. You must complete the application in full including three (3) local references for each category for which you believe you are qualified and in which you would like to appear. Call sheets, contracts or pay stubs are also acceptable.

5. 411 reserves the right to ask for additional references if those given are not verifiable or do not meet our professional guidelines.

6. References must be for film, television or commercials:
- Films must have a minimum two-week theatrical release.
- TV & commercials must be for Broadcast or Cable Networks. Local cable credits are not acceptable

Internet credits are only acceptable when produced for AMPTP affiliated companies--Studios, Broadcast Networks, certain Cable Networks and Independent Producers.

- Film & TV references are preferred but not required for a limited number of Location & Production Support categories such as Car Rentals, Travel Agencies, Notaries, etc.

7. All applicants must pay an application fee of $200 for a new application and $50 for each additional category. Applicants can pay by credit card or business check. Listings are editorial content and have no monetary value.

8. A separate application must be submitted for each 411 directory you wish to be listed in.

9. Advertising with 411 has no bearing on listing approvals. As you do not have to be a qualified listee to advertise, advertisers do not automatically qualify for listings.

10. No special provisions—such as additional text—can be provided in listings. No exceptions.

11. We only list companies by their actual business name. You may be asked to provide a copy of your state/city business license to confirm your name. A DBA or fictitious business name statement is NOT acceptable.

12. You may apply at any time. However, to be included in the next book, completed applications must be received prior to the advertised deadline. 411 will process your application as fast as possible. During season, this may take upwards of several weeks. Please be patient.

13. Applicants may be required to complete a phone interview with our editors.

14. The 411 Publishing editorial staff has final say in all matters regarding what goes into our directories and our Web sites. 411 Publishing reserves the right to review, confirm, edit and/or omit any listing or Enhanced Dedicated Page in whole or in part at our discretion.

15. NOT ALL APPLICANTS WILL QUALIFY.

16. You must provide at least three references per category AND pay your application fee BEFORE we can begin processing your application.

Applications can be found on our website la411.com. Select the "Apply to Be Listed" tab at the top of the Hompage and download a PDF of our application. You can also submit an application using our online system.

Submit your completed application and any additional materials you need to send for verification to: Application Dept., LA 411 Publishing Co., 5900 Wilshire Blvd., 31st Fl., Los Angeles, CA 90036

Or fax it to us at: (678) 680-0671

If you have questions call us at: (323) 617-9404

Complete this form and send with your payment to:
Attn: Book Sales Dept. 411 Publishing, 5900 Wilshire Blvd., 31st Fl., Los Angeles, CA 90036
or order through our online store at www.la411.com

For credit card orders, air and international shipments or questions call: (323) 617-9409 or contact Maria Salcedo-Puerto at maria.salcedopuerto@reedbusiness.com. Credit card orders received by 12:00 noon PST will be shipped via FedEx that day. Please allow five working days for delivery on all orders.

Quantity	Item		Price	Tax	Shipping	Total
	LA 411 2013	(CA or NY orders)	$79.00	$6.91	$9.00	
		(Elsewhere)		$0.00	$9.00	
	New York 411	(CA or NY orders)	$59.00	$5.16	$6.00	
	2012/2013	(Elsewhere)		$0.00	$6.00	

Make checks payable to 411 Publishing Company.

_____

Name/Title

_____

Company/Profession

_____

Address (No P.O. Boxes Please)   City

_____

State   Zip Code   Telephone

Explore Opportunities to be a
Corporate Partner and Sponsor of

PRODUCERS GUILD OF AMERICA

Associate with the industry's only organization representing more than 5,300 producers of Film, Television and New Media

Benefits of associations include:

* Communication to and interaction with Producers Guild members in Los Angeles, New York, San Francisco, Washington D.C. and elsewhere

* Exposure at premier entertainment industry events such as the PGA Awards and Produced By Conference, as well as seminars, screenings and networking programs throughout the year

* Product seeding and product/service demonstrations for membership

* Inclusion in national and worldwide publicity generated at events

* Exposure in Produced By magazine, mailed to more than 5,700 people

* Logo and link on producersguild.org

Producers are the engine at the heart of the entertainment industry.

**To discuss how an association with the
Producers Guild of America can support
your sales, marketing and branding objectives, contact:**

Diane Salerno/Six Degrees Global
Corporate Partnership and Sponsorship Specialist
310-440-7804
diane@sixdegreesglobal.com

The Los Angeles region is the entertainment production capital of the world—with good reason. No other area can match the talent of L.A.'s casts and crews, its industry resources, diverse locations and great weather. Add to this a permit coordination process streamlined by FilmL.A., and it's no wonder why the region sees more days of film production than anywhere else.

Working with FilmL.A., Inc.

FilmL.A. is a private, not-for-profit organization that coordinates and processes permits for on-location motion picture, television and commercial production under contract to the City of Los Angeles, Los Angeles County, and the cities of Diamond Bar, La Habra Heights, Lancaster, Palmdale, South Gate, Vernon, and The City of Industry. Non-municipal clients include the Angeles National Forest, the Burbank Unified School District, Glendale Unified School District, La Cañada Unified School District, Lawndale Elementary School District, Los Angeles Unified School District, Norwalk/La Mirada Unified School District and San Gabriel Unified School District.

Ongoing community relations is a key component of the service FilmL.A. provides. The organization works to strike a balance between the needs and interests of the entertainment industry and the neighborhoods affected by on-location production.

FilmL.A.'s services help the region stay competitive in today's global entertainment production market. The organization coordinates tens of thousands of days of permitted production each year.

Determining if You Need a Permit to Film

A permit is required for filming any commercial motion picture, television program, advertisement, music video, or other similar production outside of the confines of a certified studio. A permit is also required for commercial still photography.

Obtaining a Permit

FilmL.A.'s website (www.filmla.com) provides the most up-to-date source of information on how to obtain an on-location production permit. A short guide highlighting key elements of the permit process is reprinted here for your convenience. Comprehensive process guides are also available on the "Film Permits" page in the "For Filmmakers" section of FilmL.A.'s website.

Insurance

Every permit application must include a valid certificate of insurance naming specific "additional insureds." Minimum coverage requirements are specified by City, County or other permit jurisdictions. FilmL.A. staff members are available to help you identify your film insurance needs.

Application

Film permit applicants may apply for permits online through FilmL.A.'s state-of-the-art Online Permit System (OPS), which allows users to track permit progress and status of agency approvals in real-time and download paid-for and finalized permits at their convenience. Applications may also be submitted in person, via fax or by email.

Your Production Coordinator

Once your application has been accepted, a FilmL.A. Production Coordinator will be assigned to your project. Your coordinator will be available to assist you from pre-production through wrap on the last day of your permit. He/she will collaborate with local authorities, making every effort to ensure that your permit is fulfilled, while minimizing the impact your activities could cause to the surrounding community.

Other Planning Resources

FilmL.A.'s Production Planning Team is available to help filmmakers navigate a host of pre-permitting location issues. Staffed by experienced production coordinators, the team is standing by to help you deal with planning issues long before you're ready to apply for your next permit. The team can provide immediate answers to questions involving: parking, lane and street closures, reservations at City Hall, Los Angeles County Beaches and many other issues. FilmL.A. also maintains LocoScout (www.locoscout.com), an online location library focused on schools and municipal properties available for filming.

Special Accommodations

In the areas served by FilmL.A., standard production days are Monday through Friday, and the normal hours of film activity are from 7 a.m. to 10 p.m. in residential areas. The hours noted on every film permit specify arrival and departure times for production company personnel. Any filming activity outside of normal production hours usually requires that affected residents be surveyed to identify specific concerns or problems with the proposed activities. Surveys may also be required when filmmakers request to film on weekends in residential areas, seek permits to film at locations for extended durations, close streets or potentially interfere with merchant activity, or conduct exceptional activities (e.g., gunfire, explosions, aerial work, etc.). FilmL.A. does not provide survey services but does require that surveys be performed with specific forms. Typically, a production company will have its staff go door-to-door in the affected area and collect the surrounding neighbors' specific concerns, which will then be addressed in the permit process.

Application Fees

The easiest way to pay for and take delivery of your permit is to take advantage of FilmL.A.'s Permits on Account program, which allows credit-worthy customers to receive permits and be invoiced at a later time. FilmL.A.'s coordination fees, as well as fees required for official personnel (e.g., Fire Department staff) may be paid together in a single transaction, and non-credit customers can pay by cash, cashier's check, or money order. Business checks are also accepted from production companies that hold long-term insurance.

Neighborhood Notification

FilmL.A.'s permit coordination service includes notifying local residents and businesses about upcoming on-location production. In addition, FilmL.A. serves as a central contact for all neighborhood inquiries and complaint resolution.

FilmL.A. employs a team of experienced notification personnel, many of whom are bilingual. They make sure that FilmL.A.'s familiar door hangers are distributed to every neighbor within 500 feet of permitted filming activity and within 200 feet of production-related parking. Unusual activities such as gunfire, explosions and helicopter work often require notification on a larger scale, depending on the extent of the activities requested. FilmL.A. also offers eNotification in select areas for those who prefer to receive notices electronically.

FilmL.A.'s goal is to perform notification two days before production activity is scheduled to begin. This includes any substantial prep work that requires more than one large equipment vehicle parked on the street.

Other Locations

Some incorporated cities within L.A. County operate their own film offices, while others coordinate filming through their respective city departments. Requirements for filming in these areas differ, but as a courtesy to the industry, FilmL.A. will provide contact information for other Southern California permit offices.

FilmL.A., Inc.
1201 W. 5th St., Ste. T-800
Los Angeles, CA 90017
Tel: (213) 977-8600
Fax (main): (213) 977-8610
Fax (permits): (213) 977-8601
www.filmla.com

This is just a small sampling of groups that offer assistance to those in need in the L.A area. Some of these organizations work to get excess food to the area's hungry. With the help of this list, if there is more food on set than your crew could eat, you can give one of these organizations a call.

AIDS Project Los Angeles
(213) 201-1600
www.apla.org

American Humane Association
(818) 501-0123
www.americanhumane.org

Angel Harvest
(323) 256-6881
www.angelharvest.org

Audrey Hepburn Children's Fund
(626) 304-1380
 www.audreyhepburn.com/menu/index.php

Autism Speaks
(323) 549-0500
www.autismspeaks.org

Camp Laurel
(626) 683-0800
www.laurel-foundation.org

Children of the Night
(818) 908-4470
www.childrenofthenight.org

Childrens Hospital Los Angeles
(323) 660-2450
www.chla.org

City of Hope
(626) 359-8111
www.cityofhope.org

Covenant House California
(323) 461-3131
www.covenanthouse.org

Daniel Pearl Foundation
(310) 441-1400
www.danielpearl.org

Food Forward
(818) 530-4125
www.foodforward.org

Elizabeth Glaser Pediatric AIDS Foundation
(310) 314-1459
www.pedaids.org

Heal the Bay
(310) 451-1500
www.healthebay.org

Hollywood for Habitat for Humanity
(310) 323-4663
www.habitatla.org

The Humane Society of the United States
(202) 452-1100
www.hsushollywood.org

Inner-City Arts
(213) 627-9621
www.inner-cityarts.org

Jewish Family Service of Los Angeles (JFS)
(877) 275-4573
www.jfsla.org

The Leeza Gibbons Memory Foundation
(888) 655-3392
www.leezasplace.org

Literacy Network of Greater Los Angeles
(213) 237-6643
www.literacynetwork.org

Make-a-Wish Foundation of Greater Los Angeles
(310) 788-9474
www.wishla.org

Much Love Animal Rescue
(310) 636-9115
www.muchlove.org

National Multiple Sclerosis Society (Southern CA Chapter)
(310) 479-4456
www.nationalmssociety.org/cal or

Operation Blankets of Love (Comfort Items for Homeless Animals)
(818) 402-6586
www.operationblanketsoflove.com

PAWS/LA
(213) 741-1950
www.pawsla.org

A Place Called Home (APCH)
(323) 232-7653
www.apch.org

Project Angel Food
922 Vine St.
(323) 845-1800
www.angelfood.org

St. Jude Children's Research Hospital
(800) 822-6344
www.stjude.org

spcaLA (Society for the Prevention of Cruelty to Animals LA)
(323) 730-5303
www.spcaLA.com

Union Rescue Mission
(213) 347-6300
www.unm.org

411 Publishing promotes listees that have incorporated green standards into their organization and consumer output. Companies highlighted as Green Listees are incorporating elements from the following four areas into their day to day business practices and services: Recylce/Reuse, Reduce Waste, Utilizing Sustainable Products and Educate/Encourage.

Adapt Consulting, Inc
13618 Lemay St.
Van Nuys, CA 91401
888-782-6974

Affordable Sound Stages
1708 Hale St.
Glendale, CA 91201
818-563-3456

BBC Motion Gallery, Los Angeles
4144 Lankershim Blvd., Ste. 200
North Hollywood, CA 91602
818-299-9720

Caviar Content
900 Pacific Ave.
Venice, CA 90291
310-396-3400

CBS Studio Center
4024 Radford Ave
Studio City, CA 91604
818-665-5665

Cinnabar
4571 Electronics Pl.
Los Angeles, CA 90039
818-842-8190

Dozar Office Furnishings
9937 Jefferson Blvd., Ste. 100
Culver City, CA 90232
310-559-9292

Empress
306 W. 38th St., Ninth Fl.
New York, NY 10018
888-683-6773

Fox Studios
10201 W. Pico Blvd.
Los Angeles, CA 90035
310-369-2786

GoTV Studios, Inc.
14144 Ventura Blvd, Ste. 300
Sherman Oaks, CA 91423
818-933-2122

Hero Productions, Inc.
805 S. San Fernando Blvd., Ste. 55
Burbank, CA 91502
323-257-0454

Instant Karma Films
212 Marine St.
Santa Monica, CA 90405
310-526-7703

King Kong Production Vehicles, Inc,
4000 Cohasset St..
Burbank, CA 91505
949-673-1999

LA City Biodiesel
9009 Independence Ave.
Canoga Park, CA 91304
818-701-6845

Mat Men
P.O. Box 60204
Pasadena, CA 91116
323-632-4368

National Promotions & Advertising Inc.
3434 Overland Ave, Los Angeles, CA 90034
310-558-8555

NBC Universal Stages
100 Universal City Plaza, Bldg. 4250-3
Universal City, CA 91608
818-777-3000

New Deal Studios, Inc
4105 Readwood Ave.
Los Angeles, CA 90066
310-578-9929

Oakwood Temporary Housing
3600 Barham Blvd.
Los Angeles, CA 90068
888-745-3429

Paramount Studios
Backlot Operations, 5555 Melrose Ave.
Hollywood, CA 90038
323-956-5284

Quixote Production Vehicles
1021 N. Lillian Way
Hollywood, CA 90038
323-960-9191

SirReel - LA & San Diego
Burbank, CA
760-672-5522

Sony Pictures Studio
10202 W. Washington Blvd.
Culver City, CA 90232
310-244-6926

Warner Bros. Studio Facilities-Operations
4000 Warner Blvd.
Burbank, CA 91522
818-954-2577

For information on becoming a Green Listee, please visit our webpage: www.resourse411.com/Green

EVERYONE loved the Streetlights PA's. Not only did they have great work skills, they were a total pleasure and asset to have with us and will certainly be called and recommended for future jobs. — Beth, Production Supervisor

20
1992 - 2012
STREETLIGHTS
creating ethnic diversity in the entertainment industry

For over 20 years Streetlights has impacted the Entertainment Industry by providing skilled ethnic minority workers to thousands of productions.

Wonderful attitude - very sharp - extremely helpful... You guys do a terrific job vetting and training Production Assistants. — Mike, UPM

STREETLIGHTS
(323) 960-4540
streetlights@streetlights.org
www.streetlights.org

This table is based on sunrise and sunset times for Los Angeles, California. LA 411 recommends that the reader double-check any sunrise or sunset time with the day's ocal newspaper or with a weather service.

	JANUARY Rise A.M.	JANUARY Set P.M.	FEBRUARY Rise A.M.	FEBRUARY Set P.M.	MARCH Rise A.M.	MARCH Set P.M.	APRIL Rise A.M.	APRIL Set P.M.	MAY Rise A.M.	MAY Set P.M.	JUNE Rise A.M.	JUNE Set P.M.
1	6:59	4:55	6:50	5:24	6:21	5:50	6:40	7:14	6:03	7:37	5:43	4:29
2	6:59	4:56	6:49	5:25	6:20	5:51	6:39	7:15	6:02	7:38	5:42	4:29
3	6:59	4:57	6:48	5:26	6:19	5:51	6:37	7:16	6:01	7:39	5:42	4:29
4	6:59	4:57	6:48	5:27	6:18	5:52	6:36	7:16	6:00	7:39	5:42	4:29
5	6:59	4:58	6:47	5:28	6:16	5:53	6:35	7:17	6:00	7:40	5:42	4:29
6	6:59	4:59	6:46	5:29	6:15	5:54	6:33	7:18	5:59	7:41	5:41	4:28
7	6:59	5:00	6:45	5:30	6:14	5:55	6:32	7:19	5:58	7:42	5:41	4:28
8	6:59	5:01	6:44	5:31	6:12	5:55	6:31	7:19	5:57	7:43	5:41	4:28
9	6:59	5:02	6:43	5:32	6:11	5:56	6:29	7:20	5:56	7:43	5:41	4:29
10	6:59	5:03	6:42	5:33	7:10	6:57	6:28	7:21	5:55	7:44	5:41	4:29
11	6:59	5:03	6:41	5:34	7:08	6:58	6:27	7:22	5:54	7:45	5:41	4:29
12	6:59	5:04	6:40	5:34	7:07	6:59	6:25	7:22	5:53	7:46	5:41	4:29
13	6:59	5:05	6:39	5:35	7:06	6:59	6:24	7:23	5:53	7:46	5:41	4:29
14	6:59	5:06	6:38	5:36	7:04	7:00	6:23	7:24	5:52	7:47	5:41	4:29
15	6:58	5:07	6:37	5:37	7:03	7:01	6:22	7:25	5:51	7:48	5:41	4:30
16	6:58	5:08	6:36	5:38	7:02	7:02	6:16	7:25	5:51	7:49	5:41	4:30
17	6:58	5:09	6:35	5:39	7:00	7:03	6:19	7:26	5:50	7:49	5:41	4:30
18	6:57	5:10	6:34	5:40	6:59	7:03	6:18	7:27	5:49	7:50	5:42	4:31
19	6:57	5:11	6:33	5:41	6:58	7:04	6:17	7:28	5:49	7:51	5:42	4:31
20	6:57	5:12	6:32	5:42	6:56	7:05	6:16	7:29	5:48	7:52	5:42	4:32
21	6:56	5:13	6:31	5:43	6:55	7:06	6:14	7:29	5:47	7:52	5:42	4:32
22	6:56	5:14	6:30	5:44	6:54	7:06	6:13	7:30	5:47	7:53	5:42	4:33
23	6:55	5:15	6:29	5:44	6:52	7:07	6:12	7:31	5:46	7:54	5:43	4:33
24	6:55	5:16	6:27	5:45	6:51	7:08	6:11	7:32	5:46	7:54	5:43	4:34
25	6:54	5:17	6:26	5:46	6:49	7:09	6:10	7:32	5:45	7:55	5:43	4:34
26	6:54	5:18	6:25	5:47	6:48	7:10	6:09	7:33	5:45	7:56	5:44	4:35
27	6:53	5:19	6:24	5:48	6:47	7:10	6:08	7:34	5:44	7:56	5:44	4:36
28	6:53	5:20	6:23	5:49	6:45	7:11	6:07	7:35	5:44	7:57	5:44	4:36
29	6:52	5:21			6:44	7:12	6:05	7:36	5:44	7:58	5:45	4:37
30	6:51	5:22			6:43	7:13	6:04	7:36	5:43	7:58	5:45	4:38
31	6:51	5:23			6:41	7:13			5:43	7:59		

This table is based on sunrise and sunset times for Los Angeles, California. LA 411 recommends that the reader double-check any sunrise or sunset time with the day's local newspaper or with a weather service.

	JULY		AUGUST		SEPTEMBER		OCTOBER		NOVEMBER		DECEMBER	
	Rise A.M.	Set P.M.	Rise A.M.	Set P.M.	Rise A.M.	Set P.M.	Rise A.M.	Set P.M.	Rise A.M.	Set P.M.	Rise A.M.	Set P.M.
1	5:45	8:08	6:05	7:54	6:27	7:18	6:48	6:37	7:13	6:00	6:41	4:44
2	5:46	8:08	6:05	7:53	6:27	7:17	6:48	6:35	7:14	5:59	6:42	4:44
3	5:46	8:08	6:06	7:52	6:28	7:16	6:49	6:34	6:15	4:58	6:42	4:43
4	5:47	8:08	6:07	7:51	6:29	7:14	6:50	6:33	6:16	4:57	6:43	4:43
5	5:47	8:08	6:08	7:50	6:30	7:13	6:51	6:31	6:17	4:56	6:44	4:43
6	5:48	8:08	6:08	7:49	6:30	7:12	6:51	6:30	6:18	4:55	6:45	4:44
7	5:48	8:07	6:09	7:48	6:31	7:10	6:52	6:29	6:18	4:55	6:46	4:44
8	5:49	8:07	6:10	7:47	6:32	7:09	6:53	6:27	6:19	4:54	6:46	4:44
9	5:49	8:07	6:10	7:46	6:32	7:07	6:54	6:26	6:20	4:53	6:47	4:44
10	5:50	8:07	6:11	7:45	6:33	7:06	6:54	6:25	6:21	4:52	6:48	4:44
11	5:51	8:07	6:12	7:44	6:34	7:05	6:55	6:23	6:22	4:52	6:49	4:44
12	5:51	8:06	6:13	7:43	6:34	7:03	6:56	6:22	6:23	4:51	6:49	4:44
13	5:52	8:06	6:13	7:42	6:35	7:02	6:57	6:21	6:24	4:50	6:50	4:45
14	5:52	8:05	6:14	7:41	6:36	7:00	6:58	6:20	6:25	4:50	6:51	4:45
15	5:53	8:05	6:15	7:39	6:36	6:59	6:58	6:18	6:26	4:49	6:51	4:45
16	5:54	8:04	6:15	7:38	6:37	6:58	6:59	6:17	6:27	4:49	6:52	4:46
17	5:54	8:04	6:16	7:37	6:38	6:56	7:00	6:16	6:28	4:48	6:53	4:46
18	5:55	8:03	6:17	7:36	6:39	6:55	7:01	6:15	6:29	4:47	6:53	4:46
19	5:56	8:03	6:18	7:35	6:39	6:53	7:02	6:14	6:30	4:47	6:54	4:47
20	5:56	8:02	6:18	7:34	6:40	6:52	7:03	6:12	6:31	4:47	6:54	4:47
21	5:57	8:02	6:19	7:32	6:41	6:51	7:03	6:11	6:32	4:46	6:55	4:48
22	5:58	8:01	6:20	7:31	6:41	6:49	7:04	6:10	6:33	4:46	6:55	4:48
23	5:58	8:00	6:20	7:30	6:42	6:48	7:05	6:09	6:33	4:45	6:56	4:49
24	5:59	8:00	6:21	7:29	6:43	6:46	7:06	6:08	6:34	4:45	6:56	4:49
25	6:00	7:59	6:22	7:27	6:43	6:45	7:07	6:07	6:35	4:45	6:57	4:50
26	6:00	7:58	6:23	7:26	6:44	6:44	7:08	6:06	6:36	4:44	6:57	4:51
27	6:01	7:58	6:23	7:25	6:45	6:42	7:08	6:05	6:37	4:44	6:57	4:51
28	6:02	7:57	6:24	7:24	6:46	6:41	7:09	6:04	6:38	4:44	6:58	4:52
29	6:02	7:56	6:25	7:22	6:46	6:40	7:10	6:03	6:39	4:44	6:58	4:53
30	6:03	7:55	6:25	7:21	6:47	6:38	7:11	6:02	6:40	4:44	6:58	4:53
31	6:04	7:54	6:26	7:20			7:12	6:01			6:58	4:54

January 1	New Year's Day (IA/SAG)
January 21	Martin Luther King, Jr. Day (IA/SAG)
February 13	Ash Wednesday
February 18	President's Day (IA/SAG)
March 26*	Passover
March 29	Good Friday (SAG)
March 31	Easter Sunday
May 12	Mother's Day
May 27	Memorial Day (IA/SAG)
June 16	Fathers Day
July 4	Independence Day (IA/SAG)
July 9	Ramadan Begins
September 2	Labor Day (IA/SAG)
September 5*	Rosh Hashanah
September 14*	Yom Kippur
November 5	Islamic New Year Begins
November 11	Veterans Day
November 28	Thanksgiving (IA/SAG)
November 28*	Chanukah Begins
December 25	Christmas (IA/SAG)

* Begins at previous sundown

3D Int'l Film Festival   (323) 785-2389
1641 N. Ivar   www.3dff.org
Los Angeles, CA 90028
September, 2013

Academy Awards   (310) 247-3000
Academy of Motion Picture   FAX (310) 859-9619
Arts & Sciences   www.oscars.org/awards
8949 Wilshire Blvd.
Beverly Hills, CA 90211
February 24, 2013

AFCI Locations Trade Show   (323) 461-2324
Association of Film Commissioners Int'l FAX (413) 375-2903
8530 Wilshire Blvd., Ste. 210   www.afci.org
Beverly Hills, CA 90211
June, 2013

AFI Los Angeles Int'l. Film Festival   (323) 856-7600
The American Film Institute   FAX (323) 467-4578
2021 N. Western Ave.   www.afifest.com
Los Angeles, CA 90027
November, 2013

AICP Shows   (323) 960-4763
National LA   FAX (323) 960-4766
650 N. Bronson Ave. Ste. 223B   www.aicp.com
Los Angeles, CA 90004
October, 2013

American Film Market   (310) 446-1000
10850 Wilshire Blvd., Ninth Fl.   FAX (310) 446-1600
Los Angeles, CA 90024   www.americanfilmmarket.com
Fall, 2013

Ann Arbor Film Festival   (734) 995-5356
308 1/2 S. State St., Ste. 22   FAX (734) 995-5396
Ann Arbor, MI 48104   www.aafilmfest.org
March 19-24, 2013

Annie Awards   (818) 842-8330
ASIFA-Hollywood, 2114 Burbank Blvd. FAX (818) 842-5645
Burbank, CA 91502   www.annieawards.org
February 2, 2013

Artios Awards   (323) 463-1925
Casting Society of America   FAX (323) 463-5753
606 N. Larchmont Blvd., Ste. 4-B   www.castingsociety.com
Los Angeles, CA 90004
November, 2013

   (323) 969-4333
ASC Awards   (800) 448-0145
c/o American Society of   FAX (323) 882-6391
Cinematographers   www.theasc.com
P.O. Box 2230
Los Angeles, CA 90078
February, 2013

Aspen FilmFest   (970) 925-6882
110 E. Hallam St., Ste. 102   FAX (970) 925-1967
Aspen, CO 81611   www.aspenfilm.org
Fall, 2013

BAFTA Awards   44 20 7734 0022
British Academy of Film & TV Arts   FAX 44 20 7734 1792
195 Piccadily   www.bafta.org/awards
London W1J 9LN United Kingdom
February 10, 2013

Berlinale/Berlin Int'l Film Festival   49 30 259 20 0
Potsdamer Strabe 5   FAX 49 30 259 20 299
Berlin 10785 Germany   www.berlinale.de
February 7-17, 2013

The Black Maria
Film & Video Festival   (201) 200-2043
c/o Department of Media Arts   FAX (201) 200-3490
Fries Hall New Jersey City University
2039 Kennedy Blvd.   www.blackmariafilmfestival.org
Jersey City, NJ 07305
Touring year-round, 2013

Cannes Film Festival   33 1 53 59 61 00
Three, rue Amélie   FAX 33 1 53 59 61 10
Paris F-75007 France   www.festival-cannes.org
May 15-26, 2013

Cannes Lions International
Advertising Festival   44 0 20 7728 4040
Greater London House   FAX 44 0 20 7728 4040
Hampstead Rd.   www.canneslions.com
London, NW1 7EJ United Kingdom
June 16-22, 2013

Chicago Int'l. Children's
Film Festival   (773) 281-9075
c/o Facets Multi-Media   FAX (773) 929-0266
1517 W. Fullerton Ave.   www.cicff.org
Chicago, IL 60614
October, 2013

Ⓐ Cine Gear Expo   (310) 472-0809
P.O. Box 492296   FAX (310) 471-8973
Los Angeles, CA 90049   www.cinegearexpo.com
May 30-June 2, 2013

CineQuest   (408) 295-3378
P.O. Box 720040   FAX (408) 995-5713
San Jose, CA 95172   www.cinequest.org
February 26-March 10, 2013

   (800) 946-2546
Clio Awards   (212) 683-4300
770 Broadway, Seventh Fl.   FAX (212) 683-4796
New York, NY 10003   www.clioawards.com
May, 2013

Comic-Con   (619) 491-2475
P.O. Box 128458   FAX (619) 414-1022
San Diego, CA 92112   www.comic-con.org
July 18-21, 2013

Ⓐ Createasphere Entertainment
and Technology Expo   (818) 842-6611
November 6-7, 2013   FAX (818) 842-6624
   www.createasphere.com

Creative Arts Emmy Awards   (818) 754-2800
Academy of Television Arts & Sciences FAX (818) 761-2827
5220 Lankershim Blvd.   www.emmys.org
North Hollywood, CA 91601
September, 2013

Directors Guild of America Awards   (310) 289-2000
7920 Sunset Blvd.   FAX (310) 289-2029
Los Angeles, CA 90046   www.dga.org/awards
February 2, 2013

DV Expo   (212) 378-0400
c/o NewBay Media   www.dvexpo.com
28 E. 28th St., 12th Fl.
New York, NY 10016
September 24-26, 2013

Emmy Awards   (818) 754-2800
Academy of Television Arts & Sciences FAX (818) 761-2827
5220 Lankershim Blvd.   www.emmys.org
North Hollywood, CA 91601
September, 2013

Film Independent   (310) 432-1240
Los Angeles Film Festival   (866) 345-6337
9911 W. Pico Blvd.   FAX **(310) 432-1203**
Los Angeles, CA 90035   **www.lafilmfest.com**
June 13-23, 2013

Film Independent's Spirit Awards   (310) 432-1240
Film Independent/Los Angeles   FAX **(310) 432-1234**
9911 W. Pico Blvd.   **www.filmindependent.org**
Los Angeles, CA 90035
February 23, 2013

Golden Globes   (310) 657-1731
c/o Hollywood Foreign Press Association   FAX **(310) 657-5576**
646 N. Robertson Blvd.   **www.goldenglobes.org**
West Hollywood, CA 90069
January 13, 2013
President: Lorenzo Soria

The Gotham Awards   (212) 465-8200
68 Jay St., Ste. 425   FAX **(212) 465-8525**
Brooklyn, NY 11201   **www.gotham.ifp.org**
November, 2013

GRAMMY Awards   (310) 392-3777
The Recording Academy   FAX **(310) 392-2187**
3030 Olympic Blvd.   **www.grammy.com**
Santa Monica, CA 90404
February 10, 2013

The Hamptons Int'l. Film Festival   (631) 324-4600
Three Newtown Mews   FAX **(631) 607-0444**
East Hampton, NY 11937   **www.hamptonsfilmfest.org**
October 13-17, 2013

Heartland Film Festival   (317) 464-9409
Truly Moving Pictures   FAX **(317) 464-8409**
1043 Virginia Ave., Ste. 2   **www.heartlandfilmfestival.org**
Indianapolis, IN 46203
October, 2013

Hollywood Film Festival   (310) 288-1882
433 N. Camden Dr., Ste. 600   FAX **(310) 288-0060**
Beverly Hills, CA 90210   **www.hollywoodawards.com**
October, 2013

HPA Awards Sponsored by
the Hollywood Post Alliance   (213) 614-0860
846 S. Broadway, Ste. 601   FAX **(213) 614-0890**
Los Angeles, CA 90014   **www.hpaawards.net**
November, 2013

Independent Film Week
    www.ifp.org/independent-film-week/
B-Side Entertainment
327 Congress Ave., Ste. 650
Austin, TX 78701
September, 2013

The Jackson Hole
Wildlife Film Festival   (307) 733-7016
P.O. Box 3940   FAX **(307) 733-7376**
240 S. Glenwood, Ste. 112   **www.jhfestival.org/**
Jackson, WY 83001
September 23-27, 2013

Just for Laughs   (514) 845-3155
2101 St-Laurent Blvd.   FAX **(514) 845-4140**
Montreal, QC H2X 2T5 Canada   **www.hahaha.com**
Check website for dates

Long Island Int'l Film Expo   (516) 783-3199
c/o Bellmore Movies   **www.liifilmexpo.org**
222 Petit Ave., Side Entrance
Bellmore, NY 11710
July 11-18, 2013

Miami Int'l Film Festival   (305) 237-3456
Miami Dade College   FAX **(305) 257-7344**
25 NE Second St., Ste. 5501   **www.miamifilmfestival.com**
Miami, FL 33132
March 1-10, 2013

Mill Valley Film Festival   (415) 383-5256
1001 Lootens Pl., Ste. 220   FAX **(415) 383-8606**
San Rafael, CA 94901   **www.mvff.com**
October, 2013

Mobius Awards   (310) 540-0959
713 S. Pacific Coast Hwy., Ste. B   FAX **(310) 316-8905**
Redondo Beach, CA 90277   **www.mobiusawards.com**
January, 2013

    (212) 258-8000
MTV Movie Awards   (310) 752-8000
1515 Broadway   FAX **(212) 846-1804**
New York, NY 10036   **www.mtv.com**
April 14, 2013

    (212) 258-8000
MTV Music Video Awards   (310) 752-8000
1515 Broadway   FAX **(212) 846-1804**
New York, NY 10036   **www.mtv.com**
September, 2013

NABSHOW/   (202) 429-5300
National Association of Broadcasters   (800) 342-2460
1771 N St. NW   FAX **(202) 429-5493**
Washington, DC 20036   **www.nabshow.com**
April 6-11, 2013

Nashville Film Festival   (615) 742-2500
P.O. Box 24330   FAX **(615) 742-1004**
Nashville, TN 37202   **www.nashvillefilmfestival.org**
April 18-25, 2013

NATPE Market & Conference   (310) 453-4440
5757 Wilshire Blvd., Penthouse 10   FAX **(310) 453-5258**
Los Angeles, CA 90036   **www.natpe.org**
January 28-30, 2013

New Directors/New Films   (212) 875-5610
The Film Society @ Lincoln Center   **www.filmlinc.com**
70 Lincoln Center Plaza
New York, NY 10023
March, 2013

New York Festivals
Int'l Advertising in All Media Awards   (212) 643-4800
260 W. 39th St., 10th Fl.   FAX **(212) 643-0170**
New York, NY 10018   **www.newyorkfestivals.com**
Check website for dates

New York Festivals
Int'l. Film & Video Awards   (212) 643-4800
260 W. 39th St., 10th Fl.   FAX **(212) 643-0170**
New York, NY 10018   **www.newyorkfestivals.com**
April 9, 2013

New York Festivals
Int'l. Television Broadcasting Awards   (212) 643-4800
260 W. 39th St., 10th Fl.   FAX **(212) 643-0170**
New York, NY 10018   **www.newyorkfestivals.com**
April 9, 2013

New York Film Festival   (212) 875-5600
The Film Society of Lincoln Center
70 Lincoln Center Plaza   **www.filmlinc.com/nyff2012**
New York, NY 10023
September/October, 2013

The One Show Festival   (212) 979-1900
The One Club For Art & Copy   FAX **(212) 979-5006**
21 E. 26th St., Fifth Fl.   **www.enter.oneclub.org**
New York, NY 10010
May, 2013

Palm Springs Int'l Film Festival   (760) 322-2930
1700 E. Tahquitz Canyon Way, Ste. 3   FAX **(760) 322-4087**
Palm Springs, CA 92262   **www.psfilmfest.org**
January 3-14, 2013

PGA Produced By Conference   (310) 358-9020
8530 Wilshire Blvd., Ste. 450   FAX **(310) 358-9520**
Los Angeles, CA 90036   **www.producedbyconference.com**
June, 2013

Cine Gear Expo 2013
May 30 - June 2, 2013 Expo & Conference
The Studios at Paramount, Hollywood, CA

May 30 Film Competition + Screenings
May 31 - June 1 Exhibition + Seminars
June 2 Master Class Seminars

phone: 310.472.0809
fax: 310.471.8973
email: info@cinegearexpo.com

www.cinegearexpo.com

Producers Guild Awards   **(310) 358-9020**
8530 Wilshire Blvd., Ste. 450   FAX **(310) 358-9520**
Beverly Hills, CA 90211   **www.producersguild.org**
January 26, 2013

Rocky Mountain VidExpo   **(303) 771-2000**
8002 S. Oneida Court   **www.avxpo.biz**
Centennial, CO 80112
October, 2013

San Francisco Int'l Film Festival   **(415) 561-5020**
39 Mesa St., Ste. 110, The Presidio   **www.sffs.org**
San Francisco, CA 94129
April 25-May 9, 2013

Santa Barbara Int'l Film Festival   **(805) 963-0023**
1528 Chapala St., Ste. 203   FAX **(805) 962-2524**
Santa Barbara, CA 93101   **www.sbiff.org**
January 24-February 3, 2013

Seattle Int'l Film Festival   **(206) 464-5830**
400 Ninth Ave., North   FAX **(206) 264-7919**
Seattle, WA 98109   **www.siff.net**
May 16-June 9, 2013

ShowEast   **(646) 654-7680**
770 Broadway   FAX **(646) 654-7694**
New York, NY 10003   **www.showest.com**
November, 2013

Showbiz Expo   **(212) 404-2345**
440 Ninth Ave., Eighth Fl.   FAX **(212) 253-4123**
New York, NY 10001   **www.theshowbizexpo.com**
See website for dates

SIGGRAPH   **(212) 869-7440**
One Commerce Valley Dr. East   **www.siggraph.org**
Markhan, ON L5T 7X6 Canada
July 21-25, 2013

Slamdance Int'l Film Festival   **(323) 466-1786**
5634 Melrose Ave.   FAX **(323) 466-1784**
Los Angeles, CA 90038   **www.slamdance.com**
January 18-24, 2013

South By Southwest
Music & Media Conference   **(512) 467-7979**
SXSW Headquarters, Box 4999   FAX **(512) 451-0754**
Austin, TX 78765   **www.sxsw.com**
March 8-17, 2013

    (435) 658-3456
Sundance Film Festival   **(310) 360-1981**
P.O. Box 684429   FAX **(435) 658-3457**
Park City, UT 84068   **www.sundance.org**
January 17-27, 2013

Telluride Film Festival   **(510) 655-9494**
800 Jones St.   FAX **(510) 665-9589**
Berkeley, CA 94710   **www.telluridefilmfestival.org**
August 29-September 2, 2013

Toronto Int'l Film Festival   **(416) 967-7371**
Two Carlton St.   FAX **(877) 968-3456**
Toronto, ON M5B1J3 Canada   **www.tiff.net**
September, 2013

Tribeca Film Festival   **(212) 941-2400**
375 Greenwich St.   FAX **(212) 941-3539**
New York, NY 10013   **www.tribecafilm.com/festival**
April 17-29, 2013

U.S. Int'l Film & Video Festival   **(310) 540-0959**
713 S. Pacific Coast Hwy, Ste. A   FAX **(310) 316-8905**
Redondo Beach, CA 90277   **www.filmfestawards.com**
June, 2013

UNAFF-United Nations
Association Film Festival   **(650) 724-5544**
P.O. Box 19369   **www.unaff.org**
Stanford, CA 94309
October, 2013

Visual Effects Society (VES) Awards (310) 981-7681
5535 Balboa Blvd., Ste. 206   FAX **(310) 981-0179**
Encino, CA 91316   **www.vesawards.com**
February 5, 2013

The Webby Awards   **(212) 675-4890**
22 West 21st St., 7th Fl.   **www.webbyawards.com**
New York, NY 10010
May 20, 2013

Woods Hole Film Festival   **(508) 495-3456**
87B Water St.   **www.woodsholefilmfestival.org**
Woods Hole, MA 02543
July 27-August 3, 2013

WorldFest/
Houston Int'l Film & Video Fest   **(713) 965-9955**
9898 Bissonnet St., Ste. 650   FAX **(713) 965-9960**
Houston, TX 77036   **www.worldfest.org**
April 12-21, 2013

Industry Expertise with a Global Reach

With Createasphere, you can explore the world of content creation, asset management and preservation — and you'll get a preview of all the new and emerging technologies.
We converge the best of the creative, technology and marketing communities — both online with our Coalition sites and in person with our industry-defining expos.

- **The Entertainment Technology Expo**
  The entertainment and media industry's leading annual showcase that unveils the newest production gear, ground-breaking advances in technology and the latest tools for content creation and post.
  Burbank November 6-7, 2013

- **Digital Asset Management Conference**
  The premier event on managing digital assets, this Conference continues to dominate as the leading voice exploring the urgent global issues of asset management in the sectors of advertising, entertainment, media, publishing, sports, museums and higher education.
  Los Angeles February 27-28, 2013
  New York October 7-8, 2013

- **Post Production Master Class**
  In this essential half-day class, the post production community meets with industry leaders for intensive seminars, keynote sessions and one-on-one demos. Attendees get the information and networking opportunities they need to expand their skills and move their careers forward.
  New York October 7, 2013
  Burbank November 7, 2013

- **Executive Marketplace**
  Imagine connecting directly with a group of senior-level buyers who are ready to make enterprise-level purchases. The Executive Marketplace is an exclusive event featuring face-to-face, personal sales conversations with a targeted group of buyers who have been hand-selected and personally invited to attend.
  Chicago July 2013

- **Createasphere's Online Coalitions**

  PRO VIDEO COALITION: The leading resource for digital content professionals. This award-winning site provides comprehensive information on all facets of this multi-dimensional industry. providocoalition.com

  PRO PHOTO COALITION: As digital technology continues to erase the boundaries between still and motion photography, Pro Photo Coalition serves as a guiding beacon in this brave new world. prophotocoalition.com

  DAM COALITION: The exclusive global online resource for up-to-date solutions, technology, expertise and industry trends on all things DAM. damcoalition.com

the future in hand | createasphere.com | 818.842.6611

LA 411 FEATURE

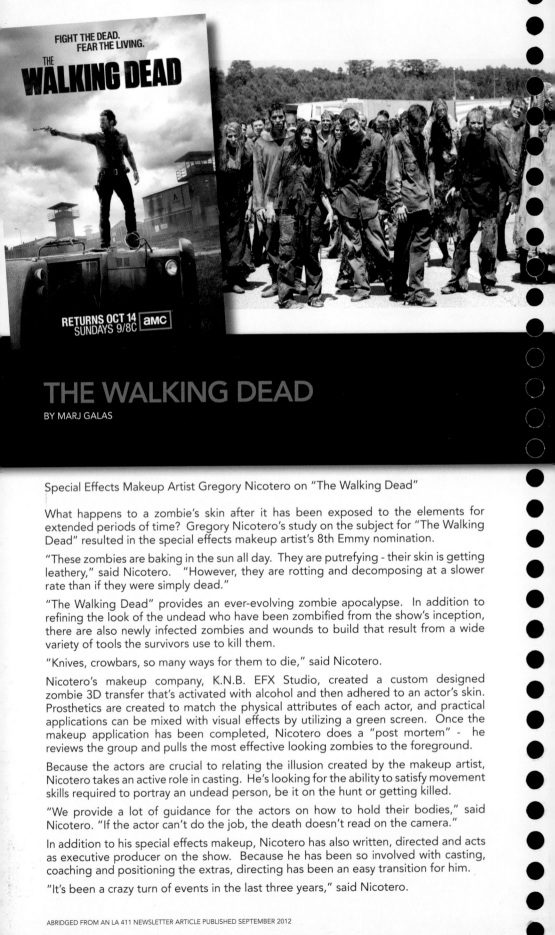

**FIGHT THE DEAD.
FEAR THE LIVING.**

THE
WALKING DEAD

RETURNS OCT 14 **aMC**
SUNDAYS 9/8C

THE WALKING DEAD

BY MARJ GALAS

Special Effects Makeup Artist Gregory Nicotero on "The Walking Dead"

What happens to a zombie's skin after it has been exposed to the elements for extended periods of time? Gregory Nicotero's study on the subject for "The Walking Dead" resulted in the special effects makeup artist's 8th Emmy nomination.

"These zombies are baking in the sun all day. They are putrefying - their skin is getting leathery," said Nicotero. "However, they are rotting and decomposing at a slower rate than if they were simply dead."

"The Walking Dead" provides an ever-evolving zombie apocalypse. In addition to refining the look of the undead who have been zombified from the show's inception, there are also newly infected zombies and wounds to build that result from a wide variety of tools the survivors use to kill them.

"Knives, crowbars, so many ways for them to die," said Nicotero.

Nicotero's makeup company, K.N.B. EFX Studio, created a custom designed zombie 3D transfer that's activated with alcohol and then adhered to an actor's skin. Prosthetics are created to match the physical attributes of each actor, and practical applications can be mixed with visual effects by utilizing a green screen. Once the makeup application has been completed, Nicotero does a "post mortem" - he reviews the group and pulls the most effective looking zombies to the foreground.

Because the actors are crucial to relating the illusion created by the makeup artist, Nicotero takes an active role in casting. He's looking for the ability to satisfy movement skills required to portray an undead person, be it on the hunt or getting killed.

"We provide a lot of guidance for the actors on how to hold their bodies," said Nicotero. "If the actor can't do the job, the death doesn't read on the camera."

In addition to his special effects makeup, Nicotero has also written, directed and acts as executive producer on the show. Because he has been so involved with casting, coaching and positioning the extras, directing has been an easy transition for him.

"It's been a crazy turn of events in the last three years," said Nicotero.

ABRIDGED FROM AN LA 411 NEWSLETTER ARTICLE PUBLISHED SEPTEMBER 2012

Advertiser Index

Covers & Tabs

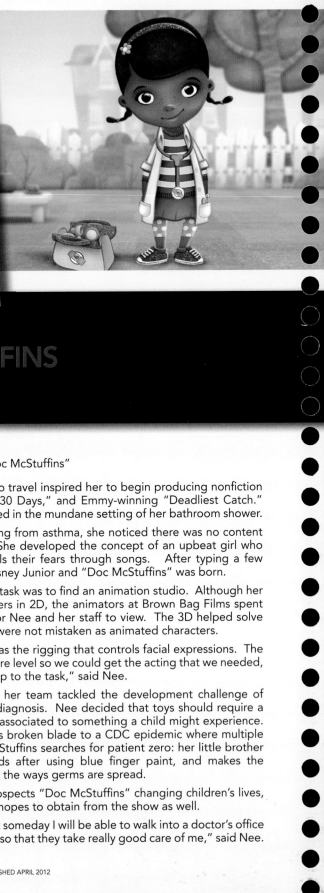

DOC MCSTUFFINS

BY MARJ GALAS

Writer/Producer Chris Nee on "Doc McStuffins"

Writer/producer Chris Nee's itch to travel inspired her to begin producing nonfiction fare such as Morgan Spurlock's "30 Days," and Emmy-winning "Deadliest Catch." Nee's latest creation was formulated in the mundane setting of her bathroom shower.

Being the parent of a child suffering from asthma, she noticed there was no content that demystifies a doctor's visit. She developed the concept of an upbeat girl who diagnosis toy's ailments and quells their fears through songs. After typing a few pages she pitched the show to Disney Junior and "Doc McStuffins" was born.

As executive producer, Nee's first task was to find an animation studio. Although her initial pitch illustrated the characters in 2D, the animators at Brown Bag Films spent time modeling characters in 3D for Nee and her staff to view. The 3D helped solve the problem of ensuring the toys were not mistaken as animated characters.

"A concern for us regarding 3D was the rigging that controls facial expressions. The rigging had to be almost at a feature level so we could get the acting that we needed, and amazingly they just stepped up to the task," said Nee.

With the look in place, Nee and her team tackled the development challenge of how the toys benefit from Doc's diagnosis. Nee decided that toys should require a mechanical condition that can be associated to something a child might experience. Ailments range from a helicopter's broken blade to a CDC epidemic where multiple toys develop blue spots. Doc McStuffins searches for patient zero: her little brother who neglected to wash his hands after using blue finger paint, and makes the correlation between the paint and the ways germs are spread.

While Nee is excited with the prospects "Doc McStuffins" changing children's lives, there is one personal change she hopes to obtain from the show as well.

"I may have an ulterior motive that someday I will be able to walk into a doctor's office and say 'I created Doc McStuffins' so that they take really good care of me," said Nee.

ABRIDGED FROM AN LA 411 NEWSLETTER ARTICLE PUBLISHED APRIL 2012

AD AGENCIES & PRODUCTION COS.
Advertising Agencies
Advertising Agency Freelance Producers
Animation Production Companies
Bidders
Commercial Directors
Commercial Production Companies
Corporate & Video Production Companies
Independent Sales Reps
Infomercial Production Companies
Motion Picture Production Companies
Movie & TV Marketing Companies
Music Video Directors
Music Video Production Companies
Production Offices
Promo Production Companies
Public Relations
Storyboard Artists
Television Production Companies
Trailer Production Companies
Web Production Companies
Web Broadcasting & Streaming Media

POST PRODUCTION
3D Computer Animation
Audio Post Facilities
Color Correction/Color Grading
Commercial Editorial Houses
Composers/Sound Designers & Sound Editors
Compositing
Computer Graphics & Visual FX
Digital Dailies
Digital Intermediates
Duplication
DVD/Blu-Ray, Authoring & Replication
Editing Equipment Rentals & Sales
Editing Equipment & Software Manufacturers
Editors
Film & Tape Storage
Film & Video Transfers
Film Laboratories—Motion Picture
Film Laboratories—Still Photography
Mobile Video Units, Satellite &
  Transmission Services
Music Libraries & Publishing
Music Production & Sound Design
Post Houses
Post Production Supervisors
Pre-Visualization
Quality Control (QC)
Screening Rooms
Stereoscopic Visual FX
Stock Footage & Photos
Titling, Captioning & Broadcast Design
Visual FX Artists
Visual FX Supervisors & Producers

SETS & STAGES
Aviation Mock-Ups & Props
Backings & Scenic Artists
Green Screens
Rehearsal Studios
Set Design, Construction & Rentals
Set Sketchers
Still Photography Studios & Lofts
Stages
Stages—Portable
Standing Sets
TV Studios
Virtual Sets

LOCATION SERVICES & EQUIPMENT
Air Charters
Air Freight & Courier Services
Airlines
Airport Shuttles
Airports
Bus Charters
Car Dealerships
Car Rentals
Caterers
Communications Equipment
Consulates General
Crating & Packing
Custom Brokers & Carnets
Film Commissions &
  Permit Offices—California
Film Commissions—International
Film Commissions—North America
Hotels & Short-Term Housing
Limousine & Car Services
Location Libraries
Location Management & Scouts
Locations/Ranches

LOCATION SVCS & EQUIP (cont)
Motorhomes & Portable
  Dressing Rooms
Moving, Storage & Transportation
Permit Services
Portable Restrooms
Production Services—International
Production Services—North America
Security & Bodyguards
Specialty Transportation
Theaters & Stadiums
Traffic Control & Barricades
Travel Agencies
Weather

PRODUCTION SUPPORT
Acting/Dialect Coaches
Animals & Trainers
Budgeting & Scheduling
Casting Directors
Casting Facilities
Choreographers
Computer Consultants & Software
Computers, Office Equipment &
  Supplies
Directories & Trade Publications
Entertainment Attorneys
Extras Casting Agencies
Finance
Hand & Leg Models
Insurance Brokers & Guarantors
Janitorial & Strike Services
Large Scale Event Planning
Libraries, Research & Clearance
Massage Therapists
Messenger Services
Nautical Film Services & Coordination
Notaries
Payroll, Bus. Affairs & Prod. Accountants
Printing Services
Promotional Products
Stunt Coordinators—Aerial & Specialty
Stunt Coordinators &
  Performance Drivers
Stunt Equipment
Talent & Modeling Agencies
Tax Incentive Services
Technical Advisors
Transcription & Secretarial Services
Translation & Interpretation Services
Webcasting, Digital Casting &
  Video Conferencing
Wrap Party Locations

CAMERA & SOUND EQUIPMENT
Aerial Equipment
Aerial—Fixed Wing & Helicopter Pilots
Camera & Sound Equipment
  Manufacturers
Camera Cars & Tracking Vehicles
Camera Rentals—Motion Picture
Camera Rentals—Still Photography
Motion Control
Music Playback Services
Raw Stock
Sound Equipment Rentals & Sales
Teleprompting & Cue Card Services
Video Assist Services
Video Cameras & Equipment
Video Display, Playback & Projection

HIGH DEF, DIGITAL CINEMA & 3D
Digital Cinema/3D Exhibition
Digital Cinema Content Mgmt. &
  Storage Manufacturers
Digital Cinema Packages/Post
HD/3D Cameras & Equipment
HD Duplication
HD Editing Equipment
HD Equipment Manufacturers
HD Post Houses
HD Screening Rooms
HD Stock Footage
HD Tape Stock & Hard Drives

GRIP & LIGHTING EQUIPMENT
Booms, Cranes & Camera Support
Climate Control Systems
Construction Equipment Rentals
Grip & Lighting Equipment Manufacturers
Grip & Lighting Expendables
Grip Equipment
Lift Equipment, Cherry Pickers &
  Scaffolding

GRIP & LIGHTING EQUIP (cont)
Lighting Equipment & Generators
Production Equipment & Accessories
Trucks & Vans

PROPS & WARDROBE
Aerial Picture Vehicles
Animatronics, Puppets &
  Makeup FX
Art Fabrication, Licensing & Rentals
Arts & Crafts Supplies
Atmospheric/Lighting FX & Pyrotechnics
Boats & Nautical Props
Building/Surface Materials & Hardware
Canopies & Tents
Car Prep, Rigging & Prototypes
Color-Correct Props
Costume Makers & Rentals
Draperies & Window Treatments
Dry Cleaners
Eyewear & Jewelry
Fabrics
Firearms & Weapons
Flags, Graphics & Signage
Flowers, Greens & Plants
Foam
Furniture Rentals & Accessories
Games, Toys & Amusements
Glass
Hair, Makeup & Wardrobe Supplies
Ice
Medical & Scientific Props
Musical Instrument Rentals
Neon
Photo, Video & Electronic Props
Picture Vehicles
Plastics, Plexiglas & Fiberglass
Product Placement
Prop Fabrication & Mechanical FX
Prop Houses
Restaurant & Kitchen Equipment
Specialty Props
Sport Vehicle Rentals
Sporting Goods
Studio Prop Rentals
Studio Services
Tailoring & Alterations
Uniforms & Surplus
Vintage Clothing & Accessories
Water Trucks

CREW
Agents, Reps & Job Referral Services
Ambulance/Paramedics & Nurses
Art Directors/Production Designers
Baby Wranglers
Camera Assistants
Camera Operators
Camera Operators—Steadicam
Craft Service
Digital Imaging Technicians
Directors of Photography
First Assistant Directors
Food Stylists & Home Economists
Gaffers & Lighting Directors
Grips
Hair & Makeup Artists
Producers
Production Coordinators
Production Managers
Production Stills Photographers
Prop Masters
Prosthetics
Script Supervisors
Second Assistant Directors
Set Decorators
Sound Mixers
Studio Teachers/Welfare Workers
Trade Associations/Unions
Transportation Captains
Underwater Technicians
VTR Operators
Wardrobe Stylists/Costume Designers

General Index

G

T

General Index

the first motion picture from the creator of
family guy

mark **wahlberg** mila **kunis**

seth **macfarlane**

ted

this summer

www.tedisreal.com

TED
BY MARJ GALAS

Jason Clark, Producer, Jenny Fulle, VFX Producer and Blair Clark, VFX Supervisor on "Ted"

When Jason Clark read the script for "Ted," a live-action buddy story featuring an innocent talking teddy bear who evolves into a foul-mouthed, lewd bachelor, he laughed. "It was the funniest thing I've ever read," said Clark.

Taken by McFarlane's witty social and political commentary, Clark was excited to work with McFarlane on the animator's live-action directorial debut. McFarlane, who supplied the voice of Ted the teddy bear, also wanted to infuse his creation with his own mannerisms and gestures. Working with a tight budget, Clark's first step was to enlist the help of Jenny Fulle at The Creative-Cartel to oversee all visual effects on "Ted."

"Seth knew he wanted motion capture so he could infuse his personality, gestures and facial expressions into Ted," said Fulle. "It was up to The Creative-Cartel to understand how to make that process work."

Fulle wanted to help MacFarlane fluidly transition from the motion capture process to his directorial duties. A moven suit proved to be the best option - the suit consists of bands and straps placed on the legs, body and head. Unlike the more commonly used Lycra suits, the moven suit was something MacFarlane could wear over his street clothing.

"We did the motion capture directly on set," said Clark. "We brought the suit and trained someone to operate the interface, putting us in charge of our own destiny."

In addition to its use for the visual effects team, the suit was also kept in the editorial suite and used during post vis. Animation could be re-recorded to ensure Ted's placement within the frame was always spot on prior to the final edit.

Fulle reached out to Blair Clark to act as Visual Effects Supervisor on "Ted." While he had dabbled in motion capture years previously, "Ted" also provided him with his first hands-on opportunity.

"With key frame animation, the animator gets to be the actor; in motion capture the actor is posing," said Clark. "Motion capture put us further ahead of the game. There was still a lot of work, but we were able to skip a step."

ABRIDGED FROM AN LA 411 NEWSLETTER ARTICLE PUBLISHED MAY 2012

Company/Crew Index

Symbols

A

B

C

D

Company/Crew Index

Company/Crew Index

F

Company/Crew Index

H

J

M

N

O

P

S

Company/Crew Index

FROM THE NETWORK THAT BRINGS YOU **MAD MEN** AND THE PRODUCERS OF **UNDERCOVER BOSS**

amc

THE PITCH

BY MARJ GALAS

Joel Stillerman, SVP of Original Programming, AMC, Aaron Saidman, Executive Producer, and Brad Dean, Editor on "The Pitch"

On AMC's "The Pitch," the cameras begin capturing the action before the brand's first campaign meeting. Story producers with single cameras follow the creative heads from the moment they obtain the assignment through the aftermath of the pitch. The challenge editor Brad Dean shares with the editorial team is sifting through roughly 350 hours of footage per an episode to find images that convey the stories behind the process.

"You can't set up a camera and tell someone to be creative," said Dean. "You have only 42 minutes to express the stress and tension, you find every little shot that tells the story."

Eager to change the visual format many associate with reality shows, executive producer Aaron Saidman wanted each episode of "The Pitch" to have a cinematic style akin to documentary filmmaking. Saidman carefully considered every aspect of storytelling necessary to illustrate the subject matter, depicting the ad agencies' creative processes as the glue that binds the series while simultaneously presenting each episode as a stand alone unit.

"We felt this show needed to break new ground, and we were happy to violate all sorts of 'rules' from our industry," said Saidman. "Whether it's being on a shot longer than in a typical reality show, or in the way that it was scored, and that we didn't ask everyone to speak in the present tense, that was very liberating for us."

Due to the high volume of material shot for "The Pitch," digital HD cameras are used, going against the grain of the majority of AMC's original series. AMC's SVP of Programing Joel Stillerman feels the quality of the footage seen in "The Pitch" illustrates a sense of care and attention to detail that normally is not seen in reality programming.

"(The Pitch) is very composed and very cinematic," said Stillerman. "It's kind of cliché to say it, but the technology has come so far. I think the cinephile might be able to tell the difference, but in the right hands digital can be incredibly beautiful."

ABRIDGED FROM AN LA 411 NEWSLETTER ARTICLE PUBLISHED MAY 2012

A ADVERTISER SYMBOL

**Refer to the General Index for
cross-referencing items in this section.**

1124 Design Advertising
(310) 821-1775
(310) 902-0808
322 Culver Blvd.
FAX (310) 821-1972
Playa del Rey, CA 90293
www.1124design.com

72andSunny
(310) 215-9009
6300 Arizona Circle
FAX (310) 215-9012
Los Angeles, CA 90045
www.72andsunny.com

Admarketing, Inc.
(310) 203-8400
1801 Century Park East, Ste. 2000
FAX (310) 277-7621
Century City, CA 90067
www.admarketing.com

Bramson + Associates
(323) 938-3595

Campbell-Ewald
(310) 358-4800
8687 Melrose Ave., Ste. G510
www.cecom.com
West Hollywood, CA 90069

Dailey
(310) 360-3100
8687 Melrose Ave., Ste. G300
FAX (310) 360-0810
West Hollywood, CA 90069
www.daileyideas.com

davidandgoliath
(310) 445-5200
909 N. Sepulveda
FAX (310) 445-5201
El Segundo, CA 90245
www.dng.com

DavisElen
(213) 688-7000
865 S. Figueroa St., 12th Fl.
FAX (213) 688-7288
Los Angeles, CA 90017
www.daviselen.com

DDB Worldwide
Communications Group, Inc.
(310) 907-1500
www.ddb.com

Dentsu America
(310) 586-5600
2001 Wilshire Blvd., Ste. 600
FAX (310) 586-5894
Santa Monica, CA 90403
www.dentsuamerica.com

Deutsch, Inc.
(310) 862-3000
FAX (310) 862-3100
www.deutschinc.com

DNA Studio
(323) 463-2826
6535 Santa Monica Blvd.
FAX (323) 463-2535
Hollywood, CA 90038
www.dnala.com

Draft FCB
(949) 851-3050
17600 Gillette Ave.
FAX (949) 567-9465
Irvine, CA 92614
www.fcb.com

Dreamentia, Inc.
(213) 347-6000
453 S. Spring St., Ste. 1101
FAX (213) 347-6001
Los Angeles, CA 90013
www.dreamentia.com

The Gary Group/2g Studios
(310) 264-1800
2048 Broadway
FAX (310) 264-1804
Santa Monica, CA 90404
www.2gstudios.com

Kovel/Fuller
(310) 841-4444
9925 Jefferson Blvd.
FAX (310) 841-4599
Culver City, CA 90232
www.kovelfuller.com

La Agencia de Orci & Asociados
(310) 444-7300
11620 Wilshire Blvd., Ste. 600
FAX (310) 478-3587
West Los Angeles, CA 90025
www.laagencia.com

LatinSphere Advertising, LLC
(562) 983-5103
115 Pine Ave., Ste. 200
FAX (562) 983-5167
Long Beach, CA 90802
www.latinsphere.com

Leo Burnett, USA
(323) 866-6020
6500 Wilshire Blvd., Ste. 1950
FAX (323) 866-6033
Los Angeles, CA 90048

McCann-Erickson, Inc.
(323) 900-7100
5700 Wilshire Blvd., Ste. 225 www.universalmccann.com
Los Angeles, CA 90036

MeadsDurket, Inc.
(619) 574-0808
6863 Friars Rd.
FAX (619) 574-1664
San Diego, CA 92108
www.meadsdurket.com

The Miller Group Advertising, Inc.
(310) 442-0101
1516 S. Bundy Dr., Ste. 200
FAX (310) 442-0107
Los Angeles, CA 90025 www.millergroupmarketing.com

MOB Media Inc./MOB Media Studios (949) 222-0220
27121 Towne Centre Dr., Ste. 260
FAX (949) 222-0243
Foothill Ranch, CA 92610
www.mobmedia.com

Ogilvy & Mather, Inc.
(310) 280-2200
3530 Hayden Ave.
FAX (310) 280-2699
Culver City, CA 90232
www.ogilvy.com

(213) 977-0440
Oskoui+Oskoui, Inc.
(213) 977-0400
1201 W. Fifth St., Ste. T-430   www.oskoui-oskoui.com
Los Angeles, CA 90017
(Consultation, Design, Development, Digital Campaigns, Online
Ad Traffic, Online Banners, Print & Testing)

Planet 3 Entertainment Group, LLC (310) 392-4600
10844 Burbank Blvd.   www.planet3entertainment.com
N. Hollywood, CA 91601

Project X Media
(858) 792-9685
P.O. Box 783
www.projectxmedia.com
Solana Beach, CA 92075

R&R Partners, Inc.
(310) 321-3900
300 N. Continental Blvd., Ste. 410
FAX (310) 321-3890
El Segundo, CA 90245
www.rrpartners.com

(310) 227-8200
Red Marketing
(310) 678-7601
345 Richmond St.
FAX (310) 227-8205
El Segundo, CA 90245
www.redm33.com

Riester
(310) 392-4244
1960 E Grand Ave., Ste. 260
FAX (310) 392-2595
Los Angeles, CA 90025
www.riester.com

Rubin Postaer and Associates
(310) 394-4000
2525 Colorado Ave.
www.rpa.com
Santa Monica, CA 90404

Saatchi & Saatchi/LA
(310) 214-6000
3501 Sepulveda Blvd.
FAX (310) 214-6160
Torrance, CA 90505
www.saatchila.com

Saeshe, Inc.
(213) 683-2100
FAX (213) 683-2103
www.saeshe.com

(310) 575-4441
Sagon-Phior
(818) 262-1838
2107 Sawtelle Blvd.
FAX (310) 575-4995
Los Angeles, CA 90025
www.sagon-phior.com

TBWA Chiat/Day Advertising
(310) 305-5000
5353 Grosvenor Blvd.
FAX (310) 305-6000
Los Angeles, CA 90066
www.tbwachiat.com

Team One Advertising
(310) 615-2000
1960 E. Grand Ave., Ste. 700
FAX (310) 322-7565
El Segundo, CA 90245
www.teamone-usa.com

TVA Marketing & Advertising	(818) 505-8300
	(818) 322-4296
	FAX (818) 505-8370
	www.tvaproductions.com

Young & Rubicam Brands	(949) 754-2000
2010 Main St., Fourth Fl.	FAX (949) 754-2001
Irvine, CA 92614	www.yr.com

Wongdoody	(310) 280-7800
8500 Steller Dr., Ste. 5	FAX (310) 280-7780
Culver City, CA 90232	www.wongdoody.com

LA 411   Advertising Agency Freelance Producers   LA 411

Christine Anthony	(323) 376-6463
Linda Arett	(323) 650-5605
Bryan Barker	(310) 869-9765
	web.mac.com/bbarker/
Shari Becker	(310) 254-6794
	web.mac.com/sharibecker
Jackie Bombeck	(310) 701-5898
John Brooks	(310) 418-6708
Patrick Collins	(310) 474-2780
	(310) 849-4599
	FAX (310) 474-7582
Jackye Cruz	(323) 460-4432
Bill Curran	(310) 392-1035
	(310) 729-4701
Juliet Diamond	(310) 994-7935
	www.julietdiamond.com
Brian Donnelly	(310) 880-9400
Marla Friedler	(949) 813-2450
	www.bluetangoproductions.com
Bruce Fritzberg	(818) 231-2260
	(972) 735-9878
Debbie Galloway	(818) 424-2353
Ellen J. Goldfarb	(818) 342-9026
	FAX (818) 342-9827
	www.ellenthetvproducer.com
Jerry Grant	(503) 914-9672
	(818) 882-3990
Joan M. Gringer	(310) 842-3281
	(888) 436-2168
	www.myspace.com/JGringer
Chantal Houle	(310) 953-9166
(French)	www.chantalhoule.com
Brad Johnson	(949) 302-3318
Erwin Kramer	(310) 446-1866
	(310) 266-8146
	FAX (310) 446-1856
	www.erwinkramer.com
Ilene Kramer	(310) 446-1866
	FAX (310) 446-1856
Anne Kurtzman	(818) 512-3889
	www.annekurtzman.com
Mariann Kwiat	(424) 237-2761
	(312) 399-1155
	FAX (424) 237-2761
	web.mac.com/mariann.kwiat

Rick Lieberman	(310) 709-4832
	(305) 321-3556
Jane Liepshutz	(310) 365-9998
	www.seejaneproduce.tv
Stephania Lipner	(310) 739-1469
Lynn M. Luckoff	(310) 463-2201
Patty Lum	(310) 376-8088
	(310) 989-7003
Patricia Matus	(310) 216-7268
Kathy McGoff	(310) 493-2718
Melanie Coventry McKinnell	(818) 957-0708
	(626) 688-2956
Jim Miller	(213) 503-5448
Tena Montoya	(310) 733-7369
	www.tenamontoya.com
Tony Osiecki	(310) 600-5823
Ronnie Reade	(310) 820-7939
Rickmon Media	(310) 503-5402
	www.rickmonmedia.com
Lyra Rider	(323) 309-7800
Kristin Roberts	(310) 397-8850
Nancy Rose	(818) 439-2126
	www.nancyrose.ws
Cat Sautter	(760) 439-6600
	FAX (760) 439-6688
Michael Shores	(323) 791-9433
	www.heavenanimage.com
Jacob Silver	(310) 994-7600
	(347) 855-5270
Nancy Skenderian Montgomery	(310) 753-1962
Brian Stashick	(310) 487-6044
	FAX (310) 275-6995
Dan Tarver	(310) 433-5143
Steven Tobenkin	(310) 621-1122
	FAX (310) 388-1403
Kathie Van Kerckhoven	(310) 968-6875
	(310) 395-9899
Susan Vogelfang	(310) 306-2648
Ree Whitford	(818) 424-9988
	www.reewhitford.com

Allen Williams	(310) 652-1393 (213) 308-8466	Randall Zook	(310) 753-5733 www.randallzook.com

Kelly Wood	(310) 600-1035
	www.kellywoodproducer.com

	(818) 762-4346
Leslie Zurla	(818) 207-1743
	FAX (818) 506-8483

Kathleen Yip	(310) 746-6302
	kathleenyip.com

Animation Production Companies

Acme Filmworks, Inc. (323) 464-7805
6525 Sunset Blvd., Ste. G-10   FAX (323) 464-6614
Hollywood, CA 90028   **www.acmefilmworks.com**
(2D/3D Animation, CGI, Character Cel Animation, Clay
Animation, Computer Animation & Stop-Motion)
Executive Producer: Ron Diamond
Producer: Pernille D'Avolio
Directors: Aixsponza, Gil Alkabetz, Claire Armstrong-Parod,
Danny Cannizzaro, Peter Chung, Evert de Beijer, Paul and
Menno De Nooijer, Michael Dudok De Wit, John Dilworth,
Paul Driessen, Piotr Dumala, Daniel Guyonnet, Chris Hinton,
Greg Holfeld, Aleksandra Korejwo, Igor Kovalyov, Torill Kove,
Raimund Krumme, Chris Landreth, Christopher and Wolfgang
Lauenstein, Caroline Leaf, Susan Loughlin, Frank and Caroline
Mouris, Oury and Thomas, Luc Perez, Janet Perlman, Afonso
Poyart, Robert Proch, Barry Purves, Daniel Guvonnet, Gitaniali
Rao, Rosto, Erica Russell, Michael Socha, Michael Sormannx,
Pam Stalker, Tiger Hare, Wendy Tilby/Amanda Forbis, Gianluigi
Toccafondo, Sarah van Den Boom, Solweig von Kleist,
Wachtenheim/Marianetti, David Wasson, Koji Yamamura, Yuval
and Merav Nathan & Juan Pablo Zaramella
East Coast Sales Rep: Mark Mirsky
Midwest Sales Rep: Tim Harwood
West Coast Sales Rep: Toni Saarinen

Acorn Entertainment (323) 238-4650
Hollywood Production Center
121 W. Lexington Dr., Ste. V100
Glendale, CA 91203   **www.acornentertainment.com**
(2D/3D Animation & Character Design)
Executive Producers: Evan Ricks & Thad Weinlein
Producer: Mary Wall

Animax Entertainment (818) 787-4444
6627 Valjean Ave.   FAX (818) 374-9140
Van Nuys, CA 91406   **www.animaxent.com**
(2D/3D Computer Animation, Character Animation, Character
Design, Compositing & Motion Graphics)

Berkos & Associates (310) 940-1329
(2D and 3D Animation & Stop-Motion Animation)

Bill Melendez Productions, Inc. (818) 382-7382
13400 Riverside Dr., Ste. 201   **www.billmelendez.tv**
Sherman Oaks, CA 91463
(2D/3D & Character Animation)
Business Affairs: Joanna Coletta
Animation Supervisor: Larry Leichliter
Sales Rep: Jeff Arnold

DUCK Studios,
a.k.a. Duck Soup Studios (310) 478-0771
2205 Stoner Ave.   FAX (310) 478-0773
Los Angeles, CA 90064   **www.duckstudios.com**
(2D/3D Computer Animation, Cel Animation, Character and
Illustrative Design, Compositing, Digital Ink and Paint, Live
Action Integration & Stop Motion)
Executive Producer: Mark Medernach
President/Director: Roger Chouinard
Directors: abstract: groove, B and C Wall, Simon Blake, Jamie
Caliri, Roger Chouinard, Paul Cummings, Delicatessen, Eric
Goldberg, James Hackett, Chris Harding, Impactist, JL Design,
Kompost, Lane and Jan, Main Frame, Meindbender, Monkmus,
Yorico Murakami, NMA, Nina Paley, Daniel Peacock, Hsin Ping
Pan, Corky Quakenbush, Chris Romano, Maureen Selwood,
Kang Seong, SMOG, Tiny Inventions, Brian Williams &
Yellow Shed
Sales Rep: Andrew Halpern
Music Video Rep: Randi Wilens

Duncan Studio (626) 578-1587
35 N. Arroyo Parkway, Ste. 200   FAX (626) 578-1327
Pasadena, CA 91103   **www.duncanstudio.com**

The Ebeling Group (310) 577-9963
628 California Ave.   FAX (212) 239-9069
Venice, CA 90291   **www.theebelinggroup.com**

Elektrashock, Inc. (310) 399-4985
1320 Main St.   FAX (310) 399-4972
Venice, CA 90291   **www.elektrashock.com**
(3D Animation)

Epoch Ink Animation (310) 823-0577
2918 Grayson Ave.   **www.epochinkanimation.com**
Venice, CA 90291

Fred Wolf Films (818) 846-0611
4222 W. Burbank Blvd.   FAX (818) 846-0979
Burbank, CA 91505   **www.fredwolffilms.com**
(Cel Animation)

	(917) 351-0520
Hornet, Inc.	(310) 641-9464
3962 Ince Blvd.	FAX (917) 314-2117
Culver City, CA 90232	**www.hornetinc.com**
(2D/3D Computer Animation)
CEO: Jon Slusser
President: Greg Harvey
Vice President: Greg Bedard
Executive Producer: Michael Feder

Klasky Csupo, Inc. (323) 468-2600
1238 Highland Ave.   FAX (323) 468-2808
Los Angeles, CA 90038   **www.klaskycsupo.com**

Kurtz & Friends (818) 841-8188
1023 N. Hollywood Way, Ste. 103   FAX (818) 841-6263
Burbank, CA 91505   **www.kurtzandfriends.com**
(2D/3D Computer Animation, Cel Animation, Character Design,
Compositing, Digital Ink and Paint, Live Action Integration &
Storyboards)
Producer: Kenneth Smith
Director: Bob Kurtz

Prana Studios, Inc. (323) 645-6500
1145 N. McCadden Pl.   **www.pranastudios.com**
Los Angeles, CA 90038

Renegade Animation, Inc. (818) 551-2351
111 E. Broadway, Ste. 208   FAX (818) 551-2350
Glendale, CA 91205   **www.renegadeanimation.com**
(Cel Animation)
Producer: Ashley Postlewaite
Animation Director: Darrell Van Citters
Sales Rep: Andy Arkin

Rhythm + Hues Design　　　(310) 448-7500
2100 E. Grand Ave.　　FAX **(310) 448-7600**
El Segundo, CA 90245　　**www.rhythm.com**
(Cel and Character Animation)
Executive Producer: Paul Babb
Head of Production, Commercial Digital: Lisa White
Animation/FX Directors: Clark Anderson, John-Mark Austin,
Steve Beck, Robert Caruso, Mark Dippé, Bill Kroyer, Craig
Talmy & Michael Wright
Visual FX Supervisors: Eric DeHaven, John Heller, Tim Miller &
Bill Westenhofer
East Coast Sales Rep: Henry Hagerty
Midwest/Detroit Sales Rep: Marci Miles
Los Angeles Sales Rep: Connie Mellors

Ring of Fire　　　(310) 966-5055
1538 20th St.　　FAX **(310) 966-5056**
Santa Monica, CA 90404　　**www.ringoffire.com**
(2D/3D Computer Animation, Compositing, HD Visual FX &
Visual FX Supervision)

Shadedbox, Inc.　　　(626) 356-3663
1137 Huntington Dr., Bldg. D　　**www.shadedbox.com**
South Pasadena, CA 91030
(3D Animation, 3D Modeling, Animatics, CGI, Character
Animation, Character Design, Computer Animation,
Previsualizations & Stop-Motion Animation)

STEELE Studios　　　(310) 656-7770
5737 Mesmer Ave.　　FAX **(310) 391-9055**
Culver City, CA 90230　　**www.steelevfx.com**
(2D/3D Animation, 2D Paint, 3D Digitizing, 3D Modeling,
Animatics, Blue Screen Compositing, Broadcast Design,
CGI, Character Animation, Character Design, Compositing,
Computer Animation, Digital FX, Digital Matte Painting, Digital
Paint, Digital Restoration, Editorial, Graphic Design, Green
Screen Compositing, Live Action Integration, Morphing,
Motion Graphics, Pre-Production Planning, Previsualizations,
Rotoscoping, Stereoscopic 3D, Storyboards, Visual FX & Visual
FX Supervision)

Storyheads Entertainment　　　(310) 487-6011
924 Calle Ruiz　　**www.storyheads.com**
Thousand Oaks, CA 91360
(2D/3D Animation, Cel Animation & Character Animation)
Founder/Creative Director: David Smith
Co-Founder/Executive Producer: Donna Smith

　　　(888) 577-4045
Synthespian Studios　　　**(413) 458-0202**
3050 Runyon Canyon Rd.　　**www.synthespians.net**
Los Angeles, CA 90046
President: Diana Walczak
COO: Michael Van Himbergen
Executive Producer: Amanda Roth
Producers: Wendy Gipp & Tom Leeser
Directors: Jeff Kleiser & Diana Walczak

Toon Makers, Inc.　　　(818) 832-8666
17333 Ludlow St.　　**www.toonmakers.com**
Granada Hills, CA 91344
(Cel Animation, CGI & Character Design)
Producer: Rocky Solotoff

Madelyn Curtis	(310) 459-8976
Kat Dillon	(310) 399-7839
Dale Dreher	(310) 600-5020
	www.mavericklocations.com
Peggy Dunn	(310) 200-3979
	(310) 398-4867
Leslie M. Evers	(310) 600-7373
Franny Faull	(310) 614-0992
Katy Greene	(310) 406-8800
Tracy Hauser	(310) 293-2752
Lisa Hollingshead	(310) 880-7556
	(310) 454-0861
Craig Houchin	(818) 951-5959
	www.craighouchin.com
Holly D. Hughes	(818) 951-6889
Alexis Ignatieff	(323) 664-6417
Jan Katz Black	(310) 821-2221
	(310) 804-0913
Jodi Kemper	(213) 507-8045
Brooke Lawrence	(310) 560-9787

Darcy Leslie-Parsons	(310) 963-6629
	(310) 736-1663
	www.brewsterparsons.com
Martha Lucas	(323) 376-9699
Judy May	(818) 883-4909
Susan McGonigle	(310) 770-7715
Colleen O'Donnell	(818) 591-1953
	(818) 437-1133
Kim Shapiro	(818) 389-6888
Kathleen E. Simons	(818) 497-8889
	(423) 239-4949
Jay Sisson	(213) 820-3075
	(213) 210-1961
(Spanish)	
Lindsay Skutch	(805) 341-3554
	(805) 687-9852
Debby Timmons	(818) 203-5655
Allan Wachs	(310) 589-4841
	(310) 467-5131
Ree Whitford	(818) 424-9988

Nasar Abich Jr.	(310) 652-8778 www.lspagency.net	Chris Applebaum	(323) 645-1000 www.believemedia.com
Neil Abramson	(323) 860-8030 www.chelsea.com	Michael Apted	(310) 659-3503 www.independentmediainc.com
abstract:groove	(310) 478-0771 www.duckstudios.com	Dante Ariola	(310) 826-6200 www.mjz.com
Brian Ades	(310) 503-8080	Ken Arlidge	(310) 396-3636 www.aerofilm.tv
Ben Affleck	(310) 659-3503 www.independentmediainc.com	Bozena Armstrong	(310) 289-6650 FAX (310) 289-6658
Aixsponza	(323) 464-7805 www.acmefilmworks.com	Claire Armstrong-Parod	(323) 464-7805 www.acmefilmworks.com
Francois Alaux	(310) 659-1577 www.littleminx.tv	Arni and Kinski	(323) 969-0555 www.awhitelabelproduct.com
Claudia Alberdi	(310) 858-7204 www.labandafilms.com	Guillermo Arriaga	(310) 659-3503 www.independentmediainc.com
Jaron Albertin	(323) 817-3300 www.smugglersite.com	Miguel Arteta	(310) 396-7333 www.bobcentral.com
Sebastian Alfie	(310) 823-5400 www.carbofilms.com	Charles Ashira	(323) 931-1782 www.backhomepictures.com
Gil Alkabetz	(323) 464-7805 www.acmefilmworks.com	Renato Assad	(818) 788-0153 www.fjproductions.com
Debbie Allen	(310) 315-1750 www.30secondfilms.com	Shona Auerbach	(310) 899-1700 www.gartner.tv
John Alper	(310) 659-0010 www.newhousefilms.com	Enrique Aular	(323) 932-6588 www.acatch22production.com
Ambitious Entertainment (Reps for Commercial Directors)	(818) 990-8993 www.ambitiousent.com	Sam Auster	(818) 843-5040 www.austerproductions.com
Mitchell Amundsen	(310) 559-5404 www.banditobrothers.com	Jesse Austin	(323) 464-2406 www.47pictures.com
Philip Andelman	(323) 468-0123 www.partizan.com	John-Mark Austin	(310) 448-7900 www.rhythm.com
Brad Anderson	(310) 659-3503 www.independentmediainc.com	Mazik-Self Aviary	(310) 288-8000 www.paradigmagency.com
Clark Anderson	(310) 448-7900 www.rhythm.com	Pedro Avila	(310) 823-5400 www.carbofilms.com
Wes Anderson	(310) 857-1000 www.moxiepictures.com	Awesome and Modest	(310) 558-3667 www.anonymouscontent.com
Philippe Andre	(310) 277-7001 (323) 856-9200 www.companyfilms.net	AXIS	(310) 659-1577 www.littleminx.tv
Daniel Andreas	(310) 986-3370 www.24pcine.com	Steve Ayson	(310) 826-6200 www.mjz.com
Tim Angulo	(310) 798-6332 www.wyomingfilms.com	Amin Azali	(310) 822-2147 www.residentfilms.tv
Animal	(323) 645-1000 www.believemedia.com	B and C Wall	(310) 478-0771 www.duckstudios.com
Steven Antin	(310) 828-8989 www.tateusa.com	Matthew Badger	(310) 275-9333 www.epochfilms.com
Debbie Anzalone	(323) 468-0123 www.partizan.com	Rebecca Baehler	(310) 656-4900 www.greendotfilms.com
		Brian Bain	(310) 295-0848 www.blueyedpictures.com

Grant Baird	(310) 260-6100 www.motivfilms.com	Trudy Bellinger	(310) 659-6220 www.crossroadsfilms.com
Bob Balaban	(323) 465-9494 www.helloandcompany.com	Daniel Benmayor	(310) 558-3667 www.anonymouscontent.com
Agust Baldursson	(310) 319-1990 www.curiouspictures.com	Mark Raymon Bennett	(310) 917-9191 www.untitled.tv
Thomas Balmes	(310) 659-3503 www.independentmediainc.com	Anthea Benton	(323) 645-1000 www.believemedia.com
Joe Baratelli	(310) 899-0335 www.tuesdayfilms.com	Adam Berg	(323) 817-3300 www.smugglersite.com
Bryan Barber	(323) 957-5400 www.picrow.com	Stu Berg	(310) 827-3336
Alejandro Barbosa	(310) 823-5400 www.carbofilms.com	Patrik Bergh	(323) 468-0123 www.partizan.com
Hector Barboza	(323) 932-6588 www.acatch22production.com	Michael Bernard	(323) 645-1000 www.believemedia.com
Antoine Bardou-Jacquet	(323) 468-0123 www.partizan.com	Bert and Bertie	(323) 463-2826 www.dnala.com
Hernan Bargman	(310) 559-8333 www.boxerfilms.net	Christian Bevilacqua	(310) 558-3667 www.anonymouscontent.com
Tom Barham	(310) 319-1990 www.curiouspictures.com	Nico Beyer	(310) 659-6220 (323) 468-0123 www.crossroadsfilms.com
Geoff Barish	(310) 917-9191 www.untitled.tv	Alan Bibby	(310) 399-6047 www.stardust.tv
Howard Barish	(818) 789-6777 www.kandoofilms.com	Scott Bibo	(323) 461-0101 www.altavistafilms.com
Raymond Bark	(310) 899-1700 www.gartner.tv	Tim Bieber	(310) 399-9910 www.mrbigfilm.com
Nicholas Barker	(323) 860-8030 www.chelsea.com	Big Machine	(818) 906-0006 www.thedirectorsnetwork.com
David Barnard	(323) 969-0555 www.awhitelabelproduct.com	Michael Bigelow	(310) 899-1700 www.gartner.tv
Thomas Barron	(818) 761-6644 www.imageg.com	Brian Billow	(310) 264-3000 www.hungryman.com
Lenny Bass	(323) 463-2826 www.dnala.com	Scott Billups	(818) 990-8993 www.ambitiousent.com
Gabriel Bassio	(310) 305-8200 www.900frames.tv	Michael Bindlechner	(310) 828-8989 www.tateusa.com
Jason Bateman	(310) 558-7100 www.hsiproductions.com	Robb Bindler	(323) 860-8030 www.chelsea.com
Russell Bates	(310) 659-6220 www.crossroadsfilms.com	Ozan Biron	(310) 659-1577 www.rsafilms.com
Christopher Bean	(310) 550-6990 www.macguffin.com	Henry Bjoin	(818) 846-1650 www.bjoinfilms.com
Marina Belaustegui	(323) 932-6588 www.acatch22production.com	Richard Black	(818) 760-8707
Brian Beletic	(323) 817-3300 www.smugglersite.com	Robert Black	(323) 653-0404 www.form.tv
Mark Belincula	(310) 314-1618 www.blind.com	Stephen Blackman	(310) 577-0700 www.slim-pictures.com
Greg Bell	(310) 275-9333 www.epochfilms.com	Simon Blake	(310) 478-0771 www.duckstudios.com
Katie Bell	(310) 659-6220 www.crossroadsfilms.com	Robert Blalack	(323) 460-4393
		M Blash	(323) 465-5299 www.thedirectorsbureau.com

Saul Blinkoff	(310) 319-1990	Kerry Shaw Brown	(818) 906-0006
	www.curiouspictures.com		www.thedirectorsnetwork.com
Blue Source	(310) 826-6200	PR Brown	(323) 465-9494
	www.mjz.com		www.helloandcompany.com
Armando Bo	(310) 558-3667	Sam Brown	(323) 465-5299
	www.anonymouscontent.com		www.thedirectorsbureau.com
James Bobin	(310) 857-1000	Bill Bruce	(310) 659-1577
	www.moxiepictures.com		www.rsafilms.com
Arlene Bogna	(323) 841-7464	Andy Bruntel	(323) 465-5299
	cargocollective.com/arlenebogna		www.thedirectorsbureau.com
David Bojorquez	(310) 986-3370	James Bryce	(310) 659-1577
	www.24pcine.com		www.rsafilms.com
Carlos Bolado	(310) 858-7204	Bua	(310) 917-9191
	www.labandafilms.com		www.untitled.tv
Fredrik Bond	(310) 826-6200	Bryan Buckley	(310) 264-3000
	www.mjz.com		www.hungryman.com
John Bonito	(818) 906-0006	Frank Budgen	(310) 558-3667
	www.thedirectorsnetwork.com		www.anonymouscontent.com
Gillian Bonner	(323) 874-8888	Richard Bullock	(310) 264-3000
	www.blackdragon.com		www.hungryman.com
Borgato and Berte	(323) 860-8030	Tim Bullock	(310) 264-3000
	www.chelsea.com		www.hungryman.com
Kevin Bourland	(310) 305-8200	Neil Burger	(310) 264-3000
	www.900frames.tv		www.hungryman.com
Gavin Bowden	(310) 559-5404	Don Burgess	(310) 828-8443
	www.banditobrothers.com		www.tuesdayfilms.com
Mike Brady	(310) 338-0580	Marcelo Burgos	(323) 645-1000
	www.utopiafilms.com		www.believemedia.com
Zach Braff	(310) 319-1990	Nanette Burstein	(310) 264-3000
	www.curiouspictures.com		www.hungryman.com
Eddie Brakha	(310) 288-8000	Kinga Burza	(323) 468-0123
	www.paradigmagency.com		www.partizan.com
	(323) 658-6541	Carlao Busato	(310) 264-3000
Moshe Brakha	(310) 288-8000		www.hungryman.com
	www.commercialhead.com	Matthaus Bussmann	(310) 854-0647
Kevin Bray	(323) 463-2826		www.sandwickmedia.com
	www.dnala.com	Eric Bute	(310) 260-6100
Gary Breslin	(310) 956-3500		www.motivfilms.com
	www.sdintegrated.com	Erik Buth	(310) 314-1618
Dom Bridges	(310) 396-7333		www.blind.com
	www.bobcentral.com	Adam Byrd	(323) 464-3080
Alain Briere	(310) 656-4900		www.moostudios.com
	www.greendotfilms.com	Scott Caan	(310) 288-8000
David Briggs	(866) 711-5195		www.paradigmagency.com
	www.jspcreative.com	Juan Cabral	(310) 826-6200
Mark Brinster	(818) 990-8993		www.mjz.com
	www.ambitiousent.com	Nelson Cabrera	(310) 699-3133
Adrien Brody	(310) 956-3500		www.nelsoncabrera.com
	www.sdintegrated.com	Marc Cadieux	(310) 880-2493
James Brown	(310) 453-9244		FAX (818) 788-4168
	www.toolofna.com		www.sirreelfilms.com
Jerry Brown	(310) 396-5796	Reto Caduff	(310) 986-3370
	www.detourfilms.com		www.24pcine.com
Jonathan Brown	(310) 828-8989	Stephen Cafiero	(323) 468-0123
	www.tateusa.com		www.partizan.com

Nicolas Caicoya	(310) 577-0700 www.slim-pictures.com	Peter Chung	(323) 464-7805 www.acmefilmworks.com
Joshua Caine	(323) 874-8888 www.blackdragon.com	Curtis Clark	(323) 703-1333 wp-a.com
Chris Cairns	(323) 468-0123 www.partizan.com	Mark Claywell	(818) 906-0006 www.thedirectorsnetwork.com
Nicolas Calcoya	(310) 858-7204 www.labandafilms.com	Chuck Clemens	(310) 305-8200 www.900frames.tv
Jamie Caliri	(310) 478-0771 www.duckstudios.com	Danny Clinch	(323) 468-0123 www.partizan.com
David Cameron	(323) 650-4722	Harry Cocciolo	(310) 396-7333 www.bobcentral.com
Danny Cannizzaro	(323) 464-7805 www.acmefilmworks.com	The Coen Brothers	(310) 277-7001 www.companyfilms.net
Ric Cantor	(323) 785-6500 www.gofilm.net	Omri Cohen	(310) 656-4900 www.greendotfilms.com
Peter Care	(310) 396-7333 (323) 951-0010 www.bobcentral.com	Robert Cohen	(310) 659-1577 www.rsafilms.com
Rey Carlson	(323) 465-9494 www.helloandcompany.com	Isabel Coixet	(310) 823-5400 www.carbofilms.com
Bob Carmichael	(310) 739-0650 FAX (303) 955-7064 www.bobcarmichael.com	Barney Cokeliss	(310) 659-1577 www.rsafilms.com
Joe Carnahan	(310) 659-1577 www.rsafilms.com	Jack Cole	(323) 860-8030 www.chelsea.com
Luis Carone	(310) 659-6220 www.crossroadsfilms.com	Simon Cole	(310) 558-7100 www.hsiproductions.com
Dick Carruthers	(323) 465-9494 www.helloandcompany.com	Todd Cole	(323) 465-5299 www.thedirectorsbureau.com
Carter and Blitz	(310) 558-3667 www.anonymouscontent.com	Jim Collins	(310) 550-6990 www.macguffin.com
Mac Carter	(310) 314-1122 www.backyard.com	Collision	(310) 275-9333 www.epochfilms.com
Tom Carty	(310) 558-3667 www.anonymouscontent.com	Pete Commins	(323) 468-0123 www.partizan.com
Bruce Caulk	(310) 882-2100 www.intelliscape.com	Michel Comte	(323) 653-0404 www.form.tv
Trevor Cawood	(310) 558-3667 www.anonymouscontent.com	Kevin Connolly	(310) 558-7100 www.hsiproductions.com
Tano Celentano	(310) 858-7204 www.labandafilms.com	Gil Cope	(323) 460-2077 www.darklightpictures.com
Jerry Chan	(310) 876-2278 www.ringleaderproductions.com	Roman Coppola	(323) 465-5299 www.thedirectorsbureau.com
Peter Chelsom	(310) 659-3503 www.independentmediainc.com	Sofia Coppola	(323) 465-5299 www.thedirectorsbureau.com
Alison Chernick	(323) 969-0555 www.awhitelabelproduct.com	Mark Coppos	(310) 656-4900 www.greendotfilms.com
Lisa Cholodenko	(323) 468-0123 www.partizan.com	Ericson Core	(310) 823-7445 www.wildplum.tv
Gotham Chopra	(310) 319-1990 www.curiouspictures.com	David Cornell	(323) 653-0404 www.form.tv
Roger Chouinard	(310) 478-0771 www.duckstudios.com	Alex Courtes	(323) 468-0123 www.partizan.com
Dana Christiaansen	(818) 906-0006 (310) 422-5044 www.thedirectorsnetwork.com	Gabriela Cowperthwaite	(310) 956-3500 www.sdintegrated.com

Brian Coyne	(818) 906-0006	Jan de Bont	(310) 823-7445
	www.thedirectorsnetwork.com		www.wildplum.tv
Simon Cracknell	(310) 526-7703	Feliz Fernandez de Castro	(310) 823-5400
	www.instantkarmafilms.tv		www.carbofilms.com
Simon Crane	(310) 659-3503	Tom De Cerchio	(310) 566-6733
	www.independentmediainc.com		www.incubatorfilms.com
Sam Crawford	(310) 659-6220	Michael J. DeCourcey	(310) 480-4031
	www.crossroadsfilms.com		www.decourcey.com
Rudy Crew	(323) 930-0101	Herve De Crecy	(310) 659-1577
	www.altavistafilms.com		www.littleminx.tv
Pablo Croce	(323) 932-6588	Augusto de Fraga	(310) 823-5400
	www.acatch22production.com		www.carbofilms.com
Jeff Cronenweth	(310) 917-9191	Lorenzo De Guia	(323) 790-1732
	www.untitled.tv		www.maneaterproductions.com
Tim Cronenweth	(310) 917-9191	Leslie Dektor	(323) 466-3455
	www.untitled.tv		www.the-cartel.tv
Paul Crowder	(310) 399-9600	Mark Dektor	(323) 466-3455
	www.nonfictionunlimited.com		www.the-cartel.tv
Cameron Crowe	(310) 857-1000	Paul Dektor	(323) 466-3455
	www.moxiepictures.com		www.the-cartel.tv
Michael Cuesta	(323) 650-4722	Delicatessen	(310) 478-0771
			www.duckstudios.com
Paul Cummings	(310) 478-0771		
	www.duckstudios.com	Carole Denis	(323) 645-1000
			www.believemedia.com
Dean Cundey	(626) 584-4000		
	www.danwolfe.com	David Denneen	(323) 653-0404
			www.form.tv
John Curran	(310) 854-0647		
	www.sandwickfilms.com	Paul and Menno De Nooijer	(323) 464-7805
			www.acmefilmworks.com
Victor Currie	(877) 741-5990		
	www.currie.tv	Alex De Rakoff	(323) 465-9494
			www.helloandcompany.com
	(323) 466-3455		
Werner Damen	(310) 260-6100	Caleb Deschanel	(323) 460-2077
	www.the-cartel.tv		www.darklightpictures.com
Tim Damon	(310) 632-4092	Gerard De Thame	(323) 645-1000
	FAX (310) 632-4092		www.believemedia.com
	www.squareplanetmedia.com		
		Martin De Thurah	(323) 465-9494
Greg Daniels	(310) 659-3503		www.helloandcompany.com
	www.independentmediainc.com		
		Alfred de Villa	(310) 858-7204
Jon Danovic	(310) 876-2278		www.labandafilms.com
	www.ringleader.pro		
		Rob Devor	(310) 399-9600
DarkFibre	(323) 957-5400		www.nonfictionunlimited.com
	www.picrow.com		
		Michael Dudok De Wit	(323) 464-7805
Jeffrey Darling	(323) 465-9494		www.acmefilmworks.com
	www.helloandcompany.com		
		Tom Dey	(310) 659-1577
Jakob Daschek	(310) 659-1577		www.rsafilms.com
	www.rsafilms.com		
		Jun Diaz	(323) 817-3300
Patrick Daughters	(323) 465-5299		www.smugglersite.com
	www.thedirectorsbureau.com		
		Nigel Dick	(323) 463-2826
Garth Davis	(310) 558-3667		www.dnala.com
	www.anonymouscontent.com		
		Brandon Dickerson	(310) 578-9383
Jake Davis	(323) 465-9494		www.kaboomproductions.com
	www.helloandcompany.com		
			(310) 659-1577
Jonathan Dayton	(310) 396-7333	Ben Dickinson	(323) 951-4400
	www.bobcentral.com		www.rsafilms.com
Evert de Beijer	(323) 464-7805	Devon Dickson	(818) 906-0006
	www.acmefilmworks.com		www.thedirectorsnetwork.com

Diego and Vlady	(323) 930-0101	Steve Dunning	(818) 906-0006
	www.altavistafilms.com		www.thedirectorsnetwork.com
Ray Dillman	(310) 826-6200	Claudio Duran	(323) 932-6588
	www.mjz.com		www.acatch22production.com
Matt Dilmore	(310) 275-9333	Jesse Dylan	(323) 951-0010
	www.epochfilms.com		www.wondros.com
John Dilworth	(323) 464-7805	Richard E.	(323) 464-5111
	www.acmefilmworks.com		www.showreel.com
The Directors Network	(818) 906-0006	Timothy Eaton	(866) 535-1972
(Reps for Commercial Directors)	FAX (818) 906-0007		www.veritestudios.com
	www.thedirectorsnetwork.com	Jared Eberhardt	(323) 468-0123
Abby Dix	(310) 567-2240		www.partizan.com
Jon Dixon	(310) 288-8000	Robert Eberlein	(310) 277-0070
	www.paradigmagency.com	Ryan Ebner	(310) 558-7100
Chris Do	(310) 314-1618		www.hsiproductions.com
	www.blind.com	Paul Edwards	(310) 288-8000
John Dolan	(323) 468-0123		www.paradigmagency.com
	www.partizan.com	Eagle Egilsson	(310) 857-7745
Kevin Dole	(310) 470-0491		www.attackads.tv
	FAX (310) 388-1399	Sean Ehringer	(310) 453-9244
Roger Donaldson	(310) 659-3503		www.toolofna.com
	www.independentmediainc.com	Chad Einbinder	(323) 464-3080
Andrew Douglas	(310) 558-3667		www.moostudios.com
	www.anonymouscontent.com	Mona El Monsouri	(310) 854-0647
Tony Dow	(310) 315-1750		www.sandwickmedia.com
	www.30secondfilms.com	Nabil Elderkin	(310) 659-1577
Bruce Dowad	(323) 645-1000		www.littleminx.tv
	www.believemedia.com	Filip Engstrom	(323) 817-3300
Michael Downing	(310) 275-9333		www.smugglersite.com
	www.epochfilms.com	Jesper Ericstam	(310) 314-1122
Niall Downing	(323) 468-0123		www.backyard.com
	www.partizan.com	Daniel Eskils	(323) 468-0123
Dr. Garry	(310) 857-7745		www.partizan.com
	www.attackads.tv	Bill Everett	(310) 314-8770
Shane Drake	(310) 823-7445		www.wyomingfilms.net
	www.wildplum.tv	Everynone	(310) 275-9333
Pau Driessen	(323) 464-7805		www.epochfilms.com
	www.acmefilmworks.com	Linus Ewers	(310) 917-9191
	(310) 450-1220		www.untitled.tv
David Dryer	(818) 906-0006	Matt Fackrell	(310) 578-9383
	www.thedirectorsnetwork.com		www.kaboomproductions.com
Rick Dublin	(323) 240-6736	Lauri Faggioni	(310) 659-1577
	www.motelfilms.com		www.rsafilms.com
Danny Ducovny	(310) 396-7778	Tenney Fairchild	(310) 899-9100
	www.cucoloris.com		www.m80films.com
Paul Dugdale	(323) 969-0555	Adriano Falconi	(323) 860-8030
	www.awhitelabelproduct.com		www.chelsea.com
Piotr Dumala	(323) 464-7805	Trey Fanjoy	(310) 260-6100
	www.acmefilmworks.com		www.motivfilms.com
Scott Duncan	(310) 319-1990	Darren Fanton	(414) 810-7851
	www.curiouspictures.com	Amir Farhang	(323) 860-8686
Laurence Dunmore	(310) 659-1577		www.ubercontent.com
	www.rsafilms.com	Valerie Faris	(310) 396-7333
Sean Dunne	(310) 399-9600		www.bobcentral.com
	www.nonfictionunlimited.com		

Richard Farmer	(310) 656-4900 www.greendotfilms.com	Raphael Frydman	(323) 468-0123 www.partizan.com
Jason Farrand	(310) 396-3636 www.aerofilm.tv	Paul Fuentes	(818) 990-8993 www.ambitiousent.com
Aaron Fedor	(310) 295-0848 www.blueyedpictures.com	Nick Fuglestad	(310) 550-6990 www.macguffin.com
Roderick Fenske	(310) 264-3000 www.hungryman.com	Nicolai Fuglsig	(310) 826-6200 www.mjz.com
Rafael Fernandez	(310) 656-4900 www.greendotfilms.com	Steve Fuller	(323) 785-6500 www.gofilm.net
Jeff Feuerzeig	(310) 659-1577 www.rsafilms.com	Antoine Fuqua	(323) 951-0010 www.wondros.com
David Fincher	(310) 558-3667 www.anonymouscontent.com	Andy G.	(310) 399-6630 www.rebelrobot.tv
Rod Findley	(310) 208-2324 www.c-2k.com	Jim Gable	(310) 979-4333 www.gandb.tv
Mauro Fiore	(310) 659-3503 www.independentmediainc.com	Stephen Gaghan	(323) 653-0404 www.form.tv
Matt Fischman	(323) 466-3455 www.the-cartel.tv	Mark Galanty	(310) 451-2525
Mo Fitzgibbon	(323) 469-6800 www.walkerfitzgibbon.com	Sidney Galanty	(310) 451-2525
		Andy Gallerani	(310) 399-6630
Ohav Flantz	(310) 828-8989 www.tateusa.com	Damon Gameau	(323) 464-3080 www.moostudios.com
Jeffrey Fleisig	(323) 860-8686 www.ubercontent.com	Pico Garcez	(818) 788-0153 www.fjproductions.com
E.J. Foerster	(310) 448-7900 www.rhythm.com	Elma Garcia	(323) 860-8686 www.ubercontent.com
Tom Foley	(310) 659-3503 www.independentmediainc.com	Rodrigo Garcia	(310) 858-7204 www.labandafilms.com
Roger Fonts	(310) 823-5400 www.carbofilms.com	Victor Garcia	(310) 826-6200 www.mjz.com
Brett Foraker	(310) 659-1577 www.rsafilms.com	Rodrigo Garcia-Saiz	(310) 559-8333 www.boxerfilms.net
Amanda Forbis	(323) 464-7805 www.acmefilmworks.com	Anthony Garth	(323) 790-1732 www.maneaterproductions.com
Danny Forster	(310) 319-1990 www.curiouspictures.com	James Gartner	(310) 899-1700 www.gartner.tv
Marc Forster	(310) 659-3503 www.independentmediainc.com	Francisco Garuti	(310) 858-7204 www.labandafilms.com
Claudia Forsthoevel	(310) 399-3456 www.cwuw.com	Tucker Gates	(310) 659-3503 www.independentmediainc.com
Ken Fox	(323) 930-0101 www.altavistafilms.com	Romain Gavras	(323) 465-5299 www.thedirectorsbureau.com
Justin Francis	(323) 465-9494 www.helloandcompany.com	Larry Gebhardt	(818) 906-0006 www.thedirectorsnetwork.com
David Frankel	(310) 659-3503 www.independentmediainc.com	Kim Geldenhuys	(310) 396-7333 www.bobcentral.com
David Frankham	(323) 817-3300 www.smugglersite.com	Michael Geoghegan	(323) 468-0123 www.partizan.com
Larry Frey	(310) 277-7001 www.companyfilms.net	Tryan George	(323) 645-1000 www.believemedia.com
Liz Friedlander	(323) 645-1000 www.believemedia.com	Luis Gerard	(323) 860-8686 www.ubercontent.com

Alex Gibney	(323) 860-8030 www.chelsea.com	Matt Goodman	(310) 559-5404 www.banditobrothers.com
Mark Gilbert	(323) 465-9494 www.helloandcompany.com	Dennie Gordon	(323) 785-6500 www.gofilm.net
Jim Gilchrist	(310) 826-6200 www.mjz.com	Seth Gordon	(310) 857-1000 www.moxiepictures.com
Stuart Gillard	(310) 288-8000 www.paradigmagency.com	Paul Gore	(323) 463-2826 www.dnala.com
Craig Gillespie	(310) 826-6200 www.mjz.com	Jeff Gorman	(310) 854-0647 www.sandwickfilms.com
Tony Gilroy	(310) 659-3503 www.independentmediainc.com	Neil Gorring	(310) 857-1000 www.moxiepictures.com
Bob Giraldi	(310) 274-6102 www.giraldi.com	Chris Gosch	(818) 729-0000 www.goschproductions.com
Francois Girard	(310) 659-3503 www.independentmediainc.com	Fred Goss	(310) 277-7001 www.companyfilms.net
Maxime Giroux	(310) 526-7703 www.instantkarmafilms.tv	Mike Goubeaux	(310) 823-7445 www.wildplum.tv
Michael Givens	(310) 444-7055 www.blueyedpictures.com	Alain Gourrier	(310) 526-7703 www.instantkarmafilms.tv
Peter Glanz	(323) 969-0555 www.awhitelabelproduct.com	Michael Gracey	(323) 468-0123 www.partizan.com
Jonathan Glazer	(323) 465-9494 www.helloandcompany.com	Chris Graham	(310) 828-8989 www.tateusa.com
Tim Godsall	(310) 275-9333 www.biscuitfilmworks.com	John Grammatico	(310) 277-7001 www.companyfilms.net
Eric Goldberg	(310) 478-0771 www.duckstudios.com	Paulo Grandra	(310) 264-3000 www.hungryman.com
Robert Golden	(818) 906-0006 www.thedirectorsnetwork.com	Martin Granger	(310) 857-1000 www.moxiepictures.com
Paul Goldman	(323) 468-0123 www.partizan.com	Evin Grant	(310) 444-7055 www.blueyedpictures.com
Adam Goldstein	(310) 453-2600 www.harvestfilms.com	Grapefruit	(310) 659-0010 www.newhousefilms.com
Tony Goldwyn	(310) 659-3503 www.independentmediainc.com	Michael Grasso	(310) 458-0663 www.passportfilms.com
Fabio Golombek	(818) 788-0153 www.fjproductions.com	David Gordon Green	(323) 860-8030 www.chelsea.com
Alfonso Gomez-Rejon	(310) 659-1577 www.rsafilms.com	Steph Green	(310) 659-1577 www.littleminx.tv
Michel Gondry	(323) 468-0123 www.partizan.com	Lauren Greenfield	(323) 860-8030 www.chelsea.com
Olivier Gondry	(323) 969-0555 www.awhitelabelproduct.com	David Griffiths	(310) 319-1990 www.curiouspictures.com
Sunu Gonera	(310) 288-8000 www.paradigmagency.com	James Griffiths	(310) 857-1000 www.moxiepictures.com
Alejandro González Inárritu	(310) 558-3667 www.anonymouscontent.com	Kamp Grizzly	(310) 823-7445 www.wildplum.tv
Gonzo	(310) 823-5400 www.carbofilms.com	Robert Groenwold	(310) 559-8333 www.boxerfilms.net
Miles Goodall	(323) 785-6500 www.gofilm.net	Ron Gross	(323) 658-6893 www.bluegoose.tv
James Gooding	(310) 264-3000 www.hungryman.com	Todd Grossman	(310) 295-0848 www.blueyedpictures.com

Commercial Directors

The Guard Brothers	(323) 817-3300 www.smugglersite.com	Jim Hardy	(323) 969-8822 www.illuminatehollywood.com
Christopher Guest	(323) 860-5400 www.gofilm.net	Rachel Harms	(310) 917-9191 www.untitled.tv
Davis Guggenheim	(310) 396-7333 www.bobcentral.com	Neil Harris	(323) 817-3300 www.smugglersite.com
Guillaume	(323) 650-4722	Ben Hartenstein	(310) 526-7703 www.instantkarmafilms.tv
Max Gutierrez	(310) 809-1778 www.maxgutierrez.net	Kent Harvey	(310) 699-3674 www.kentharvey.com
Ben Gutteridge	(323) 969-0555 www.awhitelabelproduct.com	Michael Haussman	(310) 558-7100 www.hsiproductions.com
Daniel Guyonnet	(323) 464-7805 www.acmefilmworks.com	James Haworth	(310) 264-3000 www.hungryman.com
Gonzalo Guzman	(323) 930-0101 www.altavistafilms.com	Blair Hayes	(323) 653-0404 www.form.tv
Banner Gwin	(323) 465-9494 www.helloandcompany.com	Todd Haynes	(310) 857-1000 www.moxiepictures.com
Jon Gwyther	(310) 526-7703 www.instantkarmafilms.tv	Peter Hedges	(310) 659-3503 www.independentmediainc.com
James Hackett	(310) 478-0771 www.duckstudios.com	Hannah Hempstead	(310) 306-3088 FAX (310) 306-3088
Norman Hafezi	(818) 906-0006 (310) 659-6220 www.thedirectorsnetwork.com	Stewart Hendler	(310) 559-5404 www.banditobrothers.com
Francois Halard	(323) 464-3080 www.moostudios.com	Henry and Rel	(310) 857-1000 www.moxiepictures.com
Robert Hales	(323) 465-9494 www.helloandcompany.com	Doug Henry	(323) 466-2490 www.kavichreynolds.com
Henrik Hallgren	(310) 695-3741 www.interrogate.com	Alvaro Hernandez	(310) 559-8333 www.boxerfilms.net
Jim Hallowes	(310) 390-4767 www.jimhallowes.com	Marshall Herskovitz	(310) 395-5022
Tim Hamilton	(323) 860-5400 www.gofilm.net	Jared Hess	(310) 857-1000 www.moxiepictures.com
Sanaa Hamri	(310) 659-6220 www.crossroadsfilms.com	Scott Hicks	(310) 659-3503 www.independentmediainc.com
Sean Hanish	(626) 395-7700 FAX (626) 395-7722 www.seanhanish.com	Fluorescent Hill	(323) 785-6500 www.gofilm.net
Henrik Hansen	(310) 659-1577 www.rsafilms.com	Laurie Hill	(310) 659-3503 www.independentmediainc.com
Pamela Hanson	(323) 464-3080 www.moostudios.com	Thomas Hilland	(323) 468-0123 www.partizan.com
Happycamper	(310) 319-1990 www.curiouspictures.com	Chris Hinton	(323) 464-7805 www.acmefilmworks.com
Alex Hardcastle	(310) 659-3503 www.independentmediainc.com	Cameron Hird	(310) 458-0663 www.passportfilms.com
Phil Harder	(310) 396-7333 www.bobcentral.com	Steven M. Hirohama	(310) 204-0520 FAX (310) 202-1386 www.applebox.com
Chris Harding	(310) 478-0771 www.duckstudios.com	Kris Hixson	(310) 871-1506 www.i40films.com
Johnny Hardstaff	(310) 659-1577 www.littleminx.com	The Hodges	(310) 798-6332 www.wyomingfilms.com
Corin Hardy	(323) 465-9494 www.helloandcompany.com	Matthias Hoene	(323) 468-0123 www.partizan.com

The Hoffman Brothers	(310) 453-2600	Jesse Jacobs	(310) 717-0708
	www.harvestfilms.com		www.jessestudio.com
Andreas Hoffman	(310) 854-0647	Kim Jacobs	(310) 656-4900
	www.sandwickmedia.com		www.greendotfilms.com
Florian Hoffmeister	(323) 957-5400	Enno Jacobsen	(310) 828-8989
	www.picrow.com		www.tateusa.com
Greg Holfeld	(323) 464-7805	Price James	(310) 659-1577
	www.acmefilmworks.com		www.rsafilms.com
King Hollis	(323) 665-4198	Steve James	(310) 399-9600
	www.alteregofilms.com		www.nonfictionunlimited.com
Wayne Holloway	(323) 645-1000	Michael Patrick Jann	(323) 465-9494
	www.believemedia.com		www.helloandcompany.com
David Holm	(310) 956-3500	Mikael Jansson	(323) 969-0555
	www.sdintegrated.com		www.awhitelabelproduct.com
Nicole Holofcener	(310) 659-3503		(310) 558-3667
	www.independentmediainc.com	Garth Jennings	(323) 969-0555
			www.anonymouscontent.com
Chris Hooper	(323) 860-8686	Joe Jennings	(310) 305-8200
	www.ubercontent.com		www.900frames.tv
Tom Hooper	(323) 817-3300	Charles Jensen	(323) 785-6500
	www.smugglersite.com		www.gofilm.net
Cameron Hopkins	(323) 464-2406	Robert Jitzmark	(310) 656-4900
	www.47pictures.com		www.greendotfilms.com
Jason House	(323) 957-5400	JL Design	(310) 478-0771
	www.picrow.com		www.duckstudios.com
Arturo Hoyos	(310) 338-0580	Phil Joanou	(310) 826-6200
	www.utopiafilms.com		www.mjz.com
Ricardo Hoyos	(310) 338-0580	Bryan Johnson	(323) 938-8080
	www.utopiafilms.com		
Andy Huang	(323) 464-3080	Erich Joiner	(310) 453-9244
	www.moostudios.com		www.toolofna.com
Steve Hudson	(310) 264-3000	Bronston Jones	(310) 857-7745
	www.hungryman.com		www.attackads.tv
Maureen Hufnagel	(310) 559-8333	Jeff Jones	(818) 906-0006
	www.boxerfilms.net		www.thedirectorsnetwork.com
Allen Hughes	(323) 645-1000	Kirk Jones	(323) 466-3455
	www.believemedia.com		www.the-cartel.tv
Greg Hughs	(310) 305-8200	Nick Jones	(310) 277-7001
	www.900frames.tv		www.companyfilms.net
Mat Humphrey	(310) 828-8989	Tomas Jonsgarden	(310) 558-3667
	www.tateusa.com		www.anonymouscontent.com
Bruce Hunt	(323) 860-8030	Arni Thor Jonsson	(310) 392-7333
	www.chelsea.com		www.thomaswintercooke.com
Anthony Hurd	(323) 464-7805	Spike Jonze	(310) 826-6200
	www.acmefilmworks.com		www.mjz.com
Bruce Hurwit	(310) 659-6220	Anton Josef	(310) 559-8333
	www.crossroadsfilms.com		www.boxerfilms.net
Impactist	(310) 478-0771	Jaci Judelson	(310) 558-7100
	www.duckstudios.com		www.hsiproductions.com
Wayne Isham	(323) 951-0010	Gil Junger	(310) 288-8000
	www.wondros.com		www.paradigmagency.com
Michael Ivey	(310) 314-8770	Laszlo Kadar	(310) 392-7333
	www.wyomingfilms.net		www.thomaswintercooke.com
Eric Jackson	(323) 464-5111	Joseph Kahn	(310) 558-7100
	www.showreel.com		www.hsiproductions.com

Janusz Kaminski	(310) 659-3503
	www.independentmediainc.com
	(323) 468-0123
Nadav Kander	(323) 860-8030
	www.partizan.com
Kang/Seong	(310) 478-0771
	www.duckstudios.com
Shekhar Kapur	(310) 319-1990
	www.curiouspictures.com
Michael Karbelnikoff	(323) 465-9494
	www.helloandcompany.com
Dean Karr	(323) 876-3331
	www.wildindigo.tv
Geoffrey Katar	(818) 225-1541
	www.mcreativegroup.net
David Katz	(818) 533-1937
	FAX (310) 589-1565
	davidkatzproductions.com
Jeff Kaumeyer	(310) 396-5796
	www.detourfilms.com
Lance Kelleher	(323) 653-0404
	www.form.tv
Rory Kelleher	(323) 645-1000
	www.believemedia.com
Rory Kelleher	(323) 645-1000
	www.believemedia.com
David Kellogg	(310) 558-3667
	www.anonymouscontent.com
Richard Kelly	(310) 659-3503
	www.independentmediainc.com
Timothy Kendall	(310) 448-7900
	www.rhythm.com
Billy Kent	(818) 906-0006
	www.thedirectorsnetwork.com
Darius Khondji	(323) 969-0555
	www.awhitelabelproduct.com
Eric Kiel	(310) 260-6100
	www.motivfilms.com
Karl Kimbrough	(323) 665-4198
	www.alteregofilms.com
Jim Kimura	(323) 559-1110
	FAX (626) 398-1387
	www.tdnartists.com
Justin Klarenbeck	(310) 559-8333
	www.boxerfilms.net
Ariel Kleiman	(323) 468-0123
	www.partizan.com
Isaac Klotz	(323) 620-6925
	www.halfelement.com
Rick Knief	(310) 917-9191
	www.untitled.tv
Rene Kock	(310) 399-3456
	www.cwuw.com
Tom Koh	(310) 314-1618
	www.blind.com

Jason Kohn	(323) 860-8686
	www.ubercontent.com
Kompost	(310) 478-0771
	www.duckstudios.com
Jeremy Konner	(323) 468-0123
	www.partizan.com
Barbara Kopple	(310) 399-9600
	www.nonfictionunlimited.com
Aleksandra Korejwo	(323) 464-7805
	www.acmefilmworks.com
Harmony Korine	(310) 826-6200
	www.mjz.com
Joe Kosinski	(310) 558-3667
	www.anonymouscontent.com
Jesper Kouthoofd	(310) 659-1577
	www.littleminx.tv
Igor Kovalyov	(323) 464-7805
	www.acmefilmworks.com
Torill Kove	(323) 464-7805
	www.acmefilmworks.com
Bo Krabbe	(310) 526-7703
	www.instantkarmafilms.tv
Rob Kraetsch	(323) 620-6925
	www.halfelement.com
Brandon Kraines	(310) 288-8000
	www.paradigmagency.com
Randy Krallman	(323) 817-3300
	www.smugglersite.com
Johan Kramer	(323) 860-8030
	www.chelsea.com
Sue Kramer	(212) 674-1400
	www.curiouspictures.com
Bob Kronovet	(310) 315-1750
	www.30secondfilms.com
Raimund Krumme	(323) 464-7805
	www.acmefilmworks.com
Chuck Kuhn	(310) 314-8770
	www.wyomingfilms.net
Tom Kuntz	(310) 826-6200
	www.mjz.com
Warren Kushner	(310) 393-4200
	www.kfilms.us
Jeff Labbe	(310) 695-3741
	www.interrogate.com
David LaChapelle	(310) 558-7100
	www.hsiproductions.com
Dave Laden	(310) 264-3000
	www.hungryman.com
Richard LaGravenese	(310) 659-3503
	www.independentmediainc.com
Adri Laham	(310) 858-7204
	www.labandafilms.com
Brian Lai	(310) 526-7703
	www.instantkarmafilms.tv

Christian Lamb	(323) 969-0555	Elyse Lewin	(213) 798-3320
	www.awhitelabelproduct.com		www.elyselewin.com
Ken Lambert	(310) 392-7333	Taron Lexton	(310) 288-8000
	www.thomaswintercooke.com		www.paradigmagency.com
Lou La Monte	(310) 656-9100	Leslie Libman	(323) 653-0404
	www.epixfilms.com		www.form.tv
Luis Lance	(323) 930-0101	Mark Liddell	(323) 465-9494
	www.altavistafilms.com		www.helloandcompany.com
Chris Landreth	(323) 464-7805	Ron Lieberman	(323) 653-0404
	www.acmefilmworks.com		www.form.tv
Lane and Jan	(310) 478-0771	Doug Liman	(310) 659-3503
	www.duckstudios.com		www.independentmediainc.com
Rocky Lane	(818) 906-0006	Peter Lindbergh	(323) 969-0555
	www.thedirectorsnetwork.com		www.awhitelabelproduct.com
Marcel Langenegger	(310) 899-1700	Scott Evans Lindsay	(310) 291-4999
	www.gartner.tv		www.youtube.com/SevansLindsay#p/u
Lance Larson	(310) 883-7800	William Linsman	(310) 450-1220
	www.japanesemonster.com		www.oceanparkpix.com
Axel Laubscher	(310) 396-7333	Steven Lippman	(323) 790-1732
	www.bobcentral.com		www.maneaterproductions.com
Christoph and Wolfgang Lauenstein	(323) 464-7805	Little Fluffy Clouds	(310) 319-1990
	www.acmefilmworks.com		www.curiouspictures.com
Francis Lawrence	(323) 463-2826	Henry Littlechild	(310) 695-3741
	www.dnala.com		www.interrogate.com
Tom Lazarevich	(310) 274-6102	Nick Livesey	(310) 659-1577
	www.giraldi.com		www.rsafilms.com
Caroline Leaf	(323) 464-7805	Walt Lloyd	(818) 729-0000
	www.acmefilmworks.com		www.goschproductions.com
Ringan Ledwidge	(323) 817-3300	Brent Loefke	(866) 711-5195
	www.smugglersite.com		www.jspcreative.com
Rich Lee	(323) 463-2826	Robert Logevall	(310) 956-3500
	www.dnala.com		www.sdintegrated.com
Rob Legato	(310) 857-1000	Loki	(323) 969-0555
	www.moxiepictures.com		www.awhitelabelproduct.com
Danny Leiner	(310) 659-3503	Mike Long	(310) 275-9333
	www.independentmediainc.com		www.epochfilms.com
Gregory Lemkin	(310) 450-1220 (310) 991-9595	Peter Long	(323) 957-5400
	www.oceanparkpix.com		www.picrow.com
Rick LeMoine	(323) 860-8030	Christian Loubek	(310) 558-3667
	www.chelsea.com		www.anonymouscontent.com
Yoann Lemoine	(310) 558-7100	Susan Loughlin	(323) 464-7805
	www.hsiproductions.com		www.acmefilmworks.com
Matt Lenski	(310) 956-3500	Jeff Low	(323) 856-9200
	www.sdintegrated.com		www.biscuitfilmworks.com
Dana Leshem	(310) 986-3370	Henry Lu	(310) 857-1000
	www.24pcine.com		www.moxiepictures.com
K. Asher Levin	(323) 465-9494	Julien Lutz	(323) 463-2826
	www.helloandcompany.com		www.dnala.com
James Levine	(818) 817-4341 (818) 554-8019 FAX (818) 728-6785	Reynir Lyngdal	(310) 578-9383
			www.kaboomproductions.com
	www.typecastinginc.com	Eric Lynne	(323) 468-0123
			www.partizan.com
Dan Levinson	(310) 857-1000	Scott Lyon	(310) 695-3741
	www.moxiepictures.com		www.interrogate.com

Commercial Directors

m-i-e	(310) 264-3000	Allen Martinez	(323) 362-2660
	www.hungryman.com		allen_martinez.prosite.com
M.I.X.	(310) 338-0580	Vanessa Marzaroli	(310) 314-1618
	www.utopiafilms.com		www.blind.com
Toby Macdonald	(323) 468-0123	Renny Maslow	(323) 817-3300
	www.partizan.com		www.smugglersite.com
Asa Mader	(323) 969-0555	Adam Massey	(310) 917-9191
	www.awhitelabelproduct.com		www.untitled.tv
	(323) 465-5299	Zach Math	(310) 396-7333
Mike Maguire	(323) 856-9200		www.bobcentral.com
	www.thedirectorsbureau.com	Tim Matheson	(310) 396-3636
Main Frame	(310) 478-0771		www.aerofilm.tv
	www.duckstudios.com	Camilo Matiz	(323) 932-6588
Margaret Malandruccolo	(323) 957-5400		www.acatch22production.com
	www.picrow.com	Michael Maxxis	(323) 463-2826
Samir Mallal	(323) 817-3300		www.dnala.com
	www.smugglersite.com	Albert Maysles	(310) 399-9600
Marcel Mallio	(310) 581-1100		www.nonfictionunlimited.com
	www.filmplanet.com	Ross McCanse	(818) 506-4715
Malloys	(310) 558-7100	Jeffrey McCarthy	(323) 464-3080
	www.hsiproductions.com		www.moostudios.com
Jorge Malpica	(310) 823-5400	Wayne McClammy	(310) 264-3000
	www.carbofilms.com		www.hungryman.com
Luis Mandoki	(310) 858-7204	David McClister	(323) 463-2826
	www.labandafilms.com		www.dnala.com
Carlos Manga Jr.	(323) 969-0555	Marcus McCollum	(323) 465-9494
	www.awhitelabelproduct.com		www.helloandcompany.com
James Mangold	(310) 396-3636	Mike McCoy	(310) 559-5404
	www.aerofilm.tv		www.banditobrothers.com
Vesa Manninen	(310) 695-3741	Scott McCullough	(310) 437-3518
	www.interrogate.com		www.scottmccullough.com
Mattieu Mantovani	(310) 828-8989	Melodie McDaniel	(323) 465-5299
	www.tateusa.com		www.thedirectorsbureau.com
Maurice Marable	(323) 645-1000	Craig McDean	(323) 969-0555
	www.believemedia.com		www.awhitelabelproduct.com
Marandi/Heath	(310) 277-7001	Kevin McDonald	(323) 860-8030
	www.companyfilms.net		www.chelsea.com
Gregory Marquette	(818) 990-8993	Geoff McFetridge	(323) 465-5299
	www.ambitiousent.com		www.thedirectorsbureau.com
Stephen Marro	(310) 305-8200		(323) 653-0404
	www.900frames.tv	Gary McKendry	(310) 396-3636
Chris Marrs Piliero	(323) 465-9494		www.form.tv
	www.helloandcompany.com	David McNally	(310) 277-7001
Joel Marsden	(310) 458-0663		www.companyfilms.net
	www.passportfilms.com	Charles Mehling	(323) 860-8030
Rob Marshall	(310) 857-1000		www.chelsea.com
	www.moxiepictures.com	Robert Mehnert	(626) 584-4000
Diane Martel	(310) 558-7100		www.danwolfe.com
	www.hsiproductions.com	Amit Mehta	(310) 695-3741
Glenn Martin	(310) 917-9191		www.interrogate.com
	www.untitled.tv	Meindbender	(310) 478-0771
Jay Martin	(323) 463-2826		www.duckstudios.com
	www.dnala.com	Theodore Melfi	(310) 899-1700
Patricia Martinez de Velasco	(310) 858-7204		www.gartner.tv
	www.labandafilms.com		

Rob Meltzer	(323) 466-2490
	www.kavichreynolds.com
	(323) 876-5123
Nick Mendoza	(323) 842-3004
	www.mendozagomez.com
Hugo Menduina	(310) 314-1122
	www.backyard.com
Dave Merhar	(323) 462-1220
	www.mortarinc.com
E. Elias Merhige	(310) 659-3503
	www.independentmediainc.com
Matt Miadich	(310) 396-5796
	www.detourfilms.com
David Michalek	(323) 969-0555
	www.awhitelabelproduct.com
Paul Middleditch	(323) 969-0555
	www.awhitelabelproduct.com
Thomas Mignone	(310) 927-6661
	www.doominc.com
	(323) 817-3300
Bennett Miller	(310) 264-3000
	www.smugglersite.com
Jefferson Miller	(323) 876-3331
	www.wildindigo.tv
Josh Miller	(310) 659-1577
	www.littleminx.com
Mike Miller	(818) 990-8993
	www.ambitiousent.com
Robin Miller	(818) 225-1541
	www.mcreativegroup.net
Paul Minor	(323) 466-3455
	www.the-cartel.tv
Monty Miranda	(310) 458-0663
	www.passportfilms.com
Bo Mirosseni	(323) 468-0123
	www.partizan.com
John Cameron Mitchell	(323) 969-0555
	www.awhitelabelproduct.com
Adrian Moat	(310) 659-1577
	www.rsafilms.com
Francis Mohajerin	(310) 727-2600
	www.megahertzpictures.com
Hans Moland	(310) 392-7333
	www.thomaswintercooke.com
Jean-Baptiste Mondino	(323) 463-2826
	www.dnala.com
Monkmus	(310) 478-0771
	www.duckstudios.com
Ben Mor	(310) 659-1577
	www.littleminx.tv
Flavia Moraes	(310) 581-1100
	www.filmplanet.com
Andy Morahan	(323) 645-1000
	www.believemedia.com
Brett Morgan	(310) 558-3667
	www.anonymouscontent.com

Jay P. Morgan	(818) 957-9002
Errol Morris	(310) 857-1000
	www.moxiepictures.com
Brad Morrison	(310) 577-0700
	www.slim-pictures.com
Phil Morrison	(310) 275-9333
	www.epochfilms.com
David R. Morton	(323) 665-4198
	www.alteregofilms.com
Rocky Morton	(310) 826-6200
	www.mjz.com
Caroline Mouris	(323) 464-7805
	www.acmefilmworks.com
Frank Mouris	(323) 464-7805
	www.acmefilmworks.com
David Mueller	(310) 727-2600
	www.megahertzpictures.com
Michael Muller	(323) 860-8030
	www.chelsea.com
Alan Munro	(310) 394-0110
	www.movingtargetla.com
Yorico Murakami	(310) 478-0771
	www.duckstudios.com
Steven Murashige	(323) 650-4722
Dom Murgia	(818) 906-0006
	www.thedirectorsnetwork.com
Dominic Murphy	(323) 468-0123
	www.partizan.com
Scott Murphy	(866) 711-5195
	www.jspcreative.com
Malcolm Murray	(323) 856-9200
	www.biscuitfilmworks.com
Noam Murro	(323) 856-9200
	www.biscuitfilmworks.com
Ken Musen	(310) 208-2324
	www.c-2k.com
Thomas Napper	(310) 558-7100
	www.hsiproductions.com
Jake Nava	(323) 645-1000
	www.believemedia.com
Joshua Neale	(323) 817-3300
	www.smugglersite.com
Chris Neilson	(310) 558-7100
	www.hsiproductions.com
Mike Nelesen	(310) 659-6220
	www.crossroadsfilms.com
Rich Newey	(310) 288-8000
	www.paradigmagency.com
Nic and Sune	(310) 854-0647
	www.sandwickfilms.com
Doug Nichol	(323) 468-0123
	www.partizan.com
Max Nichols	(323) 465-9494
	www.helloandcompany.com

Dewey Nicks	(310) 888-8900
	www.villains.com
Nico and Martin	(310) 659-1577
	www.littleminx.tv
Nicolas	(310) 338-0580
	www.utopiafilms.com
Andreas Nilsson	(323) 856-9200
	www.biscuitfilmworks.com
Marcus Nispel	(310) 826-6200
	www.mjz.com
NMA	(310) 478-0771
	www.duckstudios.com
Alex Noble	(310) 822-2147
	www.residentfilms.tv
Nobuhito Noda	(310) 752-7183
Guy Norman Bee	(310) 828-8443
	www.tuesdayfilms.com
Mehdi Norowzian	(323) 465-9494
	www.helloandcompany.com
Ace Norton	(323) 468-0123
	www.partizan.com
Nima Nourizadeh	(323) 468-0123
	www.partizan.com
David Nutter	(310) 453-2600
	www.harvestfilms.com
Peter Nydrle	(310) 659-8844
	www.nydrle.com
Steve Oakes	(310) 319-1990
	www.curiouspictures.com
Klaus Obermeyer	(310) 396-3636
	www.aerofilm.tv
Bob Odenkirk	(310) 396-7333
	www.bobcentral.com
Matt Ogens	(310) 453-9244
	www.toolofna.com
John O'Hagan	(310) 659-1577
	www.rsafilms.com
Sam O'Hare	(310) 396-3636
	www.aerofilm.tv
Jarl Olsen	(323) 240-6736
	www.motelfilms.com
James O'Neil	(323) 876-6853
Jim O'Neil	(310) 470-0491
Opel	(310) 526-7703
	www.instantkarmafilms.tv
Alex Oqus	(310) 392-7333
	www.thomaswintercooke.com
Estevan Oriol	(310) 823-5400
	www.carbofilms.com
Oury and Thomas	(323) 464-7805
	www.acmefilmworks.com
Jim Owen	(323) 468-0123
	www.partizan.com

Angelo Pacifici	(310) 313-3762
	(818) 990-8993
	FAX (310) 745-1949
	www.ambitiousent.com
Nina Paley	(310) 478-0771
	www.duckstudios.com
Chris Palmer	(310) 558-3667
	www.anonymouscontent.com
Hsin-Ping Pan	(310) 478-0771
	www.duckstudios.com
Scott Papera	(310) 809-1910
	www.alteregofilms.tv/scottpapera
Brian Papierski	(310) 305-8200
	www.900frames.tv
Brad Parker	(310) 396-7333
	www.bobcentral.com
Harry Patramanis	(323) 653-0404
	(310) 277-7001
	www.form.tv
Chris Patterson	(310) 209-8974
	www.ranchexitfilms.com
Alexander Paul	(310) 314-1122
	www.backyard.com
Charlie Paul	(323) 464-2406
	www.47pictures.com
Daniel Peacock	(310) 478-0771
	www.duckstudios.com
Sam Peacocke	(310) 396-7333
	www.bobcentral.com
Rob Pearlstein	(323) 860-5400
	www.gofilm.net
Barbara Peeters	(818) 729-0000
	www.goschproductions.com
Mark Pellington	(323) 951-0010
	www.wondros.com
Stacy Peralta	(310) 399-9600
	www.nonfictionunlimited.com
Jesse Peretz	(310) 659-1577
	www.rsafilms.com
John Perez	(310) 260-6100
	www.motivfilms.com
Luc Perez	(323) 464-7805
	www.acmefilmworks.com
Hank Perlman	(310) 264-3000
	www.hungryman.com
Janet Perlman	(323) 464-7805
	www.acmefilmworks.com
PES	(310) 558-3667
	www.anonymouscontent.com
Suthon Petchsuwan	(310) 392-7333
	www.thomaswintercooke.com
Adria Petty	(323) 969-0555
	www.awhitelabelproduct.com
Wally Pfister	(310) 659-3503
	www.independentmediainc.com

Todd Philips	(310) 857-1000	Psyop	(323) 817-3300
	www.moxiepictures.com		www.smugglersite.com
Sean MacLeod Phillips	(310) 395-4739	Gualter Pupo	(310) 264-3000
			www.hungryman.com
Kevin Pike	(818) 808-9321	Purchase Brothers	(310) 558-3667
	www.filmtrix.com		www.anonymouscontent.com
James Pilkington	(323) 969-0555	Bob Purman	(310) 857-1000
	www.awhitelabelproduct.com		www.moxiepictures.com
Marco Pinesi	(310) 526-7703	Barry Purves	(323) 464-7805
	www.instantkarmafilms.tv		www.acmefilmworks.com
Nick Piper	(310) 314-1122	Joe Pytka	(310) 392-9571
	www.backyard.com		
Valerie Pirson	(323) 468-0123	The Brothers Quay	(323) 465-9494
	www.partizan.com		www.helloandcompany.com
Martin Pitts	(323) 931-9962	Christopher Quinn	(323) 860-8030
			www.chelsea.com
Jeffery Plansker	(310) 956-3500	Joanna Quinn	(323) 464-7805
	www.sdintegrated.com		www.acmefilmworks.com
Bo Platt	(323) 645-1000	Marcus Raboy	(323) 463-2826
	www.believemedia.com		www.dnala.com
Pleix	(310) 826-6200	Jamie Rafn	(323) 817-3300
	www.mjz.com		www.smugglersite.com
Hervé Plumet	(323) 468-0123	Fred Raimondi	(818) 990-8993
	www.partizan.com		www.ambitiousent.com
Michael Polish	(310) 559-5404	Paul Raimondi	(760) 837-1093
	www.banditobrothers.com		www.raimondifilms.com
Tim Pope	(323) 969-0555	Lynne Ramsay	(323) 465-9494
	www.awhitelabelproduct.com		www.helloandcompany.com
David Popescu	(310) 828-8989	David Ramser	(323) 650-4722
	www.tateusa.com		(310) 823-5400
Greg Popp	(310) 956-3500		www.theartistscompany.com
	www.sdintegrated.com	Scott Randall	(323) 930-0101
Popular Society	(323) 464-2406		www.altavistafilms.com
	www.47pictures.com	Gitaniali Rao	(323) 464-7805
Afonso Povart	(323) 464-7805		www.acmefilmworks.com
	www.acmefilmworks.com	Mark Rasmussen	(323) 224-9051
William Powloski	(310) 376-7870	Brett Ratner	(310) 558-7100
	www.velocityfx.com		www.hsiproductions.com
Jose Antonio Pray	(310) 858-7204	Eliot Rausch	(323) 860-8686
	www.labandafilms.com		www.ubercontent.com
Jeff Preiss	(310) 275-9333	Juston Reardon	(310) 558-3667
	www.epochfilms.com		www.anonymouscontent.com
Mac Premo	(310) 956-3500	Eugenio Recuenco	(323) 969-0555
	www.sdintegrated.com		www.awhitelabelproduct.com
Claudio Prestia	(310) 559-8333	Adam Reed	(310) 917-9191
	www.boxerfilms.net		www.untitled.tv
Leland Price	(310) 915-0366	Peyton Reed	(310) 857-1000
	www.lelandprice.com		www.moxiepictures.com
Sarah Price	(310) 659-3503	Sebastian Reed	(310) 659-1577
	www.independentmediainc.com		www.littleminx.tv
Rodrigo Prieto	(310) 659-1577	Matt Reeves	(310) 659-3503
	www.littleminx.tv		www.independentmediainc.com
Rob Pritts	(310) 314-1122	Richard Reiss	(818) 906-0006
	www.backyard.com		www.thedirectorsnetwork.com
Joel Pront	(323) 645-1000	Jason Reitman	(310) 828-8989
	www.believemedia.com		www.tateusa.com

Commercial Directors

Trent Reznor	(323) 951-0010 www.wondros.com	Roger Roth	(818) 901-1178 (310) 963-4812 FAX (818) 901-1179
Scott Rhea	(310) 260-6100 www.motivfilms.com	James Rouse	(310) 695-3741 www.interrogate.com
Leonardo Ricagni	(310) 559-5404 www.banditobrothers.com	Jorge Rubia	(323) 932-6588 www.acatch22production.com
Paul Riccio	(310) 854-0647 www.sandwickmedia.com	Henry-Alex Rubin	(323) 817-3300 www.smugglersite.com
Tony Richards	(818) 990-8993 www.ambitiousent.com	Ondrej Rudavsky	(818) 990-8993 www.ambitiousent.com
Robert Richardson	(310) 453-9244 www.toolofna.com	Aaron Ruell	(323) 856-9200 www.biscuitfilmworks.com
Tim Richardson	(323) 969-0555 www.awhitelabelproduct.com	George Marshall Ruge	(310) 288-8000 www.paradigmagency.com
Branscombe Richmond	(310) 315-1750 www.30secondfilms.com	Mike Ruiz	(323) 463-2826 www.dnala.com
Thomas Richter	(310) 559-8333 www.boxerfilms.net	Mark Russel	(310) 260-6100 www.motivfilms.com
Ricki and Annie	(310) 578-9383 www.kaboomproductions.com	David O. Russell	(323) 951-0010 www.wondros.com
Stuart Rideout	(310) 659-6220 www.crossroadsfilms.com	Erica Russell	(323) 464-7805 www.acmefilmworks.com
Terry Rietta	(310) 392-7333 www.thomaswintercooke.com	Saboteur	(310) 458-0663 www.passportfilms.com
Christopher Riggert	(323) 856-9200 www.biscuitfilmworks.com	Saint & Mather	(323) 969-0555 www.awhitelabelproduct.com
Carl Erik Rinsch	(310) 659-1577 www.rsafilms.com	Jorge Salinas	(323) 932-6588 www.acatch22production.com
Randy Roberts	(310) 319-1990 www.curiouspictures.com	Salmon	(310) 854-0647 www.sandwickmedia.com
Gary Robinson	(310) 247-0818 FAX (310) 858-2254 www.sharpcut.com	Ari Sandel	(310) 458-0663 www.passportfilms.com
Ruairi Robinson	(323) 969-0555 www.awhitelabelproduct.com	Jessica Sanders	(310) 275-9333 www.epochfilms.com
Roenberg	(310) 854-0647 www.sandwickfilms.com	Rupert Sanders	(310) 826-6200 www.mjz.com
Steve Rogers	(323) 856-9200 www.biscuitfilmworks.com	Albert Saquer	(310) 823-5400 www.carbofilms.com
Mark Romanek	(310) 558-3667 www.anonymouscontent.com	Fernando Sarinana	(323) 461-0101 www.altavistafilms.com
Chris Romano	(310) 478-0771 www.duckstudios.com	Fred Savage	(323) 860-8686 www.ubercontent.com
Aaron Rose	(323) 465-5299 www.thedirectorsbureau.com	Malik H. Sayeed	(310) 659-1577 www.littleminx.com
Anthony Rose	(323) 464-3080 www.moostudios.com	Rocky Schenck	(323) 463-2826 www.dnala.com
Jocob Rosenberg	(310) 559-5404 www.banditobrothers.com	Paul Schneider	(323) 465-9494 www.helloandcompany.com
Brent Roske	(310) 867-5366 www.roskefilm.com	Marc Schölermann	(323) 860-8686 www.ubercontent.com
Rosto	(323) 464-7805 www.acmefilmworks.com	Ludovic Schorno	(310) 577-0700 www.slim-pictures.com
David Adam Roth	(310) 559-8333 www.boxerfilms.net	Luc Schurgers	(310) 656-4900 www.greendotfilms.com

Bob Schwartz	(323) 851-5151	Marcos Siega	(310) 264-3000
			www.hungryman.com
Daniel Schweizer	(323) 969-0555	Thomas Sigel	(310) 854-0647
	www.awhitelabelproduct.com		www.sandwickfilms.com
Bradley Scott	(323) 790-1732	Floria Sigismondi	(323) 645-1000
	www.maneaterproductions.com		www.believemedia.com
Corbett Scott	(310) 883-7800	Brian Silva	(323) 620-6925
	www.japanesemonster.com		www.halfelement.com
Jake Scott	(310) 659-1577	Evan Silver	(310) 453-9244
	www.rsafilms.com		www.toolofna.com
Jordan Scott	(310) 659-1577	Marc Silver	(323) 957-5400
	www.rsafilms.com		www.picrow.com
Luke Scott	(310) 659-1577		(310) 739-7356
	www.rsafilms.com	Tim Silver	(310) 399-5122
Tony Scott	(310) 659-1577	Jay Silverman	(323) 466-6030
	www.rsafilms.com		www.jaysilverman.com
Stephane Sednaoui	(323) 969-0555	Sabrina D. Simmons	(323) 939-5711
	www.awhitelabelproduct.com		
Kosai Sekine	(818) 906-0006	Christopher Sims	(323) 463-2826
	www.thedirectorsnetwork.com		www.dnala.com
The Selby	(310) 399-9600	John Singleton	(310) 659-3503
	www.nonfictionunlimited.com		www.independentmediainc.com
Maureen Selwood	(310) 478-0771	Johan Skoq	(310) 392-7333
	www.duckstudios.com		www.thomaswintercooke.com
Shaun Sewter	(323) 464-3080	Holly Goldberg Sloan	(310) 450-1220
	www.moostudios.com		www.oceanparkpix.com
Toben Seymour	(310) 659-1577	Baker Smith	(310) 453-2600
	www.littleminx.tv		www.harvestfilms.com
Dawn Shadforth	(310) 659-1577	Carter Smith	(323) 969-0555
	www.littleminx.com		www.awhitelabelproduct.com
Gary Shaffer	(310) 578-9383	Chris Smith	(323) 817-3300
	www.kaboomproductions.com		www.smugglersite.com
Jerry Shanks	(818) 506-0502	Jim Field Smith	(310) 659-1577
	FAX (818) 506-0502		www.littleminx.tv
Guy Shelmerdine	(323) 817-3300		(310) 314-1122
	www.smugglersite.com	Kevin Smith	(310) 857-1000
Jim Sheridan	(310) 857-1000		www.backyard.com
	www.moxiepictures.com	Austin Smithard	(310) 396-3636
Larry Shiu	(310) 526-7703		www.aerofilm.tv
	www.instantkarmafilms.tv	SMOG	(310) 478-0771
Gary Shore	(310) 558-3667		www.duckstudios.com
	www.anonymouscontent.com	Roberto Sneider	(310) 858-7204
Wade Shotter	(323) 969-0555		www.labandafilms.com
	www.awhitelabelproduct.com	Skott Snider	(818) 906-0006
Ed Shumacher	(310) 883-7800		www.thedirectorsnetwork.com
	www.japanesemonster.com	Snorri Bros.	(310) 695-3741
Shynola	(323) 465-5299		www.interrogate.com
	www.thedirectorsbureau.com	Zack Snyder	(323) 645-1000
Si & Ad	(323) 465-9494		www.believemedia.com
	www.helloandcompany.com	Michael Socha	(323) 464-7805
Alastair Siddons	(323) 468-0123		www.acmefilmworks.com
	www.partizan.com	Marcus Soderlund	(323) 465-9494
Trish Sie	(310) 396-7333		www.helloandcompany.com
	www.bobcentral.com	Peter Sollett	(310) 857-1000
			www.moxiepictures.com

Patrick Solomon	(310) 659-0010 www.newhousefilms.com	Anibal Suarez	(818) 906-0006 FAX (818) 301-2780 www.thedirectorsnetwork.com
Bruce Somers	(310) 566-6701 www.sincbox.com	Kevin Summers	(323) 468-0123 www.partizan.com
Michael Somoroff	(310) 550-6990 www.macguffin.com	Jake Sumner	(323) 465-9494 www.helloandcompany.com
Michael Sormannx	(323) 464-7805 www.acmefilmworks.com	Spencer Susser	(310) 396-7333 www.bobcentral.com
Nick Spanos	(323) 465-9494 www.helloandcompany.com	Syd/Eric	(310) 396-7333 www.bobcentral.com
Abraham Spear	(310) 319-1990 www.curiouspictures.com	Jeremy Sykes	(619) 435-0888 www.sykesfilm-tv.com
Randy Spear	(310) 822-2147 www.residentfilms.tv	Josh Taft	(310) 956-3500 www.sdintegrated.com
Scott Speer	(323) 463-2826 www.dnala.com	Picky Talarico	(310) 581-1100 www.filmplanet.com
Jake Springfield	(310) 295-0848 www.blueyedpictures.com	Hideyuki Tanaka	(310) 264-3000 www.hungryman.com
Bruce St. Clair	(323) 645-1000 (323) 653-0404 www.believemedia.com	Tano	(323) 930-0101 www.altavistafilms.com
Pam Stalker	(323) 464-7805 www.acmefilmworks.com	Johan Tappert	(310) 854-0647 www.sandwickmedia.com
Chris Stanford	(310) 396-5796 www.detourfilms.com	Julie Taymor	(310) 659-3503 www.independentmediainc.com
Ty Stanford	(310) 828-8443 www.tuesdayfilms.com	Tell No One	(323) 969-0555 www.awhitelabelproduct.com
Jerry Stanley	(866) 711-5195 www.jspcreative.com	Julien Temple	(323) 969-0555 www.awhitelabelproduct.com
David Steinberg	(323) 460-2077 www.darklightpictures.com	Jonathan Teplitzky	(310) 828-8989 www.tateusa.com
Geordie Stephens	(310) 453-9244 www.toolofna.com	Jessy Terrero	(310) 823-5400 www.carbofilms.com
David P. Stern	(818) 788-7876 (818) 907-7012	Dinh Long Thai	(626) 688-5818 (818) 906-0006 www.chopstickninja.com
Dylan Stern	(818) 901-1178	Jean-Claude Thibaut	(310) 659-1577 www.littleminx.tv
Walter Stern	(323) 465-9494 www.helloandcompany.com	Gary Thieltges	(310) 449-1300
Adam Stevens	(323) 468-0123 www.partizan.com	Brent Thomas	(310) 656-4900 www.greendotfilms.com
Jacques Steyn	(310) 396-3636 www.aerofilm.tv	Claire Thomas	(310) 656-4900 www.greendotfilms.com
Aaron Stoller	(323) 856-9200 www.biscuitfilmworks.com	Jeff Thomas	(310) 277-7001 www.companyfilms.net
Paul Street	(323) 931-3300 FAX (323) 931-3307 www.streetlightfilms.net	Pam Thomas	(310) 857-1000 www.moxiepictures.com
Tobias Stretch	(323) 969-0555 www.awhitelabelproduct.com	Virgil P. Thompson	(310) 838-7783 www.addressone.tv
Chace Strickland	(310) 314-1122 www.backyard.com	Sean Thonson	(310) 956-3500 www.sdintegrated.com
Jakob Strom	(323) 785-6500 www.gofilm.net	Three Legged Legs	(310) 314-1618 www.blind.com
Stylewar	(323) 817-3300 www.smugglersite.com	Jorn Threlfall	(310) 695-3741 www.interrogate.com

Peter Thwaites	(310) 558-3667	Phillip Van	(310) 659-1577
	www.anonymouscontent.com		www.littleminx.com
Tiger Hare	(323) 464-7805	Sarah van Den Boom	(323) 464-7805
	www.acmefilmworks.com		www.acmefilmworks.com
Wendy Tilby	(323) 464-7805	Matthijs Van Heijningen	(310) 826-6200
	www.acmefilmworks.com		www.mjz.com
Bart Timmer	(310) 695-3741	Matthew Vaughn	(323) 969-0555
	www.interrogate.com		www.awhitelabelproduct.com
Tiny Inventions	(310) 478-0771	Nicolas Veiga	(310) 659-1577
	www.duckstudios.com		www.littleminx.tv
Gianluigi Toccafondo	(323) 464-7805	Malcolm Venville	(310) 558-3667
	www.acmefilmworks.com		www.anonymouscontent.com
Frank Todaro	(310) 857-1000	Gore Verbinski	(310) 558-3667
	www.moxiepictures.com		www.anonymouscontent.com
Mark Toia	(310) 559-8333	Scott Vincent	(310) 264-3000
	www.boxerfilms.net		www.hungryman.com
Sam Tootal	(310) 264-3000	Max Vitali	(310) 558-7100
	www.hungryman.com		www.hsiproductions.com
Salvatore Totino	(310) 395-9550	Art Vitarelli	(949) 548-4524
	www.skouras.com		www.reelorange.com
Lars Tovik	(323) 785-6500	Jordan Vogt-Roberts	(310) 659-1577
	www.gofilm.net		www.rsafilms.com
Seth Townsend	(310) 314-1122	Liz Von Hoene	(323) 860-8030
	www.backyard.com		www.chelsea.com
Traktor	(323) 468-0123	Solweig von Kleist	(323) 464-7805
	www.partizan.com		www.acmefilmworks.com
Pete Travis	(323) 969-0555	Ellen Von Unwerth	(323) 464-3080
	www.awhitelabelproduct.com		www.moostudios.com
Joachim Trier	(310) 659-1577	Wachtenheim/Marianetti	(323) 464-7805
	www.rsafilms.com		www.acmefilmworks.com
Tronic	(310) 558-7100	The Wade Brothers	(310) 396-7333
	www.hsiproductions.com		www.bobcentral.com
Neil Tsai	(310) 399-6047	James Wahlberg	(310) 448-7900
	www.stardust.tv		www.rhythm.com
Steven Tsuchida	(323) 860-8686	Wong Kar Wai	(310) 558-3667
	www.ubercontent.com		www.anonymouscontent.com
Brad Tucker	(310) 399-6047	David Wain	(310) 659-3503
	www.stardust.tv		www.independentmediainc.com
Chris Turner	(310) 264-3000	Taika Waititi	(310) 264-3000
	www.hungryman.com		www.hungryman.com
David Turnley	(310) 319-1990	Lucy Walker	(310) 956-3500
	www.curiouspictures.com		www.sdintegrated.com
Gregory Tuzin	(310) 230-5253	Robert W. Walker	(323) 469-6800
	www.tuzin.com		www.walkerfitzgibbon.com
Dana Tynan	(310) 396-5796	Markus Walter	(310) 558-3667
	www.detourfilms.com		www.anonymouscontent.com
UFO	(310) 399-6047	Derek Wan	(323) 788-3883
	www.stardust.tv		FAX (323) 780-8887
			www.allinone-usa.com
Frank Underwood	(818) 729-0000		
	www.goschproductions.com	David Wasson	(323) 464-7805
			www.acmefilmworks.com
Antonio Urrutia	(310) 858-7204		
	www.labandafilms.com	John Waters	(310) 857-1000
			www.moxiepictures.com
Sebastian Valino	(310) 823-5400		
	www.carbofilms.com	Jon Watts	(323) 817-3300
			www.smugglersite.com

Commercial Directors

Scott Waugh	(310) 559-5404	Clay Williams	(310) 826-6200
	www.banditobrothers.com		www.mjz.com
Margo Weathers	(310) 956-3500	Michael Williams	(323) 468-0123
	www.sdintegrated.com		www.partizan.com
Marc Webb	(323) 463-2826	Theresa Wingert	(323) 790-0440
	www.dnala.com		www.sticks.tv
Christian Weber	(323) 951-0010	Henning Winkelmann	(310) 652-8778
	www.wondros.com		www.lspagency.net
Cole Webley	(323) 860-8686	Max Winkler	(310) 659-3503
	www.ubercontent.com		www.independentmediainc.com
Curtis Wehrfritz	(310) 526-7703	David Winning	(818) 729-0000
	www.instantkarmafilms.tv		www.goschproductions.com
Clay Weiner	(323) 856-9200	Dan Wolfe	(626) 584-4000
	www.biscuitfilmworks.com		www.danwolfe.com
Benji Weinstein	(323) 785-6500	Andrew Wonder	(310) 659-6220
	www.gofilm.net		www.crossroadsfilms.com
Jeff Weiser	(818) 906-0006	Anthony Wonke	(323) 468-0123
	www.thedirectorsnetwork.com		www.partizan.com
Martin Weisz	(323) 465-9494	Bille Woodruff	(323) 653-0404
	www.helloandcompany.com		www.form.tv
Doug Werby	(310) 578-9383	Edgar Wright	(323) 463-2826
	www.kaboomproductions.com		www.dnala.com
Julian West	(310) 550-6990	Koji Yamamura	(323) 464-7805
	www.macguffin.com		www.acmefilmworks.com
Alan White	(310) 396-7333	Jon Yarbrough	(310) 899-0335
	www.bobcentral.com		www.tuesdayfilms.com
Bill White	(818) 400-9878	Yellow Shed	(310) 478-0771
	FAX (818) 845-1756		www.duckstudios.com
	www.billwhitemedia.com		
Declan Whitebloom	(310) 659-1577	Jessica Yu	(310) 399-9600
	www.rsafilms.com		www.nonfictionunlimited.com
Whitey	(310) 264-3000	Yuval and Merav Nathan	(323) 464-7805
	www.hungryman.com		www.acmefilmworks.com
	(818) 985-1582	Ivan Zacharias	(323) 817-3300
	(818) 425-8310		www.smugglersite.com
Kenneth Wiatrak	FAX (818) 766-4584	Jason Zada	(310) 453-9244
	www.wiatrak.us		www.toolofna.com
Michael Wiehart	(310) 319-1990	Leo Zahn	(818) 981-0252
	www.curiouspictures.com		www.picturepaleprod.com
Mark Wilkinson	(310) 566-6701	ZCDC	(310) 577-0700
	www.sincbox.com		www.slim-pictures.com
Eric Will	(310) 392-7333	Matthias Zentner	(310) 453-2600
	www.thomaswintercooke.com		www.harvestfilms.com
Kenneth Willardt	(323) 969-0555	Craig Zisk	(310) 659-3503
	www.awhitelabelproduct.com		www.independentmediainc.com
Brendan Williams	(310) 458-0663	Zoink Animation	(310) 319-1990
	www.passportfilms.com		www.curiouspictures.com
Brian Williams	(310) 478-0771	Jim Zoolalian	(310) 559-8333
	www.duckstudios.com		www.boxerfilms.net
		Harald Zwart	(310) 277-7001
			www.companyfilms.net

24pCine   **(323) 375-4040**
www.iconspots.com
Executive Producers: Daniel Andreas & Andrea Cominato
Vice President: Josh Kameyer
Directors: Daniel Andreas, David Bojorquez, Reto Caduff &
Dana Leshem

30 Second Films   **(310) 315-1750**
3019 Pico Blvd.   FAX **(310) 315-1757**
Santa Monica, CA 90405   www.30secondfilms.com
Executive Producer: Alan J. Stamm
Directors: Debbie Allen, Tony Dow, Bob Kronovet &
Branscombe Richmond

47 Pictures   **(323) 464-2406**
6525 Sunset Blvd., Penthouse   FAX **(323) 464-2426**
Hollywood, CA 90028   www.47pictures.com
Executive Producer: Doug Kluthe
Directors: Jesse Austin, Cameron Hopkins, Charlie Paul &
Popular Society
VFX Editor: Jesse Austin

900 Frames   **(310) 305-8200**
12211 W. Washington Blvd.,   FAX **(310) 305-8240**
Second Fl.   www.900frames.tv
Los Angeles, CA 90066
Executive Producer: Sam Najah
Directors: Gabriel Bassio, Kevin Bourland, Chuck Clemens,
Greg Hughs, Joe Jennings, Stephen Marro & Brian Papierski

Acme Filmworks, Inc.   **(323) 464-7805**
6525 Sunset Blvd., Ste. G-10   FAX **(323) 464-6614**
Hollywood, CA 90028   www.acmefilmworks.com
Executive Producer: Ron Diamond
Producer: Pernille D'Avolio
Directors: Aixsponza, Gil Alkabetz, Claire Armstrong-Parod,
Danny Cannizzaro, Peter Chung, Evert de Beijer, Paul and
Menno De Nooijer, Michael Dudok De Wit, John Dilworth,
Paul Driessen, Piotr Dumala, Daniel Guyonnet, Chris Hinton,
Greg Holfeld, Aleksandra Korejwo, Igor Kovalyov, Torill Kove,
Raimund Krumme, Chris Landreth, Christopher and Wolfgang
Lauenstein, Caroline Leaf, Susan Loughlin, Frank and Caroline
Mouris, Oury and Thomas, Luc Perez, Janet Perlman, Afonso
Poyart, Robert Proch, Barry Purves, Daniel Guvonnet, Gitanjali
Rao, Rosto, Erica Russell, Michael Socha, Michael Sormannx,
Pam Stalker, Tiger Hare, Wendy Tilby/Amanda Forbis, Gianluigi
Toccafondo, Sarah van Den Boom, Solweig von Kleist,
Wachtenheim/Marianetti, David Wasson, Koji Yamamura, Yuval
and Merav Nathan & Juan Pablo Zaramella
East Coast Sales Rep: Mark Mirsky
Midwest Sales Rep: Tim Harwood
West Coast Sales Rep: Toni Saarinen

Aéro Film   **(310) 396-3636**
3000 31st St.   FAX **(310) 396-5636**
Santa Monica, CA 90405   www.aerofilm.tv
President: Skip Short
Executive Producer: Lance O'Connor
Head of Production: Rob Helphand
Directors: Ken Arlidge, Jason Farrand, James Mangold,
Tim Matheson, Gary McKendry, Klaus Obermeyer, Sam
O'Hare, Austin Smithard & Jacques Steyn

All In One Productions   **(323) 780-8880**
1111 Corporate Center Dr., Ste. 303   FAX **(323) 780-8887**
Monterey Park, CA 91754   www.allinone-usa.com
Producer: Joanna Or
Director/Camerman: Derek Wan

Alta Vista Films   **(323) 930-0101**
6615 Melrose Ave., Ste. 1   FAX **(323) 935-8181**
Hollywood, CA 90038   www.altavistafilms.com
Executive Producer: David Lozano
Directors: Scott Bibo, Rudy Crew, Diego and Vlady, Gonzalo
Guzman, Luis Lance, Fernando Sariñana & Tano
Director/Cameramen: Ken Fox & Scott Randall

Alter Ego Films   **(310) 809-1910**
FAX **(310) 356-3397**
www.alteregofilms.com
Executive Producers: Karl Kimbrough & Scott Papera
Directors: King Hollis, Karl Kimbrough, David R. Morton &
Scott Papera

Alturas Films   **(310) 230-6100**
www.alturasfilms.com
Owner/Executive Producer: Marshall Rawlings
Executive Producer/ Music Videos: Lanette Phillips
Commercial/Film Development Executive: Dannikke Walkker
Executive Producer: Roger Hunt

American Video Group   **(310) 477-1535**
2542 Aiken Ave.   www.americanvideogroup.com
Los Angeles, CA 90064
President: John Berzner

Anonymous Content   **(310) 558-3667**
3532 Hayden Ave.   FAX **(310) 558-4212**
Culver City, CA 90232   www.anonymouscontent.com
Executive Producers: Jeff Baron, Cassie Hulen,
Dave Morrison & Andy Traines
Head of Production: Sue Ellen Clair
Directors: Awesome and Modest, Daniel Benmayor, Christian
Bevilacqua, Armando Bo, Frank Budgen, Carter and Blitz, Tom
Carty, Trevor Cawood, Garth Davis, Andrew Douglas, David
Fincher, Alejandro González Iñárritu, Garth Jennings, Tomas
Jonsgarden, David Kellogg, Joe Kosinski, Christian Loubek,
Brett Morgan, Chris Palmer, PES, Purchase Brothers, Juston
Reardon, Mark Romanek, Gary Shore, Peter Thwaites, Malcolm
Venville, Gore Verbinski, Wong Kar Wai & Markus Water

Apple Box Productions, Inc.   **(310) 204-0520**
10736 Jefferson Blvd., Ste. 415   FAX **(310) 202-1386**
Culver City, CA 90230   www.applebox.com
Director: Steven M. Hirohama

The Artists Company   **(323) 650-4722** / **(212) 679-7199**
1015 N. Fairfax Ave.   FAX **(323) 650-4706**
Los Angeles, CA 90046   www.theartistscompany.com
Executive Producers: Roberto Cecchini & Lori Lober
Vice President: Sally Antonacchio
Head of Production: Susan Burton
Directors: David Cameron, Michael Cuesta, Guillaume,
Steven Murashige & David Ramser

The Association, Inc.   **(818) 841-9660**
135 N. Screenland Dr.   FAX **(818) 841-8370**
Burbank, CA 91505   www.wemakethephonering.com
Executive Producer: Fletcher Murray
Producers: Jeff Murphy & Tom Myrdahl
Social Media Strategist: Trevor Eisenman
Animator/Graphic Artist: Tom Murray

Attack Ads, Inc.   **(310) 857-7745**
578 Washington Blvd., Ste. 594   www.attackads.tv
Marina Del Rey, CA 90292
E.P.: Roberts Jones
Director/E.P.: Bronston Jones
Directors: Eagle Egilsson & Dr. Garry

Auster Productions, Inc.   **(818) 843-5040**
2607 W. Magnolia Blvd.   FAX **(818) 843-5041**
Burbank, CA 91505   www.austerproductions.com
Director/Cameraman: Sam Auster

aWHITELABELproduct (323) 969-0555
1820 Industrial St., Ste. 106 FAX (323) 512-7007
Los Angeles, CA 90021 www.awhitelabelproduct.com
Executive Producers: Annique De Caestecker, Oliver Hicks &
Ellen Jacobson-Clarke
Directors: Arni and Kinski, David Barnard, Alison Chernick, Paul
Dugdale, Peter Glanz, Olivier Gondry, Ben Gutteridge, Mikael
Jansson, Garth Jennings, Darius Khondji, Christian Lamb,
Peter Lindbergh, Loki, Asa Mader, Carlos Manga Jr., Craig
McDean, David Michalek, Paul Middleditch, John Cameron
Mitchell, James Pilkington, Tim Pope, Eugenio Recuenco, Tim
Richardson, Ruairi Robinson, Saint & Mather, Daniel Schweizer,
Stéphane Sednaoui, Wade Shotter, Carter Smith, Tell No One,
Julien Temple, Pete Travis, Matthew Vaughn & Kenneth Willardt
Head of Production: Lynn Zekanis

BackHome Pictures (323) 931-1782
Director: Charles Ashira www.backhomepictures.com
Production Office Manager: Karen Beller

Backyard Productions (310) 314-1122
248 Main St. FAX (310) 314-1123
Venice, CA 90291 www.backyard.com
Partners: Blair Stribley & Chris Zander
Executive Producers: Kris Mathur & Eric Bonnoit
Directors: Mac Carter, Jesper Ericstam, Hugo Menduina,
Alexander Paul, Nick Piper, Rob Pritts, Kevin Smith, Chace
Strickland, & Seth Townsend
Sales Reps: The Family, Them Reps & Options
Head of Production: Cori Cooperider

Bandito Brothers (310) 559-5404
3115 S. La Cienega Blvd. FAX (310) 559-5230
Los Angeles, CA 90016 www.banditobrothers.com
Chief Executive Officer & Creative Director: Mike McCoy
Co-Founder & Director: Scott Waugh
Chief Operating Officer: Max Leitman
Chief Technology Officer & Director: Jacob Rosenberg
Managing Director/Executive Producer: Jay Pollak
Managing Director/EP Commercial Division: Suzanne Hargrove
Directors: Mitchell Amundsen, Gavin Bowden, Matt Goodman,
Stewart Hendler, Mike McCoy, Michael Polish, Leonardo
Ricagni, Jacob Rosenberg & Scott Waugh
East Coast Sales Rep: Rich Shafler
Mid West Sales Reps: Tracy Bernard & Robin Stevens
West Coast Sales Reps: Holly Ross & Tracy Reed

Beard Boy Productions (714) 734-0372
14451 Chambers Rd., Ste. 250 FAX (714) 734-6031
Tustin, CA 92780 www.beardboy.com
Executive Producer: Mike Smith
Producer: Steven Rey
Writer/Producer: Joe Dinki

Beef Films (310) 576-0797
2049 Colorado Ave. www.beeffilms.com
Santa Monica, CA 90404
Executive Producers: Ashley Adams, Stephen Hens &
John Malina
Director/Partner: Nick Spooner

Believe Media (323) 645-1000
1040 N. Las Palmas Ave., Bldg. 10 FAX (323) 645-1001
Los Angeles, CA 90038 www.believemedia.com
Executive Producers: Gerard Cantor, Betsy Kelley, Liz Silver &
Luke Thornton
Directors: Animal, Chris Applebaum, Anthea Benton, Michael
Bernard, Marcelo Burgos, Gerard de Thame, Carole Denis,
Bruce Dowad, Liz Friedlander, Tryan George, Wayne Holloway,
Allen Hughes, Rory Kelleher, Maurice Marable, Andy Morahan,
Jake Nava, Bo Platt, Joel Pront, Floria Sigismondi,
Zack Snyder & Bruce St. Clair

Bill White Media (818) 400-9878
3625 Pacific Ave. FAX (818) 845-1756
Burbank, CA 91505 www.billwhitemedia.com
Producer/Production Manager: Amy Shomer
Director/Writer/Producer: Bill White

Biscuit Filmworks (323) 856-9200
7026 Santa Monica Blvd. FAX (323) 856-9300
Los Angeles, CA 90038 www.biscuitfilmworks.com
Managing Director: Shawn Lacy
Directors: Philippe Andre, Tim Godsall, Jeff Low, Mike Maguire,
Malcolm Murray, Noam Murro, Andreas Nilsson, Christopher
Riggert, Steve Rogers, Aaron Ruell, Aaron Stoller &
Clay Weiner
West Coast Sales Reps: Resource
Executive Producers: Colleen O'Donnell & Holly Vega
Midwest Sales Reps: Gay Guthrey & Assoc.
East Coast Sales Reps: Zeigler Jakubowicz
Management Group
Executive Producer (UK): Orlando Wood

Bjoin Films (818) 846-1650
121 E. Linden Ave. FAX (818) 846-1670
Burbank, CA 91502 www.bjoinfilms.com
Director/Cameraman: Henry Bjoin

Blind (310) 314-1618
1702 Olympic Blvd. FAX (310) 314-1718
Santa Monica, CA 90404 www.blind.com
Executive Producer: Tino Sladavic
Directors: Chris Do, Tom Koh & Vanessa Marzaroli

Blue Goose Productions (323) 658-6893
8350 Melrose Ave., Ste. 204 www.bluegoose.tv
Los Angeles, CA 90069
Executive Producer: Bill Hoare
Director: Ron Gross

Blueyed Pictures, Inc. (310) 295-0848
1806 Thayer Ave. FAX (310) 492-5270
Los Angeles, CA 90025 www.blueyedpictures.com
Executive Producer: Jamee Natella
Directors: Brian Bain, Aaron Fedor, Evin Grant,
Todd Grossman & Jake Springfield

Bob Industries (310) 396-7333
1313 Fifth St. FAX (310) 396-0202
Santa Monica, CA 90401 www.bobcentral.com
Executive Producers: TK Knowles, John O'Grady &
Chuck Ryant
Directors: Miguel Arteta, Dom Bridges, Peter Care, Harry
Cocciolo, Jonathan Dayton/Valerie Faris, Kim Geldenhuys,
Davis Guggenheim, Phil Harder, Alex Laubscher, Zach Math,
Bob Odenkirk, Brad Parker, Sam Peacocke, Trish Sie, Spencer
Susser, Syd/Eric, The Wade Brothers & Alan White

Boxer Films (310) 559-8333
3453 S. La Cienega Blvd., Bldg. B FAX (310) 559-6226
Los Angeles, CA 90016 www.boxerfilms.net
CEO: Kelly Clark
President: John Clark
Directors: Hernan Bargman, Robert Groenwold, Alvaro
Hernandez, Maureen Hufnagel, Anton Josef, Justin Klarenbeck,
Claudio Prestia, Thomas Richter, David Adam Roth, Rodrigo
Garcia Saiz, Mark Toia & Jim Zoolalian
Sales Reps: Ann McKallagat, Jill Reehl & Reber-Covington

Bucks Boys Productions, Inc. (310) 437-0914
578 Washington Blvd., Ste. 362 FAX (310) 437-0919
Marina Del Rey, CA 90292 www.bucksboys.com
Executive Producers: Jonathan Becker & Joshua Greenberg

Bueno Films (323) 851-5030
1011 N. Fuller Ave. FAX (323) 851-4120
West Hollywood, CA 90046 www.buenofilms.com

(310) 395-6500
Bully Pictures (310) 871-0385
1240 Sixth St. FAX (310) 395-6522
Santa Monica, CA 90401 www.bullypictures.com

c.2K Entertainment (310) 208-2324
1067 Gayley Ave. FAX (310) 208-2414
Los Angeles, CA 90024 www.c-2k.com
Directors: Rod Findley & Ken Musen

Carbo Films   (310) 823-5400
720 Hampton Dr.   FAX (310) 823-5400
Venice, CA 90291   www.carbofilms.com
Executive Producers: Javier Carbo & Dora Medrano
Producer: Soledad Ramos
Directors: Sebastian Alfie, Pedro Avila, Alejandro Barbosa,
Isabel Coixet, Feliz Fernandez de Castro, Augusto de Fraga,
Roger Fonts, Gonzo, Jorge Malpica, Estevan Oriol, David
Ramser, Albert Saquer, Jessy Terrero & Sebastian Valiño

Carey Melcher Productions, Inc./   (213) 598-3457
CMP   (818) 222-9817
Executive Producer: Carey Melcher

The Cartel   (323) 466-3455
1151 N. Highland Ave.   FAX (323) 856-8187
Hollywood, CA 90038   www.the-cartel.tv
Executive Producers: Faith Dektor & Sven Shelgren
Director: Werner Damen, Paul Dektor, Rob Feng, Matt
Fischman, Kirk Jones & Paul Minor
Director/Cameramen: Leslie Dektor & Mark Dektor

      (818) 787-7442
Castleland Productions   (818) 633-3606
5827 Cantaloupe Ave.   FAX (818) 787-7462
Van Nuys, CA 91401   www.castlelandproductions.com

      (323) 932-6588
A Catch 22 Production   (310) 863-6909
5478 Wilshire Blvd., Ste. 300   FAX (323) 932-6598
Los Angeles, CA 90036   www.acatch22production.com
Executive Producer: Todd Harter
VP of Production: Valerie Mayer
Directors: Enrique Aular, Hector Barboza, Marina Belaustegui,
Pablo Croce, Claudio Duran, Camilo Matiz, Jorge Rubia &
Jorge Salinas

CatchLight Films   (310) 295-0071
      FAX (310) 341-3806
      www.catchlightfilms.com
Producers: Rick A. Osako & Jeanette Volturno-Brill

The Cavalry Productions   (310) 966-4440
11849 W. Olympic Blvd., Ste. 204   FAX (310) 954-1414
Los Angeles, CA 90064
      www.thecavalryproductions.com

Caviar   (310) 396-3400
1265 S. Cochran Ave.   FAX (310) 396-3400
Los Angeles, CA 90019   www.caviarcontent.com
Executive Producers: Michael Sagol & Jasper Thomlinson
Executive Producer, Features & Television: Madeline Shapiro
Executive Producer, Hispanic Market: Valeria Maldini
Head of Marketing: Cathleen Kisich
Head of Production: Leigh Miller

      (323) 860-8030
Chelsea Pictures   (212) 431-3434
1040 N. Las Palmas Ave., Bldg. 15   FAX (323) 860-8035
Hollywood, CA 90038   www.chelsea.com
Owner/Executive Producers: Allison Amon & Lisa Mehling
Executive Producer: Patrick McGoldrick
Head of Production: Leslie Evers
Directors: Neil Abramson, Nicholas Barker, Robb Bindler,
Borgato and Berte, Jack Cole, Alex Gibney, David Gordon
Green, Lauren Greenfield, Bruce Hunt, Nadav Kander, Johan
Kramer, Rick LeMoine, Kevin MacDonald, Charles Mehling
Michael, Muller, Christopher Quinn, & Liz Von Hoene
West Coast Sales Rep: Ezra Burke
Midwest Sales Reps: Janice Harryman & Jim Robison
East Coast Sales Rep: Denise Blate Roederer

Cinevative Productions   (323) 852-8903
8455 Beverly Blvd., Ste. 507   FAX (323) 852-0349
Los Angeles, CA 90048   www.cinevative.com
Executive Producers: Mark Ciglar & Carrie Dobro

Commercial Head/Films   (323) 658-6541
1049 S. Alfred St.   FAX (323) 655-7650
Los Angeles, CA 90035   www.commercialhead.com
Executive Producer: Buddy Joe
Director: Moshe Brakha

Commercials While-U-Wait, Inc.   (310) 399-3456
218 Grand Blvd.   FAX (310) 396-1614
Venice, CA 90291   www.cwuw.com
Executive Producer/Directors: Claudia Forsthoevel &
Rene Kock

      (310) 823-7300
A Common Thread, Inc.   (310) 798-9007
4081 Redwood Ave.   FAX (310) 823-7305
Los Angeles, CA 90066   www.acommonthread.tv
Executive Producers: Tristan Drew & J.P. McMahon

Company   (310) 277-7001
1551 S. Robertson Blvd.   FAX (310) 277-7004
Los Angeles, CA 90035   www.companyfilms.net
Owner/Executive Producer: Robin Benson
Executive Producer: Richard Goldstein
Head of Production: Robert Nackman
Directors: Philippe Andre, The Coen Brothers, Larry Frey, Fred
Goss, John Grammatico, Nick Jones, Marandi/Heath,
David McNally, Harry Patramanis, Jeff Thomas & Harald Zwart
East Coast Sales: Laura Dane
Mid West Sales: Rich Newman
West Coast Sales: Keith Quinn

      (310) 659-6220
Crossroads Films   (212) 647-1300
8630 Pine Tree Pl.   FAX (310) 659-3105
West Hollywood, CA 90069   www.crossroadsfilms.com
Executive Producers: Carole Hughes & Camille Taylor
Directors: Russell Bates, Katie Bell, Trudy Bellinger, Nico Beyer,
Luis Carone, Sam Crawford, Norman Hafezi, Sanaa Hamri,
Bruce Hurwit, Wayne Isham, Mike Nelesen, Vadim Perelman,
Stuart Rideout & Andrew Wonder
Head of Sales/East Coast Sales Rep: Sharon Lew
Midwest Sales Rep: Janice Harryman
West Coast Rep: Tanya Cohen

Curious Pictures   (310) 319-1990
1700 Ocean Ave., Ste. 126   www.curiouspictures.com
Santa Monica, CA 90401
Executive Producer: Bill Reilly
Directors: Agust Baldursson, Tom Barham, Saul Blinkoff, Zach
Braff, Gotham Chopra, Scott Duncan, Danny Forster, David
Griffiths, Happycamper, Shekhar Kapur, Sue Kramer, Little
Fluffy Clouds, Steve Oakes, Randy Roberts, Abraham Spear,
David Turnley, Michael Wiehart & Zoink Animation
Sales Reps: Hello Tomorrow, Scout Creative Representation
Head of Production: Kimberly Bryant

Custom Video   (310) 543-4901
707 Torrance Blvd., Ste. 105   www.customvideo.tv
Redondo Beach, CA 90277
Founder & Producer: Joe Jennings
President: Michael Ude
Producers: Hugh Malay, Geoff Nathanson & Rob Vouna

Dancing Pictures LLC   (617) 771-7277
      www.thedancingpictures.com

Dark Light Pictures   (323) 460-2077
812 N. Highland Ave.   FAX (323) 460-7097
Los Angeles, CA 90038   www.darklightpictures.com
Executive Producer: Vincent Arcaro
Head of Production: Sheila Flaherty
Director: David Steinberg
Director/Cameramen: Gil Cope & Caleb Deschanel
Sales Reps: Lauran McNamara, Connie Mellors &
Schaffer Rogers

Detour Films   (310) 396-5796
1557 Seventh St.   FAX (310) 260-0911
Santa Monica, CA 90401   www.detourfilms.com
Executive Producer: Josh Canova
Directors: Jerry Brown, Jeff Kaumeyer, Matt Miadich, Chris
Stanford & Dana Tynan
East Rep: Michael Eha
Midwest Rep: Marci Miles
West Rep: Dawn Clarke
Head of Production: Rob Traill

      (714) 842-1505
Digital Studios West, Inc.   (877) 379-7058
P.O. Box 614   www.digitalstudioswest.com
Huntington Beach, CA 92648

Diligent (323) 863-6204
4214 Santa Monica Blvd. www.dodiligent.com
Los Angeles, CA 90029

                                        (323) 465-5299
The Directors Bureau   (323) 663-0500
1641 N. Ivar Ave.   FAX (323) 465-5547
Hollywood, CA 90028 www.thedirectorsbureau.com
Directors: M Blash, Sam Brown, Andy Bruntel, Todd Cole,
Roman Coppola, Sofia Coppola, Patrick Daughters, Romain
Gavras, Mike Maguire, Melodie McDaniel, Geoff McFetridge,
Aaron Rose & Shynola

DNA Studio (323) 463-2826
6535 Santa Monica Blvd. FAX (323) 463-2535
Hollywood, CA 90038 www.dnala.com
Executive Producer: Patricia Judice
Directors: Lenny Bass, Bert and Bertie, Kevin Bray, Nigel Dick,
Paul Gore, Francis Lawrence, Rich Lee, Julien Lutz, Jay Martin,
Michael Maxxis, David McClister, Jean-Baptiste Mondino,
Marcus Raboy, Mike Ruiz, Rocky Schenck, Christopher Sims,
Scott Speer, Marc Webb & Edgar Wright
Sales Rep: Michel Waxman

DOOM, Inc. (310) 927-6661
818 S. Grand Ave., Ste. 804 FAX (310) 496-2666
Los Angeles, CA 90017 www.doominc.com
Head of Production/Producer: Darci Oltman
Director: Thomas Mignone

DUCK Studios,
a.k.a. Duck Soup Studios (310) 478-0771
2205 Stoner Ave. FAX (310) 478-0773
Los Angeles, CA 90064 www.duckstudios.com
Executive Producer: Mark Medernach
President/Director: Roger Chouinard
Directors: abstract: groove, B and C Wall, Simon Blake, Jamie
Caliri, Roger Chouinard, Paul Cummings, Delicatessen, Eric
Goldberg, James Hackett, Chris Harding, Impactist, JL Design,
Kompost, Lane and Jan, Main Frame, Meindbender, Monkmus,
Yorico Murakami, NMA, Nina Paley, Daniel Peacock, Hsin Ping
Pan, Corky Quakenbush, Chris Romano, Maureen Selwood,
Kang Seong, SMOG, Tiny Inventions, Brian Williams &
Yellow Shed
Sales Rep: Andrew Halpern
Music Video Rep: Randi Wilens

DuckPunk Productions (310) 836-3818
12022 Venice Blvd., Ste. D www.duckpunk.net
Los Angeles, CA 90066
Executive Producer: Mellissa Tong

Encore Media LLC (310) 823-9233
5301 Beethoven St., Ste. 290 FAX (310) 823-9211
Los Angeles, CA 90066 www.encoremediallc.com

Epix (310) 656-9100
22631 Pacific Coast Hwy, Ste. 379 FAX (310) 656-9104
Malibu, CA 90265 www.epixfilms.com
Executive Producer/Director: Lou La Monte
Producer: Laraine Gregory

                                        (310) 275-9333
Epoch Films, Inc.   (310) 275-7938
9290 Civic Center Dr. FAX (310) 275-7696
Beverly Hills, CA 90210 www.epochfilms.com
Executive Producers: Mindy Goldberg & Jerry Solomon
Head of Production: John Duffin
Directors: Matthew Badger, Collision, Matt Dilmore, Michael
Downing, Everyone, Mike Long, Phil Morrison, Jeff Preiss &
Jessica Sanders
Sales Rep: Mal Ward

Exeter Road Films (310) 503-8080
9255 Sunset Blvd., Mezzanine www.exeterroadfilms.com
Los Angeles, CA 90069

Exploded View (818) 402-0706
743 N. Keystone St. www.explodedviewla.com
Burbank, CA 91506
Executive Producer: Therese Sherman
Director: Richard Foley

Eyestorm Productions (310) 582-3937
1522 Cloverfield Blvd., Ste. C FAX (310) 582-3939
Santa Monica, CA 90404
www.eyestormproductions.com

F. J. Productions, Inc. (818) 788-0153
14900 Ventura Blvd., Ste. 350 FAX (818) 788-0186
Sherman Oaks, CA 91403 www.fjproductions.com
Directors: Renato Assad, Pico Garcez & Fabio Golombek
Production Coordinator: Tanira Lebedeff

Film Planet (310) 581-1100
1317 Innes Pl. FAX (310) 581-1130
Venice, CA 90291 www.filmplanet.com
Executive Producers: Robyn Bensinger & Karin Stuckenschmidt
Directors: Marcel Mallio, Flavia Moraes & Picky Talarico

Film Réalité, Inc. (310) 883-8801
2017 Pacific Ave., Second Fl. FAX (310) 822-0835
Venice, CA 90291 www.filmrealite.com
Executive Producer: Richard Epstein
Head of Production: Marla Whittaker
Sales Rep: Andrew Hall Management

The Film Syndicate (323) 938-8080
7214 Melrose Ave. FAX (323) 938-8183
Los Angeles, CA 90046
Producer/Director: Bryan Johnson

Flip Films, Inc. (310) 401-6140
1639 16th St. FAX (310) 401-6149
Santa Monica, CA 90404 www.flipfilms.com

Fluid Films Productions Inc. (323) 899-3762
5708 Troost Ave. www.fluidfilms.net
North Hollywood, CA 91601

Galanty & Company, Inc. (310) 451-2525
1640 Fifth St., Ste. 203
Santa Monica, CA 90401
Executive Producers: Mark Galanty & Sidney Galanty
Senior Producer: Steve Rood
Directors: Mark Galanty & Sidney Galanty

GARTNER (310) 899-1700
1531 Colorado Ave. FAX (310) 899-1710
Santa Monica, CA 90404 www.gartner.tv
Executive Producers: Don Block & Rich Carter
Head of Production: Elaine Strom Behnken
Directors: Shona Auerbach, Raymond Bark, Michael Bigelow,
James Gartner, Marcel Langenegger & Theodore Melfi
East Coast Rep: Phillip Alden, The PTA
Midwest Rep: Renee Case & Co.
West Coast Reps: Andrea Andrews & Mark Andrews

                                        (310) 274-6102
                                        (212) 966-1212
Giraldi Media
510 N. Hillcrest Rd. FAX (310) 274-6192
Beverly Hills, CA 90210 www.giraldi.com
Executive Producer: Debbie Merlin
Directors: Bob Giraldi & Tom Lazarevich
US Rep: Dennis Loonan

Go Film (323) 785-6500
6509 De Longpre Ave. FAX (323) 785-6599
Los Angeles, CA 90028 www.gofilm.net
Partners/Executive Producers: Gary Rose &
Jonathan Weinstein
Head of Production: Sandy Newman
Production Coordinator: JoJo Nannini
Directors: Jason Alexander, John Benson, Neal Brennan, Ric
Cantor, David Dobkin, Ward Evans, Billy Frederighi, Steve
Fuller, Dennie Gordon, Christopher Guest, Tim Hamilton,
Fluorescent Hill, Charles Jensen, Kennedy, Joe Meade, Rob
Pearlstein, Nick Robertson, Roberto Schaefer, Brett Snider,
Jakob Strom, Jeff Thomsic, & Lars Tovik
East Coast/Mid West Sales Reps: Amy Jones,
Michael Lobikis & Alison Noel
West Coast/Texas Sales Rep: Stephanie Stephens
Staff Producer: Emily Malito
Executive Producer: Catherine Finkenstaedt

A Gosch Production (818) 729-0000
CEO: Rob Gosch www.goschproductions.com
Executive Producer: Pat Gosch
Directors: Chris Gosch, Walt Lloyd, Barbara Peeters, Frank
Underwood & David Winning

Graying & Balding, Inc.   **(310) 979-4333**
Executive Producer: Ann Kim   FAX **(310) 979-4334**
Director: Jim Gable   **www.gandb.tv**

Great Guns USA   **(310) 451-8150**
53 N. Venice Blvd., Ground Fl.   FAX **(310) 305-8040**
Venice, CA 90291   **www.greatgunsusa.com**
President/Executive Producer: Tom Korsan
Executive Producer: Mary Sanders
Head of Production: Ellen DeVine

Green Dot Films, Inc.   **(310) 656-4900**
1554 16th St.   FAX **(310) 656-0444**
Santa Monica, CA 90404   **www.greendotfilms.com**
Special Projects: Rick Fishbein
Directors: Rebecca Baehler, Omri Cohen, Mark Coppos,
Richard Farmer, Rafael Fernandez, Jacobsbriere, Robert
Jitzmark, Luc Schurgers, Brent Thomas & Claire Thomas
Executive Producer/Head of Production: Rich Pring
Executive Producer/Head of Sales: Darren Foldes
CFO: Beth Clark
Digital Assets Manager: Brady Spear
Office Manager: Sarah Spitzer
CEO: Jane Thomas
Staff Producer: Preston Garrett
Sales Rep: Leticia Schroeder

Habana Avenue   **(310) 857-6678**
1158 26th St., Ste. 374   **www.habanaavenue.com**
Santa Monica, CA 90403
CEO/Executive Producer: Steven J. Levy
COO: Rob Salo
East Coast Traditional Rep: Anya Zander
Exclusive Broadcast Rep: Brett Ashy
Director - Networks Division: Scott Duncan
East Coast Traditional Rep: Emilia Ferreira

Half Element Productions   **(323) 620-6925**
1911 17th St., Ste. 5   **www.halfelement.com**
Santa Monica, CA 90404
Producers: Kim Daniels & Des Escober
Directors: Isaac Klotz & Brian Silva
Director/Cameraman: Rob Kraetsch

Hallowes Productions and   **(310) 390-4767**
Advertising   **(310) 753-9381**
11260 Regent St.   FAX **(310) 745-1107**
Los Angeles, CA 90066   **www.jimhallowes.com**
Producer: Harry Mathias
Producer/Director: Jim Hallowes

harvest   **(310) 453-2600**
3002 Pennsylvania Ave.   FAX **(310) 453-2602**
Santa Monica, CA 90404   **www.harvestfilms.com**
Executive Producers: Matt Benson, Bonnie Goldfarb &
Rob Sexton
Directors: Adam Goldstein, The Hoffman Brothers, David Nutter,
Baker Smith & Matthias Zentner
East Coast Rep: Miss Smith: Jamie Scalera & Sasha Stern
Midwest Rep: David Wagner
West Coast Reps: Brooke Covington & Rebecca Reber

Hello!   **(323) 465-9494**
1641 N. Ivar Ave.   FAX **(323) 465-4203**
Hollywood, CA 90028   **www.helloandcompany.com**
Owners: Graham Henman & Michael Karbelnikoff
Head of Production: Alex Chamberlain
Executive Producers: Mike Brady & Carl Swan
Head of Film & Television: Lenny Beckerman
Directors: Bob Balaban, David Barnard, Brothers Quay, PR
Brown, Rey Carlson, Dick Carruthers, Jeffrey Darling, Jake
Davis, Alex De Rakoff, Martin De Thurah, Justin Francis, Mark
Gilbert, Jonathan Glazer, Banner Gwin, Robert Hales, Corin
Hardy, Michael Patrick Jann, Michael Karbelnikoff, K. Asher
Levin, Mark Liddell, Chris Marrs Piliero, Marcus McCollum, Max
Nichols, Mehdi Norowzian, Jeremy Rall, Lynne Ramsay, Paul
Schneider, SI and AD, Matt Smukler, Marcus Soderlund, Nick
Spanos, Bruce St. Clair, Walter Stern, Jake Sumner, Martin
Weisz & Kevin Wilson
East Coast Sales Reps: Michael Arkin & Anna Triggs
EP of Music Videos & Digital: Kerri Kleiner
Midwest Sales Reps: Chris Breneman, Marguerite Juliusson &
Paul Saylor
West Coast Sales Rep: Mark Andrews, Brad Grubaugh &
Erika Sheldon

Hokus Pokus Productions, Inc.   **(818) 879-2200**
23679 Calabasas Rd., Ste. 552   **www.tvadvertising.com**
Calabasas, CA 91302
Executive Producer: Robert Haukoos

House of Usher Films   **(310) 586-0055**
2014 Broadway   FAX **(310) 586-0065**
Santa Monica, CA 90404   **www.usherfilms.com**

The House Production Company   **(323) 851-5151**
1429 N. Spaulding Ave.   FAX **(323) 851-9598**
Los Angeles, CA 90046
Executive Producer: Bonnie Matchinga
Producer: Sue Berry
Director: Bob Schwartz

    (310) 558-7100
HSI Productions, Inc.   **(212) 627-3600**
3630 Eastham Dr.   FAX **(310) 558-7101**
Culver City, CA 90232   **www.hsiproductions.com**
President: Stavros Merjos
Executive Producer: Michael McQuhae
Directors: Jason Bateman, Simon Cole, Kevin Connolly, Ryan
Ebner, Michael Haussman, Jaci Judelson, Joseph Kahn, David
LaChapelle, Yoann Lemoine, Malloys, Diane Martel, Thomas
Napper, Chris Neilson, Casey Neistat, Brett Ratner, Jason
Smith & Max Vitali
Sales Rep: Michelle Ross
Executive Producer/VP: Rebecca Skinner

Hu-Man Element Productions, Inc.   **(213) 534-3700**
1201 W. Fifth St., Ste. F-220A   FAX **(213) 534-3711**
Los Angeles, CA 90017   **www.hu-manelement.com**
President: Rick Ojeda

    (310) 264-3000
Hungry Man   **(212) 625-5600**
3111 S. La Cienega Blvd.   FAX **(310) 264-3001**
Los Angeles, CA 90016   **www.hungryman.com**
Managing Partner: Kevin Byrne
Partners/Directors: Bryan Buckley & Hank Perlman
Executive Producer: Dan Duffy
Executive Producer/Head of Production: Cindy Becker
Directors: Brian Billow, Bryan Buckley, Richard Bullock, Tim
Bullock, Neil Burger, Nanette Burstein, Carlao Busato, Roderick
Fenske, Paulo Grandra, James Gooding, James Haworth,
Steve Hudson, Dave Laden, m-i-e, Wayne McClammy, Hank
Perlman, Gualter Pupo, Marcos Siega, Hideyuki Tanaka, Sam
Tootal, Chris Turner, Taika Waititi, Scott Vincent & Whitey
East Coast Sales Reps: Mary French & Stacie Gillman
Midwest Sales Rep: Monaghan/Halpine

I-40 Films   **(310) 871-1506**
11301 W. Olympic Blvd., Ste. 595   FAX **(919) 832-3274**
Los Angeles, CA 90064   **www.i40films.com**
Executive Producer: Kris Hixson
Senior VP of Production: David Mahanes
Director: Kris Hixson

an ideal world   **(714) 953-9501**
209 N. Bush St.   FAX **(714) 380-6311**
Santa Ana, CA 92701   **www.anidealworld.com**
Director: Robb Hart
Executive Producer: Molly Talbot Hart

Illuminate –
Arts, Media & Entertainment   **(323) 969-8822**
3575 Cahuenga Blvd. West, Fourth Fl. FAX **(323) 969-8840**
Los Angeles, CA 90068   **www.illuminatehollywood.com**
Executive Producers: Eric Geisler, Patricia Sullivan & AJ Ullman
Director: Jim Hardy

Image G   **(818) 761-6644**
28490 Westinghouse Pl.   **www.imageg.com**
Valencia, CA 91355
Director: Thomas Barron

Imaginary Forces   **(323) 957-6868**
6526 Sunset Blvd.   FAX **(323) 957-9577**
Los Angeles, CA 90028   **www.imaginaryforces.com**
Presidents: Peter Frankfurt & Chip Houghton
Head of Production: Ben Apley

Independent Media, Inc.   **(310) 659-3503**
6950 S. Centinela Ave.   FAX **(310) 659-3520**
Culver City, CA 90230   **www.independentmediainc.com**

Instant Karma Films (310) 526-7703
212 Marine St. FAX (310) 526-7076
Santa Monica, CA 90405 www.instantkarmafilms.tv
President: Tanya Hunger
Executive Producer: Craig Farkas
Directors: Simon Cracknell, Maxime Giroux, Alain Gourrier,
Ben Hartenstein, Bo Krabbe, Jon Gwyther, Opel, Marco Pinesi,
Larry Shiu & Curtis Wehrfritz
Director/Cameraman: Brian Lai

Intelliscape Films, LLC (310) 882-2100
  (800) 422-5996
Director: Bruce Caulk FAX (310) 575-1890
  www.intelliscape.com

Interrogate Inc. (310) 695-3741
6374 Arizona Circle FAX (310) 956-3501
Los Angeles, CA 90045 www.interrogate.com
Executive Producer/Founder: Jeff Miller
Staff Production Manager: Christa Miles
Directors: Henrik Hallgren, Jeff Labbe, Henry Littlechild, Scott
Lyon, Vesa Manninen, Amit Mehta, James Rouse, Snorri Bros,
Jörn Threlfall & Bart Timmer
Executive Producer: George Meeker
Head of Production: Jen Beitler

Japanese Monster (310) 883-7800
2347 Ocean Ave. FAX (310) 883-7880
Venice, CA 90291 www.japanesemonster.com
Executive Producer: Tod Feaster
Head of Production: Paula Williams
Directors: Scott Corbett, Lance Larson, Ed Shumacher &
Craig Tanimoto

Jay Silverman Productions (323) 466-6030
1541 N. Cahuenga Blvd. FAX (323) 466-7139
Hollywood, CA 90028 www.jaysilverman.com
Director: Jay Silverman
Producer: Neil Gabriel

JMP Spotlight (877) 297-8887
760 N. Cahuenga Blvd. www.jmpspotlight.com
Los Angeles, CA 90068

JSP Creative (866) 711-5195
  (714) 288-6005
229 N. Glassell St. FAX (714) 288-6014
Orange, CA 92866 www.jspcreative.com
Producers: Brian FitzGerald & Jerry Stanley
Directors: David Briggs, Brent Loefke, Scott Murphy &
Jerry Stanley

K Films (310) 393-4200
Director: Warren Kushner FAX (310) 496-0442
  www.kfilms.us

Kaboom Productions (310) 578-9383
2898 Glencoe Ave. www.kaboomproductions.com
Venice, CA 90291
Executive Producer: Lauren Schwartz
Head of Production: Mallary Weintraub
Directors: Brandon Dickerson, Matt Fackrell, Reynir Lyngdal,
Joe Meade, Ricki and Annie, Gary Shaffer, Doug Werby
East Coast Sales Rep: Mary Ford & Co.
Midwest Sales Rep: Julie Vargo & Assoc.
West Coast Sales Rep: Connie Mellors & Co.

Kandoo Films, Inc. (818) 789-6777
4515 Van Nuys Blvd., Ste. 100 FAX (818) 789-2299
Sherman Oaks, CA 91403 www.kandoofilms.com
Executive Producer/Director: Howard Barish
Producer: Al Smith
Sales Rep: Rhonda Kinosian

Karma Kollective (310) 653-1400
6334-B Wilshire Blvd. FAX (310) 653-1402
Los Angeles, CA 90048 www.karmakollective.tv

Kavich Reynolds Productions, Inc. (323) 466-2490
6381 Hollywood Blvd., Ste. 580 FAX (323) 466-3655
Hollywood, CA 90028 www.kavichreynolds.com
President/Executive Producer: John Reynolds
Senior Executive Producer: Steve Kavich
Directors: Doug Henry & Rob Meltzer

La Banda Films (310) 858-7204
329 N. Wetherly Dr., Ste. 205 FAX (310) 858-7206
Beverly Hills, CA 90211 www.labandafilms.com
President: Roberto Sneider
Executive Producers: Emilia Arau
Directors: Claudia Alberdi, Carlos Bolado, Nicolas Caicoya,
Tano Celentano, Alfredo de Villa, Rodrigo Garcia, Francisco
Garuti, Adri Laham, Luis Mandoki, Patricia Martinez de Velasco,
Roberto Sneider & Antonio Urrutia

Lewin Pictures (213) 798-3320
4423 Firmament Ave. FAX (818) 788-1601
Encino, CA 91436 www.elyselewin.com
Director: Elyse Lewin

Lightning Bolt PIX (310) 828-8239
1653 18th St., Ste. 3B FAX (310) 828-1923
Santa Monica, CA 90404 www.boltpix.com
President: Michael Barnard
Designer/Director: Morgan Barnard
Designer/Editor: Christian Knudsen

Little Minx (310) 659-1577
634 N. LaPeer Dr. FAX (310) 659-1377
West Hollywood, CA 90069 www.littleminx.tv
President: Rhea Scott
Directors: Francois Alaux, AXIS, Herve De Crecy, Nabil
Elderkin, Steph Green, Johnny Hardstaff, Martin Kalina, Jesper
Kouthoofd, Josh Miller, Ben Mor, Nico and Martin, Rodrigo
Prieto, Sebastian Reed, Malik Sayeed, Toben Seymour, Dawn
Shadforth, Jim Field Smith, Jean Claude Thibaut, Phillip Van &
Nicolas Veiga
Coordinator: Adam Lane

Locksmith (310) 287-1022
8500 Steller Dr., Bldg. 3 FAX (310) 287-1208
Culver City, CA 90232 www.locksmithcontent.com

M Creative Group, Inc. (818) 225-1541
23209 Mariano St., Ste. 100 FAX (818) 225-1476
Woodland Hills, CA 91367 www.mcreativegroup.net
Creative Director/CEO
Director/Producer: Seth Pinsker
Executive Producer/COO: Diane Glezerman
Directors: Geoffrey Katar & Robin Miller

M-80 Films (310) 899-9100
701 Santa Monica Blvd. FAX (310) 395-1750
Santa Monica, CA 90401 www.m80films.com
Director: Tenney Fairchild
Sales Reps: Stacey Altman, Marci Miles & Jennifer Warren

MacGuffin Films, Ltd. (310) 550-6990
350 N. Crescent Dr., Ste. 304 FAX (310) 550-6237
Beverly Hills, CA 90212 www.macguffin.com
President: Michael Salzer
Executive Producers: Gloria Colangelo & Sam Wool
Directors: Christopher Bean, Jim Collins, Nick Fuglestad,
Michael Somoroff & Julian West
East Coast Sales Reps: Vanessa Moseley & Maria Stenz
Office Head: Greg Pappas
Midwest Sales Rep: Jay Anderson
West Coast Sales Rep: Claire Worch
Regional Sales Rep: Sarah Lange

Make It Happen Productions, Inc. (818) 981-2327
13557 Ventura Blvd., Second Fl. FAX (818) 981-2440
Sherman Oaks, CA 91423 www.mihp.tv

Maneater Productions (323) 790-1732
  (323) 327-2793
6860 Lexington Ave. FAX (323) 460-6063
Hollywood, CA 90038 www.maneaterproductions.com
Executive Producer: Jed James
Directors: Lorenzo De Guia, Anthony Garth, Steven Lippman &
Bradley Scott
Business Development: Molly Macdonald
Representation: Yvette Lubinsky
PR: Press Kitchen

Mesita (818) 760-8707
11333 Moorpark Ave., Ste. 446
Studio City, CA 91602
Executive Producer: L.D. James
Director/Cameraman: Richard E. Black
Sales Rep: Darr Hawthorne

MJZ, Inc. (310) 826-6200
2201 Carmelina Ave. FAX (310) 826-6219
Los Angeles, CA 90064 www.mjz.com
President: David Zander
Sr. Executive Producer: Jeff Scruton
Executive Producers: Eric Stern, Emma Wilcockson
Directors: Dante Ariola, Steve Ayson, Joaquin Baca-Asay,
Blue Source, Fredrik Bond, Juan Cabral, Ray Dillman, Nicolai
Fuglsig, Victor Garcia, Craig Gillespie, Jim Gilchrist, Phil
Joanou, Spike Jonze, Harmony Korine, Tom Kuntz, Rocky
Morton, Marcus Nispel, Pleix, Rupert Sanders, Matthijs
Van Heijningen & Clay Williams

Mohr, Gallerani & More Films (310) 399-6630
1011 Pico Blvd., Ste. 9 FAX (310) 399-4876
Santa Monica, CA 90405 www.mgandm.tv
Executive Producer: Cay Mohr
Director: Andy Gallerani
Head of Production: Margot Ott
Producer: Melodie Woods

Moo Studios (323) 464-3080
746 N. Cahuenga Blvd. FAX (323) 464-3699
Hollywood, CA 90038 www.moostudios.com
Executive Producer: David Lyons
Directors: Adam Byrd, Chad Einbinder, Damon Gameau,
Francois Halard, Pamela Hanson, Andy Huang, Jeffrey
McCarthy, Anthony Rose, Shaun Sewter & Ellen von Unwerth
Head of Sales: Erika Sheldon
Head of Production: Rebecca Donaghe

Motion Theory (310) 396-9433
4235 Redwood Ave. FAX (310) 396-7883
Los Angeles, CA 90066 www.motiontheory.com
Executive Producer: Javier Jimenez
East Coast Sales Rep: Blah! Blah? (Blah..)
Director of Marketing/Sales: Caroline Gomez

Motiv Films (310) 260-6100
1630 Stewart St., Studio B1 FAX (310) 260-6111
Santa Monica, CA 90404 www.motivfilms.com
Executive Producer/Partner: Jim Rutherford
Directors: Grant Baird, Eric Bute, Werner Damen, Trey Fanjoy,
Eric Kiel, John Perez, Scott Rhea & Mark Russel

Moving Target (310) 394-0110
P.O. Box 5367 www.movingtargetla.com
Santa Monica, CA 90409
Executive Producer: Brian Jochum
Director: Alan Munro

Moxie Pictures (310) 857-1000
5890 W. Jefferson Blvd., Ste. J FAX (310) 857-1004
Los Angeles, CA 90016 www.moxiepictures.com
Executive Producers: Robby Fernandez & Lizzie Schwartz
Directors: Wes Anderson, James Bobin, Cameron Crowe,
Seth Gordon, Neil Gorring, Martin Granger, James Griffiths,
Todd Haynes, Henry and Rel, Jared Hess, Rob Legato, Dan
Levinson, Henry Lu, Rob Marshall, Errol Morris, Todd Philips,
Bob Purman, Peyton Reed, Peter Sollett, Jim Sheridan, Kevin
Smith, Pam Thomas, Frank Todaro & John Waters

Mr. Big Film (310) 399-9910
1434 Abbot Kinney Blvd. www.mrbigfilm.com
Venice, CA 90291
Director/Cinematographer: Tim Bieber
Executive Producer: Kate Zimmer
Producer: Lisa DeLeo
East Coast Sales Rep: Judy Wolff
West Coast/Midwest Sales Rep: Ellen Knable
Business Manager: Pat Standley

MRB Productions (323) 965-8881
FAX (323) 965-8882
www.mrbproductions.com

Newhouse Films (310) 659-0010
8630 Pine Tree Pl. FAX (310) 659-3105
Los Angeles, CA 90069 www.newhousefilms.com
Executive Producer: Heidi Nolting
Directors: John Alper, Grapefruit, Walter Kehr &
Patrick Solomon
East Coast Sales Rep: Roxanne & Co.
Midwest Sales Rep: Robin Pickett & Assoc.
West Coast Sales Rep: Stacey & Co.

Nobody Productions (323) 662-7976
President: Adele Baughn www.nobodyproductions.com
Sr. VP of Marketing: Tom Wilson
Development: Anadel Baughn & Craig Lachman

Noda Films, Inc. (310) 866-1594
171 Pier Ave., Ste. 259
Santa Monica, CA 90405
Director/Cameraman: Nobuhito Noda

Nonfiction Unlimited (310) 399-9600
905 Olympic Blvd. www.nonfictionunlimited.com
Santa Monica, CA 90404
Executive Producers: Michael Degan & LJ/Loretta Jeneski
Directors: Paul Crowder, Rob Devor, Sean Dunne, Steve
James, Barbara Kopple, Albert Maysles, Stacy Peralta,
The Selby & Jessica Yu

November Films (310) 230-9370
17751 Tramonto Dr. www.novemberfilms.com
Pacific Palisades, CA 90272
Executive Producer: Alan Siegel
Producer: Chris Sheffield
Head of Production: Matthew Hensley
Directors: Peter Fuszard, Simon Mestel, Stacy Toyama &
Jason Wulfsohn
Sales Rep: Andrew Halpern

Nydrle, Inc. (310) 659-8844
670 N. La Peer Dr. FAX (310) 659-7733
West Hollywood, CA 90069 www.nydrle.com
Executive Producer: Adele Amos
Director: Peter Nydrle

O'Neil & Associates (323) 876-6853
1158 N. Curson Ave.
West Hollywood, CA 90046
Director: James O'Neil
Storyboards: Justice O'Neil

Ocean Park Pictures (310) 450-1220
741A 10th St. FAX (310) 319-1392
Santa Monica, CA 90403 www.oceanparkpix.com
Executive Producer: Tim Goldberg
Directors: David Dryer, Gregory Lemkin, William Linsman &
Holly Goldberg Sloan

Oceangate Productions (323) 224-9051
1939 N. Gramercy Pl.
Los Angeles, CA 90068
Executive Producer/Director: Mark Rasmussen

ODM Inc. (323) 933-1614
5820 Wilshire Blvd., Ste. 306 www.odmproductions.com
Los Angeles, CA 90036

Onyx Productions Direct, Inc. (323) 692-9830
2355 Westwood Blvd., Ste. 401 FAX (323) 470-0190
Los Angeles, CA 90064 www.onyxprod.com
President/Executive Producer: Joan Renfrow

Order, LLC (323) 930-5900
6374 Arizona Circle FAX (323) 930-5909
Los Angeles, CA 90045 www.order.tv
Executive Producer/Managing Partner: Charles Salice
Head of Production: Jennifer Ingalls
Executive Coordinator: Matthew Turke

Original Film, Inc. (310) 445-9000
4223 Glencoe Ave., Ste. B119 FAX (310) 445-9191
Marina del Rey, CA 90292 www.originalfilm.com
Executive Producers: Jeff Devlin & Bruce Mellon
Head of Production: Robbyn Foxx
Sales Rep: Jeff Devlin

The Outfit Media Group (310) 499-0226
2148 Federal Ave., Ste. B FAX (310) 499-0235
Los Angeles, CA 90025 www.theoutfitmg.com

PAC (323) 931-9962
Producer/Director: Martin Pitts

Commercial Production Companies

Partizan (323) 468-0123
7083 Hollywood Blvd., Ste. 401 FAX (323) 468-0129
Hollywood, CA 90028 **www.partizan.com**
Executive Producer & CEO: Sheila Stepanek
East Coast Sales Rep: Melanie McEvoy
Midwest Sales Rep: Tracy Bernard
West Coast Sales Rep: Tracy Fetterman
Directors: Philip Andelman, Debbie Anzalone, Antoine Bardou-
Jacquet, Patrik Bergh, Nico Beyer, Kinga Burza, Stephen
Cafiero, Chris Cairns, Lisa Cholodenko, Alex Courtes, Karen
Cunningham, John Dolan, Niall Downing, Jared Eberhardt,
Daniel Eskils, Raphael Frydman, Michael Geoghegan, Paul
Goldman, Michel Gondry, Michael Gracey and Pete Commins,
Thomas Hilland, Matthias Hoene, Nadav Kander, Ariel Kleiman,
Jeremy Konner, Eric Lynne, Toby Macdonald, Bo Mirosseni,
Dominic Murphy, Doug Nichol, Ace Norton, Nima Nourizadeh,
Jim Owen, Valerie Pirson, Hervé Plumet, Alastair Siddons,
Adam Stevens, Kevin Summers, Traktor, Michael Williams &
Anthony Wonke

Passport Films (310) 458-0663
701 Santa Monica Blvd., Ste. 200 FAX (310) 458-9692
Santa Monica, CA 90401 **www.passportfilms.com**
Executive Producers: David Coulter & Patti Coulter
Directors: Michael Grasso, Cameron Hird, Joel Marsden, Monty
Miranda, Saboteur, Ari Sandel & Brendan Williams
West Coast Sales Rep: Chuck Silverman
East Coast Sales Rep: Cindy Velsor
Midwest Sales Rep: Julie Vargo, Julie Vargo & Associates
South Eastern Sales Rep: Cindy Velsor
Detroit Sales Rep: Chuck Silverman

Pictures In A Row (323) 957-5400
736 Seward St. FAX (323) 957-5405
Los Angeles, CA 90038 **www.picrow.com**
Directors: Bryan Barber, DarkFibre, Florian Hoffmeister, Jason
House, Peter Lang, Margaret Malandruccolo & Marc Silver

Playroom Creative (714) 969-3938
412 Indianapolis Ave. **www.playroomcreative.com**
Huntington Beach, CA 92648

Praxis Films (323) 460-4393
c/o R. Sirott, 17324 Partheia St. FAX (323) 460-4181
Northridge, CA 91325
Director: Robert Blalack

Precision Productions + Post (310) 839-4600
10718 McCune Ave. FAX (310) 839-4601
Los Angeles, CA 90034 **www.precisionpost.com**

PRETTYBIRD (310) 315-8700
9905 Jefferson Blvd. FAX (310) 315-5470
Culver City, CA 90404 **www.prettybirdus.com**

Proscenium Pictures, Ltd. (323) 650-6767
8840 Wilshire Blvd. FAX (323) 650-1345
Beverly Hills, CA 90211 **www.prosceniumpictures.com**
Executive Producer: Jeff McQueen

Pytka (310) 392-9571
858 N. Doheny Dr. FAX (310) 392-5873
West Hollywood, CA 90069
Executive Producer: Tara Fitzpatrick
Director: Joe Pytka

(310) 664-4500
@radical.media (212) 462-1500
1630 12th St. FAX (310) 664-4600
Santa Monica, CA 90404 **www.radicalmedia.com**
Executive Producers: Jon Kamen, Donna Portaro &
Frank Scherma
Sales Rep: Dominic Bernacchi

Raimondi Films, Inc. (760) 837-1093
75387 Stardust Ln. **www.raimondifilms.com**
Indian Wells, CA 92210
Executive Producer: Jane Raimondi
Director/Cameraman: Paul Raimondi

Raintree Productions (310) 827-3336
President/Executive Producer: Bob Wollin
Director: Stu Berg

Ranch Exit Media (310) 209-8974
846 S Broadway, Ste. 1003 FAX (213) 623-5349
Los Angeles, CA 90014 **www.ranchexitmedia.com**
Executive Producer: Christopher Raser
Director: Chris Patterson
Sales Reps: Kim Griswold & Doug Sherin

Raymond Entertainment Direct (323) 785-4700
3450 Cahuenga Blvd. FAX (323) 785-4701
Los Angeles, CA 90068
www.raymondentertainment.com

RebelRobot (310) 399-6630
1011 Pico Blvd., Ste. 9 FAX (310) 399-4876
Santa Monica, CA 90405 **www.rebelrobot.tv**
Producer: Melodie Woods
Head of Production: Margot Ott
Director: Andy G.

Reel Orange (949) 548-4524
316 La Jolla Dr. **www.reelorange.com**
Newport Beach, CA 92663
Director/Cameraman: Art Vitarelli

Resident Films (310) 822-2147
1180 Nelrose Ave., Ste. 3 **www.residentfilms.tv**
Venice, CA 90291
Directors: Amin Azali, Alex Noble & Randy Spear
Executive Producer (USA): David M. Bando
Sales Representative: Nelssy Bieniak
Executive Producer (Mexico): Mauricio Cisneros

Revolver Films (310) 827-2441
4040 Del Rey Ave., Ste. 5 FAX (310) 827-2661
Marina del Rey, CA 90292 **www.revolverfilmsla.com**
Producer: Mark Priola

Rhythm + Hues Commercial Studios (310) 448-7900
2100 E. Grand Ave. FAX (310) 448-7601
El Segundo, CA 90245 **www.rhythm.com**
Executive Producer: Paul Babb
Head of Production, Live Action: Kat Dillon
Head of Production, Commercial Digital: Lisa White
Directors: Clark Anderson, John-Mark Austin, EJ Foerster,
Timothy Kendall, Joe Murray & James Wahlberg
East Coast Sales: Carolyn Hill
Midwest/Detroit Sales: Marci Miles
Western Region/Texas Sales: Claire Worch
United Kingdom/Europe Sales: Georgina Poushkine
Creative Services Manager: Chad Norton

Ringleader (310) 876-2278
13101 Washington Blvd., Ste. 402 **www.ringleader.pro**
Los Angeles, CA 90066
Directors: Jerry Chan, Jon Danovic & Max Gutierrez
Producers: Mike Begovich, Sarah Craig, David Harb &
R.L. Hooker

Ross McCanse & Associates, Inc. (818) 506-4715
3315 Oakdell Rd. FAX (818) 506-4587
Studio City, CA 91604
Director: Ross McCanse

(310) 659-1577
RSA Films, Inc. (212) 343-2020
634 N. La Peer Dr. FAX (310) 659-1377
West Hollywood, CA 90069 **www.rsafilms.com**
President: Jules Daly
VP & Executive Producer: Marjie Abrahams
Executive Producers: Philip Fox-Mills & Tracie Norfleet
Directors: Ozan Biron, Bill Bruce, James Bryce, Joe Carnahan,
Robert Cohen, Barney Cokeliss, Jakob Daschek, Tom Dey, Ben
Dickinson, Laurence Dunmore, Lauri Faggioni, Jeff Feuerzeig,
Brett Foraker, Adam Goldstein, Alfonso Gomez-Rejon, Henrik
Hansen, Price James, Nick Livesey, Adrian Moat, John
O'Hagan, Jesse Peretz, Carl Erik Rinsch, The Russo Brothers,
Jake Scott, Jordan Scott, Luke Scott, Tony Scott, Joachim Trier,
Jordan Vogt-Roberts & Declan Whitebloom
East Coast Sales Reps: Philip Fox-Mills & Victoria Venantini
Midwest Sales Reps: Chris Karabas & Rob Mueller
West Coast Sales Rep: Holly Ross

Rumpus Creative (310) 390-3410
www.rumpuscreative.com

(212) 647-1310
Sandwick (310) 854-0647
8630 Pine Tree Pl. www.sandwickmedia.com
Los Angeles, CA 90069
President: Bill Sandwick
Directors: Matthaus Bussmann, John Curran, Mona El
Monsouri, Jeff Gorman, Andreas Hoffman, Keir McFarlane,
Nic and Sune, Nick Rafter, Paul Riccio, Roenberg, Salmon,
Thomas Sigel & Johan Tappert
East Coast Sales Rep: Jared Shapiro
Midwest Sales Rep: Janice Harryman
West Coast Sales Rep: Andrew Hall

Satin Sky Productions (310) 641-0756

Sean Hanish Creative (626) 395-7700
26 E. Colorado Blvd. FAX (626) 395-7722
Pasadena, CA 91105 www.seanhanish.com
President/Owner: Sean Hanish
Director: Sean Hanish
Producer: Chris Sias

Sharpcut Productions (310) 247-0088
Director: Gary Robinson FAX (310) 858-2254
www.sharpcut.com

Shine (323) 937-7470
5410 Wilshire Blvd., Ste. 204 FAX (360) 237-0542
Los Angeles, CA 90036 www.shinestudio.tv
Creative Director: Michael Riley
Executive Producer: Bob Swensen

Sincbox (310) 566-6701
12100 Wilshire Blvd., Ste. 550 FAX (310) 566-6719
Los Angeles, CA 90025 www.sincbox.com
Commercial Director/Partner: Bruce Somers
Executive Creative Director: Peter Smaha
Director of Client Services: Brigid Devine
Director, Commercial/Music Video: Mark Wilkinson
Agency Coordinator: Zach Cohen

Slim Pictures (310) 577-0700
514 Victoria Ave. FAX (310) 577-0770
Venice, CA 90291 www.slim-pictures.com
Directors: Stephen Blackman, Nicolas Caicoya, Brad Morrison,
Ludovic Schorno & ZCDC

Smith and Jones Films, Inc. (310) 948-5751
4123 Lankershim Blvd. FAX (310) 496-2635
Los Angeles, CA 91602 www.smithandjonesfilms.net

Smuggler (323) 817-3300
1715 N. Gower St. FAX (323) 817-3333
Los Angeles, CA 90028 www.smugglersite.com
Executive Producers: Brian Carmody & Patrick Milling Smith
Heads of Production: Allison Kunzman & Laura Thoel
Directors: Jaron Albertin, Brian Beletic, Adam Berg, Jun Diaz,
Filip Engstrom, David Frankham, Guard Brothers, Neil Harris,
Tom Hooper, Randy Krallman, Ringan Ledwidge, Samir Mallal,
Renny Maslow, Bennett Miller, Joshua Neale, Psyop, Jamie
Rafn, Henry-Alex Rubin, Guy Shelmerdine, Chris Smith,
Stylewar, Jon Watts & Ivan Zacharias
Chief Operating Officer: Lisa Rich

(310) 785-9100
Sonic Films, Inc. (212) 744-5333
73 Market St. FAX (310) 564-7500
Venice, CA 90291 www.sonicfilmsinc.com
Executive Producer: David Stoltz

(310) 785-9100
Sports Cinematography Group (212) 744-5333
73 Market St. FAX (310) 564-7500
Venice, CA 90291
www.sportscinematographygroup.com
Executive Producer: David Stoltz

Square Planet (310) 632-4090
20432 S. Santa Fe Ave., Ste. F FAX (310) 632-4092
Long Beach, CA 90810 www.squareplanetmedia.com

Squeeze (818) 906-0006
www.thedirectorsnetwork.com

Stardust Studios (310) 399-6047
1823 Colorado Ave. FAX (310) 399-7486
Santa Monica, CA 90404 www.stardust.tv
Creative Directors- LA: Jake Banks & Brad Tucker
Executive Producer: Josh Libitsky

Steam (310) 636-4620
3021 Airport Ave., Ste. 201 FAX (310) 636-4621
Santa Monica, CA 90405 www.steamshow.com
Contact: Scott Bryant

Sticks + Stones Studios (323) 790-0440
6615 Melrose Ave., Loft 2 FAX (323) 790-0450
Los Angeles, CA 90038 www.sticks.tv
Executive Producer: Marlon Staggs
Coordinator: Michaela Quinn
Director: Theresa Wingert

Stiles-Bishop Productions, Inc. (213) 400-1600
12652 Killion St.
Valley Village, CA 91607
Producer: D Cassidy

Streetlight Films (323) 931-3300
717 N. Highland Ave., Ste. 9 FAX (323) 931-3307
Hollywood, CA 90038 www.streetlightfilms.net

Subliminal Pictures (818) 841-2550
FAX (818) 450-0559

superstudio (310) 582-1111
2900 Olympic Blvd., Ste. 170 FAX (310) 582-1113
Santa Monica, CA 90404 www.superstudio.tv
President/Executive Producer: Dana Garman Jacobsen
Staff Producer: Nathan de la Rionda

Supply & Demand Integrated (310) 956-3500
6374 Arizona Circle FAX (310) 956-3501
Los Angeles, CA 90045 www.sdintegrated.com
Founder/Managing Partner: Tim Case
President/Managing Partner: Charles Salice
Directors: Gary Breslin, Adrien Brody, Gabriela Cowperthwaite,
David Holm, Matt Lenski, Robert Logevall, Jeffery Plansker,
Greg Popp, Mac Premo, Josh Taft, Sean Thonson,
Lucy Walker & Margo Weathers
East Coast Rep: Eby/Dickson
West Coast Sales Rep: Reber/Covington
Executive Producer/Partner: Kira Carstensen
Sr. Head Of Production: Rika Osenberg
Mid-West Sales Rep: Miller/Stephen
Co-Head Of Production: Tracy Hauser, Jennifer Ingalls &
Alexis Kaplan
Integrated Consultant: Dana Locatell

Tate USA (310) 828-8989
1913 Centinela Ave. FAX (310) 828-0707
Santa Monica, CA 90404 www.tateusa.com
Executive Producers: Hugh Bacher & David Tate
Directors: Steven Antin, Michael Bindlechner, Jonathan Brown,
Ohav Flantz, Chris Graham, Mat Humphrey, Enno Jacobsen,
Mattieu Mantovani, David Popescu, Jason Reitman &
Jonathan Teplitzky

Tempered Entertainment, LLC (323) 252-6774
1234 Sixth St., Ste. 403 FAX (323) 934-1150
Santa Monica, CA 90401
www.temperedentertainment.com

Tool of North America (310) 453-9244
2210 Broadway FAX (310) 453-4185
Santa Monica, CA 90404 www.toolofna.com
Executive Producer: Jennifer Siegel
Head of Production: Amy Delossa
Directors: James Brown, Sean Ehringer, Erich Joiner, Matt
Ogens, Robert Richardson, Evan Silver, Geordie Stephens &
Jason Zada

trio films (310) 207-7800
2023 S. Westgate Ave. FAX (310) 207-7807
Los Angeles, CA 90025 www.triofilms.com
Executive Producers: Taylor Ferguson & Erin Tauscher

Commercial Production Companies

Tuesday Films   (310) 828-8443
3025 Olympic Blvd., Ste. 300   FAX **(310) 828-4278**
Santa Monica, CA 90404   **www.tuesdayfilms.com**
Executive Producer: Mardi Minogue
Directors: Joe Baratelli, Don Burgess, Guy Norman Bee,
Ty Stanford & Jon Yarbrough
Production Supervisor: Neil Daniels

TWC   (310) 392-7333
1655 Euclid St.   FAX **(310) 392-7323**
Santa Monica, CA 90404   **www.thomaswintercooke.com**
Executive Producer/Partner: Mark Thomas
Partners: Philip Cooke & Ralph Winter
Head of Production: Jeff Snyder
Directors: Arni Thor Jonsson, Laszlo Kadar, Ken Lambert, Hans
Moland, Alex Oqus, Suthon Petchsuwan, Terry Rietta, Johan
Skoq & Eric Will
West Coast Sales Rep: Michel Waxman

Über Content   (323) 860-8686
1040 N. Las Palmas Ave., Bldg. 7N   FAX **(323) 860-8689**
Los Angeles, CA 90038   **www.ubercontent.com**
Executive Producers: Phyllis Koenig & Preston Lee
Directors: Lucia Aniello, Jeffrey Fleisig, Luis Gerard, Chris
Hooper, Jason Kohn, Eliot Rausch, Keith Rivers, Fred Savage,
Molly Schiot, Marc Scholermann, Daniel Strange,
Charlie Todd & Cole Webley

Untitled   (310) 917-9191
2241 Corinth Ave.   FAX **(310) 231-7612**
Los Angeles, CA 90064   **www.untitled.tv**
Executive Producer: Jim Evans
General Manager: Larry Edwards
Head of Production: Geoff Campbell
Directors: Geoffrey Barish, Mark Bennett, Bua, The
Cronenweths, Linus Ewers, Rachel Harms, Rick Knief, Glenn
Martin, Adam Massey & Adam Reed
West Coast Sales Rep: Siobhan McCafferty
Midwest Sales Rep: Donna D'Aguanno
East Coast Sales Rep: Sarah Jenks

Utopia Films, Inc.   (310) 338-0580
1976 S. La Cienega Blvd., Ste. 130   FAX **(313) 557-0580**
Los Angeles, CA 90034   **www.utopiafilms.com**
Directors: Mike Brady, Arturo Hoyos, Ricardo Hoyos,
M.I.X. & Nicolas

Velocity Visuals, Inc.   (310) 376-7870
Producer/Director: William Powloski   **www.velocityfx.com**

Verité Studios   (866) 535-1972
708 Westmont Rd.   **www.veritestudios.com**
Santa Barbara, CA 93108
Director: Timothy Eaton

Vihlene & Associates, Inc.   (949) 582-0937
28241 Crown Valley Pkwy, Ste. F187   **www.vihlene.com**
Laguna Niguel, CA 92677
Executive Producer: Vern Vihlene Jr.

**Walker/Fitzgibbon Television/
Film Productions**   (323) 469-6800
6565 Sunset Blvd., Ste. 417   FAX **(323) 469-6801**
Los Angeles, CA 90028   **www.walkerfitzgibbon.com**
Executive Producer: Mo Fitzgibbon
Directors: Mo Fitzgibbon & Robert W. Walker
Producer: Fernando Viquez
Production: Elissa Slovin

    (818) 901-1178
Waterline Pictures, Inc.   (310) 963-4812
P.O. Box 56387   FAX **(818) 901-1179**
Sherman Oaks, CA 91413
Director: Roger Roth
Producer/Director: Dylan Stern

Wild Indigo, LLC   (323) 876-3331
Executive Producer: Arthur Gorson   **www.wildindigo.tv**
Directors: Moses Edinborough, Dean Karr & Jefferson Miller

Wild Plum   (310) 823-7445
2128 Narcissus Court   FAX **(310) 578-1445**
Venice, CA 90291   **www.wildplum.tv**
Contact: Shelby Sexton
Directors: Ericson Core, Jan De Bont, Shane Drake, Mike
Goubeaux, Kamp Grizzly & Kieran Walsh
Executive Producer: Shelby Sexton
CFO: Alisa Allen
Head of Production: Sandy Haddad
Creative Director: Ben Ross
Associate Producer: Matt Lancaster

William Moffitt Associates   (818) 495-3106
785 New York Dr.   FAX **(626) 345-0673**
Altadena, CA 91001   **www.wmadigital.com**
President: Will Moffitt
Executive Producer: Lynne Moffitt
Sales Rep: Brooke Rothman

Windowseat Pictures   (310) 372-3650
200 Pier Ave., Ste. 124   **www.windowseatpictures.com**
El Segundo, CA 90245

Wolfe and Company Films   (626) 584-4000
39 E. Walnut St.   FAX **(626) 584-4099**
Pasadena, CA 91103   **www.danwolfe.com**
Directors: Dean Cundey, Robert Mehnert & Dan Wolfe
Sales Rep: Tony Luna

Wondros   (323) 951-0010
8330 W. Third St.   FAX **(323) 951-0710**
Los Angeles, CA 90048   **www.wondros.com**
Executive Producers: Priscilla Cohen & Gina Zapata
Directors: Peter Care, Jesse Dylan, Antoine Fuqua, Wayne
Isham, Mark Pellington, Trent Reznor, David O. Russell, Aaron
Schneider & Christian Weber
Staff Production Manager: Clark Farrell
Post Production Supervisor: Janine Criscuolo
Sales, USA East: Ann McKallagat
Sales, USA Midwest: Nikki Weiss
Sales, USA West: Jeanie DiMaggio
Music Video Executive Producer: Joe Uliano
Chief Creative Officer: Anne-Marie Mackay
Office Manager: Maggie Wagner
Chief Financial Officer: Kim MacKaye

Wright Banks/Tag Team   (310) 470-0491
1334 Westwood Blvd., Ste. 9   FAX **(310) 388-0399**
Los Angeles, CA 90024
Executive Producer: Cindie Wright
Directors: Kevin Dole & Jim O'Neil

WSR Creative   (310) 837-7001
9503 Jefferson Blvd., Ste. B   FAX **(310) 837-3680**
Culver City, CA 90232   **www.wsrcreative.com**

Wyoming Films   (310) 798-6332
    FAX **(310) 374-2082**
Executive Producer: Mark West   **www.wyomingfilms.com**
Directors: The Hodges, Michael Ivey & Chuck Kuhn
Director/Cameraman: Tim Angulo & Bill Everett
Head of Sales: Mike West

Zoo Film   (323) 871-9000
6427 W. Sunset Blvd.   FAX **(323) 962-8028**
Hollywood, CA 90028   **www.zoofilm.net**
Executive Producers: Gower Frost
Media Director: Matt Sarnecki
Office Manager: Meredith Snider

The Zoofx   (818) 535-4025
5115 Douglas Fir Rd., Ste. H   FAX **(818) 222-9483**
Calabasas, CA 91302   **www.thezoofx.com**

24pCine/PAL HD (323) 375-4040
1247 Lincoln Blvd., Ste. 151 www.palhd.com
Santa Monica, CA 90401
Contact: Julian Diamond

2K4K Talking Pictures (310) 447-8575
www.2k4ktalkingpictures.com

30 Second Films (310) 315-1750
3019 Pico Blvd. FAX (310) 315-1757
Santa Monica, CA 90405 www.30secondfilms.com
Contact: Alan J. Stamm

5th Wall (323) 461-0600
6311 Romaine St., Ste. 7135 www.5thwall.tv
Hollywood, CA 90038

Acme Events (818) 767-8888
www.acme-events.com

Ad-Lib Marketing & Advertising (909) 629-1995
One Blacksmith Circle FAX (909) 629-1995
Phillips Ranch, CA 91766
Contact: Keith N. Underwood

Alex Pitt Photography (323) 665-4492
www.alexpittphotography.com

All In One Productions (323) 780-8880
1111 Corporate Center Dr., Ste. 303 FAX (323) 780-8887
Monterey Park, CA 91754 www.allinone-usa.com
Contact: Joanna Or

Almost Midnight Productions (310) 313-4046
12240 Venice Blvd., Ste. 18 FAX (310) 313-4048
Los Angeles, CA 90066 www.almostmidnight.com

Alter Ego Films (310) 809-1910
FAX (310) 356-3397
www.alteregofilms.com

American Video Group (310) 477-1535
2542 Aiken Ave. www.americanvideogroup.com
Los Angeles, CA 90064
Contact: John Berzner

Anyes Galleani Images & Film (213) 626-6260
912 E. Third St., Ste. 203 www.galleani.com
Los Angeles, CA 90013

Arclight Productions (323) 464-7791
732 N. Highland Ave. FAX (323) 464-7406
Hollywood, CA 90038 www.arclightprods.com
Contacts: Karlo David, Steven Kochones & Steven Morales

The Association, Inc. (818) 841-9660
135 N. Screenland Dr. FAX (818) 841-8370
Burbank, CA 91505 www.wemakethephonering.com
Contacts: Trevor Eisenman, Jeff Murphy, Fletcher Murray, Tom Murray & Tom Myrdahl

Auster Productions, Inc. (818) 843-5040
2607 W. Magnolia Blvd. FAX (818) 843-5041
Burbank, CA 91505 www.austerproductions.com
Contacts: Nona Friedman & Jennifer Wetzel

Barcon Video Productions (818) 248-9161
3653 Mesa Lila Ln. FAX (818) 249-8884
Glendale, CA 91208 www.barryconrad.com

BCTV Productions (949) 495-1500
Contact: Bud W. Connell FAX (501) 851-7303
www.bctv.us

Bianco-Scott Productions (323) 467-6936
1438 Gower St., Box 52 www.biancoscott.com
Hollywood, CA 90028
Contact: Eric Scott

Bluth Enterprises, Inc. (818) 502-1414
517 Commercial St. FAX (818) 500-1137
Glendale, CA 91203 www.bluthenterprises.com

A Broad Vision Productions (323) 848-9411
(323) 401-4157
FAX (866) 247-8610
www.abroadvisionproductions.com

Buddy Systems (626) 482-3479
www.buddysystems.tv

Castleland Productions (818) 787-7442
(818) 633-3606
5827 Cantaloupe Ave. FAX (818) 787-7462
Van Nuys, CA 91401 www.castlelandproductions.com

The Cavalry Productions (310) 966-4440
11849 W. Olympic Blvd., Ste. 204 FAX (310) 954-1414
Los Angeles, CA 90064
www.thecavalryproductions.com

Cinevative Productions (323) 852-8903
8455 Beverly Blvd., Ste. 507 FAX (323) 852-0349
Los Angeles, CA 90048 www.cinevative.com
Contacts: Mark Ciglar & Carrie Dobro

Combat Film Productions (818) 618-2527
www.combatfilmproductions.com

Crash Productions (310) 489-6848
713 N. Mansfield Ave. FAX (323) 939-9622
Los Angeles, CA 90038 www.crashproductions.com

Cresta West (323) 939-7003
6815 Willoughby Ave., Ste. 102 FAX (323) 939-7002
Los Angeles, CA 90038 www.crestagroup.com
Contact: Sara Beugen

Crystal Pyramid Productions (619) 644-3000
(800) 365-8433
7323 Rondel Court FAX (619) 644-3001
San Diego, CA 92119 www.crystalpyramid.com
Contacts: Patty Mooney & Mark Schulze

Custom Video (310) 543-4901
707 Torrance Blvd., Ste. 105 www.customvideo.tv
Redondo Beach, CA 90277
Contact: Michael Ude

Defy Agency (310) 204-2340
3750 S. Robertson Blvd., Ste. 104 FAX (310) 204-2341
Culver City, CA 90232 www.defyagency.com

Diligent (323) 863-6204
4214 Santa Monica Blvd. www.dodiligent.com
Los Angeles, CA 90029

Documentary Makers (213) 570-9500
1807 Grave Ave. FAX (213) 985-3001
Los Angeles, CA 90028 www.documentarymakers.com
Contact: Adam Wilkenfeld

The Dreaming Tree (818) 845-3230
1112 Chestnut St., Ste. B FAX (818) 333 0795
Burbank, CA 91506
www.dreamingtreeproductions.com

Dynasty Films (818) 823-6088
www.dynastyfilms.com

Earl J. Beadle Productions, Inc. (626) 792-5626
(626) 688-5266
www.ejbproductions.com

Edward Pacio & Associates
(818) 880-1586
(310) 995-6037
26931 Deerweed Trail
FAX (818) 880-1001
Agoura Hills, CA 91301
Contact: Edward Pacio

Epiphany Media
(323) 819-1001
5300 Melrose Ave.
www.epiphanymedia.com
Hollywood, CA 90038

Eric Blum Productions, Inc.
(818) 707-4524
(818) 707-4526
31139 Via Colinas, Ste. 210
FAX (818) 707-0071
Thousand Oaks, CA 91362
www.ericblumproductions.com

EVIDENCE Productions
(323) 522-5298
(310) 628-5400
1819 Winona Blvd.
FAX (323) 522-5298
Hollywood, CA 90027 www.evidenceproductions.com
(Video Production Services)

Evolution L.A. Inc.
(310) 587-9191
(310) 587-9116
1510 11th St., Ste. 101
FAX (310) 564-7717
Santa Monica, CA 90401
www.evolutionla.com
Contact: Mark Shockley

eVox Productions, LLC
(310) 605-1400
2363 E. Pacifica Pl.
FAX (310) 605-1429
Rancho Dominguez, CA 90220
www.evox.com

FilmCrafter
(310) 773-1431
www.filmcrafter.com

Filmstyle Productions
(818) 993-1099
FAX (818) 993-0062

Firestone Productions
(323) 461-7500
(323) 377-9494
Contact: Scott Firestone www.firestoneproductions.com

Fluid Films Productions Inc.
(323) 899-3762
5708 Troost Ave.
www.fluidfilms.net
North Hollywood, CA 91601

Galanty & Company, Inc.
(310) 451-2525
1640 Fifth St., Ste. 203
Santa Monica, CA 90401
Contact: Mark Galanty

Golden Eagle Pix
(805) 381-9095
(805) 208-1658
Contact: Peter Good
FAX (805) 381-9096
www.goldeneaglepix.com

A Gosch Production
(818) 729-0000
Contact: Pat Gosch
www.goschproductions.com

Grainey Pictures
(310) 827-1111
4220 Glencoe Ave., Ste. 100
FAX (310) 827-1124
Marina del Rey, CA 90292
www.gpixer.com

Granbery Studios
(213) 373-1099
(949) 515-0100
200 Fairway Pl.
www.gstudios.net
Costa Mesa, CA 92627

GSM Entertainment
(310) 205-0370
309 S. Sherbourne Dr., Ste. 108
Los Angeles, CA 90048 www.gsmentertainment.com
Contact: Geoffrey S. McNeil

Healthcare Communications Group (310) 606-5700
909 N. Sepulveda Blvd., Ste. 550
FAX (310) 606-5705
El Segundo, CA 90245
www.hcg.com
Contact: Linda Kilpatrick

Highline Studios
(424) 245-4031
8842 Hollywood Blvd.
www.highlinestudios.com
Los Angeles, CA 90069

Hot Buttered Content
(310) 230-5539
1426 Main St., Ste. 201
www.hb-content.com
Venice, CA 90291

Hu-Man Element Productions, Inc. (213) 534-3700
1201 W. Fifth St., Ste. F-220A
FAX (213) 534-3711
Los Angeles, CA 90017
www.hu-manelement.com

Image Factory, Inc.
(818) 841-1515
2029 Verdugo Blvd., Ste. 1030
FAX (818) 841-2395
Montrose, CA 91020
Contact: Machiko Kobayashi

Image Line Productions, Inc.
(818) 762-2900
1220 N. Poinsettia Pl.
FAX (818) 762-2992
W. Hollywood, CA 90046
www.imagelinemedia.com
Contact: Brad D. White

Imagecraft
(818) 954-0187
3318 Burton Ave.
FAX (818) 954-0189
Burbank, CA 91504
www.imagecraft.tv

Imaginaut Entertainment
(323) 665-5274
908 Parkman Ave.
FAX (323) 693-5320
Los Angeles, CA 90026
www.imaginaut.com
Contact: Clay Westervelt

Intelliscape Films, LLC
(310) 882-2100
(800) 422-5996
Contact: Bruce Caulk
FAX (310) 575-1890
www.intelliscape.com

International Television Group (ITG) (310) 656-9100
22631 Pacific Coast Hwy, Ste. 379
FAX (310) 656-9104
Malibu, CA 90265
Contact: Laraine Gregory & Lou La Monte

Jam Media, LLC
(310) 289-4466
1800 Century Park East, Ste. 600
FAX (310) 289-2199
Los Angeles, CA 90067
www.jam-media.net

Jeffrey Markowitz Productions, Inc. (877) 297-8887
760 N. Cahuenga Blvd.
www.jeffproductions.com
Hollywood, CA 90068

JM Digital Works
(760) 476-1783
2460 Impala Dr.
FAX (760) 476-1788
Carlsbad, CA 92008
www.jmdigitalworks.com
Contact: Ken Kebow

JSP Creative
(866) 711-5195
(714) 288-6005
229 N. Glassell St.
FAX (714) 288-6014
Orange, CA 92866
www.jspcreative.com
Contact: Jerry Stanley

Kandoo Films, Inc.
(818) 789-6777
4515 Van Nuys Blvd., Ste. 100
FAX (818) 789-2299
Sherman Oaks, CA 91403
www.kandoofilms.com

LeTo Entertainment, LLC
(310) 358-3282
8840 Wilshire Blvd., Third Fl.
FAX (310) 388-1403
Beverly Hills, CA 90211
www.letoentertainment.com

M Creative Group, Inc.
(818) 225-1541
23209 Mariano St., Ste. 100
FAX (818) 225-1476
Woodland Hills, CA 91367
www.mcreativegroup.net
Contacts: Diane Glezerman & Seth Pinsker

Main Street Media, Inc.
(310) 450-1846
(213) 509-7798
185 Pier Ave., Ste. 105 www.mainstreetmediainc.com
Santa Monica, CA 90405
Contacts: Chris Blakely & Rob Newell

Make It Happen Productions, Inc.
(818) 981-2327
13557 Ventura Blvd., Second Fl.
FAX (818) 981-2440
Sherman Oaks, CA 91423
www.mihp.tv

Master Communication
(310) 832-3303
445 W. Seventh St.
FAX (310) 832-0296
San Pedro, CA 90731
www.bestmedia.com
Contact: Mary Jo Masters

Matrix Communications (310) 782-8400	**StandardVision, LLC** (323) 224-3944
2522 Torrance Blvd. www.matrixcommunications.info	2020 N. Main St., Ste. 227 FAX (323) 225-6226
Torrance, CA 90503	Los Angeles, CA 90031 www.standardsite.com
	Contact: Steven Wren
McNulty Nielsen, Inc. (310) 704-1713	
6930 1/2 Tujunga Ave. FAX (323) 372-3768	(858) 679-9303
North Hollywood, CA 91605 www.mcnultynielsen.com	**Staylor-Made Communications, Inc.** (800) 711-6699
	11835 Carmel Mountain Rd., FAX (858) 679-9373
Media Fishtank (818) 518-7283	Ste. 1304-365 www.staylor-made.com
www.mediafishtank.com	San Diego, CA 92128
MOB Media Inc./MOB Media Studios (949) 222-0220	**Steam** (310) 636-4620
27121 Towne Centre Dr., Ste. 260 FAX (949) 222-0243	3021 Airport Ave., Ste. 201 www.steamshow.com
Foothill Ranch, CA 92610 www.mobmedia.com	Santa Monica, CA 90405
Motion City Films (310) 434-1272	**Sterling Productions** (626) 675-0994
www.motioncity.com	600 N. Louise St., Ste. 8
	Glendale, CA 91206 www.sterlingproductionstv.com
New West Productions (949) 717-3444	
P.O. Box 11418 www.newwest-inc.com	**StormMaker Productions, Inc.** (818) 760-4111
Newport Beach, CA 92658	10551 Burbank Blvd. FAX (818) 760-4111
	North Hollywood, CA 91601
Pat Blessing Productions (213) 705-6978	www.stormmakerproductions.com
755 N. Lafayette Park Pl.	
Los Angeles, CA 90026	**TVP Studios** (818) 843-3188
Contact: Pat Blessing	1539 W. Magnolia Blvd. www.tvpstudiosburbank.com
	Burbank, CA 91506
Patterson Avenue Productions (818) 567-1308	Contact: Richard Tamayo
238 S. Lamer St. www.pattersonavenue.com	
Burbank, CA 91506	**Upper Diamond** (310) 936-7103
Contacts: Keith Dixon, Yvonne Harper & Lisa Holden	5225 Wilshire Blvd., Ste. 1212 www.upperdiamond.com
	Los Angeles, CA 90036
Point of Origin (818) 392-8735	
www.pointoforiginmedia.com	**Verité Studios** (866) 535-1972
	708 Westmont Rd. www.veritestudios.com
Precision Productions + Post (310) 839-4600	Santa Barbara, CA 93108
10718 McCune Ave. FAX (310) 839-4601	Contact: Timothy Eaton
Los Angeles, CA 90034 www.precisionpost.com	
	The Video Agency, Inc./ (818) 505-8300
Quest Pictures (818) 400-7533	**TVA Productions** (888) 322-4296
7625 Hayvenhurst Ave., Ste. 41 www.questpictures.com	3950 Vantage Ave. FAX (818) 505-8370
Van Nuys, CA 91406	Studio City, CA 91604 www.tvaproductions.com
	Contact: Jeffery Goddard
Rickmon Media (310) 503-5402	
www.rickmonmedia.com	**Video Production Specialists (VPS)** (866) 447-3877
	FAX (310) 577-0850
(310) 339-8382	www.videoproductionspecialists.com
RPM/Rigdon Production and Media (310) 922-7197	
Contact: Dickie Rigdon FAX (310) 424-7105	(310) 393-8754
www.rpmstudios.tv	**Videowerks** (310) 780-4156
	3435 Ocean Park Blvd., Ste. 107 FAX (310) 399-1829
Scott Films (818) 730-4900	Santa Monica, CA 90405 www.videowerks.com
www.scottfilms.com	
	Vihlene & Associates, Inc. (949) 582-0937
Screen Door Entertainment, Inc. (818) 781-5600	28241 Crown Valley Pkwy, Ste. F187 www.vihlene.com
15223 Burbank Blvd. FAX (818) 781-5601	Laguna Niguel, CA 92677
Sherman Oaks, CA 91411 www.sdetv.com	Contact: Debbie Stolpp
Seven Pictures (323) 462-0987	**Visual Concepts** (858) 598-6494
6072 Franklin Ave. www.sevenpictures.com	FAX (858) 694-0546
Los Angeles, CA 90028	www.visualconcepts.tv
Showreel International, Inc. (323) 464-5111	**Westside Media Group** (310) 979-3500
1021 N. McCadden Pl. FAX (323) 464-4216	12233 W. Olympic Blvd., Ste. 152 www.wmgmedia.com
Hollywood, CA 90038 www.showreel.com	Los Angeles, CA 90064
Contact: Lynne Jackson	Contact: Lewis Lipstone
silver lining productions, inc. (310) 289-6650	**William Moffitt Associates** (818) 495-3106
149 South Barrington Ave., Ste. 770	785 New York Dr. FAX (626) 345-0673
Los Angeles, CA 90049 www.silverliningp.com	Altadena, CA 91001 www.wmadigital.com
Contact: Bozena Armstrong	Contacts: Lynne Moffitt & Will Moffitt
(858) 759-7983	**WSR Creative** (310) 837-7001
Solana Productions (800) 745-8225	9503 Jefferson Blvd., Ste. B FAX (310) 837-3680
249 S. Highway 101, Ste. 225	Culver City, CA 90232 www.wsrcreative.com
Solana Beach, CA 92075	
	Yada/Levine Video Productions (323) 461-1616
SplendidLight Media Productions (949) 722-8485	1253 Vine St., Ste. 21A FAX (323) 461-2288
177 Riverside St. www.splendidlight.com	Hollywood, CA 90038 www.yadalevine.com
Newport Beach, CA 92663	Contact: Michael Yada
Contacts: Lynn Splendid & Clayton Light	

Corporate & Video Production Companies

Boardalicious/Lisa Schreiber-Naber	(310) 376-8656 (310) 480-4596
	www.boardalicious.com
Char & Associates/Char Noonan	(805) 338-1301
	www.char-associates.com
Kelley Class/Class Represents	(310) 823-9808 (310) 650-5357
Connie Mellors & Company	(818) 761-4520
	FAX (818) 763-2248
Directors Management	(310) 295-0223
	FAX (310) 295-0226
Ellen Knable & Associates, Inc.	(310) 829-3269
	FAX (310) 453-4035
	www.ekareps.com
The Everett Group/Patty Everett	(818) 887-6633
	FAX (818) 887-6655
Janet Gilson	(818) 708-8152 (310) 488-8055
	FAX (818) 708-1609
Hardtribe/Maria V. Elgar	(323) 793-3996
	FAX (323) 936-9553
	www.hardtribe.com
Darr Hawthorne	(818) 906-8222 (818) 424-6656
	www.burningmotorhome.com
Ron Hoffman	(323) 960-3422
	FAX (323) 960-3405
Lee+Lou Productions, Inc.	(310) 374-1918 (310) 480-5475
211 N. Dianthus St.	www.leelou.com
Manhattan Beach, CA 90266	
Yvette Lubinsky	(310) 827-2626
	www.yvettereps.com
Tony Luna	(818) 842-5490
	FAX (818) 842-5490

Lynda Woodward & Associates, Inc.	(818) 784-2168
	FAX (818) 784-8507
Nikki Weiss & Co.	(323) 651-1414
754 N. La Jolla Ave.	FAX (323) 651-2525
Los Angeles, CA 90046	www.nikkiweissandco.com
Novick & Assoc., Inc TV and	(415) 460-1626
Digital Reps	(415) 860-1055
1010 B St., Ste. 219	FAX (415) 460-1646
San Rafael, CA 94901	
Reber/Covington	(310) 459-9711 (415) 398-4944
	FAX (310) 459-4482
Red Iron/Michael Coronado	(949) 474-5390 (949) 891-5961
86 Agostino	www.red-iron.com
Irvine, CA 92614	
Saarinen	(323) 460-2320
	FAX (323) 460-2323
	www.saarinen.tv
Tom Scott	(310) 230-9932
	FAX (310) 230-9932
Sherry&Company/Sherry Howell	(310) 399-7477 (213) 999-9879
Shoreline Entertainment, Inc.	(310) 551-2060
1875 Century Park East	FAX (310) 201-0729
Los Angeles, CA 90067	
	www.shorelineentertainment.com
Stacey & Company	(310) 551-0050
10369 Tennessee Ave.	
Los Angeles, CA 90064	
Joan Webb	(818) 514-6837 (213) 703-9769
Claire Worch/Claire & Company	(310) 318-8700
	FAX (310) 318-8762
	www.claireandcompany.net

30 Second Films   (310) 315-1750
3019 Pico Blvd.   FAX (310) 315-1757
Santa Monica, CA 90405   www.30secondfilms.com
Contact: Alan J. Stamm

American Video Group   (310) 477-1535
2542 Aiken Ave.   www.americanvideogroup.com
Los Angeles, CA 90064
President: John Berzner

Custom Video   (310) 543-4901
707 Torrance Blvd., Ste. 105   www.customvideo.tv
Redondo Beach, CA 90277
Contact: Michael Ude

dapTV associates/ieditvideo.com   (310) 867-5881
820 Westbourne Dr., Ste. 4   www.daptv.com
West Hollywood, CA 90069
Contact: Don Azars

Goldmine Productions, Inc.   (424) 832-7474
11728 Wilshire Blvd., Ste. 1511   www.gpitv.com
Los Angeles, CA 90025
Contact: Bruce Gold

Hu-Man Element Productions, Inc.   (213) 534-3700
1201 W. Fifth St., Ste. F-220A   FAX (213) 534-3711
Los Angeles, CA 90017   www.hu-manelement.com

Infomercial Solutions, Inc.   (818) 879-1140
30748 Davey Jones Dr.   FAX (818) 879-1148
Agoura Hills, CA 91301   www.infomercialsolutions.com
Contact: David Schwartz

Launch DRTV   (310) 305-8342
12211 W. Washington Blvd.,   FAX (310) 305-8240
Second Fl.   www.launchdrtv.com
Los Angeles, CA 90066

Onyx Productions Direct, Inc.   (323) 692-9830
2355 Westwood Blvd., Ste. 401   FAX (310) 470-0190
Los Angeles, CA 90064   www.onyxprod.com
Contact: Joan Renfrow

Proof   (310) 592-2247
P.O. Box 1014   www.proofla.com
Los Angeles, CA 90078

Raymond Entertainment Direct   (323) 785-4700
3450 Cahuenga Blvd.   FAX (323) 785-4701
Los Angeles, CA 90068
www.raymondentertainment.com

    (714) 558-3971
Script to Screen, Inc.   (800) 453-0003
200 N. Tustin Ave., Ste. 200   FAX (714) 558-1759
Santa Ana, CA 92705   www.scripttoscreen.com
Contact: Tony Kerry

Three and Two Films, Inc.   (818) 700-8725
21363 Lassen St., Ste. 101   FAX (818) 700-8758
Chatsworth, CA 91311   www.threeandtwofilms.com

Two-D Productions   (818) 224-2097
23945 Calabasas Rd., Ste. 112   FAX (818) 224-2098
Calabasas, CA 91302   www.two-d.com
Contact: Dena Levy

The Video Agency, Inc./   (818) 505-8300
TVA Productions   (888) 322-4296
3950 Vantage Ave.   FAX (818) 505-8370
Studio City, CA 91604   www.tvaproductions.com
Contact: Jeffery Goddard

Video Production Specialists (VPS)   (866) 447-3877
FAX (310) 577-0850
www.videoproductionspecialists.com

    (310) 393-8754
Videowerks   (310) 780-4156
3435 Ocean Park Blvd., Ste. 107   FAX (310) 399-1829
Santa Monica, CA 90405   www.videowerks.com
Contact: David Werk

    (951) 659-2580
Waldorf Crawford LLC   (951) 659-6399
P.O. Box 771, 52965 Cedar Crest Dr.   FAX (951) 659-3700
Idyllwild, CA 92549   www.waldorfcrawford.com

20th Century Fox Film Corp. (310) 369-1000
10201 W. Pico Blvd. **www.foxmovies.com**
Los Angeles, CA 90035

3 Arts Entertainment (310) 888-3200
9460 Wilshire Blvd., Seventh Fl. FAX **(310) 888-3210**
Beverly Hills, CA 90212

A&E IndieFilms (310) 201-6060
www.aetv.com/indiefilms/index.jsp

Alcon Entertainment (310) 789-3040
10390 Santa Monica Blvd., Ste. 250 FAX **(310) 789-3060**
Los Angeles, CA 90025 **www.alconent.com**

Anonymous Content (310) 558-3667
3532 Hayden Ave. FAX **(310) 558-4212**
Culver City, CA 90232 **www.anonymouscontent.com**

Atlas Entertainment (310) 786-4900
9200 Sunset Blvd., 10th Fl.
Los Angeles, CA 90069

Crest Animation Productions (818) 846-0166
333 N. Glenoaks Blvd., Ste. 300 **www.crestcgi.com**
Burbank, CA 91007

Dark Castle Entertainment (818) 954-4490
4000 Warner Blvd., Bldg. 90 FAX **(818) 954-3237**
Burbank, CA 91522

DC Entertainment (818) 954-6000

Di Bonaventura Pictures (323) 956-5454
5555 Melrose Ave., DeMille Bldg., FAX **(323) 862-2288**
Second Fl.
Los Angeles, CA 90038

DreamWorks Animation (818) 695-5000
1000 Flower St. **www.dreamworksanimation.com**
Glendale, CA 91201

DreamWorks SKG (818) 733-7000
100 Universal City Plaza, Bldg. 10 FAX **(818) 733-7574**
Universal City, CA 91608 **www.dreamworks.com**

Focus Features (818) 777-7373
100 Universal City Plaza **www.focusfeatures.com**
Universal City, CA 91608

Fox 2000 Pictures (310) 369-2000
10201 W. Pico Blvd., Bldg. 78 **www.fox.com**
Los Angeles, CA 90035

Fox Searchlight Pictures (310) 369-1000
10201 W. Pico Blvd., Bldg. 38 **www.foxsearchlight.com**
Los Angeles, CA 90035

Gary Sanchez Productions (323) 465-4600
729 Seward St. FAX **(323) 465-0782**
Los Angeles, CA 90038 **www.garysanchezprods.com**

Good Universe (310) 360-1441
1601 Cloverfield Blvd., Ste. 200, FAX **(310) 360-1447**
South Tower **www.mandatepictures.com**
Santa Monica, CA 90404

Groundswell Productions (310) 385-7540
11925 Wilshire Blvd., Ste. 310 FAX **(310) 385-7541**
Los Angeles, CA 90025

Happy Madison Productions (310) 244-3100
10202 W. Washington Blvd., FAX **(310) 244-1210**
Judy Garland Bldg. **www.adamsandler.com**
Culver City, CA 90232

Illumination Entertainment (310) 593-8800
1805 Colorado Ave. FAX **(310) 593-8850**
Santa Monica, CA 90404
www.illuminationentertainment.com

Imagine Entertainment (310) 858-2000
9465 Wilshire Blvd., Seventh Fl. FAX **(310) 858-2020**
Beverly Hills, CA 90212
www.imagine-entertainment.com

Jerry Bruckheimer Films (310) 664-6260
1631 10th St. FAX **(310) 664-6261**
Santa Monica, CA 90404 **www.jbfilms.com**

Katalyst Films (323) 785-2700
6806 Lexington Ave. FAX **(323) 785-2715**
Los Angeles, CA 90038

Legendary Pictures (818) 954-3888
4000 Warner Blvd., Bldg. 76 FAX **(818) 954-3884**
Burbank, CA 91522 **www.legendarypictures.com**

Lightstorm Entertainment (310) 656-6100
919 Santa Monica Blvd. FAX **(310) 656-6102**
Santa Monica, CA 90401

Marc Platt Productions (818) 777-8811
100 Universal City Plaza, Bungalow 5163
Universal City, CA 91608

Media Rights Capital (310) 786-1600
1800 Century Park East, 10th Fl. FAX **(310) 786-1625**
Los Angeles, CA 90067 **www.mrcstudios.com**

Millennium Films (310) 388-6900
6423 Wilshire Blvd. FAX **(310) 388-6901**
Los Angeles, CA 90048 **www.nuimage.net**

Misher Films (310) 405-7999
FAX **(310) 405-7991**
www.misherfilms.com

Mosaic Media Group (310) 786-4900
9200 Sunset Blvd. FAX **(310) 777-2185**
Los Angeles, CA 90069

New Line Cinema (310) 854-5811
116 N. Robertson Blvd., Ste. 200 FAX **(310) 854-1824**
Los Angeles, CA 90048 **www.newline.com**

New Regency Pictures (310) 369-8300
10201 W. Pico Blvd., Bldg. 12 FAX **(800) 219-0491**
Los Angeles, CA 90035 **www.newregency.com**

Nickelodeon Movies (310) 752-8000
2600 Colorado Ave., Second Fl. **www.nick.com/movies/**
Santa Monica, CA 90404

Nu Image Films (310) 388-6900
6423 Wilshire Blvd. FAX **(310) 388-6901**
Los Angeles, CA 90048 **www.nuimage.net**

Overbrook Entertainment (310) 432-2400
450 N. Roxbury Dr., Fourth Fl. FAX **(310) 432-2441**
Beverly Hills, CA 90210 **www.overbrookent.com**

Ⓐ**Paramount Picutres** (323) 956-5000
5555 Melrose Ave. **www.paramount.com**
Los Angeles, CA 90038

Participant Media (310) 550-5100
331 Foothill Rd., Third Fl. **www.participantmedia.com**
Beverly Hills, CA 90210

Pixar Animation Studios (510) 922-3000
1200 Park Ave. FAX **(510) 922-3151**
Emeryville, CA 94608 **www.pixar.com**

Pressman Films   **(310) 450-9692**
1639 11th St., Ste. 251   FAX **(310) 450-9705**
Santa Monica, CA 90404   **www.pressman.com**

Regency Enterprises   **(310) 369-8300**
10201 W. Pico Blvd., Bldg. 12   FAX **(310) 969-0470**
Los Angeles, CA 90035   **www.newregency.com**

Relativity Media   **(310) 859-1250**
9242 Beverly Blvd.   **www.relativitymedia.com**
Beverly Hills, CA 90210

River Road Entertainment   **(213) 253-4610**
2000 Avenue of the Stars, Ste. 620-N
Los Angeles, CA 90067
         www.riverroadentertainment.com

Screen Gems   **(310) 244-4000**
10202 W. Washington Blvd.,   FAX **(310) 244-0046**
Jimmy Stewart Bldg., Ste. 200-F
Culver City, CA 90232

Sony Pictures Entertainment **(310) 244-4000**
10202 W. Washington Blvd.   FAX **(310) 244-2626**
Culver City, CA 90232   **www.spe.sony.com**

Spyglass Entertainment   **(310) 443-5800**
10900 Wilshire Blvd.   FAX **(310) 443-5912**
Los Angeles, CA 90024
       www.spyglassentertainment.com

Strike Entertainment   **(310) 315-0550**
3000 W. Olympic Blvd.,   FAX **(310) 315-0560**
Bldg. 5, Ste. 1250
Santa Monica, CA 90404

StudioCanal   **(310) 247-0994**
9250 Wilshire Blvd., Ste. 210 **www.studiocanal.com**
Beverly Hills, CA 90212

Temple Hill Entertainment   **(310) 270-4383**
9255 Sunset Blvd., Ste. 801   FAX **(310) 270-4395**
Los Angeles, CA 90069   **www.templehillent.com**

Universal Pictures   **(818) 777-1000**
100 Universal City Plaza
Universal City, CA 91608

Village Roadshow Pictures   **(310) 385-4300**
100 N. Crescent Dr., Ste. 323
Beverly Hills, CA 90210
      www.villageroadshowpictures.com

Walt Disney Productions   **(818) 560-1000**
500 S. Buena Vista St.   **www.disney.com**
Burbank, CA 91521

Warner Bros. Pictures   **(818) 954-6000**
4000 Warner Blvd.   **www.warnerbros.com**
Burbank, CA 91522

Ant Farm
(323) 850-0700
110 S. Fairfax Ave., Ste. 200　FAX (323) 932-6797
Los Angeles, CA 90036　www.theantfarm.net
(Print, Trailers & TV Spots)

Artphase, LLC
(310) 943-9208
FAX (310) 441-9606
www.artphase.com

BLT & Associates
(323) 860-4000
6430 Sunset Blvd., Eighth Fl.　FAX (323) 860-0890
Los Angeles, CA 90028　www.bltomato.com
(DVD Packaging, Interactive, Motion Graphics, Print & Trailers)

Cimarron Group
(323) 337-0300
6855 Santa Monica Blvd.　FAX (323) 337-0333
Hollywood, CA 90038　www.cimarrongroup.com
(Interactive, Motion Graphics, Packaging, Print, Radio and TV Spots, Trailers & Web-Based)

Creative Impact Agency
(818) 981-7656
(310) 613-3438
15315 Magnolia Blvd., Ste. 110　FAX (818) 981-7643
Sherman Oaks, CA 91403　www.cia-adv.com
(Interactive, Packaging, Posters, Print & Web-Based)

D&E Entertainment, Inc.
(323) 464-2403
6525 Sunset Blvd., Ninth Fl.　FAX (323) 464-2426
Los Angeles, CA 90028　www.dandeentertainment.com

Firestone Productions
(323) 461-7500
(323) 377-9494
www.firestoneproductions.com

Framework Studio, LLC
(310) 815-1245
3535 Hayden Ave., Ste. 300　FAX (310) 815-9821
Culver City, CA 90232　www.frameworkla.com

GSM Entertainment
(310) 205-0370
309 S. Sherbourne Dr., Ste. 108
Los Angeles, CA 90048　www.gsmentertainment.com
(Interactive, Motion Graphics, Trailers, TV Spots & Web-Based)

Haley Miranda Group
(310) 842-7369
8654 Washington Blvd.　FAX (310) 842-8932
Culver City, CA 90232　www.haleymiranda.com
(Contests, Print & Web-Based)

Hammer Creative
(323) 606-4700
6311 Romaine St., Third Fl.　FAX (323) 463-8130
Hollywood, CA 90038　www.hammercreative.com
(Motion Graphics, Print, Trailers & TV Spots)

Hurwitz Creative
(818) 487-8300
5344 Vineland Ave.　FAX (818) 467-8301
North Hollywood, CA 91601　www.hurwitzcreative.com
(Interactive, Motion Graphics, Packaging, Radio Spots, Trailers, TV Spots & Web-based)

Insight EPK
(818) 665-5451
32322 Saddle Mountain Dr.　FAX (866) 339-3959
Westlake Village, CA 91301　www.insightepk.com

KO Creative
(310) 288-3820
465 South Beverly Blvd., Third Fl.　FAX (310) 288-3837
Beverly Hills, CA 90212　www.ko-creative.com
(Interactive, Motion Graphics, Network Promotions, Packaging, Posters, Print, Radio Spots, Trailers, TV Spots & Web-Based)

Mark Woollen & Associates
(310) 399-2690
207 Ashland Ave.　FAX (310) 399-2670
Santa Monica, CA 90405　www.markwoollen.com
(Trailers, TV Spots & Web-Based)

Mighty Oak Media, Inc.
(818) 807-4225
14203 Dickens St.　www.mightyoakmedia.com
Sherman Oaks, CA 91423
(Motion Graphics, Network Promotions, Radio Spots, Trailers, TV Spots & Web-based)

MOB Media Inc./MOB Media Studios (949) 222-0220
27121 Towne Centre Dr., Ste. 260　FAX (949) 222-0243
Foothill Ranch, CA 92610　www.mobmedia.com
(Contests, Events, Interactive, Motion Graphics, Network Promotions, Packaging, Posters, Print, Radio Spots, Trailers, TV Spots & Web-based)

mOcean
(310) 481-0808
2440 S. Sepulveda Blvd., Ste. 150　FAX (310) 481-0807
Los Angeles, CA 90064　www.moceanla.com
(Interactive, Network Promotions, Print, Promos, Trailers & TV Spots)

New Wave Entertainment
(818) 295-5000
2660 W. Olive Ave.　FAX (818) 295-5002
Burbank, CA 91505　www.nwe.com
(Motion Graphics, Network Promotions, Packaging & Print)

Oskoui+Oskoui, Inc.
(213) 977-0440
(213) 977-0400
1201 W. Fifth St., Ste. T-430　www.oskoui-oskoui.com
Los Angeles, CA 90017
(DVD and Blu-Ray Menu Design, Key Art, Mobile Banners, Online Campaigns, Packaging Design, Social Media Marketing & TV Online Marketing)

Parkour Media
(310) 846-8051
(212) 845-9089
P.O. Box 1442　FAX (310) 846-8051
Los Angeles, CA 90078　www.parkourmedia.com
(Interactive, Motion Graphics, Network Promotions, Online Marketing Strategies, Packaging, Posters, Print, TV Spots & Web-based)

Playground Media Group
(310) 315-3800
1813 Centinela Ave.　FAX (310) 315-3801
Santa Monica, CA 90404　www.playgroundla.com

Studio 27
(818) 216-9026
6860 Lexington Ave.　FAX (415) 621-1875
Hollywood, CA 90038　www.studio27inc.com
(Web-Based)

SunnyBoy Entertainment
(626) 356-9020
230 E. Union St.　FAX (626) 356-9022
Pasadena, CA 91101 www.sunnyboyentertainment.com
(Interactive, Motion Graphics, Network Promotions, Trailers, TV Spots & Web-based)

Tao Creative
(323) 930-8550
955 S. Carrillo Dr., Ste. 205　FAX (323) 930-8545
Los Angeles, CA 90048　www.taocreativela.com
(Motion Graphics, Radio and TV Spots & Trailers)

The Testimonial Wrangler
(858) 735-7646
(858) 456-6180
7486 La Jolla Blvd., Ste. 164　FAX (858) 777-5418
La Jolla, CA 92037　www.testimonialwrangler.com
(Testimonials)

Trailer Park
(310) 845-3000
6922 Hollywood Blvd., 12th Fl.　FAX (310) 845-3470
Hollywood, CA 90028　www.trailerpark.com
(Motion Graphics, Print, Trailers & TV Spots)

Timothy Agoglia	(626) 442-6454
	www.absolutefilms.net
Francois Alaux	(310) 659-1577
	www.littleminx.tv
Jaron Albertin	(323) 817-3300
	www.smugglersite.com
Don Allen	(323) 644-5552
	www.revolverfilms.com
Jeff Alley	(310) 860-1771
	www.banditfilms.com
Philip Andelman	(323) 468-0123
	www.partizan.com
Animal	(323) 645-1000
	www.believemedia.com
Chris Applebaum	(323) 645-1000
	www.believemedia.com
Paul Ardolino	(323) 469-8991
	www.palardo.com
Miguel Arteta	(310) 396-7333
	www.bobcentral.com
Meiert Avis	(310) 576-1344
	www.pushermedia.com
AXIS	(310) 659-1577
	www.littleminx.tv
Matthew Badger	(310) 275-9333
	www.epochfilms.com
Eddie Barber	(818) 982-7775
	FAX (661) 339-3235
	www.barbertvp.com
Lenny Bass	(323) 463-2826
	www.dnala.com
BB Gun	(323) 468-0123
	www.partizan.com
Tom Beard	(323) 468-0123
	www.partizan.com
Ed Bell	(310) 860-1771
	www.banditfilms.com
Greg Bell	(310) 275-9333
	www.epochfilms.com
Trudy Bellinger	(310) 659-7659
	www.mergefilms.com
Anthea Benton	(323) 645-1000
	www.believemedia.com
Michael Bernard	(323) 645-1000
	www.believemedia.com
Bert and Bertie	(323) 463-2826
	www.dnala.com
Cedric Blaisbois	(323) 468-0123
	www.partizan.com
M Blash	(323) 465-5299
	www.thedirectorsbureau.com
Blue Leach	(310) 558-7100
	www.hsiproductions.com
Richard Bowen	(310) 576-1344
	www.pushermedia.com
Kevin Bray	(323) 463-2826
	www.dnala.com
Daniel Brereton	(323) 468-0123
	www.partizan.com
Dom Bridges	(310) 396-7333
	www.bobcentral.com
Sam Brown	(323) 465-5299
	www.thedirectorsbureau.com
Andy Bruntel	(323) 465-5299
	www.thedirectorsbureau.com
Marcelo Burgos	(323) 645-1000
	www.believemedia.com
Kinga Burza	(323) 468-0123
	www.partizan.com
Peter Byck	(323) 252-5272
	www.ralphtheroadie.com
Peter Care	(310) 396-7333
	www.bobcentral.com
Carter and Blitz	(310) 558-3667
	www.anonymouscontent.com
Herbert Chan	(626) 442-6454
	www.absolutefilms.net
Barney Clay	(323) 468-0123
	www.partizan.com
Harry Cocciolo	(310) 396-7333
	www.bobcentral.com
Caswell Coggins	(310) 659-7659
	www.mergefilms.com
Todd Cole	(323) 465-5299
	www.thedirectorsbureau.com
Collision	(310) 275-9333
	www.epochfilms.com
Roman Coppola	(323) 465-5299
	www.thedirectorsbureau.com
Sofia Coppola	(323) 465-5299
	www.thedirectorsbureau.com
Alisa Daglio	(310) 576-4992
	www.agogofilms.com
Patrick Daughters	(323) 465-5299
	www.thedirectorsbureau.com
Jonathan Dayton	(310) 396-7333
	www.bobcentral.com
Herve De Crecy	(310) 659-1577
	www.littleminx.tv
Lorenzo De Guia	(323) 790-1732
	www.maneaterproductions.com
Tabitha Denholm	(323) 468-0123
	www.partizan.com

Carole Denis	(323) 645-1000 www.believemedia.com	Warren Fu	(323) 468-0123 www.partizan.com
Gerard De Thame	(323) 645-1000 www.believemedia.com	Jim Gable	(310) 979-4333 www.gandb.tv
Nigel Dick	(323) 463-2826 www.dnala.com	Anthony Garth	(323) 790-1732 www.maneaterproductions.com
Ben Dickinson	(310) 659-1577 www.blackdogfilms.com	Romain Gavras	(323) 465-5299 www.thedirectorsbureau.com
Stephanie Di Giusto	(323) 468-0123 www.partizan.com	Kim Geldenhuys	(310) 396-7333 www.bobcentral.com
Matt Dilmore	(310) 275-9333 www.epochfilms.com	Tryan George	(323) 645-1000 www.believemedia.com
Diamond Dogs	(310) 558-7100 www.hsiproductions.com	Michel Gondry	(323) 468-0123 www.partizan.com
Andrew Dosunmu	(323) 650-4722	Paul Gore	(323) 463-2826 www.dnala.com
Andrew Douglas	(310) 558-3667 www.anonymouscontent.com	Michael Gracey	(323) 468-0123 www.partizan.com
Tony Dow	(310) 315-1750 www.30secondfilms.com	Gil Green	(323) 468-0123 www.partizan.com
Bruce Dowad	(323) 645-1000 www.believemedia.com	Davis Guggenheim	(310) 396-7333 www.bobcentral.com
Michael Downing	(310) 275-9333 www.epochfilms.com	Michael Haussman	(310) 558-7100 www.hsiproductions.com
Steve Drypolcher	(323) 468-0123 www.partizan.com	Simon Henwood	(310) 558-7100 www.hsiproductions.com
Michael Eckhardt	(626) 442-6454 www.absolutefilms.net	Fluorescent Hill	(323) 644-5552 www.revolverfilms.com
Moses Edinborough	(323) 876-3331 www.wildindigo.tv	Wayne Holloway	(323) 645-1000 www.believemedia.com
Charles Eganstein	(626) 442-6454 www.absolutefilms.net	Jess Holzworth	(310) 558-7100 www.hsiproductions.com
Nabil Elderkin	(310) 659-1577 www.littleminx.tv	Honey	(323) 468-0123 www.partizan.com
Filip Engstrom	(323) 817-3300 www.smugglersite.com	Allen Hughes	(323) 645-1000 www.believemedia.com
Fernando Escovar	(818) 726-7269 www.fotographer.com	Wayne Isham	(310) 659-7659 www.mergefilms.com
Daniel Eskills	(323) 468-0123 www.partizan.com	Mari Ito	(626) 442-6454 www.absolutefilms.net
Ollie Evans	(323) 468-0123 www.partizan.com	Garth Jennings	(310) 558-3667 www.anonymouscontent.com
Everynone	(310) 275-9333 www.epochfilms.com	Bryan Johnson	(323) 938-8080
Lauri Faggioni	(310) 659-1577 www.blackdogfilms.com	Noble Jones	(323) 644-5552 www.revolverfilms.com
Valerie Faris	(310) 396-7333 www.bobcentral.com	Byron Jost	(626) 442-6454 www.absolutefilms.net
David Fincher	(310) 558-3667 www.anonymouscontent.com	Joseph Kahn	(310) 558-7100 www.hsiproductions.com
Liz Friedlander	(323) 645-1000 www.believemedia.com	Dean Karr	(323) 876-3331 www.wildindigo.tv
Raphael Frydman	(323) 468-0123 www.partizan.com	David Katz	(818) 533-1937 davidkatzproductions.com

David Kellogg	(310) 558-3667	Melodie McDaniel	(323) 465-5299
	www.anonymouscontent.com		www.thedirectorsbureau.com
Arthur King	(323) 468-0123	Geoff McFetridge	(323) 465-5299
	www.partizan.com		www.thedirectorsbureau.com
Isaac Klotz	(323) 620-6925	Micah Meisner	(323) 644-5552
	www.halfelement.com		www.revolverfilms.com
Jesper Kouthoofd	(310) 659-1577	Thomas Mignone	(310) 927-6661
	www.littleminx.tv		www.doominc.com
Rob Kraetsch	(323) 620-6925	Geoff Millar	(310) 576-4992
	www.halfelement.com		www.agogofilms.com
Bob Kronovet	(310) 315-1750	Bennett Miller	(323) 817-3300
	www.30secondfilms.com		www.smugglersite.com
David LaChapelle	(310) 558-7100	Jefferson Miller	(323) 876-3331
	www.hsiproductions.com		www.wildindigo.tv
Alex Laubscher	(310) 396-7333	Josh Miller	(310) 659-1577
	www.bobcentral.com		www.littleminx.com
Francis Lawrence	(323) 463-2826	Jean-Baptiste Mondino	(323) 463-2826
	www.dnala.com		www.dnala.com
Rich Lee	(323) 463-2826	Darrin Monroe	(310) 860-1771
	www.dnala.com		www.banditfilms.com
Nancy Leiviska	(310) 454-0109	Ben Mor	(310) 659-1577
	www.stefanino.com		www.littleminx.tv
Yoann Lemoine	(310) 558-7100	Andy Morahan	(323) 645-1000
	www.hsiproductions.com		www.believemedia.com
Drew Lightfoot	(323) 644-5552	Wendy Morgan	(323) 644-5552
	www.revolverfilms.com		www.revolverfilms.com
Steven Lippman	(323) 790-1732	Phil Morrison	(310) 275-9333
	www.maneaterproductions.com		www.epochfilms.com
Mike Long	(310) 275-9333	Hiro Murai	(323) 468-0123
	www.epochfilms.com		www.partizan.com
Dan Lowe	(323) 468-0123	Steven Murashige	(323) 650-4722
	www.partizan.com		
Julien Lutz	(323) 463-2826	Tony (Nako) Nakonechnyj	(323) 848-7293
	www.dnala.com		www.reconfilms.com
Andrew MacNaughtan	(323) 644-5552	Jake Nava	(323) 645-1000
	www.revolverfilms.com		www.believemedia.com
Mike Maguire	(323) 465-5299	Nico and Martin	(310) 659-1577
	www.thedirectorsbureau.com		www.littleminx.tv
Malloys	(310) 558-7100	Ace Norton	(323) 468-0123
	www.hsiproductions.com		www.partizan.com
Lisa Mann	(323) 644-5552	Nima Nourizadeh	(323) 468-0123
	www.revolverfilms.com		www.partizan.com
Maurice Marable	(323) 645-1000	Bob Odenkirk	(310) 396-7333
	www.believemedia.com		www.bobcentral.com
Diane Martel	(310) 558-7100	Gareth O'Neil	(323) 848-7293
	www.hsiproductions.com		www.reconfilms.com
Jay Martin	(323) 463-2826	Mike Palmieri	(323) 644-5552
	www.dnala.com		www.revolverfilms.com
Nic Mathieu	(310) 558-3667	Brad Parker	(310) 396-7333
	www.anonymouscontent.com		www.bobcentral.com
Michael Maxxis	(323) 463-2826	Travis Payne	(323) 665-6680 (323) 957-6680 FAX (323) 665-6681 www.travispayne.net
	www.dnala.com		
David McClister	(323) 463-2826	Sam Peacocke	(310) 396-7333
	www.dnala.com		www.bobcentral.com

Vadim Perelman	(310) 659-7659 www.mergefilms.com		Rod S. Scott	(818) 501-3000 www.vimeo.com/screenlab
Valerie Pirson	(323) 468-0123 www.partizan.com		Tony Scott	(310) 659-1577 www.blackdogfilms.com
Martin Pitts	(323) 931-9962		Mark Seliger	(310) 659-1577 www.blackdogfilms.com
Jeff Preiss	(310) 275-9333 www.epochfilms.com		Nick Semmens	(323) 848-7293 www.reconfilms.com
Rodrigo Prieto	(310) 659-1577 www.littleminx.tv		Toben Seymour	(310) 659-1577 www.littleminx.tv
Joel Pront	(323) 645-1000 www.believemedia.com		Dawn Shadforth	(310) 659-1577 www.littleminx.com
Marcus Raboy	(323) 463-2826 www.dnala.com		Guy Shelmerdine	(323) 817-3300 www.smugglersite.com
Brett Ratner	(310) 558-7100 www.hsiproductions.com		Graydon Sheppard	(323) 644-5552 www.revolverfilms.com
Sebastian Reed	(310) 659-1577 www.littleminx.tv		Shynola	(323) 465-5299 www.thedirectorsbureau.com
Matty Rich	(310) 860-1771 www.banditfilms.com		Trish Sie	(310) 396-7333 www.bobcentral.com
Branscombe Richmond	(310) 315-1750 www.30secondfilms.com		Floria Sigismondi	(323) 645-1000 www.believemedia.com
Carl Erik Rinsch	(310) 659-1577 www.blackdogfilms.com		Brian Silva	(323) 620-6925 www.halfelement.com
Roboshobo	(323) 644-5552 www.revolverfilms.com		Christopher Sims	(323) 463-2826 www.dnala.com
Mark Romanek	(310) 558-3667 www.anonymouscontent.com		Skinny	(323) 468-0123 www.partizan.com
Aaron Rose	(323) 465-5299 www.thedirectorsbureau.com		Jim Field Smith	(310) 659-1577 www.littleminx.tv
George Marshall Ruge	(310) 288-8000 www.paradigmagency.com		Matt Smukler	(323) 465-9494 www.helloandcompany.com
Mike Ruiz	(323) 463-2826 www.dnala.com		Zack Snyder	(323) 645-1000 www.believemedia.com
Timothy Saccenti	(323) 468-0123 www.partizan.com		Speedway Films	(323) 644-5552 www.revolverfilms.com
Jessica Sanders	(310) 275-9333 www.epochfilms.com		Scott Speer	(323) 463-2826 www.dnala.com
Hank Saroyan	(323) 848-7293 www.reconfilms.com		Bruce St. Clair	(323) 645-1000 www.believemedia.com
Malik H. Sayeed	(310) 659-1577 www.littleminx.com		Stardust	(323) 644-5552 www.revolverfilms.com
Rocky Schenck	(323) 463-2826 www.dnala.com		Paul Street	(323) 931-3300 FAX (323) 931-3307 www.streetlightfilms.net
Henry Scholfield	(323) 468-0123 www.partizan.com		Stylewar	(323) 817-3300 www.smugglersite.com
Bradley Scott	(323) 790-1732 www.maneaterproductions.com		Spencer Susser	(310) 396-7333 www.bobcentral.com
Jake Scott	(310) 659-1577 www.blackdogfilms.com		Syd/Eric	(310) 396-7333 www.bobcentral.com
Jordan Scott	(310) 659-1577 www.blackdogfilms.com		Tarsem	(323) 650-4722
Luke Scott	(310) 659-1577 www.blackdogfilms.com		Ray Tintori	(323) 468-0123 www.partizan.com

Phillip Van	(310) 659-1577	Marc Webb	(323) 463-2826
	www.littleminx.com		www.dnala.com
Malcolm Venville	(310) 558-3667	Alan White	(310) 396-7333
	www.anonymouscontent.com		www.bobcentral.com
Gore Verbinski	(310) 558-3667	Declan Whitebloom	(310) 659-1577
	www.anonymouscontent.com		www.blackdogfilms.com
Robert Villalobos	(626) 442-6454	Nick Wickham	(310) 558-7100
	www.absolutefilms.net		www.hsiproductions.com
The Wade Brothers	(310) 396-7333	Edgar Wright	(323) 463-2826
	www.bobcentral.com		www.dnala.com
Wong Kar Wai	(310) 558-3667	Masaki Yokochi	(323) 848-7293
	www.anonymouscontent.com		www.reconfilms.com
Rupert Wainwright	(310) 576-1344	Ali Zamani	(310) 779-9603
	www.pushermedia.com		www.azfilmstudios.com
Jon Watts	(323) 817-3300		
	www.smugglersite.com		

30 Second Films   (310) 315-1750
3019 Pico Blvd.   FAX (310) 315-1757
Santa Monica, CA 90405   **www.30secondfilms.com**
Executive Producer: Alan J. Stamm
Directors: Tony Dow, Bob Kronovet & Branscombe Richmond

   (626) 442-6454
Absolute Films   (323) 692-1010
1441 Huntington Dr., Bldg. 301   FAX (626) 448-1930
South Pasadena, CA 91030   **www.absolutefilms.net**
Executive Producer/Director: Romeo Carey
Producers: Charles Egan, Tom Franklin, Dino Lee,
Josh Oacha & Saul Silver
Directors: Timothy Agoglia, Herbert Chan, Michael Eckhardt,
Charles Eganstein, Mari Ito, Byron Jost & Robert Villalobos

Ali Zeus Corp.   (310) 779-9603
6250 Canoga Ave., Ste. 474   **www.azfilmstudios.com**
Woodland Hills, CA 91367
Director: Ali Zamani

Almost Midnight Productions   (310) 313-4046
12240 Venice Blvd., Ste. 18   FAX (310) 313-4048
Los Angeles, CA 90066   **www.almostmidnight.com**

Anonymous Content   (310) 558-3667
3532 Hayden Ave.   FAX (310) 558-4212
Culver City, CA 90232   **www.anonymouscontent.com**
Executive Producer: Sheira Rees-Davis
Directors: Carter and Blitz, Andrew Douglas, David Fincher,
Garth Jennings, David Kellogg, Nic Mathieu, Mark Romanek,
Malcolm Venville, Gore Verbinski & Wong Kar Wai
Sales Rep: Molly Bohas

   (323) 650-4722
The Artists Company   (212) 679-7199
1015 N. Fairfax Ave.   FAX (323) 650-5150
Los Angeles, CA 90046   **www.theartistscompany.com**
Executive Producer: Roberto Cecchini
Vice President: Sally Antonacchio
Directors: Andrew Dosunmu, Steven Murashige & Tarsem
Sales Rep: Laure Scott Representation

The Association, Inc.   (818) 841-9660
135 N. Screenland Dr.   FAX (818) 841-8370
Burbank, CA 91505   **www.theassociation.tv**
Executive Producer: Fletcher Murray
Producers: Jeff Murphy & Tom Myrdahl

   (818) 982-7775
Barber Tech Video Products   (877) 887-6388
40125 20th St. West   FAX (661) 339-3235
Palmdale, CA 93551   **www.barbertvp.com**
Executive Producer/Director: Eddie Barber

Believe Media   (323) 645-1000
1040 N. Las Palmas Ave., Bldg. 10   FAX (323) 645-1001
Los Angeles, CA 90038   **www.believemedia.com**
Executive Producers: Gerard Cantor, Betsy Kelley, Liz Silver &
Luke Thornton
Directors: Animal, Chris Applebaum, Anthea Benton, Michael
Bernard, Marcelo Burgos, Gerard de Thame, Carole Denis,
Bruce Doward, Liz Friedlander, Tryan George, Wayne Holloway,
Allen Hughes, Rory Kelleher, Maurice Marable, Andy Morahan,
Jake Nava, Bo Platt, Joel Pront, Floria Sigismondi &
Bruce St. Clair

   (310) 659-1577
Black Dog Films (RSA Films)   (212) 343-2020
634 N. La Peer Dr.   FAX (310) 659-1377
Los Angeles, CA 90069   **www.blackdogfilms.com**
Executive Producer: Kim Dellara
Directors: Ben Dickinson, Lauri Faggioni, Carl Erik Rinsch, Jake
Scott, Jordan Scott, Luke Scott, Tony Scott & Mark Seliger

Bob Industries   (310) 396-7333
1313 Fifth St.   FAX (310) 396-0202
Santa Monica, CA 90401   **www.bobcentral.com**
Executive Producers: TK Knowles, John O'Grady &
Chuck Ryant
Directors: Miguel Arteta, Dom Bridges, Peter Care, Harry
Cocciolo, Jonathan Dayton, Valerie Faris, Kim Geldenhuys,
Davis Guggenheim, Alex Laubscher, Bob Odenkirk, Brad
Parker, Sam Peacocke, Trish Sie, Spencer Susser, Syd/Eric,
The Wade Brothers & Alan White

   (323) 848-9411
A Broad Vision Productions   (323) 401-4157
   FAX (866) 247-8610
www.abroadvisionproductions.com

Bucks Boys Productions, Inc.   (310) 437-0914
578 Washington Blvd., Ste. 362   FAX (310) 437-0919
Marina Del Rey, CA 90292   **www.bucksboys.com**
Executive Producers: Jonathan Becker & Joshua Greenberg

   (310) 823-7300
A Common Thread, Inc.   (310) 798-9007
4081 Redwood Ave.   FAX (310) 823-7305
Los Angeles, CA 90066   **www.acommonthread.tv**
Executive Producers: Tristan Drew & J.P. McMahon

Devil's Night   (310) 584-1086
3435 Ocean Park Blvd., Ste. 107-666   FAX (310) 584-1087
Santa Monica, CA 90405   **www.devilsnight.com**

Dice Films   (818) 726-7269
Director: Fernando Escovar

   (323) 465-5299
The Directors Bureau   (323) 663-0500
1641 N. Ivar Ave.   FAX (323) 465-5547
Hollywood, CA 90028   **www.thedirectorsbureau.com**
Executive Producer: Cayce Cole
Head of Production: Lana Kim
Directors: M Blash, Sam Brown, Andy Bruntel, Todd Cole,
Roman Coppola, Sofia Coppola, Patrick Daughters, Romain
Gavras, Mike Maguire, Melodie McDaniel, Geoff McFetridge,
Aaron Rose & Shynola

DNA Studio   (323) 463-2826
6535 Santa Monica Blvd.   FAX (323) 463-2535
Hollywood, CA 90038   **www.dnala.com**
President/Executive Producer: David Naylor
VP/Executive Producer: Sam Aslanian
Executive Producer: Missy Galanida
Directors: Lenny Bass, Bert and Bertie, Kevin Bray, Nigel Dick,
Paul Gore, Francis Lawrence, Rich Lee, Julien Lutz, Jay Martin,
Michael Maxxis, David McClister, Jean-Baptiste Mondino,
Marcus Raboy, Mike Ruiz, Rocky Schenck, Christopher Sims,
Scott Speer, Marc Webb & Edgar Wright

DOOM, Inc.   (310) 927-6661
308 N. Kenwood St., Ste. D   FAX (310) 496-2666
Burbank, CA 91505   **www.doominc.com**
Head of Production/Producer: Darci Oltman
Director: Thomas Mignone
Producer: Natasha Noramly

   (310) 275-9333
Epoch Films, Inc.   (310) 275-7938
9290 Civic Center Dr.   FAX (310) 275-7696
Beverly Hills, CA 90210   **www.epochfilms.com**
Executive Producers: Mindy Goldberg & Jerry Solomon
Directors: Matt Badger, Greg Bell, Collision, Matt Dilmore,
Michael Downing, Everynone, Mike Long, Phil Morrison, Jeff
Preiss & Jessica Sanders
Sales Rep: Mal Ward

Eyestorm Productions   (310) 582-3937
1522 Cloverfield Blvd., Ste. C   FAX (310) 582-3939
Santa Monica, CA 90404

   www.eyestormproductions.com

The Film Syndicate   (323) 938-8080
7214 Melrose Ave.   FAX (323) 938-8183
Los Angeles, CA 90046
Producer/Director: Bryan Johnson

A Go Go Films   (310) 576-4992
927 Fourth St.   www.agogofilms.com
Santa Monica, CA 90403
Producer: Art Brown
Directors: Alisa Daglio & Geoff Millar

Grainey Pictures   (310) 827-1111
4220 Glencoe Ave., Ste. 100   FAX (310) 827-1124
Marina del Rey, CA 90292   www.gpixer.com

Graying & Balding, Inc.   (310) 979-4333
Executive Producers: Ann Kim   FAX (310) 979-4334
Director: Jim Gable   www.gandb.tv

Half Element Productions   (323) 620-6925
1911 17th St., Ste. 5   www.halfelement.com
Santa Monica, CA 90404
Producers: Kim Daniels & Des Escober
Directors: Isaac Klotz & Brian Silva
Director/Cameraman: Rob Kraetsch

      (310) 558-7100
HSI Productions, Inc.   (212) 627-3600
3630 Eastham Dr.   FAX (310) 558-7101
Culver City, CA 90232   www.hsiproductions.com
President: Stavros Merjos
Executive Producers: Coleen Haynes & Rebecca Skinner
Directors: Blue Leach, Yoann Lemoine, Diamond Dogs, Michael
Haussman, Simon Henwood, Jess Holzworth, Joseph Kahn,
David LaChapelle, Malloys, Diane Martel, Brett Ratner &
Nick Wickham
Music Video Sales: Christopher Clavadetscher

Karma Kollective   (310) 653-1400
6334-B Wilshire Blvd.   FAX (310) 653-1402
Los Angeles, CA 90048   www.karmakollective.tv

Little Minx   (310) 659-1577
634 N. La Peer Dr.   FAX (310) 659-1377
Los Angeles, CA 90069   www.littleminx.tv
President: Rhea Scott
Directors: Francois Alaux, AXIS, Herve De Crecy, Nabil
Elderkin, Jim Field Smith, Johnny Hardstaff, Josh Miller,
Ben Mor, Nico and Martin, Sebastian Reed, Malik Sayeed,
Toben Seymour, Dawn Shadforth & Phillip Van
Executive Producer: Kim Dellara

      (323) 790-1732
Maneater Productions   (323) 327-2793
6860 Lexington Ave.   FAX (323) 460-6063
Hollywood, CA 90038   www.maneaterproductions.com
Directors: Lorenzo De Guia, Anthony Garth,
Steven Lippman & Bradley Scott
Executive Producer: Jed James
Business Development: Molly Macdonald
PR: Press Kitchen

Mega G Productions   (310) 574-9591
4712 Admiralty Way, Ste. 473   FAX (310) 564-7766
Marina del Rey, CA 90292   www.megagproductions.com

      (310) 659-7659
Merge@Crossroads   (212) 647-1310
8630 Pine Tree Pl.   FAX (310) 659-3105
West Hollywood, CA 90069   www.mergefilms.com
Executive Producer: Joseph Uliano
Directors: Trudy Bellinger, Caswell Coggins,
Wayne Isham & Vaidm Perelman
Head of Production & Sales: Neil Maiers

Motion Theory   (310) 396-9433
4235 Redwood Ave.   FAX (310) 396-7883
Los Angeles, CA 90066   www.motiontheory.com
Executive Producer: Javier Jimenez
Sales Rep: Caroline Gomez

PAC   (323) 931-9962
Producer/Director: Martin Pitts

      (323) 469-8991
Palardo Productions   (203) 387-0741
1807 Taft Ave., Ste. 4   FAX (323) 469-8991
Hollywood, CA 90028   www.palardo.tv
President/Director: Paul Ardolino
Senior VP of Production: Michael Ward
Production Designer: Tom Ardolino
Sound Editor: Michael Goldblatt
Music Director: Bjorn Englen
Production Manager: Tim Wilson
Director of Photography: Russell Carpenter
VP of Sales: Catherine Taylor
Associate Producer: Chip Clements
Public Relations: Deanna Palfrey
Sound Mixer Engineer: Paul Mittenberg
Assistant Mixer/Boom: Todd Skelton

Partizan   (323) 468-0123
7083 Hollywood Blvd., Ste. 401   FAX (323) 468-0129
Hollywood, CA 90028   www.partizan.com
Executive Producer & CEO: Sheila Stepanek
Executive Producer: Jeff Pantaleo
Sales Representative: Danielle Hinde
Directors: Philip Andelman, BB Gun, Tom Beard, Cédric
Blaisbois, Daniel Brereton, Kinga Burza, Canada, Barney Clay,
Alex Courtes, Tabitha Denholm, Stéphanie Di Giusto, Steve
Drypolcher, Daniel Eskills, Ollie Evans, Raphael Frydman,
Warren Fu, Michel Gondry, Michael Gracey, Honey, Arthur
King, Dan Lowe, Hiro Murai, Ace Norton, Nima Nourizadeh,
Valerie Pirson, Timothy Saccenti, Henry Scholfield, Skinny &
Ray Tintori

Peter Nydrle Productions   (310) 659-8844
672 N. La Peer Dr.   FAX (310) 659-7733
West Hollywood, CA 90069   www.nydrle.com
Head of Production: Adele Amos

PRETTYBIRD   (310) 315-8700
9905 Jefferson Blvd.   FAX (310) 315-5470
Culver City, CA 90232   www.prettybirdus.com

Railroad Studios   (818) 396-4985
1500 Railroad St.   FAX (818) 396-4986
Glendale, CA 91204   www.railroadstudios.com

Ringleader   (310) 876-2278
13101 Washington Blvd., Ste. 402   www.ringleader.pro
Los Angeles, CA 90066

Riveting Entertainment   (213) 785-5230
1010 Wilshire Blvd., Ste. 1502
Los Angeles, CA 90017   www.rivetingentertainment.com

Rockhard   (310) 659-4400
1022 Palm Ave., Ste. 1   FAX (310) 659-4402
West Hollywood, CA 90069   www.rhfilms.com

      (310) 710-6525
Sleeping Giant Films   (818) 847-1555
2819 N. San Fernando Blvd.   FAX (818) 847-1556
Burbank, CA 91504   www.sleepinggiantfilms.com

Smuggler   (323) 817-3300
1715 N. Gower St.   FAX (323) 817-3333
Los Angeles, CA 90028   www.smugglersite.com
Executive Producers: Brian Carmody & Patrick Milling Smith
Heads of Production: Allison Kunzman & Laura Thoel
Directors: Jaron Albertin, Filip Engstrom, Bennett Miller,
Guy Shelmerdine, Stylewar & Jon Watts
Chief Operating Officer: Lisa Rich

      (714) 437-9585
Sound Matrix Studios   (714) 402-7450
18060 Newhope St.   www.soundmatrixstudios.com
Orange County, CA 92708

trio films   (310) 207-7800
2023 S. Westgate Ave.   FAX (310) 207-7807
Los Angeles, CA 90025   www.triofilms.com
Executive Producers: Taylor Ferguson & Erin Tauscher

Waterline Pictures, Inc. (818) 901-1178
P.O. Box 56387 (310) 963-4812
Sherman Oaks, CA 91413 FAX (818) 901-1179
President/Director: Roger Roth

Wild Eyed Entertainment (213) 741-9301
3929 Flower Dr. (310) 466-1040
Los Angeles, CA 90007 FAX (213) 741-6301
www.wildeyedent.com

Wild Indigo, LLC (323) 876-3331
www.wildindigo.tv
Directors: Moses Edinborough, Dean Karr & Jefferson Miller
Executive Producer: Arthur Gorson

Production Offices

1st Wave Productions (310) 474-2439
2017 Pacific Ave. (310) 883-8800
Venice, CA 90291 FAX (310) 474-5282
www.1stwaveproductions.com

4-Production Space (310) 566-6710
3303 Pico Blvd., Ste. A (310) 566-6701
Santa Monica, CA 90405 FAX (310) 943-1705
www.4-productionspace.com

A-1 Production Office in Hollywood (323) 456-1706
6615 Melrose Ave., Ste. 2 FAX (323) 790-0450
Los Angeles, CA 90038
www.a1productionofficeinhollywood.com

Absolute Post Production (818) 567-6190
4119 W. Burbank Blvd. (818) 842-7966
Burbank, CA 91505 FAX (818) 567-6199
www.absoluterentals.com

Albuquerque Studios (505) 227-2000
5650 University Blvd. SE FAX (505) 227-2001
Albuquerque, NM 87106 www.abqstudios.com

ANA Special Effects, Inc. (818) 909-6999
7021 Hayvenhurst Ave. FAX (818) 782-0635
Van Nuys, CA 91406 www.anaspecialeffects.com

Associated Television International (323) 556-5600
4401 Wilshire Blvd. www.4401wilshire.com
Los Angeles, CA 90010

Audio Head (323) 850-2500
1041 N. Formosa Ave. FAX (323) 850-2771
West Hollywood, CA 90046 www.audioheadpost.com

Bill Rentals (310) 396-5937
73 Market St. (323) 715-5499
Venice, CA 90291 FAX (310) 450-4988

CatchLight Films (310) 295-0071
FAX (310) 341-3806
www.catchlightfilms.com

Century Studio Corporation (310) 287-3600
8660 Hayden Pl., Ste. 100 (888) 878-2437
Culver City, CA 90232 FAX (310) 287-3608
www.centurystudio.com

Costume Rentals Corporation (818) 753-3700
11149 Vanowen St. FAX (818) 753-3737
North Hollywood, CA 91605
www.costumerentalscorp.com

The Culver Studios (310) 202-1234
9336 W. Washington Blvd. FAX (310) 202-3201
Culver City, CA 90232 www.theculverstudios.com

Digital Jungle Post Production (323) 962-0867
6363 Santa Monica Blvd. FAX (323) 962-9960
Los Angeles, CA 90038 www.digijungle.com

e Suites, Inc. division,
Studio e Valencia (661) 702-9700
28005 Smyth Dr. FAX (661) 702-9705
Valencia, CA 91355 www.esuitesinc.com

e Suites, Inc. division, Sunset 8335 (323) 656-7100
8335 Sunset Blvd. FAX (323) 656-7155
West Hollywood, CA 90069 www.esuitesinc.com

Eastern Costume Company (818) 982-3611
7243 Coldwater Canyon Ave. FAX (818) 982-1905
North Hollywood, CA 91605
www.easterncostume.com/services/
productionoffices

Entertainment Post (818) 846-0411
639 S. Glenwood Pl. FAX (818) 846-1542
Burbank, CA 91506 www.entpost.com

eOfficeSuites, Inc. (310) 566-7000
13101 Washington Blvd., Ste. 100 FAX (310) 566-7400
Los Angeles, CA 90066 www.eofficesuites.com

Hollywood Center Studios (323) 860-0000
1040 N. Las Palmas Ave. FAX (323) 860-8105
Hollywood, CA 90038 www.hollywoodcenter.com

Hollywood Production Center (323) 785-2100
1149 N. Gower St. FAX (323) 462-8179
Los Angeles, CA 90038 www.hollywoodpc.com

Hollywood Production Center 2 (818) 480-3100
121 W. Lexington Dr. FAX (818) 480-3199
Glendale, CA 91203 www.hollywoodpc.com

Line 204 Inc. (323) 960-0113
837 N. Cahuenga Blvd. FAX (323) 960-8509
Hollywood, CA 90038 www.line204.com

Los Angeles Center Studios (213) 534-3000
1201 W. Fifth St., Ste. T-110 www.lacenterstudios.com
Los Angeles, CA 90017

The Lot (323) 850-3180
1041 N. Formosa Ave. (323) 850-2832
West Hollywood, CA 90046 www.thelotstudios.com

Motiv Films (310) 260-6100
1630 Stewart St., Studio B1 FAX (310) 260-6111
Santa Monica, CA 90404 www.motivfilms.com

Ⓐ The Studios at Paramount (323) 956-2524
The Studios at Paramount Tenant Services,
5555 Melrose Ave. www.thestudiosatparamount.com
Hollywood, CA 90038

Pasadena Production Studios (626) 584-4090	**Red Studios Hollywood** (323) 463-0808
39 E. Walnut St. FAX (626) 584-4099	846 N. Cahuenga Blvd. FAX (323) 465-8173
Pasadena, CA 91103 www.danwolfe.com	Hollywood, CA 90038 www.redstudio.com

Pasadena Production Studios   (626) 584-4090
39 E. Walnut St.   FAX (626) 584-4099
Pasadena, CA 91103   www.danwolfe.com

                 (818) 933-2100
Phunware Studios   (818) 933-2107
14144 Ventura Blvd., Ste. 300   FAX (818) 704-9386
Sherman Oaks, CA 91423   phunware.com/studio

Quixote Studios   (323) 851-5030
1011 N. Fuller Ave.   FAX (323) 851-5029
West Hollywood, CA 90046   www.quixote.com

Raleigh Studios - Hollywood   (323) 960-3456
5300 Melrose Ave.   FAX (323) 960-4712
Hollywood, CA 90038   www.raleighstudios.com

Raleigh Studios - Manhattan Beach (323) 960-3456
1600 Rosecrans Ave.   FAX (310) 727-2710
Manhattan Beach, CA 90266   www.raleighstudios.com

Raleigh Studios - Playa Vista   (323) 960-3456
5600 S. Campus Center Dr.   www.raleighstudios.com
Playa Vista, CA 90094

Red Studios Hollywood   (323) 463-0808
846 N. Cahuenga Blvd.   FAX (323) 465-8173
Hollywood, CA 90038   www.redstudio.com

Silverlake Production Annex   (323) 661-0391
4216 Santa Monica Blvd.   www.fancyfilm.com
Los Angeles, CA 90029

Sunset Bronson Studios   (323) 460-5858
5800 W. Sunset Blvd.   FAX (323) 460-3844
Los Angeles, CA 90028   www.sgsandsbs.com

Sunset Gower Studios   (323) 467-1001
1438 N. Gower St.   www.sgsandsbs.com
Los Angeles, CA 90028

Video Assist Systems, Inc.   (818) 606-8901
                   FAX (818) 222-5862
       www.videoassistsystems.com

XcitableBoy Productions, Inc.   (310) 392-8000
3313 Ocean Park Blvd.   FAX (310) 359-9202
Santa Monica, CA 90405   www.xcitableboy.com

7ate9 Entertainment (323) 464-6789
740 N. La Brea Ave. FAX (323) 937-6713
Hollywood, CA 90038 www.7ate9.com

Alternate Reality Entertainment (818) 742-7208
5701 Cantaloupe Ave. FAX (818) 782-0826
Sherman Oaks, CA 91401 www.alternatereality.tv
Contact: Michael Marconi

The Association, Inc. (818) 841-9660
135 N. Screenland Dr. FAX (818) 841-8370
Burbank, CA 91505 www.wemakethephonering.com
Contacts: Trevor Eisenman, Jeff Murphy, Fletcher Murray,
Tom Murray & Tom Myrdahl

Attack Ads, Inc. (310) 857-7745
578 Washington Blvd., Ste. 594 www.attackads.tv
Marina Del Rey, CA 90292
Contacts: Eagle Egilsson, Dr. Garry, Bronston Jones &
Roberts Jones

Autonomy, Inc. (213) 814-2919
www.autonomy.tv

Barcon Video Productions (818) 248-9161
3653 Mesa Lila Ln. FAX (818) 249-8884
Glendale, CA 91208 www.barryconrad.com

Beantown Productions, Inc. (323) 960-0290
5707 Melrose Ave. www.beantown.tv
Los Angeles, CA 90038
Contacts: David Carr, David Comtois & Judie Stillman

BloomFilm (323) 850-5575

Brainwaves Media (310) 702-6374
223 E. Thousand Oaks Blvd. FAX (801) 720-2090
Thousand Oaks, CA 91362 www.brainwavesmedia.com

Cinevative Productions (323) 852-8903
8455 Beverly Blvd., Ste. 507 FAX (323) 852-0349
Los Angeles, CA 90048 www.cinevative.com
Contacts: Mark Ciglar & Carrie Dobro

D&E Entertainment, Inc. (323) 464-2403
6525 Sunset Blvd., Ninth Fl. FAX (323) 464-2426
Los Angeles, CA 90028 www.dandeentertainment.com

Evolution Film and Tape, Inc. (818) 260-0300
3310 W. Vanowen St. FAX (818) 260-1333
Burbank, CA 91505 www.evolutionusa.com
Contact: Lisa Lettunich

Evolution L.A. Inc. (310) 587-9191
1510 11th St., Ste. 101 FAX (310) 564-7717
Santa Monica, CA 90401 www.evolutionla.com
Contact: Mark Shockley

Framework Studio, LLC (310) 815-1245
3535 Hayden Ave., Ste. 300 FAX (310) 815-9821
Culver City, CA 90232 www.frameworkla.com

Hammer Creative (323) 606-4700
6311 Romaine St., Third Fl. FAX (323) 463-8130
Los Angeles, CA 90038 www.hammercreative.com
Contact: Mark Pierce

Hieroglyphic Productions (818) 505-6050
3211 Cahuenga Blvd. West, Ste. 103 FAX (818) 505-6054
Los Angeles, CA 60068 www.hiero.net

Idea Asylum Productions, Inc. (323) 634-0434
6100 Wilshire Blvd., Ste. 1550 FAX (323) 634-0575
Los Angeles, CA 90048 www.ideaasylum.com

Ignition Post (818) 762-2210
4130 Cahuenga Blvd., Ste. 100 www.ignition-post.com
Toluca Lake, CA 91602

Jay Silverman Productions (323) 466-6030
1541 N. Cahuenga Blvd. FAX (323) 466-7139
Hollywood, CA 90028 www.jaysilverman.com

Kandoo Films, Inc. (818) 789-6777
4515 Van Nuys Blvd., Ste. 100 FAX (818) 789-2299
Sherman Oaks, CA 91403 www.kandoofilms.com
Contacts: Howard Barish & Rhonda Kinosian

Make It Happen Productions, Inc. (818) 981-2327
13557 Ventura Blvd., Second Fl. FAX (818) 981-2440
Sherman Oaks, CA 91423 www.mihp.tv

Mighty Oak Media, Inc. (818) 807-4225
14203 Dickens St. www.mightyoakmedia.com
Sherman Oaks, CA 91423

Moving Parts, Inc. (818) 557-7412
4111 W. Alameda Ave., Ste. 602 FAX (818) 557-6553
Burbank, CA 91505 www.movingpartsinc.com
Contacts: Chad Cooperman & Matt Van Buren

Planet 3 Entertainment Group, LLC (310) 392-4600
10844 Burbank Blvd. www.planet3entertainment.com
N. Hollywood, CA 91601

Play Editorial, Inc. (323) 465-3500
6464 Sunset Blvd., Ste. 600 FAX (323) 465-3511
Hollywood, CA 90028 www.playeditorial.com

Point of Origin (818) 392-8735
www.pointoforiginmedia.com

Pongo Productions (323) 850-3333
Contacts: Tom McGough & Jon Mingle FAX (323) 850-3334
www.gopongo.com

Precision Productions + Post (310) 839-4600
10718 McCune Ave. FAX (310) 839-4601
Los Angeles, CA 90034 www.precisionpost.com

Proscenium Pictures, Ltd. (323) 650-6767
8840 Wilshire Blvd. FAX (323) 650-1345
Beverly Hills, CA 90211 www.prosceniumpictures.com

Psychic Bunny (310) 862-4262
453 S. Spring St., Ste.620 FAX (213) 614-9046
Los Angeles, CA 90013 www.psychicbunny.com

Randemonium, Inc. (818) 505-0400
4555 Radford Ave. FAX (818) 505-0599
Studio City, CA 91607
Contact: Kenton Rand

Revolver Films (310) 827-2441
4040 Del Rey Ave., Ste. 5 FAX (310) 827-2661
Marina del Rey, CA 90292 www.revolverfilmsla.com
Contact: Mark Priola

Richmel Productions, Inc. (818) 719-9920
4829 Topanga Canyon Blvd., Ste. 208
Woodland Hills, CA 91364

Rickmon Media (310) 503-5402
www.rickmonmedia.com

Rumpus Creative (310) 390-3410
www.rumpuscreative.com

silver lining productions, inc. (310) 289-6650
149 S. Barrington Ave., Ste. 770 www.silverliningp.com
Los Angeles, CA 90049
Contact: Bozena Armstrong

Splat Pictures (310) 403-4267
Contact: Rob Hampton FAX (310) 231-1113
www.splatpictures.com

Studio City　　　　　　(818) 557-7777
4705 Laurel Canyon Blvd., Ste. 400　　FAX (818) 557-6777
Studio City, CA 91607　　　　www.studiocity.com

Super 78　　　　　　(323) 663-7878
2894 Rowena Ave.　　　　FAX (323) 663-7800
Los Angeles, CA 90039　　　　www.super78.com
Contact: Laurie Leitzel

Thumbwar　　　　　　(310) 910-9030
5700 Melrose Ave., Ste. 302　　FAX (310) 910-9031
Los Angeles, CA 90038　　　　thumbwar.tv

Video Production Specialists (VPS)　(866) 447-3877
　　　　　　　　FAX (310) 577-0850
www.videoproductionspecialists.com

Wholly Cow Productions, Inc.　　(310) 545-8222
3770 Highland Ave., Ste. 202　　FAX (310) 545-0144
Manhattan Beach, CA 90266　　　　www.whollycow.tv

WSR Creative　　　　　　(310) 837-7001
9503 Jefferson Blvd., Ste. B　　FAX (310) 837-3680
Culver City, CA 90232　　　　www.wsrcreative.com

LA 411　　　　Public Relations　　　　LA 411

Artisans Public Relations　　(310) 837-6008
2530 Wilshire Blvd., Ste. 300　　FAX (310) 837-2286
Santa Monica, CA 90403　　　　www.artisanspr.com

Bender/Helper Impact　　(310) 473-4147
11500 W. Olympic Blvd., Ste. 655　　FAX (310) 473-1408
West Los Angeles, CA 90064　　　　www.bhimpact.com

Bragman Nyman Cafarelli, LLC　　(310) 854-4800
8687 Melrose Ave., Eighth Fl.　　FAX (310) 854-4848
Los Angeles, CA 90069　　　　www.bncpr.com

Costa Communications　　(323) 650-3588
8265 Sunset Blvd., Ste. 101　　FAX (323) 654-5207
Los Angeles, CA 90046　　　　www.costacomm.com

Ed Baran Publicity　　　　(213) 482-4696
1114 Echo Park Ave.　　　　FAX (213) 482-4616
Los Angeles, CA 90026　　　　www.edbaran.com

Goldfish Public Relations　　(818) 688-1502
2232 1/4 Mira Vista Ave.　　　　www.goldfishpr.com
Montrose, CA 91020

Henri Bollinger Associates　　(818) 784-0534
P.O. Box 57227　　　　FAX (818) 789-8862
Sherman Oaks, CA 91413　　　www.bollingerpr.com

The Honig Company, LLC　　(818) 986-4300
4804 Laurel Canyon Blvd., Ste. 828
Studio City, CA 91607　　www.honigcompany.com

Hype　　　　　　(323) 938-8363
6380 Wilshire Blvd., Ste. 1010　　www.hypeworld.com
Los Angeles, CA 90048

Julian Myers Public Relations　　(310) 827-9089
13900 Panay Way, Ste. R217　　FAX (310) 827-9838
Marina del Rey, CA 90292

Kallista　　　　　　(818) 566-9769
　　　　　　　　FAX (310) 356-7234
　　　　　　　　www.kallistapr.com

PMK, Inc.　　　　　　(310) 854-4800
8687 Melrose Ave., Eighth Fl.　　FAX (310) 854-4848
Los Angeles, CA 90069　　　　www.pmkbnc.com

Press Kitchen PR　　　　(310) 392-6682
15B Brooks Ave.　　　　FAX (310) 392-6680
Venice, CA 90291　　　www.presskitchen.com

Public Relations Associates　　(323) 653-0380
8455 Beverly Blvd., Ste. 304　　FAX (323) 653-0381
Los Angeles, CA 90048

Rogers & Cowan, Inc.　　(310) 854-8100
8687 Melrose Ave., Seventh Fl.　　FAX (310) 854-8106
Los Angeles, CA 90069　　www.rogersandcowan.com

Smoke & Mirrors Communications　(213) 250-4603
1825 Park Dr., Ste. 4　　　　www.sampr.net
Los Angeles, CA 90026

Spelling Communications　　(310) 838-4010
10460 Cheviot Dr.　　　　www.spellcom.com
Los Angeles, CA 90064

Wolfson Entertainment, Inc.　　(818) 615-0499
22201 Ventura Blvd., Ste. 207　　FAX (818) 615-0498
Woodland Hills, CA 91364　　　www.wolfsonent.com

310 Artists Agency (310) 278-4787
3500 W. Olive Ave., Ste. 300 www.310artists.com
Burbank, CA 91505
(Reps for Storyboard Artists)

Action Artists (323) 337-4666
(Reps for Storyboard Artists) www.action-artists.com

Mike Alden (310) 393-5300
www.storyboardsinc.com

Cassie R. Anderson (310) 943-9208
FAX (310) 441-9606
www.artphase.com

(818) 585-7719
Andy Lee Storyboards (818) 991-9186
www.andyleearts.com

Bill Angresano (310) 642-2721
www.famousframes.com

(818) 842-0800
Animatic Media, Inc. (954) 462-4000
1907 W. Burbank Blvd., Second Fl. FAX (818) 842-0864
Burbank, CA 91506 www.animaticmedia.com
(Animated Test Spots)

Dave Arkle (310) 393-5300
www.storyboardsinc.com

(310) 581-6677
Artwrist (310) 739-0280
www.artwrist.com

Andrew Baron (310) 339-9558
www.baronwork.com

Patrick Barrett (818) 489-9465
www.patrickbarrettart.com

Laurent Ben-Mimoun (818) 876-9618
rocketsciencetalent.com

Kathy Berry (310) 642-2721
www.famousframes.com

Paul Bonanno (310) 642-2721
www.famousframes.com

Jarid Boyce (310) 642-2721
www.famousframes.com

(310) 398-8150
Georgia Bragg (310) 345-8817
FAX (310) 398-4340

BrainForest Digital (818) 865-8333
5743 Corsa Ave., Ste. 220 FAX (818) 865-9333
Westlake Village, CA 91362 www.brain4est.com
(Animatics)

Tim Burgard (310) 393-5300
www.storyboardsinc.com

Ray Cadd (310) 393-5300
www.storyboardsinc.com

Dan Caplan (310) 393-5300
www.storyboardsinc.com

Peter Carpenter (310) 393-5300
www.storyboardsinc.com

(310) 581-4050
Ivan Cat (800) 289-0109
www.storyboardsinc.com

Bernard Chang (310) 642-2721
www.famousframes.com

Jiye Choi (310) 393-5300
www.storyboardsinc.com

Jeff Coatney (310) 642-2721
www.famousframes.com

Phillipe Collot (310) 642-2721
www.famousframes.com

Elizabeth Colomba (310) 393-5300
www.storyboardsinc.com

Ronald M. Croci (310) 642-2721
www.famousframes.com

Federico D'Alessandro (310) 393-5300
www.storyboardsinc.com

Jesse D'Angelo (310) 642-2721
www.famousframes.com

Tony Daniel (310) 393-5300
www.storyboardsinc.com

Danelle Davenport (818) 590-8586
www.danelledavenport.com

Malcomb Davis (562) 537-8020
www.malcomb.com

Joe Dea (818) 990-8993
www.ambitiousent.com

Stephen DeBonrepos (310) 642-2721
www.famousframes.com

(310) 985-1733
Alex DeLeon (310) 473-0775
FAX (310) 473-0775
www.stayup.com/artwork.html

Maurice DePas (818) 292-6531

Juan Diaz (310) 642-2721
www.famousframes.com

Hugo Dipietro (310) 642-2721
www.famousframes.com

Cash Donovan (310) 642-2721
www.famousframes.com

Alex Echevarria (310) 393-5300
www.storyboardsinc.com

Tomoki Echigo (310) 642-2721
www.famousframes.com

Edward Cook Storyboards (818) 620-8624
edcookstoryboards.blogspot.com

(310) 642-2721
Famous Frames, Inc. (800) 530-3375
5839 Green Valley Circle, Ste. 104 FAX (310) 642-2728
Culver City, CA 90230 www.famousframes.com
(Reps for Storyboard Artists)

Kevin Farrell (310) 642-2721
www.famousframes.com

John Fox (310) 383-3773
www.johnfoxart.com

Frameworks Artists	(323) 665-7736	**Lance Leblanc**	(310) 393-5300
983 Manzanita St.	www.frameworks-la.com		www.storyboardsinc.com
Los Angeles, CA 90029			
(Reps for Storyboard Artists)		**Jason Lee**	(310) 642-2721
			www.famousframes.com
Matt Fuller	(310) 393-5300		
	www.storyboardsinc.com	**Michael Lee**	(310) 642-2721
			www.famousframes.com
Roger Gana	(310) 393-5300		
	www.storyboardsinc.com	**Anthony Liberatore**	(310) 393-5300
			www.storyboardsinc.com
Jonathan Gesinski	(310) 642-2721		
	www.famousframes.com	**Wes Louie**	(310) 642-2721
			www.famousframes.com
Craig Gilmore	(310) 642-2721		
	www.famousframes.com	**Franck Louis-Marie**	(310) 642-2721
			www.famousframes.com
Jacob Glaser	(310) 642-2721		
	www.famousframes.com	**Jim Magdaleno**	(714) 356-3765
Chad Glass	(310) 393-5300	**Ernie Marjoram**	(310) 393-5300
	www.storyboardsinc.com		www.storyboardsinc.com
Lyle Grant	(310) 393-5300	**Adolfo Martinez**	(310) 393-5300
	www.storyboardsinc.com		www.storyboardsinc.com
Zack Grossman	(310) 393-5300	**Steven Martinez**	(310) 642-2721
	www.storyboardsinc.com		www.famousframes.com
Eric Hamlin	(323) 350-2578	**Eddy Mayer**	(310) 383-3152
	www.erichamlin.com		FAX (310) 209-8480
			www.eddymayer.com
Ray Harris	(818) 219-8970		
	www.rayharrisstudio.com	**Philip Mayor**	(310) 591-9910
			www.philipmayor.com
Adrian Hashimi	(310) 642-2721		
	www.famousframes.com	**Gabe McIntosh**	(310) 642-2721
			www.famousframes.com
Josh Hayes	(310) 393-5300		
	www.storyboardsinc.com	**Ernesto Melo**	(310) 642-2721
			www.famousframes.com
Trevor Hoier	(310) 422-0596		
	s76.photobucket.com/albums/j39/thoier/	**Martin Mercer**	(310) 415-7535
			www.martinmercer.com
Tim Holtrop	(310) 642-2721		
	www.famousframes.com	**Marc Michelon**	(949) 290 5066
			FAX (949) 497-8831
David Hudnut	(310) 642-2721		www.michelondrawings.com
	www.famousframes.com		
		Mark Millicent	(310) 642-2721
	(310) 641-9319		www.famousframes.com
Robert Hunt/Studio E Design	(310) 486-8551		
	FAX (310) 641-3926	**Yori Mochizuki**	(310) 642-2721
	www.setsketch.com		www.famousframes.com
Mark Hurtado	(310) 642-2721	**Alex Morris**	(310) 642-2721
	www.famousframes.com		www.famousframes.com
Patrick James	(310) 393-5300	**Brian Murray**	(310) 642-2721
	www.storyboardsinc.com		www.famousframes.com
Zeke Johnson	(310) 393-5300	**John Killian Nelson**	(310) 642-2721
	www.storyboardsinc.com		www.famousframes.com
Robert Kalafut	(310) 642-2721	**Rick Newsome**	(310) 393-5300
	www.famousframes.com		www.storyboardsinc.com
Merle Keller	(310) 642-2721	**Mark S. Pacella**	(310) 642-2721
	www.famousframes.com		www.famousframes.com
Brian Koons	(310) 393-5300	**Ivan Pavlovits**	(310) 642-2721
	www.storyboardsinc.com		www.famousframes.com
Turner Lange	(310) 642-2721		(818) 763-0995
	www.famousframes.com	**Chris Pechin/Peach Productions**	(818) 903-2560
			FAX (818) 763-0995
Phil Langone	(310) 642-2721		www.peachprods.com
	www.famousframes.com		
		Elizabeth Perez	(323) 666-5452
David Larks	(310) 642-2721		
	www.famousframes.com	**Khang Pham**	(310) 642-2721
			www.famousframes.com

Richard Poulain	(323) 307-1490	Timothy Spain	(818) 240-0500
			FAX (818) 240-5515
Charles Ratteray	(310) 642-2721		
	www.famousframes.com	Eric Stewart	(310) 393-5300
			www.storyboardsinc.com
Renee Reeser	(310) 642-2721		
	www.famousframes.com	Chris Stiles	(310) 642-2721
			www.famousframes.com

Reinman Illustration/Design (805) 640-7393
4612 Thacher Rd.
Ojai, CA 93023

Storyboards Online (818) 842-0800
1907 W. Burbank Blvd., Second Fl. FAX (818) 842-0864
Burbank, CA 91506 www.storyboardsonline.com

David Reuss (310) 642-2721
www.famousframes.com

  (310) 393-5300
Storyboards, Inc. (800) 289-0109
1207 Fourth St., Ste. 250 FAX (310) 393-5311
Santa Monica, CA 90401 www.storyboardsinc.com

Robin Richesson (310) 633-0306
www.robinrichesson.com

William Rosado (310) 642-2721
www.famousframes.com

Dan Sweetman (310) 642-2721
www.famousframes.com

Rosenthal Represents (818) 222-5445
(Reps for Storyboard Artists) FAX (818) 222-5650
www.rosenthalrepresents.com

TellAVision (310) 230-5303
1060 20th St., Ste. 8 FAX (310) 388-5550
Santa Monica, CA 90403 www.tellavisionagency.com
(Reps for Storyboard Artists)

Peter Rubin (818) 876-9618
rocketsciencetalent.com

Ruben Ter Sarkissian (310) 642-2721
www.famousframes.com

Marc Sandroni (310) 393-5300
www.storyboardsinc.com

Tom Tonkin (310) 642-2721
www.famousframes.com

Mark Sasway (310) 642-2721
www.famousframes.com

Bob Towner (310) 642-2721
www.famousframes.com

Gerry Schelly (213) 687-3720
www.gerryschelly.t35.com

Transcontinuity Studios, Inc. (818) 980-8852
4710 W. Magnolia Blvd. FAX (818) 980-8974
Burbank, CA 91505 www.nealadamsentertainment.com

Joe Schiettino (310) 642-2721
www.famousframes.com

Ed Traquino (310) 642-2721
www.famousframes.com

  (323) 316-6809
Mitt Seely (310) 457-6111
www.mittseely.com

Keith Turner (310) 569-5444
www.keithturner.info

David Selvadurai (310) 393-5300
www.storyboardsinc.com

Joel Venti (310) 642-2721
www.famousframes.com

  (323) 573-1234
Josh Sheppard (323) 258-4661
www.thestoryboardartist.com

Kaleo Welborn (310) 642-2721
www.famousframes.com

Jeremy Shires (310) 642-2721
www.famousframes.com

Steve Werblum (310) 642-2721
www.famousframes.com

Joseph Simon (818) 206-0144
www.allcrewagency.com

Shari Wickstrom (310) 642-2721
www.famousframes.com

Serg Souleiman (310) 642-2721
www.famousframes.com

Brian Wilcox (310) 642-2721
www.famousframes.com

Aaron Sowd (310) 642-2721
www.famousframes.com

Jonathan Woods (310) 642-2721
www.famousframes.com

Jeff Zugale (310) 642-2721
www.famousframes.com

20th Century Fox Television (310) 369-1000
10201 W. Pico Blvd.
Los Angeles, CA 90035
www.newscorp.com/operations/television.html

3 Arts Entertainment (310) 888-3200
9460 Wilshire Blvd., Seventh Fl. FAX (310) 888-3210
Beverly Hills, CA 90212

A&E Television Network (310) 556-7500
www.aetv.com

ABC Entertainment (818) 973-4042
500 S. Buena Vista St. abc.go.com
Burbank, CA 91521

ABC Family (818) 560-1000
3800 West Alameda Ave. abcfamily.go.com
Burbank, CA 91505

Alloy Entertainment (323) 937-7070
6300 Wilshire Blvd., Ste. 2150 FAX (323) 801-1355
Los Angeles, CA 90048 www.alloyentertainment.com

American Movie Classics (AMC) (212) 324-8500
11 Penn Plaza, 15th Fl. www.amctv.com
New York, NY 10001

Anonymous Content (310) 558-3667
3532 Hayden Ave. FAX (310) 558-4212
Culver City, CA 90232 www.anonymouscontent.com

Bad Robot (310) 664-3456
FAX (310) 664-3457
www.badrobot.com

BBC America (310) 405-8205
10351 Santa Monica Blvd., Ste. 250
Los Angeles, CA 90025 www.bbcamerica.com

Beacon Pictures (310) 260-7000
FAX (310) 260-7096
www.beaconpictures.com

Bunim-Murray Productions (818) 756-5100
6007 Sepulveda Blvd. FAX (818) 756-5140
Van Nuys, CA 91411 www.bunim-murray.com

CBS Productions (323) 575-2345
7800 Beverly Blvd. www.cbs.com
Los Angeles, CA 90036

CBS Television Studios (818) 655-5000
4024 Radford Ave. www.cbstelevisionstudios.com
Studio City, CA 91604

Centro Net Productions (310) 237-5653
2740 California St. FAX (310) 294-3691
Torrance, CA 90503 www.centronetproductions.com

The Disney Channel (818) 569-7500
3800 W. Alameda Ave. home.disney.go.com/tv/
Burbank, CA 91505

eOne Television (310) 407-0960
9465 Wilshire Blvd., Ste. 500 www.e1entertainment.com
Beverly Hills, CA 90212

Film Roman Productions (818) 748-4000
2950 N. Hollywood Way, Third Fl. FAX (818) 748-4600
Burbank, CA 91505 www.filmroman.com

Grammnet Productions (310) 317-4231
22631 Pacific Coast Hwy, Ste. 350 FAX (310) 317-4200
Malibu, CA 90265

Happy Madison Productions (310) 244-3100
10202 W. Washington Blvd., FAX (310) 244-1210
Judy Garland Bldg. www.adamsandler.com
Culver City, CA 90232

HBO (310) 382-3000
2500 Broadway, Ste. 400 www.hbo.com
Santa Monica, CA 90404

Imagine Television (310) 858-2000
9465 Wilshire Blvd., Seventh Fl. FAX (310) 858-2020
Beverly Hills, CA 90212
www.imagine-entertainment.com

itv Studios America (818) 455-4600
15303 Ventura Blvd., Bldg. C, Ste. 800
Sherman Oaks, CA 91403 www.itvstudios.com

Jerry Bruckheimer Television (310) 664-6260
1631 10th St. FAX (310) 664-6261
Santa Monica, CA 90404 www.jbfilms.com

Katalyst Films (323) 785-2700
6806 Lexington Ave. FAX (323) 785-2715
Los Angeles, CA 90038

Leverage Management (310) 526-0320
3030 Pennsylvania Ave. FAX (310) 526-0834
Santa Monica, CA 90404

Mark Burnett Productions (310) 903-5400
3000 Olympic Blvd. FAX (310) 903-5566
Santa Monica, CA 90404

NBC Universal Television (818) 840-4444
100 Universal City Plaza www.nbcuni.com
Universal City, CA 91608

Nickelodeon Network (310) 752-8000
2600 Colorado Ave. www.nick.com
Santa Monica, CA 90404

Principato Young Management (310) 274-4474
9465 Wilshire Blvd., Ste. 900 FAX (310) 274-4108
Beverly Hills, CA 90212

(310) 659-1577
RSA Films, Inc. (212) 343-2020
634 N. La Peer Dr. FAX (310) 659-1377
West Hollywood, CA 90069 www.rsafilms.com

Ryan Murphy Productions (323) 956-5000
5555 Melrose Ave., Chevalier Bldg. FAX (323) 862-1014
Los Angeles, CA 90038

Showtime Networks Inc. (310) 234-5000
10880 Wilshire Blvd., Ste. 1600 www.sho.com
Los Angeles, CA 90036

Sony Pictures Television (310) 244-4000
10202 W. Washington Blvd.
Culver City, CA 90232

Universal Media Studios (818) 777-1000
100 Universal City Plaza, www.nbcuni.com
Bldg. 1320, Fourth Fl.
Universal City, CA 91608

USA Network (818) 777-1000
100 Universal City Plaza www.usanetwork.com
Universal City, CA 91608

Warner Bros. Television (818) 954-6000
4000 Warner Blvd. www.warnerbros.com
Burbank, CA 91522

Wonderland Sound & Vision (310) 659-4451
8739 Sunset Blvd. FAX (310) 659-4451
Los Angles, CA 90069
www.wonderlandsoundandvision.com

Alternate Reality Entertainment (818) 742-7208
5701 Cantaloupe Ave. FAX (818) 782-0826
Sherman Oaks, CA 91401 www.alternatereality.tv
Contact: Michael Marconi

Ant Farm (323) 850-0700
110 S. Fairfax Ave., Ste. 200 FAX (323) 932-6797
Los Angeles, CA 90036 www.theantfarm.net

BloomFilm (323) 850-5575
Contact: Jon Bloom

BLT AV (323) 860-4000
6430 Sunset Blvd., Eighth Fl. FAX (323) 860-0890
Los Angeles, CA 90028 www.bltomato.com

Buddha Jones (323) 962-5100
910 N. Sycamore Ave. FAX (323) 962-5105
Los Angeles, CA 90038 www.buddhajonestrailers.com

Cimarron Group (323) 337-0300
6855 Santa Monica Blvd. FAX (323) 337-0333
Hollywood, CA 90038 www.cimarrongroup.com
Contact: Bob Farina

Eyestorm Productions (310) 582-3937
1522 Cloverfield Blvd., Ste. C FAX (310) 582-3939
Santa Monica, CA 90404
www.eyestormproductions.com

(323) 461-7500
Firestone Productions (323) 377-9494
Contact: Scott Firestone www.firestoneproductions.com

Fix It In Post, Inc. (818) 344-7944
www.fixitinpost.net

Goodspot (310) 453-5550
6565 Sunset Blvd. www.goodspot.com
Hollywood, CA 90028

The Grossmyth Company (310) 202-0211
9750 Braddock Dr. FAX (310) 202-0238
Los Angeles, CA 90232 www.grossmyth.com
Contact: Caddie Hastings

Hammer Creative (323) 606-4700
6311 Romaine St., Third Fl. FAX (323) 463-8130
Los Angeles, CA 90038 www.hammercreative.com
Contact: Mark Pierce

Hurwitz Creative (818) 487-8300
5344 Vineland Ave. FAX (818) 467-8301
North Hollywood, CA 91601 www.hurwitzcreative.com

Ignition Creative (310) 315-6300
3211 Olympic Blvd. FAX (310) 315-6399
Santa Monica, CA 90404 www.ignitionla.com

Illusion Factory (818) 598-8400
21800 Burbank Blvd., Ste. 225 www.illusionfactory.com
Woodland Hills, CA 91367
Contact: Brian Weiner

In Sync Advertising (323) 965-4810
6135 Wilshire Blvd. FAX (323) 965-8155
Los Angeles, CA 90048 www.insyncad.com

Intralink Film (310) 859-7001
155 N. LaPeer Dr. FAX (310) 859-0738
Los Angeles, CA 90048 www.intralinkfilm.com

Kandoo Films, Inc. (818) 789-6777
4515 Van Nuys Blvd., Ste. 100 FAX (818) 789-2299
Sherman Oaks, CA 91403 www.kandoofilms.com
Contacts: Howard Barish & Rhonda Kinosian

KO Creative (310) 288-3820
465 South Beverly Blvd., Third Fl. FAX (310) 288-3837
Beverly Hills, CA 90212 www.ko-creative.com
Contact: Kristi Kilday

Mark Woollen & Associates (310) 399-2690
207 Ashland Ave. FAX (310) 399-2670
Santa Monica, CA 90405 www.markwoollen.com

mOcean (310) 481-0808
2440 S. Sepulveda Blvd., Ste. 150 FAX (310) 481-0807
Los Angeles, CA 90064 www.moceanla.com

Mojo, LLC (323) 932-7700
5750 Wilshire Blvd., Ste. 600 FAX (323) 932-7701
Los Angeles, CA 90036 www.mojohouse.com

Precision Productions + Post (310) 839-4600
10718 McCune Ave. FAX (310) 839-4601
Los Angeles, CA 90034 www.precisionpost.com

(323) 465-3900
Reality Check Studios, Inc. (323) 908-7000
6100 Melrose Ave. FAX (323) 465-3600
Los Angeles, CA 90038 www.realityx.com

Seismic Productions (323) 957-3350
7010 Santa Monica Blvd. www.seismicproductions.com
Los Angeles, CA 90038

Studio 27 (818) 216-9026
6860 Lexington Ave. FAX (415) 621-1875
Hollywood, CA 90038 www.studio27inc.com

Tao Creative (323) 930-8550
955 S. Carrillo Dr., Ste. 205 FAX (323) 930-8545
Los Angeles, CA 90048 www.taocreativela.com

Trailer Park (310) 845-3000
6922 Hollywood Blvd., 12th Fl. FAX (310) 845-3470
Los Angeles, CA 90028 www.trailerpark.com

TriCoast Studios (310) 458-7707
11124 W. Washington Blvd. FAX (310) 204-2450
Culver City, CA 90232 www.tricoast.com

Adap.TV   **(818) 636-2996**
8611 Washington Blvd.   **www.adap.tv**
Culver City, CA 90232

AEG Digital Media Group   **(310) 751-1911**
800 W. Olympic Blvd.   FAX **(310) 751-1901**
Los Angeles, CA 90015   **www.aegdigitalmedia.com**
(Live Encoding & On-Demand Encoding)

ChinaCache   **(866) 998-3399**
21700 Copley Dr., Ste. 300   FAX **(213) 403-6155**
Diamond Bar, CA 91765   **www.chinacache.com**
(Live, On Demand & Webcast)

    (514) 334-5445
Haivision Network Video   **(514) 334-0088**
13975 Polo Trail Dr.   **www.haivision.com**
Lake Forest, IL 60045

Harmonic Inc.   **(800) 788-1330**
4300 North First St.   FAX **(408) 542-2511**
San Jose, CA 95134   **www.harmonicinc.com**
(Real-Time, On-Demand & Bandwith Optimization)

Media Excel   **(408) 800-1502**
5201 Great America Pkwy, Ste. 456 **www.mediaexcel.com**
Santa Clara, CA 95054
(SD, HD, Mobile TV & Multi-Screen)

ON24, Inc.   **(415) 369-8000**
201 3rd St., 3rd Fl.   FAX **(415) 369-8388**
San Francisco, CA 94103   **www.on24.com**

Onstream Media Corp.   **(415) 274-8800**
901 Battery St.   **www.onstreammedia.com**
San Francisco, CA 94111

VBC Broadcasting   **(832) 615-5045**
2150 Town Square Pl., Ste. 200   FAX **(832) 615-5049**
Sugar Land, TX 77479   **www.vbcbroadcasting.com**
(Internet Broadcasting & VT Network Platform)

ABC Family (818) 560-1000
3800 W. Alameda Ave. abcfamily.go.com
Burbank, CA 91505

Avalon Television (323) 930-6010
8332 Melrose Ave., 2nd Fl. FAX (323) 930-6018
West Hollywood, CA 90069 www.avalonuk.com

Babelgum (310) 469-6392
3212 Nebraska Ave. www.babelgum.com
Santa Monica, CA 90404

BET (310) 481-3700
10635 Santa Monica Blvd. www.bet.com
Los Angeles, CA 90025

CBS Studios (323) 575-2345
7800 Beverly Blvd. www.cbs.com/video/index.php
Los Angeles, CA 90036

College Humor LA (310) 360-2424
8800 W. Sunset Blvd., 5th Fl. www.collegehumor.com
West Hollywood, CA 90069

Crackle (310) 845-2626
9336 W. Washington Blvd. www.crackle.com
Culver City, CA 90232

Electus (310) 360-4500
8800 W. Sunset Blvd., 7th Fl. FAX (310) 360-3408
West Hollywood, CA 90069 www.electus.com

FishBowl Worldwide Media (310) 826-4912
www.fbwmedia.com

Funny or Die (323) 460-7007
1710 N. La Brea Ave. www.funnyordie.com
Los Angeles, CA 90046

Hulu (310) 571-4700
12312 W. Olympic Blvd. www.hulu.com
Los Angeles, CA 90064

KoldCast TV (949) 861-8949
P.O. Box 17569 www.koldcast.tv
Irvine, CA 92623

My Damn Channel (310) 647-6216
2121 Rosencrans Ave., Ste. 4310
El Segundo, CA 90245 www.mydamnchannel.com

Odenkirk Provissiero (323) 960-4777
650 N. Bronson Ave., Ste. B-145 FAX (323) 960-4772
Los Angeles, CA 90004 www.odenkirktalent.com

Revision3 (415) 734-3500
2415 3rd St., Ste. 232 revision3.com
San Francisco, CA 94107

Sander/Moses (818) 560-4500
c/o ABC Studios, FAX (818) 560-8777
500 S. Buena Vista St., Animation 1E13
Burbank, CA 91521 www.sandermoses.com

Studio 8 Entertainment (225) 278-2032
2450 Valentine St. www.studio8.net
Los Angeles, CA 90026

TBS Burbank (818) 977-5500
3500 W. Olive, 15th Fl. www.tbs.tv
Burbank, CA 91505

Vuguru (310) 229-1210
315 S. Beverly Dr., Ste. 315 FAX (310) 229-1207
Beverly Hills, CA 90212 www.vuguru.com

Warner Bros.
Interactive Entertainment (818) 977-0102
4000 W. Alameda Ave., Ste. 4050 FAX (818) 977-8974
Burbank, CA 91505 www.wbie.com

Wonderland Sound & Vision (310) 659-4451
8739 Sunset Blvd.
West Hollywood, CA 90069
www.wonderlandsoundandvision.com

LA 411 FEATURE

THE AMAZING SPIDERMAN

BY MARJ GALAS

Visual Effects Supervisor Jerome Chen on "The Amazing Spiderman"

The first order of business in rebooting the Spiderman story was determining how visual effects would bring this newly defined character to life. Visual Effects Supervisor Jerome Chen worked alongside Director Marc Webb in their "mission" to transform Peter Parker into his super-hero alter-ego.

"In our early concepts we wanted this Spiderman to have more of a natural and organic vibe to it," said Chen. "This was also going to be photographed in native stereo, so combining these two things alone gave this version a new look."

Chen and his team combined the web-slinging in the comic books with natural movements of the body. Attention to positive and negative space along with the perspective of distance to objects during flight were important ingredients used through the action sequences. Additionally, video references were used to determine how Spiderman's webbing would connect to buildings, and how his body would elevate from the ground to a building's surface. This data was then incorporated into motion capture technology.

"He has to appear that he is defying gravity," said Chen. "Motion capture has created many more advances in the way we use optic data to allow people to move in an unnatural existence."

In addition to the complexity of Spiderman's movements, Chen and his team also had to create a realistic metamorphosis of the villain into his alter ego The Lizard. They studied a variety of lizard species to define how the scales should be patterned on the body. Some scales had to be retractable and smaller while others, such as on the back, were larger and hard like armor. Once the scales were defined, the rigging and musculature of The Lizard was constructed.

"We had to create the illusion of the look of the skin, the way light reflects on it, the weight of it, how the muscles move together; there are so many different components," said Chen. "The most important thing was that The Lizard was a transformed version of a human, so we had to keep the proportions of his face closely human."

ABRIDGED FROM AN LA 411 NEWSLETTER ARTICLE PUBLISHED JULY 2012

A ADVERTISER SYMBOL

**Refer to the General Index for
cross-referencing items in this section.**

Baked FX (323) 937-6200
3750 Robertson Bl., Ste. 200 FAX (323) 937-6201
Culver City, CA 90232 **www.bakedfx.com**

Gradient Effects (310) 821-3177
4120 Del Rey Ave. FAX (310) 821-0584
Marina del Rey, CA 90292 **www.gradientfx.com**

(818) 524-2600
Merlan Creative Studios (818) 620-3617
5723 Auckland Ave. **www.merlancreative.com**
N. Hollywood, CA 91601

Monkeyhead (310) 836-7600
8553 Washington Blvd. FAX (310) 836-7611
Culver City, CA 90232 **www.monkeyhead.com**

STEELE Studios (310) 656-7770
5737 Mesmer Ave FAX (310) 391-9055
Culver City, CA 90230 **www.steelevfx.com**

SunnyBoy Entertainment (626) 356-9020
230 E. Union St. FAX (626) 356-9022
Pasadena, CA 91101 **www.sunnyboyentertainment.com**

(310) 659-5959
World of Video & Audio (WOVA) (866) 900-3827
8717 Wilshire Blvd. **www.wova.com**
Beverly Hills, CA 90211

1 Mix Productions   (310) 237-6438
www.1mixproductions.com
(ADR, Foreign Language Dubbing, Mixing, Synching & Voice
Over Services)

48 Windows Music and Mix   (310) 392-9545
1661 Lincoln Blvd., Ste. 220   FAX (310) 392-9445
Santa Monica, CA 90404   www.48windows.com
(ADR, Audio Laybacks, Digital Sound Editing, Dubbing, Foley,
Sound FX Library, Synching & Transmission Services)

5.1 Audio/iPost LLC   (323) 932-6300
5757 Wilshire Blvd., Ste. 401   FAX (323) 932-7084
Los Angeles, CA 90036   www.ipostllc.com
(5.1 Surround, ADR, Audio Laybacks, Audio Laybacks to
High Def, Digital Editing, Dolby Surround, ISDN, Laybacks,
Mastering, Mixing, Music, Music Composition, Sound Design,
Sound Editing, Sound FX Editing & Voice Over Services)
Contacts: Bob Grey, Michael Kross, Justin Lebens Laurence,
Michael Senescu & Sheldon II

740 Sound Design   (310) 574-0740
12509 Beatrice St.   FAX (310) 306-0744
Los Angeles, CA 90066   www.740sounddesign.com

AB Audio Visual Ent., Inc.   (562) 429-1042
FAX (562) 429-2401
www.abaudio.com
(ADR, Audio Laybacks, Digital Sound Editing, Dubbing, Foley,
Mastering, Music, Sound FX Library, Synching, Transfers &
Voice Over Services)

Absolute Post   (818) 567-6190
(818) 842-7966
4119 W. Burbank Blvd.   FAX (818) 567-6199
Burbank, CA 91505   www.absoluterentals.com
(ADR, Foley, Mixing, Sound Editing, Synching & Transfers)

Advantage Audio/Jim Hodson   (818) 566-8555
1026 N. Hollywood Way   FAX (818) 566-8963
Burbank, CA 91505   www.advantageaudio.com
(Digital Sound Editing, Dubbing, Foley, Laybacks, Mixing &
Sound FX Library)
Contacts: Jim Hodson, Heather Holbrook, Bob Poole &
Paca Thomas

Aftershock Digital   (323) 658-5700
8222 Melrose Ave., Ste. 304   FAX (323) 658-5200
Los Angeles, CA 90046   www.editkings.com
(Sound FX Library)
Contact: Fritz Feick

Alan Audio Works   (310) 753-1564
4720 W. Magnolia Blvd.   FAX (562) 408-6821
Burbank, CA 91505   www.alanaudioworks.com
(5.1 Surround, ADR, Audio Laybacks, Dolby Surround,
Dubbing, Foley, Foreign Dubbing, Mastering, Mixing, Music,
Music Composition, Music/Sound FX Library, Pre-Dubbing,
Restoration, Sound Design, Sound Editing, Synching &
Voice Over Services)

Allied Post Audio   (310) 392-8280
1158 26th St., Ste. 272   www.alliedpost.com
Santa Monica, CA 90403
(ADR, Audio Laybacks, Foley, Mixing, Pre-Dubbing, Sound
Design, Sound Editing, Sound FX Library &
Voice Over Services)

AlphaDogs, Inc.   (818) 729-9262
1612 W. Olive Ave., Ste. 200   FAX (818) 729-8537
Burbank, CA 91506   www.alphadogs.tv
(5.1 Surround, Audio Laybacks, Audio Laybacks to High Def,
Dialogue Cleanup/Advanced NR (LB Labs), Digital Editing,
Dolby Surround, Laybacks, Mixing, Sound Design, Sound
Editing, Sound FX Editing, Sound FX Library & Synching)

(805) 955-7742
AMP Studios   (805) 955-7770
101 W. Cochran St.   FAX (805) 955-7705
Simi Valley, CA 93065   www.ampstudios.com
(Dolby Surround, Laybacks, Mixing, Music/Sound FX Library,
Remote Sessions, Sound Editing, Synching & Transfers)

Anarchy Post   (818) 334-3300
1811 Victory Blvd.   FAX (818) 334-3305
Glendale, CA 91201   www.anarchypost.net
(5.1 Surround, ADR, Dialogue Cleanup/Advanced NR [LB Lab],
Digital Editing, Dolby Surround, Domestic Dubbing, Dubbing,
Foley, Foreign Dubbing, Mixing, Pre-Dubbing, Sound Design,
Sound Editing, Sound FX Editing, Sound FX Library, Synching,
THX Certified 5.1 Mixing & Voice Over Services)

Atlantis Group   (310) 458-9098
429 Santa Monica Blvd., Ste. 250   FAX (310) 458-9048
Santa Monica, CA 90401
www.atlantisgrouprecording.com
(5.1 Surround, ADR, Audio Laybacks, Digital Sound Editing,
ISDN, Mixing, Music, Restoration, Sound Design, Sound
Editing, Sound FX Editing, Synching & Voice Over Services)

Audio Gadgets   (818) 567-2080
210 N. Pass Ave., Ste. 106   FAX (818) 567-2011
Burbank, CA 91505
(5.1 Surround, ADR, Digital Editing, Dolby Surround, ISDN,
Laybacks, Mixing, Real Time Internet Streaming, Sound Editing,
Sound FX Editing, Sound FX Library, Source Connect &
Voice Over Services)
Contact: John Jackson

Audio Head   (323) 850-2500
1041 N. Formosa Ave.   FAX (323) 850-2771
West Hollywood, CA 90046   www.audioheadpost.com
(5.1 Surround, 6.1 Surround, 7.1 Surround, ADR, Archiving,
Audio Laybacks, Audio Laybacks to High Def, Digital Editing,
Dolby Surround, Domestic Dubbing, Dubbing, Foley, Foreign
Dubbing, ISDN, Laybacks, Mixing, Pre-Dubbing, Remote
Sessions, Sound Design, Sound Editing, Sound FX Editing,
Sound FX Library, Synching, Transfers & Voice Over Services)
Contact: Ricky Delena

LA's Voice-Over Studio of Choice for over 35 years
PAL • NTSC • HD • RADIO

• NARRATION
• ADR
• COMMENTARY
• NEW MEDIA
• GAMES
• ANIMATION

BUZZY'S
R E C O R D I N G

ISDN • SOURCE CONNECT/IP • PHONE PATCH • FTP
323-931-1867   www.BuzzysRecording.com

Audio Mechanics (818) 846-5525
1200 W. Magnolia Blvd. FAX (818) 846-5501
Burbank, CA 91506 www.audiomechanics.com
(Digital Sound Editing, Mastering, Mixing, Restoration,
Synching & Transfers)

Audio Post & Picture (818) 562-6444
3619 W. Magnolia Blvd. www.audiopostpicture.com
Burbank, CA 91505
(5.1 Surround, ADR, Dialogue Cleanup/Advanced NR (LB
Labs), Digital Editing, Dolby, Dubbing, Foley, Mixing,
Pre-Dubbing, Sound Design, Sound Editing &
Voice Over Services)

AudioKut Digital Audio Post (818) 665-8266
www.audiokut.com

(714) 731-8883
AudioVision Production Services (888) 731-8883
14731 Franklin Ave., Ste. D www.audiovisionps.com
Tustin, CA 92780
(5.1 Surround, ADR, Audio Laybacks, Dialog Cleanup, Dolby E
Encoding, Domestic Dubbing, DTS Encoding, Foreign Dubbing,
ISDN, Laybacks, Mastering, Mixing, Music Composition,
Music Editing, Music FX Library, Pre-Dubbing, Preservation,
Restoration, Sound Design, Sound Editing, Sound FX Editing,
Sound FX Library, Transfers, Transmission Services &
Voice Over Services)

Bang Zoom! Studios (818) 295-3939
1100 N. Hollywood Way www.bangzoomstudios.com
Burbank, CA 91505
(5.1 Surround, AC3/dts Encoding (LB Labs), ADR, Audio
Laybacks, Digital Editing, Dolby Surround, Domestic Dubbing,
Dubbing, Foley, Foreign Dubbing, Laybacks, Mastering,
Mixing, Music Composition, Music FX Library, Pre-Dubbing,
Restoration, Sound Design, Sound Editing, Sound FX Editing,
Sound FX Library, Synching, Transfers & Voice Over Services)
Contact: Jonathan Sherman

Bell Sound Studios (323) 461-3036
916 N. Citrus Ave. FAX (323) 461-8764
Los Angeles, CA 90038 www.bellsound.com
(5.1 Surround, ADR, Audio Laybacks, Audio Laybacks to High
Def, Dialogue Cleanup/Advanced NR (LB Labs), Digital Editing,
Dolby Surround, Domestic Dubbing, Dubbing, Foreign Dubbing,
ISDN, Laybacks, Mixing, Music, Music FX Library, Remote
Sessions, Sound Design, Sound Editing, Sound FX Editing,
Sound FX Library, Transfers, Transmission Services, Video
Services & Voice Over Services)
Contact: Keefe Kaupanger-Swacker

The Bennett Group (310) 442-6630
2032 Armacost Ave. FAX (310) 442-8235
Los Angeles, CA 90025 www.bennettproductions.com
(ADR, Audio Laybacks, Digital Sound Editing, Dubbing, Mixing,
Music/Sound FX Library, Transfers & Transmission Services)
Contact: Cindy Casillas

Blague Communications (866) 769-5661
11417 Moorpark St. FAX (818) 232-9295
North Hollywood, CA 91602 www.blague-studio.com
(ADR, Audio Laybacks, Dubbing, Foreign Dubbing, Mixing,
Laybacks, Remote Sessions, Sound Design, Sound Editing,
Synching, Transfers & Voice Over Services)
Contacts: Mariela Fernandez & Blas Kisic

BluWave Audio (818) 777-3171
100 Universal City Plaza, FAX (818) 866-2274
Bldg. 1220-LL www.bluwaveaudio.com
Universal City, CA 91608
(Digital and Analog Archiving, Digital Mastering, Mixing,
Preservation, Restoration & Transfers)
Contact: Richard LeGrand

BritMix Audio Post (323) 252-8891
6020 Seabluff Dr. www.britmix.com
Playa Vista, CA 90094
(5.1 Surround, ADR, Audio Laybacks, Digital Sound Editing,
Foley, Mixing, Remote Sessions, Sound Design, Sound FX
Editing & Voice Over Services)

Ⓐ Buzzy's Recording (323) 931-1867
6900 Melrose Ave. FAX (323) 931-9681
Los Angeles, CA 90038 www.buzzysrecording.com
(ADR, Digital Sound Editing, Interactive Voice-Over, Mixing &
Music/Sound FX Library)
Contact: Andrew Morris

Capitol Studios (323) 871-5001
1750 N. Vine St. FAX (323) 871-5058
Hollywood, CA 90028 www.capitolstudios.com
(Audio Laybacks, Digital Sound Editing, Dubbing, Mixing,
Scoring/Sound Stage, Sound FX Library, Synching & Transfers)

CCI Digital, Inc. (818) 562-6300
2921 W. Alameda Ave. FAX (818) 562-6222
Burbank, CA 91505 www.ccidigital.com
(ADR, Dubbing, Laybacks, Mixing, Music/Sound FX Library &
Sound Editing)

CMI Media Management
(Cine Magnetics Digital & (818) 623-2560
Video Laboratories) (800) 431-1102
3765 Cahuenga Blvd. West
Studio City, CA 91604
www.cinemagnetics.com/post-production.html
(ADR, Audio Laybacks, Digital Sound Editing, Dolby Surround,
Dubbing, Foreign and Domestic Dubbing, Laybacks, Mastering,
Mixing, Sound Editing, Sound FX Library, Synching, THX
Certified 5.1 Mixing, Transfers, Transmission Services &
Voice Over Services)

(818) 842-8346
Chace Audio by Deluxe (800) 842-8346
201 S. Victory Blvd. FAX (818) 842-8353
Burbank, CA 91502 www.chace.com
(5.1 Surround, 6.1 Surround, 7.1 Surround, ADR, AC3/dts
Encoding (LB Labs), ADR, Archiving, Audio Laybacks, Audio
Laybacks to High Def, Dialogue Cleanup/Advanced NR (LB
Labs), Digital Editing, Digital Sound Editing, Dolby E, Dolby
Surround, Domestic Dubbing, Dubbing, Foley, Foreign Dubbing,
ISDN, Laybacks, Mastering, Mixing, Restoration, Sound Editing,
Sound FX Editing, Synching,
THX Certified 5.1 Mixing & Transfers)
Contacts: James Eccles, Bob Heiber & Doug Johnson

(818) 882-3300
Command Post (818) 882-1315
8400 Keokuk Ave. www.command-post.com
Winnetka, CA 91306
(ADR, Dolby Surround, Dubbing, Foley, Laybacks, Mixing,
Music/Sound FX Library, Sound Editing, Synching & Transfers)

The Complex Studios (310) 477-1938
2323 Corinth Ave. FAX (310) 607-9631
West Los Angeles, CA 90064
www.thecomplexstudios.com
(ADR, Mixing, Sound Editing & Transmission Services)

Costa Mesa Studios (949) 515-9942
711 W. 17th St., Ste. D10 www.costamesastudios.com
Costa Mesa, CA 92627
(Digital Sound Editing, ISDN, Foley, Mastering, Mixing, Mobile
Facilities, Music, Music Composition, Music/Sound FX Library,
Remote Sessions, Scoring/Sound Stage, Sound Design, Sound
Editing, Sound FX Library & Voice Over Services)

Creative Media Recording (714) 892-9469
11105 Knott Ave., Ste. G
Cypress, CA 90630 www.creativemediarecording.com
(ADR, Audio Laybacks, Digital Sound Editing, Dubbing,
Foley, ISDN Capabilities, Mixing, Music, Sound FX Library &
Translation and Transmission Services)
Contact: Tim Keenan

Daily Post (310) 417-4844
6701 Center Dr. West, Ste. 1111 FAX (310) 410-1543
Los Angeles, CA 90045 www.dailypost.tv

Danetracks, Inc. (323) 512-8160
7356 Santa Monica Blvd. FAX (323) 512-8163
West Hollywood, CA 90046 www.danetracks.com
(Editing, Mixing & Sound Design)
Contact: Ann Marie Wachel

Audio Post Facilities

Dangerous Waters Music   (310) 839-9444
www.dwmusic.com
(Dialogue Cleanup/Advanced NR (LB Labs), Digital Editing, Dubbing, Mastering, Music, Music FX Library, Sound Design, Sound Editing & Voice Over Services)

Different by Design   (310) 689-2470
12233 W. Olympic Blvd., Ste. 120   FAX (310) 689-2471
Los Angeles, CA 90064   www.dxdproductions.com
(ADR, Audio Laybacks, Digital Sound Editing & Mixing)
Contact: Matt Radecki

Digital Jungle Post Production   (323) 962-0867
6363 Santa Monica Blvd.   FAX (323) 962-9960
Hollywood, CA 90038   www.digijungle.com
(5.1 Surround, ADR, Archiving, Audio Laybacks to High Def, Dolby Surround, ISDN, Mastering, Mixing, Pre-Dubbing, Sound Editing, Sound FX Editing, Sound FX Library, Synching, Transfers & Voice Over Services)

Digital Sound Recording   (323) 258-6741
607 N. Ave. 64   www.vanwebster.com
Los Angeles, CA 90042
(Archiving, Digital Editing, Mastering, Mixing, Music, Preservation, Restoration, Sound Editing, Sound FX Library & Voice Over Services)
Contact: Van Webster

The Surround Factory   (818) 620-3030
FAX (805) 578-8767
www.Surroundfactory.com
(5.1 Surround, ADR, Audio Laybacks, Digital Editing, Dialogue Cleanup/Advanced NR (LB Labs), Dolby Surround, Domestic and Foreign Dubbing, Foley, Laybacks, Mastering, Mixing, Music, Music Composition, Music FX Library, Pre-Dubbing, Restoration, Sound Design, Sound Editing, Sound FX Editing, Sound FX Library, Synching & Voice Over Services)

Ear to Ear Music & Sound Design   (310) 581-1660
1660 Ninth St.   FAX (310) 581-1661
Santa Monica, CA 90404   www.eartoear.com
(ADR, Audio Laybacks, Digital Sound Editing, Dubbing, Foley, Mixing, Music/Sound FX Library & Synching)
Contacts: Amy Lyngos & Charlie Pomykal

Eleven   (310) 526-2911
1231 Lincoln Blvd.   FAX (310) 526-2929
Santa Monica, CA 90401   www.elevensound.com
(ADR, Dolby Surround, Dubbing, Foley, ISDN, Laybacks, Mixing, Music/Sound FX Library, Sound Editing, Synching & Transfers)
Contacts: Kristin Felt & D. J. Fox-Engstrom

Encompass Digital Media   (323) 344-4500
3030 Andrita St.   FAX (323) 344-4800
Los Angeles, CA 90065   www.encompass-m.com
(ADR, Audio Laybacks, Digital Sound Editing, Dubbing, Foley, Foreign and Domestic Dubbing, Laybacks, Mastering, Mixing, Sound Editing, Sound FX Library, Synching, Transfers, Transmission Services & Voice Over Services)

Fox Studios   (310) 369-7678
(310) 369-4636
10201 W. Pico Blvd.   FAX (310) 369-4407
Los Angeles, CA 90035   www.foxpost.com

Gold Street   (818) 567-1911
Bethany Rd.   www.goldstreetpost.com
Burbank, CA 91504
(5.1 Surround, ADR, Dialogue/Music Editing, Domestic/Foreign Dubbing, Mastering, Mixing, Music Composition, Noise Reduction, Sound Design/Editing & Voice Over Services)
Contact: Eric Michael Cap

Gray Martin Studios   (310) 449-4007
3000 Olympic Blvd., Ste. 2520   FAX (310) 449-4008
Santa Monica, CA 90404   www.graymartinstudios.com
(5.1 Surround, ADR, Audio Laybacks, Digital Editing, ISDN, Mixing, Sound Design & Sound FX Library)

Happy Feet Foley   (818) 564-4924
6099 Crape Myrtle Court   www.happyfeetfoley.com
Woodland Hills, CA 91367
(Foley)

Hieroglyphic Productions   (818) 505-6050
3211 Cahuenga Blvd. West, Ste. 103   FAX (818) 505-6054
Los Angeles, CA 90068   www.hiero.net

Hollywood Voice Over Service   (323) 202-3675
(Voice Over Services)   www.dcdouglas.com

iProbe Multilingual Solutions, Inc.   (888) 489-6035
www.iprobesolutions.com
(5.1 Surround, ADR, Audio Laybacks, Audio Laybacks to High Def, Digital Editing, Dolby Surround, Domestic Dubbing, Dubbing, Foley, Foreign Dubbing, ISDN, Laybacks, Mastering, Mixing, Pre-Dubbing, Remote Sessions, Restoration, Sound Design, Sound Editing, Sound FX Editing, Sound FX Library, Sound Stage, Synching, Transfers, Transmission Services & Voice Over Services)

J.E. Sound Productions   (323) 850-0765
www.jesound.com
(Analog, CD Duplication, Digital Editing, Engineering, Mastering, Mixing, Music, Post Production, Pro Tools, Sound Design, Sound Editing, Sound Recording, Transfers & Voice Over Services)
Contact: John Goodenough

(323) 883-0123
Jet Stream Sound   (310) 770-2439
www.jetstreamsound.com
(5.1 Surround, AC3/dts Encoding (LB Labs), ADR, Archiving, Audio Laybacks, Audio Laybacks to High Def, Dialogue Cleanup/Advanced NR (LB Labs), Digital Editing, Dolby Surround, Domestic Dubbing, Dubbing, Foley, Foreign Dubbing, Laybacks, Mastering, Mixing, Music Composition, Music FX Library, Pre-Dubbing, Preservation, Remote Sessions, Restoration, Scoring Stage, Sound Design, Sound Editing, Sound FX Editing, Sound FX Library, Synching, Transfers & Voice Over Services)

Juice   (310) 460-7830
1648 10th St.   FAX (310) 460-7845
Santa Monica, CA 90404
Contact: Oscar Morales

Juniper Post   (818) 841-1244
932 N. Ford   FAX (818) 972-4966
Burbank, CA 91505   www.juniperpost.com
(ADR, Foley, Mixing & Sound Editing)

Kappa Studios, Inc.   (818) 843-3400
3619 W. Magnolia Blvd.   FAX (818) 559-5684
Burbank, CA 91505   www.kappastudios.com
(ADR, Digital Sound Editing, Mixing, Restoration, Sound FX Library, Sound Stage & Transfers)
Contact: Paul Long

LA Studios, Inc.   (323) 851-6351
3453 Cahuenga Blvd. West   FAX (323) 876-5347
Los Angeles, CA 90068   www.lastudios.com
(ADR, Audio Laybacks, Digital Sound Editing, Dubbing, ISDN, Mixing, Music/Sound FX Library, Synching, Transfers & Transmission Services)
Contact: Jane Curry

LA3D   (323) 817-4466
6337 Santa Monica Blvd.   www.thela3d.com
Hollywood, CA 90038
(5.1 Surround, AC3/dts Encoding (LB Labs), ADR, Audio Laybacks, Audio Laybacks to High Def, Dialogue Cleanup/Advanced NR (LB Labs), Digital Editing, Dolby Surround, Domestic Dubbing, Dubbing, Foley, Foreign Dubbing, Laybacks, Mastering, Mixing, Music, Music Composition, Music FX Library, Pre-Dubbing, Restoration, Sound Design, Sound Editing, Sound FX Editing, Sound FX Library, Synching, Transfers, Transmission Services & Voice Over Services)

Larson Studios   (323) 469-3986
6520 Sunset Blvd.   FAX (323) 469-8507
Hollywood, CA 90028   www.larson.com
(ADR, Audio Laybacks, Digital Sound Editing, Dubbing, Foley, Mixing, Music/Sound FX Library, Synching & Transfers)
Contact: Scott Turner

LB Labs (818) 363-9395
www.lb-labs.com
(7.1 Surround, Dialogue Cleanup/Advanced NR (LB Labs),
Dolby E, AC3 and DTS Encoding, Mastering, Mixing,
Restoration, Transfers & Upmix to Surround)

Levels Audio (323) 461-3333
1026 N. Highland Ave. FAX (323) 461-3364
Los Angeles, CA 90038 www.levelsaudio.com

Lightpost Productions (818) 955-7678
1811 Victory Blvd. FAX (818) 334-3305
Glendale, CA 91201 www.renthd.com
(5.1 Surround, ADR, Audio Laybacks, Audio Laybacks to
High Def, Digital Sound Editing, Foley, Foreign and Domestic
Dubbing, Laybacks, Mastering, Mixing, Sound Design &
Sound Editing)

Lime Studios (310) 829-5463
1528 20th St. FAX (310) 829-5048
Santa Monica, CA 90404 www.limestudios.tv
(5.1 Surround, ADR, Archiving, Audio Laybacks, Audio
Laybacks to High Def, Digital Editing, Dolby Surround,
Domestic/Foreign Dubbing, ISDN, Laybacks, Mixing, Music,
Music Composition, Music FX Library, Pre-Dubbing, Remote
Sessions, Sound Design, Sound Editing, Sound FX Editing,
Sound FX Library, Synching, Transfers, Transmission
Services & Voice Over Services)

Margarita Mix de Santa Mónica (310) 396-3333
1661 Lincoln Blvd., Ste. 101 FAX (310) 396-9633
Santa Monica, CA 90404 www.lastudios.com
(5.1 Surround Sound, ADR, Audio Laybacks, Digital Encoding,
Digital Sound Editing, Dubbing, Foley, High Def, ISDN, Mixing,
Sound Design, Sound FX Network, Synching, Transfers &
Transmission Services)
Contacts: Jack Aurora, Jimmy Hite, Jeff Levy, Michele Millard,
Whitney Warren & Jonathan Whitehead

Margarita Mix Hollywood (323) 962-6565
6838 Romaine St. FAX (323) 962-8662
Hollywood, CA 90038 www.lastudios.com
(5.1 Surround Sound, ADR, Audio Laybacks,
Digital Sound Editing, Dubbing, High Def, ISDN, Mixing,
Sound FX Library & Transfers)
Contact: Veneta Butler

Media City Sound (818) 508-3311
12711 Ventura Blvd., Ste. 110 FAX (818) 508-3314
Studio City, CA 91604 www.mcsound.com
(7.1 Surround, AC3/dts Encoding (LB Labs), ADR, Audio
Laybacks, Audio Laybacks to High Def, Digital Sound Editing,
Dubbing, Mixing, Music/Sound FX Library, Sound Design,
Synching, Transmission Services & Voice Over Services)
Contact: Marvin Rich

Mercury Sound Studios (818) 545-8090
632 Thompson Ave. FAX (818) 545-8641
Glendale, CA 91201 www.mercurysoundstudios.com
(5.1 Surround, ADR, Digital Editing, Dolby Surround, Domestic
Dubbing, Dubbing, Foley, Foreign Dubbing, Mixing, Pre-
Dubbing, Sound FX Library, Sound Design, Sound Editing,
Sound FX Editing, THX Certified 5.1 Mixing & Transfers)

(818) 849-5085
Michael Hamilton Co. (818) 205-3246
spikey01.com
(5.1 Surround, ADR, Audio Laybacks, Audio Laybacks to
High Def, Digital Editing, Dolby Surround, Dubbing, Foreign
Dubbing, ISDN, Laybacks, Mastering, Mixing, Music FX Library,
Restoration, Sound Design, Sound Editing, Sound FX Editing,
Sound FX Library, Synching, Transfers & Voice Over Services)

(323) 804-1993
Mint Mix (310) 301-1800
316 S. Venice Blvd. www.mintmix.net
Venice, CA 90291
(5.1 Surround, AC3/dts Encoding (LB Labs), ADR, Audio
Laybacks, Audio Laybacks to High Def, Dialogue Cleanup/
Advanced NR (LB Labs), Digital Editing, Dolby Surround,
Domestic Dubbing, Dubbing, Foley, Foreign Dubbing, ISDN,
Laybacks, Mastering, Mixing, Pre-Dubbing, Remote Sessions,
Restoration, Sound Design, Sound Editing, Sound FX Editing,
Sound FX Library, Sound Stage, Synching, Transfers &
Voice Over Services)

Mixers Inc. (323) 799-4707
1330 Vine St. FAX (909) 625-0050
Hollywood, CA 90028 www.mixersinc.com
(5.1 Surround, 7.1 Surround, AC3/dts Encoding (LB Labs),
ADR, Audio Laybacks, Audio Laybacks to High Def, Dialogue
Cleanup/Advanced NR (LB Labs), Digital Editing, Dolby
Surround, Domestic Dubbing, Dubbing, Foley, Foreign Dubbing,
ISDN, Laybacks, Mastering, Mixing, Music Composition, Pre-
Dubbing, Preservation, Remote Sessions, Restoration, Sound
Design, Sound Editing, Sound FX Editing, Sound FX Library,
Sound Stage, Synching, THX Certified 5.1 Mixing, Transfers,
Transmission Services & Voice Over Services)

Monkeyland Audio, Inc. (818) 553-0955
4620 West Magnolia Blvd. FAX (818) 553-1155
Burbank, CA 91505 www.monkeylandaudio.com
(5.1 Surround, ADR, Archiving, Audio Laybacks, Audio
Laybacks to High Def, Digital Editing, Dolby Surround,
Domestic Dubbing, Dubbing, Foley, Foreign Dubbing, HD and
SD Laybacks, ISDN, Mixing, Pre-Dubbing, Sound Design,
Sound Editing, Sound FX Editing, Sound FX Library, Sound
Stage, Sound Supervision, Synching, THX Certified 5.1 Mixing,
Transfers & Voice Over Services)
Contact: Melissa Strater

NL3 Audio (213) 268-4226
1984 N. Main St., Ste. 300 www.nl3audio.com
Los Angeles, CA 90031
(ADR, Digital Sound Editing, Dolby Surround, Dubbing,
Foley, Laybacks, Mastering, Mixing, Music, Music/Sound FX
Library, Predubbing, Remote Sessions, Restoration, Scoring
Stage, Scoring/Soundstage, Sound Editing, Sound FX Library,
Synching & THX Certified 5.1 Mixing)

ON Music and Sound (310) 264-0407
2042-A Broadway FAX (310) 264-0381
Santa Monica, CA 90404 www.onmusicandsound.com
(ADR, Dolby Surround, Dubbing, Foley, Laybacks, Mixing,
Music/Sound FX Library, Remote Systems & Sound Editing)

OneWorld Language Solutions (323) 848-7993
3940 Laurel Canyon Blvd., Ste. 501 FAX (323) 848-7995
Studio City, CA 91604 www.oneworldlanguage.com

Oracle Post (818) 752-2800
4720 W. Magnolia Blvd. FAX (818) 769-2624
Burbank, CA 91505 www.oraclepost.com
(AC3/dts Encoding (LB Labs), ADR, Audio Laybacks, Digital
Mixing, Dolby Surround, Digital Sound Editing, Foley, Mixing,
Music FX Library, Scoring Stage, Sound Design, Sound FX
Library, THX Certified 5.1 Mixing & Transfers)
Contacts: James Lifton & Paulette Lifton

Outlaw Sound (323) 462-1873
1608 N. Argyle Ave. FAX (323) 957-2733
Hollywood, CA 90028 www.outlawsound.com
(5.1 Surround, ADR, Dialogue Cleanup/Advanced NR (LB
Labs), Digital Sound Editing, ISDN, Mixing, Music, Music
Composition, Music FX Library, Pre-Dubbing, Sound Design,
Sound Editing, Sound FX Editing, Sound FX Library, Synching,
Transmission Services & Voice Over Services)
Contact: Steve Pierson

**The Outpost Sound
Mixing Company** (323) 466-7937
4101 Lankershim Blvd. www.outpostsound.com
Noth Hollywood, CA 91602
(5.1 Surround, ADR, Audio Laybacks, Dialogue Cleanup/
Advanced NR (LB Labs), ISDN, Laybacks, Mastering, Mixing,
Music, Music Composition, Restoration, Sound Design,
Sound Editing, Sound FX Editing & Transfers)
Contacts: Tony Friedman & Eva Friedman

Paramount Recording Studios (323) 465-4000
6245 Santa Monica Blvd. FAX (323) 469-1905
Hollywood, CA 90038 www.paramountrecording.com
(Mixing, Scoring Stage, Sound Editing,
Sound FX Library & Transfers)
Contacts: Adam Beilenson & Mike Kerns

Ⓐ The Studios at Paramount (323) 956-3991
The Studios at Paramount Post Production Services,
5555 Melrose Ave. www.thestudiosatparamount.com
Los Angeles, CA 90038
(5.1 Surround, ADR, Archiving, Audio Laybacks, Audio
Laybacks to High Def, Digital Editing, Dolby Surround,
Domestic Dubbing, Dubbing, ISDN, Foley, Laybacks, Mastering,
Mixing, Pre-Dubbing, Remote Sessions, Restoration, Sound
Editing, Sound FX Editing, Sound FX Library, Sound Stage,
Transfers, Transmission Services & Voice Over Services)

Pixel Plantation (818) 566-7777
4111 W. Alameda Ave., www.pixelplantation.com
Ste. 301
Burbank, CA 91505
(5.1 Surround, Audio Laybacks, Audio Laybacks to High Def,
ISDN, Mixing, Sound Design, Sound Editing &
Voice Over Services)

Play (310) 576-0066
1447 Second St., Fourth Fl. FAX (310) 576-0063
Santa Monica, CA 90401 www.playsound.com
(5.1 Surround, ADR, Audio Laybacks, Audio Laybacks to
High Def, Digital Editing, Dolby Surround, Domestic Dubbing,
Dubbing, Foley, ISDN, Laybacks, Mastering, Mixing, Music,
Music Composition, Music FX Library, Remote Sessions, Sound
Design, Sound Editing, Sound FX Editing, Sound FX Library,
Synching, Transfers & Voice Over Services)

(818) 556-5700
Point360 (866) 968-4336
1133 N. Hollywood Way FAX (818) 556-5753
Burbank, CA 91505 www.point360.com
(ADR, Audio Laybacks, Audio Restoration, Digital Sound
Editing, Foley, Foreign Language Dubbing, Mixing, Sound FX
Library, Synching & Transfers)

Point360 (310) 481-7000
12421 W. Olympic Blvd. FAX (310) 207-8408
Los Angeles, CA 90064 www.point360.com
(ADR, Audio Laybacks, Digital Sound Editing, Dubbing, Foley,
Mixing, Sound FX Library, Synching & Transfers)

POP Sound (310) 587-1200
625 Arizona Ave. FAX (310) 587-1222
Santa Monica, CA 90401 www.popsound.com
(ADR, Digital Sound Editing & Mixing)

Post Haste Media, Inc. (818) 232-7556
11115 Magnolia Blvd., Second Fl. FAX (818) 237-5838
North Hollywood, CA 91601 www.posthastemedia.com
(5.1 Surround, Audio Laybacks, Audio Restoration Services,
Digital Sound Editing, Domestic Dubbing, Foley, Foreign
Dubbing, ISDN, Laybacks, Mixing, Music Composition, Music
FX Library, Pre-Dubbing, Sound Design, Sound Editing, Sound
FX Library & Voice Over Services)

Post Logic Studios (323) 461-7887
1800 N. Vine St., Ste. 100 FAX (323) 461-7790
Los Angeles, CA 90028 www.postlogic.com
(ADR, Digital Sound Editing, Dubbing, Foley, Mixing,
Sound FX Library & Transfers)

Post Modern Creative, LLC (949) 608-8700
2941 Alton Pkwy FAX (949) 608-8729
Irvine, CA 92606 www.postmoderncreative.com
(5.1 Surround, AC3/dts Encoding (LB Labs), ADR, Archiving,
Audio Laybacks, Audio Laybacks to High Def, Dialogue
Cleanup/Advanced NR (LB Labs), Digital Editing, Dolby
Surround, Domestic and Foreign Dubbing, Laybacks,
Mastering, Mixing, Music/Sound FX Library, Remote Sessions,
Sound Editing, Sound Stage, Synching, Transmission Services,
Transfers & Voice Over Services)
Contacts: Michael Boyd, Troy Burlage & Rich O'Neill

Private Island Trax (323) 856-8729
FAX (323) 965-8732
www.privateislandtrax.com
(5.1 Surround, ADR, Dialogue Cleanup/Advanced NR (LB
Labs), Dolby Surround, Foley, Laybacks, Mastering, Mixing,
Music, Restoration, Sound Design, Sound Editing &
Sound FX Editing)

Race Horse Studios (310) 280-0175
3780 Selby Ave. FAX (310) 280-0176
Los Angeles, CA 90034 www.racehorsestudios.com
(5.1 Surround, ADR, Digital Editing, Dubbing, Foley, Laybacks,
Mastering, Mixing, Music Composition, Restoration, Sound
Design, Sound Editing, Sound FX Editing, Synching, Transfers,
Transmission Services & Voice Over Services)

RavensWork (310) 392-2542
215 Rose Ave. FAX (310) 392-1222
Venice, CA 90291 www.ravenswork.com
(5.1 Mixing, ADR, Audio Laybacks, Digital Sound Editing,
Dubbing, Mixing, Music Composition, Sound Design, Sound FX
Library, Synching, Transfers & Transmission Services)

Rusk Sound Studios (323) 462-6477
1556 N. La Brea Ave.
Hollywood, CA 90028
(5.1 Surround, 6.1 Surround, 7.1 Surround, ADR, Audio
Laybacks, Dialogue Cleanup/Advanced NR (LB Labs), Digital
Sound Editing, Dubbing, Foley, Foreign Dubbing, Mastering,
Mixing, Music, Music Composition, Music FX Library, Scoring/
Sound Stage, Sound Design, Sound Editing, Sound FX Editing,
Sound FX Library, Synching & Voice Over Services)

ScreenMusic International (818) 789-2954
18034 Ventura Blvd., Ste. 450 FAX (818) 789-5801
Encino, CA 91316 www.screenmusic.com
(Digital Sound Editing, Dubbing, Mixing, Synching & Transfers)

Shoreline Studios (310) 394-4932
100 Wilshire Blvd., Ste. 150 FAX (310) 458-7802
Santa Monica, CA 90401 www.shorelinestudios.com
(ADR, Audio Laybacks, Digital Sound Editing, Mixing, Music/
Sound FX Library & Transmission Services)
Contact: Gary Zacuto

Skyline Sound (818) 754-0194
12419 Valleyheart Dr. FAX (818) 754-0194
Studio City, CA 91604 www.skylinesound.com
(5.1 Surround, AC3/dts Encoding (LB Labs), ADR, Dialogue
Cleanup/Advanced NR (LB Labs), Digital Editing, Dolby
Surround, Mastering, Mixing, Restoration & Sound Editing)

Skywalker Sound (415) 662-1000
www.skysound.com

Snap Sound (818) 432-2475
4640 Lankershim Blvd., Ste. 400 www.snapsound.tv
North Hollywood, CA 91602

Sonic Pool (323) 460-4649
6860 Lexington Ave. FAX (323) 460-6063
Los Angeles, CA 90038 www.sonicpool.com
(ADR, Digital Sound Editing, Dubbing, Foley, Mixing &
Sound FX Library)

Sony Pictures Studios (310) 244-5722
10202 W. Washington Blvd. FAX (310) 244-2303
Culver City, CA 90232 www.sonypicturesstudios.com
Contact: Richard Branca

The Sound Shop, Inc.   **(310) 237-6438**
1315 1/2 Westwood Blvd.   **www.postsoundshop.com**
Los Angeles, CA 90024
(ADR, Digital Sound Editing, Foreign Language Dubbing and
Voice Over Services & Synching)

Soundelux   **(323) 603-3200**
7080 Hollywood Blvd., Ste. 1100   FAX **(323) 603-3233**
Hollywood, CA 90028   **www.soundelux.com**
(ADR, Digital Sound Editing, Dubbing, Foley, Laybacks, Mixing,
Music/Sound FX Library, Restoration, Sound Design, Sound
Editing, Sound FX Editing, Sound FX Library,
Synching & Transfers)
Contact: Jeffrey Eisner

Soundmine   **(818) 767-4226**
8457 Petaluma Dr.   **www.soundmine.com**
Sun Valley, CA 91352

Soundscape Productions   **(818) 456-1051**
7543 Loma Verde Ave.   FAX **(818) 456-1046**
Canoga Park, CA 91303   **www.soundscapepost.com**
(5.1 Surround, AC3/dts Encoding (LB Labs), ADR, Audio
Laybacks, Dialogue Cleanup/Advanced NR (LB Labs), Digital
Sound Editing, Dubbing, Mixing, Mobile Facilities, Remote
Sessions, Restoration, Sound Design, Sound FX Library,
Transfers, Transmission Services & Voice Over Services)
Contact: Gregg Hall

Soundworks   **(818) 567-2000**
3401 W. Burbank Blvd.   FAX **(818) 567-2228**
Burbank, CA 91505   **www.soundworks.tv**
(5.1 Surround, ADR, Archiving, Dialogue Cleanup/Advanced NR
(LB Labs), Digital Editing, Domestic Dubbing, Dubbing, Foreign
Dubbing, ISDN, Mastering, Mixing, Music, Music Composition,
Music FX Library, Pre-Dubbing, Preservation , Remote
Sessions, Restoration, Sound Design, Sound Editing, Sound
FX Editing, Sound FX Library, Transfers, Transmission
Services & Voice Over Services)
Contacts: Vince Colivetti, Bridget Gardiner, Dan Montes &
Jeff Sheridan

Stampede Post Productions   **(323) 463-8000**
931 N. Citrus Ave.   FAX **(323) 463-8010**
Hollywood, CA 91104   **www.stampedepost.com**
(ADR, Dubbing & MIxing)

Station 22 Edit & Effects   **(310) 488-7726**
3614 Overland Ave.   **www.station22.com**
Los Angeles, CA 90034

Stewart Sound   **(714) 973-3030**
204 N. Broadway, Ste. N   FAX **(714) 973-2530**
Santa Ana, CA 92701   **www.stewartsound.com**
(5.1 Surround, ADR, Audio Laybacks, Audio Laybacks to
High Def, Audio Restoration Services, Digital Sound Editing,
Dolby Surround, Domestic and Foreign Dubbing, Foley, ISDN,
Laybacks, Mastering, Mixing, Music, Music Composition, Music
FX Library, Remote Sessions, Restoration, Sound Design,
Sound Editing, Sound FX Editing, Sound FX Library, Synching,
THX Certified 5.1 Mixing, Transfers & Voice Over Services)

**STS Foreign Language Services/a division
of STS Media Services, Inc.**   **(818) 563-3004**
P.O. Box 10213   **www.stsmedia.com**
Burbank, CA 91510
(5.1 Surround, ADR, Audio Laybacks, Digital Sound Editing,
Dolby Surround, Dubbing, Foley, Mixing, Foreign Dubbing,
Scoring/Sound Stage, Sound FX Library, Synching, Transfers &
Voice Over Services)

Studio City Sound   **(818) 505-9368**
4412 Whitsett Ave.   FAX **(818) 761-4744**
Studio City, CA 91604   **www.studiocitysound.com**
(ADR, Audio Laybacks, Audio Restoration Services, Digital
Sound Editing, Dolby Surround, Dubbing, ISDN, Foley, Foreign
and Domestic Dubbing, Laybacks, Mastering, Mixing, Mobile
Facilities, Music, Music Composition, Music/Sound FX Library,
Pre-Dubbing, Remote Sessions, Restoration, Scoring Stage,
Scoring/Sound Stage, Sound Design, Sound Editing, Sound FX
Library, Synching, Transfers & Voice Over Services)

Studiopolis   **(818) 753-2680**
11700 Ventura Blvd.   FAX **(818) 753-7830**
Studio City, CA 91604   **www.studiopolisinc.com**
(ADR, Audio/Video Editing, Dialogue Record, Dubbing, Foley,
ISDN, Laybacks, Mixing, Music/Sound FX Library, Remote
Sessions, Sound Editing, Synching & Transfers)
Contacts: Laura Lopez & Jamie Simone

Switch Studios   **(310) 301-1800**
316 S. Venice Blvd.   FAX **(310) 496-1964**
Venice, CA 90291   **www.switch-studios.com**
(5.1 Surround, ADR, Audio Laybacks to High Def, Dolby
Surround, Laybacks, Mixing, Sound Design, Sound Editing,
Sound FX Editing, Sound FX Library & Voice Over Services)

**Technicolor Creative
Services - Glendale**   **(818) 500-9090**
1631 Gardena Ave.   FAX **(818) 500-4099**
Glendale, CA 91204   **www.technicolor.com**
(Audio Restoration Services)
Contact: Jim Feeney

Technicolor Creative   **(323) 860-7600**
Services - Hollywood   **(323) 860-7816**
1438 N. Gower St., Box 50, Bldg. 48   FAX **(323) 860-7801**
Hollywood, CA 90028   **www.technicolor.com**
(ADR, Foley, Laybacks, Mixing, Sound Editing,
Synching & Transfers)
Contact: Mark Kaplan

**Damon A. Tedesco/
Mobile Disc Music Inc.**   **(310) 670-6155**
8726 S. Sepulveda Blvd.   **www.scoringmixer.com**
Los Angeles, CA 90045
(Digital Sound Editing, Mixing, Mobile Facilities &
Scoring Stage)

Terra Vista Media, Inc.   **(310) 237-6438**
   www.media-movers.com
(ADR, Domestic Dubbing, Foreign Language Dubbing, Foreign
Language Voice Over Services, Sound Editing & Synching)

Thunder Recording + Sound Design **(310) 829-4765**
3211 Olympic Blvd.   FAX **(310) 615-6399**
Santa Monica, CA 90404   **www.thunder-sound.com**

Timecode Multimedia   **(310) 826-9199**
12340 Santa Monica Blvd., Ste. 230
West Los Angeles, CA 90025
   www.timecodemultimedia.com
(5.1 Surround, ADR, Archiving, Audio Laybacks, Audio
Laybacks to High Def, Dialogue Cleanup, Digital Editing,
Domestic Dubbing, Dubbing, Foley, Foreign Dubbing,
Laybacks, Mastering, Mixing, Music, Music Composition, Music
FX Library, Pre-Dubbing, Sound Design, Sound Editing, Sound
FX Editing, Synching, Transfers & Voice Over Services)

Todd-AO Burbank   **(818) 295-5300**
2901 W. Alameda Ave., Second Fl.   **www.toddao.com**
Burbank, CA 91505
(5.1 Surround, ADR, Audio Laybacks, Digital Editing, Domestic
Dubbing, Dubbing, Foley, Laybacks, Mastering, Mixing,
Pre-Dubbing, Remote Sessions, Sound Design, Sound Editing,
Sound FX Editing, Sound FX Library, Synching, Transfers &
Voice Over Services)
Contact: Duke Lim

Todd-AO Hollywood   **(323) 962-4000**
900 N. Seward   FAX **(323) 466-2327**
Hollywood, CA 90038   **www.toddao.com**
(5.1 Surround, ADR, Archiving, Audio Laybacks, Audio
Laybacks to High Def, Dialogue Cleanup/Advanced NR (LB
Labs), Digital Editing, Domestic Dubbing, Dubbing, Foreign
Dubbing, ISDN, Laybacks, Mastering, Mixing, Pre-Dubbing,
Preservation, Remote Sessions, Restoration, Sound Design,
Sound Editing, Sound FX Editing, Sound FX Library, Sound
Stage, Transfers & Voice Over Services)
Contacts: Richard Burnette & Jeffrey Eisner

Todd-AO West   **(310) 315-5000**
3000 Olympic Blvd., Bldg. 1   FAX **(310) 315-5099**
Santa Monica, CA 90404   **www.toddao.com**
(5.1 Surround, ADR, Audio Laybacks, Audio Laybacks to High
Def, Domestic Dubbing, Dubbing, Foley, Foreign Dubbing,
ISDN, Laybacks, Mastering, Mixing, Pre-Dubbing, Remote
Sessions, Sound Design, Sound Editing, Sound FX Editing,
Sound FX Library, Sound Stage, Transfers &
Voice Over Services)
Contacts: Matt Dubin & Shelly Hovland

Tree Falls Post   **(323) 851-0299**
3131 Cahuenga Blvd. West   FAX **(323) 851-0277**
Los Angeles, CA 90068   **www.tfpost.com**
(5.1 Surround, ADR, Audio Laybacks, Audio Laybacks to High
Def, DaVinci Resolve, Digital Editing, Dolby Surround, Dubbing,
ISDN, Laybacks, Mixing, Pre-Dubbing, Sound Design, Sound
Editing, Sound FX Library, Synching, Transfers, Transmission
Services & Voice Over Services)

Union Editorial   **(310) 481-2200**
12200 W. Olympic Blvd., Ste. 140   FAX **(310) 481-2248**
Los Angeles, CA 90064   **www.unioneditorial.com**
(ADR, Dolby Surround, Laybacks, Mixing, Music/Sound FX
Library, Remote Sessions & Sound Editing)
Contact: Dona Richardson

       (818) 777-0169
Universal Studios Sound   **(800) 892-1979**
100 Universal City Plaza   FAX **(818) 866-1494**
Universal City, CA 91608
    www.filmmakersdestination.com
(ADR, Audio Layback, Audio Restoration and Preservation,
Digital and Analog Archiving, Digital Mastering, Foley, Mix
Stages, Mixing, Sound Design and Editing & Sound Transfers)
Contacts: Chris Jenkins & Steve Williams

The Village Recorder   **(310) 478-8227**
1616 Butler Ave.   FAX **(310) 479-1142**
Los Angeles, CA 90025   **www.villagestudios.com**
(ADR & Mixing)
Contact: Darren Frank

Virtual Mix   **(818) 209-6176**
    www.virtualmix.com
(ADR, Digital Editing, Dolby Surround, Domestic Dubbing,
Dubbing, Foley, Foreign Dubbing, Mixing, Pre-Dubbing,
Restoration, Sound Design, Sound Editing, Sound FX Editing,
Sound Stage, Synching, THX Certified 5.1 Mixing & Transfers)

Vitello Productions   **(818) 955-9930**
4224 Beck Ave.   **www.vitello.com**
Studio City, CA 91604
(ADR, Foley, Mixing & Sound Editing)
Contact: Paul Vitello

       (800) 993-3660
Voice Over There, Inc.   **(310) 880-0241**
    www.voiceoverthere.com
(ADR, ADR Trailer, Domestic Dubbing, Foreign Dubbing, ISDN,
Mobile ADR, Mobile Facilities, Sound Editing, Sound Stage &
Voice Over Services)
Contacts: Tony Schmitz & Amir Soleimani

The Walt Disney Studios   **(818) 560-2731**
500 S. Buena Vista St.   FAX **(818) 562-3262**
Burbank, CA 91521   **www.buenavistapost.com**

Warner Bros. Studio Facilities -   **(818) 954-1625**
Post Production Services   **(818) 954-2515**
4000 Warner Blvd.   FAX **(818) 954-4138**
Burbank, CA 91522   **www.wbsound.com**
(ADR, Digital Sound Editing, Dubbing, Foley, Mixing, Sound FX
Library, Synching & Transfers)

Warrenwood Sound Studios   **(818) 563-1263**
3825 W. Burbank Blvd.   FAX **(818) 526-8963**
Burbank, CA 91505   **www.warrenwood.com**
(ADR, APT-X, Avid DS/Symphony NITRIS Rental, Dolby
Surround, Foley, HDCAM SR, ISDN Dolby Fax, Laybacks,
Mixing, Re-Recording Stage, Sound Editing,
Sound FX Library & Zypher)

Wildfire Studios   **(323) 951-1700**
640 S. San Vicente Blvd.   **www.wildfirepost.com**
Los Angeles, CA 90048
(ADR & Foley)

William Sound Service   **(323) 461-5321**
1343 N. Highland Ave.
Hollywood, CA 90028
(ADR, Audio Laybacks, Digital Sound Editing, Dubbing, Foley,
Mixing, Sound FX Library, Synching & Transfers)
Contact: William Wang

4K Finish	**(323) 365-1221**
1149 N. Gower St., Ste. 281	**www.4kfinish.com**
Los Angeles, CA 90038	

AlphaDogs, Inc.	**(818) 729-9262**
1612 W. Olive Ave., Ste. 200	FAX **(818) 729-8537**
Burbank, CA 91506	**www.alphadogs.tv**

Bell Sound Studios	**(323) 461-3036**
916 N. Citrus Ave.	FAX **(323) 461-8764**
Los Angeles, CA 90038	**www.bellsound.com**

Company 3 LA	**(310) 255-6600**
1661 Lincoln Blvd., Ste. 400	FAX **(310) 255-6602**
Santa Monica, CA 90404	**www.company3.com**

Digital Jungle Post Production	**(323) 962-0867**
6363 Santa Monica Blvd.	FAX **(323) 962-9960**
Hollywood, CA 90038	**www.digijungle.com**

Hueman Interest	**(310) 765-4051**
531 Main St., Ste. 101	FAX **(310) 765-4052**
El Segundo, CA 90245	**www.huemaninterest.com**

	(818) 459-6630
Laurel Canyon Productions	**(310) 738-4184**
1101 S. Flower Ave.	FAX **(818) 450-0916**
Burbank, CA 91502	**www.lcproductions.tv**

Light Iron	**(323) 472-8300**
6381 De Longpre Ave.	FAX **(323) 832-8432**
Los Angeles, CA 90028	**www.lightiron.com**

New Hat	**(310) 401-2220**
1819 Colorado Ave.	FAX **(310) 401-2224**
Santa Monica, CA 90404	**www.newhat.tv**

Oasis Imagery	**(323) 469-9800**
6500 Sunset Blvd.	FAX **(323) 462-4620**
Hollywood, CA 90028	**www.oasisimagery.com**

Post Modern Edit, LLC	**(949) 608-8700**
2941 Alton Pkwy	FAX **(949) 608-8729**
Irvine, CA 92606	**www.postmodernedit.com**

Station 22 Edit & Effects	**(310) 488-7726**
3614 Overland Ave.	**www.station22.com**
Los Angeles, CA 90034	

STEELE Studios	**(310) 656-7770**
5737 Mesmer Ave.	FAX **(310) 391-9055**
Culver City, CA 90230	**www.steelevfx.com**

Timecode Multimedia	**(310) 826-9199**
12340 Santa Monica Blvd., Ste. 230	
West Los Angeles, CA 90025	
	www.timecodemultimedia.com

Tree Falls Post	**(323) 851-0299**
3131 Cahuenga Blvd. West	FAX **(323) 851-0277**
Los Angeles, CA 90068	**www.tfpost.com**

	(310) 979-3500
Westside Media Group	**(818) 779-8600**
12233 W. Olympic Blvd., Ste. 152	
West Los Angeles, CA 90064	
	www.westsidemediagroup.com

	(310) 659-5959
World of Video & Audio (WOVA)	**(866) 900-3827**
8717 Wilshire Blvd.	FAX **(310) 659-8247**
Beverly Hills, CA 90211	**www.wova.com**

30 Second Films (310) 315-1750
3019 Pico Blvd. FAX (310) 315-1757
Santa Monica, CA 90405 www.30secondfilms.com
(Non-Linear Offline and Online)
Contact: Alan J. Stamm

47 Pictures (323) 464-2406
6525 Sunset Blvd., Penthouse FAX (323) 464-2426
Hollywood, CA 90028 www.47pictures.com
(Computer Animation, Computer Graphics, Film Editing, Non-
Linear Offline, Post Production Supervision & Sound Design)

5th Wall (323) 461-0600
6311 Romaine St., Ste. 7135 www.5thwall.tv
Hollywood, CA 90038
(Color Correction, Digital Offline, Digital Online, Film Editing,
HD Editing, Non-Linear Offline, Non-Linear Online &
Post Production Supervision)
Post Producer, Editor, Colorist, Color Correction & Online
Editor: Michael Garber

Aaron & Le Duc (310) 452-2034
www.leducdesign.com
(Digital Online & Linear/Non-Linear Offline)
Editors: Bruce Abrams, Arlan Boll & Greg Le Duc

Aftershock Digital (323) 658-5700
8222 Melrose Ave., Ste. 304 FAX (323) 658-5200
Los Angeles, CA 90046 www.editkings.com
(Non-Linear Offline and Online)
Editors: Fritz Feick & Scott Tetti

All In One Productions (323) 780-8880
1111 Corporate Center Dr., Ste. 303 FAX (323) 780-8887
Monterey Park, CA 91754 www.allinone-usa.com
(Non-Linear Offline and Online)
Post Production Supervisor: Joanna Or

Alternate Reality Entertainment (818) 742-7208
5701 Cantaloupe Ave. FAX (818) 782-0826
Sherman Oaks, CA 91401 www.alternatereality.tv
(Computer Animation, Computer Graphics, Digital Offline,
Digital Online, DVD Authoring, HD Editing, Non-Linear Offline,
Non-Linear Online & Sound Design)
President: Michael Marconi

American Video Group (310) 477-1535
2542 Aiken Ave. www.americanvideogroup.com
Los Angeles, CA 90064
(Digital Non-Linear Offline and Online)
Executive Producer: John Berzner

Atomic Post (310) 922-2167
3025 W. Olympic Blvd., Ste. 124 www.atomicpost.us
Santa Monica, CA 90404
(Non-Linear Offline and Online)
Editor: Paul Belanger

Beam Universal (323) 363-2999
www.beamuniversal.com
(Non-Linear Offline & Post-Production Supervision)
Executive Producers/Editors: Bella Erikson & Stuart Robertson

Beast (310) 576-6300
1222 Sixth St. FAX (310) 576-6305
Santa Monica, CA 90401 www.beast.tv
(Digital Offline, HD Editing, Linear Offline, Non-Linear Offline &
Post Production Supervision)
Managing Director: Valerie Petrusson
Editors: Andy Ames, David Baxter, Rebecca Beluk, Sean
Berringer, David Blackburn, Tim Brooks, Andrew Cahn, Chris
Chynoweth, Michelle Czukar, John Dingfield, Michael Elliot,
Lucas Eskin, Tim Fender, Kevin Garcia, Jean Kawahara,
Paul Kelly, Matthew Kett, Igor Kovalik, Brian Lagerhausen,
Charlie Lee, Connor McDonald, Amanda Moreau, Paul Norling,
Ariel Quintans, Adam Schwartz, Sam Selis, Stewart Shevin,
Jai Shukla, Richard Smith, Adam Svatek, Derek Swanson,
Val Thrasher, Jim Ulbrich, Jason Uson, Angelo Valencia,
Doug Walker & Rob Watzke
Executive Producer: Sybil McCarthy
Senior Producer: Yole Barrera
Producer: Joanna Hall

Blissium (310) 453-7070
1630 Stewart St., Ste. B1 FAX (310) 260-6111
Santa Monica, CA 90404 www.blissium.com
(Compositing, Computer Animation, Computer Graphics, Digital,
Digital Offline, Digital Online, DVD Authoring, HD Editing,
Non-Linear Offline, Non-Linear Online & Visual FX)

Bonch, Inc. (323) 944-0286
7471 Melrose Ave., Ste. 1 FAX (323) 944-0289
Los Angeles, CA 90046 www.bonch.tv
(Analog, Compositing, Computer Graphics, Digital, Digital
Offline, Digital Online, Duplication, Film Editing, HD Editing,
Linear Offline, Linear Online, Non-Linear Offline, Non-Linear
Online, Post Production Supervision, Sound Design, Standards
Conversions & Visual FX)
Editors: Rich Alarcon, Chris Davis, Farah X, Jarrett Fijal, Steve
Forner, Jackie London, Bill Pollock & Jeff Selis

Burbank Post (818) 953-8919
3619 W. Magnolia Blvd.
Burbank, CA 91505
(Non-Linear Offline and Online)
Executive Producer/Editor: Jim Settlemoir

BUTCHER editorial (310) 829-9333
2601 Colorado Ave. FAX (310) 829-5157
Santa Monica, CA 90404 www.butcheredit.com
Executive Producer: Rob Van
Producer: Chrissy Hamilton
Editors: Gordon Carey, Teddy Gersten, Dave Henegar, Cory
Livingston, Keith Salmon & Chris Scheer

Chainsaw (323) 785-1550
940 N. Orange Dr., Second Fl. FAX (323) 785-1555
Hollywood, CA 90038 www.chainsawedit.com
(Analog, Compositing, Digital, Digital Offline and Online,
Duplication, DVD Authoring, HD Editing, Non-Linear Offline and
Online, Post Production Supervision & Standards Conversions)

Cosmo Street (310) 828-6666
2036 Broadway FAX (310) 453-9699
Santa Monica, CA 90404 www.cosmostreet.com
(Non-Linear Offline)
Producers: Yvette Cobarrubias & Jerry Sukys
Editors: Kevin Anderson, Steve Bell, Tiffany Burchard, Bill
Chessman, Tessa Davis, Katz, Aaron Langley, Ken Rosenberg,
Billy Sacdalam, Tom Scherma, Justin Trovato & Asako Ushio

Cut + Run (310) 909-8801
2044 Broadway FAX (310) 264-9701
Santa Monica, CA 90404 www.cutandrun.tv
(Non-Linear Offline and Online)
Producer: Christie Price
Editors: Isaac Chen, Alex Dondero, Steve Gandolfi, Jon Grover,
Ty Herrington, Akiko Iwakana, Gary Knight, Joel Miller, Jay
Nelson, James Rose & Dayn Williams
Managing Director/Executive Producer: Michelle Burke

Cutters Editorial (310) 309-3780
1657 Euclid St. www.cutters.com
Santa Monica, CA 90404
(HD Editing & Non-Linear Offline)
Producer: Sasha Grubor
West Coast Rep: Will Kneip

DaveOneal.com (818) 584-6470
www.daveoneal.com
(Compositing, Computer Graphics, Digital Offline, Duplication,
DVD Authoring, Linear Offline and Online & Visual FX)
Editor: Dave Oneal

The Edit Bay (714) 978-7878
571 N. Poplar St., Ste. I FAX (714) 978-7858
Orange, CA 92868 www.theeditbay.com

Foundation   **(424) 238-0381**
3583 Hayden Ave.   **www.foundationcontent.com**
Culver City, CA 90232
(Compositing, Computer Animation, Computer Graphics, Film
Editing, HD Editing, Linear Online, Non-Linear Offline and
Online, Post Production Supervision, Sound Design &
Visual FX)
Co-Owner/Editor/Director: James Lipetzky
President/Co-Owner: Samantha Hart
Editors: Andrew Hall, Suzie Moore, Anna Patel, Ben Poster &
Christina Stumpf

A Gosch Production   **(818) 729-0000**
    www.goschproductions.com
(Non-Linear Offline and Online)
Contact: Pat Gosch
Executive Producer: Rob Gosch
Directors/Editors: Cindia Perez & Jimmie Rhee
Producer: Barbara Peeters

an ideal world   **(714) 953-9501**
209 N. Bush St.   FAX **(714) 380-6311**
Santa Ana, CA 92701   **www.anidealworld.com**
(Autodesk Flame Finishing, Color Correction, Compositing,
Computer Animation, Computer Graphics, Digital Offline, Digital
Online, HD Editing, Post Production Supervision, Stereoscopic
Post & Visual FX)
Executive Producer: Molly Talbot Hart
Editors/Flame Artists: Sharon Diaz & Robb Hart

Ignition Post   **(818) 762-2210**
4130 Cahuenga Blvd., Ste. 100   **www.ignition-post.com**
Toluca Lake, CA 91602

JM Digital Works   **(760) 476-1783**
2460 Impala Dr.   FAX **(760) 476-1788**
Carlsbad, CA 92008   **www.jmdigitalworks.com**
(Digital Offline and Online)
Contact: Ken Kebow
Editor: Dave Graack

JR Post   **(818) 557-0200**
2501 W. Burbank Blvd., Ste. 311   FAX **(818) 557-0201**
Burbank, CA 91505   **www.jrmediaservices.com**
(Negative Cutting & Non-Linear Offline)
Post Supervisor: Robert Troy

Jump   **(310) 202-7474**
3123 S. La Cienega Blvd.   FAX **(310) 202-7475**
Los Angeles, CA 90016   **www.jumpla.tv**
(Composition, Computer Graphics, Digital Offline, Digital
Online, Film Editing, HD Editing, Non-Linear Offline, Non-Linear
Online, Post Production Supervision, Sound Design &
Visual FX)
Editors: Jack Douglas, Mark Imgrund, Nick Lofting, Troy
Mercury, Richard Mettler, Luis Moreno, Lin Polito, Michael Saia,
David Trachtenberg & Terence Ziegler

Lost Planet Editorial, Inc.   **(310) 396-7272**
2515 Main St.   FAX **(310) 450-8696**
Santa Monica, CA 90405   **www.lostplanet.com**
(Digital Online, Film Editing, HD Editing, Offline, Post
Production Supervision & Sound Design)
Editors: Hank Corwin, Bruce Herrman, Chris Huth, Charlie
Jonston, Saar Klein, Max Koepke, Paul Snyder &
Jaime Valdueza

Massive Post Productions   **(310) 306-7678**
13114 W. Washington Blvd.   **www.massivepost.com**
Culver City, CA 90066
(Film Editing, HD Editing, Non-Linear Offline, Non-Linear
Online, Post Production Supervision, Sound Design &
Visual FX)
Editors: Michael Alberts & Steve Swersky
Producers: Greg Conway & Steve Swersky

Migrant Editors   **(310) 345-1301**
Editor: Nate Hubbard   **www.migranteditors.com**

Miller Wishengrad Post/MWP   **(310) 587-3300**
1335 Fourth St., Ste. 400   FAX **(310) 587-3387**
Santa Monica, CA 90401   **www.mwpost.com**
(Compositing, Computer Graphics, Film Editing, HD Editing,
Non-Linear Offline and Online & Sound Design)
Executive Producer: Gary Le Vine
Editors: Sean Leute, Mike Miller & Jeff Wishengrad
Graphics: Josh Oram

    (310) 396-4663
Mind Over Eye, LLC   **(310) 968-4259**
1639 11th St., Ste. 117   FAX **(310) 396-0663**
Santa Monica, CA 90404   **www.mindovereye.com**
(HD and SD Offline and Online & Standards Conversions)

Nomad Editing Company   **(310) 828-4999**
1661 19th St.   FAX **(310) 828-3950**
Santa Monica, CA 90404   **www.nomadedit.com**
(Non-Linear Offline)
Contact: Susye Idema

Oasis Imagery   **(323) 469-9800**
6500 Sunset Blvd.   FAX **(323) 462-4620**
Los Angeles, CA 90028   **www.oasisimagery.com**
(Digital Offline and Online, Duplication, HD Editing, Linear
Online, Linear/Non-Linear Offline & Post Supervision)

Optimus   **(310) 917-2761**
1237 Seventh St.   FAX **(310) 917-2762**
Santa Monica, CA 90401   **www.optimus.com**
(Non-Linear Offline)
Executive Producer: Therese Hunsberger
Editors: Justin Amore, Erin Nordstrom & Jim Staskauskas

Oracle Post   **(818) 752-2800**
4720 W. Magnolia Blvd.   FAX **(818) 769-2624**
Burbank, CA 91505   **www.oraclepost.com**
(Digital Non-Linear Offline and Online)
Executive Producer: James Lifton
CEO/Post Supervisor: Paulette Lifton

PIC Agency   **(323) 461-2900**
6161 Santa Monica Blvd., Ste. 300   FAX **(323) 461-2909**
Hollywood, CA 90038   **www.picagency.com**
(Compositing, Computer Animation, Computer Graphics, Digital,
Digital Offline, Film Editing, HD Editing, Non-Linear Offline &
Post Production Supervision)

Pistolera Post   **(310) 451-9499**
530 Wilshire Blvd., Ste. 308   FAX **(310) 451-7416**
Santa Monica, CA 90401   **www.pistolerapost.com**
(Analog, Compositing, Computer Graphics, Digital, Digital
Online and Offline, Non-Linear Online and Offline, Post
Production Supervision, Standards Conversions & Visual FX)

Play Editorial, Inc.   **(323) 469-3500**
6464 Sunset Blvd., Ste. 600   FAX **(323) 469-3511**
Hollywood, CA 90028   **www.playeditorial.com**
(Compositing, Digital Offline and Online, Film Editing,
Non-Linear Offline and Online, Post Production Supervision &
Visual FX)

Playroom Creative   **(714) 969-3938**
412 Indianapolis Ave.   **www.playroomcreative.com**
Huntington Beach, CA 92648
(Compositing, Computer Animation, Computer Graphics,
Digital, Digital Offline, Digital Online, DVD Authoring, HD
Editing, Non-Linear Offline, Non-Linear Online, Post Production
Supervision & Visual FX)

Point360   **(310) 481-7000**
12421 W. Olympic Blvd.   **www.point360.com**
Los Angeles, CA 90064
(Compositing, Computer Animation, HD Editing, Non-Linear
Offline, Non-Linear Online, Post Production Supervision, Sound
Design & Visual FX)

Post Factory
(714) 705-6099
(877) 411-4446
630 The City Dr., Ste. 100 FAX (714) 705-6090
Orange, CA 92868 www.postfactory.com
(Compositing, Computer Animation, Computer Graphics,
Digital, Digital Offline, Digital Online, Duplication, DVD
Authoring, Film Editing, HD Editing, Non-Linear Offline,
Non-Linear Online, Post Production Supervision, Sound
Design, Standards Conversions & Visual FX)
Avid/FCP/Smoke/Editor & Colorist: Chris Gendrin
Executive Producer: Jeremy Kientz
Editors: Bruce Bockman, dB Bracamontes, Nahum Chiappa,
Ellen Crocker, Noel Oliver & Serena Tupper

Post Modern Creative, LLC (949) 608-8700
2941 Alton Pkwy FAX (949) 608-8729
Irvine, CA 92606 www.postmoderncreative.com
(Analog, Compositing, Computer Graphics, Digital, Duplication,
DVD Authoring, HD Editing, Linear Online, Non-Linear Offline
and Online, Post Production Supervision, Sound Design,
Standards Conversions & Visual FX)
Producer: Rich O'Neill
Executive Producer: Michael Boyd
VP of Sales: Troy Burlage

Precision Productions + Post (310) 839-4600
10718 McCune Ave. FAX (310) 839-4601
Los Angeles, CA 90034 www.precisionpost.com
(Non-Linear Offline and Online)
Executive Producer: Joseph Arnao

Razor Edits (310) 968-1172
2996 Hyperion Ave. www.razoredits.com
Los Angeles, CA 90026
(Non-Linear Offline)
Executive Producer: Woody Pobiega
Editor: David Frame

The Reel Thing, Inc. (310) 828-9555
2425 Colorado Ave., Ste. 100 FAX (310) 828-9544
Santa Monica, CA 90404 www.thereelthinginc.com
(HD Editing & Non-Linear Offline and Online)
Executive Producer: Doug Klekner
Editors: Sally Banta, Todd Betts, Moody Glasgow &
Mark Goodman
Smoke Artist: Mutalib Glasgow

ReX Edit (310) 314-8110
221 Rose Ave. FAX (310) 314-8115
Venice, CA 90291 www.rexedit.com
(Non-Linear Offline)
Executive Producer: Bill Fortney
Producer: Chanel Boyd
Editors: Paul Bertino, Bill Marmor, Igor Patalas &
Drew Thompson
Director of Marketing & Sales: Jeanie DiMaggio

Rock Paper Scissors (310) 586-0600
2308 Broadway FAX (310) 586-0601
Santa Monica, CA 90404 www.rockpaperscissors.com
(Linear/Non-Linear Offline)
CEO/Owner: Linda Carlson
Executive Producer: Carol Lynn Weaver
Editors: Carlos Arias, Kirk Baxter, David Brodie, Terence "Biff"
Butler, Damion Clayton, Elliot Graham, Ted Guard, Adam
Pertofsky, The Quarry, Frank Snider & Angus Wall

Roush Media (818) 559-8648
84 E. Santa Anita Ave. www.roush-media.com
Burbank, CA 91502
(Computer Graphics, Digital Non-Linear Offline and Online &
Duplication)
Contact: Keith Roush

Rye (213) 361-1391
10523 Kling St. FAX (818) 760-7855
Toluca Lake, CA 91602 www.ryefilms.com
(Computer Graphics & Non-Linear Offline)
Editor: Rye Dahlman

Spot Welders, Inc. (310) 399-3350
825 Hampton Dr. FAX (310) 399-1228
Venice, CA 90291 www.spotwelders.com
(Non-Linear)
CEO: David Glean
Editors: Catherine Bull, Robert Duffy, Sarah Flack, Dick Gordon,
Haines Hall, Dahkil Hausif, Michael Heldman, Dan Maloney,
Pam Martin, Livio Sanchez, Lucas Spaulding,
Jon Stefansson & Brad Waskewich

Spring Media Group (818) 804-8741
www.springmediagroup.com
(Non-Linear Offline and Online)
Contact: Joseph Conarkov
Editors: Joseph Conarkov, Laurence Prophet & Sean Prophet

StandardVision, LLC (323) 224-3944
2020 N. Main St., Ste. 227 FAX (323) 225-6226
Los Angeles, CA 90031 www.standardsite.com
(3D Visualizations, Computer Graphics, Film Editing, HD
Editing, Non-Linear Offline and Online, Post Production
Supervision & Visual FX)
Producer: Steven Wren

Stitch (310) 450-1116
1635 12th St. FAX (310) 450-1166
Santa Monica, CA 90404 www.stitchediting.tv
(Analog, CompositingComputer Graphics, Digital, Digital
Offline, Digital Online, HD Editing, Linear Online, Non-Linear
Offline, Non-Linear Online, Post Production Supervision, Sound
Design & Visual FX)

(323) 467-8550
Sunset Edit (818) 679-4014
849 N. Seward St. FAX (323) 467-8545
Los Angeles, CA 90038 www.sunsetedit.com
(Audio, HD Editing, Offline, Online & Visual FX)
Editors: Mandy Brown, Hank Friedmann, Ken Mowe, Jake
Pushinsky, Steve Rees, Declan Whitebloom & Bill Yukich
VFX: Howard Shur

TEDS (310) 237-6438
www.tedsla.com
(Compositing, DVD Authoring, Non-Linear Offline and Online,
Post Production Supervision, Sound Design, Standards
Conversions, Telecine & Visual FX)

Tonawanda Pictures, Inc. (323) 525-0151
8075 W. Third St., Ste. 406 FAX (323) 395-5574
Los Angeles, CA 90048
(Computer Graphics & Non-Linear Offline)

Undertow Productions (310) 497-8020
(DVD Authoring & Non-Linear Offline and Online)
Contact: Dave Poncia

Union Editorial (310) 481-2200
12200 W. Olympic Blvd., Ste. 140 FAX (310) 481-2248
Los Angeles, CA 90064 www.unioneditorial.com
(Non-Linear Offline and Online)
President/Executive Producer: Michael Raimondi
President of Entertainment: Jijo Reed
Vice President/Sr. Producer: Megan Dahlman
Editors: Nico Alba, Geordie Anderson, Eric Argiro, Mike Colao,
Einar, Jay Friedkin, Jinx Godfrey, Alex Hagen, Jim Haygood,
Sloane Klevin, Laura Milstein, Marco Perez, Paul Plew, &
Nicholas Wayman-Harris

Venice Beach Editorial (310) 305-5777
5353 Grosvenor St. FAX (310) 305-4892
Los Angeles, CA 90066 www.venicebeacheditorial.com
(Linear/Non-Linear Offline)
Executive Producer: Hunter Conner
Producer: Cristy Pacheco
Editors: Dan Bootzin, Billy Sacdalan, Rick Shambaugh &
Greg Young

Via Verde Productions & Post (310) 458-3778
22631 Pacific Coast Hwy, Ste. 480 FAX (310) 496-2992
Malibu, CA 90265 www.viaverdedigital.com
(Non-Linear Offline & Post Supervision)
Executive Producer: Mari Ciravolo
Director/Editor: Melissa Landini

Victory Studios LA (818) 769-1776
10911 Riverside Dr., Ste. 100 FAX (818) 760-1280
North Hollywood, CA 91602 www.victorystudiosla.com
(Digital Offline, Digital Online, HD Editing, Non-Linear Offline,
Non-Linear Online & Sound Design)

Visual Concepts (858) 598-6494
  FAX (858) 694-0546
  www.visualconcepts.tv
(Compositing, Computer Graphics, Digital, Digital Offline and
Online, DVD Authoring, HD Editing, Non-Linear Offline and
Online & Post Production Supervision)
Director of Photography: Mark Nelson
Post-Production Manager: Leslie Nelson

  (818) 901-1178
Waterline Pictures, Inc. (310) 963-4812
P.O. Box 56387 FAX (818) 901-1179
Sherman Oaks, CA 91413
Editor: Roger Roth

Wheelhouse Editorial & Effects (213) 595-4144
  www.wheelhouseedit.com
(Compositing, Computer Animation, Computer Graphics, Digital
Offline and Online, HD Editing, Post Production Supervision &
Sound Design)
Executive Producer: CJ Edwards

the Whitehouse (310) 319-9908
530 Wilshire Blvd., Ste. 400 FAX (310) 319-9905
Santa Monica, CA 90401 www.whitehousepost.com
Director of Post Production: Sue Dawson
Editors: Nick Allix, Heidi Black, Josh Bodnar, David Brixton, Jen
Dean, Ian Davies, Corky DeVault, Trish Fuller, Brian Gannon,
Sam Gunn, Lisa Gunning, Charlie Harvey, Jon Hopp, Russell
Icke, Stephen Jess, Alaster Jordan, Meg Kubicka, Paul La
Calandra, Marc Langley, Rick Lawley, Carlos Lowenstein,
Adam Marshall, Gareth McEwen, Crandall Miller, Ethan
Mitchell, James Norris, Dan Oberle, Nathan Petty, Steve
Prestemon, Sam Puglise-Kipley, Adam Robinson, John Smith,
Ben Stephens, Nikki Vapensky, Glorily Velez, Tim Warmanen,
Christine Wolf & Matthew Wood
Represented Editors: Filip Malasek, Alex Rodriguez &
Greg Snider

Why Not Coco, Inc. (323) 798-4497
7959 Hollywood Blvd. FAX (323) 798-4497
Los Angeles, CA 90046 www.whynotcoco.com
(Compositing, Computer Animation, Computer Graphics, Digital
Offline, Digital Online, HD Editing, Post Production Supervision,
Sound Design & Visual FX)
Executive Producer: Angela Galletta
Editors: George Artope, Javier Bermudez & Joe Linton

Wild Pictures (310) 526-7225
100 Market St., Third Fl. www.wildpictures.com
Venice, CA 90291
(Compositing, Computer Animation, Computer Graphics, Digital,
Digital Offline, Digital Online, Duplication, DVD Authoring, Film
Editing, HD Editing, Non-Linear Offline, Non-Linear Online, Post
Production Supervision, Sound Design & Visual FX)

William Moffitt Associates (818) 495-3106
785 New York Dr. FAX (626) 345-0673
Altadena, CA 91001 www.wmadigital.com
(DVD Authoring, Computer Graphics, Digital Online, DVD
Authoring, HD Editing & Non-Linear Editing)
Post Production Supervisor: Will Moffitt
Executive Producer: Lynne Moffitt

WSR Creative (310) 837-7001
9503 Jefferson Blvd., Ste. B FAX (310) 837-3680
Culver City, CA 90232 www.wsrcreative.com
Editors: Jose Delgado & Pablo Garrahan

Commercial Editorial Houses

John Adair (310) 399-6900	**Bill Bodine** (310) 459-6500
www.emotomusic.com	www.billbodinemusic.com

Neil Argo (323) 854-2555
(818) 505-9600
(Composer) www.neilargo.com

Norman Arnold (310) 654-4060
www.amimusicgroup.com

Shane August (310) 651-6233
www.halfpipemusic.com

Laura B. (310) 237-6438
www.mixinpixls.com
(ADR Editor, Dialogue Editor, Foreign Language Track Editor,
Sound Editor, Sound Effects Editors & Voice Over Editor)

Klaus Badelt (310) 478-8227
www.primalscreammusic.com

Brian Banks (310) 581-1660
www.eartoear.com

James Barth (818) 903-3680
www.jamesbarth.com
(ADR Editor, Composer, Dialogue Editor, Music Editor, Music
Supervisor, Re-Recording Mixer, Sound Designer, Sound
Editor, Sound Effects Editor, Supervising Sound Editor &
Voice Over Editor)

Hugh Barton (310) 478-2120
FAX (310) 478-2130
www.glueaudio.com

Tom Batoy (323) 466-4696
www.monadavis.com

John Beal (818) 762-1640
www.composerjohnbeal.com

Chris Bell (707) 363-1000
www.cbmsd.com
(ADR Editor, Composer, Dialogue Editor, Music Editor, Music
Supervisor, Re-Recording Mixer, Sound Designer, Sound
Editor, Sound Effects Editor, Supervising Sound Editor &
Voice Over Editor)

Sean Benaim (310) 828-2292
www.beatmusiclibrary.com

Michael Benghiat (661) 338-4749
www.themusickitchen.com

Scott Bennett (323) 857-7299
(323) 851-9623
www.blastmanagement.com

Joe Berardi (323) 222-1082
www.jhuck.com

Paul Bessenbacher (310) 399-6900
www.emotomusic.com

Garret Bever (818) 505-8787
(Sound Editor) www.kingklong.com

Onnalee Blank (310) 210-6769
(310) 393-5340
www.fingermusic.tv
(Re-Recording Mixer, Sound Designer, Sound Effects Editor &
Supervising Sound Editor)

Blue Jay Productions/Bill Johnson (310) 306-7968
(Composer)

Bill Bodine (310) 459-6500
www.billbodinemusic.com

Rick Boston (323) 857-7299
(310) 393-5340
www.blastmanagement.com

Roddy Bottum (323) 222-1082
www.jhuck.com

Brad Breeck (323) 481-4581
www.audibleshift.com

Danny Brin (323) 655-2560

Benedikt Brydern (310) 451-8075
www.consordino.com

Scott Burton (310) 478-8227
www.primalscreammusic.com
(Sound Designer & Supervising Sound Editor)

Cadesky/Dyer (323) 857-7299
www.blastmanagement.com

Dustin Camilleri (310) 392-8393
(Sound Designer) www.machinehead.com

Chris Campanaro (310) 581-6500
www.eliasarts.com

Marc Cashman (661) 222-9300
www.cashmancommercials.com

Sonia Castro (310) 392-9545
www.48windows.com

Michael Chandler (310) 392-9545
www.48windows.com

Garron Chang (310) 392-0369
www.soundbath.com

Simon Changer (310) 285-0303
(Music Editor) www.sandramarsh.com

Brad Chiet (310) 640-3435
www.ifuelmusic.com

Meredith Chinn (310) 651-6233
www.halfpipemusic.com

Barbara Cohen (323) 856-3000
www.easterntalent.net

Contraband (323) 933-1614
5820 Wilshire Blvd., Ste. 306 www.contrabandusa.com
Los Angeles, CA 90036

Bruno Coon (323) 857-7299
(Composer & Music Editor) www.blastmanagement.com

Michael Coulter (310) 393-7577
www.confidencehead.com

Hal Cragin (310) 568-3355
www.bluemusicla.com

Dan Crane (323) 222-1082
www.jhuck.com

Bobby Crew (858) 254-6779
(Sound Editor)

Raja Das (323) 481-4581
www.audibleshift.com

Steve Davis (310) 260-9838 www.themixsantamonica.com	**Sam Glaser** (310) 204-6111 www.samglaser.com
Reinhard Denke (310) 460-0123 www.stimmung.tv	**Scott Glenn** (310) 260-4949 www.humit.com
Richard Devine (310) 393-5340 www.fingermusic.tv	**Godhead** (310) 478-8227 www.primalscreammusic.com
Stephen Dewey (310) 392-8393 (Sound Designer) www.machinehead.com	**Rich Goldman** (310) 437-4380 (Music Supervisor) www.riptidemusic.com
James DiSalvio (310) 393-5340 www.fingermusic.tv	**Manoj Gopinath** (818) 505-8787 www.kingklong.com
Ramin Djuadi (310) 478-8227 www.primalscreammusic.com	**Brett Grant-Grierson** (818) 606-5700 (Sound Editor) www.ears4hire.com
Dom and Ant (310) 393-5340 www.fingermusic.tv	**John Graves** (818) 882-3300 www.command-post.com/music (Foley Artist, Re-Recording Mixer, Sound Designer, Sound Effects Editor & Supervising Sound Editor)
Larry Dunn (818) 990-8993 www.ambitiousent.com	**Robert Grieve** (310) 788-3918 www.d-a-a.com (ADR Editor, Sound Designer & Supervising Sound Editor)
Eastern Talent Agency (323) 856-3000 849 S. Broadway, Ste. 811 FAX (323) 856-3009 Los Angeles, CA 90014 www.easterntalent.net	
Josh Eichenbaum (310) 260-9838 (Sound Designer) www.themixsantamonica.com	**Greg Griffith** (310) 460-0123 www.stimmung.tv
Ryan Elder (310) 399-6900 www.emotomusic.com	**Grizzly Bear** (310) 652-8778 www.lspagency.net
Jeff Elmassian (310) 566-1463 www.endlessnoise.com	**Andrew Hagen** (310) 828-5189 (Composer & Sound Designer) www.schtungmusic.com
The Engine Room (310) 478-8227 www.primalscreammusic.com	**Marlene Hajdu** (818) 762-0635
Jim Ervin (800) 579-9157 www.laeg.net	**Wes Hambright** (818) 448-9262 www.orangedogmusic.com
Charles Etienne (818) 399-6992 www.charlesetienne.com	**Johannes Hammers** (310) 392-8393 www.machinehead.com
Alan Ett (818) 508-3303 www.themusiccollective.com	**Steve Hampton** (310) 399-6900 www.emotomusic.com
Christopher Faizi (310) 651-6233 www.halfpipemusic.com	**Craig Harris** (323) 851-8510 (Sound Effects Editor) www.craigharrismusic.com
Mitchell Forman (310) 568-3355 www.bluemusicla.com	**Dan Hart** (310) 260-4949 www.humit.com
Carey Fosse (323) 222-1082 www.jhuck.com	**Jud Haskins** (310) 260-9939 www.horriblemusic.net
Jill Fraser (818) 908-9083 (Composer) www.jillfrasermusic.com	**Jimmy Haun** (310) 581-6500 www.eliasarts.com
Mike Freedman (310) 597-3600 www.bigears.com	**Emanuel Heinstein** (323) 250-0708 www.emanuelheinstein.com (Composer, Music Editor, Music Supervisor, Sound Designer, Sound Editor, Sound Effects Editor & Supervising Sound Editor)
Eddie Freeman (562) 925-4514 www.icarusmusic.com	**Sean Hennessy** (310) 651-6233 www.halfpipemusic.com
Christopher Garcia (310) 478-8227 www.primalscreammusic.com	**Dino Herrmann** (323) 222-1082 www.jhuck.com (Re-Recording Mixer & Supervising Sound Editor)
Eric Garcia (310) 392-9545 www.48windows.com	**Peter Himmelman** (310) 478-8227 www.primalscreammusic.com
Michelle Garuik (818) 565-5565 www.grindinc.com (Re-Recording Mixer, Sound Designer, Sound Editor & Sound Effects Editor)	**Dave Hodge** (310) 393-5340 www.fingermusic.tv
Adam Giorgoni (310) 568-3355 www.bluemusicla.com	**Jim Hodson** (818) 566-8555 www.advantageaudio.com (Re-Recording Mixer & Sound Effects Editor)

Composers/Sound Designers & Editors

Paul Hoffman (310) 568-3355 www.bluemusicla.com	Chris Lennertz (310) 578-9686 www.sonicfuel.net
Heather Holbrook (818) 566-8555 www.advantageaudio.com	Daniel Lenz (310) 393-5340 www.fingermusic.tv
Sean Holt (310) 478-2120 FAX (310) 478-2130 www.glueaudio.com	Geoff Levin (818) 841-6607 www.geofflevin.com
Les Hooper (818) 501-2727 (Composer & Sound Designer)	Marc Levisohn (310) 597-3600 (ADR Supervisor & Dialogue Editor) www.bigears.com
Hein Hoven (310) 393-5340 www.fingermusic.tv	Scott Liggett (818) 508-3303 (818) 645-2364 (Composer & Producer) www.themusiccollective.com
Jon Huck (323) 222-1082 (Music Supervisor) www.jhuck.com	Ted Lobinger (310) 260-9838 www.themixsantamonica.com (Dialogue Editor & Sound Designer)
Nick Huntington (310) 285-0303 (Composer) www.sandramarsh.com	David A. Logan (310) 393-5340 www.fingermusic.tv
Marc Jackson (818) 955-5268 FAX (818) 295-5001 www.zoostreet.com	Robert Lopez (310) 260-4949 www.humit.com
Mark Jasper (310) 264-0407 www.onmusicandsound.com (Re-Recording Mixer, Sound Designer & Sound Effects Editor)	Steve Love (310) 568-3355 www.bluemusicla.com
Jeff Martin/Idaho (323) 857-7299 www.blastmanagement.com	Curtis S.D. Macdonald (805) 390-1910 www.linkedin.com/in/curtismacdonald (Composer, Dialogue Editor, Music Editor & Sound Editor)
Chip Jenkins (310) 581-6500 www.eliasarts.com	Wendy MaHarry (323) 857-7299 www.blastmanagement.com
Jason Johnson (310) 460-0123 www.stimmung.tv	Billy Mallery (323) 462-4862 www.billymallery.com
Tobias Johnston (310) 393-7577 www.confidencehead.com	Anthony Marinelli (323) 461-4646 www.musicforever.com
Jeffery Alan Jones (310) 753-1564 4720 W. Magnolia Blvd. FAX (562) 408-6821 Burbank, CA 91505 www.jeffjonesmusic.com (Composer, Foley Artist, Music Editor, Music Supervisor, Sound Designer, Re-Recording Mixer & Supervising Sound Editor)	Ric Markmann (818) 505-8505 www.mattermusic.com
dj JUN (310) 651-6233 www.halfpipemusic.com	Jeff Martin (310) 651-6233 www.halfpipemusic.com
Kent Karlsson (310) 651-6233 www.halfpipemusic.com	Hirotaka Matsuoka (310) 260-4949 www.humit.com
Christopher Kemp (310) 581-6500 www.eliasarts.com	John McCarthy (323) 466-7056 www.mccarthymusic.com
Daniel Kolton (323) 857-7299 (310) 651-6233 www.blastmanagement.com	Stephen McCarthy (310) 651-6233 www.halfpipemusic.com
Kathryn Korniloff (310) 291-1122 (Sound Editor & Sound Effects Editor) www.sonicfruit.com	Steve McClure (323) 481-4581 www.audibleshift.com
Gus Koven (310) 460-0123 (Sound Editor & Sound Effects Editor) www.stimmung.tv	Dan McNamara (818) 789-0226 www.jinglefactory.com
Kadet Kuhne (323) 481-4581 www.audibleshift.com	Alex Menck (323) 466-4696 www.monadavis.com (Composer, Music Editor & Music Supervisor)
Hao Lam (310) 566-1463 www.endlessnoise.com	Dean Menta (310) 337-9727 (Music Editor) www.bendymusic.com
Garron R. Larcombe (310) 477-7195 www.soundtrackstudio.com	Mark Mercury (323) 349-5580 (Composer & Sound Designer) www.markmercury.com
Bernie Larsen (323) 856-3000 www.easterntalent.net	Nick Michaud (310) 260-9838 (Sound Designer) www.themixsantamonica.com
Latin Music Artist Alliance (323) 857-7299 www.blastmanagement.com	Bryan E. Miller (818) 985-3300 www.sensory-overload.com
	Robert Miller (310) 460-0123 www.stimmung.tv

Scott Miller (310) 378-8633 FAX (310) 793-2625 www.thehithouse.com (Composer, Re-Recording Mixer & Sound Designer)	**Luis Resto** (323) 857-7299 www.blastmanagement.com
The Millionaire (323) 222-1082 www.jhuck.com	**Eddie Reyes** (310) 828-5189 www.schtungmusic.com
Monster Music (323) 857-7299 www.blastmanagement.com	**David Rolfe** (310) 568-3355 www.bluemusicla.com
Guy Moon (310) 568-3355 www.bluemusicla.com	**Spookey Ruben** (310) 393-5340 www.fingermusic.tv
Mophonics (310) 452-0331 200 Westminister Ave. FAX (310) 452-0356 Venice, CA 90291 www.mophonics.com	**Joey Rubenstien** (310) 393-5340 www.fingermusic.tv
Tony Morales (310) 399-6900 www.emotomusic.com	**Boris Salchow** (818) 260-8530 www.borissalchow.com
Sean Morris (323) 852-9991 www.seanmorris.com	**Adam Sanborne** (310) 312-3329 www.s3mx.com
Sunday Morzeno (818) 314-8314 (Composer) www.sunofz.com	**Andrea Saparoff** (310) 455-1950 www.saparoffmusic.com
Tim Mosher (323) 656-0197 www.mosherandstoker.com	**Adam Schiff** (310) 392-8393 www.machinehead.com
Mark Mothersbaugh (310) 360-0561 www.mutato.com	**Erik Schuiten** (310) 566-1463 (Supervising Sound Editor) www.endlessnoise.com
The Newton Brothers (310) 651-6233 www.halfpipemusic.com	**Robert J. Schuster** (818) 706-6375 www.hodads.com
John O (310) 651-6233 www.halfpipemusic.com	**David Schwartz** (310) 459-1419 FAX (310) 459-7448 www.davidschwartzmusic.com
Tommy O'Brien (310) 902-4784	**Mike Semple** (310) 651-6233 www.halfpipemusic.com
John Paesano (323) 857-7299 www.blastmanagement.com	**Kiran Shahani** (310) 651-6233 www.halfpipemusic.com
dj Chris Paul (323) 857-7299 www.blastmanagement.com	**Michael Sherwood** (310) 581-6500 www.eliasarts.com
Joey Peters (310) 651-6233 www.halfpipemusic.com	**Dan Silver** (310) 437-4380 (Composer & Sound Designer) www.riptidemusic.com
Howard Pfeifer (818) 505-8787 www.mixinpixls.com	**Anna Sitko** (323) 481-4581 www.audibleshift.com
Maggie Phillips (310) 652-8778 (Music Supervisor) www.lspagency.net	**Josh Sklair** (310) 337-9727 www.bendymusic.com
Photek (310) 393-5340 www.fingermusic.tv	**Gregory Darryl Smith** (323) 856-3000 www.easterntalent.net
Dan Pinella (818) 505-8505 www.mattermusic.com	**Nathan Smith** (213) 268-4226 www.nl3audio.com (Re-Recording Mixer, Sound Designer & Supervising Sound Editor)
Bob Poole (818) 566-8555 www.advantageaudio.com	**Andy Snavley** (310) 337-9727 www.bendymusic.com (Composer, Dialogue Editor, Re-Recording Mixer, Sound Designer & Supervising Sound Editor)
Popular Beat Combo (323) 857-7299 www.blastmanagement.com	
Michael Portis (818) 216-2841	**Bruce Somers** (310) 568-3355 www.bluemusicla.com
Alec Puro (818) 508-3303 (Composer) www.themusiccollective.com	**Sound Design Digital Post/** **Sean Fahimian** (310) 210-7133 www.sounddesigndigitalpost.com (ADR Editor, Composer, Dialogue Editor, Foley Artist, Foley Editor, Music Editor, Music Supervisor, Re-Recording Mixer, Sound Designer, Sound Editor, Sound Effects Editor, Supervising Sound Editor & Voice Over Editor)
Dan Radlauer (310) 440-0055	
Scott Rea (866) 630-6372 www.scottreamusic.com	
Andy Rehfeldt (310) 566-1463 www.endlessnoise.com	

Composers/Sound Designers & Editors

Sounddogs.com, Inc.
(877) 315-3647
(714) 783-3096
FAX (310) 496-3135
4712 Admiralty Way, Ste. 497
Marina del Rey, CA 90292
www.sounddogs.com
(ADR Editor, Sound Designer, Sound Editor, Sound Effects
Editor, Supervising Sound Editor & Voice Over Editor)

David Steinberg (323) 467-2529

Shepard Stern (310) 439-1903
www.sternworld.net

Bob Stewart (714) 973-3030
(Dialogue Editor & Music Editor) www.stewartsound.com

Chris Stills (310) 651-6233
www.halfpipemusic.com

Stoker (323) 656-0197
www.mosherandstoker.com

Andreas Straub (310) 392-9545
www.48windows.com

David Streefkerk (323) 466-4696
www.monadavis.com
(Sound Designer & Supervising Sound Editor)

Andy Sturmer (310) 651-6233
www.halfpipemusic.com

Michael Suby (310) 312-3329
www.s3mx.com

Summerfield Music, Inc./
Trailer Trash Music Library (818) 905-0400
(Reps for Composers) FAX (818) 905-0488
www.summerfieldmusic.com

Stanislas Syrewicz (310) 285-0303
www.sandramarsh.com

Kathie Talbot (310) 651-6233
www.halfpipemusic.com

John Tartaglia (323) 666-6550

Danny Tate (310) 651-6233
www.halfpipemusic.com

Paca Thomas (818) 566-8555
www.advantageaudio.com
(Sound Designer & Supervising Sound Editor)

Scott Thomas (310) 651-6233
www.halfpipemusic.com

Rick Torres (310) 279-2388
www.ricktorres.com
(ADR Editor, Composer, Dialogue Editor, Music Editor, Music
Supervisor, Re-Recording Mixer, Sound Designer, Sound
Editor, Sound Effects Editor, Supervising Sound Editor &
Voice Over Editor)

Franco Tortora (323) 466-4696
www.monadavis.com

dj True:129 (310) 651-6233
www.halfpipemusic.com

Neil Uchitel (323) 737-6995
www.audio.slappo.com
(Sound Editor, Sound Effects Editor & Supervising
Sound Editor)

Kubilay Uner (323) 428-8429
(Composer) www.kubilayuner.com

Bill Ungerman (323) 222-1082
www.jhuck.com

Marta Victoria (562) 925-4514
www.icarusmusic.com

Bill Wadsworth (310) 396-4663
www.mindovereye.com

Chris Wagner (818) 505-8505
www.mattermusic.com

Michael Wandmacher (310) 478-8227
www.primalscreammusic.com

Adam Watkins (818) 505-8787
www.kingklong.com

Jim Watson (310) 828-5189
www.schtungmusic.com
(Re-Recording Mixer & Sound Designer)

Billy White Acre (818) 909-9222
www.bigplanetmusic.com

Danny Wilde (323) 857-7299
www.blastmanagement.com

Rob Winch (310) 828-5189
www.schtungmusic.com

David Winer (310) 460-0123
www.stimmung.tv

Chris Winston (310) 264-0407
www.onmusicandsound.com
(Music Editor, Re-Recording Mixer & Sound Editor)

Dave Wittman (310) 581-6500
www.eliasarts.com

Roger Wojahn (310) 829-6200
www.wojahn.com

Scott Wojahn (310) 829-6200
www.wojahn.com

Art Wright (310) 829-4765
www.thunder-sound.com
(Foley Artist, Sound Designer & Sound Editor)

Timothy Michael Wynn (310) 578-9686
www.sonicfuel.net

John Zuker (818) 500-9288
www.johnzuker.com

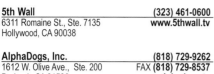

5th Wall   (323) 461-0600
6311 Romaine St., Ste. 7135   **www.5thwall.tv**
Hollywood, CA 90038

AlphaDogs, Inc.   (818) 729-9262
1612 W. Olive Ave., Ste. 200   FAX **(818) 729-8537**
Burbank, CA 91506   **www.alphadogs.tv**

Blue Room Post   (310) 727-2600
1600 Rosecrans Ave., Bldg. 5A   FAX **(310) 727-2601**
Manhattan Beach, CA 90266   **www.blueroompost.com**

Company 3 LA   (310) 255-6600
1661 Lincoln Blvd., Ste. 400   FAX **(310) 255-6602**
Santa Monica, CA 90404   **www.company3.com**

ICO VFX, LLC   (818) 531-7200
727 S. Main St.   FAX **(818) 531-7299**
Burbank, CA 91506   **www.icovfx.com**

Post Modern Edit, LLC   (949) 608-8700
2941 Alton Pkwy   FAX **(949) 608-8729**
Irvine, CA 92606   **www.postmodernedit.com**

Station 22 Edit & Effects   (310) 488-7726
3614 Overland Ave.   **www.station22.com**
Los Angeles, CA 90034

STEELE Studios   (310) 656-7770
5737 Mesmer Ave.   FAX **(310) 391-9055**
Culver City, CA 90230   **www.steelevfx.com**

11:11 MediaWorks — (818) 780-4466
6611 Valjean Ave., Ste. 108   FAX (818) 780-4467
Van Nuys, CA 91406   **www.1111mediaworks.com**
(2D/3D and Stop-Motion Animation, Blue/Green Screen
Compositing, Digital Matte Painting, Miniatures & Visual FX)

3 Ring Circus — (323) 466-5300
1040 N. Sycamore Ave.   FAX (323) 466-5310
Hollywood, CA 90038   **www.3ringcircus.tv**
(Broadcast Design)

3dBob Productions — (818) 559-9700
21601 Devonshire St., Ste. 112   FAX (818) 559-9768
Chatsworth, CA 91311   **www.3dbob.com**
(2D/3D Computer Animation, Digital FX & Motion Graphics)

A52 — (310) 586-0650
2308 Broadway   FAX (310) 586-0651
Santa Monica, CA 90404   **www.a52.com**
(2D/3D Computer Animation, Compositing, Digital and Visual
FX & Matte Painting)
Executive Producer: Mark Tobin
VFX Artists: Pat Murphy
3D Supervisor: Andrew Hall
Sales: Steven Monkarsh

The Aaron Sims Company — (323) 332-7316
www.aaron-sims.com
(2D Animation, 3D Animation, 3D Modeling, Character
Animation, Compositing, Matte Painting, Previsualizations &
Visual FX)

ACME Digital Content
(310) 217-0688
(310) 569-2263
20434 S. Santa Fe Ave., Ste. 206   **www.acmedc.com**
Long Beach, CA 90810
(3D Scanning, 3D Modeling, 3D Digitizing, CAD Conversion,
Computer Animation & Rendering)

Acme Filmworks, Inc. — (323) 464-7805
6525 Sunset Blvd., Ste. G-10   FAX (323) 464-6614
Hollywood, CA 90028   **www.acmefilmworks.com**
(2D/3D Animation, CGI, Character Cel Animation, Computer
Animation & Stop-Motion)
Executive Producer: Ron Diamond
Producer: Pernille D'Avolio
Directors: Aixsponza, Gil Alkabetz, Claire Armstrong-Parod,
Danny Cannizzaro, Peter Chung, Evert de Beijer, Paul and
Menno De Nooijer, Michael Dudok De Wit, John Dilworth,
Paul Driessen, Piotr Dumala, Daniel Guyonnet, Chris Hinton,
Greg Holfeld, Aleksandra Korejwo, Igor Kovalyov, Torill Kove,
Raimund Krumme, Chris Landreth, Christopher and Wolfgang
Lauenstein, Caroline Leaf, Susan Loughlin, Frank and Caroline
Mouris, Oury and Thomas, Luc Perez, Janet Perlman, Afonso
Poyart, Robert Proch, Barry Purves, Daniel Guvonnet, Gitaniali
Rao, Rosto, Erica Russell, Michael Socha, Michael Sormannx,
Pam Stalker, Tiger Hare, Wendy Tilby/Amanda Forbis, Gianluigi
Toccafondo, Sarah van Den Boom, Solweig von Kleist,
Wachtenheim/Marianetti, David Wasson, Koji Yamamura, Yuval
and Merav Nathan & Juan Pablo Zaramella
East Coast Sales Rep: Mark Mirsky
Midwest Sales Rep: Tim Harwood
West Coast Sales Rep: Toni Saarinen

Acorn Entertainment — (323) 238-4650
Hollywood Production Center
121 W. Lexington Dr.,   **www.acornentertainment.com**
Ste. V100
Glendale, CA 91203
(2D and 3D Animation, 3D Modeling, Animatics, Broadcast
Design, Cel Animation, CGI, Character Animation and Design,
Computer Animation, Graphic Design, Live Action Integration,
Previsualizations, Rotoscoping & Storyboards)
Executive Producers: Evan Ricks & Thad Weinlein
Producer: Mary Wall
Broadcast Graphics: Bill Hastings
Client Services: Nikki Auckerman

Altered Illusions — (818) 471-0044
www.alteredillusions.com
(2D Animation, Broadcast Design, Compositing, Editorial,
Motion Graphics, Stereoscopic 3D, Visual FX &
Visual FX Supervision)

Amalgamated Pixels, Inc. — (818) 865-8423
2475 Townsgate Rd., Ste. 220   FAX (818) 575-9032
Westlake Village, CA 91361   **www.apixels.com**
(2D/3D Computer Animation, Compositing, Digital FX, Digital
Matte Painting, Previsualizations & Rotoscoping)
Head of Production: Derry Frost
Executive Producer: Bonnie Kanner & Michael Morreale

Animal Logic
(310) 664-8765
(310) 945-8765
2644 30th St., Ste. 100   FAX (310) 664-9355
Santa Monica, CA 90405   **www.animallogic.com**
(3D Animation, Blue Screen Compositing, CGI, Character
Design, Compositing, Green Screen Compositing, Matte
Painting, Stereoscopic 3D, Visual FX & Visual FX Supervision)
VP of Operations and Production: Katherine Concepcion

Animax Entertainment — (818) 787-4444
6627 Valjean Ave.   FAX (818) 374-9140
Van Nuys, CA 91406   **www.animaxentertainment.com**
(2D/3D Computer Animation, Character Design &
Motion Graphics)

Antifreeze Design — (619) 795-2940
www.antifreezedesign.com
(Broadcast Design, Compositing & Rotoscoping)

Area 51 — (626) 791-7151
1299 Boston St.   **www.area51fx.com**
Altadena, CA 91001
(Animatics, CGI, Character Animation, Compositing &
Digital Matte Painting)
Visual FX Supervisors: Glenn Campbell & Tim McHugh
Visual FX Co-Producer: Michelle Massie

Arsenal FX — (310) 453-5400
1620 Euclid St.   **www.arsenalfx.tv**
Santa Monica, CA 90404
(2D Animation, 2D Paint, 3D Animation, 3D Digitizing, 3D
Modeling, Animatics, Blue Screen Compositing, Broadcast
Design, CGI, Character Animation, Character Design,
Compositing, Computer Animation, Digital FX, Digital Matte
Painting, Digital Paint, Digital Restoration, Editorial, Graphic
Design, Green Screen Compositing, Illustrative Design, Image
Processing, Live Action Integration, Matte Painting, Morphing,
Motion Control, Motion Graphics, Photography, Pre-Production
Planning, Previsualizations, Real Time Motion Control,
Rotoscoping, Scanning and Recording, Stop-Motion Animation,
Ultimatte, Visual FX & Visual FX Supervision)

At The Post VFX
(310) 452-4600
(502) 585-9500
1200 S. Pacific Coast Highway, Ste. F FAX (310) 733-1797
Redondo Beach, CA 90277   **www.atthepost.net**
(2D Animation, 2D Paint, 3D Animation, 3D Modeling,
Animatics, Blue Screen Compositing, Broadcast Design, CGI,
Compositing, Computer Animation, Digital FX, Digital Matte
Painting, Digital Paint, Editorial, Graphic Design, Green Screen
Compositing, Image Processing, Live Action Integration,
Matte Painting, Motion Graphics, Pre-Production Planning,
Previsualizations, Rotoscoping, Visual FX &
Visual FX Supervision)
VFX Supervisor: Wayne A. Shepherd

AvatarLabs — (818) 784-2200
16030 Ventura Blvd.   FAX (818) 784-2204
Encino, CA 91436   **www.avatarlabs.com**
(Motion Graphics)

Baked FX — (323) 937-6200
3750 Robertson Blvd., Ste. 200   FAX (323) 937-6201
Culver City, CA 90232   **www.bakedfx.com**
(2D Animation, 3D Animation, 3D Modeling, Animatics, Blue
Screen Compositing, Broadcast Design, CGI, Character
Animation, Character Design, Compositing, Computer
Animation, Digital Film Mastering, Digital FX, Digital Matte
Painting, Digital Paint, Digital Restoration, Editorial, Green
Screen Compositing, Graphic Design, Illustrative Design, Image
Processing, Live Action Integration, Matte Painting, Morphing,
Motion Graphics, Photography, Pre-Production Planning,
Rotoscoping, Previsualizations, Stereoscopic 3D, Ultimatte,
Visual FX & Visual FX Supervision)

Beau Studio   **(310) 857-6696**
3215 La Cienega Ave.   FAX **(310) 861-5970**
Culver City, CA 90232   **www.beaustudio.com**
(2D Animation, 2D Paint, 3D Animation, 3D Modeling,
Animatics, Blue Screen Compositing, CGI, Character
Animation, Character Design, Compositing, Computer
Animation, Digital FX, Digital Matte Painting, Digital Paint,
Green Screen Compositing, Live Action Integration, Matte
Painting, Morphing, Pre-Production Planning, Previsualizations,
Rotoscoping, Time-Lapse Photography, Ultimatte, Visual FX &
Visual FX Supervision)

Berkos & Associates   **(310) 940-1329**
(2D and 3D Animation, Computer Animation, Blue and Green
Screen Compositing, Stop-Motion & Time-Lapse Photography,
Visual FX & Visual FX Supervision)
Producer/Director: Craig Berkos

Bill Melendez Productions, Inc.   **(818) 382-7382**
13400 Riverside Dr., Ste. 201   **www.billmelendez.tv**
Sherman Oaks, CA 91463
(2D/3D & Character Animation)
Business Affairs: Joanna Coletta
Animation Supervisor: Larry Leichliter
Sales Rep: Jeff Arnold

Blind   **(310) 314-1618**
1702 Olympic Blvd.   FAX **(310) 314-1718**
Santa Monica, CA 90404   **www.blind.com**
(2D/3D Computer Animation, Character Design &
Digital and Visual FX)
Executive Producer: David Kleinman

Blissium   **(310) 453-7070**
1630 Stewart St., Ste. B1   FAX **(310) 260-6111**
Santa Monica, CA 90404   **www.blissium.com**
(2D Animation, 3D Animation, 3D Modeling, Animatics, Blue
Screen Compositing, Broadcast Design, Cel Animation, CGI,
Character Design, Compositing, Computer Animation, Digital
FX, Digital Matte Painting, Editorial, Graphic Design, Green
Screen Compositing, Illustrative Design, Image Processing,
Live Action Integration, Matte Painting, Morphing, Motion
Capture, Motion Control, Motion Control Photography,
Motion Graphics, Photography, Pre-Production Planning,
Previsualizations, Real Time Motion Control, Rotoscoping,
Stop-Motion Animation, Storyboards, Time-Lapse Photography,
Ultimatte, Visual FX & Visual FX Supervision)

Blue Room Post   **(310) 727-2600**
1600 Rosecrans Ave., Bldg. 5A   FAX **(310) 727-2601**
Manhattan Beach, CA 90266   **www.blueroompost.com**
(Blue/Green Screen Compositing, Broadcast Design,
Compositing, Computer Animation, Digital FX, Digital
Matte Painting, Digital Paint, Digital Restoration, Editorial,
Graphic Design, Pre-Production Planning, Previsualizations,
Rotoscoping, Visual FX & Visual FX Supervision)

BlueScreen, LLC/Bob Kertesz   **(323) 467-7572**
     www.bluescreen.com
(Blue/Green Screen, Graphics, Live Action
Integration & Ultimatte)
Visual FX Supervisor: Bob Kertesz

Blur Studio, Inc.   **(310) 581-8848**
589 Venice Blvd.   FAX **(310) 581-8850**
Venice, CA 90291   **www.blur.com**
(2D/3D Computer Animation and Visual Effects)
President/Creative Director: Tim Miller
Executive Producer: Al Shier

BrainForest Digital   **(818) 865-8333**
5743 Corsa Ave., Ste. 220   FAX **(818) 865-9333**
Westlake Village, CA 91362   **www.brain4est.com**
(2D/3D Computer Animation, Animatics & Previsualizations)
Director: Joe Matamales
Production Coordinator: Merrilee Newman

Brewster Parsons   **(310) 736-1663**
1117 Abbot Kinney Blvd.   FAX **(310) 396-3299**
Venice, CA 90291   **www.brewsterparsons.com**

Brickyard VFX   **(310) 453-5722**
2054 Broadway   FAX **(310) 453-5744**
Santa Monica, CA 90404   **www.brickyardvfx.com**
(3D Animation, FX and Modeling, Animatics, Compositing,
Pre-Production Planning, Rotoscoping & Visual FX)
Executive Producer: Jeff Blodgett

     (323) 512-6000
Buf, Inc.   **(323) 791-8914**
7720 W. Sunset Blvd., Ground Fl.   FAX **(323) 512-6075**
Los Angeles, CA 90046   **www.buf.com**
President: Pierre Buffin
Producer: Vanessa Fourgeaud
General Manager: Giacun Caduff
Visual FX Supervisor: Olivier Dumont

Bully Bros. Post   **(310) 874-7000**
1240 Sixth St.   **www.bullybrospost.com**
Santa Monica, CA 90401

Camera Control, Inc.   **(310) 581-8343**
3317 Ocean Park Blvd.   FAX **(310) 581-8340**
Santa Monica, CA 90405   **www.cameracontrol.com**
(Portable Live Action and Miniature Motion Control Systems)
Head of Production: Jason Rau
Motion Control Operators: Tim Donlevy, George Hladky, Chris
Toth & Simon Wakley

Carbon VFX   **(310) 319-9908**
530 Wilshire Blvd., Ste. 400   FAX **(310) 319-9905**
Santa Monica, CA 90401   **www.carbonvfx.com**

CBS Digital   **(323) 575-2310**
7800 Beverly Blvd., Ste. 112A   FAX **(323) 575-4450**
Los Angeles, CA 90036   **www.cbsdvfx.com**
(Animatics, Broadcast Design, CGI, Previsualizations,
Rotoscoping & Ultimatte)

CCI Digital, Inc.   **(818) 562-6300**
2921 W. Alameda Ave.   FAX **(818) 562-8222**
Burbank, CA 91505   **www.ccidigital.com**
(Broadcast Design, Compositing & Digital Ink and Paint)

Charlie Company   **(310) 264-7100**
1758 Berkeley St.   FAX **(310) 264-7104**
Santa Monica, CA 90404   **www.charlieco.tv**
(2D Animation, 2D Paint, 3D Animation, 3D Digitizing, 3D
Modeling, Animatics, Blue Screen Compositing, Broadcast
Design, Cel Animation, CGI, Character Animation, Character
Design, Compositing, Computer Animation, Graphic Design,
Green Screen Compositing, Illustrative Design, Live Action
Integration, Rotoscoping & Storyboards)

Chiodo Bros. Productions, Inc.   **(818) 842-5656**
110 W. Providencia Ave.   FAX **(818) 848-0891**
Burbank, CA 91502   **www.chiodobros.com**
(Miniature Photography & Stop Motion)
Producer: Edward Chiodo
Designer: Charles Chiodo
Director: Steven Chiodo

Christopher Nibley Cinematography   **(818) 850-0096**
     www.nibley.com
(Blue Screen Compositing, Green Screen Compositing,
Miniatures, Miniature Motion Control, Previsualizations, Real
Time Motion Control, Stereoscopic 3D & Visual FX)

Christov Effects & Design, Inc.   **(818) 842-0238**
3805 W. Magnolia Blvd.   **www.christovfx.com**
Burbank, CA 91505
(2D/3D Animation and FX, 3D Modeling, Animatics, Character
Animation, Compositing, Digital Matte Painting & Visual FX)

     (310) 455-2490
Cinergy Creative   **(818) 623-6558**
     www.cinergycreative.com
(2D/3D Computer Animation, Compositing, Digital and Visual
FX & Live Action Integrating)
Creative Director: Leslie Allen
Producer: Elizabeth Lough

Comen VFX   (310) 399-2828
1750 14th St., Ste. B   www.comenvfx.com
Santa Monica, CA 90404
(2D Animation, 2D Paint, 3D Animation, 3D Digitizing, 3D
Modeling, Animatics, Blue Screen Compositing, Broadcast
Design, Cel Animation, CGI, Character Design, Compositing,
Computer Animation, Digital Film Mastering, Digital FX, Digital
Matte Painting, Digital Paint, Digital Restoration, Editorial,
Graphic Design, Green Screen Compositing, Illustrative
Design, Live Action Integration, Matte Painting, Morphing,
Motion Graphics, Photography, Pre-Production Planning,
Previsualizations, Rotoscoping, Scanning and Recording,
Storyboards, Time-Lapse Photography, Ultimatte, Visual FX &
Visual FX Supervision)

Contraband   (323) 933-1614
5820 Wilshire Blvd., Ste. 306   www.contrabandusa.com
Los Angeles, CA 90036
(2D/3D Computer Animation, Compositing, Live Action
Integration & Visual FX)

CostFX   (805) 455-7574
    FAX (805) 965-6991
    www.costfx.com
(2D Animation, 2D Paint, 3D Animation, 3D Digitizing, 3D
Modeling, Animatics, Blue Screen Compositing, Broadcast
Design, Cel Animation, CGI, Character Animation, Character
Design, Clay Animation, Compositing, Computer Animation,
Digital Film Mastering, Digital FX, Digital Ink, Digital Matte
Painting, Digital Paint, Digital Restoration, Graphic Design,
Green Screen Compositing, Illustrative Design, Image
Processing, Live Action Integration, Matte Painting, Miniature
Motion Control, Miniatures, Morphing, Motion Control
Photography, Motion Graphics, Photography, Pre-Production
Planning, Previsualizations, Rotoscoping, Scanning and
Recording, Stop-Motion Animation, Storyboards, Time-Lapse
Photography, Ultimatte, Visual FX & Visual FX Supervision)

Creative Character Engineering   (818) 901-0507
16110 Hart St.   FAX (818) 901-8417
Van Nuys, CA 91406   www.creativecharacter.com
(3D Animation, Character Animation & Compositing)
Creative Director: Andrew Clement

The Creative-Cartel, Inc.   (310) 279-5566
    www.the-cartel.com
(2D Paint, 2D/3D Animation, 3D Modeling, Animatics, Blue/
Green Screen Compositing, CGI, Character Animation,
Compositing, Computer Animation, Digital Film Mastering,
Digital FX, Digital Ink and Paint, Digital Restoration, Editorial,
Live Action, Live Action Integration, Morphing, Pre-Production
Planning, Previsualizations, Rotoscoping, Scanning and
Recording, Stereoscopic and 3D Conversion Management and
Consulting, Visual FX & Visual FX Supervision)
Contact: Jenny Fulle

    (310) 326-4500
Cutting Edge Productions, Inc.   (818) 503-0400
22904 Lockness Ave.   FAX (310) 326-4715
Torrance, CA 90501   www.cuttingedgeproductions.tv
(Blue/Green Screen, Broadcast Design & Visual FX)
Founder & CEO: Bill Dedes

Daily Post   (310) 417-4844
6701 Center Dr. West, Ste. 1111   FAX (310) 410-1543
Los Angeles, CA 90045   www.dailypost.tv

    (323) 874-3003
Desert 66/Barbed Wire FX   (323) 774-4303
6362 Hollywood Blvd., Ste. 310   www.desert66.com
Santa Monica, CA 90028
(2D/3D Computer Animation, Animatics, Compositing, Matte
Painting, Motion Graphics, Previsualizations, Storyboards &
Visual FX Supervision)

Digiscope   (310) 315-6060
1447 Cloverfield Blvd.   FAX (310) 828-5856
Santa Monica, CA 90404   www.digiscope.com
(3D Animation and Modeling, Compositing & Pre-Visualization)
Visual FX Executive Producer: Mary Stuart
Visual FX Supervisor: Dion Hatch

Digital Dimension   (818) 929-5644
P.O. Box 572800   www.digitaldimension.com
Tarzana, CA 91357
(2D/3D Computer Animation, Animatics, Compositing, Digital
Matte Painting, Live Action Integration, Motion Graphics,
Previsualizations & Rotoscoping)

Digital Domain   (310) 314-2800
300 Rose Ave.   FAX (310) 314-2888
Venice, CA 90291   www.digitaldomain.com
(2D/3D Computer Animation, Compositing, Digital and Visual
FX, Image Processing, Live Action Integration, Matte Painting &
Miniature and Motion Control Photography)
VP/Head of Production: Ed Ulbrich

Digital Jungle Post Production   (323) 962-0867
6363 Santa Monica Blvd.   FAX (323) 962-9960
Los Angeles, CA 90038   www.digijungle.com

Doglight Studios, LLC   (626) 798-3151
37 Silver Spruce Ln.   www.doglight.com
Altadena, CA 91001
(2D/3D Computer Animation and Graphic Design)
Creative Director: Tony Honkawa

DUCK Studios,
a.k.a. Duck Soup Studios   (310) 478-0771
2205 Stoner Ave.   FAX (310) 478-0773
Los Angeles, CA 90064   www.duckstudios.com
(2D/3D Computer Animation, Cel Animation, Character and
Illustrative Design, Compositing, Digital Ink and Paint, Live
Action Integration & Stop Motion)
Executive Producer: Mark Medernach
President/Director: Roger Chouinard
Directors: abstract: groove, B and C Wall, Simon Blake, Jamie
Caliri, Roger Chouinard, Paul Cummings, Delicatessen,
Eric Goldberg, James Hackett, Chris Harding, Impactist, JL
Design, Kompost, Lane and Jan, MAIN FRAME, Meindbender,
Monkmus, Yorico Murakami, NMA, Nina Paley, Daniel Peacock,
Hsin Ping Pan, Chris Romano, Maureen Selwood, Kang Seong,
SMOG, Tiny Inventions, Brian Williams & YELLOWSHED
Sales Representative: Andrew Halpern
Music Video Rep: Randi Wilens

Duncan Studio   (626) 578-1587
35 N. Arroyo Parkway, Ste. 200   FAX (626) 578-1327
Pasadena, CA 91103   www.duncanstudio.com
(2D Animation, 2D Paint, 3D Animation, 3D Modeling,
Animatics, Cel Animation, CGI, Character Animation, Character
Design, Compositing, Computer Animation, Digital Ink, Digital
Paint, Graphic Design, Compositing, Computer Animation,
Digital Ink, Digital Paint, Graphic Design, Matte Painting,
Pre-Visualizations & Storyboards)

Eden FX   (310) 481-7002
12421 W. Olympic Blvd.   FAX (310) 207-8408
Santa Monica, CA 90064   www.edenfx.com
(2D/3D Animation, 3D Modeling, Animatics, Blue/Green Screen
Compositing, CGI, Character Animation, Character Design,
Compositing, Computer Animation, Digital FX, Digital Matte
Painting, Live Action Integration, Matte Painting, Pre-Production
Planning, Previsualizations, Rotoscoping, Visual FX &
Visual FX Supervision)
Creative Director/President: John Gross
Executive Producer: Andrea D'Amico

Eight VFX   (310) 828-9628
1712 Berkeley St.   FAX (310) 828-9631
Santa Monica, CA 90404   www.eightvfx.com
(2D/3D Computer Animation, Compositing, Digital Matte
Painting, Previsualization & Visual FX Supervisors)

Elektrashock, Inc.   (310) 399-4985
1320 Main St.   FAX (310) 399-4972
Venice, CA 90291   www.elektrashock.com
(3D Animation)

Encore Hollywood   (323) 466-7663
6344 Fountain Ave.   FAX (323) 467-5539
Hollywood, CA 90028   www.encorehollywood.com
(2D/3D Computer Animation and Modeling, Character Design,
Compositing & Rotoscoping)
Producers: Stephan Fleet, Jon Howard, Tom Kendall &
Sarah McGrail

Engine Room   (323) 860-5100
1040 N. Las Palmas, Bldg. 5U   FAX (323) 860-5111
Los Angeles, CA 90038
        www.engineroomhollywood.com
(2D/3D Computer Animation & Compositing)
Executive Producer: Michael Caplan
Visual FX Supervisor: Dan Schmit

Entity FX   (310) 899-9779
1437 Seventh St., Ste. 300   FAX (310) 899-3113
Santa Monica, CA 90401   www.entityfx.com
(2D/3D Animation and FX, 3D Modeling, Character Animation,
Compositing, Digital Matte Painting, Live Action Integration,
Model/Miniature Shoots, Morphing, Previsualizations,
Rotoscoping, Stereoscopic 3D, Visual FX &
Visual FX Supervision)
President: Mat Beck
General Manager: Ellyn Lewis
Senior Producer: Trent Smith
Executive Producer: Dan Ruscinski

EP Graphic Productions   (818) 953-9375
                  (818) 953-4027
3921 W. Magnolia Blvd.   FAX (818) 953-2833
Burbank, CA 91505   www.ep-graphics.com
(2D/3D Computer Animation and Graphics)
President/Creative Director: Eddie Pong

Eyestorm Productions   (310) 582-3937
1522 Cloverfield Blvd., Ste. C   FAX (310) 582-3939
Santa Monica, CA 90404
        www.eyestormproductions.com
(2D Animation, 2D Paint, 3D Animation, 3D Modeling,
Animatics, Blue/Green Screen Compositing, Broadcast Design,
CGI, Character Animation, Character Design, Compositing,
Computer Animation, Digital FX, Editorial, Graphic Design,
Illustrative Design, Live Action Integration, Morphing, Motion
Graphics, Previsualizations, Rotoscoping, Stop-Motion
Animation, Storyboards, Time-Lapse Photography, Ultimatte &
Visual FX)

Eyetronics Media & Studios   (310) 371-6600
16861 Ventura Blvd., Ste. 310   FAX (310) 371-8700
Encino, CA 91436   www.eyetronics.com
(3D Digitizing, 3D Modeling, CGI, Character Animation,
Character Design, Computer Animation, Motion Capture,
Scanning and Recording & Visual FX)

Filmworks/FX, Inc.   (310) 577-3213
4121 Redwood Ave., Ste. 101   FAX (310) 577-3215
Los Angeles, CA 90066   www.filmworksfx.com
(2D/3D Computer Graphics, Compositing & Digital FX)
Visual FX Supervisor: Ken Locsmandi

FISH EGGS   (310) 452-8251
1261 Electric Ave.   FAX (310) 452-8364
Venice, CA 90291   www.fisheggs.tv
(2D/3D Animation and FX, Broadcast Design, Compositing,
Graphic Design, Green Screen Compositing, Motion Capture,
Motion Graphics, Pre-Production Planning, Rotoscoping &
Visual FX)

Framework Studio, LLC   (310) 815-1245
3535 Hayden Ave., Ste. 300   FAX (310) 815-9821
Culver City, CA 90232   www.frameworkla.com
(2D Animation and Paint, 3D Animation, Digitizing and
Modeling, Animatics, Blue/Green Screen Compositing,
Broadcast Design, CGI, Compositing, Computer Animation,
Digital FX, Digital Matte Painting, Graphic Design, Illustrative
Design, Live Action Integration, Motion Graphics,
Pre-Production Planning, Previsualizations, Rotoscoping,
Stop-Motion Animation, Storyboards, Ultimatte, Visual FX &
Visual FX Supervision)

Fred Wolf Films   (818) 846-0611
4222 W. Burbank Blvd.   FAX (818) 846-0979
Burbank, CA 91505   www.fredwolffilms.com
(Cel Animation)
President: Fred Wolf

Gentleman Scholar   (310) 593-2988
530 Wilshire Blvd., Ste. 400   FAX (310) 319-9905
Santa Monica, CA 90401   www.gentscholar.com
(2D Animation, 2D Paint, 3D Animation, 3D Digitizing, 3D
Modeling, Animatics, Blue Screen Compositing, Broadcast
Design, Cel Animation, CGI, Character Animation, Character
Design, Compositing, Computer Animation, Digital FX, Digital
Ink, Digital Matte Painting, Digital Paint, Digital Restoration,
Editorial, Graphic Design, Green Screen Compositing,
Illustrative Design, Live Action Integration, Matte Painting,
Morphing, Motion Graphics, Photography, Pre-Production
Planning, Previsualizations, Real Time Motion Control,
Rotoscoping, Stop-Motion Animation, Storyboards, Time-Lapse
Photography, Ultimatte, Visual FX & Visual FX Supervision)

Giant Studios   (310) 839-1999
1600 Rosecrans Ave.,   FAX (310) 862-5122
Bldg. 6A, Third Fl.   www.giantstudios.com
Manhattan Beach, CA 90266
(Motion Capture)

Giantsteps   (310) 382-1523
                  (310) 415-6320
100 Market St., Third Fl.   FAX (310) 496-3228
Venice, CA 90291   www.giantsteps.us

Gork Enterprises, Inc.   (818) 837-7984
233 N. Maclay Ave., Ste. 169   FAX (818) 365-1964
San Fernando, CA 91340   www.gork.com
(2D/3D Animation and FX, 3D Modeling, Animatics, Blue/
Green Screen, Character Animation, Compositing, Digital Matte
Painting, Morphing, Rotoscoping & Visual FX)

Gradient Effects   (310) 821-3177
4120 Del Rey Ave.   FAX (310) 821-0584
Marina del Rey, CA 90292   www.gradientfx.com
(2D Animation, 2D Paint, 3D Animation, 3D Digitizing, 3D
Modeling, Animatics, Blue Screen Compositing, CGI, Character
Animation, Character Design, Compositing, Computer
Animation, Digital Film Mastering, Digital FX, Digital Matte
Painting, Digital Paint, Editorial, Green Screen Compositing,
Image Processing, Live Action Integration, Matte Painting,
Morphing, Motion Capture, Pre-Production Planning,
Previsualizations, Rotoscoping, Visual FX &
Visual FX Supervision)

Hal   (310) 659-4400
1022 Palm Ave.   FAX (310) 659-4402
West Hollywood, CA 90069   www.hal.tv

Hammerhead Productions   (818) 986-5535
                FAX (818) 986-5545
          www.hammerhead.com
(3D Modeling, Character Animation, Compositing &
Digital Matte Painting)

Heaven - an Image Company, Ltd.   (323) 791-9433
          www.heavenanimage.com
(Broadcast Design, Graphic Design, Motion Graphics, Pre-
Production Planning & Visual FX Supervision)

Hi-Ground Media   (310) 845-9500
8579 Higuera St.   FAX (310) 845-9559
Culver City, CA 90232   www.hi-ground.com
(CGI, Offline, Online, Pre-Production Planning, Stereoscopic
3D, Visual Effects, Visual FX Compositing &
Visual FX Supervision)
Executive Producer/Founder: Gregg Katano

Hieroglyphic Productions   (818) 505-6050
3211 Cahuenga Blvd. West, Ste. 103   FAX (818) 505-6054
Los Angeles, CA 90068   www.hiero.net

HOAX Films   **(310) 426-8732**
5541 W. Washington Blvd.   FAX **(310) 426-8731**
Los Angeles, CA 90016   **www.hoaxfilms.com**
(2D Paint, 3D Animation, 3D Digitizing, 3D Modeling, Animatics, Blue Screen Compositing, Broadcast Design, CGI, Character Animation, Character Design, Compositing, Computer Animation, Digital FX, Digital Ink, Digital Matte Painting, Digital Paint, Editorial, Graphic Design, Green Screen Compositing, Illustrative Design, Live Action Integration, Matte Painting, Motion Capture, Motion Control, Motion Control Photography, Motion Graphics, Photography, Pre-Production Planning, Previsualizations, Real Time Motion Control, Rotoscoping, Stereoscopic 3D, Storyboards, Time-Lapse Photography, Visual FX & Visual FX Supervision)

                 (917) 351-0520
Hornet, Inc.   **(310) 601-1355**
3962 Ince Blvd.   FAX **(310) 641-2117**
Culver City, CA 90232   **www.hornetinc.com**
(2D/3D Computer Animation & Digital and Visual FX)
CEO: Jon Slusser
President: Greg Harvey
Vice President: Greg Bedard
Executive Producer: Michael Feder

House of Moves, Inc.   **(310) 306-6131**
5419 McConnell Ave.   FAX **(310) 437-4229**
Los Angeles, CA 90066   **www.moves.com**
(Motion Capture)
CEO: Tom Tolles
Executive Producer: Scott Gagain
COO: Matt Lawrence

Humunculus   **(310) 827-1800**
529 Victoria Ave.   **www.humunculus.com**
Venice, CA 90291
(3D Animation & Broadcast Design)

[hy*drau'lx]   **(310) 319-2300**
1447 Second St.   FAX **(310) 319-2305**
Santa Monica, CA 90401   **www.hydraulx.com**
(2D/3D Animation and FX, 3D Modeling, Character Animation, Compositing, Digital Matte Painting, Morphing & Visual FX)
President: David Strause
Visual FX Supervisors: Colin Strause & Greg Strause
Executive Producer: Scott Michelson

                 (310) 216-5678
I.E. Effects   **(866) 540-3287**
6076 Bristol Pkwy, Ste. 100   FAX **(310) 216-5616**
Culver City, CA 90230   **www.ieeffects.com**
(3D Animation, 3D Conversion, 3D Modeling, CGI, Compositing, Digital Production, Editorial, Green Screen, Live Action Integration, Motion Graphics, Pre-Production Planning, Rotoscoping, Stereoscopic 3D Post Services, Visual FX & Visual FX Supervision)
Executive Producer: David Kenneth
VFX Supervisor: Dennis Michel
Line Producer: Kris Murphy
Director of Regional Operations: Clover Keyes Roy
VFX Coordinator: Sarah Smith

ICO VFX, LLC   **(818) 531-7200**
727 S. Main St.   FAX **(818) 531-7299**
Burbank, CA 91506   **www.icovfx.com**

an ideal world   **(714) 953-9501**
209 N. Bush St.   FAX **(714) 380-6311**
Santa Ana, CA 92701   **www.anidealworld.com**
(2D/3D Animation, 3D Modeling, Animatics, Broadcast Design, Compositing, Blue Screen Compositing, CGI, Digital FX, Digital Restoration, Editorial, Graphic Design, Green Screen Compositing, Live Action Integration, Morphing, Motion Graphics, Pre-Production Planning, Previsualizations, Rotoscoping, Ultimatte, Visual FX & Visual FX Supervision)

Ignite Rentals   **(310) 702-7955**
(2D/3D Animation & Compositing)
President: Laurie Shearing

Ignition Post   **(818) 762-2210**
4130 Cahuenga Blvd., Ste. 100   **www.ignition-post.com**
Toluca Lake, CA 91602

Image G/Ikonographics   **(818) 761-6644**
28490 Westinghouse Pl., Ste. 160   **www.imageg.com**
Valencia, CA 91355
(Miniature Photography, Portable Real Time Motion Control, Stop Motion & Time-Lapse Photography)
Director: Thomas Barron

Imaginal Cells, Inc.   **(818) 785-0051**
6314 Ethel Ave.   FAX **(818) 782-3756**
Van Nuys, CA 91401   **www.imaginalcellsinc.com**
(2D Paint, 2D/3D Animation, 3D Modeling, Broadcast Design, Compositing, Computer Animation, Editorial, Graphic Design, Green Screen Compositing, Motion Graphics & Photography)

The Institution Post   **(818) 566-7801**
423 N. Fairview St.   **www.the-institution.com**
Burbank, CA 91505
(2D Animation, 2D Paint, 3D Animation, 3D Digitizing, 3D Modeling, Blue Screen Compositing, Broadcast Design, CGI, Compositing, Computer Animation, Digital Film Mastering, Digital FX, Digital Ink, Digital Matte Painting, Digital Paint, Digital Restoration, Editorial, Graphic Design, Green Screen Compositing, Illustrative Design, Image Processing, Live Action Integration, Matte Painting, Morphing, Motion Graphics, Pre-Production Planning, Previsualizations, Rotoscoping, Storyboards, Ultimatte, Visual FX & Visual FX Supervision)

Khaos Digital   **(323) 762-2260**
6007 Waring Ave.   **www.khaosdigital.com**
Hollywood, CA 90038
(Editorial, Graphic Design, Green Screen Compositing, Photography, Pre-Production Planning & Rotoscoping)

Klasky Csupo, Inc.   **(323) 468-2600**
1238 Highland Ave.   FAX **(323) 468-2808**
Los Angeles, CA 90038   **www.klaskycsupo.com**
(Animation)

Kurtz & Friends   **(818) 841-8188**
1023 N. Hollywood Way, Ste. 103   FAX **(818) 841-6263**
Burbank, CA 91505   **www.kurtzandfriends.com**
(2D/3D Computer Animation, Cel Animation, Character Design, Compositing, Digital Ink and Paint, Live Action Integration & Storyboards)
Producer: Kenneth Smith
Director: Bob Kurtz

Lightcraft Technology   **(310) 386-7293**
612 Venice Blvd.   **www.lightcrafttech.com**
Venice, CA 90291

Liquid Images   **(310) 392-8900**
                 www.liquidimages.tv
(Compositing, Digital FX, Digital Matte Painting, Live Action Integration, Previsualization, Rotoscoping & Visual FX Supervision)

Liquid Light Studios   **(323) 851-5550**
8039 Hemet Pl.   FAX **(323) 214-8339**
Los Angeles, CA 90046   **www.liquidlightstudios.com**
(Computer Animation)
Executive Producer: Julie Pesusich

Liquid VFX   **(310) 392-1212**
215 Rose Ave.   FAX **(310) 392-1222**
Venice, CA 90291   **www.laliquid.com**
(Blue Screen Compositing, Compositing, Digital FX, Graphic Design, Green Screen Compositing, Morphing, Motion Graphics, Rotoscoping, Visual FX & Visual FX Supervision)
Visual FX Artist: James Bohn
Producer: Terry O'Gara

Look! Effects, Inc.   **(323) 469-4230**
6834 Hollywood Blvd., Ste. 200   FAX **(323) 469-4931**
Los Angeles, CA 90028   **www.lookfx.com**
(2D/3D Computer Animation, Compositing & Visual FX)
President/Visual FX Supervisor: Mark Driscoll
Visual FX Supervisors: Henrik Fett & Max Ivins

MacLeod Productions   **(310) 395-4739**
502 10th St.
Santa Monica, CA 90402
(Computer Animation, Live Action Integration, Motion Control &
Stereoscopic Visual FX)
Producer/Director: Sean MacLeod Phillips

Majikmaker Effects   **(818) 558-6400**
www.majikmaker.com
(3D Animation, Animatics, Blue Screen Compositing, Broadcast
Design, CGI, Compositing, Computer Animation, Digital FX,
Green Screen Compositing, Live Action Integration, Pre-
Production Planning, Previsualizations, Rotoscoping,
Visual FX & Visual FX Supervision)

    (818) 662-0300
Mechnology   **(661) 714-2604**
121 W. Lexington Dr., Ste. B101   **www.mechnology.com**
Glendale, CA 91203
(2D Animation, 2D Paint, 3D Animation, 3D Digitizing,
3D Modeling, Animatics, Blue Screen Compositing, CGI,
Character Animation, Character Design, Compositing,
Computer Animation, Digital FX, Digital Matte Painting, Digital
Paint, Digital Restoration, Graphic Design, Green Screen
Compositing, Illustrative Design, Image Processing, Matte
Painting, Morphing, Motion Graphics, Pre-Production Planning,
Previsualizations, Rotoscoping, Storyboards, Visual FX &
Visual FX Supervision)
Owner/Executive Producer: Chip Potter
Owner/VFX Supervisor: Stephen Lebed

    (818) 842-2600
Merlan Creative Studios   **(818) 620-3617**
5723 Auckland Ave.   **www.merlancreative.com**
N. Hollywood, CA 91601

Method   **(310) 434-6500**
730 Arizona Ave.   FAX **(310) 434-6501**
Santa Monica, CA 90401   **www.methodstudios.com**
(2D/3D Computer Animation, Compositing, Digital Matte
Painting, Previsualizations & Visual FX Supervision)
Executive Producer: Gabby Gourrier
VP, Operations: Patrick Davenport

MFX   **(323) 969-1011**
3400 Barham Blvd.   FAX **(323) 969-1015**
Los Angeles, CA 90068   **www.mfxdesign.com**
(2D/3D Computer Graphics & Compositing)
Visual FX Designer: Scott Milne

Michael Busch Digital Media/
TVart Inc.   **(213) 281-0264**
www.michaelbusch.com
(2D Animation, 3D Animation, 3D Modeling, Broadcast Design,
CGI, Character Animation, Compositing, Computer Animation,
Digital FX, Editorial, Motion Graphics, Visual FX &
Visual FX Supervision)
Visual FX Supervisor/Director: Michael Busch

    (310) 396-4663
Mind Over Eye, LLC   **(310) 968-4259**
1639 11th St., Ste. 117   FAX **(310) 396-0663**
Santa Monica, CA 90404   **www.mindovereye.com**
(2D/3D Animation and FX, 2D Paint, 3D Modeling, Animatics,
Compositing, Morphing & Rotoscoping)

Mirada   **(424) 216-7470**
4235 Redwood Ave.   **www.mirada.com**
Los Angeles, CA 90066
(2D/3D Animation and FX, CGI, Character Animation,
Compositing, Editorial, Motion Graphics & Visual FX)

Mixin Pixls   **(310) 237-6438**
www.mixinpixls.com
(2D to 3D Conversion, 2D/3D Computer Animation,
Compositing, Digital FX, Digital Restoration, Rotoscoping,
Stereoscopic 3D & Visual FX)

Monkeyhead   **(310) 836-7600**
8553 Washington Blvd.   FAX **(310) 836-7611**
Culver City, CA 90232   **www.monkeyhead.com**
(2D Animation, 2D Paint, 3D Animation, 3D Modeling,
Animatics, Blue Screen Compositing, Broadcast Design, Cel
Animation, CGI, Character Animation, Character Design,
Compositing, Computer Animation, Digital FX, Editorial,
Graphic Design, Green Screen Compositing, Illustrative
Design, Live Action Integration, Morphing, Motion Graphics,
Previsualizations, Rotoscoping, Stereoscopic 3D, Stop-Motion
Animation, Storyboards, Ultimatte, Visual FX &
Visual FX Supervision)

Motion Analysis Studios   **(323) 802-1850**
(Motion Capture)   FAX **(323) 802-1889**
www.mastudios.com

Motion City Films   **(310) 434-1272**
www.motioncity.com
(2D/3D Computer Animation, Blue/Green Screen Compositing,
CGI, Compositing, Digital FX, Editorial, Motion Graphics &
Visual FX)
Producer/Director: Jerry Witt

NBC Universal Artworks   **(212) 664-5972**
30 Rockefeller Plaza, Ste. 514E   **www.nbcartworks.com**
New York, NY 10012

New Deal Studios, Inc.   **(310) 578-9929**
15392 Cobalt St.   FAX **(310) 578-7370**
Sylmar, CA 91342   **www.newdealstudios.com**
(3D Environments, Animation, Compositing, Matte Painting,
Pre-Production Planning & Rotoscope Tracking)
Contact: David Sanger

Nitrous Visual Effects   **(818) 536-7991**
5000 N. Parkway Calabasas, Ste. 305
Calabasas, CA 91302   **www.nitrousvfx.com**
(2D Animation, 2D Paint, 3D Animation, 3D Digitizing, 3D
Modeling, Animatics, Blue Screen Compositing, CGI, Character
Animation, Character Design, Compositing, Computer
Animation, Digital FX, Digital Matte Painting, Digital Paint,
Digital Restoration, Green Screen Compositing, Live Action
Integration, Matte Painting, Morphing, Pre-Production Planning,
Previsualizations, Rotoscoping, Stereoscopic 3D, Storyboards,
Visual FX & Visual FX Supervision)
Visual FX Supervisors & Producers: Jonathan Bourgoine, Kerry
Bourgoine & Geoff Leavitt
Visual FX Artists: Matt DiNardo, Geoff Leavitt & Joe Spano

Ntropic   **(310) 806-4950**
2332 S. Centinela St., Ste. B   FAX **(310) 806-4959**
Los Angeles, CA 90064   **www.ntropic.com**
(Animatics, Blue/Green Screen Compositing,
Previsualizations & Rotoscoping)

Ocean Visual FX   **(714) 258-6678**
8462 Gilford Circle   **www.oceanvisualfx.com**
Huntington Beach, CA 92646
(3D Animation, 3D Modeling, Animatics, Blue/Green Screen
Compositing, Broadcast Design, CGI, Character Animation,
Character Design, Compositing, Computer Animation, Digital
FX, Editorial, Graphic Design, Motion Capture, Motion
Graphics, Pre-Production Planning, Previsualizations,
Rotoscoping, Storyboards, Ultimatte, Visual FX & Visual FX
Supervision)
Vice President/Technical Director: Rudy Sarzo
Head of 3D Character Animation: Jeff Clifton
President/VFX Supervisor: Robbie Robfogel

OOOii   **(323) 960-9275**
1604 N. Cahuenga Blvd.   **www.oooii.us**
Hollywood, CA 90028
(2D/3D Computer Animation & Compositing)

Opticam, Inc.   **(310) 403-6691**
810 Navy St.
Santa Monica, CA 90405
(Animation Camera, Cel Animation, Large Format Film, Motion
Control, Motion Graphics & Rotoscoping)
Director: Annette Buehre-Nickerson

     Computer Graphics & Visual FX

Pacific Motion Control, Inc.   (818) 768-1573
   (661) 644-1516
9812 Glenoaks Blvd.   FAX **(818) 768-1575**
Sun Valley, CA 91352   **www.pacificmotion.net**
(Blue/Green Screen Facilities, Miniature Motion Control, Motion
Control, Motion Control Photography, Real Time Motion Control,
Stop-Motion Animation, Time-Lapse Photography & Visual FX)

Pacific Vision Productions, Inc.   **(626) 441-4869**
210 Pasadena Ave.   **www.pacificvision.com**
South Pasadena, CA 91030
(2D/3D Computer Animation, Compositing, Digital and Visual
FX, Green Screen, Live Action Integration & Matte Painting)

Perpetual Motion Pictures   **(661) 294-0788**
16654 Soledad Canyon Rd., Ste. 198   FAX **(661) 294-0786**
Santa Clarita, CA 91387   **www.pmpfx.com**
(2D/3D Computer Animation, Blue/Green Screen Compositing,
Miniature Photography & Motion Control Photography)

Picture Mill   **(323) 465-8800**
6422 Homewood Ave.   FAX **(323) 465-8875**
Los Angeles, CA 90028   **www.picturemill.com**
(Broadcast Design)

Pixel Liberation Front   **(310) 396-9854**
1285 Electric Ave.   FAX **(310) 396-9874**
Venice, CA 90291   **www.thefront.com**
(2D/3D Computer Animation & Previsualization)
President: Colin Green

Pixel Magic   **(818) 760-0862**
10635 Riverside Dr.   FAX **(818) 760-4983**
Toluca Lake, CA 91602   **www.pixelmagicfx.com**
(2D/3D Computer Animation, Animatics, Compositing, Digital
Matte Painting, Previsualization & Restoration)

Pixel Playground   **(818) 205-9910**
   FAX **(818) 501-0343**
   www.pixelplaygroundinc.com
(2D/3D Animation and FX, 2D Paint, 3D Modeling, Character
Animation, Compositing, Digital Matte Painting, Morphing,
Rotoscoping, Ultimatte, Visual FX & Visual FX Supervision)

PixelMonger Inc./Scott Billups   **(818) 990-8993**
   www.pixelmonger.com/esbindex.html
(2D Painting, 3D Modeling, Blue/Green Screen Compositing &
Digital Matte Painting)

Pixomondo   **(310) 394-0555**
903 Colorado Ave., Ste. 100   **www.pixomondo.com**
Santa Monica, CA 90401
(CGI, Character Animation, Previsualizations, Visual FX &
Visual FX Supervision)

Planet Blue   **(310) 899-3877**
1250 Sixth St., Ste. 102   FAX **(310) 899-3787**
Santa Monica, CA 90401   **www.planetblue.com**
(2D/3D Computer Animation, Compositing & Image Processing)
President: Maury Rosenfeld
Executive Producer: Milt Alvarez

Playground Media Group   **(310) 315-3800**
1813 Centinela Ave.   FAX **(310) 315-3801**
Santa Monica, CA 90404   **www.playgroundla.com**
(2D/3D Computer Animation, Character Design & Compositing)

Point of Origin   **(818) 392-8735**
   www.pointoforiginmedia.com

Post Logic Studios   **(323) 461-7887**
1800 N. Vine St., Ste. 100   FAX **(323) 461-7790**
Hollywood, CA 90028   **www.postlogic.com**
(2D/3D Computer Animation, Digital and Visual FX & Live
Action Integration)

Prana Studios, Inc.   **(323) 645-6500**
1145 N. McCadden Pl.   **www.pranastudios.com**
Los Angeles, CA 90038

Praxis Films   **(323) 460-4393**
c/o R. Sirott, 17324 Partheia St.   FAX **(323) 460-4181**
Northridge, CA 91325
(3D Animation, Compositing, Miniature Photography &
Motion Control)

Psychic Bunny   **(310) 862-4262**
453 S. Spring St., Ste. 620   FAX **(213) 614-9046**
Los Angeles, CA 90013   **www.psychicbunny.com**

Public VFX   **(310) 450-6969**
69 Market St.   FAX **(310) 450-6999**
Venice, CA 90291   **www.publicvfx.com**
(2D Animation, 3D Computer Animation, Editorial & Visual FX)
Executive Producer: Sam Swisher

R.C. Gear   **(323) 465-3900**
   (800) 714-8099
6100 Melrose Ave.   FAX **(323) 465-3600**
Los Angeles, CA 90038   **www.rc-gear.com**
(Broadcast Design, Graphic Design & Motion Graphics)

Radium   **(310) 264-6440**
2115 Colorado Ave.   **www.radium.com**
Santa Monica, CA 91404

Ratched Graphics   **(310) 696-4600**
7920 Sunset Blvd., Ste. 200   FAX **(310) 696-4891**
Los Angeles, CA 90046   **www.asylument.com**

Reality Check Studios, Inc.   **(323) 465-3900**
   (323) 908-7000
6100 Melrose Ave.   FAX **(323) 465-3600**
Los Angeles, CA 90038   **www.realityx.com**
(2D/3D Animation, 3D Modeling, Animatics, Blue/Green Screen
Compositing, Broadcast Design, CGI, Character Animation
and Design, Compositing, Computer Animation, Digital FX,
Digital Matte Painting, Editorial, Graphic Design, Live Action
Integration, Matte Painting, Motion Graphics, Previsualizations,
Visual FX & Visual FX Supervision)
Contact: Andrew Heimbold

RenderCore   **(866) 627-3149**
(3D Animation and FX & Visual FX)   FAX **(213) 623-3149**
   www.rendercore.com

Renegade Animation, Inc.   **(818) 551-2351**
111 E. Broadway, Ste. 208   FAX **(818) 551-2350**
Glendale, CA 91205   **www.renegadeanimation.com**
(Cel Animation)
Producer: Ashley Postlewaite
Animation Director: Darrell Van Citters
Sales Rep: Andy Arkin

Rhythm + Hues Commercial Studios (310) 448-7900
2100 E. Grand Ave.   FAX **(310) 448-7601**
El Segundo, CA 90245   **www.rhythm.com**
(2D Compositing, 3D Animation, Broadcast Design, CGI,
Character Animation, Digital FX, Digital Matte Painting,
Scanning and Recording, Stereoscopic 3D, Stop-Motion
Animation & Visual FX)
Executive Producer: Paul Babb
Head of Production, Commercial Digital: Lisa White
Animation/FX Directors: Clark Anderson, John-Mark Austin,
Mark Dippé, Bill Kroyer, Bud Myrick, Craig Talmy &
James Wahlberg
Visual FX Supervisors: Eric DeHaven, John Heller, Tim Miller,
Nik Titmarsh & Bill Westenhofer
East Coast Sales: Carolyn Hill
Midwest/Detroit Sales: Marci Miles
Western Region/Texas Sales: Claire Worch
United Kingdom/Europe Sales: Georgina Poushkine
Creative Services Manager: Chad Norton

Ring of Fire   **(310) 966-5055**
1538 20th St.   FAX **(310) 966-5056**
Santa Monica, CA 90404   **www.ringoffire.com**
(2D/3D Computer Animation, Compositing, HD Visual FX &
Visual FX Supervision)
Executive Producer: John Myers
Creative Director: Jerry Spivack
Director of Sales: Amy Grgich

Rocket Films   **(310) 405-2011**
2106 W. Glen Ave.   **www.rocketfilms.com**
Anaheim, CA 92801
(Blue Screen, Miniature Photography, Motion Control,
Rotoscoping & Stop Motion)
Executive Producer/Visual FX Supervisor: Jon Tucker

Rocket Science Motion
Capture Studios   (323) 247-7862
5320 McConnell Ave.
Los Angeles, CA 90066
(Motion Capture) **www.rocketsciencemotioncapture.com**

Rundell Filmworks   **(818) 314-7560**
5309 Wilkinson Ave.   FAX **(818) 760-3221**
Valley Village, CA 91607   **www.rundellfilmworks.com**
Producer: Courtney Rundell
Editor: Matt Rundell

Shine   **(323) 937-7470**
5410 Wilshire Blvd., Ste. 204   FAX **(360) 237-0542**
Los Angeles, CA 90036   **www.shinestudio.tv**

          (818) 768-9778
Sir Reel Pictures   **(818) 415-7326**
8036 Shadyglade Ave.   **www.sirreelpictures.com**
North Hollywood, CA 91605
(Compositing & Matte Painting)

SoftMirage   **(949) 474-2002**
17922 Fitch, First Fl.   FAX **(949) 474-2011**
Irvine, CA 92614   **www.softmirage.com**
(3D Animation and Modeling, Animatics, Graphic Design,
Illustrative Design, Motion Graphics & Previsualizations)

Sony Pictures Imageworks   **(310) 840-8000**
9050 W. Washington Blvd.   FAX **(310) 840-8100**
Culver City, CA 90232   **www.imageworks.com**
(3D Character Animation & Visual FX)
Executive VP, Production Infrastructure/Executive Producer:
Debbie Denise
Visual FX Supervisor: Jim Berney

StandardVision, LLC   **(323) 224-3944**
          FAX **(323) 225-6226**
          www.standardsite.com
(3D Animation, 3D Computer Graphics, 3D Modeling,
Broadcast Design, Compositing, Digital FX, Editorial, Graphic
Design & Visual FX)
Producer: Steven Wren

Stargate Digital   **(626) 403-8403**
1001 El Centro St.   FAX **(626) 403-8444**
South Pasadena, CA 91030   **www.stargatestudios.net**
(2D/3D Computer Animation, Blue Screen, Compositing, Laser
Animation FX, Miniature Photography & Motion Control)

Steam   **(310) 636-4620**
3021 Airport Ave., Ste. 201   FAX **(310) 636-4621**
Santa Monica, CA 90405
          www.steamshow.com

STEELE Studios   **(310) 656-7770**
5737 Mesmer Ave.   FAX **(310) 391-9055**
Culver City, CA 90230   **www.steelevfx.com**
(2D Paint, 2D/3D Animation, 3D Digitizing, 3D Modeling,
Animatics, Blue Screen Compositing, Broadcast Design,
CGI, Character Animation, Character Design, Compositing,
Computer Animation, Digital FX, Digital Matte Painting, Digital
Paint, Digital Restoration, Editorial, Green Screen Compositing,
Live Action Integration, Motion Capture, Motion Control,
Motion Graphics, Pre-Production Planning, Previsualizations,
Rotoscoping, Stereoscopic 3D, Storyboards, Visual FX &
Visual FX Supervision)

Stokes/Kohne Associates, Inc.   **(323) 468-2340**
742 Cahuenga Blvd.   FAX **(323) 468-2345**
Hollywood, CA 90038   **www.stokeskohne.com**
(2D Animation, Blue Screen Compositing, Broadcast Design,
Cel Animation, Clay Animation, Compositing, Graphic Design,
Green Screen Compositing, Miniature Motion Control,
Miniatures, Motion Control, Motion Control Photography, Motion
Graphics, Pre-Production Planning, Stop-Motion Animation,
Time-Lapse Photography, Visual FX & Visual FX Supervision)
Visual FX Supervisor/Director: Dan Kohne

Storyheads Entertainment   **(310) 487-6011**
924 Calle Ruiz   **www.storyheads.com**
Thousand Oaks, CA 91360
(2D/3D Animation and FX, Animatics, Cel Animation, Character
Animation, Storyboards & Visual FX)
Founder/Creative Director: David Smith
Co-Founder/Executive Producer: Donna Smith

The Studio at   **(818) 295-5000**
New Wave Entertainment   **(818) 295-8060**
2660 W. Olive Ave.   **www.nwe.com**
Burbank, CA 91505
(3D Computer Animation & Visual FX)
VP/Creative Director: Gary Lister
Director of Business Development: Bruce Greenberg

Subtext Studio   **(323) 550-8190**
2451 Colorado Blvd., Ste. 2   **www.subtextstudio.com**
Los Angeles, CA 90041
(2D Animation, 3D Animation, 3D Modeling, Animatics, Blue
Screen Compositing, Broadcast Design, CGI, Compositing,
Computer Animation, Digital FX, Editorial, Graphic Design,
Green Screen Compositing, Live Action Integration, Motion
Graphics, Visual FX & Visual FX Supervision)
Executive Producer: Kirk Cameron

SunnyBoy Entertainment   **(626) 356-9020**
230 E. Union St.   FAX **(626) 356-9022**
Pasadena, CA 91101 **www.sunnyboyentertainment.com**
(2D Animation, 3D Animation, 3D Modeling, Animatics,
Broadcast Design, CGI, Character Animation, Character
Design, Compositing, Computer Animation, Digital FX, Editorial,
Graphic Design, Green Screen Compositing, Illustrative Design,
Live Action Integration, Motion Graphics, Previsualizations,
Rotoscoping, Storyboards & Visual FX)

Super 78   **(323) 663-7878**
2894 Rowena Ave.   FAX **(323) 663-7800**
Los Angeles, CA 90039   **www.super78.com**
(2D/3D Animation and FX, Character Animation,
Compositing & Editorial)

          (310) 310-8383
Svengali FX   **(310) 709-2836**
228 Main St., Ste. 1   FAX **(310) 943-1833**
Venice, CA 90291   **www.svengali-fx.com**
(2D/3D Animation and FX, 3D Modeling, Animatics, Blue/
Green Screen Facilities, Compositing, Digital Matte Painting,
Model/Miature Shoots, Pre-Production Planning, Rotoscoping,
Ultimatte & Visual FX)

          (888) 577-4045
Synthespian Studios   **(413) 458-0202**
3050 Runyon Canyon Rd.   **www.synthespians.net**
Los Angeles, CA 90046
(2D Paint, CGI, Character Animation, Character Design,
Compositing, Computer Animation, Digital FX, Green Screen
Compositing, Live Action Integration, Morphing, Stereoscopic
3D, Visual FX & Visual FX Supervision)
President: Diana Walczak
Directors: Jeff Kleiser & Diana Walczak

TeamWorks Digital   **(310) 991-5442**
          www.teamworksdigital.com
(2D/3D Animation and FX, 2D Paint, 3D Modeling, Animatics,
Blue/Green Screen Facilities, Character Animation,
Compositing, Morphing, Pre-Production Planning, Rotoscoping,
Ultimatte & Visual FX)

Technicolor Creative
Services - Hollywood   **(323) 817-6600**
6040 Sunset Blvd.   **www.technicolor.com**
Hollywood, CA 90028
(2D/3D Computer Animation, Compositing &
Live Action Integration)
Contact: Jennifer Tellefsen

The Third Floor Previs Studios   **(323) 931-6633**
5410 Wilshire Blvd., Ste. 1000   FAX **(323) 931-9928**
Los Angeles, CA 90036   **www.thethirdfloorinc.com**
(3D Animation, 3D Modeling, CGI, Character Animation,
Compositing, Computer Animation, Motion Capture,
Previsualizations & Virtual Production)

Tigar Hare Studios (818) 907-6663
4485 Matilija Ave. FAX (818) 907-0693
Sherman Oaks, CA 91423 www.tigarhare.com
(3D Computer Animation, Animatics, Blue Screen Compositing,
Broadcast Design, CGI, Character Animation, Compositing,
Digital FX, Editorial, Green Screen Compositing, Matte
Painting, Motion Capture, Motion Graphics, Previsualizations,
Rotoscoping, Stereoscopic 3D, Storyboards, Visual FX &
Visual FX Supervision)
Executive Producer: Rhonda Cox
Creative Directors/Visual FX Supervisors: Dave Hare &
Michael Tigar

Toon Makers, Inc. (818) 832-8666
17333 Ludlow St. www.toonmakers.com
Granada Hills, CA 91344
(Cel Animation, CGI & Character Design)
Producer: Rocky Solotoff

Trance (323) 651-1114
449 N. Edinburgh Ave. www.trancedesigns.com
Los Angeles, CA 90048

Trans FX, Inc. (805) 485-6110
2361 Eastman Ave. FAX (805) 751-0149
Oxnard, CA 93030 www.transfx.com
(Scanning)

Transcontinuity Studios, Inc. (818) 980-8852
4710 W. Magnolia Blvd. FAX (818) 980-8974
Burbank, CA 91505 www.nealadamsentertainment.com
President/Creative Director: Neal Adams
VP/Executive Producer: Marilyn Adams
Head of Sales: Eric Knight

Ultimatte-Rentals.com (323) 512-1542
www.ultimatte-rentals.com
(Blue Screen Compositing, Compositing, Digital FX, Green
Screen Compositing, Previsualizations, TriCaster Streaming,
TriCaster Virtual Sets, Ultimatte & Visual FX)

Van Guard Animation (310) 360-8039
8703 W. Olympic Blvd. FAX (310) 360-8059
Los Angeles, CA 90035 www.vanguardanimation.com
(2D/3D Computer Animation, Compositing, Digital and Visual
FX & Visual FX Supervision)

Velocity Visuals, Inc. (310) 376-7870
www.velocityfx.com
(2D Animation, 3D Animation, 3D Modeling, Animatics, Blue
Screen Compositing, CGI, Character Animation, Character
Design, Computer Animation, Digital FX, Digital Matte
Painting, Green Screen Compositing, Live Action Integration,
Matte Painting, Pre-Production Planning, Previsualizations,
Rotoscoping, Visual FX & Visual FX Supervision)
Executive Producer/Creative Director: William Powloski
Computer Animation Director: Steward Burris

View Studio, Inc. (805) 745-8814
385 Toro Canyon Rd. www.viewstudio.com
Carpinteria, CA 93013
(2D/3D Computer Animation and Graphics, Compositing, Visual
FX & Visual FX Supervision)
President/Creative Director: Bob Engelsiepen

Virtualsets.com (323) 512-1542
www.virtualsets.com
(Blue Screen Compositing, Compositing, Green Screen
Compositing, TriCaster and Streaming, Ultimatte &
Virtual Set Design)

(805) 991-9866
Vital Distraction, LLC (888) 339-4927
2045 Royal Ave., Ste. 234 FAX (805) 991-9866
Simi Valley, CA 93065 www.vitaldistraction.com
(2D/3D Animation, 3D Modeling, Animatics, CGI, Character
Animation, Computer Animation, Digital FX, Digital Matte
Painting, Live Action Integration, Pre-Production Planning,
Previsualizations & Visual FX)

Wicked Liquid FX (949) 250-8786
20342 SW Acacia St., Ste. 210 FAX (949) 250-8701
Newport Beach, CA 92660 www.wickedliquidfx.com
(2D Paint, 2D/3D Animation and FX, 3D Modeling, Animatics,
Character Animation, Compositing, Digital Matte Painting,
Morphing, Motion Capture, Pre-Production Planning,
Ultimatte & Visual FX)

Wut It Is (323) 467-3300
6121 Santa Monica Blvd., Ste. 201 FAX (323) 467-7480
Los Angeles, CA 90038 www.wutitis.com
(2D Animation, 2D Paint, 3D Animation, 3D Modeling, Blue
Screen Compositing, Broadacst Design, Cel Animation,
CGI, Character Animation, Character Design, Compositing,
Computer Animation, Digital FX, Digital Ink, Digital Paint,
Editorial, Graphic Design, Green Screen Compositing,
Illustrative Design, Image Processing, Live Action Integration,
Matte Painting, Morphing, Motion Graphics, Rotoscoping, Stop-
Motion Animation, Ultimatte, Visual FX & Visual FX Supervision)

yU+co. (323) 606-5050
941 N. Mansfield Ave. FAX (323) 606-5040
Los Angeles, CA 90038 www.yuco.com
(2D/3D Computer Animation, Broadcast Design, Digital and
Visual FX, Logo and Type Design & Motion Graphics)

Zak/Paperno (323) 937-2517
7000 Beverly Blvd.
Los Angeles, CA 90036
(Computer Graphics, FX Animation, Image Processing &
Storyboards)
Executive Producer/Creative Director: Michael Zak
Creative Director: Lisa Paperno

Zoic, Inc. (310) 838-0770
3582 Eastham Dr. FAX (310) 838-1169
Culver City, CA 90232 www.zoicstudios.com
(2D/3D Animation and FX, 3D Modeling, Animatics, Character
Animation, Compositing, Digital Matte Painting, Morphing, Pre-
Production Planning, Rotoscoping & Visual FX)

The Zoofx (818) 535-4025
5115 Douglas Fir Rd., Ste. H FAX (818) 222-9483
Calabasas, CA 91302 www.thezoofx.com

Blue Room Post   (310) 727-2600
1600 Rosecrans Ave., Bldg. 5A   FAX (310) 727-2601
Manhattan Beach, CA 90266   **www.blueroompost.com**

Brewster Parsons   (310) 736-1663
1117 Abbot Kinney Blvd.   FAX (310) 396-3299
Venice, CA 90291   **www.brewsterparsons.com**

      (323) 785-1550
Chainsaw   (323) 785-1555
940 N. Orange Dr., Second Fl.   **www.chainsawedit.com**
Hollywood, CA 90038

Company 3 LA   (310) 255-6600
1661 Lincoln Blvd., Ste. 400   FAX (310) 255-6602
Santa Monica, CA 90404   **www.company3.com**

Digital Jungle Post Production   (323) 962-0867
6363 Santa Monica Blvd.   FAX (323) 962-9960
Los Angeles, CA 90038   **www.digijungle.com**

Encore Hollywood   (323) 466-7663
6344 Fountain Ave.   FAX (323) 467-5539
Hollywood, CA 90028   **www.encorehollywood.com**

      (818) 846-3101
FotoKem   (818) 846-3102
2801 W. Alameda Ave.   FAX (818) 841-2130
Burbank, CA 91505   **www.fotokem.com**

Gradient Effects   (310) 821-3177
4120 Del Rey Ave.   FAX (310) 821-0584
Marina del Rey, CA 90292   **www.gradientfx.com**

Hip Films   (323) 467-2897
1622 Gower St.   FAX (323) 469-8251
Hollywood, CA 90028   **www.hipfilms.com**

Hollywood-DI   (323) 850-3550
1041 N. Formosa Ave.,   FAX (323) 850-3551
Fairbanks Bldg., Ste. 7   **www.hollywooddi.com**
West Hollywood, CA 90046

      (323) 969-8822
HTV - High Technology Video   (818) 760-7600
3575 Cahuenga Blvd. West, Fourth Fl. FAX (323) 969-8860
Los Angeles, CA 90068   **www.htvinc.net**

Illuminate –
Arts, Media & Entertainment   (323) 969-8822
3575 Cahuenga Blvd. West, Fourth Fl. FAX (323) 969-8840
Los Angeles, CA 90068   **www.illuminatehollywood.com**

iProbe Multilingual Solutions, Inc.   (888) 489-6035
     www.iprobesolutions.com

Laser Pacific Media Corporation   (323) 462-6266
809 N. Cahuenga Blvd.   FAX (323) 464-3233
Hollywood, CA 90038   **www.laserpacific.com**

Light Iron   (323) 472-8300
6381 De Longpre Ave.   FAX (323) 832-8432
Los Angeles, CA 90028   **www.lightiron.com**

      (818) 662-0300
Mechnology   (661) 714-2604
121 W. Lexington Dr., Ste. B101   **www.mechnology.com**
Glendale, CA 91203

New Hat   (310) 401-2220
1819 Colorado Ave.   FAX (310) 401-2224
Santa Monica, CA 90404   **www.newhat.tv**

Oasis Imagery   (323) 469-9800
6500 Sunset Blvd.   FAX (323) 462-4620
Hollywood, CA 90028   **www.oasisimagery.com**

STEELE Studios   (310) 656-7770
5737 Mesmer Ave.   FAX (310) 391-9055
Culver City, CA 90230   **www.steelevfx.com**

Technicolor Creative
Services - Hollywood   (323) 817-6600
6040 Sunset Blvd.   **www.technicolor.com**
Hollywood, CA 90028

Acutrack (888) 234-3472
FAX (925) 579-5001
www.acutrack.com

Affordable Sound Stages (818) 563-3456
1708 Hale St. www.affordablesoundstages.com
Glendale, CA 91201
(Video Tape Recycling and Evaluating)

AGF Media Services (818) 780-7400
(323) 467-1234
14932 Delano St. FAX (818) 904-9905
Van Nuys, CA 91411 www.agfmedia.com
(All Formats)

Antarctica Productions (925) 899-8909
5027 Colfax Ave., Studio 5
Valley Village, CA 91607
www.antarcticaproductions.com

Archetype DVD (310) 613-6654
www.archetypedvd.com

Bitmax, LLC (323) 978-7878
6255 Sunset Blvd., Ste. 1515 FAX (323) 978-7879
Los Angeles, CA 90028 www.bitmax.net
(All Formats, DVD, DVDR & Standards Conversion)

Clonetown HD (323) 850-6608
(323) 851-0299
3131 Cahuenga Blvd. West FAX (323) 851-0277
Los Angeles, CA 90068 www.clonetownhd.com
(¾", 1", 8mm, Beta SP & SX, Betacam SP, CD-Audio, CD-ROM, Composer Dubs, D2, Digibeta, DV, DVCAM, DVC Pro, HDCAM, HDCAM SR, HDV, Hi-8mm, High Def, NTSC, Standards Conversions & VHS)

Complete Media Services (310) 306-5074
4240 Via Marina, Ste. 16 FAX (310) 306-5124
Marina del Rey, CA 90292
(All Formats, CD-ROM & DVD)

Copy Right Video (818) 786-3000
14932 Delano St. FAX (818) 786-3007
Van Nuys, CA 91411 www.copyrightvideo.com
(All Formats)

Custom Video (310) 543-4901
707 Torrance Blvd., Ste. 105 www.customvideo.tv
Redondo Beach, CA 90277
(¾", ¾" SP, 8mm, All Formats, Beta SP, Betacam SP, Blu Ray, CD-Audio, CD-ROM, DV, DVCAM, DVD, DVD-5, DVD-9, DVD-R, Hi-8mm, HD D5, High Def, Laserdisc, NTSC, Standards Conversions, Super 8, S-VHS, Tape Cloning & VHS)

Deck Hand, Inc. (818) 557-8403
1905 Victory Blvd., Ste. 8 FAX (818) 557-8406
Glendale, CA 91201 www.deckhand.com
(All Video Formats, Beta SP, Digital Betacam, DV, DV-5, DVCAM, DVCPRO, DVCPRO HD, DVD-R, HDCAM & HDV)

Disc Makers (800) 731-8009
(323) 876-1411
3445 Cahuenga Blvd. West FAX (323) 876-6724
Los Angeles, CA 90068 www.discmakers.com

Dubscape, Inc. (818) 456-1051
7543 Loma Verde Ave. FAX (818) 456-1046
Canoga Park, CA 91303 www.dubscape.com
(1", 1/2", 3/4", Beta SP, Digibeta, Digital Betacam, D2, DV & DVCAM)

Duplitech Corporation (310) 781-1101
2639 Manhattan Beach Blvd., Ste. A FAX (310) 781-1109
Redondo Beach, CA 90278 www.duplitech.com
(Blu Ray, CD, DVD & DVD-R)

DVD-IT Media Consulting (818) 985-9570
(888) 993-8248
11031 Tiara St. FAX (866) 467-3145
North Hollywood, CA 91601 www.dvd-replication.com
(CD-ROM, DVD, DVD-R & VHS)

The Edit Bay (714) 978-7878
571 N. Poplar St., Ste. I FAX (714) 978-7858
Orange, CA 92868 www.theeditbay.com
(3/4", 1", 8mm, Betacam SP, CD-ROM, Digital Betacam, DVD, Standards Conversion, S-VHS & VHS)

Filmcore Distribution/Vault Services (818) 526-3700
2130 N. Hollywood Way FAX (818) 526-3701
Burbank, CA 91505 www.filmcore.net
(1", 1/2", 3/4", Beta, Beta SP, D1, D2 & Digibeta)

Flow Motion, Inc. (888) 818-3569
20 N. Aviador St., Ste. B FAX (888) 818-3569
Camarillo, CA 93010 www.flowmotioninc.com
(CD-Audio, CD-ROM, DVD, DVD-5, DVD-9, DVD-R, Blu Ray, DVCAM & DV)

Hellman Production, Inc. (323) 456-0446
6404 Wilshire Blvd., Ste. 700
Los Angeles, CA 90048 www.hellmanproduction.com

Home Run Software Services, Inc. (714) 901-0109
15562 Chemical Ln. FAX (714) 901-0102
Huntington Beach, CA 92649 www.home-run.com
(All Formats)

Imperial Media Services, Inc. (310) 396-2008
(800) 736-8273
3202 Pennsylvania Ave. FAX (310) 396-8894
Santa Monica, CA 90404 www.imperialmedia.com
(All Formats, Authoring, Duplication, DVD, DVDR, Replication, Standards Conversions, Transfers & VHS)

iProbe Multilingual Solutions, Inc. (888) 489-6035
www.iprobesolutions.com
(¾", ¾" SP, 1", Beta SP, Beta SX, Betacam SP, CD-Audio, CD-ROM, Composer Dubs, D1, D2, D3, D5, Digibeta, Digital Betacam, DV, DVC Pro, DVCAM, DVD, DVD-5, DVD-9, DVD-R, HD D5, HD Digibeta, HD DVC Pro, High Def, Laserdisc, NTSC, Standards Conversions, Super 8, S-VHS & VHS)

JR Media Services, Inc. (818) 557-0200
2501 W. Burbank Blvd., Ste. 200 FAX (818) 557-0201
Burbank, CA 91505 www.jrmediaservices.com

Level 3 Post (818) 840-7200
(818) 840-7889
2901 W. Alameda, Third Fl. www.level3post.com
Burbank, CA 91505

Lightning Media (323) 957-9255
1415 N. Cahuenga Blvd. www.lightningmedia.com
Hollywood, CA 90028
(All Formats, High Def & Standards Conversion)

New & Unique Videos (619) 644-3000
(800) 365-8433
7323 Rondel Court FAX (619) 644-3001
San Diego, CA 92119 www.newuniquevideos.com
(All Video Formats, CD-ROM & DVD)

OneWorld Language Solutions (323) 848-7993
3940 Laurel Canyon Blvd., Ste. 501 FAX (323) 848-7995
Studio City, CA 91604 www.oneworldlanguage.com

Ⓐ The Studios at Paramount (323) 956-3991
The Studios at Paramount
Post Production Services,
5555 Melrose Ave. www.thestudiosatparamount.com
Los Angeles, CA 90038
(All Formats)

Point360 (323) 957-5500
1147 Vine St. FAX **(323) 466-7406**
Hollywood, CA 90038 **www.point360.com**
(All Video Formats)

(818) 569-4949
Point360 (IVC) (866) 968-4336
2777 N. Ontario St. **www.point360.com**
Burbank, CA 91504
(All Video Formats)

Post and Beam (310) 828-1128
1623 Stanford St. **www.postandbeam.tv**
Santa Monica, CA 90404
(All Video Formats, Blu Ray, DVD & HD and SD
Digitizing and Encoding)

Post Digital Services (323) 845-0812
1258 N. Highland Ave., Ste. 210 FAX **(323) 845-0812**
Hollywood, CA 90038 **www.postdigitalservices.com**
(¾", ¾" SP, 1", 2K, 4K, 8mm, 16mm, 35mm, All Formats,
All Video Formats, Beta SP, Beta SX, Blu Ray, CD, Digibeta,
DVD, HD D5, HD Digibeta, HD DVC Pro, Hi-8mm, High Def,
Standards Conversions, Super 8, S-VHS, Tape Cloning & VHS)

Post Media Group, Inc. (310) 289-5959
337 S. Robertson Blvd., Ste. 201
Beverly Hills, CA 90211 **www.postmediagroup.tv**

Post Modern Edit, LLC (949) 608-8700
2941 Alton Pkwy FAX **(949) 608-8729**
Irvine, CA 92606 **www.postmodernedit.com**
(All Video Formats, High Def & Standards Conversions)

Prime Digital Media Services (661) 964-0220
28111 Avenue Stanford FAX **(661) 964-0550**
Valencia, CA 91355 **www.primedigital.com**

(310) 451-0333
Santa Monica Video, Inc. (800) 843-3827
1505 11th St. FAX **(310) 458-3350**
Santa Monica, CA 90401 **www.smvcompletemedia.com**
(All Formats)

SpeedMedia (310) 822-8182
200 Mildred Ave. FAX **(310) 822-8923**
Venice, CA 90291 **www.speedmedia.com**
(3/4" SP, 1", 8mm, All Formats, All Video Formats, Beta
SP, Beta SX, Betacam SP, Blu Ray, CD-Audio, CD-ROM,
Composer Dubs, D1, D2, D3, D5, Digibeta, Digital Betacam,
DV, DVC Pro, DVCAM, DVD, DVD-5, DVD-9, DVD-R,
HDD5, HD Digibeta, HD DVC Pro, Hi-8mm, High Def, NTSC,
Standards Conversion, S-VHS, Super 8, Tape Cloning & VHS)

**Technicolor Creative
Services - Glendale** (818) 500-9090
1631 Gardena Ave. FAX **(818) 500-4099**
Glendale, CA 91204 **www.technicolor.com**
(1", 1/2", 3/4", 3/4" SP, Beta SP, Beta SX, CD-Audio, Composer
Dubs, D1, D2, D3, D5, DVCAM, DVD, DVD-5, DVD-9,
DVD-R, Digibeta/Digital Betacam, Motion Vector, Standards
Conversions, S-VHS & VHS)

TEDS (310) 237-6438
(All Formats & Standards Conversion) **www.tedsla.com**

Timecode Multimedia (310) 826-9199
12340 Santa Monica Blvd., Ste. 230
West Los Angeles, CA 90025
www.timecodemultimedia.com
(All Video Formats, Beta SP, Beta SX, CD-Audio, Composer
Dubs, Digibeta, DV, DVC Pro, DVCAM, DVCPro, DVD, HD D5,
High Def, NTSC, Standards Conversions, Tape Cloning & VHS)

Tylie Jones & Associates, Inc. (818) 955-7600
58 E. Santa Anita Ave. FAX **(818) 955-8551**
Burbank, CA 91502 **www.tylie.com**
(1", 1/2", 3/4", Beta, Beta SP, CD-Audio, CD-ROM, D1, D2, D3,
D5, Digibeta, DVC Pro, DVD, HD D5, HD DVC Pro & High Def)

VFX Technologies (310) 593-4848
3916 Sepulveda Blvd. **www.vfxtechnologies.com**
Culver City, CA 90230
(CD-ROM & DVD)

Victory Studios LA (818) 769-1776
10911 Riverside Dr., Ste. 100 FAX **(818) 760-1280**
North Hollywood, CA 91602 **www.victorystudiosla.com**
(3/4" SP, Betacam SP, CD-ROM, Digibeta, DV, DVC Pro, DVD,
HD DVC Pro, Standards Conversions, S-VHS & VHS)

(310) 979-3500
Westside Media Group (818) 779-8600
12233 W. Olympic Blvd., Ste. 152 **www.wmgmedia.com**
West Los Angeles, CA 90064
(¾", ¾" SP, 1", 8mm, All Formats, All Video Formats, Beta
SP, Beta SX, Betacam SP, Blu Ray, CD-Audio, CD-ROM,
Composer Dubs, D2, D5, Digibeta, Digital Betacam, DV,
DVC Pro, DVCAM, DVD, DVD-5, DVD-9, DVD-R, HD D5, HD
Digibeta, HD DVC Pro, Hi-8mm, High Def, Laserdisc, NTSC,
Standards Conversions, Super 8, S-VHS, Tape Cloning & VHS)

(310) 659-5959
World of Video & Audio (WOVA) (866) 900-3827
8717 Wilshire Blvd. FAX **(310) 659-8247**
Beverly Hills, CA 90211 **www.wova.com**
(8mm, All Formats, Betacam SP, CD-Audio, Digibeta, Digital
Betacam, Digital Services, DVCPro, DVCAM, DVD, HD DVC
Pro, HDCam, High Def, Film, Standards Conversions,
Super 8 & Tape Cloning)

Acutrack	**(888) 234-3472**
	FAX **(925) 579-5001**
	www.acutrack.com

Beat Music Library	**(310) 828-2292**
7806 Denrock Ave.	**www.beatmusiclibrary.com**
Los Angeles, CA 90045	

Bitmax, LLC	**(323) 978-7878**
6255 Sunset Blvd., Ste. 1515	FAX **(323) 978-7879**
Los Angeles, CA 90028	**www.bitmax.net**

Blue Room Post	**(310) 727-2600**
Raleigh Manhattan Beach Studios,	FAX **(310) 727-2601**
1600 Rosecrans Ave., Bldg. 5A	**www.blueroompost.com**
Manhattan Beach, CA 90266	

Cinevision Digital	**(213) 617-7200**
424 Bamboo Ln.	FAX **(213) 617-7300**
Los Angeles, CA 90012	**www.cinevisiondigital.com**

	(323) 850-6608
Clonetown HD	**(323) 851-0299**
3131 Cahuenga Blvd. West	FAX **(323) 851-0277**
Los Angeles, CA 90068	**www.clonetownhd.com**

	(310) 839-5400
Cloud 19	**(310) 717-7819**
3767 Overland Ave., Ste. 103	FAX **(310) 839-5404**
Los Angeles, CA 90034	**www.cloud19.com**

Complete Media Services	**(310) 306-5074**
4240 Via Marina, Ste. 16	FAX **(310) 306-5124**
Marina del Rey, CA 90292	
(Replication)	

Copy Right Video	**(818) 786-3000**
14932 Delano St.	FAX **(818) 786-3007**
Van Nuys, CA 91411	**www.copyrightvideo.com**

	(323) 860-1300
Crest National	**(800) 961-8273**
1000 Highland Ave.	FAX **(323) 461-2598**
Hollywood, CA 90038	**www.crestdigital.com**

Custom Video	**(310) 543-4901**
707 Torrance Blvd., Ste. 105	
Redondo Beach, CA 90277	www.customvideodiscs.com

	(800) 731-8009
Disc Makers	**(323) 876-1411**
3445 Cahuenga Blvd. West	FAX **(323) 876-6724**
Los Angeles, CA 90068	**www.discmakers.com**

Dogma Studios	**(310) 838-2973**
10559 Jefferson Blvd.	FAX **(310) 356-3603**
Culver City, CA 90232	**www.dogmastudios.com**

drotardesign.com	**(310) 399-5700**
236 Main St.	**www.drotardesign.com**
Venice, CA 90291	
(Authoring)	

Duplitech Corporation	**(310) 781-1101**
2639 Manhattan Beach Blvd., Ste. A	FAX **(310) 781-1109**
Redondo Beach, CA 90278	**www.duplitech.com**

	(818) 985-9570
DVD-IT Media Consulting	**(888) 993-8248**
11031 Tiara St.	FAX **(866) 467-3145**
North Hollywood, CA 91601	**www.dvd-replication.com**
(Replication)	

Flow Motion, Inc.	**(888) 818-3569**
20 N. Aviador, Ste. B	FAX **(888) 818-3569**
Camarillo, CA 93010	**www.flowmotioninc.com**
(Authoring Only, Blu-Ray & Rentals)	

FXF Productions, Inc.	**(310) 577-5009**
1024 Harding Ave., Ste. 201	FAX **(310) 577-1960**
Venice, CA 90291	**www.fxfproductions.com**

Hellman Production, Inc.	**(323) 456-0446**
6404 Wilshire Blvd., Ste. 700	
Los Angeles, CA 90048	**www.hellmanproduction.com**

Illusion Factory	**(818) 598-8400**
21800 Burbank Blvd., Ste. 225	**www.illusionfactory.com**
Woodland Hills, CA 91367	

	(310) 396-2008
Imperial Media Services, Inc.	**(800) 736-8273**
3202 Pennsylvania Ave.	FAX **(310) 396-8894**
Santa Monica, CA 90404	**www.imperialmedia.com**

JR Media Services, Inc.	**(818) 557-0200**
2501 W. Burbank Blvd., Ste. 200	FAX **(818) 557-0201**
Burbank, CA 91505	**www.jrmediaservices.com**

Kappa Studios, Inc.	**(818) 843-3400**
3619 W. Magnolia Blvd.	FAX **(818) 559-5684**
Burbank, CA 91505	**www.kappastudios.com**

Lightning Media	**(323) 957-9255**
1415 N. Cahuenga Blvd.	**www.lightningmedia.com**
Hollywood, CA 90028	

	(323) 466-6655
LightSoundImagination	**(310) 497-9456**
(Authoring)	**www.lightsoundimagination.com**

	(310) 396-4663
Mind Over Eye, LLC	**(310) 968-4259**
1639 11th St., Ste. 117	FAX **(310) 396-0663**
Santa Monica, CA 90404	**www.mindovereye.com**

	(619) 644-3000
New & Unique Videos	**(800) 365-8433**
7323 Rondel Court	FAX **(619) 644-3001**
San Diego, CA 92119	**www.newuniquevideos.com**

OneWorld Language Solutions	**(323) 848-7993**
3940 Laurel Canyon Blvd., Ste. 501	FAX **(323) 848-7995**
Studio City, CA 91604	**www.oneworldlanguage.com**

Ⓐ The Studios at Paramount	**(323) 956-3991**
The Studios at Paramount	
Post Production Services	
5555 Melrose Ave.	**www.thestudiosatparamount.com**
Los Angeles, CA 90038	

Post and Beam	**(310) 828-1128**
1623 Stanford St.	**www.postandbeam.tv**
Santa Monica, CA 90404	

Post Digital Services	**(323) 845-0812**
1258 N. Highland Ave., Ste. 210	FAX **(323) 845-0812**
Hollywood, CA 90038	**www.postdigitalservices.com**
(Authoring, Blu-Ray & Replication)	

Post Modern Digital, LLC	**(949) 608-8700**
2941 Alton Pkwy	FAX **(949) 608-8760**
Irvine, CA 92606	**www.postmoderndigital.com**
(Authoring & Replication)	

Precision Productions + Post	**(310) 839-4600**
10718 McCune Ave.	FAX **(310) 839-4601**
Los Angeles, CA 90034	**www.precisionpost.com**

Prime Digital Media Services	**(661) 964-0220**
28111 Avenue Stanford	FAX **(661) 964-0550**
Valencia, CA 91355	**www.primedigital.com**

Santa Monica Video, Inc.	**(310) 451-0333**
1505 11th St.	FAX **(310) 458-3350**
Santa Monica, CA 90401	www.smvcompletemedia.com

Station 22 Edit & Effects   **(310) 488-7726**
3614 Overland Ave.   **www.station22.com**
Los Angeles, CA 90034

Technicolor Creative Services   **(818) 260-1200**
2233 N. Ontario St., Ste. 300   FAX **(818) 260-1201**
Burbank, CA 91504   **www.technicolor.com**
(Authoring)

Timecode Multimedia   **(310) 826-9199**
12340 Santa Monica Blvd., Ste. 230
West Los Angeles, CA 90025
(Authoring)   **www.timecodemultimedia.com**

Transistor Studios   **(310) 613-3090**
(Authoring)   **www.transistorstudios.com**

VFX Technologies   **(310) 593-4848**
3916 Sepulveda Blvd.   **www.vfxtechnologies.com**
Culver City, CA 90230

Video Symphony   **(800) 871-2843**
266 E. Magnolia Blvd.   FAX **(818) 845-1951**
Burbank, CA 91502   **www.videosymphony.com**
(Authoring)

           (626) 633-0883
Viking Video Cassettes, Inc.   **(818) 262-8250**
5620 Ayala Ave.   FAX **(626) 633-0884**
Irwindale, CA 91706   **www.myvikingvideo.com**
(Replication)

           (310) 979-3500
Westside Media Group   **(818) 779-8600**
12233 W. Olympic Blvd., Ste. 152   **www.wmgmedia.com**
West Los Angeles, CA 90064

           (310) 659-5959
World of Video & Audio (WOVA)   **(866) 900-3827**
8717 Wilshire Blvd.   FAX **(310) 659-8247**
Beverly Hills, CA 90211   **www.wova.com**

Zoo Digital   **(310) 220-3939**
2201 Park Pl., Ste. 100   FAX **(310) 220-3958**
El Segundo, CA 90245   **www.zoodigital.com**
(Authoring)

A Frame (818) 339-7390
www.aframepost.net
(24P Editing Systems, 35mm, Analog, Analog Decks, Avid Systems, Digibeta, Digital Decks, Digital Editing Systems, Digital Non-Linear, Editing Suites, Editing Supplies, Fiber, Film, Final Cut Pro Systems, Hard Drive Rentals, HD Decks, High Def, Linear Offline, Linear Online, Macintosh-Based Non-Linear Offline, Magnetic Hard Drives, Monitors, Non-Linear Hard Drives, Non-Linear Offline, Non-Linear Online, Video, Video Tape Monitors & Video Tape Recorders)

Aaron & Le Duc (310) 452-2034
www.leducdesign.com
(High Def & Non-Linear Offline and Online)

Absolute Rentals (818) 842-2828
2633 N. San Fernando Blvd. FAX (818) 842-8815
Burbank, CA 91504 www.absoluterentals.com
(24P Editing Systems, Analog Decks, Audio Edit Rooms, Avid Systems, Digibeta, Digital Decks, Digital Editing Systems, Editing Suites, Final Cut Pro Systems, Hard Drive Rentals, HD Decks, HD Video Decks, Monitors, Non-Linear Hard Drives, Non-Linear Offline, Pro Tools Edit Systems, Re-Recording Mix Stage & Video Tape Recorders)

Alternative Rentals (310) 204-3388
5805 W. Jefferson Blvd. FAX (310) 204-3384
Los Angeles, CA 90016 www.alternativerentals.com
(24P Editing Systems, AVID, Final Cut Pro & HD Online)

Artistic Resources Corporation (323) 965-5200
535 N. Brand Blvd., Ste. 235 FAX (323) 965-5209
Glendale, CA 91203 www.artisticresources.com

Atomic Post (310) 922-2167
3025 W. Olympic Blvd., Ste. 124 www.atomicpost.us
Santa Monica, CA 90404

Audio Video Systems International (818) 888-7625
5101 Tendilla Ave. FAX (818) 888-9862
Woodland Hills, CA 91364
www.provideoequipment.com
(Linear/Non-Linear Offline & Online Rentals)

Avid (818) 557-2520
(800) 949-2843
101 S. First St., Ste. 200 FAX (818) 557-2558
Burbank, CA 91502 www.avid.com
(Digital Non-Linear Offline and Online)

B2 Services, Inc. (818) 566-8769
2312 W. Burbank Blvd. FAX (818) 566-1378
Burbank, CA 91506 www.b2services-inc.com
(24P Editing Systems, Analog Decks, Avid Systems, Digibeta, Digital Decks, Digital Editing Systems, Digital Non-Linear, Final Cut Pro Systems, Hard Drive Rentals, HD Decks, High Def, MacIntosh-Based Non-Linear Offline, Magnetic Hard Drive Monitors, Non-lInear Hard Drives, Non-Linear Offline and Online, Rentals Only & Video Tape Monitors and Recorders)

Big Time Picture Company, Inc. (310) 207-0921
1629 Stanford St. FAX (310) 826-0071
Santa Monica, CA 90404 www.bigtimepic.com
(Avid Systems, Digibeta, Digital Decks, Digital Editing Systems, Digital Non-Linear, Editing Suites, Final Cut Pro Systems, Hard Drive Rentals, High Def, Macintosh-Based Non-Linear Offline, Monitors & Non-Linear Offline)

Broadcast Store (818) 998-9100
9420 Lurline Ave., Ste. C FAX (818) 998-9106
Chatsworth, CA 91311 www.broadcaststore.com
(Video)

Catalyst Post Services (818) 841-4952
3029 W. Burbank Blvd. FAX (818) 566-4175
Burbank, CA 91505 www.catalystpost.com
(Analog Decks, Avid Systems, Digibeta, Digital Editing Systems, Editing Suites, Fiber, Final Cut Pro Systems, Hard Drive Rentals, HD Decks, High Def, Monitors & Non-Linear Offline and Online)

CET Universe (818) 432-4330
801 S. Main St., Ste. 101 FAX (818) 755-7748
Burbank, CA 91506 www.cetuniverse.com

(818) 845-1755
Christy's Editorial (800) 556-5706
3625 W. Pacific Ave. FAX (818) 845-1756
Burbank, CA 91505 www.christys.net
(Editing Supplies)

(800) 427-2382
CRE - Computer & A/V Solutions (888) 444-1059
5732 Buckingham Pkwy FAX (877) 440-5252
Culver City, CA 90230 www.computerrentals.com/
products/Mac/Mac_rentals_Specialist.php
(Hard Drive Rentals, HD Decks, Monitors & Rentals Only)

Deck Hand, Inc. (818) 557-8403
1905 Victory Blvd., Ste. 8 FAX (818) 557-8406
Glendale, CA 91201 www.deckhand.com
(Analog Decks, Digibeta, Digital Decks, HD Decks, HD and SD Video Tape Recorders, High Def, Monitors, Rentals Only, Video Tape Monitors & Video Tape Recorders)

The Digital Difference (310) 581-8800
1201 Olympic Blvd. FAX (310) 581-8808
Santa Monica, CA 90404 www.digdif.com
(Avid, Editing Suites, Final Cut Pro, Non-Linear Offline and Online & Pro Tools)

(949) 215-7151
Digital Systems Media (877) 629-7810
17702 Mitchell North, Ste. 110 FAX (949) 215-6399
Irvine, CA 92614 www.digitalsystemsmedia.com
(Non-Linear Offline and Online)

Digital Vortechs (800) 900-2843
1546 Victory Blvd., Ste. B www.digitalvortechs.com
Glendale, CA 91201

editSource (310) 572-7230
12044 Washington Blvd. FAX (310) 572-7238
Los Angeles, CA 90066 www.theeditsource.com
(24P Editing Systems, Analog Decks, Avid Systems, Digibeta, Digital Decks, Digital Editing Systems, Digital Non-Linear, Editing Suites, Final Cut Pro Systems, Digibeta, HD Decks, High Def, Macintosh-Based Non-Linear Offline, Monitors, Non-Linear Hard Drives, Non-Linear Offline, Non-Linear Online, Video, Video Tape Monitors & Video Tape Recorders)

EPS-Cineworks (818) 766-5000
3753 Cahuenga Blvd. West FAX (818) 623-7547
Studio City, CA 91604
(Non-Linear Offline) www.electricpicturesolutions.com

Entertainment Post (818) 846-0411
639 S. Glenwood Pl. FAX (818) 846-1542
Burbank, CA 91506 www.entpost.com
(Digibeta, Digital Non-Linear Offline and Online, Editing Suites, Hard Drive Rentals & Non-Linear Offline and Online)

Firestarter Rentals (310) 420-5146
880 W. First St., Ste. 513 FAX (866) 450-6716
Los Angeles, CA 90012
(D5 High Def Tape Deck Rentals)

(818) 846-3101
Fotokem Nonlinear Services (800) 368-6536
2801 W. Alameda Ave. www.fotokem.com
Burbank, CA 91505

Global Entertainment Partners/GEP (818) 380-8133
3747 Cahuenga Blvd. West FAX (818) 979-8133
Studio City, CA 91604 www.gepartners.com
(24P Editing Systems, Analog Decks, Avid Systems, Digibeta, Digital Decks, Digital Editing Systems, Digital Non-Linear, Editing Suites, Final Cut Pro Systems, Hard Drive Rentals, HD Decks, High Def, Monitors & Non-Linear Offline)

Go Edit, Inc. — (818) 284-6260
5614 Cahuenga Blvd. — FAX (818) 985-6260
North Hollywood, CA 91601 — www.goedit.tv

Hula Post Production — (818) 954-0200
1111 S. Victory Blvd. — FAX (818) 954-0211
Burbank, CA 91502 — www.hulapost.com
(24P Editing Systems, Analog, Digital and HD Decks, Avid
Systems, Digibeta, Digital Editing Systems, Digital Non-Linear,
Editing Suites, Final Cut Pro, Hard Drive Rentals, High Def,
Linear/Non-Linear Offline and Online, Monitors, Non-Linear
Hard Drive Rentals & Video Tape Recorders & Monitors)

J/KAM Digital — (818) 705-2986 / (818) 753-2923
FAX (818) 705-5475
www.jkamdigital.com
(24P Editing Systems, Avid Systems, Digibeta, Digital Editing
Systems, Digital Non-Linear, Editing Suites, Final Cut Pro
Systems, Hard Drive Rentals, HD Decks, High Def, Linear
Offline, Non-Linear Offline, Non-Linear Online & Rentals Only)

JuRifilm Entertainment, Inc. — (310) 915-9559
4404 Westlawn Ave. — FAX (310) 391-4217
Los Angeles, CA 90066 — www.jurifilm.com
(24P Editing Systems, Avid Systems, Digibeta, Digital Decks,
HD Decks, High Def & Non-Linear Offline and Online)

Kasdin Productions — (310) 914-4847
www.kasdin.com
(Digibeta, Digital Non-Linear Offline and Online &
Hard Drive Rentals)

Key Code Media, Inc. — (818) 303-3900
270 S. Flower St. — FAX (818) 303-3901
Burbank, CA 91502 — www.keycodemedia.com
(Non-Linear Offline and Online)

LA Digital Post, Inc. — (310) 954-8650 / (818) 487-5000
2260 Centinela Ave. — FAX (310) 954-8686
West Los Angeles, CA 90064 — www.ladigital.com
(Avid Systems, Digital Decks, Digital Editing Systems, Digital
Non-Linear Offline and Online, Editing Suites, Final Cut Pro
Systems, HD Decks, Linear/Non-Linear Offline and Online &
Non-Linear Hard Drives)

LA Digital Post, Inc. — (818) 487-5000 / (310) 954-8650
11311 Camarillo St. — FAX (818) 487-5015
Toluca Lake, CA 91602 — www.ladigital.com
(Avid Systems, Digital Decks, Digital Editing Systems, Digital
Non-Linear Offline and Online, Editing Suites, Final Cut Pro
Systems, HD Decks, Linear/Non-Linear Offline and Online &
Non-Linear Hard Drives)

Laurel Canyon Productions — (818) 459-6630 / (310) 738-4184
FAX (818) 450-0916
www.lcproductions.tv
(24P Editing Systems, Analog, Analog Decks, Avid Systems,
Digibeta, Digital Decks, Digital Editing Systems, Digital Non-
Linear, Editing Suites, Fiber, HD Decks, High Def, Non-Linear
Offline, Non-Linear Online & Video Tape Recorders)

LJK Consult, LLC — (323) 896-7541
FAX (323) 655-0549
www.ljkconsult.com

M.G. Digital, Inc. — (310) 558-3907 / (310) 558-3424
8549 Higuera St., Ste. 101 — FAX (310) 559-7800
Culver City, CA 90232 — www.mgdigital.us

Midtown Edit — (323) 782-7900 / (323) 801-2300
8489 W. Third St. — FAX (323) 651-1240
Los Angeles, CA 90048 — www.midtownedit.com
(Avid and Final Cut Pro, Decks, Editing Suites &
Storage Rentals)

Moviola/J & R Film Company — (323) 467-1116 / (800) 468-3107
1135 N. Mansfield Ave. — FAX (323) 464-1518
Hollywood, CA 90038 — www.moviola.com

Ⓐ **The Studios at Paramount**
Post Production Services — (323) 956-3991
5555 Melrose Ave. — www.thestudiosatparamount.com
Los Angeles, CA 90038
(24P Editing Systems, 35mm, Analog, Analog Decks, Avid
Systems, Digibeta, Digital Decks, Digital Editing Systems,
Digital Non-Linear, Editing Suites, Fiber, Film, Linear/Non-
Linear Offline and Online, Macintosh-Based Non-Linear Offline,
Magnetic Hard Drives, Monitors, Non-Linear Hard Drives, Video
Tape Monitors & Video Tape Recorders)

Pivotal Post — (818) 760-6000 / (818) 760-6007
4142 Lankershim Blvd. — FAX (818) 760-6012
North Hollywood, CA 91602 — www.pivotalpost.com

Planet Post — (619) 723-6690 / (619) 435-0888
(Non-Linear Online) — www.planetpost.net

Post Media Group, Inc. — (310) 289-5959
337 S. Robertson Blvd., Ste. 201 www.postmediagroup.tv
Beverly Hills, CA 90211

Post-Op Video, Inc. — (818) 840-9100
126 E. Alameda Ave., Ste. 101 — www.postop.com
Burbank, CA 91502
(Fiber, Final Cut Pro Systems, Non-Linear Editing Systems and
Components & Non-Linear Hard Drives)

Precision Productions + Post — (310) 839-4600
10718 McCune Ave. — FAX (310) 839-4601
Los Angeles, CA 90034 — www.precisionpost.com
(Non-Linear Offline and Online)

Promax Systems, Inc. — (949) 727-3977 / (800) 977-6629
18241 McDurmott West, Ste. A — FAX (949) 727-3546
Irvine, CA 92614 — www.promax.com

QSR Systems — (323) 200-2155 / (661) 294-3999
FAX (661) 257-6380
www.qsrsystems.com
(Analog, Digital and HD Decks, Avid Systems, Digibeta, Digital
Non-Linear, Final Cut Pro Systems, Hard Drive Rentals,
Macintosh-Based Non-Linear Offline, Non-Linear Offline and
Online, Non-Linear Hard Drives & Video)

Runway — (310) 636-2000
1415 N. Cahuenga Blvd. — FAX (310) 636-2034
Los Angeles, CA 90028 — www.runway.com
(Non-Linear Offline and Online)

Sim Video Los Angeles — (323) 978-9000
738 Cahuenga Blvd. — FAX (323) 978-9018
Hollywood, CA 90038 — www.simvideola.com
(Non-Linear Offline and Online)

Sonnet Technologies, Inc. — (949) 587-3500
Eight Autry — FAX (949) 457-6349
Irvine, CA 92618 — www.sonnettech.com

TV Magic, Inc. — (818) 841-6886
107 W. Valencia Ave. — www.tvmagic.tv
Burbank, CA 91502

TV Pro Gear — (818) 246-7100 / (877) 887-7643
1630 Flower St. — FAX (818) 246-1945
Glendale, CA 91201 — www.tvprogear.com
(Editing Suites, Fiber, Final Cut Pro Systems, HD Decks, Mobile
Video, Rentals & Sales)

Universal Studios
Editorial Facilities   (818) 777-4728
100 Universal City Plaza   FAX (818) 733-4290
Bldg. 2282, Ste. 154   **www.filmmakersdestination.com**
Universal City, CA 91608
(35mm, Avid Systems, Digital Editing Systems, Editing Suites,
Final Cut Pro Systems, High Def, Macintosh-Based Non-Linear
Offline & Non-Linear Offline)

                                                    (818) 956-1444
Video Equipment Rentals   (800) 794-1407
912 Ruberta Ave.   FAX (818) 241-4519
Glendale, CA 91201   **www.verrents.com**
(24P Editing Systems, 35mm, Analog, Analog Decks, Digibeta,
Digital Non-Linear, Fiber, Film, Final Cut Pro Systems, Hard
Drive Rentals, HD Decks, High Def, Monitors, Rentals Only,
Video & Video Tape Recorders)

Visionary Forces
Broadcast Equipment Rentals   (818) 562-1960
148 S. Victory Blvd.   FAX (818) 562-1270
Burbank, CA 91502   **www.visionaryforces.com**
(3D Monitors, Analog Decks, Digibeta, Digital Decks, DVS
Clipster, Encoding, HD Decks, Monitors, Rentals Only,
Streaming, Transcoding, Video Tape Monitors &
Video Tape Recorders)

                                                    (310) 979-3500
Westside Media Group   (818) 779-8600
12233 W. Olympic Blvd., Ste. 152   FAX (310) 979-3503
West Los Angeles, CA 90064   **www.wmgmedia.com**
(24P Editing Systems, Analog Decks, Avid Systems, Digibeta,
Digital Decks, Digital Editing Systems, Digital Non-Linear,
Editing Suites, Final Cut Pro Systems, Hard Drive Rentals,
HD Decks, High Def, Non-Linear Offline, Non-Linear Online,
Video Tape Monitors & Video Tape Recorders)

                                                    (818) 846-9381
Wexler Video   (800) 939-5371
1111 S. Victory Blvd.   FAX (818) 846-9399
Burbank, CA 91502   **www.wexlervideo.com**
(Linear/Non-Linear Offline)

Zero One Media Center   (310) 651-8488
7625 Havenhurst Ave., Ste. 27   FAX (310) 651-8493
Van Nuys, CA 91406   **www.01mediacenter.com**
(24P Editing Systems, Analog, Analog Decks, Apple Reseller,
Avid Systems, Digibeta, Digital Decks, Digital Editing Systems,
Digital Non-Linear, Editing Supplies, Fiber, Final Cut Pro
Systems, Hard Drive Rentals, HD Decks, High Def, iPads,
Macintosh-Based Non-Linear Offline, Monitors, Non-Linear
Hard Drives, Non-Linear Offline, Non-Linear Online &
Rentals Only)

9 Agency   (310) 430-9902
(Reps for Editors)   FAX (310) 469-7899
www.9-agency.com

Roberto Abby   (818) 468-7807
FAX (818) 244-4294
www.izonstudios.com/portfolio.html

Bruce Abrams   (818) 343-2743
(818) 321-3710

Edward Abroms   (818) 726-9128
(818) 769-6723
FAX (818) 450-0514
web.mac.com/eabroms/iweb

Bruce Adams   (310) 452-2034
www.leducdesign.com

Tracy Adams   (310) 288-8000
www.paradigmagency.com

Anthony Adler   (310) 288-8000
www.paradigmagency.com

Rich Alarcon   (323) 944-0286
www.bonch.tv

Nico Alba   (310) 481-2200
www.unioneditorial.com

Ross Albert   (310) 288-8000
www.paradigmagency.com

Jonathan Alberts   (323) 468-2240
www.nyoffice.net

Michael Alberts   (310) 306-7678
www.massivepost.com

Sean Albertson   (310) 623-5500
www.montanartists.com

Michel Aller   (323) 856-3000
www.easterntalent.net

Nick Allix   (310) 319-9908
www.whitehousepost.com

Jon Alloway   (323) 270-8854
www.intothezonemovie.com

Craig Alpert   (310) 288-8000
www.paradigmagency.com

Javier Alvarez   (310) 902-2876
FAX (509) 984-2876
www.baysevenedit.com

Timothy Alverson   (310) 656-5151
www.innovativeartists.com

Giacomo Ambrosini   (323) 468-2240
www.nyoffice.net

Andy Ames   (310) 576-6300
www.beast.tv

Justin Amore   (310) 917-2761
www.optimus.com

Peter Amundson   (310) 288-8000
www.paradigmagency.com

Erik C. Andersen   (818) 206-0144
www.allcrewagency.com

Geordie Anderson   (310) 481-2200
www.unioneditorial.com

Kevin Anderson   (310) 828-6666
www.cosmostreet.com

Lance E. Anderson   (818) 284-6423
www.italentco.com

Michael Andrews   (310) 656-5151
www.innovativeartists.com

Eric Argiro   (310) 481-2200
www.unioneditorial.com

Carlos Arias   (310) 586-0600
www.rockpaperscissors.com

Sylvette Artinian   (818) 515-9011
www.threepointlanding.com

John Axelrad   (310) 395-9550
www.skouras.com

Carole Kravetz Aykanian   (310) 652-8778
www.lspagency.net

Stuart Baird   (310) 282-9940
www.mirisch.com

Zene Baker   (310) 273-6700
www.utaproduction.com

Scott Balcerek   (310) 623-5500
www.montanartists.com

Jason Ballantine   (310) 273-6700
www.utaproduction.com

Sally Banta   (310) 828-9555
www.thereelthinginc.com

Matt Barber   (310) 656-5151
www.innovativeartists.com

Phillip Bartell   (323) 468-2240
www.nyoffice.net

Roger Barton   (310) 282-9940
www.mirisch.com

Will Barton   (323) 468-2240
www.nyoffice.net

Daryl Baskin   (818) 206-0144
www.allcrewagency.com

Ned Bastille   (310) 656-5151
www.innovativeartists.com

Sam Bauer   (310) 274-6611
www.gershagency.com

David Baxter   (310) 576-6300
www.beast.tv

Kirk Baxter   (310) 586-0600
www.rockpaperscissors.com

Eric Beason   (310) 288-8000
www.paradigmagency.com

Nicholas Beauman   (310) 395-9550
www.skouras.com

Carsten Becker   (323) 440-6007

Megan Bee	(310) 829-9333	Bruce Bockman	(714) 705-6099
	www.butcheredit.com		www.postfactory.com
Paul Belanger	(310) 315-7245	Josh Bodnar	(310) 319-9908
	www.atomicpost.us		www.whitehousepost.com
Alan E. Bell	(310) 395-9550	Arlan Boll	(310) 452-2034
	www.skouras.com		www.leducdesign.com
Steve Bell	(310) 828-6666	Elisa Bonora	(310) 652-8778
	www.cosmostreet.com		www.lspagency.net
Rebecca Beluk	(310) 576-6300	Dan Bootzin	(310) 305-5777
	www.beast.tv		www.venicebeacheditorial.com
Brian Berdan	(310) 395-9550	Charles Bornstein	(310) 656-5151
	www.skouras.com		www.innovativeartists.com
Peter Berger	(310) 288-8000	George Bowers	(310) 288-8000
	www.paradigmagency.com		www.paradigmagency.com
Debbie Berman	(310) 282-9940	Sarah Boyd	(310) 285-9000
	www.mirisch.com		www.wmeentertainment.com
Javier Bermudez	(323) 798-4497	dB Bracamontes	(714) 705-6099
	www.whynotcoco.com		www.postfactory.com
Sean Berringer	(310) 576-6300	Keith Brachmann	(323) 856-3000
	www.beast.tv		www.easterntalent.net
Paul Bertino	(310) 314-8110	Robert Brakey	(310) 288-8000
	www.rexedit.com		www.paradigmagency.com
Jeff Betancourt	(818) 284-6423	Maryann Brandon	(310) 273-6700
	www.italentco.com		www.utaproduction.com
Todd Betts	(310) 828-9555	Randy Bricker	(310) 288-8000
	www.thereelthinginc.com		www.paradigmagency.com
Avril Beukes	(310) 652-8778	Wendy Greene Bricmont	(310) 282-9940
	www.lspagency.net		www.mirisch.com
Kent Beyda	(818) 284-6423	Brad Briggs	(213) 458-3463
	www.italentco.com		www.linkedin.com/in/bradleyjbriggs
Joe Bini	(310) 652-8778	Geraud Brisson	(310) 652-8778
	www.lspagency.net		www.lspagency.net
Heidi Black	(310) 319-9908	David Brixton	(310) 319-9908
	www.whitehousepost.com		www.whitehousepost.com
David Blackburn	(818) 284-6423 (310) 576-6300	Don Brochu	(310) 288-8000
	www.italentco.com		www.paradigmagency.com
Ken Blackwell	(310) 288-8000	David Brodie	(310) 586-0600
	www.paradigmagency.com		www.rockpaperscissors.com
Sue Blainey	(310) 656-5151	Lisa Bromwell	(310) 282-9940
	www.innovativeartists.com		www.mirisch.com
Christopher Blakely	(310) 450-1846 (213) 509-7798 FAX (310) 399-9227 www.mainstreetmediainc.com	Tim Brooks	(310) 576-6300 www.beast.tv
		Mandy Brown	(323) 467-8550
David Blanchard	(818) 415-4978		www.sunsetedit.com
	www.davidblanchardeditor.com	Ryan Brown	(323) 856-3000
Gena Bleier	(323) 856-3000		www.easterntalent.net
	www.easterntalent.net	Jessica Brunetto	(323) 468-2240
			www.nyoffice.net
Edie Bleiman	(310) 282-9940	Norman Buckley	(310) 288-8000
	www.mirisch.com		www.paradigmagency.com
Andy Blumenthal	(323) 856-3000	Bradley Buecker	(310) 285-9000
	www.easterntalent.net		www.wmeentertainment.com
Larry Bock	(310) 656-5151	Conrad Buff	(310) 282-9940
	www.innovativeartists.com		www.mirisch.com

Catherine Bull	(310) 399-3350	Pernille Bech Christensen	(310) 395-9550
	www.spotwelders.com		www.skouras.com
Kurt Bullinger	(310) 623-5500	Lisa Zeno Churgin	(310) 282-9940
	www.montanartists.com		www.mirisch.com
Tiffany Burchard	(310) 828-6666	Chris Chynoweth	(310) 576-6300
	www.cosmostreet.com		www.beast.tv
Edgar Burcksen	(310) 656-5151	Louis Cioffi	(310) 285-9000
	www.innovativeartists.com		www.wmeentertainment.com
Anita Brandt Burgoyne	(310) 282-9940	Julian Clarke	(310) 285-9000
	www.mirisch.com		www.wmeentertainment.com
Terence (Biff) Butler	(310) 586-0600	Curtiss Clayton	(310) 652-8778
	www.rockpaperscissors.com		www.lspagency.net
Peter Byck	(323) 252-5272	Damion Clayton	(310) 586-0600
	www.ralphtheroadie.com		www.rockpaperscissors.com
Andrew Cahn	(310) 576-6300	Anne V. Coates	(310) 273-6700
	www.beast.tv		www.utaproduction.com
Shawna Callahan	(323) 468-2240	David Codron	(310) 656-5151
	www.nyoffice.net		www.innovativeartists.com
Malcolm Campbell	(310) 652-8778	Alan Cody	(310) 623-5500
	www.lspagency.net		www.montanartists.com
Alan Canant	(323) 468-2240	Steven Cohen	(310) 285-0303
	www.nyoffice.net		www.sandramarsh.com
Jeff W. Canavan	(310) 656-5151	Mike Colao	(310) 481-2200
	www.innovativeartists.com		www.unioneditorial.com
Bruce Cannon	(310) 288-8000	Richard Comeau	(310) 623-5500
	www.paradigmagency.com		www.montanartists.com
Christopher S. Capp	(310) 395-9550	Joseph Conarkov	(818) 804-8741
	www.skouras.com		www.springmediagroup.com
Luis Carballar	(310) 652-8778	Dana Congdon	(310) 285-9000
	www.lspagency.net		www.wmeentertainment.com
Gordon Carey	(310) 829-9333	John Coniglio	(310) 288-8000
	www.butcheredit.com		www.paradigmagency.com
John Carter	(310) 288-8000	Scott Conrad	(818) 206-0144
	www.paradigmagency.com		www.allcrewagency.com
Ryan Case	(310) 285-9000	Mark Conte	(310) 288-8000
	www.wmeentertainment.com		www.paradigmagency.com
Jay Cassidy	(310) 652-8778	Tricia Cooke	(310) 273-6700
	www.lspagency.net		www.utaproduction.com
David Checel	(310) 274-6611	Dany Cooper	(310) 285-0303
	www.cutandrun.tv		www.sandramarsh.com
Isaac Chen	(310) 909-8801	Jonathan Corn	(310) 285-9000
	www.cutandrun.tv		www.wmeentertainment.com
Bill Chessman	(310) 828-6666	Hank Corwin	(310) 395-9550
	www.cosmostreet.com		(310) 396-7272
			www.skouras.com
Scott Chestnut	(310) 395-9550	Glenn Cote	(818) 301-5651
	www.skouras.com		FAX (818) 301-2681
			www.glenncote.com
Richard Chew	(310) 395-9550		
	www.skouras.com	David Coulson	(310) 288-8000
			www.paradigmagency.com
Nahum Chiappa	(917) 972-8299		
	www.postauthority.com	Olivier Bugge Coutte	(310) 395-9550
			www.skouras.com
Debra Chiate	(310) 652-8778		
	www.lspagency.net	Paul Covington	(310) 285-9000
			www.wmeentertainment.com
John Chimples	(323) 468-2240		
	www.nyoffice.net		

Jacob Craycroft	(646) 734-0765 (310) 652-8778
Douglas Crise	(310) 652-8778 www.lspagency.net
Ellen Crocker	(714) 705-6099 www.postfactory.com
Michelle Czukar	(310) 576-6300 www.beast.tv
Rye Dahlman	(213) 361-1391 www.ryefilms.com
Robert Dalva	(310) 288-8000 www.paradigmagency.com
Raul Davalos	(310) 288-8000 www.paradigmagency.com
Annette Davey	(310) 652-8778 www.lspagency.net
Freeman Davies	(310) 288-8000 www.paradigmagency.com
Ian Davies	(310) 319-9908 www.whitehousepost.com
Chris Davis	(323) 944-0286 www.bonch.tv
Roderick Davis	(310) 288-8000 www.paradigmagency.com
Tessa Davis	(310) 828-6666 www.cosmostreet.com
Jennifer Dean	(310) 319-9908 www.whitehousepost.com
Monty DeGraff	(323) 856-3000 www.easterntalent.net
Jose Delgado	(310) 391-9181 www.wsrcreative.com
Jay Deuby	(310) 273-6700 www.utaproduction.com
Corky DeVault	(310) 319-9908 www.whitehousepost.com
John Dingfield	(310) 576-6300 www.beast.tv
Paul Dixon	(310) 288-8000 www.paradigmagency.com
Alex Dondero	(310) 909-8801 www.cutandrun.tv
Dody Dorn	(310) 285-9000 www.wmeentertainment.com
Jack Douglas	(310) 202-7474 www.jumpla.tv
Victor DuBois	(310) 285-9000 www.wmeentertainment.com
Robert Ducsay	(310) 395-9550 www.skouras.com
Orlando Duenas	(310) 288-8000 www.paradigmagency.com
Robert Duffy	(310) 395-9550 (310) 399-3350 www.skouras.com

Duwayne R. Dunham	(323) 856-3000 www.easterntalent.net
Eastern Talent Agency 849 S. Broadway, Ste. 811 Los Angeles, CA 90014 (Reps for Editors)	(323) 856-3000 FAX (323) 856-3009 www.easterntalent.net
Lance Edmands	(310) 652-8778 www.lspagency.net
Steve Edwards	(310) 285-9000 www.wmeentertainment.com
Peggy Eghbalian	(310) 288-8000 www.paradigmagency.com
Einar	(310) 481-2200 www.unioneditorial.com
Andrew Eisen	(818) 434-9904
Tom Elkins	(310) 623-5500 www.montanartists.com
Michael Elliot	(310) 576-6300 www.beast.tv
Michael Ellis	(310) 288-8000 www.paradigmagency.com
Peter Ellis	(310) 623-5500 www.montanartists.com
Ken Eluto	(310) 623-5500 www.montanartists.com
Nicholas Erasmus	(310) 274-6611 www.gershagency.com
Bella Erikson	(213) 908-5106 www.beamuniversal.com
Lucas Eskin	(310) 576-6300 www.beast.tv
Marta Evry	(310) 288-8000 www.paradigmagency.com
Jennifer Fah	(818) 588-8662 FAX (818) 908-8082 www.jennifermfah.com
Farah X	(323) 944-0286 www.bonch.tv
Gregg Featherman	(818) 284-6423 www.italentco.com
Kaja Fehr	(310) 623-5500 www.montanartists.com
Fritz Feick	(323) 658-5700 www.editkings.com
Tim Fender	(310) 576-6300 www.beast.tv
Tod Feuerman	(310) 282-9940 www.mirisch.com
Chris Figler	(323) 856-3000 www.easterntalent.net
Jarrett Fijal	(323) 944-0286 www.bonch.tv
David Finfer	(310) 274-6611 www.gershagency.com

Sarah Flack (310) 395-9550
(310) 399-3350
www.skouras.com

Peter Devaney Flanagan (323) 856-3000
www.easterntalent.net

Seth Flaum (310) 288-8000
www.paradigmagency.com

Jim Flynn (310) 474-4585
www.ddatalent.com

George Folsey (310) 288-8000
www.paradigmagency.com

Jeff Ford (310) 288-8000
www.paradigmagency.com

Steve Forner (323) 944-0286
www.bonch.tv

Billy Fox (310) 288-8000
www.paradigmagency.com

David Frame (310) 968-1172
www.razoredits.com

Jo Francis (310) 656-5151
www.innovativeartists.com

Richard Francis-Bruce (310) 395-4600
www.murthaagency.com

Peter Frank (818) 284-6423
www.italentco.com

Patrick Fraser (323) 363-6125
www.editedbypatrick.com

Robert Frazen (310) 395-9550
www.skouras.com

Jeff Freeman (310) 288-8000
www.paradigmagency.com

Jay Friedkin (310) 481-2200
www.unioneditorial.com

Matt Friedman (310) 273-6700
www.utaproduction.com

Hank Friedmann (323) 467-8550
www.sunsetedit.com

Trish Fuller (310) 319-9908
www.whitehousepost.com

Nigel Galt (310) 652-8778
www.lspagency.net

Steve Gandolfi (310) 909-8801
www.cutandrun.tv

Brian Gannon (310) 319-9908
www.whitehousepost.com

Michael Garber (323) 461-0600
www.5thwall.tv

Kevin Garcia (310) 576-6300
www.beast.tv

Glenn Garland (323) 856-3000
www.easterntalent.net

Pablo Garrahan (310) 837-7001
FAX (310) 837-3680
www.wsrcreative.com

Nicholas Gaster (310) 652-8778
www.lspagency.net

Christian Gazal (310) 395-9550
www.skouras.com

Francois Gedigier (310) 652-8778
www.lspagency.net

Chris Gendrin (714) 705-6099
www.postfactory.com

David George (213) 999-4003
www.davidsgeorge.com

The Gersh Agency (310) 274-6611
(212) 997-1818
9465 Wilshire Blvd., Sixth Fl. www.gershagency.com
Beverly Hills, CA 90212
(Reps for Editors)

Teddy Gersten (310) 829-9333
www.butcheredit.com

John Gilbert (310) 395-9550
www.skouras.com

Chris Gill (310) 285-9000
www.wmeentertainment.com

Megan Gill (310) 395-9550
www.skouras.com

Moody Glasgow (310) 828-9555
www.thereelthinginc.com

Dana Glauberman (310) 395-9550
www.skouras.com

Jinx Godfrey (310) 481-2200
www.unioneditorial.com

Mark Goldblatt (310) 282-9940
www.mirisch.com

William Goldenberg (310) 395-9550
www.skouras.com

Jordan Goldman (310) 623-5500
www.montanartists.com

Affonso Gonclaves (310) 288-8000
www.paradigmagency.com

Conrad Gonzalez (818) 284-6423
www.italentco.com

Timothy A. Good (310) 656-5151
www.innovativeartists.com

Mark Goodman (310) 828-9555
www.thereelthinginc.com

Margie Goodspeed (310) 282-9940
www.mirisch.com

Dick Gordon (310) 399-3350
www.spotwelders.com

Yana Gorskaya (310) 652-8778
www.lspagency.net

Anne Goursaud (310) 282-9940
www.mirisch.com

Dave Graack (760) 476-1783
www.jmdigitalworks.com

Elliot Graham (310) 586-0600
(310) 288-8000
www.rockpaperscissors.com

Jacques Gravett (310) 656-5151
www.innovativeartists.com

Scott Gray	(310) 274-6611 www.gershagency.com	Lee Haxall	(310) 288-8000 www.paradigmagency.com
Bruce Green	(310) 273-6700 www.utaproduction.com	James Haygood	(310) 273-6700 (310) 481-2200 www.utaproduction.com
Jerry Greenberg	(310) 273-6700 www.utaproduction.com	Shon Hedges	(310) 282-9940 www.mirisch.com
Joe Gressis	(323) 856-3000 www.easterntalent.net	Alan Heim	(310) 288-8000 www.paradigmagency.com
Kevin Greutert	(310) 273-6700 www.utaproduction.com	Michael Heldman	(310) 399-3350 www.spotwelders.com
Jamie Gross	(818) 284-6423 www.italentco.com	Mark Helfrich	(310) 288-8000 www.paradigmagency.com
Jeff Groth	(323) 468-2240 www.nyoffice.net	Keith Henderson	(310) 285-9000 www.wmeentertainment.com
Jon Grover	(310) 909-8801 www.cutandrun.tv	Dave Henegar	(310) 829-9333 www.butcheredit.com
Ted Guard	(310) 586-0600 www.rockpaperscissors.com	Evan Henke	(310) 288-8000 www.paradigmagency.com
Sam Gunn	(310) 319-9908 www.whitehousepost.com	James Herbert	(310) 282-9940 www.mirisch.com
Lisa Gunning	(310) 319-9908 (310) 273-6700 www.whitehousepost.com	Craig Herring	(310) 288-8000 www.paradigmagency.com
Michael Hackett	(310) 429-7640 www.hackettcuts.com	Ty Herrington	(310) 909-8801 www.cutandrun.tv
Alex Hagen	(310) 481-2200 www.unioneditorial.com	Bruce Herrman	(310) 396-7272 www.lostplanet.com
Celia Haining	(818) 206-0144 www.allcrewagency.com	Emma E. Hickox	(310) 273-6700 www.utaproduction.com
Alexander Hall	(323) 468-2240 www.nyoffice.net	Michael Hill	(310) 288-8000 www.paradigmagency.com
Andrew Hall	(424) 238-0381 www.foundationcontent.com	Scott Hill	(310) 282-9940 www.mirisch.com
Haines Hall	(310) 399-3350 www.spotwelders.com	Kathryn Himoff	(310) 282-9940 www.mirisch.com
Justine Halliday	(323) 856-3000 www.easterntalent.net	Suzanne Hines	(310) 623-5500 www.montanartists.com
Richard Halsey	(310) 656-5151 www.innovativeartists.com	Paul Hirsch	(310) 656-5151 www.innovativeartists.com
Eddie Hamilton	(310) 288-8000 www.paradigmagency.com	Joe Hobeck	(310) 285-9000 www.wmeentertainment.com
Dan Hanley	(310) 288-8000 www.paradigmagency.com	Tracy Hof	(310) 210-6627 www.tracyhof.com
Dorian Harris	(310) 656-5151 www.innovativeartists.com	Robert Hoffman	(818) 284-6423 www.italentco.com
Nicholas Wayman Harris	(310) 481-2200 www.unioneditorial.com	Sabine Hoffman	(310) 288-8000 www.paradigmagency.com
Philip Harrison	(323) 856-3000 www.easterntalent.net	Peter Honess	(310) 395-4600 www.murthaagency.com
Mark Hartzell	(310) 656-5151 www.innovativeartists.com	Hal Honigsberg	(310) 264-9700 www.chrome.tv
Charlie Harvey	(310) 319-9908 www.whitehousepost.com	Benjamin Hopkins	(310) 765-4051 (310) 717-9493 FAX (310) 765-4052 www.huemaninterest.com
Dahkil Hausif	(310) 399-3350 www.spotwelders.com		

Jon Hopp	(310) 319-9908	Dino Jonsater	(310) 273-6700
	www.whitehousepost.com		www.utaproduction.com
Doug Hovey	(310) 625-7688	Charlie Jonston	(310) 396-7272
	www.dougedit.com		www.lostplanet.com
Niven Howie	(310) 288-8000	Alaster Jordan	(310) 319-9908
	www.paradigmagency.com		www.whitehousepost.com
Maysie Hoy	(310) 656-5151	Lawrence Jordan	(310) 288-8000
	www.innovativeartists.com		www.paradigmagency.com
William Hoy	(310) 288-8000	David Kaldor	(310) 652-8778
	www.paradigmagency.com		www.lspagency.net
Darin Hubbard	(818) 207-3608	Mako Kamitsuna	(310) 652-8778
	(818) 279-8308		www.lspagency.net
Nate Hubbard	(310) 345-1301	Gary Katz	(310) 828-6666
	www.migranteditors.com		www.cosmostreet.com
Sean Hubbert	(323) 856-3000	Rachel Goodlett Katz	(310) 623-5500
	www.easterntalent.net		www.montanartists.com
Ray Hubley	(323) 468-2240	Robin Katz	(323) 856-3000
	www.nyoffice.net		www.easterntalent.net
Martin Hunter	(310) 288-8000	Virginia Katz	(310) 282-9940
	www.paradigmagency.com		www.mirisch.com
Chris Huth	(310) 396-7272	Jean Kawahara	(310) 576-6300
	www.lostplanet.com		www.beast.tv
Russell Icke	(310) 319-9908	Jessica Kehrhahn	(323) 856-3000
	www.whitehousepost.com		www.easterntalent.net
Mark Imgrund	(310) 592-8271	Andy Keir	(310) 288-8000
	www.markimgrund.com		www.paradigmagency.com
Chris Innis	(818) 755-9822	Alan Kelley	(310) 984-6927
			FAX (310) 984-6927
Innovative Artists	(310) 656-5151		www.chrysalides.tv
1617 Broadway, Third Fl.	FAX (310) 656-5156	Paul Kelly	(310) 576-6300
Santa Monica, CA 90404	www.innovativeartists.com		www.beast.tv
(Reps for Editors)			
		Melissa Kent	(310) 288-8000
International Creative			www.paradigmagency.com
Management - ICM	(310) 550-4000		
10250 Constellation Blvd.	www.icmtalent.com	Myron Kerstein	(310) 273-6700
Los Angeles, CA 90067			www.utaproduction.com
(Reps for Editors)			
		Matthew Kett	(310) 576-6300
iTalent Company	(818) 284-6423		www.beast.tv
522 Wilshire Blvd., Ste. K	FAX (866) 755-0708		
Santa Monica, CA 90401	www.italentco.com	Jamie Kirkpatrick	(310) 395-9550
(Reps for Editors)			www.skouras.com
Robert Ivison	(310) 652-8778	Saar Klein	(310) 395-9550
	www.lspagency.net		(310) 396-7272
			www.skouras.com
Akiko Iwakana	(310) 909-8801		
	(818) 284-6423	Sloane Klevin	(818) 284-6423
	www.cutandrun.tv		(310) 481-2200
			www.italentco.com
Michael Jablow	(310) 282-9940		
	www.mirisch.com	Elizabeth Kling	(310) 395-4600
			www.murthaagency.com
Gib Jaffe	(310) 623-5500		
	www.montanartists.com	Lynzee Klingman	(310) 273-6700
			www.utaproduction.com
Malcolm Jamieson	(310) 623-5500		
	www.montanartists.com	Gary Knight	(310) 909-8801
			www.cutandrun.tv
Stephen Jess	(310) 319-9908		
	www.whitehousepost.com	Michael N. Knue	(310) 656-5151
			www.innovativeartists.com
Allyson C. Johnson	(310) 395-4600		
	www.murthaagency.com	Max Koepke	(310) 396-7272
			www.lostplanet.com
Art Jones	(310) 274-6611		
	www.gershagency.com		

Robert Komatsu	(310) 285-9000
	www.wmeentertainment.com
Igor Kovalik	(310) 576-6300
	www.beast.tv
Bill Kruzykowski	(818) 284-6423
	www.italentco.com
Meg Kubicka	(310) 319-9908
	www.whitehousepost.com
Paul La Calandra	(310) 319-9908
	www.whitehousepost.com
Brian Lagerhausen	(310) 576-6300
	www.beast.tv
Frank Lagnese	(310) 387-7773
	www.allegropost.com
Robert K. Lambert	(310) 273-6700
	www.utaproduction.com
Melissa Landini	(310) 458-3778
	www.viaverdedigital.com
Sylvie Landra	(310) 273-6700
	www.unitedtalent.com
Aaron Langley	(310) 828-6666
	www.cosmostreet.com
Marc Langley	(310) 319-9908
	www.whitehousepost.com
Sarah LaSpisa	(310) 210-3141
Lisa Lassek	(310) 285-9000
	www.wmeentertainment.com
Rick Lawley	(310) 319-9908
	www.whitehousepost.com
Greg Le Duc	(310) 452-2034
	www.leducdesign.com
Charlie Lee	(310) 576-6300
	www.beast.tv
Robert Leighton	(310) 395-9550
	www.skouras.com
David Leonard	(310) 474-4585
	www.ddatalent.com
Sean Leute	(310) 587-3300
	www.mwpost.com
Martin Levenstein	(323) 468-2240
	www.nyoffice.net
Farrel Levy	(310) 652-8778
	www.lspagency.net
Gary Levy	(310) 623-5500
	www.montanartists.com
Robert Levy	(310) 393-7109
	www.whynotcoco.com
Stuart Levy	(310) 395-9550
	www.skouras.com
Joe Linton	(323) 798-4497
	www.whynotcoco.com
Susan Littenberg	(818) 284-6423
	www.italentco.com

Carol Littleton	(310) 273-6700
	www.utaproduction.com
Mark Livolsi	(818) 284-6423
	www.italentco.com
Adam Lobel	(310) 351-4764
Nick Lofting	(310) 202-7474
	www.jumpla.tv
Tony Lombardo	(310) 652-8778
	www.lspagency.net
Jackie London	(323) 944-0286
	www.bonch.tv
Melody London	(310) 652-8778
	www.lspagency.net
Jeffrey M. Long	(818) 206-0144
	www.allcrewagency.com
Richard Lowe	(323) 468-2240
	www.nyoffice.net
Carlos Lowenstein	(310) 319-9908
	www.whitehousepost.com
Jonathan Lucas	(323) 856-3000
	www.easterntalent.net
Patrick Lussier	(310) 288-8000
	www.paradigmagency.com
Aimée Lyde	(323) 468-2240
	www.nyoffice.net
Andrew MacRitchie	(310) 288-8000
	www.paradigmagency.com
Larry Madaras	(310) 623-5500
	www.montanartists.com
Dan Maloney	(310) 399-3350
	www.spotwelders.com
Neil Mandelberg	(310) 282-9940
	www.mirisch.com
Ethan Maniquis	(310) 288-8000
	www.paradigmagency.com
Mark Manos	(310) 652-8778
	www.lspagency.net
Jeff Marcello	(323) 468-2240
	www.nyoffice.net
Pamela March	(310) 656-5151
	www.innovativeartists.com
Andrew Marcus	(310) 282-9940
	www.mirisch.com
Stephen Mark	(323) 856-3000
	www.easterntalent.net
Mary Jo Markey	(310) 288-8000
	www.paradigmagency.com
Richard Marks	(310) 288-8000
	www.paradigmagency.com
Bill Marmor	(310) 314-8110
	www.rexedit.com
Adam Marshall	(310) 319-9908
	www.whitehousepost.com

Nicholas Martin	(323) 468-2240
	www.nyoffice.net
	(310) 399-3350
Pam Martin	(310) 274-6611
	www.spotwelders.com
Kelly Matsumoto	(310) 395-9550
	www.skouras.com
Jim May	(310) 395-9550
	www.skouras.com
Frank Mazzola	(310) 282-9940
	www.mirisch.com
Tom McArdle	(323) 856-3000
	www.easterntalent.net
Connor McDonald	(310) 576-6300
	www.beast.tv
Jeff McEvoy	(310) 274-6611
	www.gershagency.com
Gareth McEwen	(310) 319-9908
	www.whitehousepost.com
Padraic McKinley	(310) 288-8000
	www.paradigmagency.com
Patrick McMahon	(323) 856-3000
	www.easterntalent.net
Peter McNulty	(310) 395-9550
	www.skouras.com
Robert Mead	(310) 395-9550
	www.skouras.com
Troy Mercury	(310) 202-7474
	www.jumpla.tv
Richard Mettler	(310) 202-7474
	www.jumpla.tv
Crandall Miller	(310) 319-9908
	www.whitehousepost.com
Joel Miller	(310) 909-8801
	www.cutandrun.tv
Michael R. Miller	(310) 395-4600
	www.murthaagency.com
Mike Miller	(310) 587-3300
Todd E. Miller	(310) 282-9940
	www.mirisch.com
Paul Millspaugh	(310) 656-5151
	www.innovativeartists.com
Laura Milstein	(310) 481-2200
	www.unioneditorial.com
The Mirisch Agency	(310) 282-9940
8840 Wilshire Blvd., Ste. 100	FAX (310) 282-0702
Los Angeles, CA 90211	www.mirisch.com
(Reps for Editors)	
Steve Mirkovich	(310) 285-9000
	www.wmeentertainment.com
Timothy Mirkovich	(310) 623-5500
	www.montanartists.com
Ethan Mitchell	(310) 319-9908
	www.whitehousepost.com

Cindy Mollo	(310) 652-8778
	www.lspagency.net
Montana Artists Agency	(310) 623-5500
9150 Wilshire Blvd., Ste. 100	FAX (310) 623-5515
Beverly Hills, CA 90212	www.montanartists.com
(Reps for Editors)	
Suzie Moore	(424) 238-0381
	www.foundationcontent.com
Jane Moran	(310) 282-9940
	www.mirisch.com
Amanda Moreau	(310) 576-6300
	www.beast.tv
Luis Moreno	(310) 202-7474
	www.jumpla.tv
	(323) 855-4382
Bob Mori	(323) 855-4382
	www.bobmori.com
Susan Morse	(310) 273-6700
	www.utaproduction.com
Karl Morton IV	(310) 623-5500
	www.montanartists.com
Ken Mowe	(323) 467-8550
	www.sunsetedit.com
Walter Murch	(310) 282-9940
	www.mirisch.com
The Murtha Agency	(310) 395-4600
1025 Colorado Ave., Ste. B	FAX (310) 395-4622
Santa Monica, CA 90401	www.murthaagency.com
(Reps for Editors)	
Grant Myers	(323) 468-2240
	www.nyoffice.net
Robert Nassau	(310) 652-8778
	www.lspagency.net
Darrin Navarro	(310) 652-8778
	www.lspagency.net
Joel Negron	(310) 395-9550
	www.skouras.com
Jay Nelson	(310) 909-8801
	www.cutandrun.tv
	(323) 468-2240
New York Office	(212) 545-7895
6605 Hollywood Blvd., Ste. 200	FAX (323) 468-2244
Los Angeles, CA 90028	www.nyoffice.net
(Reps for Editors)	
Mat Newman	(310) 273-6700
	www.utaproduction.com
Martin Nicholson	(310) 282-9940
	www.mirisch.com
Mikkel E. G. Nielsen	(310) 652-8778
	www.lspagency.net
Aram Nigoghossian	(310) 288-8000
	www.paradigmagency.com
Tia Nolan	(310) 288-8000
	www.paradigmagency.com
Richard Nord	(310) 288-8000
	www.paradigmagency.com
Tom Nordberg	(310) 288-8000
	www.paradigmagency.com

Editors

Erin Nordstrom (310) 917-2761 www.optimus.com	Greg Perler (310) 288-8000 www.paradigmagency.com
Paul Norling (310) 576-6300 www.beast.tv	Michael Perlmutter (310) 313-4046 FAX (310) 313-4048 www.almostmidnight.com
James Norris (310) 319-9908 www.whitehousepost.com	Heather Persons (310) 288-8000 www.paradigmagency.com
Dan Oberle (310) 319-9908 www.whitehousepost.com	Adam Pertofsky (310) 586-0600 www.rockpaperscissors.com
Dan O'Brien (818) 284-6423 www.italentco.com	Fred Peterson (818) 206-0144 www.allcrewagency.com
Brendan O'Carroll (310) 458-9661 www.oasiseditorial.com	Nathan Petty (310) 319-9908 www.whitehousepost.com
Juliette Olavarria (310) 820-5254 (310) 625-5254	Alex Pitt (323) 665-4492 www.alexpittphotography.com
Noel Oliver (714) 705-6099 www.postfactory.com	Paul Plew (310) 481-2200 www.unioneditorial.com
Charles Olivier (323) 468-2240 www.nyoffice.net	Gregory Plotkin (310) 288-8000 www.paradigmagency.com
Dave Oneal (818) 584-6470 www.daveoneal.com	Lin Polito (310) 202-7474 www.jumpla.tv
Conor O'Neill (310) 395-9550 www.skouras.com	Steve Polivka (310) 623-5500 www.montanartists.com
Craig Ordelheide (818) 843-1553 (818) 429-0688 FAX (818) 843-1553	Bill Pollock (323) 944-0286 www.bonch.tv
Valdis Oskarsdottir (310) 395-9550 www.skouras.com	Roy C. Poole (310) 623-5500 www.montanartists.com
Tina Pacheco (323) 468-2240 www.nyoffice.net	Ben Poster (424) 238-0381 www.foundationcontent.com
Daniel Padgett (323) 856-3000 www.easterntalent.net	Scott Powell (310) 623-5500 www.montanartists.com
Jim Page (310) 285-9000 www.wmeentertainment.com	Steve Prestemon (310) 319-9908 www.whitehousepost.com
Bill Pankow (310) 273-6700 www.utaproduction.com	Peck Prior (310) 288-8000 www.paradigmagency.com
Shawn Paper (310) 652-8778 www.lspagency.net	Jamie Proctor (310) 394-1048
Adam Parker (310) 264-9700 www.chrome.tv	Laurence Prophet (818) 804-8741 www.springmediagroup.com
Colby Parker Jr. (310) 285-9000 www.wmeentertainment.com	Sean Prophet (818) 804-8741 www.springmediagroup.com
Joel Pashby (323) 856-3000 www.easterntalent.net	Dallas Puett (310) 282-9940 www.mirisch.com
Igor Patalas (310) 314-8110 www.rexedit.com	Sam Puglise-Kipley (310) 319-9908 www.whitehousepost.com
Anna Patel (424) 238-0381 www.foundationcontent.com	Jake Pushinsky (310) 656-5151 (323) 467-8550 www.innovativeartists.com
Vikash Patel (310) 623-5500 www.montanartists.com	The Quarry (310) 586-0600 www.rockpaperscissors.com
Lance Pereira (310) 264-9700 www.chrome.tv	Jeremy Quayhackx (213) 840-0811 www.q-edit.com
Cindia Perez (818) 729-0000 www.goschproductions.com	Ariel Quintas (310) 576-6300 www.beast.tv
Marco Perez (310) 481-2200 www.unioneditorial.com	Todd Ramsay (310) 623-5500 www.montanartists.com

Matt Ramsey (310) 656-5151 www.innovativeartists.com	**Patricia Rommel** (310) 273-6700 www.utaproduction.com
Gary Ras (626) 437-5346 www.garyras.com	**Elisabet Ronaldsdottir** (310) 285-9000 www.wmeentertainment.com
Fred Raskin (310) 395-9550 www.skouras.com	**Ron Roose** (310) 288-8000 www.paradigmagency.com
Irit Raz (818) 206-0144 www.allcrewagency.com	**James Rose** (310) 909-8801 www.cutandrun.tv
Keith Reamer (310) 623-5500 www.montanartists.com	**Ken Rosenberg** (310) 828-6666 www.cosmostreet.com
Anthony Redman (310) 282-9940 www.mirisch.com	**David Rosenbloom** (310) 288-8000 www.paradigmagency.com
Mark Rees (310) 829-9333 www.butcheredit.com	**Steven Rosenblum** (310) 395-9550 www.skouras.com
Steve Rees (323) 467-8550 www.sunsetedit.com	**Harvey Rosenstock** (310) 395-4600 www.murthaagency.com
John Refoua (310) 285-9000 www.wmeentertainment.com	**Roger Roth** (818) 901-1178 (310) 963-4812 FAX (818) 901-1179
James Renfroe (323) 856-3000 www.easterntalent.net	**Maynard Rothchild** (213) 434-1800 www.maynardrothchild.com
David Rennie (323) 856-3000 www.easterntalent.net	**Steve Rotter** (310) 288-8000 www.paradigmagency.com
Jimmie Rhee (818) 729-0000 www.goschproductions.com	**Kiran Rouzie** (310) 394-1048
Billy Rich (310) 274-6611 www.gershagency.com	**Geoffrey Rowland** (310) 656-5151 www.innovativeartists.com
Nancy Richardson (310) 285-0303 www.sandramarsh.com	**Matt Rundell** (818) 314-7560
Geoff Richman (310) 395-9550 www.skouras.com	**Michael Ruscio** (310) 656-5151 www.innovativeartists.com
Tatiana S. Riegel (310) 656-5151 www.innovativeartists.com	**Billy Sacdalan** (310) 305-5777 www.venicebeacheditorial.com
Josh Rifkin (323) 468-2240 www.nyoffice.net	**Michael Saia** (310) 202-7474 www.jumpla.tv
David Riggs (310) 463-0115 FAX (818) 779-0571	**Michael L. Sale** (310) 282-9940 www.mirisch.com
Stephen Rivkin (310) 288-8000 www.paradigmagency.com	**Keith Salmon** (310) 394-1048
Jane Rizzo (310) 623-5500 www.montanartists.com	**Livio Sanchez** (310) 399-3350 www.spotwelders.com
Stuart Robertson (213) 908-5106 www.beamuniversal.com	**Ronald Sanders** (310) 395-4600 www.murthaagency.com
Adam Robinson (310) 319-9908 www.whitehousepost.com	**Todd Sandler** (818) 206-0144 www.allcrewagency.com
Alex Rodriguez (310) 652-8778 www.lspagency.net	**Sandra Marsh & Associates** (310) 285-0303 9150 Wilshire Blvd., Ste. 220 FAX (310) 285-0218 Beverly Hills, CA 90212 www.sandramarsh.com (Reps for Editors)
Julie Rogers (310) 652-8778 www.lspagency.net	**Mark Sanger** (310) 395-4600 www.murthaagency.com
David Rogow (818) 284-6423 www.italentco.com	**Lara Sarkissian** (310) 780-1352 FAX (818) 366-6514 www.aleraenterprises.com
Tom Rolf (310) 288-8000 www.paradigmagency.com	**Pietro Scalia** (310) 395-9550 www.skouras.com
Mario Roman (213) 842-1009 sketchtv.com/PP/Mario_Roman_Avid_Editor.htm	**Glen Scantlebury** (310) 273-6700 www.utaproduction.com

Lauren Schaffer	(310) 656-5151	Alec Smight	(310) 282-9940
	www.innovativeartists.com		www.mirisch.com
Dan Schalk	(310) 285-9000	Bud Smith	(310) 282-9940
	www.wmeentertainment.com		www.mirisch.com
Mark Scheib	(310) 623-5500	Howard E. Smith	(310) 273-6700
	www.montanartists.com		www.utaproduction.com
Tom Scherma	(310) 828-6666	John Smith	(310) 319-9908
	www.cosmostreet.com		www.whitehousepost.com
Ian Schiff	(310) 702-6374	Lee Smith	(310) 274-6611
	FAX (801) 720-2090		www.gershagency.com
Hervé Schneid	(310) 273-6700	Paul Martin Smith	(310) 282-9940
	www.utaproduction.com		www.mirisch.com
Richard Schwadel	(310) 623-5500	Richard Smith	(310) 576-6300
	www.montanartists.com		www.beast.tv
Adam Schwartz	(310) 576-6300	Scott Smith	(310) 282-9940
	www.beast.tv		www.mirisch.com
Jon Schwartz	(310) 623-5500	Wyatt Smith	(310) 288-8000
	www.montanartists.com		www.paradigmagency.com
John Scott	(310) 285-0303	Frank Snider	(310) 586-0600
	www.sandramarsh.com		www.rockpaperscissors.com
Eric Sears	(323) 856-3000	Paul Snyder	(310) 396-7272
	www.easterntalent.net		www.lostplanet.com
Sam Seig	(310) 652-8778	Joan Sobel	(310) 656-5151
	www.lspagency.net		www.innovativeartists.com
Andrew Seklir	(310) 623-5500	Tony Solomons	(323) 856-3000
	www.montanartists.com		www.easterntalent.net
Jeff Selis	(323) 944-0286	Sandy Solowitz	(323) 856-3000
	www.bonch.tv		www.easterntalent.net
Sam Selis	(310) 576-6300	Suzanne Spangler	(323) 856-3000
	www.beast.tv		www.easterntalent.net
Jim Settlemoir	(818) 953-8919	Lucas Spaulding	(310) 399-3350
	www.burbankpost.tv		www.spotwelders.com
Rick Shaine	(310) 656-5151	Tim Squyres	(310) 273-6700
	www.innovativeartists.com		www.utaproduction.com
Rick Shambaugh	(310) 305-5777	Zach Staenberg	(310) 395-9550
	www.venicebeacheditorial.com		www.skouras.com
Stewart Shevin	(310) 576-6300	James Stanton	(323) 856-3000
	www.beast.tv		www.easterntalent.net
Trudy Ship	(310) 282-9940	Jim Staskauskas	(310) 917-2761
	www.mirisch.com		www.optimus.com
Mark Shockley	(310) 587-9191	Jon Stefansson	(310) 399-3350
	(310) 587-9116		www.spotwelders.com
	www.evolutionla.com	Paula Stein	(310) 430-9642
Terilyn Shropshire	(310) 656-5151		www.paulastein.net
	www.innovativeartists.com	William Steinkamp	(310) 652-8778
Wendy Shuey	(213) 999-3790		www.lspagency.net
	www.wendyshuey.com	Ben Stephens	(310) 319-9908
Jai Shukla	(310) 576-6300		www.whitehousepost.com
	www.beast.tv	Mark Stevens	(310) 288-8000
Cara Silverman	(310) 656-5151		www.paradigmagency.com
	www.innovativeartists.com	Kevin Stitt	(310) 282-9940
Beatrice Sisul	(310) 285-0303		www.mirisch.com
	www.sandramarsh.com	Eric Strand	(310) 282-9940
Conrad Smart	(323) 856-3000		www.mirisch.com
	www.easterntalent.net		

Crispin Struthers	(818) 284-6423 www.italentco.com	Nicolas Trembasiewicz	(310) 623-5500 www.montanartists.com
Zac Stuart-Pontier	(310) 274-6611 www.gershagency.com	Michael Trent	(310) 285-9000 www.wmeentertainment.com
Christina Stumpf	(424) 238-0381 www.foundationcontent.com	Leo Trombetta	(310) 395-9550 www.skouras.com
Robb Sullivan	(310) 395-9550 www.skouras.com	Justin Trovato	(310) 828-6666 www.cosmostreet.com
Adam Svatek	(310) 576-6300 www.beast.tv	Ann Trulove	(323) 468-2240 www.nyoffice.net
Derek Swanson	(310) 576-6300 www.beast.tv	Barbara Tulliver	(310) 282-9940 www.mirisch.com
Dan Sweitlik	(310) 652-8778 www.lspagency.net	Serena Tupper	(714) 705-6099 www.postfactory.com
Steve Swersky	(310) 306-7678 www.massivepost.com	Jim Ulbrich	(310) 576-6300 www.beast.tv
Vincent Tabaillon	(310) 652-8778 www.lspagency.net	Frank J. Urioste	(310) 282-9940 www.mirisch.com
Craig Tanner	(310) 288-8000 www.paradigmagency.com	Asako Ushio	(310) 828-6666 www.cosmostreet.com
David Tedeschi	(310) 656-5151 www.innovativeartists.com	Jason Uson	(310) 576-6300 www.beast.tv
Kevin Tent	(323) 856-3000 www.easterntalent.net	Susan Vaill	(818) 284-6423 www.italentco.com
Michelle Tesoro	(310) 623-5500 www.montanartists.com	Jaime Valdueza	(310) 396-7272 www.lostplanet.com
Scott Tetti	(323) 658-5700 www.editkings.com	Angelo Valencia	(310) 576-6300 www.beast.tv
Dinh Long Thai	(626) 688-5818 www.chopstickninja.com	John Valerio	(310) 656-5151 www.innovativeartists.com
Andy Thomas	(323) 468-2240 www.nyoffice.net	Randy Vandegrift	(310) 447-8575 2k4ktalkingpictures.com
Drew Thompson	(310) 314-8110 www.rexedit.com	Henk Van Eeghen	(310) 288-8000 www.paradigmagency.com
Frederic Thoraval	(310) 285-9000 www.wmeentertainment.com	Nikki Vapensky	(310) 319-9908 www.whitehousepost.com
Val Thrasher	(310) 576-6300 www.beast.tv	Glorily Velez	(310) 319-9908 www.whitehousepost.com
Dylan Tichenor	(310) 273-6700 www.utaproduction.com	Tara Veneruso	(323) 463-1996
Jennifer Tiexiera	(323) 468-2240 www.nyoffice.net	Ivan Victor	(310) 652-8778 www.lspagency.net
Greg Tillman	(323) 856-3000 www.easterntalent.net	Fernando Villena	(310) 273-6700 www.utaproduction.com
Tara Timpone	(310) 274-6611 www.gershagency.com	Christian Wagner	(310) 288-8000 www.paradigmagency.com
Tim Tommasino	(310) 282-9940 www.mirisch.com	Wayne Wahrman	(310) 288-8000 www.paradigmagency.com
Camilla Toniolo	(310) 395-4600 www.murthaagency.com	Doug Walker	(310) 576-6300 www.beast.tv
David Trachtenberg	(310) 202-7474 www.jumpla.tv	Joe Walker	(310) 285-9000 www.wmeentertainment.com
Paul Trejo	(310) 623-5500 www.montanartists.com	Jonah Walker	(323) 791-3153 www.whaleofatale.net

Lesley Walker	(310) 285-0303
	www.sandramarsh.com
Angus Wall	(310) 586-0600
	www.rockpaperscissors.com
Chris Walter	(310) 930-8118
	FAX (310) 496-0776
	www.chriswalteredits.com
Tim Warmanen	(310) 319-9908
	www.whitehousepost.com
Edward A. Warschilka	(310) 282-9940
	www.mirisch.com
Brad Waskewich	(310) 399-3350
	www.spotwelders.com
	(310) 576-6300
Rob Watzke	(310) 828-7500
	www.beast.tv
Debra Weinfeld	(310) 623-5500
	www.montanartists.com
Steven Weisberg	(310) 282-9940
	www.mirisch.com
Steve Welch	(310) 395-9550
	www.skouras.com
Juliette Welfling	(310) 652-8778
	www.lspagency.net
Jeff Werner	(310) 656-5151
	www.innovativeartists.com
Dirk Westervelt	(818) 284-6423
	www.italentco.com
Declan Whitebloom	(323) 467-8550
	www.sunsetedit.com
John Wesley Whitton	(818) 284-6423
	www.italentco.com
Kim Wilcox	(310) 623-5500
	www.montanartists.com
Brad Wilhite	(310) 623-5500
	www.montanartists.com
Dayn Williams	(310) 909-8801
	www.cutandrun.tv
Chris Willingham	(310) 285-9000
	www.wmeentertainment.com
Scott C. Wilson	(619) 663-7579
	www.metalogicmusic.com/resume.htm
Pam Wise	(310) 623-5500
	www.montanartists.com
	(310) 587-3300
Jeff Wishengrad	(818) 284-6423
	www.italentco.com

Christine Wolf	(310) 319-9908
	www.whitehousepost.com
Jeffrey Wolf	(310) 285-9000
	www.wmeentertainment.com
Michael Wolf	(310) 357-7211
	www.wildpictures.com
Julia Wong	(310) 288-8000
	www.paradigmagency.com
Craig Wood	(310) 288-8000
	www.paradigmagency.com
Matthew Wood	(310) 319-9908
	www.whitehousepost.com
John Wright	(310) 288-8000
	www.paradigmagency.com
Justine Wright	(310) 273-6700
	www.utaproduction.com
Miklos Wright	(310) 652-8778
	www.lspagency.net
Gabriel Wrye	(310) 285-0303
	www.sandramarsh.com
Steve Wystrach	(213) 369-6903
Bill Yahruas	(310) 282-9940
	www.mirisch.com
Toby Yates	(310) 656-5151
	www.innovativeartists.com
William Yeh	(310) 656-5151
	www.innovativeartists.com
Jake York	(310) 282-9940
	www.mirisch.com
Mark Yoshikawa	(310) 395-9550
	www.skouras.com
Greg Young	(310) 305-5777
	www.venicebeacheditorial.com
Gary Youngman	(310) 477-9668
Bill Yukich	(323) 467-8550
	www.sunsetedit.com
Terence Ziegler	(310) 202-7474
	www.jumpla.tv
Dan Zimmerman	(310) 273-6700
	www.utaproduction.com
Dean Zimmerman	(310) 273-6700
	www.unitedtalent.com
Don Zimmerman	(310) 273-6700
	www.utaproduction.com
Paul Zucker	(310) 395-9550
	www.skouras.com

Bonded Services, Inc.
(818) 848-9766
3205 Burton Ave.
FAX (818) 848-9849
Burbank, CA 91504
www.bonded.com

FilmCore Distribution/Vault Services (818) 526-3700
2130 N. Hollywood Way
FAX (818) 526-3701
Burbank, CA 91505
www.filmcore.net

(323) 461-6464
Hollywood Vaults, Inc.
(800) 569-5336
742 Seward St.
FAX (323) 461-6479
Los Angeles, CA 90038
www.hollywoodvaults.com

Iron Mountain Film &
Sound Archives
(800) 899-4766
www.ironmountain.com

KISS Media Vaults & Self Storage
(818) 769-5477
4444 Vineland Ave.
FAX (818) 769-1639
Toluca Lake, CA 91602
www.kissvaults.com

Los Angeles Fine Arts &
Wine Storage Company
(310) 447-7700
2290 Centinela Ave.
www.lafineart.com
West Los Angeles, CA 90064

Pacific Title Archives
(818) 239-1960
3520 Valhalla Dr.
FAX (818) 972-9724
Burbank, CA 91505
www.pacifictitlearchives.com

Pacific Title Archives
(323) 938-3711
4800 W. San Vicente
FAX (323) 938-6364
Los Angeles, CA 90019
www.pacifictitlearchives.com

Pacific Title Archives
(818) 760-4223
10717 Vanowen St.
FAX (818) 760-1704
North Hollywood, CA 91605
www.pacifictitlearchives.com

(323) 653-4390
Seward Film & Tape Vaults
(818) 209-0516
1010 N. Seward St.
FAX (818) 508-7958
Los Angeles, CA 90038

SpeedMedia
(310) 822-8182
200 Mildred Ave.
FAX (310) 822-8923
Venice, CA 90291
www.speedmedia.com

Williams Data and
Film Protection Services
(323)-234-3453
1925 E. Vernon Ave.
Los Angeles, CA 90058
www.williamsdatamanagement.com

Bang Zoom! Studios
(818) 295-3939
1100 N. Hollywood Way
www.bangzoomstudios.com
Burbank, CA 91505

Digital Jungle Post Production
(323) 962-0867
6363 Santa Monica Blvd.
FAX (323) 962-9960
Hollywood, CA 90038
www.digijungle.com

(818) 459-6630
Laurel Canyon Productions
(310) 738-4184
1101 S. Flower Ave.
FAX (818) 450-0916
Burbank, CA 91502
www.lcproductions.tv

STEELE Studios
(310) 656-7770
5737 Mesmer Ave.
FAX (310) 391-9055
Culver City, CA 90230
www.steelevfx.com

(310) 979-3500
Westside Media Group
(818) 779-8600
12233 W. Olympic Blvd., Ste. 152
West Los Angeles, CA 90064
www.westsidemediagroup.com

(310) 659-5959
World of Video & Audio (WOVA)
(866) 900-3827
8717 Wilshire Blvd.
FAX (310) 659-8247
Beverly Hills, CA 90211
www.wova.com

Cinetech (661) 222-9073
27200 Tourney Rd., Ste. 100 FAX (661) 253-3722
Valencia, CA 91355 www.cinetech.com

(323) 960-8622
Deluxe Laboratories (323) 960-8438
5433 Fernwood Ave. FAX (323) 960-7016
Hollywood, CA 90027 www.bydeluxe.com
(35mm Black/White & Color)
Cutoffs: 10pm Fri & 4am Sun–Thurs

Filmworks/FX, Inc. (310) 577-3213
4121 Redwood Ave., Ste. 101 FAX (310) 577-3215
Los Angeles, CA 90066 www.filmworksfx.com
(16mm, 35mm & Super 16)
Contact: Sean Main

(818) 846-3101
FotoKem (818) 846-3102
2801 W. Alameda Ave. FAX (818) 841-2130
Burbank, CA 91505 www.fotokem.com
Hours: 24 Hours Mon–Fri

Laser Pacific Media Corporation (323) 462-6266
809 N. Cahuenga Blvd. FAX (323) 464-3233
Hollywood, CA 90038 www.laserpacific.com
Cutoffs: 2am Mon–Fri & Midnight Sun
Contact: Peter McEvoy

NT Audio Video Film Labs (310) 828-1098
1833 Centinela Ave. www.ntaudio.com
Santa Monica, CA 90404
(Film Preservation & Restoration)

Pro8mm (818) 848-5522
2805 W. Magnolia Blvd. FAX (818) 848-5956
Burbank, CA 91505 www.pro8mm.com
(16mm, Super 8 & Super 16)

Spectra Film & Video (818) 762-4545
5626 Vineland Ave. FAX (818) 762-5454
North Hollywood, CA 91601
www.spectrafilmandvideo.com
(16mm, 35mm, Super 8 & Telecine)
Cut Off: 10:30am Mon–Fri

30 Min Foto (323) 463-1678
5834 Santa Moncia Blvd.
Hollywood, CA 90038
(Full Service Processing)

(323) 856-5280
A & I Hollywood (800) 883-9088
933 N. Highland Ave. FAX **(323) 856-5110**
Los Angeles, CA 90038 **www.aandi.com**
(Black/White and Color Processing, Digital Imaging,
Film Output, Printing, Quantity Duplication, Restoration,
Retouching & Scanning)

A & I Santa Monica (310) 264-2622
1550 17th St. FAX **(310) 453-8463**
Santa Monica, CA 90404 **www.aandi.com**
(Black and White, Color, Digital Imaging, Film Output,
Full Service Processing, Printing, Quantity Duplication,
Retouching & Scanning)

Cinetech (661) 222-9073
27200 Tourney Rd., Ste. 100 FAX **(661) 253-3722**
Valencia, CA 91355 **www.cinetech.com**

Goldencolor Photo Lab (310) 274-3445
9020 W. Olympic Blvd. FAX **(310) 274-6260**
Beverly Hills, CA 90211 **www.goldencolor.com**

GP Color (818) 504-1200
8211 Lankershim Blvd. FAX **(818) 504-1220**
North Hollywood, CA 91605 **www.gpcolor.com**
(Digital Imaging, Mural Prints, Processing,
Restoration & Retouching)

Isgo Hollywood (323) 876-8085
933 N. Highland Ave., (inside A&I) **www.isgophoto.com**
Hollywood, CA 90038
(Black and White, Color, Digital Imaging, Film Output,
Full Service Processing, Printing, Quantity Duplication,
Retouching & Scanning)

Lightbox (323) 933-2080
7122 Beverly Blvd. FAX **(323) 933-5992**
Los Angeles, CA 90036 **www.lightboxstudio.com**
(Black and White, Color, Digital Imaging, Processing &
Retouching)

One Hour Photo Center (818) 501-1234
14535 Ventura Blvd. **www.1hrphotoctr.com**
Sherman Oaks, CA 91403

Photomax Lab Corp. (323) 850-0200
7190 Sunset Blvd. FAX **(323) 850-0206**
Los Angeles, CA 90046 **www.photomaxlab.net**
(Digital Imaging, Commercial Printing, Full Service Processing,
One Hour Processing, Quantity Duplication,
Restoration & Retouching)

Prolab Digital Imaging (310) 625-4411
5441 W. 104th St. FAX **(310) 846-4496**
Los Angeles, CA 90045 **www.prolabdigital.com**
(Digital Imaging, Mural Prints, Processing, Quantity Duplication,
Restoration & Retouching)

Richard Photo Lab (323) 939-8893
979 N. La Brea Ave. FAX **(323) 937-0431**
Hollywood, CA 90038 **www.richardphotolab.com**
(Black and White, Digital Imaging, Full Service Processing,
Printing, Processing, Restoration, Retouching & Scanning)

Warner Bros. Studio
Facilities - Photo Lab (818) 954-7118
4000 Warner Blvd., Bldg. 44LL FAX **(818) 954-6732**
Burbank, CA 91522 **www.wbphotolab.com**
(Digital Imaging & Full Service Processing)

Coastal Media Group   (818) 880-9800
26660 Agoura Rd.   FAX **(818) 579-9026**
Calabasas, CA 91302   **www.coastalmediagroup.com**

Encompass Digital Media   (323) 344-4500
3030 Andrita St.   FAX **(323) 344-4800**
Los Angeles, CA 90065   **www.encompass-m.com**

Envision Studios   (310) 451-1515
1528 Sixth St., Ste. 100   FAX **(310) 393-2697**
Santa Monica, CA 90401   **www.envisionstudios.tv**

    (818) 841-3888
Fastlane Broadcast Studio   **(562) 335-7400**
3062 N. Lima St.   FAX **(818) 841-3188**
Burbank, CA 91504   **www.fastlanebroadcast.com**

Pacific Television Center   (310) 287-3800
3440 Motor Ave., Circular Bldg.   FAX **(310) 287-3808**
Los Angeles, CA 90034   **www.pactv.com**
(Satellite Uplink)

Post Modern
Broadcast Studios, LLC   (949) 608-8700
2941 Alton Pkwy   FAX **(949) 608-8729**
Irvine, CA 92606   **www.postmodernstudios.com**
(Domestic Satellite Uplink, Fiber Optic Network, International
Satellite Uplink & Video Transmission Coordination)

Prime Digital Media Services   (661) 964-0220
28111 Avenue Stanford   FAX **(661) 964-0550**
Valencia, CA 91355   **www.primedigital.com**
(Domestic/International Satellite Uplink & Fiber Optic Network)

Selak Entertainment, Inc.   (626) 584-8110
1200 Lida St.   **www.selakentertainment.com**
Pasadena, CA 91103
(Domestic Satellite Uplink, Fiber Optic Network, International
Satellite Uplink, Marine Satellite Broadcasts, Satellite Uplink,
Shipboard Satellite Broadcasts &
Video Transmission Coordination)

Strategic Television, Inc.   (310) 575-4400
7030 Havenhurst Ave.   FAX **(310) 575-4451**
Van Nuys, CA 91406   **www.pssi-usa.com**
(Domestic/International Video Transmission Coordination)

    (818) 246-7100
TV Pro Gear   **(877) 877-7643**
1630 Flower St.   FAX **(818) 246-1945**
Glendale, CA 91201   **www.tvprogear.com**
(Domestic Satellite Uplink, Mobile Satellite &
Video Transmission Coordination)

Video Production Specialists (VPS)   (866) 447-3877
    FAX **(310) 577-0850**
    www.videoproductionspecialists.com
(Domestic/International Video Transmission Coordination)

5 Alarm Music (626) 304-1698
FAX (626) 795-2058
www.5alarmmusic.com
(Acoustic, Backgrounds, Clearance, Contemporary, Ethnic,
Holiday Music, Licensing, Music Library & Vintage)

7-Out-Music (323) 650-0767
2355 Westwood Blvd., Ste. 190 FAX (323) 544-6677
Los Angeles, CA 90064 www.7outmusic.com

AE Music Publishing (310) 696-4600
15303 Ventura Blvd., Ste. 240 www.asylument.com
Encino, CA 91436
(Music Library)

(323) 461-3211
Associated Production Music (800) 543-4276
6255 Sunset Blvd., Ste. 820 FAX (323) 461-9102
Hollywood, CA 90028 www.apmmusic.com

Atrium Music Group (626) 529-3066
995 E. Green St., Ste. 509 www.atriummusicgroup.com
Pasadena, CA 91106
(Acoustic, Backgrounds, Clearance, Contemporary, Custom,
Ethnic, Holiday Music, Licensing, Music Library,
Sound FX & Vintage)

AudioMicro, Inc. (620) 842-8346
13351-D Riverside Dr., Ste 219 www.audiomicro.com
Sherman Oaks, CA 91423

Beyond (323) 856-9900
1545 N. Wilcox Ave., Ste. 101 www.musicbeyond.com
Hollywood, CA 90028
(Music Library)

Big Planet Music, Inc. (818) 909-9222
www.bigplanetmusic.com
(Acoustic, Backgrounds, Contemporary, Licensing, Music
Library, Pop Songs & Vocals)

BMG Chrysalis (323) 969-0988
6100 Wilshire Blvd., Ste. 1600 www.bmgchrysalis.com
Los Angeles, CA 90048

Brand X Music (323) 651-2816
(Music Library, Licensing & Sound FX) FAX (323) 651-2946
www.brandxmusic.net

Christmas and Holiday Music (949) 859-1615
26642 Via Noveno www.christmassongs.com
Mission Viejo, CA 92691
(Holiday Music)

Cinetrax (323) 874-9590
P.O. Box 46003 FAX (323) 874-9592
Los Angeles, CA 90046 www.cinetrax.com

(323) 666-7968
CSS Music/Dawn Music (800) 468-6874
1948 Riverside Dr. www.cssmusic.com
Los Angeles, CA 90039
(Music & Sound FX)

EMI Music Publishing-
Film Soundtrack Div. (310) 586-2700
2700 Colorado Ave., Ste. 450 FAX (310) 586-2758
Santa Monica, CA 90404 www.emimusicpub.com

Evolution Music Partners, LLC (323) 790-0525
1680 N. Vine St., Ste. 500 FAX (323) 790-0520
Hollywood, CA 90028
www.evolutionmusicpartners.com

(310) 395-0408
Extreme Music (310) 985-1126
1531 14th St. www.extrememusic.com
Santa Monica, CA 90404

(310) 395-0408
Extreme Production Music (800) 542-9494
1531 14th St. FAX (310) 395-0409
Santa Monica, CA 90404 www.extrememusic.com

(310) 865-4477
FirstCom Music (800) 858-8880
2110 Colorado Ave., Ste. 110 FAX (310) 865-4454
Santa Monica, CA 90404 www.firstcom.com
(Acoustic, Backgrounds, Clearance, Contemporary, Ethnic,
Holiday Music, Licensing, Music Library, Sound FX & Vintage)

Fundamental Music (310) 285-9808
302B S. Doheny Dr. FAX (310) 274-4511
Beverly Hills, CA 90211 www.fundamentalmusic.com
(Acoustic, Contemporary, Licensing & Music Library)

Gefen, Inc. (818) 772-9100
20600 Nordoff St. FAX (818) 772-9120
Chatsworth, CA 91311 www.gefen.com
(Backgrounds & Sound FX)

(310) 260-2626
Grooveworx (800) 400-6767
(Acoustic & Contemporary) FAX (310) 260-2662
www.grooveworx.com

The Hit House (310) 378-8633
4611 Milne Dr. FAX (310) 793-2625
Torrance, CA 90505 www.thehithouse.com
(Acoustic, Backgrounds, Contemporary, Ethnic, Holiday Music,
Licensing & Music Library)

(323) 603-3252
The Hollywood Edge (800) 292-3755
7080 Hollywood Blvd., Ste. 619 FAX (323) 603-3298
Los Angeles, CA 90028 www.hollywoodedge.com

Hum (310) 260-4949
1547 Ninth St. FAX (310) 260-4944
Santa Monica, CA 90401 www.humit.com

Indart Music (818) 774-1441
P.O. Box 573351 www.indartmusic.com
Tarzana, CA 91357

JED (949) 290-2157

(888) 578-6874
JRT Music (888) 578-6874
FAX (718) 228-9157
www.jrtmusic.com
(Acoustic, Backgrounds, Clearance, Contemporary, Ethnic,
Licensing, Music Library & Vintage)

Killer Tracks (310) 865-4455
9255 W. Sunset Blvd., Ste. 200 FAX (310) 865-4470
Los Angeles, CA 90069 www.killertracks.com
(Contemporary)

Like Dat Music (858) 254-6779
P.O. Box 9476 FAX (858) 225-0864
Rancho Santa Fe, CA 92067 www.tjknowles.com

(818) 255-7100
Megatrax Production Music (888) 634-2555
7629 Fulton Ave. FAX (818) 255-7199
North Hollywood, CA 91605 www.megatrax.com

MGM Music (310) 586-8905
10250 Constellation Blvd. mgmmusic.songcatalog.com
Los Angeles, CA 90067

Mophonics (310) 452-0331
200 Westminister Ave. FAX (310) 452-0356
Venice, CA 90291 www.mophonics.com
(Acoustic, Backgrounds, Clearance, Contemporary, Ethnic,
Holiday Music, Licensing, Music Library, Sound FX & Vintage)

Music For The Masses (323) 874-1170
7510 Sunset Blvd., Ste. 1022   FAX (323) 874-5570
Los Angeles, CA 90046

Non-Stop Music Library (818) 238-6300
3400 W. Olive Ave., Fourth Fl.   FAX (818) 238-6330
Burank, CA 91505   www.nonstopmusic.com

(323) 461-2701
OGM Music, a Division of OGM, Inc. (800) 421-4163
6464 Sunset Blvd, Ste. 790   FAX (323) 461-1543
Hollywood, CA 90028   www.ogmmusic.com

Opus 1 Music (818) 508-2040
Production Library, LLC (888) 757-6787
12711 Ventura Blvd., Ste. 170   FAX (818) 508-2044
Studio City, CA 91604   www.opus1musiclibrary.com

(760) 416-0805
Premier Tracks (866) 777-0805
1775 E. Palm Canyon Dr., Ste. H239   FAX (760) 416-1855
Palm Springs, CA 92264   www.premiertracks.com

Quincy Jones Music Publishing (323) 957-6601
6671 Sunset Blvd., Ste. 1574A   FAX (323) 962-5231
Los Angeles, CA 90028   www.quincyjonesmusic.com

Riptide Music, Inc. (310) 437-4380
4121 Redwood Ave., Ste. 202   FAX (310) 437-4384
Los Angeles, CA 90066   www.riptidemusic.com
(Licensing & Music Library)

S3 Music + Sound (310) 312-3329
11681 Gateway Blvd.   FAX (310) 312-8827
Los Angeles, CA 90064   www.s3mx.com

ScreenMusic International (818) 789-2954
18034 Ventura Blvd., Ste. 450   FAX (818) 789-5801
Encino, CA 91316   www.screenmusic.com
(Music Clearance, Library and Licensing)

Songs To Your Eyes, Ltd. (323) 988-9725
22817 Ventura Blvd., Ste. 839   FAX (323) 201-2045
Woodland Hills, CA 91364   www.songstoyoureyes.com

(818) 247-6219
Sonic Safari Music (800) 259-6004
663 W. California Ave.   FAX (818) 241-1333
Glendale, CA 91203   www.sonicsafarimusic.com
(Ethnic & Tribal)

(877) 315-3647
Sounddogs.com, Inc. (714) 783-3096
4712 Admiralty Way, Ste. 497   FAX (310) 496-3135
Marina del Rey, CA 90292   www.sounddogs.com
(Acoustic, Backgrounds, Contemporary, Ethnic, Holiday Music,
Licensing, Music Library & Sound FX)

Soundtrack Marketing (323) 274-3800
1641 Riverside Dr.   FAX (818) 500-7390
Glendale, CA 91201   www.soundtrackmarketing.com

Stock Music Store (323) 345-2806
109-260 Adelaide St. East   FAX (416) 551-9092
Toronto, ON M5A 1N1 Canada
www.stockmusicstore.com

Summerfield Music, Inc./
Trailer Trash Music Library (818) 905-0400
14024 Roblar Rd.   FAX (818) 905-0488
Sherman Oaks, CA 91423   www.summerfieldmusic.com

Syncofy (323) 250-0708
www.syncofy.com
(Acoustic, Backgrounds, Clearance, Contemporary, Ethnic,
Holiday Music, Licensing, Music Library, Sound FX & Vintage)

Uncommon Trax (312) 266-3611
610 N. Fairbanks Court, Third Fl.   FAX (312) 640-2860
Chicago, IL 60611   www.uncommontrax.com
(Acoustic, Backgrounds, Contemporary, Licensing & Sound FX)

Zoo Street Music (818) 955-5268
2701 W. Willow St.   FAX (818) 295-5001
Burbank, CA 91505   www.zoostreet.com

48 Windows Music and Mix   (310) 392-9545
1661 Lincoln Blvd., Ste. 220   FAX (310) 392-9445
Santa Monica, CA 90404   www.48windows.com
Contact: Eric Garcia
Sound Designers: Sonia Castro & Michael Chandler
Composers: Eric Garcia & Andreas Straub

740 Sound Design   (310) 574-0740
12509 Beatrice St.   FAX (310) 306-0744
Los Angeles, CA 90066   www.740sounddesign.com

AB Audio Visual Ent., Inc.   (562) 429-1042
3765 Marwick Ave.   FAX (562) 429-2401
Long Beach, CA 90808   www.abaudio.com
Creative Director: Linda Rippee
Executive Producer/Composer: Arlan H. Boll

Advantage Audio/Jim Hodson   (818) 566-8555
1026 N. Hollywood Way   FAX (818) 566-8963
Burbank, CA 91505   www.advantageaudio.com
President/Sound Designer: Jim Hodson
Sound Designers: Heather Holbrook, Bob Poole &
Paca Thomas

Alan Audio Works   (310) 753-1564
   (323) 906-8700
4720 W. Magnolia Blvd.   FAX (562) 408-6821
Burbank, CA 91505   www.alanaudioworks.com

Audible Shift   (323) 481-4581
Raleigh Studios,   www.audibleshift.com
662 N. Van Ness Ave., Ste. 200
Los Angeles, CA 90004
Creative Director/Sound Designer: Kadet Kuhne
Composers: Brad Breeck, Raja Das, Steve McClure &
Anna Sitko

Bang Zoom! Studios   (818) 295-3939
1100 N. Hollywood Way   www.bangzoomstudios.com
Burbank, CA 91505
Contact: Jonathan Sherman

Barbara Marshall Music   (818) 222-7771
Contact: Barbara Marshall

Bell Sound Studios   (323) 461-3036
Contact: John Osiecki   FAX (323) 461-8764
   www.bellsound.com

Bendy   (310) 337-9727
   (310) 753-9702
   FAX (310) 645-2708
Executive Producer: Bob Gannon   www.bendymusic.com
Composers/Sound Designers: Dean Menta & Andy Snavley
Composer: Josh Sklair

Big Planet Music, Inc.   (818) 909-9222
   www.bigplanetmusic.com
Creative Director & Chief Composer: Billy White Acre
Producer: Kharin Gilbert

Blue Music & Sound Design   (323) 810-5588
5839 Green Valley Circle,   www.bluemusicla.com
Ste. 200
Culver City, CA 90230
Executive Producer/Creative Director: Paul Hoffman
Composers: Hal Cragin, Mitchell Forman, Adam Giorgoni,
Steve Love, Guy Moon & David Rolfe
Composer/Sound Designers: Paul Hoffman & Bruce Somers

Braincloud   (415) 888-8691
385 Pine Hill Rd., Ste. G   www.braincloudsound.com
Mill Valley, CA 94941

Cashman Commercials   (661) 222-9300
26136 N. Twain Pl.   www.cashmancommercials.com
Stevenson Ranch, CA 91381
Composer: Marc Cashman

Chace   (818) 842-8346
   (800) 842-8346
201 S. Victory Blvd.   FAX (818) 842-8353
Burbank, CA 91502   www.chace.com
Contact: James Eccles

Chris Bell Music and Sound Design   (707) 363-1000
Composer/Sound Designer: Chris Bell   www.cbmsd.com

Cloud 19   (310) 839-5400
   (310) 717-7819
3767 Overland Ave., Ste. 103   FAX (310) 839-5404
Los Angeles, CA 90034   www.cloud19.com

Confidence Head   (310) 393-7577
1316 Third Street Promenade,   FAX (310) 584-1534
Ste.109   www.confidencehead.com
Santa Monica, CA 90401
Contact: Michael Coulter
Composers: Michael Coulter & Tobias Johnston

Craig Harris Music   (323) 851-8510
P.O. Box 1508   www.craigharrismusic.com
Los Angeles, CA 90078
Composer/Sound Designer: Craig Harris

DeepMix   (323) 769-3500
6255 Sunset Blvd., Ste. 1024   FAX (323) 417-5134
Hollywood, CA 90028   www.deepmix.com
Partner/Executive Producer: Brad Colerick
Managing Partner/Creative Director: Dave Curtin
Producer/NY: Marc Morris
Production Manager: Nate Fisher-Shaffer
Assistant Producer: Bobbi Hamilton
Accountant: Takayo Horikoshi

E-Records   (310) 279-2388
c/o Rick Torres, P.O. Box 352065   www.ricktorres.com
Los Angeles, CA 90035

Ear to Ear Music & Sound Design   (310) 581-1660
1660 Ninth St.   FAX (310) 581-1661
Santa Monica, CA 90404   www.eartoear.com
Contact: Amy Lyngos
Composer/Sound Designer: Brian Banks

Elias Arts LA   (310) 581-6500
2219 Main St.   FAX (310) 581-4800
Santa Monica, CA 90405   www.eliasarts.com
Executive VP & General Manager: Ann Haugen
Creative Director: Dave Gold
Composers: Chris Campanaro, Jimmy Haun, Chip Jenkins,
Christopher Kemp, Michael Sherwood & Dave Wittman
Director of Sound: Dean Hovey
Sr. VP of Sales and Business Development: Scott Cymbala
Producer: Kala Sherman

EMOTO   (310) 399-6900
1615 16th St.   FAX (310) 399-5333
Santa Monica, CA 90404   www.emotomusic.com
Executive Producer: Paul Schultz
Composers: John Adair, Paul Bessenbacher, Ryan Elder, Steve
Hampton & Tony Morales
Sound Designer: Soundwell.tv

Endless Noise   (310) 694-8251
1825 Stanford St.   www.endlessnoise.com
Santa Monica, CA 90404
Producer: Mary Catherine Finney
Creative Director/Composer: Jeff Elmassian
Composers: Chris Guardino & Andy Rehfeldt
Sound Mixer/Engineer: Bob DeMaa

Finger Music (310) 393-5340
618 Venezia Ave. FAX (310) 399-5398
Venice, CA 90291 www.fingermusic.tv
Executive Producer: Tania Thiele
Creative Directors: Dave Hodge & Hein Hoven
Composers: Rick Boston, James DiSalvio, Dom and Ant,
Dave Hodge, Daniel Lenz, David A. Logan, Photek,
Spookey Ruben & Joey Rubenstien
Sound Designers: Onnalee Blank, Richard Devine,
Dave Hodge & Hein Hoven

Fuel Music (310) 640-3435
www.ifuelmusic.com
Composer/Sound Designer: Brad Chiet

Geoff Levin Music (818) 841-6607
719 S. Main St. FAX (818) 841-2520
Burbank, CA 91506 www.geofflevin.com
Composer: Geoff Levin

(213) 999-4003
David George (323) 936-3006
www.davidsgeorge.com

(310) 204-6111
Glaser Musicworks (800) 972-6694
1941 Livonia Ave. FAX (310) 204-6222
Los Angeles, CA 90034 www.samglaser.com
Contacts: Marcia Baron
Executive Producer/Composer: Sam Glaser

Glue Audio (310) 478-2120
3111 S. Barrington Ave., Ste. 14 FAX (310) 478-2130
Los Angeles, CA 90006 www.glueaudio.com

Grind Music & Sound (818) 565-5565
4804 Laurel Canyon Blvd., Ste. 716 www.grindinc.com
Valley Village, CA 91607
Composer/Sound Designer: Michelle Garuik

GrooveWorx LLC (310) 260-2626
1420 Second St. FAX (310) 260-2662
Santa Monica , CA 90401 www.grooveworx.com
Executive Producer/Composer: Dain Blair
Composers: Tori Amos, Craig Armstrong, David Arnold, Angelo
Badalamenti, Luis Balcov, John Barry, Steve Bartek, Tyler
Bates, Christophe Beck, Byron Brizuela, Jon Brion, BT, Al
Capps, Teddy Castellucci, Stanley Clarke, George Clinton,
Harry Cody, Stewart Copeland, Don Davis, John Debney, Ann
Dudley, Rob Dougan, The Dust Brothers, Cliff Eidelman, Danny
Elfman, Nick Glenne-Smith, Joel Goldsmith, Paul Haslinger,
Mark Isham, Alexander Janko, Maurice Jarre, Rolfe Kent,
Wojciech Kilar, Chris Lennertz, Joel McNeely, Jonathan Miller,
Paul Mirkovich, David Newman, John Ottman, Howard Pfeifer,
Tony Phillips, Nicholas Pike, Nicola Piovani, Basil Poledouris,
Rachel Portman, John Powell, Trevor Rabin, Graeme Revell,
Stan Ridgeway, Lalo Schifrin, Marc Shaiman, Mark Snow,
Shirley Walker, Bruce Watson, Timothy Michael Wynn, Phil-X,
Gabriel Yared & Christopher Young
Sound Designers: Kim B. Christensen, Jonathan Miller &
Robert Wear

Halfpipe Music (310) 651-6233
P.O. Box 10534 FAX (323) 851-9648
Beverly Hills, CA 90213 www.halfpipemusic.com
Composers: Shane August, Scott Bennett, Rick Boston,
Meredith Chinn, dj JUN, dj True: 129, Christopher Faizi, Sean
Hennessy, Kent Karlsson, Daniel Kolton, Jeff Martin, Stephen
McCarthy, The Newton Brothers, John O, Joey Peters, Mike
Semple, Kiran Shahani, Chris Stills, Andy Sturmer, Kathie
Talbot, Danny Tate, Scott Thomas & Rick Torres

The Hit House (310) 378-8633
4611 Milne Dr. FAX (310) 793-2625
Torrance, CA 90505 www.thehithouse.com
Executive Producer: Sally House
Creative Director/Composer: Scott Miller
Engineer/Mixer: Jeff Kanan
Sound Designer: Chad Hughes
Arranger/Orchestrator: Bill Conn
Assistant Composer/Producer: Tyge Møller Christiansen

Horrible Music, LLC (310) 260-9939
13101 Addison St. www.horriblemusic.net
Sherman Oaks, CA 91423
Composer/Sound Designer: Jud Haskins

HUM Music + Sound Design (310) 260-4949
1547 Ninth St. www.humit.com
Santa Monica, CA 90401
Executive Producer: Debbi Landon
Producer: Chanel Scott
Associate Producer: Kristina Iwankiw
Creative Director: Jeff Koz
Associate Creative Director: Alex Kemp
Composers: Scott Glenn, Robert Lopez & Hirotaka Matsuoka
Sound Designer: Dan Hart
West Coast Sales Rep: Reber/Covington
Midwest Sales Rep: Nikki Weiss
Texas and East Coast Sales Rep: Unique Koz

Icarus Music (562) 925-4514
4954 Briercrest Ave. www.icarusmusic.com
Lakewood, CA 90713
Composers: Eddie Freeman & Marta Victoria

IM Sound and Music (323) 573-2896
P.O. Box 931493 www.reverbnation.com/johnmassari
Los Angeles, CA 90093
Composer: John Massari

Indart Music (818) 774-1441
P.O. Box 573351 www.indartmusic.com
Tarzana, CA 91357
Contact: Sara Traina

(323) 883-0123
Jet Stream Sound (310) 770-2439
4130 Cahuenga Blvd., Ste. 100
Universal City, CA 91602 www.jetstreamsound.com

Jill Fraser Music (818) 908-9083
www.jillfrasermusic.com
Composer/Sound Designer: Jill Fraser

(818) 789-0226
The Jingle Factory (818) 943-2668
13964 La Maida St. FAX (818) 789-0250
Sherman Oaks, CA 91423 www.jinglefactory.com
Composer: Dan McNamara

Jon Huck Music & Sound Design (323) 222-1082
Composer/Sound Designer: Jon Huck www.jhuck.com
Composers: Joe Berardi, Roddy Bottum, Dan Crane, Carey
Fosse, Dino Herrmann, The Millionaire & Bill Ungerman

L.A. Entertainment, Inc. (800) 579-9157
7095 Hollywood Blvd., Ste. 826 FAX (323) 924-1095
Hollywood, CA 90028 www.warriorrecords.com
Composer/Sound Designer: Jim Ervin

Les Hooper Music (818) 501-2727
4526 Rubio Ave. FAX (818) 995-6773
Encino, CA 91436
Composer/Sound Designer: Les Hooper

Like Dat Music (858) 254-6779
P.O. Box 9476 FAX (858) 225-0864
Rancho Santa Fe, CA 92067 www.tjknowles.com
Executive Producer/Creative Director: T.J. Knowles
Composer/Sound Designer: Bobby Crew
Producer: Jay Knowles

(949) 675-4790
Lyon Studios (323) 962-6117
222 21st St. FAX (949) 675-2139
Newport Beach, CA 92663 www.lyonstudios.com
Contact: Curt Lyon

Machine Head (310) 392-8393
1641 20th St. FAX (310) 392-9676
Santa Monica, CA 90404 www.machinehead.com
Head of Production: Vicki Ordeshook
Creative Director/Sound Designer: Stephen Dewey
Composer: Adam Schiff
Music Supervisor: Jason Bentley
Composer/Sound Designer: Johannes Hammers
Sound Designer: Dustin Camilleri
Engineer: Kip Smedley

MalleryScores (323) 462-4862
FAX (323) 462-6842
www.malleryscores.com
Creative Director/Composer/Sound Designer: Billy Mallery
Producer: Franchesca Free
Music Supervisor: Kristin Hooks

Margarita Mix Hollywood (323) 962-6565
6838 Romaine St. FAX (323) 962-8662
Hollywood, CA 90038 www.lastudios.com
Contact: Veneta Butler

Margarita Mix Santa Monica (310) 396-3333
1661 Lincoln Blvd., Ste. 101 FAX (310) 396-9633
Santa Monica, CA 90404 www.lastudios.com
Contacts: Jennifer Bowman, Michele Millard & Whitney Warren
Mixers: Nathan Dubin, Jimmy Hite, Jeff Levy & Scott Rader

Matter Music (818) 505-8505
FAX (818) 505-9241
www.mattermusic.com
Composers: Ric Markmann, Dan Pinella & Chris Wagner

Mental Music Productions (213) 713-8868
P.O. Box 57311 www.mental-music.com
Sherman Oaks, CA 91413

(310) 396-4663
Mind Over Eye, LLC (310) 968-4259
1639 11th St., Ste. 117 FAX (310) 396-0663
Santa Monica, CA 90404 www.mindovereye.com
Composer: Bill Wadsworth

Mona Davis Music, Inc. (323) 270-270
2633 Lincoln Blvd., Ste. 602 www.monadavis.com
Santa Monica, CA 90405
Producers: Dany Crusius & Alex Menck
Sound Designer: David Streefkerk
Composers: Tom Batoy, Alex Menck & Franco Tortora

(310) 452-0331
Mophonics (212) 260-8183
200 Westminster Ave. www.mophonics.com
Venice, CA 90291
Partner/Head of Production: Shelley Altman
Partner/Composer/Creative Director: Stephan Altman
Producer: Jean Scofield
Music Supervisor/Producer: Josh Marcy

(323) 656-0197
Mosher Music (323) 578-3868
Composers: Tim Mosher & Stoker FAX (323) 656-0197
www.mosherandstoker.com

The Music Collective (818) 508-3303
12711 Ventura Blvd., Ste. 110 FAX (818) 508-3314
Studio City, CA 91604 www.themusiccollective.com
Composers: Alan Ett, Scott Liggett & Alec Puro

Music Forever (323) 461-4646
Executive Producer: David Streja FAX (323) 461-1904
Composer: Anthony Marinelli www.musicforever.com
Head Engineer: Clint Bennett

The Music Kitchen, Inc. (661) 338-4749
12400 Connery Way www.themusickitchen.com
Bakersfield, CA 93312
Composer/Sound Designer: Michael Benghiat

Musikvergnuegen (323) 856-5900
1545 N. Wilcox Ave., Ste. 202 FAX (323) 856-5917
Hollywood, CA 90028 www.musikv.com
Owner: Walter Werzowa

Mutato Muzika (310) 360-0561
8760 Sunset Blvd. FAX (310) 360-0837
West Hollywood, CA 90069 www.mutato.com
Composer/Sound Designer: Mark Mothersbaugh
Contact: Robert Miltenberg

ON Music and Sound (310) 264-0407
2042-A Broadway FAX (310) 264-0381
Santa Monica, CA 90404 www.onmusicandsound.com
Composer: Chris Winston
Sound Designer: Mark Jasper

Orange Dog Music (818) 448-9262
6434 Whitman Ave. www.orangedogmusic.com
Lake Balboa, CA 91406
Composer/Sound Designer: Wes Hambright

Pacific Coast Presentations, Inc. (949) 548-9432
6100 West Coast Hwy, Ste. C FAX (949) 548-1622
Newport Beach, CA 92663 www.pcpmusic.com
Contact: Edo Guidotti

Peter Rotter Music Services (818) 876-7500
4766 Park Granada, Ste. 106 FAX (818) 876-7503
Calabasas, CA 91302 www.prmusicservices.com

Portis Music (818) 216-2841
4300 Shadyglade Ave.
Studio City, CA 91604
Composer/Sound Designer: Michael Portis

Rad Music (310) 440-0055
501 Hanley Pl. FAX (310) 476-5106
Los Angeles, CA 90049 www.radmusic.net
Composer/Sound Designer: Dan Radlauer

Radius360 (818) 926-6704
13547 Ventura Blvd., Ste. 612 www.radius360.com
Sherman Oaks, CA 91423
Owner/Sound Supervisor: Bo Bennike
Accounting: Shania Warren-Bennike

Riptide Music, Inc. (310) 437-4380
4121 Redwood Ave., Ste. 202 FAX (310) 437-4384
Los Angeles, CA 90066 www.riptidemusic.com
Executive Producer: Bob Kaminsky
Executive Producer/Composer: Rich Goldman
Composer: Dan Silver

S3 Music + Sound (310) 312-3329
11681 Gateway Blvd. FAX (310) 312-8827
Los Angeles, CA 90064 www.s3mx.com
Composers: Adam Sanborne & Michael Suby
Producer: Steve Schemerhorn

Saparoff Music (310) 455-1950
19709 Horseshoe Dr. FAX (310) 455-0827
Topanga, CA 90290 www.saparoffmusic.com
Owner/Composer/Sound Designer: Andrea Saparoff

Schtung Music (310) 828-5189
1825 Stanford St. FAX (310) 828-4189
Santa Monica, CA 90404 www.schtungmusic.com
Contact: Susanna Kalliomaki
Composers: Andrew Hagen, Eddie Reyes, Jim Watson & Rob
Winch (Plus World Group)
Sound Designer: Andrew Hagen
Chief Engineer: Jim Watson
Producer: Andrew Hagen

Scott Rea Music (866) 630-6372
P.O. Box 691522 www.scottreamusic.com
West Hollywood, CA 90069
Composer/Sound Designer: Scott Rea

ScreenMusic International (818) 789-2954
18034 Ventura Blvd., Ste. 450 FAX (818) 789-5801
Encino, CA 91316 www.screenmusic.com
Contact: Melissa Bree

Sensory Overload Music (818) 985-3300
2461 Santa Monica Blvd., Ste. 452 FAX (818) 761-3934
Santa Monica, CA 90404 www.sensory-overload.com
Composer: Bryan E. Miller
Audio Post Supervisor: Mike Bouska
Music Editor: Kayla Mashburn

Slappo Music & Sound Design (323) 737-6995
2554 Lincoln Blvd., Ste. 1086 FAX (323) 737-6990
Venice, CA 90291 www.audio.slappo.com
Senior Composer/Sound Designer: Neil Uchitel

Sonic Fuel (310) 578-9686
Composers: Chris Lennertz & Tim Wynn FAX (310) 578-0442
www.sonicfuel.net

Music Production & Sound Design

Sonicfruit Music & Sound Design (310) 291-1122
www.sonicfruit.com
Executive Producer, Composer & Sound Designer:
Kathryn Korniloff

Sound Design Digital Post (310) 210-7133
www.sounddesigndigitalpost.com

(310) 392-0369
Soundbath Music & Sound (310) 990-0202
675A Rose Ave. www.soundbath.com
Venice, CA 90291
Composer: Garron Chang

Soundelux Design Music Group (323) 603-3203
7080 Hollywood Blvd., Ste. 100 FAX (323) 603-3287
Hollywood, CA 90028 www.soundeluxdmg.com
Creative Director: Scott Martin Gershin

Soundmine (818) 767-4226
8457 Petaluma Dr. www.soundmine.com
Sun Valley, CA 91352

SoundTrack Studio (310) 477-7195
www.soundtrackstudio.com
Composer: Garron R. Larcombe

Sternworld Productions, Inc. (310) 439-1903
923 Marco Pl. www.sternworld.net
Venice, CA 90291
Composer/Producer: Shepard Stern

Stewart Sound Factory (714) 973-3030
204 N. Broadway, Ste. N FAX (714) 973-2530
Santa Ana, CA 92701 www.stewartsound.com
Contact: Suzi Alderson
Composer: Bob Stewart

Stimmung (310) 460-0123
2052 Broadway FAX (310) 460-0122
Santa Monica, CA 90404 www.stimmung.tv
Executive Producer: Ceinwyn Clark
Producer: Jack Catlin
Sound Designers: Reinhard Denke & Gus Koven
Composers: Greg Griffith, Jason Johnson, Robert Miller &
David Winer
Music Supervisor: Liza Richardson
Contact: Jessica Ampikapon

Summerfield Music, Inc./
Trailer Trash Music Library (818) 905-0400
14024 Roblar Rd. FAX (818) 905-0488
Sherman Oaks, CA 91423 www.summerfieldmusic.com
Composer: Bobby Summerfield

Sun of Z Music Production LLC (818) 314-8314
www.sunofz.com

Tartaglia Music Productions (323) 666-6550
3854 Shannon Rd. FAX (323) 666-6599
Los Angeles, CA 90027
Composer/Sound Designer: John Tartaglia
Production Coordinator: Odile Ledoux

Technicolor Creative (323) 860-7600
Services - Hollywood (323) 860-7816
1438 N. Gower St., Box 50, Bldg. 48 FAX (323) 860-7801
Hollywood, CA 90028 www.technicolor.com

Thunder Music + Sound Design (310) 829-4765
3211 Olympic Blvd. FAX (310) 315-6399
Santa Monica, CA 90404 www.thunder-sound.com

TommyMusic (310) 902-4784
4028 Albright Ave.
Los Angeles, CA 90066
Executive Producer/Composer: Tommy O'Brien

Trivers/Myers Music, Inc. (310) 640-9166
550 N. Continental, Ste. 100 FAX (310) 647-5869
El Segundo, CA 90245 www.triversmyersmusic.com

The V Group (310) 395-0252
359 21st St. FAX (310) 319-2030
Santa Monica, CA 90402 www.thevgroup.net

Volume (310) 578-8277
624 Milwood Ave.
Venice, CA 90291
Music Supervisor: Maureen Thompson

The Walt Disney Studios (818) 560-2731
500 S. Buena Vista St. FAX (818) 562-3262
Burbank, CA 91521 www.buenavistapost.com

Warner Bros. Studio Facilities - (818) 954-1625
Post Production Services (818) 954-2515
4000 Warner Blvd. FAX (818) 954-4138
Burbank, CA 91522 www.wbsound.com

Wojahn Bros. Music (310) 829-6200
1524-D Cloverfield Blvd. FAX (310) 829-6222
Santa Monica, CA 90404 www.wojahn.com
Composers: Roger Wojahn & Scott Wojahn

Zane Smythe Music (310) 722-9244
www.zanesmythe.com

Zoo Street Music (818) 955-5268
FAX (818) 295-5001
www.zoostreet.com
Music Supervisor: Omar Herrera & Yosuke Kitazawa

30 Second Films   **(310) 315-1750**
3019 Pico Blvd.   FAX **(310) 315-1757**
Santa Monica, CA 90405   **www.30secondfilms.com**
(Computer Graphics & Non-Linear Offline and Online)
Contact: Alan J. Stamm

303 Post   **(818) 231-8132**
7309 Paso Robles   **www.303post.com**
Lake Balboa, CA 91406
(Avid Systems, Editing, Film Editing, Finishing, HD Editing, HD
Finishing & Non-Linear Offline and Online)

310 Studios   **(818) 566-3083**
419 S. Flower St.   FAX **(818) 747-7637**
Burbank, CA 91502   **www.310studios.com**
(All Formats)

5th Wall   **(323) 461-0600**
6311 Romaine St., Ste. 7135   **www.5thwall.tv**
Hollywood, CA 90038
(All Formats, Color Correction, Compositing, Digital Editing
Systems, Digital Online, Final Cut Pro Systems, Finishing, HD
Editing, HD Finishing, HD Online, Non-Linear Offline, Non-
Linear Online & Post Supervision)

Aaron & Le Duc   **(310) 452-2034**
     www.leducdesign.com
(Computer Graphics, Digital Online, Duplication, High Def &
Linear/Non-Linear Offline and Online)
Contact: Greg Le Duc

      (626) 442-6454
Absolute Films   **(323) 692-1010**
1441 Huntington Dr., Bldg. 301   FAX **(626) 448-1930**
South Pasadena, CA 91030   **www.absolutefilms.net**
(Duplication, HD Editing, Non-Linear Offline and Online &
Standards Conversion)

      (818) 567-5190
Absolute Post   **(818) 842-7966**
4119 W. Burbank Blvd.   FAX **(818) 567-6199**
Burbank, CA 91505   **www.absoluterentals.com**
(5.1 Audio Mixing, Avid Systems, FCP Edit Suites, Flame & SD
and HD Online)

Advanced Video, Inc.   **(323) 469-0707**
723 N. Cahuenga Blvd.
Hollywood, CA 90038
(3D Conversion From All Aormats, Captions, Color Correction,
Compositing, Digital Intermediate Services, Recording,
Restoration & Subtitles)

Aftershock Digital   **(323) 658-5700**
8222 Melrose Ave., Ste. 304   FAX **(323) 658-5200**
Los Angeles, CA 90046   **www.editkings.com**
(High Def & Non-Linear Offline and Online)
Contact: Fritz Feick

Alera Enterprises, Inc.   **(323) 660-7710**
     www.aleraenterprises.com
(Authoring, HD Editing, HD Finishing, HD Online, Non-Linear
Offline and Online & Post Supervision)

AlphaDogs, Inc.   **(818) 729-9262**
1612 W. Olive Ave., Ste. 200   FAX **(818) 729-8537**
Burbank, CA 91506   **www.alphadogs.tv**
(Avid Systems, Color Correction, Compositing, Digital Media
Transfers, Duplication, DVD Design, DVD Menus, Final Cut Pro
Systems, Finishing, Graphic Design, Graphics, HD Editing, HD
Finishing, HD Online, Motion Graphics, Non-Linear Offline &
Non-Linear Online)

American Video Group   **(310) 477-1535**
2542 Aiken Ave.   **www.americanvideogroup.com**
Los Angeles, CA 90064
(Digital Non-Linear Offline and Online)
Contacts: John Berzner & Alison Kearney

Arsenal FX   **(310) 453-5400**
1620 Euclid St.   **www.arsenalfx.tv**
Santa Monica, CA 90404
(All Formats, Color Correction, Compositing, Computer
Animation, Computer Graphics, Digital Colorization, Digital
Editing Systems, Digital Film Mastering, Digital Media
Transfers, Digital Online, DVD Design, DVD Menus,
Edge Coding, Final Cut Pro Systems, Finishing, Graphic
Design, Graphics, HD Editing, HD Finishing, HD Online,
HD Remastering, HD Telecine, Mastering, Motion Graphics,
Non-Linear Offline, Non-Linear Online, Post Supervision, Pre-
Visualization, Tape to Tape Color Correction, Tape to Tape Film,
Simulation, Tape to Tape Transfers & Video to Still Transfers)

Atomic Post   **(310) 922-2167**
3025 W. Olympic Blvd., Ste. 124   **www.atomicpost.us**
Santa Monica, CA 90404
(Avid and Final Cut Pro Editing)

Autonomy, Inc.   **(213) 814-2919**
     www.autonomy.tv
(Computer Graphics & Digital Non-Linear Offline and Online)

Avenue Digital, LLC   **(818) 559-6553**
4403 W. Magnolia Blvd.   **www.avenuedigital.com**
Burbank, CA 91505
(Avid Systems, Color Correction, Digital Intermediate Services,
Duplication, Final Cut Pro Systems, Finishing, HD Editing, HD
Finishing, HD Online, HD Remastering, New Media Encoding,
Non-Linear Online, Post Supervision & Quality Control)

Bang Zoom! Studios   **(818) 295-3939**
1100 N. Hollywood Way   **www.bangzoomstudios.com**
Burbank, CA 91505
Contact: Jonathan Sherman

Beat Music Library   **(310) 828-2292**
7806 Denrock Ave.   **www.beatmusiclibrary.com**
Los Angeles, CA 90045
(Duplication & Non-Linear Online)

Bell Sound Studios   **(323) 461-3036**
916 N. Citrus Ave.   FAX **(323) 461-8764**
Los Angeles, CA 90038   **www.bellsound.com**

Big Time Picture Company, Inc.   **(310) 207-0921**
1629 Stanford St.   FAX **(310) 826-0071**
Santa Monica, CA 90404   **www.bigtimepic.com**
(Avid and Final Cut Pro Systems, Film Editing & Non-Linear
Offline and Online)

Bitmax, LLC   **(323) 978-7878**
6255 Sunset Blvd., Ste. 1515   FAX **(323) 978-7879**
Los Angeles, CA 90028   **www.bitmax.net**
(DVD Duplication)

Blue Room Post   **(310) 727-2600**
1600 Rosecrans Ave., Bldg. 5A   FAX **(310) 727-2601**
Manhattan Beach, CA 90266   **www.blueroompost.com**
(Authoring, Captions, Compositing, Computer Graphics,
Digital, Digital Editing Systems, Digital Intermediate Services,
Digital Online, Duplication, DVD Design, DVD Menus, Editing,
Final Cut Pro Systems, Finishing, High Def, HD Editing, HD
Finishing, HD Remastering, HD Online, New Media Encoding,
Non-Linear Offline and Online, Non-Linear Editing, Offline,
Online, Post Supervision, Pre-Visualization, Standards
Conversions, Subtitles & Tape to Tape Color Correction)

Bobine Telecine Post   **(310) 582-1240**
1447 Cloverfield Blvd., Ste. 101   FAX **(310) 582-1245**
Santa Monica, CA 90404   **www.bobinetelecine.com**
(Color Correction, Duplication, Film to Tape Transfers, Tape to
Tape Correction & Telecine)
Contacts: Julie Airale & Jais Lamaire

Brickyard VFX   **(310) 453-5722**
2054 Broadway   FAX **(310) 453-5744**
Santa Monica, CA 90404   **www.brickyardvfx.com**
(Computer Graphics & Non-Linear Online)

Burbank Post (818) 953-8919
3619 W. Magnolia Blvd.
Burbank, CA 91505
(DVD Authoring, DVD Design, DVD Duplication, DVD Menus,
HD Editing & Finishing)
Contact: Chris Settlemoir & Jim Settlemoir

CCI Digital, Inc. (818) 562-6300
2921 W. Alameda Ave. FAX (818) 562-8222
Burbank, CA 91505 www.ccidigital.com
(Compositing, Computer Graphics, Digital Online, Duplication,
High Def, Non-Linear Offline & Telecine)
Contact: Craig Barnes

  (323) 785-1550
Chainsaw (323) 785-1555
940 N. Orange Dr., Second Fl. www.chainsawedit.com
Hollywood, CA 90038
(All Formats, Authoring, Avid Systems, Color Correction,
Colorizations, Compositing, Digital Colorization, Digital
Editing Systems, Digital Intermediate Services, Digital Online,
Duplication, Finishing, HD Editing, HD Finishing, HD Online,
Mastering, Mobile Facility, New Media Encoding, Non-Linear
Offline and Online, Post Supervision, Standards Conversions &
Tape to Tape Transfers)

Chemical Effects (310) 587-9100
225 Santa Monica Blvd., Ninth Fl. FAX (310) 587-9299
Santa Monica, CA 90401 www.chemicaleffects.tv
(Computer Graphics & Non-Linear Online)

Christopher Gray
Post Production Services (310) 395-9845
3918 Michael Ave. www.cgpost.com
Los Angeles, CA 90066
(Duplication & Non-Linear Offline and Online)

  (818) 845-1755
Christy's Editorial (800) 556-5706
3625 W. Pacific Ave. FAX (818) 845-1756
Burbank, CA 91505 www.christys.net
(Film Editing & Non-Linear Offline and Online)

Cinema Libre Studio (818) 349-8822
8328 DeSoto Ave. FAX (818) 349-9922
Canoga Park, CA 91304 www.cinemalibrestudio.com
(Computer Graphics, Linear Online, Non-Linear Offline and
Online, Subtitles & Tape to Film Transfers)

  (323) 850-6608
Clonetown HD (323) 851-0299
3131 Cahuenga Blvd. West FAX (323) 851-0277
Los Angeles, CA 90068 www.clonetownhd.com
(All Formats, Authoring, Avid Systems, Captions, Digital Editing
Systems, Digital Media Transfers, Duplication, Final Cut Pro
Systems, HD Editing, HD Finishing, HD Online, New Media
Encoding, Non-Linear Offline and Online, Non-Linear Editing,
Recording, Standards Conversions & Tape to Tape Transfers)

  (310) 839-5400
Cloud 19 (310) 717-7819
3767 Overland Ave., Ste. 103 FAX (310) 839-5404
Los Angeles, CA 90034 www.cloud19.com

Company 3 LA (310) 255-6600
1661 Lincoln Blvd., Ste. 400 FAX (310) 255-6602
Santa Monica, CA 90404 www.company3.com
(Compositing, DI Services, Film Scanning and Recording, HD
and SD Tape to Tape Correction & Telecine)

The Complex Studios (310) 477-1938
2323 Corinth Ave. FAX (310) 607-9631
West Los Angeles, CA 90064
  www.thecomplexstudios.com

  (323) 860-1300
Crest Digital (800) 961-8273
1000 Highland Ave. FAX (323) 461-2598
Hollywood, CA 90038 www.crestdigital.com
(Analog/Digital Online, Computer Graphics, Duplication, Edge
Coding, Standards Conversion & Telecine)
Contact: John M. Walker

Daily Post (310) 417-4844
6701 Center Dr. West, Ste. 1111 FAX (310) 410-1543
Los Angeles, CA 90045 www.dailypost.tv

Defy Agency (310) 204-2340
3750 S. Robertson Blvd., Ste. 104 FAX (310) 204-2341
Culver City, CA 90232 www.defyagency.com

  (310) 689-2470
Different by Design (310) 569-8038
12233 W. Olympic Blvd., Ste. 120 FAX (310) 689-2471
Los Angeles, CA 90064 www.dxdproductions.com
(Duplication & HD and SD Non-Linear Online)

Digiscope (310) 315-6060
1447 Cloverfield Blvd. FAX (310) 828-5856
Santa Monica, CA 90404 www.digiscope.com
(Compositing, Editing & Pre-Visualization)

Digital Jungle Post Production (323) 962-0867
6363 Santa Monica Blvd. FAX (323) 962-9960
Hollywood, CA 90038 www.digijungle.com
(Color Correction, Compositing, Digital Intermediate Services,
Digital Media Transfers, Digital Online, Finishing, Graphics,
Mastering, Post Production Services & Post Supervision)

Digital Vortechs (800) 900-2843
903 Colorado Blvd., Ste. 220 www.digitalvortechs.com
Santa Monica, CA 90401

Dogma Studios (310) 838-2973
10559 Jefferson Blvd. FAX (310) 356-3603
Culver City, CA 90232 www.dogmastudios.com
(Encoding, HD Editing & New Media)

The Dreaming Tree (818) 845-3230
1112 Chestnut St., Ste. B FAX (818) 333 0795
Burbank, CA 91506
  www.dreamingtreeproductions.com

  (818) 566-4151
DVS Intelestream (818) 841-6750
2625 W. Olive FAX (818) 566-4453
Burbank, CA 91505 www.dvs.tv
(Duplication, Telecine & Standards Conversion)

  (310) 572-7230
editSource (310) 466-3624
12044 Washington Blvd. FAX (310) 572-7230
Los Angeles, CA 90066 www.theeditsource.com
(All Formats, Avid Systems, Color Correction, Compositing,
Digital Editing Systems, Digital Film Mastering, Intermediate
Services, Digital Online, Duplication, DVD Design, Film Editing,
Final Cut Pro Systems, Finishing, HD Editing, HD Finishing,
HD Online, HD Remastering, New Media Encoding, Non-Linear
Offline, Non-Linear Online, Post Supervision &
Standards Conversions)

Encore Hollywood (323) 466-7663
6344 Fountain Ave. FAX (323) 467-5539
Hollywood, CA 90028 www.encorehollywood.com
(Compositing, Computer Graphics, Digital Intermediate
Services, Digital Online, Digital Telecine, Duplication, HD Online
and Telecine, Standards Conversion & Tape to Tape
Color Correction)
Contact: Barry Goldscher

Entertainment Post (818) 846-0411
639 S. Glenwood Pl. FAX (818) 846-1542
Burbank, CA 91506 www.entpost.com

  (818) 707-4524
Eric Blum Productions, Inc. (818) 707-4526
31139 Via Colinas, Ste. 210 FAX (818) 707-0071
Thousand Oaks, CA 91362
  www.ericblumproductions.com
(Compositing, Computer Graphics, Duplication &
Linear/Non-Linear Online)

Film Technology Company, Inc. (323) 464-3456
726 N. Cole Ave. FAX (323) 464-7439
Hollywood, CA 90038 www.filmtech.com/
(Duplication, Tape to Tape Color Correction & Telecine)
Contact: Alan Stark

FILMLOOK Media and Post/
FILMLOOK Inc.　　　　　　　　**(818) 845-9200**
2917 W. Olive Ave.　　　　　　FAX **(818) 845-9238**
Burbank, CA 91505　　　　　**www.filmlook.com**
(Authoring, Avid Systems, Captions, Color Correction,
Computer Graphics, Digital Editing Systems, Duplication, DVD
Design, DVD Menus, Final Cut Pro Systems, Finishing, Graphic
Design, Graphics, HD Editing, HD Finishing, HD Online, HD
Remastering, Linear Offline, Linear Online, Mastering, Motion
Graphics, New Media Encoding, Non-Linear Offline, Non-Linear
Online & Tape to Tape Film Simulation)
Contacts: Anna Cordova & Robert Faber

　　　　　　　　　　　　　　　(818) 846-3101
FotoKem　　　　　　　　　　**(818) 846-3102**
2801 W. Alameda Ave.　　　FAX **(818) 841-2130**
Burbank, CA 91505　　　　　**www.fotokem.com**
(All Formats, Digital Intermediate Services, Digital Telecine,
Duplication, DVD, Online & Standards Conversion)

　　　　　　　　　　　　　　　(310) 369-7678
Fox Studios　　　　　　　　　**(310) 369-4636**
10201 W. Pico Blvd.　　　　FAX **(310) 369-4407**
Los Angeles, CA 90035　　　**www.foxpost.com**

Framework Post　　　　　　**(310) 696-4600**
7920 Sunset Blvd., Ste. 200　FAX **(310) 696-4891**
Los Angeles, CA 90046　　**www.asylument.com**
(Avid Systems, Color Correction, Compositing, Computer
Animation, Computer Graphics, Digital Editing Systems,
Digital Online, Duplication, DVD Design, DVD Menus, Graphic
Design, Graphics, HD Editing, HD Finishing, HD Online, Motion
Graphics, Non-Linear Offline and Online, Post Supervision,
Recording, Scanning, Tape to Tape Transfers &
Video to Still Transfers)

Full Moon & High Tide Studios　　**(310) 647-1958**
424 Main St.　　　　　　　FAX **(310) 647-1960**
El Segundo, CA 90245　　　　**www.fmht.net**
(Duplication & Non-Linear Offline and Online)

FXF Productions, Inc.　　　**(310) 577-5009**
1024 Harding Ave., Ste. 201　FAX **(310) 577-1960**
Venice, CA 90291　　　**www.fxfproductions.com**
(All Formats, Color Correction, Computer Graphics, Digital
Editing Systems, Graphic Design, Non-Linear Offline and
Online & Subtitles)
Contacts: Eric Alan Donaldson & L. Lonnie Peralta

GDC Digital Services　　　　**(818) 972-4370**
1016 W. Magnolia Blvd.　　FAX **(877) 643-2872**
Burbank, CA 91506　**www.gdc-digitalservices.com**
(Avid Systems, Color Correction, Colorizations, Digital
Colorization, Digital Editing Systems, Digital Film Mastering,
Digital Intermediate Services, Digital Media Transfers, Digital
Online, Duplication, Final Cut Pro Systems, Finishing, HD
Editing, HD Finishing, HD Online, HD Remastering, Mastering,
New Media Encoding & Post Supervision)

A Gosch Production　　　　**(818) 729-0000**
　　　　　　　　www.goschproductions.com
(Non-Linear Offline and Online)

Grainey Pictures　　　　　　**(310) 827-1111**
4220 Glencoe Ave., Ste. 100　FAX **(310) 827-1124**
Marina del Rey, CA 90292　　　**www.gpixer.com**

HD Pictures & Post, Inc.　　**(310) 264-2575**
12233 W. Olympic Blvd., Ste.120 FAX **(310) 689-2471**
Los Angeles, CA 90064
(3D Conversion From All Formats, Captions, Color Correction,
Compositing, Digital Intermediate Services, Film Restoration,
Post Supervision, Recording & Subtitles)

Hieroglyphic Productions　　**(818) 505-6050**
3211 Cahuenga Blvd. West, Ste. 103　FAX **(818) 505-6054**
Los Angeles, CA 90068　　　　**www.hiero.net**

Hip Films　　　　　　　　　**(323) 467-2897**
1622 Gower St.　　　　　　FAX **(323) 469-8251**
Hollywood, CA 90028　　　　**www.hipfilms.com**
(Avid Systems, Color Correction, Computer Animation,
Computer Graphics, Digital Film Mastering, Digital Intermediate
Services, Digital Online, Digital Telecine, DVD Designs and
Menus, Film to Tape Transfers, Final Cut Pro Systems,
Finishing, High Def, HD Editing, HD Finishing, HD Remastering,
HD Telecine, HD Online, Mastering, Mobile Facility &
Motion Graphics)

Home Planet Post, Inc.　　　**(805) 201-2618**
　　　　　　　　　　　　FAX **(805) 965-2329**
　　　　　　www.homeplanetproductions.com

　　　　　　　　　　　　　　　(323) 969-8822
HTV - High Technology Video　**(818) 760-7600**
3575 Cahuenga Blvd. West, Fourth Fl. FAX **(323) 969-8860**
Los Angeles, CA 90068　　　　**www.htvinc.net**
(Computer Graphics, Digital Intermediate Services, Digital
Offline and Online, Duplication, HD Online and Telecine &
Standards Conversion)
Contacts: Jim Hardy, Mark Shore & Steve Tannen

an ideal world　　　　　　**(714) 953-9501**
209 N. Bush St.　　　　　　FAX **(714) 380-6311**
Santa Ana, CA 92701　　**www.anidealworld.com**
(Color Correction, Compositing, Computer Animation,
Computer Graphics, Digital Editing Systems, Digital Online,
Film Restoration, Final Cut Pro Systems, Finishing, Graphic
Design, Graphics, HD Editing, HD Finishing, HD Online,
Motion Graphics, Non-Linear Offline, Non-Linear Online, Post
Supervision, Pre-Visualization, Tape to Tape Color Correction &
Tape to Tape Film Simulation)
Contact: Molly Talbot Hart

Ignite Rentals　　　　　　　**(310) 702-7955**
(Computer Graphics & Non-Linear Offline)

Ignition Post　　　　　　　**(818) 762-2210**
4130 Cahuenga Blvd., Ste. 100　**www.ignition-post.com**
Toluca Lake, CA 91602

Illuminate –
Arts, Media & Entertainment　　**(323) 969-8822**
3575 Cahuenga Blvd. West, Fourth Fl. FAX **(323) 969-8840**
Los Angeles, CA 90068　**www.illuminatehollywood.com**
(All Formats, Authoring, Avid Systems, Captions, Color
Correction, Colorizations, Compositing, Computer Animation,
Computer Graphics, Digital Colorization, Digital Editing
Systems, Digital Film Mastering, Digital Intermediate Services,
Digital Online, Digital Telecine, Duplication, DVD Design,
DVD Menus, Edge Coding, Film Editing, Film Preservation
and Restoration, Film Recording, Final Cut Pro Systems,
Finishing, Graphic Design, Graphics, HD Editing, HD Finishing,
HD Remastering, HD Telecine, HD Online, Linear Offline and
Online, Mastering, Mobile Facility, Motion Graphics, Negative
Cutting, New Media Encoding, Non-Linear Offline and Online,
Post Supervision, Pre-Visualization, Recording, Scanning,
Standards Conversions, Subtitles, Tape to Tape Color
Correction, Tape to Tape Film Simulation, Tape to Tape and Film
to Tape Transfers, Telecine, Training for Computer Graphics &
Video to Still Transfers)
Contacts: Eric Geisler, James Hardy, Patricia Sullivan &
AJ Ullman

In A Place Post Production　　**(323) 656-8412**
2044 Laurel Canyon Rd.　　FAX **(323) 848-8716**
Los Angeles, CA 90046　　　**www.inaplacepost.com**
(Boutique Post House, Color Correction, Compositing, Digital
Intermediate, FCP Suite Rentals, HD Online, Pablo 4K, RED
Camera Rental & Visual Effects)

The Institution Post　　　　**(818) 566-7801**
423 N. Fairview St.　　　**www.the-institution.com**
Burbank, CA 91505
(All Formats, Authoring, Avid Systems, Color Correction,
Compositing, Computer Animation, Computer Graphics, Digital
Editing Systems, Digital Film Mastering, Digital Intermediate
Services, Digital Media Transfers, Digital Online, DVD
Design, DVD Menus, Film Editing, Final Cut Pro Systems,
Finishing, Graphic Design, Graphics, HD Editing, HD
Finishing, HD Online, HD Remastering, Linear Offline, Linear
Online, Mastering, Motion Graphics, New Media Encoding,
Non-Linear Offline, Non-Linear Online, Post Supervision &
Pre-Visualization)

Inter Video (818) 843-3624
2211 N. Hollywood Way FAX **(818) 843-6884**
Burbank, CA 91505 **www.intervideo24.com**
(Computer Graphics & Standards Conversion)
Contact: Richard Clark

iProbe Multilingual Solutions, Inc. (888) 489-6035
www.iprobesolutions.com
(All Formats, Authoring, Avid Systems, Captions, Color
Correction, Colorizations, Compositing, Computer Animation,
Computer Graphics, Digital Colorization, Digital Editing
Systems, Digital Film Mastering, Digital Intermediate Services,
Digital Online, Digital Telecine, Duplication, DVD Design, DVD
Menus, Edge Coding, Film Editing, Film to Tape Transfers,
Final Cut Pro Systems, Finishing, Graphic Design, Graphics,
HD Editing, HD Finishing, HD Remastering, HD Telecine,
HD Online, Linear/Non-Linear Offline and Online, Mastering,
Motion Graphics, Negative Cutting, New Media Encoding, Post
Supervision, Pre-Visualization, Recording, Scanning, Standards
Conversions, Subtitles, Tape to Tape Color Correction, Tape to
Tape Film Simulation, Tape to Tape Transfers, Telecine, Training
for Computer Graphics & Video to Still Transfers)

Izon Studios (818) 468-7807
www.izonstudios.com/portfolio.html

Jetty Studios, Inc. (818) 260-9261
1612 W. Olive Ave., Ste. 304 FAX **(818) 260-9701**
Burbank, CA 91506 **www.jettystudios.com**
(Captions, Color Correction, Computer Graphics, Duplication &
Non-Linear Offline)

JM Digital Works (760) 476-1783
2460 Impala Dr. FAX **(760) 476-1788**
Carlsbad, CA 92008 **www.jmdigitalworks.com**
(Digital Online, Duplication & Offline)
Contact: Ken Kebow

Kappa Studios, Inc. (818) 843-3400
3619 W. Magnolia Blvd. FAX **(818) 559-5684**
Burbank, CA 91505 **www.kappastudios.com**
(Duplication & Non-Linear Offline and Online)
Contact: Paul Long

(310) 954-8650
LA Digital Post, Inc. (818) 487-5000
2260 Centinela Ave. FAX **(310) 954-8686**
West Los Angeles, CA 90064 **www.ladigital.com**
(Avid Systems, Color Correction, Compositing, Duplication,
Final Cut Pro Systems, Graphics, HD Editing, HD Online, HD/
SD Finishing, Offline, Standards Conversions & Visual FX)

(818) 487-5000
LA Digital Post, Inc. (310) 954-8650
11311 Camarillo St. FAX **(818) 487-5015**
Toluca Lake, CA 91602 **www.ladigital.com**
(Avid Systems, Color Correction, Compositing, Duplication,
Final Cut Pro Systems, Graphics, HD Editing, HD Online, HD/
SD Finishing, Offline, Standards Conversions & Visual FX)

Laser Pacific Media Corporation (323) 462-6266
809 N. Cahuenga Blvd. FAX **(323) 464-3233**
Hollywood, CA 90038 **www.laserpacific.com**
(Digital Intermediate Services, High Def, Online & Telecine)
Contact: Hawk Hamilton

(818) 459-6630
Laurel Canyon Productions (310) 738-4184
1101 S. Flower Ave. FAX **(818) 450-0916**
Burbank, CA 91502 **www.lcproductions.tv**
(All Formats, Avid Systems, Color Correction, Colorizations,
Computer Graphics, Digital Editing Systems, Digital
Intermediate Services, Digital Media Transfers, Digital Online,
Duplication, Film Editing, Finishing, Graphics, HD Editing, HD
Finishing, HD Online, Motion Graphics, Non-Linear Offline,
Non-Linear Online, Post Supervision & Tape to Tape Transfers)

(818) 840-7200
Level 3 Post (818) 840-7889
2901 W. Alameda, Third Fl. **www.level3post.com**
Burbank, CA 91505
(Digital Online and Telecine, Duplication, HD Online and
Telecine, Standards Conversion & Tape to Tape
Color Correction)

Libertad Soul, LLC (323) 447-7810
1732 Aviation Blvd., Ste. 323 FAX **(310) 802-3866**
Redondo Beach, CA 90278 **www.libertadsoul.com**
(Color Correction, Dailies, Digital Telecine, Film to Tape
Transfers, HD Telecine & Telecine)

Light Iron (323) 472-8300
6381 De Longpre Ave. FAX **(323) 832-8432**
Los Angeles, CA 90028 **www.lightiron.com**
(Color Correction, Digital Colorization, Digital Film Mastering,
Digital Intermediate Services, Digital Media Transfers,
Digital Online, Digital Telecine, Finishing, HD Editing, HD
Finishing, HD Online, HD Remastering, HD Telecine, Mastering,
Mobile Facility, Motion Graphics, Non-Linear Online,
Post Supervision & Video to Still Transfers)

Lightning Media (323) 957-9255
1415 Cahuenga Blvd. **www.lightningmedia.com**
Hollywood, CA 90028
(Compositing, Digital Online, Duplication, HD Telecine,
Standards Conversion, Tape to Tape
Color Correction & Telecine)

Liquid VFX (310) 392-1212
215 Rose Ave. FAX **(310) 392-1222**
Venice, CA 90291 **www.laliquid.com**
(All Formats, Color Correction, Compositing, Computer
Graphics, Digital Online, Duplication, Finishing, Graphics, HD
Finishing, HD Online, Motion Graphics, Post Supervision &
Standards Conversions)
Contacts: James Bohn & Terry O'Gara

Los Feliz Post (818) 859-3500
905 East Mountain St. **www.lfpost.com**
Glendale, CA 91207
(Color Correction, Duplication, High Def, Non-Linear Offline and
Online, Standards Conversion, Subtitles &
Tape to Tape Correction)

Madrik Multimedia, LLC (818) 802-7719
www.madrik.com
(All Formats, Avid and Final Cut Pro Systems, Computer/Motion
Graphics, Editing & High Def Editing)

Master Communication (310) 832-3303
445 W. Seventh St. FAX **(310) 832-0296**
San Pedro, CA 90731 **www.bestmedia.com**
(Non-Linear Offline and Online)
Contact: Mary Jo Masters

(818) 662-0300
Mechnology (661) 714-2604
121 W. Lexington Dr., Ste. B101 **www.mechnology.com**
Glendale, CA 91203

Media Fishtank (818) 518-7283
www.mediafishtank.com
(Authoring, Avid Systems, Color Correction, Colorizations,
Compositing, Computer Graphics, Digital Editing Systems,
Digital Media Transfers, Duplication, DVD Design, DVD Menus,
Graphics, HD Editing, Non-Linear Offline and Online, Subtitles,
Tape To Tape Color Correction & Video to Still Transfers)

(805) 658-3339
Media International (800) 477-7575
5740 Ralston St., Ste. 304 FAX **(805) 658-3331**
Ventura, CA 93003 **www.mediainternational.com**
(Duplication & Offline and Online Editing)
Contacts: John Hasbrouck & Jolene Jackson

Mega Mace Creative (323) 730-0175
www.megamace.com

Metro Encoding (818) 558-7800
4425 W. Riverside Dr., Ste. 202 **www.metroencoding.com**
Burbank, CA 91505
(Authoring, Digital Media Transfers, Digital Online, HD Online,
New Media Encoding, Training for Computer Graphics & Video
to Still Transfers)

(323) 782-7900
Midtown Edit (323) 801-2300
8489 W. Third St. FAX **(323) 651-1240**
Los Angeles, CA 90048 **www.midtownedit.com**
(Avid and Final Cut Pro, Decks, Editing Suites &
Storage Rentals)

Mind Over Eye, LLC
(310) 396-4663
(310) 968-4259
1639 11th St., Ste. 117
FAX (310) 396-0663
Santa Monica, CA 90404
www.mindovereye.com
(HD and SD Offline and Online)

Mixin Pixls
(310) 237-6438
www.mixinpixls.com
(Captions, Final Cut Pro Systems, Non-Linear Online,
Recording & Subtitles)

Motion City Films
(310) 434-1272
www.motioncity.com
(Computer Animation, Computer/Motion Graphics, Editing &
Non-Linear Offline and Online)

NBC Universal Artworks
(212) 664-5972
30 Rockefeller Plaza, Ste. 514E
www.nbcartworks.com
New York, NY 10012
(Computer Graphics, Graphic Design, Graphics, Motion
Graphics & New Media Encoding)

Ntropic
(310) 806-4950
2332 S. Centinela St., Ste. B
FAX (310) 806-4959
Los Angeles, CA 90064
www.ntropic.com

Oasis Imagery
(323) 469-9800
6500 Sunset Blvd.
FAX (323) 462-4620
Los Angeles, CA 90028
www.oasisimagery.com
(Color Correction, Colorization, Digital Online, Final Cut Pro
Systems, High Def, HD Editing, HD Finishing, HD Online,
Linear/Non-Linear Offline and Online, Online &
Post Supervision)

Oracle Post
(818) 752-2800
4720 W. Magnolia Blvd.
FAX (818) 769-2624
Burbank, CA 91505
www.oraclepost.com
(Non-Linear Offline and Online)
Contacts: James Lifton & Paulette Lifton

Outpost Digital
(310) 752-2300
1620 Euclid St.
FAX (310) 752-2299
Santa Monica, CA 90404
www.outpostdigital.com
(Color Correction, Design, High Def & Non-Linear
Offline and Online)
Contacts: Brody McHugh & Evan Schechtman

Ⓐ The Studios at Paramount
(323) 956-3991
The Studios at Paramount
Post Production Services,
5555 Melrose Ave.
www.thestudiosatparamount.com
Los Angeles, CA 90038
(All Formats, Avid Systems, Captions, Color Correction,
Colorizations, Compositing, Computer Graphics, Digital Editing
Systems, Digital Film Mastering, Digital Online, Duplication,
DVD Design, DVD Menus, Edge Coding, Film Editing, Film
Recording, Finishing, Graphic Design, Graphics, HD Editing,
HD Finishing, HD Online, Linear/Non-Linear Offline and Online,
Mastering, Mobile Facility, Motion Graphics, Negative Cutting,
New Media Encoding, Standards Conversions, Tape to Tape
Color Correction, Tape to Tape Film Simulation &
Tape to Tape Transfers)

Pixel Blues, Inc.
(818) 766-4600
411 W. Alameda Blvd., Ste. 401
FAX (818) 953-9696
North Hollywood, CA 91602
www.pixelblues.com
(Computer Graphics & Online Editing)

Pixel Plantation
(818) 566-7777
4111 W. Alameda Ave., Ste. 301
Burbank, CA 91505
www.pixelplantation.com
(All Formats, Avid Systems, Color Correction, Compositing,
Digital Online, Duplication, Finishing, Graphics, HD Editing, HD
Finishing, HD Online, Non-Linear Offline & Non-Linear Online)

Point360
(818) 556-5700
(866) 968-4336
1133 N. Hollywood Way
FAX (818) 556-5753
Burbank, CA 91505
www.point360.com
(Avid Systems, Captions, Color Correction, Digital Film
Mastering, Digital Intermediate Services, Digital Media
Transfers, Digital Online, Digital Telecine, Duplication, Film
Recording, Film Restoration, Film Scanning, Film to Tape
Transfers, Final Cut Pro Systems, Finishing, HD Editing,
HD Finishing, HD Online, HD Remastering, HD Telecine,
Linear Online, Mastering, New Media Encoding, Standards
Conversions, Subtitles, Tape to Tape Color Correction, Tape to
Tape Transfers & Telecine)

Point360
(323) 957-5500
1147 Vine St.
FAX (323) 466-7406
Hollywood, CA 90038
www.point360.com
(Captions, Digital Editing Systems, Digital Film Mastering,
Digital Online, Digital Telecine, Duplication, Finishing, HD
Editing, HD Finishing, HD Online, HD Remastering, HD
Telecine, New Media Encoding & Standards Conversions)

Point360
(310) 481-7000
12421 W. Olympic Blvd.
FAX (310) 207-8404
Los Angeles, CA 90064
www.point360.com
(Avid Systems, Color Correction, Compositing, Computer
Animation, Final Cut Pro Systems, HD Editing, HD Online, HD
Remastering, Non-Linear Offline, Non-Linear Online &
Post Supervision)

Post and Beam
(310) 828-1128
1623 Stanford St.
www.postandbeam.tv
Santa Monica, CA 90404
(Captions, Color Correction, HD Editing, HD Finishing, HD
Online & Motion Graphics)

Post Digital Services
(323) 845-0812
1258 N. Highland Ave., Ste. 210
FAX (323) 845-0812
Hollywood, CA 90038
www.postdigitalservices.com
(All Formats, Authoring, Avid Systems, Blu-Ray, Captions, CGI,
Color Correction, Compositing, Computer Animation, Computer
Graphics, Digital Colorization, Digital Editing Systems, Digital
Film Mastering, Digital Intermediate Services, Digital Media
Transfers, Digital Online, Duplication, DVD Design, DVD
Menus, Film Editing, Film Preservation, Film Recording, Film
Restoration, Film Scanning, Film to Tape Transfers, Final Cut
Pro Systems, Finishing, Graphic Design, Graphics, HD Editing,
HD Finishing, HD Online, HD Remastering, Linear Offline,
Mastering, Motion Graphics, New Media Encoding, Non-Linear
Offline, Non-Linear Online, Post Supervision, Pre-Visualization,
Recording, Scanning, Standards Conversions, Subtitles, Tape
to Tape Color Correction, Tape to Tape Film Simulation, Tape to
Tape Transfers & Video to Still Transfers)

Post Logic Studios
(323) 461-7887
1800 N. Vine St., Ste. 100
FAX (323) 461-7790
Los Angeles, CA 90028
www.postlogic.com
(Computer Graphics, Digital Online, Duplication,
Film Transfers & Standards Conversion)

Post Media Group, Inc.
(310) 289-5959
337 S. Robertson Blvd., Ste. 201
Beverly Hills, CA 90211
www.postmediagroup.tv

Post Modern Edit, LLC
(949) 608-8700
2941 Alton Pkwy
FAX (949) 608-8729
Irvine, CA 92606
www.postmodernedit.com
(Authoring, Captions, Color Correction, Compositing, Computer
Animation, Computer Graphics, Digital Editing Systems, Digital
Media Transfers, Digital Online, Duplication, DVD Design, DVD
Menus, Final Cut Pro Systems, Finishing, Graphic Design, HD
Editing, HD Finishing, HD Online, Linear Online, Mastering,
Motion Graphics, New Media Encoding, Non-Linear Online,
Post Supervision, Standards Conversion, Subtitles & Tape to
Tape Transfers)
Contacts: Kelli Alvarado, Michael Boyd, Troy Burlage &
Rich O'Neill

Precision Productions + Post (310) 839-4600
10718 McCune Ave. FAX (310) 839-4601
Los Angeles, CA 90034 www.precisionpost.com

Prime Digital Media Services (661) 964-0220
  (323) 864-8331
28111 Avenue Stanford FAX (661) 964-0550
Valencia, CA 91355 www.primedigital.com
(Color Correction, Duplication, HD Online, Non-Linear Offline,
Standards Conversion, Telecine & Transmission Services)
Contact: Brigitte Prouty

Qube Cinema, Inc. (818) 392-8155
601 S. Glenoaks Blvd., Ste. 102 FAX (818) 301-0401
Burbank, CA 91502 www.qubecinema.com
(Digital Cinema Servers and Software & Digital Film Mastering)

Quest Pictures (818) 400-7533
7625 Hayvenhurst Ave., Ste. 41 www.questpictures.com
Van Nuys, CA 91406
(All Formats, Authoring, Color Correction, Colorizations,
Compositing, Computer Graphics, Digital Colorization, Digital
Editing Systems, Digital Film Mastering, Duplication, DVD
Design, DVD Menus, Film Editing, Final Cut Pro Systems,
Graphic Design, Graphics, HD Editing, HD Online, Mastering,
Motion Graphics, Non-Linear Offline and Online, Post
Supervision, Pre-Visualization, Recording &
Video to Still Transfers)

Raleigh Studios - Manhattan Beach (323) 960-3456
1600 Rosecrans Ave. FAX (310) 727-2710
Manhattan Beach, CA 90266 www.raleighstudios.com
Contact: Walter Canton

Raleigh Studios Post Production (323) 871-5649
5300 Melrose Ave. FAX (323) 871-5629
Hollywood, CA 90038 www.raleighstudios.com
(Digital Non-Linear Offline & Film Editing)
Contact: Walter Canton

Raycom Media (818) 846-0101
2901 W. Alameda Ave. FAX (818) 846-0277
Burbank, CA 91505 www.raycompost.com
(Avid Systems, Captions, Color Correction, Downconversions,
Duplication, Graphics, HD Editing, High Def, Non-Linear
Online & Standards Conversion)

Red Dog Post & Design (310) 237-6438
  www.reddogpost.com
(All Language Captioning and Subtitling, Color Correction,
Compositing, Digital Intermediate Services & Film Restoration)
Contact: Jeff Miller

RentHD.com/Lightpost Productions (818) 955-7678
1701 W. Burbank Blvd., Ste. 201 FAX (818) 955-5181
Burbank, CA 91506 www.renthd.com
(Authoring, Color Correction, Film Restoration, Film to Tape
Transfers, Final Cut Pro Systems, HD Online & Mastering)

Ring of Fire (310) 966-5055
1538 20th St. FAX (310) 966-5056
Santa Monica, CA 90404 www.ringoffire.com
(High Def & Non-Linear Online)

Roush Media (818) 559-8648
84 E. Santa Anita Ave. www.roush-media.com
Burbank, CA 91502
(Color Correction, Digital Intermediate Services, Digital Media
Transfers, Duplication, Final Cut Pro Systems, Hard Drive
to Tape Transfers, HD Editing, HD Finishing, HD Online,
Mastering, New Media Encoding &
Tape to Tape Color Correction)

Rundell Filmworks (818) 314-7560
5309 Wilkinson Ave. FAX (818) 760-3221
Valley Village, CA 91607 www.rundellfilmworks.com

Runway (310) 636-2000
1415 N. Cahuenga Blvd. FAX (310) 636-2034
Los Angeles, CA 90028 www.runway.com
(Avid Systems, Digital Editing Systems, Final Cut Pro Systems,
HD Editing, HD Finishing, HD Online & Non-Linear
Offline and Online)
Contact: Daniel Bernato

Santa Monica Video, Inc. (310) 451-0333
  (800) 843-3827
1505 11th St. FAX (310) 458-3350
Santa Monica, CA 90401 www.smvcompletemedia.com
(Duplication)

Screen Door Entertainment, Inc. (818) 781-5600
15223 Burbank Blvd. FAX (818) 781-5601
Sherman Oaks, CA 91411 www.sdetv.com

Secret Headquarters, Inc. (323) 677-2092
5767 W. Adams Blvd. FAX (323) 677-2096
Los Angeles, CA 90016 www.secrethq.com
(All Formats, Authoring, Avid Systems, Color Correction, Digital
Film Mastering, Digital Media Transfers, Duplication, DVD
Menus, Final Cut Pro Systems, Finishing, HD Editing, HD
Finishing, HD Online, Mastering, Offline, Online &
Post Supervision)
Contacts: Dave Bogosian, Greg Huson & Lance Mueller

Shapeshifter (323) 876-3444
3405 Cahuenga Blvd. West FAX (323) 876-1444
Los Angeles, CA 90068 www.shapeshifterpost.com
(HD Avid, Nitris and Final Cut Pro Systems & Standard and
HD Offline and Online)
Contact: Russo Anastasio

Solventdreams (323) 906-9700
227 N. Avenue 66 FAX (323) 225-5235
Los Angeles, CA 90042 www.solventdreams.com
(Computer Graphics, HD and Online Editing)

Sonic Pool (323) 460-4649
6860 Lexington Ave. FAX (323) 460-6063
Los Angeles, CA 90038 www.sonicpool.com
(Duplication & Non-Linear Offline and Online)

Sony Pictures Studios (310) 244-5722
10202 W. Washington Blvd. FAX (310) 244-2303
Culver City, CA 90232 www.sonypicturesstudios.com
(Telecine & Video Transfers)
Contact: Tom McCarthy

SpeedMedia (310) 822-8182
200 Mildred Ave. FAX (310) 822-8923
Venice, CA 90291 www.speedmedia.com
(All Formats, Authoring, Avid Systems, Captions, Color
Correction, Computer Animation, Computer Graphics, Digital
Editing Systems, Digital Intermediate Services, Digital
Media Transfers, Digital Online, Duplication, DVD Design,
DVD Menus, Final Cut Pro Systems, Finishing, Graphic
Design, Graphics, HD Editing, HD Finishing, HD Online, HD
Remastering, Mastering, Mobile Facility, Motion Graphics,
New Media Encoding, Non-Linear Offline, Non-Linear Online,
Post Supervision, Pre-Visualization, Recording, Standards
Conversions, Subtitles & Video to Still Transfers)

SSI/Advanced Post Services (323) 969-9333
7165 Sunset Blvd. FAX (323) 969-8333
Los Angeles, CA 90046 www.ssipost.com

Stampede Post Productions (323) 463-8000
931 N. Citrus Ave. FAX (323) 463-8010
Hollywood, CA 91104 www.stampedepost.com
(Editing, Graphics, High Def, Online & Standards Conversion)

StandardVision, LLC (323) 224-3944
  www.standardsite.com
(Color Correction, Colorizations, Compositing, Computer
Animation, Computer Graphics, Computer/Motion Graphics,
Digital, Digital Colorization, Digital Editing Systems, Digital
Film Mastering, Digital Online, DVD, DVD Menus and Design,
Editing, Final Cut Pro Systems, Finishing, Graphic Design,
Graphics, High Def, HD Editing, HD Finishing, HD Online,
Non-Linear Offline and Online, Online & Post Supervision)

Stargate Digital (626) 403-8403
1001 El Centro St. FAX (626) 403-8444
South Pasadena, CA 91030 www.stargatestudios.net
(Compositing, Digital Online & Non-Linear Offline)
Contact: Darren Frankel

Station 22 Edit & Effects   **(310) 488-7726**
3614 Overland Ave.   **www.station22.com**
Los Angeles, CA 90034
(Authoring, Color Correction, Compositing, Computer
Animation, Computer Graphics, Digital Editing Systems, Digital
Online, Duplication, DVD Design, DVD Menus, Film Editing,
Final Cut Pro Systems, Graphic Design, Graphics, HD Editing,
HD Online, Motion Graphics, New Media Encoding & Non-
Linear Offline and Online)
Contacts: Noah Clark, Michael Degnan, Paul McConville &
Gregg Orenstein

STEELE Studios   **(310) 656-7770**
5737 Mesmer Ave.   FAX **(310) 391-9055**
Culver City, CA 90230   **www.steelevfx.com**
(3D Stereoscopic, All Formats, Authoring, Color Correction,
Compositing, Computer Animation, Computer Graphics,
Computer/Motion Graphics, Digital Colorization, Digital Editing
Systems, Digital Intermediate Services, Digital Media Transfers,
Digital Online, Duplication, DVD Design, DVD Menus, Film
Editing, Final Cut Pro Systems, Finishing, Graphic Design, HD
Editing, HD Finishing, HD Online, HD Remastering, Linear,
Linear/Non-Linear Offline and Online, Motion Graphics, Post
Supervision, Pre-Visualization, RED DI Services, Standards
Conversions, Tape to Tape Color Correction, Tape to Tape
Transfers, Visual Effects & Video to Still Transfers)

Stitch   **(310) 450-1116**
1635 12th St.   FAX **(310) 450-1166**
Santa Monica, CA 90404   **www.stitchediting.tv**
(All Formats, Color Correction, Compositing, Computer
Graphics, Digital Colorization, Digital Editing Systems, Digital
Online, Finishing, Graphic Design, Graphics, HD Editing,
HD Finishing, HD Online, Mastering, Motion Graphics,
Non-Linear Online, Post Supervision, Pre-Visualization,
Subtitles & Video to Still Transfers)

     (323) 467-8550
Sunset Edit   **(818) 679-4014**
849 N. Seward St.   FAX **(323) 467-8545**
Los Angeles, CA 90038   **www.sunsetedit.com**

Switch Studios   **(310) 301-1800**
316 S. Venice Blvd.   FAX **(310) 496-1964**
Venice, CA 90291   **www.switch-studios.com**
(Color Correction, Computer Graphics, DVD Design, Editing,
HD Finishing, Mastering, New Media Encoding, Non-Linear
Offline and Online & Post Supervision)

Technicolor Creative
Services - Hollywood   **(323) 817-6600**
6040 Sunset Blvd.   **www.technicolor.com**
Hollywood, CA 90028
(Color Correction, Digital Intermediate Services,
Film Restoration and Preservation & Telecine)
Contact: Jennifer Tellefsen

TEDS   **(310) 237-6438**
     www.tedsla.com
(All Language Closed-Captioning and Subtitling, Color
Correction, Compositing, Digital Intermediate Services &
Film Restoration)

Timecode Multimedia   **(310) 826-9199**
12340 Santa Monica Blvd., Ste. 230
West Los Angeles, CA 90025
     www.timecodemultimedia.com
(Authoring, Captions, Color Correction, Colorizations, Computer
Graphics, Digital Colorization, Digital Online, Duplication,
DVD Design, DVD Menus, Final Cut Pro Systems, Finishing,
Graphics, HD Editing, HD Online,
HD Remastering, Linear Online, Mastering, Motion Graphics,
Non-Linear Offline, Non-Linear Online, Post Supervision,
Standards Conversions, Tape to Tape Transfers &
Video to Still Transfers)
Contacts: Marc Cabaniss & Stuart Ferreyra

Tree Falls Post   **(310) 399-1899**
3435 Ocean Park Blvd., Ste. 113   FAX **(310) 399-1887**
Santa Monica, CA 90405   **www.tfpost.com**

Tree Falls Post   **(323) 851-0299**
3131 Cahuenga Blvd. West   FAX **(323) 851-0277**
Los Angeles, CA 90068   **www.tfpost.com**
(All Formats, Authoring, Avid Systems, Captions, Color
Correction, Digital Editing Systems, Digital Online, Duplication,
Final Cut Pro Systems, Finishing, HD Editing, HD Finishing,
HD Online, Mastering, New Media Encoding, Standards
Conversions, Subtitles & Tape to Tape Transfers)

Tunnel Post   **(310) 260-1208**
233 Wilshire Blvd.   FAX **(310) 260-1209**
Santa Monica, CA 90403   **www.tunnelpost.com**

Universal Studios Digital Services   **(818) 777-4728**
100 Universal City Plaza, Bldg. 3153
Universal City, CA 91608
     www.filmmakersdestination.com
(Color Correction, Duplication, Editing, Encoding & Telecine)
Contact: Ron Silveira

Victory Studios LA   **(818) 769-1776**
10911 Riverside Dr., Ste. 100   FAX **(818) 760-1280**
North Hollywood, CA 91602   **www.victorystudiosla.com**
(Avid Systems, Color Correction, Digital Editing Systems,
Duplication, Final Cut Pro Systems, Graphics, HD Editing,
HD Online, Non-Linear Offline, Non-Linear Online &
Standards Conversions)

The Video Agency, Inc./   **(818) 505-8300**
TVA Productions   **(888) 322-4296**
3950 Vantage Ave.   FAX **(818) 505-8370**
Studio City, CA 91604   **www.tvaproductions.com**
(Computer Graphics, Duplication & Linear/Non-Linear
Offline and Online)
Contact: Jeffery Goddard

Video Symphony   **(800) 871-2843**
266 E. Magnolia Blvd.   FAX **(818) 845-1951**
Burbank, CA 91502   **www.videosymphony.com**
(Digital Online, Linear/Non-Linear Offline & Training For
Computer Graphics)
Contact: Mike Flanagan

View Studio, Inc.   **(805) 745-8814**
385 Toro Canyon Rd.   **www.viewstudio.com**
Carpinteria, CA 93013

     (818) 558-3363
Visual Data Media Services, Inc.   **(888) 418-4782**
145 W. Magnolia Blvd.   FAX **(818) 558-3368**
Burbank, CA 91502   **www.visualdatainc.com**
(Authoring, Captions, Digital Intermediate Services, Duplication,
DVD Design, DVD Menus, HD Editing, Non-Linear Offline,
Non-Linear Online, Standards Conversions, Subtitles &
Tape to Tape Color Correction)

Visual Image   **(323) 962-2233**
1015 N. Cahuenga Blvd., Ste. 4200
Hollywood, CA 90038   **www.visualimagehollywood.com**
(Digital Non-Linear Online and Offline, Duplication, Graphics &
New Media Encoding)
Contact: Steve Goodwin

Vitello Productions   **(818) 955-9930**
4224 Beck Ave.   **www.vitello.com**
Studio City, CA 91604
(Color Correction, Computer Graphics, Non-Linear Offline and
Online & Standards Conversion)

Warner Bros. Studio Facilities -   **(818) 954-1625**
Post Production Services   **(818) 954-2515**
4000 Warner Blvd.   FAX **(818) 954-4138**
Burbank, CA 91522   **www.wbsound.com**

West Post Digital   **(310) 857-5000**
1703 Stewart St.   FAX **(310) 857-5060**
Santa Monica, CA 90404   **www.westpostdigital.com**
(Authoring, Color Correction, Duplication,
DVD Design & Finishing)
Contacts: Todd Brown & Kenny Fields

Westside Media Group　　　(310) 979-3500
　　　　　　　　　　　　　　　(818) 779-8600
12233 W. Olympic Blvd., Ste. 152
West Los Angeles, CA 90064
　　　　　　　www.westsidemediagroup.com
(Authoring, Avid Systems, Captions, Color Correction,
Colorizations, Computer Graphics, Digital Colorization, Digital
Online, Duplication, DVD Authoring, DVD Design, DVD Menus,
Film Transfers, Final Cut Pro Systems, Finishing, Graphics,
HD Editing, HD Finishing, HD Online, HD Remastering,
Non-Linear Offline, Non-Linear Online, Post Supervision,
Standards Conversions, Subtitles, Tape to Tape Transfers &
Video to Still Transfers)
Contacts: Dan Gitlin, Lewis Lipstone & Shirley Lipstone

Wild Pictures　　　　　　　(310) 526-7225
100 Market St., Third Fl.　　www.wildpictures.com
Venice, CA 90291
(Avid Systems, Color Correction, Compositing, Computer
Animation, Computer Graphics, Digital Editing Systems, Digital
Online, Duplication, Film Editing, Final Cut Pro Systems,
Finishing, Graphic Design, HD Editing, HD Finishing,
HD Online, Motion Graphics, New Media Encoding, Non-Linear
Offline, Non-Linear Online & Post Supervision)

Windowseat Pictures　　　　(310) 937-3650
746 Fourth St.　　www.windowseatpictures.com
Hermosa Beach, CA 90254
(All Formats, Authoring, Avid Systems, Color Correction,
Colorizations, Compositing, Computer Animation, Computer
Graphics, Digital Colorization, Digital Editing Systems, Digital
Film Mastering, Digital Intermediate Services, Digital Media
Transfers, Digital Online, Duplication, DVD Design, DVD
Menus, Film Editing, Film to Tape Transfers, Final Cut Pro
Systems, Finishing, Graphic Design, Graphics, HD Editing,
HD Finishing, HD Online, HD Remastering, Mastering, Mobile
Facility, Motion Graphics, New Media Encoding, Non-Linear
Offline, Non-Linear Online, Post Supervision, Pre-Visualization,
Recording, Scanning, Standards Conversions, Subtitles, Tape
to Tape Color Correction, Tape to Tape Film Simulation, Tape to
Tape Transfers, Telecine & Video to Still Transfers)
Contact: Emiliano Haldeman

World of Video & Audio (WOVA)　(310) 659-5959
　　　　　　　　　　　　　　　　(866) 900-3827
8717 Wilshire Blvd.　　　　FAX (310) 659-8247
Beverly Hills, CA 90211　　　　www.wova.com
(All Formats, Authoring, Color Correction, Digital Media
Transfers, Duplication, DVCPro, Film Editing, Film to Tape
Transfers, Final Cut Pro Systems, HD Editing, HDCam and
HDV Downconversions, Linear and Non-Linear Editing,
New Media Encoding, Standards Conversions, Tape to Tape
Transfers & Video to Still Transfers)

World Television Productions　(323) 469-5638
5757 Wilshire Blvd., Ste. 470　FAX (323) 469-2193
Los Angeles, CA 90036
(Duplication & Linear/Non-Linear Offline and Online)
Contact: Hugo Morales

Yada/Levine Video Productions　(323) 461-1616
1253 Vine St., Ste. 21A　　FAX (323) 461-2288
Hollywood, CA 90038　　www.yadalevine.com
(Computer Graphics & Non-Linear Offline)
Contact: Michael Yada

Terra Abroms	(818) 426-0019
	FAX (818) 450-0514
Ada Anderson	(310) 270-7121
Brad Arensman	(818) 445-3536
Bryan Barker	(310) 869-9765
	web.mac.com/bbarker/
Scott Carrey	(310) 765-4967
	(310) 985-1303
	FAX (310) 765-4967
	www.scarrey.com
Ed Chapman	(213) 200-9952
	FAX (818) 980-9788
	www.edchapman.com
Shawn Dury	(310) 200-7593
Edy H. Enriquez	(310) 836-9011
	(323) 252-0904
	FAX (310) 836-9010
	www.x1fx.com
Franny Faull	(310) 614-0992
Robert Hackl	(818) 207-1753
	(818) 986-4876
	www.imdb.com/name/nm0352531/

Benjamin Hopkins	(310) 765-4051
	(310) 717-9493
	FAX (310) 765-4052
	www.huemaninterest.com
Peter Lauritson	(310) 374-3980
	(310) 729-3763
	FAX (310) 937-0974
David McCann	(310) 282-9940
	www.mirisch.com
David Persoff	(323) 791-3840
Eliza Pelham Randall	(310) 962-9463
	(323) 525-1225
	www.queenofspades.com
Jason Reeves	(310) 668-1601
Jim Rygiel	(310) 273-6700
	www.unitedtalent.com
Jim Sterling	(310) 503-5590
	www.postwise.com
Bradley Van Herbst	(213) 700-2664
	www.vimeo.com/bradherbst
Marc Wielage	(818) 486-7747
	www.cinesound.tv

Digiscope (310) 315-6060
1447 Cloverfield Blvd. FAX (310) 828-5856
Santa Monica, CA 90404 www.digiscope.com

(818) 459-6630
Laurel Canyon Productions (310) 738-4184
1101 S. Flower Ave. FAX (818) 450-0916
Burbank, CA 91502 www.lcproductions.tv

Majikmaker Effects (818) 558-6400
www.majikmaker.com

Post Modern Edit, LLC (949) 608-8700
2941 Alton Pkwy FAX (949) 608-8729
Irvine, CA 92606 www.postmodernedit.com

STEELE Studios (310) 656-7770
5737 Mesmer Ave. FAX (310) 391-9055
Culver City, CA 90230 www.steelevfx.com

100% QC Central (323) 316-8298
www.qccentral.com

CCI Digital, Inc. (818) 562-6300
FAX (818) 562-8222
www.ccidigital.com

Post Logic Studios (323) 461-7887
1800 N. Vine St., Ste. 100 FAX (323) 461-7790
Los Angeles, CA 90028 www.postlogic.com

(310) 451-0333
Santa Monica Video, Inc. (800) 843-3827
1505 11th St. FAX (310) 458-3350
Santa Monica, CA 90401 www.smvcompletemedia.com

Alternative Rentals (310) 204-3388
FAX (310) 204-3384
www.alternativerentals.com

American Film Institute (AFI) (323) 856-7600
2021 N. Western Ave. FAX (323) 467-4578
Los Angeles, CA 90027 www.afi.com
(16mm, 35mm, 70mm, Dolby SR Stereo & Video Projection)

American Hi Definition, Inc. (818) 222-0022
7635 Airport Business Pkwy FAX (818) 222-0818
Van Nuys, CA 91406 www.hi-def.com

Arenas (323) 785-5535
3375 Barham Blvd. FAX (323) 785-5560
Los Angeles, CA 90068
www.arenasgroup.com/info-screen.html
(5.1, Beta, Betacam SP, Digital Betacam, Digital Projection,
Dolby, DVCAM, DVCPRO, DVCPRO HD, DVD, HDCAM,
HDCAM SR, High Def, Panasonic D-5, Video Projection,
XDCAM & XDCAM-HD)

Audio Head (323) 850-2500
1041 N. Formosa Ave. FAX (323) 850-2771
West Hollywood, CA 90046 www.audioheadpost.com
(5.1, Anamorphic/3D Projection, D-Cinema, Digibeta, Digital
Projection, DLP, Dolby, DV CAM, DVD, Film, HDCAM, HDDVD,
High Def, Mini DV, SR, SRD, SRW-5000, Video Projection &
VistaVision)

The Cahuenga Theater (323) 822-7237
1415 N. Cahuenga Blvd. www.cahuengatheater.com
Hollywood, CA 90028
(½", ¾", 5.1, Beta, D-Cinema, Digibeta, Digital Projection,
Dolby, Dolby A, Dolby SR, DTS, DV CAM, DVD, DVS Clipster,
Film, HDCAM, HDDVD, High Def, Mini DV, SR, SRW-5000,
THX, VHS & Video Projection)

The Charles Aidikoff
Screening Room (310) 274-0866
150 S. Rodeo Dr., Ste. 140 FAX (310) 550-1794
Beverly Hills, CA 90212 www.aidikoff.tv
(35mm, Dolby A/SR/SRD, DTS, Satellite Teleconferencing &
Video Projection)

Cinespace (323) 817-3456
6356 Hollywood Blvd., Second Fl. FAX (323) 860-9794
Hollywood, CA 90028 www.cinespace.info
(Beta, DVD, High Def, Mini DV & VHS)

The Clip Joint for Film (818) 842-2525
833-B N. Hollywood Way FAX (818) 842-2644
Burbank, CA 91505

Complete Actors Place/CAP (818) 990-2001
13752 Ventura Blvd. completeactorsplace.com
Sherman Oaks, CA 91423

The Culver Studios (310) 202-1234
9336 W. Washington Blvd. FAX (310) 202-3536
Culver City, CA 90232 www.theculverstudios.com
(Film and D-Cinema Video Projection)

Delicate Productions, Inc. (805) 388-1800
874 Verdulera St. FAX (805) 388-1037
Camarillo, CA 93010 www.delicate.com

Dick Clark Screening Room (310) 255-4699
2900 Olympic Blvd., First Fl.
Santa Monica, CA 90404
www.dickclarkproductionstheater.com

(310) 369-2406
Fox Studios (310) 369-4636
10201 W. Pico Blvd. FAX (310) 369-0503
Los Angeles, CA 90035 www.foxpost.com
(16mm, 35mm, 70mm, Digibeta 3/4" and 1/2", DLP Video
Projection, Dolby A/SR/SRD, DTS, DVCAM, DVD, HDCAM,
MMR8 Hard Drives, QC Software All Formats, SDDS,
SRW-5000 & THX Sound and Video Facilities)

Goethe-Institut (323) 525-3388
5750 Wilshire Blvd., Ste. 100 FAX (323) 934-3597
Los Angeles, CA 90036 www.goethe.de/losangeles

Hollywood-DI (323) 850-3550
1041 Formosa Ave., FAX (323) 850-3551
Fairbanks Bldg., Ste. 7 www.hollywooddi.com
West Hollywood, CA 90046
(35mm, 5.1, D-Cinema, Digibeta, Digital Projection, DLP, Dolby,
DVD, Final Cut Pro, HDCAM SR & QT and DPX Playback &
SRW-5000)

The Jim Henson Company (323) 802-1500
1416 N. La Brea Ave. FAX (323) 802-1825
Hollywood, CA 90028 leasing.henson.com/events.html

LACMA (The Los Angeles (323) 857-6039
County Museum Of Art) (323) 857-4768
5905 Wilshire Blvd. FAX (323) 857-6021
Los Angeles, CA 90036 www.lacma.org
(35mm, 70mm, DTS, SDDS & Video Projection)

Los Angeles Center Studios (213) 534-3000
1201 W. Fifth St., Ste. T-110 FAX (213) 534-3001
Los Angeles, CA 90017 www.lacenterstudios.com
(35mm, Digital Projection, Satellite Teleconferencing, VHS &
Video Projection)

Los Angeles Film School Theater (323) 860-0789
6363 Sunset Blvd. www.lafilm.edu
Los Angeles, CA 90028
(High Def & THX)

New Deal Studios, Inc. (310) 578-9929
15392 Cobalt St. FAX (310) 578-7370
Sylmar, CA 91342 www.newdealstudios.com
(35mm, 70mm, Anamorphic/3D Projection, Digital Video &
VistaVision)

Oasis Imagery (323) 469-9800
6500 Sunset Blvd. FAX (323) 462-4620
Los Angeles, CA 90028 www.oasisimagery.com
(Beta, D-Cinema, Digibeta, Digital Projection, DV CAM, DVD,
High Def, HDCAM, SRW-5000, THX & Video Projection)

Pacific Design Center/
SilverScreen Theater (310) 657-0800
8687 Melrose Ave. FAX (310) 652-8576
West Hollywood, CA 90069
(35mm & High Def) www.pacificdesigncenter.com

Ⓐ The Studios at Paramount (323) 956-5520
The Studios at Paramount
Post Production Services,
5555 Melrose Ave. www.thestudiosatparamount.com
Los Angeles, CA 90038
(¾", 35mm, 5.1, 70mm, Anamorphic/3D Projection, Beta,
Blu-ray, D-Cinema, Digibeta, Digital Projection, DLP, Dolby,
Dolby A, Dolby SR and SRD, DTS, DV CAM, DVD, Film,
HDCAM, High Def, Mini DV, Multi-Media Presentations, Satellite
Teleconferencing, SDDS, SR, SRD, SRW-5000, THX,
Video Projection & VistaVision)

Raleigh Studios - Hollywood (323) 960-3456
5300 Melrose Ave. FAX (323) 960-4712
Hollywood, CA 90038 www.raleighstudios.com
(16mm, 35mm, Dolby SR Digital Stereo, HD Projection,
Multitrack Printmasters & Video Projection)

Raleigh Studios - Manhattan Beach (323) 960-3456
1600 Rosecrans Ave. FAX (310) 727-2710
Manhattan Beach, CA 90266 www.raleighstudios.com

Renberg Theatre (323) 860-7336
The Village at Ed Gould Plaza, FAX (323) 308-4103
1125 N. McCadden Pl. www.lagaycenter.org
Los Angeles, CA 90038
(16mm, 35mm, Dolby Surround, DVD & VHS)

Santa Monica Screening   (323) 325-4501
1526 14th St., Ste. 102   www.smscreening.com
Santa Monica, CA 90404
(¾", BetaSP, BluRay, DVCam, DVD, HD-DVD, HDCam, HDV, Laptop Feed, MiniDV & VHS)

Sony Pictures Studios   (310) 244-5721
10202 W. Washington Blvd.   FAX (310) 244-2303
Culver City, CA 90232   www.sonypicturesstudios.com
(16mm, 35mm, 70mm, DTS, Dolby A/SR Stereo, SDDS, SRD & Video Facilities)

Spartan Mobile Suites, Inc.   (310) 587-3377
3727 W. Magnolia Blvd., Ste. 156   FAX (661) 702-0550
Burbank, CA 91505   www.spartanmobilesuites.com
(35mm Mobile Facilities)

    (310) 701-8925
SSG - Screening Services Group   (310) 659-3875
8670 Wilshire Blvd., Ste. 112   FAX (310) 861-9005
Beverly Hills, CA 90211   www.studioscreenings.com
(35mm, 5.1, Anamorphic/3D Projection, Beta, D-Cinema, Digibeta, DLP, Dolby A, Dolby SR, Dolby SRD, DV CAM, DVD, Film, HDCAM, HDDVD, High Def, Mini DV, SR, SRD & Video Projection)

Sunset Bronson Studios   (323) 460-5858
5800 W. Sunset Blvd.   FAX (323) 460-3844
Los Angeles, CA 90028   www.sgsandsbs.com

Sunset Gower Studios   (323) 467-1001
1438 N. Gower St.   www.sgsandsbs.com
Los Angeles, CA 90028

Sunset Screening Rooms   (310) 652-1933
2212 W. Magnolia Blvd.   FAX (310) 652-3828
Burbank, CA 91506   www.sunsetscreeningrooms.com
(3D, 16mm, 35mm, 70mm, Dolby SRD, DTS & Video Facilities)

Sunset Screening Rooms   (310) 652-1933
8730 Sunset Blvd.   FAX (310) 652-3828
West Hollywood, CA 90069
    www.sunsetscreeningrooms.com

Switch Studios   (310) 301-1800
316 S. Venice Blvd.   FAX (310) 496-1964
Venice, CA 90291   www.switch-studios.com
(Digital Projection & HD Video Projection)

Theatrical Concepts, Inc.   (818) 597-1100
3030 Triunfo Canyon Rd.   FAX (818) 597-0202
Agoura Hills, CA 91301   www.theatrical.com
(5.1, Dolby & HD Mobile Facilities)

    (310) 392-8508
    (310) 392-8509
Vidiots Annex   FAX (310) 392-0099
302 Pico Blvd.   www.vidiotsannex.com
Santa Monica, CA 90405
(½", ¾", Digital Projection, DLP, DVD, HDDVD, High Def, VHS & Video Projection)

Visionary Forces Broadcast
Equipment Rentals   (818) 562-1960
148 S. Victory Blvd.   FAX (818) 562-1270
Burbank, CA 91502   www.visionaryforces.com

Warner Bros.
Studio Facilities - Projection   (818) 954-2144
4000 Warner Blvd.   FAX (818) 954-7915
Burbank, CA 91522   www.wbpostproduction.com
(16mm, 35mm, 70mm, Dolby A/SR/SRD, Stereo & Video Facilities)

Baked FX
(323) 937-6200
3750 Robertson Bl., Ste. 200
FAX (323) 937-6201
Culver City, CA 90232
www.bakedfx.com

Hi-Ground Media
(310) 845-9500
8579 Higuera St.
FAX (310) 845-9779
Culver City, CA 90232
www.hi-ground.com

(310) 426-8732
HOAX Films
(310) 422-4558
5541 W. Washington Blvd.
FAX (310) 426-8731
Los Angeles, CA 90016
www.hoaxfilms.com

ICO VFX, LLC
(818) 531-7200
727 S. Main St.
FAX (818) 531-7299
Burbank, CA 91506
www.icovfx.com

MacLeod Productions
(310) 395-4739
502 10th St.
Santa Monica, CA 90402

Nitrous Visual Effects
(818) 536-7991
5000 N. Parkway Calabasas, Ste. 305
Calabasas, CA 91302
www.nitrousvfx.com

STEELE Studios
(310) 656-7770
5737 Mesmer Ave.
FAX (310) 391-9055
Culver City, CA 90230
www.steelevfx.com

(888) 577-4045
Synthespian Studios
(413) 458-0202
3050 Runyon Canyon Rd.
www.synthespians.net
Los Angeles, CA 90046

ABCNews VideoSource
(212) 456-5421
(800) 789-1250
125 West End Ave.
FAX (212) 456-5428
New York, NY 10023   www.abcnewsvidsource.com
Footage: ABC News 1963–Present

Action Footage/
Warren Miller Entertainment   (800) 729-3456
www.wmefootage.com
Footage: Extreme/Adventure Sports, Scenics,
Time-Lapse & Vintage

Action Sports/Scott Dittrich Films
(310) 459-2526
(212) 681-6565
P.O. Box 301   FAX (310) 456-1743
Malibu, CA 90265   www.actionsportsstockfootage.com
Footage: Aerials, Animals, Cities, Clouds, Natural Disasters,
People, Pollution, Professional and Extreme Sports, Scenics,
Sunsets, Time-Lapse & Waves

AeronauticPictures.com   (805) 985-2320
www.aeronauticpictures.com/
royalty-free-stock-footage/
Footage: Film, High Def and Video: Aerial & Location

All-Stock
(310) 317-9996
(800) 323-0079
P.O. Box 1705   www.all-stock.com
Pacific Palisades, CA 90272
Footage: All Subjects

AM Stock-Cameo Film Library   (818) 762-7865
10513 Burbank Blvd.   FAX (818) 762-6480
North Hollywood, CA 91601
Footage: 35mm and HD, Aerials, Buildings, Cities,
Nature & Skylines

Ambient Images   (310) 312-6640
4550 Overland Ave., Ste. 227   FAX (310) 876-1885
Culver City, CA 90030   www.ambientimages.com
Photos: Aerials, Agriculture, Beaches, California Cityscapes,
City, National and State Parks, Landscapes, Museums,
Neighborhoods, New York Panoramics, Rural Scenes &
Sports and Recreation

America by Air
Stock Footage Library   (800) 488-6359
154 Euclid Blvd.   FAX (413) 235-1462
Lantana, FL 33462   www.americabyair.com
Footage: 35mm and High Def, Aerials,
Contemporary & International

American Playback Images   (818) 427-8292
27748 Caraway Ln., Ste. 1   FAX (661) 263-2387
Santa Clarita, CA 91350   www.americanplayback.com
Footage: Americana, Cartoons, Commercials, Historical,
Movie Clips, News & Playback

Animation Trip   (619) 825-8875
38030 La Mesa Blvd., Ste. 200
La Mesa, CA 91942   www.animationtrip.com/licensing
Footage and Photos: Computer Animation and Illustrations,
High-Tech Imagery & Special FX

Apex Stock   (818) 890-0444
13240 Weidner St.   FAX (818) 890-7041
Los Angeles, CA 91331   www.apexstock.com

ARC Science Simulations
(970) 667-1168
(800) 759-1642
P.O. Box 1955   FAX (970) 667-1105
Loveland, CO 80539   www.arcscience.com
Footage: High Resolution 2D and 3D Earth-From-Space
AnimationPhotos: Earth Textures, Earth-From-Space & High
Resolution Cloud Layers

Archive Films by Getty Images   (800) 462-4379
6300 Wilshire Blvd., 16th Fl.   www.gettyimages.com
Los Angeles, CA 90048
Footage: Americana, Business/Industry, Cartoons, Celebrities,
Destinations, Educational, Events, Film Genres, Home Movies,
Lifestyle, News, Newsreels, Political, Sports & Travel

Artbeats
(541) 863-4429
(800) 444-9392
1405 N. Myrtle Rd.   FAX (541) 863-4547
Myrtle Creek, OR 97457   www.artbeats.com
Footage: Aerials, Animals, Archival, Backgrounds,
Lifestyles & Nature

Axiom Images, Inc.   (661) 713-6671
10500 Airpark Way, Ste. M2   www.axiomimages.com
Pacoima, CA 91331
Aerial Stock Footage: 5K to 1080

Battlegrounds
(502) 339-7934
(502) 235-5648
9801 Somerford Rd.   FAX (502) 339-7934
Louisville, KY 40242   www.battlegroundsvideo.com
Footage: Military and Generic

BBC Motion Gallery, Los Angeles
(818) 299-9720
(818) 432-4000
4144 Lankershim Blvd., Ste. 200   FAX (818) 299-9763
North Hollywood, CA 91602 www.bbcmotiongallery.com
Footage: Arts, Bloopers, Communications, Current Events,
Destinations, Entertainment, Historical, Leisure, Lifestyles,
Medicine, Music, Natural History, News, Politics, Reality,
Science, Stock, Technology, Travel and Locations, Universal
Newsreels & Wildlife

BBC Motion Gallery, New York
(212) 705-9399
(917) 267-5460
747 Third Ave., Sixth Fl.   FAX (212) 705-9342
New York, NY 10017   www.bbcmotiongallery.com
Footage: Arts, Bloopers, Communications, Current Events,
Destinations, Entertainment, Historical, Leisure, Lifestyles,
Medicine, Music, Natural History, News, Politics, Reality,
Science, Stock, Technology, Travel and Locations, Universal
Newsreels & Wildlife

Bill Bachmann Studios   (407) 333-9988
www.billbachmann.com
Photos: Abstracts, Beaches, Business, Caribbean, Lifestyle,
Medical, Minorities, Sports & World Travel

BlackLight Films
(323) 436-7070
(323) 436-2229
3371 Cahuenga Blvd. West   FAX (323) 436-2230
Hollywood, CA 90068   www.blacklightfilms.com
Footage: Aerials, Agriculture, Americana, Animals, Architecture,
Cityscapes, Clouds, Contemporary, Cultures, Deserts, Flowers,
Historical Landmarks, International People and Scenery,
Landscapes, Lifestyles, Moons, Mountains, Nature, Oceans,
Rivers, Rural, Scenic, Seasons, Skies, Storms, Suns, Sunsets,
Time-Lapse, Transportation, Travel & Wildlife

Blue Fier Photography/Blue Fier
(818) 344-5527
(818) 726-5527
7450 Beckford Ave.   FAX (818) 344-5556
Reseda, CA 91335   www.bluefier.com
Photos: Clouds, Deserts, Forests, Landscapes, Mountains,
Panoramics, Roads, Scenics, Skies, Skylines, Sunsets &
WaterTime Lapse: Cities, National Parks & Skies

Blue Sky Stock Footage/Bill Mitchell (310) 305-8384
(877) 992-5477
FAX (310) 823-0924
www.blueskyfootage.com
Footage: 35mm, High Def and Super 16mm Time-Lapse and
Real-Time, Aerials, Agriculture, Airplanes, Americana, Animals,
Architecture, Cityscapes, Clouds, Deserts, Driving Shots,
Eclipses, Experimental, Flowers, Fires, Forests, Highways,
Historical Landmarks, International People and Scenery,
Landscapes, Lighting, Motion Control, Mountains, Nature,
Oceans, Rivers, Rural, Seasons, Space, Skies,
Stars/Comets/Planets, Storms, Suns and Moons, Traffic, Trains,
Transportation & Underwater

Boeing Image Licensing (206) 662-6628
P.O. Box 3707, M/C 14-84 FAX (206) 662-0598
Seattle, WA 98124 www.boeingimages.com
Footage: Aerials, Aerospace, Airplanes, Archival, Cityscapes,
Computer Graphics, Contemporary, Deserts, Experimental,
Helicopters, Historical Landmarks, Jets, Landscapes,
Manufacturing, Military, Missiles, Mountains, Oceans, Rockets,
Satellites, Skies, Space, Suns and Moons, Technology,
Transportation, Travel & Weapons

The Bridgeman Art Library (212) 828-1238
65 E. 93rd St. FAX (212) 828-1255
New York, NY 10128 www.bridgemanart.com
Photos: Fine Art and History

Bruce Manning
Stock Footage and Production (805) 419-5080
3007 Washington Blvd., Ste. 220
Marina Del Rey, CA 90292 www.bruceamanning.com
Footage: 35mm Motion Picture Images, Aerials, Backgrounds,
Beaches, Cityscapes, Clouds, Contemporary, Kids, Landmarks,
Scenics & Suns

Budget Films, Inc. (323) 660-0187
4427 Santa Monica Blvd. FAX (323) 660-5571
Los Angeles, CA 90029 www.budgetfilms.com
Footage: Beauty, Current Events, Technology & Vintage
Black/White and Color

Camera One (206) 523-3456
8523 15th Ave. NE FAX (206) 523-3668
Seattle, WA 98115 www.cameraone.us
Footage: Aerials, Archeology, Caribbean, Cities, Clouds,
Eclipse, Europe, Landscapes, Lightning, Moons, National
Parks, Nature, Natural and Traffic/Urban Time-Lapse,
Northwest, Outdoor Sports, Scenics, Southwest, Storms,
Sunrises and Sunsets, Underwater, Whitewater & Wildlife

Carl Barth Images (805) 969-2346
(805) 637-0881
P.O. Box 5325 carlbarthimages.com
Santa Barbara, CA 93150
Footage: Aerials, Contemporary Establishing Shots,
Scenics & Skylines

Carter Productions (303) 499-9430
(303) 589-8881
P.O. Box 3537 FAX (303) 499-6130
Boulder, CO 80307
Footage: Cityscapes, Hawaii, North American Wildlife & Rocky
Mountain Scenery

CelebrityFootage (310) 360-9600
320 S. Almont Dr. www.celebrityfootage.com
Beverly Hills, CA 90211
Footage: Award Ceremonies, Celebrities, Entertainment,
Events, High Def, Hollywood, Movie Premieres, People,
Red Carpet Arrivals & Stars

Channel Sea Television (714) 299-9309
124 Tustin Ave.
Newport Beach, CA 92663
Footage: Sailing & Yacht Racing

Chicagoland News Footage (312) 455-1212
1613 W. Huron St. www.redwagonproductions.tv
Chicago, IL 60622
Footage: Chicagoland Rescues, Crimes, Fires, Gangs,
Medical Emergencies & Natural Disasters

Classic Images (310) 277-0400
(800) 949-2547
469 S. Bedford Dr. FAX (310) 277-0412
Beverly Hills, CA 90212 www.classicimg.com
Footage: 16mm, 35mm, 1890s–Present, Aerials, Americana,
Archival, Cartoons, Cityscapes, Commercials, Educational,
High Def, Historical, Hollywood, Industry, Music, Nature,
Newsreel, Sports, Technology, Time-Lapse, Travel, Underwater,
Vintage TV and Film & Wildlife

Clay Lacy Aviation, Inc. (818) 989-2900
(800) 423-2904
7435 Valjean Ave. FAX (818) 909-9537
Van Nuys, CA 91406 www.claylacy.com
Footage: Aerials

The Clip Joint for Film (818) 842-2525
833-B N. Hollywood Way FAX (818) 842-2644
Burbank, CA 91505
Footage: All Subjects

CNN ImageSource (404) 827-3326
One CNN Center www.cnnimagesource.com
Atlanta, GA 30303
Footage: 1980–Present Current Events

The Communications Group, Inc. (919) 828-4086
P.O. Box 50157 FAX (919) 832-7797
Raleigh, NC 27650 www.cgfilm.com
Footage: Aerials, Boston, High Def, North Carolina Cities,
Farms and Landscapes & The Big Dig

Compro Productions, Inc. (770) 918-8163
2055 Boar Tusk Rd. NE www.compro-atl.com
Conyers, GA 30012
Footage: Cities, European and Asian Landscapes,
Landmarks & People

Corbis (310) 342-1500
(800) 260-0444
6060 Center Drive West, Ste. 100 FAX (310) 342-1501
Los Angeles, CA 90045 www.corbis.com
Photos: Backgrounds, Classic Illustrations, Computer Graphics,
Maps, People, Textures & Worldwide Locations

Corbis (212) 375-7700
(800) 260-0444
250 Hudson St., Fourth Fl. FAX (212) 777-7240
New York, NY 10013 www.corbis.com
Photos: All Subjects

Corbis Motion (212) 375-7622
(866) 473-5264
902 Broadway FAX (212) 807-0221
New York, NY 10010 www.corbismotion.com
Footage: All Subjects

CTV Television, Inc. (416) 384-7389
(800) 628-7780
Nine Channel 9 Court FAX (416) 384-7384
Toronto, ON M1S 4B5 Canada
tinyurl.com/ctvarchivesales
Footage: Classic News, Documentary and Sports

Custom Medical Stock Photo, Inc. (773) 267-3100
(800) 373-2677
3660 W. Irving Park Rd. FAX (773) 267-6071
Chicago, IL 60618 www.cmsp.com
Footage & Photos: Medical & Science

dick clark productions
Media Archives (310) 255-4654
2900 Olympic Blvd. www.dickclark.com
Santa Monica, CA 90404
Footage: 1950s–1900s Pop/Rock Music Performances

Documentary (617) 926-0491
Educational Resources (800) 569-6621
101 Morse St. FAX (617) 926-9519
Watertown, MA 02472 www.der.org
Footage: Anthropology, Cultures & People

Stock Footage & Photos

Doubletime Productions (516) 869-1170
(866) 226-4474
162 Pond View Dr. FAX (516) 869-1171
Port Washington, NY 11050
www.doubletimeproductions.com
Footage: AMTRAK Official Licensing, Animals, Beaches and
Sunsets, Chicago, Cityscapes, Deserts, Florida, Landscapes,
Lifestyles, Mountains, New York Panoramic and Rural Scenes,
North American Wildlife, Northwest, Rocky Mountain Scenery,
Scenics, Southwest, Traffic, Trains, Transportation & Travel

Dynasty Films (818) 823-6088
(Time-Lapse) www.dynastyfilms.com

eFootage, LLC (626) 395-9593
87 N. Raymond, Ste. 850 FAX (626) 792-5394
Pasadena, CA 91103 www.efootage.com
Footage: All Subjects

eVox Productions, LLC (310) 605-1400
2363 E. Pacifica Pl. FAX (310) 605-1429
Rancho Dominguez, CA 90220 www.evox.com
Footage: Cars

FILM Archives, Inc. (212) 696-2616
35 W. 35th St., Ste. 504 www.filmarchivesonline.com
New York, NY 10001
Footage: 1890s–Present, Contemporary, Educational,
Feature Films, People, Sports, Travel & Vintage

Fish Films Footage World (818) 905-1071
4548 Van Noord Ave. www.footageworld.com
Studio City, CA 91604
Footage: Aerials, Americana, Archival, Cartoons, Cities, Classic
TV, Commericals, Computer Graphics, Contemporary, Cultures,
Educational, Extreme Sports, High Def, Historical, Landmarks,
Lifestyles, Nature, Newsreels, Oddities, Scenics, Time-Lapse,
Travel, Underwater, Wildlife & Worldwide Locations

FishBowl Licensing (310) 442-5685
12233 W. Olympic Blvd., Ste. 170 FAX (310) 442-5683
Los Angeles, CA 90064 funnyhomevideofootage.com
Footage: Clip Library of America's Funniest Home Videos

The Footage Store (818) 326-3344
Footage: All Subjects www.footagestore.com

(310) 822-1400
FootageBank HD (888) 653-1400
13470 Washington Blvd., Ste. 210 FAX (310) 822-4100
Marina del Rey, CA 90292 www.footagebank.com
Footage: Large Format and High Def, Aerials, Animals, Archival,
CGI, Landscapes, Lifestyle, Playback Content, Space, Sports,
Technology, Time-Lapse, Travel, Underwater, Wildlife &
Worldwide Locations

(775) 323-0965
FootageFinder (800) 852-2330
1775 Kuenzli St. FAX (775) 323-1055
Reno, NV 89502 www.footagefinder.com
Footage: Fighter Jets, Ghost Towns, Las Vegas and
Reno Nevada, Outdoor Activities, Steam Locomotives,
Western States & WWII Aircraft

Framepool Inc. (800) 331-1314
150 Alhambra Circle, Ste. 800 FAX (866) 928-6637
Miami, FL 33134 www.framepool.com
Footage: Aerials, Aerospace, Agriculture, Animals, Cityscapes,
Clouds, Commercials, Contemporary, Cultures, Deserts,
Flowers, International People and Scenery, Landscapes,
Lightning, Lifestyles, Mountains, Nature, Scenic, Seasons,
Space, Stars/Comets/Planets, Storms, Time-Lapse, Traffic,
Transportation, Underwater & Wildlife

(310) 402-4626
Framepool Inc. (800) 331-1314
1480 Vine St., Ste. 704 FAX (866) 928-6637
Los Angeles, CA 90028 www.framepool.com
Footage: Aerials, Aerospace, Agriculture, Animals, Cityscapes,
Clouds, Commercials, Contemporary, Cultures, Deserts,
Flowers, International People and Scenery, Landscapes,
Lightning, Lifestyles, Mountains, Nature, Scenics, Seasons,
Space, Stars/Comets/Planets, Storms, Time-Lapse, Traffic,
Transportation, Underwater & Wildlife

Freewheelin' Films Stock Footage (970) 925-2640
44895 Hwy 82 FAX (970) 925-9369
Aspen, CO 81611 www.fwf.com
Footage: Aerials, Cityscapes, Motor Sports, Scenics,
Sports & Travelogues

(323) 202-4200
Getty Images (800) 462-4379
6300 Wilshire Blvd., 16th Fl. www.gettyimages.com
Los Angeles, CA 90048
Photos: All Subjects, Illustration & Film

Global ImageWorks, LLC (201) 384-7715
65 Beacon St. FAX (201) 501-8971
Haworth, NJ 07641 www.globalimageworks.com
Footage: 9/11, Aerials, Cityscapes, Contemporary,
Entertainment, Global Conflict, Historic, Interviews, Lifestyles,
Music, Nature, Politics, Pop Culture, Science, Technology,
Terrorism, Time Lapse, Underwater & World locations

Great Waves/Delaney Films (805) 653-2699
473 Mariposa Dr. FAX (805) 653-2699
Ventura, CA 93001
Footage: Ocean Scenes & Surfing

(310) 622-4487
Greenscreen Animals (877) 563-8023
1510 11th St., Ste. 101 FAX (310) 496-1237
Santa Monica, CA 90401 www.greenscreenanimals.com
(Animal, Entertainment, Feature Films, High Def, High
Resolution, Technology, Television & Wildlife)

GregHensley.com (970) 984-3158
www.greghensley.com
Footage: High Def, Time-Lapse & Wildlife

(212) 512-7171
HBO Archives (877) 426-1121
1100 Avenue of the Americas FAX (212) 512-5225
New York, NY 10036 www.hboarchives.com
Footage: Entertainment News Collection, Contemporary
Stock From HBO Films, High Def, Iconic Sports, Newsreels &
Royalty-Free Wildlife Footage

(631) 477-9700
(800) 249-1940
Historic Films FAX (631) 477-9800
211 Third St.
Greenport, NY 11944 www.historicfilms.com
Footage: 1895–Present, All Subjects, Historical, Hollywood,
Musical Performances & Newsreels

The Hollywood Film Registry (310) 456-8184
5473 Santa Monica Blvd., Ste. 408 FAX (323) 957-2159
Los Angeles, CA 90029
Footage: Current & Historical

Image Bank Films and
Archive Films by Getty Images (800) 462-4379
6300 Wilshire Blvd., 16th Fl. FAX (323) 202-4207
Los Angeles, CA 90048 www.gettyimages.com
Footage: Archival & Contemporary

Inter Video 3D (818) 843-3624
2211 N. Hollywood Way FAX (818) 843-6884
Burbank, CA 91505 www.intervideo24.com
3D HD, 4K, and 4K HD Footage: Aerial, Underwater, News,
Space, Sports, Travel & Weather

International Travel Films (213) 841-6335
3710 Lowery Rd. www.internatinaltravelfilms.com
Los Angeles, CA 90027
Footage: People, Ships, Trains & Worldwide Locations

ITN Source (646) 723-9793
48 Wall St., Ste. 1100 FAX (646) 792-4668
New York, NY 10005 www.itnsource.com
Footage: News

Joan Kramer & Associates, Inc. (310) 446-1866
10490 Wilshire Blvd., Ste. 1701 FAX (310) 446-1856
Los Angeles, CA 90024 www.erwinkramer.com
Photos: Corporate, Glamour, Industry, Leisure, People, Scenics,
Underwater & World Travel

John Sandy Productions, Inc. (303) 721-6121
P.O. Box 5104 FAX (303) 721-0466
Englewood, CO 80155 www.jsptv.com
Footage: Business, Extreme Sports, Medical, Mountain Biking,
Outdoor Sports & Skiing

Jupiterimages (800) 764-7427
(312) 980-6111
Photos: Food www.jupiterimages.com

Linear Cycle Productions (818) 347-9880
P.O. Box 2608 FAX (818) 347-9880
North Hills, CA 91393 www.linearcycleproductions.com
Footage: People & Vintage–1990

Louis Wolfson II
Florida Moving Image Archive (305) 375-1505
101 W. Flagler St. FAX (305) 375-4436
Miami, FL 33130 www.fmia.org
Footage: The Caribbean, Cuba, Florida, Miami &
Space Program

Jay Maisel (212) 431-5013
FAX (212) 925-6092
www.jaymaisel.com
Photos: Africa, Europe, Landscapes, People, Travel & U.S.

March of Time Newsreels and (212) 512-7171
Documentaries (212) 512-5664
1100 Avenue of the Americas FAX (212) 512-7040
New York, NY 10036 www.themarchoftime.net
Footage: 1935-1967 The March of Time Documentary Series;
SD & HD

Maxx Images, Inc. (604) 985-2560
(888) 511-3939
1433 Rupert St., Ste. 3A FAX (604) 985-2590
N. Vancouver, BC V7J 1G1 Canada
www.maxximages.com
Footage: Aerials, British Columbia, Killer Whales, Mountains,
Oceans, Underwater & Wildlife

Media Bakery, LLC (805) 682-9325
(888) 899-6809
3905 State St., Ste. 7-510 FAX (805) 682-9327
Santa Barbara, CA 93105 www.mediabakery.com
Footage & Photos: All Subjects

Ned Miller (847) 816-9020
P.O. Box 7160 FAX (847) 975-9020
Libertyville, IL 60048 www.nedmiller.com
Footage: Chicago

Moe DiSesso Film Library (661) 255-7969
24233 Old Rd. FAX (661) 255-8179
Santa Clarita, CA 91321
Footage: Animals

National Geographic Digital Motion (866) 523-9097
(720) 212-0820
www.ngdigitalmotion.com
Footage: Archeology, Architecture, Ceremonies, Cities,
Landmarks, Natural Disasters, Natural History, People,
Wildlife & World Scenes

NBC News Archives (818) 840-4249
(212) 664-3797
3000 W. Alameda Ave., Ste. 3352 FAX (818) 840-4388
Burbank, CA 91523 www.nbcnewsarchives.com
Footage: NBC News from 1940s–Present

New & Unique Videos (619) 644-3000
(800) 365-8433
7323 Rondel Court FAX (619) 644-3001
San Diego, CA 92119 www.newuniquevideos.com
Footage: Aerials, Animals, Archival Film, Beaches and Sunsets,
Bloopers, Cities, Contemporary, Corporate/Industrial, Current
Events, High Def and Betacom SP, International, Lifestyles,
Medical, Military, People, Scenics, Sports, Travel and Locations,
Technological, Underwater & Wildlife

Oddball Film + Video (415) 558-8112
(415) 558-8122
275 Capp St. FAX (415) 558-8116
San Francisco, CA 94110 www.oddballfilm.com
Footage: Archival, Contemporary & Offbeat

Odyssey Productions, Inc. (503) 223-3480
2800 NW Thurman St. FAX (503) 223-3493
Portland, OR 97210 www.odysseypro.com
Footage: All Subjects

Omega Media Group, Inc. (770) 449-8870
3100 Medlock Bridge Rd., Ste. 100
Norcross, GA 30071 www.omegamediagroup.com
Footage: All Subjects

Pan American Video (707) 822-3800
(800) 726-2634
Footage: All Subjects 1900s–1970s FAX (707) 822-0800
www.panamvideo.com

Photodisc by Getty Images (323) 202-4200
(800) 462-4379
6300 Wilshire Blvd., 16th Fl. www.gettyimages.com
Los Angeles, CA 90048
Footage: All Subjects; Royalty-Free

PicturesNow.com (415) 435-1076
Digital Photos: Historic Photo Library FAX (415) 435-5027
www.picturesnow.com

Producers Library (818) 752-9097
(800) 944-2135
10832 Chandler Blvd. FAX (818) 752-9196
North Hollywood, CA 91601 www.producerslibrary.com
Footage: 35mm and High Def: Cities, Feature Film Outtakes,
Historic, Hollywood, Locations, Newsreels & Scenics

Pyramid Media (800) 421-2304
P.O. Box 1048 FAX (310) 398-7869
Santa Monica, CA 90406 www.pyramidmedia.com
Footage: Animals, Geography, Medical, Nature, Safety,
Science, Sports & Vintage Educational

Questar, Inc. (312) 266-9400
(800) 544-8422
Footage: Travel FAX (312) 266-9523
www.questar1.com

Reel Orange (949) 548-4524
316 La Jolla Dr. www.reelorange.com
Newport Beach, CA 92663
Footage: Aerials, Environmental & Grand Canyon

Robertstock/ClassicStock (800) 786-6300
4203 Locust St. FAX (800) 786-1920
Philadelphia, PA 19104 www.classicstock.com
Photos: 1920s-1990s Lifestyles

Shooting Star International (323) 469-2020
1441 N. McCadden Pl. FAX (323) 464-0880
Los Angeles, CA 90028 www.shootingstaragency.com
Photos: Celebrities, Entertainment, Geography, Glamour,
Historical, Human Interest, Movie Stills & News

Ⓐ Shutterstock (866) 663-3954
60 Broad St., 30th Fl. FAX (347) 402-0710
New York, NY 10004 footage.shutterstock.com

Silverman Stock Footage (804) 338-2234
210 Douglass St. FAX (718) 764-4411
Brooklyn, NY 11217 www.silvermanstockfootage.com
Footage: Aerials, Airplanes, Americana, Animals, Architecture,
Archival, Cityscapes, Clouds, Contemporary, Cultures, Deserts,
Extreme Sports, Flowers, International People, Landscapes,
Lifestyles, Nature, Oceans, Scenics, Space, Storms, Suns and
Moons, Time-Lapse, Traffic & Underwater

Sony Pictures Stock Footage (310) 244-3704
(866) 275-6919
10202 W. Washington Blvd., Capra 170
Culver City, CA 90232
www.sonypicturesstockfootage.com
Footage: Action, Aerials, Aerospace, Airplanes, Americana, Animals, Architecture, Cityscapes, Clouds, Contemporary, Cultures, Deserts, Driving Shots, Explosions, Fires, Forests, Futuristic, Highways, Historical Landmarks, International People and Scenery, Landscapes, Lightning, Mountains, Nature, Oceans, Rivers, Rural, Scenic, Seasons, Skies, Space, Stars/Comets/Planets, Storms, Suns and Moons, Traffic, Trains, Transportation, Travel, Underwater & Wildlife; All Digital Formats

The Source
Stock Footage Library, Inc. (520) 298-4810
140 S. Camino Seco, Ste. 308   FAX (520) 290-8831
Tucson, AZ 85710   www.sourcefootage.com
Footage: Aerials, Business, Clouds, Destinations, Lifestyles, Sports, Technology, Time-Lapse & Underwater

(310) 785-9100
Sports Cinematography Group (212) 744-5333
73 Market St.   FAX (310) 564-7500
Venice, CA 90291
www.sportscinematographygroup.com
Footage: Extreme Sports, Motor Racing, Nature, Sports & Wildlife

Storm Video (262) 443-0352
P.O. Box 161   www.stormvideo.com
Cross Plains, WI 53528
Footage: Blizzard, Clouds, Hurricanes, Lightning, Storm Chasing, Supercells & Tornadoes

StormStock (817) 276-9500
P.O. Box 122020   FAX (817) 795-1132
Arlington, TX 76012   www.stormstock.com
Footage: 16mm, 35mm, Blizzards, Beaches, Caribbean, Clouds, Disasters, Environmental, Fires, Flash Floods, Hail, High Def, High Resolution, Hurricane Katrina, Hurricanes, Landscapes, Lightning, Microbursts, Natural Disasters, Natural History, Nature, Oceans, Radar, Science, Seasons, Skies, Storm Clouds, Storms, Sunrises, Sunsets, Time-Lapse, Tornadoes, Traffic & Waves

T3Media (Thought Equity Motion) (818) 432-4000
4130 Cahuenga Blvd., Ste. 315   FAX (818) 760-0820
Universal City, CA 91602   www.t3licensing.com
Footage: 16mm, 35mm, Abstracts, Adventure Sports, Aerials, Agriculture, Air Force, Airplanes, Airports, Americana, Animals, Anthropology, Archeology, Architecture, Archival, Arts, Aviation, Award Ceremonies, Bald Eagles, Beaches, Blizzards, Bloopers, Business, Caribbean, Celebrities, Ceremonies, Cityscapes, Clearance, Clouds, College Sports, Comedy, Commercials, Communications, Computer Graphics, Contemporary, Conventions, Crimes, Crowds, Cultures, Current Events, Deserts, Disasters, Driving Shots, Eclipses, Educational, Entertainment, Environmental, Events, Experimental, Explosions, Extreme Sports, Film, Feature Films, Fires, Flash Floods, Flowers, Forests, Gangs, Geography, Grand Canyon, Hail, HBO, High Def, High Resolution, High-Speed, Highways, Historical, Historical Landmarks, Hollywood, Home Movies, Hurricanes, Icons, Industry, International, Jets, Killer Whales, Landmarks, Landscapes, Leisure, Lifestyles, Lightning, Medical Emergencies, Medicine, Military, Minorities, Moons, Motion Control, Motor Racing, Mountains, Music, National Geographic, National Parks, Natural Disasters, Natural History, Nature, Nautical, NBC News, NCAA, Neighborhoods, News, North American Wildlife, Oceans, Outdoor Sports, Outtakes, People, Photos, Planets, Police, Political, Pollution, Pop Culture, Radar, Research, Rights and Clearances, Rivers, Rocky Mountains, Royalty-Free, Rural, Sailing, Scenics, Science, Seasons, Skies, Sony, Space, Space Program, Sports, Stars, Storm Clouds, Storms, Stunts, Sunrises, Suns, Sunsets, Technology, Television, Time-Lapse, Tornadoes, Traffic, Trains, Transportation, Travel, Underwater, Vintage, Waves, Whitewater, Wildlife, World War I, World War II & Yacht Racing

Third Millennium Films (212) 675-8500
220 Madison Ave.   www.thirdmillenniumfilms.net
New York, NY 10016
Footage: Archival, Animals, Lifestyles, New York City Aerials, Time-Lapse, Vintage & World Locations

Tim Allen Photography (850) 763-5795
1118 Jenks Ave.   FAX (850) 785-3508
Panama City, FL 32401 www.timallenphotography.com
Photos: All Subjects

UCLA Film and Television Archive (323) 466-8559
Footage: 1900s–1980s Newsreels   FAX (323) 461-6317
www.cinema.ucla.edu

Universal Studios
Stock Footage Library (818) 777-1695
100 Universal Plaza,   FAX (818) 866-0763
Bldg. 2313A, Lower Level
Universal City, CA 91608
Footage: All Subjects   www.filmmakersdestination.com

(310) 235-7522
US Air Force Motion Picture Office (310) 235-7511
10880 Wilshire Blvd., Ste. 1240   FAX (310) 235-7500
Los Angeles, CA 90024 www.airforcehollywood.af.mil
Footage: Air Force

(310) 235-7621
US Army Office of Public Affairs (310) 235-7622
10880 Wilshire Blvd., Ste. 1250   FAX (310) 235-6075
Los Angeles, CA 90024
www.defenselink.mil/faq/pis/PC12FILM.html
Footage: U.S. Army

WGBH Stock Sales (617) 300-3901
One Guest St.   FAX (617) 300-1056
Brighton, MA 02135   www.wgbhstocksales.org
Footage: American Experience, Antiques Roadshow, Frontline, Julia Child & NOVA

(206) 682-5417
White Rain Films, Ltd. (800) 816-5244
2009 Dexter Ave. North   FAX (206) 682-3038
Seattle, WA 98109   www.whiterainfilms.com
Footage: Aerials, Icons, People, Time-Lapse, Travel & Wildlife

Wings Wildlife Production, Inc. (877) 542-1355
www.wingswildlife.com
Footage: 35mm African and North American Wildlife

(800) 323-0442
WPA Film Library (708) 460-0555
16101 S. 108th Ave.   FAX (708) 460-0187
Orland Park, IL 60467   www.wpafilmlibrary.com
Footage: 1895-21st Century, Americana, Classic Commercials and Industrial Films, High Def, Historic, Music, Politics & UFO Collection

WTTW Digital Archives (773) 509-5412
5400 N. St. Louis Ave.   FAX (773) 509-5307
Chicago, IL 60625   www.wttwdigitalarchives.com
Footage: Aerials, Airplanes, Americana, Architecture, Archival, Cityscapes, Contemporary, Cultures, Deserts, Flowers, Historical Landmarks, International People and Scenery, Landscapes, Lifestyles, Mountains, Nature, Oddities, Rural, Scenic, Seasons, Sports, Trains & Transportation

11:11 MediaWorks (818) 780-4466
6611 Valjean Ave., Ste. 108 FAX (818) 780-4467
Van Nuys, CA 91406 www.1111mediaworks.com
(Feature Film Titles, Logos, Station ID Packages, TV Network/
Cable ID's and Packages & TV Show Titles and Opens)

3 Ring Circus (323) 466-5300
1040 N. Sycamore Ave. FAX (323) 466-5310
Los Angeles, CA 90038 www.3ringcircus.tv
(Animated Logos, Cable ID's, Cable Packages, Feature Film,
ID's, Logos, Opens, Station ID Packages, TV Network ID's,
TV Network Packages & TV Show)

A52 (310) 586-0650
2308 Broadway FAX (310) 586-0651
Santa Monica, CA 90404 www.a52.com
(Feature Film Titles, Logos, Station ID Packages, TV Network/
Cable ID's and Packages & TV Show Titles and Opens)

(949) 858-4463
Aberdeen Captioning, Inc. (800) 688-6621
22362 Gilberto, Ste. 120 FAX (949) 858-4405
Rancho Santo Margarita, CA 92688 www.abercap.com
(Closed Captioning, DVD Subtitles, Foreign, Real Time
Captioning & Subtitles)

Acme Filmworks, Inc. (323) 464-7805
6525 Sunset Blvd., Ste. G-10 FAX (323) 464-6614
Hollywood, CA 90028 www.acmefilmworks.com
(Captions, Feature Film Titles, Logos, Station ID Packages,
Subtitles, TV Network/Cable ID's and Packages & TV Show
Titles and Opens)

Acorn Entertainment (323) 238-4650
Hollywood Production Center,
121 W. Lexington Dr., Ste. V100
Glendale, CA 91203 www.acornentertainment.com
(Feature Film Titles, Logos, Station ID Packages, TV Network/
Cable ID's and Packages & TV Show Titles and Opens)

Altered Illusions (818) 471-0044
www.alteredillusions.com
(Feature Film Titles, Logos, Station ID Packages, TV Network/
Cable ID's and Packages & TV Show Titles and Opens)

Animax Entertainment (818) 787-4444
6627 Valjean Ave. FAX (818) 374-9140
Van Nuys, CA 91406 www.animaxent.com
(Feature Film Titles, Logos, Station ID Packages, TV Network/
Cable ID's and Packages & TV Show Titles and Opens)

Antifreeze Design (619) 795-2940
www.antifreezemotiongraphics.com
(Feature Film Titles, Logos, Station ID Packages, TV Network/
Cable ID's and Packages & TV Show Titles and Opens)

Autonomy, Inc. (213) 814-2919
www.autonomy.tv
(Logos, Station ID Packages, TV Network/Cable ID's and
Packages & TV Show Titles and Opens)

AvatarLabs (818) 784-2200
16030 Ventura Blvd. FAX (818) 784-2204
Encino, CA 91436 www.avatarlabs.com
(Feature Film Titles, Logos, Station ID Packages, TV Network/
Cable ID's and Packages & TV Show Titles and Opens)

Berkos & Associates (310) 940-1329
(Feature Film Titles, Logos, Station ID Packages, TV Network/
Cable ID's and Packages & TV Titles and Opens)

Big Machine Design (818) 841-2226
201 N. Hollywood Way FAX (323) 372-3926
Burbank, CA 91505 www.bigmachine.net

Blind (310) 314-1618
1702 Olympic Blvd. FAX (310) 314-1718
Santa Monica, CA 90404 www.blind.com
(Feature Film Titles, Logos, Station ID Packages, TV Network/
Cable ID's and Packages & TV Show Titles and Opens)

BloomFilm (323) 850-5575
FAX (323) 850-7304

Blue 105 (818) 563-4335
2600 W. Olive Ave., Fifth Fl. www.blue105.com
Burbank, CA 91505
(Domestic and Foreign Language Captions and Subtitles)

Blur Studio, Inc. (310) 581-8848
589 Venice Blvd. FAX (310) 581-8850
Venice, CA 90291 www.blur.com
(Feature Film Titles, Logos, Station ID Packages, TV Network/
Cable ID's and Packages & TV Show Titles and Opens)

Brand New School (310) 315-9959
2415 Michigan Ave., Bldg. H, Ste. 100 FAX (310) 315-9939
Santa Monica, CA 90404 www.brandnewschool.com
(Feature Film Titles, Logos, Station ID Packages, TV Network/
Cable ID's and Packages & TV Show Titles and Opens)

Brewster Parsons (310) 736-1663
1117 Abbot Kinney Blvd. FAX (310) 396-3299
Venice, CA 90291 www.brewsterparsons.com

Buck (213) 623-0111
515 W. Seventh St., Fourth Fl. FAX (213) 623-0117
Los Angeles, CA 90014 www.buck.tv

Buena Vista Imaging (818) 560-1558
500 S. Buena Vista St., Camera Bldg.
Burbank, CA 91521 www.studioservices.go.com
(Feature Film Titles, Opticals & Subtitles)

Bully Bros. Post (310) 874-7000
1813 Centinela Ave. FAX (310) 745-1645
Santa Monica, CA 90404 www.bullybrospost.com

(818) 295-2500
CaptionMax (612) 341-3566
441 N. Varney St. FAX (818) 295-2509
Burbank, CA 91502 www.captionmax.com
(Audio Description, Closed Captioning, Domestic, DVD
Subtitles, Foreign, Real Time Captioning, Subtitles &
Video Subtitles)

(818) 260-2700
Captions, Inc. (800) 227-8466
640 S. Glenwood Pl. FAX (818) 260-2850
Burbank, CA 91506 www.captionsinc.com
(Captions & Subtitles)

Charlie Company (310) 264-7100
1758 Berkeley St. FAX (310) 264-7104
Santa Monica, CA 90404 www.charlieco.tv

(310) 455-2490
Cinergy Creative (818) 623-6558
www.cinergycreative.com
(Feature Film Titles, Logos, Station ID Packages, TV Network/
Cable ID's and Packages & TV Show Titles and Opens)

Cinetyp, Inc. (323) 463-8569
843 Seward St. FAX (323) 463-4129
Hollywood, CA 90038 www.cinetyp.com
(Captions & Subtitles)

Closed Captioning Services, Inc. (818) 848-8826
4450 Lakeside Dr., Ste. 350 FAX (818) 848-2023
Burbank, CA 91505
(Captions, Feature Film Titles, Subtitles & Video Description)

CTS LanguageLink (800) 208-2620
9920 Jordan Circle, Ste. A FAX (360) 693-9292
Santa Fe Springs, CA 90670 www.ctslanguagelink.com
(Captions & Subtitles)

Daily Post/Transcripts (310) 417-4844
6701 Center Dr. West, Ste. 1111 FAX (310) 410-1543
Los Angeles, CA 90045 www.dailypost.tv

Deborah Ross Film Design (310) 559-5600
3452 Beethoven St. www.drfilmdesign.com
Los Angeles, CA 90066
(Feature Film Titles, Logos & TV Show Titles and Opens)

Digiscope (310) 315-6060
1447 Cloverfield Blvd. FAX (310) 828-5856
Santa Monica, CA 90404 www.digiscope.com
(Captions, Feature Film Titles, Logos & Subtitles)

Digital Dimension (818) 929-5644
P.O. Box 572800 www.digitaldimension.com
Tarzana, CA 91357
(Captions, Feature Film Titles, Logos, Station ID Packages,
TV Network/Cable ID's and Packages & TV Show
Titles and Opens)

Digital Jungle Post Production (323) 962-0867
6363 Santa Monica Blvd. FAX (323) 962-9960
Hollywood, CA 90038 www.digijungle.com
(Animated Logos, Cable ID's, Cable Packages, DVD Subtitles,
Feature Film, ID's, Logos, Opens, Station ID Packages,
Subtitles, Titles, TV Network ID's, TV Network Packages,
TV Show & Video Subtitles)

Doglight Studios, LLC (626) 798-3151
37 Silver Spruce Ln. www.doglight.com
Altadena, CA 91001
(Logos & TV Show Titles and Opens)

Dubscape, Inc. (818) 456-1051
7543 Loma Verde Ave. FAX (818) 456-1046
Canoga Park, CA 91303 www.dubscape.com
(Captions)

DUCK Studios,
a.k.a. Duck Soup Studios (310) 478-0771
2205 Stoner Ave. FAX (310) 478-0773
Los Angeles, CA 90064 www.duckstudios.com
(Feature Film Titles, Logos, Station ID Packages &
TV Show Titles and Opens)

Elektrashock, Inc. (310) 399-4985
1320 Main St. FAX (310) 399-4972
Venice, CA 90291 www.elektrashock.com
(Feature Film Titles, Logos, Station ID Packages, TV Network/
Cable ID's and Packages & Show Titles and Opens)

Filmworks/FX, Inc. (310) 577-3213
4121 Redwood Ave., Ste. 101 FAX (310) 577-3215
Los Angeles, CA 90066 www.filmworksfx.com
(Feature Film Titles & TV Show Titles and Opens)

FISH EGGS (310) 452-8251
1261 Electric Ave. FAX (310) 452-8364
Venice, CA 90291 www.fisheggs.tv
(Captions, Feature Film Titles, Logos, Station ID Packages,
Subtitles, TV Network/Cable ID's and Packages &
TV Show Opens and Titles)

Framework Studio, LLC (310) 815-1245
3535 Hayden Ave., Ste. 300 FAX (310) 815-9821
Culver City, CA 90232 www.frameworkla.com
(Animated Logos, Cable ID's and Packages, Domestic,
Feature Film, ID's, Logos, Opens, Station ID Packages, Titles,
TV Show & TV Network ID's and Packages)

FutureCircus (310) 592-8948
www.futurecircus.com
(Feature Film Titles, Logos, Station ID Packages, TV Network/
Cable ID's and Packages & TV Show Titles and Opens)

Hollywood Title (310) 394-3300
1526 14th St., Ste. 106 www.hollywoodtitle.com
Santa Monica, CA 90404
(Feature Film Titles, Logos, Opticals, Subtitles &
TV Show Titles and Opens)

(917) 351-0520
Hornet, Inc. (310) 601-1355
3962 Ince Blvd. FAX (310) 641-2117
Culver City, CA 90232 www.hornetinc.com
(Feature Film Titles, Logos, Station ID Packages, TV Network/
Cable ID's and Packages & TV Show Titles and Opens)

Humunculus (310) 827-1800
529 Victoria Ave. www.humunculus.com
Venice, CA 90291
(Animated Logos, Cable ID's, Feature Film Titles, Logos,
Station ID Packages, Titles, TV Network/Cable ID's and
Packages & TV Show Titles and Opens)

Ignition Post (818) 762-2210
4130 Cahuenga Blvd., Ste. 100 www.ignition-post.com
Toluca Lake, CA 91602

Imaginary Forces (323) 957-6868
6526 Sunset Blvd. FAX (323) 957-9577
Los Angeles, CA 90028 www.imaginaryforces.com
(Feature Film Titles, Logos, Station ID Packages, TV Network/
Cable ID's and Packages & TV Show Titles and Opens)

iProbe Multilingual Solutions, Inc. (888) 489-6035
www.iprobesolutions.com
(Animated Logos, Audio Description, AVI Subtitles, Cable
ID's, Cable Packages, Closed Captioning, Domestic, DVD
Subtitles, Feature Film, Foreign, ID's, Logos, Opens, Real Time
Captioning, Station ID Packages, Subtitles, Titles, TV Show,
Visual Description, Video Subtitles, TV Network ID's &
TV Network Packages)

JBI Studios (818) 592-0056
21432 Wyandotte FAX (818) 592-6994
Canoga Park, CA 91303 www.jbistudios.com
(Captions & Subtitles)

JR Media Services, Inc. (818) 557-0200
2501 W. Burbank Blvd., Ste. 200 FAX (818) 557-0201
Burbank, CA 91505 www.jrmediaservices.com
(Audio Description, AVI Subtitles, Closed Captioning, Domestic,
DVD Subtitles, Feature Film, Foreign, Subtitles, Titles, TV
Network Packages, TV Show, Video Subtitles &
Visual Description)

The Kitchen,
a TM Systems Company (818) 306-5300
4119 W. Burbank Blvd. FAX (305) 415-6201
Burbank, CA 91505 www.thekitchen.tv
(Closed Captioning, DVD Subtitles, Feature Film & Subtitles)

Kurtz & Friends (818) 841-8188
1023 N. Hollywood Way, Ste. 103 FAX (818) 841-6263
Burbank, CA 91505 www.kurtzandfriends.com
(Feature Film Titles, Logos & TV Show Titles and Opens)

Lava Creative, Inc. (310) 829-5282
953 Fourth St., Ste. 304 FAX (310) 496-1295
Santa Monica, CA 90403 www.lavacreative.tv
(Animated Logos, Cable ID's, Cable Packages, ID's, Logos,
Opens, Packages, Titles, TV Show, TV Network ID's &
TV Network Packages)

(818) 840-7200
Level 3 Post (818) 840-7889
2901 W. Alameda, Third Fl. www.level3post.com
Burbank, CA 91505

Marcland
International Communications (818) 557-6677
www.marcland.com
(Domestic and Foreign DVD and Video Subtitles)

Media Access at Group WGBH/
The Caption Center (818) 562-3344
300 E. Magnolia Blvd., Second Fl. FAX (818) 562-3388
Burbank, CA 91502 www.wgbh.org/caption
(Captions & Subtitles)

MFX (323) 969-1011
3400 Barham Blvd. FAX (323) 969-1015
Los Angeles, CA 90068 www.mfxdesign.com
(Feature Film Titles, Logos, Station ID Packages, TV Network/
Cable ID's and Packages & TV Show Titles and Opens)

Michael Kelley Motion Graphics (310) 450-4594
1223 Wilshire Blvd., Ste. 577 FAX (310) 450-3594
Santa Monica, CA 90403 www.michael-kelley.com
(Feature Film Titles, Logos, Station ID Packages, TV Network/
Cable ID's and Packages & TV Show Titles and Opens)

Mind Over Eye, LLC
(310) 396-4663
(310) 968-4259
1639 11th St., Ste. 117 FAX (310) 396-0663
Santa Monica, CA 90404 **www.mindovereye.com**
(Captions, Feature Film Titles, Logos, Station ID Packages, TV
Network/Cable ID's and Packages & TV Show
Titles and Opens)

Mixin Pixls (310) 237-6438
www.mixinpixls.com
(Audio Description, AVI Subtitles, Closed Captioning, DVD
Subtitles, Feature Film, Foreign, Real Time Captioning,
Subtitles, Video Subtitles & Visual Description)

mOcean (310) 481-0808
2440 S. Sepulveda Blvd., Ste. 150 FAX (310) 481-0807
Los Angeles, CA 90064 **www.moceanla.com**
(Feature Film Titles, Logos, Station ID Packages, TV Network/
Cable ID's and Packages & TV Show Titles and Opens)

Montgomery & Co. Creative (310) 558-4914
8611 Washington Blvd. FAX (310) 558-4915
Culver City, CA 90232 **www.montgomerycreative.com**
(Captions, Feature Film Titles, Logos, Station ID Packages,
Subtitles, TV Network/Cable ID's and Packages &
TV Show Titles and Opens)

National Captioning Institute (818) 238-0068
303 N. Glenoaks Blvd., Ste. 200
Burbank, CA 91502
(Audio Description, Closed Captioning, DVD Subtitles, Real
Time Captioning & Subtitles)

NBC Universal Artworks (212) 664-5972
30 Rockefeller Plaza, Ste. 514E **www.nbcartworks.com**
New York, NY 10012

Oasis Imagery (323) 469-9800
6500 Sunset Blvd. FAX (323) 462-4620
Los Angeles, CA 90028 **www.oasisimagery.com**
(Feature Film, Opens & TV Show)

OneWorld Language Solutions (323) 848-7993
3940 Laurel Canyon Blvd., Ste. 501 FAX (323) 848-7995
Studio City, CA 91604 **www.oneworldlanguage.com**
(Captions & Subtitles)

OOOii (323) 960-9275
1604 N. Cahuenga Blvd. **www.oooii.us**
Hollywood, CA 90028
(Feature Film Titles, Logos, Station ID Packages, TV Network/
Cable ID's and Packages & TV Show Titles and Opens)

Opticam, Inc. (310) 403-6691
810 Navy St.
Santa Monica, CA 90405
(Feature Film Titles, Logos, Subtitles & TV Show
Titles and Opens)

Pacific Vision Productions, Inc. (626) 441-4869
210 Pasadena Ave. **www.pacificvision.com**
South Pasadena, CA 91030
(Feature Film Titles, Logos & TV Show Titles and Opens)

Dan Perri/Movie Titles (323) 259-1800
1472 Silverwood Dr.
Los Angeles, CA 90041
(Feature Film Titles, Logos & TV Show Titles and Opens)

Picture Mill (323) 465-8800
6422 Homewood Ave. FAX (323) 465-8875
Los Angeles, CA 90028 **www.picturemill.com**
(Animated Logos, Feature Film Titles, Logos, Station ID
Packages, TV Network/Cable and Packages, Opens, Station ID
Packages, Titles, TV Network ID's, TV Network Packages &
TV Show Titles and Opens)

PixelMonger Inc./Scott Billups (818) 990-8993
www.pixelmonger.com/esbindex.html
(Feature Film Titles, Logos, Station ID Packages, TV Network/
Cable ID's and Packages & TV Show Titles and Opens)

Planet Blue (310) 899-3877
1250 Sixth St., Ste. 102 FAX (310) 899-3787
Santa Monica, CA 90401 **www.planetblue.com**
(Feature Film Titles, Logos, Station ID Packages, TV Network/
Cable ID's and Packages & TV Show Titles and Opens)

Point of Origin (818) 392-8735
www.pointoforiginmedia.com

Post Logic Studios (323) 461-7887
1800 N. Vine St., Ste. 100 FAX (323) 461-7790
Los Angeles, CA 90028 **www.postlogic.com**
(Captions, Feature Film Titles, Logos, Station ID Packages,
Subtitles, TV Network/Cable ID's and Packages &
TV Show Titles and Opens)

Post Modern Edit, LLC (949) 608-8700
2941 Alton Pkwy FAX (949) 608-8729
Irvine, CA 92606 **www.postmodernedit.com**
(Animated Logos, Cable ID's, Closed Captioning, Domestic,
DVD Subtitles, Feature Film, Foreign Language, Logos, Station
ID Packages, TV Show & Video Subtitles)

Prime Digital Media Services (661) 964-0220
28111 Avenue Stanford FAX (661) 964-0550
Valencia, CA 91355 **www.primedigital.com**

Psychic Bunny (310) 862-4262
453 S. Spring St., Ste. 620 FAX (213) 614-9046
Los Angeles, CA 90013 **www.psychicbunny.com**

Radium (310) 264-6440
2115 Colorado Ave. **www.radium.com**
Santa Monica, CA 91404
(Captions, Feature Film Titles, Logos, Station ID Packages,
Subtitles, TV Network/Cable ID's and Packages &
TV Show Titles and Opens)

(323) 465-3900
Reality Check Studios, Inc. (323) 908-7000
6100 Melrose Ave. FAX (323) 465-3600
Los Angeles, CA 90038 **www.realityx.com**
(Feature Film, Foreign and Domestic, ID's, Logos, Opens,
Packages, Station ID Packages, Titles, TV Network/
Cable & TV Show)

Renegade Animation, Inc. (818) 551-2351
111 E. Broadway, Ste. 208 FAX (818) 551-2350
Glendale, CA 91205 **www.renegadeanimation.com**
(Feature Film Titles, Logos, TV Network/Cable ID's and
Packages & TV Show Titles and Opens)

Ring of Fire (310) 966-5055
1538 20th St. FAX (310) 966-5056
Santa Monica, CA 90404 **www.ringoffire.com**
(Feature Film Titles, Logos, Station ID Packages, TV Network/
Cable ID's and Packages & TV Show Titles and Opens)

Scratch Films (323) 664-9509
www.scratchfilms.net

SDI Media (310) 388-8800
(Captions & Subtitles) **www.sdimedia.com**

Shine (323) 937-7470
5410 Wilshire Blvd., Ste. 204 FAX (360) 237-0542
Los Angeles, CA 90036 **www.shinestudio.tv**

(818) 768-9778
Sir Reel Pictures (818) 415-7326
8036 Shadyglade Ave. **www.sirreelpictures.com**
North Hollywood, CA 91605
(Feature Film Titles, Logos, Station ID Packages, TV Network/
Cable ID's and Packages & TV Show Titles and Opens)

Paul Soady (323) 939-8785
(Captions, Feature Film Titles, Logos, Station ID Packages,
Subtitles & TV Network/Cable ID's and Packages)

Sony Pictures Imageworks (310) 840-8000
9050 W. Washington Blvd. FAX (310) 840-8100
Culver City, CA 90232 **www.imageworks.com**
(Feature Film Titles & Logos)

StandardVision, LLC   **(323) 224-3944**
FAX **(323) 225-6226**
www.standardsite.com
(Captions, Feature Film Titles, Logos, Station ID Packages,
Subtitles, TV Network/Cable ID's and Packages & TV Show
Titles and Opens)

Stardust Studios   **(310) 399-6047**
1823 Colorado Ave.   FAX **(310) 399-7486**
Santa Monica, CA 90405   **www.stardust.tv**
(Captions, Feature Films Titles, Logos, Station ID Packages,
TV Network/Cable ID's and Packages & TV Show
Opens and Titles)

Stargate Digital   **(626) 403-8403**
1001 El Centro St.   FAX **(626) 403-8444**
South Pasadena, CA 91030   **www.stargatestudios.net**
(Feature Film Titles, Logos & TV Show Titles and Opens)

STEELE Studios   **(310) 656-7770**
5737 Mesmer Ave.   FAX **(310) 391-9055**
Culver City, CA 90230   **www.steelevfx.com**
(Animated Logos, Cable ID's, Cable Packages, Feature Film,
Foreign, ID's, Logos, Station ID Packages, TV Network ID's,
TV Network Packages & TV Show)

Stokes/Kohne Associates, Inc.   **(323) 468-2340**
742 Cahuenga Blvd.   FAX **(323) 468-2345**
Hollywood, CA 90038   **www.stokeskohne.com**
(Animated Logos, Cable ID's, Cable Packages, Feature Film,
ID's, Logos, Opens, Titles, TV Network ID's & TV Show)

STS Foreign Language Services/a division
of STS Media Services, Inc.   **(818) 563-3004**
P.O. Box 10213   **www.stsforeignlanguage.com**
Burbank, CA 91510
(Closed Captioning, DVD Subtitles & Foreign Subtitles)

The Studio at   **(818) 295-5000**
New Wave Entertainment   **(818) 295-8060**
2660 W. Olive Ave.   **www.nwe.com**
Burbank, CA 91505
(Feature Film Titles, Logos, Station ID Packages, TV Network/
Cable ID's and Packages & TV Show Titles and Opens)

Subtext Studio/Subtext Semantics   **(323) 550-8190**
2451 Colorado Blvd., Ste. 2   **www.subtextstudio.com**
Los Angeles, CA 90041
(Animated Logos, Cable ID's, Cable Packages, Feature Film,
ID's, Logos, Opens, Station ID Packages, Titles, TV Network
ID's, TV Network Packages & TV Show)

TeamWorks Digital   **(310) 991-5442**
www.teamworksdigital.com
(Feature Film Titles, Logos, Station ID Packages, TV Show
Titles and Opens & TV Network/Cable ID's and Packages)

Technicolor Creative   **(818) 480-5100**
Services - Burbank   **(310) 801-7300**
www.technicolor.com

The Thomas Cobb Group   **(310) 822-1515**
4051 Glencoe Ave., Studio 1   FAX **(310) 822-5015**
Venice, CA 90292   **www.tcgstudio.com**
(Feature Film Titles, Logos, Station ID Packages, TV Network/
Cable ID's and Packages & TV Show Titles and Opens)

Tigar Hare Studios   **(818) 907-6663**
4485 Matilija Ave.   FAX **(818) 907-0693**
Sherman Oaks, CA 91423   **www.tigarhare.com**
(Feature Film Titles, Station ID Packages, TV Network/Cable
ID's and Packages & TV Show Titles and Opens)

Titra California, Inc.   **(818) 244-3663**
733 Salem St.   FAX **(818) 244-6205**
Glendale, CA 91203   **www.titra.com**
(Captions & Subtitles)

Toon Makers, Inc.   **(818) 832-8666**
17333 Ludlow St.   **www.toonmakers.com**
Granada Hills, CA 91344
(Feature Film Titles, Logos, Station ID Packages, TV Network/
Cable ID's and Packages & TV Show Titles and Opens)

Trance   **(323) 651-1114**
449 N. Edinburgh Ave.   **www.trancedesigns.com**
Los Angeles, CA 90048
(Logos & TV Show Titles and Opens)

Velocity Visuals, Inc.   **(310) 376-7870**
www.velocityfx.com

    (818) 736-5446
Video Caption Corporation   **(800) 705-1203**
300 E. Magnolia, Ste. 506   FAX **(800) 705-1207**
Burbank, CA 91502   **www.vicaps.com**
(Audio Description, AVI Subtitles, Cable Packages, Closed
Captioning, Domestic, DVD, Feature Film, Foreign, Internet
Captioning, Internet Subtitling, NLE Direct, Subtitles,
TV Network Packages, TV Show, Video Subtitles &
Visual Description)

View Studio, Inc.   **(805) 745-8814**
385 Toro Canyon Rd.   **www.viewstudio.com**
Carpinteria, CA 93013
(Feature Film Titles, Logos, Station ID Packages, TV Network/
Cable ID's and Packages & TV Show Titles and Opens)

Visions Optical Effects   **(323) 854-0399**
3257 N. Knoll Dr.   FAX **(323) 850-8138**
Los Angeles, CA 90068
(Opticals)

    (818) 558-3363
Visual Data Media Services, Inc.   **(888) 418-4782**
145 W. Magnolia Blvd.   FAX **(818) 558-3368**
Burbank, CA 91502   **www.visualdatainc.com**

    (818) 755-0410
VITAC   **(888) 528-4822**
4605 Lankershim Blvd., Ste. 250 FAX **(818) 755-0411**
North Hollywood, CA 91602   **www.vitac.com**
(Audio Description, Captions, Closed Captioning, DVD
Subtitles, Real Time Captioning, Subtitles, Video Subtitles &
Visual Description)

Viva Broadcast
Design & Production   **(805) 969-9933**
701 Coyote Rd.   FAX **(805) 969-4482**
Santa Barbara, CA 93108   **www.vivadesign.com**
(Logos, Station ID Packages, TV Network/Cable ID's and
Packages & TV Show Titles and Opens)

Wicked Liquid FX   **(949) 250-8786**
20342 SW Acacia St., Ste. 210 FAX **(949) 250-8701**
Newport Beach, CA 92660   **www.wickedliquidfx.com**
(Captions, Feature Film Titles, Logos, Station ID Packages,
Subtitles, TV Network/Cable ID's and Packages & TV Show
Titles and Opens)

Wut It Is   **(323) 467-3300**
6121 Santa Monica Blvd., Ste. 201 FAX **(323) 467-7480**
Los Angeles, CA 90038   **www.wutitis.com**
(Animated Logos, Cable ID's, Cable Packages, Domestic,
Feature Film, Foreign, ID's, Logos, Opens, Station ID Packages,
Titles, TV Network ID's, TV Network Packages, TV Show &
Visual Description)

yU+co.   **(323) 606-5050**
941 N. Mansfield Ave.   FAX **(323) 606-5040**
Los Angeles, CA 90038   **www.yuco.com**
(Feature Film Titles, Logos, Station ID Packages, TV Network/
Cable ID's and Packages & TV Show Titles and Opens)

Zak/Paperno   **(323) 937-2517**
7000 Beverly Blvd.
Los Angeles, CA 90036
(Feature Film Titles, Logos, Station ID Packages, TV Network/
Cable ID's and Packages & TV Show Titles and Opens)

Zoic, Inc.   **(310) 838-0770**
3582 Eastham Dr.   FAX **(310) 838-1169**
Culver City, CA 90232   **www.zoicstudios.com**
(Feature Film Titles)

Gerald Abraham	(818) 990-8993
	www.ambitiousent.com
Dominik Bauch	(310) 788-3918
	www.d-a-a.com
Brian Begun	(310) 788-3918
	www.d-a-a.com
Javier Bello	(310) 788-3918
(3D)	www.d-a-a.com
Vlad Bina	(310) 788-3918
	www.d-a-a.com
James Bohn	(310) 392-1212
	www.laliquid.com
Simon Brewster	(310) 736-1663
	FAX (310) 396-3299
	www.brewsterparsons.com
Thomas Briggs	(310) 788-3918
(3D)	www.d-a-a.com
Steven Browning	(310) 788-3918
	www.d-a-a.com
Kevin Cahill	(310) 450-3448
	FAX (310) 450-3448
	www.luminetik.com
Kevin Carr	(310) 788-3918
	www.d-a-a.com
R. Kevin Clarke	(310) 788-3918
(3D)	www.d-a-a.com
Matt Collorafice	(310) 788-3918
	www.d-a-a.com
Brandon Davis	(310) 788-3918
(3D)	www.d-a-a.com
Matt DiNardo	(818) 536-7991
	www.nitrousvfx.com
Andrew Edwards	(310) 788-3918
(2D)	www.d-a-a.com
Tyler Esselstrom	(310) 788-3918
	www.d-a-a.com
Jim Gorman	(310) 788-3918
	www.d-a-a.com
Robin Graham	(310) 788-3918
(2D)	www.d-a-a.com
Sarah Grossmann	(310) 788-3918
(2D)	www.d-a-a.com
Christophe Gwynne	(310) 788-3918
(3D)	www.d-a-a.com
Kevin Tod Haug	(323) 703-1333
	wp-a.com
Brad Hayes	(310) 788-3918
(3D)	www.d-a-a.com
Tim Hedegaard	(323) 512-1542
(2D, 3D & Virtual Set Design)	www.ultimatte-rentals.com

Jeff Heusser	(310) 788-3918
(2D)	www.d-a-a.com
Peter Hjorth	(323) 703-1333
	wp-a.com
Lyndsey Horton	(310) 788-3918
	www.d-a-a.com
Chris Howard	(310) 788-3918
	www.d-a-a.com
Joshua LaCross	(310) 788-3918
(2D)	www.d-a-a.com
Giancarlo Lari	(310) 788-3918
(3D)	www.d-a-a.com
Geoff Leavitt	(818) 536-7991
(2D)	www.nitrousvfx.com
Chris Ledoux	(310) 788-3918
	www.d-a-a.com
Soyoun Lee	(310) 788-3918
	www.d-a-a.com
Ken Littleton	(310) 788-3918
(2D)	www.d-a-a.com
Lawrence Littleton	(310) 788-3918
(2D)	www.d-a-a.com
Daniel Loeb	(310) 788-3918
(3D)	www.d-a-a.com
David Lombardi	(310) 788-3918
(3D)	www.d-a-a.com
Scott Milne	(323) 969-1011
	www.mfxdesign.com
Pat Murphy	(310) 586-0650
	www.a52.com
Chris Nolan	(310) 788-3918
	www.d-a-a.com
Jeremy Lei Ontiveros	(310) 788-3918
	www.d-a-a.com
Todd Sheridan Perry	(310) 788-3918
(3D)	www.d-a-a.com
Scott Rader	(310) 788-3918
(2D)	www.d-a-a.com
D. Ryan Reeb	(310) 420-0970
	www.ryanreeb.com
Rick Rische	(310) 788-3918
(Digital Matte Painting)	www.d-a-a.com
Toshihiro Sakamaki	(310) 788-3918
	www.d-a-a.com
Greg Scribner	(310) 788-3918
(2D)	www.d-a-a.com
Marcos Shih	(310) 788-3918
	www.d-a-a.com
Howard Shur	(323) 467-8550
	www.sunsetedit.com

Alan Sonneman	(310) 788-3918
(Digital Matte Painting)	www.d-a-a.com

Joe Spano	(818) 536-7991
	www.nitrousvfx.com

TellAVision	(310) 230-5303
1060 20th St., Ste. 8	FAX (310) 388-5550
Santa Monica, CA 90403	www.tellavisionagency.com
(Reps for 3D Artists)	

Taylor Tulip-Close	(323) 703-1333
	wp-a.com

	(310) 788-3918
Adam Watkins	(818) 505-8787
(3D)	www.d-a-a.com

Mark Wurts	(310) 788-3918
(3D)	www.d-a-a.com

Paal Anand   (323) 874-3003
www.blingimaging.com

Peter Anderson   (818) 951-6066
(Visual FX Supervisor/Producer)

Scott E. Anderson   (310) 827-6470
(213) 399-1600
FAX (310) 591-8830
www.digitalsandbox.org
(2D, 3D, S3D Stereographer, Visual FX Consultant &
Visual FX Supervisor)

Wenden K. Baldwin   (213) 713-1381
(Visual FX Producer)   www.wendenbaldwin.com

James Balsam   (323) 660-5580
(Motion Control and VFX Camera Operator)

Michael Baltazar   (310) 788-3918
www.d-a-a.com

Mat Beck   (310) 899-9779
FAX (310) 899-3113
www.entityfx.com

Steve Begg   (818) 876-9618
rocketsciencetalent.com

Jim Berney   (310) 840-8000
www.imageworks.com

John Berton   (818) 876-9618
rocketsciencetalent.com

Angus Bickerton   (818) 876-9618
rocketsciencetalent.com

Scott Billups   (818) 990-8993
www.ambitiousent.com

R. Edward Black   (818) 640-6814
(Visual FX Supervisor)

Jonathan Bourgoine   (818) 536-7991
www.nitrousvfx.com

Kerry Bourgoine   (818) 536-7991
www.nitrousvfx.com

Jake Braver   (310) 623-5500
www.montanartists.com

Phil Brennan   (310) 273-6700
www.utaproduction.com

Tim Burke   (818) 876-9618
rocketsciencetalent.com

David Burton   (310) 788-3918
(3D)   www.d-a-a.com

André Bustanoby   (310) 788-3918
(Visual FX Supervisor)   www.d-a-a.com

Glenn Campbell   (818) 238-9660
www.area51fx.com

Mike Chambers   (310) 488-6270
www.mrcvfx.com
(Visual FX Consultant, Producer & Supervisor)

Ed Chapman   (213) 200-9952
FAX (818) 980-9788
www.edchapman.com

Josh Comen   (310) 285-9000
(310) 399-2828
www.wmeentertainment.com

Joyce Cox   (323) 664-7294
(323) 377-5806

Joshua Cushner   (323) 650-8750
(Motion Control Operator & Visual FX Consultant)

Michael J. DeCourcey   (310) 480-4031
www.decourcey.com

Eric DeHaven   (310) 448-7900
www.rhythm.com

Jean-Marc Demmer   (310) 828-9628
www.eightvfx.com

D.J. Des Jardin   (310) 273-6700
www.utaproduction.com

Digital Artists Agency/DAA   (310) 788-3918
13323 Washington Blvd., Ste. 304   FAX (310) 788-3415
Los Angeles, CA 90066   www.d-a-a.com
(Reps for Visual FX Artists)

Mark Driscoll   (323) 469-4230
www.lookfx.com

Olivier Dumont   (323) 512-6000
www.buf.com

Art Durinski   (310) 440-3896
(310) 665-6982
FAX (310) 440-3896
(2D, 3D, Visual FX Consultant, Visual FX Producer &
Visual FX Supervisor)

Shawn Dury   (310) 200-7593
(213) 501-1499

Chris Edwards   (323) 931-6633
(Previsualization Supervisor)   FAX (323) 931-9928
www.thethirdfloorinc.com

Volker Engel   (310) 788-3918
(Visual FX Supervisor)   www.d-a-a.com

Edy H. Enriquez   (310) 836-9011
(323) 252-0904
FAX (310) 836-9010
www.x1fx.com

Jonathan Erland   (323) 257-1163
(323) 243-8999
(Composite Photography Consultant)   FAX (323) 257-0604
www.digitalgreenscreen.com

Jon Farhat   (310) 282-9940
www.mirisch.com

Henrik Fett   (323) 469-4230
www.lookfx.com

Michael Fink   (818) 876-9618
rocketsciencetalent.com

Brenton Fletcher   (323) 251-6495
www.clever-monkey.com

Mark Forker   (310) 788-3918
www.d-a-a.com

Brian Fortune	(310) 788-3918
	www.d-a-a.com
Scott Friedman	(310) 566-1463
	www.endlessnoise.com
Sari Gennis	(323) 965-9555
	FAX (323) 965-1133
	www.anim8trix.com
(Animation Supervision, Compositing & Live Action and Animation Integration)	
Charlie Gibson	(310) 273-6700
	www.utaproduction.com
Yvain Gnabro	(310) 788-3918
	www.d-a-a.com
Chris Godfrey	(310) 273-6700
	www.utaproduction.com
Karen Goulekas	(310) 273-6700
	www.unitedtalent.com
Matthew Gratzner	(310) 578-9929
	FAX (310) 578-7370
	www.newdealstudios.com
Robin Griffin	(818) 876-9618
	rocketsciencetalent.com
John Gross	(310) 481-7002
	FAX (310) 207-8408
	www.edenfx.com
Ben Grossman	(310) 788-3918
(2D)	www.d-a-a.com
Chris Guardino	(310) 566-1463
	www.endlessnoise.com
Shari Hanson	(415) 370-9600
(Visual FX Producer)	
David Hare	(818) 907-6663
	www.tigarhare.com
Joe Harkins	(818) 876-9618
(Visual FX Supervisor)	rocketsciencetalent.com
Robb Hart	(714) 953-9501
	www.anidealworld.com
(Visual FX Consultant, Producer and Supervisor)	
Dion Hatch	(310) 315-6060
	(818) 284-6423
	www.digiscope.com
Daniel Hayes	(310) 788-3918
	www.d-a-a.com
John Heller	(310) 448-7900
	www.rhythm.com
Matt Hightower	(310) 788-3918
	www.d-a-a.com
Kelle Holland	(323) 874-3003
	www.blingimaging.com
Edward Irastorza	(310) 788-3918
(3D)	www.d-a-a.com
Max Ivins	(323) 469-4230
	www.lookfx.com
Evan Jacobs	(310) 282-9940
	(310) 613-6164
(Visual FX Supervisor)	www.mirisch.com

Joni Jacobson	(310) 497-7225
Julie Jang	(310) 788-3918
	www.d-a-a.com
Chas Jarrett	(310) 285-0303
	www.sandramarsh.com
Davey Jones	(310) 788-3918
	www.d-a-a.com
Dan Kaufman	(310) 273-6700
	www.utaproduction.com
Tamara Watts Kent	(818) 363-6149
(Visual FX Producer)	FAX (818) 363-2449
	www.stormcloudvfx.com
Bob Kertesz	(323) 467-7572
	www.bluescreen.com
(Visual FX Consultant & Visual FX Supervisor)	
John Kilkenny	(310) 369-5880
(Visual FX Producer/Supervisor)	
Marc Kolbe	(818) 876-9618
	rocketsciencetalent.com
Neil Krepela	(310) 452-2488
(Visual FX Consultant & Visual FX Supervisor)	
Tim Landry	(818) 768-9778
	www.timlandry.com
Geoff Leavitt	(818) 536-7991
	www.nitrousvfx.com
Gregory Lemkin	(310) 788-3918
	www.d-a-a.com
Rick Lieberman	(310) 709-4832
	(305) 321-3556
Ken Locsmandi	(310) 577-3213
	www.filmworksfx.com
Gray Marshall	(310) 788-3918
	www.d-a-a.com
Keegan Martin	(818) 990-8993
	www.ambitiousent.com
Michelle Massie	(818) 238-9660
	www.area51fx.com
Tim McGovern	(310) 788-3918
(Visual FX Supervisor)	www.d-a-a.com
Tim McHugh	(818) 238-9660
	www.area51fx.com
Dennis Michel	(310) 216-5678
	www.ieeffects.com
Bill Millar	(310) 623-5500
	www.montanartists.com
Tim Miller	(310) 448-7900
	www.rhythm.com
Jeb Milne	(310) 788-3918
(Visual FX Producer)	www.d-a-a.com
The Mirisch Agency	(310) 282-9940
8840 Wilshire Blvd., Ste. 100	FAX (310) 282-0702
Beverly Hills, CA 90211	www.mirisch.com
(Reps for Visual FX Supervisors)	

Montana Artists Agency (310) 623-5500 9150 Wilshire Blvd., Ste. 100 FAX **(310) 623-5515** Beverly Hills, CA 90212 **www.montanartists.com** (Reps for Visual FX Supervisors)	**Scott Siegal** (213) 713-0154 (Visual FX Producer)
George Murphy (818) 876-9618 (Visual FX Supervisor) rocketsciencetalent.com	**Kathy Siegel** (323) 644-8814 (323) 578-1591 (Animation and Visual FX Supervisor) **www.fxgal.com**
Karen Murphy (310) 282-9940 **www.mirisch.com**	**Ron Simonson** (818) 876-9618 rocketsciencetalent.com
Roger Nall (818) 780-4466 FAX **(818) 780-4467** **www.1111mediaworks.com**	**Elan Soltes** (323) 533-6226 (Visual FX Consultant, Producer & Supervisor)
	Ellen Somers (661) 644-5848
Gary Nolin (661) 255-8486	**Scott Squires** (818) 876-9618 rocketsciencetalent.com
Jeffrey A. Okun (310) 273-6700 **www.utaproduction.com**	**Jerry Steele** (310) 656-7770 FAX **(310) 391-9055** **www.steelevfx.com**
Michael Owens (818) 876-9618 rocketsciencetalent.com	**Bruce Steinheimer** (310) 285-0303 **www.sandramarsh.com**
William Powloski (310) 376-7870 **www.velocityfx.com** (Visual FX Consultant, Producer and Supervisor)	**Mark Stetson** (310) 377-7239
Ted Rae (310) 788-3918 (Visual FX Supervisor) **www.d-a-a.com**	**Marcus Stokes** (310) 788-3918 **www.d-a-a.com**
Fred Raimondi (818) 990-8993 **www.ambitiousent.com**	**Colin Strause** (310) 319-2300 **www.hydraulx.com**
Eliza Pelham Randall (310) 962-9463 (323) 525-1225 **www.queenofspades.com** (Data Documentation, Stereo 3D Conversion and Supervision, Visual Effects Set Supervision, Visual FX Consultant, Visual FX Producer & Visual FX Supervisor)	**Greg Strause** (310) 319-2300 **www.hydraulx.com** **Jacques Stroweis** (310) 770-3235 (3D & Stereoscopic Supervisor)
Kelley R. Ray (323) 371-6745 **www.kelleyray.com** (2D, 3D, Visual FX Consultant, Visual FX Producer & Visual FX Supervisor)	**Mary Stuart** (818) 284-6423 (310) 315-6060 **www.italentco.com**
Chris Reynolds (310) 285-0303 (Special FX Producer) **www.sandramarsh.com**	**David G. Stump** (323) 650-5662 FAX **(323) 650-5663** (Blue/Green Screen, CGI & Matte Photography Technician)
Eric J. Robertson (310) 623-5500 **www.montanartists.com**	**Eric Swenson** (888) 965-4321 FAX **(888) 965-4321** **www.ericvfx.com**
Robbie Robfogel (714) 258-6678 **www.oceanvisualfx.com**	(Shoot Supervisor, Visual FX Consultant, Visual FX Director of Photography, Visual FX Stereography & Visual FX Supervisor)
Lesley Robson-Foster (310) 395-4600 (917) 621-7202 (Visual FX Supervisor) **www.robsonfoster.com**	**Gurvand Tanneu** (310) 788-3918 **www.d-a-a.com**
Rocket Science Talent (818) 876-9618 5023 N. Parkway Calabasas FAX **(818) 876-8501** Calabasas, CA 91302 rocketsciencetalent.com (Reps for Visual FX Supervisors and Producers)	**Bill Taylor** (310) 282-9940 **www.mirisch.com** **Michael Tigar** (818) 907-6663 **www.tigarhare.com**
Mark Russell (310) 273-6700 **www.utaproduction.com**	**Nik Titmarsh** (310) 448-7900 **www.rhythm.com**
Robert Scopinich (310) 592-9362 (2D, 3D, Reps for Visual FX Producers, Virtual Set Designer, Visual FX Consultant, Visual FX Producer & Visual FX Supervisor)	**Jon Tojek** (310) 788-3918 **www.d-a-a.com**
Ariel Velasco Shaw (310) 273-6700 **www.unitedtalent.com**	**Jon Tucker** (310) 405-2011 **www.rocketfilms.com**
Chris Shaw (818) 876-9618 rocketsciencetalent.com	**Kendrick Wallace** (818) 876-9618 (Visual FX Producer) rocketsciencetalent.com
Wayne A. Shepherd (310) 452-4600 **www.atthepost.net**	**Marc Weigert** (310) 788-3918 (Visual FX Producer) **www.d-a-a.com**
Janette Shew (323) 692-0115 (323) 791-6318 (Digital FX Producer)	**Mark Weingartner** (818) 222-5200 **www.schneiderentertainment.com**

Visual FX Supervisors & Producers

Phyllis Weisband-Fibus	(818) 726-2611
	(818) 760-8111
(Visual FX Producer/Supervisor)	FAX (818) 760-8112

Bill Westenhofer	(310) 448-7900
	www.rhythm.com

	(323) 882-8322
Terry Whiteside	(323) 646-5235
(Visual FX Producer)	

Steffen Wild	(310) 788-3918
	www.d-a-a.com

Eddie Williams	(310) 623-5500
	www.montanartists.com

Troy Williams	(310) 788-3918
	www.d-a-a.com

Dean Wright	(818) 876-9618
	rocketsciencetalent.com

Riccardo Zanettini	(310) 788-3918
	www.d-a-a.com

Vit Zelich	(310) 788-3918
	www.d-a-a.com

Fernando Zorrilla	(323) 874-3003
	www.blingimaging.com

Susan Zwerman	(818) 760-4242
(Visual FX Producer)	www.crystalrain.biz

MAD MEN

BY MARJ GALAS

Editor Christopher Gay on "Mad Men"

"Mad Men" editor Christopher Gay owes a bit of gratitude towards Oscar-winning editor Walter Murch. When Gay, a former cinematographer, was studying editing, he read everything about Murch's approach to the craft, especially Murch's understanding of sound.

"He was a sound guy, and this really brought to light the importance of sound to me," said Gay. "Whenever I am doing an episode, I always create a sound design in Avid. It's not just about the look of the storytelling, but to momentarily guide the audience's experience."

The attention to sound in editing proved especially beneficial during season five's episode "Far Away Places." Gay had to find a way to incorporate an LSD experience that didn't stray too far from the show's signature look. "Mad Men" creator Matthew Weiner had researched LSD use and discovered some users claimed they could listen to two different songs playing simultaneously. To achieve this effect, Gay laid down one music track then carefully trimmed frames of the second song so both songs could be clearly distinguished. Gay also used an auditory cue to inform viewers that the lead character in the scene was about to enter an altered state.

A key objective for editors working on "Mad Men" is to play out the wide shots and let the audience absorb the atmosphere of the scenes. Gay's goal is to use all aspects of the composition captured in conjunction with the best performances of each scene. While wide shots are an important visual element in "Mad Men," Gay also integrates varying degrees of tight shots to emphasis specific tones.

Unlike the indie films and documentaries that constituted Gay's earliest editing experience, episodic television must adhere to a strict time limit. Gay has embraced this practice, feeling that the time crunch helps him become specific in telling the story.

"It's the best possible thing. Everyone editing features should have the challenge of cutting for a specific time," said Gay. "That little bit of time is when tough choices are made. You may lose some lines or detail, but those choices benefit the story."

ABRIDGED FROM AN LA 411 NEWSLETTER ARTICLE PUBLISHED SEPTEMBER 2012

Ⓐ ADVERTISER SYMBOL

**Refer to the General Index for
cross-referencing items in this section.**

Aero Associates/Aircraft Mockups (310) 337-1938
(310) 332-4383
8033 Emerson Ave.
Los Angeles, CA 90045

Ⓐ Aero Mock-Ups, Inc. (818) 982-7327
(888) 662-5877
13126 Saticoy St. FAX (818) 982-0122
North Hollywood, CA 91605 www.aeromockups.com

Air Hollywood (818) 890-0444
13240 Weidner St. FAX (818) 890-7041
Los Angeles, CA 91331 www.airhollywood.com
(Airline Mock Ups, Airplane Mock Ups, Airplane Props, Airport
Props, Cockpit, Jet Interior, Props, Security Props, Signage &
X-Ray Machines)

ARIS Helicopters/Heli-Flite (951) 359-5016
(800) 340-1969
6871 Airport Dr. FAX (951) 359-5019
Riverside, CA 92504 www.arishelicopters.com

Aviation Warehouse (760) 388-4215
20020 El Mirage Airport Rd. FAX (760) 388-4236
El Mirage, CA 92301 www.aviationwarehouse.net

Jets & Props (818) 505-0199
(818) 324-0884
5436 Cleon Ave. FAX (818) 505-0199
North Hollywood, CA 91601 www.jetsandprops.com

Producers Air Force (818) 845-5970
(818) 795-7463
One Orange Grove Terrace FAX (818) 845-4033
Burbank, CA 91501 www.producersairforce.com
(Airplane Mock-Ups & Cockpit)

Ⓐ Scroggins Aviation (702) 348-7731
Corporate Office: FAX (702) 953-7307
5840 W. Craig Rd., Stes. 120-262
Las Vegas, NV 89130 www.scrogginsaviation.com
(Mock-ups and Props of Commercial Aircraft, Cockpits, Crash
Wreckage & Passenger Cabins)

Silver Dream Factory, Inc. (714) 836-1853
(714) 225-3708
1181 N. Knollwood Circle www.standingsets.com
Anaheim, CA 92801

Syncro Aviation, Inc./Hanger 902 (818) 901-9828
7701 Woodley Ave. FAX (818) 988-5851
Van Nuys, CA 91406 www.syncroaircraftinteriors.com

Art Pic   (818) 503-5999
6826 Troost Ave.   FAX (818) 503-5995
North Hollywood, CA 91605   www.artpic2000.com
(Faux Finishes & Murals)

Brainworks, Inc.   (323) 782-1425
5364 West Pico Blvd.   www.brainworksart.com
Los Angeles, CA 90019
(Backdrops, Faux Finishes & Murals)

Castex Rentals   (323) 462-1468
1044 Cole Ave.   FAX (323) 462-3719
Hollywood, CA 90038   www.castexrentals.com
(Backings, Blue Screens, Chroma Key Drops, Green Screens,
Muslin, Rigging & Scrims)

Cinnabar (818) 842-8190
4571 Electronics Pl. FAX (818) 842-0563
Los Angeles, CA 90039 www.cinnabar.com
(Backings, Decorative Painting, Faux Finishes, Murals, Painted
Backings, Scenic Artist, Textured & Trompe L'Oeil)

(323) 257-1163
A Composite Components Company (323) 243-8999
134 N. Avenue 61, Ste. 102/3 FAX (323) 257-0604
Los Angeles, CA 90042 www.digitalgreenscreen.com
(Blue, Green and Red Screens, Chroma Key Drops,
Paint & Rentals)

Continental Scenery, Inc. (818) 768-8075
7802 Clybourn Ave. FAX (818) 768-6939
Sun Valley, CA 91352 www.continentalscenery.com

(310) 980-0634
DammannART Scenic Backdrops (888) 957-0320
www.backdrops.net

Dapper Cadaver (818) 771-0818
www.dappercadaver.com

(818) 287-3800
Dazian Fabrics (877) 432-9426
7120 Case Ave. FAX (818) 287-3810
North Hollywood, CA 91605 www.dazian.com

(323) 938-5826
Demar Feldman Studios, Inc. (213) 760-0271
241 S. Norton Ave. FAX (323) 938-4368
Los Angeles, CA 90004
(Custom Backings, Decorative Painting, Faux Finishes &
Trompe L'Oeil)

(310) 675-2715
Bridget Duffy (310) 422-2910
www.duffyart.com
(Airbrushing, Custom Backings, Custom Fine Art Oil Paintings,
Decorative Painting, Faux Finishes, Murals, Painted Backings,
Scenic Artist & Trompe L'Oeil)

(310) 717-9034
Sean Falkner (562) 799-1514
mysite.verizon.net/resv3n82/
(Airbrushing, Backdrops, Backings, Chroma Key Drops,
Custom, Cycloramas, Decorative Painting, Faux Finishes,
Flameproofing, Murals, Paint, Painted Backings, Patinas,
Scenic Artist, Scrims, Textured & Trompe L'Oeil)

Fauve Creations (818) 481-2019
6553 Randi Ave. www.fauveassociates.com
Woodland Hills, CA 91303
(Airbrushing, Backdrops, Backings, Custom, Decorative
Painting, Faux Finishes, Murals, Paint, Painted Backings,
Patinas, Scenic Artist, Scrims & Trompe L'Oeil)

(323) 460-4192
Fore-Peak (407) 649-9937
1040 N. Las Palmas Ave. FAX (323) 871-8141
Los Angeles, CA 90038 www.fore-peak.com

(323) 662-1134
Grosh Scenic Rentals (877) 363-7998
4114 Sunset Blvd. FAX (323) 664-7526
Los Angeles, CA 90029 www.grosh.com

Hollywood Rentals/ESS/Olesen (818) 407-7800
12800 Foothill Blvd. FAX (818) 407-7875
Sylmar, CA 91342 www.hollywoodrentals.com
(Gauze, Muslin, Nets, Screens & Scrims)

A JC Backings Corporation (310) 244-5830
5905 Smiley Dr. FAX (310) 244-7949
Culver City, CA 90232 www.jcbackings.com
(Backdrops, Backings, Custom, Digital Imaging, Digital Print,
Painted and Photo Backings & Rentals)

(805) 259-6772
Ed Lister (805) 637-7969
(Custom Backings & Murals) www.edlisterscenic.com

Los Angeles Rag House (818) 276-1130
100 E. Santa Anita Ave. FAX (818) 842-2150
Burbank, CA 91502 www.laraghouse.com

(818) 994-6693
Lund Background Pictures (818) 231-5863
www.lundpix.com
(Backdrops, Backings, Custom, Cycloramas, Digital Imaging,
Murals, Muslin, Photo Backings, Rentals, Scrims, Video
Backdrops & Virtual Sets)

Keith Neely (310) 395-4600
www.murthaagency.com

Pacific Studios, Inc. (323) 653-3093
8315 Melrose Ave. FAX (323) 653-9509
Los Angeles, CA 90069 www.pacificstudiosinc.com
(Backdrops, Backings, Custom, Digital Imaging,
Photo Backings & Rentals)

(310) 820-3197
photowow.com (800) 453-9333
11950 Wilshire Blvd. FAX (310) 820-3175
Los Angeles, CA 90025 www.photowow.com
(Digital Imaging & Mural Prints)

Prolab Digital Imaging (310) 625-4411
5441 W. 104th St. FAX (310) 846-4496
Los Angeles, CA 90045 www.prolabdigital.com

The Rag Place, Inc. (818) 765-3338
13160 Raymer St. FAX (818) 765-3860
North Hollywood, CA 91605 www.theragplace.com
(Material Backings)

Ragtime Rentals, Inc. (818) 837-7077
11970 Borden Ave. FAX (818) 837-5096
San Fernando, CA 91340 www.ragtimerentals.com
(Backings, Blue and Green Screens & Rigging)

Really Fake Digital (800) 761-6995
518 N. Lake Ave. FAX (626) 666-3338
Pasadena, CA 91101 www.reallyfake.com
(Backdrops, Backings, Custom, Digital Imaging, Murals, Photo
Backings & Printed Scrims and Fabrics)

Rent What? Inc. (310) 639-7000
1978 Gladwick St. FAX (310) 639-7015
Rancho Dominguez, CA 90220 www.rentwhatinc.com
(Backdrops, Backings, Custom, Cycloramas, Flameproofing,
Muslin, Rentals, Scrims, Stage/Studio Drapes & Textured)

(818) 543-6700
Rosco Backdrops (323) 474-8795
1265 Los Angeles St. FAX (818) 662-9470
Glendale, CA 91204 www.roscodigital.com

(818) 505-6290
Rose Brand (800) 360-5056
10616 Lanark St. FAX (818) 505-6293
Sun Valley, CA 91352 www.rosebrand.com
(Chroma Key Drops, Custom Backings, Muslin, Scenery
Paint & Scrims)

Scenic Express, Inc. (323) 254-4351
3019 Andrita St. FAX (323) 254-4411
Los Angeles, CA 90065 www.scenicexpress.net

Schmidli Backdrops (323) 938-2098
5830 W. Adams Blvd. FAX (323) 938-2486
Culver City, CA 90232 www.schmidli.com
(Digital, Scenic and Textured Backdrops)

Sew What? Inc. (310) 639-6000
1978 Gladwick St. FAX (310) 639-6036
Rancho Dominguez, CA 90220 www.sewwhatinc.com

Sky Drops Inc. (818) 633-2639
999 N. Mission Rd. www.skydrops.com
Los Angeles, CA 90033
(Airbrushing, Backdrops, Backings, Chroma Key Drops,
Custom, Decorative Painting, Faux Finishes, Flameproofing,
Green Screens, Murals, Paint, Painted Backings, Patinas,
Photo Backings, Rentals, Scenic Artist, Scrims, Textured,
Trompe L'Oeil & Video Backdrops)

Snow Scenic, LLC
(310) 455-0360
(310) 877-6769
19722 Grand View Dr.
www.snowscenic.co
Topanga, CA 90290

Solbrook Display Corporation   (818) 761-3297
8700 De Soto Ave., Ste. 210
Canoga Park, CA 91304

Studio Dynamics
(562) 531-6700
(800) 595-4273
7703 Alondra Blvd.
FAX (562) 531-6769
Paramount, CA 90723   www.studiodynamics.com
(Backdrops, Backings, Blue Screens, Chroma Key Drops,
Custom, Green Screens,   Muslin, Painted Backings,
Rentals & Textured)

Theatrical Concepts, Inc.   (818) 597-1100
3030 Triunfo Canyon Rd.   FAX (818) 597-0202
Agoura Hills, CA 91301   www.theatrical.com
(Video Backgrounds & Virtual Sets)

Triangle Scenery   (323) 662-8129
1215 Bates Ave.   FAX (323) 662-8120
Los Angeles, CA 90029   www.tridrape.com
(Stage & Studio Drapes)

UVFX Scenic Productions   (310) 821-2657
171 Pier Ave.   FAX (310) 392-6817
Santa Monica, CA 90405   www.uvfx.com
(Airbrushing, Backdrops, Backings, Custom, Decorative
Painting, Murals, Painted Backings & Scenic Artist)

Virtualsets.com   (323) 512-1542
www.virtualsets.com
(Blue Screens, Chroma Key Drops, Cycloramas, Digital
Imaging, Green Screens, Red Screens, Rentals, Video
Backdrops & Virtual Sets)

**Warner Bros. Studio Facilities -
Design Studio/Sign & Scenic Art**   (818) 954-1815
4000 Warner Blvd.   FAX (818) 954-2806
Burbank, CA 91522   www.wbsignandscenic.com

West Coast Backings   (818) 772-0069
9718 Variel Ave.   FAX (818) 772-0097
Chatsworth, CA 91311   www.westcoastbackings.com

3555 Hayden Studios (310) 430-7550
3555 Hayden Ave. www.3555hayden.com
Culver City, CA 90232

Affordable Sound Stages (818) 641-0220
1708 Hale St. www.affordablesoundstages.com
Glendale, CA 91201

(805) 955-7742
AMP Studios (805) 955-7770
101 W. Cochran St. FAX (805) 955-7705
Simi Valley, CA 93065 www.ampstudios.com

Associated Television International (323) 556-5600
4401 Wilshire Blvd. www.4401wilshire.com
Los Angeles, CA 90010

(310) 779-9603
AZ Studios (310) 383-5484
1201 S. La Brea Ave. www.azfilmstudios.com
Los Angeles, CA 90036

Basso Design Scenery and Props (323) 401-8801
www.bassodesign.com

Ⓐ **Ben Kitay Studios LLC** (323) 466-9015
1015 N. Cahuenga Blvd. FAX (323) 466-4421
Hollywood, CA 90038 www.benkitay.com

Centro Net Productions (310) 237-5653
2740 California St. FAX (310) 294-3691
Torrance, CA 90503 www.centronetproductions.com

(818) 763-3650
Chandler Valley Center Studios, Inc. (818) 424-4551
FAX (818) 990-4755
www.cvcstudios.com

Coastal Media Group (818) 880-9800
26660 Agoura Rd. FAX (818) 579-9026
Calabasas, CA 91302 www.coastalmediagroup.com

(323) 257-1163
Composite Components Company (323) 243-8999
134 N. Avenue 61, Ste. 102/3 FAX (323) 257-0604
Los Angeles, CA 90042 www.digitalgreenscreen.com

Costa Mesa Studios (949) 515-9942
711 W. 17th St., Ste. D10 www.costamesastudios.com
Costa Mesa, CA 92627

(310) 326-4500
Cutting Edge Productions, Inc. (818) 503-0400
22904 Lockness Ave. FAX (310) 326-4715
Torrance, CA 90501 www.cuttingedgeproductions.tv

Digital Film Studios (818) 771-0019
11800 Sheldon St., Ste. C-D FAX (818) 351-1155
Sun Valley, CA 91352 www.digitalfilmstudios.com

Dirt Cheap Sound Stage (310) 401-3171
3019 Olympic Blvd., Stage B FAX (310) 496-0530
Santa Monica, CA 90404
www.dirtcheapsoundstage.com

The Dreaming Tree (818) 845-3230
1112 Chestnut St., Ste. B FAX (818) 333-0795
Burbank, CA 91506
www.dreamingtreeproductions.com

Epiphany Media (323) 819-1001
5300 Melrose Ave. www.epiphanymedia.com
Hollywood, CA 90038

(323) 522-5298
EVIDENCE Productions (310) 628-5400
1819 Winona Blvd. FAX (323) 522-5298
Los Angeles, CA 90027 www.evidenceproductions.com

(818) 552-4590
EVS (800) 238-8480
1819 Victory Bl. FAX (818) 552-4591
Glendale, CA 91201 www.evsonline.com

(323) 460-4192
Fore-Peak (407) 649-9937
1040 N. Las Palmas Ave. FAX (323) 871-8141
Los Angeles, CA 90038 www.fore-peak.com

Galileo Studio (626) 969-5359
392 N. Citrus Ave. FAX (626) 969-4017
Azusa, CA 91702 apu.edu/clas/galileofilmstudio

Greenery Studios (818) 253-9990
7764 San Fernando Rd., Ste. 2 greenerystudios.com
Burbank, CA 91352

HD Vision Broadcast Center (818) 769-4500
10900 Ventura Blvd. FAX (818) 769-7150
Studio City, CA 91604 www.hdvisionbc.com

(323) 467-2897
Hip Studios (323) 833-5920
6121 Sunset Blvd. FAX (323) 469-8251
Hollywood, CA 90028 www.hipfilms.com

Hollywood Center Studios (323) 860-0000
1040 N. Las Palmas Ave. FAX (323) 860-8105
Hollywood, CA 90038 www.hollywoodcenter.com

Independence Studio (818) 788-3467
6431 Independence Ave. www.independencestudio.com
Woodland Hills, CA 91367

Laurel Canyon Stages (818) 768-8935
9337 Laurel Canyon Blvd. FAX (818) 768-6852
Arleta, CA 91331 www.lcstages.com

Loyal Studios (818) 450-1115
1448 19th St. www.loyalstudios.tv
Santa Monica, CA 90404

Loyal Studios (818) 450-1115
2201 N. Hollywood Way www.loyalstudios.tv
Burbank, CA 91505

Mack Sennett Stage/Triangle (323) 660-8466
1215 Bates Ave. www.macksennettstage.com
Los Angeles, CA 90029

McNulty Nielsen, Inc. (310) 704-1713
6930 1/2 Tujunga Ave. FAX (323) 372-3768
North Hollywood, CA 91605 www.mcnultynielsen.com

Monkeyhead (310) 836-7600
8553 Washington Blvd. FAX (310) 836-7611
Culver City, CA 90232 www.monkeyhead.com

New Deal Studios, Inc. (310) 578-9929
FAX (310) 578-7370
www.newdealstudios.com

Occidental Studios, Inc. (213) 384-3331
201 N. Occidental Blvd. FAX (213) 384-2684
Los Angeles, CA 90026 www.occidentalstudios.com

(818) 768-1573
Pacific Motion Control, Inc. (661) 644-1516
9812 Glenoaks Blvd. FAX (818) 768-1575
Sun Valley, CA 91352 www.pacificmotion.net

(818) 933-2100
Phunware Studios (818) 933-2107
14144 Ventura Blvd., Ste. 300 FAX (818) 704-9386
Sherman Oaks, CA 91423 phunware.com/studio

Post Modern
Broadcast Studios, LLC   (949) 608-8700
                            FAX (949) 608-8729
                        www.postmodernstudios.com

The Production Group Studios   (323) 469-8111
1330 N. Vine St.   FAX (323) 962-2182
Los Angeles, CA 90028   www.productiongroup.tv

Prospect Studios   (323) 671-4044
4151 Prospect Ave.   FAX (818) 841-8328
Los Angeles, CA 90027   www.disneystudios.com

Quixote Studios   (323) 960-9191
1000 N. Cahuenga Blvd.   FAX (323) 960-3366
Los Angeles, CA 90038   www.quixote.com

The Rag Place, Inc.   (818) 765-3338
13160 Raymer St.   FAX (818) 765-3860
North Hollywood, CA 91605   www.theragplace.com

Railroad Studios   (818) 396-4985
1500 Railroad St.   FAX (818) 396-4986
Glendale, CA 91204   www.railroadstudios.com

Raleigh Studios - Hollywood   (323) 960-3456
5300 Melrose Ave.   FAX (323) 960-4712
Hollywood, CA 90038   www.raleighstudios.com

Raleigh Studios - Manhattan Beach (323) 960-3456
1600 Rosecrans Ave.   FAX (310) 727-2710
Manhattan Beach, CA 90266   www.raleighstudios.com

Revolutionary Productions   (310) 770-9250
2525 W. Seventh St.
Los Angeles, CA 90057
                    www.revolutionary-productions.com

ShowBiz Studios   (818) 989-7007
15541 Lanark St.   FAX (818) 989-8272
Van Nuys, CA 91406   www.showbizstudios.com

                                     (323) 467-3559
Siren Studios   (323) 960-9045
6063 W. Sunset Blvd.   FAX (323) 461-6744
Hollywood, CA 90028   www.sirenstudios.com

                                     (818) 240-1893
Solar Studios   (310) 489-7801
1601 S. Central Ave.   FAX (818) 240-4187
Glendale, CA 91204   www.solarstudios.com

                                     (714) 437-9585
Sound Matrix Studios   (714) 402-7450
18060 Newhope St.   www.soundmatrixstudios.com
Orange County, CA 92708

Source Film Studio   (323) 463-5555
1111 N. Beachwood Dr.   FAX (323) 463-5556
Los Angeles, CA 90038   www.sourcefilmstudio.com

                                     (818) 287-7274
Stage 101   (818) 505-6050
4101 Lankershim Blvd., Ste. 100/101 FAX (818) 505-6054
North Hollywood, CA 91602   www.stage101.net

                                     (626) 403-8403
Stargate Stage   (818) 778-0851
1001 El Centro St.   FAX (626) 403-8444
Pasadena, CA 91030   www.stargatestudios.net

studio/stage   (323) 463-3900
520 N. Western Ave.   FAX (323) 463-3933
Los Angeles, CA 90004   www.studio-stage.com

Universal Virtual Stage 1   (818) 777 3000
100 Universal City Plaza
Universal City, CA 91608
                        www.filmmakersdestination.com

Warner Bros. Studio
Facilities - Operations   (818) 954-2577
4000 Warner Blvd.   FAX (818) 954-4467
Burbank, CA 91522   www.wbsf.com

                                     (323) 692-5360
Westside Media Center Studios   (323) 697-0951
12312 W. Olympic Blvd.
Los Angeles, CA 90064
                www.westsidemediastudios.weebly.com

Rehearsal Studios

CenterStaging LLC   (818) 559-4333
3407 Winona Ave.   FAX (818) 848-4016
Burbank, CA 91504   www.centerstaging.com

Evolution Studios   (818) 754-1760
4200 Lankershim Blvd.   FAX (818) 754-1781
Universal City, CA 91602
(Dance Studio)   www.evolutiondancestudios.com

Prospect Studios   (323) 671-4044
4151 Prospect Ave.   FAX (818) 841-8328
Los Angeles, CA 90027   www.disneystudios.com

ShowBiz Studios   (818) 989-7007
15541 Lanark St.   FAX (818) 989-8272
Van Nuys, CA 91406   www.showbizstudios.com
Contact: Scott Webley

Universal Studios Stages   (818) 777-3000
100 Universal City Plaza, Bldg. 4250-3 FAX (818) 866-0293
Universal City, CA 91608
                        www.filmmakersdestination.com

Warner Bros. Studio
Facilities - Operations   (818) 954-2577
4000 Warner Blvd.   FAX (818) 954-4467
Burbank, CA 91522   www.wbstagesandsets.com

360 Designworks/
360 Propworks Inc.   **(310) 863-5984**
www.360designworks.com
(Custom Fabrication, High-Tech Sets, Landscapes, Set
Construction, Steel Fabrication, Turnkey Art & Welding)

41 Sets   **(323) 860-2442**
1040 N. Las Palmas Ave., Bldg. 42   FAX **(323) 860-2441**
Los Angeles, CA 90038   **www.41sets.com**
(Custom Fabrication, Foam Sculpting, Grading, High-Tech Sets,
Landscapes, Ramps, Recycled Sets, Set Construction, Steel
Fabrication, Turnkey Art & Welding)

    (310) 324-1040
Accurate Staging   **(310) 327-5049**
1820 W. 135th St.   FAX **(310) 324-1017**
Gardena, CA 90249   **www.accuratestaging.com**

Acme Design Group   **(818) 767-8888**
www.acme-designgroup.com

Ⓐ Action Sets and Props   **(818) 992-8811**
7231 Remmet Ave.   FAX **(818) 347-4330**
Canoga Park, CA 91303   **www.wonderworksweb.com**
(Hi-Tech Sets & Space Shuttle Cockpit)

Air Hollywood   **(818) 890-0444**
13240 Weidner St.   FAX **(818) 890-7041**
Los Angeles, CA 91331   **www.airhollywood.com**

All Access Staging & Productions   **(310) 784-2464**
1320 Storm Pkwy   FAX **(310) 517-0899**
Torrance, CA 90501   **www.allaccessinc.com**

    (310) 430-0971
All Sets   **(310) 430-0970**
2529 N. San Fernando Rd.   FAX **(323) 221-9600**
Los Angeles, CA 90065   **www.allsets.com**

Basso Design Scenery and Props   **(818) 759-5536**
11478 Hart St.   **www.bassodesign.com**
North Hollywood, CA 91605

    (310) 244-1945
Beachwood Services, Inc.   **(310) 244-5457**
10202 W. Washington Blvd.
Culver City, CA 90232   **www.beachwoodservices.com**

Benchmark Scenery, Inc.   **(818) 507-1351**
1757 Standard Ave.   FAX **(818) 507-1354**
Glendale, CA 91201   **www.benchmarkscenery.com**

    (323) 255-1144
California Paving & Grading   **(818) 956-5939**
3253 Verdugo Rd.   FAX **(323) 255-3473**
Los Angeles, CA 90065   **www.calpave.com**
(Grading & Paving)

Carthay Set Services   **(818) 762-3566**
5539 Riverton Ave.   FAX **(818) 762-3707**
North Hollywood, CA 91601   **www.carthay.com**

    (310) 287-3600
Century Studio Corporation   **(888) 878-2437**
8660 Hayden Pl., Ste. 100   FAX **(310) 287-3608**
Culver City, CA 90232   **www.centurystudio.com**

Cinnabar   **(818) 842-8190**
4571 Electronics Pl.   FAX **(818) 842-0563**
Los Angeles, CA 90039   **www.cinnabar.com**
(Custom Fabrication, Set Construction,
Steel Fabrication & Welding)

Company Inc. Sets   **(818) 679-2401**
5934 Noble Ave.   FAX **(818) 988-8440**
Van Nuys, CA 91411   **www.companyincsets.com**

    (626) 932-0082
Concept Design   **(800) 846-0717**
718 Primrose Ave.   FAX **(626) 932-0072**
Monrovia, CA 91016   **www.conceptdesigninc.com**

Continental Scenery, Inc.   **(818) 768-8075**
7802 Clybourn Ave.   FAX **(818) 768-6939**
Sun Valley, CA 91352   **www.continentalscenery.com**

David Weller Design   **(818) 506-7817**
4804 Laurel Canyon Blvd., Ste. 366   FAX **(818) 506-8875**
Valley Village, CA 91607   **www.wellerdesign.com**

Depict, Inc.   **(323) 222-1001**
www.depict33.com

Elden Sets, Props and Backdrops   **(323) 550-8922**
2767 W. Broadway   www.eldenworks.com/rickelden
Eagle Rock, CA 90041

Executive Set   **(310) 456-8833**
3951 Ridgemont Dr.   FAX **(310) 456-5692**
Malibu, CA 90265

    (626) 334-9388
Festival Artists, Inc.   **(626) 303-6042**
120 N. Aspan Ave.   FAX **(626) 969-8595**
Azusa, CA 91702   **www.festivalartists.org**
(Foam Sculpting)

    (310) 369-2712
Fox Studios   **(310) 369-2713**
Staff Shop, 10201 W. Pico Blvd.   FAX **(310) 969-1006**
Los Angeles, CA 90035   **www.foxstudiosstaff.com**
(Custom Fabrication)

Global Entertainment Industries   **(818) 567-0000**
2948 N. Ontario St.   FAX **(818) 567-0007**
Burbank, CA 91504   **www.globalentind.com**

Goathouse and TTS Studios   **(818) 982-9872**
7303 Ethel Ave.   FAX **(818) 982-9199**
North Hollywood, CA 91605
www.filmlocationlosangeles.com

Good Sets, Inc.   **(323) 665-9983**
5337 Cahuenga Blvd.   FAX **(818) 760-8166**
North Hollywood, CA 91601

    (714) 453-0970
Gothic Moon Productions, Inc.   **(714) 210-5840**
535 W. Palm Ave.   FAX **(714) 210-5841**
Orange, CA 92868   **www.gothicmoon.com**

Hollywood Flats & Risers   **(323) 660-8466**
1215 Bates Ave.   **www.macksennettstage.com**
Los Angeles, CA 90029
(Recycled Sets & Set Construction)

I.D.F. Studio Scenery   **(818) 982-7433**
6844 Lankershim Blvd.   FAX **(818) 982-7435**
North Hollywood, CA 91605   www.idfstudioscenery.com

Imagivations   **(818) 767-6767**
11314 Sheldon St.   FAX **(818) 767-3637**
Sun Valley, CA 91352   **www.imagivations.com**

Industrial Artists   **(626) 355-1913**
803 Woodland Dr.
Sierra Madre, CA 91024

Ironwood   **(818) 265-2055**
1514 Flower St.   FAX **(818) 265-1680**
Glendale, CA 91201   **www.ironwoodscenic.com**

Isolated Ground   **(818) 551-1399**
918 Justin Ave.   FAX **(818) 551-1018**
Glendale, CA 91201   **www.isolatedground.com**

Jet Sets
(818) 764-5644
(800) 717-7387
6910 Farmdale Ave.
FAX (818) 764-6655
North Hollywood, CA 91605
www.jetsets.com

KCW Studios
(626) 698-0029
816 S. Date Ave.
FAX (626) 872-2377
Alhambra, CA 91803
www.kcwstudios.com
(Custom Fabrication, Foam Sculpting, High-Tech Sets, Landscapes, Ramps, Recycled Sets, Set Construction, Steel Fabrication, Turnkey Art & Welding)

L.A. Propoint, Inc.
(818) 767-6800
10870 La Tuna Canyon
FAX (818) 767-3900
Sun Valley, CA 91352
www.lapropoint.com
(Custom Fabrication, High-Tech Sets, Set Construction, Steel Fabrication & Welding)

Lexington Design & Fabrication
(818) 768-5768
12660 Branford St.
FAX (818) 768-4217
Arleta, CA 91331
www.lex-usa.com
(Action Sports Ramps and Sets, CNC Renting, Custom Fabrication, High-Tech Sets, Landscapes, Set Construction, Space Shuttle Cockpit & Steel Fabrication)

Maxsets Inc.
(323) 401-2746
(562) 531-3056
14042 Orange Ave., Ste. 7
www.maxsets.com
Paramount, CA 90723
(Custom Fabrication, Foam Sculpting, High-Tech Sets, Recycled Sets, Set Construction, Steel Fabrication & Welding)

**Ⓐ The Studios at Paramount
Wood Moulding/Millwork**
(323) 956-4242
5555 Melrose Ave.
www.thestudiosatparamount.com
Hollywood, CA 90038

Powerhouse Entertainment
(818) 765-1200
11461-A Hart St.
FAX (818) 765-1209
North Hollywood, CA 91605
www.powerhousesets.com

Pro Sets West
(866) 776-7381
(818) 563-1800
1205 S. Flower St.
FAX (818) 563-1811
Burbank, CA 91502
www.prosetswest.net

Prop Masters, Inc.
(818) 846-3915
2721 W. Empire Ave.
FAX (818) 846-1278
Burbank, CA 91504
www.propmastersinc.com
(Set Construction)

Rain For Rent
(805) 525-3306
(805) 331-0175
333 S. 12th St.
FAX (805) 525-7663
Santa Paula, CA 93061
www.rainforrent.com
(Filtration Systems, Pipes, Pumps & Tanks)

Reel Orange
(949) 548-4524
316 La Jolla Dr.
www.reelorange.com
Newport Beach, CA 92663

Renmark Entertainment Engineering (310) 457-2148
327 E. Harry Bridges Blvd.
Wilmington, CA 90744
www.renmarkentertainmentengineering.com

Alan Roderick-Jones
(310) 457-3029
(310) 985-4265
29630 Cuthbert Rd.
www.alanrjstudios.com
Malibu, CA 90265

Safe Sets Recycling Corp.
(310) 359-0754
2118 Wilshire Blvd., Ste. 314
FAX (310) 853-1820
Santa Monica, CA 90403
www.safesetsrecycling.org
(Recycled Sets)

Scenic Design Works, Inc.
(310) 367-9571
(310) 216-1561
6020 W. 76th St.
Los Angeles, CA 90045
(Custom Fabrication & Set Construction)

Scenic Express, Inc.
(323) 254-4351
3019 Andrita St.
FAX (323) 254-4411
Los Angeles, CA 90065
www.scenicexpress.net

Scenic Highlights, Inc.
(818) 252-7760
11759 Sheldon St.
FAX (818) 252-7766
Sun Valley, CA 91352
www.scenichighlights.com

Set Design, Construction & Rentals

The Scenic Route, Inc.   (818) 896-6006
(818) 381-7529
13516 Desmond St.   FAX (818) 896-6709
Pacoima, CA 91331   www.the-scenic-route.com
(Custom Fabrication, Foam Sculpting, High-Tech Sets, Set
Construction, Steel Fabrication & Welding)

Scroggins Aviation   (702) 348-7731
FAX (702) 953-7307
www.scrogginsaviation.com

Sculptors Pride Design Studios   (626) 256-4779
902 S. Primrose Ave.
Monrovia, CA 91016
(Landscapes)

Set Logic   (310) 450-4018
P.O. Box 755   FAX (310) 450-4018
Venice, CA 90291
(Set Construction)

Set Masters   (818) 982-1506
(818) 238-0868
11650 Hart St.   FAX (818) 982-1508
North Hollywood, CA 91605   www.setmasters.com
(Set Construction)

The Set Shop   (310) 486-1741
(213) 680-1668
428 Colyton St.   www.thesetshop.tv
Los Angeles, CA 90013
(Set Construction)

Sew What? Inc.   (310) 639-6000
1978 Gladwick St.   FAX (310) 639-6036
Rancho Dominguez, CA 90220   www.sewwhatinc.com

Snow Park Technologies   (530) 550-2636
(530) 550-2600
FAX (530) 550-2621
www.snowparktech.com
(Custom Fabrication, Grading, Landscapes, Set Construction,
Snow Settings & Welding)

So Cal Production Source   (310) 699-2787
FAX (310) 618-0129
www.scpsunlimited.com
(Custom Fabrication, Foam Sculpting, Grading, High-Tech Sets,
Landscapes, Paving, Ramps, Recycled Sets, Set Construction,
Steel Fabrication, Turnkey Art & Welding)

Sony Pictures Studios   (310) 244-5541
10202 W. Washington Blvd.
Culver City, CA 90232   www.sonypicturesstudios.com

Spohn Ranch, Inc.   (877) 489-3539
15131 Clark Ave., Ste. B   FAX (626) 330-5503
City of Industry, CA 91745   www.spohnranch.com
(Action Sports Ramps and Sets)

Steeldeck, Inc.   (323) 290-2100
(800) 507-8243
3339 Exposition Pl.   FAX (323) 290-9600
Los Angeles, CA 90018   www.steeldeck.com

(951) 674-0998
Storyland Studios/Foam Works   (800) 218-1932
590 Crane St.   FAX (951) 674-0245
Lake Elsinore, CA 92530   www.foamworks.com

Tractor Vision   (323) 235-2885
340 E. Jefferson Blvd.   www.tractorvision.com
Los Angeles, CA 90011

Tribal Scenery   (818) 558-4045
3216 Vanowen St.   FAX (818) 558-4356
Burbank, CA 91505   www.tribalscenery.com

(714) 688-2555
Turntable Works   (800) 773-9442
650 S. Jefferson Ave., Ste. D   FAX (714) 688-2553
Placentia, CA 92870   www.turntable-works.com
(Automobile Turntable Sales and Rentals, Custom
Fabrication & Steel and Aluminum Welding)

United Pacific Studios   (213) 489-2001
729 E. Temple St.   FAX (213) 489-2098
Los Angeles, CA 90012   www.unitedpacificstudios.com

Universal Studios Moulding Shop   (818) 777-5551
100 Universal City Plaza, Stage 747   FAX (818) 733-2305
Universal City, CA 91608
www.filmmakersdestination.com

Universal Studios Set Rentals   (818) 777-5163
100 Universal City Plaza   FAX (818) 866-2587
Bldg. 4250, Third Fl., Ste. D   www.nbcunisetrentals.com
Universal City, CA 91608
(Full Set and Stock Unit Rental)

Universal Studios Stock Units   (818) 777-1126
100 Universal City Plaza, Bldg. 3156   FAX (818) 866-1363
Universal City, CA 91608
www.filmmakersdestination.com

🅐 **Vision Scenery Corporation**   (818) 567-2818
26 E. Providencia Ave.   FAX (818) 567-2839
Burbank, CA 91502   www.visionscenery.com

The Walt Disney Studios -
Set Construction   (818) 560-5488
500 S. Buena Vista St.   studioservices.go.com
Burbank, CA 91521

Warner Bros. Studio Facilities -
Construction Services   (818) 954-7820
4000 Warner Blvd., Bldg. 44   FAX (818) 954-4635
Burbank, CA 91522   www.wbsf.com

🅐 **WonderWorks**   (818) 992-8811
7231 Remmet Ave.   FAX (818) 347-4330
Canoga Park, CA 91303   www.wonderworksweb.com
(Hi-Tech Sets & Space Shuttle Cockpit)

Action Artists Agency (323) 337-4666
(Reps for Set Sketchers) www.action-artists.com

Daniel Alvarado (626) 676-4079

Artistfoundry (323) 309-0868
www.artistfoundry.net

Ted Baumgart (818) 957-1071

Concept Design (626) 932-0082
(800) 846-0717
718 Primrose Ave. FAX (626) 932-0072
Monrovia, CA 91016 www.conceptdesigninc.com

Cameron Crockett (310) 567-2777
FAX (562) 997-0971
www.ultra-unit.com

Thomas Drotar (310) 399-5700
www.thomasdrotar.com

Bob Einfrank (310) 893-4241

John Hansen (917) 855-1188
(310) 288-8000
www.hansendesigninc.com

Robert Hunt/Studio E Design (310) 641-9319
(310) 500-9619
www.setsketch.tv

Brian Johnson/Live Brain Studio (323) 574-8088
(818) 488-1179
www.livebrainstudio.com/Galleries

Kasya Design (877) 527-9233
www.kasyadesign.com

Brian Kelly (619) 517-8101
www.brooklynartdept.com

Jacqui Masson (213) 220-3530

Reinman Illustration/Design (805) 640-7393
4612 Thacher Rd.
Ojai, CA 93023

Gerry Schelly (213) 687-3720
www.gerryschelly.t35.com

Storyboards, Inc. (310) 393-5300
(800) 289-0109
1207 Fourth St., Ste. 250 FAX (310) 393-5311
Santa Monica, CA 90401 www.storyboardsinc.com

James Vaughn (323) 376-2075
www.greatbigspots.com

1 Big Cyc & Stage
(855) 345-6244
(323) 515-5034
1328 Lake Shore Ave.   FAX (818) 279-0571
Los Angeles, CA 90026   www.1bigstage.com

1020 Studios
(323) 874-8764
1020 N. Sycamore Ave.   FAX (323) 874-6330
Los Angeles, CA 90038   www.1020studios.com
(Insert Stage)

1140 The Notion Studio
(213) 745-7111
(310) 384-4356
1140 S. Hope St.   www.thenotionstudio.com
Los Angeles, CA 90015

240 Studio
(805) 845-8870
One N. Calle Cesar Chavez, Ste. 240   FAX (805) 845-6555
Santa Barbara, CA 93103   www.240studio.com
Contact: Albert DiPadova

30th Street Garage
(619) 234-4325
3335 30th St.   FAX (619) 234-2055
San Diego, CA 92104   www.30thstreetgarage.com

3555 Hayden Studios
(310) 430-7550
3555 Hayden Ave.   www.3555hayden.com
Culver City, CA 90232

360 Designworks/
360 Propworks Inc.
(310) 863-5984
www.360designworks.com
Contacts: Kevin Boyle, Peter McKinney & Randy Young

5th & Sunset Los Angeles
(310) 979-0212
12322 Exposition Blvd.   FAX (310) 979-0214
Los Angeles, CA 90064   www.5thandsunsetla.com

ABC 7 Broadcast Center
(818) 560-7450
500 Circle Seven Dr.   FAX (818) 841-8328
Glendale, CA 91201   www.studioservices.go.com

Affordable Sound Stages
(818) 641-0220
1708 Hale St.   www.affordablesoundstages.com
Glendale, CA 91201

Albuerne, Inc.
(323) 665-1307
(213) 926-0444
2990 Allesandro St.   FAX (323) 665-7034
Los Angeles, CA 90039   www.albuerneinc.com

Albuquerque Studios
(505) 227-2000
5650 University Blvd. SE   FAX (505) 227-2001
Albuquerque, NM 87106   www.abqstudios.com

Alley Kat Studio
(323) 462-1755
(323) 462-4546
1455 N. Gordon St.   FAX (323) 962-3693
Hollywood, CA 90028   www.alleykatstudios.com
Contact: Rayna Vonk

Alva's Dance Studio
(310) 519-1314
(800) 403-3447
1417 W. Eighth St.   FAX (310) 831-6110
San Pedro, CA 90732
www.alvas.com/performance_gallery
(Dance and Rehearsal Studio)
Contact: Matt Lincir

STAGES & EXTERIOR SETS

35 SOUND STAGES

ASHLEY BLVD.
(BROWNSTONE STREET)

EMBASSY COURTYARD

FRENCH STREET

JUNGLE/LAGOON

MIDWEST STREET

NEW YORK

STREET/PARK

PARK PLACE

WARNER VILLAGE

BLONDIE STREET

PARK BLVD.

PRODUCTION SERVICES

Set Lighting • Grip • Special FX • Production Sound & Video Services • Set Construction
Sign Shop • Scenic Art • Large Format Digital Printing • Metal • Staff Shop • Paint • Hardware Rentals
Property/Set Dressing/Hand Props • Drapery • Upholstery • Floor Coverings • Designer Collection
Furniture Repair & Refinishing • Costume Department • Photo Lab: Film & Digital • Expendable Store
Lumberyard • Transportation • Courier • Production Catering • Post Production Services... and more!

www.wbsf.com • 818.954.3000

AMP Studios
(805) 955-7742
(805) 955-7770
FAX (805) 955-7705
101 W. Cochran St.
Simi Valley, CA 93065
www.ampstudios.com

Apache Rental Group
(818) 842-9944
(323) 440-7799
FAX (818) 842-9269
www.apacherentalgroup.com

Associated Television International (323) 556-5600
4401 Wilshire Blvd. www.4401wilshire.com
Los Angeles, CA 90010

Avenue Six Studios
(818) 781-6600
(818) 933-0818
FAX (818) 781-6611
7900 Haskell Ave.
Van Nuys, CA 91406 www.avenuesixstudios.com

AZ Studios
(310) 779-9603
(310) 383-5484
1201 S. La Brea Ave. www.azfilmstudios.com
Los Angeles, CA 90036

Barcode
(310) 287-0066
FAX (310) 287-0066
8763 Washington Blvd.
Culver City, CA 90232 www.barcodephotostudio.com

The Barker Hangar/
Santa Monica Air Center
(310) 390-9071
(310) 666-6103
FAX (310) 391-8824
3021 Airport Ave., Ste. 203
Santa Monica, CA 90405 www.barkerhangar.com
Contacts: Judi Barker & Joe Loving

Bellevarado Studios
(213) 413-9611
(213) 503 0661
FAX (213) 413-9601
2107 Bellevue Ave.
Los Angeles, CA 90026 www.bellevaradostudios.com

Ⓐ Ben Kitay Studios
(323) 466-9015
FAX (323) 466-4421
1015 N. Cahuenga Blvd.
Hollywood, CA 90038 www.benkitay.com
Contact: Ben Kitay

Big Picture Soundstage
(818) 842-6060
FAX (818) 842-6066
3050 North Lima St.
Burbank, CA 91504 www.bigpicturesoundstage.com

Big Vision Studios
(818) 841-4008
(702) 493-9292
FAX (323) 372-3937
www.bigvision.com

California City Studios, Inc.
(760) 373-4966
(866) 966-3456
FAX (760) 373-8565
1610 Pesch Dr.
Mojave, CA 93501 www.californiacitystudios.com
Contact: Russell Michael

Canoga Village Studios
(818) 700-7500
(323) 855-1520
FAX (818) 709-9141
8431 Canoga Ave., Ste. C
Canoga Park, CA 91304 www.cv3dstudios.com

Casablanca Studios, Inc.
(760) 275-7908
FAX (760) 251-9878
66321 Pierson Blvd.
Desert Hot Springs, CA 92240
www.casablancastudios.com

CBS Studio Center
(818) 655-5000
FAX (818) 655-8000
4024 Radford Ave.
Studio City, CA 91604 www.cbssc.com
Contact: Brian Lovell

Centinela Studios
(310) 396-3688
FAX (310) 396-1984
3401 Exposition Blvd.
Santa Monica, CA 90401 www.centinelastudios.com
Contacts: Roger Webster & Bernard Perloff

Centro Net Productions   (310) 237-5653
2740 California St.   FAX (310) 294-3691
Torrance, CA 90503   www.centronetproductions.com

    (310) 287-3600
Century Studio Corporation   (888) 878-2437
8660 Hayden Pl., Ste. 100   FAX (310) 287-3608
Culver City, CA 90232   www.centurystudio.com
Contact: Trish Benson

    (818) 763-3650
Ⓐ Chandler Valley Center Studios, Inc. (818) 424-4551
13927 Saticoy St.   FAX (818) 990-4755
Van Nuys, CA 91402   www.cvcstudios.com
Contact: Claudette Fillet

    (818) 566-3000
CineLUX Sound Services Inc.   (888) 246-3589
4300 W. Victory Blvd.   www.cinelux.tv
Burbank, CA 91505

Civic Center Studios   (213) 394-4226
207 S. Broadway, Ste. 1   FAX (213) 261-4625
Los Angeles, CA 90012   www.civiccenterstudios.com

Coastal Media Group   (818) 880-9800
26660 Agoura Rd.   FAX (818) 579-9026
Calabasas, CA 91302   www.coastalmediagroup.com

Complete Actors Place/CAP   (818) 990-2001
13752 Ventura Blvd.   completeactorsplace.com
Sherman Oaks, CA 91423

Ⓐ The Culver Studios   (310) 202-1234
9336 W. Washington Blvd.   FAX (310) 202-3201
Culver City, CA 90232   www.theculverstudios.com
Contacts: Laural Ayala & Rob Vaupel

    (310) 326-4500
Cutting Edge Productions, Inc.   (818) 503-0400
22904 Lockness Ave.   FAX (310) 326-4715
Torrance, CA 90501   www.cuttingedgeproductions.tv
Contact: Bill Dedes

    (213) 629-5434
DC Stages & Sets   (310) 804-5712
1360 E. Sixth St.   FAX (213) 629-5155
Los Angeles, CA 90021   dcstages.com
Contact: Diane Markoff

    (818) 361-2421
Delfino Studios   (877) 512-0400
12501 Gladstone Ave.   FAX (818) 361-5891
Sylmar, CA 91342   www.delfinostudios.com
Contact: Linda Masino

Digital Film Studios   (818) 771-0019
11800 Sheldon St., Ste. C-D   FAX (818) 351-1155
Sun Valley, CA 91352   www.digitalfilmstudios.com

    (310) 401-3171
Dirt Cheap Sound Stage   (909) 856-4939
3019 Olympic Blvd., Stage B   FAX (310) 496-0530
Santa Monica, CA 90404
    www.dirtcheapsoundstage.com

CHANDLER VALLEY CENTER

America's premiere hi-tech studios, Chandler Valley Center Studios are centrally located with easy access from Interstate 405 and the 170 and 101 Freeways, just minutes from CBS, NBC, Universal, Warner Bros and Disney Studios. Designed to produce the finest commercials, sitcoms and movies, we offer two studios, one with over 20,000 square feet of space, and the other featuring over 18,000 square feet of space. Both studios feature state of the art Cyclorama's and 33 to 35 foot ceilings for maximum production space. With over 4800 Amps of power at your disposal, you will have power to spare. Our state of the art studios are just 5 years old and we will provide you with maximum comfort while filming with over 175 tons of air conditioning. Our complex also features the convenience of parking for over 300 vehicles to accommodate your needs. Chandler Valley Center Studios awaits your production call!

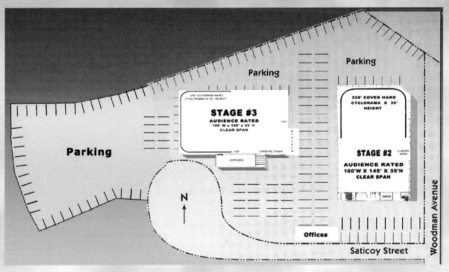

BENKITAYSTUDIOS
FILM & VIDEO STAGE RENTALS

OFFICES: 6309 Eleanor Ave Hollywood CA 90038
(323)466-9015 (323)466-4421 fax
POSTAL ADDRESS: 1015 N.Cahuenga Blvd Hollywood CA 90038

COMPLETE LIGHTING & GRIP PACKAGES
WI-FI EQUIPPED PRODUCTION OFFICES
SILENT AIR CONDITIONING

Sink | Kitchen

10' x 12' Drive-in Access
Equipment Entrance

Additional
Outside
Parking

Power

24'

NEW!
A PERMANENTLY PAINTED
GREEN SCREEN
CYCLORAMA
STAGE 5
50'x75'
17' to Grid
← 74' →

37'

Stage Mgr.

Grip Room

Parking

Restroom
Restroom

Darkroom | Front Door

Make-Up | Make-Up | Prod. Office

second floor

Production Offices

Restroom

Rest Room

Lounge | Green Room

Lounge | Dressing Room | Production / Dressing Room | Kitchen

← 41' →

ALL NEW COMPLETELY RE-MODELED

49'

STAGE 10
55' x 87'
17' to Grid

← 30' →

Power | Rear Entrance | Dark Room

Control Room
Janitor
Men
Women

Cooridor | Front Entrance

Executive Offices | Interior Parking

Drive-in Access
11'6"w x 12'h

Restroom & Shower | Restroom
Star Dressing Room

Lounge

Dressing Room
Dressing Room

Equipment

Prod. Office | Make-Up Wardrobe | Make-Up Wardrobe

Client Lounge & Kitchen
Men's Restroom
Women's Restroom

Star Dressing Room

Front Door

9'6"w x 11'5" Drive-in Access
Equipment Entrance

Additional Outside Parking

← 30' →

STAGE 15
45'x72'
20' to Grid

NEW!
A PERMANENTLY PAINTED
GREEN SCREEN
CYCLORAMA

45'

Paint Sink | Elec-trical | Power

← 52' →

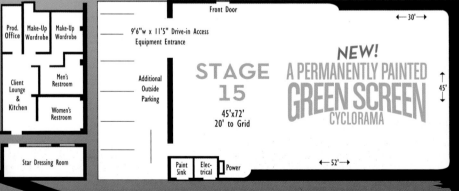

GAME & TALK SHOWS PHOTO SHOOTS
INFOMERCIALS COMMERCIALS MUSIC VIDEOS

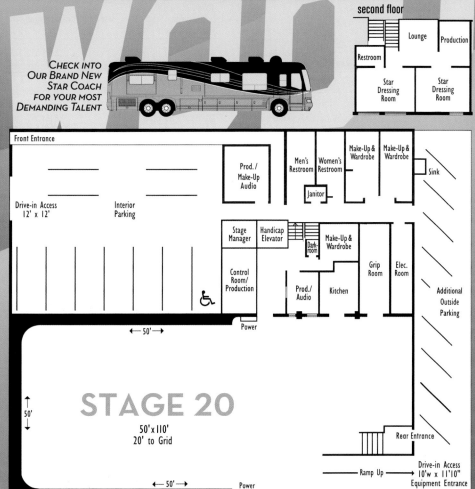

CHECK INTO
OUR BRAND NEW
STAR COACH
FOR YOUR MOST
DEMANDING TALENT

second floor

Restroom · Lounge · Production

Star Dressing Room · Star Dressing Room

Front Entrance

Drive-in Access 12' x 12'

Interior Parking

Prod./Make-Up Audio

Men's Restroom · Women's Restroom · Make-Up & Wardrobe · Make-Up & Wardrobe

Sink

Janitor

Stage Manager · Handicap Elevator · Dark-room · Make-Up & Wardrobe

Control Room/Production

Prod./Audio · Kitchen

Grip Room · Elec. Room

Additional Outside Parking

Power

← 50' →

STAGE 20

50' x 110'
20' to Grid

50'

← 50' →

Rear Entrance

Ramp Up

Drive-in Access
10'w x 11'10"
Equipment Entrance

Power

COMPLETE LIGHTING & GRIP PACKAGES
MULTIPLE MAKE-UP & WARDROBE ROOMS
WI-FI EQUIPPED PRODUCTION OFFICES
SEPARATE CELEBRITY ACCESS
STAGE 20 AUDIENCE RATED
AMPLE SECURE PARKING
STAR DRESSING ROOMS
EXPENDABLE SUPPLIES
DRIVE-IN ACCESS
24 HR SECURITY
PREP KITCHENS
24/7 ACCESS

HOLLYWOOD

Santa Monica Blvd
N. Cahuenga Blvd
Lilian Way
Vine St
5
10
15
20
Eleanor Ave
parking
Melrose Ave

MAP NOT TO SCALE

BENKITAYSTUDIOS
FILM & VIDEO STAGE RENTALS

OFFICES: 6309 Eleanor Ave Hollywood CA 90038
(323)466-9015 (323)466-4421 fax
POSTAL ADDRESS: 1015 N.Cahuenga Blvd Hollywood CA 90038

BENKITAY.COM

Encompass Digital Media   **(323) 344-4500**
3030 Andrita St.   FAX **(323) 344-4800**
Los Angeles, CA 90065   **www.encompass-m.com**

Epiphany Media   **(323) 819-1001**
5300 Melrose Ave.   **www.epiphanymedia.com**
Hollywood, CA 90038

    (323) 522-5298
EVIDENCE Productions   **(310) 628-5400**
1819 Winona Blvd.   FAX **(323) 522-5298**
Los Angeles, CA 90027   **www.evidenceproductions.com**

Evolution Studios   **(818) 754-1760**
4200 Lankershim Blvd.   FAX **(818) 754-1781**
Universal City, CA 91602
    www.evolutiondancestudios.com

Eyeboogie   **(323) 315-5750**
6425 Hollywood Blvd., Ste. 315   FAX **(323) 315-5760**
Hollywood, CA 90028   **www.eyeboogie.com**

Fantasy II Film Effects   **(818) 252-5781**
(Water Tank)   FAX **(818) 252-5995**
    www.fantasy2filmeffects.com

    (818) 841-3888
Fastlane Broadcast Studio   **(562) 335-7400**
3062 N. Lima St.   FAX **(818) 841-3188**
Burbank, CA 91504   **www.fastlanebroadcast.com**

The Focus Studio   **(310) 399-9400**
Four Rose Ave.   FAX **(310) 399-1180**
Venice, CA 90291   **www.thefocusstudio.com**

    (310) 369-2786
Ⓐ Fox Studios   **(310) 369-4636**
10201 W. Pico Blvd.   FAX **(310) 369-8858**
Los Angeles, CA 90035   **www.foxstudiosstages.com**
Contact: Kimberly Fine

    (310) 312-9772
Future Lighting   **(310) 346-1649**
626 Oxnard Blvd.   **www.futurelighting.net**
Oxnard, CA 93030

    (818) 550-6000
Glendale Studios   **(818) 317-7887**
1239 S. Glendale Ave.   FAX **(818) 550-6111**
Glendale, CA 91205   **www.glendalestudios.com**
Contact: Steve Makhanian

GMT Studios   **(310) 649-3733**
5751 Buckingham Pkwy   FAX **(310) 216-0056**
Culver City, CA 90230   **www.gmtstudios.com**

    (714) 453-0970
Gothic Moon Productions, Inc.   **(714) 210-5840**
535 W. Palm Ave.   FAX **(714) 210-5841**
Orange, CA 92868   **www.gothicmoonstudio.com**

Grant McCune Design, Inc.   **(818) 779-1920**
6836 Valjean Ave.   FAX **(818) 781-9108**
Van Nuys, CA 91406   **www.gmdfx.com**
Contacts: Monty Shook & Michael Yost

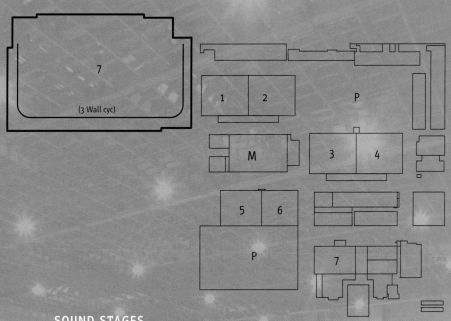

SOUND STAGES
LIGHTING AND GRIP RENTAL
PRODUCTION OFFICE SPACE
EDITORIAL SUITES
EXPENDABLES AND OFFICE SUPPLIES
HIGH SPEED DATA AND VOICE CONNECTIVITY
MILL AND STORAGE SPACE
SCREENING ROOMS
GLOBAL CUISINE BY GARY ARABIA, RESTAURANT
CATERING AND EVENT PRODUCTION
PARKING STRUCTURE W/BASECAMP
3 WALL CYCLORAMA; 50' X 100' X 25'H

STAGE SPECS:

STAGE 1	127' x 105' x 35'	*(13,335 Sq.Ft.)*
STAGE 2	127' x 105' x 35'	*(13,335 Sq.Ft.)*
STAGE 3	127' x 105' x 35'	*(13,335 Sq.Ft.)*
STAGE 4	127' x 105' x 35'	*(13,335 Sq.Ft.)*
STAGE 3/4	254' X 105' X 35'	*(26,670 sq.ft.)*
STAGE 5	112' x 92'6" x 35'	*(10,360 sq.ft.)*
STAGE 6	98' x 92'6" x 35'	*(9,065 sq.ft.)*
STAGE 7	112' x 72'6" x 27'	*(8,120 sq.ft.)*, 3 Wall cyc
MILL		*(19,110 sq.ft.)*

THE LOT

www.thelotstudios.com

TEL 323.850.3180 / **FAX** 323.850.3190

THE LOT 1041 N. Formosa Ave. West Hollywood, Ca 90046

HALA Studios
(818) 883-4771
(818) 288-6004
FAX (818) 883-4871
15844 Strathern St.
Van Nuys, CA 91406
www.halastudios.com

Hayvenhurst & Saticoy Stages
Hollywood Mobile Systems, Inc.
(818) 909-6999
7021 Hayvenhurst Ave.
FAX (818) 782-0635
Van Nuys, CA 91406
www.hmsstages.com
Contacts: Judy or Gladys

HD Vision Broadcast Center
(818) 769-4500
FAX (818) 769-7150
www.hdvisionbc.com

The Henson Soundstage
(323) 802-1587
1416 N. La Brea Ave.
FAX (323) 802-1825
Hollywood, CA 90028
leasing.henson.com
Contact: Howard Sharp

Hip Studios
(323) 467-2897
(323) 833-5920
1622 Gower St.
FAX (323) 469-8251
Hollywood, CA 90028
www.hipfilms.com

Hollywood Camera, Inc.
(818) 972-5000
3100 N. Damon Way
FAX (818) 972-5010
Burbank, CA 91505
www.hollywoodcamera.com
Contact: Serge

Hollywood Center Studios
(323) 860-0000
1040 N. Las Palmas Ave.
FAX (323) 860-8105
Hollywood, CA 90038
www.hollywoodcenter.com
Contact: Richard Schnyder

Hollywood Dance Center
(323) 467-0825
817 N. Highland Ave.
FAX (323) 467-1525
Hollywood, CA 90038 www.hollywooddancecenter.com
(Dance Rehearsal Studios)
Contact: Pamela Phillips

Hollywood Locations
(213) 534-3456
1201 W. Fifth St., Ste. F-170
Los Angeles, CA 90017 www.hollywoodlocations.com

Hollywood Loft
(323) 957-9398
6161 Santa Monica Blvd., Ste. 400
Hollywood, CA 90038
www.hollywoodloft.com
Contact: Michael Lohr

HTV Illuminate
(323) 969-8822
3575 Cahuenga Blvd. West, Ste. 490 FAX (323) 969-8860
Los Angeles, CA 90068 www.illuminatehollywood.com

Huron SubStation
(323) 225-8909
2640 Huron St.
FAX (800) 650-1522
Los Angeles, CA 90065 www.huronsubstation.com

Image G
(818) 761-6644
28490 Westinghouse Pl.
www.imageg.com
Valencia, CA 91355

Jay Silverman Productions
(323) 466-6030
1541 N. Cahuenga Blvd.
FAX (323) 466-6030
Hollywood, CA 90028
www.silvermanstages.com

The Jim Henson Company
(323) 802-1500
1416 N. La Brea Ave.
FAX (323) 802-1825
Hollywood, CA 90028 leasing.henson.com/events.html

Kappa Studios, Inc.   (818) 843-3400
3619 W. Magnolia Blvd.   FAX **(818) 559-5684**
Burbank, CA 91505   **www.kappastudios.com**
Contact: Paul Long

     (323) 953-5258
KCET Studios   **(818) 692-5766**
4401 Sunset Blvd.   FAX **(323) 953-5496**
Los Angeles, CA 90027   **www.kcetstudios.com**
Contact: Joe Keaney

KCW Studios   **(626) 698-0029**
816 S. Date Ave.   FAX **(626) 872-2377**
Alhambra, CA 91803   **www.kcwstudios.com**

KESSPRO Studios   **(213) 253-2623**
435 S. Molino St.   FAX **(213) 253-2629**
Los Angeles, CA 90013   **www.kessprostudios.com**

     (310) 442-2340
KSCI TV   **(310) 430-5200**
1990 S. Bundy Dr., Ste. 850   FAX **(310) 479-8118**
Los Angeles, CA 90025   **www.la18.tv**

The LA Lofts   **(323) 462-5880**
6442 Santa Monica Blvd.   FAX **(323) 462-7858**
Hollywood, CA 90038   **www.thelalofts.com**
Contact: Wendy

Lacy Street Production Center   **(323) 222-8872**
2630 Lacy St.   FAX **(323) 222-1258**
Los Angeles, CA 90031   **www.lacystreet.com**
Contacts: Austin Lander & Don Randles

Laurel Canyon Stages   **(818) 768-8935**
9337 Laurel Canyon Blvd.   FAX **(818) 768-6852**
Arleta, CA 91331   **www.lcstages.com**
Contact: Mary Claypool

Lightbox   **(323) 933-2080**
7122 Beverly Blvd.   FAX **(323) 933-5992**
Los Angeles, CA 90036   **www.lightboxstudio.com**

Line 204 Studios   **(323) 960-0113**
1034 N. Seward St.   FAX **(323) 960-8509**
Hollywood, CA 90038   **www.line204.com**
Contact: Alton Butler

Los Angeles Center Studios   **(213) 534-3000**
1201 W. Fifth St., Ste. T-110   FAX **(213) 534-3001**
Los Angeles, CA 90017   **www.lacenterstudios.com**
Contact: Ken Johnson

Lot 613   **(323) 934-7777**
613 N. Imperial St.   FAX **(323) 934-6582**
Los Angeles, CA 90021   **www.lot613.com**

     (323) 850-3180
Ⓐ The Lot   **(323) 850-2832**
1041 N. Formosa Ave.   **www.thelotstudios.com**
West Hollywood, CA 90046
Contact: Tricia Bodak-Smith

Loyal Studios   **(818) 450-1115**
2201 N. Hollywood Way   **www.loyalstudios.tv**
Burbank, CA 91505

Loyal Studios   **(818) 450-1115**
     www.loyalstudios.tv

Mack Sennett Stage/Triangle   **(323) 660-8466**
1215 Bates Ave.   **www.macksennettstage.com**
Los Angeles, CA 90029
Contact: Stephen Collins

UNIVERSAL STUDIOS
The Filmmakers Destination

UNIVERSAL STUDIOS STAGES

STAGE 1
137'W x 100'L x 30'H
(13,700 SQ. FT.)

STAGE 3
80'W x 154'L x 27'2"H
(12,320 SQ. FT.)
••

STAGE 4
69'W x 154'L x 27'10"H
(10,626 SQ. FT.)
••

STAGE 5
64'W x 139'L x 23'4"H
(8,896 SQ. FT.)

STAGE 6
63'W x 139'L x 19'10"H
(8,757 SQ. FT.)

STAGE 16
80'W x 144'L x 28'8"H
(11,520 SQ. FT.)
••

STAGE 17
70'W x 144'L x 28'10"H
(10,080 SQ. FT.)
••

STAGE 18
74'W x 144'L x 29'1"H
(10,656 SQ. FT.)
••

STAGE 19 *
74'W x 144'L x 27'10"H
(9,934 SQ. FT.)

STAGE 20
74'W x 144'L x 27'1"H
(10,656 SQ. FT.)

STAGE 22
74'W x 157'L x 27'H
(11,618 SQ. FT.)
••

STAGE 23
76'W x 157'L x 28'1"H
(11,932 SQ. FT.)
••

STAGE 24
112'W x 157'L x 33'4"H
(17,584 SQ. FT.)
••

STAGE 25
112'W x 157'L x 33'4"H
(17,584 SQ. FT.)

STAGE 12 w-fire
68'W x 99'L x 28'2"H
(6,732 SQ. FT.)

STAGE 12
146'W x 199'L x 49'2"H
(29,054 SQ. FT.)
••

* actual usable
floor space

•• stages with pits

••• silent air stages

FEATURING:

Universal Studios Production Services
- Stages & Backlot Locations
- Universal Virtual Stage 1
- Property & Drapery
- Costume
- Transportation
- Lighting & Grip
- Staff & Moulding Shops
- Graphic Design & Sign Shop
- Greens
- Production Office Services

Universal Studios Post Production Media Services
- Sound Mixing
- Sound Editorial & Design
- Picture Editorial & Avid Rentals
- Music Editorial
- Digital Mastering
- Screening & Projection
- ADR & Foley
- Audio Preservation & Restoration
- Music Replacement
- Archival Services
- Music Visual Media Services
- EFILM® and Company 3® DI Suite
- Remote Review/Playback

Universal Studios

**Studio Special Events
Stock Footage Library**

**Additional services at
NBC New York:**

FILMMAKERSDESTINATION.COM

UNIVERSAL STUDIOS STAGES

STAGE 27
99'W x 199'L x 39'10"H
(19,701 SQ. FT.)

STAGE 41
102'W x 140'L x 30'1"H
(14,280 SQ. FT.)
•••

STAGE 42
102'W x 140'L x 30'H
(14,280 SQ. FT.)
•••

STAGE 43
102'W x 140'L x 30'3"H
(14,280 SQ. FT.)
•••

STAGE 44
102'W x 140'L x 30'H
(14,280 SQ. FT.)
••
•••

STAGE 28
98'W x 142'L x 43'11"H
(13,916 SQ. FT.)
••

STAGE 29
97'W x 141'L x 27'H
(13,677 SQ. FT.)
•••

STAGE 31
97'W x 141'L x 27'H
(13,677 SQ. FT.)
••
•••

STAGE 33
69'W x 99'L x 25'H
(6,831 SQ. FT.)

STAGE 35
69'W x 99'L x 25'H
(6,831 SQ. FT.)

STAGE 37
100'W x 140'L x 30'H
(14,000 SQ. FT.)
•••

STAGE 34
69'W x 99'L x 25'H
(6,831 SQ. FT.)

UVS1
69'W x 99'L x 24'11"H
(6,831 SQ. FT.)

STAGE 30
88'W x 141'L x 30'H
(12,408 SQ. FT.)

STAGE 32
89'W x 141'L x 30'H
(12,549 SQ. FT.)

NBC CHICAGO STAGES

CHICAGO STAGE A
119'W x 86'L x 31'H
(10,234 SQ. FT.)

CHICAGO STAGE B
56'6"W x 75'L x 18'H
(4,087 SQ. FT.)

California Tax Film & Television Tax Credit Program

NY Tax Incentive Qualified Stages

Illinois Film Services Tax Credit

Additional services at NBC Chicago:
• Production Office Services
• Set Design & Carpentry Shops
• Paint Shop
• Electric
• Audio/Visual Services
• Transmission

Visit us online for downloadable stage charts

NBCUniversal
OPERATIONS and TECHNICAL SERVICES

UNIVERSAL
A COMCAST COMPANY

800 892 1979   Find Us   f ▶   Download 📱 at mobile.filmmakersdestination.com   Scan to Scout with your mobile

McNulty Nielsen, Inc. (310) 704-1713
6930 ½ Tujunga Ave. FAX (323) 372-3768
North Hollywood, CA 91605 www.mcnultynielsen.com

Modern Art Pictures (626) 793-0600
101 E. Green St., Ste. 7 FAX (626) 793-8599
Pasadena, CA 91105 www.modernartpictures.com

NBC Chicago Stages (312) 836-5557
454 N. Columbus Dr.
Chicago, IL 60611
nbcchicago.filmmakersdestination.com
Contact: Trisha Hockings

New Deal Studios, Inc. (310) 578-9929
15392 Cobalt St. FAX (310) 578-7370
Sylmar, CA 91342 www.newdealstudios.com
Contact: David Sanger

New Masters Studio (310) 615-3070
1142 E. Grand Ave. www.newmastersstudio.com
El Segundo, CA 90245

North Field Properties/Hangar 8 (310) 392-8844
3100 Donald Douglas Loop North FAX (310) 392-9105
Santa Monica, CA 90405 www.hangar8.net
Contacts: Jay Becker & Kurt Sebesta

Occidental Studios, Inc. (213) 384-3331
7333 Radford Ave. FAX (213) 384-2684
North Hollywood, CA 91605 www.occidentalstudios.com

Occidental Studios, Inc. (213) 384-3331
7700 Balboa Ave. FAX (213) 384-2684
Van Nuys, CA 91406 www.occidentalstudios.com
Contact: Ricky Stoutland

Occidental Studios, Inc. (213) 384-3331
201 N. Occidental Blvd. FAX (213) 384-2684
Los Angeles, CA 90026 www.occidentalstudios.com
Contact: Ricky Stoutland

OneTake Studio (213) 627-1866
821 Mateo St. FAX (213) 254-0556
Los Angeles, CA 90021 www.onetakestudio.com

Orange County Studio (213) 760-6423
14450 Hoover St. www.orangecountystudio.com
Los Angeles, CA 90004
Contact: Jeff Burke

(818) 768-1573
Pacific Motion Control, Inc. (661) 644-1516
9812 Glenoaks Blvd. FAX (818) 768-1575
Sun Valley, CA 91352 www.pacificmotion.net

Paladin Stage
(323) 851-8222
(323) 851-0900
FAX (323) 851-7328
1001 N. Poinsettia Pl.
Los Angeles, CA 90046
Contact: Darrin Scane

Panavision
(818) 316-1000
FAX (818) 316-1111
www.panavision.com
Corporate Headquarters
6219 DeSoto Ave.
Woodland Hills, CA 91367
Contact: Heather Mayer

Ⓐ **The Studios at Paramount**
Client Services
(323) 956-8811
5555 Melrose Ave.   www.thestudiosatparamount.com
Hollywood, CA 90038

Pasadena Production Studios
(626) 584-4090
FAX (626) 584-4099
www.danwolfe.com
39 E. Walnut St.
Pasadena, CA 91103
Contact: Richard Ivler

Phunware Studios
(818) 933-2100
(818) 933-2107
FAX (818) 704-9386
phunware.com/studio
14144 Ventura Blvd., Ste. 300
Sherman Oaks, CA 91423

Pier 59 Studios West
(310) 829-5959
FAX (310) 829-9550
www.pier59studioswest.com
2415 Michigan Ave.
Santa Monica, CA 90404

Pointe Studios
(310) 675-7870
(888) 907-0568
FAX (310) 675-7872
www.pointestudios.com
19801 Nordhoff Pl.
Chatsworth, CA 91311

Pollution Studios
(323) 380-8033
www.pollutionstudios.com
3239 Union Pacific Ave.
Los Angeles, CA 90023

Post Modern
Broadcast Studios, LLC
(949) 608-8700
FAX (949) 608-8729
www.postmodernstudios.com
2941 Alton Pkwy
Irvine, CA 92606
Contacts: Jay Antonos & John Reynolds

Prefix Studios
(310) 815-1951
(800) 801-7484
FAX (310) 815-1935
www.petemcarthur.com
8735 W. Washington Blvd.
Culver City, CA 90232

The Production Group Studios
(323) 469-8111
FAX (323) 962-2182
www.productiongroup.tv
1330 N. Vine St.
Los Angeles, CA 90028
Contact: Carol Noorigian

Prospect Studios
(323) 671-4044
FAX (818) 841-8328
www.disneystudios.com
4151 Prospect Ave.
Los Angeles, CA 90027

Quixote Studios
(323) 851-5030
FAX (323) 851-5029
www.quixote.com
1011 N. Fuller Ave.
West Hollywood, CA 90046

Quixote Studios - Griffith Park
(323) 957-9933
FAX (323) 957-9944
www.quixote.com
4585 Electronics Pl.
Griffith Park, CA 90039

FOX STUDIOS PRODUCTION SERVICES

Stages / Exteriors

Sound Stages:
A variety of sizes ranging from
14,000sq. ft. to over 28,000sq. ft.

New York Street

Additional Backlot Locations:
- Avenue D Walkway
- Cafeteria Courtyard
- Music Hall of Fame

(See website for other historical backlot locations)

FOX STUDIOS PRODUCTION SERVICES • 10201 W. Pico Blvd., Los Angeles, CA 90035

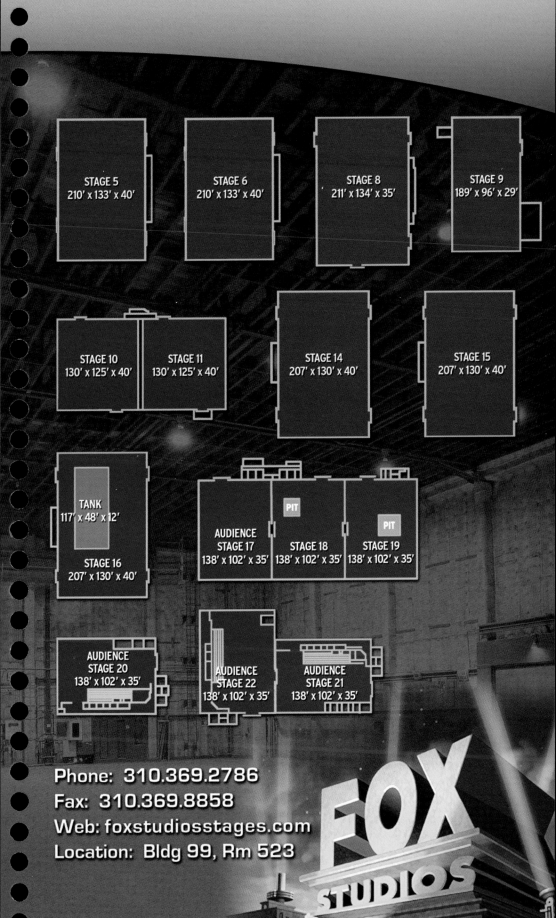

Railroad Studios   (818) 396-4985
1500 Railroad St.   FAX (818) 396-4986
Glendale, CA 91204   www.railroadstudios.com

Ⓐ Raleigh Studios - Hollywood   (323) 960-3456
5300 Melrose Ave.   FAX (323) 960-4712
Hollywood, CA 90038   www.raleighstudios.com
Contact: Yolanda Montellano

Raleigh Studios - Manhattan Beach   (310) 960-3456
1600 Rosecrans Ave.   FAX (310) 727-2710
Manhattan Beach, CA 90266   www.raleighstudios.com
Contact: Dana Bromley

Raleigh Studios - Playa Vista   (323) 960-3456
5600 S. Campus Center Dr.   www.raleighstudios.com
Playa Vista, CA 90094
Contact: Willi Schmidt

    (213) 413-9300
RecCenter Studio   (323) 868-4226
1161 Logan St.   FAX (213) 413-9301
Los Angeles, CA 90026   www.reccenterstudio.com

    (714) 342-3259
Red Gum Creative Campus   (714) 458-7003
2983 Miraloma   FAX (714) 632-8929
Anaheim, CA 92806   redgumcreativecampus.com

Red Studios Hollywood   (323) 463-0808
846 N. Cahuenga Blvd.   FAX (323) 465-8173
Hollywood, CA 90038   www.redstudio.com
Contact: Carol Cassella

    (818) 590-0042
Redemption Stages   (818) 404-9779
2980 & 2982 N. Ontario St.   FAX (818) 238-0095
Burbank, CA 91504   www.redemptionstages.com

Revolutionary Productions   (310) 770-9250
2525 W. Seventh St.
Los Angeles, CA 90057
Contact: Dr. Jeff   www.revolutionary-productions.com

S.I.R. Rehearsal Studios   (323) 957-5460
6465 Sunset Blvd.   FAX (323) 957-5472
Hollywood, CA 90028   www.sir-usa.com
(Music Performance Stages)
Contact: Rich Samore

Santa Clarita Studios   (661) 294-2000
25135 Anza Dr., Ste. C   FAX (661) 294-2020
Santa Clarita, CA 91355   www.sc-studios.com

Screenland Studios   (818) 508-2288
10501 Burbank Blvd.   www.screenlandstudios.com
North Hollywood, CA 91601
Contacts: Karen Apostolina & Steve Apostolina

Sessions West Studios, Inc.   (310) 450-9228
2601 Ocean Park Blvd., Ste. 120   FAX (310) 450-7794
Santa Monica, CA 90405
(Insert Stage)   www.sessionsweststudios.com

ShowBiz Studios   (818) 989-7007
15521 Lanark St.   FAX (818) 989-8272
Van Nuys, CA 91406   www.showbizstudios.com
Contact: Scott Webley

    (714) 836-1853
Silver Dream Factory, Inc.   (714) 225-3708
1181 N. Knollwood Circle   www.standingsets.com
Anaheim, CA 92801

    (323) 467-3559
Siren Studios   (323) 960-9045
6063 W. Sunset Blvd.   FAX (323) 461-6744
Hollywood, CA 90028   www.sirenstudios.com
Contact: Monica Macdonald

SirReel Studios (888) 477-7335
1001 Chestnut St. FAX (888) 477-7313
Burbank, CA 91506 www.sirreelstudios.com

A Small Stage (310) 488-7726
3614 Overland Ave. www.asmallstage.com
Los Angeles, CA 90034

Smashbox Studios (323) 851-5030
8549 Higuera St. FAX (323) 851-5029
Los Angeles, CA 90232 www.smashboxstudios.com
Contacts: Rebecca Cabage & Dee Delara

Smashbox Studios (323) 851-5030
1011 N. Fuller Ave. FAX (323) 851-5029
West Hollywood, CA 90046 www.smashboxstudios.com
Contacts: Rebecca Cabage & Dee Delara

(818) 240-1893
Solar Studios (310) 489-7801
1601 S. Central Ave. FAX (818) 240-4187
Glendale, CA 91204 www.solarstudios.com
Contact: Peter Cohn

Sony Pictures Studios (310) 244-6926
10202 W. Washington Blvd. FAX (310) 244-8090
Culver City, CA 90232 www.sonypicturesstudios.com

Sound City Center Stage (818) 304-0573
15464 Cabrito Rd. FAX (818) 304-0578
Van Nuys, CA 91406 www.soundcitycenterstage.com

(714) 437-9585
Sound Matrix Studios (714) 402-7450
18060 Newhope St. www.soundmatrixstudios.com
Orange County, CA 92708

Source Film Studio (323) 463-5555
1111 N. Beachwood Dr. FAX (323) 463-5556
Los Angeles, CA 90038 www.sourcefilmstudio.com
Contact: Bobby Naidu

South Bay Studios (310) 762-1360
20434 S. Santa Fe Ave. FAX (310) 639-2055
Long Beach, CA 90810 www.southbaystudios.com
Contact: Ron Kusumi

Stage 1 On Lemona (818) 787-5294
5920 Lemona Ave. www.stage1onlemona.com
Sherman Oaks, CA 91411

(310) 936-4802
The Stage 22 (310) 614-8408
2111 Bellevue Ave. www.thestage22.com
Los Angeles, CA 90026

Stage THIS (818) 726-2240
11273 Gross St. www.stagethisla.com
Sun Valley, CA 91352

(626) 403-8403
Stargate Stage (818) 778-0851
1001 El Centro St. FAX (626) 403-8444
Pasadena, CA 91030 www.stargatestudios.net

Stu Segall Productions (858) 974-8988
4705 Ruffin Rd. FAX (858) 974-8978
San Diego, CA 92123 www.stusegall.com

Studio 12000 (626) 298-4375
12000 E. Washington Blvd. www.studio12000.com
Whittier, CA 90606
Contact: Scott C. Hassel

Studio 34 (323) 223-1234
141 W. Ave. 34 www.studio34.com
Los Angeles, CA 90031
Contact: Eric Ortiz

(626) 799-3430
Studio C2 (310) 761-1767
1605 Mahalo Pl. FAX (626) 799-3506
Rancho Dominguez, CA 90220 www.studio-c2.com

studio/stage (323) 463-3900
520 N. Western Ave. FAX (323) 463-3933
Los Angeles, CA 90004 www.studio-stage.com

Sunset Bronson Studios (323) 460-5858
5800 W. Sunset Blvd. FAX (323) 460-3844
Los Angeles, CA 90028 www.sgsandsbs.com
Contact: Beth Talbert

Sunset Gower Studios (323) 467-1001
1438 N. Gower St. FAX (323) 467-2717
Hollywood, CA 90028 www.sgsandsbs.com
Contact: Terri Melkonian

THE STUDIOS
★★★★ at ★★★★
Paramount

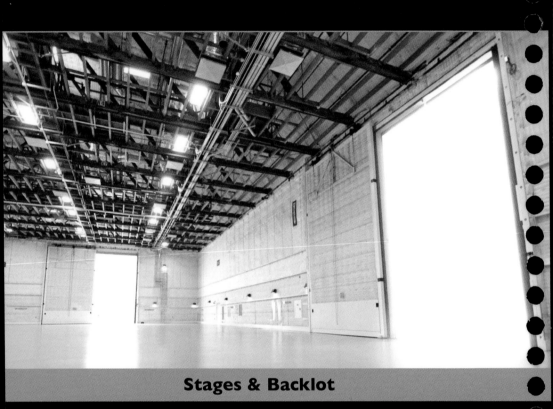

Stages & Backlot

Digital Stages
30 Stages
12 Stages Over 15,000 sq. ft.
Wireless Networking and Internet Access on All Stages
13 Audience Rated Stages
8 Stages with Pits
16 Stages Over 35' Tall

Backlot Locations
NY Street
The Alley
Blue Sky Tank
Scenic Parks
Numerous Architectural Structures and Facades

Stage Reference Guide

Stage	Length	Width	Grid Height	Area (Square Feet)	Audience Rated
1	146	73	25	10,658	Yes
2	148	57	26	8,436	No
3	94	59	37	5,546	No
4	195	71	26	13,845	No
5	247	76	34	18,772	No
6	109	69	30	7,521	No
7	167	69	30/65	11,523	No
8	147	113	30	16,611	No
9	147	113	30	16,611	No
11	95	64	38	6,080	No
12	95	65	38	6,175	No
14	217	95/64	38	17,328	No
15	164	110	56	18,040	No
16	170	105	40	17,850	No
17	186	68	36	12,648	No
18	185	99	40	18,315	Yes
19	153	99	35	15,147	Yes
20	153	99	35	15,147	Yes
21	97	92	35	8,924	Yes
23	170	75	28	12,750	Yes
24	170	75	28	12,750	Yes
25	170	75	28	12,750	Yes
26	100	68	28	6,800	No
27	127	83	32	10,541	Yes
28	99	84	33	8,316	No
29	145	108	35	15,660	Yes
30	107	90	35	9,630	Yes
31	145	107	35	15,515	Yes
32	144	109	46	15,696	Yes

All Stages Have Wi-Fi Internet Access

5555 Melrose Avenue, Hollywood, CA 90038
323.956.8811 • Studio_Operations@paramount.com
www.TheStudiosAtParamount.com

Syncro Aviation, Inc./Hanger 902   **(818) 901-9828**
7701 Woodley Ave.   FAX **(818) 988-5851**
Van Nuys, CA 91406   **www.syncroaircraftinteriors.com**

TAN Broadcast Center   **(323) 465-0411**
6430 Sunset Blvd., Ste. 1200   FAX **(323) 957-6583**
Los Angeles, CA 90028   **tanbroadcastcenter.com**
Contact: John Kim

Towards 2000, Inc.   **(818) 557-0903**
215 W. Palm Ave., Ste. 101   FAX **(866) 836-5725**
Burbank, CA 91502   **www.t2k.com**
Contact: Mark Rowlands

UCLA Dept. of Film & TV   **(310) 825-2503**
225 E. Melnitz Hall, Box 951622   FAX **(310) 206-1686**
Los Angeles, CA 90095   **www.tft.ucla.edu**

UFO-The Poodle Parlor   **(213) 694-0556**
2476 Hunter St.   **www.ufo-thepoodleparlor.com**
Los Angeles, CA 90021
Contact: Joel Unangst

Ⓐ Universal Studios Stages   **(818) 777-3000**
100 Universal City Plaza, Bldg. 4250-3 FAX **(818) 866-0293**
Universal City, CA 91608
Contact: Jeff Berry   **www.filmmakersdestination.com**

The Walt Disney Studios   **(818) 560-7450**
500 S. Buena Vista St.   FAX **(818) 841-8328**
Burbank, CA 91521   **studioservices.go.com**
Contact: Tim Schmidt

Ⓐ Warner Bros. Studio
Facilities - Operations   **(818) 954-2577**
4000 Warner Blvd.   FAX **(818) 954-4467**
Burbank, CA 91522   **www.wbstagesandsets.com**
Contact: Perry Husman

                                         (323) 692-5360
Westside Media Center Studios   **(323) 697-0951**
12312 W. Olympic Blvd.
Los Angeles, CA 90064
             www.westsidemediastudios.weebly.com
Contacts: Lauren Bowes, Kenneth Falcon & Tammy McCann

World Television Productions   **(323) 469-5638**
5757 Wilshire Blvd., Ste. 470   FAX **(323) 469-2193**
Los Angeles, CA 90036
Contact: Hugo Morales

Serving Creativity and Success

Stage & Office Rentals	Stage	W	L	H	SF
	2	54	119	40	6,426
Lighting & Grip	3	219	119	35	26,061
	2-3	273	119	35-40	32,214
Expendables	5	102	131	30	13,362
	6	102	142	30	14,484
Set Rentals	7	80	70	30	5,600
	8	80	70	30	5,600
Commissary & Catering	9	80	70	30	5,600
	10	79	39	20	3,081
Screening Rooms	11	98	136	40	13,328
	12	99	136	40	13,464
Athletic Club	14	101	136	40	13,736
	15	132	129	43	17,028
Special Events	14-15	233	129-136	40-43	30,764
	16	131	129	46	16,899

THE CULVER STUDIOS

A FULL-SERVICE PRODUCTION STUDIO

310 202 3400   www.theculverstudios.com

John Edward Linden Photography

A Technology leader throughout our long History!

Accurate Staging

(310) 324-1040
(310) 327-5049
1820 W. 135th St.   FAX (310) 324-1017
Gardena, CA 90249   www.accuratestaging.com
(Platforms, Portable Stages & Rolling Risers)

All Access Staging & Productions   (310) 784-2464
1320 Storm Pkwy   FAX (310) 517-0899
Torrance, CA 90501   www.allaccessinc.com
(Platforms, Portable Stages & Risers)

(818) 549-9915
Astro Audio Video Lighting, Inc.   (800) 427-8768
6615 San Fernando Rd.   FAX (818) 549-0681
Glendale, CA 91201   www.astroavl.com
(Platforms, Portable Stages, Risers & Step Units)

Bartle International Group   (818) 252-5806
www.bigprod.com

(310) 532-3933
Beckman Rigging/BRS Rigging   (661) 510-2518
13516 S. Mariposa Ave.   FAX (310) 532-3993
Gardena, CA 90247   www.brsrigging.com
(Disabled Persons' Lifts and Ramps, Platforms, Portable
Stages, Ramps & Step Units)

Bill Ferrell Co.   (818) 767-1900
10556 Keswick St.   FAX (818) 767-2901
Sun Valley, CA 91352   www.billferrell.com
(Ferrellels, Portable Stages & Steeldeck)

Brown-United   (800) 442-7696
Grandstands & Staging   (626) 357-1161
P.O. Box 362   FAX (626) 358-3064
Monrovia, CA 91017   www.brownunited.com
(Bleachers, Disabled Persons Lifts and Ramps, Platforms,
Portable Stages, Risers & Theater Seats)

Fuller Street Productions   (877) 637-8733
10702 Hathaway Dr., Ste. 2   FAX (877) 637-8733
Santa Fe Springs, CA 90670   www.fullerstreet.com
(Bleachers, Disabled Persons' Lifts and Ramps, Flats, Getaway
Stairs, Platforms, Portable Stages, Ramps, Risers, Rolling
Risers, Step Units, Theater Seats & Wagons)

Hollywood Flats & Risers   (323) 660-8466
1215 Bates Ave.   www.macksennettstage.com
Los Angeles, CA 90029
(Flats and Risers Only)

HSG, Inc.   (323) 733-8552
4845 Exposition Blvd.   FAX (323) 733-3306
Los Angeles, CA 90016   www.hsg-inc.com
(Platforms & Swing Stages)

Merrill Carson Entertainment   (818) 780-1735
7905 Lloyd Ave.   www.merrillcarson.com
North Hollywood, CA 91605
(Bleachers, Chair and Choir Risers & Portable Stages)

Mike Brown Grandstands, Inc.   (800) 266-2659
(Bleachers, Platforms & Portable Stages) FAX (626) 303-5115
www.mbgs.com

(323) 993-8750
The Photobubble Company   (310) 467-5131
1641 N. Ivar Ave.   www.photobubblecompany.com
Los Angeles, CA 90028

Precision Turntable Services   (661) 252-8444
28155 La Veda Ave.   www.precisionturntables.com
Santa Clarita, CA 91387
(Turntables)

(818) 762-0884
Premier Lighting & Production Co.   (800) 770-0884
12023 Victory Blvd.   FAX (818) 762-0896
North Hollywood, CA 91606   www.premier-lighting.com

Scenic Express, Inc.   (323) 254-4351
3019 Andrita St.   FAX (323) 254-4411
Los Angeles, CA 90065   www.scenicexpress.net
(Platforms & Portable Stages)

ShowBiz Enterprises, Inc.   (818) 989-7007
15541 Lanark St.   FAX (818) 989-8272
Van Nuys, CA 91406   www.showbizenterprises.com

Stage Tech   (562) 407-1133
14523 Marquardt Ave.   FAX (562) 407-1306
Santa Fe Springs, CA 90630   www.stage-tech.com

(323) 290-2100
🅐 **Steeldeck, Inc.**   (800) 507-8243
3339 Exposition Pl.   FAX (323) 290-9600
Los Angeles, CA 90018   www.steeldeck.com
(Platforms, Portable Stages & Risers)

Studio City Rentals   (818) 543-0300
100 E. Cedar Ave.   FAX (818) 955-9683
Burbank, CA 91502   www.studiocityrental.com

Universal Studios Stages   (818) 777-3000
100 Universal City Plaza, Bldg. 4250-3 FAX (818) 866-0293
Universal City, CA 91608
www.filmmakersdestination.com

(818) 247-1149
Upstage Parallels, Inc.   (866) 387-7824
4000 Chevy Chase Dr.   FAX (818) 244-4835
Los Angeles, CA 90039   www.upstageparallels.com
(Getaway Stairs, Risers & Wagons)

Aero Associates/Aircraft Mockups (310) 337-1938
(310) 332-4383
8033 Emerson Ave.
Los Angeles, CA 90045
(Airplane Mock-Ups)

Ⓐ Aero Mock-Ups, Inc. (818) 982-7327
(888) 662-5877
13126 Saticoy St. FAX (818) 982-0122
North Hollywood, CA 91605 www.aeromockups.com
(Airplane Mock-Ups & Airport Terminals)

Air Hollywood (818) 890-0444
13240 Weidner St. FAX (818) 890-7041
Los Angeles, CA 91331 www.airhollywood.com
(Airplane Mock-Ups, Airport Terminals, Bar, Cockpit,
Interrogation Room, Office, Parking Lot & Warehouse)

Avenue Six Studios (818) 781-6600
7900 Haskell Ave. FAX (818) 781-6611
Van Nuys, CA 91406 www.avenuesixstudios.com
(Meeting/Conference Room, Office, Parking Lot & Warehouse)

Aviation Warehouse (760) 388-4215
20020 El Mirage Airport Rd. FAX (760) 388-4236
El Mirage, CA 92301 www.aviationwarehouse.net

California City Studios, Inc. (760) 373-4966
(866) 966-3456
1610 Pesch St. FAX (760) 373-8565
Mojave, CA 93501 www.californiacitystudios.com
(Courtyards, Deserts, Diner, Farm House, Gas Station,
Iraqi Village, Mexican Village, Resturant, Water Tanks &
Western Town)

Central City Studio (310) 295-7751
737 Terminal St., Bldg. C FAX (213) 622-6292
Los Angeles, CA 90021 www.centralcitystudiola.com
(Hospital, Jail Cell, Kitchen, Prisoner Visitation,
Secretarial Pool & Warehouse)

Centro Net Productions (310) 237-5653
2740 California St. FAX (310) 294-3691
Torrance, CA 90503 www.centronetproductions.com

Club Ed (661) 946-1515
42848 150th St. East FAX (661) 946-0454
Lancaster, CA 93535 www.avlocations.com
(Bar, Diner, Gas Station, Market & Motel)

DC Stages & Sets (213) 629-5434
(310) 804-5712
1360 E. Sixth St. FAX (213) 629-5155
Los Angeles, CA 90021 dcstages.com
(City Hall/Rotunda, Courtrooms/Superior and Municipal,
D.A.'s Office, Detective's Office, Doctor's Office, Drunk Tank,
Elevators, Emergency Room, FBI Headquarters, Hospital,
Hotel Suite, Interrogation Rooms, Jail, Judge's Chambers, Law
Library/Mezzanine, Line-up Rooms, Lobby, Mayor's Office,
Meeting/Conference Room, Modern Home and Cottage, New
York House, Parking Lots/Alleys, Patient Exam Room/Lab,
Police Precinct/Booking Room, Restaurant/Bar &
Warehouse/Dock Offices)
Contact: Diane Markoff

Family Amusement Corporation (323) 660-8180
(800) 262-6467
876 N. Vermont Ave. FAX (323) 660-8976
Los Angeles, CA 90029 www.familyamusement.com
(Video Game Arcade)

Four Aces (310) 396-2211
14499 E. Avenue Q FAX (310) 396-5993
Palmdale, CA 93591 www.4-aces.com
(Diner/Bar, Gas Station and Motel Interiors and Exteriors)

GMT Studios (310) 649-3733
5751 Buckingham Pkwy FAX (310) 216-0056
Culver City, CA 90230 www.gmtstudios.com
(Courtroom, Detective Office, Interrogation Room & Prison)
Contact: Morgan Denton

Ⓐ Golden Oak Ranch (661) 259-8717
19802 Placerita Canyon Rd. www.goldenoakranch.com
Newhall, CA 91321

Hip Films (323) 467-2897
1622 Gower St. FAX (323) 469-8251
Hollywood, CA 90028 www.hipfilms.com
(Alley, Bar, Bedroom, Hospital, Interrogation Room, Nightclub,
Parking Lot, Restaurant, Spaceship Interior & Warehouse)

Hollywood Production Center (818) 480-3100
121 W. Lexington Dr. FAX (818) 480-3199
Glendale, CA 91203 www.hollywoodpc.com
(D.A.'s Office, Detective's Office, Doctor's Office, Elevator
Lobby, Elevators, FBI Headquarters, Interrogation Room,
Judge's Chambers, Line-up Rooms, Lobby, Mayor's Office,
Meeting/Conference Room, Office & Parking Lot)

Jets & Props (818) 505-0199
(818) 324-0884
(Airplane Mock-Ups) FAX (818) 505-0199
www.jetsandprops.com

Jon S. Clark Private Rail Cars (323) 497-1830
P.O. Box 3613
Cerritos, CA 90703
(Railroads, Streamlined Railroad Passenger Cars & Trains)

Kevin Mcateer Reel Locations (818) 970-0469
(805) 241-0992
(Diner)

Lacy Street Production Center (323) 222-8872
2630 Lacy St. FAX (323) 222-1258
Los Angeles, CA 90031 www.lacystreet.com
(Apartment, Church, Courtroom, Diner, Hotel, House,
Interrogation Room, Jail Cell, Mechanic's Shop, Nightclub &
Police Station)
Contacts: Austin Lander & Don Randles

Laurel Canyon Stages (818) 768-8935
9337 Laurel Canyon Blvd. FAX (818) 768-6852
Arleta, CA 91331 www.lcstages.com
(Spaceship Interior)
Contact: Mary Claypool

Los Angeles Center Studios (213) 534-3000
FAX (213) 534-3001
www.lacenterstudios.com
(Bar, City Street Facades, Courtroom, Diner, Elevator Lobby,
Elevators, Interrogation Room, Lobby, Morgue, Office, Parking
Lot, Police Station, Prison, Restaurant & Warehouse)

Melody Ranch Studio (661) 259-9669
(661) 810-9898
P.O. Box 220597 FAX (661) 259-3788
Newhall, CA 91322 www.melodyranchstudio.com
(Western Town)

Monad Railway Equipment Co. (562) 404-8641
(562) 522-7894
15220 Valley View Ave. FAX (562) 404-8541
La Mirada, CA 90638 www.monadrailway.com
(Locomotives, Passenger Rail Cars & Train Mock-Ups)
Contact: Lon Orlenko

The Studios at Paramount (323) 956-8811
The Studios at Paramount New York Streets,
5555 Melrose Ave. www.thestudiosatparamount.com
Hollywood, CA 90038

Producers Air Force (818) 845-5970
(818) 795-7463
One Orange Grove Terrace FAX (818) 845-4033
Burbank, CA 91501 www.producersairforce.com
(Airplane Mock-Ups & Cockpit)

Riverfront Stages, Inc.   **(818) 364-7250**
13100 Telfair Ave.   FAX **(818) 364-7251**
Sylmar, CA 91342   **www.riverfrontstages.com**
(Apartment, Bar, Bedroom, Church, City Hall, Conference
Room, Courtroom, D.A.'s Office, Detective's Office, Diner,
Doctor's Office, Elevator, Elevator Lobby, FBI Headquarters,
Hospital, Hotel, House, Interrogation Room, Jail Cell, Judge's
Chambers, Lobby, Mayor's Office, Morgue, Office, Police
Station, Prison, Restaurant & Warehouse)
Contact: Christine Johnson

Scroggins Aviation   **(702) 348-7731**
(Airplane Mock-Ups and Props)   FAX **(702) 953-7307**
                  www.scrogginsaviation.com

                        (714) 836-1853
Silver Dream Factory, Inc.   **(714) 225-3708**
1181 N. Knollwood Circle   **www.standingsets.com**
Anaheim, CA 92801
(Airplane Mock-Ups, Bedroom, Detective's Office, Hospital,
Interrogation Room, Medical Facility, Morgue, Office, Police
Station & Prison)

                        (818) 240-1893
Solar Studios   **(310) 489-7801**
1601 S. Central Ave.   FAX **(818) 240-4187**
Glendale, CA 91204   **www.solarstudios.com**

Syncro Aviation, Inc./Hanger 902   **(818) 901-9828**
7701 Woodley Ave.   FAX **(818) 988-5851**
Van Nuys, CA 91406 **www.syncroaircraftinteriors.com**
(Airplane & Ramp)

United Pacific Studios   **(213) 489-2001**
729 E. Temple St.   FAX **(213) 489-2098**
Los Angeles, CA 90012 **www.unitedpacificstudios.com**
(Bar, Detective's Office, Diner, Doctor's Office, Elevator,
Hospital, Hotel Room, House, Interrogation Room, Lawyer's
Office, Line-up Room, Lobby, Meeting/Conference Room,
Modern Home, Motel, Nightclub, Office, Parking Lots/Alleys,
Patient Exam Room, Prison/Jail Cells,
Restaurant/Bar & Warehouse)

Universal Studios Stages   **(818) 777-3000**
100 Universal City Plaza, Bldg. 4250-3 FAX **(818) 866-0293**
Universal City, CA 91608
           www.filmmakersdestination.com
(City Street Facades, Gas Station, House, Parking Lot,
Passenger Rail Cars, Warehouse & Western Town)
Contact: Jeff Berry

Veluzat Motion Picture Ranch   **(661) 810-9898**
P.O. Box 220597   FAX **(661) 294-6814**
Newhall, CA 91322
       www.veluzatmotionpictureranch.com
(Bar, Church, Diner & Gas Station)

                        (213) 625-5771
Willow Studios   **(310) 849-5452**
1333-1335 Willow St.   FAX **(213) 613-0708**
Los Angeles, CA 90013   **www.willowstudios.net**
(Alley, Bar, Bedroom, City Street Facades, D.A.'s Office,
Detective's Office, Diner, Doctor's Office, Elevators, Emergency
Room, FBI Headquarters, Hotel Suite, House, Interrogation
Room, Judge's Chambers, Line-up Rooms, Mayor's Office,
Mechanic's Shop, Meeting/Conference Room, Morgue, Motel,
Nightclub, Office, Parking Lot, Police Station, Prison,
Restaurant & Warehouse)

                                                    Standing Sets

Create
any place in one place.

BUSINESS DISTRICT

🎬 42 unique store fronts
🎬 Architecture ranging from 1920s to present

🎬 Urban alleyway
🎬 Multiple intersections

NATURAL & RURAL SETTINGS

🎬 Heavily wooded areas
🎬 Two lakes with waterfalls

🎬 Acres of meadows kept green year-round
🎬 Mutliple barns, bridges, cabins and houses

RESIDENTIAL STREET

🎬 Styles from across the U.S.
🎬 14 architecturally unique houses

🎬 Multiple backyards
🎬 Fully landscaped

661-259-8717

Golden Oak Ranch™

goldenoakranch.com

240 Studio (805) 845-8870
One N. Calle Cesar Chavez, Ste. 240 FAX (805) 845-6555
Santa Barbara, CA 93103 www.240studio.com

(818) 380-6616
Avenue Six Studios (818) 933-0818
7900 Haskell Ave FAX (818) 781-6611
Van Nuys, CA 91406 www.avenuesixstudios.com

Hollywood Loft (323) 957-9398
6161 Santa Monica Blvd., Ste. 400
Hollywood, CA 90038 www.hollywoodloft.com

(818) 240-1893
Solar Studios (310) 489-7801
1601 S. Central Ave. FAX (818) 242-1691
Glendale, CA 91204 www.solarstudios.com

The LA Lofts (323) 462-5880
6442 Santa Monica Blvd. FAX (323) 462-7858
Hollywood, CA 90038 www.thelalofts.com

3555 Hayden Studios (310) 430-7550
3555 Hayden Ave. www.3555hayden.com
Culver City, CA 90232

(323) 665-1307
Albuerne, Inc. (213) 926-0444
2990 Allesandro St. FAX (323) 665-7034
Los Angeles, CA 90039 www.albuerneinc.com

(805) 955-7742
AMP Studios (805) 955-7770
101 W. Cochran St. FAX (805) 955-7705
Simi Valley, CA 93065 www.ampstudios.com

Associated Television International (323) 556-5600
4401 Wilshire Blvd. www.4401wilshire.com
Los Angeles, CA 90010

Ⓐ **Ben Kitay Studios** (323) 466-9015
1015 N. Cahuenga Blvd. FAX (323) 466-4421
Hollywood, CA 90038 www.benkitay.com

Centro Net Productions (310) 237-5653
2740 California St. FAX (310) 294-3691
Torrance, CA 90503 www.centronetproductions.com

(310) 287-3600
Century Studio Corporation (888) 878-2437
8660 Hayden Pl., Ste. 100 FAX (310) 287-3608
Culver City, CA 90232 www.centurystudio.com

(818) 763-3650
Chandler Valley Center Studios, Inc. (818) 424-4551
13927 Saticoy St. FAX (818) 990-4755
Van Nuys, CA 91402 www.cvcstudios.com

Coastal Media Group (818) 880-9800
26660 Agoura Rd. FAX (818) 579-9026
Calabasas, CA 91302 www.coastalmediagroup.com

Costa Mesa Studios (949) 515-9942
711 W. 17th St., Ste. D10 www.costamesastudios.com
Costa Mesa, CA 92627

Encompass Digital Media (323) 344-4500
3030 Andrita St. FAX (323) 344-4800
Los Angeles, CA 90065 www.encompass-m.com

(818) 841-3888
Fastlane Broadcast Studio (562) 335-7400
3062 N. Lima St. FAX (818) 841-3188
Burbank, CA 91504 www.fastlanebroadcast.com

(310) 369-2786
Fox Studios (310) 369-4636
10201 W. Pico Blvd. FAX (310) 369-8858
Los Angeles, CA 90035 www.foxstudiosstages.com

Hollywood Center Studios (323) 860-0000
1040 N. Las Palmas Ave. FAX (323) 860-8105
Hollywood, CA 90038 www.hollywoodcenter.com

(323) 953-5258
KCET Studios (818) 692-5766
4401 Sunset Blvd. FAX (323) 953-5496
Los Angeles, CA 90027 www.kcetstudios.com

Lacy Street Production Center (323) 222-8872
2630 Lacy St. FAX (323) 222-1258
Los Angeles, CA 90031 www.lacystreet.com

Los Angeles Center Studios (213) 534-3000
1201 W. Fifth St., Ste. T-110 FAX (213) 534-3001
Los Angeles, CA 90017 www.lacenterstudios.com

(323) 850-3180
The Lot (323) 850-2832
1041 N. Formosa Ave. www.thelotstudios.com
West Hollywood, CA 90046

Ⓐ **The Studios at Paramount** (323) 956-8811
The Studios at Paramount Client Services
5555 Melrose Ave. www.thestudiosatparamount.com
Hollywood, CA 90038

(818) 933-2100
Phunware Studios (818) 933-2107
14144 Ventura Blvd., Ste. 300 phunware.com/studio
Sherman Oaks, CA 91423

The Production Group Studios (323) 469-8111
1330 N. Vine St. FAX (323) 962-2182
Hollywood, CA 90028 www.productiongroup.tv

Quixote Studios - Griffith Park (323) 957-9933
4585 Electronics Pl. FAX (323) 957-9944
Griffith Park, CA 90039 www.quixote.com

Raleigh Studios - Hollywood (323) 960-3456
5300 Melrose Ave. FAX (323) 960-4712
Hollywood, CA 90038 www.raleighstudios.com
Contact: Yolanda Montellano

Raleigh Studios - Manhattan Beach (310) 960-3456
1600 Rosecrans Ave. FAX (310) 727-2710
Manhattan Beach, CA 90266 www.raleighstudios.com
Contact: Dana Bromley

Red Studios Hollywood (323) 463-0808
846 N. Cahuenga Blvd. FAX (323) 465-8173
Hollywood, CA 90038 www.redstudio.com

(818) 590-0042
Redemption Stages (818) 404-9779
2980 & 2982 N. Ontario St. FAX (818) 238-0095
Burbank, CA 91504 www.redemptionstages.com

DOWNLOAD NOW!

LA 411

iPhone App

LA 411's dedicated app will bring all the qualified production listings you have come to rely on right to the palm of your hand.

This FREE dedicated app provides a graphical representation of LA 411's twelve production sections. You'll find full contact information including email, web address and complete company descriptions for each listing. You'll also be able to directly dial the company through the listing, initiate GPS mapping coordinates, and set favorites for those listings you love.

Staying connected to the below-the-line production community is also easier by accessing our Facebook, Twitter, and 411 News and Update pages through this comprehensive app.

TO LEARN MORE AND DOWNLOAD THE FREE LA 411 APP VISIT:

www.la411.com/iPhone

South Bay Studios (310) 762-1360
20434 S. Santa Fe Ave. FAX (310) 639-2055
Long Beach, CA 90810 www.southbaystudios.com

Sunset Bronson Studios (323) 460-5858
5800 W. Sunset Blvd. FAX (323) 460-3844
Los Angeles, CA 90028 www.sgsandsbs.com
Contact: Beth Talbert

Sunset Gower Studios (323) 467-1001
1438 N. Gower St. FAX (323) 467-2717
Los Angeles, CA 90028 www.sgsandsbs.com
Contact: Terri Melkonian

Warner Bros. Studio
Facilities - Operations (818) 954-2577
4000 Warner Blvd. FAX (818) 954-4467
Burbank, CA 91522 www.wbstagesandsets.com

(818) 597-4000
Westlake Village Studios (818) 597-4027
Two Dole Dr. FAX (818) 597-4037
Westlake Village, CA 91362 www.wlvstudios.com

(323) 692-5360
Westside Media Center Studios (323) 697-0951
12312 W. Olympic Blvd.
Los Angeles, CA 90064
www.westsidemediastudios.weebly.com

Virtual Sets

3555 Hayden Studios (310) 430-7550
3555 Hayden Ave. www.3555hayden.com
Culver City, CA 90232

All Access Staging & Productions (310) 784-2464
1320 Storm Pkwy FAX (310) 517-0899
Torrance, CA 90501 www.allaccessinc.com

Centro Net Productions (310) 237-5653
2740 California St. FAX (310) 294-3691
Torrance, CA 90503 www.centronetproductions.com

(323) 257-1163
Composite Components Company (323) 243-8999
134 N. Avenue 61, Ste. 102/3 FAX (323) 257-0604
Los Angeles, CA 90042 www.digitalgreenscreen.com

Hollywood Center Studios (323) 860-0000
1040 N. Las Palmas Ave. FAX (323) 860-8105
Hollywood, CA www.hollywoodcenter.com

Lightcraft Technology (310) 386-7293
612 Venice Blvd. www.lightcrafttech.com
Venice, CA 90291

Post Modern
Broadcast Studios, LLC (949) 608-8700
2941 Alton Pkwy FAX (949) 608-8729
Irvine, CA 92606 www.postmodernstudios.com

Universal Virtual Stage 1 (818) 777 3000
100 Universal City Plaza
Universal City, CA 91608
www.filmmakersdestination.com

STANDING SETS

STANDING SETS	Willow Studios	Veluzat Motion Picture Ranch	Universal Studios Stages	United Pacific Studios	Syncro Aviation/Hanger 902	Silver Dream Factory	Scroggins Aviation, Inc.	Riverfront Stages, Inc.	Ready Set Studio	Producers Air Force	Pointe Studios	The Studios At Paramount	Monad Railway Equipment Co.	Melody Ranch	Los Angeles Center Studios	Laurel Canyon Stages	Lacy Street Production Center	Kevin Mcateer Locations	Jon S. Clark Private Rail Cars	Jets & Props	Hip Films	GMT Studios	Four Aces	D.C. Stages & Sets	Club Ed	Aviation Warehouse	Art Scholl Aviation	Air Hollywood	Aero Mock-Ups, Inc.
AIRPLANE					•				•		•								•							•	•	•	•
AIRPORT TERMINAL					•																							•	•
APARTMENT								•						•			•												
ARMY CAMP														•															
BAR/RESTAURANT	•	•		•				•			•	•				•	•					•		•	•	•		•	•
CELL BLOCK																	•					•							
CHURCH		•																							•				
CITY HALL																									•				
CITY STREET FACADES	•													•															
CLASSROOM					•			•									•								•				
CONFERENCE ROOM	•		•	•				•						•			•							•	•				
COURTROOM								•	•		•			•			•					•		•	•				
D.A.'S OFFICE	•			•				•	•		•						•							•	•				
DETECTIVE'S OFFICE	•			•				•			•						•							•	•				
DINER	•	•		•		•		•			•						•	•						•				•	
DINING RAIL CAR	•			•		•		•			•						•								•				
DOCTOR'S OFFICE													•																
DRUNK TANK								•									•								•				
ELEVATOR	•		•	•				•						•			•								•				
ELEVATOR LOBBY			•	•				•	•					•			•												
EMERGENCY ROOM	•							•									•								•				
EXAM ROOM/LAB	•			•				•									•								•				
FARMHOUSE	•																•												
FBI HEADQUARTERS		•	•											•								•		•					
GAS STATION																													
HELICOPTER					•																								
HOSPITAL				•													•								•				
HOTEL	•		•	•				•			•						•								•				
HOUSE	•		•	•				•	•								•								•				
INTERROGATION ROOM	•		•	•				•									•							•				•	•
JAIL	•			•				•									•								•				
JAIL CELL	•			•				•									•								•				
JET FIGHTER										•																			
JUDGE'S CHAMBERS	•							•	•		•						•							•	•				
LIBRARY	•																•							•	•				
LINE-UP ROOM	•			•										•			•							•	•				
LOBBY			•	•		•						•		•			•								•				
LOCOMOTIVE																													
MARKET														•													•		
MAYOR'S OFFICE	•								•	•																			
MECHANICS SHOP	•			•										•			•	•											
MILITARY AIRCRAFT																													
MILITARY BARRACKS				•																									
MORGUE	•																							•	•				
MOTEL	•		•	•													•												
NIGHTCLUB	•		•	•																		•							
OFFICE	•		•	•	•	•		•	•		•	•		•			•					•				•		•	•
OCTAGONAL OFFICE																										•			
PARKING LOT	•		•	•					•					•			•												
PASSENGER RAIL CAR		•																											
POLICE STATION									•				•													•			
PRISON	•							•						•			•							•					
SPACESHIP	•			•													•							•	•				
WAREHOUSE																	•	•											
WESTERN TOWN	•		•	•	•					•				•	•										•				

STAGE NAME	PHONE	STAGE NUMBER	LENGTH	WIDTH	HEIGHT	AREA SQUARE FEET	SOUND STAGE	INSERT	POWER/AMPS	CYCLORAMAS
Raleigh Studios - Playa Vista	323-960-3456	31	741	102	72	75582	•		24000 Amps	
Raleigh Studios - Playa Vista	323-960-3456	32	741	102	72	75582	•		24000 Amps	
Sony Pictures Studios	310-224-6926	15	311	135	40	41985	•		9000 Amps	
Quixote Studios Griffith Park	323-957-9933	8	220	180	42	39600	•		2400 Amps	
The Barker Hangar/SM Air Center	310-390-9071	A	234	150	45	35100			Unlimited	
Occidental Studios, Inc.	213-384-3335	5	180	180	16	32400	•		4600 Amps	
Warner Bros. Studio Facilities	818-954-2577	16	238	135	65	32130	•		Unlimited	
Sony Pictures Studios	310-244-6926	27	237	134	80	31758	•		9600 Amps	
The Walt Disney Studios	818-560-7450	2	240	130	40	31200	•		Unlimited	
Sony Pictures Studios	310-244-6926	30	236	132	50	31152	•		9600 Amps	
1 Big Cyc & Stage	855-345-5244	1	290	71	24	30590			400 Amps	2 wall
Centinela Studios	310-396-3688	A	200	150	22	30000			600AC/320DC	
Universal Studios	818-777-3000	12	199	146	49' 2	29054	•		Unlimited	
Fox Studios	310-369-2786	6	210	134	40	28140	•		9000AC Avail.	
Fox Studios	310-369-2786	8	211	133	35	28063	•		9000AC Avail.	
Fox Studios	310-369-2786	5	210	133	40	27930	•		9000AC Avail.	
Fox Studios	310-369-2786	14&15	207	130	40	26910	•		9000AC Avail.	
Fox Studios	310-369-2786	16	207	129	40	26703	•		9000AC Avail.	
The Lot	323-850-3184	3/4	254	105	35	26670	•		4800 Amps	
The Culver Studios	310-202-3400	3	219	119	35	26061	•		7200AC	
Raleigh Studios - Manhattan Beach	310-727-2700	23	130	195	45	25350	•		7200AC	
Raleigh Studios - Manhattan Beach	310-727-2700	24	130	195	45	25350	•		7200AC	
Raleigh Studios - Manhattan Beach	310-727-2700	25	130	195	45	25350	•		7200AC	
Raleigh Studios - Manhattan Beach	310-727-2700	26	130	195	45	25350	•		7200AC	
Raleigh Studios - Manhattan Beach	310-727-2700	27	130	195	45	25350	•		7200AC	
Warner Bros. Studio Facilities	818-954-2577	29	182	139	45	25298	•		Unlimited	
Red Studios	323-463-0808	8/9	215	117	38	25155	•		9000AC	
CBS Studio Center	818-655-5665	21	190	130	45	24700	•		7200AC	
CBS Studio Center	818-655-5665	W21	190	130	19	24700	•		6000AC	
D.C. Stages & Sets	213-629-5434	III	360	68	19' 6	24480	•	•	500 Amps	
Occidental Studios, Inc.	213-384-3337	7	187	130	22	24310	•		4800 Amps	
CBS Studio Center	818-655-5665	3	200	120	41	24000	•		9000AC/9000DC	
Albuquerque Studios	505-227-2000	3	178	134	55	23852	•		6400 Amps	
Albuquerque Studios	505-227-2000	4	178	134	55	23852	•		6400 Amps	
Albuquerque Studios	505-227-2000	7	178	134	55	23852	•		6400 Amps	
Albuquerque Studios	505-227-2000	8	178	134	55	23852	•		6400 Amps	
Sony Pictures Studios	310-244-6926	29	197	118	40	23246	•		9600 Amps	
Sony Pictures Studios	310-244-6926	28	197	117	40	23049	•		9600 Amps	
Sony Pictures Studios	310-244-6926	26	196	117	40	22932	•		9600 Amps	
Century Studio Corporation	888-878-2437	3/4	198	115	23	22770	•	•	1800AC	
Sony Pictures Studios	310-244-6926	25	194	117	40	22698	•		9600 Amps	
Warner Bros. Studio Facilities	818-954-2577	15	206	110	35	22660	•		Unlimited	

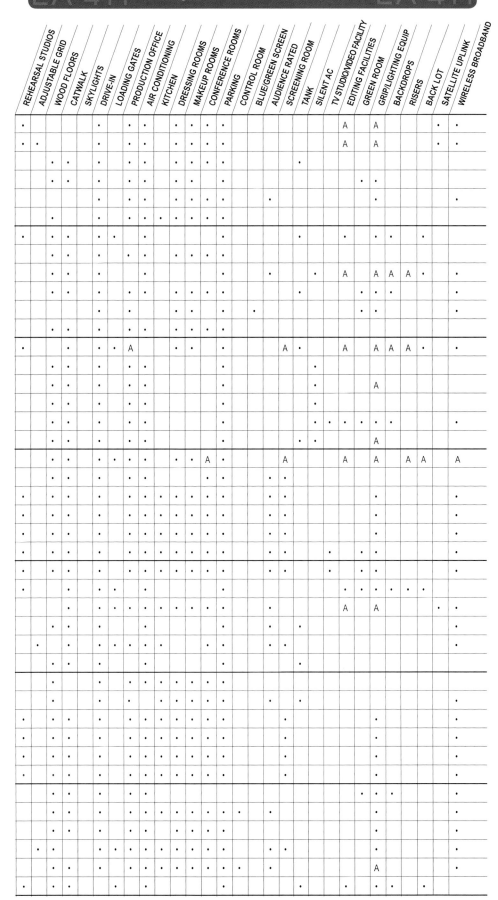

REHEARSAL STUDIOS	ADJUSTABLE GRID	WOOD FLOORS	CATWALK	SKYLIGHTS	DRIVE-IN	LOADING GATES	PRODUCTION OFFICE	AIR CONDITIONING	KITCHEN	DRESSING ROOMS	MAKEUP ROOMS	CONFERENCE ROOMS	PARKING	CONTROL ROOM	BLUE/GREEN SCREEN	AUDIENCE RATED	SCREENING ROOM	TANK	SILENT AC	TV STUDIO/VIDEO FACILITY	EDITING FACILITIES	GREEN ROOM	GRIP/LIGHTING EQUIP	BACKDROPS	RISERS	BACK LOT	SATELLITE UPLINK	WIRELESS BROADBAND
•		•		•	•		•	•		•	•	•	•							A		A					•	•
•	•			•			•	•		•	•	•	•							A		A					•	•
		•	•				•			•	•	•	•				•											
		•					•			•	•	•	•									•	•					
		•					•				•	•	•		•													•
		•					•			•	•	•	•															•
•		•	•				•					•					•				•	•	•	•		•		
		•	•				•			•	•	•																
		•	•				•		•			•				•			•	A		A	A	A	•			•
		•	•				•			•	•	•					•				•	•	•					
		•					•			•	•		•		•						•	•						•
		•	•				•	•		•	•	•																
•			•			•	A			•	•		•			A	•			A		A	A	A	•			•
		•	•				•	•				•					•											
		•	•				•	•				•					•					A						
		•	•				•	•				•					•											
		•	•				•	•				•						•	•	•	•	•	•					•
		•	•				•	•				•							•	•		A						
		•	•		•	•	•				•	•	A	•			A			A		A		A	A			A
		•	•				•	•				•	•					•	•									
•		•	•				•	•	•	•	•	•	•				•	•				•						•
•		•	•				•	•	•	•	•	•	•				•	•				•						•
•		•	•				•	•	•	•	•	•	•				•	•				•						•
		•	•	•			•	•	•	•	•	•	•				•	•		•		•	•					•
•		•	•				•	•	•	•	•	•	•				•	•				•						•
•			•		•	•	•					•						•			•	•	•	•	•	•		
		•		•	•	•	•	•	•	•	•	•					•			A		A					•	•
		•	•				•					•					•	•										•
	•		•		•			•			•	•					•	•										•
		•	•				•					•						•										
		•	•			•	•	•	•	•		•				•		•					•					•
		•	•				•					•			•		•											•
•		•	•				•	•	•	•	•	•					•					•						•
		•	•				•	•	•	•	•	•					•					•						•
•		•	•				•	•	•	•	•	•					•					•						•
		•	•				•					•											•	•	•				•
		•	•			•	•	•	•	•	•	•	•	•		•						•						•
		•	•				•	•	•	•	•	•	•									•						•
	•		•	•			•	•				•		•	•							•						•
	•		•				•	•	•	•	•	•	•	•		•						A						•
•		•	•			•		•				•						•			•		•	•		•		

A = Available to Rent

STAGE NAME	PHONE	STAGE NUMBER	LENGTH	WIDTH	HEIGHT	AREA SQUARE FEET	SOUND STAGE	INSERT	POWER/AMPS	CYCLORAMAS
CBS Studio Center	818-655-5665	2	200	110	33	22000	•		9000AC/9000DC	
CBS Studio Center	818-655-5665	9	200	110	31	22000	•		5000AC/8000DC	
CBS Studio Center	818-655-5665	10	200	110	31	22000	•		8000AC/11200DC	
Warner Bros. Studio Facilities	818-954-2577	19	160	135	35	21600	•		Unlimited	
Warner Bros. Studio Facilities	818-954-2577	20	160	135	35	21600	•		Unlimited	
Warner Bros. Studio Facilities	818-954-2577	21	160	135	35	21600	•		Unlimited	
Warner Bros. Studio Facilities	818-954-2577	22	160	135	35	21600	•		Unlimited	
Warner Bros. Studio Facilities	818-954-2577	23	160	135	45	21600	•		Unlimited	
Warner Bros. Studio Facilities	818-954-2577	24	160	135	35	21600	•		Unlimited	
Warner Bros. Studio Facilities	818-954-2577	25	160	135	35	21600	•		Unlimited	
Warner Bros. Studio Facilities	818-954-2577	26	160	135	35	21600	•		Unlimited	
Prospect Studios	818-560-7450	4	216	97	40	20952	•	•	Unlimited	
Sony Pictures Studios	310-244-6926	11	201	103	31	20703	•		7200 Amps	
Sunset Bronson Studios	323-460-5858	9	247	87	29	20189	•		7200 Amps	
Prospect Studios	818-560-7450	6w	144	137	19	19728	•	•	Unlimited	
Universal Studios	818-777-3000	27	199	99	39' 10	19701	•		Unlimited	
Hollywood Center Studios	323-860-0000	3/8	194	100	30	19400	•		4800 amps	
Pointe Studios	310-675-7870	1	82	114.6	30	19,338	•		800 AC	
Encompass Digital Media	323-344-4500	1	160	120	18	19200	•			
Delfino Studios	818-361-2421	3	213	90	34' 8	19170	•		1800AC	
Century Studio Corporation	888-878-2437	8	176	108	25	19008	•	•	1200AC	2 wall hard
The Walt Disney Studios	818-560-7450	3	190	100	39	19000	•		Unlimited	
The Studios At Paramount	323-956-8811	5	247	76	34	18,772			120-208V / 3,840A	
Sony Pictures Studios	310-244-6926	12	179	104	37	18616	•		7200 Amps	
Century Studio Corporation	888-878-2437	7	118	156	23	18408	•	•	1800AC	
The Studios At Paramount	323-956-8811	18	185	99	40	18,315			120-208V / 4,800A	
Fox Studios	310-369-2786	9	189	96	29	18144	•		9000AC Avail.	
The Studios At Paramount	323-956-8811	15	164	110	56	18,040			120-208V / 9,600A	
CBS Studio Center	818-655-5665	22	150	120	35	18000	•		6000AC	
CBS Studio Center	818-655-5665	23	150	120	35	18000	•		6000AC	
CBS Studio Center	818-655-5665	W22	150	120	19	18000	•		6000AC	
CBS Studio Center	818-655-5665	W23	150	120	19	18000	•		6000AC	
Los Angeles Center Studios	213-534-3000	1	150	120	43	18000	•		Unlimited	
Los Angeles Center Studios	213-534-3000	2	150	120	43	18000	•		Unlimited	
Los Angeles Center Studios	213-534-3000	3	150	120	35	18000	•		Unlimited	
Los Angeles Center Studios	213-534-3000	4	150	120	35	18000	•		Unlimited	
Los Angeles Center Studios	213-534-3000	5	150	120	35	18000	•		Unlimited	
Los Angeles Center Studios	213-534-3000	6	150	120	35	18000	•		Unlimited	
Raleigh Studios - Manhattan Beach	310-727-2700	15	120	150	35	18000	•		7200AC	
Raleigh Studios - Manhattan Beach	310-727-2700	16	120	150	35	18000	•		7200AC	
Raleigh Studios - Manhattan Beach	310-727-2700	17	120	150	35	18000	•		7200AC	
Raleigh Studios - Manhattan Beach	310-727-2700	18	120	150	35	18000	•		7200AC	

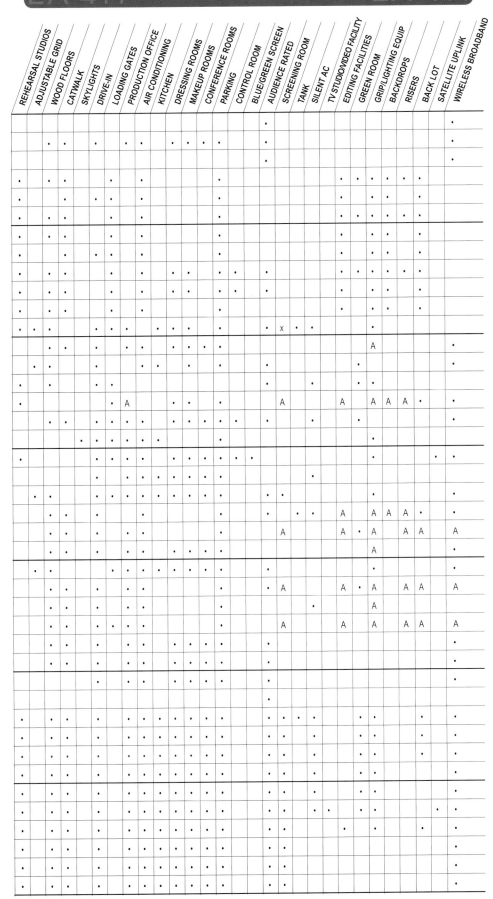

Rehearsal Studios	Adjustable Grid	Wood Floors	Catwalk	Skylights	Drive-In	Loading Gates	Production Office	Air Conditioning	Kitchen	Dressing Rooms	Makeup Rooms	Conference Rooms	Parking	Control Room	Blue/Green Screen	Audience Rated	Screening Room	Tank	Silent AC	TV Studio/Video Facility	Editing Facilities	Green Room	Grip/Lighting Equip	Backdrops	Risers	Back Lot	Satellite Uplink	Wireless Broadband
															•													•
	•	•			•		•	•		•	•	•	•		•													•
															•													•
•			•			•		•			•									•		•	•	•	•	•		
•		•	•		•	•		•			•									•		•	•	•				
•		•	•			•		•			•									•	•	•	•	•				
•		•	•			•		•			•									•		•	•	•				
•		•			•	•		•		•	•		•							•		•	•	•				
•		•				•		•		•	•	•	•							•		•	•	•				
•		•				•		•			•									•		•	•	•				
•	•	•			•		•	•			•	•	•		•	x	•	•				•						
	•	•		•	•	•	•	•		•	•	•	•								A							•
	•	•			•		•	•		•	•	•	•		•							•						•
•		•			•	•		•						•			•				•	•						
•				•	A			•	•		•		•			A				A		A	A	A	A	•		•
	•	•			•	•	•	•		•	•	•	•	•		•						•						
			•			•	•	•	•		•											•						
•		•			•	•	•		•	•	•	•	•	•	•							•				•	•	•
					•		•	•		•	•	•	•									•						•
	•	•			•	•		•		•	•	•	•		•	•						•						•
	•	•			•			•			•				•		•	•		A		A	A	A	•			•
	•	•			•	•	•				•				A					A	•	A		A	A			A
	•	•			•	•		•		•	•									A								•
	•	•			•	•	•	•			•				•							•						•
	•	•			•	•		•			•				•	A				A	•	A		A	A			A
	•	•			•	•		•			•								•			A						
	•	•			•	•	•	•			•					A				A		A		A	A			A
	•	•			•			•		•	•	•	•		•							•						•
	•	•			•			•			•				•							•						•
		•			•	•		•		•	•	•			•													•
															•													
•		•	•		•	•	•	•	•		•		•		•	•	•	•				•	•			•		•
•		•	•		•	•	•	•	•		•		•		•	•		•				•	•			•		•
•		•	•		•	•	•	•	•		•		•		•	•			•			•	•			•		•
•		•	•		•	•	•	•			•		•		•	•												•
•		•	•		•	•	•	•	•		•		•		•	•						•	•				•	•
•		•	•		•	•	•	•	•		•		•		•	•										•	•	•
•		•	•		•	•	•	•	•		•	•	•		•	•			•				•			•		•
•		•	•		•	•	•	•	•		•	•	•		•	•						•	•					•
•	•	•	•		•	•	•	•	•		•	•	•		•	•							•					•

A = Available to Rent

STAGE NAME	PHONE	STAGE NUMBER	LENGTH	WIDTH	HEIGHT	AREA SQUARE FEET	SOUND STAGE	INSERT	POWER/AMPS	CYCLORAMAS
Raleigh Studios - Manhattan Beach	310-727-2700	19	120	150	35	18000	•		7200AC	
Raleigh Studios - Manhattan Beach	310-727-2700	20	120	150	35	18000	•		7200AC	
Raleigh Studios - Manhattan Beach	310-727-2700	21	120	150	35	18000	•		7200AC	
Raleigh Studios - Manhattan Beach	310-727-2700	22	120	150	35	18000	•		7200AC	2 wall hard
Raleigh Studios - Manhattan Beach	310-727-2700	28	120	150	35	18000	•		7200AC	
Red Studios	323-463-0808	4	100	180	30	18000	•		6500AC	
The Studios At Paramount	323-956-8811	16	170	105	40	17,850			120-208V / 9,600A	
Albuquerque Studios	505-227-2000	5	149	119	35	17731	•		2400 Amps	
Albuquerque Studios	505-227-2000	6	149	119	35	17731	•		2400 Amps	
Albuquerque Studios	505-227-2000	1	148	119	45	17612	•		4000 Amps	
Albuquerque Studios	505-227-2000	2	148	119	45	17612	•		4000 Amps	
Universal Studios	818-777-3000	24	157	112	33' 4	17584	•		Unlimited	
Universal Studios	818-777-3000	25	157	112	33' 4	17584	•		Unlimited	
Sunset Gower Studios	323-467-1001	7	143	107	29	17559	•		4800AC	
Red Studios	323-463-0808	5	100	175	30	17500	•		6500AC	
Hollywood Center Studios	323-860-0000	4	174	100	35	17400	•		7200 amps	
The Studios At Paramount	323-956-8811	14	217	95/64	38	17,328			120-208V / 9,600A	
Sunset Gower Studios	323-467-1001	14	128	131	35	17028	•		4800AC	
The Culver Studios	310-202-3400	15	132	129	43	17028	•		7200AC	
The Culver Studios	310-202-3400	16	131	129	46	16899	•		9600AC	
Warner Bros. Studio Facilities	818-954-2577	8	125	135	35	16875	•		Unlimited	
Warner Bros. Studio Facilities	818-954-2577	9	125	135	35	16875	•		Unlimited	
Warner Bros. Studio Facilities	818-954-2577	10	125	135	35	16875	•		Unlimited	
Warner Bros. Studio Facilities	818-954-2577	12	125	135	35	16875	•		Unlimited	
Warner Bros. Studio Facilities	818-954-2577	4	124	135	35	16740	•		Unlimited	
Warner Bros. Studio Facilities	818-954-2577	17	124	135	35	16740	•		Unlimited	
The Studios At Paramount	323-956-8811	8	147	113	30	16,611			120-208V / 13,200A	
The Studios At Paramount	323-956-8811	9	147	113	30	16,611			120-208V / 13,200A	
Sunset Gower Studios	323-467-1001	12	128	129	35	16459	•		4800AC	
Raleigh Studios - Hollywood	323-960-FILM	11	136	120	45	16320	•		6000 Amps	
Raleigh Studios - Hollywood	323-960-FILM	12	136	120	45	16320	•		8000 Amps	
Sunset Gower Studios	323-467-1001	9	149	107	35	16275	•		7200AC	
Fox Studios	310-369-2786	11	125	130	40	16250	•		7200AC Avail.	
Sony Pictures Studios	310-244-6926	23	157	102	35	16014	•		7200 Amps	
Sony Pictures Studios	310-244-6926	24	157	102	35	16014	•		7200 Amps	
South Bay Studios	310-762-1360	3	160	100	25	16000		•	Unlimited	3 wall hard
D.C. Stages & Sets	213-629-5434	II	232	68	19' 6	15776	•	•	500 Amps	
Fox Studios	310-369-2786	10	121	130	40	15730	•		7200AC Avail.	
Sunset Bronson Studios	323-460-5858	6	132	119	30	15708	•		12400 Amps	
The Studios At Paramount	323-956-8811	32	144	109	46	15,696			120-208V / 7,200A	
The Studios At Paramount	323-956-8811	29	145	108	35	15,660			120-208V / 9,600A	
Sony Pictures Studios	310-244-6926	14	88	177	34	15576	•		9600 Amps	

REHEARSAL STUDIOS	ADJUSTABLE GRID	WOOD FLOORS	CATWALK	SKYLIGHTS	DRIVE-IN	LOADING GATES	PRODUCTION OFFICE	AIR CONDITIONING	KITCHEN	DRESSING ROOMS	MAKEUP ROOMS	CONFERENCE ROOMS	PARKING	CONTROL ROOM	BLUE/GREEN SCREEN	AUDIENCE RATED	SCREENING ROOM	TANK	SILENT AC	TV STUDIO/VIDEO FACILITY	EDITING FACILITIES	GREEN ROOM	GRIP/LIGHTING EQUIP	BACKDROPS	RISERS	BACK LOT	SATELLITE UPLINK	WIRELESS BROADBAND
•		•		•		•	•	•	•	•	•	•			•	•							•					•
•		•		•		•	•	•	•	•	•	•			•	•							•					•
•		•		•		•	•	•	•	•	•	•			•	•					•		•					•
•		•		•		•	•	•	•	•	•	•			•	•			•	•	•	•	•					•
•		•			•	•	•	•	•	•	•	•			•					•	A		A				•	•
	•	•		•		•	•					•				A					A		A		A	A		A
•		•		•		•	•	•	•			•			•								•					•
•		•		•		•	•	•	•			•			•								•					•
•		•		•		•	•	•	•			•			•								•					•
•		•		•		•	•	•	•			•			•								•					•
•		•			•	A				•	•		•			A	•					A		A	A	A	•	
•		•			•	A				•	•		•			A						A		A	A	A	•	
•		•		•		•	•	•	•	•	•												•			•		•
•		•		•		•	•	•	•	•	•	•			•				•			A		A			•	•
•		•		•		•	•	•	•	•	•				•			•	•			•		•			•	•
	•	•		•		•	•					•			A							A		A		A	A		A
•		•		•		•	•	•	•	•	•												•			•		•
	•	•		•		•	•					•	•		•							•		•	•	•		
	•	•		•		•	•					•	•		•							•		•	•	•		
•		•			•		•			•	•		•	•		•						•		•	•			•
•		•			•		•			•	•		•	•		•						•		•	•			•
•		•	•			•				•	•		•	•		•						•		•	•			•
•		•	•			•				•	•		•	•		•						•		•	•	•		•
•		•			•		•			•	•	•	•			•						•		•	•	•		•
•		•			•							•										•						
	•	•		•		•	•					•			A							A		A		A	A		A
	•	•		•		•	•					•			A				•		A	•	A		A	A		A
•		•		•		•	•	•	•	•	•												•			•		•
	•	•		•		•	•			•	•	•	•										•			•		•
	•	•		•		•	•			•	•	•	•										•			•		•
	•	•		•		•	•			•	•		•							•	•		•	•	•		•	•
	•	•		•		•	•			•	•	•	•							•			A					•
	•	•		•		•	•			•	•	•	•						•				A					•
	•	•			•	•	•			•	•	•	•	A	•								A	A				•
•	•	•		•		•	•			•	•	•																
	•	•		•		•	•			•	•	•							•									•
	•	•		•		•	•			•	•	•									•							•
	•	•		•		•	•			•	•	•	•		A							A		A	A	A		A
	•	•		•		•	•			•	•	•	•		A							A		A	A	A		A
	•	•		•		•	•			•	•								•				A					•

A = Available to Rent

STAGE NAME	PHONE	STAGE NUMBER	LENGTH	WIDTH	HEIGHT	AREA SQUARE FEET	SOUND STAGE	INSERT	POWER/AMPS	CYCLORAMAS
Hollywood Center Studios	323-860-0000	10	154	101	35	15554	•		7200 amps	
Hollywood Center Studios	323-860-0000	11	154	101	35	15554	•		7200 amps	
The Studios At Paramount	323-956-8811	31	145	107	35	15,515			120-208V / 4,800A	
Sony Pictures Studios	310-244-6926	21	152	102	28	15504	•		7200 Amps	
Sony Pictures Studios	310-244-6926	22	152	102	28	15504	•		7200 Amps	
Sunset Gower Studios	323-467-1001	15	138	99	35	15271	•		4800AC	
The Studios At Paramount	323-956-8811	20	153	99	35	15,147			120-208V / 9,600A	
The Walt Disney Studios	818-560-7450	5	127	119	40	15113	•		Unlimited	
Sunset Gower Studios	323-467-1001	1	152	93.5	22	15083	•		7200AC	
Chandler Valley Center Studios, Inc.	818-763-3650	3	150	100	33	15000	•		4800AC	3 wall hard
North Field Properties/Hangar 8	310-392-8844	Hgr 8	100	150	30	15000			3PH/208V	
Prospect Studios	818-560-7450	7	150	100	42	15000	•	•	Unlimited	
Prospect Studios	818-560-7450	9	150	100	42	15000	•	•	Unlimited	
Stu Segall Productions	858-974-8988	3	100	150	14	15000	•	•	400AC	
The Walt Disney Studios	818-560-7450	6	150	100	40	15000	•		Unlimited	
The Walt Disney Studios	818-560-7450	7	150	100	40	15000	•		Unlimited	
The Studios At Paramount	323-956-8811	19	153	98	35	14,994			120-208V / 7,200A	
Warner Bros. Studio Facilities	818-954-2577	6	110	135	35	14850	•		Unlimited	
Warner Bros. Studio Facilities	818-954-2577	14	110	135	35	14850	•		Unlimited	
Warner Bros. Studio Facilities	818-954-2577	7	109	135	35	14715	•		Unlimited	
Warner Bros. Studio Facilities	818-954-2577	11	109	135	35	14715	•		Unlimited	
Warner Bros. Studio Facilities	818-954-2577	18	109	135	35	14715	•		Unlimited	
Warner Bros. Studio Facilities	818-954-2577	5	108	135	35	14580	•		Unlimited	
Chandler Valley Center Studios, Inc.	818-763-3650	2	145	100	35	14500	•		4800AC	3 wall hard
The Culver Studios	310-202-3400	6	142	102	30	14484	•		7200AC	
Hollywood Center Studios	323-860-0000	5	160	90	25	14400	•		3000 amps	1 wall hard
Quixote Studios Griffith Park	323-957-9933	7	120	120	42	14400	•		2400 Amps	
Raleigh Studios - Hollywood	323-960-FILM	1	125	115	35	14375	•		4800 Amps	
The Walt Disney Studios	818-560-7450	4	127	113	40	14351	•		Unlimited	
CBS Studio Center	818-655-5665	12	130	110	29	14300	•		6000AC/4800DC	
Raleigh Studios - Hollywood	323-960-FILM	14	130	110	30	14300	•		8000 Amps	
Universal Studios	818-777-3000	41	140	102	30' 1	14280	•		Unlimited	
Universal Studios	818-777-3000	42	140	102	30	14280	•		Unlimited	
Universal Studios	818-777-3000	43	140	102	30' 3	14280	•		Unlimited	
Universal Studios	818-777-3000	44	140	102	30	14280	•		Unlimited	
Sunset Gower Studios	323-467-1001	16	138	102	35	14143	•		4800AC	
Santa Clarita Studios	661-294-2000	7	94	150	35	14100	•		3600 Amps	
Santa Clarita Studios	661-294-2000	8	94	150	35	14100	•		3600 Amps	
Fox Studios	310-369-2786	17	138	102	35	14076	•		9000AC Avail.	
Fox Studios	310-369-2786	18	138	102	35	14076	•		6000AC Avail.	
Fox Studios	310-369-2786	19	138	102	35	14076	•		9000AC Avail.	
Fox Studios	310-369-2786	20	138	102	35	14076	•		3840AC Avail.	

REHEARSAL STUDIOS	ADJUSTABLE GRID	WOOD FLOORS	CATWALK	SKYLIGHTS	DRIVE-IN	LOADING GATES	PRODUCTION OFFICE	AIR CONDITIONING	KITCHEN	DRESSING ROOMS	MAKEUP ROOMS	CONFERENCE ROOMS	PARKING	CONTROL ROOM	BLUE/GREEN SCREEN	AUDIENCE RATED	SCREENING ROOM	TANK	SILENT AC	TV STUDIO/VIDEO FACILITY	EDITING FACILITIES	GREEN ROOM	GRIP/LIGHTING EQUIP	BACKDROPS	RISERS	BACK LOT	SATELLITE UPLINK	WIRELESS BROADBAND
	•	•		•	•	•	•		•	•	•	•	•						•	•		•	•				•	•
	•	•		•	•	•	•		•	•	•	•	•						•	•	•	•		•				•
	•	•		•	•	•	•		•	•	•		•		•	A					A	A		A	A			A
	•	•		•	•	•	•		•	•	•	•										A						•
	•	•		•	•	•	•		•	•	•	•								•	A							•
		•		•	•	•	•	•	•	•	•	•	•									•				•		•
	•	•		•		•						•		•	A						A	A		A	A			A
	•	•		•			•					•						•			A	A	A	A	•			•
	•	•		•		•		•	•	•	•	•										•		•	•			•
•				•		•	•		•	•	•			•	•		•			•		•	•					
•	•	•		•		•	•		•	•	•			•	•		•					•	•					
•	•	•		•		•	•		•	•	•			•	•	•				•		•						
•	•				•	•	•	•		•		•			•	•						•	•					•
•		•	•		•		•	•		•	•	•	•		•			•		A	•	A	A	A	A	•		•
•		•	•		•		•	•		•	•	•	•		•			•		A	•	A	A	A	A	•		•
•		•	•		•	•		•		•	•		•		•	A		•		A		A	A		A	A		A
•						•	•		•	•	•	•			•													
•		•				•			•			•																
•		•				•			•	•	•	•	•															
•		•				•			•			•																
•		•				•			•	•	•	•	•		•													
•						•		•	•		•		•	•						•		•	•					•
	•	•				•		•	•	•	•	•	•		•					•	•		•					•
	•	•				•		•	•	•	•	•	•		•					•	•	•	•					•
		•				•	•		•	•					•						•		•					
	•	•			•		•	•		•	•	•			•					•		•				•		•
	•				•		•				•				•	•					•	A	A	A	A	•		
	•	•			•			•		•	•				•							•				•		
	•	•			•		•	•		•	•	•			•	•					•		•				•	
•					•	A				•	•		•				A	•	•	A		A	A	A	•			
•		•			•	A				•	•		•				A	•	•	A		A	A	A	•			
•		•			•	A				•	•		•				A	•	•	A		A	A	A	•			
•		•			•	A				•	•		•				A	•		A		A	A	A	•			
		•			•			•	•	•	•	•										•		•	•			
•	•	•			•			•	•	•	•	•										•						•
	•	•			•		•	•	•	•	•	•									•	•						•
	•	•			•	•			•	•		•	•		•				•			A						
	•	•			•	•			•	•		•										A						
	•	•			•				•	•		•										A						
	•	•			•	•		•	•	•	•	•	•		•				•									

A = Available to Rent

STAGE NAME	PHONE	STAGE NUMBER	LENGTH	WIDTH	HEIGHT	AREA SQUARE FEET	SOUND STAGE	INSERT	POWER/AMPS	CYCLORAMAS
Fox Studios	310-369-2786	21	138	102	35	14076	•		3840AC Avail.	
Fox Studios	310-369-2786	22	138	102	35	14076	•		4800AC Avail.	
CBS Studio Center	818-655-5665	14–16	140	100	35	14000	•		5000AC/4800DC	
CBS Studio Center	818-655-5665	17	140	100	35	14000	•		5000AC/4800DC	
CBS Studio Center	818-655-5665	18	140	100	24	14000	•		6000AC/3200DC	
CBS Studio Center	818-655-5665	19	140	100	24	14000	•		6000AC/3200DC	
CBS Studio Center	818-655-5665	20	140	100	24	14000	•		3600AC/3200DC	
Occidental Studios, Inc.	213-384-3331	1	111	125	54	14000			7200 Amps	
Universal Studios	818-777-3000	37	140	100	30	14000	•		Unlimited	
Warner Bros. Ranch	818-954-2577	30	101	138	35	13938	•		Unlimited	
Universal Studios	818-777-3000	28	142	98	43' 11	13916	•		Unlimited	
The Studios At Paramount	323-956-8811	4	195	71	26	13,845			120-208V / 4,800A	
Studio 34	323-223-1234	2	192	72	20	13824	•		8600AC	
The Culver Studios	310-202-3400	14	136	101	39	13736	•		7200AC	
Universal Studios	818-777-3000	1	100	137	30	13700	•		Unlimited	
Universal Studios	818-777-3000	29	141	97	27	13677	•		Unlimited	
Universal Studios	818-777-3000	31	141	97	27	13677	•		Unlimited	
The Culver Studios	310-202-3400	12	136	99	40	13464	•		7200AC	
The Culver Studios	310-202-3400	5	131	102	30	13362	•		7200AC	
The Lot	323-850-3184	1	127	105	35	13335	•		4800 Amps	
The Lot	323-850-3184	2	127	105	35	13335	•		4800 Amps	
The Lot	323-850-3184	3	127	105	35	13335	•		4800 Amps	
The Lot	323-850-3184	4	127	105	35	13335	•		4800 Amps	
The Culver Studios	310-202-3400	11	136	98	40	13328	•		7200AC	
Raleigh Studios - Hollywood	323-960-FILM	5	148	90	35	13320	•		5600 Amps	3 wall hard
Century Studio Corporation	888-878-2437	1	125	105	22	13125	•	•	1800AC	2 wall hard
Century Studio Corporation	888-878-2437	2	125	144	22	13000	•	•	1200AC	
Saticoy Stage	818-909-6999	3	115'6	112'6	35	12994	•		12000AC	
The Studios At Paramount	323-956-8811	23	170	75	28	12,750			120-208V / 4,800A	
The Studios At Paramount	323-956-8811	24	170	75	28	12,750			120-208V / 7,200A	
The Studios At Paramount	323-956-8811	25	169	75	28	12,675			120-208V / 9,600A	
The Studios At Paramount	323-956-8811	17	186	68	36	12,648			120-208V / 7,200A	
Sony Pictures Studios	310-244-6926	10	144	86	29	12384	•		4800 Amps	
Sunset Gower Studios	323-467-1001	2	138	89	24	12383	•		7200AC	
Warner Bros. Ranch	818-954-2577	31	78	158	35	12324	•		Unlimited	
Universal Studios	818-777-3000	3	154	80	27' 2	12320	•		Unlimited	
CBS Studio Center	818-655-5665	4	120	100	26	12000	•		5000AC/11200DC	
CBS Studio Center	818-655-5665	5	120	100	26	12000	•		5000AC/9600DC	
Universal Studios	818-777-3000	23	157	76	28	11932	•		Unlimited	
Stu Segall Productions	858-974-8988	4	110	108	16	11880	•	•	400AC	
Delfino Studios	818-361-2421	4	163	72	14	11736	•		1800AC	
Sunset Gower Studios	323-467-1001	4	158	73	24	11678	•		4800AC	

REHEARSAL STUDIOS	ADJUSTABLE GRID	WOOD FLOORS	CATWALK	SKYLIGHTS	DRIVE-IN	LOADING GATES	PRODUCTION OFFICE	AIR CONDITIONING	KITCHEN	DRESSING ROOMS	MAKEUP ROOMS	CONFERENCE ROOMS	PARKING	CONTROL ROOM	BLUE/GREEN SCREEN	AUDIENCE RATED	SCREENING ROOM	TANK	SILENT AC	TV STUDIO/VIDEO FACILITY	EDITING FACILITIES	GREEN ROOM	GRIP/LIGHTING EQUIP	BACKDROPS	RISERS	BACK LOT	SATELLITE UPLINK	WIRELESS BROADBAND
		•	•		•		•	•	•	•		•	•		•													
		•	•		•		•	•	•			•	•		•							•						•
		•	•		•		•	•	•	•	•		•		•													•
		•	•		•		•	•	•	•			•		•									•				•
		•			•		•	•	•	•			•		•													•
		•	•		•		•	•	•	•			•		•									•				•
		•			•		•	•	•	•	•		•		•			•										•
•		•	•		•	•	A			•	•	•		•		A	•	•		A		A	A	A	•			
•		•			•		•		•				•							•	•	•	•	•	•	•		
•		•			•	•	A			•	•	•		•		A				A		A	A	A	A	•		
		•	•		•		•	•					•		A		•			A		A		A	A	A		A
		•	•		•		•	•				•	•								•	•						•
		•	•		•		•	•				•	•		•	•					•	•	•					•
•		•			•	•	A	•	•	•	•	•	•	•	•	•	•	•	A		•		A	A	A	•		
•		•			•	•	A	•		•			•		A	•				A		A	A	A	•			•
•		•	•		•	•	A	•		•			•		A	•				A		A	A	A	•			
		•	•		•	•	•	•		•	•		•		•	•				A		•						
		•	•		•	•	•	•		•			•		•	•				A		•						
		•	•		•	•	•	•		•	•	A	•		A					A		A	A		A	A		A
		•	•		•	•	•	•		•	•	A	•		A					A		A	A		A	A		A
		•	•		•	•	•	•		•	•	A	•		A					A		A	A		A	A		A
		•	•		•	•	•	•		•	•	A	•		A					A		A	A		A	A		A
		•	•		•	•	•	•		•	•		•		•	•			•	A		•						•
		•	•		•		•	•		•	•		•		•	•				•		•						•
	•	•			•		•	•		•	•		•		•	•				•		•						•
	•	•			•		•	•		•	•		•		•	•				•		•						•
•		•	•		•		•	•		•	•		•		•	•			•	•		•						•
		•	•		•		•	•					•		•	•	A		•	A		A		A	A		A	
		•	•		•		•	•					•		•	•	A		•	A		A		A	A		A	
		•	•		•		•	•	•				•		•	A												
		•	•		•		•	•				•	•		A											•		•
		•	•		•		•			•	•	•	•															
		•	•		•		•	•				•	•									•				•		•
•		•				•	A			•	•		•							A	•		A	A	A	•		•
					•		•	•		•	•		•		•							•	•					
					•		•	•		•	•		•		•													•
•	•	•			•		•	•			•		•							A	•		A	A	A	•		•
•	•			•			•	•			•		•						•			•	•			•		•
	•	•			•		•	•	•			•	•								•							
	•	•		•			•	•	•			•	•		•							•			•		•	

A = Available to Rent

STAGE NAME	PHONE	STAGE NUMBER	LENGTH	WIDTH	HEIGHT	AREA SQUARE FEET	SOUND STAGE	INSERT	POWER/AMPS	CYCLORAMAS
Century Studio Corporation	888-878-2437	6	111	105	13	11655	•	•	600AC	
Universal Studios	818-777-3000	22	157	74	27	11618	•		Unlimited	
The Studios At Paramount	323-956-8811	7	167	69	23/65	11,523			120-208V / 7,200A	
Santa Clarita Studios	661-294-2000	1	90	128	24	11520	•		3600 Amps	
Santa Clarita Studios	661-294-2000	2	90	128	24	11520	•		3600 Amps	2 wall hard
Santa Clarita Studios	661-294-2000	3	90	128	24	11520	•		3600 Amps	
Santa Clarita Studios	661-294-2000	4	90	128	24	11520	•		4800 Amps	
Santa Clarita Studios	661-294-2000	5	90	128	24	11520	•		3600 Amps	
Santa Clarita Studios	661-294-2000	6	90	128	24	11520	•		3600 Amps	
Universal Studios	818-777-3000	16	144	80	28' 8	11520	•		Unlimited	
Sunset Gower Studios	323-467-1001	3	157	72	24	11395	•		4800AC	
Sony Pictures Studios	310-244-6926	9	152	74	32	11248	•		7200 Amps	3 wall hard
Occidental Studios, Inc.	213-384-3338	8	187	60	22	11220	•		4800 Amps	
Red Studios	323-463-0808	6	70	160	30	11200	•		6500AC	
Stu Segall Productions	858-974-8988	6	80	140	14	11200	•	•	400AC	
GMT Studios	310-649-3733	7	116	96	25	11136	•		3600AC	
Encompass Digital Media	323-344-4500	2	110	100	18	11000	•			
South Bay Studios	310-762-1360	14	110	100	25	11000		•	Unlimited	3 wall hard
The Walt Disney Studios	818-560-7450	1	154	71	40	10934	•		Unlimited	
Sunset Gower Studios	323-467-1001	8	126.5	83	35	10915	•		7200AC	
Delfino Studios	818-361-2421	1	120	90	23	10800	•		Generator Req.	2 wall hard
Hollywood Center Studios	323-860-0000	6	120	90	26	10800	•		3000 amps	3 wall hard
Warner Bros. Studio Facilities	818-954-2577	1	109	99	35	10791	•		Unlimited	
Warner Bros. Studio Facilities	818-954-2577	3	109	99	35	10791	•		Unlimited	
Raleigh Studios - Playa Vista	323-960-3456	30	220	49	31	10780	•		2400 Amps	
Warner Bros. Studio Facilities	818-954-2577	2	109	98	35	10682	•		Unlimited	
The Studios At Paramount	323-956-8811	27	127	84	32	10,668			120-208V / 9,600A	
Warner Bros. Studio Facilities	818-954-2577	27	79	135	35	10665	•		Unlimited	
Warner Bros. Studio Facilities	818-954-2577	27a	79	135	35	10665	•		Unlimited	
Warner Bros. Studio Facilities	818-954-2577	28	79	135	35	10665	•		Unlimited	
Warner Bros. Studio Facilities	818-954-2577	28a	79	135	35	10665	•		Unlimited	
The Studios At Paramount	323-956-8811	1	146	73	25	10,658			120-208V / 7,200A	
Universal Studios	818-777-3000	18	144	74	29' 1	10656	•		Unlimited	
Universal Studios	818-777-3000	19	144	74	27' 10	10656	•		Unlimited	
Universal Studios	818-777-3000	20	144	74	27' 1	10656	•		Unlimited	
Universal Studios	818-777-3000	4	154	69	27' 10	10626	•		Unlimited	
Prospect Studios	818-560-7450	5	87	121	56	10527	•	•	Unlimited	
Sunset Bronson Studios	323-460-5858	9B	126	87	29	10420	•		4800 Amps	
The Lot	323-850-3184	5	112	92.5	35	10360	•		4800 Amps	
Lacy Street Production Center	323-222-8872	12	190	54	12	10260	•		400AC/3 Phase	
Universal Studios	818-777-3000	17	144	70	28' 10	10080	•		Unlimited	
Raleigh Studios - Manhattan Beach	310-727-2700	3A	94	107	25	10058	•		3600AC	

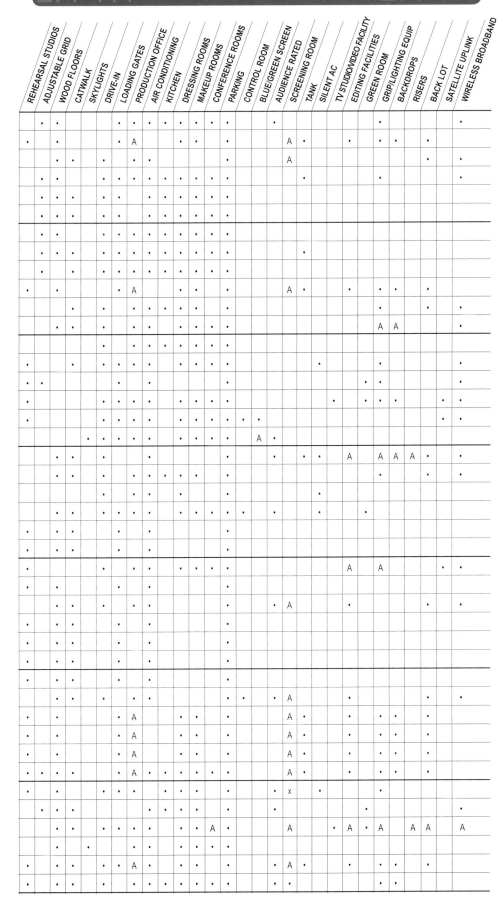

Rehearsal Studios	Adjustable Grid	Wood Floors	Catwalk	Skylights	Drive-In	Loading Gates	Production Office	Air Conditioning	Kitchen	Dressing Rooms	Makeup Rooms	Conference Rooms	Parking	Control Room	Blue/Green Screen	Audience Rated	Screening Room	Tank	Silent AC	TV Studio/Video Facility	Editing Facilities	Green Room	Grip/Lighting Equip	Backdrops	Risers	Back Lot	Satellite Uplink	Wireless Broadband
	•	•				•	•	•	•	•	•	•			•					•								•
•		•				•	A			•	•	•			A	•				•			•	•	•		•	
	•	•	•		•		•	•	•	•	•	•			A									•			•
	•	•	•			•	•	•	•	•	•	•															•	
	•	•	•			•	•	•	•	•	•	•																
	•	•	•			•	•	•	•	•	•	•																
	•	•	•		•		•	•	•	•	•	•					•											
	•		•			•	•	•	•	•	•	•																
•		•				•	A			•	•	•			A	•				•			•	•	•		•	
	•	•			•		•	•	•	•	•	•											•		•		•	
	•	•			•		•	•	•	•	•	•										A	A					•
		•			•		•	•	•	•	•	•																
•		•			•	•	•	•	•	•	•	•										•						•
•	•					•	•	•				•										•	•					•
•		•				•	•	•				•						•				•	•	•		•	•	
•						•	•	•	•	•	•	•	•	•												•	•	
			•		•	•	•	•				•		A	•													
	•	•		•		•		•				•		•		•	•		A		A	A	A	•				•
	•	•		•		•		•	•	•	•	•										•			•			•
		•			•	•	•			•		•			•			•										
		•	•		•	•	•			•		•		•			•			•								
•		•	•			•		•				•																
•		•	•			•		•				•																
•		•				•		•				•								A		A				•	•	
•		•				•		•				•								A		A						
	•	•			•		•	•			•	•		•	A					•					•		•	
	•	•			•		•	•				•																
	•	•			•		•					•																
	•	•			•		•					•																
•		•				•	•					•																
	•	•			•		•	•		•	•	•		•	A					•					•		•	•
•		•			•	A		•	•	•		•		A	•					•			•	•	•		•	
•		•			•	A		•	•	•		•		A	•					•			•	•	•		•	
•		•			•	A		•	•	•		•		A	•					•			•	•	•		•	
•	•	•			•	A	•	•	•	•	•	•		A	•					•			•	•	•		•	
•		•			•		•	•	•	•	•	•		•	x	•				•								
	•	•	•			•	•	•	•	•	•			•								•						•
	•	•		•	•	•	•	•		•	•	A	•		A		•	A	•	A	A	A		A				A
	•	•	•		•	•	•	•		•	•	•																
•		•	•		•	•	A	•		•	•	•		•	A	•				•			•	•	•		•	
•		•	•		•		•	•	•	•	•	•		•	•					•	•							

A = Available to Rent

STAGE NAME	PHONE	STAGE NUMBER	LENGTH	WIDTH	HEIGHT	AREA SQUARE FEET	SOUND STAGE	INSERT	POWER/AMPS	CYCLORAMAS
Centinela Studios	310-396-3688	B	200	50	22	10000			200AC/160DC	
GMT Studios	310-649-3733	1	100	100	18	10000	•	•	1200AC	2 wall hard
Hollywood Center Studios	323-860-0000	9	99	100	24	9900	•		4800 amps	
GMT Studios	310-649-3733	6	112	88	24	9856	•	•	3600AC	2 wall hard
Raleigh Studios - Playa Vista	323-960-3456	29	200	49	31	9800	•		5500 Amps	
Sunset Bronson Studios	323-460-5858	9A	118	87	29	9769	•		4800 Amps	
The Studios At Paramount	323-956-8811	30	107	90	35	9,630			120-208V / 7,200A	
Raleigh Studios - Hollywood	323-960-FILM	2	148	65	25	9620	•		2000 Amps	3 wall hard
Warner Bros. Ranch	818-954-2577	32	82	117	35	9594	•		Unlimited	
Stu Segall Productions	858-974-8988	5	106	90	14	9540	•	•	400AC	
The Lot	323-850-3184	6	98	92.5	35	9065	•		4800 Amps	
Laurel Canyon Stages	818-768-8935	A	133	68	18	9044	•	•	600-1200AC	2 wall hard
Delfino Studios	818-361-2421	2	100	90	28	9000	•		1800AC	
ShowBiz Studios	818-989-7007	2	100	90	18-12	9000	•		4800	1 Wall
The Production Group Studios	323-469-8111	1	100	90	18	9000	•		2000AC	3 hard, 4 soft
GMT Studios	310-649-3733	3	96	93	23	8928	•		1800AC	
The Studios At Paramount	323-956-8811	21	97	92	35	8,924			120-208V / 4,800A	
Universal Studios	818-777-3000	5	139	64	23' 4	8896	•		Unlimited	
Sunset Bronson Studios	323-460-5858	4	117	76	30	8892	•		9600 Amps	
Universal Studios	818-777-3000	6	139	63	19' 10	8757	•		Unlimited	
Century Studio Corporation	888-878-2437	9	80	108	25	8640	•	•	1200AC	
Raleigh Studios - Hollywood	323-960-FILM	3	148	58	28	8584	•		2800 Amps	
The Studios At Paramount	323-956-8811	2	148	57	26	8,436			120-208V / 7,200A	
D.C. Stages & Sets	213-629-5434	I	123	68	19' 6	8364	•	•	500Amps	
The Studios At Paramount	323-956-8811	28	99	84	33	8,316			120-208V / 2,400A	2 wall hard
Occidental Studios, Inc.	213-384-3332	2	108	76	26	8208	•		3600 Amps	
Universal Studios	818-777-3000	747	139	59	21'2	8201	•		Unlimited	
The Lot	323-850-3184	7	112	72.5	27	8120	•		4800 Amps	3 wall hard
Occidental Studios, Inc.	213-384-3333	3	130	62	19	8060	•		3600 Amps	
Glendale Studios	818-550-6000	1	100	80	18	8000	•	•	5000AC	4 wall soft
Hayvenhurst Stage	818-909-6999	2	100	80	28	8000	•		5000AC/750DC	3 wall hard
Hollywood Center Studios	323-860-0000	7	100	80	24	8000	•		2400 amps	
Occidental Studios, Inc.	213-384-3336	6	100	80	14	8000	•		2400 Amps	
Prospect Studios	818-560-7450	2	106	74	22	7844	•	•	Unlimited	
KCET Studios	323-953-5258	2	110	70	25' 6	7700	•		1200AC	180 white/black
Redemption Stages	818-238-0012	1	120	64	18	7680	•		2400	
Sunset Bronson Studios	323-460-5858	1	108	72	30	7655	•		4800 Amps	
Warner Bros. Ranch	818-954-2577	34	78	98	20	7644	•	•	Unlimited	
Sunset Bronson Studios	323-460-5858	5	101	75	30	7575	•		9600 Amps	
The Studios At Paramount	323-956-8811	6	109	69	30	7,521			120-208V / 9,600A	
The Henson Soundstage	323-856-2682	1	100	75	26	7500	•	•	1200 Amps	3 wall hard
Quixote Studios Griffith Park	323-957-9933	6	120	60	21'8"-17'	7200	•		1200amps	3 wall hard

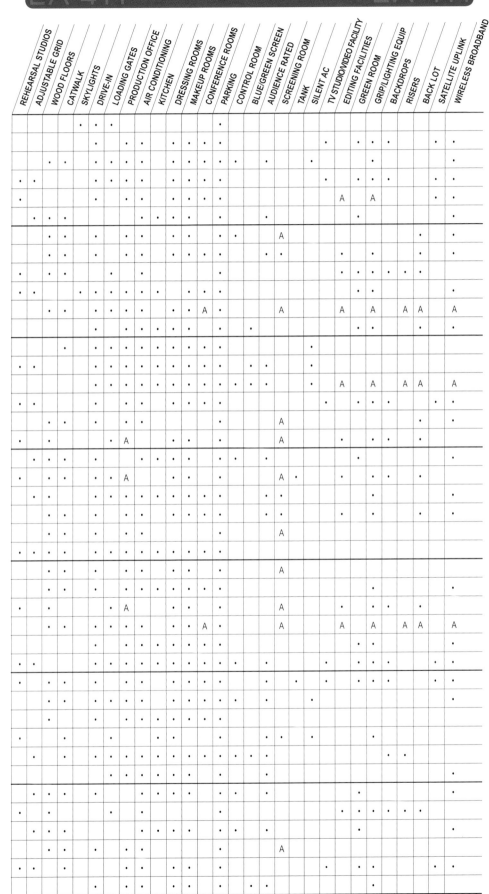

REHEARSAL STUDIOS	ADJUSTABLE GRID	WOOD FLOORS	CATWALK	SKYLIGHTS	DRIVE-IN	LOADING GATES	PRODUCTION OFFICE	AIR CONDITIONING	KITCHEN	DRESSING ROOMS	MAKEUP ROOMS	CONFERENCE ROOMS	PARKING	CONTROL ROOM	BLUE/GREEN SCREEN	AUDIENCE RATED	SCREENING ROOM	TANK	SILENT AC	TV STUDIO/VIDEO FACILITY	EDITING FACILITIES	GREEN ROOM	GRIP/LIGHTING EQUIP	BACKDROPS	RISERS	BACK LOT	SATELLITE UPLINK	WIRELESS BROADBAND
				•	•	•							•															
					•		•		•		•	•	•	•					•			•	•	•			•	•
	•	•			•	•	•	•		•	•	•	•	•		•			•			•	•	•			•	•
•	•				•		•		•	•	•	•	•							A		A					•	•
	•	•	•				•		•	•		•	•		•							•						•
	•	•			•		•		•	•		•	•			A									•			•
	•	•			•		•		•	•		•	•		•	•						•			•			•
•		•	•			•		•		•			•							•	•	•	•	•	•	•		
•	•	•			•		•		•	•	•	•	•									•	•					•
	•	•			•		•		•	•	•	•	•	A	•		A			A		A		A	A			A
					•		•	•	•	•	•		•			•			•			•	•			•		•
			•		•		•		•	•	•	•	•	•				•										
•	•				•		•		•	•	•	•	•	•		•	•			•								
	•	•			•		•	•	•	•	•	•	•	•	•	•	•				•	A		A		A	A		A
•		•			•		•		•	•		•	•					•			•	•	•	•			•	•
	•	•		•		•	•			•		•			A						•						•	•
•		•			•		A		•	•		•			A					•		•	•	•			•	
	•	•	•		•				•	•	•	•		•	•							•						
	•	•	•		•		A		•	•		•			A	•				•		•	•	•			•	
	•	•			•		•	•	•	•	•	•	•		•	•					•		•			•		•
	•	•			•		•		•	•	•	•	•		•	•				•		•			•			•
	•	•			•		•	•	•			•			A													
•	•	•			•		•	•	•	•	•	•	•		•	•												
	•	•			•		•		•	•		•	•		A													
	•	•			•		•		•	•		•										•						•
•		•			•		A		•	•		•			A					•		•	•	•		•		
	•	•			•	•	•			•	A	•			A					A		A		A	A			A
					•		•	•	•		•	•	•			•						•	•	•				
•	•				•		•			•			•	•					•			•	•	•			•	•
•		•	•		•		•		•	•		•				•		•				•	•	•			•	•
	•	•			•		•		•	•	•	•	•					•										•
	•	•			•		•		•	•	•	•	•															
	•	•			•		•				•	•		•								•						
•		•			•				•	•		•		•	•		•					•						
	•		•		•		•			•		•		•	•	•	•											•
	•				•				•	•		•		•								•						•
	•		•		•		•			•	•		•			•						•						•
•	•	•			•				•	•		•			•	•						•	•					
	•	•			•		•		•	•		•										•						•
	•	•			•		•	•			•			•		A						•	•					
•	•	•			•		•			•	•		•							•		•	•				•	•
					•		•	•			•	•		•	•							•						

A = Available to Rent

STAGE NAME	PHONE	STAGE NUMBER	LENGTH	WIDTH	HEIGHT	AREA SQUARE FEET	SOUND STAGE	INSERT	POWER/AMPS	CYCLORAMAS
South Bay Studios	310-762-1360	1	120	60	19	7200	•	•	Unlimited	3 wall hard
CBS Studio Center	818-655-5665	11	110	65	27	7150	•		3600AC/4800DC	
Solar Studios	818-240-1893	1	110	65	14-22	7150	•	•	1200 Amps	2 wall hard
Redemption Stages	818-238-0012	2	110	64	18	7040	•		2400	2 wall
ShowBiz Studios	818-989-7007	4	105	67	30	7035	•		4800	2 Wall
Line 204 Studios	323-960-0113	B/West	100	70	27	7000	•		1200AC	
South Bay Studios	310-762-1360	2	140	50	25	7000		•	Unlimited	3 wall hard
Sunset Bronson Studios	323-460-5858	2	94	75.5	30	6935	•		9600 Amps	
Sunset Bronson Studios	323-460-5858	3	100	76	30	6916	•		9600 Amps	
UFO - The Poodle Parlor	213-694-0556	1	88	78	15	6864			400AC	
Universal Studios	818-777-3000	33	99	69	25	6831	•		Unlimited	
Universal Studios	818-777-3000	34	99	69	25	6831	•		Unlimited	
Universal Studios	818-777-3000	35	99	69	25	6831	•		Unlimited	
Universal Studios	818-777-3000	UVS1	99	69	24' 11	6831	•		Unlimited	green hard
The Studios At Paramount	323-956-8811	26	100	68	28	6,800			120-208V / 9,600A	
Hollywood Center Studios	323-860-0000	1	97	70	24	6790	•		4800 amps	3 wall hard
Hollywood Center Studios	323-860-0000	2	97	70	24	6790	•		4800 amps	
D.C. Stages & Sets	213-629-5434	MILL	169	40	19' 6	6760	•	•	500 Amps	
Raleigh Studios - Hollywood	323-960-FILM	7	90	75	20	6750	•		2000 Amps	2 wall hard
Avenue Six Studios	818-781-6600	East (1)	81	81	16	6561	•		400 Amps	2 walls hard
KCET Studios	323-953-5258	1	92	70	25' 6	6440	•		1200AC	180 white/black
The Culver Studios	310-202-3400	2	54	119	40	6426	•		120/208V	
Apache Studios	818-842-9944	1	70	90	21	6300	•	•	2400 Amps	3 wall soft
Gothic Moon Studio	714-453-0970	1	90	70	14	6300	•		800 Amps	2 wall hard
Line 204 Studios	323-960-0113	A/East	90	70	25	6300	•		1200AC	2 wall hard
Studio C2	310-761-1767	1	105	60	24	6300			1200AC	3 wall hard
Laurel Canyon Stages	818-768-8935	B	93	67	18	6231			600-1200AC	
The Studios At Paramount	323-956-8811	12	95	65	38	6,175		•	120-208V / 2,400A	
Warner Bros. Ranch	818-954-2577	33	78	78	20	6084	•	•	Unlimited	
Raleigh Studios - Hollywood	323-960-FILM	10	79	77	20	6083	•		3600 Amps	
The Studios At Paramount	323-956-8811	11	95	64	38	6,080		•	120-208V / 2,400A	
Line 204 Studios	323-960-0113	South	100	60	24	6000	•		1200AC	2 wall hard
Raleigh Studios - Hollywood	323-960-FILM	8	100	60	20	6000	•		1200 Amps	
Mack Sennett Stage/Triangle	323-660-8466	1	100	55	23	5800	•		1200AC	3 wall hard
AMP Studios	805-955-7742	A	85	68	26	5780	•		5640 Amps	3 wall soft
Century Studio Corporation	888-878-2437	5	114	50	23	5700	•	•	1800AC	
Sunset Bronson Studios	323-460-5858	10	81	76	29	5600	•		2400 Amps	
The Culver Studios	310-202-3400	7	80	70	30	5600	•		2400AC	
The Culver Studios	310-202-3400	8	80	70	29	5600	•		2400AC	
The Culver Studios	310-202-3400	9	80	70	30	5600	•		2400AC	
The Studios At Paramount	323-956-8811	3	94	59	37	5,546		•	120-208V / 7,200A	
Ben Kitay Studios	323-466-9015	20	110	50	20	5500	•	•	2400AC	3 wall hard

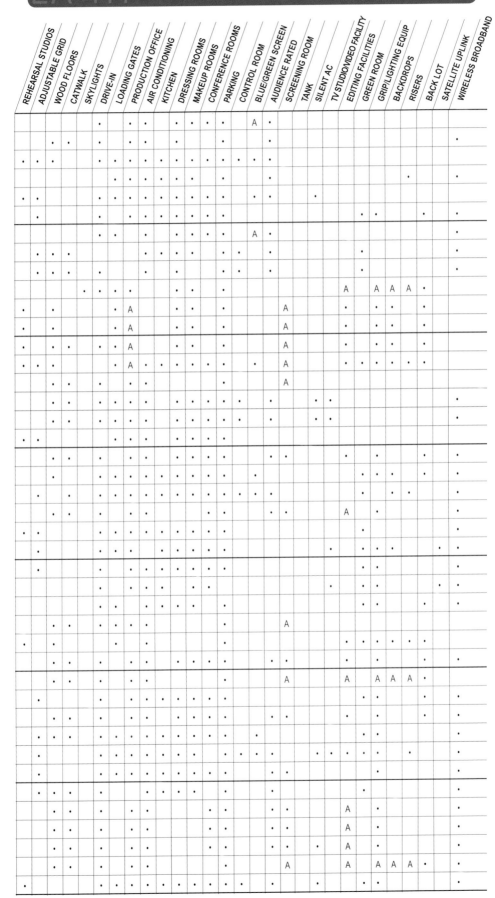

REHEARSAL STUDIOS	ADJUSTABLE GRID	WOOD FLOORS	CATWALK	SKYLIGHTS	DRIVE-IN	LOADING GATES	PRODUCTION OFFICE	AIR CONDITIONING	KITCHEN	DRESSING ROOMS	MAKEUP ROOMS	CONFERENCE ROOMS	PARKING	CONTROL ROOM	BLUE/GREEN SCREEN	AUDIENCE RATED	SCREENING ROOM	TANK	SILENT AC	TV STUDIO/VIDEO FACILITY	EDITING FACILITIES	GREEN ROOM	GRIP/LIGHTING EQUIP	BACKDROPS	RISERS	BACK LOT	SATELLITE UPLINK	WIRELESS BROADBAND
		•			•	•		•		•	•	•	•	A	•													
	•	•			•	•		•			•			•														•
•	•	•			•	•	•	•	•	•	•	•	•	•	•													•
					•	•	•	•		•	•	•	•	•														
•	•				•		•	•		•		•	•	•			•											•
	•				•		•			•		•		A	•													
•	•		•		•	•	•	•	•	•	•		•			•					•	•						•
•	•				•		•			•		•		•			•				•							•
			•	•	•	•	•			•	•		•							A		A	A	A	•			
•		•			•	A		•	•		•		A							•		•	•		•			
•		•			•	A		•	•		•		A							•		•	•		•			
•	•	•		•	•	A		•	•		•		A							•		•	•		•			
•	•	•		•	•	A	•	•	•	•		•	A							•		•	•	•	•			
	•	•		•		•	•			•		A																
	•	•	•	•	•		•	•	•		•							•	•									•
	•	•	•	•	•		•	•	•		•							•	•									•
•	•				•	•		•	•	•	•																	
	•	•		•	•	•	•	•	•	•	•			•	•					•		•			•			
	•			•	•	•	•	•	•	•	•	•	•	•						•	•	•						•
	•			•	•	•	•	•	•	•	•	•	•	•						•	•	•	•	•				•
	•	•		•	•	•		•	•	•	•			•	•					A		•					•	
•	•				•	•	•	•	•	•	•	•	•									•	•					•
	•			•	•	•	•	•	•	•	•	•	•								•	•	•	•			•	•
	•				•	•	•	•	•	•	•		•							•		•	•					•
	•				•		•	•	•	•	•	•									•	•						•
	•				•	•	•	•	•		•		•							•		•	•					•
•	•			•	•		•		•			•		A								•	•	•	•	•		
	•	•			•	•	•		•		•									•		•	•					•
	•	•		•	•		•	•		•			•							•	•	•						
	•	•		•	•		•	•	•	•	•		•									A		A	A	A	•	
	•			•	•		•	•	•	•	•	•	•									•						•
	•			•	•		•	•	•	•	•	•			•	•						•						•
•	•			•	•		•	•	•	•	•	•	•	•								•	•					•
•	•			•	•		•	•	•	•	•	•	•						•	•	•	•						•
	•				•	•	•	•	•	•	•	•			•	•						•						•
	•	•		•	•		•			•		•								•		•						•
	•	•		•	•		•		•		•		•							A		•						•
	•	•		•	•		•		•		•		•							A		•						•
	•	•		•	•		•		•	•		•			•				•		A		•					•
	•			•	•	•		•	•	•	•	•			•		A			A		A	A	A	•			•
•					•	•		•	•	•	•	•	•	•					•			•	•					•

A = Available to Rent

STAGE NAME	PHONE	STAGE NUMBER	LENGTH	WIDTH	HEIGHT	AREA SQUARE FEET	SOUND STAGE	INSERT	POWER/AMPS	CYCLORAMAS
Stu Segall Productions	858-974-8988	1	55	100	16	5500	•	•	400AC	
Avenue Six Studios	818-781-6600	South (3)	137	40	15	5480				
Quixote Studios Griffith Park	323-957-9933	10	94	58	18-16	5452	•		1200 Amps	3 wall hard
Sunset Gower Studios	323-467-1001	5	86	60	19	5160	•		4800AC	
Prospect Studios	818-560-7450	1	74	68	35	5032	•	•	Unlimited	
Raleigh Studios - Hollywood	323-960-FILM	9	100	50	20	5000	•		3200 Amps	3 wall hard
South Bay Studios	310-762-1360	10-12	100	50	25	5000		•	Unlimited	2 & 3 wall hard
GMT Studios	310-649-3733	4	70	70	24	4900	•	•	1200AC	2 wall hard
Grant McCune Design, Inc.	818-779-1920	3	100	49	16	4900			600AC	
Paladin Stage	323-851-8222	1	80	60	24	4800	•		1600AC	2 wall hard
South Bay Studios	310-762-1360	5	80	60	19	4800	•	•	Unlimited	3 wall hard
Ben Kitay Studios	323-466-9015	10	80	59	17	4720	•	•	1200AC	3 wall hard
Siren Studios	323-467-3559	2	55	85	16	4675	•		1400 Amps	4 wall soft
Orange County Studio	323-965-8881		70	66		4620	•	•		
Occidental Studios, Inc.	213-384-3341	12	74	62	20	4588	•		2400 Amps	2 wall hard
BelleVarado Studios	213-503-0661	22	40	40	18	4500	•		200/200 Amps	3 wall
Hip Studios	323-467-2897	B	90	50	17	4500	•		600Amps	3 wall hard
Occidental Studios, Inc.	213-384-3339	9	80	55	17	4400	•		1600 Amps	
Avenue Six Studios	818-781-6600	North (2)	75	57	17	4275	•		240 Amps	2 walls hard
Occidental Studios, Inc.	213-384-3341	11	75	55	16	4125	•		2400 Amps	2 wall hard
Studio 34	323-223-1234	1	84	48	19	4032	•		8600AC	
Big Vision Studios	818-841-4008	1	80	50	24	4000	•	•	400AC	2 wall grn scrn
Cutting Edge Productions	310-326-4500	1	80	50	17	4000	•	•	2500AC	2 wall hard
GMT Studios	310-649-3733	2	80	50	17	4000	•	•	600AC	3 wall hard
Hollywood Center Studios	323-860-0000	12	80	50	20	4000	•		2400 amps	3 wall green
Stargate Stage	626-403-8403	1	80	50	25	4000		•		1 wall hard
Stu Segall Productions	858-974-8988	2	80	50	16	4000	•	•	400AC	
Studio C2	310-761-1767	2	80	50	24	4000			400AC	
SmashBox Studios	310-558-7660	STG	80	49	22	3920	•	•	1200AC	2 wall hard
Sunset Bronson Studios	323-460-5858	7	80	49	21	3920	•			
Raleigh Studios - Hollywood	323-960-FILM	6	95	38	18	3800	•		2800 Amps	3 wall hard
Ben Kitay Studios	323-466-9015	5	75	50	17	3750	•	•	1200AC	3 wall hard
Big Picture Soundstage	818-842-6060		75	50	25	3750	•		1200 Amps	2 wall
Glendale Studios	818-550-6000	2	75	50	18	3750	•	•	5000AC	4 wall soft
Red Studios	323-463-0808	7	63	58	38	3654	•	•	4000AC	3 wall hard
Apache Studios	818-842-9944	2	90	40	15	3600	•	•	2400 Amps	
HD Vision Broadcast Center	818-769-4500	A	60	60	16	3600	•	•	400 Amps	
Source Film Studio	323-463-5555	2	71	46	27	3266	•	•	2000 Amps	3 wall
5th & Sunset Los Angeles	310-979-0212	XXL	50	65	13	3250			900AC	2 wall hard
Ben Kitay Studios	323-466-9015	15	72	45	20	3240	•	•	1800AC	3 wall hard
Sanders Studio	714-444-3000	1	30	24	12	3200			300	8 corners
Image G - HD Broadcast Center	818-769-4500	A	60	52	17	3120	•		400AC	1 wall hard

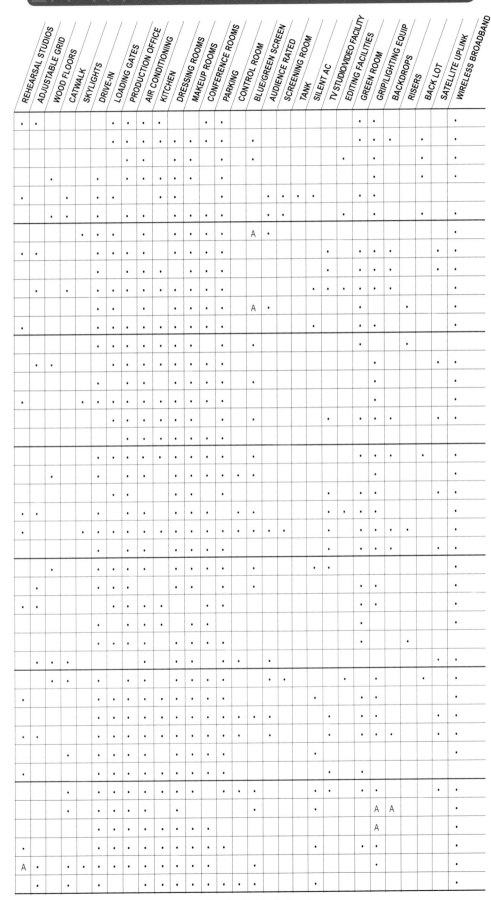

REHEARSAL STUDIOS	ADJUSTABLE GRID	WOOD FLOORS	CATWALK	SKYLIGHTS	DRIVE-IN	LOADING GATES	PRODUCTION OFFICE	AIR CONDITIONING	KITCHEN	DRESSING ROOMS	MAKEUP ROOMS	CONFERENCE ROOMS	PARKING	CONTROL ROOM	BLUE/GREEN SCREEN	AUDIENCE RATED	SCREENING ROOM	TANK	SILENT AC	TV STUDIO/VIDEO FACILITY	EDITING FACILITIES	GREEN ROOM	GRIP/LIGHTING EQUIP	BACKDROPS	RISERS	BACK LOT	SATELLITE UPLINK	WIRELESS BROADBAND
•	•					•	•	•	•			•	•									•	•					•
						•	•	•	•	•	•		•	•								•	•	•		•		•
						•	•		•	•		•	•								•	•				•		•
		•			•		•	•	•	•		•										•				•		•
•			•			•	•		•	•		•			•		•	•	•			•				•		•
		•	•		•		•		•	•		•		A	•							•						•
•	•					•	•	•	•		•	•	•						•			•	•	•		•	•	•
						•	•	•	•	•	•		•						•			•	•	•		•	•	•
		•				•	•	•	•	•		•							•	•		•				•	•	•
						•	•	•	•	•	•		•	A	•							•			•			•
•						•	•	•	•	•		•										•	•					•
						•	•	•	•	•	•		•		•							•			•			•
	•		•			•	•	•	•	•		•										•				•		•
						•	•	•	•	•	•		•		•							•				•		•
•		•				•	•	•	•	•	•		•								•				•		•	•
						•	•	•	•	•	•		•						•			•				•		•
						•	•	•	•													•						•
						•	•	•	•		•	•	•	•								•		•	•	•		•
		•				•	•	•	•	•		•							•			•						•
						•	•	•	•	•	•		•		•						•	•			•		•	•
•					•	•	•	•	•	•	•	•	•		•						•	•	•	•	•		•	•
•				•		•	•	•	•	•	•	•	•	•	•							•	•	•	•		•	•
						•	•	•	•	•		•	•		•						•	•	•	•	•		•	•
	•					•	•	•	•	•	•		•	•			•	•				•	•					•
	•	•				•	•	•	•	•		•			•							•	•					•
•	•					•	•	•	•			•	•									•	•				•	•
						•	•	•	•	•	•		•									•				•		•
		•				•	•	•	•	•		•	•									•		•				•
						•	•	•	•	•		•	•									•					•	•
	•	•				•	•	•	•	•			•	•								•	•				•	•
•						•	•	•	•	•	•	•	•									•	•					•
						•	•	•	•	•	•		•	•		•						•	•				•	•
•	•					•	•	•	•	•	•		•		•							•	•	•			•	•
		•				•	•	•	•	•	•		•						•			•					•	•
•						•	•	•	•	•	•		•									•						•
		•				•	•	•	•	•			•	•	•							•	•				•	•
		•				•	•	•	•	•		•	•									A	A					•
						•	•	•	•	•		•	•									A						•
•						•	•	•	•	•		•							•			•	•					•
A	•				•	•	•	•	•	•		•	•		•							•						•
	•			•		•		•	•	•	•	•	•	•					•									•

A = Available to Rent

STAGE NAME	PHONE	STAGE NUMBER	LENGTH	WIDTH	HEIGHT	AREA SQUARE FEET	SOUND STAGE	INSERT	POWER/AMPS	CYCLORAMAS
The Culver Studios	310-202-3400	10	79	39	20	3081	•		2400AC	
Dirt Cheap Sound Stage	310-401-3171		60	50	22	3000	•	•	600 Amps	2 wall soft
Evidence Productions	323-522-5298	Green	60	50	16	3000			100	1 Wall
Solar Studios	818-240-1893	2	75	40	19	3000		•	600 Amps	3 wall hard
The L.A. Lofts	323-462-5880	2	70	30	12	3000			200 Amps	
30th Street Garage	619-234-4325		62	48	18	2976			200 Amps	
Coastal Media Group	310-775-7362	1	48	62	18	2976	•	•	600 Amps	2 wall hard
UFO - The Poodle Parlor	213-694-0556	2	99	29	12	2871			400AC	
Panavision	818-316-1080	1	51	54	16	2754	•	•	1200Amps	2 wall hard
AMP Studios	805-955-7742	B	60	45	22	2700	•		4300 Amps	3 wall soft
Hollywood Center Studios	323-860-0000	2A	57	48	20	2700	•		4800 amps	2 wall hard
SmashBox Studios	310-558-7660	SB	55	48	22	2640			200AC	1 wall hard
The Production Group Studios	323-469-8111	2	60	43	18	2580	•		400AC	3 wall soft,hard
Hollywood Loft	323-957-9398	1	35	32	15	2500	•	•	200AC	1 wall hard
The L.A. Lofts	323-462-5880	1	50	30	12	2500			200 Amps	
The L.A. Lofts	323-462-5880	4	30	45	12	2500		•	200 Amps	1 wall
5th & Sunset Los Angeles	310-979-0212	XL	40	60	12	2400			300AC	1 wall
Epiphany Media	323-960-4000	6	60	40	15	2400	•	•	2000	3 wall
SmashBox Studios	310-558-7660	LB	75	32	18	2400			200AC	
5th & Sunset Los Angeles	310-979-0212	L	42	53	15	2226			600AC	1 wall
Sunset Bronson Studios	323-460-5858	8	50	42	21	2100	•			
UCLA Dept of Film & TV	310-267-5369	1&2	37	56	25	2072	•		100AC	
Siren Studios	323-467-3559	1	50	40	25	2000			1400 Amps	4 wall hard
Stage 1 on Lemona	818-787-5294	1	40	50	14	2000		•	800 Amps	1 wall both
5th & Sunset Los Angeles	310-979-0212	M	36	54	15	1944			300AC	1 wall
Digital Film Studios	818-771-0019	1	55	35	15.5	1925		•	600 Amps	3 wall
SmashBox Studios	310-558-7660	BB	48	38	22	1824			200AC	2 wall hard
Mack Sennett Stage/Triangle	323-660-8466	2	60	35	23	1800		•	600AC	
Screenland Studios	818-508-2288	D	60	30	14' 6	1800			220AC	
Sound Matrix Studios	714-437-9696	A	38	47	18	1786	•		450 Amps	2 hard w/catwalk
Sound Matrix Studios	714-437-9696	B	38	44	18	1672	•		450 Amps	
The Focus Studio	310-399-9400	1	43	37	12	1591			250 Amps	
Encompass Digital Media	323-344-4500	3	36	44	11	1584	•			
Silver Dream Factory	714-836-1853	2	45	35	16	1575	•	•	400AC	
Avenue Six Studios	818-781-6600	Backlot	128	11.5		1472				
Huron Substation	323-225-8909		46	32	45	1472			200AC	
UFO - The Poodle Parlor	213-694-0556	3	49	29	18	1421			400AC	
5th & Sunset Los Angeles	310-979-0212	S	35	40	18	1400			300AC	1 wall
The L.A. Lofts	323-462-5880	3	28	30	12	1400			120 Amps	
SmashBox Studios	310-558-7660	Sky	35	39	13	1365			200AC	
SmashBox Studios	310-558-7660	SM	42	32	14	1344		•	200AC	1 wall hard
South Bay Studios	310-762-1360	6–9	40	32	27	1280		•	Unlimited	

REHEARSAL STUDIOS	ADJUSTABLE GRID	WOOD FLOORS	CATWALK	SKYLIGHTS	DRIVE-IN	LOADING GATES	PRODUCTION OFFICE	AIR CONDITIONING	KITCHEN	DRESSING ROOMS	MAKEUP ROOMS	CONFERENCE ROOMS	PARKING	CONTROL ROOM	BLUE/GREEN SCREEN	AUDIENCE RATED	SCREENING ROOM	TANK	SILENT AC	TV STUDIO/VIDEO FACILITY	EDITING FACILITIES	GREEN ROOM	GRIP/LIGHTING EQUIP	BACKDROPS	RISERS	BACK LOT	SATELLITE UPLINK	WIRELESS BROADBAND
		•	•		•	•						•	•		•	•				A		•						•
•		•					•	•	•				•		•							•	•					•
			•		•	•	•	•	•				•		•							•						•
•	•		•		•	•	•	•	•				•	•	•							•						•
		•			•	•	•	•	•										•			•	•					•
			•		•				•				•									•						•
•	•				•	•	•	•	•	•	•	•	•	•	•			•	•	•		•	•			•	•	•
			•		•	•	•	•		•	•		•							A		A	A	A	•			
			•		•	•	•	•		•	•		•				•		•			•						
			•		•	•	•	•		•	•	•	•					•	•			•		•				•
		•	•	•				•		•	•	•	•	•								•						
			•		•	•		•		•	•	•	•									•						
			•		•	•	•	•		•	•	•	•						•		A		A		A	A		A
•		•		•		•	•	•	•		•	•	•									•						•
		•		•		•	•	•	•		•	•	•	•							A		A		A	A		A
		•		•		•	•	•	•		•		•								A		A		A	A		A
													•								A							•
	•	•			•			•		•			•						•			•	•				•	•
			•		•	•		•		•			•															
			•		•	•	•	•		•			•								A							•
	•	•			•			•		•		•	•		•							•				•		•
	•		•		•	•	•	•		•			•								A		A	A	A	•		
			•		•	•		•		•			•	•					•			•	•					•
			•		•			•		•			•									•						•
		•			•	•		•		•			•								A							•
•	•				•	•		•		•			•		•							•						•
			•		•	•		•		•			•															
	•	•			•	•		•		•		•	•		•				•		•		•	•			•	•
•			•		•	•		•		•			•		•							•						•
		•		•		•	•		•		•		•		•				•			•	A	A				•
•		•			•	•	•	•	•		•		•		•							•	A	A				•
			•		•			•		•			•						•			•	•				•	•
			•		•	•	•	•	•		•		•		•												•	•
					•	•					•		•															
			•		•			•		•			•									•	•	•		•		•
•				•	•	•		A		•	•																	
			•		•			•	•		•		•								A		A	A	A	•		
		•			•			•	•		•	•									A		A					•
		•			•			•	•		•	•									A		A		A	A		A
			•		•	•		•		•	•	•										•		•				•
			•		•			•		•	•	•																
			•		•	•		•	•	•	•		A									•	•					•

A = Available to Rent

STAGE NAME	PHONE	STAGE NUMBER	LENGTH	WIDTH	HEIGHT	AREA SQUARE FEET	SOUND STAGE	INSERT	POWER/AMPS	CYCLORAMAS
Affordable Sound Stages	818-563-3456	1	40	30	18	1200		•	200 Amps	2 wall hard
Apache Studios	818-842-9944	3	30	40	20	1200	•	•		
The Production Group Studios	323-469-8111	3	40	30	13	1200	•		800AC	3 wall hard
Source Film Studio	323-463-5555	1	45	25	15	1125	•	•	300 Amps	4 wall
Occidental Studios, Inc.	213-384-3334	4	36	31	14	1116	•		1200 Amps	
Railroad Studios	888-662-3647	1	38	29	19	1102	•		450 Amps	2 wall hard
Albuerne, Inc.	323-665-1307	1	35	30	12	1050	•	•	600 Amps	2 wall covered
Hollywood Camera, Inc.	818-972-5000	1	30	35	16	1050	•	•	600AC	
Occidental Studios, Inc.	213-384-3340	10	32	32	17	1024	•		400 Amps	
Silver Dream Factory	714-836-1853	1	40	25	16	1000	•	•	240AC	1 wall
Pacific Motion Control, Inc.	818-768-1573	1	25	39	16	975		•	200 Amps	
UCLA Dept of Film & TV	310-267-5369	TV2	33	29	15	957	•		100AC	
RecCenter Studio	213-413-9300	1	38	24	19	912				
Digital Film Studios	818-771-0019	2	35	24	15	840		•	200-400 Amps	1 wall
Revolutionary Productions	310-613-8094	1	30	25	10	750			100 Amps	3 wall soft
CAP, Complete Actors Place	818-990-2001		30	24	18	720				
Screenland Studios	818-508-2288	E	35	20	10	700			220AC	
studio/stage	323-463-3900	1	29	22	14	638	•	•	400 Amps	3 wall hard
Hollywood Center Studios	323-860-0000	Virtual	26	20	11	520	•		300 amps	3 wall green
Image G - HD Broadcast Center	818-769-4500	Stage B	20	20	17	400	•		400AC	

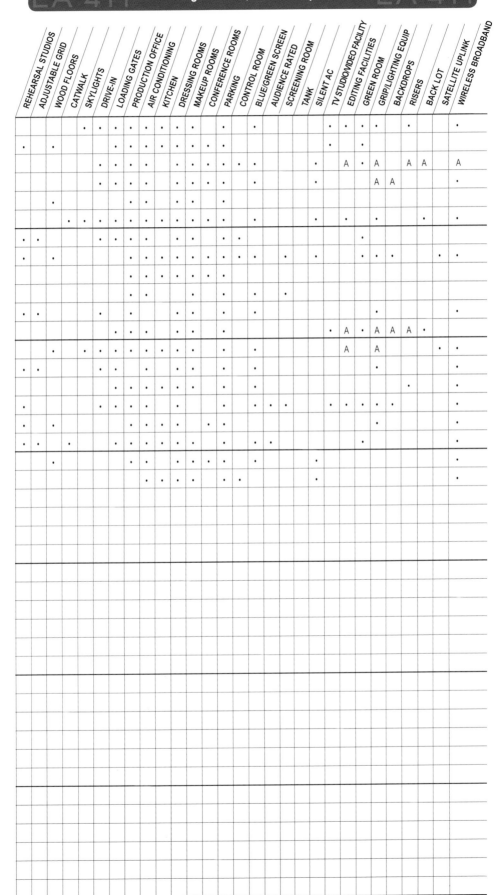

Rehearsal Studios	Adjustable Grid	Wood Floors	Catwalk	Skylights	Drive-In	Loading Gates	Production Office	Air Conditioning	Kitchen	Dressing Rooms	Makeup Rooms	Conference Rooms	Parking	Control Room	Blue/Green Screen	Audience Screen	Screening Rated	Tank	Silent AC	TV Studio/Video Facility	Editing Facilities	Green Room	Grip/Lighting Equip	Backdrops	Risers	Back Lot	Satellite Uplink	Wireless Broadband
				•	•	•	•	•	•	•		•		•						•	•	•	•		•			•
•		•				•	•	•	•	•	•	•							•		•							
				•	•	•	•	•		•	•	•	•	•	•	•			•		A	•	A		A	A		A
				•	•	•	•	•		•	•	•		•		•			•			A	A					•
		•				•	•	•		•	•	•		•														
			•	•	•	•	•	•		•	•	•		•					•		•		•			•		•
•	•					•	•	•		•	•			•	•							•						
•		•				•	•	•		•	•	•	•	•	•	•			•			•	•	•			•	•
						•	•	•		•	•	•		•														
						•	•			•		•			•		•		•									
•	•	•			•			•		•		•		•									•					
				•	•	•	•	•		•	•			•					•	A	•	A	A	A		•		
		•		•	•	•	•	•		•	•			•						A		A					•	•
•	•					•	•	•		•	•			•								•						•
				•	•	•	•		•	•	•			•										•				•
•		•				•	•	•		•	•			•			•	•	•	•		•	•					•
•		•				•	•	•		•	•	•		•								•						•
•	•		•			•	•	•		•	•			•			•	•				•						•
		•				•	•	•	•	•	•	•		•					•									•
						•	•	•	•	•		•	•						•									•

A = Available to Rent

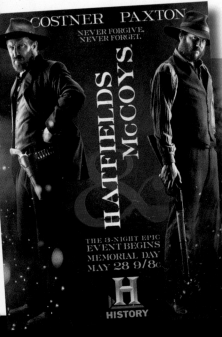

HATFIELDS & MCCOYS

BY MARJ GALAS

Director of Photography Arthur Reinhart on "Hatfields & McCoys"

Arthur Reinhart knew very little about the Civil War and American history when he agreed to shoot the History Channel's "Hatfields & McCoys." A German director of photography living in Poland, Reinhart was attracted to the dynamics of the feuding families and immediately immersed himself in researching the period. With only 69 days to shoot a three part mini-series, knowing exactly how he would achieve the series' very specific look was the first safely crossed hurdle on a challenging course.

Shooting on location in Romania presented a number of aesthetic problems. Many trees in Romania are not indigenous to the US, and with roughly two hours of daylight each day, there was little room for error. Many of the film's mid-day interior shots actually occurred in the darkness. Reinhart helped the design team incorporate light spaces and rigging throughout constructed sets where lights could be mounted or holes where they could pass through.

"We pre-rigged lights then covered the lights with set dressing," said Reinhart. "Pre-rigging really helped save time and overcome problems."

Prior to shooting, Reinhart anticipated some digital replacements would be required, such as masking modern and non-American buildings. However, green screens were also instrumental in replacing the windows in buildings to represent daytime scenes during night time shoots. Reinhart relied upon his previous experience with CG and was able to set up trackers accurately.

"The wind would make the screens move and bend. There was not a single chance to fix them," said Reinhart. "I was worried the movement might affect keying but it all worked out."

Some found locations were not configured well for shooting. While it is not unusual for a cinematographer to have to adapt to a location, the structure used for the saloon was extremely annoying to Reinhart. He didn't expect a great return but it ended up providing an exceptional result.

"I hated the saloon; it wasn't built for us but we adapted the location and it turned out nice," said Reinhart. "It's funny, what I hated the most gave me the biggest wow!"

ABRIDGED FROM AN LA 411 NEWSLETTER ARTICLE PUBLISHED JULY 2012

Ⓐ ADVERTISER SYMBOL

**Refer to the General Index for
cross-referencing items in this section.**

Action Air Express
(310) 390-8802
(866) 390-8802
FAX (323) 464-3507
2501 Airport Ave.
Santa Monica, CA 90405
www.actionairexpress.com

Air Charter Guru
(866) 501-4878
FAX (972) 931-4878
www.aircharterguru.com

Air One Charter
(310) 743-0103
(877) 247-1359
FAX (310) 743-0140
6101 W. Centinela Ave., Ste. 375
Culver City, CA 90230
www.aironecharter.com
(24-Hour Service)

Air Royale International
(310) 289-9800
(800) 776-9253
FAX (310) 289-9804
5757 Wilshire Blvd., Ste. 315
Los Angeles, CA 90036
www.airroyale.com
(24-Hour Service)

Altitude Aviation
(310) 379-4448
(310) 489-8938
FAX (310) 937-7112
200 Pier Ave., Ste. 128
Hermosa Beach, CA 90254
www.altitudeaviation.com
(24-Hour Service)

ARIS Helicopters/Heli-Flite
(951) 359-5016
(800) 340-1969
FAX (951) 359-5019
6871 Airport Dr.
Riverside, CA 92504
www.arishelicopters.com

Behind the Scenes
(818) 222-4007
FAX (818) 222-4036
23934 Craftsman Rd.
Calabasas, CA 91302
www.btsfreight.com

Briles Wing & Helicopter, Inc.
(818) 994-1445
FAX (818) 994-1447
16303 Waterman Dr.
Van Nuys, CA 91406
www.toflyla.com

Celebrity Helicopters
(877) 999-2099
FAX (877) 999-2099
961 W. Alondra Blvd.
Compton, CA 90220
www.celebheli.com

Charter Services/
CSI Aviation Services, Inc.
(800) 765-9464
(505) 761-9000
FAX (505) 342-7377
(24-Hour Service)
www.aircharter travel.com

Chrysler Aviation, Inc.
(818) 989-7900
FAX (818) 989-0116
7120 Hayvenhurst Ave., Ste. 309
Van Nuys, CA 91406
www.chrysleraviation.com

Clay Lacy Aviation, Inc.
(818) 989-2900
(800) 423-2904
FAX (818) 909-9537
7435 Valjean Ave.
Van Nuys, CA 91406
www.claylacy.com

Corporate America Aviation, Inc.
(818) 953-7206
(800) 521-8585
FAX (818) 563-2368
P.O. Box 1978
Burbank, CA 91507
www.privatebizjets.com

Cove Aviation Partners LLC
(310) 479-1890
FAX (310) 479-1360
11845 W. Olympic Blvd., Ste. 1080W
Los Angeles, CA 90064

Dreamline Aviation LLC
(877) 457-5241
(818) 988-0029
FAX (818) 779-8682
16461 Sherman Way, Ste. 210
Van Nuys, CA 91406
www.dreamlineaviation.com

Elite Aviation, Inc.
(818) 988-5387
FAX (818) 988-2111
7501 Hayvenhurst Pl.
Van Nuys, CA 91406
www.eliteaviation.com

Global Exec Aviation
(562) 424-0663
(888) 878-0788
FAX (562) 424-1144
3250 Airflite Way
Long Beach, CA 90807
www.globalexecaviation.com

Hangar 1 Productions
(323) 810-7560
1910 W. Sunset Blvd., Ste. 900 www.hangar1project.com
Los Angeles, CA 90026

Heli-USA
(818) 994-1445
(877) 863-5952
FAX (818) 994-1447
16303 Waterman Dr.
Van Nuys, CA 91406
www.toflyla.com

Helinet Aviation Services
(818) 902-0229
(800) 221-8389
FAX (818) 902-9278
16644 Roscoe Blvd.
Van Nuys, CA 91406
www.helinet.com

Hosking Aviation
(661) 251-5151
FAX (661) 414-8048

Island Express Helicopter
(310) 510-2525
(800) 228-2566
FAX (310) 510-9671
1175 Queens Hwy South
Long Beach, CA 90802
www.islandexpress.com

Jet Productions
(818) 781-4742
(877) 895-1790
FAX (818) 781-4743
7240 Hayvenhurst Ave., Ste. 243C
Van Nuys, CA 91406
www.jetproductions.net

JetStream International
(800) 891-0456
(786) 202-8884
FAX (305) 447-1919
www.jetstreamintl.com

Le Bas International
(805) 593-0510
(800) 331-5466
FAX (805) 593-0509
3440 Empresa Dr., Ste. B
San Luis Obispo, CA 93401
www.lebas.com

Maguire Aviation
(818) 989-2300
(800) 451-7270
FAX (818) 902-9386
7155 Valjean Ave.
Van Nuys, CA 91406

MC Aviation
(818) 904-9860
FAX (818) 904-0324
7415 Havenhurst Pl.
Van Nuys, CA 91406
www.mcaviationcorp.com

Metro-Jet, LLC
(562) 869-4128
(888) 682-6227
FAX (562) 923-7181
12101 S. Crenshaw Blvd., Ste. 1
Hawthorne, CA 90250

Orbic Air, LLC
(818) 988-6532
www.orbicair.com
16700 Roscoe Blvd.
Van Nuys, CA 91406

Orbic Helicopters, Inc.
(805) 389-1070
FAX (805) 389-1020
777 Aviation Dr.
Camarillo, CA 93010
www.orbichelicopters.com

Rock-It Air Charter, Inc.
(310) 702-6770
LA International Airport
www.rockitair.com
5438 W. 104th St.
Los Angeles, CA 90045
(24-Hour Service)

Rotor Aviation
(562) 595-6867
FAX (562) 595-5323
3250 Airflite Way
Long Beach, CA 90807
www.rotoraviation.com

Studio Jet
(818) 769-3535
(24-Hour Service)
FAX (818) 301-2536
www.studiojet.com

Style Aviation Services, Inc. (818) 988-2931
7415 Hayvenhurst Pl. FAX (818) 988-2953
Van Nuys, CA 91406 www.styleair.com

Sun Air Jets (805) 389-9301
Camarillo Airport, 855 Aviation Dr. FAX (805) 987-4720
Camarillo, CA 93010 www.sunairjets.com

Sun Quest (818) 778-6520
(800) 529-7595
7415 Hayvenhurst Pl. FAX (818) 778-6526
Van Nuys, CA 91406 www.sunquestexec.com

TwinAir (818) 988-7573
7552 Hayvenhurst Pl. FAX (818) 988-7578
Van Nuys, CA 91406 www.twinair.net

Worldwide Jet (856) 825-4540
(800) 354 4481
www.worldwidejet.com

Xpeditious Unlimited (310) 885-8001
610 Carob St. www.xpeditiousunlimited.com
Compton, CA 90220

LA 411   Air Freight & Couriers   LA 411

Advanced Express, Inc. (310) 640-8400
(800) 767-2326
1750 E. Holly Ave. FAX (310) 640-9413
El Segundo, CA 90245 www.advancedexpress.com
(24-Hour Service)

Air Charter Guru (866) 501-4878
FAX (972) 931-4878
www.aircharterguru.com

Air France Cargo (310) 646-3621
FAX (310) 646-1002
www.airfrancecargo.com

Alliance Air Freight, Inc. (818) 504-3900
(800) 684-6359
9022 Glen Oaks Blvd. FAX (818) 504-3924
Sun Valley, CA 91352 www.shipalliance.com

Anchor News Courier (800) 747-6397
P.O. Box 7083 FAX (818) 841-3809
Burbank, CA 91510 www.anchornewscourier.com

Art Pack, Inc. (310) 328-0300
www.artpack.us

Atlant USA, Inc. (310) 631-1810
FAX (310) 631-1830
www.atlant.com

Atlas Worldwide Transportation (310) 968-2090
(310) 798-9467
505 Earle Ln. FAX (310) 318-6497
Redondo Beach, CA 90278
www.atlasworldwidetrans.com

Behind the Scenes (818) 222-4007
23934 Craftsman Rd. FAX (818) 222-4036
Calabasas, CA 91302 www.btsfreight.com

Bellair Express (310) 216-9200
(800) 888-7785
5140 W. 106th St., Stes. J & K FAX (310) 216-7124
Inglewood, CA 90304 www.bellairlax.com
(24-Hour Service)

Bluebird Express, LLC (310) 645-0300
5261B W. Imperial Hwy www.bluebird-courier.com
Los Angeles, CA 90045

Bonded Services, Inc. (310) 680-6830
441 N. Oak St. FAX (310) 680-9099
Inglewood, CA 90302 www.bonded.com

British Airways World Cargo (213) 785-3465
(213) 785-3460
FAX (310) 641-6958
www.baworldcargo.com

DB Schenker (323) 908-4800
(800) 541-6261
2815 W. El Segundo Blvd. FAX (323) 908-4874
Hawthorne, CA 90250 www.dbschenkerusa.com

Delta Air Logistics (800) 352-2746

Delta Dash (800) 352-2746
(Small Package Express) www.deltacargo.com

DHL Global Forwarding (310) 297-4400
(800) 354-1743
FAX (310) 417-8057

DHL Worldwide Express (800) 225-5345
www.dhl-usa.com

Distribution by Air, Inc. (DBA) (800) 272-1379
www.dbaco.com

Efficient Delivery Service (818) 817-2700
7065 Hayvenhurst Ave., Ste. 7 FAX (818) 205-9883
Van Nuys, CA 91406
www2.efficientdeliveryservice.com/entrack/index.asp

ETC International Freight System (800) 383-3157
21039 S. Figueroa St., Ste. 101 FAX (310) 632-3044
Carson, CA 90745 www.etcinternational.com

Excalibur International Couriers (310) 568-1000
235 S. Glasgow Ave. FAX (310) 568-1604
Inglewood, CA 90301 www.excaliburintl.com

Federal Express (800) 463-3339
www.fedex.com

FedEx Custom Critical (800) 762-3787
(800) 255-2421
(24-Hour Service) FAX (234) 310-4172
www.fedexcustomcritical.com

Graf Air Freight (424) 205-1000
(24-Hour Service) FAX (424) 205-1006
www.grafairfreight.com

Karmel Courier & (714) 670-3480
Messenger Service (888) 995-7433
FAX (714) 670-3496
www.karmel.com

Lufthansa Cargo (800) 542-2746
FAX (877) 543-2948
www.lhcargo.com

Marken (310) 641-8393
(800) 627-5361
FAX (310) 641-8396
www.marken.com

Midnite Express (310) 330-2300
(800) 643-6483
FAX (310) 330-2358
www.mnx.com

MPA International (310) 590-1660
(866) 744-7672
10121 Pinehurst Ave. FAX (310) 590-1688
Southgate, CA 90280 www.mpasite.com

Norman Kreiger, Inc. (310) 668-5700
921 W. Artesia Blvd. FAX (310) 668-5800
Rancho Dominguez, CA 90220 www.nkinc.com

(650) 380-3300
Omni Logistics, Inc. (310) 644-4274
4949 W. 145th St. FAX (650) 618-8713
Hawthorne, CA 90250 www.omnilogistics.com

Pacific Express (800) 322-9521
FAX (714) 992-1026

Pack Air (310) 337-0529
FAX (310) 337-0669
www.packair.com

Paramount Courier Inc. (310) 693-0503
601 Hindry Ave. FAX (310) 670-4640
Inglewood, CA 90301 www.paramountcourier.com

(800) 834-7579
ProCourier, Inc. (949) 251-1777
www.procourier.com

Qantas Cargo, Ltd. (800) 227-0290
FAX (310) 665-2201
www.qantas.com.au/freight

(310) 414-9211
Quick International Courier (800) 788-4529
FAX (310) 414-0659
www.quickintl.com

(877) 576-6300
Reels On Wheels Unlimited (914) 576-6300
FAX (914) 633-6932
www.reelsonwheels.com

Rock-It Cargo USA, Inc. (310) 410-0935
FAX (310) 410-0628
www.rockitcargo.com

(323) 779-1230
Saturn Freight Systems (800) 660-4076
12333 S. Van Ness Ave. FAX (323) 779-1277
Hawthorne, CA 90250 www.saturnfreight.com

(818) 789-3999
Security Couriers, Inc. (323) 464-2673
13351-D Riverside Dr., Ste. 671 FAX (818) 789-3888
Sherman Oaks, CA 91423 www.securitycouriers.com
(24-Hour Service)

(252) 635-1400
SOS Global Express, Inc. (800) 628-6363
www.sosglobal.com

TBI/Truck Brokers, Inc. (800) 900-3572
FAX (407) 876-8691
www.truckbrokersinc.com

(213) 975-9850
Time Machine Courier (800) 734-8463
FAX (213) 975-9858
www.timemachinenetwork.com

(310) 337-0515
Total Transportation Concept, Inc. (800) 582-7110
8728 Aviation Blvd. FAX (310) 337-7901
Inglewood, CA 90301 www.totaltrans.com

U.S. Postal Service (800) 275-8777
Express Mail (LAX) (310) 649-7400

(800) 822-2746
United Airlines Cargo (310) 342-8391
FAX (310) 342-8361
www.unitedcargo.com

UPS Logistics (800) 528-6070
www.upslogistics.com

USAir Cargo (888) 300-0099
www.usairways.com

(310) 410-7230
World Courier (800) 221-6600
FAX (310) 410-7247
www.worldcourier.com

Xpeditious Unlimited (310) 885-8001
610 Carob St. www.xpeditiousunlimited.com
Compton, CA 90220

Aerolineas Argentinas	(800) 333-0276
	www.aerolineas.com.ar
Aeromexico	(800) 237-6639
	www.aeromexico.com
Air Canada	(888) 247-2262
	FAX (888) 422-7533
	www.aircanada.ca
Air France	(800) 237-2747
	www.airfrance.com
Air Jamaica	(800) 523-5585
	www.airjamaica.com
Air New Zealand	(800) 262-1234
	www.airnz.com
Alaska Airlines	(800) 252-7522
	www.alaskaair.com
Alitalia	(800) 223-5730
	www.alitaliausa.com
American Airlines	(800) 433-7300
	www.aa.com
ANA All Nippon Airways	(800) 235-9262
	www.anaskyweb.com
Asiana Airlines	(800) 227-4262
	(213) 365-4500
	www.flyasiana.com
Avianca	(800) 284-2622
	www.avianca.com
British Airways	(800) 247-9297
	www.britishairways.com
Cathay Pacific	(310) 615-1113
	(800) 233-2742
	www.cathaypacific.com
China Airlines	(800) 227-5118
	www.china-airlines.com
Delta Airlines	(800) 241-4141
	www.delta.com
Egypt Air	(800) 334-6787
	www.egyptair.com
El Al Israel Airlines	(800) 223-6700
	(323) 852-1252
	www.elal.com
Finnair	(800) 950-5000
	www.finnair.com
Frontier Airlines	(800) 432-1359
	www.frontierairlines.com
Garuda-Indonesia	(800) 342-7832
	www.garuda-indonesia.com
Grupo Taca	(800) 327-9832
	(800) 225-2272
	www.taca.com
Hawaiian Airlines	(800) 367-5320
	www.hawaiianair.com
Iberia Airlines	(800) 772-4642
	www.iberia.com
Japan Airlines	(800) 525-3663
	www.jal.com
Korean Air	(310) 646-4866
	(800) 438-5000
	www.koreanair.com
Lan Airlines	(310) 416-9061
	(866) 435-9526
	www.lan.com
LOT Polish Airlines	(212) 789-0970
	www.lot.com
LTU	(866) 266-5588
	FAX (407) 831-2470
	www.airberlin.com
Malaysia Airlines	(800) 552-9264
	www.malaysiaairlines.com.my
Martinair-Holland	(800) 627-8462
	FAX (561) 391-2188
	www.martinairusa.com
Philippine Airlines	(800) 435-9725
	www.philippineairlines.com
Qantas	(800) 227-4500
	www.qantas.com.au
SAS Scandinavian Airlines	(800) 221-2350
	www.flysas.com
Singapore Airlines	(800) 742-3333
	www.singaporeair.com/americas
Southwest	(800) 435-9792
	www.iflyswa.com
Swiss	(877) 359-7947
	www.swiss.com
Taca International	(800) 400-8222
	www.taca.com
Thai Airways International	(800) 426-5204
	www.thaiair.com
United Airlines/United Express	(800) 864-8331
	www.ual.com
US Airways	(800) 428-4322
	www.usairways.com
USAirways/USAirways Express	(800) 428-4322
	www.usairways.com
Varig Brazilian Airlines	(800) 468-2744
	www.varig.com.br
Virgin Atlantic Airways	(800) 862-8621
	www.virgin-atlantic.com

1800Fly1800
(310) 330-7500
(800) 359-1800
FAX (310) 419-8129
www.1800fly1800.com

Amour Way Luxury Transportation
(310) 591-8690
(866) 261-6651
P.O. Box 661749 FAX (310) 390-9315
Los Angeles, CA 90066 www.amourway.com

Emerald Limousine Service
(310) 591-6060
1601 N. Sepulveda Blvd., Ste. 630 FAX (310) 921-5624
Manhattan Beach, CA 90266 www.limobyemerald.com

Express Shuttle/Limousine
(800) 427-7483
(800) 310-8267
www.expressshuttle.com

Prime Time Airport Shuttle
(800) 733-8267
www.primetimeshuttle.com

RPM Limos Inc.
(949) 521-4383
23272 Arroyo Vista FAX (949) 888-8544
Rancho Santa Margarita, CA 92688 www.rpmlimos.com

Shuttle 2000
(800) 977-7872
www.shuttle2000.com

Southern California Coach
(800) 995-7433
www.karmel.com

SuperShuttle
(800) 258-3826
www.supershuttle.com

Van Nuys Fly-Away Bus Service
(866) 435-9529
7610 Woodley Ave. www.lawa.org/vny
Van Nuys, CA 91406

Agua Dulce Airport (661) 268-8835
33638 Agua Dulce Canyon Rd. FAX (661) 268-7662
Agua Dulce, CA 91390
Contacts: Kristen Hicks & Barry Kirshner

Bob Hope Airport (818) 840-8840
2627 Hollywood Way FAX (818) 848-1173
Burbank, CA 91505 www.bobhopeairport.com

Brackett Field Airport (909) 593-1395
1615 McKinley Ave. FAX (909) 593-5224
La Verne, CA 91750 www.americanairports.net
Contact: Jared Fox-Tuck

Camarillo Airport (805) 388-4246
555 Airport Way, Ste. B FAX (805) 388-4366
Camarillo, CA 93010 portal.countyofventura.org
Contact: Tad Dougherty

Chino Airport (909) 597-3910
7000 Merrill Ave., Box 1 FAX (909) 597-0274
Chino, CA 91710
Contact: James Jenkins

Compton Airport (310) 631-8140
901 W. Alondra Blvd. FAX (310) 762-9801
Compton, CA 90220 www.americanairports.net
Contact: Rafael Herrera

El Monte Airport (626) 448-6129
Contact: Richard Smith FAX (626) 448-6179
www.americanairports.net

Fox Airfield (661) 940-1709
Contact: Steve Irving FAX (661) 942-6754

Fullerton Municipal Airport (714) 738-6323
Contact: Rod Propst FAX (714) 738-3112
www.ci.fullerton.ca.us

Hawthorne Municipal Airport (310) 349-1637
12101 S. Crenshaw Blvd., Ste. 3 FAX (310) 978-9144
Hawthorne, CA 90250
Contact: Don Knechtel

Inyokern Airport (760) 377-5844
Contact: Scott Seymour FAX (760) 377-4194
www.inyokernairport.com

John Wayne Airport - (949) 252-5171
Orange County (949) 252-5182
3160 Airway Ave. FAX (949) 252-5178
Costa Mesa, CA 92626 www.ocair.com
Contact: Ann McCarley

LAX - Airfield Operations Bureau/
Film Office (424) 646-6843
7333 World Way West, Ste. 311
Los Angeles, CA 90045

(562) 570-2600
Long Beach Airport (562) 570-2619
4100 Donald Douglas Dr. FAX (562) 570-2601
Long Beach, CA 90808 www.lgb.org

McClellan-Palomar Airport (760) 431-4646
2198 Palomar Airport Rd. FAX (760) 931-5713
Carlsbad, CA 92008
Contact: Floyd Best

(661) 824-2433
Mojave Airport (661) 824-2434
1434 Flightline, Bldg. 58 FAX (661) 824-2914
Mojave, CA 93501 www.mojaveairport.com
Contact: Debbie Roth

(858) 573-1440
Montgomery Field (858) 573-1441
FAX (858) 279-0536

(909) 975-5344
Ontario International Airport (909) 975-5340
Operations Center FAX (909) 937-2800
1940 E. Moore Way www.lawa.org
Ontario, CA 91761
Contact: Kim Ellis

(805) 382-3022
(805) 382-3024
Oxnard Airport
Contact: Chris Hastert FAX (805) 382-9845
www.iflyoxnard.com

Palm Springs International Airport (760) 318-3800
3400 E. Tahquitz Canyon Way FAX (760) 318-3815
Palm Springs, CA 92262 www.palmspringsca.gov

Palmdale Airport (661) 266-7602
41000 20th St. East www.lawa.org
Palmdale, CA 93550
Contact: Sgt. Curtis Thompson

Perris Valley Airport (951) 657-3904
2091 Goetz Rd. FAX (951) 657-6178
Perris, CA 92570 www.skydiveperris.com
Contacts: Patrick Conaster & Melanie Conaster

Riverside Municipal Airport (951) 351-6113
6951 Flight Rd. FAX (951) 359-3570
Riverside, CA 92504 www.riversideca.gov/airport
Contacts: Mark Kranenburg & Barbara McIlwaine

San Diego International Airport -
Lindberg Field (619) 400-2400
Contact: Bryan Enarson FAX (619) 400-2549
www.san.org

Santa Monica Airport (310) 458-8591
3223 Donald Douglas Loop South FAX (310) 572-4495
Ste. 3 www.santamonicaairport.org
Santa Monica, CA 90405
Contact: Bob Trimborn

Santa Ynez Valley Airport (805) 688-8390
900 Airport Rd. FAX (805) 688-6105
Santa Ynez, CA 93460 www.santaynezairport.com
Contact: Kim Joos

Southern California
Logistics Airport (760) 243-1900
18374 Phantom FAX (760) 243-1929
Victorville, CA 92394 www.globalaccessvcv.com

Torrance Municipal Airport (310) 784-7900
FAX (310) 784-7930

Van Nuys Airport (818) 442-6500
FAX (818) 442-6560
www.lawa.org

Whiteman Airport (818) 896-5271
12653 Osborne St. FAX (818) 897-2654
Pacoima, CA 91331
Contact: Andrew Marino

Avalon Transportation, Inc.
(310) 391-6161
(800) 528-2566
5239 Sepulveda Blvd.   FAX (310) 391-8017
Culver City, CA 90230   www.avalontrans.com

Coach America
(562) 634-7969
(800) 642-3287
FAX (562) 634-5818
www.coachamerica.com

Coast to Coast Coach
(661) 268-0404
FAX (661) 268-0666
www.coasttocoastcoach.com

Fast Deer Bus Charters
(323) 201-8988
FAX (323) 201-8900
fastdeerbus.com

Fleetwood Limousine
(310) 645-6092
(800) 283-5893
FAX (310) 645-1245
www.fleetwoodlimousine.com

Greyhound Bus Lines
(213) 629-8401
(213) 629-8536
www.greyhound.com

KLS Limousine Service Inc.
(310) 247-0804
(877) 936-5466
9663 Santa Monica Blvd., Ste. 773   FAX (310) 247-0805
Beverly Hills, CA 90210   www.klsla.com

LA VIP Bus
(310) 855-2236
150 S. Glenoaks Blvd., Ste. 9166   FAX (818) 352-2857
Burbank, CA 91502   www.lavipbus.com

RPM Limos Inc.
(949) 521-4383
23272 Arroyo Vista   FAX (949) 888-8544
Rancho Santa Margarita, CA 92688   www.rpmlimos.com

Silverado Coach Company, Inc.
(818) 251-9700
(800) 544-7999
FAX (818) 884-4997
www.silveradocoach.com

Special Events Services, SES Inc.
(310) 831-1761
(800) 738-6739
1891 N. Gaffey St., Ste. M   FAX (310) 831-2528
Los Angeles, CA 90731
www.specialeventsservices.com

Starline
(323) 463-3333
(800) 959-3131
www.starlinetours.com

Sunrize Plaza
Transportation Co./SPT
(310) 406-3115
(800) 564-5806
FAX (310) 406-3119

Tourcoach Charter Service
(323) 262-1114
(323) 463-3131
www.tourcoach.com

Transportation
Charter Services, Inc.
(714) 637-4300
(800) 833-5773
FAX (714) 637-4377
www.tcsbus.com

Audi of Downtown LA
(213) 745-7200
1900 S. Figueroa St.   FAX (213) 222-1263
Los Angeles, CA 90007   www.audiofdtla.com
(Audi)

Beverly Hills BMW
(866) 849-3816
5070 Wilshire Blvd.   www.beverlyhillsbmw.com
Los Angeles, CA 90036
(BMW)

Browning Auto Group
(562) 924-1414
www.browningautogroup.com
(Acura, Chevrolet, Dodge, Honda, Kia, Mazda, Mitsubishi,
Oldsmobile & Toyota)

Calstar Motors
(818) 630-6410
700 S. Brand Blvd.   www.calstarmercedes.com
Glendale, CA 91204
(Mercedes-Benz)

Cerritos Auto Square
(888) 364-2288
10900 Auto Square Dr.   www.cerritosautosquare.com
Cerritos, CA 90703
(Acura, Buick, Chevrolet, Chrysler, Dodge, Ford, GMC, Honda,
Hummer, Hyundai, Infinity, Isuzu, Kia, Lexus, Lincoln, Mazda,
Mercury, Mitsubishi, Nissan, Pontiac, Saturn, Suzuki,
Toyota & Volvo)

Circle Imports
(562) 597-3663
(800) 675-2472
(Audi, Porsche & Volkswagen)   www.circleimports.com

Culver City Volvo
(888) 786-9472
11201 Washington Blvd.   FAX (310) 398-2814
Culver City, CA 90230   www.culvercityvolvo.com
(Volvo)

Downtown LA Motors
(888) 835-8640
(888) 854-2969
1801 S. Figueroa St.   www.dtlamotors.com
Los Angeles, CA 90015
(Audi, Buick, Chevrolet, Mercedes-Benz, Nissan,
Porsche & Volkswagen)

Felix Chevrolet
(213) 748-6141
3330 S. Figueroa St.   www.felixautos.com
Los Angeles, CA 90007
(Chevrolet)

Galpin Ford
(800) 256-7137
15505 Roscoe Blvd.   www.galpinford.com
North Hills, CA 91343
(Aston Martin, Ford, Jaguar, Lincoln, Mazda, Mercury,
Saturn & Volvo)

Honda of Hollywood
(323) 466-7191
(800) 371-3718
6525 Santa Monica Blvd.   FAX (323) 372-3200
Hollywood, CA 90038   www.hondaofhollywood.com
(Honda)

Huntington Beach Dodge
(866) 554-8590
(888) 895-7193
16701 Beach Blvd.   www.hbchryslerdodgejeepram.com
Huntington Beach, CA 92647
(Dodge)

Jaguar Newport Beach (949) 640-6445
1540 Jamboree Rd. FAX **(949) 759-3528**
Newport Beach, CA 92660
(Jaguar) **www.jaguarnewportbeach.com**

Jessup Auto Plaza (760) 904-0525
68-111 E. Palm Canyon **www.jessupautoplaza.com**
Cathedral City, CA 92234
(Buick, Cadillac, GMC, Hummer, Pontiac & Saab)

  (310) 274-5200
Jim Falk Lexus of Beverly Hills **(888) 860-7618**
9230 Wilshire Blvd. FAX **(310) 275-3248**
Beverly Hills, CA 90210
(Lexus) **www.jimfalkbeverlyhillslexus.com**

Keyes Automotive Group (800) 768-6105
  www.keyescars.com
(Acura, Audi, Lexus, Mercedes-Benz, Scion & Toyota)

Kirby Auto (888) 442-5017
2350 First St. **www.kirbyauto.com**
Simi Valley, CA 93065
(Jeep, Oldsmobile & Suzuki)

Land Rover South Bay (310) 975-6999
900 N. Pacific Coast Hwy **www.landroversouthbay.com**
Redondo Beach, CA 90277
(Land Rover)

Mark Christopher Auto Center (909) 509-8299
2131 Convention Center Way FAX **(909) 390-8174**
Ontario, CA 91764 **www.markchristopher.com**
(Cadillac, Chevrolet, Hummer & Oldsmobile)

Martin Automotive Group (800) 601-5063
12101 W. Olympic Blvd. FAX **(310) 826-3717**
Los Angeles, CA 90064 **www.martinautogroup.com**
(Cadillac, GMC, Isuzu & Pontiac)

Miller Automotive (800) 730-8966
  www.millerautomotive.com
(Honda, Infinity, Mitsubishi, Nissan & Toyota)

Newport Beach Auto Center (949) 478-0590
445 East Coast Hwy **www.newportautocenter.com**
Newport Beach, CA 92660
(Audi, Bentley & Porsche)

Norm Reeves Honda Superstore **(888) 725-6611**
18500 Studebaker Rd. FAX **(562) 402-4584**
Cerritos, CA 90703 **www.normreevescerritos.com**

Penske Automotive Group (626) 580-6000
3534 N. Peck Rd. FAX **(626) 580-6158**
El Monte, CA 91731 **www.penskeautomotive.com**
(Audi, Honda, Lexus, Maybach, Merecedes-Benz & Toyota)

Phillips Auto of Newport Beach (949) 574-7777
1220 W. Coast Hwy FAX **(949) 631-2192**
Newport Beach, CA 92663 **www.phillipsauto.com**
(Aston Martin, BMW, Chevrolet, Dodge, Ferrari & Ford)

Sierra Autocars, Inc. (800) 404-2886
1450 S. Shamrock Ave. **www.sierraauto.com**
Monrovia, CA 91016
(Acura, Buick, Chevrolet, Honda, Isuzu, Saturn & Subaru)

  (888) 421-0348
Silver Star Auto Group (805) 371-5400
3905 Auto Mall Dr. FAX **(805) 371-5488**
Thousand Oaks, CA 91362 **www.silverstarauto.com**
(Buick, Cadillac, GMC, Honda, Hummer, Jaguar, Land Rover,
Lexus, Lotus, Mazda, Mercedes-Benz, Mitsubishi, Nissan,
Saab & Subaru)

Toyota of Hollywood (323) 300-5026
(Lincoln, Mercury, Scion & Toyota) FAX **(323) 860-5628**
  www.hollywoodtoyota.com

Tustin Auto Center (888) 449-6414
  www.tustinautocenter.com
(Acura, Buick, Cadillac, Chevrolet, Chrysler, Dodge, Ford,
GMC, Infinity, Jeep, Lexus, Lincoln, Mazda, Mercury, Mitsubishi,
Nissan, Pontiac & Toyota)

  (866) 301-1111
Universal City Nissan (866) 245-8623
3550 Cahuenga Blvd. West FAX **(818) 755-7380**
Los Angeles, CA 90068 **www.universalcitynissan.com**
(Nissan)

  (866) 918-3702
Volkswagen Santa Monica (866) 469-6576
2440 Santa Monica Blvd. FAX **(310) 829-3906**
Santa Monica, CA 90404 **www.vw-sm.com**
(Volkswagen)

1800Fly1800
(310) 330-7500
(800) 359-1800
FAX (310) 419-8129
www.1800fly1800.com

310 Picture Cars
6709 La Tijera Blvd., Ste. 247
Los Angeles, CA 90045
(310) 678-8007
FAX (310) 878-0338
facebook.com/picturecardivision

AAA Limousine Service
(818) 704-4746
(800) 232-4133
FAX (818) 888-1280
www.aaalimo.net

Absolute Transportation Service
(310) 270-5253
(800) 966-5753
www.americanlimousine.us

Affordable West, Inc.
1040 N. La Brea Ave.
Hollywood, CA 90038
(323) 467-7182
FAX (323) 467-6520

Alamo
9020 Aviation Blvd.
Inglewood, CA 90301
(See Web Site for Additional Locations)
(800) 327-9633
(310) 649-2242
www.alamo.com

Aloha Limousine
P.O. Box 352
Hawthorne, CA 90251
(310) 641-1811
(323) 464-2456
FAX (310) 978-6366

Avalon Transportation, Inc.
5239 Sepulveda Blvd.
Culver City, CA 90230
(310) 391-6161
(800) 528-2566
FAX (310) 391-8017
www.avalontrans.com

Avis
9217 Airport Blvd.
Los Angeles, CA 90045
(See Web Site for Additional Locations)
(310) 342-9200
www.avis.com

Avon Studio Transportation
7080 Santa Monica Blvd.
Los Angeles, CA 90038
(323) 850-0826
(800) 432-2866
FAX (323) 467-4239
www.avonrents.com

Beverly Hills Rent-A-Car
9732 S. Santa Monica Blvd.
Beverly Hills, CA 90210
(310) 274-6969
(855) 818-6969
FAX (310) 550-1700
www.bhrentacar.com

Blue Moon Limousine & Sedan
(714) 546-6737
(800) 726-1837
FAX (714) 546-7048

Budget
(866) 767-8143
(310) 274-9174
www.budgetbeverlyhills.com

Budget of Beverly Hills
9815 Wilshire Blvd.
Beverly Hills, CA 90212
(310) 966-0642
FAX (310) 578-1068
www.budgetbeverlyhills.com

California Rent-A-Car
1033 N. Fuller Ave.
Los Angeles, CA 90046
(310) 477-2727
FAX (310) 477-9176
www.productioncarrental.com

Classic Car Rental Connection
17514 Ventura Blvd.
Encino, CA 91316
(818) 728-0607
(800) 494-8092
FAX (818) 728-0684
www.101classiccarrental.com

Crown Limousine L.A.
(310) 737-0888
(800) 933-5466
FAX (310) 737-0890
www.crownlimola.com

Dollar
(See Web Site for Locations)
(800) 800-3665
(866) 434-2226
www.dollar.com

Dream One
(800) 538-8799
(310) 670-5466
FAX (310) 670-0558
www.dreamonesedans.com

ELS Transportation
(800) 940-6482
FAX (888) 371-1997
www.elstransportation.com

Empire CLS Worldwide Chaufferured Services
(800) 266-2577
FAX (310) 414-8126
www.empirecls.com

Enterprise
8734 Bellanca Ave.
Los Angeles, CA 90045
(See Web Site for Locations)
(800) 261-7331
(310) 216-0100
www.enterprise.com

Exclusive Sedan Service
12580 Saticoy St.
North Hollywood, CA 91605
(818) 765-7311
(800) 400-7332
FAX (818) 765-0183
www.exclusivesedan.com

Executive Productions
3957 Ridgemont Dr.
Malibu, CA 90265
(310) 456-8833
FAX (310) 456-5692

Exquisite Limo and Sedan Service
10834 S. Freeman Ave.
Inglewood, CA 90304
(310) 674-3326
(310) 420-0277
FAX (310) 412-0079
www.exquisitelimoandsedanservice.com

Fleetwood Limousine
(310) 645-6092
(800) 283-5893
FAX (310) 645-1245
www.fleetwoodlimo.com

Galpin Studio Rentals
1763 N. Ivar Ave.
Hollywood, CA 90028
(323) 957-3333
(800) 256-6219
FAX (323) 856-6790
www.galpinstudiorentals.com

Galpin Studio Rentals
3200 La Cienega Blvd.
Los Angeles, CA 90016
(323) 857-0111
(800) 256-6219
FAX (323) 964-6234
www.galpinstudiorentals.com

Gemstar Limousine Service
(310) 457-7307
(800) 922-5466
FAX (310) 457-6307
www.gemstarlimo.com

Hertz
9000 Airport Blvd.
Los Angeles, CA 90045
(See Web Site for Additional Locations)
(800) 654-3131
(310) 568-5100
FAX (310) 568-3461
www.hertz.com

Integrated Transportation Services
9740 W. Pico Blvd.
Los Angeles, CA 90034
(310) 551-3159
(800) 487-4255
FAX (310) 551-3061
www.itslimo.com

Marathon Car Rental
12903 Washington Blvd.
Los Angeles, CA 90066
(800) 586-4004
(310) 827-5600
FAX (310) 823-6526
www.marathonrentacar.com

Midway Car Rentals
1800 S. Sepulveda Blvd.
West Los Angeles, CA 90025
(310) 445-4355
(800) 824-5260
FAX (310) 445-4368
www.midwaycarrental.com

National
(See Web Site for Locations)
(888) 826-6890
(310) 338-8200
FAX (310) 641-4587
www.nationalcar.com

Olympic Rent A Car
9230 W. Olympic Blvd., Ste. 200
Beverly Hills, CA 90212
(310) 751-6501
FAX (310) 274-1271
www.olympicrentacar.com

Red Carpet Limousine Service, Inc. (866) 398-9700
FAX (310) 398-9750
www.rcllimo.com

Rent-A-Wreck
12333 W. Pico Blvd.
West Los Angeles, CA 90064
(See Web Site for Additional Locations)
(310) 826-7555
(800) 995-0994
FAX (310) 207-0681
www.rentawreck.com

Secure Transportation
13111 Meyer Rd.
Whittier, CA 90605
(562) 941-0107
(800) 856-9994
FAX (562) 906-2947
www.securetransportation.com

Silverado Coach Company, Inc.
(818) 251-9700
(800) 544-7999
FAX (818) 884-4997
www.silveradocoach.com

Thrifty
5440 W. Century Blvd.
Los Angeles, CA 90045
(See Web Site for Additional Locations)
(877) 283-0898
(310) 645-1881
www.thrifty.com

1st To Roll Catering, Inc. (818) 345-6562 / (818) 209-2626
FAX (818) 345-6562
www.1sttorollcatering.com
(24-Hour Service & Mobile Kitchen Facilities)

24 Hr. Production Catering (818) 321-7403 / (818) 703-2275
FAX (818) 477-2151
www.productioncatering.com
(24-Hour Service, Breakfasts, Drop Off Services, Lunch & Second Meals)

A & M Catering (818) 709-5385 / (818) 535-9411
19201 Halstead St. FAX (818) 709-5385
Northridge, CA 91324 www.aandmcatering.net
(Mobile Kitchen Facilities)

Abbey Road Catering (310) 649-4040
www.abbeyroadfilmcatering.com

**Above & Beyond
The Culinary Experience** (310) 995-9353
www.aandbcatering.com

Aki Catering (818) 266-9912
www.classiccateringshowroom.com
(Dim-Sum, Second Meals, Sushi & Tempura)

Alex's Gourmet Catering (818) 775-0590 / (818) 355-8218
20928 Itasca FAX (818) 775-0591
Chatsworth, CA 91311

All American Softy & Coffee (818) 881-8890
(24-Hour Service) www.allamericansofty.com

Allstar Catering LLC (818) 262-6197
(Mobile Kitchen Facilities)

Ammo Catering & Cafe (323) 871-2666 / (323) 467-3293
1155 N. Highland Ave. www.ammocafe.com
Hollywood, CA 90038

Ann & Mario Catering (818) 262-1750 / (818) 262-2727
FAX (818) 353-7953
www.annandmariocatering.com

Apple Spice Junction (310) 885-5222
801 W. Victoria St., Ste. E FAX (310) 885-5228
Rancho Dominguez, CA 90220 www.applespice.com
(Drop-Off Lunches and On-Site Catering)

Auntie Em's Kitchen (323) 255-0800
4616 Eagle Rock Blvd. FAX (323) 259-6424
Los Angeles, CA 90041 www.auntieemskitchen.com

Bella Events (323) 436-0082
(24-Hour Service) FAX (323) 784-2004
www.ilbellaevents.com

Benny's Tacos & Chicken Rotisserie (310) 396-8749 / (818) 612-3875
427 Lincoln Blvd. FAX (310) 396-8778
Venice, CA 90291 www.bennystacos.com

Best Boy espresso (323) 665-2378
www.myspace.com/bestboy
(24 Hour Service, Mobile Cappuccino, Coffee & Smoothie Service)

Big Picture Catering (661) 296-5303

Big Screen Cuisine Catering (818) 345-0009 / (818) 881-0009
18420 Hart St. www.bigscreencuisine.com
Reseda, CA 91335
(Mobile Kitchen Facilities)

**Black Tie Event Services, Inc./
Bar Catering** (310) 337-9900
5741 Buckingham Pkwy, Ste. D FAX (310) 337-9916
Los Angeles, CA 90230 www.blacktieevent.com
(Mobile Kitchen Facilities)

**Blended Drink Catering/
California Brain Chill** (818) 635-2262 / (888) 525-8423
FAX (818) 972-3952
www.californiabrainchill.com
(Blended Drinks, Smoothies & Sundae Bar)

Bobby Weisman Caterers (818) 843-9999
736 S. Glenwood Pl. FAX (818) 843-9995
Burbank, CA 91506 www.bobbyweisman.com
(Mobile Kitchen Facilities)

Bonne Bouffe Catering (310) 629-7423 / (310) 397-1660
1521 Venice Blvd.
Venice, CA 90291

Boyz In The Kitchen (818) 845-1200
FAX (818) 845-1209
www.boyzinthekitchen.com

Breakfast Rendezvous (818) 787-5502 / (818) 349-5211
(24-Hour Service)

**Breakfast! Rise & Shine/
Rise & Shine Lunch Catering** (310) 649-0906
7401 W. 88th Pl. FAX (310) 649-0264
Los Angeles, CA 90045 www.riseandshinecatering.com
(24-Hour Service, Breakfasts, Drop Off Services, Lunch and Second Meal & Mobile Kitchen Facilities)

Bruce's Gourmet Catering, Inc. (818) 376-1288
13631 Saticoy St. FAX (818) 376-1505
Panorama City, CA 91402
(Mobile Kitchen Facilities)

Café on Location, Inc. (818) 758-9858
19451 Ventura Blvd. FAX (818) 758-9754
Tarzana, CA 91356
(Mobile Kitchen Facilities)

California Catering (323) 216-6210
(Mobile Kitchen Facilities)

Camille's (626) 202-5214 / (626) 791-4081
FAX (866) 222-7760
www.camilleskitchen.com

Cappuccino Connection (800) 270-0188 / (800) 270-0188
FAX (805) 969-7295
www.capbar.com

Cappuccino On Call (323) 481-6575
(Cappuccino & Espresso) www.cappuccinooncall.com

The Cast Supper, Inc. (818) 908-0069
(Mobile Kitchen Facilities) FAX (818) 908-9737
www.thecastsupper.com

CateringUnlimited.com (805) 782-8070 / (805) 544-5777
2990 Dairy Creek Rd. FAX (805) 782-8071
San Luis Obispo, CA 93405 www.cateringunlimited.com

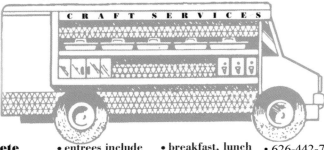

chefs on location catering, inc.
www.chefsonlocation.com

CRAFT SERVICES

- **a complete catering service**
- short notice
- 24 hour service
- vegetarian menu

- entrees include a full salad bar, desserts & drinks
- truck rental
- table & chairs

- breakfast, lunch & second meal
- linen/silverware
- **WE DO BBQ!**

- 626-442-7331 OFFICE
- 626-309-9042
- 626-448-4379 FAX
- 626-437-9153 CELL

Chef 2 Go	(805) 698-0465
	www.chef2go.us

	(818) 686-6449
Chef Robért Motion Picture Catering	(323) 864-6605
7336 Santa Monica Blvd., Ste. 692	FAX (818) 686-6602
West Hollywood, CA 90046	
	www.chefrobertcatering.com

	(626) 442-7331
Ⓐ Chefs on Location	(626) 437-9153
(Mobile Kitchen Facilities)	

Crepes of Paris	(323) 679-4973
6399 Wilshire Blvd., Ste. 101	www.cafeofparis.com
Los Angeles, CA 90048	

Cross Culture Cuisine	(661) 713-5392
43941 Blue Sky Court	FAX (661) 723-6925
Lancaster, CA 93536	

	(818) 901-8041
Curbside Café	(818) 744-4742
15410 Runnymede St.	www.thecurbsidecafe.com
Van Nuys, CA 91406	
(24-Hour Mobile Espresso Service & Smoothie Bar)	

	(818) 625-5850
Dean's Catering	(818) 999-5850
	FAX (818) 999-5851
	www.deanscatering.co

Debbie's Dinners	(323) 936-4545
6051 David Ave.	FAX (323) 936-4358
Los Angeles, CA 90034	www.debbiesdinners.com

	(800) 985-9069
Deluxe Motion Picture Catering	(818) 985-9069
(Mobile Kitchen Facilities)	FAX (818) 979-9069

Dine With 9 Catering	(818) 769-1883
	www.dinewith9.com

El Cholo Catering	(323) 737-7718
1121 S. Western Ave.	FAX (323) 737-1873
Los Angeles, CA 90006	
(24-Hour Service & Mobile Kitchen Facilities)	

Encore Catering	(213) 700-1616
	FAX (818) 222-3834
	www.encorecateringca.com

	(562) 773-0402
Entertainment Catering	(626) 582-8449
1500 Chico Ave., Ste. F	
South El Monte, CA 91733	

Espresso Express	(310) 200-7274
10600 Culver Blvd.	www.eemobile.com
Culver City, CA 90232	
(24-Hour Moble Cappuccino Coffee Bar)	

Famous Dave's BBQ	(866) 408-7427
	FAX (949) 421-5110
	www.famousdaves.com/catering

	(818) 516-8956
Final Cut Catering	(818) 704-6219
5223 Alhama Dr.	
Woodland Hills, CA 91364	
(Mobile Kitchen Facilities)	

Creative Catering For The Entertainment Industry
FEDERICO BARBIER
(323) 733-5544
(323) 733-5545 Fax
toucancatering.com
TOUCAN

First Take Catering Services (805) 577-1554
950 Enchanted Way, Ste. 101 (800) 318-7797
Simi Valley, CA 93065 FAX (805) 584-5147
(Mobile Kitchen Facilities)

Fit Food (323) 848-7996
7998 Santa Monica Blvd., Ste. C (925) 785-6372
West Hollywood, CA 90046 FAX (323) 848-7950
(24-Hour Service) www.fitfoodla.com

Flatbush & J Gourmet (310) 312-3632
Company, Inc. (310) 283-3043
11058 Santa Monica Blvd. FAX (310) 312-3679
Los Angeles, CA 90025 www.flatbushandj.com

Flava Catering (323) 291-1570
(Caribbean Creole Cuisine) (323) 445-7296
www.flavalady.com

Food Fetish (818) 762-7850
(24-Hour Service) FAX (818) 762-8470
www.foodfetishcatering.com

Food Lab Catering, LLC (323) 851-7120
7253 Santa Monica Blvd. FAX (323) 461-7837
West Hollywood, CA 90046 www.foodlabcatering.com

For Stars Express Catering (310) 322-1972
www.forstarscatering.com

George Studio Catering (661) 309-9034
17789 Sierra Hwy (310) 505-6676
Santa Clarita, CA 91351 www.georgestudiocatering.com

Global Cuisine by Gary Arabia (323) 850-2600
1041 N. Formosa Ave. (323) 668-0855
West Hollywood, CA 90046 FAX (323) 850-2652
www.globalcuisinecatering.com

Green Truck (310) 204-0477
3315 Helms Ave., Ste. B FAX (310) 204-0377
Culver City, CA 90232 www.greentruckonthego.com

Greenz on Wheelz/Hungry Nomad (877) 666-2310
(818) 246-8002
FAX (818) 572-8744
www.nomadgreenz.com

Hat Trick Catering (818) 968-4403
10953 San Fernando Rd.
Pacoima, CA 91331
(Mobile Kitchen Facilities)

Hollywood Caterers (818) 345-6718
7527 Reseda Blvd., Ste. B FAX (818) 345-6719
Reseda, CA 91335 www.hollywood-caterers.com
(24-Hour Service & Mobile Kitchen Facilities)

J.R.'s Gourmet Catering (805) 688-0086
1210 Mission Dr., Ste. 110 (805) 245-0953
Solvang, CA 93463 FAX (805) 688-5396
www.jrscatering.net

Java The Truck -
Entertainment Coffee Service (310) 717-6967
8180 Manitoba St., Ste. 333 FAX (818) 994-4228
Playa Del Rey, CA 90293 www.javathetruck.com

Jennie Cook Catering (323) 982-0052
3048 Fletcher Dr. FAX (323) 982-9180
Los Angeles, CA 90065 www.jenniecooks.com

Joe's Studio Services (818) 469-9047
(866) 671-5637
FAX (661) 729-9480
www.joesstudioservices.com

Johnny Pacific (818) 885-6927
www.johnnypacificeats.com

Jolly Brothers Catering (805) 687-2023
423 W. Victoria St. (805) 969-5656
Santa Barbara, CA 93101 FAX (805) 969-5656

Karen's Espresso (818) 342-8400
(818) 770-8826
www.karensespresso.com
(24-Hour Mobile Espresso and Smoothie Service)

Leave It To Linda Catering (310) 848-4197
www.leaveittolinda.com

Let's Have A Cart Party (310) 246-1230
FAX (310) 786-1719
www.letshaveacartparty.com
(24-Hour Service & Mobile Kitchen Facilities)

Lidia's Dominican Kitchen (323) 967-3310
(718) 809-7968
www.lidiasdominicankitchen.com

Life In The Food Chain/Patty Domay (661) 255-3625
(661) 222-8334
(Breakfasts)

Little Next Door (323) 951-1010
8142 W. Third St. FAX (323) 951-0487
Los Angeles, CA 90048 www.thelittledoor.com

Lori's Kitchen (310) 473-5783
FAX (818) 787-5066

M.B.'s Food/Mary Beth Pape (310) 398-3653
(Breakfasts) FAX (310) 398-3653

Mario Guzman Catering (818) 421-1876
14053 Lanark St. (818) 997-7478
Panorama, CA 91402 FAX (818) 997-7478

Matt's Coffee Express (805) 388-5035
P.O. Box 675 (805) 377-3630
Somis, CA 93066 FAX (805) 484-3503
www.mattscoffeeexpress.com
(24-Hour Mobile Coffee Service)

Michael's Epicurean Catering (818) 360-7626
P.O. Box 33965 (818) 262-5702
Granada Hills, CA 91394
www.michaelsepicurean.com/filmtvprodcatering.html
(24-Hour Service)

Nagomi LLC (310) 923-8515

Neil Richardson's Premier Breakfast (323) 651-5121
P.O. Box 36745 (310) 849-6463
Los Angeles, CA 90036

New Frontier Espresso Bar Catering (310) 839-3423
12021 Wilshire Blvd., Ste. 352 (800) 949-5282
Los Angeles, CA 90025 FAX (310) 839-3453
www.nfcoffee.com
(Mobile Espresso Bar)

Off The Shelf Catering (310) 440-0794
9854 National Blvd., Ste. 234 (310) 936-5665
Los Angeles, CA 90034 FAX (310) 494-0794
(Mobile Kitchen Facilities)

Oranges/Sardines (323) 256-6172
(Breakfast) www.orangessardines.com/Breakfast

Panini Di Ambra, I
(323) 463.1200
(323) 459-1541
www.thepaninilady.com
5633 Hollywood Blvd.
Los Angeles, CA 90028
(24-Hour Service)

Patrick's Location Catering
(805) 388-5544
FAX (805) 388-5544
(24-Hour Service & Mobile Kitchen Facilities)

Piknic
(310) 496-3966
FAX (310) 862-5762
www.piknic.us
13020 Pacific Promenade, Ste. 1
Playa Vista, CA 90094
(24-Hour Service)

Playland Concessions Inc.
(714) 396-7000
(714) 471-5015
www.socaleventrentals.com
8961 Bedel Dr.
Huntington Beach, CA 92646
(Mobile Kitchen Facilities)

Raleigh Studios Special Events & Catering
(323) 871-4430
(323) 960-3456
FAX (323) 871-5600
www.raleighstudios.com
5300 Melrose Ave.
Hollywood, CA 90038

Red Balls Rock & Roll Pizza
(818) 348-1524
(818) 431-0115
FAX (818) 348-1574
www.redballs.com
6551 Topanga Canyon Blvd.
Woodland Hills, CA 91303

Reel Chefs Catering
(310) 613-6986
(310) 397-5405
FAX (310) 398-3436
www.reelchefscatering.com

Richard Friedman Catering
(310) 450-4377
FAX (323) 932-1499
1326 Pico Blvd.
Santa Monica, CA 90405

Ruisseau Espresso
(213) 663-9455
www.ruisseau.biz
819 N. Florence St.
Burbank, CA 91506
(Cappuccino Bar)

Sam Choy's Pineapple Express
(310) 746-7163
(818) 881-4852
www.samchoyspx.com
6027 ¼ Reseda Blvd.
Tarzana, CA 91356
24-Hour Service, Mobile Kitchen Facilities

Sandmarsh Coffee Lady
(310) 429-4633
720 Angelus Pl.
Venice, CA 90291
(Coffee Service, Smoothies & Teas)

Charlie Scola/PartyCharlie
(310) 214-9158
www.charliescola.com

Silver Grill Catering
(818) 255-2085
(818) 314-9696
FAX (818) 255-2084

Smoke City Market
(818) 855-1280
FAX (818) 855-1281
www.smokecitymarket.com
5242 Van Nuys Blvd.
Sherman Oaks, CA 91401

Some Like It Hot Catering
(818) 765-5663
(323) 934-3330
FAX (323) 934-3393
www.somelikeithotcatering.com

Stonefire Grill
(818) 991-4054
(888) 649-5783
FAX (818) 338-8757
www.stonefiregrill.com

Sunlight Catering, Inc.
(818) 441-8177
(323) 304-3680

Taco-Man! LLC
(310) 784-1399
(310) 784-1396
FAX (310) 784-1396
www.taco-man.com
P.O. Box 1483
Torrance, CA 90505

Taste Catering, Inc.
(949) 215-7373
FAX (949) 215-7494
www.tastecateringcafe.com
(24-Hour Service & Mobile Kitchen Facilities)

TomKats, Inc.
(800) 670-2248
FAX (615) 256-5055
www.tomkats.com

Too Tasty Catering
(818) 335-2096
(818) 355-5431
FAX (818) 549-0848
www.tootasty-catering.com
329 Winchester Ave.
Glendale, CA 91201

Ⓐ Toucan Catering, Inc.
(323) 733-5544
FAX (323) 733-5545
(24-Hour Service)

Truly Yours Catering
(818) 753-9100
FAX (818) 753-6777
www.trulyyourscatering.com
10940 Burbank Blvd.
N. Hollywood, CA 91601

What's Cooking Good Looking Caterers
(818) 349-0926
FAX (818) 349-1492

Wild Wild West Catering
(818) 317-3015
FAX (818) 989-5890
6552 Greenbush Ave.
Valley Glen, CA 91401

Wolfgang Puck Catering
(323) 491-1250
www.wolfgangpuck.com
6801 Hollywood Blvd.
Ste. 5013
Los Angeles, CA 90028

AAA Communications
(626) 813-7580
(888) 925-5437
16025 Arroyo Hwy, Ste. H   FAX (626) 813-7460
Irwindale, CA 91706   www.aaacomm.com
(Cellular Phones, Multi-Line Phone Systems, Pagers &
Walkie Talkies)

AAAAAA-You! Walkie Rentals   (310) 383-6572
(Walkie Talkies)

Airwaves Cellular
(818) 501-8200
(800) 400-9929
13400 Riverside Dr., Ste. 103   FAX (818) 528-7686
Sherman Oaks, CA 91423
(Cellular Phones, Nextels, Walkie Talkies & Wireless Internet)

American Radio
(619) 239-5020
(877) 247-8866
2907 Shelter Island Dr., Ste. 105   FAX (619) 239-5925
San Diego, CA 92106   www.americanradio.us
(Base Stations, Cellular Phones, Repeaters & Walkie Talkies)

**Anytime Production
Equipment Rentals, Inc.**   (323) 461-8483
755 N. Lillian Way   FAX (323) 461-2338
Hollywood, CA 90038   www.anytimerentals.com
(Bullhorns, Helicopter Headsets & Walkie Talkies)

Apache Rental Group
(818) 842-9944
(818) 842-9875
3910 W. Magnolia Blvd.   FAX (818) 842-9269
Burbank, CA 91505   www.apacherentalgroup.com
(Base Stations, Bullhorns, Cellular Phones, Pagers,
Repeaters & Walkie Talkies)

Atomic Production Supplies   (818) 566-8811
2621 N. Ontario St.   FAX (818) 566-8311
Burbank, CA 91504
                www.atomicproductionsupplies.com
(Cellular Phones, Nextels & Walkie Talkies)

AVS   (818) 954-8842
712 S. Main St.   FAX (818) 954-9122
Burbank, CA 91506   www.aerialvideo.com
(Miniature Talent Cueing Systems, Repeaters, Walkie Talkies &
Wired/Wireless Intercom Systems)

C3 Communications   (818) 787-6700
Cabling Consulting   (818) 231-3079
7737 Densmore Ave.   FAX (818) 787-6701
Van Nuys, CA 91406   www.c-3usa.com
(Fax Installation, Internet Connection, Office Phones, Rental
Phones, Telephone Systems, Temporary Land Lines, Voice/
Data Cabling & VOIP Phone Systems)

Cellular Abroad
(310) 862-7100
(800) 287-5072
425 Culver Blvd.   FAX (310) 919-2820
Playa del Rey, CA 90293   www.cellularabroad.com
(Cellular Phones)

CineLUX Sound Services Inc.
(818) 566-3000
(888) 246-3589
4300 W. Victory Blvd.   www.cinelux.tv
Burbank, CA 91505

CloudCasters Satellite &   (866) 978-7555
Cellular Internet Solutions   (360) 944-9842
13825 Vanowen St., Ste. 4
Van Nuys, CA 91405
                www.cloudcasters.com/onset_wifi
(Cellular Wifi Internet & Location Satellite Services)

**Coffey Sound &
Communications, Inc.**   (323) 876-7525
3325 Cahuenga Blvd. West   FAX (323) 876-4775
Hollywood, CA 90068   www.coffeysound.com
(Bullhorns, Cellular Phones, Fax Machines, Repeaters &
Walkie Talkies)

COMMLine Inc.   (310) 390-8003
5563 Sepulveda Blvd., Ste. D   FAX (310) 390-4393
Culver City, CA 90230   www.commlineinc.com
(Radios, Rentals, Repeaters & Walkie Talkies)

Day Wireless Systems
(818) 557-7390
(800) 235-7011
1801 W. Burbank Blvd.   FAX (818) 557-0254
Burbank, CA 91504   www.daywireless.com
(Base Stations, Cellular Phone/Fax Equipment, Nextels,
Pagers, Repeaters, Walkie Talkies & Wireless Systems)

Ⓐ **Exchange Communications**
(888) 679-6111
(505) 501-1029
8217 Lankershim Blvd., Ste. 43   FAX (888) 694-8111
North Hollywood, CA 91605   www.exchangecom.net
(Internet Connectivity, Office Phone Systems, Satellite Internet
Connection, Temporary Land Lines & Wireless Internet)

Heavy Artillery Production Rentals (310) 295-1202
3200 S. La Cienega Blvd.   FAX (310) 295-1202
Los Angeles, CA 90016 www.heavyartilleryrentals.com
(Base Stations, Bullhorns, Mobile Services & Walkie Talkies)

**Hollywood Telephone/
Will Communications**   (310) 536-9777
2627 Manhattan Beach Blvd., Ste. 211 FAX (310) 536-9276
Redondo Beach, CA 90278
                www.willcommunications.com
(Digital Phone Systems, Panasonic System IP Wireless
Handsets (128) on PBX, Rental Phone Systems and
Installation & Telephone Systems)

J & R Productions
(818) 845-6440
(800) 818-7234
201 N. Hollywood Way, Ste. 102   FAX (818) 557-0270
Burbank, CA 91505
(Bullhorns, Cellular Phones, Pagers & Walkie Talkies)

J. Dolan Communications   (818) 487-7203
11331 Ventura Blvd., Ste. 1A   FAX **(818) 487-7208**
Studio City, CA 91604 **www.dolancommunications.com**
(2-Ways, Base Stations, Bullhorns, Helicopter Headsets,
Intercom Systems, Internet Connectivity, Radios, Rentals,
Repair, Repeaters, Walkie Talkies, Wired/Wireless Intercom
Systems & Wireless Internet)

JLH Communications   (310) 398-7430
12549 Everglade St.   FAX **(310) 398-7430**
Los Angeles, CA 90066
(Digital Phone Systems, Installation, Office Phone Systems and
Installation & Telephone Systems)

                                     (310) 476-8380
LCS   (310) 740-0995
2554 Lincoln Blvd., Ste. 421   FAX **(818) 789-6435**
Venice, CA 90291
(Acoustic Coupler Systems, Base Stations, Bullhorns, Cellular
Data Interfaces and Phone/Fax Equipment, Nextels, Office
Phone Systems, Pagers, Repeaters, Satellite Systems &
Walkie Talkies)

                                     (310) 476-8380
LCS   (310) 740-0995
15445 Ventura Blvd., Ste. 3312 FAX **(818) 789-6435**
Sherman Oaks, CA 91403

**Lighthouse
CommunicationsEquipment**   (818) 571-9738
            www.communicationsequipment.net
(2-Ways Radios, Base Stations, Bullhorns, Helicopter
Headsets, Installation, Intercom Systems, Internet Connectivity,
Interpretation Equipment, Mobile Services, Radios, Rentals,
Repair, Repeaters, Speaker Mics, Walkie Talkies,
Wired/Wireless Intercom Systems & Wireless Internet)

Line 204 Inc.   (323) 960-0113
837 N. Cahuenga Blvd.   FAX **(323) 960-0163**
Hollywood, CA 90038   **www.line204.com**
(Base Stations, Cellular Phones, Repeaters & Walkie Talkies)

                                     (800) 818-8324
Location Connect   (626) 792-0000
200 E. Del Mar Blvd., Ste. 300 FAX **(626) 844-1001**
Pasadena, CA 91105   **www.locationconnect.com**
(Digital Phone Systems, Fax Equipment, Installation, Intercom
Systems, Internet Connectivity, Internet Streaming, Mobile
Services, Radios, Remote Video Village, Rentals, Repeaters,
Satellite Internet Connection, Satellite Phones, Satellite-Based
Service, Telephone Systems, Temporary Land Lines, Wired/
Wireless Intercom Systems & Wireless Internet)

                                     (818) 980-9891
Location Sound Corporation   (800) 228-4429
10639 Riverside Dr.   FAX **(818) 980-9911**
North Hollywood, CA 91602 **www.locationsound.com**
(2-Way Radios, Base Stations, Bullhorns, Intercom Systems,
Radios, Rentals, Repair, Repeaters, Walkie Talkies, Wired/
Wireless Intercom Systems & Wireless Mics)

**Los Angeles
Telemedia Associates, Inc.**   (818) 386-2013
3609 Meadville Dr.   **www.losangelestelemedia.com**
Sherman Oaks, CA 91403
(Installation, Internet Connectivity, Rental Phone Systems &
Telephone Systems)

Loud and Clear Communications (310) 350-1717
2118 Wilshire Blvd., Ste. 164   FAX **(310) 496-3247**
Santa Monica, CA 90403
(2-Ways, Bullhorns, Cellular Phones, Helicopter Headsets,
Radios, Rentals, Repeaters & Walkie Talkies)

                                     (323) 254-7466
The Neighborhood Phone Co.   (323) 376-4232
5260 Dahlia Dr.   FAX **(323) 258-7646**
Los Angeles, CA 90041
(Digital Phone Systems, Installation, Telephone Systems &
Temporary Land Lines)

                                     (949) 566-8140
Newport Audio and Video   (949) 650-4445
480 Old Newport Blvd., Ste. B   FAX **(949) 650-4674**
Newport Beach, CA 92663   **www.newportav.com**
(Digital Phone Systems, Intercom Systems, Loudspeakes,
Internet Connectivity, Satellite Television, Telephone Systems,
Temporary Land Lines, Wired/Wireless Intercom Systems &
Wireless Mics)

On Set Communications, Inc.   (818) 512-1918
(Walkie-Talkies)   FAX **(818) 260-0225**
            www.onsetcommunications.net

Out of Frame Communications   (323) 462-1898
1124 N. Citrus Ave.   FAX **(323) 462-1897**
Hollywood, CA 90038   **www.outofframela.com**
(2-Ways, Base Stations, Bullhorns, Helicopter Headsets,
Radios, Rentals, Walkie Talkies, Wired/Wireless Intercom
Systems & Wireless Internet)

The Production Truck, Inc.   (818) 459-0425
711 Ruberta Ave.   FAX **(818) 459-0427**
Glendale, CA 91201   **www.theproductiontruck.com**
(Walkie Talkies)

Quixote Studios   (323) 461-1408
1000 N. Cahuenga Blvd.   FAX **(323) 461-5517**
Los Angeles, CA 90038   **www.quixote.com**

                                     (818) 455-8300
Reliable Telephone & Data, Inc. (800) 942-7200
16742 Stagg St., Ste. 105   FAX **(818) 920-1202**
Van Nuys, CA 91406   **www.latelephone.com**
(Digital Phone Systems & Telephone Systems)

                                     (310) 315-2600
Rock Bottom Rentals   (800) 794-5444
1310 Westwood Blvd.   FAX **(310) 582-1178**
Los Angeles, CA 90024   **www.rockbottomrentals.com**
(4G Hot Spots, Base Stations, Bullhorns, Cellular Phone/Fax
Equipment, International Phones, Junxion Boxes, Pagers,
Repeaters, Satellite Phones, Verizon, Walkie Talkies & WiFi)

                                     (877) 447-6253
Rocket Internet   (310) 532-9216
200 Oceangate, Eighth Fl.   FAX **(562) 432-6096**
Long Beach, CA 90802   **www.rocketinternet.net**
(Internet Connectivity)

                                     (818) 645-3390
Rockstar Communications, Inc   (323) 578-6088
1920 N. Hillhurst Ave., Ste. 108 FAX **(323) 662-3233**
Los Angeles, CA 90027
(Base Stations, Bullhorns, Cellular Phones, Internet
Connectivity, Rentals, Repeaters, Walkie Talkies &
Wireless Internet)

S&W Communications, Inc.   (818) 786-7050
14714 Lull St.   FAX **(818) 786-3289**
Van Nuys, CA 91405   **www.swphonedata.com**
(Phone Installation and Systems)

                                     (323) 938-2420
Samy's Camera   (800) 321-4726
431 S. Fairfax Ave.   FAX **(323) 937-2919**
Los Angeles, CA 90036   **www.samys.com**
(Walkie Talkies)

Samy's Camera   (310) 450-4551
4411 Sepulveda Blvd.   FAX **(310) 450-8590**
Culver City, CA 90230   **www.samys.com**

Selak Entertainment, Inc.   (626) 584-8110
1200 Lida St.   **www.selakentertainment.com**
Pasadena, CA 91103
(Internet Connectivity, Satellite-Based Service, Satellite Internet
Connection, Satellite Phones, Temporary Land Lines &
Wireless Internet)

Set Stuff, Inc.   (323) 993-9500
1105 N. Sycamore Ave.   FAX **(323) 993-9506**
Hollywood, CA 90038   **www.setstuffrentals.com**
(40-Watt Base Stations, Cellular Phones, Helicopter Headsets,
Nextels, Pagers, Repeaters & Walkie Talkies)

SJM Industrial Radio (310) 640-2700
(800) 688-1653
1212 E. Imperial Ave. FAX **(310) 640-9635**
El Segundo, CA 90245 **www.sjmradio.com**
(2-Ways, Authorized Motorola Dealer, Base Stations, Bullhorns,
Cellular Phones, Installation, Mobile Services, Radios, Rentals,
Repeaters, Repair, Satellite Phones & Walkie Talkies)

Skye Rentals **(323) 462-5934**
1016 Mansfield Ave. FAX **(323) 462-5935**
Hollywood, CA 90038 **www.skyerentals.com**
(2-Ways, Base Stations, Bullhorns, Helicopter Headsets,
Internet Connectivity, Radios, Rentals, Repeaters, Satellite
Phones, Walkie Talkies & Wireless Internet)

Star Communications, Inc. **(310) 659-3232**
9107 Wilshire Blvd., Ste. 500 FAX **(310) 659-3377**
Beverly Hills, CA 90210 **www.starcommunicationsinc.net**
(Cellular Phones)

TCH/The Camera House **(818) 997-3802**
7351 Fulton Ave. FAX **(818) 997-3885**
North Hollywood, CA 91605 **www.thecamerahouse.com**

Theatrical Concepts, Inc. **(818) 597-1100**
3030 Triunfo Canyon Rd. FAX **(818) 597-0202**
Agoura Hills, CA 91301 **www.theatrical.com**
(Walkie Talkies)

Vision Communications (800) 778-2275
(818) 844-8480
FAX **(562) 494-1106**
www.2viscom.com
(2-Ways, Base Stations, Bullhorns, CCTV, Cellular Phones,
Installation, Pagers, Rentals, Repair, Repeaters, Satellite
Phones & Walkie Talkies)

Walkietalkie.com (818) 782-5705
(800) 400-5705
16844 Saticoy FAX **(818) 782-5817**
Van Nuys, CA 91406 **www.walkietalkie.com**
(2-Ways, Base Stations, Bullhorns, Radios, Rentals, Repair,
Repeaters & Walkie Talkies)

Warner Bros. Studio Facilities -
Production Sound & Video **(818) 954-2511**
4000 Warner Blvd., Bldg. 43 FAX **(818) 954-2491**
Burbank, CA 91522 **www.wbsoundandvideo.com**

Wilcox Sound and Communications **(818) 504-0507**
7680 Clybourn Ave., Ste. B FAX **(818) 504-0921**
Sun Valley, CA 91352 **www.wilcoxsound.net**

Wired Accessories, Inc. (818) 344-9998
(877) 947-3352
9601 Owensmouth Ave., Ste. 1 FAX **(818) 344-9991**
Chatsworth, CA 91311 **www.wiredaccessories.com**
(Cellular Phones, Nextels & Walkie Talkies)

Wright Communications (818) 340-5481
(818) 307-7224
4558 Don Pio Dr. **www.themobilehotspot.com**
Woodland Hills, CA 91364
(Cellular Phones, Internet Connectivity, Portable Faxing,
Rentals, Repeaters, Sales & Wireless Internet)

Xela Communications **(323) 636-1910**
www.xelallc.com
(Cellular Phones, Digital Phone Systems, Intercom Systems,
Internet Connectivity, Mobile Services, Internet Connection,
Satellite Phones, Telephone, Wired/Wireless
Intercom Systems & Wireless Internet)

Argentina Consulate General (323) 954-9155
FAX **(323) 934-9076**
www.clang.mrecic.gob.ar/en

Australian Consulate General (310) 229-2300
2029 Century Park East, Ste. 3150   FAX **(310) 229-2380**
Los Angeles, CA 90067
www.losangeles.consulate.gov.au

Austrian Consulate General (310) 444-9310
FAX **(310) 477-9897**
www.austria-la.org

Barbados Consulate General (800) 221-9831
www.barbados.org

Belgian Consulate General (323) 857-1244
FAX **(323) 936-2564**
www.diplomatie.be/losangeles

Brazilian Consulate General (323) 651-2664
8484 Wilshire Blvd., Ste. 711   FAX **(323) 651-1274**
Beverly Hills, CA 90211   **www.brazilian-consulate.org**

Canadian Consulate General (213) 346-2700
FAX **(213) 346-2767**
www.losangeles.gc.ca

Chile Consulate General (323) 933-3697
FAX **(323) 933-3842**

China Consulate General (213) 807-8088
FAX **(213) 807-8091**
www.losangeles.china-consulate.org/eng/

(213) 380-7915
Costa Rica Consulate General (213) 380-6031
FAX **(213) 380-5639**
www.costarica-embassy.org

Finland Consulate General (310) 203-9903
1801 Century Park East, Ste. 2100   FAX **(310) 203-9186**
Los Angeles, CA 90067   **www.finland.org**

French Consulate General (310) 235-3200
FAX **(310) 479-4813**
www.consulfrance-losangeles.org

German Consulate General (323) 930-2703
FAX **(323) 930-2805**
www.germany.info/losangeles.org

Great Britain Consulate General (310) 481-0031
FAX **(310) 481-2960**
www.ukinusa.fco.gov.uk

Greek Consulate General (310) 826-5555
12424 Wilshire Blvd., Ste. 1170   FAX **(310) 826-8670**
Los Angeles, CA 90025
www.greekembassy.org/losangeles/

Guatemala Consulate General (213) 365-9251
3540 Wilshire Blvd., Ste. 100   FAX **(213) 365-9245**
Los Angeles, CA 90010   **www.consulaxgt.com**

Honduras Consulate General (213) 995-6406
3550 Wilshire Blvd., Ste. 410   FAX **(213) 383-9306**
Los Angeles, CA 90010   **www.hondurasemb.org**

Israeli Consulate General (323) 852-5500
11766 Wilshire Blvd., Ste. 1600   FAX **(323) 852-5556**
Los Angeles, CA 90025   **www.israeliconsulatela.org**

Italy Consulate General (310) 820-0622
12400 Wilshire Blvd., Ste. 300   FAX **(310) 820-0727**
Los Angeles, CA 90025   **sedi.esteri.it/losangeles/**

Japanese Consulate General (213) 617-6700
350 S. Grand Ave., Ste. 1700   FAX **(213) 617-6727**
Los Angeles, CA 90071   **www.la.us.emb-japan.go.jp**

Malaysia Consulate General (213) 892-1238
550 S. Hope St., Ste. 400   FAX **(213) 892-9031**
Los Angeles, CA 90071 **www.malaysianconsulatela.com**

Mexico Consulate General (213) 351-6800
www.sre.gob.mx/losangeles

(310) 268-1598
The Netherlands Consulate General (877) 388-2443
11766 Wilshire Blvd., Ste. 1150   FAX **(310) 312-0989**
Los Angeles, CA 90025   **www.ncla.org**

New Zealand Consulate General (310) 566-6555
2425 Olympic Blvd., Ste. 600E   FAX **(310) 566-6556**
Santa Monica, CA 90404   **www.nzcgla.com**

Nicaragua Consulate General (213) 252-1170
3550 Wilshire Blvd., Ste. 200   FAX **(213) 252-1177**
Los Angeles, CA 90010
www.consuladodenicaragua.com

Peruvian Consulate General (213) 252-5910
3450 Wilshire Blvd., Ste. 800   FAX **(213) 252-8130**
Los Angeles, CA 90010   **www.peruvianembassy.us**

Philippines Consulate General (213) 639-0980
3600 Wilshire Blvd., Ste. 500   FAX **(213) 639-0990**
Los Angeles, CA 90010   **www.philippineconsulatela.org**

Saudi Arabia Consulate General (310) 479-6000
2045 Sawtelle Blvd.   FAX **(310) 479-2752**
West Los Angeles, CA 90025   **www.saudiembassy.net**

South African Consulate General (323) 651-0902
6300 Wilshire Blvd., Ste. 600   FAX **(323) 651-5969**
Los Angeles, CA 90048   **www.link2southafrica.com**

South Korea Consulate General (213) 385-9300
FAX **(213) 385-1849**
usa-losangeles.mofat.go.kr

Spanish Consulate General (323) 938-0158
FAX **(323) 938-0112**

Sweden Consulate General (858) 271-1573
9625 Black Mountain Rd., Ste. 306
San Diego, CA 92126   **www.sweden-sandiego.org**

Switzerland Consulate General (310) 575-1145
11766 Wilshire Blvd., Ste. 1400   FAX **(310) 575-1982**
Los Angeles, CA 90025   **www.eda.admin.ch/la**

Thailand Consulate General (323) 962-9574
611 N. Larchmont Blvd., Second Fl.   FAX **(323) 962-2128**
Los Angeles, CA 90004   **www.thaiconsulatela.org**

Turkey Consulate General (323) 655-8832
6300 Wilshire Blvd., Ste. 2010   FAX **(323) 655-8681**
Los Angeles, CA 90048 **www.losangeles.cg.mfa.gov.tr/**

Uruguay Consulate General (310) 394-5777
429 Santa Monica Blvd., Ste. 400   FAX **(310) 394-5140**
Santa Monica, CA 90401   **www.uruwashi.org**

Art Pack, Inc.   (310) 328-0300
www.artpack.us

Banner Packing   (310) 276-0804
FAX (310) 659-9887

Beverly Packing, Inc.   (323) 658-8365
645 N. Fairfax Ave.   FAX (323) 658-5815
Los Angeles, CA 90036   www.beverlypacking.com

Box Brothers   (310) 478-4008
(800) 842-6937
FAX (310) 478-0667
www.boxbros.com

Cooke's Crating   (323) 268-5101
FAX (323) 262-2001
www.cookescrating.com

Dynamic L.A., Inc.   (818) 771-1111
11755 Sheldon St.   FAX (818) 771-1159
Sun Valley, CA 91352   www.dynamicla.com

ETC International Freight System   (800) 383-3157
21039 S. Figueroa St., Ste. 101   FAX (310) 632-3044
Carson, CA 90745   www.etcinternational.com
(24-Hour Service)

Fine Art Shipping   (310) 677-0011
(800) 421-7464
404 N. Oak St.   FAX (310) 677-8586
Inglewood, CA 90302   www.fineartship.com

LA Packing, Crating & Transport   (323) 937-2669
(800) 852-9836
5722 W. Jefferson Blvd.   FAX (323) 937-9012
Los Angeles, CA 90016   www.lapacking.com

Packaging Store   (818) 956-1137
4525 San Fernando Rd.   FAX (818) 763-2050
Glendale, CA 91204   www.gopackagingstore.com

Packaging Store   (818) 763-1808
10218 Riverside Dr.   FAX (818) 763-2050
Toluca Lake, CA 91602   www.gopackagingstore.com

UsedCardboardboxes.com   (888) 269-3788
(323) 724-2500
4032 Wilshire Blvd., Ste. 402   FAX (323) 315-4194
Los Angeles, CA 90010   www.usedcardboardboxes.com
(24-Hour Service, New, Surplus and Used Boxes)

Customs Brokers & Carnets

Atlant USA, Inc.   (310) 631-1810
FAX (310) 631-1830
www.atlant.com

DB Schenker   (323) 908-4800
(800) 541-6261
2815 W. El Segundo Blvd.   FAX (323) 908-4874
Hawthorne, CA 90250   www.dbschenkerusa.com

ETC International Freight System   (800) 383-3157
21039 S. Figueroa St., Ste. 101   FAX (310) 632-3044
Carson, CA 90745   www.etcinternational.com
(24-Hour Service)

Hahn International   (310) 216-6691
(24-Hour Service)   FAX (310) 216-1681
www.hahnintl.com

MPA International   (310) 590-1660
(866) 744-7672
10121 Pinehurst Ave.   FAX (310) 590-1688
Southgate, CA 90280   www.mpasite.com
(24-Hour Service)

Rock-It Cargo USA, Inc.   (310) 410-0935
FAX (310) 410-0628
www.rockitcargo.com

Total Transportation Concept, Inc.   (310) 337-0515
(800) 582-7110
8728 Aviation Blvd.   FAX (310) 337-7901
Inglewood, CA 90301   www.totaltrans.com

Alhambra (626) 570-5021
111 S. First St. FAX (626) 308-4868
Alhambra, CA 91801 www.cityofalhambra.org
(Issues Permits)
Contact: Kim Johnson

Anaheim (714) 765-5183
Traffic Engineering Division FAX (714) 765-4667
200 S. Anaheim Blvd.
Anaheim, CA 92805
Contact: Cyndee Blake

(661) 723-6090
Antelope Valley (661) 510-4231
44933 Fern Ave. FAX (661) 723-5914
Lancaster, CA 93534 www.avfilm.com

Arcadia (626) 574-5430
P.O. Box 60021 FAX (626) 821-4336
Arcadia, CA 91066 www.ci.arcadia.ca.us
Contact: Silva Vergel

Bell (323) 588-6211
6330 Pine Ave. FAX (323) 771-9473
Bell, CA 90201

(562) 806-7700
Bell Gardens (562) 806-7740
7100 Garfield Ave. FAX (562) 806-7720
Bell Gardens, CA 90201 www.bellgardens.org
(Issues Permits)
Contact: Carmen Morales

Bellflower (562) 804-1424
16600 Civic Center Dr. FAX (562) 925-8660
Bellflower, CA 90706 www.bellflower.org
(Issues Permits)

(510) 549-7040
Berkeley (800) 847-4823
Berkeley Film Office FAX (510) 644-2052
2030 Addison St., Ste. 102 www.filmberkeley.com
Berkeley, CA 94704
(Issues Permits)

Beverly Hills (310) 285-2408
455 N. Rexford Dr., Ste. G10 FAX (310) 273-0972
Beverly Hills, CA 90210 www.beverlyhills.org
(Issues Permits)
Contact: Benita Miller

Bradbury (626) 358-3218
600 Winston Ave. FAX (626) 303-5154
Bradbury, CA 91010 www.cityofbradbury.org
(Issues Permits)
Contacts: Claudia Saldana & Jennifer Vasquez

Burbank (818) 238-3105
200 N. Third St. FAX (818) 238-3109
Burbank, CA 91502
www.ci.burbank.ca.us/police/filmpermits.html
(Issues Permits)
Contact: Norma Brolsma

Bureau of Land Management (760) 252-6000
2601 Barstow Rd. FAX (760) 252-6098
Barstow, CA 92311 www.filminlandempire.com
(Issues Permits)
Contacts: Sheri Davis & Dan Taylor

Calabasas (805) 495-7521
Calabasas Film Office FAX (805) 495-7621
25 W. Rolling Oaks Dr., Ste. 201 www.cityofcalabasas.com
Thousand Oaks, CA 91361
(Issues Permits)

(800) 225-3764
Calaveras County (209) 736-0049
P.O. Box 637, 1192 S. Main St. FAX (209) 736-9124
Angels Camp, CA 95222 www.filmcalaveras.org
Contact: Lisa Reynolds

(323) 860-2960
A California (800) 858-4749
California Film Commission FAX (323) 860-2972
7080 Hollywood Blvd., Ste. 900 www.film.ca.gov
Los Angeles, CA 90028
Contact: Amy Lemisch

Carson (310) 952-1748
701 E. Carson St. FAX (310) 518-2874
Carson, CA 90745 ci.carson.ca.us
(Issues Permits)
Contact: Yuko Dunham

Catalina Island (310) 510-7649
P.O. Box 217 FAX (310) 510-7607
Avalon, CA 90704
(Issues Permits)
www.catalinachamber.com/mediafilming/contact

Cerritos (562) 916-8513
18125 S. Bloomfield Ave. www.filmcerritos.com
Cerritos, CA 90703
(Issues Permits)
Contact: Cynthia Doss

Claremont (909) 399-5497
207 Harvard Ave. FAX (909) 399-5492
Claremont, CA 91711
(Issues Permits)
Contact: Aileen Flores www.ci.claremont.ca.us/
ps.businessservices.cfm?ID=1719

Clovis
(559) 299-7273
(559) 299-7363
FAX (559) 299-2969
325 Pollasky Ave.
Clovis, CA 93612
www.clovischamber.com
(Issues Permits)

Covina
(626) 384-5430
(626) 384-5400
City of Covina, 125 E. College St.   www.ci.covina.ca.us
Covina, CA 91723
(Issues Permits)
Contact: Kathy Cordova

Culver City
(310) 253-6212
Culver City Police Dept.   FAX (310) 253-6220
4040 Duquesne Ave.
Culver City, CA 90232 www.culvercity.org/Government/
PublicSafety/Police/FilmingInCulverCity.aspx
(Issues Permits)
Contact: Lt. Danjou

Downey
(562) 904-7345
11111 Brookshire Ave.
Downey, CA 90241
(Issues Permits)
Contact: Louretta Horton

Duarte
(626) 357-7931
1600 E. Huntington Dr.   www.accessduarte.com
Duarte, CA 91010
(Issues Permits)
Contact: Pat Razavi

El Dorado County Lake Tahoe
(530) 626-4400
(800) 457-6279
542 Main St.   www.filmtahoe.com
Placerville, CA 95667
(Issues Permits)
Contact: Kathleen Dodge

El Monte
(626) 580-2131
(Issues Permits)   FAX (626) 454-3220
Contact: Mark Sullivan

Fresno
(559) 908-0539
Fresno Film Commission   FAX (559) 354-5980
5241 E. Townsend Ave.   www.fresnofilm.com
Fresno, CA 93727
(Issues Permits)
Contact: Ray Arthur

Fresno County
(559) 600-4271
Fresno County Film Commission   FAX (559) 600-4573
2220 Tulare St., Ste. 800   www.filmfresno.com
Fresno, CA 93721
Contacts: Gigi Gibbs & Kristi Johnson

Glendale
(818) 548-2090
(818) 548-4000
613 E. Broadway, Ste. 110   FAX (818) 241-5386
Glendale, CA 91206   www.ci.glendale.ca.us
(Issues Permits)
Contact: Judy Herwig

Glendora
(626) 914-8244
116 E. Foothill Blvd.   FAX (626) 852-9650
Glendora, CA 91741   www.ci.glendora.ca.us
(Issues Permits)
Contact: Kay Dudley

Hawthorne
(310) 349-2935
4455 W. 126th St.   FAX (310) 978-9858
Hawthorne, CA 90250   www.cityofhawthorne.com
(Issues Permits)

Hermosa Beach
(310) 318-0239
(310) 318-0280
710 Pier Ave.   FAX (310) 372-4333
Hermosa Beach, CA 90254
www.hermosabch.org/index.aspx?page=250
(Issues Permits)
Contact: Shaunna Miller Donahue

Humboldt County
(707) 444-6633
(800) 338-7352
520 E St.   FAX (707) 443-5115
Eureka, CA 95501   www.filmhumboldt.org
(Issues Permits)
Contact: Mary Cruse

Huntington Beach   (714) 969-3492
Huntington Beach Film Commission
301 Main St., Ste. 208   www.filmhuntingtonbeach.com
Huntington Beach, CA 92648
(Issues Permits)
Contact: Briton Saxton

Inglewood
(310) 412-5500
(310) 412-5257
One Manchester Blvd.   FAX (310) 330-5735
Inglewood, CA 90301   www.cityofinglewood.org
(Issues Permits)

Inland Empire
(951) 377-7849
(951) 232-1271
Inland Empire Film Commission   FAX (909) 382-6066
1601 E. Third St.   www.filminlandempire.com
San Bernardino, CA 92408
(Issues Permits)
Contacts: Sheri Davis & Dan Taylor

Kern County
(661) 868-5376
(800) 500-5376
2101 Oak St.   FAX (661) 861-2017
Bakersfield, CA 93301   www.filmkern.com
(Issues Permits)
Contacts: Rick Davis & Dave Hook

La Cañada Flintridge   (818) 790-8880
1327 Foothill Blvd.   FAX (818) 790-7536
La Cañada Flintridge, CA 91011   www.lcf.ca.gov
(Issues Permits)

La Habra Heights   (562) 694-6302
1245 N. Hacienda Rd.   FAX (562) 694-4410
La Habra Heights, CA 90631
(Issues Permits)
Contact: Amy Smith-Parker

La Mirada   (562) 943-0131
13700 La Mirada Blvd.   FAX (562) 943-3666
La Mirada, CA 90638   www.cityoflamirada.org
(Issues Permits)
Contact: Karen Bufkin

Lake County   (707) 263-2277
255 N. Forbes St.   FAX (707) 263-1012
Lakeport, CA 95453   www.lakecounty.com
(Issues Permits)
Contact: Debra Sommerfield

Lake Tahoe (South)   (530) 542-6004
1052 Tata Ln.   www.cityofslt.us
South Lake Tahoe, CA 96150
(Issues Permits)
Contact: Angela Peterson

Lakewood   (562) 866-9771
5050 Clark Ave.   FAX (562) 866-0505
Lakewood, CA 90712   www.lakewoodcity.org
(Issues Permits)
Contact: Doug Butler

Livermore Valley   (925) 447-1606
Livermore Valley Film Commission   FAX (925) 447-1641
2157 First St.   www.livermorechamber.org
Livermore, CA 94550
(Issues Permits)

Lomita   (310) 325-7110
24300 Narbonne Ave.   FAX (310) 325-4024
Lomita, CA 90717   www.lomita.com/cityhall
(Issues Permits)
Contact: Pat Negrete

Long Beach
(562) 570-5399
(562) 570-5333
211 E. Ocean Blvd., Ste. 410   FAX (562) 570-5335
Long Beach, CA 90802   www.filmlongbeach.com
(Issues Permits)
Contacts: Tasha Day & Andy Witherspoon

Los Angeles City & County -
Film L.A., Inc.   (213) 977-8600
1201 W. Fifth St., Ste. T800   FAX (213) 977-8610
Los Angeles, CA 90017   www.filmlainc.com
(Issues Permits)

Los Angeles County
Department of Parks & Recreation   (213) 738-2961
433 S. Vermont Ave.   FAX (213) 738-6444
Los Angeles, CA 90020   parks.lacounty.gov
(Issues Permits)
Contacts: Sheila Ortega & Rosanna Franco

Los Padres National Forest -
Monterey   (831) 385-5434
406 S. Mildred   FAX (831) 385-0628
King City, CA 93930   www.fs.fed.us/r5/lospadres
Contact: Manny Madrigal

Los Padres National Forest -
Mt. Pinos   (805) 967-3481
34580 Lockwood Valley Rd.   FAX (805) 967-7312
Frazier Park, CA 93225   Contact: Loreigh Brannan
www.fs.usda.gov/main/lpnf/passes-permits/
event-commercial

Los Padres National Forest - Ojai   (805) 646-4348
1190 E. Ojai Ave.   FAX (805) 646-0484
Ojai, CA 93023   www.fs.fed.us/r5/lospadres
Contact: Al Hess

Los Padres National Forest -
Santa Barbara   (805) 967-3481
3505 Paradise Rd.   FAX (805) 967-7312
Santa Barbara, CA 93105   www.fs.fed.us/r5/lospadres
Contact: Tony Martinez

Los Padres National Forest -
Santa Lucia   (805) 925-9538
1616 N. Carlotti Dr.   FAX (805) 961-5781
Santa Maria, CA 93454   www.fs.fed.us/r5/lospadres
Contacts: Jill Evans & Michael Crain

Malibu   (805) 495-7521
23815 Stuart Ranch Rd.   FAX (805) 495-7621
Malibu, CA 90265   www.ci.malibu.ca.us
(Issues Permits)

Mammoth Lakes & Mono County   (800) 845-7922
P.O. Box 603   www.monocounty.org/static/
Mammoth Lakes, CA 93546   index. cfm?contentID=688
(Issues Permits)
Contact: James Vanko

Manhattan Beach
(310) 802-5561
(310) 802-5555
1400 Highland Ave.   FAX (310) 802-5551
Manhattan Beach, CA 90266   www.citymb.info
(Issues Permits)
Contacts: Steve Charelian & Colette Bellavance

Mendocino County (Film Office)   (707) 961-6302
217 S. Main St.   FAX (707) 964-2056
Fort Bragg, CA 95437   www.filmmendocino.com
Contact: Debra DeGraw

Mendocino County (Permit Office)   (707) 463-4441
501 Low Gap Rd., Ste. 1010   FAX (707) 463-5649
Ukiah, CA 95482 www.mendocinocoast.com/filmoffice/
Contact: Denice Brown

Modesto
(209) 526-5588
(888) 640-8467
1150 Ninth St., Ste. C   FAX (209) 526-5586
Modesto, CA 95354   www.visitmodesto.com
(Issues Permits)

Modoc County   (530) 233-6406
203 W. Fourth St.   FAX (530) 233-6420
Alturas, CA 96101
(Issues Permits)
Contact: Scott Kessler

Monrovia
(626) 932-5586
(626) 932-5550
415 S. Ivy Ave.   FAX (626) 932-5569
Monrovia, CA 91016   www.ci.monrovia.ca.us
(Issues Permits)
Contact: Sheila Spicer-Batice

Montebello   (323) 887-1490
1600 W. Beverly Blvd.   FAX (323) 887-1488
Montebello, CA 90640
(Issues Permits)
Contact: Lynda Carter

Monterey (Permit Office)
(831) 646-3805
(831) 646-3830
Monterey Police Dept.   FAX (831) 646-3802
351 Madison Ave.
Monterey, CA 93940

Monterey County   (831) 646-0910
801 Lighthouse Ave., Ste. 104   FAX (831) 655-9250
Monterey, CA 93940   www.filmmonterey.org
Contact: Karen Nordstrand

Monterey Park
(626) 307-1338
(626) 307-1371
320 W. Newmark Ave.   FAX (626) 307-0753
Monterey Park, CA 91754   www.ci.montereypark.ca.us
(Issues Permits)
Contact: Film Liaison

Napa County Public Works   (707) 253-4351
1195 Third St., Ste. 201   FAX (707) 279-2979
Napa, CA 94559   www.countyofnapa.org
(Issues Permits)

Newport Beach
(949) 644-3309
(949) 644-3300
1624 W. Oceanfront Walk   www.newportbeachca.gov
Newport Beach, CA 92663
(Issues Permits)
Contact: Joseph Cleary

Norwalk   (562) 929-5713
12700 Norwalk Blvd.   FAX (562) 929-5056
Norwalk, CA 90650   www.ci.norwalk.ca.us
(Issues Permits)
Contact: Finance Department - Business License Section

Oakland
(510) 238-4734
(510) 238-3456
One Frank H. Ogawa Plaza, Ninth Fl. FAX (510) 238-6149
Oakland, CA 94612   www.filmoakland.com
(Issues Permits)

Orange County   (714) 278-7569
CSUF, P.O. Box 6850   FAX (714) 278-7521
Fullerton, CA 92834   www.filmorangecounty.org

Orange County -
Unincorporated Area (Permit Office) (714) 667-8888
(714) 667-8866
300 N. Flower St.   FAX (714) 835-7425
Santa Ana, CA 92703   www.ocpermits.com
Contact: Carolyn Uribe

Oxnard
(805) 385-7444
(800) 422-6332
400 E. Esplanade Dr., Ste. 301   FAX (805) 385-7452
Oxnard, CA 93036   www.filmventuracounty.com
(Issues Permits & Location Assistance)
Contact: Brittany Green

Pacific Palms
(626) 810-4455
(800) 524-4557
One Industry Hills Pkwy   www.pacificpalmsresort.com
City of Industry, CA 91744
(Issues Permits)
Contact: Michael Swyney

Palm Springs (951) 377-7849
(951) 232-1271
401 S. Pavilion Way www.palmspringsfilm.com
Palm Springs, CA 92262
(Issues Permits)
Contact: Lois Ware

Palm Springs/Coachella Valley (909) 888-9011
(760) 864-1313
201 A N. E St. FAX (909) 888-9073
Riverside, CA 92507 www.filminlandempire.com

Palmdale (661) 267-5115
Palmdale Film, FAX (661) 267-5122
Convention & Visitors Bureau, www.cityofpalmdale.org
38300 Sierra Hwy, Ste. A
Palmdale, CA 93550
(Issues Permits)
Contact: Barbara Vilardo

Palos Verdes Estates (310) 378-0383
340 Palos Verdes Dr. West FAX (310) 378-7820
Palos Verdes Estates, CA 90274
Contact: Vickie Kroneberger www.palosverdes.com/pve
(Issues Permits)

Paramount (562) 220-2048
(562) 220-2000
16400 Colorado Ave. FAX (562) 220-2051
Paramount, CA 90723 www.paramountcity.com
(Issues Permits)
Contact: John Carver

Pasadena (626) 744-3964
100 N. Garfield Ave., Ste. 116 FAX (626) 396-7567
Pasadena, CA 91101 www.filmpasadena.com
(Issues Permits)
Contact: Kristin Dewey

Placer-Lake Tahoe (530) 889-4091
(877) 228-3456
175 Fulweiler Ave. FAX (530) 889-4095
Auburn, CA 95603 www.placer.ca.gov/films
(Issues Permits)
Contact: Beverly Lewis

Pomona (909) 620-2051
505 S. Garey Ave. www.ci.pomona.ca.us
Pomona, CA 91766
(Issues Permits)
Contact: Tracy Radcliffe

Rancho Palos Verdes (310) 544-5205
30940 Hawthorne Blvd. FAX (310) 544-5291
Rancho Palos Verdes, CA 90275
(Issues Permits) www.palosverdes.com/rpv
Contact: Toni Harris

Redding/Shasta County (530) 225-4105
(800) 874-7562
777 Auditorium Dr. FAX (530) 225-4354
Redding, CA 96001 www.visitredding.org
(Issues Permits)
Contact: Sherry Ferguson

Redondo Beach (310) 318-0603
(310) 372-1171
415 Diamond St., Ste. C FAX (310) 937-6666
Redondo Beach, CA 90277 www.redondo.org
(Issues Permits)
Contact: Ron Brown

Ridgecrest (760) 375-8202
(800) 847-4830
139 Balsam St., Ste. 1700 FAX (760) 375-9850
Ridgecrest, CA 93555 www.filmdeserts.com
(Issues Permits)

Riverside (877) 748-7433
3900 Main St. FAX (951) 826-5744
Riverside, CA 92522 www.riversideca.gov
(Issues Permits)
Contacts: Simone McFarland & Sherry Shimshock

Riverside County (951) 377-7849
1201 Research Park Dr., Ste. 100
Riverside, CA 92507 www.filminlandempire.com
(Issues Permits)

Rolling Hills Estates (310) 377-1577
4045 Palos Verdes Dr. North FAX (310) 377-4468
Rolling Hills Estates, CA 90274
(Issues Permits)
Contact: Kelley Thom

Rosemead (626) 569-2100
8838 E. Valley Blvd. FAX (626) 307-9218
Rosemead, CA 91770 www.cityofrosemead.org
(Issues Permits)
Contacts: Bill Crowe & Don Wagner

Sacramento (916) 808-7777
(916) 808-5553
Sacramento Film Commission FAX (916) 808-7788
1608 I St. www.filmsacramento.com
Sacramento, CA 95814
Contact: Lucy Steffens

San Bernardino County (951) 377-7849
1201 Research Park Dr., Ste. 100
Riverside, CA 92507 www.filminlandempire.com
(Issues Permits)
Contact: Sheri Davis

San Diego (619) 234-3456
2508 Historic Decatur Rd., Ste. 200 FAX (619) 234-4631
San Diego, CA 92106 www.sdfilm.com
(Issues Permits)
Contacts: Rob Dunson, Carrie Heath & Stephen Scott

San Fernando (818) 898-1211
117 Macneil St. FAX (818) 365-8090
San Fernando, CA 91340 www.ci.san-fernando.ca.us
(Issues Permits)
Contact: Sandra Huicochea

San Francisco (415) 554-6241
San Francisco Film Commission FAX (415) 554-6503
One Dr. Carlton B. Goodlett Pl., Ste. 473 www.filmsf.org
San Francisco, CA 94102
(Issues Permits)
Contacts: Laurel Barsotti, Stefanie Coyote & Christine Munday

San Jose (408) 792-4111
(800) 726-5673
408 Almaden Blvd. FAX (408) 277-3535
San Jose, CA 95110 www.sanjose.org
Contact: Kate Manley

San Luis Obispo (800) 634-1414
San Luis Obispo County FAX (805) 543-9498
Film Commission www.sanluisobispocounty.com
811 El Capitan, Ste. 200
San Luis Obispo, CA 93401
Contact: Dave Kastner

San Marino (626) 300-0781
(626) 300-0700
2200 Huntington Dr. FAX (626) 300-0709
San Marino, CA 91108
(Issues Permits)
Contacts: Rob Wishner & Matthew Ballantyne

San Mateo County (650) 348-7600
(800) 288-4748
San Mateo County FAX (650) 348-7687
Film Commission www.filmsanmateocounty.com
111 Anza Blvd., Ste. 410
Burlingame, CA 94010
(Issues Permits)

Santa Barbara City (Permit Office) (805) 897-2300
(805) 897-3747
Santa Barbara Police Dept. FAX (805) 897-2434
215 E. Figueroa St. www.filmsantabarbara.com
Santa Barbara, CA 93101
Contact: Scott Naganuma

Santa Barbara County (805) 966-9222
Santa Barbara County FAX **(805) 966-1728**
Film Commission, **www.filmsantabarbara.com**
1601 Anacapa St.
Santa Barbara, CA 93101
Contact: Geoff Alexander

Santa Barbara County (805) 897-1945
(Permit Office) (805) 966-9222
123 E. Anapamu St. FAX **(805) 568-3103**
Santa Barbara, CA 93101 **www.filmsantabarbara.com**
Contact: Jim Norris

Santa Clarita (661) 284-1425
23920 Valencia Blvd., Ste. 100 FAX **(661) 286-4001**
Santa Clarita, CA 91355 **www.filmsantaclarita.com**
(Issues Permits)

(831) 425-1234
(800) 833-3494
Santa Cruz County
Santa Cruz County Film Commission FAX **(831) 425-1260**
303 Water St., Ste. 100 **www.santacruzfilm.org**
Santa Cruz, CA 95060
Contact: Christina Glynn

Santa Fe Springs (562) 868-0511
11710 E. Telegraph Rd. FAX **(562) 868-7112**
Santa Fe Springs, CA 90670 **www.santafesprings.org**
(Issues Permits)
Contact: Julie Herrera

Santa Monica (310) 458-8737
1685 Main St., Ste. 113 FAX **(310) 576-3598**
Santa Monica, CA 90401
(Issues Permits)
Contacts: Kathy Ruff & Vee Gomez
www.smgov.net/Departments/PublicWorks/
ContentAdminSvcs.aspx?id=7290

Santa Monica Mountains (805) 370-2308
401 W. Hillcrest Dr. FAX **(805) 370-1851**
Thousand Oaks, CA 91360 **www.nps.gov/samo/**
(Issues Permits)
Contact: Alice Allen

Simi Valley (805) 583-6842
Simi Valley Film Permitting Office FAX **(805) 583-6399**
2929 Tapo Canyon Rd. **www.simivalley.org/filming**
Simi Valley, CA 93063
(Issues Permits)

Sonoma County (707) 565-7170
Sonoma County Film Program FAX **(707) 565-7231**
401 College Ave., Ste. D **www.sonomacountyfilm.com**
Santa Rosa, CA 95401
(Issues Permits)
Contact: Colette Thomas

South Gate (323) 563-9500
8650 California Ave. FAX **(323) 357-5818**
South Gate, CA 90280 **www.cityofsouthgate.org**
(Issues Permits)
Contact: Diane Warden

South Pasadena (626) 403-7263
1414 Mission St. **www.ci.south-pasadena.ca.us**
South Pasadena, CA 91030

Temple City (626) 285-2171
9701 Las Tunas Dr. FAX **(626) 285-8192**
Temple City, CA 91780 **www.templecity.us**
(Issues Permits)
Contact: Mary Flandrick

Torrance (310) 618-5923
Business License Office **www.torranceca.gov**
3031 Torrance Blvd.
Torrance, CA 90503
(Issues Permits)
Contact: Jill Weldin

(559) 624-7187
Tulare County (559) 786-5339
Tulare County Film Commission FAX **(559) 730-2591**
5961 S. Mooney Blvd. **www.filmtularecounty.com**
Visalia, CA 93277
(Permit Assistance)
Contact: Eric Coyne

(209) 533-4420
Tuolumne County (800) 446-1333
Tuolumne County Film Commission FAX **(209) 533-0956**
542 West Stockton Rd. **www.tcfilm.org**
Sonora, CA 95370
(Issues Permits)
Contact: Jerry Day

Two Harbors (310) 510-4205
P.O. Box 2530
Avalon, CA 90704
(Issues Permits)
Contact: Gina Long

(707) 642-3653
Vallejo/Solano County (800) 482-5535
289 Mare Island Way FAX **(707) 644-2206**
Vallejo, CA 94590
www.visitvallejo.com/film-office/index.php

Ventura County (Film Office) (805) 384-1800
1601 Carmen Dr., Ste. 215 FAX **(805) 384-1805**
Camarillo, CA 93010 **www.filmventuracounty.com**

Ventura County (Permit Office) (805) 654-2406
Attn: Film Permits FAX **(805) 477-7168**
800 S. Victoria Ave., L-1740
Ventura, CA 93009
Contacts: Dan Price & Pat Richards
www.ventura.org/rma/planning/film.html

(323) 583-8811
Vernon Fire Dept. (323) 583-4821
4305 Santa Fe Ave. FAX **(323) 826-1407**
Vernon, CA 90058 **www.cityofvernon.org**
(Issues Permits)
Contact: Capt. Dan Armellini

Walnut (909) 595-7543
21201 La Puente Rd. FAX **(909) 595-6095**
Walnut, CA 91789 **www.ci.walnut.ca.us**
(Issues Permits)
Contacts: Tony Ramos & Bevin Handel

West Covina (626) 939-8400
1444 W. Garvey Ave.
West Covina, CA 91790
(Issues Permits)
Contact: Cmdr Myrick

West Hollywood (323) 848-6489
8300 Santa Monica Blvd., Third Fl. FAX **(323) 848-6561**
West Hollywood, CA 90069 **www.weho.org**
(Issues Permits)
Contact: Terry House

Westlake Village (818) 706-1613
31200 Oak Crest Dr. FAX **(818) 706-1391**
Westlake Village, CA 91361 **www.wlv.org**
(Issues Permits)
Contact: Kerry Kallman

Whittier (562) 567-9500
13230 E. Penn St. FAX **(562) 567-2874**
Whittier, CA 90602 **www.whittierpd.org**
(Issues Permits)
Contact: Helen Gonzalez

Yosemite/Madera County (559) 760-1143
Yosemite/Madera County FAX **(559) 658-2851**
Film Commission **www.yosemitefilm.com**
Box 3690
Oakhurst, CA 93644

Yreka (530) 841-2386
701 Fourth St. FAX **(530) 842-4836**
Yreka, CA 96097
(Issues Permits)
Contacts: Pam Hayden & Brian W. Meek

Alabama (334) 242-4195
Alabama Film Office FAX **(334) 242-2077**
401 Adams Ave., Ste. 170 **www.alabamafilm.org**
Montgomery, AL 36104
Contact: Courtney Murphy

Alabama-Mobile (251) 438-7102
Mobile Film Office FAX **(251) 438-7104**
164 Saint Emanuel St. **www.mobilefilmoffice.com**
Mobile, AL 36602

Alaska (907) 269-8190
Alaska Film Office FAX **(907) 269-5666**
550 W. Seventh Ave., Ste. 1770 **www.film.alaska.gov**
Anchorage, AK 99501
Contact: Dave Worrell

(602) 771-1116
(800) 523-6695
Arizona
Arizona Film Office FAX **(602) 771-1211**
1700 W. Washington St. Ste. 220
Phoenix, AZ 85007 **www.azcommerce.com/film**
Contact: Ken Chapa

(800) 288-3861
Arizona-Cochise County (520) 432-9215
Cochise County Film Office FAX **(520) 432-5016**
1415 Melody Ln., Bldg. G **www.explorecochise.com**
Bisbee, AZ 85603

(928) 425-4495
Arizona-Globe (800) 804-5623
The Globe-Miami Regional Film Office FAX **(928) 425-3410**
1360 N. Broad St. **www.globemiamichamber.com**
Globe, AZ 85501

(928) 645-2741
Arizona-Page-Lake Powell (888) 261-7243
Page-Lake Powell Film Office FAX **(928) 645-3181**
P.O. Box 727 **www.pagechamber.com**
Page, AZ 86040

Arizona-Phoenix (602) 262-4850
Phoenix Film Office FAX **(602) 534-2295**
200 W. Washington St. **www.filmphoenix.com**
Phoenix, AZ 85003

(928) 777-1204
Arizona-Prescott (866) 878-2489
Prescott Film Office, 201 S. Cortez St. FAX **(928) 777-1255**
Prescott, AZ 86302
www.cityofprescott.net/business/film/

Arizona-Sedona (928) 204-1123
Sedona Film Office, P.O. Box 478 FAX **(928) 204-1064**
Sedona, AZ 86339 **www.sedonafilmoffice.com**
Contact: Lori Reinhart

(520) 770-2151
Arizona-Tucson (877) 311-2489
Tucson Film Office FAX **(520) 629-0160**
100 S. Church Ave. **www.filmtucson.com**
Tucson, AZ 85701

(928) 684-5479
Arizona-Wickenburg (928) 684-0977
Wickenburg Film Office FAX **(928) 684-5470**
216 N. Frontier St. **www.wickenburgchamber.com**
Wickenburg, AZ 85390

Arizona-Yuma (928) 314-9247
Yuma Film Commission FAX **(928) 314-2280**
2600 S. Fourth Ave. **www.filmyuma.com**
Yuma, AZ 85364
Contacts: Yvonne Taylor

Arkansas (501) 682-7676
Arkansas Film Commission FAX **(501) 682-7394**
900 W. Capitol Ave., Ste. 400 **www.arkansasedc.com**
Little Rock, AR 72201
Contact: Christopher Crane

Association of
Film Commissioners International (323) 461-2324
8530 Wilshire Blvd., Ste. 210 FAX **(413) 375-2903**
Beverly Hills, CA 90211 **www.afci.org**

NEVADA FILM OFFICE
Your Imagination. Our Locations.

877.638.3456 • 702.486.2711 • nevadafilm.com

Concrete jungle
to blue boulevards.

(And every dusty road, picket fence and alligator alley in between.)

sunny.org/film

greater FORT LAUDERDALE

Bahamas (242) 322-8744 / (242) 322-4374
Bahamas Film Commission www.bahamasfilm.com
P.O. Box N-3701
The Nassau Bahamas
Contact: Grace Caron

British Virgin Islands (800) 835-8530
British Virgin Islands Film Commission FAX (284) 494-8138
P.O. Box 134, Wickham's Cay 1
Road Town, Tortola Virgin Islands (British)
www.bvitourism.com/FilmCommission.aspx

Ⓐ California (323) 860-2960 / (800) 858-4749
California Film Commission FAX (323) 860-2972
7080 Hollywood Blvd., Ste. 900 www.film.ca.gov
Los Angeles, CA 90028
Contact: Amy Lemisch

Canada-Alberta (780) 422-8584 / (888) 813-1738
Alberta Film Commission FAX (780) 422-8582
140 Whitemud Crossing, 4211 106th St.
Edmonton, AB T6J 6L7 Canada www.albertafilm.ca
Contact: Jeff Brinton

Canada-Argenteuil Laurentians (450) 562-2446
Argenteuil-Laurentians FAX (450) 562-1911
Film Commission www.filmlaurentides.ca
430 Grace St.
Lachute, QC J8H 1M6 Canada

Canada-British Columbia (604) 660-2732
BC Film Commission FAX (604) 660-4790
201-865 Hornby St. www.bcfilmcommission.com
Vancouver, BC V6Z 2G3 Canada

Canada-Calgary (403) 221-7831 / (888) 222-5855
Calgary Film Commission FAX (403) 221-7828
731 First St. SE
Calgary, AB T2G 2G9 Canada
www.calgaryeconomicdevelopment.com
Contact: Beth Thompson

Canada-Cariboo Chilcotin (250) 392-2226 / (800) 663-5885
Cariboo Chilcotin Film Commission FAX (250) 392-2838
204-350 Barnard St. cccfr.landwithoutlimits.com
Williams Lake, BC V2G 4T9 Canada

Canada-Columbia Shuswap (250) 833-5928 / (250) 832-8194
Columbia Shuswap Film Commission FAX (250) 832-3375
P.O. Box 978 www.filmcolumbiashuswap.com
Salmon Arm, BC V1E 4P1 Canada

Canada-Edmonton (780) 917-7627 / (800) 463-4667
Edmonton Film Commission, World Trade Center
9990 Jasper Ave., Third Fl.
Edmonton, AB T5J 1P7 Canada
Contact: Patti Tucker www.edmonton.com/for-business/edmonton-film-office.aspx

Canada-Manitoba (204) 947-2040
Manitoba Film & Sound FAX (204) 956-5261
410-93 Lombard Ave. www.mbfilmsound.ca
Winnipeg, MB R3B 3B1 Canada
Contact: Carole Vivier

Canada-Montreal (514) 872-2883
Montreal Film & TV Commission FAX (514) 872-3409
801 rue Brennan, Fifth Fl. www.montrealfilm.com
Montreal, QC H3C 0G4 Canada
Contact: Andre LaFord

Canada-New Brunswick (506) 453-2555
New Brunswick Film FAX (506) 453-2416
Place 2000, P.O. Box 6000 www.nbfilm.com
Fredericton, NB E1B 5H1 Canada
Contact: Roger Cyr

Canada-Newfoundland (709) 738-3456 / (877) 738-3456
Newfoundland & Labrador Film FAX (709) 739-1680
12 King's Bridge Rd. www.nlfdc.ca
St. John's, NL A1C 3K3 Canada
Contact: Chris Bonnell

Canada-Northwest Territories (867) 920-8793
NWT Film Commission, P.O. Box 1320 FAX (867) 873-0101
Yellowknife, NT X1A 2L9 Canada www.nwtfilm.com
Contact: Camilla MacEachern

Canada-Nova Scotia (902) 424-7177
Collins Bank Building, Third Fl. FAX (902) 424-0617
1869 Upper Water St. www.filmnovascotia.com
Halifax, NS B3J 1S9 Canada
Contact: Ann MacKenzie

Canada-Okanagan (250) 717-0087
Okanagan Film Commission FAX (250) 868-0512
1450 KLO Rd. www.okanaganfilm.com
Kelowna, BC V1W 3Z4 Canada

Canada-Ontario (416) 314-6858
Ontario Media Development FAX (416) 314-6876
175 Bloor St. East, South Tower, Ste. 501
Toronto, ON M4W 3R8 Canada www.omdc.on.ca
Contact: Gail Thomson

Canada-Prince Edward Island (902) 368-5336
PEI Film Commission FAX (902) 368-6255
P.O. Box 34, 94 Euston St. www.peifilm.net
Charlottetown, PE C1A 7K7 Canada
Contact: Nancy Roberts

Canada-Quebec (866) 320-3456 / (514) 499-7070
Quebec Film & Television Council FAX (514) 499-7018
204 Saint-Sacrement St., Ste. 500 www.filmquebec.com
Quebec H2Y 1W8 Canada
Contacts: Lorraine Boily, Geneviève Doré & Karine Latulippe

Canada-Saskatchewan (306) 798-9800
Sask Film, 1831 College Ave. FAX (306) 798-7768
Regina, SK S4P 3V5 Canada www.saskfilm.com
Contact: Susanne Bell

Canada-Thompson-Nicola (250) 377-8673
Thompson-Nicola Film Commission FAX (250) 372-5048
300-465 Victoria St. www.tnrdfilm.com
Kamloops, BC V2C 2A9 Canada
Contact: Victoria Weller

Canada-Toronto (416) 338-3456
Toronto Film & TV Office, City Hall, FAX (416) 392-0675
Rotunda North, 100 Queen St. West www.toronto.ca/tfto
Toronto, ON M5H 2N2 Canada
Contact: Rhonda Silverstone

Canada-Victoria BC (250) 386-3976
Greater Victoria Film Commission FAX (250) 386-3967
P.O. Box 34, 794 Fort St. www.filmvictoria.com
Victoria, BC V8W 1H2 Canada
Contact: Jo Anne Walton

Canada-Yukon (867) 667-5400
Yukon Film & Sound Commission FAX (867) 393-7040
P.O. Box 2703 www.reelyukon.com
Whitehorse, YT Y1A 2C6 Canada
Contact: Iris Merritt

Colorado (303) 592-4075 / (800) 726-8887
Colorado Office of Film, Television & Media
1625 Broadway, Ste. 2700 www.coloradofilm.org
Denver, CO 80202
Contact: Donald Zuckerman

Colorado-Boulder (303) 442-2911 / (303) 938-2066
Boulder Film Commission FAX (303) 938-2098
2440 Pearl St. www.bouldercoloradousa.com/film
Boulder, CO 80302

Colorado-Clear Creek County (303) 567-4660
(866) 674-9237
Chamber & Tourism Bureau of FAX (303) 569-6296
Clear Creek County, www.clearcreekcounty.org
2060 Miner St., P.O. Box 100
Idaho Springs, CO 80452

Colorado-Colorado Springs (719) 685-7630
(800) 888-4748
Colorado Springs Film Commission FAX (719) 635-4968
515 S. Cascade Ave. www.filmcoloradosprings.com
Colorado Springs, CO 80903
Contact: Ms. Floy Kennedy

Colorado-Fremont/Custer County (719) 275-2331
Fremont/Custer County Film Office FAX (719) 275-2332
403 Royal Gorge Blvd.
Canon City, CO 81212 www.coloradofilm.org/
production/community/details.html?id=56

Colorado-Southwest (970) 887-2536
Southwest Colorado Travel Region FAX (970) 385-7884
295-A Girard www.swcolotravel.org
Durango, CO 81303

Colorado-Telluride (310) 994-9753
Telluride Film Commission FAX (970) 728-4720
P.O. Box 1592 www.filmtelluride.com
Telluride, CO 81435

Connecticut (860) 270-8198
Connecticut Film Office FAX (860) 270-8032
505 Hudson St., Fourth Fl. www.ctfilm.com
Hartford, CT 06106
Contacts: Mark Dixon & Ellen Woolf

Delaware (302) 739-4271
(866) 284-7483
Delaware Tourism Office FAX (302) 739-5749
99 Kings Hwy www.visitdelaware.com
Dover, DE 19901

District of Columbia (202) 727-6608
DC Office of Motion Picture and FAX (202) 727-3246
Television Development www.film.dc.gov
2025 M St. NW
Washington, DC 20036
Contact: Crystal Palmer

Dominican Republic (809) 687-2166
Mayor's Film Office www.dgcine.gob.do
Cayetano Rodriguez, Ste. 154
Gazcue 10205 Dominican Republic
Contact: Tracey Cuesta

Florida (818) 508-7772
(877) 352-3456
Governor's Office of FAX (818) 508-7747
Film & Entertainment www.filminflorida.com
5426 Simpson Ave.
North Hollywood, CA 91607
Contact: Paul Sirmons

Florida-Cape Canaveral (877) 572-3224
Space Coast Film Commission FAX (321) 433-4476
430 Brevard Ave., Ste. 150 www.space-coast.com
Cocoa Village, FL 32922

Florida-Central Florida (863) 551-4709
Central Florida Motion Picture/TV FAX (863) 551-4740
2701 Lake Myrtle Park
Auburndale, FL 33823
www.visitcentralflorida.org/film-tv/production-guide

Florida-Collier County (239) 659-3456
Collier County Film Commission FAX (239) 213-3053
755 Eighth Ave. South www.shootinparadise.com
Naples, FL 34102

Florida-Emerald Coast (850) 651-7644
(800) 322-3319
Emerald Coast Film Commission FAX (850) 651-7149
P.O. Box 609 www.destin-fwb.com/film
Fort Walton Beach, FL 32549

Ⓐ **Florida-Greater Fort Lauderdale/** (954) 767-2440
Broward (954) 767-2467
Greater Fort Lauderdale/ FAX (954) 767-2468
Broward Office of Film & Entertainment
110 E. Broward Blvd., Ste. 200 www.sunny.org/film
Fort Lauderdale, FL 33301
Contact: Noelle P. Stevenson

Florida-Jacksonville (904) 630-7247
Jacksonville Film & TV Office FAX (904) 630-2919
One W. Adams St., Ste. 200 www.filmjax.com
Jacksonville, FL 32202

Florida-Key West (305) 293-1800
(800) 345-6539
Florida Keys & FAX (305) 296-0788
Key West Film Commission www.filmkeys.com
1201 White St., Ste. 102
Key West, FL 33040

Florida-Miami (305) 539-3000
Greater Miami Convention & Visitors Bureau
701 Brickell Ave., Ste. 2700
Miami, FL 33131
www.miamiandbeaches.com/visitors/filmiami.asp

Florida-Miami Beach (305) 673-7070
Miami Beach Film Commission FAX (305) 673-7063
1700 Convention Center Dr. www.miamibeachfl.gov
Miami, FL 33139

Florida-Miami-Dade (305) 375-3288
Miami-Dade County Office of FAX (305) 375-3266
Film & Entertainment www.filmiami.org
111 NW First St., Ste. 2200
Miami, FL 33128
Contacts: Dorothea "Dee" Belz & Sandy Lighterman

Florida-Orlando (407) 422-7159
Metro Orlando Film & FAX (407) 841-9069
Entertainment Commission www.filmorlando.com
301 E. Pine St., Ste. 900
Orlando, FL 32801

Florida-Palm Beach County (561) 233-1000
(800) 745-3456
Palm Beach County Film & FAX (561) 233-3113
Television Commission www.pbfilm.com
1555 Palm Beach Lakes Blvd., Ste. 900
West Palm Beach, FL 33401

Florida-Tampa Bay (813) 223-1111
(800) 826-8358
Tampa Bay Film Commission FAX (813) 223-0083
401 E. Jackson St., Ste. 2100 www.filmtampabay.com
Tampa, FL 33602
Contact: Lindsey Norris

Georgia (404) 962-4052
Georgia Film, Video & Music Office FAX (404) 962-4053
75 Fifth St., Ste. 1200 www.georgia.org
Atlanta, GA 30308

Georgia-Savannah (912) 651-2360
Savannah Film Commission FAX (912) 651-0982
P.O. Box 1027 www.savannahfilm.org
Savannah, GA 31402

Hawaii (808) 586-2570
Hawaii Film Office, P.O. Box 2359 FAX (808) 586-2572
Honolulu, HI 96804 www.hawaiifilmoffice.com
Contact: Donne Dawson

Hawaii-Big Island (808) 323-4705
Big Island Film Office FAX (808) 323-4701
74-5044 Ane Keohokalole Hwy. www.filmbigisland.com
Bldg C-204
Kailua-Kona, HI 96720
Contact: Marilyn Killeri

Hawaii-Honolulu (808) 768-6108
Honolulu Film Office FAX (808) 527-6102
530 S. King St., Ste. 306 www.filmhonolulu.com
Honolulu, HI 96813

Hawaii-Kauai   **(808) 241-4948**
Kauai Film Commission   **www.filmkauai.com**
4444 Rice St., Ste. 200
Lihue, HI 96766
Contact: Tiffani Lizama

Hawaii-Maui   **(808) 270-8237**
Contact: Benita Brazier   FAX **(808) 270-8228**
    www.filmmaui.com

    (208) 334-2470
Idaho   **(800) 942-8338**
Idaho Film Office   FAX **(208) 334-2631**
700 W. State St., Box 83720   **www.filmidaho.com**
Boise, ID 83720
Contacts: Diane Norton & Peg Owens

Illinois   **(312) 814-3600**
Illinois Film Office   FAX **(312) 814-8874**
100 W. Randolph St., Third Fl.   **www.illinoisfilm.biz**
Chicago, IL 60601
Contact: Betsy Steinberg

Illinois-Chicago   **(312) 744-6415**
Chicago Film Office   **egov.cityofchicago.org**
121 N. LaSalle St., Ste. 806
Chicago, IL 60602

Indiana   **(317) 234-2087**
Film Indiana   FAX **(317) 232-4146**
One N. Capitol Ave., Ste. 700   **www.filmindiana.com**
Indianapolis, IN 46204
Contact: Erin Newell

Iowa   **(515) 725-3024**
Iowa Film Office, 200 E. Grand Ave.
Des Moines, IA 50309
   www.iowaeconomicdevelopment.com/film/
Contact: Steven Schott

    (319) 398-5009
Iowa-Cedar Rapids   **(800) 735-5557**
Cedar Rapids Convention &   FAX **(319) 398-5089**
Visitors Bureau, 119 First Ave. SE **www.cedar-rapids.com**
Cedar Rapids, IA 52406

    (876) 978-7755
Jamaica-Kingston   **(888) 468-3785**
Jamaica Film Commission   FAX **(876) 978-0140**
18 Trafalgar Rd.   **www.filmjamaica.com**
Kingston 10 Jamaica
Contact: Del Crooks

Kansas   **(785) 296-2178**
Kansas Film Commission   FAX **(785) 296-3490**
1000 SW Jackson St., Ste. 100   **www.filmkansas.com**
Topeka, KS 66612
Contact: Peter Jasso

Kansas-Wichita   **(800) 288-9424**
Go Wichita Convention & Visitors Bureau/
Wichita Film Commission   **www.gowichita.com**
100 S. Main St., Ste. 100
Wichita, KS 67202

    (502) 564-3456
Kentucky   **(800) 345-6591**
Kentucky Film Office   FAX **(502) 564-7588**
500 Mero St., 2200 Capital Plaza Tower
Frankfort, KY 40601   **www.kyfilmoffice.com**

    (225) 342-5403
Louisiana   **(225) 342-3456**
LED Entertainment, P.O. Box 94185
Baton Rouge, LA 70804   **louisianaentertainment.gov**
Contact: Alex Schott

Louisiana-Lafayette   **(337) 291-3456**
P.O. Box 4017-C   FAX **(337) 291-8309**
Lafayette, LA 70502   **www.lafayetteentertainment.org**

Louisiana-New Orleans   **(504) 658-0923**
Film New Orleans, 1340 Poydras, Ste. 1000
New Orleans, LA 70112   **www.filmneworleans.org**
Contact: Katie Williams

Louisiana-Northeast   **(800) 843-1872**
Northeast Louisiana Film Commission   **www.nelafilm.com**
400 Lea Joyner Memorial Expressway
P.O. Box 14092
Monroe, LA 71201
Contact: C.J. Sartor

Louisiana-Shreveport   **(318) 673-7515**
505 Travis St., Ste. 200   FAX **(318) 673-5085**
Shreveport, LA 71101 **www.shreveport-bossierfilm.com**

Maine   **(207) 624-9828**
Maine Film Office   FAX **(207) 287-8070**
59 State House Station   **www.filminmaine.com**
Augusta, ME 04333
Contact: Lea Girardin

    (410) 767-6340
Maryland   **(800) 333-6632**
Maryland Film Office   FAX **(410) 333-0044**
401 E. Pratt St., 14th Fl.   **www.marylandfilm.org**
Baltimore, MD 21202
Contact: Jack Gerbes

Maryland-Baltimore   **(410) 752-8632**
Baltimore County Film Commission   FAX **(410) 887-5781**
400 Washington Ave.   **www.baltimorefilm.com**
Baltimore, MD 21204

Massachusetts   **(617) 973-8400**
Massachusetts Film Office   FAX **(617) 973-8525**
10 Park Plaza, Ste. 4510   **www.mafilm.org**
Boston, MA 02116

    (617) 635-3911
Massachusetts-Boston   **(617) 635-4455**
City of Boston Film Bureau   FAX **(617) 635-4428**
One City Hall Square, Ste. 802
Boston, MA 02201   **www.cityofboston.gov/film**

Mexico   **52 (55) 5488 5383**
Mexican Film Commission/   FAX **52 (55) 5448 5381**
Mexican Film Institute
Insurgentes Sur, Ste. 674, Second Fl.
Col. Del Valle 03300 Mexico City Mexico
Contact: Jorge Santoyo
   www.comefilm.gob.mx/indexIng.php

Mexico-Baja California   **(52) 664 682 3367**
P.O. Box 2448   FAX **(52) 664 682 3331**
Chula Vista, CA 91912   **www.bajafilm.com**

    (800) 477-3456
Michigan   **(517) 373-3456**
Michigan Film Office   FAX **(517) 241-0867**
300 N. Washington Square, Third Fl.
Lansing, MI 48913   **www.michiganfilmoffice.org**
Contact: Alice Florida

Minnesota   **(612) 767-0095**
Minnesota Film & TV Board   FAX **(612) 767-2425**
401 N. Third St., Ste. 440   **mnfilmtv.org**
Minneapolis, MN 55401
Contact: Lucinda Winter

Mississippi   **(601) 359-3297**
Mississippi Film Office, P.O. Box 849   FAX **(601) 359-5048**
Jackson, MS 39205   **www.filmmississippi.org**

    (662) 453-9197
Mississippi-Greenwood   **(800) 748-9064**
Greenwood Film Office   FAX **(662) 453-5526**
P.O. Drawer 739   **www.greenwoodms.org**
Greenwood, MS 38935

Mississippi-Natchez   **(800) 647-6724**
Natchez Film Commission   **www.visitnatchez.org**
640 S. Canal St., Box C
Natchez, MS 39120

    (662) 841-6599
Mississippi-Tupelo   **(800) 533-0611**
Tupelo Film Commission, P.O. Box 47   FAX **(662) 841-6558**
Tupelo, MS 38802   **www.tupelo.net**

Mississippi-Vicksburg (601) 636-9421
Vicksburg Convention & FAX **(601) 636-9475**
Visitors Bureau, P.O. Box 110 **www.visitvicksburg.com**
Vicksburg, MS 39181

Missouri (573) 751-4962
Missouri Department of Economic Development
301 W. High St., Ste. 720
Jefferson City, MO 65101
Contact: Jerry Jones **www.missouribusiness.net/film/**

Missouri-Kansas City (816) 210-6556
Film Commission of FAX **(816) 472-0991**
Greater Kansas City **www.kcfilm.com**
1906 Wyandotte
Kansas City, MO 64108

Montana (406) 841-2876
  (800) 553-4563
Montana Film Office, 301 S. Park Ave. FAX **(406) 841-2877**
Helena, MT 59620 **www.montanafilm.com**
Contacts: Sten Iversen

Montana-Southcentral (406) 222-0438
Montana Film Center, P.O. Box 253
Livingston, MT 59047

Navajo Nation (928) 871-6647
Navajo Nation Office of FAX **(928) 871-6637**
Broadcast Services, P.O. Box 2520
Window Rock, AZ 86515 **navajonationparks.org**
Contact: Kee Long

Nebraska (402) 471-3746
  (800) 228-4307
Nebraska Film Office, P.O. Box 94666 FAX **(402) 471-3778**
Lincoln, NE 68509 **www.filmnebraska.org**

Nebraska-Omaha (402) 444-4631
  (402) 444-4660
Omaha Film Office FAX **(402) 444-4511**
1001 Farnam St. Ste. 200 **www.visitomaha.com**
Omaha, NE 68102

Ⓐ Nevada (702) 486-2711
  (877) 638-3456
Nevada Film Office Las Vegas FAX **(702) 486-2712**
555 E. Washington Ave., Ste. 5400 **www.nevadafilm.com**
Las Vegas, NV 89101
Contact: Charles Geocaris

New Hampshire (603) 271-2220
New Hampshire Film & TV Office **www.nh.gov/film**
19 Pillsbury St.
Concord, NH 03301
Contact: Matthew Newton

New Jersey (973) 648-6279
New Jersey Motion FAX **(973) 648-7350**
Picture Commission **www.njfilm.org**
153 Halsey St. P.O. Box 47023
Newark, NJ 07101
Contact: Joseph Friedman

New Jersey-Fort Lee (201) 592-3663
  (201) 693-2763
Fort Lee Film Commission FAX **(201) 585-7222**
309 Main St. **www.fortleefilm.org**
Fort Lee, NJ 07024

New Mexico (505) 476-5600
  (800) 545-9871
New Mexico Film Office FAX **(505) 476-5601**
1600 Saint Michael's Dr. **www.nmfilm.com**
Santa Fe, NM 87505
Contact: Lisa Stroot

New Mexico-Albuquerque (505) 768-3283
Albuquerque Film Office FAX **(505) 768-3280**
P.O. Box 1293 **www.filmabq.com**
Albuquerque, NM 87103

New Mexico-Rio Rancho (505) 891-7258
  (888) 746-7262
Rio Rancho Convention & FAX **(505) 892-8328**
Visitors Bureau **www.rioranchonm.org/film.php**
3200 Civic Center Circle
Rio Rancho, NM 87174
Contact: Judi Snow

New York State (212) 803-2330
Governor's Office for Motion FAX **(212) 803-2339**
Picture & Television Development
633 Third Ave., 33rd Fl. **www.nylovesfilm.com/index.asp**
New York, NY 10017
Contact: Pat Swinney Kaufman

New York-Columbia County (518) 828-3375
  (518) 567-2247
Columbia County Tourism FAX **(518) 828-2825**
Department and Film Office
401 State St. **www.filmcolumbiacountyny.com**
Hudson, NY 12534

New York-Nassau County (516) 571-3168
Nassau County Film Office FAX **(516) 571-6195**
County Executive Bldg. **www.longislandfilm.com**
One West St., Ste. 326A
Mineola, NY 11501

New York-New York City (212) 489-6710
NYC Mayor's Office of Film, FAX **(212) 307-6237**
Theatre & Broadcasting **www.nyc.gov/film**
1697 Broadway, Ste. 602
New York, NY 10019

New York-Rochester (585) 279-8308
Rochester/Finger Lakes Film Office FAX **(585) 232-4822**
45 East Ave., Ste. 400 **www.filmrochester.org**
Rochester, NY 14604

New York-Suffolk County (631) 853-4800
Suffolk County Film Office FAX **(631) 853-4888**
H. Lee Dennison Bldg.,
Second Fl. 100 Veterans Hwy
Hauppauge, NY 11788
  www.suffolkcountyfilmcommission.com

New York-Upstate (518) 584-3255
  (800) 526-8970
Capital-Saratoga Film Commission FAX **(518) 587-0318**
28 Clinton St. **www.capital-saratogafilm.com**
Saratoga Springs, NY 12866

North Carolina (919) 733-9900
  (866) 468-2273
North Carolina Film Office FAX **(919) 715-0151**
4324 Mail Service Center **www.ncfilm.com**
Raleigh, NC 27699
Contact: Aaron Syrett

North Carolina-Charlotte (704) 347-8942
  (800) 554-4373
Charlotte Regional Film Commission FAX **(704) 347-8981**
550 South Caldwell St., Ste. 760 **www.charlottefilm.com**
Charlotte, NC 28202

North Carolina-Durham (919) 680-8313
Durham Film Office FAX **(919) 683-8353**
101 E. Morgan St. **www.durham-nc.com**
Durham, NC 27701

North Carolina-Greensboro (336) 393-0001
Piedmont Triad Film Commission FAX **(336) 668-3749**
416 Gallimore Dairy Rd., Ste. M **www.piedmontfilm.com**
Greensboro, NC 27409

North Carolina-Northeast (252) 482-4333
  (888) 872-8562
Northeast Partnership Film Office FAX **(252) 482-3366**
119 W. Water St. **www.ncnortheast.com**
Edenton, NC 27932

**North Carolina-
Western North Carolina** (828) 687-7234
Western North Carolina FAX **(828) 687-7552**
Film Commission, 134 Wright Brothers Way
Fletcher, NC 28732 **www.wncfilm.com**

| North Carolina-Wilmington | (910) 343-3456 |
Wilmington Regional | FAX (910) 343-3457
Film Commission, Inc., 1223 N. 23rd St.
Wilmington, NC 28405 | **www.wilmingtonfilm.com**

North Dakota | (701) 328-2509
| (800) 435-5663
North Dakota Film Commission | FAX (701) 328-4878
1600 E. Century Ave., Ste. 2 | **www.ndtourism.com**
Bismarck, ND 58502
Contact: Tourism Director

Ohio | (614) 644-5156
| (800) 848-1300
Ohio Film Office | **www.ohiofilmoffice.com**
77 S. High St., 29th Fl.
Columbus, OH 43216

Ohio-Cincinnati | (513) 784-1744
Cincinnati & Northern | FAX (513) 768-8963
Kentucky Film Commission | **www.film-cincinnati.org**
602 Main St., Ste. 712
Cincinnati, OH 45202

Ohio-Cleveland | (216) 623-3910
Greater Cleveland Film Commission | FAX (216) 623-0876
812 Huron Rd. East, Ste. 690 | **www.clevelandfilm.com**
Cleveland, OH 44115
Contacts: Sara Dering, Kammeron Hughes, Erin Kaminski & Ivan Schwarz

Ohio-Columbus | (614) 450-0264
Greater Columbus Film Commission, P.O. Box 12735
Columbus, OH 43212
www.columbusfilmcommission.com
Contact: Steve Cover

Ohio-Dayton | (800) 221-8235
One Chamber Plaza, Ste. A | **www.daytoncvb.com**
Dayton, OH 45402

Oklahoma | (405) 230-8440
| (800) 766-3456
Oklahoma Film & Music Office | FAX (405) 230-8640
120 N. Robinson, Sixth Fl. | **www.oklahomafilm.org**
Oklahoma City, OK 73102
Contact: Jill Simpson

Oregon | (503) 229-5832
Oregon Film & Video Office | FAX (503) 229-6869
1001 SE Water Ave., Ste. 430 | **www.oregonfilm.org**
Portland, OR 97214

Pennsylvania | (717) 783-3456
Pennsylvania Film Office | FAX (717) 787-0687
Commonwealth Keystone Bldg. 400 North St., Fourth Fl.
Harrisburg, PA 17120 | **www.filminpa.com**
Contact: Jane Shecter

Pennsylvania-Philadelphia | (215) 686-2668
Greater Philadelphia Film Office | FAX (215) 686-3659
1515 Arch St., 11th Fl. | **www.film.org**
Philadelphia, PA 19102

Pennsylvania-Pittsburgh | (412) 261-2744
| (888) 744-3456
Pittsburgh Film Office | FAX (412) 471-7317
130 Seventh St., Ste. 1000 | **www.pghfilm.org**
Pittsburgh, PA 15222

Puerto Rico | (787) 758-4747
Puerto Rico Film Commission | FAX (787) 756-5706
355 F.D. Roosevelt Ave., Ste. 106
P.O. Box 362350 | **www.puertoricofilm.com**
Hato Rey 00918 Puerto Rico
Contacts: Cristina Caraballo & Luis Rief Kohl

Rhode Island | (401) 222-3456
| (401) 222-6666
Rhode Island Film & TV Office | FAX (401) 222-3018
One Capitol Hill, Third Fl. | **www.film.ri.gov**
Providence, RI 02908
Contact: Steven Feinberg

South Carolina | (803) 737-0490
South Carolina Film Commission | FAX (803) 737-3104
1205 Pendleton St., Ste. 225 | **www.filmsc.com**
Columbia, SC 29201
Contact: Jeff Monks

South Dakota | (605) 773-3301
| (800) 952-3625
South Dakota Film Office | FAX (605) 773-3256
711 E. Wells Ave. | **www.filmsd.com**
Pierre, SD 57501
Contact: Emily Currey

Tennessee | (615) 741-3456
| (877) 818-3456
Tennessee Film, Entertainment and | FAX (615) 741-5554
Music Commission | **tn.gov/film/con_flm.htm**
312 Rosa L. Parks Ave., Tennessee Tower 10th Fl.
Nashville, TN 37243

Tennessee-Memphis | (901) 527-8300
Memphis & Shelby County | FAX (901) 527-8326
Film Commission | **www.filmmemphis.org**
50 Peabody Pl., Ste. 250
Memphis, TN 38103

Tennessee-Nashville | (615) 862-6024
Mayor's Office of Film | **www.filmnashville.com**
222 Second Ave. North, Ste. 418
Nashville, TN 37201

Texas | (512) 463-9200
Texas Film Commission | FAX (512) 463-4114
P.O. Box 13246 | **www.texasfilmcommission.com**
Austin, TX 78711
Contact: Evan Fitzmaurice

Texas-Austin | (512) 583-7229
| (512) 583-7230
Austin Film Commission | FAX (512) 583-7281
301 Congress Ave., Ste. 200 | **www.austintexas.org**
Austin, TX 78701

Texas-Dallas/Fort Worth | (214) 671-9821
| (877) 817-3456
Dallas Film Commission | FAX (214) 670-4773
1500 Marilla St., 2C North
Dallas, TX 75201 | **www.dallasfilmcommission.com**

Texas-El Paso | (915) 534-0698
| (800) 351-6024
El Paso Film Commission | FAX (915) 534-0687
One Civic Center Plaza | **www.visitelpaso.com/film**
El Paso, TX 79901

Texas-Houston | (713) 437-5251
| (800) 446-8786
| FAX (713) 223-3816
www.houstonfilmcommission.com

Texas-San Antonio | (210) 207-6730
| (800) 447-3372
San Antonio Film Commission | FAX (210) 207-9731
203 S. St. Mary's St., Second Fl.
San Antonio, TX 78205 | **www.filmsanantonio.com**

Texas-South Padre Island | (956) 761-3005
| (800) 767-2373
South Padre Island Film Commission | **www.sopadre.com**
7355 Padre Blvd.
Port Isabel, TX 78597

U.S. Virgin Islands | (340) 774-8784
U.S. Virgin Island | FAX (340) 774-4390
Film Promotion Office, P.O. Box 6400 | **www.filmusvi.com**
St. Thomas 00804 Virgin Islands (US)
Contact: Caroline Simon

Utah | (801) 538-8740
| (800) 453-8824
Utah Film Commission | FAX (801) 538-1397
Council Hall/Capitol Hill | **www.film.utah.gov**
300 N. State St.
Salt Lake City, UT 84114
Contact: Marshall Moore

Utah-Kane County
(435) 644-5033
(800) 733-5263
Kane County Film Commission
FAX (435) 644-5923
78 South 100 East
www.kaneutah.com
Kanab, UT 84741

Utah-Moab
(435) 259-4341
(435) 260-1575
Moab to Monument Valley
FAX (435) 259-4135
Film Commission, 217 E. Center St.
www.filmmoab.com
Moab, UT 84532

Utah-Park City
(435) 649-6100
(800) 453-1360
Park City Film Commission
FAX (435) 649-4132
1910 Prospector Ave., Ste. 103
www.parkcityinfo.com
Park City, UT 84060

Ute Mountain Ute Tribe
(970) 564-5725
Ute Mountain Ute Tribe Film Office
FAX (970) 564-5401
110 Mike Wash Rd., P.O. Box 248
Towaoc, CO 81334
Contact: Lynn Hartman

Vermont
(802) 828-3618
Vermont Film Commission
FAX (802) 828-3383
One National Life Dr., Sixth Fl.
www.vermontfilm.com
Montpelier, VT 05602
Contacts: Joe Bookchin & Perry Schafer

Virginia
(804) 545-5530
(800) 854-6233
Virginia Film Office
FAX (804) 545-5531
901 E. Byrd St., West Tower, 19th Fl.
Richmond, VA 23219
www.film.virginia.org

Washington
(206) 264-0667
Washington State Film Office
FAX (206) 382-4343
1411 Fourth Ave., Ste. 420
Seattle, WA 98101
www.washingtonfilmworks.org

Washington-Seattle
(206) 684-0903
(206) 684-5030
Seattle Film & Music Office
FAX (206) 684-0379
700 Fifth Ave., Ste. 5752, P.O. Box 94708
Seattle, WA 98124
www.seattle.gov/filmandmusic

West Virginia
(800) 982-3386
(304) 558-2234
West Virginia
FAX (304) 558-1189
Department of Commerce
www.wvfilm.com
Capitol Complex, Bldg. 6, Ste. 525
Charleston, WV 25305
Contact: Pamela Haynes

Wisconsin
(414) 287-4251
Wisconsin Film Office
www.filmwisconsin.net
3770 S. Pennsylvania Ave., Ste. 8
Milwaukee, WI 53235
Contact: Melissa Musante

Wyoming
(307) 777-3400
(800) 458-6657
Wyoming Film Office
FAX (307) 777-2877
1520 Etchepare Circle
www.filmwyoming.com
Cheyenne, WY 82007
Contact: Michell Howard

Australia-Melbourne
61 3 9660 3240
61 3 9660 3200
Melbourne Film Office/Film Victoria   FAX 61 3 9660 3201
Level 7, 189 Flinders Ln.   www.film.vic.gov.au
Melbourne, Victoria 3000 Australia

Australia-New South Wales   61 2 8222 4844
Screen NSW, Level 43, MLC Centre   FAX 61 2 8222 4840
19 Martin Pl.   www.screen.nsw.gov.au
Sydney, NSW 2000 Australia

Australia-Queensland   61 7 3224 4114
Screen Queensland, P.O. Box 15094
City East, Queensland 4002 Australia
www.screenqueensland.com.au

Austria   43 1 588 580
Opernring 3/2   FAX 43 1 586 8659
1010 Vienna Austria   www.location-austria.at

Austria-Cine Tirol   43 512 53 20 182
Cine Tirol Film Commission   FAX 43 512 53 20 200
Maria-Theresien-Strasse 55   www.cinetirol.com
Innsbruck, Österreich 90254 Austria

France   33 1 53 83 98 98
33, rue des Jeûneurs, 75002   FAX 33 1 53 83 98 99
Paris, France   www.filmfrance.net

Germany-Bavaria
49 89 544 60 216
49 89 544 60 217
Sonnenstrasse 21   FAX 49 89 544 60 223
Munich, Bavaria 80331 Germany
www.location-bayern.com

Germany-Berlin
49 331 743 8730
49 331 743 8731
Berlin Brandenburg Film Commission FAX 49 331 743 8799
August-Bebel-Strasse 26-53   www.bbfc.de
14482 Postdam-Babelsberg
Germany

Ireland   353 91 561 398
Irish Film Board, Queensgate   FAX 353 91 561 405
23 Dock Rd.   www.irishfilmboard.ie
Galway Ireland

Italy-Campania   39 081 420 6071
Calata Trinità, Maggiore 53   FAX 39 081 790 4221
Naples 80134 Italy   www.fcrc.it

Netherlands-Rotterdam   31 10 436 0747
Lloydstraat 9F   FAX 31 10 436 0553
Rotterdam 3024 EA Netherlands   www.rmf.rotterdam.nl

New Zealand   64 4 385 0766
P.O. Box 24142   FAX 64 4 384 5840
Wellington 6142 New Zealand   www.filmnz.com

Northern Ireland   44 28 9023 2444
21 Alfred St., Third Fl.   FAX 44 28 9023 9918
Belfast BT2 8ED Ireland
www.northernirelandscreen.co.uk

Norway   47 2247 4500
P.O. Box 482, Sentrum   www.norwegianfilm.com
Oslo 0105 Norway

Peru Film Commission   (310) 954-6407
P.O. Box 661266   www.filmperu.com
Los Angeles, CA 90066

Portugal   351 21 3230800
Rua S. Pedro de Alcantara, 45-1   FAX 351 21 3431952
Lisboa 1269-138 Portugal   www.icam.pt

Scotland-Edinburgh   44 131 622 7337
63 George St.   FAX 44 131 622 7338
Edinburgh EH2 2JG United Kingdom   www.edinfilm.com

Scotland-Glasgow   0141 287 0424
Glasgow Film Office, Exchange House FAX 0141 287 0311
231 George St.   www.glasgowfilm.com
Glasgow, Scotland G1 1RX United Kingdom

Scotland-Highlands & Islands   44 1463 702 955
Glenurquhart Rd.   FAX 44 1463 702 298
Inverness, Scotland   www.scotfilm.org
IV3 5NX United Kingdom

Spain-Barcelona   34 934 548 066
Barcelona Plató Film Commission   FAX 34 933 238 048
Roselló, 184, 5°   www.bcncatfilmcommission.com
Barcelona - Catalunya 08008 Spain
Contact: Júlia Goytisolo

Spain-Canary Islands
34 647 346 462
34 922 237 875
Tenerife Film Commission   FAX 34 922 237894
Avda. Constitución, 12 - 38005   www.tenerifefilm.com
Santa Cruz de Tenerife - Canary Islands
Andalucia 38005 Spain

Sweden-Stockholm   46 70 323 77 71
Greta Garbos väg 11   www.stofilm.com
Solna 169 40 Sweden

Sweden-West Sweden
46 (0) 520 49 09 00
46 (0) 727 49 15 00
Box 134   FAX 46 (0) 520 49 09 01
Trollhattan 461 23 Sweden
www.filmivast.se/sv/Film-i-Vast/Film-i-Vast/

UK   44 (0) 20 7255 1444
British Film Institute, 21 Stephen St.   www.bfi.org.uk
London W1T 1LN United Kingdom

UK-East Midlands   44 115 993 23 33
Antenna Media Centre, Beck St.   www.em-media.org.uk
Nottingham NG1 1EQ United Kingdom

UK-Isle of Main   44 1624 687173
Department of   FAX 44 1624 687171
Economic Development   www.gov.im/dti/iomfilm
St Georges Court, Upper Church St.
Douglas IMI 5EP United Kingdom

UK-Liverpool   +44 (0)151 233 6380
P.O. Box 2008   www.liverpool.gov.uk
Municipal Buildings, Dale St.
Liverpool L22DH United Kingdom

UK-London   44 207 613 7676
Film London, Ste. 6.10   AX 44 207 613 7677
The Tea Building 56 Shoreditch High St.
London E1 6JJ United Kingdom   www.filmlondon.org.uk

UK-South West Screen   44 117 952 9977
St. Bartholomews Court   FAX 44 117 952 9988
Lewins Mead   www.swscreen.co.uk
Bristol BS1 5BT United Kingdom

UK-Yorkshire   44 (0) 113 294 4410
Studio 22, 46 The Calls   FAX 44 (0) 113 294 4989
Leeds LS2 7EY United Kingdom
www.screenyorkshire.co.uk

1st Wave Productions   (310) 474-2439
2017 Pacific Ave.   FAX (310) 474-5282
Venice, CA 90291   www.1stwaveproductions.com
(Short-Term Housing)

Airtel Plaza Hotel &   (818) 997-7676
Conference Center   (800) 224-7835
7277 Valjean Ave.   FAX (818) 785-8864
Van Nuys, CA 91406   www.airtelplaza.com
(Monthly Rates)

The Anabelle Hotel   (800) 782-4373
2011 W. Olive Ave.   www.coastanabelle.com
Burbank, CA 91506

   (323) 656-1234
Andaz West Hollywood   (888) 591-1234
8401 W. Sunset Blvd.   FAX (323) 650-7024
West Hollywood, CA 90069   westhollywood.hyatt.com

Bamboo Retreats   (323) 962-0270
   www.bambooretreats.com
(Monthly Rates & Short and Long Term Housing)

   (310) 472-1211
Bel-Air Hotel   (800) 648-4097
   FAX (310) 476-5890
   www.hotelbelair.com

The Belamar Hotel   (310) 750-0300
3501 Sepulveda Blvd.   FAX (310) 750-0307
Manhattan Beach, CA 90266   www.thebelamar.com

   (310) 677-7733
Best Western   (800) 424-5005
(See Web Site for Locations)   FAX (310) 671-7722
   www.bestwestern.com

Best Western Heritage Inn   (909) 466-1111
8179 Spruce Ave.   FAX (908) 466-3876
Rancho Cucamonga, CA 91730
www.bestwestern.com/heritageinnranchocucamonga

Beverly Garland's Holiday Inn   (818) 980-8000
Universal Studios Hollywood   (800) 238-3759
4222 Vineland Ave.   FAX (818) 766-5230
North Hollywood, CA 91602   www.beverlygarland.com

   (310) 276-2251
Beverly Hills Hotel   (800) 283-8885
9641 Sunset Blvd.   FAX (310) 887-2887
Beverly Hills, CA 90210   www.beverlyhillshotel.com

Beverly Hills Plaza Hotel   (310) 275-5575
   FAX (310) 278-3325
   www.beverlyhillsplazahotel.com

Breeze Suites   (310) 656-0311
609 Broadway   FAX (310) 656-0360
Santa Monica, CA 90401   www.breezesuites.com
(Monthly Rates)

Broadcast Center (AIMCO)   (323) 602-0248
7660 Beverly Blvd.   www.broadcastcenterapts.com
Los Angeles, CA 90036
(Short-Term Housing)

   (805) 884-0300
Canary Hotel   (805) 879-9142
31 W. Carrillo St.   FAX (805) 879-9145
Santa Barbara, CA 93101   www.canarysantabarbara.com
(Pet Friendly)

   (310) 275-4445
The Carlyle Inn   (800) 322-7595
   FAX (310) 859-0496
   www.carlyle-inn.com

Carriage Inn   (760) 446-7910
901 N. China Lake Blvd.   FAX (760) 446-6408
Ridgecrest, CA 93555   www.carriageinn.biz
(Extended Stay, Pet Friendly & Short-Term Housing)

   (310) 657-7400
Chamberlain Hotel   (800) 210-9693
1000 Westmount Dr.   FAX (310) 854-6744
West Hollywood, CA 90069   www.korhotelgroup.com

Channel Road Inn   (310) 459-1920
219 W. Channel Rd.   FAX (310) 454-9920
Santa Monica, CA 90402   www.channelroadinn.com

Chateau Marmont Hotel   (323) 656-1010
8221 Sunset Blvd.   FAX (323) 655-5311
Hollywood, CA 90046   www.chateaumarmont.com

Cinema Suites Bed & Breakfast   (323) 272-3160
925 S. Fairfax Ave.   FAX (323) 272-3162
Los Angeles, CA 90036   www.cinemasuites.biz
(Extended Stay, Monthly Rates, Pet Friendly &
Short-Term Housing)

Citrus Suites, LLC   (866) 995-2618
1915 Ocean Way   www.citrussuites.com
Santa Monica, CA 90405
(Short-Term Housing)

The Country Inn and   (818) 222-5300
Suites by Carlson   (800) 596-2375
(See Web Site for Locations)   FAX (818) 591-0870
   www.countryinns.com

Courtyard by Marriott   (310) 484-7000
Los Angeles Westside   (800) 736-2593
6333 Bristol Pkwy   FAX (310) 590-2593
Culver City, CA 90230   www.marriott.com/laxcv

Courtyard Marriott Marina del Rey   (310) 822-8555
13480 Maxella Ave.   www.marriott.com/laxcm
Marina del Rey, CA 90292

the Crescent   (310) 247-0505
403 N. Crescent Dr.   FAX (310) 247-9053
Beverly Hills, CA 90210   www.crescentbh.com

Crowne Plaza of Beverly Hills   (310) 553-6561
1150 S. Beverly Dr.   FAX (310) 277-4469
Los Angeles, CA 90035   www.ichotelsgroup.com
(See Web Site for Additional Locations)

Custom Hotel Los Angeles   (310) 645-0400
8639 Lincoln Blvd.   FAX (310) 645-0700
Los Angeles, CA 90045   www.customhotel.com

Days Inn   (661) 824-2421
16100 Sierra Hwy   FAX (661) 824-2345
Mojave, CA 93501   www.the.daysinn.com/mojave19743

Disneyland Hotel   (714) 778-6600
   FAX (714) 956-6597
   www.disneyland.com

Doubletree Hotels & Guest Suites   (310) 395-3332
(See Web Site for Locations)   FAX (310) 458-6493
   www.doubletree.com

   (323) 658-6663
Élan Hotel   (866) 203-2212
8435 Beverly Blvd.   FAX (323) 658-6640
Los Angeles, CA 90048   www.elanhotel.com

   (858) 454-3001
Empress Hotel of La Jolla   (888) 369-9900
   FAX (858) 454-6387
   www.empress-hotel.com

Fairmont Miramar Hotel   (310) 576-7777
101 Wilshire Blvd.   FAX **(310) 458-7912**
Santa Monica, CA 90401   **www.fairmont.com**

   (323) 937-3930
Farmer's Daughter   **(800) 334-1658**
115 S. Fairfax Ave.   FAX **(323) 932-1608**
Los Angeles, CA 90036   **www.farmersdaughterhotel.com**

   (213) 627-8971
Figueroa Hotel   **(800) 421-9092**
939 S. Figueroa St.   FAX **(213) 689-0305**
Los Angeles, CA 90015   **www.figueroahotel.com**

   (310) 273-2222
The Four Seasons   **(800) 786-2227**
300 S. Doheny Dr.   FAX **(310) 859-3824**
Los Angeles, CA 90048   **www.fourseasons.com**
(See Web Site for Additional Locations)

   (310) 275-5200
The Four Seasons   **(800) 545-4000**
9500 Wilshire Blvd.   FAX **(310) 274-2851**
Beverly Hills, CA 90212   **www.fourseasons.com**

   (805) 969-2261
The Four Seasons   **(800) 819-5053**
The Four Seasons Biltmore   FAX **(805) 565-8323**
1260 Channel Dr.   **www.fourseasons.com**
Santa Barbara, CA 93108
(See Web Site for Additional Locations)

   (310) 395-9945
The Georgian   **(800) 538-8147**
1415 Ocean Ave.   FAX **(310) 656-0904**
Santa Monica, CA 90401   **www.georgianhotel.com**

   (323) 654-4600
The Grafton on Sunset   **(800) 821-3660**
8462 Sunset Blvd.   FAX **(323) 654-5918**
West Hollywood, CA 90069   **www.graftononsunset.com**

   (714) 750-4321
Hilton Hotels   **(800) 445-8667**
Anaheim Hilton, 777 Convention Way   FAX **(714) 740-4460**
Anaheim, CA 92802   **www.hilton.com**
(See Web Site for Additional Locations)

Hilton Hotels   **(310) 274-7777**
Beverly Hilton, 9876 Wilshire Blvd.   FAX **(310) 285-1313**
Beverly Hills, CA 90210   **www.hilton.com**
(See Web Site for Additional Locations)

Hilton Hotels   **(213) 624-0000**
Hilton Checkers, 535 S. Grand Ave.   FAX **(213) 626-9906**
Los Angeles, CA 90071   **www.hilton.com**
(See Web Site for Additional Locations)

   (310) 410-6128
Hilton Los Angeles Airport Hotel   **(310) 410-4000**
5711 W. Century Blvd.   FAX **(310) 410-6177**
Los Angeles, CA 90045
   www.losangelesairport.hilton.com
(Extended Stay, Monthly Rates, Pet Friendly; See Web Site for
Additional Locations)

   (310) 649-5151
Holiday Inn   **(800) 972-2576**
9901 La Cienega Blvd.   FAX **(310) 670-3619**
Los Angeles, CA 90045   **www.holiday-inn.com**
(See Web Site for Additional Locations)

Holiday Inn Express Century City   **(310) 553-1000**
(See Web Site for Additional Locations)   FAX **(310) 277-1633**
   www.ihg.com

   (323) 466-7000
Hollywood Roosevelt   **(800) 950-7667**
7000 Hollywood Blvd.   FAX **(323) 462-8056**
Hollywood, CA 90028   **www.hollywoodroosevelt.com**

   (800) 377-7855
The Horizon Hotel   **(760) 409-6199**
1050 E. Palm Canyon Dr.   **www.thehorizonhotel.com**
Palm Springs, CA 92264

   (310) 472-1211
Hotel Bel-Air   **(800) 648-4097**
   www.hotelbelair.com

   (310) 581-5533
Hotel Casa Del Mar   **(800) 898-6999**
1910 Ocean Way   FAX **(310) 581-5503**
Santa Monica, CA 90405   **www.hotelcasadelmar.com**

   (310) 393-0486
Hotel Oceana   **(800) 777-0758**
849 Ocean Ave.   FAX **(310) 458-1182**
Santa Monica, CA 90403
   www.hoteloceanasantamonica.com

Hotel Sofitel Los Angeles   **(310) 278-5444**
8555 Beverly Blvd.   FAX **(310) 657-2816**
Los Angeles, CA 90048   **www.sofitel.com**

   (323) 852-6920
The Hotel Wilshire   **(323) 852-6000**
6317 Wilshire Blvd.   FAX **(323) 852-6921**
Los Angeles, CA 90048   **www.hotelwilshire.com**

Housing Solutions   **(213) 793-0320**
(Short-Term Housing)   FAX **(323) 665-3007**
   www.villawest.com

   (310) 277-1234
Hyatt Regency   **(800) 233-1234**
2025 Avenue of The Stars   FAX **(310) 551-3355**
Century City, CA 90067   **www.hyatt.com**
(See Web Site for Additional Locations)

Hyatt Regency Huntington Beach
Resort & Spa   **(714) 845-4902**
21500 Pacific Coast Hwy   FAX **(714) 845-4620**
Huntington Beach, CA 92648
   www.huntingtonbeach.hyatt.com

   (310) 642-1111
ITT Sheraton Hotels   **(800) 325-3535**
Sheraton Gateway Hotel   FAX **(310) 645-4048**
6101 W. Century Blvd.   **www.sheraton.com**
Los Angeles, CA 90045
(See Web Site for Additional Locations)

ITT Sheraton Hotels   **(818) 980-1212**
Sheraton Universal Hotel   FAX **(818) 985-4980**
333 Universal Hollywood Dr.   **www.sheraton.com**
Universal City, CA 91608
(See Web Site for Additional Locations)

   (310) 823-5333
Jamaica Bay Inn   **(888) 823-5333**
4175 Admiralty Way   FAX **(310) 823-1325**
Marina del Rey, CA 90292   **www.jamaicabayinn.com**

Kyoto Grand Hotel & Gardens   **(213) 629-1200**
120 S. Los Angeles St.   FAX **(213) 622-0980**
Los Angeles, CA 90012   **www.kyotograndhotel.com**

   (310) 617-4546
L.A. Residence   **(323) 650-5565**
1416 Havenhurst Dr.   **www.lafurnishedapartments.com**
West Hollywood, CA 90046
(Short-Term Housing)

LA Furnished Apartments   **(323) 788-4483**
(Extended Stay, Monthly Rates,   FAX **(323) 965-9963**
Pet Friendly & Short-Term Housing)   **www.furnapt.com**

   (858) 551-2001
La Jolla Village Lodge   **(877) 551-2001**
1141 Silverado St.   FAX **(858) 551-3277**
La Jolla, CA 92037   **www.lajollavillagelodge.com**

The Langham Huntington, Pasadena **(626) 568-3900**
1401 S. Oak Knoll Ave.   FAX **(626) 568-3700**
Pasadena, CA 91106   **www.filmlangham.com**
(See Web Site for Additional Locations)

Le Merigot   **(310) 395-9700**
1740 Ocean Ave.   FAX **(310) 395-9200**
Santa Monica, CA 90401   **www.lemerigothotel.com**

Le Montrose Suite Hotel (310) 855-1115 (800) 776-0666	**Mondrian** (323) 650-8999 (800) 606-6090
900 Hammond St. FAX (310) 657-9192 West Hollywood, CA 90069 www.lemontrose.com	8440 W. Sunset Blvd. FAX (323) 650-5215 West Hollywood, CA 90069 www.mondrianhotel.com

Le Montrose Suite Hotel (310) 855-1115
(800) 776-0666
900 Hammond St. FAX (310) 657-9192
West Hollywood, CA 90069 www.lemontrose.com

Le Parc (310) 855-8888
(800) 578-4837
733 N. West Knoll Dr. FAX (310) 659-7812
West Hollywood, CA 90069 www.leparcsuites.com

Loews Santa Monica Beach Hotel (310) 458-6700
(800) 235-6397
1700 Ocean Ave. FAX (310) 458-6761
Santa Monica, CA 90401 www.loewshotels.com

The London West Hollywood (866) 282-4560
1020 N. San Vicente Blvd.
West Hollywood, CA 90069
www.thelondonwesthollywood.com
(See Web Site for Additional Locations)

Los Angeles Guest Suites (310) 289-0220
FAX (310) 289-0221
www.losangelesguestsuites.com
(Extended Stay, Monthly Rates, Pet Friendly &
Short-Term Housing)

Los Angeles Marriott-Downtown (213) 617-1133
333 S. Figueroa St. FAX (213) 613-0291
Los Angeles, CA 90071 www.marriott.com
(See Web Site for Additional Locations)

Los Feliz Lodge (323) 660-4150
1507 N. Hoover St. FAX (323) 660-0447
Los Angeles, CA 90027 www.losfelizlodge.com

Luxe Hotel Rodeo Drive (310) 273-0300
(800) 589-3711
360 N. Rodeo Dr. FAX (310) 859-8730
Beverly Hills, CA 90210 www.luxehotels.com
(See Web Site for Additional Locations)

Maison 140 Hotel (310) 281-4000
(800) 670-6182
140 S. Lasky Dr. FAX (310) 281-4001
Beverly Hills, CA 90212 www.maison140.com

Marriott (310) 641-5700
(800) 228-9290
LAX Marriott, 5855 W. Century Blvd. FAX (310) 337-5358
Los Angeles, CA 90045 www.marriott.com
(See Web Site for Additional Locations)

Marriott (310) 301-3000
Marina Beach Marriott FAX (310) 448-4870
4100 Admiralty Way www.marriott.com
Marina del Rey, CA 90292

Marriott (760) 341-2211
(800) 331-3112
Desert Springs Resort & Spa FAX (760) 341-1872
74855 Country Club Dr. www.marriott.com
Palm Desert, CA 92260

Marriott (310) 556-2777
Courtyard by Marriott FAX (310) 203-0563
10320 W. Olympic Blvd. www.marriott.com
West Los Angeles, CA 90064

Marriott (310) 546-7511
Manhattan Beach Marriott FAX (310) 939-1486
1400 Parkview Ave. www.marriott.com
Manhattan Beach, CA 90266

Marriott (310) 421-3100
(310) 421-3102
Marriott Residence Inn www.marriott.com
1700 N. Sepulveda Blvd.
Manhattan Beach, CA 90266

Millennium Biltmore Hotel (213) 624-1011
(800) 245-8673
506 S. Grand Ave. FAX (213) 612-1545
Los Angeles, CA 90071 www.thebiltmore.com

Mondrian (323) 650-8999
(800) 606-6090
8440 W. Sunset Blvd. FAX (323) 650-5215
West Hollywood, CA 90069 www.mondrianhotel.com

Motel 6 (323) 464-6006
(See Web Site for Locations) FAX (323) 464-4645
www.motel6.com

Northwoods Resort (909) 866-3121
(800) 866-3121
40650 Village Dr. FAX (909) 878-2122
Big Bear Lake, CA 92315 www.northwoodsresort.com
(Extended Stay, Pet Friendly & Short-Term Housing)

Oakwood Worldwide (877) 603-4406
3600 Barham Blvd. www.oakwood.com/LA411
Los Angeles, CA 90068
(Extended Stay, Monthly Rates, Pet Friendly &
Short-Term Housing)

Omni Hotel (213) 617-3300
(800) 843-6664
FAX (213) 617-3399
www.omnihotels.com

The Orlando (323) 658-6600
(800) 624-6835
8384 W. Third St. FAX (323) 653-3464
Los Angeles, CA 90048 www.theorlando.com

The Palmdale Hotel (661) 273-1200
(800) 272-6232
FAX (661) 947-9593
www.thepalmdalehotel.com
(Extended Stay, Monthly Rates, Pet Friendly & Short-Term
Housing; See Web Site for Additional Locations)

Peninsula Beverly Hills Hotel (310) 551-2888
(800) 462-7899
9882 S. Santa Monica Blvd. FAX (310) 788-2319
Beverly Hills, CA 90212 www.peninsula.com

Queen Mary Hotel (877) 342-0742
1126 Queen's Hwy www.queenmary.com
Long Beach, CA 90802

Radisson Hotels (310) 670-9000
6225 W. Century Blvd. www.radisson.com
Los Angeles, CA 90045
(See Web Site for Additional Locations)

Ramada (310) 419-1011
(See Web Site for Additional Locations) FAX (310) 412-1294
www.ramada.com

Renaissance Hotels (323) 856-1200
(800) 468-3571
1755 N. Highland Ave. FAX (323) 856-1205
Hollywood, CA 90028 www.renaissancehotels.com
(See Web Site for Additional Locations)

The Ritz-Carlton (310) 823-1700
(800) 542-8680
4375 Admiralty Way FAX (310) 823-2403
Marina del Rey, CA 90292 www.ritzcarlton.com
(See Web Site for Additional Locations)

The Ritz-Carlton, Laguna Niguel (949) 240-2000
(800) 542-8680
One Ritz-Carlton Dr. FAX (949) 240-0829
Dana Point, CA 92629 www.ritzcarlton.com
(See Web Site for Additional Locations)

Royal Equestrian (818) 843-2441
1200 Riverside Dr. FAX (818) 843-0948
Burbank, CA 91506
(Short-Term Housing)

Royal Palace Westwood (310) 208-6677
(800) 631-0100
FAX (310) 824-3732
www.royalpalacewestwood.com

San Ysidro Ranch
(805) 565-1700
(800) 368-6788
900 San Ysidro Ln.
Santa Barbara, CA 93108
FAX (805) 565-1995
www.sanysidroranch.com

SeaCastle
(310) 917-1998
(800) 295-0022
1725 Ocean Front Walk
Santa Monica, CA 90401
(Extended Stay)
FAX (310) 917-1178
www.theseacastle.com

Shangri-La
(310) 394-2791
1301 Ocean Ave.
Santa Monica, CA 90401
FAX (310) 451-3351
www.shangrila-hotel.com

Sheraton Delfina
(310) 399-9344
(888) 627-8532
530 W. Pico Blvd.
Santa Monica, CA 90405
FAX (310) 399-2504
www.sheratonsantamonica.com

Shutters on the Beach
(310) 458-0030
(800) 334-9000
One Pico Blvd.
Santa Monica, CA 90405
FAX (310) 458-4589
www.shuttersonthebeach.com

SLS Hotel of Beverly Hills
(310) 247-0400
465 S. La Cienega Blvd.
Los Angeles, CA 90048
FAX (310) 247-0315
www.slshotels.com

Sportsmen's Lodge Hotel
(818) 769-4700
(800) 821-8511
12825 Ventura Blvd.
Studio City, CA 91604
FAX (818) 769-4798
www.slhotel.com

The Standard
(323) 650-9090
8300 Sunset Blvd.
West Hollywood, CA 90069
FAX (323) 650-2820
www.standardhotel.com

Sunset Marquis Hotel
(310) 657-1333
(800) 858-9758
1200 N. Alta Loma Rd.
West Hollywood, CA 90069
FAX (310) 652-5300
www.sunsetmarquishotel.com

Sunset Tower Hotel
(323) 654-7100
8358 W. Sunset Blvd.
West Hollywood, CA 90069
www.sunsettowerhotel.com

TENTEN Wilshire, LLC
(877) 338-1010
1010 Wilshire Blvd.
Los Angeles, CA 90017
(Short-Term Housing)
FAX (213) 482-4722
www.1010wilshire.com

Town House Motel
(661) 942-1195
(661) 496-6607
44125 N. Sierra Hwy
Lancaster, CA 93534
FAX (661) 945-2084
www.townhouselancaster.com

Trump International Hotel
Las Vegas
(702) 982-0000
(866) 939-8786
2000 Fashion Show Dr.
Las Vegas, NV 89109
FAX (702) 476-8450
www.trumplasvegashotel.com

Viceroy Hotel
(310) 260-7500
(800) 670-6185
1819 Ocean Ave.
Santa Monica, CA 90401
FAX (310) 260-7515
www.viceroysantamonica.com

Villa Malibu Luxury Rentals
(888) 526-6096
6487 Cavalleri Rd., Ste. 224
Malibu, CA 90265
www.villamalibuliving.com

The W Hotel
(310) 208-8765
FAX (310) 824-0355
www.whotels.com

The Westin Bonaventure
(213) 624-1000
(See Web Site for Locations)
FAX (213) 612-4800
www.westin.com

Wilshire Grand Hotel & Centre
(213) 688-7777
930 Wilshire Blvd.
Los Angeles, CA 90017
FAX (213) 612-3989
www.wilshiregrand.com

Limousine & Car Services

1800Fly1800
(310) 330-7500
(800) 359-1800
FAX (310) 419-8129
www.1800fly1800.com

310 Picture Cars
(310) 678-8007
6709 La Tijera Blvd., Ste. 247
Los Angeles, CA 90045
FAX (310) 878-0338
facebook.com/picturecardivision

AAA Limousine Service
(818) 704-4746
(800) 232-4133
FAX (818) 888-1280
www.aaalimo.net

Absolute Transportation Service
(310) 270-5253
(800) 966-5753
www.americanlimousine.us

Ace Limousine
(866) 429-5466
(310) 452-7083
P.O. Box 5431
Santa Monica, CA 90409
www.ace-limo.com

Affordable West, Inc.
(323) 467-7182
1040 N. La Brea Ave.
Hollywood, CA 90038
FAX (323) 467-6520

Allways Chauffeurs & Bodyguards
(310) 385-9088
FAX (310) 385-9038
www.allwaysdrivers.com

Aloha Limousine
(310) 641-1811
(323) 464-2456
P.O. Box 352
Hawthorne, CA 90251
FAX (310) 978-6366

AM-PM Limousine Service
(323) 876-2676
(800) 995-2676
FAX (323) 876-1507
www.am-pmlimo.com

American Limousine
(310) 665-0999
(310) 623-5999
5230 W. Century Blvd., Ste. 212
Los Angeles, CA 90045
FAX (310) 665-9020
www.americanlimos.org

Amour Way Amour Way
Luxury Transportation
(310) 591-8690
(866) 261-6651
P.O. Box 661749
Los Angeles, CA 90066
FAX (310) 390-9315
www.amourway.com

AMS/Pacific Limousine &
Transportation, Inc.
(310) 649-5466
(310) 838-4727
2006 S. La Cienega
Los Angeles, CA 90034
FAX (310) 838-9208
www.amspacific.com

Anytime Limousine Service
(818) 764-9116
(800) 760-5466
6844 Bellaire Ave.
North Hollywood, CA 91605
FAX (818) 765-4756
www.anytimelimousines.com

Avalon Transportation, Inc.
(310) 391-6161
(800) 528-2566
5239 Sepulveda Blvd.
Culver City, CA 90230
FAX (310) 391-8017
www.avalontrans.com

Avectra Global Transportation
(888) 928-3287
www.avectralimo.com

Avenue LS Inc.
(818) 335-3303
(310) 882-3279
FAX (818) 786-0792
www.lalimousin.com

Avon Studio Transportation	(323) 850-0826
	(800) 432-2866
7080 Santa Monica Blvd.	FAX (323) 467-4239
Los Angeles, CA 90038	www.avonrents.com

	(866) 759-6929
Baron Limousine	(818) 719-0155
	FAX (818) 774-1333
	www.labaronlimo.com

	(310) 274-6969
Beverly Hills Rent-A-Car	(855) 818-6969
9732 S. Santa Monica Blvd.	FAX (310) 550-1700
Beverly Hills, CA 90210	www.bhrentacar.com

	(714) 546-6737
Blue Moon Limousine & Sedan	(800) 726-1837
	FAX (714) 546-7048

	(800) 527-7000
Budget	(310) 642-4500
(See Web Site for Locations)	www.budget.com

California Rent-A-Car	(310) 477-2727
1033 N. Fuller Ave.	FAX (310) 477-9176
Los Angeles, CA 90046	www.productioncarrental.com

	(310) 670-1166
Carey Limousine Service	(800) 262-5070
	FAX (310) 665-5110
	www.careyint.com

	(818) 728-0607
Classic Car Rental Connection	(800) 494-8092
17514 Ventura Blvd.	FAX (818) 728-0684
Encino, CA 91316	www.101classiccarrental.com

	(800) 550-3125
Classic Limos	(949) 495-3125
30251 Golden Lantern, E-510	FAX (949) 495-1652
Laguna Niguel, CA 92677	www.classiclimousines.com

CPS Worldwide	(888) 277-2776
12400 Wilshire Blvd., Ste. 400	FAX (866) 636-6977
Los Angeles, CA 90025	
	www.californiaprotectiveservices.com

	(310) 737-0888
Crown Limousine L.A.	(800) 933-5466
	FAX (310) 737-0890
	www.crownlimola.com

	(310) 642-6666
Dav-El Limousines	(800) 922-0343
	www.davel.com

Diva Limousine, Ltd.	(800) 427-3482
	www.divalimo.com

	(800) 538-8799
Dream One	(310) 670-5466
	FAX (310) 670-0558
	www.dreamonesedans.com

ELS Transportation	(800) 940-6482
	FAX (888) 371-1997
	www.elstransportation.com

Emerald Limousine Service	(310) 591-6060
1601 N. Sepulveda Blvd., Ste. 630	FAX (310) 921-5624
Manhattan Beach, CA 90266	www.limobyemerald.com

Empire CLS Worldwide	
Chaufferured Services	(800) 266-2577
	FAX (310) 414-8126
	www.empirecls.com

	(818) 765-7311
Exclusive Sedan Service	(800) 400-7332
12580 Saticoy St.	FAX (818) 765-0183
North Hollywood, CA 91605	www.exclusivesedan.com

Executive Limousine	(310) 823-5466
4330 Lincoln Blvd.	FAX (310) 822-5528
Marina del Rey, CA 90292	www.ezeclimo.com

Executive Productions	(310) 456-8833
3957 Ridgemont Dr.	FAX (310) 456-5692
Malibu, CA 90265	

	(310) 674-3326
Exquisite Limo and Sedan Service	(310) 420-0277
10834 S. Freeman Ave.	FAX (310) 412-0079
Inglewood, CA 90304	
	www.exquisitelimoandsedanservice.com

	(310) 645-6092
Fleetwood Limousine	(800) 283-5893
	FAX (310) 645-1245
	www.fleetwoodlimo.com

	(310) 457-7307
Gemstar Limousine Service	(800) 922-5466
	FAX (310) 457-6307
	www.gemstarlimo.com

Green CLS Car Service and	
Limousine	(800) 505-0405
	FAX (323) 908-6080
	www.greencls.com

	(310) 657-5800
Greenwich Limousine	(888) 777-4611
P.O. Box 321	FAX (818) 957-8078
Beverly Hills, CA 90213	www.greenwichlimoservice.com

	(310) 551-3159
Integrated Transportation Services	(800) 487-4255
9740 W. Pico Blvd.	FAX (310) 551-3061
Los Angeles, CA 90034	www.itslimo.com

	(323) 734-9955
Jackson Limousine Service	(800) 522-9955
	FAX (323) 291-2669
	www.jacksonlimo.com

	(310) 247-0804
KLS Limousine Service Inc.	(877) 936-5466
9663 Santa Monica Blvd., Ste. 773	FAX (310) 247-0805
Beverly Hills, CA 90210	www.klsla.com

Lokie Limousine Service	(310) 815-9228
13428 Maxella Ave.	www.lokielimousine.com
Marina del Rey, CA 90292	

	(818) 845-1502
Music Express	(800) 255-4444
	FAX (818) 845-1738
	www.musiclimo.com

Red Carpet Limousine Service, Inc.	(866) 398-9700
	FAX (310) 398-9750
	www.rcllimo.com

	(310) 446-0041
Regal Limousine Service	(800) 383-7028
P.O. Box 321	FAX (818) 957-8078
Beverly Hills, CA 90213	www.regallimousineservice.com

RPM Limos Inc.	(949) 521-4383
23272 Arroyo Vista	FAX (949) 888-8544
Rancho Santa Margarita, CA 92688	www.rpmlimos.com

	(562) 941-0107
Secure Transportation	(800) 856-9994
13111 Meyer Rd.	FAX (562) 906-2947
Whittier, CA 90605	www.securetransportation.com

	(818) 251-9700
Silverado Coach Company, Inc.	(800) 544-7999
	FAX (818) 884-4997
	www.silveradocoach.com

	(877) 856-9898
Winn Limousine Service, Inc.	(818) 332-8809
12400 Ventura Blvd., Ste. 245	FAX (818) 647-0212
Studio City, CA 91604	www.911limos.com

Limousine & Car Services

12:01 Afterdark Locations   (323) 424-0871
P.O. Box 1294   **www.afterdarklocations.com**
Venice, CA 90294
(Architectural Properties, Bar and Restaurant Locations,
Castles, Churches, Coastal and Marine Locations, Colleges/
Schools, Deserts, Estates, Historic Properties, Houses,
International Locations, Licensed Broker, Mountain
Locations, Museums, Office Buildings, Retail Spaces,
Stages & Warehouses)

21st Century Locations, Inc.   (661) 255-0911
25458 Via Novia   **www.21centurylocations.com**
Valencia, CA 91355

       (818) 376-6506
24/7 Plan-It Locations   **(310) 770-8458**
15500 Erwin St., Ste. 4009   FAX **(818) 376-7606**
Van Nuys, CA 91411   **www.planitlocations.com**

       (323) 654-3900
5 Star Film Locations Inc.   **(818) 970-0422**
11244 Briarcliff Ln.   FAX **(323) 654-8838**
Studio City, CA 91604   **www.5starfilmlocations.com**

A2Z Locations, Inc.   **(323) 667-3456**
3171 Los Feliz Blvd., Ste. 308   FAX **(323) 667-3434**
Los Angeles, CA 90039   **www.a2zlocations.com**
(Architectural Properties, Bar and Restaurant, Castles,
Churches, Coastal and Marine Locations, Colleges/Schools,
Deserts, Estates, Historic Properties, Houses, International
Locations, Museums, Office Buildings, Retail Spaces,
Stages & Warehouses)

Access Locations, Inc.   **(310) 601-0644**
24797 W. Saddle Peak   FAX **(310) 317-9508**
Malibu, CA 90265   **www.accesslocationsinc.com**

       (626) 243-0456
All Pictures Media Locations   **(323) 377-3804**
15 S. Raymond Ave., Ste. 200   FAX **(626) 243-0455**
Pasadena, CA 91105   **www.allpicturesmedia.com**
(Malibu to Los Angeles to Palm Springs Locations; Architectural
Properties, Bar and Restaurant Locations, Estates, Houses,
Office Buildings, Retail Spaces & Warehouses)

Alpha Film Locations, LLC   **(818) 554-8940**
5460 White Oak Ave., Ste. J108   FAX **(818) 990-0387**
Encino, CA 91316   **www.alphafilmlocations.com**

       (818) 207-4524
Amazing Film Locations   **(818) 634-6808**
8507 Browns Creek Ln.   **www.amazinglocations.com**
Canoga Park, CA 91307
(Architectural Properties, Bar and Restaurant Locations,
Castles, Churches, Estates, Houses, Licensed Broker &
Warehouses)

       (818) 906-8945
America Film Network, Inc.   **(818) 613-5962**
4225 Woodman Ave.   FAX **(818) 267-5717**
Sherman Oaks, CA 91423 **www.americafilmnetwork.com**
(Architectural Properties, Bar and Restaurant Locations,
Castles, Churches, Marine Locations, Colleges/Schools,
Deserts, Estates, Historic Properties, Houses, International
Locations, Mountain Locations, Museums, Office Buildings,
Retail Spaces, Stages & Warehouses)

       (818) 723-0099
Angela's Locations   **(818) 231-9626**
4141 Falling Leaf Dr.   FAX **(818) 881-3049**
Encino, CA 91316   **www.angelaslocations.com**
(Apartments, Architectural Properties, Bar and Restaurant
Locations, Beach Houses, Churches, Collages, Commercial
Properties, Gardens, Gyms, Hospitals, Hotels, Houses, Lobby,
Mansions, Medical Buildings, Motels, Office Buildings,
Rooftops, Schools & Warehouses)

Ascot Locations Service, Inc.   **(818) 843-3210**
       FAX **(818) 833-7080**
       www.ascotlocations.com
(Coachella Valley and Palm Springs, Long Beach, Los Angeles
and Ventura Counties & West Valley)

BEBworld.com   **(323) 400-5587**
       www.bebworld.com
(Architectural Properties, Bar and Restaurant Locations,
Castles, Coastal and Marine Locations, Estates, Historic
Properties, Houses, International Locations, Mountain
Locations, Museums, Office Buildings, Retail Spaces & Stages)

Blockbuster Locations   **(818) 219-8101**
17451 Oak Creek Ct.   FAX **(818) 501-8659**
Encino, CA 91316   **www.blockbusterlocations.com**

California Film Commission   **(323) 860-2960**
Location Resource Center   **(800) 858-4749**
7080 Hollywood Blvd., Ste. 900   FAX **(323) 860-2972**
Los Angeles, CA 90028   **www.film.ca.gov**

Cast Locations   **(323) 469-6616**
536 N. Larchmont Blvd.   FAX **(323) 466-4482**
Los Angeles, CA 90004   **www.castlocations.com**
(Architectural Properties, Castles, Churches, Estates, Historic
Properties, Houses, Office Buildings, Retail Spaces,
Stages & Warehouses)

CBAV, Inc./World Locations   **(310) 659-0599**
8533 Sunset Blvd., Ste. 203   FAX **(310) 659-3292**
West Hollywood, CA 90069   **www.worldlocations.com**

Central Locations   **(818) 312-1137**
P.O. Box 260-231   **www.filmlocations.la**
Encino, CA 91426
(Architectural Properties, Bar and Restaurant Locations,
Castles, Churches, Coastal and Marine Locations, Estates,
Houses, Licensed Broker, Mountain Locations, Office Buildings,
Stages & Warehouses)

Chinatown Film Bridge   **(310) 576-9250**
       www.filmbridge.com

       (949) 675-8888
Cinemafloat   **(714) 801-5553**
1624 W. Oceanfront Walk   FAX **(949) 644-3073**
Newport Beach, CA 92663
(Houses, Marine Locations & Piers)

       (562) 803-3701
Clean Strike Locations   **(562) 879-2207**
12214 Lakewood Blvd., Bldg. 9   FAX **(562) 803-3702**
Downey, CA 90242   **www.cleanstrikelocations.com**

Cypress Sea Cove   **(310) 589-3344**
33572 Pacific Coast Hwy **www.malibufilmlocations.com**
Malibu, CA 90265

Dennis Morgan Locations Inc.   **(818) 718-1734**
       FAX **(866) 715-5545**
       www.dennismorganlocations.com
(Architectural Properties, Bar and Restaurant Locations,
Castles, Churches, Coastal and Marine Locations, Colleges/
Schools, Deserts, Estates, Houses, International Locations,
Mountain Locations, Museums, Office Buildings, Retail Spaces,
Stages & Warehouses)

       (323) 769-3550
EastWest Locations, Inc.   **(213) 509-1699**
8491 Sunset Blvd., Ste. 477   FAX **(323) 656-6324**
West Hollywood, CA 90069 **www.eastwestlocations.com**

Elite Film Locations (818) 207-6410
4335 Van Nuys Blvd., Ste. 263   FAX (818) 530-7795
Sherman Oaks, CA 91403   www.elitefilmlocations.net
(Greater Los Angeles: Architectural Properties, Bar and
Restaurant Locations, Beach Locations, Castles, Churches,
Coastal and Marine Locations, Colleges/Schools, Deserts,
Estates, Historic Properties, Hotels, Houses, Lofts, Map
Services, Office Buildings, Ranches, Retail Spaces, Stages,
Theatres & Warehouses)

Estate Weddings and Events, Inc. (888) 662-8360
893 Felspar St.   FAX (858) 270-0788
San Diego, CA 92109
www.estateweddingsandevents.com

The Event Division (310) 424-5112
9903 Santa Monica Blvd., Ste. 960   FAX (866) 477-2516
Beverly Hills, CA 90212   www.theeventdivision.net
(Bar and Restaurant Locations, Estates, Houses,
Museums & Warehouses)

Exclusive Filming Locations (424) 200-4091
www.exclusivefilminglocations.com
(All American, Architectual Properties, Auto Repair, Bars, Beach
Font, Bungalow, Churches, Colleges, Craftsman, Dilapidated/
Distressed Properties, Diners, Estates, Gallery and Museum,
Hotels, Log Cabin, Mansions, Mid Century Modern, Modern,
Nightclubs, Offices, Period, Restaurants, Retail, Schools,
Stages, State Buildings, Theaters, Theme Parks,
Victorian & Warehouses)

Far West Locations (310) 287-8310
3835-R E. Thousand Oaks Blvd.   FAX (805) 446-6597
Ste. 319   www.farwestlocations.com
Thousand Oaks, CA 91362

Fergusons' Film LA Property (310) 858-7727
Management Co. (760) 399-9682
78710 Via Sonata   FAX (760) 399-9685
La Quinta, CA 92253   www.locations2film.com
(Licensed Broker, L.A. Zone)

Film Friendly Locations/ (323) 461-6386
Joseph Darrell (310) 212-3243
FAX (310) 212-3242
www.jdls.com
(Architectural Properties, Bar and Restaurant Locations,
Castles, Churches, Coastal and Marine Locations, Colleges/
Schools, Deserts, Estates, Historic Properties, Mountain
Locations, International Locations, Mountain Locations, Museums, Office
Buildings, Retail Spaces, Stages & Warehouses)

Film Westside Locations (310) 710-2833
www.filmwestside.com

FilmWerx Locations, Inc. (323) 525-0008
4525 Wilshire Blvd., Ste. 204   FAX (323) 525-0009
Los Angeles, CA 90010   www.filmwerx.com
(Architectural Properties, Bar and Restaurant Locations,
Castles, Churches, Coastal and Marine Locations, Colleges/
Schools, Deserts, Estates, Historic Properties, Houses, Office
Buildings, Retail Spaces, Stages & Warehouses)

Fresno Film Commission (559) 908-0539
5241 E. Townsend Ave.   FAX (559) 354-5980
Fresno, CA 93727   www.fresnofilm.com
(Architectural Properties, Bar and Restaurant Locations,
Churches, Colleges/Schools, Historic Properties, Houses,
Museums, Office Buildings, Retail Spaces,
Stages & Warehouses)

Golden Locations (310) 820-3312
P.O. Box 16251   www.goldenlocations.com
Beverly Hills, CA 90209
(Churches)

Hollywood Locations (213) 534-3456
1201 W. Fifth St., Ste. F-170   FAX (213) 534-3459
Los Angeles, CA 90017   www.hollywoodlocations.com
(Licensed Broker)

HomeShootHome (626) 794-1616
FAX (626) 737-6047
www.homeshoothome.com

(310) 871-8004
Image Locations, Inc. (888) 411-2344
9663 Santa Monica Blvd., Ste. 842   FAX (213) 674-2098
Beverly Hills, CA 90210   www.imagelocations.com

Independent Locations (818) 222-5744
22655 DeKalb Dr.   FAX (818) 332-7079
Calabasas, CA 91302   www.independentlocations.com
(Architectural Properties, Bar and Restaurant Locations,
Castles, Churches, Coastal and Marine Locations, Colleges/
Schools, Deserts, Estates, Historic Properties, Houses, Map
Service, Mountain Locations, Office Buildings, Retail Spaces,
Stages & Warehouses)

Kodevco Locations/ (323) 852-1817
Richard Korngute (213) 300-1817
www.kodevco.com
(Architectural Properties, Houses, Office Buildings, Retail
Spaces & Warehouses)

(310) 826-9660
Landmark Locations, Inc. (805) 908-1797
11726 San Vicente Blvd., Ste. 223   FAX (805) 496-1406
Los Angeles, CA 90049   www.landmark.locations.org
(Licensed Broker)

Legend Locations, LLC (323) 467-9265
6735 Yucca St., Ste. 311   FAX (323) 467-9266
Hollywood, CA 90028   www.legendlocations.com
(Architectural Properties, Bar and Restaurant Locations,
Castles, Churches, Coastal and Marine Locations, Colleges/
Schools, Deserts, Estates, Historic Properties, Houses,
International Locations, Map Service, Mountain Locations,
Museums, Office Buildings, Retail Spaces,
Stages & Warehouses)

(310) 376-9797
The Location Connection, Inc. (818) 422-8127
Raleigh Studios Manhattan Beach   FAX (888) 837-4643
1600 Rosecrans Ave. Bldg. Five, Second Fl.
Manhattan Beach, CA 90266
www.locationconnection.com
(Coachella Valley, Los Angeles, Malibu, Orange County, San
Fernando Valley, South Bay & Ventura County)

(818) 845-9600
Location Network/Geoff White (818) 426-2600
P.O. Box 81   FAX (818) 845-9606
Burbank, CA 91503   www.locationnetwork.com

Locations Plus (805) 969-0887
755 Romero Canyon Rd.   FAX (805) 695-0861
Santa Barbara, CA 93108   www.locationsplus.net
(Coastal and Marine Locations, Estates, Houses, Mountain
Locations, Santa Barbara and Ventura Counties &
Santa Ynez Valley)

Malibu Locations (310) 457-3926
29575 Pacific Coast Hwy, Ste. E   FAX (310) 457-9308
Malibu, CA 90265   www.malibu-locations.com

(323) 939-1912
Media Locations, Inc. (323) 202-8884
139 N. Highland Ave.   FAX (323) 965-1088
Los Angeles, CA 90036   www.medialocationsinc.com
(Los Angeles County)

Meyler & Co. (310) 276-5717
8899 Beverly Blvd., Ste. 618   FAX (310) 276-5718
Los Angeles, CA 90048   www.meylerandco.com

Miles of Files/Bianca Gonzalez (805) 895-1325
817 Kentia Ave.
Santa Barbara, CA 93101

MNM Locations   (310) 600-3011
FAX **(310) 821-5506**
www.mnmlocations.com
(Architects Offices, Architectural Properties, Art Galleries, Auto Mechanic Shops, Banks, Bar and Restaurant Locations, Campgrounds, Churches, Coastal and Marine Locations, Colleges/Schools, Estates, Golf Courses, Gyms, Historic Properties, International Locations, Licensed Broker, Mountain Locations, Office Buildings, Retail Spaces, Sports Facilities, Stages, Tennis Courts, Theaters, Vineyards, Warehouses & Yoga and Dance Studios)

National Film Locations/   (310) 231-7045
National Special Event Locations   **(310) 231-7828**
11740 Wilshire Blvd., Ste. A2306   FAX **(310) 231-7047**
Los Angeles, CA 90025

         (310) 657-0800
Pacific Design Center   **(310) 360-6423**
8687 Melrose Ave., Ste. M60   FAX **(310) 652-8576**
West Hollywood, CA 90069
www.pacificdesigncenter.com

         (323) 874-0404
ProductionLocations.com   **(310) 561-2430**
9663 Santa Monica Blvd., Ste. 490   FAX **(323) 843-9808**
Beverly Hills, CA 90210   **productionlocations.com**
(Architectural Properties, Bar and Restaurant Locations, Estates, Houses, Office Buildings, Retail Spaces & Warehouses)

Rancho Simi Recreation &   **(805) 584-4400**
Park District   **(805) 584-4453**
1692 Sycamore Dr.   FAX **(805) 527-2495**
Simi Valley, CA 93065   **www.rsrpd.org**
(Oak Park, Simi Valley; Churches, Colleges/Schools, Historic Properties, Houses, Lakes, Mountain Locations, Parking Lots, Parks, Picnic Pavilions, Sports Fields/Facilities, Trails)

Real to Reel Locations   **(818) 785-7075**
16118 Sherman Way   FAX **(818) 785-9817**
Van Nuys, CA 91406   **www.rtrlocations.com**
(Licensed Broker)

Ridgecrest Film Commission   **(760) 375-8202**
Location Library   **(800) 847-4830**
139 Balsam St., Ste. 1700   FAX **(760) 375-9850**
Ridgecrest, CA 93555   **www.filmdeserts.com**
(Mojave High Desert)

San Luis Obispo County
Location & Casting   **(805) 547-9000**
128 La Colina   FAX **(805) 969-9595**
Pismo Beach, CA 93449
www.sanluisobispocounty.com/film-commission/

Santa Barbara Location Services/
aka Location Production   **(805) 565-1562**
Coordination   **(805) 969-5555**
110 Olive Mill Ln.   FAX **(805) 969-9595**
Santa Barbara, CA 93108
www.santabarbaralocations.com
(Ojai, San Luis Obispo, Santa Barbara, Santa Ynez Valley & Ventura)

Sight to Site Film Locations   **(818) 758-3456**
5938 Aldea Ave.   FAX **(818) 758-0004**
Encino, CA 91316   **www.sighttositelocations.com**
(Architectural Properties, Bar and Restaurant Locations, Castles, Churches, Coastal and Marine Locations, Colleges/Schools, Estates, Historic Properties, Houses, Licensed Broker, Mountain Locations, Office Buildings, Retail Spaces, Stages & Warehouses)

Skyline Locations   **(213) 680-7400**
915 Wilshire Blvd., Ste. 1780   FAX **(213) 680-7401**
Los Angeles, CA 90017   **www.skylinelocations.com**

         (323) 464-5360
Sources Location Library, Inc.   **(323) 493-8844**
FAX **(323) 395-5575**
www.locationlibrary.com

South Bay Locations   **(310) 600-5020**
www.southbaylocations.net
(Architectural Properties, Bar and Restaurant Locations, Churches, Coastal and Marine Locations, Colleges/Schools, Deserts, Houses, Office Buildings, Retail Spaces & Warehouses)

Stuart Raven Barter & Associates   **(323) 931-2177**
5576 W. First St.   **www.srba.com**
Los Angeles, CA 90036

         (888) 994-6786
(A) **Sunrise Locations Inc.**   **(818) 489-8889**
23679 Calabasas Rd., Ste. 798   FAX **(310) 388-0893**
Calabasas, CA 91302   **www.sunriselocations.net**

Sunset Locations, Inc.   **(310) 360-1306**
8730 Sunset Blvd., Ste. 485   FAX **(310) 360-1362**
West Hollywood, CA 90069   **www.sunsetlocations.com**
(Architectural Properties, Estates, Historic Properties, Houses, Licensed Broker, Office Buildings & Warehouses)

Toni Maier-On Location, Inc.   **(323) 469-9941**
6253 Hollywood Blvd., Ste. 309   FAX **(323) 469-9943**
Hollywood, CA 90028   **www.onlocation.com**
(Architectural Properties, Malibu Locations, Office Buildings, Stages & Warehouses)

Universal Locations, Inc.   **(661) 505-4150**
24791 Valley St.   FAX **(661) 505-4157**
Santa Clarita, CA 91321   **www.universallocations.com**
(Estate Rentals; Licensed Broker)

Unreel Locations   **(323) 953-6189**
2950 Los Feliz Blvd., Ste. 206   FAX **(323) 953-1637**
Los Angeles, CA 90039   **www.unreellocations.com**
(Architectural Properties, Churches, Coastal and Marine Locations, Colleges/Schools, Historic Properties, Houses, Licensed Broker, Museums & Retail Spaces)

Ventura County Location &   **(805) 641-3456**
Casting Services   **(805) 565-1562**
1791 Tanager St.   FAX **(805) 969-9595**
Ventura, CA 93003
santabarbara-locations.com/venturalocations

James Abke	(323) 937-1010
	www.zenobia.com

	(310) 394-6066
Ronald Abrams	(310) 880-5007
	FAX (310) 458-0858
	www.ronabrams.org

Ron Adams/Hero Locations -
Scouting & Management (323) 461-1231
1245 N. Vine St., Ste. 300
Hollywood, CA 90038

All Major Productions Location (818) 344-5454
21221 Pacific Coast Hwy   FAX (310) 456-5692
Malibu, CA 90265
(Bar and Restaurant Locations & Retail Spaces)

Dennis C. Alpert (818) 985-2739
4945 Coldwater Canyon Ave.
Sherman Oaks, CA 91423

	(818) 723-0099
Angela's Locations	(818) 231-9626
4141 Falling Leaf Dr.	FAX (818) 881-3049
Encino, CA 91316	www.angelaslocations.com

(Apartments, Architectural Properties, Bars/Restaurants, Beach
Houses, Churches, Collages, Commercial Properties, Gardens,
Gyms, Hospitals, Hotels, Houses, Mansions, Medical Buildings,
Motels, Office Buildings, Rooftops, Schools & Warehouses)

	(661) 723-6090
Antelope Valley Film Office	(661) 510-4231
44933 Fern Ave.	FAX (661) 723-5914
Lancaster, CA 93534	www.avfilm.com

(Lancaster, City of Palmdale & North Los Angeles County)

Jonathan Arroyo	(323) 828-7664
	FAX (213) 381-1980
	www.creativescouts.com

Roger Barth (310) 877-3063

Steve Beimler/locationcompass (310) 877-3032
(Japanese & Spanish)   www.locationcompass.com

Brad Bemis	(310) 991-0959
	www.bradbemis.com

Rob Benson (818) 760-0222

	(818) 554-8940
Alex Berechet	(818) 783-4423
5460 White Oak Ave., Ste. J108	FAX (818) 990-0387
Encino, CA 91316	www.alphafilmlocations.com

(Architectural Properties, Bar and Restaurant Locations,
Castles, Churches, Coastal and Marine Locations, Colleges/
Schools, Estates, Houses, Office Buildings & Warehouses)

Mike Bergemann	(310) 849-2296
	FAX (310) 919-3612
	www.bergie.locations.org

Mike Besoli	(626) 836-2225
	www.mikebesoli.com

Beth Tate Locations (310) 396-0305
(International Locations)   www.bethtate.com

Dorsey Bethune (310) 904-3115

Big Bear Locations	(818) 321-0091
	FAX (909) 584-8527
	www.bigbearlocations.com

	(818) 219-8101
Blockbuster Locations	(818) 501-8649
17451 Oak Creek Ct.	FAX (310) 501-8659
Encino, CA 91316	www.blockbusterlocations.com

Bruce Boehner	(213) 925-5379
	FAX (213) 250-5379

Robert Bonk	(213) 361-0746
	FAX (626) 303-1277

Alasdair Boyd	(213) 618-2643
	boyd.locations.org

Kenny Brant (310) 871-8675
(Central, Northern and Southern California)

	(310) 322-4499
Laura Brown	(310) 592-1774

	(818) 902-9646
Michael J. Burmeister	(818) 400-4406
6540 Hayvenhurst Ave., Ste. 30	www.burmco.com
Lake Balboa, CA 91406	

	(310) 403-9332
Jordan Burwick	(323) 668-1959
	www.jordanburwick.com

California Location Scouting/
Ken Campbell (818) 503-0035
www.calocationscouting.com

Chinatown Film Bridge (310) 576-9250
www.filmbridge.com

Bruce Chudacoff	(213) 300-4321
	FAX (310) 827-2660
zenobia.com/location/location_chudacoff_la_f400.html	

(Architectural, Bars/Restaurants, Castles, Churches, Coastal/
Marine, Colleges/Schools, Deserts, Estates, Historic, Houses,
International, Los Angeles, Mountains, Museums, NY Office
Buildings, Retail Spaces, Stages & Warehouses)

	(949) 675-8888
Cinemafloat	(714) 801-5553
1624 W. Oceanfront Walk	FAX (949) 644-3073
Newport Beach, CA 92663	

(Houses, Marine Locations & Piers)

Zack Clark	(818) 642-7341
	www.zclocations.com

	(310) 514-7579
Clean Wrap	(213) 217-0241
	FAX (818) 507-5626
	www.cleanwrap.biz

(Architectural, Bars/Restaurants, Castles, Churches, Coastal/
Marine, Colleges/Schools, Deserts, Estates, Historic, Houses,
International, Mountains, Museums, Office Buildings, Retail
Spaces, Stages & Warehouses)

Club Ed	(661) 946-1515
42848 150th St. East	FAX (661) 946-0454
Lancaster, CA 93535	www.avlocations.com

(Desert Landscapes)

Peter Cohn/	(818) 240-1893
Solar Studios & Location Services	(310) 489-7801
1601 S. Central Ave.	FAX (818) 240-4187
Glendale, CA 91204	www.solarstudios.com

	(626) 590-9339
Joni Coyote	(626) 791-0087

	(818) 986-9869
Carey Crews	(818) 800-0913
3940 Laurel Canyon Blvd., Ste. 154	
Studio City, CA 91604	www.locationcrews.smugmug.com

	(435) 645-5314
Steven Currie/Scout!	(310) 505-9342
	FAX (435) 645-8036
	www.scoututah.com

Rad Daly	(818) 203-9709
	www.radscouting.com

Dennis Morgan Locations Inc.	(818) 718-1734
	FAX (866) 715-5545
	www.dennismorganlocations.com

(Architectural Properties, Bars/Restaurants Locations, Castles, Churches, Coastal and Marine Locations, Colleges/Schools, Deserts, Estates, Houses, International Locations, Mountains, Office Buildings, Retail Spaces, Stages & Warehouses)

	(323) 697-7464
Mark DeRobertis	(626) 296-8655
	www.locationinvestigation.com

	(323) 666-6740
Scott Dewees	(310) 995-6740
	www.scottdewees.com

Direct2 Locations	(323) 766-1733
	FAX (323) 372-3948
	www.direct2pro.com

	(818) 406-3433
Paul Dirks	(626) 394-3759

	(310) 315-1800
Clay Dodder	(310) 729-0665
	FAX (310) 315-1831
	www.clayscout.com

Wendy Donovan	(323) 240-1188
	www.wendydonovan.com

Tim Down	(626) 437-7078

Robert Doyle	(310) 394-0935

Dale Dreher	(310) 600-5020
	www.mavericklocations.com

(Architectural Properties, Churches, Coastal/Marine Locations, Deserts, Houses, Mountains, Museums & Warehouses)

Randall Duryea	(310) 489-0547
	www.nationscout.com

	(323) 650-9850
Jack R. English	(323) 219-4387

P.O. Box 2081
Beverly Hills, CA 90213

Albert Maximilian Epps	(213) 479-7975
	www.epps.locations.org

	(949) 362-0727
Liz Ervin	(949) 280-7695
	www.pacificlocationsearch.com

Thomas A. Farmer	(310) 458-6025

David S. Ferdig	(818) 398-3271
	www.lunchwithdave.com

James J. Fitzpatrick	(818) 506-8051

:

Chris Foels	(818) 209-9787
	www.creativescouts.com

Andrew Gardiner	(323) 972-9624
4450 W. 165th St.	www.scout4locations.com
Lawndale, CA 90260	

	(323) 963-3496
Jon Gentry	(323) 908-3563
	www.imageevent.com/jongentry

(Architectural Properties, Bar and Restaurant Locations, Churches, Coastal and Marine Locations, Colleges/Schools, Deserts, Estates, Historic Properties, Houses, International Locations, Las Vegas Locations, Mountain Locations, Museums, Office Buildings & Retail Spaces)

Peter Gluck	(323) 466-7722
	www.petergluck.com

Marie-Paule Goislard	(323) 661-0610
(French)	FAX (323) 644-1897
	www.mpglocations.com

	(310) 801-9899
David T. Golden	(310) 837-4038
	FAX (310) 919-3004
	www.pixx.org

Bianca Gonzalez	(805) 895-1325

Jimmy Griffin	(818) 681-1250

Donna Gross	(213) 219-1959
	www.donnascout.com

Bryan Grossmann	(323) 228-5486
817 S. Los Angeles St.	www.modernlocations.net
Fourth Fl. Penthouse	
Los Angeles, CA 90014	

	(213) 500-7515
Cale Hanks	(323) 222-5144
	FAX (323) 225-7726

Jof Hanwright/scout911	(310) 452-7660
	www.scout911.com

	(310) 397-2800
Paul Hargrave	(310) 415-8870
	FAX (310) 397-2867

Howard Harnett	(818) 355-1891

	(951) 312-9009
Hart Brothers Livestock	(951) 677-6810
P.O. Box 514	FAX (951) 600-3805
Temecula, CA 92593	
(Ranches)	

David Henriksen	(818) 599-9823

	(213) 705-8500
Tom Holaday	(626) 798-9700

	(323) 876-6522
Ron Hugo	(323) 839-6047
	www.ronhugo.com

	(951) 377-7849
Inland Empire Film Commission	(951) 232-1271
1601 E. Third St.	FAX (909) 382-6066
San Bernardino, CA 92408	www.filminlandempire.com

(Agriculture Properties, Airports, Bar and Restaurant Locations, Bridges, Casinos, Castles, Churches, Colleges/Schools, Deserts, Estates, Historic Properties, Houses, International Locations, Lakes, Mountain Locations, Museums, Office Buildings, Retail Spaces, Rivers, Riverside and San Bernardino Counties, Stages, Warehouses & Western Settings)

	(714) 892-5858
ITC Barricades, Inc.	(661) 816-6270
P.O. Box 858	FAX (714) 892-5887
Westminster, CA 92684	mysite.verizon.net/itcbarricades/

(Street Closures & Traffic Plans)

Jerry Jaffe	(310) 403-4925
1603 Linden Ave.	FAX (310) 861-1774
Venice, CA 90291	www.jerryjaffe.net

JCL Barricade Company	(213) 622-9775
2334 E. Eighth St.	FAX (213) 622-9790
Los Angeles, CA 90021	www.jclbarricade.com

(Street Closures & Traffic Plans)

John Richard Massengill	(831) 588-2572
Photography	(800) 330-3064
289 Madrona Way	FAX (831) 609-6098
Ben Lomond, CA 95005	www.filminthesierras.com

(Architectural Properties, Bar and Restaurant Locations, Coastal and Marine Locations, Colleges/Schools, Deserts, Inyo and Mono Counties & Mountain Locations)

John A. Johnston	(323) 646-7226

Fred Jové/Locations Etcetera	(661) 433-1138
	(661) 269-2640

Geoff Juckes/Location America	(626) 791-3484
	(626) 484-4145
www.locationamerica.com	

(Aerials, Deserts, Mountains, Remote Areas & Tropical Islands)

Stephen Kardell	(323) 770-6567
2436 E. Fourth St., Box 26	FAX (562) 683-0409
Long Beach, CA 90814	www.stephenkardell.com

Larry Kelly	(818) 620-4155
	(818) 783-8050
	FAX (818) 783-8051
	www.larrykelly.tv

Halli Kristjansson	(310) 980-2806

La Classe Locations, Inc.	(818) 845-9600
	(818) 426-2600
P.O. Box 81	FAX (818) 845-9606
Burbank, CA 91503	www.locationnetwork.com

Simon Lampard	(310) 455-2203
	(310) 963-2203
	FAX (310) 455-1393
www.lampardlocations.com	

Nancy Lazarus	(310) 207-9878
	(213) 500-7000
www.lazaruslocations.com	

Greg Lazzaro	(310) 850-2249
www.greglazzaro.com	

Location Association/Bob Heberly	(213) 507-4640
3206 Wyoming Ave.	www.locationassociation.com
Burbank, CA 91505	

The Location Connection, Inc.	(310) 376-9797
	(818) 422-8127
Raleigh Studios Manhattan Beach	FAX (888) 837-4643
1600 Rosecrans Ave. Bldg. Five, Second Fl.	
Manhattan Beach, CA 90266	
www.locationconnection.com	

(Coachella Valley, Los Angeles, Malibu, Orange County, San Fernando Valley & South Bay)

Location Network/Geoff White	(818) 845-9600
	(818) 426-2600
P.O. Box 81	FAX (818) 845-9606
Burbank, CA 91503	www.locationnetwork.com

Scott Allen Logan	(310) 571-1555
	(310) 433-0337
Loganfilm, Inc., 12100 Wilshire Blvd., Ste. 200	
Los Angeles, CA 90025	www.loganfilm.com

Long Beach Locations	(562) 951-0306
	(562) 900-1928
235 E. Broadway, Ste.220	FAX (562) 951-0347
Long Beach, CA 90802	www.filmlb.com

Lorin Miller Locations	(916) 600-8442
	(530) 888-6625

Bill Lose	(310) 386-9919

Charlie Love	(323) 646-7826

John C. Lowe	(818) 355-5602
www.creativescouts.com	

Melissa MacCracken	(310) 344-3080
86 Dapplegray Ln.	
Palos Verdes, CA 90274	

Jim Maceo	(626) 398-3000
	(818) 424-4577
	FAX (626) 398-6557

Flint Maloney	(323) 254-3715
www.flintman.com	

Nik Mansoor	(818) 822-9292

Edward Mazurek	(310) 980-4142
	(310) 936-4606
1320 Pico Blvd., Ste. D	www.3dlocations.com
Santa Monica, CA 90406	

David McKinney	(310) 990-9404
	(310) 534-3463
www.prophotoscout.com	

Beth Melnick	(310) 779-5683
	(503) 281-4741
northlight.locations.org	

Robert Mendel/Location Scouting	(213) 591-0510
www.mendel.locations.org	

Michael N. Marks, Inc.	(310) 600-3011
7352 Trask Ave.	FAX (310) 821-5506
Playa del Rey, CA 90293	www.mnmlocations.com

(Architectural Properties, Bars/Restaurants, Churches, Coastal/Marine, Colleges/Schools, Estates, Historic, Houses, Office Buildings, Retail, Stages & Warehouses)

Miles of Files/Bianca Gonzalez	(805) 895-1325
817 Kentia Ave.	
Santa Barbara, CA 93101	

(Santa Barbara; Spanish Speaking)

Aaron Millar	(310) 278-8957
	(310) 780-3547
128 S. Camden Dr., Ste. 205	FAX (310) 271-3547
Beverly Hills, CA 90212	www.aaronmillar.com

Barbara Miller	(213) 393-5555
	(626) 356-9913
(Domestic/International Locations) www.millerlocations.com	

David Moate/Reconnoitre	(626) 794-8552

Judy Montgomery	(323) 377-2336

Dennis Morley	(310) 963-9400
	FAX (323) 660-8997
www.dennismorley.com	

Nick Morley	(323) 848-7762
	(213) 716-4298
	FAX (323) 210-7153

Jeff Morris/LA Scout Planet	(213) 798-7676
	(661) 254-8650
	FAX (661) 254-2853
www.lascoutplanet.com	

(Architectural, Bars/Restaurants, Coastal/Marine, Deserts, Estates, Historic, Houses, Mountains, Office Buildings, Retail Spaces & Warehouses)

David Nakata	(818) 355-5517
www.creativescouts.com	

Keith Nakata	(323) 653-0455
811 N. Croft Ave.	
Los Angeles, CA 90069	

Galidan Nauber	(213) 705-3212

Michael Neale	(818) 371-2300

Elizabeth Nicole	(323) 937-1010
www.zenobia.com	

Kevin Noonan	(310) 251-6880

Pacific Production Services, Inc.	(323) 260-4777
	(213) 360-7844
1481 E. Fourth St.	FAX (323) 415-6180
Los Angeles, CA 90033	www.lafilmpermits.com

(Street Closures & Traffic Plans)

Michael Paolillo   (310) 493-1671

Pat Parrish   (310) 652-5585
      (310) 291-6618
8642 Gregory Way   www.scout4ads.com
Los Angeles, CA 90035

Marino Pascal   (323) 254-9272
      www.locationscout.com

Osceola Refetoff/
Red Eye Productions   (213) 300-1300
859 N. Las Palmas Ave.
Los Angeles, CA 90038
(International and Domestic Locations)

Will Regan   (626) 441-8066
      (626) 827-9800
      FAX (626) 263-7630
      www.willscout.com

Errol Reichow   (805) 404-7871
      FAX (818) 707-1940

Patrick Reinoso   (818) 606-3081
      (818) 883-3081
(Architectural Properties, Castles, Coastal/Marine, Deserts,
Historic Properties, International Locations, Mountains, Office
Buildings & Stages in Arizona, California, Nevada and Utah)

Renaissance Locations/   (310) 779-6221
Paul Kruhm & Richard Latarewicz   (310) 466-0485
P.O. Box 66663   FAX (212) 859-7344
Los Angeles, CA 90066 www.renaissancelocations.com

Richard Muessel Company   (310) 245-1990
7336 Santa Monica Blvd., Ste. 762 FAX (323) 512-5374
Los Angeles, CA 90046

Greg Robinson   (562) 420-2276
      (213) 895-8105
      FAX (562) 420-2276

Santiago Romeo   (818) 254-7110
      (310) 666-5012
      FAX (626) 380-1617

Gregg Ross   (626) 840-2484
      FAX (626) 398-8779
      www.greggrosslocations.com

Albie Salsich   (310) 930-3620
      (310) 446-6268

Santa Barbara Location Co.   (805) 203-0611
212 Cottage Grove
Santa Barbara, CA 93101
(Architectural, Bars/Restaurants, Castles, Churches, Coastal/
Marine, Colleges/Schools, Deserts, Estates, Historic, Houses,
International, Mountains, Museums, Offices, Retail Spaces,
Stages & Warehouses)

Santa Barbara Location Services/
aka Location Production   (805) 969-5555
Coordination   (805) 565-1562
110 Olive Mill Ln.   FAX (805) 969-9595
Santa Barbara, CA 93108
      www.santabarbaralocations.com
(Architectural Properties, Coastal and Marine Locations,
Colleges/Schools, Estates, Houses, Office Buildings; Ojai, San
Luis Obispo, Santa Barbara, Santa Ynez Valley & Ventura)

The Scoutmaster/Jerry Tomson   (310) 363-5097

John Shaughnessy   (818) 512-1658
      www.creativescouts.com

Adam Silver   (213) 709-8273
      www.adamsilverpictures.com

Skyline Locations   (213) 680-7400
915 Wilshire Blvd., Ste. 1780 FAX (213) 860-7401
Los Angeles, CA 90017 www.skylinelocations.com

Carol Smith   (626) 437-3060
      (626) 395-9574

Jeff Smith   (310) 617-9147
      (323) 876-5240
      www.witsendlocations.com

Maria Smith   (323) 937-1010
      www.zenobia.com

Susan Snyder/Amazing Locations   (310) 570-0047
      (310) 470-2208
2023 Manning Ave.
West Los Angeles, CA 90025

Gregory M. Strait   (323) 630-7824

Stuart Raven Barter & Associates   (323) 931-2177
5576 W. First St.   www.srba.com
Los Angeles, CA 90036

Sunset Locations, Inc.   (310) 360-1306
8730 Sunset Blvd., Ste. 485 FAX (310) 360-1362
West Hollywood, CA 90069 www.sunsetlocations.com

Team Halprin, Inc.   (310) 842-7000
9190 W. Olympic Blvd., Ste. 304 FAX (310) 842-7014
Beverly Hills, CA 90212 www.teamhalprin.com

Russ Thomas   (818) 437-2560
      (818) 753-8117
      www.russfoundit.com

Danny Thomsen   (626) 419-7766
      www.dtlocations.com

Tom Lackey, Scott Bigbee &   (310) 395-8817
Associates   (310) 613-7322
      FAX (310) 395-8817

Traffic Management, Inc.   (800) 763-3999
2435 Lemon Ave.   FAX (562) 424-0266
Signal Hill, CA 90755 www.trafficmanagement.com
(Street Closures & Traffic/Pedestrian Control)

Scott Trimble   (310) 528-1241
      FAX (310) 362-8920
      www.ststlocations.com

Vertical Adventures   (949) 854-6250
      (800) 514-8785
P.O. Box 7548   FAX (949) 854-5249
Newport Beach, CA 92658
(Deserts & Mountains)

Vincent Vanni   (310) 713-8084
      FAX (866) 227-7589
      www.creativescouts.com

Capt. Troy Waters   (310) 713-9193
(Coastal, Harbor and Marine Locations) FAX (310) 943-3328

Willie's On & Off Road Center   (760) 257-3734
      (760) 953-3303
48301 National Trails Hwy   FAX (760) 257-3335
Newberry Springs, CA 92365 www.williesoffroad.com

Mel Wilson   (213) 591-0719
      (323) 936-3666
      FAX (815) 550-8565
      wilson.locations.org

Frank Yoshikane   (714) 273-3103

Mark Zekanis   (805) 512-4161

Zenobia Agency, Inc.   (323) 937-1010
      (888) 639-6917
130 S. Highland Ave.   FAX (323) 937-1133
Los Angeles, CA 90036 www.zenobia.com
(Reps for Location Managers and Scouts)

30th Street Garage   **(619) 234-4325**
3335 30th St.   FAX **(619) 234-2055**
San Diego, CA 92104   www.30thstreetgarage.com
(Historic Auto Garage)

Agua Dulce Airport   **(661) 268-8835**
33638 Agua Dulce Canyon Rd.   FAX **(661) 268-7662**
Agua Dulce, CA 91390

    (661) 251-2365
Agua Dulce Movie Ranch   **(661) 510-6958**
34855 Petersen Rd.   FAX **(661) 268-7680**
Agua Dulce, CA 91390   www.sosfilmworks.com

Andresen's Rancho Rosita   **(805) 491-3242**
    www.ranchorosita.com

Angelus Mountain Center/   **(626) 577-9979**
Summerkids Camp   **(626) 398-1426**
3697 N. Fair Oaks Ave.   FAX **(626) 577-9974**
Altadena, CA 91001   www.angelusmountaincenter.com

Auto Club Speedway   **(909) 429-5000**
Contact: Phil Tucker   FAX **(909) 429-5500**
    www.autoclubspeedway.com

Bothwell Ranch   **(818) 347-9000**
5300 Oakdale Ave.   FAX **(818) 587-9215**
Woodland Hills, CA 91364

    (818) 636-5754
Break Room Cafe   **(323) 963-5500**
3244 Cahuenga Blvd. West www.thebreakroomcafe.com
Universal City, CA 90068

Bridges Auditorium   **(909) 607-8580**
450 N. College Way   www.cuc.claremont.edu/bridges
Claremont, CA 91711

California State University   **(818) 677-2744**
Northridge   **(818) 677-2628**
18111 Nordhoff St.   FAX **(818) 677-3017**
Northridge, CA 91330   www.csun.edu/licensing

    (805) 371-0097
Canyon Ranch   **(805) 358-9545**
368 E. Carlisle Rd.   FAX **(805) 371-0091**
Thousand Oaks, CA 91361
    www.canyonranchfilmlocation.com

Ⓐ Caravan West Productions   **(661) 268-8300**
35660 Jayhawker Rd.   FAX **(661) 268-8301**
Agua Dulce, CA 91390   www.caravanwest.com

Chic Little Devil Style House   **(310) 403-6929**
1206 Maple Ave., 11th Fl.
Los Angeles, CA 90015
    www.chiclittledevilstylehouse.com

Cinespace   **(323) 817-3456**
    FAX **(323) 860-9794**
    www.cinespace.info

City Loft   **(818) 613-5962**
1275 E. Sixth St.   www.cityloftfilmlocation.com
Los Angeles, CA 90021
(Basement, Loft, Parking Lot, Rooftop & Warehouse)

Cojo - Jalama Ranch   **(805) 736-7300**
P.O. Box 1177   FAX **(805) 736-8084**
Lompoc, CA 93438   www.cojoranch.com

Cypress Sea Cove   **(310) 589-3344**
33572 Pacific Coast Hwy www.malibufilmlocations.com
Malibu, CA 90265

Dance Studio No. 1   **(310) 979-9929**
12121 W. Pico Blvd., Ste. 2C   FAX **(310) 979-9920**
Los Angeles, CA 90064   www.dancestudiono1.com

    (213) 629-5434
DC Stages & Sets   **(310) 804-5712**
1360 E. Sixth St.   FAX **(213) 629-5155**
Los Angeles, CA 90021   dcstages.com
(Standing Sets)

Depict, Inc.   **(323) 222-1001**
    www.depict33.com

The Derby Dolls   **(310) 428-4238**
1910 W. Temple St.   www.derbydolls.com
Los Angeles, CA 90026

Disney Ice   **(714) 535-7465**
300 W. Lincoln Ave.   FAX **(714) 518-3220**
Anaheim, CA 92805   www.anaheimice.com

Downtown Office Location   **(323) 273-0636**
529 E. Sixth St.
Los Angeles, CA 90021   www.kodakgallery.com/gallery/
    sharing/shareRedirectSwitchBoard.jsp?token
    =926400292213%3A1121719219

    (310) 457-3807
Dry Gulch Ranch - Malibu   **(310) 589-8311**
12420 Yellow Hill Rd.   FAX **(310) 457-3807**
Malibu, CA 90265   www.drygulchlodge.com

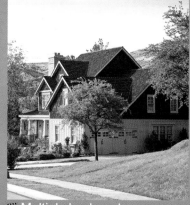

Dusty Oak Ranch   **(805) 495-9543**
670 E. Carlisle Canyon Rd.
Westlake Village, CA 91361

Ebony Repertory Theatre @
The Nate Holden   **(323) 964-9768**
4718 W. Washington Blvd. **www.ebonyrep.org**
Los Angeles, CA 90016

El Campeon Farms/   **(805) 497-2766**
Windy Hill Ranch   **(805) 732-9163**
999 W. Potrero Rd.   FAX **(805) 497-0377**
Thousand Oaks, CA 91361 **www.elcampeonfarms.com**
(Farm/Ranch Location)

El Capitan Theatre &   **(323) 467-7674**
Entertainment Centre   **(818) 845-3110**
6838 Hollywood Blvd.   FAX **(323) 467-0922**
Los Angeles, CA 90028 **www.elcapitantickets.com**

Epicenter Stadium -
City of Rancho Cucamonga   **(909) 477-2760**
10500 Civic Center Dr.   FAX **(909) 477-2761**
Rancho Cucamonga, CA 91730 **www.rcepicenter.com**

Esprit   **(310) 305-3700**
13900 Marquesas Way   FAX **(310) 305-1743**
Marina del Rey, CA 90292 **www.espritmdr.com**

Fairplex   **(909) 865-4042**
           (909) 226-8813
1101 W. Mckinley Ave.   FAX **(909) 623-9599**
Pomona, CA 91768 **www.fairplex.com**

The Forum   **(310) 330-7300**
3900 W. Manchester Blvd. **www.thelaforum.com**
Inglewood, CA 90305
Contact: Devon Mackey

Gallery 1018   **(310) 804-3372**
         www.gallery1018.com

Gallery de Soto   **(323) 253-2255**

Goathouse and TTS Studios   **(818) 982-9872**
7303 Ethel Ave.   FAX **(818) 982-9199**
North Hollywood, CA 91605
(Loft & Stage) **www.filmlocationlosangeles.com**

Gold Creek Ranch   **(818) 378-9609**
8807 Gold Creek Rd. **www.goldcreekranch.com**
Lake View Terrace, CA 91342

A Golden Oak Ranch   **(661) 259-8717**
19802 Placerita Canyon Rd. **www.goldenoakranch.com**
Newhall, CA 91321

Goldspirit Farm   **(818) 834-1272**
12682 Kagel Canyon Rd.   FAX **(818) 834-1902**
San Fernando, CA 91342 **www.goldspiritfarm.com**

Greek Theatre   **(323) 665-5857**
2700 N. Vermont Ave.   FAX **(323) 666-8202**
Los Angeles, CA 90027 **www.greektheatrela.com**

The Grove   **(323) 900-8142**
         (323) 900-8100
101 The Grove Dr.   FAX **(323) 900-8001**
Los Angeles, CA 90036 **www.carusoaffiliated.com/film**

Hart Brothers Livestock   **(951) 312-9009**
         (951) 677-6810
P.O. Box 514   FAX **(951) 600-3805**
Temecula, CA 92593

Hollywood Park   **(310) 419-1500**
Box 369   **www.hollywoodpark.com**
Inglewood, CA 90306
Contact: Deann Fruhling

Hollywood Production Center **(818) 480-3100**
121 W. Lexington Dr.   FAX **(818) 480-3199**
Glendale, CA 91203 **www.hollywoodpc.com**

Honda Center   **(714) 704-2422**
2695 E. Katella Ave.   FAX **(714) 704-2610**
Anaheim, CA 92806 **www.hondacenter.com**
Contact: Jo-Ann Armstrong

House of Blues   **(323) 848-5100**
8430 Sunset Blvd.   **www.hob.com**
West Hollywood, CA 90069
Contact: Maureen McGrath

Hummingbird Nest Ranch   **(805) 579-8000**
2940 Kuehner Dr.   FAX **(805) 583-1527**
Simi Valley, CA 93063
   www.hummingbirdnestranch.com

The Huntington Library, Art Collections and
Botanical Gardens   **(626) 405-2215**
         www.filmhuntington.org

Huron SubStation   **(323) 225-8909**
2640 Huron St.   FAX **(800) 650-1522**
Los Angeles, CA 90065 **www.huronsubstation.com**

Ice Chalet   **(310) 541-6630**
550 Deep Valley Dr.   FAX **(310) 541-8674**
Avenue of the Peninsula Mall
Rolling Hills Estates, CA 90274
   www.palosverdesicechalet.com

Inner-City Arts Campus   **(213) 627-9621**
720 Kohler St.   FAX **(213) 627-6469**
Los Angeles, CA 90021
   www.inner-cityarts.org/images.html

A JMJ Ranch   **(805) 497-3018**
930 W. Potrero Rd.   FAX **(805) 497-2122**
Thousand Oaks, CA 91361 **www.jmjranch.com**

Jody Domingue Studios   **(818) 577-9737**
5770 Melrose Ave., Ste. 204
Los Angeles, CA 90038 **www.jodydominguestudios.com**

Knightsbridge Theatre   **(323) 667-0955**
         (323) 394-1584
1944-1952 Riverside Dr. **www.knightsbridgetheatre.com**
Los Angeles, CA 90039

La Mirada Theatre for the   (714) 994-6310
Performing Arts   (562) 944-9801
14900 La Mirada Blvd.   FAX **(714) 994-5796**
La Mirada, CA 90638   www.lamiradatheatre.com
Contact: Laura Moore

     (213) 972-7211
LA Music Center   (213) 972-3335
Contact: John Vassiliou   www.musiccenter.org

Lane Ranch & Company   (661) 942-0435
42220 10th St. West, Ste. 101   FAX **(661) 942-7485**
Lancaster, CA 93534   www.laneranch.net
(Desert Landscape)

Limoneira Orchards   (866) 242-1828
1141 Cummings Rd.   FAX **(805) 525-8761**
Santa Paula, CA 93060   www.limoneiraorchards.com

Los Angeles County Metropolitan
Transportation Authority (Metro)   (213) 922-6000
One Gateway Plaza   www.metro.net
Los Angeles, CA 90012

Madera Design House   (415) 407-8440
1503 S. Central Ave.   FAX **(213) 747-2412**
Los Angeles, CA 90021   www.maderadesign.org
(Photography Studio)

Mid-Century Modern House   (310) 274-7440
    FAX **(310) 274-9809**
    www.simonhousela.com

National Aerospace Training and
Research Center/NASTAR   (866) 482-0933
Contact: Brienna Henwood   www.nastarcenter.com

     (805) 625-3309
The Newhall Mansion at Piru   (805) 521-0866
829 N. Park St., P.O. Box 26   www.pirumansion.com
Piru, CA 93040

     (619) 231-1941
The Old Globe   (619) 234-5623
1363 Old Globe Way   FAX **(619) 231-9518**
San Diego, CA 92101   www.theoldglobe.org
Contact: Debbie Ballard

     (877) 677-4386
Orpheum Theatre   (213) 626-5321
842 S. Broadway   www.laorpheum.com
Los Angeles, CA 90014
Contact: Steve Needleman

Pacific Earth Resources/   (805) 987-8456
Rogers Ranch   (800) 942-5296
305 W. Hueneme Rd.   FAX **(805) 986-5210**
Camarillo, CA 93012   www.pacificearth.com

     (562) 863-4567
Paddison Farm   (562) 972-4126
11951 E. Imperial Hwy   www.paddisonfarm.com
Norwalk, CA 90650

Paramount Ranch Locations   (805) 530-1967
8800 Grimes Canyon Rd.   FAX **(805) 523-1903**
Moorpark, CA 93021   www.movielocationsca.com
Contact: Lisa Francey

Ⓐ The Studios at Paramount   (323) 956-8811
The Studios at Paramount New York Streets
5555 Melrose Ave.   www.thestudiosatparamount.com
Hollywood, CA 90038

Pier 59 Studios West   (310) 829-5959
2415 Michigan Ave.   FAX **(310) 829-9550**
Santa Monica, CA 90404   www.pier59studioswest.com

The Polsa Rosa Ranch   (661) 257-3456
    www.polsarosa.com

     (805) 521-0511
Rancho Temescal   (805) 889-1114
P.O. Box 378   FAX **(805) 521-0559**
Piru, CA 93040   www.ranchotemescal.com

     (213) 413-9300
RecCenter Studio   (323) 868-4226
1161 Logan St.   FAX **(213) 413-9301**
Los Angeles, CA 90026   www.reccenterstudio.com

REDCAT   (213) 237-2800
631 W. Second St.   FAX **(213) 237-2811**
Los Angeles, CA 90012   www.redcat.org

Renberg Theatre   (323) 860-7336
The Village at Ed Gould Plaza   FAX **(323) 308-4103**
1125 N. McCadden Pl.   www.lagaycenter.org
Los Angeles, CA 90038

     (909) 797-7534
Riley's Farm & Apple Orchard   (909) 790-8463
12261 Oak Glen Rd.   FAX **(909) 790-2552**
Oak Glen, CA 92399   www.rileysfarm.com

     (818) 348-6000
Rock Star Properties   (661) 803-5822
19855 Ventura Blvd.   FAX **(818) 348-6666**
Woodland Hills, CA 91364

     (626) 577-3130
Rose Bowl   (626) 577-3206
1001 Rose Bowl Dr.   FAX **(626) 405-0992**
Pasadena, CA 91103   www.rosebowlstadium.com
Contacts: Julie Granillo & Erika Samarzich

Saddle Peak Lodge   (818) 222-3888
419 Cold Canyon Rd.   www.saddlepeaklodge.com
Calabasas, CA 91302

Saddlerock Ranch   (818) 889-0008
31727 Mulholland Hwy   FAX **(818) 889-5349**
Malibu, CA 90265   www.malibufamilywines.com

Santa Anita Park   (626) 574-7223
285 W. Huntington Dr.   FAX **(626) 821-1530**
Arcadia, CA 91007   www.santaanita.com
Contact: Pete Siberell

     (323) 896-3017
Santino Bros Wrestling Academy   (323) 767-3577
5640 Shull St., Ste. S   www.santinobros.net
Bell Gardens, CA 90201
(Wrestling Ring)

     (949) 489-9000
SC Village   (562) 867-9600
8900 McCarty Rd.   FAX **(562) 804-1514**
Chino, CA 91710   www.scvillage.com
(Paintball Park)

The Shrine Auditorium   (213) 748-5116
649 W. Jefferson Blvd.   FAX **(213) 742-9922**
Los Angeles, CA 90007   www.shrineauditorium.com

Sky Drops Inc.   (818) 633-2639
999 N. Mission Rd.   www.skydrops.com
Los Angeles, CA 90033

     (818) 240-1893
Solar Studios   (310) 489-7801
1601 S. Central Ave.   FAX **(818) 240-4187**
Glendale, CA 91204   www.solarstudios.com

The Solomon Loft   (626) 388-8342
    www.filmdowntown.com

Staples Center   (213) 742-7100
1111 S. Figueroa St.   www.staplescenter.com
Los Angeles, CA 90015

Summit (818) 909-7933
(818) 458-4495

Sunset Plaza House (323) 365-6606
(310) 360-1634
1870 Sunset Plaza Dr. FAX (310) 360-1634
Los Angeles, CA 90069 www.sunsetplazahouse.com

Tank One Studios (562) 988-3400
(310) 717-8717
2549 N. Palm Dr. FAX (562) 988-3433
Signal Hill, CA 90755 www.tankonestudios.com
(Underwater Filming Studio, Water Sets & Water Tank)

Teatro Theater (310) 312-9772
(310) 346-1649
626 Oxnard Blvd. www.futurelighting.net
Oxnard, CA 93030

Tejon Ranch (661) 248-6890
(661) 203-6261
4436 Lebec Rd., P.O. Box 1000 FAX (661) 248-6773
Lebec, CA 93243 www.tejonfilm.com

Tierra Rejada Ranch (805) 529-1766
15191 Read Rd. FAX (805) 529-1470
Moorpark, CA 93021

**Universal Studios
Hollywood Theme Park** (818) 622-5453
FAX (818) 622-5897
www.universalstudioshollywood.com/production/

Vasa Park (818) 889-3336
(818) 889-2224
2854 Triunfo Canyon Rd. FAX (818) 889-2416
Agoura Hills, CA 91301 www.vasa-park.com

Veluzat Motion Picture Ranch (661) 810-9898
FAX (661) 294-6814
P.O. Box 220597
Newhall, CA 91322
www.veluzatmotionpictureranch.com

Ventura Farms (805) 496-0767
235 W. Potrero Rd. www.venturafarms.com
Thousand Oaks, CA 91361

Vess House (619) 795-4300
10636 Snyder Rd. www.vesshouse.com
La Mesa, CA 91941

Villa Malibu Luxury Rentals (888) 526-6096
6487 Cavalleri Rd., Ste. 224 www.villamalibuliving.com
Malibu, CA 90265

Westfield, LLC (310) 689-2635
6600 Topanga Canyon Blvd., Ste. 1M www.westfield.com
Canoga Park, CA 91304
(Multiple Locations)

**Westside Loft & Art Studio/
Spanish Style Home** (310) 822-4504
3918 Alla Rd. FAX (310) 822-4504
Los Angeles, CA 90066 www.amadeabailey.com

Willow Studios (213) 625-5771
(310) 849-5452
1333-1335 Willow St. FAX (213) 625-0101
Los Angeles, CA 90013 www.willowstudios.net

Winnetka Ranch (619) 468-9127
P.O. Box 915 FAX (619) 468-9128
Jamul, CA 91935 www.winnetkaranch.com

Writers Guild Theater (323) 782-4525
135 S. Doheny Dr. www.wga.org
Beverly Hills, CA 90211

5th & Sunset Los Angeles (310) 979-0212
12322 Exposition Blvd. FAX (310) 979-0214
Los Angeles, CA 90064 www.5thandsunsetla.com

5th Wheel Production Trailers (661) 256-2991
(661) 406-2325
(Motorhomes & Production Trailers) www.bobspt.com

A & J Restroom Rentals (562) 507-1466
www.ajportabletoilets.com
(Portable Restrooms, Portable Toilets & V.I.P. Restrooms)

A-1 Portables (760) 949-4111
(800) 554-7723
17491 Lilac St. FAX (760) 949-4224
Hesperia, CA 92345
(Motorhomes & VIP Restrooms)

Al's Production Trailers (760) 373-5771
(805) 490-4399
P.O. Box 2442 FAX (760) 373-5771
California City, CA 93504 www.pridept.com
(Production Trailers)

All Day And Knight (818) 262-6568
(818) 262-3467
P.O. Box 3053
Chatsworth, CA 91313

Aloha Studio Rentals (661) 993-5393
30402 Clover Court FAX (661) 414-8090
Castaic, CA 91384 www.alohastudiorentals.com
(Honeywagons, Portable Restrooms/Toilets & V.I.P. Restrooms)

Andy Gump, Inc. (661) 251-7721
(800) 992-7755
26954 Ruether Ave. FAX (661) 251-7729
Santa Clarita, CA 91351 www.andygump.com
(Portable Toilets, Restrooms & Shower Trailers)

**Anytime Production
Equipment Rentals, Inc.** (323) 461-8483
755 N. Lillian Way FAX (323) 461-2338
Hollywood, CA 90038 www.anytimerentals.com

Apache Rental Group (818) 842-9944
(818) 842-9875
3910 W. Magnolia Blvd. FAX (818) 842-9269
Burbank, CA 91505 www.apacherentalgroup.com
(Motorhomes)

Base Camp Mobile Offices (818) 352-5750
1317 N. San Fernando Blvd., Ste. 503 FAX (818) 743-7882
Burbank, CA 91504
(Honeywagons & Makeup Trailers)

BBL Mobile, Inc. (800) 848-4140
(Honeywagons & Makeup Trailers) FAX (805) 241-8793
www.bblmobile.com

Bertrand Enterprises (760) 446-6600
1210 Graaf Ave. FAX (760) 446-2669
Ridgecrest, CA 93555
(Motorhomes)

Bill's Motorhome Rentals (818) 219-6162
9555 Via Ricardo
Burbank, CA 91504

Blue Sky Production Equipment (818) 591-1761
(818) 253-6152
25734 Punto De Vista Dr.
Calabasas, CA 91302
www.blueskyproductionequipment.com

Buboosky Production Vehicles (661) 993-9022
FAX (661) 513-9776
www.buboosky.com

Century Studio Corporation (310) 287-3600
(888) 878-2437
8660 Hayden Pl., Ste. 100 FAX (310) 287-3608
Culver City, CA 90232 www.centurystudio.com
(Trailers)

Characters on Wheels (909) 393-6575
(310) 650-7046
15506 Dupont Ave. FAX (909) 393-6275
Chino, CA 91710 www.stardeckrvs.com

Cinewagon, LLC (818) 822-0786
(818) 534-6402
P.O. Box 573511 FAX (818) 366-1102
Tarzana, CA 91357 www.cinewagon.com

**D. Aguire Production
Service Vehicles** (310) 925-0967
(888) 527-7381
2542 Norte Vista Dr. FAX (909) 628-7708
Chino Hills, CA 91709

**Diamond Environmental
Services, LLC** (888) 744-7191
1801 Villa Burton, Ste. B FAX (760) 290-3365
Fullerton, CA 92831 www.diamondprovides.com
(Honeywagons, Makeup Trailers, Mobile Offices, Motorhomes,
Portable Restrooms/Toilets, Shower Trailers, Star Trailers &
V.I.P. Restrooms)

Easy Rider Productions, Inc. (818) 822-8782
(877) 982-3279
P.O. Box 222034 FAX (661) 288-1958
Newhall, CA 91322 www.easyriderprod.com
(Honeywagons, Makeup Trailers, Mobile Offices, Motorhomes,
Portable Restrooms/Toilets, Production Trailers, Shower
Trailers, Star Trailers, V.I.P. Restrooms & Wardrobe Trailers)

El Monte RV (800) 337-2150
(562) 483-4983
6323 Sepulveda Blvd. FAX (818) 787-3612
Van Nuys, CA 91411 www.elmonterv.com/studio
(Honeywagons, Makeup Trailers, Motorhomes, Star Trailers &
Wardrobe Trailers)

Elliott Location Equipment (310) 915-1744
(505) 328-0909
www.elliottlocationequipment.com
(Honeywagons, Makeup Trailers, Mobile Offices, Production
Trailers, Star Trailers, V.I.P. Restrooms & Wardrobe Trailers)

Genie Production Vehicles (323) 447-0622
(909) 917-9859
12188 Central Ave., Ste. 195 FAX (909) 591-2045
Chino, CA 91710 www.geniepv.com
(Makeup Trailers, Mobile Offices, Motorhomes, Portable Toilets,
Production Trailers, Star Trailers & Wardrobe Trailers)

Holiday Studio Rentals (818) 252-7722
11473 Penrose St. www.holidaysr.com
Sun Valley, CA 91352

**Hollywood Honeywagon &
Production Vehicles** (818) 763-1966
(818) 535-9648
11160 Victory Blvd. FAX (818) 760-0551
North Hollywood, CA 91606
www.hollywoodhoneywagon.com
(Honeywagons, Makeup and Wardrobe Trailers, Motorhomes,
Portable Restroom Units & Production Trailers)

King Kong Production Vehicles (323) 462-6646
(949) 673-1999
FAX (800) 513-9354
www.kingkongtrailers.com
(Airstream, Honeywagons, Makeup Trailers, Mobile Offices,
Motorhomes, People Mover, Portable Restrooms/Toilets,
Production Trailers, Star Trailers, V.I.P. Restrooms &
Wardrobe Trailers)

Kohler Rental
(310) 518-5118
(310) 600-3063
766 Gifford Ave.
FAX (920) 459-1846
San Bernardino, CA 92408
www.kohlerrental.com
(Portable Restrooms)

LBS Rentals
(818) 768-6170
(818) 652-5784
11323 Sheldon St.
FAX (818) 768-6079
Sun Valley, CA 91352
www.lbsrentals.com

Line 204/Angstrom Lighting
(323) 960-0113
837 N. Cahuenga Blvd.
FAX (323) 960-0163
Hollywood, CA 90038
www.line204.com

Mike Green RV's
(818) 317-7099
(541) 619-3934
1137 E. California Ave., Ste. 5
FAX (323) 927-1546
Glendale, CA 91206
www.mikegreenrv.com
(Motorhomes, Portable Restrooms, Toilets & V.I.P. Restrooms)

Moe's Motorhome
(805) 526-9252
(805) 794-2500
2465 Pinewood Pl.
www.moesmotorhome.com
Simi Valley, CA 93065

Moho to Go/MTG Trailers
(562) 572-1565
4268 Jackson Ave., Ste. A
FAX (424) 603-4058
Culver City, CA 90232
www.mtgtrailers.com

Motionpv
(714) 454-6249
www.motionpv.com

Movie Movers
(818) 252-7722
Transportation Equipment
(276) 650-3378
11473 Penrose St.
FAX (818) 252-7723
Sun Valley, CA 91352
www.moviemovers.com

Moving Stars Production Vehicles
(818) 549-9595
(626) 815-2770
15 Aspendale Court
FAX (626) 815-2771
Azusa, CA 91702

N.W. Production Services &
RV Rental
(949) 212-9735
190 Avenida La Cuesta
FAX (949) 361-2836
San Clemente, CA 92672
www.nwproduction.com

No Boundary Productions
(305) 491-2433
(619) 981-0508
www.nbpro.biz

On Location Motorhomes
(323) 465-5600
P.O. Box 3087
FAX (909) 394-7423
San Dimas, CA 91773 www.onlocationmotorhomes.com
(Honeywagons, Makeup Trailers, Mobile Offices, Motorhomes,
Portable Restrooms, Production Trailers, Star Trailers &
Wardrobe Trailers)

Premiere Transportation
(888) 771-0588
FAX (615) 261-2108
www.myluxurybus.com
(Makeup Trailers, Mobile Offices, Mobile Screening Rooms,
Motorhomes & Star Trailers)

Prestige Star Trailers
(818) 426-5280
6933 Whitaker Ave.
Lake Balboa, CA 91406
(Production Trailers & Talent/Production Motorhomes)

Production On Wheels
(562) 882-8504
(424) 247-9166
2301 Belmont Ln.
FAX (424) 247-9166
Redondo Beach, CA 90278
www.productiononwheels.com
(Makeup Trailers, Motorhomes, Star Trailers & Wardrobe Trailers)

Quixote Studios
(323) 857-5050
1011 N. Fuller Ave.
FAX (323) 851-5029
West Hollywood, CA 90046
www.quixote.com
(Motorhomes & Production Trailers)

Ray's Production Services
(805) 649-9064
1187 Coast Village Rd., Ste. 362
Santa Barbara, CA 93108
www.raysmotorhomes.com

Redline RV Productions, LLC
(866) 720-1930
7251 E. Lewis Dr.
www.redlinervp.com
Orange, CA 92869
(Honeywagons & Star Trailers)

Reyes RV Rentals, LLC
(855) 739-3700
(818) 642-4940
20832 Valerio St., Ste. 7
FAX (818) 337-2194
Winnetka, CA 91306
www.reyesrvrentals.com
(Mobile Offices, Motorhomes, Star Trailers & Wardrobe Trailers)

Royal Restrooms
(877) 922-9980
FAX (877) 922-9980
www.royalrestroomsca.com
(Honeywagons, Portable Restrooms/Toilets, Shower Trailers &
V.I.P. Restrooms)

Silverstar Rentals
(909) 322-4392
www.silverstarrentals.net

SirReel - LA & San Diego
(888) 477-7335
(818) 859-7766
(Production Trailers)
FAX (888) 477-7313
www.sirreel.us

Sony Pictures Studios
(310) 244-7016
10202 W. Washington Blvd.
FAX (310) 244-7995
Culver City, CA 90232
www.sonypicturesstudios.com

Spartan Mobile Suites, Inc.
(310) 587-3377
3727 W. Magnolia Blvd., Ste. 156
FAX (661) 702-0550
Burbank, CA 91505
www.spartanmobilesuites.com
(Mobile Screening Rooms & Star Trailers)

Star Waggons Production Trailers
(818) 367-5946
(888) 367-5946
13334 Ralston Ave.
FAX (818) 362-1448
Sylmar, CA 91342
www.starwaggons.com
(Trailers)

StaR.V. Rentals
(323) 864-8332
28109 Avenue Stanford
FAX (661) 964-0550
Valencia, CA 91355

Steelgrave Production Services
(818) 652-7377
(661) 298-8912
www.pmfarms.biz
(Honeywagons, Makeup Trailers, Production Trailers,
Star Trailers & Wardrobe Trailers)

Suite Water Studio Enterprises, LLC
(661) 510-7319
(661) 510-9260
11531 Davenport Rd.
Agua Dulce, CA 91390

Susie's Production Vehicles
(661) 260-3500
(800) 299-6949
21226 Placerita Canyon Rd.
FAX (866) 472-1450
Newhall, CA 91321
www.productionvehicles.com
(Production Motorhomes)

T&D Studio Support Services
(818) 285-6667
8001 Langdon Ave., Ste. 1
FAX (818) 787-6480
Van Nuys, CA 91406
(Shower Trailers)

United Site Services
(626) 831-4517
(800) 864-5387
4511 Rowland Ave.
www.unitedsiteservices.com
El Monte, CA 91734
(Portable Restrooms, Portable Toilets, Shower Trailers &
V.I.P. Restrooms)

VJ's Studio Equipment Rentals
(818) 621-0701
12854 El Dorado Ave.
FAX (818) 367-3048
Sylmar, CA 91342
www.vjstudiorentals.com

Zio Rentals
(818) 504-2809
9046 Sunland Blvd.
FAX (818) 504-2816
Sun Valley, CA 91352
www.ziorentals.com
(Honeywagons, Makeup Trailers, Mobile Offices, Motorhomes,
Portable Restrooms, Production Trailers, Star Trailers, V.I.P.
Restrooms & Wardrobe Trailers)

Motorhomes & Portable Dressing Rooms

247 Delivers Inc.
(818) 843-1954
(800) 773-9947
8541 Lankershim Blvd.
FAX (818) 683-1034
Sun Valley, CA 91352 www.247delivers.com/cartage.html
(Rush Jobs, Storage of Editing, Sound, Musical Equipment and Props & Transportation of Editing, Sound Equipment, Musical Equipment and Props)

Advanced Records Management (323) 727-7277
1540 Church Rd.
FAX (323) 727-7070
Montebello, CA 90640 www.advancedrecords.com
(Information Management, Retrieval and Storage)

Agua Dulce Water Trucks (818) 216-3680
14854 Lassen St.
FAX (818) 892-7710
Mission Hills, CA 91345
(Transportation of Equipment and Picture Vehicles)

Baker Corp.
(805) 525-1710
(Portable Storage Tanks)
FAX (805) 525-7861
www.bakertanks.com

Bekins Moving & Storage
(714) 736-6160
(800) 223-3146
6300 Valley View St.
www.bekins.com
Buean Park, CA 90620

Cor-O-Van Moving & Storage (888) 544-3929
www.corovan.com

Dynamic L.A., Inc.
(818) 771-1111
11755 Sheldon St.
FAX (818) 771-1159
Sun Valley, CA 91352
www.dynamicla.com

File Keepers, LLC
(323) 728-3133
(800) 332-3453
6277 E. Slauson Ave.
FAX (323) 728-1349
Los Angeles , CA 90040
www.filekeepers.com
(Document Copying/Imaging, File Management (Digital Solutions), Information Management/Retrieval, Scan On Demand & Temperature-Controlled Storage and Delivery)

Fine Art Shipping
(310) 677-0011
(800) 421-7464
404 N. Oak St.
FAX (310) 677-8586
Inglewood, CA 90302
www.fineartship.com

Flat Rate Moving
(213) 404-1080
3255 E. Slauson Ave.
FAX (213) 404-1086
Los Angeles, CA 90058
www.flatrate.com/la

Gilbert Production Service, Inc. (323) 871-0006
4578 Worth St.
FAX (323) 264-2501
Los Angeles, CA 90063 www.gilbertproductionservice.com
(Storage/Transportation of Equipment and Props)

Holiday Transfer Co./
Holiday Moving & Storage
(310) 515-0900
1829 W. El Segundo Blvd., Ste. A FAX (310) 515-5566
Compton, CA 90222
www.holidaytransferco.com

Hollywood Parts
(818) 255-0617
12580 Saticoy St., Bldg. C
FAX (818) 255-0613
North Hollywood, CA 91605 www.hollywoodparts.com
(Asset Management, File Management, Storage of Props, Scenery and Vehicles, Temperature-Controlled Storage, Transportation of Props, Scenery and Vehicles & Wood Vaults)

Homer Mann Trucking
(818) 834-0481
12000 Paxton St.
FAX (818) 834-0380
Lakeview, CA 91342
www.homermann.com
(Transportation of Oversized Equipment and Props)

Lambert's Van & Storage, Inc.
(310) 652-1555
(800) 652-1555
P.O. Box 38250
FAX (818) 547-0956
Los Angeles, CA 90038 www.lambertsvanandstorage.com

Load Lock-N-Roll Moving-N-Storage
(323) 962-6683
(800) 358-6683
www.mrmove.us

Los Angeles Fine Arts &
Wine Storage Company
(310) 447-7700
2290 Centinela Ave.
www.lafineart.com
West Los Angeles, CA 90064
(Humidity and Temperature-Controlled Security Rooms)

The Mobile Storage Group (866) 891-3249
www.mobilestorage.com

Musicians Transfer
(818) 558-1052
(Transportation of Musical Equipment) FAX (818) 558-1053

NorthStar Moving Corporation
(800) 275-7767
(818) 727-0128
9120 Mason Ave.
FAX (818) 727-7527
Chatsworth, CA 91311
www.northstarmoving.com

Noteworthy Moving
(626) 441-6004
Systems & Delivery
(818) 241-4745
534 Lakeview Rd.
FAX (626) 441-5679
Pasadena, CA 91105 www.noteworthymoving.com
(Rush Jobs & Transportation of Props)

Public Storage
(800) 447-8673

Saugus Station Storage
(661) 253-0944
(818) 438-7777
FAX (661) 253-0944
www.saugusstationstorage.com
(Storage of Props, Scenery and Vehicles, & Wood Vaults)

Scenic Expressions
(818) 409-3354
4000 Chevy Chase Dr.
FAX (818) 244-4835
Los Angeles, CA 90039 www.scenicexpressions.com
(Storage/Transportation of Props and Scenery)

Schafer Bros. Piano Movers
(310) 835-7231
1981 E. 213th St.
FAX (310) 830-6615
Carson, CA 90810
www.schaferlogistics.com

Sidelifter.com
(877) 274-3354
(916) 761-2442
Satelite Yard, 1941 W. Ninth St.
FAX (916) 372-7287
Long Beach, CA 90810
www.sidelifter.com

Starving Students
(888) 931-6683
1850 W. Sawtelle, Ste. 300
FAX (800) 825-1145
West Los Angeles, CA 90025
www.ssmovers.com

Studio Express Prop Transportation
(818) 352-9402
(818) 445-8175
10333 McVine Ave.
FAX (818) 951-9883
Sunland, CA 91040
www.studioexpress.biz
(Storage/Transportation of Equipment and Props)

Studio Instrument Rentals/SIR
(323) 957-5460
6465 Sunset Blvd.
FAX (323) 957-5472
Hollywood, CA 90028
www.sirla.com
(Storage/Transportation of Musical Equipment)

Third Encore
(818) 753-0148
(800) 339-8850
10917 Vanowen St.
FAX (818) 753-0151
North Hollywood, CA 91605
www.3rdencore.com
(Transportation of Musical Equipment)

United Valet Parking, Inc.
(310) 642-7740
5839 Green Valley Circle, Ste. 202 FAX (310) 642-7753
Culver City, CA 90230
www.unitedparkinginc.com

Western Studio Services
(818) 244-2036
4561 Colorado Blvd.
FAX (818) 842-0250
Los Angeles, CA 90039 www.westernstudioservice.com
(Storage/Transportation of Props)

Xpeditious Unlimited
(310) 885-8001
610 Carob St.
www.xpeditiousunlimited.com
Compton, CA 90220

5th & Sunset Los Angeles   (310) 979-0212
12322 Exposition Blvd.   FAX (310) 979-0214
Los Angeles, CA 90064   **www.5thandsunsetla.com**

Beautiful Day Permits   (619) 749-6088
12714 Los Coches Ct.   FAX (619) 749-8870
Lakeside, CA 92040
(Notification Services, Posting Services & Signature Services)

Children In Film   (818) 901-0082
11600 Ventura Blvd.   FAX (818) 432-7405
Studio City, CA 91604   **www.childreninfilm.com**
(Children's Entertainment Work Permits)

Film Permits Unlimited, Inc./
Denise Wheeler   (818) 347-9929
22025 Ventura Blvd., Ste. 101   FAX (818) 347-9784
Woodland Hills, CA 91364   **www.filmpermits.com**

Film This Production Services, Inc.   (213) 763-9000
137 Arena St., Ste. A   FAX (213) 763-9004
El Segundo, CA 90245   **www.filmthis.net**
(Film Permits and Location Services for
All California Jurisdictions)

   (310) 979-5729
iManagement Group   (888) 549-2600
c/o Elkins Jones Insurance Agency   FAX (310) 207-5441
12100 Wilshire Blvd., Ste. 300   **www.elkinsjones.com**
Los Angeles, CA 90025
(Location Permit Insurance Requirements)

   (951) 377-7849
Inland Empire Film Commission   (951) 232-1271
1601 E. Third St.   FAX (909) 382-6066
San Bernardino, CA 92408   **www.filminlandempire.com**
(Riverside and San Bernardino Counties)
Contacts: Sheri Davis & Dan Taylor

Mammoth Location Services   (800) 845-7922
P.O. Box 603
Mammoth Lakes, CA 93546
www.monocounty.org/static/index.cfm?contentID=688

   (818) 640-8822
Don Mann   (818) 994-8822
(Notification, Posting & Signature Services)

   (323) 260-4777
🅐 **Pacific Production Services, Inc.**   (213) 360-7844
1481 E. Fourth St.   FAX (323) 415-6180
Los Angeles, CA 90033   **www.lafilmpermits.com**
(Notification, Permit, Posting and Signature Services)

Stanley Locations   (818) 706-8022
591 E. Los Angeles   FAX (888) 846-6011
Simi Valley, CA 93065

   (805) 969-5555
Tri-County Permit Services   (805) 565-1562
110 Olive Mill Ln.
Santa Barbara, CA 93108
(San Luis Obispo, Santa Barbara & Ventura Counties)

A & J Restroom Rentals   (562) 299-8582
2121 Cover St.   www.ajportabletoilets.com
Long Beach, CA 90807

    (760) 949-4111
A-1 Portables   (800) 554-7723
17491 Lilac St.   FAX (760) 949-4224
Hesperia, CA 92345

    (661) 251-7721
Andy Gump, Inc.   (800) 992-7755
26954 Ruether Ave.   FAX (661) 251-7729
Santa Clarita, CA 91351   www.andygump.com

    (562) 803-3701
Clean Strike Rental & Cleaning   (562) 879-2207
12214 Lakewood Blvd., Bldg. 9   FAX (562) 803-3702
Downey, CA 90242   www.cleanstrikerentals.com

Diamond Environmental
Services, LLC   (888) 744-7191
1801 Villa Burton, Ste. B   FAX (760) 290-3365
Fullerton, CA 92831   www.diamondprovides.com

    (310) 915-1744
Elliott Location Equipment   (505) 328-0909
www.elliottlocationequipment.com

Hollywood Honeywagon &   (818) 763-1966
Production Vehicles   (818) 535-9648
11160 Victory Blvd.   FAX (818) 760-0551
North Hollywood, CA 91606
    www.hollywoodhoneywagon.com

    (323) 462-6646
King Kong Production Vehicles   (949) 673-1999
4000 Cohasset St.   FAX (800) 513-9354
Burbank, CA 91505   www.kingkongtrailers.com

    (310) 518-5118
Kohler Rental   (310) 600-3063
766 Gifford Ave.   FAX (920) 459-1846
San Bernardino, CA 92408   www.kohlerrental.com

Line 204 Inc.   (323) 960-0113
837 N. Cahuenga Blvd.   FAX (323) 960-0163
Hollywood, CA 90038   www.line204.com

Quixote Studios   (323) 857-5050
1000 N. Cahuenga Blvd.   FAX (323) 857-0655
Los Angeles, CA 90038   www.quixote.com

Royal Restrooms   (877) 922-9980
4470 W. Sunset Blvd., Ste. 121   FAX (877) 922-9980
Los Angeles, CA 90027   www.royalrestroomsca.com

    (626) 831-4517
United Site Services   (800) 864-5387
    www.unitedsiteservices.com

Africa Film Services
(310) 273-9693
(310) 273-9698
507 N. Almont Dr.
FAX (310) 383-9699
Los Angeles, CA 90048
www.afsproductions.com
Contact: Dale Kushner

**Association of Film
Commissioners International**
(323) 461-2324
8530 Wilshire Blvd., Ste. 210
FAX (413) 375-2903
Beverly Hills, CA 90211
www.afci.org

Bajala Production Services
(310) 990-9503
(310) 862-4201
FAX 011 52 624 142 6031
www.bajalaprod.com

Box Films - Chile
(714) 849-6491
FAX (714) 849-6491
www.boxfilms.cl

CDI Virtual Brazil Films
(818) 841-9446
2219 W. Olive Ave., Ste. 263
FAX (818) 506-1654
Burbank, CA 91506
www.brazilfilms.com

Cine South de Mexico
(956) 522-7221
Pedro Sainz de Baranda
FAX (956) 584-9488
Ste. 139, Col. Avante
www.filmmexico.com
Mexico City, DF 04460 Mexico
(Belize, Guatemala & Mexico)
Contact: Mark Pittman

DMI Productions
00 44 1784 421 212
FAX 00 44 1784 421 213
www.dmiproductions.com

European Touch Productions
(310) 686-6611
011 420 602 364 345
(Czech Republic & Prague)
www.etpprague.com

Global Production Network
(323) 939-9639
(310) 570-0065
FAX (323) 417-1599
www.globalproductionnetwork.com

The Good Film Company Ltd.
(310) 228-6206
256 S. Robertson Blvd., Ste. 219
www.goodfilms.co.uk
Beverly Hills, CA 90211

Italian Film Commission
(323) 879-0950
1801 Avenue of the Stars, Ste. 700
FAX (310) 203-8335
Los Angeles, CA 90067
www.filminginitaly.com

Mexico Tourism Board
(800) 446-3942
1880 Century Park East, Ste. 511
www.visitmexico.com
Los Angeles, CA 90067
Contact: Jorge Gamboa-Patron

Milk & Honey Films
(323) 993-9600
4401 Wilshire Blvd., Ste. 250
FAX (323) 993-9333
Los Angeles, CA 90010
www.milkandhoneyfilms.com
Contact: Howard Woffinden

PPM Filmproductions
(323) 788-4132
36 1 315 1510
FAX 36 1 315 1520
www.ppm.hu

Prana Studios, Inc.
(323) 645-6500
1145 N. McCadden Pl.
www.pranastudios.com
Los Angeles, CA 90038

Stillking Films
(310) 499-3695
www.stillking.com
(Bulgaria, Chile, Czech Republic, London, South Africa & Spain)
Contact: Doug Lewis

Acme Design Group (818) 767-8888	**Epiphany Media** (323) 819-1001
www.acme-designgroup.com	5300 Melrose Ave. www.epiphanymedia.com
	Hollywood, CA 90038

Acme Design Group   (818) 767-8888
www.acme-designgroup.com

AFS Productions   (310) 273-9693
507 N. Almont Dr.   (310) 273-9698
Los Angeles, CA 90048   FAX (310) 383-9699
Contact: Dale Kushner   www.afsproductions.com

Albrecht Productions   (858) 581-3700
4687 Torrey Circle, Ste. B206
San Diego, CA 92130
Contact: Jacques Albrecht

All In One Productions   (323) 780-8880
1111 Corporate Center Dr., Ste. 303 FAX (323) 780-8887
Monterey Park, CA 91754   www.allinone-usa.com

Blueyed Pictures, Inc.   (310) 295-0848
1806 Thayer Ave.   FAX (310) 492-5270
Los Angeles, CA 90025   www.blueyedpictures.com

Bully Pictures   (310) 395-6500
1240 Sixth St.   (310) 871-0385
Santa Monica, CA 90401   FAX (310) 395-6502
www.bullypictures.com

CDI Virtual Brazil Films   (818) 841-9446
2219 W. Olive Ave., Ste. 263 FAX (818) 506-1654
Burbank, CA 91506   www.brazilfilms.com

Chiari Cook Company, Inc.   (213) 304-0053
5822 W. Washington Blvd.
Culver City, CA 90232
Contacts: Jared Cook & Chiari Endo

Coastal Media Group   (818) 880-9800
26660 Agoura Rd.   FAX (818) 579-9026
Calabasas, CA 91302   www.coastalmediagroup.com

Cobalt Blue, LLC   (818) 988-9093
15115 Lemay St.   www.cobaltbluefilms.com
Van Nuys, CA 91405
Contacts: Carl Beyer & Tracy Thomas

Concrete Images   (310) 452-9644
1301 Main St., Ste. 3   (310) 480-8738
Venice, CA 90291   FAX (310) 452-9655
www.concreteimages.com

Crash Productions   (310) 489-6848
713 N. Mansfield Ave.   FAX (323) 939-9622
Los Angeles, CA 90038   www.crashproductions.com

DCM Productions   (310) 503-1631
1611 19th St.
Manhattan Beach, CA 90266
Contact: Douglas Merrifield

Dorf Production Services   (310) 476-8380
2554 Lincoln Blvd., Ste. 421   (310) 740-0995
Venice, CA 90291   FAX (818) 789-6435
Contacts: Gary Dorf & Ilene Roberts

Dorf Production Services   (310) 476-8380
15445 Ventura Blvd., Ste. 3312   (310) 740-9885
Sherman Oaks, CA 91403   FAX (818) 789-6435
Contacts: Gary Dorf & Ilene Roberts

Encore Media LLC   (310) 823-9233
5301 Beethoven St., Ste. 290 FAX (310) 823-9211
Los Angeles, CA 90066   www.encoremediallc.com

Engine Room   (323) 860-5100
1040 N. Las Palmas, Bldg. 5U FAX (323) 860-5111
Los Angeles, CA 90038
www.engineroomhollywood.com
Contacts: Michael Caplan & Dan Schmit

Epiphany Media   (323) 819-1001
5300 Melrose Ave.   www.epiphanymedia.com
Hollywood, CA 90038

The Focus Studio   (310) 399-9400
Four Rose Ave.   FAX (310) 399-1180
Venice, CA 90291   www.thefocusstudio.com

FXF Productions, Inc.   (310) 577-5009
1024 Harding Ave., Ste. 201 FAX (310) 577-1960
Venice, CA 90291   www.fxfproductions.com
Contacts: Eric Alan Donaldson & Lonnie Peralta

Gateway Productions, Inc.   (818) 371-1135
Contact: Earl Mann

HD Republic   (310) 956-0346
FAX (310) 309-4702
www.hdrepublic.com

hi. Inc.   (323) 605-3951
1752 N. Serrano Ave., Ste. 104 FAX (323) 395-0431
Los Angeles, CA 90027   www.hi-medias.com

Jack Provost/Associates   (818) 988-8150
4570 Van Nuys Blvd., Ste. 122   (818) 422-0998
Sherman Oaks, CA 91403   FAX (818) 988-8152
Contact: Jack Provost   www.jackprovost.com

John Purdy, Inc.   (323) 874-9802
P.O. Box 616   FAX (760) 322-5400
Palm Springs, CA 92263
Contact: Jack Black

KGB Films   (323) 956-5000
5555 Melrose Ave.   FAX (323) 224-1876
Lucy Bungalow 101   www.kgbfilms.com
Los Angeles, CA 90038

Lena Production Services   (310) 990-8223
3121 Fifth St.   (310) 399-2007
Santa Monica, CA 90405   FAX (310) 399-2425
Contact: Bonnie Lena

LeTo Entertainment, LLC   (310) 358-3282
8840 Wilshire Blvd., Third Fl. FAX (310) 388-1403
Beverly Hills, CA 90211   www.letoentertainment.com

Lookout Entertainment   (310) 798-3000
54 Hermosa Ave.   FAX (310) 798-3001
Hermosa Beach, CA 90254
Contact: Yvonne Bernard www.lookoutentertainment.com

Lyon Studios   (949) 675-4790
222 21st St.   FAX (949) 675-2139
Newport Beach, CA 92663   www.lyonstudios.com
Contacts: Naomi Killian & Curt Lyon

The M Company, Inc.   (310) 577-3377
31 26th Ave.   FAX (310) 577-8877
Venice, CA 90291   www.mcompanyinc.com
Contact: Yen King

New Circuit Films, LLC   (323) 871-8122
6546 Hollywood Blvd., Ste. 213   (818) 378-0033
Los Angeles, CA 90028   FAX (818) 871-8122
www.newcircuit.com

P.I.G./Protean Image Group   (310) 399-9898
212 Main St.   FAX (310) 399-9876
Venice, CA 90291   www.pigusa.com

Patrick Stewart Productions, LLC (818) 882-3700
Contact: Jennifer Nejman   FAX (818) 882-3793
www.psptv.com

Revolver Films (310) 827-2441
4040 Del Rey Ave., Ste. 5 FAX (310) 827-2661
Marina del Rey, CA 90292 www.revolverfilmsla.com

SCG Kino (310) 717-9264
Contact: Michael Schenk www.scgkino.com

Sim Video Los Angeles (323) 978-9000
738 Cahuenga Blvd. FAX (323) 978-9018
Hollywood, CA 90038 www.simvideola.com

Sincbox (310) 566-6701
12100 Wilshire Blvd., Ste. 550 FAX (310) 566-6719
Los Angeles, CA 90025 www.sincbox.com

(323) 871-0201
Slash Productions (213) 810-5059
2086 Mound St. FAX (323) 871-0315
Los Angeles, CA 90068
Contacts: Antonia Holt & Scott Luhrsen

(800) 507-0159
Spot On Media (818) 536-7334
www.spotonmedia.tv
Contacts: Lisa Brandi, Shaun Greenspan, Igori Kamoevi &
Andrew Webb

(626) 403-8403
Stargate Stage (818) 778-0851
1001 El Centro St. FAX (626) 403-8444
Pasadena, CA 91030 www.stargatestudios.net

Team Halprin, Inc. (310) 842-7000
FAX (310) 842-7014
www.teamhalprin.com

U.S. Production Services (310) 857-7780
578 Washington Blvd., Ste. 594 FAX (310) 496-0192
Marina del Rey, CA 90292
www.usproductionservices.com

Video Production Specialists (VPS) (866) 447-3877
FAX (310) 577-0850
www.videoproductionspecialists.com

(310) 574-9385
Video Tech Services (310) 505-4015
10866 Washington Blvd., Ste. 513 FAX (310) 577-0850
Culver City, CA 90232 www.videotechservices.com
Contact: Richard Larsen

(310) 777-8828
Warped Pictures (310) 999-1219
2447 Benedict Canyon FAX (310) 777-8805
Beverly Hills, CA 90210 www.warpedpictures.com
Contact: Volker Fleck

(818) 762-3810
Western Branch Productions, Inc. (818) 642-3810
4231 Beck Ave. FAX (818) 769-2847
Studio City, CA 91604 www.western-branch.com
Contact: Pete Vanlaw

Wheelhouse Productions (213) 595-4144
Contact: C.J. Edwards

A.S.A. Security Services Division   (323) 662-9787
P.O. Box 727   FAX (323) 662-1569
Montrose, CA 91021   **www.asafilmcrew.com**
(Reps for Bodyguards, Off-Duty Police Officers, Retired
Officers, Security Guards & Set Security)

Allways Chauffeurs & Bodyguards   (310) 385-9088
                                      FAX (310) 385-9038
                             www.allwaysdrivers.com

                                          (323) 722-8585
American Security Force   (877) 722-8585
                                      FAX (323) 722-8282
                          www.americansecurityforce.com

Angel Guarding Security   (818) 482-6634
                                      FAX (323) 739-0340
(Location Security, Patrol Security, Radio Security, Special
Events Security, Stage Security, Studio Security, Unarmed
Guards & Undercover Security)

Archangel Security Services, Inc.   (800) 691-2798
46330 Sawtooth Ln.   FAX (347) 503-0975
Temecula, CA 92592   **www.security13.com**
(Armed Guards, Bodyguards, Location Bodyguards, Location
Security, Off-Duty Officers, Studio Security, Trained Law
Enforcement Officers & Unarmed Guards)

Associated Protection   (818) 527-1780
Specialists, Inc.   (855) 441-7725
            www.associatedprotectionspecialists.com
(Executive/Celebrity Protection & Red Carpet/Private Events)

                                          (323) 343-8810
Augie's Security   (323) 253-3079
533 Clifton St.   FAX (323) 345-5780
Los Angeles, CA 90031   **www.augiessecurity.com**
(Location Security, Studio Security & Unarmed Guards)

                                          (877) 776-8282
Beach Cities Protective Services   (310) 514-0576
                                      FAX (310) 831-0261
           www.beachcitiesprotectiveservices.com
(Armed Guards, Bodyguards, Location Bodyguards, Location
Security, Off-Duty Officers, Retired Officers, Studio Security,
Trained Law Enforcement Officers & Unarmed Guards)

Bonanza Solutions, Inc.   (818) 890-5951
P.O. Box 55729   FAX (661) 287-4485
Santa Clarita, CA 91385
(Location Bodyguards & Security)

                                          (818) 842-7286
Bravo Motion Picture Security   (818) 967-7795
146 N. San Fernando Blvd., Ste. 212
Burbank, CA 91502
(Armed Guards, Bodyguards, Location Bodyguards, Location
Security, Off-Duty Officers, Retired Officers, Studio Security,
Trained Law Enforcement Officers & Unarmed Guards)

Celebrity Security   (818) 469-9047
                                      FAX (661) 729-9480
                          www.joesstudioservices.com
(Armed Guards, Bodyguards, Location Bodyguards and
Security, Off-Duty Officers, Retired Officers, Studio Security &
Unarmed Guards)

CPS Worldwide   (888) 277-2776
12400 Wilshire Blvd., Ste. 400   FAX (866) 636-6977
Los Angeles, CA 90025
                www.californiaprotectiveservices.com

CSI Protective Services   (800) 965-4274
                                      FAX (800) 342-1274
                                      www.usacsi.org
(Armed Guards, Bodyguards, Celebrity Protection, Location
Bodyguards, Location Security, Off-Duty Officers, Retired
Officers, Security Only, Studio Security, Trained Law
Enforcement Officers & Unarmed Guards)

EPS Security/
Robbie Thomas Security   (562) 673-8164
P.O. Box 1273
Norwalk, CA 90650
(Location Security, Security Only & Unarmed Guards)

F.E.D. Security Armed Service   (323) 578-7330
5029 Alhambra Ave.   FAX (323) 222-5290
Los Angeles, CA 90032
(Armed Guards, Location Bodyguards, Location Security, Studio
Security & Unarmed Guards)

Galahad Protection   (818) 780-1818
23638 Lyons Ave., Ste. 444   FAX (661) 259-4848
Valencia, CA 91321   **www.galahadinc.com**
(Armed Guards, Bodyguards, Location Security, Studio
Security & Unarmed Guards)

                                          (323) 772-7377
General Security Service, Inc.   (800) 350-1944
633 N. Marine Ave.   FAX (310) 973-7627
Wilmington, CA 90744
(Armed Guards, Bodyguards, Location Bodyguards, Location
Security, Off-Duty Officers, Retired Officers, Studio Security,
Trained Law Enforcement Officers & Unarmed Guards)

                                          (323) 461-3377
Hollywood Production Security, Inc. (818) 961-7474
6520 Platt Ave., Ste. 681   FAX (818) 340-1940
West Hills, CA 91307
            www.hollywoodproductionsecurity.com

                                          (800) 496-0182
Johnson & Associates, Inc.   (866) 211-7516
8581 Santa Monica Blvd., Ste. 305   FAX (858) 793-0471
West Hollywood, CA 90069   **www.jnasecurity.com**
(Armed Guards, Bodyguards, Location Bodyguards, Location
Security, Off-Duty Officers, Security Only & Unarmed Guards)

Location Pros   (800) 278-5102
                                      FAX (800) 278-5102
                                 www.locationpros.net
(Location Bodyguards, Studio Security & Trained Law
Enforcement Officers)

Movie Guard   (818) 262-5353
3727 W. Magnolia Blvd., Ste. 230
Burbank, CA 91510
(Bodyguards, Location Security & Off-Duty/Retired Officers)

                                          (323) 634-1911
North American Security, Inc.   (310) 427-9196
1801 Beverly Blvd.   FAX (323) 634-9111
Los Angeles, CA 90026   **www.nasecurityinc.com**

Picore Worldwide   (818) 888-9659
                                      FAX (818) 475-1882
                                    www.picore.com
(Armed Guards, Bodyguards, Location Bodyguards, Location
Security, Off-Duty Officers, Retired Officers, Studio Security,
Trained Law Enforcement Officers & Unarmed Guards)

Praetorian Security Specialists   (310) 493-4620
50 Majestic Court, Ste. 1101   **www.praesecinc.com**
Moorpark, CA 93021

Reel Security Corp.   (818) 508-4750
4370 Tujunga Ave., Ste. 140   **www.reelsecurity.com**
Studio City, CA 91604
(Armed Guards, Bodyguards, Location Bodyguards, Location
Security, Off-Duty Officers, Retired Officers, Studio Security,
Trained Law Enforcement Officers & Unarmed Guards)

                                          (800) 261-8211
Security Detection Metal Detectors   (918) 629-3399
860 Carlton Privado   FAX (866) 702-9303
Ontario, CA 91762   **www.securitydetection.com**
(Location & Studio Security)

SET Security, Inc.   **(818) 360-7686**
P.O. Box 33356   FAX **(818) 876-0544**
Granada Hills, CA 91394
(Armed/Unarmed Security & Bodyguards)

SPI Entertainment Services   **(951) 205-8848**
(Armed Guards, Bodyguards, Location Bodyguards, Location
Security & Trained Law Enforcement Officers)

Starside Security &   **(310) 417-9999**
Investigation, Inc.   **(800) 782-7906**
6080 Center Dr., Ste. 677   FAX **(310) 417-9811**
Los Angeles, CA 90045   **www.starside.com**
(Armed Guards, Bodyguards, Location Bodyguards, Location
Security, Off-Duty Officers, Retired Officers, Studio Security,
Trained Law Enforcement Officers & Unarmed Guards)

StoneWall Protective Services LLC **(310) 483-3849**
23200 Sesame St., Ste. 40E   FAX **(310) 834-1591**
Torrance, CA 90502   **www.stonewallps.com**
(Armed Guards, Bodyguards, Location Bodyguards, Location
Security, Off-Duty Officers, Retired Officers, Studio Security,
Trained Law Enforcement Officers & Unarmed Guards)

Sully's Crew, Inc./Crew Protection   **(661) 250-2111**
        FAX **(661) 250-3111**
        www.crewprotection.com
(Armed Guards, Bodyguards, Location Bodyguards, Studio
Security & Unarmed Guards)

        (323) 583-8660
Westside Detectives, Inc.   **(323) 833-2383**
6230 Wilshire Blvd., Ste. 59
Los Angeles, CA 90048   **www.westsidedetectives.com**
(Bodyguards, Investigations & Security)

Adventures at Sea Charters
(949) 650-2412
(800) 229-2412
3101 West Coast Hwy
FAX (949) 548-8856
Newport Beach, CA 92663
www.boatcharter.com
(Gondolas, Sailboats & Yachts)

Air One Charter
(310) 743-0103
(877) 247-1359
6101 W. Centinela Ave., Ste. 375
FAX (310) 743-0140
Culver City, CA 90230
www.aironecharter.com
(Jets)

Aircraft Charter Holdings, LLC
(866) 359-2487
(415) 464-0400
1657 S. Spaulding Ave.
FAX (310) 492-5177
Los Angeles, CA 90019
www.aircharter.com
(Jets)

AirFlite Aviation Services
(562) 490-6200
(800) 241-3548
3250 Airflite Way
FAX (562) 490-6270
Long Beach, CA 90807
www.airflight.com
(Jets)

American Yacht Charters, Inc.
(949) 673-4453
2901 West Coast Hwy, Ste.190
FAX (949) 673-0807
Newport Beach, CA 92663
www.aycharters.com
(Yachts)

Avjet Corporation
(800) 342-8538
(818) 841-6190
4301 Empire Ave.
FAX (818) 841-6209
Burbank, CA 91505
www.avjet.com
(Jets)

Blue Water Sailing
(310) 823-5545
(Sailboats & Yachts)
FAX (310) 823-5728
www.bluewatersailing.com

California Dreamin'
(800) 373-3359
33133 Vista del Monte Rd.
www.californiadreamin.com
Temecula, CA 92591
(Hot Air Balloons)

Chrysler Aviation, Inc.
(818) 989-7900
(800) 995-0825
7120 Hayvenhurst Ave., Ste. 309
Van Nuys, CA 91406
www.chrysleraviation.com
(Jets)

Clay Lacy Aviation, Inc.
(818) 989-2900
(800) 423-2904
7435 Valjean Ave.
FAX (818) 909-9537
Van Nuys, CA 91406
www.claylacy.com
(Jets)

D & D Ballooning
(800) 510-9000
(Hot Air Balloons)
FAX (951) 303-8645
www.hotairadventures.com

Elite Aviation, Inc.
(818) 988-5387
7501 Hayvenhurst Pl.
FAX (818) 988-2111
Van Nuys, CA 91406
www.eliteaviation.com
(Jets)

Elite Yacht Charters
(310) 552-7968
468 N. Camden Dr., Ste. 200
FAX (310) 553-2551
Beverly Hills, CA 90210
www.eliteyacht.com
(Sailboats & Yachts)

FantaSea Yachts & Yacht Club
(310) 827-2220
4215 Admiralty Way
FAX (310) 827-7453
Marina del Rey, CA 90292
www.fantaseayachts.com
(Yachts)

Golf Cars - LA, Inc.
(661) 251-2201
16439 Sierra Hwy
www.golfcars-la.com
Canyon Country, CA 91351

Gondola Company Of Newport Beach
(949) 675-1212
3400 Via Oporto, Ste. 103
FAX (949) 675-8812
Newport Beach, CA 92663
www.gondolas.com
(Gondolas)

Heli-USA
(818) 994-1445
(877) 863-5952
16303 Waterman Dr.
FAX (818) 994-1447
Van Nuys, CA 91406
www.toflyla.com
(Helicopters)

Island Express Helicopter
(310) 510-2525
(800) 228-2566
1175 Queens Hwy South
FAX (310) 510-9671
Long Beach, CA 90802
www.islandexpress.com
(Helicopters)

Jet Productions
(818) 781-4742
(877) 895-1790
7240 Hayvenhurst Ave., Ste. 243C
FAX (818) 781-4743
Van Nuys, CA 91406
www.jetproductions.net
(Jets)

Maguire Aviation
(818) 989-2300
(800) 451-7270
7155 Valjean Ave.
FAX (818) 902-9386
Van Nuys, CA 91406
(Jets)

Meridian Teterboro
(800) 882-2333
(Jets)
www.meridianteb.com

Odyssey Yacht Charter, Inc.
(310) 308-4643
(Yachts)
FAX (310) 823-9917
www.odysseyyacht.com

Paradise Bound Yacht Charters
(800) 655-0850
4375 Admiralty Way
Marina del Rey, CA 90292
www.the-calculating-lady.com/captalex
(Sailboats & Yachts)

Pierpoint Landing
(562) 983-9300
(Jets)
FAX (562) 495-6252
www.pierpoint.net

Skytrails Aviation
(877) 759-8724
16233 Vanowen St.
FAX (818) 901-0272
Van Nuys, CA 91406
www.skytrails.com
(Jets)

Studio Jet
(818) 769-3535
P.O. Box 4215
FAX (818) 301-2536
Valley Village, CA 91617
www.studiojet.com
(Jets)

Summit Helicopters
(818) 890-0903
12653 Osborne St., PMB. 35
FAX (818) 890-2143
Pacoima, CA 91331
www.summithelicopter.com
(Helicopters)

Sun Quest
(818) 778-6520
(800) 529-7595
7415 Hayvenhurst Pl.
FAX (818) 778-6526
Van Nuys, CA 91406
www.sunquestexec.com
(Jets)

Trans-Exec Air Service
(310) 399-9435
www.transexec.com

Auto Club Speedway   (909) 429-5000
Contact: Phil Tucker   FAX (909) 429-5500
www.autoclubspeedway.com

Cinespace   (323) 817-3456
6356 Hollywood Blvd., Second Fl.   FAX (323) 860-9794
Hollywood, CA 90028   www.cinespace.info

Disney Ice   (714) 535-7465
300 W. Lincoln Ave.   FAX (714) 518-3220
Anaheim, CA 92805   www.anaheimice.com
Contact: Jill Legault

Ebony Repertory Theatre @ The Nate Holden
Performing Arts Center   (323) 964-9768
4718 W. Washington Blvd.   www.ebonyrep.org
Los Angeles, CA 90016

El Capitan Theatre &   (323) 467-7674
Entertainment Centre   (818) 845-3110
6838 Hollywood Blvd.   FAX (323) 467-0922
Los Angeles, CA 90028   www.elcapitantickets.com

Epicenter Stadium -
City of Rancho Cucamonga   (909) 477-2760
10500 Civic Center Dr.   FAX (909) 477-2761
Rancho Cucamonga, CA 91730   www.rcepicenter.com

     (909) 865-4042
Fairplex   (909) 865-4041
1101 W. Mckinley Ave.   FAX (909) 623-9599
Pomona, CA 91768   www.fairplex.com

The Forum   (310) 330-7300
3900 W. Manchester Blvd.   www.thelaforum.com
Inglewood, CA 90305
Contact: Devon Mackey

Greek Theatre   (323) 665-5857
2700 N. Vermont Ave.   FAX (323) 666-8202
Los Angeles, CA 90027   www.greektheatrela.com

Hollywood Park   (310) 419-1500
Box 369   www.hollywoodpark.com
Inglewood, CA 90306
Contact: Deann Fruhling

Honda Center   (714) 704-2422
2695 E. Katella Ave.   FAX (714) 704-2610
Anaheim, CA 92806   www.hondacenter.com
Contact: Jo-Ann Armstrong

House of Blues Concerts   (323) 769-4600
Contact: Ingrid Gunn   FAX (323) 769-4792
www.hob.com

Ice Chalet   (310) 541-6630
550 Deep Valley Dr.   FAX (310) 541-8674
Avenue of the Peninsula Mall
Rolling Hills Estates, CA 90274
www.palosverdesicechalet.com

     (323) 667-0955
Knightsbridge Theatre   (323) 394-1584
1944-1952 Riverside Dr. www.knightsbridgetheatre.com
Los Angeles, CA 90039

La Mirada Theatre for the   (714) 994-6310
Performing Arts   (562) 944-9801
14900 La Mirada Blvd.   FAX (714) 994-5796
La Mirada, CA 90638   www.lamiradatheatre.com
Contact: Laura Moore

     (213) 972-7211
LA Music Center   (213) 972-3335
135 N. Grand Ave.   www.musiccenter.org
Los Angeles, CA 90012
Contact: John Vassiliou

     (619) 231-1941
The Old Globe   (619) 234-5623
1363 Old Globe Way   FAX (619) 231-9518
San Diego, CA 92101   www.theoldglobe.org
Contact: Debbie Ballard

     (877) 677-4386
Orpheum Theatre   (213) 626-5321
842 S. Broadway   www.laorpheum.com
Los Angeles, CA 90014
Contact: Steve Needleman

REDCAT   (213) 237-2800
631 W. Second St.   FAX (213) 237-2811
Los Angeles, CA 90012   www.redcat.org

Renberg Theatre   (323) 860-7336
The Village at Ed Gould Plaza   FAX (323) 308-4103
1125 N. McCadden Pl.   www.lagaycenter.org
Los Angeles, CA 90038

     (626) 577-3130
Rose Bowl   (626) 577-3206
1001 Rose Bowl Dr.   FAX (626) 405-0992
Pasadena, CA 91103   www.rosebowlstadium.com
Contacts: Julie Granillo & Erika Samarzich

Santa Anita Park   (626) 574-7223
285 W. Huntington Dr.   FAX (626) 821-1530
Arcadia, CA 91007   www.santaanita.com
Contact: Pete Siberell

The Shrine Auditorium   (213) 748-5116
649 W. Jefferson Blvd.   FAX (213) 742-9922
Los Angeles, CA 90007   www.shrineauditorium.com

Staples Center   (213) 742-7100
1111 S. Figueroa St.   www.staplescenter.com
Los Angeles, CA 90015

Universal Studios
Hollywood Theme Park   (818) 622-5453
(Theme Park Show Stages)   FAX (818) 622-5897
www.universalstudioshollywood.com/production/

Writers Guild Theater   (323) 782-4525
135 S. Doheny Dr.   www.wga.org
Beverly Hills, CA 90211

Castex Rentals   (323) 462-1468
1044 Cole Ave.   FAX (323) 462-3719
Hollywood, CA 90038   www.castexrentals.com
(Equipment)

Heavy Artillery Production Rentals   (310) 295-1202
3200 S. La Cienega Blvd.   FAX (310) 295-1202
Los Angeles, CA 90016   www.heavyartilleryrentals.com
(Equipment)

   (714) 892-5858
ITC Barricades, Inc.   (661) 816-6270
P.O. Box 858   FAX (714) 892-5887
Westminster, CA 92684
(Equipment & Services) mysite.verizon.net/itcbarricades/

JCL Barricade Company   (213) 622-9775
2334 E. Eighth St.   FAX (213) 622-9790
Los Angeles, CA 90021   www.jclbarricade.com
(Equipment & Services)

   (323) 260-4777
Pacific Production Services, Inc.   (213) 360-7844
1481 E. Fourth St.   FAX (323) 415-6180
Los Angeles, CA 90033   www.lafilmpermits.com
(Equipment & Services)

Ⓐ Pacific Traffic Control, Inc.   (323) 981-0600
1481 E. Fourth St.   FAX (323) 981-0779
Los Angeles, CA 90033   www.pacifictc.com

RC Production Rentals   (626) 483-7679
13105 Saticoy St.   FAX (310) 943-0480
North Hollywood, CA 91605
(Equipment)   www.rcproductionrentals.com

   (714) 648-1919
Statewide Traffic Safety & Signs   (888) 953-8272
13261 Garden Grove Blvd.   FAX (888) 507-8549
Garden Grove, CA 92840   www.statewidesafety.com
(Equipment & Services)

Traffic Management, Inc.   (800) 763-3999
2435 Lemon Ave.   FAX (562) 424-0266
Signal Hill, CA 90755   www.trafficmanagement.com
(Equipment & Services)

Xpendable Rentals   (323) 656-0905
5925 Santa Monica Blvd.   FAX (323) 375-1711
Hollywood, CA 90038   www.xpendablerentals.com
(Equipment)

Altour
(310) 571-6000
(800) 878-5847
12100 W. Olympic Blvd., Ste. 300   FAX (310) 571-3157
Los Angeles, CA 90064   www.altour.com

Intercontinental Visa Service
(866) 552-8472
350 S. Figueroa St., Ste. 185   www.ivisaservice.com
Los Angeles, CA 90071
(Visa Service)

Judy Garland & Associates
(310) 376-1337
(310) 849-1604
1181 Cypress Ave., Ste. A
Hermosa Beach, CA 90254
(Visa Service)

Montrose Travel
(818) 553-3200
(800) 666-8767
2349 Honoluloa Ave.   FAX (818) 248-7358
Montrose, CA 91020   www.montrosetravel.com
Mon–Fri 9am–5pm

Plaza Travel
(818) 990-4053
(800) 347-4447
16530 Ventura Blvd., Ste. 106   FAX (818) 789-5405
Encino, CA 91436   www.plazatravel.com

PNR Travel
(310) 574-6800
1726 Westwood Blvd.   FAX (310) 574-6801
Los Angeles, CA 90024   www.pnrtravel.com
Mon–Fri 8:30am–5:30pm

Pothos, Inc.
(619) 546-0621
2260 El Cajon Blvd., Ste. 474   FAX (413) 723-7838
San Diego, CA 92104   www.pothos.us

Production Travel & Tours
(818) 760-0327
Mon–Fri 9am–6pm   www.adventureplanners.org

**Rand-Fields Division of
Pro-Travel Intl.**
(310) 271-9566
9171 Wilshire Blvd., Ste. 428   FAX (310) 271-9597
Beverly Hills, CA 90210   www.protravelinc.com
Mon–Fri 9am–5:30pm

Sabrina Brazil Travel
(888) 456-2224
13030 Valleyheart Dr., Ste. 102   FAX (818) 789-4523
Studio City, CA 91604   www.sabrinabraziltravel.com

The Travel Exchange
(323) 848-8022
Mon–Fri 10am–5pm   FAX (323) 848-8023

Travel Express LA
(310) 728-1831
9200 Sunset Blvd., Ste. 320   FAX (310) 728-1881
West Hollywood, CA 90069   www.travelexpressla.com

Travel of America
(626) 814-6350
(800) 228-8843
668 Arrow Grand Circle   FAX (626) 331-7051
Covina, CA 91722   www.travelofamerica.com
Mon–Fri 7am–6pm, Sat 10am–3pm

TravelStore
(310) 689-5400
11601 Wilshire Blvd., Ste. 325   FAX (310) 689-5401
Los Angeles, CA 90025   www.travelstoreusa.com
Mon–Fri 8am–5pm

Visas International
(818) 859-7101
(800) 638-1517
3005 W. Victory Blvd.   FAX (818) 859-7103
Burbank, CA 91505   www.visasintl.com
(Visa Service)
Mon–Fri 9am–5pm

**Westside International
Travel at Altour**
(310) 571-6090
FAX (310) 571-3157
www.westsideintltravel.com

Willett Travel
(818) 762-0676
(800) 994-5538
FAX (818) 763-7806
www.willetttravel.com
(Corporate, Production & Vacation Travel)
Mon–Fri 9am–5pm

California Weather &
Earth Sciences, LLC   **(760) 684-5761**
(Worldwide Forecasts)   FAX **(760) 868-0906**
                                         www.califweather.com

                                         (800) 825-4445
CompuWeather   **(323) 666-4411**
                                         FAX **(800) 825-4441**
                                         www.filmweather.com
(24-Hour Live Meteorologists, Hurricane Surveillance, Live
Forecasts, Nationwide Weather & Worldwide Weather)

Los Angeles Weather & Vicinity   **(805) 988-6610**
(Recorded Forecasts)

Metro Weather Service   **(800) 488-7866**
                                         FAX **(516) 568-8853**
                                         www.metroweather.com
(24-Hour Live Meteorologists for Nationwide and
Worldwide Weather)

Weather Watch Service   **(863) 686-6234**
                                         FAX **(863) 686-6234**
                                         www.weatherwatchservice.com
(24-Hour Live Meteorologists, Nationwide Weather &
Worldwide Weather)

CHICAGO FIRE

BY MARJ GALAS

Casting Directory Jonathan Strauss on "Chicago Fire"

The actors in "Chicago Fire" are subjected to regular endurance tests: pulling victims from overturned cars, hoisting hoses to battle raging fires, and carrying the unconscious through blinding smoke. For Jonathan Strauss, the actor's physical abilities are a small part of what he's looking for when casting each role.

"They have their fair share of fire and explosions," chuckled Strauss. "Relationships, back-stories, subtext: these are the things an audience gravitates to. Chemistry is very important."

Strauss believes having the opportunity to do chemistry tests between actors is extremely beneficial for dramatic material such as "Chicago Fire." Due to the physical challenges of their roles, the full cast was involved in a boot camp where Strauss was able to confirm that a natural chemistry was in place.

In addition to casting the leads, Strauss is very involved in casting the special guests and day players. While actors with a familiarity with Chicago are beneficial, having been a resident is not always a requirement. Chicago, like New York and many major cities, is a melting pot. Actors with unique attributes, such as a Midwestern look or British accent, can add authenticity to a scene.

"Advances in technology have made it much easier to find talent not just around the country but internationally. I have a reach I didn't have five years ago. You can really make projects come to life through today's technology."

Several of the actors cast in "Chicago Fire" were people Strauss has come to know well over the years. When he read the pilot he immediately thought of two actors he wanted to cast, David Eigenberg and Monica Raymund. Above all else, he knew he wanted to get Charlie Barnett involved. Strauss met Barnett after he graduated from Julliard and gave him his first TV credit on "Law and Order."

"I learned that Charlie Barnett was in LA for pilot season," said Strauss. "I really wanted to cast him for 'Chicago Fire.' I made it my mission to get him."

ABRIDGED FROM AN LA 411 NEWSLETTER ARTICLE PUBLISHED OCTOBER 2012

ⓐ ADVERTISER SYMBOL

Refer to the General Index for cross-referencing items in this section.

Night at the Museum

The Closer

Evan Almighty

Meet the Parents

Harry Potter

Beverly Hills Chihuahua

Mr. Popper's Penguins

Marley & Me

Marmaduke

Charlotte's Web

Movies

Partial Listing_
We Bought A Zoo
Evan Almighty
Beverly Hills Chihuahua I, II & III
Harry Potter I-VIII
Marley & Me
Dr. Dolittle I & II
Marmaduke
101 & 102 Dalmatians
Zookeeper
Hotel for Dogs
Eight Below
The Shaggy Dog
The Crow I, II & III
Ace Ventura I & II

Partial Listing_
The Closer
Two and A Half Men
CSI / CSI Miami / CSI NY
Parks & Recreation
Mike & Molly
It's Always Sunny In Philadelphia
Frasier

Birds & Animals®
Unlimited

US/CAN West Coast 661.269.0148 • US/CAN East Coast 863.439.0551 • London 01923680639
www.birdsandanimals.com

W

Accurate English   (310) 892-3556
13101 Washington Blvd., Ste. 231
Los Angeles, CA 90066   **www.accurateenglish.com**
(Accent Reduction & Dialect Coaching)

Robert Easton   (818) 985-2222

Joel Goldes/The Dialect Coach   (818) 879-1896
                          www.thedialectcoach.com
(Dialects, Pre-Production, On-Set and ADR Coaching)

Peter Kelley   (212) 431-4000
601 W. 26th St., Ste. 1762   **www.actingonfilm.com**
New York, NY 10001
(Acting Coaching)

Larry Moss Speech &
Dialect Services   (310) 395-4284

                                    (310) 584-6606
Jill Massie   (323) 533-8690
(Dialect Coaching)   FAX (951) 531-8959
                               www.jillmassie.com

Kevin McDermott   (310) 800-5691
(Acting Coaching)   **www.kevinrobertmcdermott.com**

                                    (323) 848-7993
OneWorld Language Solutions   (323) 620-7063
3940 Laurel Canyon Blvd., Ste. 501   FAX (323) 848-7995
Studio City, CA 91604   **www.oneworldlanguage.com**
(Dialect Coaching)

Strommen Language Experts   (323) 638-9787
4450 Clarissa Ave.   **www.strommentutoring.com**
Los Angeles, CA 90027
(Dialect Coaching)

Katherine Vallin/French a la Carte   (323) 493-5533
(French Dialect Coaching)   **www.french-a-la-carte.com**

Wayne Dvorak Acting Studio   (323) 462-5328
                               www.waynedvorak.com

1 All Animal Productions   (800) 926-9969
(408) 621-0620
www.bowwowproductions.com
(Birds, Cats, Dogs, Exotics & Farm Animals)

1 Benay's Bird &
Animal Source, Inc.   (818) 881-0053
FAX (818) 888-5548
www.benaysanimals.net
(Birds, Cats, Coati, Dogs, Exotics, Farm Animals, Horses,
Monkeys, Raccoons, Reptiles, Rodents, Sea Lions, Skunks,
Squirrels & Wildlife)

1st Phil's Animal Rentals   (805) 521-1100
P.O. Box 309   FAX (805) 521-0956
Piru, CA 93040   www.philsanimalrentals.com
(Baby Animals, Buffalo, Bulls, Chickens, Cows, Dogs, Donkeys,
Ducks, Goats, Horses, Livestock, Pigs, Rabbits & Sheep)

A2Z Animals   (661) 269-1999
FAX (661) 269-0989
www.a2zanimals.com

AAA Performing Animal Troupe   (661) 722-1497
4154 W. Avenue N   FAX (661) 722-1498
Palmdale, CA 93551 www.performinganimaltroupe.com
(Domestics, Exotics, Horses & Livestock)

Acting Dogs by Steven Ritt   (661) 269-3647
P.O. Box 121   www.actingdogs.com
Llano, CA 93544

Action Animal Rental   (604) 826-6115
(877) 363-3388
www.actionanimals.com

Action Bulls   (805) 878-6948
P.O. Box 5175   www.leffewbullridingworld.com
Santa Maria, CA 93456
(Rodeo Animals)

Action Reptiles   (951) 897-8317
(Alligators, Amphibians, Insects, Lizards, Snakes,
Tarantulas & Turtles)

All Stars Studio Animals   (818) 421-4327
(Dogs)   www.allstarsanimals.com

Alvin's Animal Rental   (909) 823-9437
P.O. Box CB   FAX (909) 822-2748
Bloomington, CA 92316   www.alvinanimalrentals.com
(Domestic and Wild Animals)

Amazing Animal Productions, Inc.   (310) 990-3538
16203 Cajon Blvd.
Devore Heights, CA 92407
www.amazinganimalproductions.com
(Alligators, Amphibians, Animal Colorist, Barnyard Animals,
Bears, Beavers, Bees, Birds, Birds of Prey, Black Bears, Black
Leopards, Buffalo, Bunnies, Butterflies, Camels, Cats, Cattle,
Coati, Cougars, Deer, Dogs, Domestics, Doves, Draft Animals,
Driving Horses, Eagles, Elephants, Emus, Exotics, Ferrets,
Fish, Foxes, Foxhounds, Frogs, Giraffes, Goats, Grizzly Bears,
Horses, Insects, Kangaroos, Leopards, Lions, Livestock,
Llamas, Monkeys, Mules, On Set Veterinarian, Orangutans,
Ostriches, Palominos, Panthers, Parrots, Pigeons, Ponies,
Porcupines, Primates, Raccoons, Rats, Reindeer, Reptiles,
Rhinos, Rodents, Rodeo Animals, Scorpions, Sea Lions,
Sheep, Skunks, Sloth, Small Exotics, Small Wildlife, Snakes,
Spiders, Squirrels, Tigers, Trick Horses, Turtles, Vultures,
Wasps, White Pigeons, White Tigers, Wild Animals & Wolves)

Ⓐ American Humane Association
(818) 501-0123
(800) 677-3420
11530 Ventura Blvd.   FAX (818) 501-8725
Studio City, CA 91604   www.americanhumane.org/film

Animal Actors of Hollywood, Inc.   (805) 495-2122
860 W. Carlisle Rd.   FAX (805) 496-3053
Thousand Oaks, CA 91361   www.animalactors.net
(Barnyard, Birds, Cages, Cats, Deer, Dogs, Elephants, Ferrets,
Foxes, Monkeys, Porcupines, Props, Raccoons, Rats, Reptiles,
Sloth, Squirrels & Wolves)

Animal Actors Sweet Sunshine
(951) 609-1687
(877) 609-1687
FAX (951) 609-1687
www.animal-actors.com
(Birds, Cats, Dogs, Exotics, Elephants, Farm Animals, Horses,
Insects, Livestock, Monkeys, Reptiles, Small Wildlife, Trick
Horses & Wolves)

Animal Fantasy Shows
(661) 944-1651
(661) 944-4888
P.O. Box 1260   FAX (661) 944-6773
Littlerock, CA 93543
(Dogs, Macaw Parrots & White and Bay Andalusian Horses)

Animal Savvy   (661) 492-0776
16654 Soledad Canyon Rd., Box 151 FAX (661) 298-2532
Canyon Country, CA 91387   www.animalsavvy.net
(Birds, Cats, Dogs, Exotics, Insects, Livestock,
Rabbits & Rodents)

Animal SuperModels   (805) 320-3952
P.O. Box 7004   www.animalsupermodels.com
Thousand Oaks, CA 91360
(Birds, Cats, Dogs, Farm Animals & Horses)

Animals For You/Diana Smith   (805) 521-1000
(Barnyard Animals & Livestock)   FAX (805) 521-1008
www.animalsforyou.com

INSTINCT animalsforfilm

Andrew Simpson
Animal Coordinator/Trainer
Specializing in Wolves

Worldwide Permits • Worldwide Locations
USDA Licensed/SAG Member

Toll free: 877 455 5866 • Email: info@instinctforfilm.com
www.instinctforfilm.com

Follow your instinct

Animals of a Different Color
(661) 252-3300
(805) 358-4818
16900 Forrest St.   FAX (661) 252-9870
Canyon Country, CA 91351   www.animalcolorist.com
(Animal Colorist)

Aquatic Design
(310) 822-7484
(310) 420-8379
4943 McConnell Ave., Ste. K   FAX (310) 822-8644
Los Angeles, CA 90066   www.aquatic2000.com
(Fish)

Asman & Associates, LLC
(818) 842-8444
(818) 929-9164
P.O. Box 21022   FAX (818) 842-8445
Glendale, CA 91221   www.asmanj.com
(Birds, Cats, Dogs & Horses)

Ⓐ Bear...With Us
(661) 724-0409
(661) 886-1794
P.O. Box 469   www.bearwithus.biz
Acton, CA 93510
(Bears)

Bee & Insect People Unlimited   (800) 924-3097
(Bees, Insects, Spiders & Wasps)   FAX (909) 869-7391

Berens Animals of Distinction   (661) 268-1057
P.O. Box 773
Acton, CA 93510
(Birds, Cats & Dogs)

Bill Rivers' Movieland Animals   (210) 478-8808
(American Buffaloes, Camels & Exotics) FAX (830) 535-4707
www.movielandanimals.net

Birdman   (702) 896-4274
FAX (702) 896-4275
www.birdshow.org
(Birds, Condors, Cranes, Crows, Eagles, Parrots, Reptiles,
Storks & Wild Animals)

Ⓐ Birds & Animals Unlimited
(661) 269-0148
(877) 542-1355
FAX (866) 212-7898
www.birdsandanimals.com
(Birds, Cats, Dogs, Exotics, Farm Animals, Horses, Insects,
Livestock, Primates, Reptiles, Small Animals & Snakes)

Bob Dunn's Animal Services   (818) 896-0394
16001 Yarnell St.   FAX (818) 364-0222
Sylmar, CA 91342   www.animalservices.com
(Birds, Chimps, Fish, Insects, Orangutans & Reptiles)

Boone's Animals for Hollywood, Inc. (661) 257-0630
(Birds, Cats, Dogs & Rodents)   FAX (661) 257-4274
www.boonesanimals.com

Brockett's Film Fauna, Inc.   (805) 379-3141
437 W. Carlisle Rd.   FAX (805) 379-4585
Thousand Oaks, CA 91361
www.brockettsfilmfauna.com
(Alligators, Amphibians, Birds, Cats, Crocodiles, Dogs, Insects,
Reptiles, Small Animals, Snakes & Spiders)

**Bugs Are My Business/
Steve Kutcher**   (626) 836-0322
1801 Oakview Ln.   www.bugsaremybusiness.com
Arcadia, CA 91006
(Butterflies, Insects, Small Animals & Spiders)

Caravan West Productions   (661) 268-8300
35660 Jayhawker Rd.   FAX (661) 268-8301
Agua Dulce, CA 91390   www.caravanwest.com
(Horses & Livestock)

Cats & Cockatoos of Hollywood
(866) 264-6257
(623) 205-0245
www.cats-cockatoos.com
(Amphibians, Birds, Cats, Dogs, Exotics, Fishes,
Horses & Reptiles)

Jennifer Conrad, DVM
(310) 394-5877
(310) 948-6789
P.O. Box 445   FAX (310) 394-5877
Santa Monica, CA 90406
(On Set Veterinarian)

Cougar Hill Ranch   (661) 533-3549
P.O. Box 132   FAX (661) 533-1590
Littlerock, CA 93543   www.cougarhillranch.com
(Birds, Domestics, Exotics, Farm Animals & Reptiles)

Critters of the Cinema
(661) 724-1929
(800) 233-3647
P.O. Box 378   FAX (661) 724-1868
Lake Hughes, CA 93532   www.crittersofthecinema.com
(Barnyard Animals, Birds, Cats, Dogs, Exotics & Reptiles)

Doves Trained for TV   (818) 340-4040
(Trained Doves and Pigeons)   www.traineddoves.com

Dusty Promotions, LLC   (651) 238-2017
(Horses)   www.dustypromotions.com

The Elephant Store/Cheryl Shawver (805) 796-2122
850 W. Carlisle Rd.   FAX (805) 496-3053
Thousand Oaks, CA 91361

Gentle Jungle   (661) 248-6195
P.O. Box 832   FAX (661) 248-6992
Lebec, CA 93243   www.gentlejungle.com
(Domestics, Exotics, Farm Animals & Horses)

Good Dog Animals   (661) 270-0907
FAX (661) 270-0909
www.gooddoganimals.com
(Birds, Cats, Dogs, Exotics, Fish, Insects, Livestock,
Reptiles & Small Animals)

Grisco's Animals
(951) 685-4081
(951) 215-0980
P.O. Box 54   FAX (951) 685-2142
Mira Loma, CA 91752   www.griscosanimals.com
(Alligators, Barnyard Animals, Birds of Prey, Cats & Dogs)

Hart Brothers Livestock
(951) 312-9009
(951) 677-6810
FAX (951) 600-3805
(Barnyard Animals, Buffalo, Bulls, Cattle, Driving Horses, Farm
Animals, Livestock & Riding and Trick Horses)

Have Trunk Will Travel, Inc.   (951) 943-9227
(Asian Elephants)   FAX (951) 943-9563
www.havetrunkwilltravel.com

Hollywood Animals
(323) 665-9500
(213) 842-2170
P.O.Box 2088   FAX (661) 252-4509
Santa Clarita, CA 91386   www.hollywoodanimals.com
(Domestics & Exotics)

Horses for Productions
(310) 961-1584
(310) 457-7027
2277 Decker Canyon Rd.
Malibu, CA 90265   www.horsesforproductions.com
(Horses, Hunting Hounds, Ponies & Riders)

Ⓐ Instinct   (877) 455-5866
www.instinctforfilm.com

Isis Preservation
(310) 927-4141
(310) 262-0520
www.isispreservation.com
(Animal Trainer, Dogs, Exotic Animals, Tigers & White Tigers)

**Jules Sylvester's
Reptile Rentals Inc.**
(818) 621-4101
(818) 706-0815
FAX (818) 707-3537
www.reptilerentals.com
(Frogs, Insects, Reptiles, Rodents, Scorpions,
Spiders & Tortoises)

Jungle Exotics (909) 887-3500
16215 Cajon Blvd. FAX (909) 887-0953
San Bernardino, CA 92407 www.junglexotics.com
(Cats, Dogs, Insects, Reptiles & Wild Animals)

Ⓐ**Lane Ranch & Company** (661) 942-0435
42220 10th St. West, Ste. 101 FAX (661) 942-7485
Lancaster, CA 93534 www.laneranch.net
(Draft Animals, Liberty and Trick Horses & Livestock)

Le PAWS (818) 437-1153
303 E. Walnut Ave. FAX (310) 648-7653
El Segundo, CA 90245 www.lepawsagency.com
(Dogs)

(661) 252-6140
Lundin Farm (818) 618-9959
(Farm Animals & Horses) www.rrstar.net

(714) 649-3194
Mark Jackson Animals (714) 306-9986
28252 Modjeska Grade www.mjanimals.com
Silverado, CA 92676

Merrill Carson Show & Ranch (818) 780-1735
7905 Lloyd Ave. www.merrillcarson.com
North Hollywood, CA 91605
(Palominos)

(805) 526-0321
Mike Boyle Ranches (805) 230-9315
(Livestock & Trick Horses) FAX (805) 520-8037
www.mikeboyleranches.com

Moe DiSesso Trained Animals (661) 255-7969
24233 Old Rd. FAX (661) 255-8179
Santa Clarita, CA 91321 www.animalactors4hire.com
(Domestics & Small Exotics)

(661) 252-8654
Movin' On Livestock Rental Co. (661) 816-7624
20527 Soledad St. FAX (661) 250-8843
Canyon Country, CA 91351 www.movinonlivestock.com

(951) 741-1922
Oliver Livestock (951) 767-9493
38565 San Ignacio Rd. www.oliverlivestock.com
Hemet, CA 92544
(Farm Animals)

(714) 572-8353
Omar's Exotic Birds, Inc. (949) 472-3962
903 E. Imperial Hwy FAX (714) 671-3104
Brea, CA 92821 www.omarsexoticbirds.com

(661) 724-2201
Paws For Effect (877) 729-7439
(Birds, Cats, Dogs, Exotics & Livestock) FAX (661) 724-2252
www.pawsforeffect.net

PHD Animals (310) 650-6337
www.phdanimals.com
(Aquatics, Birds, Domestics, Exotics, Horses,
Insects & Reptiles)

Randy Miller's Predators in Action (909) 585-9286
P.O. Box 1691 FAX (909) 585-9356
Big Bear City, CA 92314 www.predatorsinaction.com
(Black and Grizzly Bears, Cougars, Leopards, Lions, Tigers &
White Tigers)

(661) 252-0461
Rolling Thunder Ranch (661) 478-1616
16163 Sierra Hwy FAX (661) 250-3907
Canyon Country, CA 91351
www.rollingthunderranch.com
(Barnyard Animals, Cows, Llamas, Raccoons, Sheep &
Trick Horses)

Silver Screen Animals (661) 269-0231
34540 Brock Ln. FAX (661) 269-8041
Acton, CA 93510 www.silverscreenanimals.com
(Birds, Cats, Dogs, Exotics, Farm Animals, Raccoons, Reptiles,
Rodents & Squirrels)

Steve Martin's Working Wildlife (661) 245-2406
FAX (661) 245-3617
www.workingwildlife.com
(Bears, Black Leopards, Chimps, Dogs, Ferrets, Foxes, Lions,
Orangutans, Raccoons, Reindeer, Reptiles, Skunks,
Tigers & Wolves)

Studio Animal Services (661) 257-4798
FAX (661) 257-4892
28230 San Martinez Grande Canyon Rd.
Castaic, CA 91384 www.studioanimals.com
(Barnyard Livestock, Birds, Cats, Dogs, Exotics & Squirrels)

**Summersalt Equi-Service, Ltd./
800 Creatures** (661) 803-1531
34162 Agua Dulce Canyon Rd.
Saugus, CA 91390
(Domestics, Horses & Insects)

**A Tad Western
Production Company, Inc.** (661) 268-0658
(661) 609-2033
(Horses & Livestock) FAX (661) 268-0438
www.atadwest.com

Talented Animals (310) 858-8722
FAX (310) 215-9370
www.talentedanimals.com
(Birds, Cats, Dogs, Exotics, Horses, Livestock, Primates,
Reptiles, Rodents, Wild Animals & Wolves)

Geoffrey Vernon (310) 433-2003
(On-Set Veterinarian) FAX (310) 271-0986

**War Horse &
Militaria Heritage Foundation** (818) 694-9277
(Horses) FAX (818) 896-8310
www.warhorsefoundation.com

(831) 455-1901
Wild Things Animal Rentals, Inc. (800) 228-7382
(Domestics & Exotics) FAX (831) 455-1902
www.wildthingsinc.com

Wolves and Company (760) 244-3317
19150 Willow St.
Hesperia, CA 92345
(Domestics & Exotics)

(661) 252-2000
Worldwide Movie Animals, LLC (805) 630-5848
29264 Bouquet Canyon Rd. FAX (661) 252-2001
Santa Clarita, CA 91390
www.worldwidemovieanimals.com
(Beavers, Birds, Camels, Cats, Dogs, Emus, Foxes, Insects,
Kangaroos, Monkeys, Ostriches, Porcupines & Snakes)

Entertainment Partners (818) 955-6296
FAX (818) 450-0255
www.entertainmentpartners.com

Film Budget Pro (323) 574-9696
FAX (888) 699-9778
www.filmbudgetpro.com

KGB Films (323) 956-5000
(323) 610-0501
5555 Melrose Ave. FAX (323) 224-1876
Lucy Bungalow 101 www.kgbfilms.com
Los Angeles, CA 90038

Media Services (310) 440-9600
(800) 333-7518
500 S. Sepulveda Blvd., Fourth Fl. FAX (310) 472-9979
Los Angeles, CA 90049 www.media-services.com

ScheduALL (310) 242-5506
(310) 242-5507
FAX (310) 242-5508
www.scheduall.com

AAA Urban Casting (310) 967-9954
www.aaaurbancasting.com
(Babies, Celebrities, Children, Circus/Variety Acts,
Commercials, Film, Foreign Language Casting, Podcasting,
Real People, Reality, TV, Voice Casting & Webisodes)
Contact: Alan Armani

**ABA - Antoinette Motion Picture Production/
Casting Services** (310) 323-9028
8306 Wilshire Blvd., PMB 900   www.abaaa.com
Beverly Hills, CA 90211
(Commercials)
Contact: Antoinette Meier

Abesera Casting (323) 931-5622
400 N. Orange Dr.   www.abeseracasting.tv
Los Angeles, CA 90036
(Children, Commercials, Film, Music Videos, Real People,
Reality & TV)

**Action Casting/Jenny O'Haver &
James Levine** (818) 817-4341
On Your Mark Studios   FAX (818) 728-6785
13425 Ventura Blvd.   www.actioncasting.net
Sherman Oaks, CA 91423
(Commercial, Film, Real People & TV)

Aisha Coley Casting (323) 882-4144
7336 Santa Monica Blvd., Ste. 611
Los Angeles, CA 90046
(Commercials, Film, TV & Webisodes)

(805) 705-4110
Akimas Casting (805) 705-8179
P.O. Box 650   www.akimascasting.com
Santa Barbara, CA 93116
(Commercials)

Alice Ellis Casting (310) 314-1488
(Commercials)   FAX (310) 314-2649
www.elliscasting.com

Allison Jones Casting (323) 461-0705

**Alyson Horn Casting/
Studios@Orange** (323) 874-8764
1020 N. Sycamore Ave.   FAX (323) 874-6330
Los Angeles, CA 90038   www.alysonhorncasting.com
(Commercials)

Amy Lippens Casting (310) 369-3800
10201 W. Pico Blvd., Bldg. 1, Ste. 136
Los Angeles, CA 90035

(310) 503-1967
Annelise Collins Casting (310) 586-1936
(Commercials, Film & TV)   www.annelisecast.com

Annie Egian Casting (323) 969-8200
7700 W. Sunset Blvd.   www.annieegiancasting.com
Los Angeles, CA 90046
(Babies, Celebrities, Children, Circus/Variety Acts,
Commercials, Film, Real People, TV & Voice Casting)

April Webster Casting (818) 977-5888
6767 Forrest Lawn Dr., Ste. 100
Los Angeles, CA 90068

Aquila/Wood Casting (323) 460-6292
1680 Vine St., Ste. 806
Los Angeles, CA 90028

ASG Casting, Inc. (818) 762-0200
4144 Lankershim Blvd., Ste. 202   FAX (818) 753-9322
North Hollywood, CA 91602   www.asgcasting.com
(Commercials, Film & TV)
Contacts: Erin Murphy, Justin Radley & Arlene Schuster-Goss

AthleteSource Casting (310) 871-7956
13425 Ventura Blvd., Second Fl.   FAX (435) 645-8163
Sherman Oaks, CA 91423
www.athletesourcecasting.com
(Real People & Sports Casting)

Danielle Aufiero (323) 954-3600
5225 Wilshire Blvd., Ste. 636
Los Angeles, CA 90036

Automatic Sweat/John Papsidera (323) 934-5141
5243 W. Washington Blvd.
Los Angeles, CA 90016

AYC Casting (310) 314-7664
2234 Virginia Ave., Ste. 4   FAX (310) 452-3315
Santa Monica, CA 90404
(Reality)

Bacharach/O'Neill Casting (818) 954-3702
4000 Warner Blvd., Bldg. 183, First Fl.
Burbank, CA 91522

Bad Girls Casting (323) 468-6888
6660 Santa Monica Blvd., First Fl.   FAX (323) 468-8811
Los Angeles, CA 90038   www.badgirlscasting.com
(Commercials, Film & Music Videos)

Bang Zoom! Studios (818) 295-3939
1100 N. Hollywood Way   www.bangzoomstudios.com
Burbank, CA 91505
(Voice Casting)

Barbara Bersell Casting (310) 470-1670
(Commercials, Film & TV)

Barden/Schnee Casting, Inc. (310) 451-2278
1513 Sixth St., Ste. 105   FAX (310) 576-3456
Santa Monica, CA 90401   www.bardenschnee.com

Barry/Green-Keyes Casting (818) 759-4425
4924 Balboa Blvd., Ste. 371
Encino, CA 91316

Bass Casting (323) 848-3737
8284 Santa Monica Blvd.
Los Angeles, CA 90046
(Film & TV)

Beach/Katzman Casting (323) 468-6633

Bebe Flynn Casting (323) 252-6026
www.bebeflynncasting.com
(Commercials, Film & Real People)

(323) 956-2020
Juel Bestrop (818) 508-7451

Beth Holmes Casting, Inc. (818) 980-9803
11340 Moorpark St.   FAX (818) 980-2838
Studio City, CA 91602   www.bethholmescasting.com
(Commercials)
Contacts: Beth Holmes & Monica Lee-Eisenbeis

Betty Mae, Inc. (310) 396-6100
13375 Beach Ave.   FAX (310) 396-1313
Marina del Rey, CA 90292
(Film & TV)

Beverly Holloway Casting (310) 410-9405
5721 W. Slauson Ave., Ste. 110
Culver City, CA 90230

Beverly Long Casting (818) 754-6222
11425 Moorpark St.   FAX (818) 754-6226
Studio City, CA 91602
(Commercials, Film & TV)

Bialy/Thomas Casting   **(323) 468-4533**
1438 N. Gower St., Bldg. 5, Ste. 100
Los Angeles, CA 90028

Big House Casting   **(323) 464-0990**
4055 Lankershim Blvd., Ste. 401
Studio City, CA 91604   www.bighousecasting.com

Billik/Wood Casting   **(818) 623-1631**
14044 Ventura Blvd., Ste. 309
Shermon Oaks, CA 91423   www.billikwoodcasting.com
(Film & TV)

Billy DaMota Casting   **(818) 243-1263**
13425 Ventura Blvd., Ste. 200   www.castboy.com
Sherman Oaks, CA 91423
(Commercials, Film & TV)

Blanca Valdez Casting   **(323) 876-5700**
1001 N. Poinsettia Pl.   FAX **(323) 876-5297**
West Hollywood, CA 90046   www.blancavaldez.com
(Bilingual Casting, Celebrities, Children, Commercials, Film,
Foreign Language Casting, Industrials, Podcasting, Real
People, Reality, TV, Voice Casting & Webisodes)

Bluewater Ranch/
Casting Artists, Inc.   **(310) 395-1882**
1433 Sixth St.   www.bluewaterranch.com
Santa Monica, CA 90401
(Film & TV)

Charles Bogdan   **(323) 606-2636**
(Commercials, Film & TV)   www.charlesbogdan.com

bokcreative   **(323) 330-1020**
200 S. La Brea Ave., Second Fl.   www.bokcreative.com
Los Angeles, CA 90036
(Babies, Celebrities, Children, Circus/Variety Acts,
Commercials, Film, Foreign Language Casting,
Industrials, Podcasting, Real People, Reality, TV,
Voice Casting & Webisodes)

Judith Bouley   **(831) 252-7733**
5850 W. Third St., Ste. 326
Los Angeles, CA 90036

Brad Gilmore Casting   **(323) 464-2278**
646 N. Beachwood Ave., Ste. 1
Los Angeles, CA 90004   www.bradgilmorecasting.com

Megan Branman/Dylann Brander   **(818) 560-7499**
500 S. Buena Vista St., Props/Drapes Bldg., Ste. 110
Burbank, CA 91521

Brice/Gergely Casting   **(323) 860-3320**
1040 N. Las Palmas Ave., Bldg 33, Second Fl.
Los Angeles, CA 90038

Broad-cast   **(323) 937-0411**
7461 Beverly Blvd., Ste. 203   FAX **(323) 937-2070**
Los Angeles, CA 90036   www.broad-cast.tv
(Commercials)
Contact: Dan Cowan

Bronson/Barnes Casting   **(323) 871-4461**
650 N. Bronson Ave., Pickford Bungalow
Los Angeles, CA 90038

Bruce H. Newberg Casting   **(323) 468-6633**
     FAX **(323) 467-6175**

Krisha Bullock   **(323) 468-5010**
6230 W. Sunset Blvd.
Los Angeles, CA 90028

Bump It Casting/Balyndah Bumpus   **(213) 700-5139**
5482 Wilshire Blvd., Ste. 363   FAX **(310) 397-8905**
Los Angeles, CA 90036
(Babies, Celebrities, Children, Commercials, Film, Music Video
Models, Real People, Reality, Spanish Language, TV, Voice
Casting & Webisodes)

Melanie Burgess   **(818) 954-4080**

Burrows/Boland Casting   **(310) 503-4719**
333 W. Washington Blvd., Ste. 309
Marina del Rey, CA 90292   www.burrowsboland.com
(Film & TV)

C&C Casting   **(818) 441-1513**
     candccasting.com

Cami Patton Casting   **(818) 509-5779**
4640 Lankershim Blvd., Ste. 511
North Hollywood, CA 91602
(Film & TV)

Carol Lefko Casting   **(310) 888-0007**
P.O. Box 84509
Los Angeles, CA 90073
(Film & TV)

Carol Rosenthal Casting   **(213) 483-4200**
     www.rosenthalcasting.com
(Commercials, Film, Music Videos & PSAs)

Carrafiello Casting   **(310) 237-6438**
     www.ccasting.net
(Commercials, Film, Foreign Language Voice-Over Casting,
Industrials, Television & Web TV)
Contacts: Meghan Carrafiello

Carroll Voiceover Casting Co.   **(323) 851-9966**
6767 Forest Lawn Dr., Ste. 203   FAX **(323) 851-3973**
Los Angeles, CA 90068   www.carrollcasting.com
(Commercials)
Contact: Carroll Kimble

Casting Brothers   **(818) 763-1361**
Fifth Street Studios, 1216 Fifth St.
Santa Monica, CA 90401   www.castingbrothers.com
(Commercials, Hosts, Industrials, Infomercials, Real People &
Voice Casting)
Contacts: Alan Kaminsky & Joshua Rappaport

Casting by Lila Selik   **(310) 556-2444**
P.O. Box 66369   www.castingbylilaselik.com
Los Angeles, CA 90066
(Commercials, Film & TV)

Casting by Patrick Baca &   **(323) 683-9020**
Shana Landsburg   **(818) 981-4995**
13251 Ventura Blvd. Ste. 2
Sherman Oaks, CA 91604
     www.speedreels.com/talent/pbaca/pbaca.html
(Film, Industrials, TV & Webisodes)

The Casting Company   **(818) 487-5600**
12750 Ventura Blvd., Ste. 102   www.janeandjanet.com
Studio City, CA 91604

     (310) 924-9803
The Casting Connection   **(310) 508-3033**
5536 Carpenter Ave.
Valley Village, CA 91607
(Commercials, Film & TV)
Contacts: Mary Ann Phelps & Peter Szeliga

The Casting Couch, Inc./
Sande Alessi   **(818) 201-0555**
13731 Ventura Blvd.   www.sandealessicasting.com
Sherman Oaks, CA 91423
(Commercials, Film & TV)

Catherine Wilshire Casting   **(818) 623-9200**
11684 Ventura Blvd., Ste. 118
Studio City, CA 91604

Cathi Carlton Casting, Inc.   **(310) 581-3010**
2701 Ocean Park Blvd., Ste. 250
Santa Monica, CA 90405   www.cathicarltoncasting.com
(Babies, Celebrities, Children, Circus/Variety Acts,
Commercials, Film, Foreign Language Casting,
Industrials, Podcasting, Real People, Reality, TV,
Voice Casting & Webisodes)
Contacts: Jon Beauregard, Cathi Carlton, Raines Carr &
Marty Fortney

Cathy Henderson-Martin Casting (805) 773-2256
201 Five Cities Dr., Ste. 134
Pismo Beach, CA 93449

(415) 987-1877
Cervantes Nomad Casting (323) 330-1020
c/o 200 South Studios www.nomadcasting.com
200 S. La Brea Ave., Ste. C
Los Angeles, CA 90036
(Celebrities, Commercials, Film, Industrials, Music Videos,
Real People & TV)
Contact: Toni Cervantes

CFB Casting (323) 372-1250
(Film & TV)

Denise Chamian (323) 315-9445
1438 N. Gower St., Bldg. 35, Ste. 270
Los Angeles, CA 90028

(818) 735-7372
Charisse Glenn Casting (310) 656-4600
(Commercials) FAX (818) 735-7964

Christal Blue Casting (213) 804-4304
(Commercials, Film & TV) www.christalblue.com

Christine Sheaks Casting (323) 443-2453
4221 Wilshire Blve., Ste. 155
Los Angeles, CA 90010

Clair Sinnett Casting (310) 237-6438
www.clairsinnettcasting.com
(Foreign Language Voice-Over Casting; Film & TV)
Contacts: Jamie Boalbey & Heather Shay

Kim Coleman (323) 939-9002
5225 Wilshire Blvd., Ste. 415
Los Angeles, CA 90036

Veronica Collins Rooney (818) 526-4493
800 S. Main St., Second Fl.
Burbank, CA 91506

(818) 618-2527
Combat Casting (310) 686-2718
FAX (818) 509-9581
www.combatcasting.com

Craig Campobasso Casting (818) 503-2474
P.O. Box 800735
Santa Clarita, CA 91380

Craig Colvin & Co. (323) 785-7850
(Commercials, Film & TV)

(323) 385-6537
crashcasting & Associates (818) 817-4348
(Commercials & Real People) FAX (818) 728-6785
Contact: Rosanna

Creative Casting Services (818) 846-3200
(Children, Commercials & Real People)

Cricket Feet (310) 395-9540
P.O. Box 1417 www.cricketfeet.com/casting
Los Angeles, CA 90028

Currently Casting, Inc. (818) 613-7703
13636 Ventura Blvd., Ste. 411 FAX (818) 760-0355
Sherman Oaks, CA 91423 www.currentlycasting.net
(Babies, Celebrities, Children, Circus/Variety Acts,
Commercials, Film, Industrials, Music Videos, Podcasting,
Real People, Reality, TV, Voice Casting & Webisodes)
Contact: Michelle Metzner

Danielle Eskinazi Casting (323) 969-8200
7700 W. Sunset Blvd. FAX (323) 969-0101
West Hollywood, CA 90046 www.daniellecasting.com
(Babies, Celebrities, Children, Commercials, Film, Foreign
Language Casting, Real People, TV, Voice Casting &
Webisodes)

Dava Waite Casting (818) 428-6890
21050 Lassen St.
Chatsworth, CA 91311

David Glanzer Casting (213) 369-4345
7985 Santa Monica Blvd., Ste. 570 www.dgcasting.com
Los Angeles, CA 90046
(Film & TV)

David Kang Casting (213) 384-2404
2404 Wilshire Blvd, Ste. 12F FAX (213) 384-2408
Los Angeles, CA 90057 www.davidkangcasting.net
(Babies, Celebrities, Children, Circus/Variety Acts, Commercials, Film, Podcasting, Real People, TV & Webisodes)

David Rapaport Casting (323) 468-2090
1438 N. Gower St., Bldg. 5, Ste. 208
Los Angeles, CA 90028

Davis/Baddeley Casting (323) 436-7098

Dawn Hershey (213) 321-8213
www.dawnhershey.com

(818) 752-7052
Debe Waisman Casting (310) 535-1325
11684 Ventura Blvd., PMB 415
Studio City, CA 91604
(Commercials)

Deborah Kurtz Casting, Inc. (310) 550-5300
8899 Beverly Blvd. FAX (310) 248-5297
Los Angeles, CA 90048
(Commercials, Film & TV)

Deedra Ricketts Casting (323) 807-5825
(Commercials) www.deedeecasting.com

DeHorter Casting (323) 957-1657
1501 N. Gardner St. www.zdcasting.net
Los Angeles, CA 90046
(Commercials, Film, TV & Webisodes)

Demo/McCarthy Casting (323) 937-4493
5225 Wilshire Blvd., Ste. 400
Los Angeles, CA 90036

Dickson/Arbusto Casting (323) 871-8501
P.O. Box 27668
Los Angeles, CA 90027
(Film & TV)

(323) 651-0888
Digital Dogs Casting (323) 314-1317
P.O. Box 48229 www.digitaldogscasting.com
Los Angeles, CA 90048
(Commercials, Film and TV)
Contact: Robert B. Martin, Jr.

Dino Ladki Casting/Dino Ladki (310) 289-4962
8556 Rugby Dr. www.dinoladkicasting.com
West Hollywood, CA 90069
(Commercials, Film, Industrials, Teens, TV, Voice Casting,
Webisodes & Youth)

(323) 203-1331
Doron Ofir Casting (310) 203-1302
6207 Santa Monica Blvd. FAX (310) 943-1598
Los Angeles, CA 90038 www.popularproductions.net
(Real People, Reality & TV)

(323) 665-1776
Dowd-Roman Casting (323) 330-1020
200 S. La Brea Ave., Second Fl. FAX (323) 954-0933
Los Angeles, CA 90036
(Babies, Celebrities, Children, Commercials, Foreign Language
Casting, Industrials, Podcasting, Real People, Voice
Casting & Webisodes)

Dream Big Casting, LLC (323) 463-4554
1258 N. Highland Ave., Ste. 305
Los Angeles, CA 90038

Eastside Studios   **(323) 660-7874**
4216 Fountain Ave.   FAX **(323) 660-7875**
Los Angeles, CA 90029   **www.eastsidestudiosla.com**
(Commercials)
Contact: Doug Mangskau

Elaine Craig Voice Casting, Inc.   **(323) 469-8773**
6464 Sunset Blvd., Ste. 1100   **www.elainecraig.com**
Hollywood, CA 90028
(Commerials, Foreign Language Casting & Voice Casting)

Emily Schweber Casting   **(310) 470-9444**
10642 Santa Monica Blvd., Ste. 207
Los Angeles, CA 90025

Engine   **(310) 306-9366**
P.O. Box 1859   FAX **(310) 306-9374**
Venice, CA 90291

Eyde Belasco Casting   **(213) 388-1475**
3780 Wilshire Blvd., Seventh Fl.
Los Angeles, CA 90010

Face in the Crowd Casting/   **(310) 720-3117**
Maryclaire Sweeters   **(310) 458-1100**
    www.faceinthecrowdcasting.com
(Commercials, Film, Foreign Language Casting, Real People,
TV & Webisodes)

Felicia Fasano   **(310) 840-3540**
8621 Hayden Pl.
Culver City, CA 90232

Fenton/Frederick Casting   **(310) 277-1955**
P.O. Box 15457
Beverly Hills, CA 90209

Paula Ferguson   **(661) 297-3282**
(Commercials)   FAX **(661) 297-5580**

Fern Champion Casting   **(323) 473-0900**
11050 Santa Monica Blvd.
Los Angeles, CA 90025

Barbara Fiorentino   **(323) 954-3600**
5225 Wilshire Blvd., Ste. 678
Los Angeles, CA 90036

Firefly Casting   **(323) 857-1699**
6333 W. Third St., Ste. 915
Los Angeles, CA 90036

    (818) 216-9350
Foley/Marra Casting   **(818) 817-4319**
c/o On Your Mark Studios   **www.meganfoleycasting.com**
13425 Ventura Blvd., Ste. 200
Sherman Oaks, CA 91423
(Commercials)
Contacts: Megan Foley-Marra, Chuck Marra & Kira Shea
Smithson

Francine Maisler Casting   **(310) 244-6945**
10202 W. Washington Blvd., Jimmy Stewart Bldg., Ste. 207
Culver City, CA 90232
(Film & TV)

Dorian Frankel   **(323) 463-7676**
1617 N. El Centro, Ste. 14
Los Angeles, CA 90028

Gabrielle Schary Casting   **(310) 450-0835**
2601 Ocean Park Blvd., Ste. 120   FAX **(310) 450-7794**
Santa Monica, CA 90405
    www.gabriellescharycasting.com
(Commercials, TV, Voice Over Casting & Web)

Garalyn Flood Casting   **(323) 956-1804**

Gerrie Wormser Casting   **(310) 277-3281**
470 1/2 S. Roxbury Dr.
Beverly Hills, CA 90212
(Film & TV)

Jan Glaser   **(310) 458-7707**
11124 W. Washington Blvd.   FAX **(310) 204-2450**
Culver City, CA 90232

    (323) 762-7373
Goldwasser/Meltzer Casting   **(310) 308-4083**
5800 Sunset Blvd., Bldg. 10, Ste. 3
Los Angeles, CA 90028

Greenstein/Daniel Casting   **(323) 461-5100**
6671 W. Sunset Blvd., Ste. 1527
Los Angeles, CA 90028

Headquarters Casting   **(310) 556-9001**
3108 W. Magnolia Blvd.   FAX **(310) 861-5988**
Burbank, CA 91505   **www.headquarterscasting.com**

Heidi Levitt Casting   **(323) 525-0800**
7201 Melrose Ave., Ste. 203 **www.heidilevittcasting.com**
Los Angeles, CA 90046
(Film & TV)

Helgoth & Associates Casting   **(323) 464-5413**
1312 N. Wilton Pl.
Hollywood, CA 90028
    www.helgothandassociatescasting.com
(Commercials, Film & TV)

Hispanic Talent
Casting of Hollywood   **(323) 934-6465**
2536 Hauser Blvd., Ste. 3
Los Angeles, CA 90016
(Commercials, Film & TV)

Amber Horn   **(323) 954-3600**
5225 Wilshire Blvd., Ste. 636
Los Angeles, CA 90036

House Casting   **(323) 769-0200**
855 N. Cahuenga Blvd.   FAX **(323) 469-8901**
Los Angeles, CA 90038   **www.housecasting.com**
(Babies, Celebrities, Children, Commercials, Film, Foreign
Language Casting, Real People, TV, Voice Casting &
Webisodes)

Ian Royston Casting   **(310) 720-7242**
(Commercials, Film, Real People & Webisodes)

Idell James Casting   **(310) 230-9986**
(Commercials)   FAX **(310) 230-8233**

    (818) 623-2336
In The Twink of An Eye Casting   **(800) 821-2974**
(Commercials)   FAX **(818) 623-2637**

iProbe Multilingual Solutions, Inc.   **(888) 489-6035**
    www.iprobesolutions.com
(Foreign Language Voice Overs and Voice Casting)

Ivy Isenberg Casting   **(323) 652-0625**
741 N. Cahuenga Blvd., First Fl.
Los Angeles, CA 90038

Jane Doe Casting   **(323) 692-1800**
c/o The Casting Lounge, 1035 S. La Brea Ave.
Los Angeles, CA 90019   **www.janedoecasting.com**
(Commercials, Film & TV)

Jeanne McCarthy Casting   **(310) 396-1501**
    FAX **(310) 396-8885**

Jeff Gerrard Casting   **(818) 782-9900**
13425 Ventura Blvd., Second Fl.
Sherman Oaks, CA 91423
(Commercials, Film & TV)
Contacts: Jeff & Justin

Jeff Greenberg Casting   **(310) 369-8363**
10201 W. Pico Blvd., Bldg. 226, Ste. 115
Los Angeles, CA 90035

Jeff Hardwick Casting   (818) 752-9898
3940 Laurel Canyon Blvd., Ste. 58
Studio City, CA 91604   www.jeffhardwickcasting.com
(Commercials, Film & TV)

Jeff Rosenman Casting   (323) 330-1020
200 S. La Brea Ave., Second Fl.
Los Angeles, CA 90036   www.rosenmancasting.com

Jennifer Cooper Casting   (323) 655-5253
4024 Radford Ave., Bldg. 1, Ste. 100
Studio City, CA 91604

     (213) 841-1905
Jennifer Levy Casting   (310) 601-2371
     www.musiclevycasting.com

Jennifre DuMont Casting   (323) 270-2278

     (310) 498-6668
Jessica J Casting   (323) 330-1020
200 South Studios, 200 S. La Brea, Second Fl.
Los Angeles, CA 90036   www.jessicajcasting.com
(Babies, Celebrities, Children, Circus/Variety Acts, Commercials, Podcasting, Reality, TV & Webisodes)

Jill Anthony Thomas Casting   (818) 560-5250
15001 Calvert St.
Van Nuys, CA 91411

Joe Blake Casting   (310) 581-3009
@ Ocean Park Casting   FAX (310) 450-3758
2701 Ocean Park Blvd., Ste. 250
Santa Monica, CA 90405
(Commercials, Film & TV)

John McCarthy Casting   (323) 732-8118
1234 S. Gramercy Pl.   FAX (323) 732-8818
Los Angeles, CA 90035
(Commercials, Film & TV)

Julie Ashton Casting   (323) 856-9000
(Film & TV)   FAX (323) 856-9010

Junie Lowry-Johnson Casting   (323) 850-3171
1041 Formosa Ave., Formosa Bldg., Ste. 94
Los Angeles, CA 90046
(Film & TV)

Kalmenson & Kalmenson
Voice Casting   (818) 377-3600
P.O. Box 260207   FAX (818) 377-3636
Encino, CA 91426   www.kalmenson.com
(Voice Overs)
Contacts: Catherine & Harvey Kalmenson

Kari Peyton Casting   (323) 468-6888
6660 Santa Monica Blvd.
Los Angeles, CA 90038
(Film & TV)

Karmic Casting   (310) 295-7575
io/LA 7083 Hollywood Blvd.   www.karmiccasting.com
Los Angeles, CA 90028
(Commercials, Film & TV)

Kathy Knowles Casting   (310) 458-1100
     FAX (310) 458-7878
     www.kkcasting.com
(Commercials, Industrials, Voice Casting & Webisodes)

Lisa Miller Katz   (310) 369-7545
10201 W. Pico Blvd., Bldg. 214, Ste. 1
Los Angeles, CA 90035

Kelli Lerner Casting   (212) 459-9293
9595 Wilshire Blvd., Ste. 900
Beverly Hills, CA 90212   www.kellilernercasting.com

Kelly Wagner Casting   (323) 933-6120
6338 Wilshire Blvd.
Los Angeles, CA 90048

Lee Sonja Kissik   (805) 688-3702
1660 Cougar Ridge Rd.
Buellton, CA 93427
(Commercials, Film & TV)

Koblin/Harding Casting   (323) 424-3800

Koczara/Shevchenko Casting   (818) 954-5407
4000 Warner Blvd., Bldg. 186
Burbank, CA 91505

La La Casting   (323) 661-5252
1938 Hillhurst Ave.
Los Angeles, CA 90027

     (818) 254-3541
La Padura/Hart Casting   (323) 468-7940

Lambert/McGee Casting   (818) 480-3144
121 W. Lexington Dr., Ste. 732
Glendale, CA 91203

Landau McRae Casting   (310) 458-1100
1216 Fifth St.   FAX (310) 458-7878
Santa Monica, CA 90401   www.fifthstreetstudios.net
(Commercials, Film & TV)

Laray Mayfield   (323) 817-1190
5620 Hollywood Blvd.   www.mccoyfilms.biz
Los Angeles, CA 90028

Lauren Grey Casting   (424) 204-4025
9242 Beverly Blvd., Ste. 200
Beverly Hills, CA 90210

Leilani Music Casting   (323) 823-0921
     www.musiclevycasting.com

Matthew Lessall   (323) 965-2104
5225 Wilshire Blvd., Ste. 501   www.lessallcasting.com
Los Angeles, CA 90036
(Commercials, Film, TV & Webisodes)

John Frank Levey   (818) 954-4080

Sheryl Levine   (323) 860-8160
1040 N. Las Palmas Ave., Bldg. 2, Ste. 205
Los Angeles, CA 90038

Linda Lowy Casting   (323) 671-5438
4151 Prospect Ave., Cottages, Ste. 105
Los Angeles, CA 90027
(Film & TV)

Linda Phillips Palo Casting   (310) 396-8328
22 Paloma Ave., Ste. D
Venice, CA 90291

Lindsey Kroeger Casting   (310) 882-5800
8509 W. Washington Blvd.   www.lkcasting.com
Culver City, CA 90232

Lisa Fields Casting   (310) 775-6604
     FAX (310) 478-2100
     www.lisafieldscasting.com
(Babies, Celebrities, Children, Commercials, Film, Industrials, Podcasting, Real People, TV, Voice Casting & Webisodes)

Lisa Freiberger Casting   (818) 990-9956
(Film & TV)

Lisa Pantone Casting   (818) 552-2772
(Commercial, Film &TV)   www.lisapantone.com
Contact: Lisa Pantone

Leslie Litt   (310) 244-2822
10202 W. Washington Blvd., Gable Bldg., Ste. 209
Culver City, CA 90232

Liz Lewis Casting Partners (310) 779-4860
7700 W. Sunset Blvd. www.lizlewis.com
Los Angeles, CA 90046

LJ Casting (310) 393-3141
www.imdb.com/name/nm0421908/

London/Stroud Casting (323) 956-1838

Long/Di Matteo Casting (310) 225-5267

Loop Troop ADR Voice Casting/
Terri Douglas (818) 216-3678
827 Hollywood Way, Ste. 411 www.looptroop.com
Burbank, CA 91505
(ADR Group Voice Casting, Animation, Film, Principal
Sound-Alike, TV & Voice Casting)
Contact: Terri Douglas

(310) 492-6520
Lynne Quirion Casting (818) 606-4533
13425 Ventura Blvd. www.lynnequirioncasting.com
Sherman Oaks, CA 91423
(Commercials, Film, Print, Real People, TV, Union &
Voice Casting)
Contact: Lynne Quirion

(310) 248-5296
M Casting (213) 393-2758
8899 Beverly Blvd. FAX (310) 248-5297
Los Angeles, CA 90048
(Commercials)
Contacts: Marisa Munoz & Ray Munoz

M-O Casting (213) 281-9802
Contacts: Rosalinda Morales & Pauline O'Con

Mackey/Sandrich Casting (310) 449-4009
3000 W. Olympic Blvd., Bldg. 3, Ste. 2323
Santa Monica, CA 90404

Suzie Magrey (310) 497-7115
c/o On Your Mark Studio, 13425 Ventura Blvd., Ste. 200
Sherman Oaks, CA 91423
(Commercials)

Mambo Casting (323) 655-7200
489 S. Robertson Blvd., Ste. 104 FAX (323) 655-7221
Beverly Hills, CA 90211 www.mambocasting.com
(Commercials, Film, Hispanic Casting & TV)
Contact: Orlette Ruiz

Marci Liroff Casting (818) 784-5434
P.O. Box 57948 www.marciliroff.com
Sherman Oaks, CA 91413
(Film & TV)

(323) 401-1188
Mariko Ballentine Casting (818) 761-0774
www.marikoballentine.com
(Babies, Children, Commercials, Industrials, Non-Union, Union,
Voice Casting & Webisodes)

Marisa Ross Casting (310) 369-3970
10201 W. Pico Blvd., Bldg. 104, Second Fl.
Los Angeles, CA 90064

(323) 465-7553
Mark Randall Casting (323) 533-0572
1811 N. Whitley Ave., Ste. 401
Hollywood, CA 90028 www.markrandallcasting.com
(Celebrities, Children, Circus/Variety Acts, Commercials, Film,
Print, Real People, Reality, TV & Webisodes)
Contact: Mark Randall

Mark Sikes Casting (818) 759-7648
c/o Pioneer Valley Productions, 8909 24th St.
Los Angeles, CA 90034 www.marksikes.com
(Film & TV)

Mark Teschner Casting (323) 671-5542
c/o The Prospect Studios
4151 Prospect Ave. General Hospital Bldg.
Los Angeles, CA 90027
(Film & TV)

Mary Downey Productions (818) 563-1200
705 N. Kenwood St. FAX (818) 563-1585
Burbank, CA 91505

Massalas/Digman Casting (424) 259-3016
2013 Beloit Ave.
Los Angeles, CA 90025

(310) 581-3000
McBride Casting (310) 433-3177
2701 Ocean Park Blvd., Ste. 250 FAX (310) 450-3149
Santa Monica, CA 90405 www.mcbridecasting.com
(Babies, Children, Circus/Variety Acts, Commercials, Film, Real
People, TV & Webisodes)

Valerie McCaffrey (818) 785-1886
4924 Balboa Blvd., Ste. 172
Encino, CA 91316
(Film & TV)

Helen McCready (310) 651-0637
531-A North Hollywood Way, Ste. 162
Burbank, CA 91505 www.helenwheels.net

Mel and Liz Casting (323) 330-1020
200 S. La Brea, Second Fl. FAX (323) 954-0933
Los Angeles, CA 90036 www.melandlizcasting.com

Melissa Feliciano Casting (323) 969-8200
c/o Exclusive Casting Studios FAX (323) 969-0101
7700 W. Sunset Blvd., Ste. 200
Los Angeles, CA 90046 www.melissafcasting.com
(Commercials)

Melissa Skoff Casting (818) 760-2058
(Film & TV) www.melissaskoff.com

Howard Meltzer (213) 534-3520

Mexico Casting/Casting Valdes (818) 292-7982
1024 Iron Point Rd. www.mexicocasting.com/new
Folsom, CA 95630

Michael Donovan Casting (323) 876-9020
7805 Sunset Blvd., Ste. 200 FAX (323) 876-9021
Los Angeles, CA 90046
(Commercials, Film & TV)

Michelle Gertz Casting (310) 255-4977
2700 Colorado Ave., Second Fl.
Santa Monica, CA 90404
(Film & TV)

Monika Mikkelsen (323) 965-2104
5225 Wilshire Blvd., Ste. 501
Los Angeles, CA 90036

Rick Millikan (310) 369-4447
10201 W. Pico Blvd., Bldg. 1, Ste. 142 FAX (310) 969-0524
Los Angeles, CA 90035

(310) 452-0863
Mimi Webb Miller Casting (310) 991-0863
725 Arizona FAX (310) 581-5277
Santa Monica, CA 90401
(Commercials, Foreign Language Casting, Real People,
SAG & Non-Union)

Mindy Marin Casting (310) 395-1882
1433 Sixth St.
Santa Monica, CA 90401
(Film & TV)

Monroe Casting (818) 640-4770
3100 Damon Way www.monroecasting.com
Burbank, CA 91505
(Commercials)

Rick Montgomery (310) 474-5703
2329 Purdue Ave.
Los Angeles, CA 90064

Morman/Boling Casting   (323) 874-8965
7300 Fountain Ave.
West Hollywood, CA 90046

MTierney Casting   (213) 422-2181
FAX **(323) 262-2759**
www.mtierneycasting.com
(Commercials, Films, Real People, Reality & TV)

Nan Dutton Casting   (818) 981-3330
16161 Ventura Blvd., Ste. 212
Encino, CA 91436

Nancy Nayor Casting   (323) 857-0151
6320 Commodore Sloat Dr., Second Fl.
Los Angeles, CA 90048   **nancynayorcasting.com**
(Film & TV)

Gregory Orson/GO Casting   (323) 469-6464
6464 Sunset Blvd., Ste. 970
Los Angeles, CA 90028
(Film & TV)

Pagano/Manwiller Casting   (323) 841-4360
3815 Hughes Ave., Fourth Fl.
Culver City, CA 90232

Mark Paladini   (818) 613-3982

Pam Dixon Casting   (323) 463-4475

Pam Gilles Casting   (818) 386-9843
www.gillescasting.com
(Celebrities, Children, Commercials, Film, Foreign Language
Casting, Industrials, TV & Webisodes)
Contact: Pam Gilles

Pamela Kaplan Casting   (415) 902 6484
311 Keller St.   **www.pkcasting.com**
Petaluma, CA 94952
(Real People)

Patrick Cunningham Casting   (323) 956-5435
c/o Paramount Pictures
5555 Melrose Ave., Drier Bldg., Ste. 206
Hollywood, CA 90038
(Babies, Celebrities, Children, Commercials, Film, Foreign
Language Casting, Podcasting, Real People, Reality, TV, Voice
Casting & Webisodes)

Patrick Rush Casting   (818) 953-5129
3808 W. Riverside Dr., Ste. 201
Burbank, CA 901505   **www.patrickrushcasting.com**
(Film & TV)

Paula Rosenberg Casting   (310) 260-0129
818 12th St., Ste. 9
Santa Monica, CA 90403
(Film & TV)

Payne/Ystrom Casting   (818) 505-3762
10200 Riverside Dr., Ste. 201
Toluca Lake, CA 91602

Pemrick/Fronk Casting   (818) 325-1289
14724 Ventura Blvd., PH   **www.pfcast.com**
Sherman Oaks, CA 91403
(Film & TV)

Perry/Reece Casting   (310) 889-1660
500 S. Sepulveda Blvd., Ste. 600   FAX **(310) 889-1670**
Los Angeles, CA 90049   **www.perryreececasting.com**

Petite, A Casting Company   (310) 656-4600
725 Arizona Ave., Ste. 103
Santa Monica, CA 90401
www.petiteacastingcompany.com
(Babies, Celebrities, Children, Commercials, Film, Foreign
Language Casting, Industrials, Real People, Reality, TV, Voice
Casting & Webisodes)

Bonita Pietila   (310) 369-3632
10201 W. Pico Blvd., Bldg. 203, Ste. 2
Los Angeles, CA 90035

Pitch Casting   (323) 969-8200
7700 W. Sunset Blvd.   FAX **(323) 969-0101**
West Hollywood, CA 90046   **www.pitchcasting.com**
(Commercials & Film)

Pogo Casting   (310) 775-6606
2329 Purdue Ave.   **www.pogocasting.com**
Los Angeles, CA 90064
(Babies, Children, Commercials, Film, Foreign Language
Casting, Industrials, TV & Webisodes)
Contact: Karen Maseng

    (310) 990-4418
popcasting   (323) 692-1800
1035 S. La Brea   **www.popcastingla.com**
Los Angeles, CA 90019
(Babies, Children, Commercials, Film, Foreign Language
Casting, Podcasting, Real People, Reality Casting,
TV & Webisodes)

    (323) 962-0377
Prime Casting & Payroll   (323) 962-1455
6430 Sunset Blvd., Ste. 425   FAX **(323) 872-5050**
Hollywood, CA 90028   **www.primecasting.com**
(Babies, Children, Circus/Variety Acts, Commercials, Film,
Industrials, Real People, TV & Webisodes)
Contact: Peter Alwazzan

Real People Casting   (310) 827-9498
4732-D Villa Marina
Marina del Rey, CA 90292
(Celebrities, Commercials, Film, Industrials, Podcasting,
Real People, Reality & TV)
Contact: Sharon Lindsey

Reel Talent/Kids   (805) 969-2222
110 Olive Mill Ln.   FAX **(805) 969-9595**
Santa Barbara, CA 93108
(Commercials)

René Haynes Casting   (818) 842-0187
(Film & TV)

    (323) 939-5992
Renita Casting   (310) 775-6611
c/o 310 Casting Studios, 2329 Purdue Ave.
Los Angeles, CA 90064   **www.renitacasting.com**
(Babies, Celebrities, Children, Circus/Variety Acts,
Commercials, Film, Foreign Language Casting, Podcasting,
Real People, Reality, TV, Voice Casting & Webisodes)

Richard Delancy Casting   (818) 760-3110
11684 Ventura Blvd., Ste. 474   FAX **(818) 760-1382**
Studio City, CA 91604
(Babies, Children, Commercials, Film, Industrials, Real People,
Reality, TV, Voice Casting & Webisodes)
Contacts: Richard Delancy & Ricky Montez

Ricki Maslar Casting   (818) 433-6024
5020 Alcove Ave.   **www.rickimaslarcasting.com**
Valley Village, CA 91607
(Film & TV)

RMB Casting   (310) 880-3494
2701 Ocean Park Blvd., Ste. 250   **www.rmbcasting.com**
Santa Monica, CA 90405
(Babies, Children, Commercials, Foreign Language
Casting, Industrials, Podcasting, Real People, Voice
Casting & Webisodes)

Rodeo Casting   (323) 969-9125
7013 Willoughby Ave.   FAX **(323) 874-7729**
Hollywood, CA 90038   **www.rodeocasting.com**
(Babies, Children, Commercials, Industrials, Non-Union,
Real People & Web Video)
Contact: Britt Enggren

Roger Mussenden Casting   (310) 244-2266

Romano/Benner (310) 202-2477

Ronna Kress Casting (310) 788-5581
333 S. Beverly Dr., Ste. 109   FAX (310) 788-0060
Beverly Hills, CA 90212

Ronnie Yeskel & Associates (310) 312-5753
2013 1/2 Beloit Ave.
Los Angeles, CA 90025

Donna Rosenstein (818) 526-4230
800 S. Main St., Ste. 202
Burbank, CA 91506

Ross Lacy Casting (323) 330-1020
                         FAX (323) 954-9391
                         www.rosslacycasting.com
(Babies, Celebrities, Children, Commercials, Film,
TV & Webisodes)

Ruth Conforte Casting (818) 771-7287
P.O. Box 4474
Valley Village, CA 91617
(Commercials, Film, Industrials, TV & Voice Casting)
Contact: Ruth Conforte

Samuel Warren & Associates (323) 462-1510
International Casting Services (619) 264-4135
5205 Kearny Villa Way   www.samuelwarren.com
San Diego, CA 92123
(Commercials, Film & TV)

                         (323) 465-9999
Sanford Casting   (818) 908-1800
The Casting Underground,   FAX (818) 908-4325
1641 N. Ivar Ave.   www.sanfordcasting.com
Los Angeles, CA 90028
(Commercials)

Sara Finn Casting (323) 460-7040
588 N. Larchmont Blvd.
Los Angeles, CA 90004
(Film & TV)

The Sarah Finn Company (323) 460-7040
588 N. Larchmont Blvd., First Fl.
Los Angeles, CA 90004

Schiff/Audino Casting (213) 534-3595
1201 W. Fifth St., Ste. M230
Los Angeles, CA 90017

Scott Muller Casting (310) 369-1095
10201 W. Pico Blvd., Bldg. 795
Los Angeles, CA 90035

                         (323) 468-6888
SHANE. a casting company (323) 708-1574
Silver Layne Studios   FAX (323) 468-8811
6660 Santa Monica Blvd., First Fl.
Los Angeles, CA 90038   www.shanecasting.com
(Commercials)
Contact: Zac Dixon

Shaner/Testa Casting (310) 202-1234
9336 W. Washington Ave., Bldg. J, Second Fl.
Culver City, CA 90232
(Film & TV)

Sheila Manning Casting (310) 557-9990
332 S. Beverly Dr., Ste. 101   FAX (310) 557-9998
Beverly Hills, CA 90212
(Commercials, Film & TV)

Sherman/Knight Casting (323) 655-4000

Ava Shevitt (310) 656-4600
(Commercials, Film & TV)   FAX (310) 656-4610
                         www.villagestudio.net

Shooting From The Hip Casting (818) 506-0613
Zydeco Studios, 11317 Ventura Blvd. FAX (818) 506-8858
Studio City, CA 91604
                         www.shootingfromthehipcasting.com
(Commercials, Film & TV)
Contact: Francene Selkirk-Ackerman

Alyson Silverberg (818) 560-2081

Sitowitz/Pianko Casting (310) 712-3446

[skirts] (323) 692-1800
1035 S. La Brea Ave.   FAX (323) 692-1810
Los Angeles, CA 90019   www.skirtscasting.com

Slater/Brooksbank Casting (818) 526-4470
13100 Telfair Ave., Second Fl.
Sylmar, CA 91342

                         (323) 854-1888
Sobo Casting   (310) 248-5296
8899 Beverly Blvd., Ste. 206   www.sobocasting.com
Los Angeles, CA 90048
(Commercials, Film, Podcasting, TV & Webisodes)
Contacts: Amy Sobo & Jane Sobo

                         (323) 330-1020
Spot Casting   (323) 954-0933
200 S. La Brea Ave., Second Fl.   www.spotcasting.net
Los Angeles, CA 90036
(Babies, Celebrities, Children, Commercials & TV)

                         (323) 253-0205
Pamela Starks   (323) 330-1020
(Commercials & Film)

Steven Erdek Casting (310) 770-7226
Village Studios, 725 Arizona Ave., Ste. 103
Santa Monica, CA
(Commercials, Film & TV)

Stiner/Block Casting (213) 534-3060
1201 W. Fifth St., Ste. M120
Los Angeles, CA 90017

Stordahl/Terry Casting (323) 938-0184
5225 Wilshire Blvd., Ste. 720
Los Angeles, CA 90036

StormMaker Productions, Inc. (818) 760-4111
10551 Burbank Blvd.   FAX (818) 760-4111
North Hollywood, CA 91601
                         www.stormmakerproductions.com
(Babies, Celebrities, Children, Circus/Variety Acts,
Commercials, Film, Podcasting, Real People, Reality Casting,
TV, Voice Casting & Webisodes)

Stuart Stone Casting (323) 866-1811
8899 Beverly Blvd.   www.stonecasting.tv
Los Angeles, CA 90048
(Babies, Children, Commercials, Film, Industrials, Location
Casting, Non-Union, Real People, Street Casting, Testimonials,
TV, Union & Webisodes)
Contact: Stuart Stone

Susan Bluestein Casting (323) 463-1925
(Film & TV)

Susan Edelman Casting (818) 905-6200
13273 Ventura Blvd., Ste. 210
Studio City, CA 91604

Susan Glicksman Casting (310) 305-2222

Susan Johnston Casting (323) 969-4800
P.O. Box 1514   www.susanjohnstoncasting.com
Studio City, CA 91614

Susan Tyler Casting (818) 628-1953
(Celebrities, Commercials, Film, Foreign Language Casting,
Podcasting, Reality, TV & Voice Casting)

Suzanne Goddard-Smythe Casting   (818) 733-0933
100 Universal City Plaza, Bldg. 2128, Ste. D
Los Angeles, CA 91608

                                         (310) 313-2090
Taylor Casting   (310) 600-6339
(Commercials & Real People)

Terri Taylor Casting   (323) 956-1284
5555 Melrose Ave., Lyles Bldg., Ste. 200
Los Angeles, CA 90038

Terry Berland Casting   (310) 275-0601
2329 Purdue Ave.   www.berlandcasting.com
Los Angeles, CA 90064
(Commercials)
Contacts: Terry Berland & Karmen Leech

Mark Tillman   (310) 557-2565
9434 Gregory Way
Beverly Hills, CA 90212

TLC Booth, Inc.   (323) 464-2788
6521 Homewood Ave.   www.tlccasting.biz
Hollywood, CA 90028
(Commercials)
Contacts: Loree Booth, Kathy Carr, Pamela Scudder &
Leland Williams

                                         (323) 931-3263
Tolley Casparis Casting, Inc.   (310) 248-5296
8899 Beverly Blvd.   www.tolleycasting.com
Los Angeles, CA 90048
(Babies, Children, Circus/Variety Acts, Commercials, Film,
Foreign Language Casting, Podcasting, Real People, TV, Voice
Casting & Webisodes)

Tondino/Warren Casting   (818) 843-1902
178 S. Victory Blvd., Ste. 205   FAX (818) 843-1897
Burbank, CA 91502

Susan Turner   (818) 262-8117
13425 Ventura Blvd., Ste. 200
Sherman Oaks, CA 91423
                           www.susanturnercasting.com
(Celebrities, Children, Commercials, Film, Industrials,
Podcasting, Real People, Reality, TV, Voice Casting &
Webisodes)

Ulrich/Dawson/Kritzer Casting   (818) 623-1818
4705 Laurel Canyon Blvd., Ste. 301
North Hollywood, CA 91607
(Commercials, Film & TV)

Valko/Miller Casting   (818) 953-7743
3500 W. Olive Ave., Ste. 930
Burbank, CA 91505
(Film & TV)

Vicki Goggin & Associates Casting (818) 817-4330
13425 Ventura Blvd., Second Fl.   www.vickigoggin.com
Sherman Oaks, CA 91423
(Commercials, TV & Webisodes)

Vicki Rosenberg & Associates   (310) 369-3448
10201 W. Pico Blvd., Bldg. 80, Ste. 19
Los Angeles, CA 90035
(Film & TV)

Vickie Thomas Casting   (310) 274-5932
9021 Melrose Ave., Ste. 200B
West Hollywood, CA 90069

The Voicecaster   (818) 841-5300
1832 W. Burbank Blvd.   FAX (818) 841-2085
Burbank, CA 91506   www.voicecaster.com
(Commercials)
Contacts: Gary Giambo, Huck Liggett & Martha Mayakis

Voices Voicecasting   (818) 716-8865
11340 Moorpark St.   www.voicesvoicecasting.com
North Hollywood, CA 91602
(Commercials)
Contact: Mary Lynn Wissner

                                         (818) 652-3048
The Walkie Talkies   (818) 633-5377
P.O. Box 3233   www.trustthebeeps.com
Granada Hills, CA 91394
(ADR Group Voice Casting)
Contacts: Joey Naber & Paula Price

Weber & Associates Casting   (310) 449-3685
10250 Constellation Blvd., Ste. 2060
Los Angeles, CA 90067
(Film & TV)

                                         (310) 314-1332
Alyssa Weisberg   (310) 392-3904
1666 Euclid St.
Santa Monica, CA 90404

Wendy O'Brien Casting   (310) 473-0400
2233 Barry Ave., Second Fl.
Los Angeles, CA 90064

                                         (310) 248-5296
Anissa Williams   (323) 550-1205
c/o Castaway Studios, 8899 Beverly Blvd.
Beverly Hills, CA 90048
(Commercials)

Kim Williams   (323) 284-6416
5225 Wilshire Blvd., Ste. 526
Los Angeles, CA 90036

G. Charles Wright   (818) 977-5537
411 N. Hollywood Way., Bldg. 29-R
Burbank, CA 91505

Yumi Takada Casting   (424) 247-8522
5455 Wilshire Blvd., Ste. 800
Los Angeles, CA 90036
(Commercials, Film & TV)

Debra Zane   (323) 939-5200
5225 Wilshire Blvd., Ste. 536
Los Angeles, CA 90036
(Film & TV)

Zane/Pillsbury Casting   (323) 769-9191
585 N. Larchmont Blvd.
Los Angeles, CA 90004
(Film & TV)

Gary Zuckerbrod   (818) 954-6334
6735 Forrest Lawn Dr., Fourth Fl.
Los Angeles, CA 90068

1 Space (323) 962-1455
6430 Sunset Blvd., Ste. 425　　FAX (323) 466-4166
Hollywood, CA 90028　　www.primecasting.com

1020 Studios (323) 874-8764
1020 N. Sycamore Ave.　　FAX (323) 874-6330
Los Angeles, CA 90038　　www.1020studios.com

200 South, Inc. (323) 330-1020
200 S. La Brea Ave., Second Fl.　　FAX (323) 954-0933
Los Angeles, CA 90036　　www.200south.com

(310) 775-6600
310 Casting Studios (310) 775-6601
2329 Purdue Ave.　　FAX (310) 478-2100
Los Angeles, CA 90064　www.310castingstudios.com

5th Street Studios (310) 458-1100
1216 Fifth St.　　FAX (310) 458-7878
Santa Monica, CA 90401

(323) 462-1755
Alley Kat Studio (323) 462-4546
1455 N. Gordon St.　　FAX (323) 962-3693
Hollywood, CA 90028　　www.alleykatstudios.com

AuditionTape, Inc. (310) 289-4962
8556 Rugby Dr.　　www.audition-tape.com
West Hollywood, CA 90069

Castaway Studios (310) 248-5296
8899 Beverly Blvd., Lobby　　FAX (310) 248-5297
Los Angeles, CA 90048　　www.castawaystudios.com

Casting Cafe (310) 274-9909
668 N. La Peer Dr.　　FAX (310) 659-7733
West Hollywood, CA 90069　　www.castingcafe.us

The Casting Lounge (323) 692-1800
1035 S. La Brea Ave.　　FAX (323) 692-1810
Los Angeles, CA 90019　　www.thecastinglounge.com

The Casting Underground (323) 465-9999
1641 N. Ivar Ave.　　FAX (323) 465-6290
Hollywood, CA 90028

Complete Actors Place/CAP (818) 990-2001
13752 Ventura Blvd.　　completeactorsplace.com
Sherman Oaks, CA 91423

Eastside Studios (323) 660-7874
4216 Fountain Ave.　　FAX (323) 660-7875
Los Angeles, CA 90029　　www.eastsidestudiosla.com

Exclusive Casting Studios (323) 969-8200
7700 W. Sunset Blvd., Second Fl.　　FAX (323) 696-0101
Los Angeles, CA 90046
　　www.exclusivecastingstudios.com

Hollywood Production Center (818) 480-3100
121 W. Lexington Dr.　　FAX (818) 480-3199
Glendale, CA 91203　　www.hollywoodpc.com

Kalmenson & Kalmenson
Voice Casting (818) 377-3600
P.O. Box 260207　　FAX (818) 377-3636
Encino, CA 91426　　www.kalmenson.com

LoudMouth Studios (818) 980-9803
11340 Moorpark St.　　FAX (818) 980-2838
Studio City, CA 91602　　www.loudmouthstudios.com
Contacts: Beth Holmes, Jim Holmes & Monica Lee-Eisenbeis

MetaTheatre on Melrose (323) 852-6963
7801 Melrose Ave., Ste. 3　　FAX (323) 852-6963
Los Angeles, CA 90046　　www.anthonymeindl.com

MysticArt Pictures (818) 563-4121
1918 Magnolia Blvd., Ste. 206　　FAX (818) 563-4318
Burbank, CA 91506　　www.mysticartpictures.com
Contacts: Tim Safford & Katy Wallin

Ocean Park Casting (310) 581-3000
2701 Ocean Park Blvd., Ste. 250　　FAX (310) 450-3149
Santa Monica, CA 90405　　www.oceanparkcasting.com

On Your Mark Studios (818) 817-4300
13425 Ventura Blvd., Ste. 200　　FAX (818) 728-6785
Sherman Oaks, CA 91423
　　www.onyourmarkstudios.com

(213) 384-2404
Park View Casting Studios (917) 575-5730
2404 Wilshire Blvd., Ste. 12F　　FAX (213) 384-2408
Los Angeles, CA 90057
　　www.parkviewcastingstudios.com

Prestige Casting (310) 331-8734
6900 Santa Monica Blvd.
Los Angeles, CA 90038

Rodeo Studios (323) 969-9125
7013 Willoughby Ave.　　www.rodeostudios.com
Hollywood, CA 90038

Samuel Warren & Associates (323) 462-1510
International Casting Services (619) 264-4135
5205 Kearny Villa Way　　www.samuelwarren.com
San Diego, CA 92123

San Luis Obispo County
Location & Casting (805) 547-9000
128 La Colina　　FAX (805) 969-9595
Pismo Beach, CA 93449

Screenland Studios (818) 508-2288
10501 Burbank Blvd.　　www.screenlandstudios.com
North Hollywood, CA 91601
Contacts: Karen Apostolina & Steve Apostolina

Sessions West Studios, Inc. (310) 450-9228
2601 Ocean Park Blvd., Ste. 120　　FAX (310) 450-7794
Santa Monica, CA 90405
　　www.sessionsweststudios.com

Silver Layne Studios (323) 468-6888
6660 Santa Monica Blvd., First Fl.　　FAX (323) 468-8811
Los Angeles, CA 90038

(818) 240-1893
Solar Studios (310) 489-7801
1601 S. Central Ave.　　FAX (818) 240-4187
Glendale, CA 91204　　www.solarstudios.com

StormMaker Productions, Inc. (818) 760-4111
10551 Burbank Blvd.　　FAX (818) 760-4111
North Hollywood, CA 91601
　　www.stormmakerproductions.com

studio/stage (323) 463-3900
520 N. Western Ave.　　FAX (323) 463-3933
Los Angeles, CA 90004　　www.studio-stage.com

Talent Network (310) 570-6275
P.O. Box 642546
Los Angeles, CA 90064
　　www.talentnetworkusa.biz/studio.html

Village Studio (310) 656-4600
725 Arizona Ave., Ste. 103　　FAX (310) 656-4610
Santa Monica, CA 90401

Eddie Baytos	(818) 985-4533 (818) 304-4123 www.eddiebaytos.com
Kim Blank	(323) 935-3341 (323) 547-2970 FAX (323) 937-4975
bloc, Inc. 6100 Wilshire Blvd., Ste. 1100 Los Angeles, CA 90048 (Choreography/Dance Agency)	(323) 954-7730 FAX (323) 954-7731 www.blocagency.com
Bobby Ball Talent Agency	(818) 506-8188 FAX (818) 506-8588
Donna Boise	(562) 861-9227 FAX (562) 861-9227
Jordi Caballero	(310) 562-9340 www.latinchoreography.com
Carol Cetrone	(323) 669-8619 (213) 483-3915 www.carolcetrone.com
Clear Talent Group/CTG 10950 Ventura Blvd. Studio City, CA 91604 (Dance)	(818) 509-0121 (818) 509-0207 FAX (818) 509-7729 www.cleartalentgroup.com
DDO Artists Agency 6725 Sunset Blvd., Ste. 230 Los Angeles, CA 90028 (Reps for Choreographers)	(323) 462-8000 FAX (323) 462-0100 www.ddoagency.com
Joanne DiVito	(818) 760-3160 FAX (818) 760-3160
Entertainment Plus Productions, Inc./Doug Johnson	(323) 969-1756 (310) 770-4582 FAX (310) 287-0595 www.eplusproductions.com
Myrna Gawryn	(310) 837-9388

JoAnn F. Jansen	(323) 851-8012 FAX (323) 851-6317 www.joannjansen.com
Kazarian/Spencer/ Ruskin & Associates, Inc. 11969 Ventura Blvd., Third Fl. Studio City, CA 91604 (Reps for Choreographers)	(818) 769-9111 FAX (818) 769-9840 www.ksrtalent.com
La Premiere Productions/ Neisha Folkes 123 S. Figueroa St., Ste. 535 Los Angeles, CA 90012	(213) 999-1223 (818) 615-0400 www.neishafolkes.com
Ted Lin	(310) 440-1471 (310) 869-7361
McDonald/Selznick Associates 953 N. Cole Ave. Hollywood, CA 90038 (Reps for Choreographers)	(323) 957-6680 FAX (323) 957-6688 www.msaagency.com
Mime and Movement by Lorin Eric Salm (Mime and Movement Coach)	(310) 494-6463 (818) 300-7473 www.movement-coach.com
More Zap Productions	(310) 749-5700 www.morezap.com
Travis Payne	(323) 665-6680 (323) 957-6680 FAX (323) 665-6681 www.travispayne.net
Karen Russell-Budge	(310) 281-1956
Sebastien Stella	(323) 404-1328 www.stellartinc.net
Fred Tallaksen	(818) 753-9887 (818) 209-9887 FAX (818) 753-9810 www.fredtallaksen.com
Mic Thompson	(323) 240-2828 (800) 485-4147 www.micsmatch.com

1 On 1 Computing Technologies   (818) 992-0584 / (818) 254-5448
5824 Kentland Ave.   www.1on1comp.com
Woodland Hills, CA 91367
(Consulting, Hardware, Networking and Troubleshooting
for Mac and PC, Networks & Software, Systems Design &
Troubleshooting)

318, Inc.   (310) 581-9500
830 Colorado Ave.   FAX (310) 581-9515
Santa Monica, CA 90401   www.318.com

Acacia Systems   (562) 437-7690
FAX (562) 690-6520
www.acaciasystems.com
(Consulting, Multimedia Training & Networking)

Action Computer Service   (310) 552-2722 / (213) 703-6218
FAX (310) 286-7850
(Consulting, Networking and Troubleshooting for
Macintosh and PCs)

Agenda Media Services, Inc.   (818) 990-5343
5445 Balboa Blvd., Ste. 112   FAX (818) 990-5344
Encino, CA 91316   www.agenda.net
(Consulting, Networking & Software)

Alchemy Solutions   (310) 736-1633
www.macalchemist.com

Alpha Lex Systems Integration   (818) 407-9200
FAX (818) 337-2061
www.alphalex.com
(Consulting, Multimedia Software & Systems Design)

**Chaparral Software &
Consulting Services**   (877) 203-3109
5737 Kanan, Ste. 589   www.chapsoft.com
Agoura Hills, CA 91301
(Database and Network Consultants for Macintosh)

Christian Boyce and Associates   (310) 452-3720
3435 Ocean Park Blvd., Ste. 107   FAX (310) 392-4989
Santa Monica, CA 90405   www.christianboyce.com
(Macintosh Consultants)

Computech Support Services   (310) 237-6065
3272 Motor Ave., Ste. I   FAX (310) 845-9536
Los Angeles, CA 90035   www.computechsos.com

CrownPeak   (310) 841-5920
5880 W. Jefferson Blvd., Ste. G   www.crownpeak.com
Los Angeles, CA 90016

DriveSavers Data Recovery   (800) 440-1904
(Data Recovery)   www.drivesavers.com

egad, inc.   (818) 558-6968
434 N. Niagara   FAX (818) 954-6317
Burbank, CA 91502   www.egad.com
(Media Vault Management Systems)
Contact: Peter Zaharkiv

Empress Media, Inc.   (888) 683-6773
10777 Sherman Way   FAX (818) 255-3398
Sun Valley, CA 91352   www.empressdigital.com
(Commercial Production, Contract Software, Consulting,
Database Design, Media Vault Management Systems, Systems
Design, Television Commercial Information Database,
Training & Translation Software)

**EP's Global &
Movie Magic Applications**   (818) 955-6299
2835 N. Naomi St.   FAX (818) 845-6507
Burbank, CA 91504
(Accounting, Budgeting and Scheduling Software)

**EP's Movie Magic & Vista Accounting
Applications**   (818) 955-6296
2835 N. Naomi St.   FAX (818) 450-0255
Burbank, CA 91504   www.entertainmentpartners.com
(Budgeting, Scheduling and Accounting Software)

Final Draft, Inc.   (818) 995-8995 / (800) 231-4055
26707 W. Agoura Rd., Ste. 205   FAX (818) 995-4422
Calabasas, CA 91302   www.finaldraft.com
(Screenwriting Software)

FMS Techniques, Inc.   (323) 965-7300
13538 Cantara St.   FAX (818) 997-6541
Van Nuys, CA 91402   www.techniques.com
(Macintosh Consultants)

Go Go Techs, LLC   (800) 314-9771
2633 Lincoln Blvd., Ste. 155
Santa Monica, CA 90405

Stephen Goepel   (818) 781-7025 / (818) 404-7570
(Multimedia Consultant)

iCare4Macs   (818) 414-4051 / (310) 476-5243
17216 Saticoy St., Ste. 310   FAX (818) 301-1961
Van Nuys, CA 91406   www.icare4macs.com
(Macintosh Consulting)

ICS, Inc.   (818) 609-7648 / (800) 684-5009
6038 Tampa Ave.   FAX (818) 705-4933
Tarzana, CA 91356   www.click2tech.com
(Network Support, Networking & PC)

Illuvatar, LLC   (310) 753-1774 / (714) 965-5918
P.O. Box 8506   FAX (714) 969-5918
Fountain Valley, CA 92728   www.illuvatar.com
(Consulting, Mac, Network Support, PC, Systems Design &
Troubleshooting)

imagistic   (818) 706-9100
4333 Park Terrace Dr., Ste. 120   FAX (818) 706-9103
Westlake Village, CA 91361   www.imagistic.com

InEntertainment, Inc.   (323) 456-1580
6404 Wilshire Blvd., Ste. 960   FAX (323) 782-4900
Los Angeles, CA 90048   www.inentertainment.com
(Software)

IT4LA, Inc.   (323) 936-4900
8033 Sunset Blvd., Ste. 228   FAX (323) 937-2445
Los Angeles, CA 90046   www.it4la.com
(Hardware, Networks & Software)

JDK Consulting   (818) 705-8050
16752 Addison St.   FAX (818) 474-7012
Encino, CA 91436   www.jdkconsulting.com
(IT Consulting)

Jungle Software   (818) 456-0719 / (877) 497-3301
1792 Erringer Rd.   FAX (818) 459-9093
Simi Valley, CA 93065   www.junglesoftware.com
(Databases & Production Software for Independent
Filmmakers)

LAComputerBuddy   (818) 530-1655
www.lacomputerbuddy.com
(Accounting Software, Consulting, Mac, Network Support,
Networking, PC & Troubleshooting)

LJK Consult, LLC   (323) 896-7541
FAX (323) 655-0549
www.ljkconsult.com

The Mac Network
(866) 622-7247
(626) 583-9122
FAX (866) 309-5721
573 S. Lake Ave., Ste. 7
Pasadena, CA 91101
www.themacnetwork.com

Mac Talk
(818) 225-9327
22110 Ventura Blvd.
www.mactalk.com
Woodland Hills, CA 91364

Mac Talk
(805) 804-3009
228 E. Thompson Blvd.
www.mactalk.com
Ventura, CA 93003
(Consulting, Hardware, Networks and Software for Macintosh)

Mac Universe
(818) 876-2589
8055 Chastain Ave.
www.macorpcrepair.com
Reseda, CA 91335
(Macintosh Consultants)

MacEnthusiasts Inc.
(800) 948-6902
(800) 615-0492
FAX (310) 626-8472
10600 W. Pico Blvd.
Los Angeles, CA 90064
www.macenthusiasts.com

MacFAQulty
(310) 435-9972
137 N. Larchmont, Ste. 137
FAX (419) 715-1159
Los Angeles, CA 90004
www.macfaqulty.com
(Macintosh Consultants)

MacMan
(323) 215-5668
835 Centennial St.
www.macmannow.com
Los Angeles, CA 90012
(Consulting, Mac, Network Support, Networking, Systems Design, Training & Troubleshooting)

Mann Consulting
(415) 546-6266
(888) 746-8227
FAX (415) 546-4099
(Consulting, Hardware, Networks and Software for Macintosh and PCs)
www.mann.com

Media Services
(310) 440-9600
(800) 333-7518
FAX (310) 472-9979
500 S. Sepulveda Blvd., Fourth Fl.
Los Angeles, CA 90049
www.media-services.com
(Accounting and AICP/AICE Actualizing/Bidding Software)

Mocha Media, Inc.
(323) 462-5765
(866) 672-3813
FAX (323) 462-5766
1523 Gordon St., Ste. 5
Los Angeles, CA 90028
www.mochamedia.com

Moviola Digital Education Center
(323) 467-1116
(323) 467-3107
FAX (323) 466-2522
1135 N. Mansfield Ave.
Los Angeles, CA 90038
www.moviola.com/edu
(Education & Training)

New Agenda Inc.
(818) 355-3677
P.O. Box 251313
www.newagendainc.com
Los Angeles, CA 90025

The Personal Computer Specialists
(213) 700-4861
(949) 429-5131
www.personalcomputerspecialists.com

Production Suppliers
(818) 340-0545
(818) 439-8066
FAX (818) 340-3355
www.prosuppliers.com
(Commercial Production, Consulting, Hardware, Mac, PC, Systems Design & Troubleshooting)

Productivity Consulting
(626) 794-3637
2450 N. Lake Ave., Ste. B228
FAX (626) 794-3886
Altadena, CA 91001
www.proconsult.com
(Consulting, Database Design, Mac, Multimedia Training, Network Support, Networking, PC, Scheduling Software, Systems Design, Training & Troubleshooting)

ScheduALL
(310) 242-5506
(310) 242-5507
(Consulting & Scheduling Software)
FAX (310) 242-5508
www.scheduall.com

Showbiz Software
(310) 471-9330
(800) 333-7518
500 S. Sepulveda Blvd., Fourth Fl.
FAX (310) 472-9979
Los Angeles, CA 90049
www.showbizsoftware.com
(Accounting and AICP/AICE Actualizing/Bidding Software)

Ten Over Eight
(800) 995-2652
16350 Ventura Blvd., Ste. D150
www.10over8.com
Encino, CA 91436
(Consulting, Hardware and Software for MacIntosh and PCs)

UnderlineMedia
(303) 719-2623
www.underlinemedia.com

V.2 Consulting, Inc.
(818) 528-5394
(415) 989-9889
11132 Ventura Blvd., Ste. 420
FAX (415) 358-4085
Studio City, CA 91604
www.v2consulting.com
(Consulting, Database Design, Mac, Media Vault Management Systems, Network Support, Networking, Systems Design, Training & Troubleshooting)

Wide Screen Software LLC
(818) 764-3639
(Sun Tracking Software for Mac and PC) FAX (928) 441-8243
www.wide-screen.com

Wiredrive
(310) 823-8238
4216 ¾ Glencoe Ave.
www.wiredrive.com
Marina del Rey, CA 90292
(Online Reel Creation and Production Tools)

Wizard Consulting Group
(818) 706-8877
(818) 483-4686
4039 Liberty Canyon Rd.
FAX (888) 524-5024
Agoura Hills, CA 90301
www.wizardconsultinggroup.com
(Consulting for IBM and Mac & Database Design)

The Writers' Store
(310) 441-5151
(800) 272-8927
3510 W. Magnolia Blvd.
FAX (818) 566-8644
Burbank, CA 91505
www.writersstore.com
(Budgeting and Scriptwriting Software)

Xytech Systems Corporation
(818) 303-7800
2835 N. Naomi St., Ste. 310
FAX (818) 303-7801
Burbank, CA 91504
www.xytechsystems.com
(Facility Management Software)

All States Office Machines, Inc.   (818) 755-9568 / (800) 464-1941
10712 Valley Spring Ln.   FAX (818) 755-9569
Universal City, CA 91602
www.allstatesofficemachine.com

Alliant Event Services, Inc.   (909) 622-3306 / (800) 851-5415
196 University Pkwy   FAX (909) 622-3917
Pomona, CA 91768   www.alliantevents.com
(Audience Response Systems, Copiers, Audio Visual Equipment, Desktop Computers, Digital Signage, Exhibitor Services, Interactive Kiosks, Laptops, Monitors, PC, Printers, Projectors, Webcasting & Wireless Networking)

American Surplus   (818) 993-5355
18643 Parthenia St.
Northridge, CA 91324
(Office Furniture)

Batchelor Business Machines   (818) 222-2152
5169 Douglas Fir Rd., Ste. 6   FAX (310) 278-2117
Calabasas, CA 91302   www.ibmtypewriters.com
(Typewriters)

Burtype Office Products   (818) 843-3800
2801 W. Magnolia Blvd.   FAX (818) 843-3257
Burbank, CA 91505   www.burtype.com
(Copiers, Fax Machines, Printers & Typewriters)

C.P. Four   (323) 466-8201
706 N. Cahuenga Blvd.   FAX (323) 467-2749
Hollywood, CA 90038   www.omegacinemaprops.com
(Macintosh)

Cal Business Systems & Supply   (310) 470-3435 / (818) 980-0373
1920 Pandora Ave., Ste. 7   FAX (310) 470-3557
Los Angeles, CA 90025   www.calbusiness.us
(Copiers & Fax Machines)

Computech Support Services   (310) 237-6065
3272 Motor Ave., Ste. I   FAX (310) 845-9536
Los Angeles, CA 90035   www.computechsos.com

Copier Rental, Inc.   (714) 898-7772 / (800) 655-8802
7341 Garden Grove Blvd., Ste. C   FAX (714) 898-7705
Garden Grove, CA 92841   www.rentcopiers.com
(Copiers & Fax Machines)

Copyrite Solutions Inc.   (818) 503-0015
7532 Atoll Ave.   FAX (818) 503-0543
North Hollywood, CA 91605   www.copyritesolutions.com

Ⓐ CRE - Computer & A/V Solutions   (877) 266-7725 / (888) 444-1059
5732 Buckingham Pkwy   FAX (877) 440-5252
Culver City, CA 90230   www.computerrentals.com/products/Mac/Mac_rentals_Specialist.php
(Desktop Computers, Fax Machines, Laptops, Macintosh, Monitors, PC, Plasmas, Printers & Projectors)

Dean Security Safe Co.   (818) 997-1234 / (800) 827-7534
8616 Woodman Ave.   FAX (818) 894-0280
Arleta, CA 91331   www.deansafe.com

Docusource   (562) 447-2600 / (949) 337-7117
10450 Pioneer, Ste. 1   FAX (562) 447-2614
Santa Fe Springs, CA 90670   www.docusource.com

EcoToner   (877) 326-8663
19360 Rinaldi Ave., Ste. 355   www.ecotoner.com
Porter Ranch, CA 91326
(Fax Machines & Printers)

GreenBear Technologies Computer Rentals   (888) 292-0978 / (818) 239-1740
7524 Clybourn Ave.   FAX (818) 859-1105
Los Angeles, CA 91352   www.greenbear.us
(Computers, Copiers, Desktops, Fax Machines, Laptops, Mac, Monitors, Networking, PC, Plasmas, Printers & Projectors)

Hi-Tech Computer Rental   (818) 841-0677 / (213) 387-6861
172 W. Verdugo Ave.   FAX (818) 841-0575
Burbank, CA 91502   www.htcr.net
(Desktop Computers, Fax Machines, Laptops, Macintosh, Monitors, Printers & Projectors)

Hopper's Office & Drafting Furniture   (323) 254-7362 / (800) 762-7717
2901 Fletcher Dr.   FAX (323) 254-8226
Los Angeles, CA 90065   www.draftingfurniture.com
(Office Furniture)

House of Business Machines   (818) 980-0090 / (818) 501-2255
4652 Lankershim Blvd.   FAX (818) 985-7899
North Hollywood , CA 91602   www.hbmla.com
(Copiers, Fax Machines, Printers & Typewriters)

Lasercare   (310) 202-4200 / (800) 527-3720
3375 Robertson Pl.   FAX (310) 202-4202
Los Angeles, CA 90034   www.lasercare.com
(Printers)

LCS
(310) 476-8380
(310) 740-0995
FAX (818) 789-6435
15445 Ventura Blvd., Ste. 3312
Sherman Oaks, CA 91403

LCS
(310) 476-8380
(310) 740-0995
FAX (818) 789-6435
2554 Lincoln Blvd., Ste. 421
Venice, CA 90291
(Compact Refrigerators, Copiers, Fax Machines, Microwave
Ovens, Phone Systems, Printers & Shredders)

Line 204 Inc.
(323) 960-0113
FAX (323) 960-0163
837 N. Cahuenga Blvd.
Hollywood, CA 90038
www.line204.com

Mac Talk
(805) 804-3009
www.mactalk.com
228 E. Thompson Blvd.
Ventura, CA 93003
(Macintosh)

Mac Talk
(818) 225-9327
www.mactalk.com
22110 Ventura Blvd.
Woodland Hills, CA 91364

MacEnthusiasts Inc.
(800) 615-0492
FAX (310) 626-8472
10600 W. Pico Blvd.
Los Angeles, CA 90064 www.macenthusiasts.com
(Desktop Computers, Fax Machines, Laptops, Mac Rental,
Macintosh, Monitors, PC, Printers, Projectors & Televisions)

Marathon Services, Inc.
(818) 280-0510
(800) 325-3130
FAX (818) 280-0191
9259 Eton Ave.
Chatsworth, CA 91311 www.marathonservice.com
(Copiers, Desktop Computers, Fax Machines, Laptops,
Macintosh, Monitors, PC, Printers & Projectors)

NTS Office Machines
(818) 905-9446
FAX (818) 905-8725
4854 Van Nuys Blvd.
Sherman Oaks, CA 91403 www.ntsofficemachines.com
(Copiers, Fax Machines & Printers)

Office Furniture LA
(323) 750-6206
FAX (323) 750-6208
7625 Crenshaw Blvd.
Los Angeles, CA 90043 www.laofficefurniture.com
(Office Furniture)

Perfect Copy Products
(818) 997-9120
FAX (818) 901-9320
5914 Kester Ave.
Van Nuys, CA 91411 www.perfectcopyproducts.com
(Copiers & Fax Machines)

Quality Business Machines
(310) 330-4733
(800) 927-1601
FAX (310) 674-6145
233 E. Hillcrest Blvd.
Inglewood, CA 90301
www.qbminc.com
(Copiers & Fax Machines)

Quixote Studios
(323) 461-1408
FAX (323) 461-5517
1000 N. Cahuenga Blvd.
Los Angeles, CA 90038
www.quixote.com

R.C. Gear
(323) 465-3900
(800) 714-8099
FAX (323) 465-3600
6100 Melrose Ave.
Los Angeles, CA 90038
www.rc-gear.com
(PC Laptops and Monitors)

Rack Innovations, Inc.
(818) 847-0200
(800) 557-8861
FAX (888) 262-1726
107 W. Valencia Ave.
Burbank, CA 91502
www.marketec.com
(A/V Furniture)

RenderCore
(866) 627-3149
FAX (213) 623-3149
www.rendercore.com

Rush Computer Rentals
(800) 343-7368
(818) 781-2221
FAX (818) 374-7350
6060 Sepulveda Blvd.
Van Nuys, CA 91411 www.rushcomputer.com
(Copiers, Desktop Computers, Fax Machines, Laptops,
Macintosh, Monitors, PC, Printers & Projectors)

Santa Monica Lock & Safe Co., Inc.
(310) 450-5101
(800) 696-9499
FAX (310) 450-9563
2208 Pico Blvd.
Santa Monica, CA 90405
(Safes & Vaults)

SmartSource Rentals
(310) 237-5324
FAX (310) 237-5327
10391 Jefferson Blvd.
Los Angeles, CA 90232 www.smartsourcerentals.com
(Copiers, Desktop Computers, Fax Machines, Laptops,
Macintosh, Monitors, PC, Printers, Projectors & Televisions)

SoCal Xerox
(800) 736-7979
www.socal-office.com
15821 Ventura Blvd.
Encino, CA 91436
(Copiers, Fax Machines, Printers & Scanners)

TMG Copier Rentals
(310) 326-5100
(800) 267-9261
FAX (310) 326-4976
25018 Broadwell Ave.
Harbor City, CA 90710 www.copierrental.com
(Copiers, Desktop Computers, Fax Machines, Monitors, PC,
Printers & Projectors)

Wexler Video
(818) 846-9381
(800) 939-5371
FAX (818) 846-9399
1111 S. Victory Blvd.
Burbank, CA 91502 www.wexlervideo.com

Advertising Age (323) 522-6256
4611 La Mirada Ave. www.adage.com
Los Angeles, CA 90048

The Alternative Pick (212) 675-4176
P.O. Box 335 www.altpick.com
New York, NY 10156
(Design, Illustration & Photography for Film,
Print and Television)

Animation Magazine (818) 883-2884
26500 W. Agoura Rd., Ste. 102-651 FAX (818) 883-3773
Calabasas, CA 91302 www.animationmagazine.net

Backstage/West (323) 525-2356
5700 Wilshire Blvd., Ste. 500 www.backstage.com
Los Angeles, CA 90036

Billboard (323) 525-2237
5055 Wilshire Blvd., Ste. 700 www.billboard.com
Los Angeles, CA 90036

Breakdown Services, Ltd./
Commercial Express (310) 276-9166
2140 Cotner Ave., Third Fl. FAX (310) 276-8829
Los Angeles, CA 90025 www.breakdownservices.com
(Information Service for Talent Agents)

(805) 383-0800
Cinefex (951) 781-1917
79 Daily Dr., Ste. 309 FAX (805) 383-0803
Camarillo, CA 93010 www.cinefex.com
(Visual Effects Publication)

(626) 797-7699
Debbies Book (626) 798-7968
www.debbiesbook.com
(Advertising, Commercial Production, Film Production, Music
Video Production, Photography, Special Events, Television
Production & Video Production)

DGA Directory of Members (310) 289-2082
FAX (310) 289-5384
www.dga.org

DGA Quarterly (310) 289-5333
7920 Sunset Blvd. www.dga.org
Los Angeles, CA 90046

Digital Content Producer (913) 967-1740
www.digitalcontentproducer.com

Emmy (ATAS Magazine) (818) 754-2800
5220 Lankershim Blvd. FAX (818) 761-2827
North Hollywood, CA 91601 www.emmys.tv

(949) 362-0727
Encore (949) 280-7695
25171 La Jolla Way, Ste. A www.encoredirectory.com
Laguna Niguel, CA 92677
(Directory for Orange County and San Diego)

Entertainment Partners (818) 955-6296
2835 N. Naomi St. FAX (818) 450-0255
Burbank, CA 91504 www.entertainmentpartners.com
(Paymaster Labor Guide)

(310) 277-3001
'Extra' Work For Brain Surgeons (310) 277-1007
c/o Hollywood OS FAX (818) 333-2280
3108 West Magnolia Blvd. www.hollywoodos.com
Burbank, CA 91505
(Extras Casting and Talent Directory)

International Cinematographers
Guild (IA Local 600) (323) 876-0160
7755 Sunset Blvd. FAX (323) 876-6383
Los Angeles, CA 90046 www.cameraguild.com

(310) 277-3001
Kids' Acting for Brain Surgeons (310) 277-1007
3108 W. Magnolia Blvd. FAX (818) 333-2280
Burbank, CA 91505 www.hollywoodos.com

The Knowledge (011) 44 20 7549 2532
WBI Media & Entertainment, 6-14 Underwood St.
London N1 7JQ United Kingdom
www.theknowledgeonline.com

LA 411 (800) 357-4745
5900 Wilshire Blvd., 31st Fl. www.la411.com
Los Angeles, CA 90036
(Commercial, Film, Music Video, Television and Video
Production for Southern California)

The Mercury Production Report (855) 372-8792
www.themercuryreport.com
(Pre-Production & Development Listings)

The Musicians Atlas (973) 767-1800
www.musiciansatlas.com

(800) 357-4745
New York 411 (646) 746-6891
360 Park Ave. South, 10th Fl. FAX (646) 746-6894
New York, NY 10010 www.newyork411.com
(Commercial, Film, Music Video, Television and Video
Production for NY, NJ and CT)

P3-Production Update Magazine (323) 315-9477
c/o Sunset Gower Studios FAX (323) 297-6661
1438 N. Gower St. www.p3update.com
Hollywood, CA 90026

Players Directory (310) 247-3058
2210 W. Olive Ave. FAX (310) 601-4445
Burbank, CA 91506 www.playersdirectory.com
(Casting)

Pollstar (559) 271-7900
4697 W. Jacquelyn Ave. FAX (559) 271-7979
Fresno, CA 93722 www.pollstar.com
(Music Industry)

Production Reference Services (310) 275-8002
2140 Cotner Ave., Third Fl. www.prodrefservice.com
Los Angeles, CA 90025
(Advertising, Film Production, Marketing, Media, Multimedia
Production & Television Production)

(888) 215-5506
Production Weekly (888) 221-1161
www.productionweekly.com

The Reel Directory (415) 531-9760
P.O. Box 1910 www.reeldirectory.com
Boyes Hot Springs, CA 95416
(Advertising, Casting, Commercial Production, Design, Film
Production, Guild and Union Contracts, Illustration, Media,
Multimedia Production, Music Industry, Music Video Production,
Payroll Production Guide, Photography, Talent, Television
Production & Video Production)

(604) 451-7335
Reel West Productions, Inc. (888) 291-7335
5512 Hastings St. www.reelwest.com
Burnaby, BC V5B 1R3 Canada
(Film, Multimedia Production and Video)

Shoot Commercial (323) 960-8035
Production Directory (818) 884-2440
650 N. Bronson Ave., Ste. B140 FAX (323) 960-8036
Los Angeles, CA 90004

Shoot Magazine
(323) 960-8035
650 N. Bronson Ave., Ste. B140
FAX (323) 960-8036
Los Angeles, CA 90004
www.shootonline.com

Showbiz Labor Guide
(310) 471-9330
500 S. Sepulveda Blvd.
www.showbizsoftware.com
Los Angeles, CA 90049
(Guild and Union Contracts)

Variety, Inc.
(323) 617-9100
5900 Wilshire Blvd., 31st Fl.
www.variety.com
Los Angeles, CA 90036

(530) 891-8410
Videomaker Magazine
(800) 284-3226
1350 E. York St.
FAX (530) 891-8443
Chico, CA 95926
www.videomaker.com

Wisconsin Production Guide
(414) 312-4230
www.badgerguide.com

(323) 856-0008
Workbook
(800) 547-2688
6762 Lexington Ave.
FAX (323) 856-4368
Los Angeles, CA 90038
www.workbook.com
(Advertising, Design, Illustration & Photography)

Written By, The Magazine of the
Writers Guild of America, West
(323) 782-4522
7000 W. Third St.
FAX (323) 782-4802
Los Angeles, CA 90048
www.wga.org

Entertainment Attorneys

Blake & Wang P.A.
(310) 295-1198
1801 Century Park East, 24th Fl.
FAX (310) 943-2363
Los Angeles, CA 90067
www.blakewang.com

Leon Gladstone/Berger Kahn
Entertainment Division
(310) 821-9000
4551 Glencoe Ave., Ste. 300
www.bergerkahn.com
Marina del Rey, CA 90292

Keene Law Office
(310) 450-1745
9701 Wilshire Blvd., Ste. 1000
Beverly Hills, CA 90212

(310) 247-2790
Law Offices of Greg S. Bernstein
(310) 247-2799
9601 Wilshire Blvd., Ste. 240
FAX (310) 247-2791
Beverly Hills, CA 90210
www.thefilmlaw.com

Law Offices of Mark Litwak
(310) 859-9595
433 N. Camden Dr., Ste. 1010
FAX (310) 859-0806
Beverly Hills, CA 90210
www.marklitwak.com

Macfarlane Law
(310) 280-9445
3780 Selby Ave.
FAX (310) 280-0176
Los Angeles, CA 90034
www.macfarlane-law.com

Marc Moses Law
(310) 940-4557
445 S. Figueroa St., Ste. 2700
FAX (310) 843-9960
Los Angeles, CA 90071

Nathalie Hoffman & Assocs.
(310) 448-8885
(International Business Transactions)

Owen Sloane/Berger Kahn
Entertainment Division
(310) 821-9000
4551 Glencoe Ave., Ste. 300
www.bergerkahn.com
Marina del Rey, CA 90292

Zuber & Taillieu, LLP
(213) 516-5620
777 S. Figueroa St., 37th Fl.
FAX (213) 516-5621
Los Angeles, CA 90017
www.zuberlaw.com

AAA Urban Casting (661) 255-5097
(310) 967-9954
P.O. Box 800126 www.aaaurbancasting.com
Valencia, CA 91380
(Large Crowds, TV Audiences, Union & Non-Union)
Contacts: Alan Armani, Ursula Presley & Angel Princess

Advanced Casting & Talent/
Zach Schary (323) 645-2327
FAX (323) 395-5510

Akimas Casting (805) 705-4110
(805) 705-8179
P.O. Box 650 www.akimascasting.com
Santa Barbara, CA 93116

Alice Ellis Casting (310) 314-1488
(Large Crowds) FAX (310) 314-2649
www.elliscasting.com

Atmosphere Casting (888) 858-7090
2528 12th Ave. FAX (323) 316-9611
Los Angeles, CA 90018
(Large Crowds)

Background Artists (888) 442-2867
12021 Wilshire Blvd., Ste. 632 FAX (888) 442-2867
Los Angeles, CA 90025 www.backgroundartists.tv

Bill Dance Casting (818) 754-6639
4605 Lankershim Blvd., Ste. 110 FAX (818) 754-6643
North Hollywood, CA 91602 www.billdancecasting.com

Bump It Casting/Balyndah Bumpus (213) 700-5139
5482 Wilshire Blvd., Ste. 363 FAX (310) 397-8905
Los Angeles, CA 90036
(Large Crowds, Music Video Models & TV Audiences)

Burbank Casting/Michelle Gabriel (818) 559-2446
P.O. Box 7106 FAX (818) 480-4314
Burbank, CA 91510 www.burbankcasting.com

Caravan West Productions (661) 268-8300
35660 Jayhawker Rd. FAX (661) 268-8301
Agua Dulce, CA 91390 www.caravanwest.com

Carol Grant Casting (323) 390-9422
www.carolgrantcasting.com

The Casting Couch, Inc./
Sande Alessi (818) 201-0555
13731 Ventura Blvd. www.sandealessicasting.com
Sherman Oaks, CA 91423

Ⓐ Central Casting (818) 562-2700
220 S. Flower St. FAX (818) 562-2786
Burbank, CA 91502 www.centralcasting.org

Christal Blue Casting (213) 804-4304
www.christalblue.com

Combat Casting (818) 618-2527
(310) 686-2718
FAX (818) 509-9581
www.combatcasting.com

Creative Extras Casting (310) 391-9041
(310) 913-1310
2461 Santa Monica Blvd., Ste. 501 FAX (310) 391-9043
Santa Monica, CA 90404
www.creativeextrascasting.com

Crowd In A Box (877) 927-6939
(416) 275-0422
(Inflatable Extras) www.crowdinabox.com

Debbie Sheridan Casting (800) 820-5305
13547 Ventura Blvd., Ste. 311 FAX (800) 820-5305
Sherman Oaks, CA 91423 www.dsctalent.com
(Large Crowds & TV Audiences)

Deedra Ricketts Casting (323) 807-5825
www.deedeecasting.com

Dixie Webster-Davis Casting, Inc. (818) 281-6282
4924 Balboa Blvd., Ste. 432   www.dixiecasting.com
Encino, CA 91316
Contacts: Tammy Smith & Dixie Webster-Davis

Extra Extra Casting, Inc. (310) 552-1888
FAX (310) 728-6574
www.extraextracastings.com

Gonzo Bros. (310) 828-4989
www.gonzobrothers.com
(Cardboard Crowds & Inflatable Figures)

Headquarters Casting (310) 556-9001
3108 W. Magnolia Blvd. FAX (310) 861-5988
Burbank, CA 91505   www.headquarterscasting.com

(310) 277-3001
Hollywood OS (310) 277-1007
3108 West Magnolia Blvd. FAX (818) 333-2280
Burbank, CA 91505   www.hollywoodos.com

Ⓐ Idell James Casting (310) 230-9986
FAX (310) 230-8233

(818) 285-5462
Jeff Olan Casting, Inc. (818) 377-4475
14044 Ventura Blvd., Ste. 209 FAX (818) 285-5470
Sherman Oaks, CA 91423   www.jeffolancasting.com

L.A. Casting Group, Inc. (213) 537-6083
8335 W. Sunset Blvd., Ste. 332   www.lacgroup.com
Los Angeles, CA 90069

Magic Casting (805) 688-3702
1660 Cougar Ridge Rd.   magiccasting.mysite.com
Buellton, CA 93427
Contact: Hayley Kantor

(323) 962-0377
Prime Casting & Payroll (323) 962-1455
6430 Sunset Blvd., Ste. 425 FAX (323) 872-5050
Hollywood, CA 90028   www.primecasting.com
(Large Crowds, Stand-Ins & TV Audiences)

Star Casting/Cheryl Faye (661) 510-3466
FAX (661) 254-2853
www.cherylfaye.webs.com

Ugly Models & Unique Characters (818) 201-0466
13731 Ventura Blvd.
Sherman Oaks, CA 91423
(Commercials)

Finance

AFEX - Associated (818) 386-2702
Foreign Exchange, Inc. (888) 307-2339
16133 Ventura Blvd., Ste. 900 FAX (818) 728-3263
Encino, CA 91436   www.afex.com
(Currency Exchange)

Citibank (818) 845-9956
FAX (818) 845-0879
www.citibank.com

The Jacobson Group (310) 444-5255
11835 W. Olympic Blvd., Ste. 1285 FAX (310) 444-5256
Los Angeles, CA 90064   www.jacobsongrp.com

The Library (213) 985-4225
453 S. Spring St., Ste. 332 FAX (213) 975-9553
Los Angeles, CA 90013

Markay Financial Corporation (818) 998-6125
20407 Strathern St. FAX (818) 998-6127
Canoga Park, CA 91306   www.markay.com
(Consultants & Equipment Financing and Leasing)

(949) 955-7889
Morgan Stanley Smith Barney (800) 533-3402
1901 Main St., PH   fa.smithbarney.com
Irvine, CA 92614

Rose Greene Financial Services (310) 399-1200
2665 30th St., Ste. 111 FAX (310) 399-0911
Santa Monica, CA 90405   www.rosegreene.com

The Shindler Perspective, Inc. (818) 223-8345
16060 Ventura Blvd., Ste. 110-246   www.ishindler.com
Encino, CA 91436
(Consultants)

Union Bank of California (213) 236-7700
445 S. Figueroa St., Plaza Level FAX (213) 236-7734
Los Angeles, CA 90071   www.uboc.com
(Film Finance)

(213) 253-6600
Wells Fargo (800) 464-6027
333 S. Grand Ave., Ste. 2000   www.wellsfargo.com
Los Angeles, CA 90071

Steve Altes   (818) 434-8469 / (661) 297-4852
(Male Hand Model)   www.stevealtes.com

LáShan Anderson   (310) 729-1978 / (310) 314-3365
www.bylashan.com
(African-American Foot, Hand and Leg Model & Child-Sized Hands)

Linda Ashton   (310) 475-2111
(Female Hand Model)   www.cesdtalent.com

Elizabeth Atkins   (310) 475-2111
(Female Foot Model)   www.cesdtalent.com

Nick Ballard   (310) 475-2111
(Male Hand Model)   www.cesdtalent.com

Te-See Bender   (818) 642-5187
(Female Hand Model)   FAX (818) 988-5777

Laura-Shay Bentley   (310) 878-2897
www.laura-shay.com
(Female Foot Model, Hand Model and Leg Model & On-Camera Writing)

Body Parts Models   (310) 275-8263 / (702) 496-8469
2023 Coldwater Canyon Dr.   FAX (310) 273-5878
Beverly Hills, CA 90210   www.bodypartsmodels.com
(Reps for Body Parts Models)

Paul McCarthy Boyington   (310) 475-2111
(Male Foot Model)   www.cesdtalent.com

Ms. Marlon Braccia   (323) 696-2756
losangelesfootmodel.com
(Female Foot, Hand and Leg Model & On-Camera Writing)

Gerald Brodin   (818) 636-9842 / (818) 526-0070
(Male Hand Model)   FAX (818) 526-0070
www.geraldbrodin.com

Marc Buccola   (310) 475-2111
(Male Hand Model)   www.cesdtalent.com

C.E.S.D. Talent Agency   (310) 475-2111
10635 Santa Monica Blvd., Ste. 130   FAX (310) 475-1929
Los Angeles, CA 90025   www.cesdtalent.com
(Reps for Body Parts Models)

JC Caballero   (310) 231-7010 / (310) 201-0120
(Male Hand Model)   FAX (310) 231-7013
www.jordicaballero.com/handsbody

Brian Chase   (310) 475-2111
(Male Hand Model)   www.cesdtalent.com

Elisha Choice   (213) 804-2511
(African-American Female Hand Model)

Jenna Chong   (626) 755-5653
(Hand Model)   www.jennachong.com

Mia Crowe   (323) 428-8434
www.handsupermodel.com
(Female Foot, Hand and Leg Model & On-Camera Writing)

Mary Culmone   (310) 475-2111
(Female Hand Model)   www.cesdtalent.com

Charles Davis   (310) 475-2111
(Male Hand Model)   www.cesdtalent.com

Cheryl Dent   (310) 251-2149
(Hand Model)   www.cheryldent.com

Juliet Diamond   (310) 994-7935
(Child-Sized Hands)

Traci Dority   (310) 418-2433 / (310) 418-2433
(Female Hand Model)

Denise Feir   (818) 710-8055 / (818) 389-3789
(Child-Sized Hands & Puppeteer)

Chris Gardner   (310) 475-2111
(Male Hand Model)   www.cesdtalent.com

Mike Garibaldi   (707) 224-7370
(Hand Model)

Susan Gayle   (818) 990-8650
(Child-Sized Hands)

Paulette Gilbert   (805) 374-6090 / (805) 660-7868
(Hand Model)

Kimberly Girard   (310) 475-2111
(Female Foot Model)   www.cesdtalent.com

Laura Grayson   (323) 899-9090 / (323) 512-5332
(Hand Model)   FAX (323) 512-5332

Garon Grisby   (310) 475-2111
(Male Hand Model)   www.cesdtalent.com

Steve Harris   (310) 475-2111
(Male Hand Model)   www.cesdtalent.com

Anicka Haywood   (310) 475-2111
(Female Foot Model)   www.cesdtalent.com

Kelly Hornbaker   (310) 306-6000 / (310) 345-2331
(Male Foot and Hand Model)

Tom Howard   (661) 775-9566 / (661) 755-3839
(Hand Model)

Janine Jordae   (310) 475-7573 / (818) 415-2929
www.janinejordae.com
(Female Foot and Hand Model & On-Camera Writing)

Alison Nicole Karp   (310) 968-7370

Bill Karp   (213) 999-9890 / (323) 876-7721
(Hand Model)

Tracy Kay   (310) 475-2111
(Female Foot Model)   www.cesdtalent.com

Horace Knight   (310) 475-2111
(Male Hand Model)   www.cesdtalent.com

Linda Kruse   (818) 370-4649
(Female Hand Model)   www.tvhandmodel.com

Breney Kurylo   (714) 686-1313 / (562) 325-2030
(Child-Sized Hands)

Joel Lambert (310) 475-2111 (Male Hand Model) www.cesdtalent.com	**Simeon Russell** (310) 475-2111 (Male Hand Model) www.cesdtalent.com

Joel Lambert (310) 475-2111
(Male Hand Model) www.cesdtalent.com

Henry LeBlanc (323) 993-8615
(323) 365-3333
(Hand Model) FAX (323) 938-2156
www.henryshands.com

Rebecca Levinson-Gaither (818) 404-1069
(Child-Sized Hands)

Joycelyne Lew (323) 466-3100
(213) 999-5514
(Foot, Hand and Leg Model) FAX (323) 469-7138
www.joycelyne.com

Roger Lim (310) 475-2111
(Male Hand and Foot Model) www.cesdtalent.com

Louisa Maccan (310) 990-2704
FAX (310) 496-3008
www.ladyhands.com
(Female Hand, Foot and Leg Model & On-Camera Writing)

Susan McWilliams (310) 475-2111
(Female Hand Model) www.cesdtalent.com

Jodi Novak (310) 995-4410
(Child-Sized Hands)

Laila Odom (310) 475-2111
(Female Hand Model) www.cesdtalent.com

Linda O'Neil (310) 475-2111
(Female Hand Model) www.cesdtalent.com

Sondra Prosper (310) 475-2111
(Female Hand Model) www.cesdtalent.com

Chelsea Rangsikitpho (310) 475-2111
(Female Hand Model) www.cesdtalent.com

Tamia Richmond (310) 475-2111
(Female Hand and Foot Model) www.cesdtalent.com

Jennifer Robinson (310) 475-2111
(Female Hand Model) www.cesdtalent.com

Simeon Russell (310) 475-2111
(Male Hand Model) www.cesdtalent.com

Noah Schuffman (310) 475-2111
(Male Hand and Foot Model) www.cesdtalent.com

April Scott (310) 475-2111
(Female Hand and Foot Model) www.cesdtalent.com

Douglas Stockley (310) 475-2111
(Male Hand Model) www.cesdtalent.com

Lisa Tobin (818) 571-4499
(818) 501-2002
(Child-Sized Hands)

Adele Uddo (310) 980-2992
www.adeleuddo.com

Rick Wagner (310) 433-3900
(Hand Model) www.rickwagnerhands.com

Eric Weldon (310) 475-2111
(Male Hand Model) www.cesdtalent.com

Amy Weller (310) 475-2111
(Female Hand and Foot Model) www.cesdtalent.com

Sheri Weller (323) 253-0519
(Hand Model) FAX (323) 857-6648
www.sheriweller.com

David Lloyd Wilson (310) 475-2111
(Male Hand Model) www.cesdtalent.com

Gerold Wunstel (310) 699-4335
(Hand Model) www.geroldactor.com

Tanya York (818) 788-4050
(Child-Sized Hands) FAX (818) 788-4011
www.yorkentertainment.com

Melissa Yvonne Lewis (310) 475-2111
(Female Hand and Foot Model) www.cesdtalent.com

Abacus Insurance Brokers, Inc. **(310) 207-5432**
12300 Wilshire Blvd., Ste. 400   FAX **(310) 207-8526**
Los Angeles, CA 90025   **www.abacusins.com**

American Entertainment Insurance **(800) 555-4177**
1438 Gower St., Bldg. 1, Ste. 15-72   **www.aeweb.com**
Hollywood, CA 90028

American Entertainment
Insurance Services **(323) 464-5144**
Sunset Gower Studios   FAX **(323) 464-7348**
1438 N. Gower St., Bldg. 35, Box 71   **www.aeweb.com**
Los Angeles, CA 90028

Aon/Albert G. Ruben **(818) 742-1400**
Insurance Services, Inc. **(800) 752-9157**
15303 Ventura Blvd.,,, Ste. 1200   FAX **(847) 953-2480**
Sherman Oaks, CA 91403   **www.aonagr.com**

ASIS Entertainment Insurance **(310) 498-0866**
3835R E. Thousand Oaks Blvd.,Ste. 308
Westlake Village, CA 91362   **www.asisfinancial.com**

Brilliant Insurance Services **(818) 264-0300**
5900 Canoga Ave., Ste. 460   FAX **(818) 264-0699**
Woodland Hills, CA 91367   **www.movieinsure.com**

Cal-Surance Associates, Inc. **(800) 745-7189**
681 S. Parker, Ste. 300   **www.calsurance.com**
Orange, CA 92868

Claim Specialists International, Ltd. **(213) 347-0250**
550 South Hope St., Ste. 1625   FAX **(213) 347-0266**
Los Angeles, CA 90071

CMM Entertainment **(818) 224-6100**
21045 Califa St., Ste. 100 **www.cmmentertainment.com**
Woodland Hills, CA 91367

Dewitt Stern Of California
Insurance Services **(818) 623-5400**
801 N. Brand Blvd., Ste. 650   FAX **(818) 623-5500**
Glendale, CA 91203   **www.dewittstern.com**

Film Finances **(310) 275-7323**
9000 Sunset Blvd., Ste. 1400   FAX **(310) 275-1706**
West Hollywood, CA 90069   **www.filmfinances.com**
(Completion Bond Guarantors)

(866) 441-0321
First Tower Insurance Agency **(562) 821-0321**
P.O. Box 7325   FAX **(562) 949-7146**
Orange, CA 92863   **www.firsttower.com**

(800) 696-3023
Frankel & Associates Insurance **(310) 271-5582**
9233 W. Pico Blvd., Ste. 226   FAX **(310) 887-1758**
Los Angeles, CA 90035   **www.frankelinsurance.com**

Gallagher Entertainment **(818) 539-1220**
505 N. Brand Blvd., Sixth Fl.   FAX **(818) 539-1520**
Glendale, CA 91203   **www.ajgrms.com/entertainment**

Heffernan Insurance Brokers/ **(213) 622-6500**
InsureMyEquipment.com **(213) 785-6927**
811 Wilshire Blvd., Ste. 1801   FAX **(213) 243-1233**
Los Angeles, CA 90017 **www.insuremyequipment.com**

(310) 979-5729
iManagement Group **(888) 549-2600**
c/o Elkins Jones Insurance Agency   FAX **(310) 207-5441**
12100 Wilshire Blvd., Ste. 300   **www.elkinsjones.com**
Los Angeles, CA 90025

Infiniti Pacific Insurance Services **(800) 957-6542**
(Insurance Coverage)   FAX **(571) 323-0715**
www.infinitipacific.com

International Film Guarantors **(310) 309-5660**
2828 Donald Douglas Loop North   FAX **(310) 309-5696**
Second Fl.   **www.ifgbonds.com**
Santa Monica, CA 90405
(Completion Bond Guarantors)

John Wm. Hart III
Insurance Agency, Inc. **(310) 789-5865**
1800 Century Park East, Ste. 600   FAX **(800) 858-6693**
Los Angeles, CA 90067   **www.johnhartinsurance.com**

Kaercher Campbell &
Associates Insurance Brokerage **(310) 556-4766**
FAX **(310) 551-6874**
www.kaerchercampbell.com

Liberty Entertainment
Insurance Services **(818) 914-3983**
21820 Burbank Blvd., Ste. 330   FAX **(866) 517-7303**
Burbank, CA 91367
www.libertyentertainmentinsurance.com

Marsh Risk & Insurance Services **(213) 624-5555**
Entertainment Practice   FAX **(213) 346-5922**
777 S. Figueroa St., 23rd Fl.   **www.marsh.com**
Los Angeles, CA 90017

MIB Insurance Services **(310) 775-9020**
111 N. Sepulveda Blvd., Ste. 245   FAX **(310) 374-2305**
Manhattan Beach, CA 90266 **www.mediainsurance.com**

(818) 933-2297
Momentous Insurance Brokerage **(818) 933-2700**
5990 Sepulveda Blvd., Ste. 550   FAX **(818) 574-0871**
Van Nuys, CA 91411   **www.momentousins.com**
(Casualty, Property and Vehicle Insurance)

PacFed Benefit Administrators, Inc./
Group Health Insurance Division **(800) 753-0222**
1000 N. Central Ave., Ste. 400   FAX **(818) 549-0610**
Glendale, CA 91202   **www.pacfed.com**

Premier Class Insurance **(562) 821-0321**
Services, Inc. **(866) 441-0321**
10002 Pioneer Blvd., Ste. 104   FAX **(562) 949-7146**
Santa Fe Springs, CA 90670   **www.premierclass.net**

Sterling Grant and Associates, LLC **(877) 954-7200**
FAX **(602) 954-9624**
www.sterling-grant.com

Steven Randall Peterson **(805) 643-2477**
Commercial Insurance Services **(800) 441-7077**
21 S. California St., Ste. 407   FAX **(805) 643-3874**
Ventura, CA 93001

Robert Sulzinger/Insurance West **(805) 579-1900**
2450 Tapo St.   FAX **(805) 579-1916**
Simi Valley, CA 93063   **www.insurancewest.com**

(626) 795-9921
Supple-Merrill & Driscoll, Inc. **(800) 890-4840**
550 El Dorado St.   FAX **(626) 577-6656**
Pasadena, CA 91101   **www.productioninsurance.com**

(818) 981-9700
Taylor & Taylor, Ltd. **(212) 490-8511**
15060 Ventura Blvd., Ste. 210   FAX **(818) 981-9703**
Sherman Oaks, CA 91403   **www.taylorinsurance.com**

Tom C. Pickard & Co., Inc. **(800) 726-3701**
820 Pacific Coast Hwy   FAX **(800) 318-9840**
Hermosa Beach, CA 90254   **www.tcpinsurance.com**

Truman Van Dyke Co. **(323) 883-0012**
6767 Forest Lawn Dr., Ste. 301   FAX **(323) 883-0024**
Los Angeles, CA 90068
(Completion Bond Guarantors)

United Agencies, Inc. (800) 800-5880
100 N. First St., Ste. 301   FAX (877) 901-5522
Burbank, CA 91502   www.unitedagencies.com

USI Entertainment
Insurance Services (818) 251-3000
21600 Oxnard St., Eighth Fl.   FAX (818) 251-1800
Woodland Hills, CA 91367   www.usi.biz

Wells Fargo Insurance Services (818) 464-9300
15303 Ventura Blvd., Seventh Fl.   FAX (818) 464-9398
Sherman Oaks, CA 91403   www.wellsfargo.com

(949) 498-7017
Zeboray Insurance Services (800) 829-8445
P.O. Box 1044   efilminsurance.zeboray.com
San Clemente, CA 92674
(Production Insurance)

Janitorial & Strike Services

A+ Services Disposal (323) 703-4175
www.aplusservicesdisposal.com

(323) 469-0781
A-1 King Cleaning (323) 702-0587
1607 N. El Centro, Ste. 6   FAX (818) 547-1553
Hollywood, CA 90028   www.a1king.com
(Carpet Cleaning, Dirt Removal, Floor Service, Hauling, Hot
Pressure Washing, Janitorial Only, Layout Board, Pressure
Cleaning, Steam Cleaning, Trash Collection &
Window Cleaning)

A. Mullins Janitorial & (323) 933-8288
Floor Maintenance (310) 275-4950
5030 W. Washington Blvd.   FAX (323) 933-8107
Los Angeles, CA 90016

AK Exterior Steam Cleaning (661) 373-7727
19425 Soledad Canyon, Ste. 137
Canyon Country, CA 91351
(Steam Cleaning)

(818) 834-6555
All-Ways Steam Cleaning (800) 347-8633
10515 Foothill Blvd.
Sylmar, CA 91342
(Pressure Cleaning)

Anytime Production
Equipment Rentals, Inc. (323) 461-8483
755 N. Lillian Way   FAX (323) 461-2338
Hollywood, CA 90038   www.anytimerentals.com

(818) 786-5805
Bin Rental (877) 246-7368
9871 San Fernando Rd.
Pacoima, CA 91331
(Dirt Removal, Dumpster Rental, Hauling, Hot Pressure
Washing, Janitorial, Pressure Cleaning, Recycling Service for
Sets & Trash Collection)

Board Sily (818) 590-5878

(562) 803-3701
Clean Strike Rental & Cleaning (562) 879-2207
12214 Lakewood Blvd., Bldg. 9   FAX (562) 803-3702
Downey, CA 90242   www.cleanstrikerentals.com
(Carpet Cleaning, Dirt Removal, Dumpsters, Floor Service,
Hauling, Hot Pressure Washing, Layout Board, Location Site
Prep, Pressure Cleaning, Steam Cleaning, Trash Collection &
Window Cleaning)

(323) 962-7280
Clean Up Your Act (310) 774-1952
336 N. Bronson Ave.
Los Angeles, CA 90004
(Janitorial Only)

(310) 514-7579
Clean Wrap (213) 217-0241
FAX (818) 507-5626
www.cleanwrap.biz
(Art Strikes, Carpet Cleaning, Dirt Removal, Floor Service,
Hauling, Hot Pressure Washing, Janitorial, Layout Board
Removal, Pressure Cleaning, Recycling Service for Sets,
Steam Cleaning, Trash Collection & Window Cleaning)

(310) 346-5439
Cleaner Image Janitorial (310) 544-1028
FAX (310) 832-2097
www.cleanerimage.net
(Carpet Cleaning, Floor Service , Full Service, Hauling, Hot
Pressure Washing, Trash Collection & Window Cleaning)

(818) 767-0675
Crown Disposal (310) 773-0032
9189 De Garmo Ave.   www.crowndisposal.com/filmtv
Sun Valley, CA 91352
(Food Scrap Composting, Hauling, Recycling Reports,
Recycling Service for Sets & Trash Collection)

Diamond's Cleaning Service & (213) 884-8787
Family, Inc. (312) 823-8717
6712 Woodman Ave., Ste. 42   FAX (818) 781-1013
Van Nuys, CA 91401
www.diamondscleaningservices.com
(Art Strikes, Carpet Cleaning, Dirt Removal, Floor Service, Grip
Strikes, Hauling, Hot Pressure Washing, Location Site Prep,
Pressure Cleaning, Recycling Service for Sets,
Steam Cleaning, Trash Collection & Window Cleaning)

(888) 818-6488
Dumpstars LA (310) 745-3607
1515 Park Row Ave.   www.dumpstars.net
Los Angeles, CA 90291
Trash Collection

Executive Building Services (626) 584-5757
260 S. Los Robles Ave., Ste. 101   FAX (626) 584-0178
Pasadena, CA 91101

(661) 255-0602
Express Layout Boards, Inc. (661) 857-1715
24504 Apple St.   FAX (661) 255-0602
Santa Clarita, CA 91321

The Ground Floor (818) 887-6413
15812 Arminta St.   FAX (818) 780-8554
Van Nuys, CA 91406   www.groundfloor.org
(Floor Service, Marble Polishing & Stone Restoration)

Holt Enterprises, Inc. (213) 924-9371
FAX (323) 661-0157
www.holtfloorcare.com
(Carpet Cleaning, Floor Service, Location Site Prep, Pressure
Cleaning & Window Cleaning)

It's A Blast, Inc. (805) 955-9809
2235 First St., Ste. 119   FAX (866) 278-4847
Simi Valley, CA 93065   www.itsablastcps.com
(Hot Pressure Washing)

(626) 794-2666
Lavaughn's High Pressure System (818) 427-8820
44 W. Loma Alta Dr.   FAX (626) 794-2666
Altadena, CA 91001   www.lavaughnshighpressure.com
(Steam Cleaning)

(310) 980-0430
Layout Lou (424) 245-6336
www.layoutboard.net
(Floor Service, Layout Boards, Location Site Prep &
Trash Collection)

Location Trash and Cleaning (818) 590-2455	**Strike Force** (818) 967-9888
FAX **(818) 706-2945**	(Art Strikes, Electric Strikes, Grip Strikes & Lighting Strikes)
www.locationtrash.com	

Location Trash and Cleaning   (818) 590-2455
FAX **(818) 706-2945**
www.locationtrash.com

Metropolis Disposal   (800) 650-6165
7740 Burnet Ave.   FAX **(818) 778-1895**
Van Nuys, CA 91405   **www.metropolis-disposal.com**

     (310) 200-8228
Pacific Powerwash   (866) 987-9274
www.pacificpowerwash.net
(Hot Pressure Washing, Pressure Cleaning & Steam Cleaning)

Safe Sets Recycling Corp.   (310) 359-0754
2118 Wilshire Blvd., Ste. 314   FAX **(310) 853-1820**
Santa Monica, CA 90403   **www.safesetsrecycling.org**
(Recycling Service for Sets)

Strike Force   (818) 967-9888
(Art Strikes, Electric Strikes, Grip Strikes & Lighting Strikes)

Thoreau Janitorial   (310) 822-8017
5301 Beethovan St., Ste. 101   FAX **(310) 822-5867**
Los Angeles, CA 90066   **www.thoreauservices.com**
(Janitorial Services)

Trailer Trash   (818) 400-2455
6601 Noble Ave.   FAX **(818) 787-2577**
Van Nuys, CA 91405   **www.trailertrashla.com**
(Art Strikes, Hauling, Recycling Service for Sets, Trash Bin
Rental & Trash Collection)

Wrap Patrol   (310) 836-6321
(Grip and Lighting Strikes)   FAX **(310) 636-1020**

15/40 Productions   **(310) 848-1150**
3133 Jack Northrop Ave.   FAX **(310) 848-1121**
Hawthorne, CA 90250   **www.1540productions.com**

360 Designworks/
360 Propworks Inc.   **(310) 863-5984**
    www.360designworks.com
(Corporate Event Planning, Event Show Production &
Event Staffing)

Acme Design Group   **(818) 767-8888**
    www.acme-designgroup.com

Along Came Mary   **(323) 931-9082**
5265 W. Pico Blvd.   FAX **(323) 936-8249**
Los Angeles, CA 90019   **www.alongcamemary.com**

    (818) 549-9915
Astro Audio Video Lighting, Inc.   **(800) 427-8768**
6615 San Fernando Rd.   FAX **(818) 549-0681**
Glendale, CA 91201   **www.astroavl.com**
(Corporate Event Planning, Event Show Production & Rentals)

Bill Ferrell Co.   **(818) 767-1900**
10556 Keswick St.   FAX **(818) 767-2901**
Sun Valley, CA 91352   **www.billferrell.com**

Brent Bolthouse Productions   **(323) 848-9300**
314 N. Vista St.   FAX **(323) 525-2425**
Los Angeles, CA 90036
    www.bolthouseproductions.com

Estate Weddings and Events, Inc.   **(888) 662-8360**
893 Felspar St.   FAX **(858) 270-0788**
San Diego, CA 92109
    www.estateweddingsandevents.com

Event Management Productions   **(760) 340-6003**
73-647 Sun Ln.   **www.eventproducer.com**
Palm Desert, CA 92260
(Event Show Production)

Events in Motion   **(323) 962-7660**
6525 Sunset Blvd., Ste. G2   FAX **(323) 962-7647**
Hollywood, CA 90028   **www.eventsinmotion.com**

Fortune Entertainment   **(818) 760-0560**
11253 Peachgrove St., Ste. 104   FAX **(818) 760-0558**
North Hollywood, CA 91601   **www.efortune.com**
(Corporate Event Planning, Entertainment, Event Show
Production, Event Staffing & Party Supplies)

    (323) 850-2600
Global Cuisine by Gary Arabia   **(323) 668-0855**
1041 N. Formosa Ave.   FAX **(323) 850-2652**
West Hollywood, CA 90046
    www.globalcuisinecatering.com
(Caterers, Corporate Event Planning, Event Show Production,
Event Staffing, Party Supplies & Rentals)

    (323) 751-3486
L.A. Circus   **(323) 547-5960**
7531 La Salle Ave.   **www.lacircus.com**
Los Angeles, CA 90047

LARedCarpets.com   **(910) 431-9004**
(Red Carpets, Ropes & Stanchions) **www.laredcarpets.com**

Marilyn Jenett Locations   **(310) 475-0211**
1933 Manning Ave.   **www.marilynjenettlocations.com**
Los Angeles, CA 90025
(Location Coordinator)

Ocean Park Productions   **(310) 450-5599**
3435 Ocean Park Blvd., Ste. 107-244   FAX **(310) 450-5591**
Santa Monica, CA 90405   **www.oceanparkproductions.com**

Ⓐ **The Studios at Paramount**   **(323) 956-8398**
The Studios at Paramount Special Events
5555 Melrose Ave.   **www.paramountspecialevents.com**
Los Angeles, CA 90038

Raleigh Studios Special   **(323) 871-4430**
Events & Catering   **(323) 960-3456**
5300 Melrose Ave.   FAX **(323) 871-5600**
Hollywood, CA 90038   **www.raleighstudios.com**

Randy Fuhrman Events   **(310) 854-0155**
1500 Sunset Plaza Dr.   FAX **(310) 854-0133**
Los Angeles, CA 90069   **www.randyfuhrmanevents.com**

Charlie Scola   **(310) 214-9158**
    www.charliescola.com

    (818) 640-6100
Scott Topper Productions   **(310) 575-0200**
11684 Ventura Blvd., Ste. 870
Studio City, CA 91604   **www.scotttopperproductions.com**

Silver Birches   **(626) 796-1431**
650 S. Raymond Ave.   FAX **(626) 568-3274**
Pasadena, CA 91105   **www.silverbirches.net**

staffworkX Event Staffing   **(310) 337-9900**
5741 Buckingham Pkwy, Ste. D   FAX **(310) 337-9916**
Los Angeles, CA 90230   **www.staffworkx.com**
(ABC Permits, Alcohol Permits, Bar Catering, Beverage
Concessions, Caterers, Conference Staffing, Corporate Event
Planning, Event Staffing & Promotional Staffing)

Stoelt Productions   **(323) 463-3700**
1962 S. La Cienega   FAX **(323) 463-3303**
Los Angeles, CA 90034   **www.stoeltproductions.com**

Taste Catering, Inc.   **(949) 215-7373**
    FAX **(949) 215-7494**
    www.tastecateringcafe.com
(Caterers, Corporate Event Planning, Entertainment, Event
Show Production, Event Staffing, Party Supplies & Rentals)

Academy of Motion Picture Arts & Sciences -
Margaret Herrick Library   **(310) 247-3020**
333 S. La Cienega Blvd.
Beverly Hills, CA 90211
(Research)   **www.oscars.org/library/index.html**

Act One Script Clearance, Inc.
230 N. Maryland Ave., Ste. 201
Glendale, CA 91206
(Research & Script Clearance)
(818) 240-2416
(818) 240-2417
FAX **(818) 240-2418**
www.actonescript.com

Action Sports/Scott Dittrich Films
P.O. Box 301
Malibu, CA 90265 **www.actionsportsstockfootage.com**
(310) 459-2526
(212) 681-6565
FAX **(310) 456-1743**

Aero Associates
Aviation Research Library, 8033 Emerson Ave.
Los Angeles, CA 90045
(Aviation History)
(310) 337-1938
(310) 332-4383

American Society of Composers, Authors &
Publishers (ASCAP)   **(323) 883-1000**
7920 Sunset Blvd., Ste. 300   FAX **(323) 883-1049**
Los Angeles, CA 90046   **www.ascap.com**
(Music Research)

Munish Asnani/Visual
Research & Treatment Design   **(323) 383-5663**
                    www.munishasani.com
(Footage Research for Treatment Design)

BBC Motion Gallery, Los Angeles
4144 Lankershim Blvd., Ste. 200   FAX **(818) 299-9763**
North Hollywood, CA 91602 **www.bbcmotiongallery.com**
(Clips, Footage and Text Resource Library, Sound/Radio
Archive & Stock Footage Clearances)
(818) 299-9720
(818) 432-4000

Broadcast Music, Inc. (BMI)   **(310) 659-9109**
8730 Sunset Blvd., Third Fl. West   FAX **(310) 657-6947**
Los Angeles, CA 90069   **www.bmi.com**
(Music Research & Performance Rights)

California Film Commission   **(323) 860-2960**
Location Resource Center   **(800) 858-4749**
7080 Hollywood Blvd., Ste. 900   FAX **(323) 860-2972**
Los Angeles, CA 90028   **www.film.ca.gov**

Center for the Study of
Political Graphics   **(323) 653-4662**
8124 W. Third St., Ste. 211   FAX **(323) 653-6991**
Los Angeles, CA 90048   **www.politicalgraphics.org**
(Political Poster Archive)

Clearance Domain LLC
                    FAX **(888) 562-5120**
                    www.clearancedomain.com
(Art Clearances, Clearances, Clips, Footage Clearance,
Intellectual Property, Legal Research, Performance Rights,
Product Placement Services, Research, Script Annotations,
Script Clearance, Script Research & Title Search)
(800) 562-1231
(818) 389-5930

Clearance Unlimited   **(818) 988-5599**
6848 Firmament Ave.   FAX **(818) 988-5577**
Van Nuys, CA 91406   **www.clearances.net**
(Artist, Copyright, Footage, Music and Script Clearance &
Title Search)

Clearly Right Entertainment, Inc.   **(310) 709-7909**
5853 David Ave.   **www.clearlyrightentertainment.com**
Los Angeles, CA 90034
(Art Clearances, Clearances, Clips, Film Copyright Research,
Footage Clearance, Footage Research, Intellectual Property,
Internet, Music Clearances, Music Research, Photography
Clearances, Photography Research, Research, Stock Footage
Clearances & Talent)

Costume Rentals Corporation   **(818) 753-3700**
11149 Vanowen St.   FAX **(818) 753-3737**
North Hollywood, CA 91605
                    www.costumerentalscorp.com

Creative Clearance   **(818) 728-4622**
                    FAX **(818) 332-7070**
                    www.creativeclearance.com
(Clearances, Clips, Copyrights, Errors and Omissions, Film
Copyright Research, Footage Clearance, Music Clearances,
Music Research, Photography Clearances, Script Clearances,
Stock Footage Clearances, Talent & Title Search)

Creative Musical Services   **(818) 426-7727**
13547 Ventura Blvd., Ste. 358
Sherman Oaks, CA 91423
                    www.creativemusicalsvcs.com
(Music Clearance Library and Supervision)

Elizabeth Bardsley
Associates, Inc.   **(818) 563-4008**
3727 W. Magnolia Blvd., Ste. 450   FAX **(818) 823-1938**
Burbank, CA 91510   **www.elizabethbardsley.com**
(Research Services & Script Annotations)

Evan M. Greenspan, Inc./EMG   **(818) 762-9656**
4181 Sunswept Dr., Second Fl.   FAX **(818) 762-2624**
Studio City, CA 91604   **www.clearance.com**
(Music Clearance)

Film Art LA   **(323) 461-4900**
5870 Melrose Ave., Ste. 3300   FAX **(323) 461-4959**
Hollywood, CA 90038   **www.filmartla.com**
(Art and Photography Copyright Clearance and Research)

Film Superlist - Motion
Pictures in The Public Domain   **(323) 655-4968**
8391 Beverly Blvd., Ste. 321   **www.hfarchive.com**
Los Angeles, CA 90048
(Film Copyright Research)

Global Brainstorm Research/
Carey Ann Strelecki   **(310) 993-3700**
                    FAX **(818) 508-6635**
                    www.globalbrainstorm.com
(Art Research, Footage, Photo & Text Research and
Clearances)

Global ImageWorks, LLC   **(201) 384-7715**
65 Beacon St.   FAX **(201) 501-8971**
Haworth, NJ 07641   **www.globalimageworks.com**
(Clearances, Clips, Copyrights, Footage Clearance, Footage
Research, Music Clearances, Music Research, Music Supervi-
sion, Photography Clearances, Script Clearances & Stock
Footage Clearances)

Hollywood Script Research   **(818) 553-3633**
1012 Justin Ave.   FAX **(818) 553-3624**
Glendale, CA 91201 **www.hollywoodscriptresearch.com**
(Errors and Omissions & Legal Research)

IndieClear Script Clearance
1150 Highland Ave.   FAX **(818) 956-6059**
Glendale, CA 91202   **www.indieclear.com**
(Script Clearance and Research)
(323) 828-8280
(818) 956-6049

Joan Pearce Research Associates   **(323) 655-5464**
8111 Beverly Blvd., Ste. 308   FAX **(323) 655-4770**
Los Angeles, CA 90048
(Errors and Omissions, Research & Script Clearances)

Just Imagine Research Library, Inc. **(818) 764-5644**
6910 Farmdale Ave.   FAX **(818) 764-6655**
North Hollywood, CA 91605
(Architecture, Art & Photography)

Debra Lemonds   **(626) 844-9363**
P.O. Box 5516
Pasadena, CA 91117
(Art Research, Photography Clearances and Research &
Rare Books)

License It   **(310) 772-0984**
9903 Santa Monica Blvd., Ste. 1103   FAX **(310) 772-0985**
Beverly Hills, CA 90212
(Art Clearances, Clearances, Clips, Copyrights, Footage Clearance, Intellectual Property, Music Clearances &
Photography Clearances)

Lillian Michelson Research Library   **(818) 695-6445**
Dreamworks SKG, 1000 Flower St.   FAX **(818) 695-4545**
Glendale, CA 91201
(History; By Appointment Only)

Liquid Courage Music   **(310) 838-5656**
3002 Midvale Ave., Ste. 210   FAX **(310) 441-7558**
Los Angeles, CA 90034
(Music Supervision)

Louis B. Mayer Library/   **(323) 856-7654**
American Film Institute   **(323) 856-7600**
2021 N. Western Ave.   **www.afi.com**
Los Angeles, CA 90027

Marshall/Plumb Research
Associates, Inc.   **(818) 848-7071**
4150 Riverside Dr., Ste. 209   FAX **(818) 848-7702**
Burbank, CA 91505   **www.marshall-plumb.com**
(Script Research)

     (323) 270-9298
Miss Information   **(213) 200-4063**
P.O. Box 50291   FAX **(323) 375-0555**
Los Angeles, CA 90050   **www.miss-info.net**

Mophonics   **(310) 452-0331**
200 Westminister Ave.   FAX **(310) 452-0356**
Venice, CA 90291   **www.mophonics.com**
(Clearances, Copyrights, Intellectual Property, Internet, Music
Clearances, Music Research, Music Supervision,
Research & Talent)

Nickerson Research   **(323) 965-9990**
     FAX **(323) 965-9991**
     www.nickersonresearch.com
(Footage, Photo, Talent and Text Clearance and Research)

PAC   **(323) 931-9962**
(Historic Footage and Music Performance Research)

     (818) 506-1077
Pacifica Radio Archives   **(800) 735-0230**
3729 Cahuenga Blvd.   FAX **(818) 506-1084**
North Hollywood, CA 91604
     www.pacificaradioarchives.org
(Public Radio Programming & Sound Actualities)

The Paley Center for Media   **(310) 786-1000**
465 N. Beverly Dr.   FAX **(310) 786-1086**
Beverly Hills, CA 90210   **www.paleycenter.org**
(Archives & Research Library)

PicturesNow.com   **(415) 435-1076**
(Historic Photo Library)   FAX **(415) 435-5027**
     www.picturesnow.com

Richard J. Riordan - Central Library   **(213) 228-7000**
630 W. Fifth St.   **www.lapl.org**
Los Angeles, CA 90071
(Public Library)

Searchworks   **(323) 469-3783**
     FAX **(323) 464-0824**
     www.searchworks.com
(Footage, Photo, Script and Talent Clearance and Licensing)

Seeling-Lafferty Research, LLC   **(310) 391-1801**
12829 Rose Ave.   FAX **(310) 391-3561**
Los Angeles, CA 90066
(Permission, Script Clearance and Title Research)

Southern California Genealogical Society &
Family Research Library   **(818) 843-7247**
417 Irving Dr.   FAX **(818) 843-7262**
Burbank, CA 91504   **www.scgsgenealogy.com**

Sue Terry Associates   **(818) 506-0500**
P.O. Box 56719
Sherman Oaks, CA 91413
(Art Clearances, Art Research, Copyrights, Costume Research,
Footage Clearance, Footage Research, Historical Consulting,
Literary Research, Music Research, Photography Clearances,
Photography Research, Public Library, Research & Stock
Footage Clearances)

TellAVision   **(310) 230-5303**
1060 20th St., Ste. 8   FAX **(310) 388-5550**
Santa Monica, CA 90403   **www.tellavisionagency.com**
(Reps for Footage & Visual Research/Treatment Design
Companies)

Western Costume Co.   **(818) 760-0900**
11041 Vanowen St.   FAX **(818) 508-2190**
North Hollywood, CA 91605
     www.lawardrobesupplies.com
(Costume Research Library)

     (323) 583-8660
Westside Detectives, Inc.   **(323) 833-2383**
6230 Wilshire Blvd., Ste. 59
Los Angeles, CA 90048   **www.westsidedetectives.com**
(Intellectual Property & Trademark Infringement)

Ree Whitford   **(818) 424-9988**

Alexsasha Lauren's
Excellent Massage (310) 927-0297

(818) 762-9223
Lama Amin (818) 321-3539
www.magicfingersla.com

(818) 980-3060
An Ancient Touch (818) 437-8041
10458 1/2 Moorpark St. FAX (818) 980-3060
Toluca Lake, CA 91602 www.anancienttouch.com

Aroma Spa & Sports (213) 387-2111
3680 Wilshire Blvd. www.aromaresort.com/spa.html
Los Angeles, CA 90010

Jennifer Astman-Posen (310) 480-8855
www.jenmassagela.com

Tanja Barnes (310) 439-8754
11630 Chayote, Ste. 5 www.tanjabarnes.com
Los Angeles, CA 90049

Belle Visage Day Spa (818) 907-0502
13207 Ventura Blvd. www.bellevisage.com
Studio City, CA 91604

Beverly Hot Springs (323) 734-7000
308 N. Oxford Ave. www.beverlyhotsprings.com
Los Angeles, CA 90004

Bodies in Motion (310) 836-8000
12100 Olympic Blvd. FAX (310) 775-8650
Los Angeles, CA 90064 www.bodiesinmotion.com

Body Energizers on Location/
Diane Hubner (310) 394-4334
www.bodyenergizers.net

Jennifer L. Bratton/
A Positive Change (310) 428-0568
www.servemehere.com/jenniferlbratton

(323) 932-8854
Brooks Massage Therapy (323) 937-8781
7619-21 Beverly Blvd. www.brooksmassage.com
Los Angeles, CA 90036

Burke Williams Spa (310) 587-3366
1358 Fourth St. www.burkewilliamsspa.com
Santa Monica, CA 90405
(See Web Site for Additional Locations)

Center for Wellbeing (626) 355-2443
31 West Sierra Madre Blvd. FAX (626) 355-2445
Sierra Madre, CA 91024 www.centerwellbeing.com

(310) 838-0849
Rachel Cohen (310) 701-9191
FAX (310) 838-1922
www.cadencearts.com

Creative Chakra/Sandie West (310) 823-9378
3401 Pacific Ave., Stes. 2A & 2B
Marina del Rey, CA 90292 www.creativechakra.com

Deep Work/Kimberly Korljan (310) 542-5773
FAX (310) 542-5773
www.deepwork.com

Anna Dekker/The Dutch Touch (310) 630-7577

DuBunné Day Spa and
Massage Center (310) 326-9062
23725 Arlington Ave. FAX (310) 326-7056
Torrance, CA 90501 www.dubunnedayspa.com

Dr. Caren M. Elin, D.C. (805) 448-1424
FAX (805) 344-4255

Equinox Fitness Club & Spa (310) 552-0420
www.equinoxfitness.com

Exhale Spa (310) 319-3193
101 Wilshire Blvd. FAX (310) 899-6022
Santa Monica, CA 90401 www.exhalespa.com

Deb Fingerman (213) 400-4475

Four Seasons Hotel Spa (310) 273-2222
FAX (310) 859-3824
www.fourseasons.com

(888) 506-2772
Go Massage (312) 224-2966
www.gomassage.com

Healing Choices (805) 449-2646
901 Greenwich Dr. FAX (805) 449-2647
Thousand Oaks, CA 91360 www.chiro.net

Healing Choices (818) 266-7599
13202 Washington Blvd. FAX (805) 449-2647
Los Angeles, CA 90066 www.chiro.net
(Chiropractic)

Heidi's Fabulous Fatigue (310) 488-5297
Fighters Worldwide (917) 301-2022
FAX (212) 996-1958
www.fabulousfatiguefighters.com

Helen Hodgson/U Knead Massage (323) 573-6344
www.ukneadmassage.com

Infinite Circle/Debra Tourigny (310) 567-4445
P.O. Box 12442
Marina del Rey, CA 90295

Karen Becker-Burns (818) 543-1739
Massage Therapy (310) 282-0997
9845 S. Santa Monica Blvd. www.lamedicinewoman.com
Beverly Hills, CA 90212

Kinara Spa (310) 657-9188
656 N. Robertson Blvd. FAX (310) 657-9184
Los Angeles, CA 90069 www.kinaraspa.com

The Kneaded Experience (877) 242-4752
www.kneadedexperience-la.com

(323) 935-7464
Carole Koenig (323) 610-1997
www.ckmassagetherapy.com

LA Body Points (310) 941-8464
www.labodypoints.com/chair_massage

Le Petite Retreat day spa (323) 466-1028
331 N. Larchmont Blvd. FAX (323) 462-4008
Los Angeles, CA 90004 www.lprdayspa.com

Elaine Lew (310) 874-4768
P.O. Box 64226 elainemassage.moonfruit.com
Los Angeles, CA 90064

Lulur Day Spa (310) 659-4100
642 1/2 N. Robertson Blvd. FAX (310) 659-4117
Beverly Hills, CA 90069 www.lulurspa.com

Massage By Angie (818) 231-4094
www.massagebyangie.com

The Massage Company   **(310) 358-1999**
1106 N. La Cienega Blvd., Ste. 206
West Hollywood, CA 90069 **www.messagecoweho.com**

The Massage Express Co.   **(310) 806-0831**
    FAX **(310) 401-7748**
www.themassageexpress.com

Massage Therapy Center, Inc.   **(310) 444-8989**
2130 S. Sawtelle Blvd., Ste. 207 **www.massagenow.com**
Los Angeles, CA 90025

**Meta Touch Custom
Therapeutic Massage**   **(310) 397-3422**
4441 Sepulveda Blvd.   FAX **(310) 915-9532**
Culver City, CA 90230   **www.metatouch.com**

Mobile Massage   **(310) 210-3033**
1807 Marine St.   **www.healingacademy.net**
Santa Monica, CA 90405

Kim Moise   **(323) 360-8366**
    FAX **(310) 441-5032**
www.kimlanmoise.com

Larry Nesti/Massage for Health   **(818) 266-3833**
4149 Murietta Ave.
Sherman Oaks, CA 91423

    (310) 854-7700
Ole Henriksen Face/Body   **(800) 327-0331**
8622-A W. Sunset Blvd.   FAX **(310) 854-1869**
Los Angeles, CA 90069   **www.olehenriksen.com**

Ona Spa   **(323) 931-4442**
7373 Beverly Blvd.   FAX **(323) 931-9992**
Los Angeles, CA 90036   **www.onaspa.com**

Production Massage   **(818) 434-8874**
    FAX **(818) 688-0101**
www.productionmassage.com

Pure Bodywork   **(310) 396-6800**
    FAX **(310) 396-6855**
www.purebodywork.com/set.html

Gloria Ramos/On Set Massage   **(818) 445-1727**
P.O. Box 361223   **www.onsetmassage.com**
Los Angeles, CA 90036

Sea Mountain Inn Resort Spa   **(877) 928-2827**
Astral Ocean   **www.seamountaininn.com**
Desert Hot Springs, CA 92240

    (310) 394-6986
A Shaman in the City/Dr. Mark   **(877) 674-2626**
1431 Ocean Ave., Ste. 1118   **www.shaman.cc**
Santa Monica, CA 90401

Spa by Diane Loring, Inc.   **(805) 641-0022**
Pierpont Racquet Club 500 San Jon Rd., Four Points by
Sheraton 1050 Schooner Dr.   **www.spaventura.com**
Ventura, CA 93001

Spa Connections   **(888) 660-3636**
www.spa-connections.com

    (310) 453-0210
Spa On Location, Inc.   **(310) 497-1607**
2461 Santa Monica Blvd., Ste. 404 FAX **(310) 396-3066**
Santa Monica, CA 90404   **www.spaonlocation.com**
(Mobile Spa)

Take 5 Massage Therapy   **(818) 795-3111**
5019 Alcove Ave.   **www.t5mt.com**
Valley Village, CA 91607

Tim Ciatti Massage Therapy   **(310) 704-0806**
www.timciatti.com

Trilogy Spa   **(310) 760-0044**
451 Manhattan Beach Blvd.   FAX **(310) 760-0053**
Hermosa Beach, CA 90266   **www.trilogyspa.com**

    (323) 851-6000
Seppo J. Viljanen   **(818) 599-6056**
www.sportscentertltc.com

Deirdre Wagner   **(310) 570-0056**
www.shentherapy.info

Yada Yada Yoga   **(310) 274-2665**
www.yadayoga.com

Zykoff Bodywork & Hypnotherapy **(310) 275-7673**
517 N. La Cienega Blvd., Ste. 9
West Hollywood, CA 90048 **www.zykoffbodywork.com**

247 Delivers Inc.
(818) 843-1954
(800) 773-9947
FAX **(818) 683-1034**
www.247delivers.com

A-1 Courier
(310) 450-9000
655 S. Flower St., Ste. 280   www.a-1courier.com
Los Angeles, CA 90017

Academy Messenger Service
(323) 655-8224
FAX **(323) 655-8386**
www.academymessenger.com

Accurate Express
(323) 906-1000
FAX **(323) 906-9633**
www.accurateexpress.net

Action Messenger Service
(323) 654-2333
(800) 474-2587
1311 N. Highland Ave.   FAX **(323) 654-8889**
Los Angeles, CA 90028   www.actionmessenger.com

Ad Delivery
(323) 852-1301
FAX **(323) 852-9181**

CitySprint
(310) 258-0800
(800) 734-7328
FAX **(310) 410-9331**

Classic Couriers
(323) 461-3741
1601 N. El Centro Ave.   FAX **(323) 957-3110**
Hollywood, CA 90028   www.classic-couriers.com

Deliver LA
(310) 478-8000
(800) 653-3548
10537 Santa Monica Blvd., Ste. 200   FAX **(310) 470-4564**
Los Angeles, CA 90025   www.deliverla.com

Eclipse/Sequoia Messenger Service
(818) 906-2009
(877) 546-3001
3400 Irvine Ave., Ste. 113   FAX **(818) 906-2616**
Newport Beach, CA 92660 www.eclipsemessenger.com

Efficient Delivery Service
(818) 817-2700
7065 Hayvenhurst Ave., Ste. 7   FAX **(818) 205-9883**
Van Nuys, CA 91406
www2.efficientdeliveryservice.com/entrack/index.asp

Entertainment Delivery Group
(888) 838-2929
FAX **(661) 294-1051**
www.edgla.net

KBS Messenger Service
(310) 842-6880
3336 S. Robertson Blvd.   FAX **(310) 842-6888**
Los Angeles, CA 90034   www.kbsmessenger.com

Messenger Express
(818) 754-1234
5503 Cahuenga Blvd., Ste. 100   FAX **(818) 754-1031**
North Hollywood, CA 91601

Now Services
(818) 774-9111
(800) 648-1985
6047 Tampa Ave.   FAX **(818) 654-2900**
Tarzana, CA 91356

PDL Concepts, Inc.
(800) 995-8819
21213-B Hawthorne Blvd., Ste. 5637   FAX **(562) 948-4554**
Torrance, CA 90503   www.pdlonline.com

Reels On Wheels Unlimited
(877) 576-6300
(914) 576-6300
FAX **(914) 633-6932**
www.reelsonwheels.com

Rocket Messenger Service
(323) 469-7155
(818) 341-9786
P.O. Box 3506   FAX **(818) 734-8641**
Chatsworth, CA 91311   www.rocketmessenger.com

Santa Monica Express Messenger Service
(310) 458-6000
(800) 458-4502
11150 W. Olympic Blvd., Ste. 150   FAX **(310) 458-4500**
Los Angeles, CA 90064   www.smexpress.com

Security Couriers, Inc.
(818) 789-3999
(323) 464-2673
FAX **(818) 789-3888**
www.securitycouriers.com

Sunrise Delivery Service, Inc.
(818) 789-5121
FAX **(818) 789-5333**
www.sunrisedelivery.com

Team Delivery Systems
(310) 590-1500
5839 Green Valley Circle, Ste. 105   FAX **(310) 410-9331**
Culver City, CA 90230   www.teamdelivery.com

Time Machine
(213) 975-9850
(800) 734-8463
1533 Wilshire Blvd.   FAX **(800) 977-2077**
Los Angeles, CA 90017 www.timemachinenetwork.com

United Express
(310) 556-1883
(818) 787-1883
1801 Century Park East, Ste. 1132   FAX **(310) 556-7700**
Los Angeles, CA 90067

Universal Courier
(310) 410-4500
(323) 463-3975
5839 Green Valley Circle, Ste. 105   FAX **(310) 410-9331**
Culver City, CA 90230   www.universalcourier.com

Warner Bros. Studio Facilities - Courier Services
(818) 954-5536
4000 Warner Blvd.   FAX **(818) 954-5410**
Burbank, CA 91522   www.wbcourierservice.com

A and C Harbour Lites, Ltd.   (310) 926-9552
P.O. Box 9279   FAX (310) 356-3579
Marina Del Rey, CA 90295
(Marine Coordination)

Aquatic Cinema   (310) 864-2000
www.aquaticcinema.com

    (562) 433-2863
Aquavision   (562) 688-3038
3708 E. Fourth St.   FAX (562) 433-2863
Long Beach, CA 90814   www.aquavision.net
(Marine Coordination, Fabrication, Production & Stunt Rigging)

    (714) 330-9900
Camera Craft   (714) 964-6920
www.cameracraftonline.com

Cat Production Services/
Extreme Sports Filming   (562) 596-7105
(Marine Coordination)   www.extremesportsfilming.com

    (818) 365-7999
Cinema Aquatics   (805) 207-5797
www.cinemaaquatics.com

Cinema Safety &   (310) 614-0206
Marine Services, Inc.   (805) 207-5797
1534 N. Moorpark Rd., Ste. 108   FAX (805) 241-3954
Thousand Oaks, CA 91360   www.cinemasafety.com
(Marine Coordination)

CineMarine Team -   (661) 222-7342
Cinema Rentals, Inc.   (818) 365-7999
25876 The Old Road, Ste. 174   FAX (661) 427-0881
Stevenson Ranch, CA 91381   www.cinemarineteam.com
(Marine Coordination)

Executive Yacht Management, Inc.   (310) 306-2555
644 Venice Blvd.   FAX (310) 306-1147
Marina del Rey, CA 90291   www.yacht-management.com
(Marine Coordination)

    (305) 586-6664
Marine Crew, Inc.   (760) 889-3107
(Marine Coordination)   www.marinecrew.net

Motion Picture Marine   (310) 822-1100
616 Venice Blvd.   FAX (310) 822-2679
Marina del Rey, CA 90291
(Marine Coordination)   www.motionpicturemarine.com

    (562) 594-9276
🅐 **Nautical Film Services**   (310) 729-6920
P.O. Box 50066   FAX (562) 594-9242
Long Beach, CA 90815   www.nauticalfilmservices.com
(Marine Coordination)

    (310) 968-0549
Jimmy O'Connell   (310) 452-5774
306 Market St., Ste. A   FAX (310) 452-5774
Venice, CA 90291

Offshore Grip Marine, Inc.   (310) 547-3515
23852 Pacific Coast Hwy, Ste. 764   FAX (310) 943-3328
Malibu, CA 90265   www.offshoregripmarine.com
(Marine Coordination)

    (619) 410-5222
Premiere Yacht Charters   (619) 808-2822
1380 Harbor Island Dr.   FAX (800) 530-7668
San Diego, CA 92101   www.premiereyachtcharters.com

Privateer Lynx   (866) 446-5969
(Marine Coordination)   FAX (949) 723-1958
    www.privateerlynx.org

US Camera Boats LLC   (949) 230-9327
(On-Water Filming Platform)   FAX (949) 492-7783
    www.uscameraboats.com

Capt. Troy Waters   (310) 713-9193
(Marine Coordination)   FAX (310) 943-3328

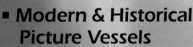

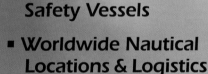

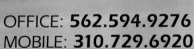
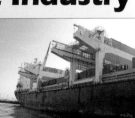

Mei-Ling Andreen
(818) 259-0821
(818) 622-9138
(Traveling Notary)
FAX (818) 622-0728

ASAP Traveling Notary Public
(818) 780-8121
(800) 266-8279
(24-Hour Service & Traveling Notary)
1800anotary.com

Film Auditors, Inc.
(213) 413-0033
849 N. Occidental Blvd.
FAX (213) 413-0088
Los Angeles, CA 90026
www.filmauditors.com

Mobile Notary
(310) 475-1764
(323) 650-3164
(24-Hour Service)

Paragon Language Services, Inc.
(323) 966-4655
(800) 499-0299
5657 Wilshire Blvd., Ste. 310
FAX (323) 651-1867
Los Angeles, CA 90036
www.paragonls.com

Traveling Notary Public/
Michele Lamorie
(310) 274-4832
(310) 691-6943
P.O. Box 66738
FAX (310) 337-1231
Los Angeles, CA 90066

ABS Payroll & Production
Accounting Services
(818) 848-9200
(877) 284-5600
2600 W. Olive Ave., Fifth Fl.
www.abspayroll.net
Burbank, CA 91505

The Accounting Group
(818) 333-4555
FAX (818) 333-4556

ARTpayroll
(603) 367-2028
14755 Diamond View Dr., Ste. A
FAX (209) 296-0627
Pioneer, CA 95666
www.artpayroll.com
(Celebrity Contracts, Payroll, SAG/AFTRA Commercial
Signatory & Union Compliance Signatory)

ARTpayroll
(805) 526-9119
1409 Kuehner Dr., Ste. 206
FAX (209) 296-0627
Simi, CA 93063
www.artpayroll.com
(Celebrity Contracts, Payroll & SAG/AFTRA Commercial
Signatory Services)

CAPS Payroll
(310) 280-0755
10600 Virginia Ave.
FAX (310) 280-0889
Culver City, CA 90232
www.capspayroll.com
(Celebrity Contracts, Payroll, Production Software, SAG/AFTRA
Commercial Signatory Services & Union Compliance Signatory)

Cast & Crew Entertainment Services (818) 848-6022
2300 Empire Ave., Fifth Fl.
www.castandcrew.com
Burbank, CA 91504

Audrey S. Cohen
(310) 993-3375
(305) 385-2204
(Production Accountant)
FAX (310) 208-6776

Daugherty Accounting Services, Inc. (818) 901-8208
FAX (818) 901-8208

Dolphingirl Productions, Inc.
(562) 688-8999
(562) 531-8999
5421 Whitewood Ave.
FAX (562) 634-3898
Lakewood, CA 90712
(SAG/AFTRA Commercial Signator Services)

EMS, Inc.
(818) 386-0905
16027 Ventura Blvd., Ste. 506
FAX (818) 386-9341
Encino, CA 91436
www.emspayroll.com

Entertainment Partners
(818) 955-6296
2835 N. Naomi St.
FAX (818) 450-0255
Burbank, CA 91504
www.entertainmentpartners.com
(Production Software)

Film Auditors, Inc.
(213) 413-0033
849 N. Occidental Blvd.
FAX (213) 413-0088
Los Angeles, CA 90026
www.filmauditors.com

Film Budget Pro
(323) 574-9696
FAX (888) 699-9778
www.filmbudgetpro.com
(Budgeting, Production Software & Scheduling)

HHG Productions, LLC
(603) 367-2024
(877) 290-2024
FAX (603) 367-2004
www.hhgproductions.com
(Celebrity Contracts, Post Production Accounting, SAG/AFTRA
Commercial Signatory Services & Union Compliance Signatory)

The Jacobson Group
(310) 444-5255
11835 W. Olympic Blvd., Ste. 1285
FAX (310) 444-5256
Los Angeles, CA 90064
www.jacobsongrp.com

Douglas W. McHenry
(310) 293-3871

Media Services
(310) 440-9600
(800) 333-7518
500 S. Sepulveda Blvd., Fourth Fl.
FAX (310) 472-9979
Los Angeles, CA 90049
www.media-services.com
(Payroll, Post Production Accounting, Production Accountant,
Production Software & SAG/AFTRA Commercial
Signatory Services)

Lisa Mitchell
(310) 801-8860
(Auditor, Controller, Personal Business Manager &
Production Accountant)

NPI Entertainment Payroll, Inc.
(818) 566-7878
(866) 296-2267
2550 Hollywood Way, Ste. 430
FAX (818) 566-7879
Burbank, CA 91505
www.npiproductionservices.com
(Union and Non-Union Payroll)

Oberman, Tivoli, Miller &
Pickert, Inc.
(310) 471-9354
(800) 333-7518
500 S. Sepulveda Blvd., Fourth Fl.
FAX (310) 472-9979
Los Angeles, CA 90049
www.media-services.com

PayReel
(800) 352-7397
(303) 526-4900
FAX (303) 526-4901
www.payreel.com

Marilyn Penn-Lindley
(310) 827-2094
(310) 780-8683
FAX (951) 361-1446
(Post Production Accounting & Production Accountant)

PES Payroll
(818) 729-0080
(800) 301-1992
4100 W. Burbank Blvd.
FAX (818) 295-3886
Burbank, CA 91505
www.pespayroll.com
(Payroll)

Prime Casting & Payroll
(323) 962-0377
(323) 962-1455
FAX (323) 872-5050
6430 Sunset Blvd., Ste. 425
Hollywood, CA 90028
www.primecasting.com

Talent Partners
(818) 556-4700
FAX (818) 955-7789
www.talentpartners.com

Randemonium, Inc.
(818) 505-0400
FAX (818) 505-0599
4555 Radford Ave.
Studio City, CA 91607
(SAG/AFTRA Commercial Signatory Services & Union
Compliance Signatory)

TEAM
(818) 558-3261
FAX (818) 558-3263
901 W. Alameda Ave., Ste. 100
Burbank, CA 91506
www.teamservices.net
(Celebrity Contracts, Payroll, SAG/AFTRA Commercial
Signatory Services & Union Compliance Signatory)

Rice Gorton Pictures, Ltd.
(323) 665-6200
FAX (323) 665-4222
2870 Los Feliz Pl., Ste. 301
Los Angeles, CA 90039
(Post Production Accounting)

Trevanna Post, Inc.
(310) 820-7678
FAX (310) 820-7679
11833 Mississippi Ave., Ste. 101
Los Angeles, CA 90025
www.trevannapost.com
(Post Production Accounting)

Sessions Payroll Management, Inc. (818) 841-5202
303 N. Glenoaks Blvd., Ste. 810
FAX (818) 841-9112
Burbank, CA 91502
www.sessionspayroll.com

Michele Varon, C.P.A.
(818) 386-1900
FAX (818) 386-1901
4064 Weslin Ave.
Sherman Oaks, CA 91423
(Production Accountant)

LA 411   Printing Services   LA 411

A & I Santa Monica
(310) 264-2622
(310) 453-8463
www.aandi.com
1550 17th St.
Santa Monica, CA 90404

Print Technology
(310) 273-9450
(877) 613-9450
FAX (310) 273-8450
8899 Beverly Blvd., Ste. 803
Los Angeles, CA 90048
www.print-technology.com

National Promotions & Advertising
(310) 558-8555
(310) 591-7389
FAX (310) 558-8558
3434 Overland Ave.
Los Angeles, CA 90034
www.npaprints.com
(Commercial Printing)

Prolab Digital Imaging
(310) 625-4411
(310) 846-4496
FAX (310) 204-6939
5441 W. 104th St.
Los Angeles, CA 90045
www.prolabdigital.com

Action Ad Specialties, Inc.   (818) 762-7680
5323 Babcock Ave.   FAX **(818) 762-2568**
North Hollywood, CA 91607   **www.actionadpromos.com**
(Apparel, Bags, Embossing, Embroidery, Hats, Merchandising, Packaging, Silkscreening & T-Shirts)

   (310) 558-3533
Active Ad Specialties   **(800) 866-8684**
10746 Francis Pl., Ste. 305   FAX **(310) 558-0503**
Los Angeles, CA 90034   **www.activeadspecialties.com**
(Merchandising)

Adapt Consulting, Inc.   **(818) 782-6974**
13618 Lemay St.   FAX **(818) 782-6975**
Van Nuys, CA 91401   **www.adaptadspecialty.com**
(Apparel, Bags, Hats, Merchandising & T-Shirts)

Art of the Gift   **(805) 581-8000**
572 Winncastle St.   FAX **(805) 581-8020**
Simi Valley, CA 93065   **www.artgiftla.com**

   (818) 349-3932
Award Winners   **(818) 943-1634**
8939 Reseda Blvd.   **www.awardwinners.net**
Northridge, CA 91324
(Silkscreening)

   (310) 719-7004
B & H Company   **(800) 996-6003**
217 E. 157th St.   FAX **(310) 719-9894**
Gardena, CA 90248   **www.bhcompany.com**
(Embroidery & Silkscreening)

   (310) 822-1706
The Bag Ladies   **(800) 359-2247**
13428 Maxella Ave., Ste. 982   FAX **(310) 574-9960**
Marina del Rey, CA 90292   **www.bag-ladies.com**
(Bags)

Banners and Flags Unlimited/
Banner Marketing Group   **(805) 528-5018**
P.O. Box 7004   FAX **(805) 528-3529**
Los Osos, CA 93412   **www.bannermarketinggroup.com**
(Apparel, Bags, Embossing, Embroidery, Hats, Laser Printing, Merchandising, Packaging, Silkscreening & T-Shirts)

Bare Reflections   **(818) 765-5304**
12547 Sherman Way, Ste. J   FAX **(818) 765-1830**
North Hollywood, CA 91605

Big 10 Industries, Inc.   **(310) 280-1610**
149 S. Barrington Ave., Ste. 812   FAX **(310) 280-1611**
Los Angeles, CA 90049   **www.big10.com**
(Embroidery, Engraving, Silkscreening & Tie-Dye)

   (323) 933-7448
Bovary and Butterfly   **(310) 430-4321**
5225 Wilshire Blvd., Ste. 100   FAX **(323) 933-1315**
Los Angeles, CA 90036   **www.bovaryandbutterfly.com**

   (800) 828-1943
Brand Central Promotions   **(800) 828-1943**
   FAX **(800) 828-1943**
www.bcpromo.com

Brand-It Promotions   **(310) 318-8585**
   FAX **(310) 318-5854**
www.branditpromotions.com

Brownstone Screen Printers   **(818) 985-7283**
5709 Cahuenga Blvd.   FAX **(818) 753-9155**
North Hollywood, CA 91601   **www.bspplus.com**
(Embroidery & Silkscreening)

Coastal Printworks, Inc.   **(818) 503-0781**
7344 Hinds Ave.   FAX **(818) 503-0977**
North Hollywood, CA 91605 **www.coastalprintworks.com**
(Crew and Promotional Apparel, Embroidery & Screenprinting)

   (805) 498-9018
Corporate Images, Inc.   **(800) 439-8939**
3563 Old Conejo Rd.   FAX **(805) 498-9017**
Newbury Park, CA 91320   **www.corporateimages.com**
(Apparel, Bags, Embossing, Embroidery, Hats, Laser Printing, Merchandising, Packaging, Silkscreening & T-Shirts)

David K's T-Shirt Printing   **(310) 204-3812**
8926 Venice Blvd.   **www.davidkla.com**
Culver City, CA 90232
(Embroidery & Silkscreening)

EKF Promotions   **(818) 786-2996**
19528 Ventura Blvd., Ste. 232   FAX **(818) 578-6439**
Tarzana, CA 91356   **www.ekfpromo.com**
(Apparel, Bags, Embossing, Hats, Merchandising, Packaging, Silkscreening & T-Shirts)

Ellen's Silkscreening &   **(626) 441-4415**
Promotional Products   **(888) 545-9711**
1506 Mission St.   FAX **(626) 441-2788**
South Pasadena, CA 91030
   www.ellenssilkscreening.com
(Embroidery & Silkscreening)

Event Apparel   **(818) 252-7622**
11355 Penrose St.   FAX **(818) 252-1112**
Sun Valley, CA 91352   **www.eventapparel.com**

Gamble Gear, LLC   **(310) 435-3307**
(Promotional Apparel Manufacturing)

Get Smart Promotions   **(818) 808-0812**
4570 Van Nuys Blvd., Ste. 313
Sherman Oaks, CA 91403
   www.getsmartpromotions.com
(Crew and Promotional Apparel & Merchandising)

Golden Fleece Designs, Inc. (818) 848-7724
441 S. Victory Blvd. (800) 468-7245
Burbank, CA 91502 FAX (818) 566-7100
(Canvas Products Manufacturing)

Hartt Trophy & Engraving Co. (323) 462-7309
319 Westbern Ave. (323) 462-3516
Los Angeles, CA 90004 FAX (323) 462-2127

I.D. Me Promotions (818) 774-9500
18401 Burbank Blvd., Ste. 116 FAX (818) 774-9510
Tarzana, CA 91356 www.idmepromotions.com
(Advertising Space, Embroidery, Merchandising, Promotional
Products & Silkscreening)

Imprint Revolution (310) 474-4472
10681 W. Pico Blvd. FAX (310) 474-1340
West Los Angeles, CA 90064
www.imprintrevolution.com
(Embroidery, Heat Pressing, Promotional Products &
Silkscreening)

Inner Circle Graphics (310) 392-9784
706 Lincoln Blvd. (800) 404-9784
Venice, CA 90291 FAX (310) 399-0359
www.innercirclegraphics.com
(Embroidery & Silkscreening)

The Logo Shop (818) 501-8000
7020 Hayvenhurst Ave., Ste. A (866) 966-5646
Van Nuys, CA 91406 FAX (818) 501-8099
www.thelogoshop.com
(Crew and Promotional Apparel)

Merch Graphics (866) 356-3724
3520 Cadillac Ave., Ste. G FAX (714) 556-2301
Costa Mesa, CA 92626 www.merchgraphics.com
(Apparel, Bags, Embossing, Embroidery, Hats, Laser Printing,
Merchandising, Packaging, Silkscreening & T-Shirts)

Perlman Creative Group (310) 709-2091
P.O. Box 4016 www.perlmancreative.com
Newport Beach, CA 92661
(Graphic Design & Packaging)

platine cookies (310) 559-9933
10850 Washington Blvd. FAX (310) 559-9934
Culver City, CA 90232 www.platinecookies.com
(Custom Cookies and Brownies)

Quick Draw (310) 477-6770
2244 Federal Ave. www.quickdraw1.com
Los Angeles, CA 90064
(Embroidery, Promotional Products & Screenprinting)

Roots (310) 858-8343
371 N. Beverly Dr. (310) 577-8026
Beverly Hills, CA 90210 FAX (310) 858-8229
www.roots.com
(Embroidery)

Sichel Embroidered Crew Apparel (818) 255-0862
11917 Vose St. (800) 729-0361
Sun Valley, CA 91352 FAX (818) 255-3913
(Embroidery)

Star Treatment Gift Services (818) 781-9016
15200 Stagg St. (800) 444-9059
Van Nuys, CA 91405 FAX (818) 781-9230
www.startreatment.com

Sweatsedo (310) 398-6845
5239 Sepulveda Blvd. FAX (310) 975-6758
Culver City, CA 90230 www.sweatsedo.com
(Apparel & Embroidery)

we-designstudio (323) 284-5130
P.O. Box 411223 FAX (561) 455-9644
Los Angeles, CA 90041 www.wedesignstudio.com

World Emblem Intl. (800) 766-0448
3465 E. Cedar Ave. FAX (800) 880-2073
Ontario, CA 91761 www.worldemblem.com
(Apparel, Bags, Embroidery, Hats, Laser Printing,
Silkscreening & T-Shirts)

A1-Stuntworld, Inc./Gianni Biasetti (310) 666-3004 (909) 797-7621
www.stuntworldinc.com

Absolute Action/Tom McComas (310) 251-6254
(Coordinator)

Dennis C. Alpert/Wheels on Film (818) 985-2739
FAX (818) 985-2739

Jim Arnett (323) 856-3000
www.easterntalent.net

Joe Bacal (310) 310-0572
www.jtgrey.com

Dean Bailey/Performance (818) 980-2123
Filmworks Edge System (310) 721-4812
(Stunt Coordination and Driving) FAX (805) 604-3398
www.performancefilmworks.com

(310) 398-2033
Bill Young's Precision Driving Team (310) 476-6229
453 S. Barrington Ave. FAX (310) 476-6229
Los Angeles, CA 90049
www.billyoungsdrivingteam.com

Bobby Ore Motorsports LLC (818) 880 5678
(Coordinator) FAX (863) 655-6262
www.bobbyoremotorsports.com

(818) 654-1055
Bondelli Driving Team (818) 795-1999
FAX (818) 957-6390
www.mbdrivingteam.com

(818) 980-2123
Eddie Braun (310) 339-7367
FAX (310) 545-4906
www.driversinc.com

Gregory Brazzel (805) 479-7446
(Coordinator)

Charlie Brewer (310) 991-7150
www.stuntsunlimited.com

Bob Brown (310) 623-5500
www.montanartists.com

(800) 400-3124
Rocky Capella (323) 462-3001
(Coordinator & Driver) www.rockycapella.com

R.J. Chambers (661) 295-6789
29034 Sheridan Rd. FAX (661) 295-0123
Val Verde, CA 91384

Cinema Drivers/
Tom Anthony's Driving Team (818) 389-5211
3418 N. Knoll Dr. www.cinemadrivers.com
Hollywood, CA 90068

Marcel Cozza (714) 981-3029
(Coordinator)

Charlie Croughwell (310) 623-5500
www.montanartists.com

(310) 913-2935
Shawn Crowder (818) 347-0671

(818) 970-0959
Tamra Crowder (818) 982-9447

Wally Crowder (805) 443-1550
FAX (805) 491-0708
www.stuntplayers.com

(323) 462-2301
Jeff Danoff/Ramp Rentals (661) 803-2210
P.O. Box 1063 FAX (661) 285-7748
Canyon Country, CA 91386 www.stuntramps.com

Peter DeMarzo/ (949) 733-8755
Performance Driving Specialists (949) 478-9152
10 Starflower
Irvine, CA 92604

(714) 847-1501
Chad Di Marco (714) 596-6952
17161 Palmdale Ln. FAX (714) 848-0561
Huntington Beach, CA 92647 www.subesports.com

Drivers East (800) 803-3992
www.driverseast.com

Ⓐ Drivers Inc. (818) 994-4199
620 Resolano Dr. FAX (310) 459-7374
Pacific Palisades, CA 90272 www.driversinc.com
(Rigging)

(818) 508-0122
Georgia Durante (818) 508-7618
FAX (818) 508-0322
www.performancetwo.com

Corey Eubanks (805) 368-0800
P.O. Box 427 FAX (805) 344-4639
Santa Ynez, CA 93460

Executive Productions (310) 456-8833
3957 Ridgemont Dr. FAX (310) 456-5692
Malibu, CA 90265
(Coordinator)

ExpertDrivers.com (949) 922-3013	(310) 922-0069
12 Genoa www.expertdrivers.com	**Hubie Kerns Jr.** (818) 980-2123
Laguna Niguel, CA 92677	(Coordinator, Referral Service & Rigging) FAX (310) 459-7374
(Referral Service)	

ExpertDrivers.com (949) 922-3013
12 Genoa www.expertdrivers.com
Laguna Niguel, CA 92677
(Referral Service)

femmefatale motorsports/
Kathy Jarvis (310) 666-4758
FAX (323) 843-9486
www.ffmotorsports.com

Mike Garibaldi (707) 224-7370

Jack Gill (310) 656-5151
www.innovativeartists.com

(714) 899-3939
Ⓐ **Sonny Goulet** (818) 774-3889
FAX (714) 899-3939
www.sonnygouletdriving.com

Allan Graf (310) 288-8000
www.paradigmagency.com

(818) 335-2130
J. Bud Graves (415) 336-6257
FAX (818) 761-8383

(661) 268-1942
John & Candace Hateley (323) 462-2301
10810 Zorro Way FAX (661) 268-1992
Santa Clarita, CA 91390

(206) 947-7126
Art Hickman (818) 825-5502

Michael Hilow (818) 554-2803
(Coordinator & Rigging)

Kelly Hine (818) 633-6175
www.driversinc.com

Hit The Mark (949) 697-4042
(Coordinator) FAX (949) 497-0157
www.thedrivingconnection.com

(805) 740-6018
Steve Holladay (323) 462-2301
FAX (805) 735-7205
www.camerabikes.com

Hollywood Picture Cars (323) 466-2277
3957 Ridgemont Dr., Ste. 101 FAX (310) 456-5692
Malibu, CA 90265 www.hollywoodpicturecars.com

(661) 775-9566
Tom Howard (661) 755-3839

Tony Hunt (310) 782-4892
www.tonyhunt.com

Gary Hymes (310) 273-6700
www.utaproduction.com

International Stunt Association (ISA) (818) 501-5225
4454 Van Nuys Blvd., Ste. 214 FAX (818) 501-5656
Sherman Oaks, CA 91403 www.isastunts.com

Jackknife King (661) 251-4200
FAX (661) 251-5165
www.jackknifeking.net

(818) 710-1186
Penny Johnson (818) 384-2429

(213) 999-9890
Bill Karp (323) 876-7721

(818) 713-0552
Steve Kelso/K4 Motorsports, Inc. (323) 462-2301
www.k4motorsports.com

---

(310) 922-0069
Hubie Kerns Jr. (818) 980-2123
(Coordinator, Referral Service & Rigging) FAX (310) 459-7374

Jim Kirby (562) 595-8886
(Coordinator) FAX (562) 595-6566
www.laprepinc.com

(818) 681-8317
Kim Robert Koscki (661) 288-1118

(818) 222-6954
L.A. Motorsports (877) 526-6867
FAX (866) 294-3266
www.lamsports.com

Terry Leonard (310) 623-5500
www.montanartists.com

(661) 821-1210
Mark Lonsdale (310) 405-2655
(Coordinator) www.sttu.com

(818) 985-2739
Freddy Lopez (818) 292-1562

Peter MacDonald (310) 273-6700
www.utaproduction.com

(661) 904-2292
Eddie Marazzito (818) 786-9030
www.rzicarprep.com

Glenn Marks (310) 623-5500
www.montanartists.com

McCabe Performance Driving (818) 519-0474
(Coordinator) FAX (818) 360-4662
www.mccabedriving.com

(818) 980-2123
Shawn McConnell (818) 985-2739

Rhys Millen (714) 847-2158
17471 Apex Circle FAX (714) 848-6821
Huntington Beach, CA 92647 www.rmrproducts.com

(714) 540-5566
Steve Millen (949) 645-1224
3176 Airway Ave. FAX (714) 540-5784
Costa Mesa, CA 92626 www.stillen.com

Rick Miller (818) 970-1099

Montana Artists Agency (310) 623-5500
9150 Wilshire Blvd., Ste. 100 FAX (310) 623-5515
Beverly Hills, CA 90212 www.montanartists.com
(Reps for Stunt Coordinators)

National Alliance of
Stunt Performers (818) 508-0122
www.performancetwo.com

(310) 709-5561
Chris Nielsen/Stunt Driver Inc. (818) 980-2123
P.O. Box 12877 www.thestuntdriver.com
Marina del Rey, CA 90295
(Coordinator, Professional Stunt Driver, Rigging & Stuntman)

Guy Norris (310) 273-6700
www.utaproduction.com

David Kent Ottenberg (805) 995-2965
P.O. Box 521 FAX (805) 995-2821
Cayucos, CA 93430 www.cayucoscreekbarn.com

Greg Pene/GP Performance Driving (909) 240-8401
1943 N. Campus Ave., Ste. B234
Upland, CA 91784

Performance Two, Inc. (818) 508-0122
(818) 508-7618
5235 Goodland Ave. FAX (818) 508-0322
North Hollywood, CA 91607 www.performancetwo.com

R.S.O. Productions (661) 803-7349
(Coordinator & Driver)

Branko Racki (310) 273-6700
www.utaproduction.com

Doriana Richman (818) 222-6954
(310) 480-5302
FAX (866) 294-3266
www.lamsports.com

Roger Richman (818) 222-6954
(310) 890-0505
FAX (866) 294-3266
www.lamsports.com

Mic Rodgers (310) 288-8000
www.paradigmagency.com

John D. Ross (310) 710-1632
P.O. Box 46130 www.johndross.com
Los Angeles, CA 90046

Markos Rounthwaite (310) 656-5151
www.innovativeartists.com

George Marshall Ruge (310) 288-8000
(Coordinator) www.paradigmagency.com

Rich Rutherford (949) 300-6029
360 One, Inc., 5401 Camino Mojado FAX (949) 218-7864
San Clemente, CA 92673 www.richrutherford.com

Errol Sack (661) 252-7629
(805) 432-9149
12059 Davenport Rd. FAX (661) 251-5165
Agua Dulce, CA 91390 www.errolsack.com

Eric Schwab (310) 623-5500
(2nd Unit Director) www.montanartists.com

Ben Scott (805) 279-0229
(Coordinator, Referral Service & Rigging)

Jeff Scott (213) 709-9190
(323) 469-9980
(Coordinator)

Kevin Scott (310) 656-5151
www.innovativeartists.com

Mike Smith (310) 623-5500
www.montanartists.com

Peter Stader (805) 559-4995
(818) 886-8687
(Coordinator)

Gregg Stern (310) 292-0915
FAX (505) 982-0163

Tom Struthers (310) 273-6700
www.unitedtalent.com

Stunt Coordinators, Inc. (818) 254-7270
2016 Rayshire St. www.stuntcoordinatorsinc.com
Thousand Oaks, CA 91362
(Coordinator)

**Stuntmen's Association of
Motion Pictures** (818) 766-4334
5200 Lankershim Blvd., Ste. 190 FAX (818) 766-5943
North Hollywood, CA 91601 www.stuntmen.com
(Referral Service)

Stunts for Commercials (661) 295-6789
29034 Sheridan Rd. FAX (661) 295-0123
Val Verde, CA 91384

Stunts In Trucks (661) 295-7711
(818) 404-8230
25111 Rye Canyon Loop FAX (661) 295-7721
Santa Clarita, CA 91321 www.fastrucks.com
(Coordinator)

**Stuntwomen's Association of
Motion Pictures** (818) 762-0907
12457 Ventura Blvd., Ste. 208 FAX (818) 762-9534
Studio City, CA 91604 www.stuntwomen.com
(Referral Service)

Olivia Summers (818) 970-4108
(Precision/Stunt Driver) www.oliviasummers.com

Greg Tracy (562) 714-7191
FAX (562) 856-8187
www.driversinc.com

**United Stuntwomen's
Association, Inc. (USA)** (818) 508-4651
FAX (818) 508-7074
www.usastunts.com

Shelly Ward (805) 358-5784
FAX (877) 401-1525
www.shellywardent.com

Jack Weimer (818) 504-4131
(818) 448-2000

Max Werk (805) 878-3201
www.youtube.com/user/MaxWerk1

Webster Whinery (310) 623-5500
www.montanartists.com

T.J. White (877) 377-8868
P.O. Box 2832 www.t-minusproductions.com
Toluca Lake, CA 91610

Audrey Williams (818) 985-2739
(818) 219-1568

Josh Wood (435) 901-1674
www.stuntphone.com/viewprofiledetail.php?id=338
(Performance Driver)

John Woodward (310) 288-8000
www.paradigmagency.com

Stephen Woolfenden (310) 288-8000
www.paradigmagency.com

1-Stuntworld, Inc./   (310) 666-3004
Gianni Biasetti   (909) 797-7621
www.stuntworldinc.com

Absolute Action/Tom McComas   (310) 251-6254
(General Stunts & Skydiving)

Adrenaline Nation/Scott Smith   (310) 686-0778
FAX (818) 509-1751
www.adrenalinenation.com
(Aerial, Aerial Coordination, BASE Jumping, Coordination,
Rigging, Skydiving, Skysurfing, Stunt Coordination, Wingsuit
Skydiving & Wingwalking)

Aerial Stunt Service/Joe Jennings   (310) 543-2222
3128 Via La Selva   www.skydive.tv
Palos Verdes Estates, CA 90274
(Aerial Coordination, BASE Jumping, Paragliding, Skydiving
Stunts, Skysurfing, Stunt Coordination & Wingsuit Skydiving)

     (562) 433-2863
Aquavision/Bob Anderson   (562) 688-3038
3708 E. Fourth St.   FAX (562) 433-2863
Long Beach, CA 90814   www.aquavision.net
(Aquatic, Extreme Rigging, Fight Choreography, General
Stunts, Marine Coordination and Equipment, Rigging, Scuba
Diving & Stunt Coordination and Equipment)

Jim Arnett   (323) 856-3000
www.easterntalent.net

     (626) 434-3636
ATS Filmworks   (951) 202-4303
417-B W. Foothill Blvd., Ste. 528   FAX (626) 857-0252
Glendora, CA 91741   www.atsfilmworks.com
(Canyoneering, Extreme Rigging, General Stunts, Kayaking,
Rigging, Rock Climbing, Rope Rescue & Wirework)

Dave Barlia   (818) 207-9696
www.davebarlia.com
(BASE and Bungee Jumping & Wingsuit Skydiving)

     (310) 532-3933
Beckman Rigging/BRS Rigging   (661) 510-2518
13516 S. Mariposa Ave.   FAX (310) 532-3993
Gardena, CA 90247   www.brsrigging.com

     (818) 885-6474
Branam Enterprises   (877) 295-3390
9152 Independence Ave.   www.branament.com
Chatsworth, CA 91311
(Flying & General Stunts)

     (818) 701-9239
Brand X Action Specialists   (818) 903-3314
FAX (818) 886-8754
www.brandxstunts.org

     (818) 980-2123
Eddie Braun   (310) 339-7367
FAX (310) 545-4906

Charlie Brewer   (310) 991-7150
(General Stunts)   www.stuntsunlimited.com

Bungee America, Inc./Ron Jones   (310) 322-8892
P.O. Box 8925   www.bungeeamerica.com
Calabasas, CA 91302
(Bungee Jumping & Rope Rescue)

California Dreamin'   (800) 373-3359
33133 Vista del Monte Rd.   www.californiadreamin.com
Temecula, CA 92591

     (800) 400-3124
Rocky Capella/RCP-SF Stunt Group   (323) 462-2301
www.rockycapella.com
(Coordination, Fight Choreography, General Stunts, Multi-
Vehicle Coordinator, Stunt Coordination & Wirework)

R.J. Chambers   (661) 295-6789
29034 Sheridan Rd.   FAX (661) 295-0123
Val Verde, CA 91384

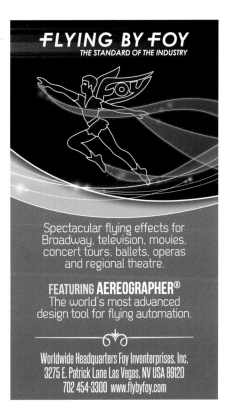

Eric Chen (714) 900-9974
(Martial Arts) www.usawushu.com

Andy Cheng (310) 288-8000
www.paradigmagency.com

Benjamin Cooke (310) 656-5151
www.innovativeartists.com

Wally Crowder (805) 443-1550
FAX (805) 491-0708
www.stuntplayers.com
(Fight Choreography, General Stunts, Marine Coordination, Rigging & Scuba Diving)

Ian Eyre (323) 363-6225
(818) 774-3889
www.imdb.com/name/nm0264226/
(General Stunts & Rigging)

Hartley Folstad (909) 597-8511
(Aerial & Wingwalking) FAX (909) 597-8511
www.silverwingswingwalking.com

Ⓐ Foy Inventerprises, Inc. (702) 454-3300
3275 E. Patrick Ln. www.flybyfoy.com
Las Vegas, NV 89120
(Aerial, Aerial Coordination, Aquatic, Coordination, Extreme Rigging, General Stunts, Hang Gliding, Paragliding, Rigging, Skiing, Skydiving & Skysurfing)

Frogmen Unlimited/Mark Lonsdale (661) 821-1210
(310) 405-2655
(Aquatic) www.sttu.com

Got Rigging?/Michael Li & Norbert Phillips (818) 391-4883
20040 Curassow Court FAX (661) 250-8133
Canyon Country, CA 91351
(Extreme Rigging)

Got Stunts Inc. (310) 766-5867
www.gotstunts.com
(Aerial Advertising, Aerial Coordination, BASE Jumping, General Stunts, Skydiving, Skysurfing, Stunt Coordination & Wirework)

Piergiorgio Gusso/TwinAir (818) 988-7573
7552 Hayvenhurst Pl. FAX (818) 988-7578
Van Nuys, CA 91406 www.twinair.net

Hang Gliding Aerobatics, Inc. (760) 822-5667
(Hang Gliding) www.johnheiney.com

Helifilms USA, Inc. (310) 487-0065
1299 Ocean Ave., Ste. 333 FAX (310) 496-0405
Santa Monica, CA 90401 www.helifilmsusa.com
(Aerial & Aerial Coordination)

Hollywood Stuntworks (818) 419-5661
28261 W. Parker Rd. FAX (661) 295-8956
Castaic, CA 91384 www.hollywoodstuntworks.com
(General Stunts)

Craig Hosking (661) 251-5151
(Aerial) FAX (661) 414-8048
www.hoskingaviation.com

International Stunt Association (ISA) (818) 501-5225
4454 Van Nuys Blvd., Ste. 214 FAX (818) 501-5656
Sherman Oaks, CA 91403 www.isastunts.com

Capt. Lance Julian (808) 224-0801
(323) 856-3000
(Marine Coordinator) FAX (323) 856-3009
www.easterntalent.net

Kim K. Kahana Jr. (818) 888-2935
(323) 462-2301
P.O. Box 6214 FAX (818) 888-2951
Woodland Hills, CA 91365 www.dttrampolines.com
(Aerial Coordination, General Stunts, Rigging, Stunt Coordination & Trampolines)

KCW Studios (626) 698-0029
816 S. Date Ave. FAX (626) 872-2377
Alhambra, CA 91803 www.kcwstudios.com
(BASE Jumping, Bungee Jumping, Coordination, Extreme Rigging, Fencing, General Stunts, Referral Service, Rigging, Rope Rescue, Skydiving, Skysurfing, Stunt Coordination, Sword Fighting, Trampolines & Trick Horseback Riding)

Hubie Kerns Jr. (310) 922-0069
(818) 980-2123
FAX (310) 459-7374
(General Stunts Coordinaton, Referral and Rigging)

L.A. Motorsports (818) 222-6954
(877) 526-6867
FAX (866) 294-3266
www.lamsports.com

Lane Leavitt/Leavittation, Inc. (661) 252-7551
25982 Sand Canyon Rd. FAX (661) 250-8526
Santa Clarita, CA 91387 www.stuntrev.com
(Flying & General Stunts)

Ray Lykins (310) 922-3852
(General Stunts) www.raylykins.com

Peter J. McKernan Jr. (310) 458-9176
(310) 993-4486
(Aerial) FAX (310) 496-0744

Mike Ryan Stunt Services (661) 295-7711
(818) 404-8230
25111 Rye Canyon Loop FAX (661) 295-7721
Santa Clarita, CA 91321 www.fastrucks.com

Victor Paul (626) 284-3432
(323) 469-9980
(Sword Master)

Jimmy Romano (818) 980-2123
(818) 430-6411
(General Stunts)

John Ross (310) 710-1632
P.O. Box 46130 www.johndross.com
Los Angeles, CA 90046
(Coordination, General Stunts, Rigging, Scuba Diving, Skiing & Trampolines)

John D. Sarviss (661) 270-0565
(661) 810-9456
39120 Bouquet Canyon Rd. www.radicalcameracars.com
Leona Valley, CA 93551
(Aerial)

Peter Stader (805) 559-4995
(818) 886-8687
(General Stunts)

Steve Stafford/Studio Wings, Inc. (805) 320-9500
855 Aviation Dr. FAX (805) 987-4720
Camarillo, CA 93010 www.studiowings.com
(Aerial & Aerial Coordination)

Stunt Coordinators, Inc. (818) 254-7270
2016 Rayshire St. www.stuntcoordinatorsinc.com
Thousand Oaks, CA 91362

Stunt Wings/Adventure Sports (818) 367-2430
(818) 266-0874
12623 Gridley St. FAX (818) 367-5363
San Fernando, CA 91342 www.stuntwings.com
(Aerial Coordination, Hang Gliding, Paragliding, Stunt Coordination & Ultralight Aviation)

Stuntmen's Association of Motion Pictures (818) 766-4334
5200 Lankershim Blvd., Ste. 190 FAX (818) 766-5943
North Hollywood, CA 91601 www.stuntmen.com
(Referral Service)

Stunts for Commercials (661) 295-6789
29034 Sheridan Rd. FAX (661) 295-0123
Val Verde, CA 91384
(Stunt Coordination)

Stuntwomen's Association of
Motion Pictures   (818) 762-0907
12457 Ventura Blvd., Ste. 208   FAX **(818) 762-9534**
Studio City, CA 91604   **www.stuntwomen.com**
(Referral Service)

                        (818) 421-2926
SwordPlay/Tim Weske   **(818) 980-2123**
64 E. Magnolia Blvd.   FAX **(818) 566-4357**
Burbank, CA 91502   **www.timweske.com**

John Tamburro   **(661) 713-6671**
(Aerial Coordination)   FAX **(877) 272-4764**
     www.blackstarhelicopters.com

Thornton Aircraft Company **(818) 787-0205**
7520 Hayvenhurst Ave.   FAX **(818) 787-9334**
Van Nuys, CA 91406   **www.thorntonaircraft.com**
(Aerial)

Stuart Thorp   **(310) 656-5151**
     www.innovativeartists.com

United Stuntwomen's
Association, Inc. (USA)   **(818) 508-4651**
         FAX **(818) 508-7074**
     www.usastunts.com

               (949) 854-6250
Vertical Adventures/Bob Gaines **(800) 514-8785**
P.O. Box 7548   FAX **(949) 854-5249**
Newport Beach, CA 92658 **www.verticaladventures.com**
(Extreme Rigging, Mountain Climbing, Rigging, Rope Rescue,
Stunt Coordination & Wirework)

Dick Ziker   **(323) 462-2301**

A1-Stuntworld, Inc./   **(310) 666-3004**
Gianni Biasetti   **(909) 797-7621**
www.stuntworldinc.com

       (661) 775-8530
Action Specialists   **(818) 915-4691**
28313 Industry Dr.   FAX **(661) 775-8531**
Valencia, CA 91355   www.actionspecialists.com
(Flying and Stunt Rigging Equipment)

       (310) 532-3933
Beckman Rigging/BRS Rigging   **(661) 510-2518**
13516 S. Mariposa Ave.   FAX **(310) 532-3993**
Gardena, CA 90247   www.brsrigging.com
(Flying and Stunt Rigging Equipment)

Bikes..Camera..Action!   **(310) 995-2084**
1105 Bonilla
Topanga, CA 90290
(Adjustable Jump Ramps for Bikes, Skateboards and Skates)

       (818) 885-6474
Branam Enterprises   **(877) 295-3390**
9152 Independence Ave.   www.branament.com
Chatsworth, CA 91311
(Flying and Stunt Rigging Equipment)

       (909) 949-1601
CA Rampworks   **(707) 235-4230**
273 N. Benson Ave.   FAX **(707) 264-6503**
Upland, CA 91786   www.carampworks.com
(Adjustable Jump Ramps, BMX, Jump/Stunt Ramps, Mats,
Moto Cross, Pads, Rental and Manufacturing, Safety Gear,
Skate Boards & Trampolines)

       (818) 888-2935
Ⓐ DT Trampolines Inc.   **(800) 649-4945**
P.O. Box 6214   FAX **(818) 888-2951**
Woodland Hills, CA 91365   www.dttrampolines.com
(Mats, Pads, Stunt Rigging Equipment & Trampolines)

       (702) 997-1939
Fisher Technical Services Rentals   **(866) 942-4098**
www.ftsrentals.com

Freshpark LLC   **(714) 369-2495**
7412 Count Circle   FAX **(714) 369-2185**
Huntington Beach, CA 92647   www.freshpark.com
(Adjustable Jump Ramps, Automotive Ramps, Bike, Skateboard
and Snowboard Ramps and Rails, Hardware Fasteners, Jump/
Stunt Ramps & Remote Control Car Ramps)

Got Rigging?/Michael Li &
Norbert Phillips   **(818) 391-4883**
20040 Curassow Court   FAX **(661) 250-8133**
Canyon Country, CA 91351
(Flying and Stunt Rigging Equipment)

Hollywood Stuntworks   **(818) 419-5661**
28261 W. Parker Rd.   FAX **(661) 295-8956**
Castaic, CA 91384   www.hollywoodstuntworks.com
(Flying and Stunt Rigging Equipment)

Icarus Rigging   **(323) 660-4112**
3531 Casitas Ave.   FAX **(323) 660-6135**
Los Angeles, CA 90039   www.icarusrigging.com

International Stunt Association (ISA) **(818) 501-5225**
4454 Van Nuys Blvd., Ste. 214   FAX **(818) 501-5656**
Sherman Oaks, CA 91403   www.isastunts.com
(Mats, Pads & Stunt Rigging Equipment)

Jack Rubin & Sons, Inc.   **(818) 562-5100**
520 S. Varney St.   FAX **(818) 562-5101**
Burbank, CA 91502   www.wirerope.net
(Cord, Hardware Fasteners, Harnesses, Flying Equipment,
Safety Gear, Stunt Rigging Equipment and Supplies,
Velcro & Webbing)

Leavittation, Inc.   **(661) 252-7551**
25982 Sand Canyon Rd.   FAX **(661) 250-8526**
Santa Clarita, CA 91387   www.stuntrev.com
(Articulated Crash Dummies, Mats, Pads & Stunt
Rigging Equipment)

Lowy Enterprises, Inc.   **(310) 763-1111**
1970 E. Gladwick St.   FAX **(310) 763-1112**
Rancho Dominguez, CA 90220   www.lowyusa.com
(Cord, Elastic, Hardware Fasteners, Harnesses, Safety and
Stunt Rigging, Thread, Velcro & Webbing)

Rick's Stunt Car Service/   **(818) 341-9526**
Motion Picture Driving Clinic   **(818) 796-1497**
8560 Variel Ave.
Canoga Park, CA 91304
       www.rickseamanstuntdrivingschool.com
(Articulated Stunt Mannequins)

       (818) 980-2123
S & S Stunt Equipment Rental, Inc.   **(818) 681-1348**
26943 Ruether Ave., Ste. R   www.stuntequipment.com
Santa Clarita, CA 91351
(Mats, Pads & Stunt Rigging Equipment)

Spohn Ranch, Inc.   **(877) 489-3539**
15131 Clark Ave., Ste. B   FAX **(626) 330-5503**
City of Industry, CA 91745   www.spohnranch.com
(BMX, MX, Skateboard and Stunt Ramps)

       (818) 567-3000
VER Sales, Inc.   **(800) 229-0518**
2509 N. Naomi St.   FAX **(818) 567-3018**
Burbank, CA 91504   www.versales.com
(Safety and Stunt Rigging Equipment & Supplies)

       (818) 344-4231
Yerkes Productions   **(323) 462-2301**
(Mats, Pads & Stunt Rigging Equipment)

Above The Line Agency   (310) 859-6115
468 N. Camden Dr., Ste. 200
Beverly Hills, CA 90210   www.abovethelineagency.com

     (310) 859-0625
Abrams Artists Agency   (310) 859-1417
9200 Sunset Blvd., Ste. 1130   FAX (310) 276-6193
West Hollywood, CA 90069   www.abramsartists.com
(Talent Only)

     (323) 525-1221
Affinity Artists Agency   (323) 525-0577
5724 W. Third St., Ste. 511   www.affinityartists.com
Los Angeles, CA 90036
(Children, Comedians, Commercial Talent, Film and Television
Talent, Models, Talent & Voice-Over Artists)

**Agency for the
Performing Arts., Inc.**   (310) 888-4200
405 S. Beverly Dr.   FAX (310) 888-4242
Beverly Hills, CA 90212   www.apa-agency.com

AKA Talent Agency   (323) 965-5600
6310 San Vicente Blvd., Ste. 200   FAX (323) 965-5601
Los Angeles, CA 90048   www.akatalent.com

**Amatruda Benson &
Associates/ABA**   (310) 276-1851
9107 Wilshire Blvd., Ste. 500   FAX (310) 276-3517
Beverly Hills, CA 90210

Amsel, Eisenstadt & Frazier   (323) 939-1188
5055 Wilshire Blvd., Ste. 865   FAX (323) 939-0630
Los Angeles, CA 90036

Angel City Talent   (323) 656-5489
     www.angelcitytalent.biz

The Ann Waugh Talent Agency   (818) 980-0141
4741 Laurel Canyon Blvd., Ste. 210
North Hollywood, CA 91607

Aqua Talent Agency   (310) 859-8889
9000 W. Sunset Blvd., Ste. 700   FAX (310) 859-8898
West Hollywood, CA 90069   www.aquatalent.com

Arlene Thornton & Associates, Inc.   (818) 760-6688
12711 Ventura Blvd., Ste. 490   FAX (818) 760-1165
Studio City, CA 91604   www.arlenethornton.com

     (714) 558-7373
Artist Management Agency   (619) 233-6655
2102 Business Center Dr., Ste. 220-F
Irvine, CA 92612   www.artistmanagementagency.com
(Commercial Talent, Talent & Voice-Overs)

AthleteSource Casting   (310) 871-7956
13425 Ventura Blvd., Second Fl.   FAX (435) 645-8163
Sherman Oaks, CA 91423
(Athletes)   www.athletesourcecasting.com

Atlas Talent Agency   (310) 324-9800
8721 W. Sunset Blvd., Ste. 205   www.atlastalent.com
West Hollywood, CA 90069

Avalon Artists Group   (323) 692-1700
5455 Wilshire Blvd., Ste. 900   FAX (323) 692-1722
Los Angeles, CA 90036   www.avalonartists.com

AVO Talent   (310) 360-7680
5670 Wilshire Blvd., Ste. 1930   FAX (310) 360-7681
Los Angeles, CA 90036
(Voice-Over Artists)

Baier/Kleinman International   (323) 874-9800
16917 Ventura Blvd., Ste. 9
Encino, CA 91316

Baldwin Talent, Inc.   (310) 827-2422
8055 W. Manchester Ave., Ste. 550
Playa del Rey, CA 90293
(Commercial Talent)

Baron Entertainment   (323) 969-1000
13848 Ventura Blvd., Ste. A   FAX (818) 933-0798
Sherman Oaks, CA 91423

     www.baronentertainment.com

Bauman, Redanty & Shaul   (323) 857-6666
5757 Wilshire Blvd., Ste. 659   FAX (323) 857-0368
Los Angeles, CA 90036   www.brsagency.com

Bicoastal Talent & Literary   (818) 845-0150
210 N. Pass Ave., Ste. 204   FAX (818) 845-0512
Burbank, CA 91505   www.bicoastaltalent.com

The Blake Agency   (310) 456-2022
23411 Malibu Colony Rd.   FAX (310) 456-9994
Malibu, CA 90265   www.theblakeagency.com

bloc, Inc.   (323) 954-7730
6100 Wilshire Blvd., Ste. 1100   FAX (323) 954-7731
Los Angeles, CA 90048   www.blocagency.com

BMG Models   (323) 692-0900
5455 Wilshire Blvd., Ste. 900   www.bmgmodels.com
Los Angeles, CA 90036

Bobby Ball Talent Agency   (818) 506-8188
4116 W. Magnolia Blvd., Ste. 205   FAX (818) 506-8588
Burbank, CA 91505   www.bobbyballagency.com
(Athletes, Body Parts Models, Children, Commercial Talent,
Models, Talent, TV Hosts & Voice-Over Artists)

     (310) 275-8263
Body Parts Models   (702) 496-8469
2023 Coldwater Canyon Dr.   FAX (310) 273-5878
Beverly Hills, CA 90210   www.bodypartsmodels.com
(Body Parts Models)

Brady, Brannon, Rich   (323) 852-9559
5670 Wilshire Blvd., Ste. 820   FAX (323) 852-9579
Los Angeles, CA 90036
(Commercial Talent)

Brand Model & Talent Agency, Inc.   (714) 850-1158
601 N. Baker   FAX (714) 850-0806
Santa Ana, CA 92703   www.brandmodelandtalent.com

Bresler Kelly & Associates   (310) 479-5611
11500 W. Olympic Blvd., Ste. 352
Los Angeles, CA 90064

The Brogan Agency   (310) 450-9700
1517 Park Row   FAX (310) 450-9600
Venice, CA 90291   www.thebroganagency.com

C.E.S.D. Talent Agency   (310) 475-2111
10635 Santa Monica Blvd., Ste. 130   FAX (310) 475-1929
Los Angeles, CA 90025   www.cesdtalent.com

Carry Company   (213) 388-0770
3875 Wilshire Blvd., Ste. 402   www.carrycompany.com
Los Angeles, CA 90010

Cassell-Levy, Inc./CL, Inc.   (323) 461-3971
843 N. Sycamore Ave.   FAX (323) 461-1134
Hollywood, CA 90038   www.clinc.com
(Talent & Voice-Overs)

Castle Hill Entertainment   (323) 653-3535
1101 S. Orlando Ave.   www.castlehillagency.com
Los Angeles, CA 90035

Cavaleri & Associates   (818) 955-9300
178 S. Victory Blvd., Ste. 205   FAX (818) 955-9399
Burbank, CA 91502

The Chasin Agency   (310) 278-7505
8899 Beverly Blvd., Ste. 716   FAX (310) 275-6685
Los Angeles, CA 90048

The Cindy Romano Talent Agency   (760) 323-3333
P.O. Box 1951   www.cindyromanotalent.com
Palm Springs, CA 92263

                  (310) 496-4501
Circle Talent Associates   (310) 496-4502
520 Broadway, Ste. 350   www.circletalent.com
Santa Monica, CA 90401

                  (818) 509-0121
Clear Talent Group/CTG   (818) 509-0207
10950 Ventura Blvd.   FAX (818) 509-7729
Studio City, CA 91604   www.cleartalentgroup.com
(Choreographers)

Click Models Management   (310) 246-0800
9057 Nemo St.   FAX (310) 858-1701
West Hollywood, CA 90069   www.clickmodel.com
(Models Only)

Coast to Coast Talent Group, Inc.   (323) 845-9200
3350 Barham Blvd.   FAX (323) 845-9212
Los Angeles, CA 90068   www.ctctalent.com

Colleen Cler Agency   (818) 841-7943
178 S. Victory Blvd., Ste. 108   FAX (818) 841-4541
Burbank, CA 91502   www.colleencler.com
(Children Through Young Adults)

Commercial Talent, Inc.   (310) 247-1431
9255 W. Sunset Blvd., Ste. 505   FAX (310) 247-1327
Los Angeles, CA 90069
     www.commercialtalentagency.com

Creative Artists Agency (CAA)   (424) 288-2000
                  FAX (424) 288-2900
                  www.caa.com

                  (310) 820-1020
D2 Models   (888) 820-1001
11693 San Vicente Blvd., Ste. 823   FAX (323) 372-3948
Los Angeles, CA 90049   models.direct2pro.com
(Children, Commercial Talent, Models & Talent)

Daniel Hoff Agency   (323) 932-2500
5455 Wilshire Blvd., Ste. 1100   FAX (323) 932-2501
Los Angeles, CA 90036   www.danielhoffagency.com

David Shapira & Associates   (310) 967-0480
193 N. Robertson Blvd.   FAX (310) 659-4177
Beverly Hills, CA 90211

DDO Artists Agency   (323) 462-8000
6725 Sunset Blvd., Ste. 230   FAX (323) 462-0100
Los Angeles, CA 90028   www.ddoagency.com
(Athletes, Children, Choreographers, Commercial Talent,
Models & Talent)

Defining Artists   (818) 753-2405
10 Universal City Plaza, 20th Fl.   FAX (818) 753-2403
Universal City, CA 91608   www.definingartists.com

Diverse Talent Group   (310) 201-6565
9911 Pico Blvd., Ste. 350W   FAX (310) 201-6572
Los Angeles, CA 90035   www.diversetalentgroup.com

Dominique Model and Talent   (310) 430-4301
(Talent)   www.dominiquemodelandtalent.com

Don Buchwald & Associates, Inc.   (323) 655-7400
6500 Wilshire Blvd., Ste. 2200   FAX (323) 655-7470
Los Angeles, CA 90048   www.buchwald.com

Dramatic Artists   (818) 288-1859
103 W. Alameda Ave., Ste. 139 www.dramaticartists.com
Burbank, CA 91502

Elite Model Management   (310) 274-9395
345 N. Maple Dr., Ste. 397   FAX (310) 278-7520
Beverly Hills, CA 90210   www.elitemodel.com
(Models Only)

Ellis Talent Group   (818) 980-8072
4705 Laurel Canyon Blvd., Ste. 300
Valley Village, CA 91607   www.ellistalentgroup.com

Envy Model & Talent   (310) 694-8567
930 S. Robertson Blvd., Ste. 502   FAX (310) 598-5619
Los Angeles, CA 90035

         www.envymodelmanagement.com

Film Artists Associates   (818) 883-5008
21044 Ventura Blvd., Ste. 215
Woodland Hills, CA 91364
(Talent Only)

Flick   (310) 271-9111
9057 Nemo St.   www.flickcommercials.com
West Hollywood, CA 90069

The Ford Agency   (310) 276-8100
9200 W. Sunset Blvd.   FAX (310) 276-9299
Hollywood, CA 90029   www.fordmodels.com

The Gage Group   (818) 905-3800
14724 Ventura Blvd., Ste. 505   FAX (818) 905-3322
Sherman Oaks, CA 91403

The Geddes Agency   (323) 848-2700
8430 Santa Monica Blvd., Ste. 200   www.geddes.net
West Hollywood, CA 90069

The Gersh Agency   (310) 274-6611
9465 Wilshire Blvd., Sixth Fl.   FAX (310) 274-4035
Beverly Hills, CA 90212   www.gershagency.com

Greene & Associates Talent Agency (310) 550-9333
1901 Avenue of the Stars, Ste. 130   FAX (310) 550-9334
Los Angeles, CA 90067

Hervey/Grimes Talent Agency   (310) 475-2010
10561 Missouri Ave., Ste. 2   FAX (310) 475-5851
Los Angeles, CA 90025   www.herveygrimes.com

Hollander Talent Group   (818) 382-9800
14011 Ventura Blvd., Ste. 202W
Sherman Oaks, CA 91423   www.hollandertalent.com
(Children)

                  (310) 961-1584
Horses for Productions   (310) 457-7027
2277 Decker Canyon Rd.
Malibu, CA 90265   www.horsesforproductions.com
(Champions, Jockeys & Riders)

The House of Representatives   (310) 451-2345
1434 Sixth St., Ste. 1   FAX (310) 451-3451
Santa Monica, CA 90401

Howard Talent West   (818) 766-5300
10657 Riverside Dr.   FAX (818) 760-3328
Toluca Lake, CA 91602

HRI Talent   (818) 733-2424
100 Universal City Plaza   FAX (818) 733-4307
Bungalow 7152   www.hritalent.com
Universal City, CA 91608

Imperium 7 Talent Agency   (323) 931-9099
5455 Wilshire Blvd., Ste. 1706   FAX (323) 931-9084
Los Angeles, CA 90036   www.imperium-7.com

Independent Artists   (310) 550-5000
9601 Wilshire Blvd., Ste. 750   FAX (310) 550-5005
Beverly Hills, CA 90210

Innovative Artists   (310) 656-0400
1505 10th St.   FAX (310) 656-0456
Santa Monica, CA 90401   www.innovativeartists.com

International Creative
Management - ICM   (310) 550-4000
10250 Constellation Blvd.   www.icmtalent.com
Los Angeles, CA 90067
(Talent & Voice-Overs)

Jack Scagnetti Talent & Literary   (818) 761-0580
5118 Vineland Ave., Ste. 106
North Hollywood, CA 91601

Jaime Ferrar Agency/JFA   (818) 506-8311
4741 Laurel Canyon Blvd., Ste. 110 FAX (818) 506-8334
Valley Village, CA 91607   www.jfala.com

Jana Luker Agency   (310) 441-2822
1923 ½ Westwood Blvd., Ste. 3   FAX (310) 441-2823
Los Angeles, CA 90025

Jet Set Talent Agency   (858) 551-9393
1316 Third St., Ste. 109   FAX (858) 551-9392
Santa Monica, CA 90401   www.jetsetmodels.com

JS Represents   (323) 462-3246
6815 Willoughby Ave., Ste. 102 www.jsrepresents.com
Los Angeles, CA 90038

Kathleen Schultz Associates   (818) 760-3100
6442 Coldwater Canyon, Ste. 117   FAX (818) 760-3125
Valley Glen, CA 91606

Kazarian/Spencer/
Ruskin & Associates, Inc.   (818) 769-9111
11969 Ventura Blvd., Third Fl.   FAX (818) 769-9840
Studio City, CA 91604   www.ksrtalent.com
(Talent & Voice-Overs)

The Kohner Agency   (310) 550-1060
9300 Wilshire Blvd., Ste. 555   FAX (310) 276-1083
Beverly Hills, CA 90212

LA Models & LA Talent   (323) 436-7700
7700 W. Sunset Blvd.   FAX (323) 436-7755
Los Angeles, CA 90046   www.lamodels.com
(Models Only)

Linda McAlister Talent   (310) 561-2688
530 S. Lake Ave., Ste. 335   FAX (866) 816-3042
Pasadena, CA 91101   www.lmtalent.com

                                    (310) 601-2532
LW1 Light/Wilhelmina Talent Agency (323) 653-5700
9378 Wilshire Blvd., Ste. 310   FAX (323) 653-2255
Los Angeles, CA 90212   www.wilhelmina.com
(Commercial Talent & Talent)

Mademoiselle Talent &
Modeling Agency   (213) 387-9994
3550 Wilshire Blvd., Ste. 1610   FAX (213) 387-9991
Los Angeles, CA 90010

Mavrick Artists Agency   (323) 931-5555
6100 Wilshire Blvd., Ste. 550   FAX (323) 931-5554
Los Angeles, CA 90048   www.mavrickartists.com

McDonald/Selznick Associates   (323) 957-6680
953 N. Cole Ave.   FAX (323) 957-6688
Hollywood, CA 90038   www.msaagency.com
(Choreographers, Dancers, Models, Production Designers,
Singers & Talent)

Media Artists Group   (323) 658-5050
8255 Sunset Blvd.   FAX (866) 805-8621
Los Angeles, CA 90046 www.mediaartistsgroup.com

Metropolitan Talent Agency   (323) 857-4500
7020 La Pesa Dr.   FAX (323) 857-4599
Los Angeles, CA 90068   www.mta.com

MGA/Mary Grady Agency   (818) 763-8400
269 S. Beverly Dr., Ste. 1088   www.mgatalent.com
Los Angeles, CA 90212

Mitchell K. Stubbs & Associates   (310) 838-1200
8695 W. Washington Blvd., Ste. 204 FAX (310) 838-1245
Culver City, CA 90232   www.mksagency.com

Momentum Talent & Literary Agency (310) 858-6655
9401 Wilshire Blvd., Ste. 501   FAX (310) 858-6651
Beverly Hills, CA 90212   www.momentumtal.com

Nancy Chaidez Agency &
Association   (323) 467-8954
6340 Coldwater Canyon, Ste. 214   FAX (323) 467-8963
North Hollywood, CA 91606

Nous Model Management, Inc./   (310) 385-6900
Nu Talent Agency   (310) 385-6907
117 N. Robertson Blvd.   FAX (310) 385-6910
Los Angeles, CA 90048   www.nousmodels.com

Nouveau Model & Talent   (858) 456-1400
7825 Fay Ave., Ste. 200   FAX (858) 456-1969
La Jolla, CA 92037   www.nouveaumodels.com

O'Neill Talent Group   (818) 566-7717
4150 Riverside Dr., Ste. 212   www.oneilltalent.com
Burbank, CA 91505

Origin Talent   (818) 487-1800
4705 Laurel Canyon Blvd., Ste. 306 FAX (818) 487-9788
Studio City, CA 91607   www.origintalent.com

Osbrink Talent Agency   (818) 760-2488
4343 Lankershim Blvd., Ste. 100   FAX (818) 760-0991
Universal City, CA 91602   www.osbrinkagency.com

Otto Models & Talent   (323) 650-2200
(Commercial Talent, Models & Talent) www.ottomodels.com

Pakula/King & Associates   (310) 281-4868
9229 W. Sunset Blvd., Ste. 400   FAX (310) 281-4866
Los Angeles, CA 90069

Paradigm, A Talent &
Literary Agency   (310) 288-8000
360 N. Crescent Dr.   FAX (310) 288-2000
Beverly Hills, CA 90210   www.paradigmagency.com

Peak Models & Talent   (661) 294-1100
25852 McBean Pkwy, Ste. 190   FAX (661) 294-9311
Valencia, CA 91355   www.peakmodels.com

Periwinkle Entertainment
Productions   (714) 776-5820
P.O. Box 2486   FAX (714) 635-1711
Anaheim, CA 92814
(Circus and Variety Acts)

Peter Rotter Music Services   (818) 876-7500
4766 Park Granada., Ste. 106   FAX (818) 876-7503
Calabasas, CA 91302   www.prmusicservices.com

Peter Strain & Associates, Inc.   (323) 525-3391
5455 Wilshire Blvd., Ste. 1812   FAX (323) 525-0881
Los Angeles, CA 90036

Pinnacle Commercial Talent   (323) 939-5440
5055 Wilshire Blvd., Ste. 865   FAX (323) 939-0630
Los Angeles, CA 90036

The Premier Talent Group   (818) 752-5911
4370 Tujunga Ave., Ste. 110   FAX (866) 469-0944
Studio City, CA 91604 www.thepremiertalentgroup.com

Premier West Entertainment/   (818) 231-1491
Divas in Training   (888) 340-7444
10700 Centura Blvd., Ste. 8   www.premierwest.net
Universal City, CA 91601

Privilege Talent Agency   (818) 386-2377
P.O. Box 260860
Encino, CA 91426

Progressive Artists Agency (323) 850-2992
1041 N. Formosa Ave.
West Hollywood, CA 90046

PTI Talent Agency, Inc. (818) 386-1310
14724 Ventura Blvd., PH
Sherman Oaks, CA 91403

Q Model Management (310) 205-2888
8618 W. Third St. FAX (310) 205-6920
Los Angeles, CA 90048 www.qmodels.com

Rage Models & Talent (818) 225-0526
23679 Calabasas Rd., Ste. 501 FAX (818) 225-1736
Calabasas, CA 91302 www.ragemodels.com

Rebel Entertainment Partners, Inc. (323) 935-1700
5700 Wilshire Blvd., Ste. 456 FAX (323) 932-9901
Los Angeles, CA 90036 www.reptalent.com

Rogers Orion Talent Agency (818) 789-7064
13731 Ventura Blvd., Ste. D FAX (818) 301-2090
Sherman Oaks, CA 91423 rogersorionagency.com

(619) 296-1018
San Diego Model Management (619) 296-2373
438 Camino del Rio South, Ste. 116 FAX (619) 296-3422
San Diego, CA 92108 www.sdmodel.com
(Athletes, Body Parts Models, Children, Commercial Talent,
Models & Talent)

The Savage Agency (323) 461-8316
6212 Banner Ave. FAX (323) 461-2417
Hollywood, CA 90038

Schiowitz Connor Ankrum Wolf, Inc. (323) 463-8355
1680 N. Vine St., Ste. 1016
Los Angeles, CA 90028

Scott Stander & Associates (818) 905-7000
4533 Van Nuys Blvd., Ste. 401 FAX (818) 990-0582
Sherman Oaks, CA 91403 www.scottstander.com

SDB Partners (310) 785-0060
1801 Avenue of the Stars, Ste. 902 FAX (310) 785-0071
Los Angeles, CA 90067

Shamon Freitas Agency (619) 325-1180
3916 Oregon St. FAX (619) 325-1183
San Diego, CA 92104 www.shamonfreitas.com

Sharon Kemp Talent Agency (310) 858-7200
865 Comstock Ave., Ste. 11C FAX (310) 550-1131
Los Angeles, CA 90024

Shirley Wilson & Associates (323) 857-6977
5410 Wilshire Blvd., 510 FAX (323) 857-6980
Los Angeles, CA 90036

SMS Talent, Inc. (310) 289-0909
8730 W. Sunset Blvd., Ste. 440 FAX (310) 289-0990
Los Angeles, CA 90069 www.smstalent.net

Special Artists Agency (310) 859-9688
9465 Wilshire Blvd., Ste. 820
Beverly Hills, CA 90212

Stage 9 Talent (323) 460-6006
1249 N. Lodi Pl. FAX (323) 462-3535
Hollywood, CA 90038 www.stage9talent.com

Starcraft Talent Agency (818) 403-1105
27525 Newhall Ranch Rd. FAX (323) 845-4783
Ste 7D, Second Fl.
Valencia, CA 91355

Stone Manners Salners Agency (323) 655-1313
9911 W. Pico Blvd., Ste. 1400 FAX (323) 389-1577
Los Angeles, CA 90035 www.smsagency.com

Susan Nathe & Associates (323) 653-7573
8281 Melrose Ave., Ste. 200 FAX (323) 653-1179
Los Angeles, CA 90046
(Commercial Talent & Theatrical Talent)

Sutton, Barth & Vennari (323) 938-6000
145 S. Fairfax Ave., Ste. 310 FAX (323) 935-8671
Los Angeles, CA 90036 www.sbvtalent.com
(Talent & Voice-Overs)

**Tisherman Gilbert Motley Drozdoski
Talent Agency/TGMD** (323) 850-6767
6767 Forest Lawn Dr., Ste. 101 FAX (323) 850-7340
Los Angeles, CA 90068 www.tgmdtalent.com
(Voice-Over Artists)

Trio Talent Agency (323) 851-6886
1502 Gardner St. FAX (323) 851-6882
Los Angeles, CA 90046 www.triotalentagency.com
(Choreographers & Talent)

United Talent Agency (310) 273-6700
9560 Wilshire Blvd., Ste. 500 FAX (310) 247-1111
Beverly Hills, CA 90212 www.unitedtalent.com

Venture IAB (213) 381-1900
3211 Cahuenga Blvd. West, Ste. 104 FAX (213) 908-2194
Los Angeles, CA 90068 www.ventureiab.com

VOX, Inc. (323) 655-8699
6420 Wilshire Blvd., Ste. 1080 FAX (323) 852-1472
Los Angeles, CA 90048 www.voxusa.net
(Talent & Voice-Overs)

The Wallis Agency (818) 953-4848
210 N. Pass Ave., Ste. 205 www.wallisagency.com
Burbank, CA 91505

William Kerwin Agency (323) 469-5155
1605 N. Cahuenga Blvd., Ste. 202
Los Angeles, CA 90028 www.kerwinagency.com

William Morris Endeavor (310) 285-9000
9601 Wilshire Blvd. FAX (310) 285-9010
Beverly Hills, CA 90210 www.wmeentertainment.com
(Talent & Voice-Overs)

Entertainment Partners   (818) 955-6216
2835 N. Naomi St.   FAX (818) 559-2517
Burbank, CA 91504   www.entertainmentpartners.com

The Incentives Office   (310) 982-1340
1507 Seventh St., Ste. 157www.theincentivesoffice.com
Santa Monica, CA 90401

Tax Credits, LLC   (866) 652-3170
45 Knightsbridge Rd.   www.taxcreditsllc.com
Piscataway, NJ 08854

                                    (949) 768-7110
A & D Music Incorporated   (949) 500-6307
22322 Colonna Dr.   FAX (949) 716-7667
Laguna Hills, CA 92653   www.admusic.net
(Music)

A and C Harbour Lites, Ltd.   (310) 926-9552
P.O. Box 9279   FAX (310) 356-3579
Marina Del Rey, CA 90295
(Boat Handling, Marine, Nautical, Scuba Diving & Water Safety)
Contact: Capt. Seth Chase

Abacus Consulting &   (626) 487-8909
Chinese Translation Services   (877) 800-8832
401 N. Garfield Ave., Ste. 1   FAX (626) 282-9252
Alhambra, CA 91801
(Chinese Culture) www.certifiedchinesetranslation.com

Adam Williams, Magic & Illusion   (310) 289-9852
(Illusion & Magic)   FAX (310) 271-4822
                                    www.magicsnow.com

Aerial Action Productions/
Reel Orange   (949) 548-4524
316 La Jolla Dr.   www.reelorange.com
Newport Beach, CA 92663
(Aerial & White Water)
Contact: Art Vitarelli

Airboyd.tv/Boyd Kelly   (818) 535-2693
                                    www.airboyd.com
(Aviation, Commercial Airline Pilot & SAG Airplane Pilot)
Contact: Boyd Kelly

                                    (626) 354-4421
Andersen Physical Therapy   (626) 568-4997
(Physical Therapy)   www.callthept.com

                                    (562) 433-2863
Aquavision   (562) 688-3038
3708 E. Fourth St.   FAX (562) 433-2863
Long Beach, CA 90814   www.aquavision.net
(Marine Coordination, Rigging, Scuba Diving &
Stunt Coordination)
Contact: Bob Anderson

                                    (310) 273-9190
Julie Armstrong, RN PsyD   (310) 666-9190
4519 Admiralty Way, Ste. 202
Marina del Rey, CA 90212
                www.psychologyexpertwitness.com
(Forensic Psychology, Hospital, Medications, Nursing, Psychia-
try, Psychoanalysis, Psychology, Psychosis, Therapy &
Workers Compensation)

                                    (818) 842-8444
Asman & Associates, LLC   (818) 929-9164
P.O. Box 21022   FAX (818) 842-8445
Glendale, CA 91221   www.asmanj.com
(Animal-Related Events and Programs)

AthleteSource Casting   (310) 871-7956
13425 Ventura Blvd., Second Fl.   FAX (435) 645-8163
Sherman Oaks, CA 91423
                www.athletesourcecasting.com
(Action and Olympic Sports)

                                    (310) 227-8200
Carrie Becks/A-1 Medical Advisor (310) 678-7601
345 Richmond St.   FAX (310) 227-8205
El Segundo, CA 90245   www.redm33.com

Bikes..Camera..Action!   (310) 995-2084
1105 Bonilla
Topanga, CA 90290
(Bicycle Racing & Rollerblading)
Contact: Rick Denman

Bob Marriott's Flyfishing Store   (714) 525-1827
2700 W. Orangethorpe Ave.   FAX (714) 525-5783
Fullerton, CA 92833   www.bobmarriotts.com
(Fly-Fishing)

                                    (310) 301-9426
Paul K. Bronston, M.D.   (310) 503-0347
One Jib St., Ste. 202   FAX (310) 823-2433
Marina del Rey, CA 90292
(Medical)

Call the Cops   (530) 305-3558
(Homicide, Narcotics, Patrol and Vice Procedure, Police
Dialogue & SWAT Tactics)
Contact: Randy Walker

Cannon's Great Escapes   (818) 385-7092
35358 Rancho Rd.   FAX (818) 581-4130
Yucaipa, CA 92399   www.cannonsgreatescapes.com
(Escapes, Illusion & Magic)

Caravan West Productions   (661) 268-8300
35660 Jayhawker Rd.   FAX (661) 268-8301
Agua Dulce, CA 91390   www.caravanwest.com
(Firearms Instructor, Westerns - 1860-1910)
Contact: Peter Sherayko

                                    (818) 365-7999
Cinema Aquatics   (805) 207-5797
(Marine)   www.cinemaaquatics.com

                                    (661) 222-7342
Cinema Rentals, Inc.   (818) 365-7999
25876 The Old Road, Ste. 174   FAX (661) 427-0881
Stevenson Ranch, CA 91381   www.cinemarentals.com
(Marine and Underwater Safety)
Contact: Jim Pearson

Cinema Safety &   (310) 614-0206
Marine Services, Inc.   (805) 207-5797
1534 N. Moorpark Rd., Ste. 108   FAX (805) 241-3954
Thousand Oaks, CA 91360   www.cinemasafety.com
(Medical, Scuba Diving, Underwater & Water Safety)

Cinemafloat
(949) 675-8888
(714) 801-5553
1624 W. Oceanfront Walk FAX (949) 644-3073
Newport Beach, CA 92663
(Marine)
Contact: Joseph Cleary

Combat Casting
(818) 618-2527
(310) 686-2718
(Military, Police & SWAT) FAX (818) 509-9581
www.combatcasting.com

Cynthia Crothers
(310) 691-9388
14126 Marquesas Way, Ste. A www.kidzseatz.com
Marina Del Rey, CA 90292
(Child Passenger Safety Children's Car Seat Specialist)

Customs by Eddie Paul, A Division (310) 322-8035
of EP Industries, Inc. (310) 259-0542
1330 E. Franklin Ave. FAX (310) 322-8044
El Segundo, CA 90245 www.deadlinetv.net
(Automotive, Motorcycle & Underwater)

Debbie Merrill's Skate Great USA
(310) 625-0059
(888) 866-6121
P.O. Box 3452 www.skategreat.com
Santa Monica, CA 90408
(Ice, In-Line and Roller Skating)
Contact: Debbie Merrill

Don Wayne Magic, Inc. (818) 763-3192
(Illusion & Magic) www.donwaynemagic.com

Doves Trained for TV (818) 340-4040
(Magic Cosultant) FAX (818) 340-2432
www.amosmagic.com

DT Trampolines Inc.
(818) 888-2935
(800) 649-4945
P.O. Box 6214 FAX (818) 888-2951
Woodland Hills, CA 90365 www.dttrampolines.com
Contact: Kim Kahana, Jr.

Donna Duffy, R.N.
(310) 545-2895
(310) 704-9131
(Medical)

The Etiquette Company (949) 493-6700
29 St. Kitts FAX (949) 493-6700
Dana Point, CA 92629 www.theetiquettecompany.com
(Etiquette)

Executive Yacht Management, Inc. (310) 306-2555
644 Venice Blvd. FAX (310) 306-1147
Marina del Rey, CA 90291 www.yacht-management.com
(Marine)
Contact: L. Ring

Art Fransen (951) 736-9440
FAX (951) 453-3580
www.supertrap.com
(Homicide, Narcotics, Police Procedure & SWAT Tactics)

Franz Harary Productions
(323) 871-1796
(323) 855-9886
(Illusion & Magic) www.harary.com

Gary Fredo (310) 686-0460
FAX (818) 761-5184
www.ghprocutions.com
(Con Games, Criminal Law, Firearms Instruction, Homicide,
Intelligence, Military, Missing Persons Procedures, Narcotics,
Patrol and Vice Procedure, Police & Police Dialogue)

Frogmen Unlimited/Mark Lonsdale
(661) 821-1210
(310) 405-2655
(Aquatic Action & Diving) www.sttu.com

Steven Guerrero (310) 864-2000
(Marine) www.aquaticcinema.com

Bob Hamer, FBI (310) 801-0083
(FBI & Law Enforcement)

Harlan's Heroes (818) 439-9664
(Military: Korea, Vietnam, World War I & World War II)

Hollywoodivers.com
(323) 969-9875
(877) 657-2822
(Diving & Marine) FAX (323) 969-9734
www.hollywoodivers.com

Interorbital Systems
(661) 965-0771
(323) 463-6529
1394 Barnes St., Bldg. 7 www.interorbital.com
Mojave Spaceport
Mojave, CA 93501
(Aerospace, Rocket and Space Systems)
Contact: Randa Milliron

Steve Kutcher (626) 836-0322
1801 Oakview Ln. www.bugsaremybusiness.com
Arcadia, CA 91006
(Biology, Entomology & Science)

Edward Lear, Esq.
(310) 642-6900
(866) 522-2642
5200 W. Century Blvd., Ste. 345 FAX (310) 642-6910
Los Angeles, CA 90045
(Civil and Criminal Law & Trial Scenes)

Gary Leffew/Anything Rodeo (805) 878-6948
P.O. Box 517
Santa Maria, CA 93456
(Rodeo)

Los Angeles Police Department
(213) 972-2971
(213) 485-9899
1358 N. Wilcox Ave. www.lapdonline.org
Hollywood, CA 90028

The Magic Castle (323) 851-3313
7001 Franklin Ave. FAX (323) 851-4899
Hollywood, CA 90028 www.magiccastle.com
(Magic)
Contact: James G. Williams

Nina Marino, ESQ (310) 557-0007
9454 Wilshire Blvd., Ste. 500 FAX (310) 557-0008
Beverly Hills, CA 90212 www.kaplanmarino.com
(Criminal Law)

Robin McCarthy (818) 883-6223
(Ice Skating)
Contacts: Robin McCarthy & Bonnie Harris

Bobbi McRae
(310) 922-2777
(818) 767-2121
(Figure and Hockey Skating) www.bobbimcrae.com

Mime and Movement by (310) 494-6463
Lorin Eric Salm (818) 300-7473
(Mime and Movement) www.movement-coach.com

Brandon Molale
(310) 493-5158
(818) 774-3889
(Football) www.brandonmolale.com

Monad Railway Equipment Co.
(562) 404-8641
(562) 522-7894
15220 Valley View Ave. FAX (562) 404-8541
La Mirada, CA 90638 www.monadrailway.com
(Railroads & Trains)
Contact: Lon Orlenko

Motion Picture Marine (310) 822-1100
616 Venice Blvd. FAX (310) 822-2679
Marina del Rey, CA 90291
(Marine Coordination) www.motionpicturemarine.com

Next Level Sailing
(858) 922-3522
(800) 644-3454
Embarcadero at Harbor Dr. www.stars-stripes.com
San Diego, CA 92101
(Marine & Sailing)

Jimmy O'Connell (310) 968-0549
306 Market St., Ste. A (310) 452-5774
Venice, CA 90291 FAX (310) 452-5774

David O'Leary (805) 558-6754
3211 Winterbrook Court
Thousand Oaks, CA 91360
(Firefighting & Medical)

Stephen Patt, M.D. (310) 582-1114
2001 Santa Monica Blvd., Ste. 888-W
Santa Monica, CA 90404
(Medical)

Perris Valley Skydiving (951) 657-3904
2091 Goetz Rd. FAX (951) 657-6178
Perris, CA 92570 www.skydiveperris.com
Contact: Patrick Conaster

Reel Deal Technical Advisors (310) 780-0618
P.O. Box 1444
Manhattan Beach, CA 90266
(Homicide, Military, Narcotics, Police-Patrol, Special Ops,
SWAT & Vice)
Contact: Chic Daniel

Howard Richman (818) 344-3306
soundfeelings.com/products/music_instruction/
(Piano) piano_lessons.htm

John Sakas (310) 908-9198
2408 Carnegie Ln., Ste. 3 FAX (310) 376-7872
Redondo Beach, CA 90278
(Martial Arts)

Schwartz Oil Company, Inc. (661) 259-4000
27241 Henry Mayo Dr. (818) 365-9214
Valencia, CA 91355 FAX (661) 257-0137
(HAZWOPER) www.socifuel.com

Sigloch Military-Tactical (818) 414-5381
26873 Sierra Hwy, Ste. 421 www.sigloch-mt.com
Santa Clarita, CA 91321
(Military & Tactical)

State Fire Marshal -
Motion Picture/Entertainment Unit (626) 305-1908
602 E. Huntington Dr., Ste. A FAX (626) 305-5173
Monrovia, CA 91016 www.fire.ca.gov
Contact: Deputy Adams

Studio Sea Management, Inc. (818) 519-4399
(Marine) FAX (888) 297-5947
Contact: Ransom Walrod

Stunt Wings/Joe Greblo (818) 367-2430
12623 Gridley St. (818) 266-0874
Sylmar, CA 91342 FAX (818) 367-5363
(Hang Gliding, Paragliding & Ultralight Aircraft) www.stuntwings.com

SwordPlay/Tim Weske (818) 421-2926
64 E. Magnolia Blvd. (818) 980-2123
Burbank, CA 91502 FAX (818) 566-4357
(Fencing and Sword Fight Choreography) www.timweske.com

Tactical Media Group (310) 880-6018
578 Washington Blvd., Ste. 346
Marina del Rey, CA 90292 www.tacticalmediagroup.net
(Military Technical Advisors & Combat Weapon Trainers)

Richard Theiss/RTSea Prods. (949) 645-4304
P.O. Box 51417 FAX (949) 645-4304
Irvine, CA 92619 www.rtsea.com
(Marine Action & Scuba Diving)

US Air Force Motion Picture Office (310) 235-7522
10880 Wilshire Blvd., Ste. 1240 (310) 235-7511
Los Angeles, CA 90024 FAX (310) 235-7500
Contact: Charles Davis www.airforcehollywood.af.mil

US Army Office of Public Affairs (310) 235-7621
10880 Wilshire Blvd., Ste. 1250 (310) 235-7622
Los Angeles, CA 90024 FAX (310) 235-6075
www.defenselink.mil/faq/pis/PC12FILM.html

US Coast Guard Motion
Picture & Television Office (310) 235-7817
10880 Wilshire Blvd., Ste. 1210 FAX (310) 235-7851
Los Angeles, CA 90024
www.defenselink.mil/faq/pis/PC12FILM.html

US Marine Corps Motion
Picture & Television Liason Office (310) 235-7272
10880 Wilshire Blvd., Ste. 1230 FAX (310) 235-7274
Los Angeles, CA 90024

US Navy Office Entertainment (310) 235-7481
Industry Liason (310) 235-6266
10880 Wilshire Blvd., Ste. 1220 FAX (310) 235-7856
Los Angeles, CA 90024
Contacts: Rosalie Clark & Robert Anderson

Vertical Adventures (949) 854-6250
P.O. Box 7548 (800) 514-8785
Newport Beach, CA 92658 FAX (949) 854-5249
(Mountain Climbing and Safety, Rigging, Rock Climbing &
Stunt Safety)
Contact: Bob Gaines

War Horse & Militaria
Heritage Foundation (818) 694-9277
(Military Cavalry) FAX (818) 896-8310
www.warhorsefoundation.com

Warriors, Inc. (818) 349-6640
16129 Tupper St. FAX (818) 688-3939
North Hills, CA 91343 www.warriorsinc.com
(Firearms Instruction, History, Intelligence, Korean War,
Marines, Martial Arts, Military, Special Operations, Vietnam War,
World War I & World War II)

Westside Detectives, Inc. (323) 583-8660
6230 Wilshire Blvd., Ste. 59 (323) 833-2383
Los Angeles, CA 90048 www.westsidedetectives.com
(Missing Persons and Private Detective Procedures)

WW2 Military Vehicle Rentals, Ltd. (949) 632-4345
www.ww2militaryvehiclerentals.com
(WW II Armored Fighting Vehicles, Equipment, Military
History & Uniforms)

1st Choice Transcription (818) 742-5189
2416 W. Victory Blvd., Ste. 262 **www.rnkproductions.com**
Burbank, CA 91506
(Scripts & Transcription)

a+ The Employment Company, Inc. (818) 840-0998
3500 West Olive Ave., Ste. 300 FAX **(661) 834-3194**
Burbank, CA 91505 **www.theemploymentco.com**

AD Personnel (310) 284-3939
12100 Wilshire Blvd., Ste. 860 **www.adpersonnel.com**
Los Angeles, CA 90025
(Foreign Language Transcription, Permanent Personnel,
Temporary Personnel, Transcription & Word Processing)

Alpha Dog Transcriptions (818) 785-6818
6314 Ethel Ave. FAX **(818) 937-6888**
Van Nuys, CA 91401 **www.alphadogtranscriptions.com**
(Foreign Language Transcription, Scripts & Transcription)

BAM Transcription
(818) 505-0990
(310) 600-6595
10061 Riverside Dr., Ste. 917 FAX **(818) 506-1462**
Toluca Lake, CA 91602 **www.bamtranscription.com**
(Scripts & Transcription)

Brocato Transcription Services (818) 846-1128
3607 W. Magnolia Blvd., Ste. 8
Burbank, CA 91505 **www.brocatotranscriptions.com**
(As-Broadcast Scripts, Audio, Video Tape and Digital Transcription, Dialogue Lists & Foreign Language Transcription)

Comar Agency (310) 248-2700
6500 Wilshire Blvd., Ste. 2240 FAX **(310) 288-0205**
Los Angeles, CA 90048 **www.comaragency.com**
(Permanent and Temporary Personnel)

The Continuity Company (310) 968-4302
8726D S. Sepulveda Blvd., Ste. B22
Los Angeles, CA 90045
(Scripts & Transcription)

Daily Transcripts
(310) 734-8853
(888) 515-7143
6701 Center Dr. West, Ste. 1111 FAX **(424) 203-3072**
Los Angeles, CA 90045 **www.dailytranscription.com**
(Foreign Language Transcription, Script Coordinator, Scripts,
Transcription & Word Processing)

Echotext (818) 985-1887
3621 Lankershim Blvd. FAX **(818) 985-1889**
Los Angeles, CA 90068 **www.echotext.com**
(Scripts, Transcription & Word Processing)

Flying Fingers Transcripts (818) 557-0580
927 W. Olive Ave., Ste. B FAX **(818) 557-0590**
Burbank, CA 91506 **www.flyingfingerstranscripts.com**
(Foreign Language Transcription, Scripts, Transcription &
Word Processing)

Hollywood Transcribing (818) 437-9970
hottranscribe.com
(Temporary Personnel, Transcription Services &
Word Processing)

Hollywood Transcriptions (818) 559-1562
847 N. Hollywood Way, Ste. 200 FAX **(818) 559-1362**
Burbank, CA 91505 **www.hollywoodtranscriptions.com**
(Scripts, Transcription & Word Processing)

Huntington Court Reporters &
Transcription, Inc.
(626) 792-7250
(800) 586-2988
301 N. Lake Ave., Ste. 150 FAX **(626) 792-8760**
Pasadena, CA 91101 **www.huntingtoncr.com**
(Transcription & Foreign Language Transcription)

iProbe Multilingual Solutions, Inc. (888) 489-6035
www.iprobesolutions.com
(Foreign Language Transcription)

JR Media Services, Inc.
(818) 557-0200
(818) 398-9306
2501 W. Burbank Blvd., Ste. 200 FAX **(818) 557-0201**
Burbank, CA 91505 **www.jrmediaservices.com**

Brenda Marshall (818) 766-8735
www.brendamarshall.net
(Resumes, Scripts & Word Processing)

MSG LLC Transcription Service
(310) 826-4563
(310) 288-6598
2118 Wilshire Blvd., Ste. 1003
Santa Monica, CA 90403
(Transcription)

Production Transcripts
(818) 265-1541
(888) 349-3022
3736 San Fernando Rd. FAX **(213) 947-1585**
Glendale, CA 91204 **www.productiontranscripts.com**
(Transcription)

Script Changes (310) 995-3098
11979 Iowa Ave., Ste. C **www.scriptchanges.com**
Los Angeles, CA 90025
(Script Coordinator, Scripts, Transcription & Word Processing)

The Script Specialists (818) 380-3090
15303 Ventura Blvd., Ste. 900 FAX **(818) 804-3662**
Sherman Oaks, CA 91403
(Scripts & Transcription) **www.thescriptspecialists.com**

Sound Transcription Service (818) 908-2404
7336 Santa Monica Blvd., Ste. 603
West Hollywood, CA 90046
(Transcribing & Dialogue Continuity Scripts)

Studio Transcription Services, a division
of STS Media Services, Inc. (818) 563-3004
P.O. Box 10213 **www.studiotranscription.com**
Burbank, CA 91510
(Foreign Language Transcription and Translation, Continuity
Scripts and Multiple Script Formats & Timecoded Transcription)

Talk 2 TYPE Transcriptions (818) 986-6982
FAX **(818) 986-1343**
www.talk2type.net

The Transcription House (818) 557-7293
2174 Pine Ave. **www.thetranscriptionhouse.tv**
Long Beach, CA 90806

Transcriptions Overnight (310) 995-3098
11979 Iowa Ave., Ste. C
Los Angeles, CA 90025
www.transcriptionsovernight.com
(Script Coordinator, Scripts, Transcription & Word Processing)

Word of Mouth
Transcription Services
(818) 904-9044
(818) 780-7346
6710 Calhoun Ave. FAX **(818) 780-7346**
Van Nuys, CA 91405
www.wordofmouthtranscripts.com
(Scripts & Transcription)

Word Factory
Transcription Services, Inc.
(323) 684-5488
(323) 684-5411
FAX **(888) 908-6199**
www.wordfactorytranscriptioncom
(Foreign Language Transcription, Permanent Personnel,
Scripts, Temporary Personnel, Transcription &
Word Processing)

Words Plus (866) 456-2095
6621 W. Fifth St. FAX **(323) 655-2048**
Los Angeles, CA 90048 **www.wordsplus1.com**

WP Plus (323) 255-5515
2858 El Roble Dr.
Los Angeles, CA 90041
(Scripts & Transcription)

1-Stop Translation (213) 480-0011
3700 Wilshire Blvd., Ste. 630 FAX (213) 232-3223
Los Angeles, CA 90010 www.1stoptr.com

Abacus Consulting & (626) 487-8909
Chinese Translation Services (877) 800-8832
401 N. Garfield Ave., Ste. 1 FAX (626) 282-9252
Alhambra, CA 91801
www.certifiedchinesetranslation.com
(Cantonese, Mandarin & Spanish)

ABC WordExpress Worldwide
Language Services (310) 260-0700
8306 Wilshire Blvd., Ste. 200 FAX (310) 260-7705
Beverly Hills, CA 90211 www.wordexpress.net
(Localization, Subtitling & Transcription)

Agnew Tech-II (805) 494-3999
741 Lakefield Rd., Ste. C FAX (805) 494-1749
Westlake Village, CA 91361 www.agnew.com

Jose Albertini (323) 252-4948
3752 Meier St. FAX (323) 252-4948
Los Angeles, CA 90066
(Spanish)

Lisa Azuma (310) 430-3143
(Japanese, Localization & Transcription)

Philippe Bergeron (818) 932-9491
(French & French-Canadian) www.pbergeron.com

Blague Communications (818) 769-5661
11417 Moorpark St. FAX (818) 232-9295
North Hollywood, CA 91602
www.blaguecommunications.com
(Language and Cultural Consulting, Localization &
Transcription)

Blue 105 (818) 563-4335
2600 W. Olive Ave., Fifth Fl. www.blue105.com
Burbank, CA 91505
(Arabic, Brazilian Portuguese, Chinese, Danish, Dutch, French,
German, Greek, Hebrew, Italian, Japanese, Korean,
Norwegian, Spanish & Swedish)

Marina Brodskaya (650) 387-3168
(Russian)

Claudette Roland
Translation Services (310) 475-4347
P.O. Box 24035
Los Angeles, CA 90024
(Adaptation, Localization, Transcription & Translation)

(213) 484-4984
Bernadette Colomine (213) 247-9414
(French; Localization) FAX (213) 484-4984
www.bernatettecolomine.com

Communicate Japan (818) 842-6506
P.O. Box 4253 FAX (818) 842-5106
Burbank, CA 91503 www.communicatejapan.com
(Japanese)

Cosmos Lingua (323) 935-4100
Translation Services (323) 459-9531
269 S. Beverly Dr., Ste. 542 FAX (323) 935-4446
Beverly Hills, CA 90212 www.cosmoslingua.com

CTS LanguageLink (800) 208-2620
9920 Jordan Circle, Ste. A FAX (360) 693-9292
Santa Fe Springs, CA 90670 www.ctslanguagelink.com

Laura D'Auri, Esq. (310) 270-5779
(Italian)

(310) 376-1409
Executive Linguist Agency, Inc. (800) 522-2320
500 S. Sepulveda Blvd., Ste. 300 FAX (310) 376-9285
Manhattan Beach, CA 90266
www.executivelinguist.com

Exotic Languages Agency (949) 222-2760
18101 Von Karmen Ave., Ste. 550 FAX (949) 222-9961
Irvine, CA 92612 www.ela1.com

French a la Carte/Katherine Vallin (323) 493-5533
1632 N. Laurel Ave., Ste. 116 www.french-a-la-carte.com
West Hollywood, CA 90046
(French & Spanish)

A Frenchman in LA (310) 237-6438
www.afrenchman.com
(African, Asian, European, Indian and Middle-Eastern
Languages Localization, Transcription and Translation)

Gilmour Translations (626) 355-5257
(French & Italian) home.earthlink.net/~ngilmour

Nanette Gobel (310) 801-2164
(French, German & Localization)

Esther M. Hermida (310) 890-3129
(Spanish) www.certifiedspanishinterpreter.com

In Other Words (323) 697-8130
818 N. Doheny Dr., Ste. 407 FAX (310) 446-3022
Los Angeles, CA 90069 www.iowtrans.com

iProbe Multilingual Solutions, Inc. (888) 489-6035
www.iprobesolutions.com
(6912 Languages & Transcription Including Arabic, Dutch,
Finnish, French, French Canadian, Cantonese, Chinese,
Danish, German, Greek, Hebrew, Hindi, Italian, Japanese,
Korean, Mandarin, Norwegian, Polish, Portuguese, Russian,
Spanish, Swedish, Turkish, Urdu & Vietnamese)

Japanese Media Translation (323) 229-9161
(Japanese)

JBI Studios (818) 592-0056
21432 Wyandotte FAX (818) 592-6994
Canoga Park, CA 91303 www.jbistudios.com
(Asian and European Languages)

(818) 557-0200
JR Media Services, Inc. (818) 398-9306
2501 W. Burbank Blvd., Ste. 200 FAX (818) 557-0201
Burbank, CA 91505 www.jrmediaservices.com

The Kitchen,
a TM Systems Company (818) 306-5300
4119 W. Burbank Blvd. FAX (305) 415-6201
Burbank, CA 91505 www.thekitchen.tv
(Localization, Transcription & Translation)

Language.net (310) 399-1790
804 Main St. FAX (310) 399-1901
Venice, CA 90291 www.language.net
(All Languages, Localization & Transcription)

(818) 549-9591
Linguatheque (800) 440-5344
FAX (818) 479-9731
www.linguatheque.com

Melissa MacCracken (310) 344-3080
(Spanish Interpretation, Transcription & Translation)

Marcland International
Communications (818) 557-6677
www.marcland.com

My Own Private Japan (310) 749-9091
(888) 909-9185
(Japanese) FAX (888) 909-9185

OneWorld Language Solutions (323) 848-7993
3940 Laurel Canyon Blvd., Ste. 501 FAX (323) 848-7995
Studio City, CA 91604 www.oneworldlanguage.com
(Asian and European Languages)

Paragon Language Services, Inc. (323) 966-4655
(800) 499-0299
5657 Wilshire Blvd., Ste. 310 FAX (323) 651-1867
Los Angeles, CA 90036 www.paragonls.com

Post Modern Edit, LLC (949) 608-8700
2941 Alton Pkwy FAX (949) 608-8729
Irvine, CA 92606 www.postmodernedit.com
(Arabic, Chinese, Danish, Dutch, French, German, Greek,
Hebrew, Hindi, Italian, Japanese, Korean, Norwegian,
Portuguese, Spanish, Swedish & Tamil)

The Sign Language Company (818) 763-1215
12050 Guerin St., Ste. 204 FAX (818) 763-3708
Studio City, CA 91604 www.signlanguageco.com

Jacqueline Stine (661) 298-9243
(818) 209-0070
18637 Nathan Hill Rd.
Santa Clarita, CA 91351
(Spanish)

**Strommen Translations and
Language Experts** (323) 638-9787
4450 Clarissa Ave. www.strommentutoring.com
Los Angeles, CA 90027
(Afrikaans, Albanian, Arabic, Armenian, Azerbaijani, Basque,
Belarusian, Bulgarian, Catalan, Chinese, Croatian, Czech,
Danish, Dutch, English, Estonian, Filipino, Finnish, French,
Galician, Georgian, German, Greek Haitian Creole, Hebrew,
Hindi, Hungarian, Icelandic, Indonesian, Irish, Italian, Japanese,
Korean, Latvian, Lithuanian, Macedonian, Malay, Maltese,
Mandarin, Norwegian, Persian, Polish, Portuguese, Romanian,
Russian, Serbian, Slovak, Slovenian, Spanish, Swahili,
Swedish, Thai, Turkish, Ukrainian, Urdu, Vietnamese,
Welsh & Yiddish)

**STS Foreign Language Services/a division
of STS Media Services, Inc.** (818) 563-3004
P.O. Box 10213 www.stsforeignlanguage.com
Burbank, CA 91510
(Arabic, Armenian, Bengali, Chinese, Dutch, Finnish, French,
German, Greek, Haitian French Creole, Hebrew, Hindi, Italian,
Japanese, Khmer, Korean, Latin, Portuguese, Russian,
Spanish, Swedish, Tamil, Thai & Ukrainian)

Technicolor Creative (818) 480-5100
Services - Burbank (310) 801-7300
www.technicolor.com

Toro Bravo (323) 363-7746
www.torobravo.us

Addie Akemi Tosto (818) 207-2555
(Japanese Localization)

(310) 822-1781
V & L International, LLC (212) 292-4228
4111 W. Sunset Blvd., Ste. 549 FAX (310) 822-1761
Los Angeles, CA 90029 www.vnli.com

Voicegroup, Inc. (818) 973-2770
3500 W. Olive Ave., Third Fl. FAX (818) 998-2770
Burbank, CA 91505 www.voicegroup.com

Marie Zelenka-Hootsmans (310) 237-6438
www.baesjou.net
(African, Asian, European, Indian and Middle-Eastern
Languages Localization, Transcription and Translation)

1020 Studios (323) 874-8764
1020 N. Sycamore Ave. FAX **(323) 874-6330**
Los Angeles, CA 90038 **www.1020studios.com**

(310) 775-6600
310 Casting Studios **(310) 775-6601**
2329 Purdue Ave. FAX **(310) 478-2100**
Los Angeles, CA 90064 **www.310castingstudios.com**
(Digital Casting & Video Conferencing)

(310) 451-1515
Beth Melsky Satellite Casting **(212) 505-5000**
1528 Sixth St., Ste. 100 FAX **(310) 393-2697**
Santa Monica, CA 90401 **www.bethmelsky.com**
(Video Conferencing)

The Casting Frontier (323) 300-6129
P.O. Box 291640 **www.castingfrontier.com**
Los Angeles, CA 90029
(Digital Casting)

Coastal Media Group (818) 880-9800
26660 Agoura Rd. FAX **(818) 579-9026**
Calabasas, CA 91302 **www.coastalmediagroup.com**
(Video Conferencing)

Eastside Studios (323) 660-7874
4216 Fountain Ave. FAX **(323) 660-7875**
Los Angeles, CA 90029 **www.eastsidestudiosla.com**

Encompass Digital Media (323) 344-4500
3030 Andrita St. FAX **(323) 344-4800**
Los Angeles, CA 90065 **www.encompass-m.com**

Envision Studios (310) 451-1515
1528 Sixth St., Ste. 100 FAX **(310) 293-2697**
Santa Monica, CA 90401 **www.envisionstudios.tv**

Exclusive Studios (323) 969-8200
7700 W. Sunset Blvd. FAX **(323) 969-0101**
Los Angeles, CA 90046
www.exclusivecastingstudios.com

Hollywood Telephone/
Will Communications **(310) 536-9777**
2627 Manhattan Beach Blvd., Ste. 211 FAX **(310) 536-9276**
Redondo Beach, CA 90278
(Video Conferencing) **www.willcommunications.com**

Nydrle, Inc. **(310) 659-8844**
670 N. La Peer Dr. FAX **(310) 659-7733**
West Hollywood, CA 90069 **www.nydrle.com**

ON24, Inc. **(415) 369-8000**
201 3rd St., 3rd Fl. **www.on24.com**
San Francisco, CA 94103

Onstream Media Corp. **(415) 274-8800**
901 Battery St. **www.onstreammedia.com**
San Francisco, CA 94111
(Web Conferencing & Webinars)

Pacific Television Center **(310) 287-3800**
3440 Motor Ave., Circular Bldg. FAX **(310) 287-3808**
Los Angeles, CA 90034 **www.pactv.com**
(Video Conferencing)

Sample Digital, Inc. **(310) 895-9550**
100 Corporate Point, Ste. 350 FAX **(424) 543-5110**
Culver City, CA 90230 **www.sampledigital.com**

Ava Shevitt **(310) 656-4600**
FAX **(310) 656-4610**
www.villagestudio.net

(832) 615-5045
VBC Broadcasting **(832) 615-5049**
2150 Town Square Pl., Ste. 200
Sugar Land, TX 77479 **www.vbcbroadcasting.com**
(Video Conferencing & Webcasting)

(877) 294-9910
Voicebank.net **(661) 294-9912**
9190 Olympic Blvd., Ste. 318 FAX **(661) 294-9764**
Beverly Hills, CA 90212 **www.voicebank.net**

Air Hollywood (818) 890-0444
13240 Weidner St. FAX (818) 890-7041
Los Angeles, CA 91331 www.airhollywood.com

Autry National Center (323) 667-2000
4700 Western Heritage Way FAX (323) 660-5721
Los Angeles, CA 90027 www.autrynationalcenter.org
Contact: Special Events Coordinator

Avalon (323) 462-6031
(323) 462-8900
1735 Vine St. FAX (323) 462-0579
Hollywood, CA 90028 www.avalonhollywood.com
Contact: Barney Holm

Boardner's (323) 462-9621
1652 N. Cherokee Ave. FAX (323) 462-8858
Hollywood, CA 90028 www.boardners.com
Contact: Tricia La Belle

Cafe-Club Fais Do-Do (323) 931-4636
5257 W. Adams Blvd. www.faisdodo.com
Los Angeles, CA 90016

Calamigos (818) 972-5940
LA Equestrian Center FAX (818) 972-5946
480 Riverside Dr. www.calamigosequestrian.com
Burbank, CA 91506
Contact: Alison Court

Cinespace (323) 817-3456
6356 Hollywood Blvd., Second Fl. FAX (323) 860-9794
Hollywood, CA 90028 www.cinespace.info

El Cid (323) 668-0318
4212 W. Sunset Blvd. www.elcidla.com
Los Angeles, CA 90029
Contact: Tobin Shea

El Rey Theatre (323) 936-6400
Contact: Tessa Swallow FAX (323) 936-5657
www.theelrey.com

Equestrian Center (818) 972-5940
480 Riverside Dr. FAX (818) 972-5946
Burbank, CA 91506 www.calamigosequestrian.com
Contact: Mina Behboudei

Fox Studios (310) 369-3663
(310) 369-4636
10201 W. Pico Blvd. FAX (310) 369-3978
Los Angeles, CA 90035 www.foxstudios.com

Gallery 1018 (310) 804-3372
1018 S. Santa Fe Ave. www.gallery1018.com
Los Angeles, CA 90021

The Highlands (323) 461-9800
6801 Hollywood Blvd., Ste. 433 FAX (323) 461-9802
Hollywood, CA 90028
www.thehighlandshollywood.com

House of Blues (323) 848-5100
8430 Sunset Blvd. www.hob.com
West Hollywood, CA 90069
Contact: Maureen McGrath

Jillian's Universal (818) 985-9213
(818) 985-8234
1000 Universal Studios Blvd. FAX (818) 985-9513
Ste. G103 www.jilliansbilliards.com
Universal City, CA 91608

The Jim Henson Company (323) 802-1500
1416 N. La Brea Ave. FAX (323) 802-1825
Hollywood, CA 90028 leasing.henson.com/events.html

Joseph's Cafe (323) 462-8697
1775 N. Ivar Ave. FAX (323) 462-0614
Los Angeles, CA 90028 www.josephscafe.com

LACMA (The Los Angeles County (323) 857-6039
Museum Of Art) (323) 857-4768
5905 Wilshire Blvd. FAX (323) 857-6021
Los Angeles, CA 90036 www.lacma.org

Laugh Factory (323) 656-1336
8001 Sunset Blvd. FAX (323) 656-2563
Los Angeles, CA 90046 www.laughfactory.com

Lucky Strike Lanes (323) 467-7776
6801 Hollywood Blvd., Ste. 143 FAX (323) 467-9997
Hollywood, CA 90028 www.bowlluckystrike.com

Lucky Strike Lanes (714) 937-5263
20 City Blvd. West www.bowlluckystrike.com
Bldg. G, Ste. 2
Orange, CA 92868

Maggiano's Little Italy Banquets (323) 965-2777
189 The Grove Dr. FAX (323) 965-8662
Los Angeles, CA 90036
www.maggianos.com/en/Pages/Banquets.aspx

The Magic Castle (323) 851-3313
7001 Franklin Ave. FAX (323) 851-4899
Hollywood, CA 90028 www.magiccastle.com
Contact: James G. Williams

My House (323) 525-2453
7080 Hollywood Blvd. www.myhousehollywood.com
Hollywood, CA 90028
Contact: Billie Jo Neidlinger

Pacific Design Center (310) 657-0800
(310) 360-6423
8687 Melrose Ave., Ste. M60 FAX (310) 652-8576
West Hollywood, CA 90069
Contact: Diana Arone www.pacificdesigncenter.com

Pacific Park (310) 260-8744
380 Santa Monica Pier FAX (310) 899-1826
Santa Monica, CA 90401 www.pacpark.com
Contact: Kristin Wasiluk

The Paley Center for Media (310) 786-1000
465 N. Beverly Dr. FAX (310) 786-1086
Beverly Hills, CA 90210 www.paleycenter.org

Ⓐ The Studios at Paramount (323) 956-8398
The Studios at Paramount Special Events
5555 Melrose Ave. www.paramountspecialevents.com
Los Angeles, CA 90038

Pickwick Bowl/Pickwick Ice Center (818) 845-5300
1001 Riverside Dr. FAX (818) 846-6424
Burbank, CA 91506 www.pickwickgardens.com
Contact: Sherrie Dickinson

Pinz Bowling Center (818) 769-7600
12655 Ventura Blvd. FAX (818) 509-1284
Studio City, CA 91604 www.pinzbowlingcenter.com
Contact: Eleda Cohen

Raleigh Studios Special (323) 871-4430
Events & Catering (323) 960-3456
5300 Melrose Ave. FAX (323) 871-5600
Hollywood, CA 90038 www.raleighstudios.com
Contact: Taylor Peeples

(213) 413-9300
RecCenter Studio (323) 868-4226
1161 Logan St. FAX (213) 413-9301
Los Angeles, CA 90026 www.reccenterstudio.com

(818) 348-6000
Rock Star Properties (661) 803-5822
FAX (818) 348-6666

Smoke House Restaurant (818) 845-3731
4420 Lakeside Dr. FAX (818) 845-3181
Burbank, CA 91505 www.smokehouse1946.com
Contact: Israel Aviles

Three Clubs (323) 462-6441
1123 N. Vine St. www.threeclubs.com
Los Angeles, CA 90038

Union Station (213) 617-0111
800 N. Alameda St., Ste. 100 FAX (213) 617-0171
Los Angeles, CA 90012
www.hollywoodlocations.com/property_details.cfm?
pID=597&catID=4&propTypeID=111

(818) 777-9466
Universal Studios Special Events (800) 892-1979
100 Universal City Plaza FAX (818) 866-0293
Bldg. 1280-10 www.filmmakersdestination.com
Universal City, CA 91608

Villa Malibu Luxury Rentals (888) 526-6096
6487 Cavalleri Rd., Ste. 224 www.villamalibuliving.com
Malibu, CA 90265

(310) 395-3648
World Cafe (310) 392-1661
2820 Main St. FAX (310) 392-8440
Santa Monica, CA 90405 www.worldcafela.com
Contact: Leslie Paonessa

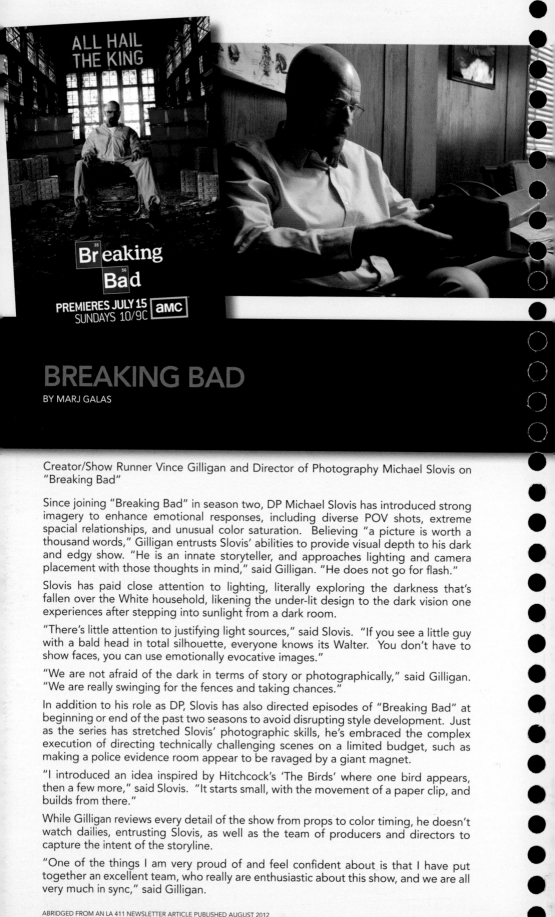

ALL HAIL
THE KING

Breaking
Bad

PREMIERES JULY 15 amc
SUNDAYS 10/9C

BREAKING BAD

BY MARJ GALAS

Creator/Show Runner Vince Gilligan and Director of Photography Michael Slovis on "Breaking Bad"

Since joining "Breaking Bad" in season two, DP Michael Slovis has introduced strong imagery to enhance emotional responses, including diverse POV shots, extreme spacial relationships, and unusual color saturation. Believing "a picture is worth a thousand words," Gilligan entrusts Slovis' abilities to provide visual depth to his dark and edgy show. "He is an innate storyteller, and approaches lighting and camera placement with those thoughts in mind," said Gilligan. "He does not go for flash."

Slovis has paid close attention to lighting, literally exploring the darkness that's fallen over the White household, likening the under-lit design to the dark vision one experiences after stepping into sunlight from a dark room.

"There's little attention to justifying light sources," said Slovis. "If you see a little guy with a bald head in total silhouette, everyone knows its Walter. You don't have to show faces, you can use emotionally evocative images."

"We are not afraid of the dark in terms of story or photographically," said Gilligan. "We are really swinging for the fences and taking chances."

In addition to his role as DP, Slovis has also directed episodes of "Breaking Bad" at beginning or end of the past two seasons to avoid disrupting style development. Just as the series has stretched Slovis' photographic skills, he's embraced the complex execution of directing technically challenging scenes on a limited budget, such as making a police evidence room appear to be ravaged by a giant magnet.

"I introduced an idea inspired by Hitchcock's 'The Birds' where one bird appears, then a few more," said Slovis. "It starts small, with the movement of a paper clip, and builds from there."

While Gilligan reviews every detail of the show from props to color timing, he doesn't watch dailies, entrusting Slovis, as well as the team of producers and directors to capture the intent of the storyline.

"One of the things I am very proud of and feel confident about is that I have put together an excellent team, who really are enthusiastic about this show, and we are all very much in sync," said Gilligan.

ABRIDGED FROM AN LA 411 NEWSLETTER ARTICLE PUBLISHED AUGUST 2012

Ⓐ ADVERTISER SYMBOL

Refer to the General Index for cross-referencing items in this section.

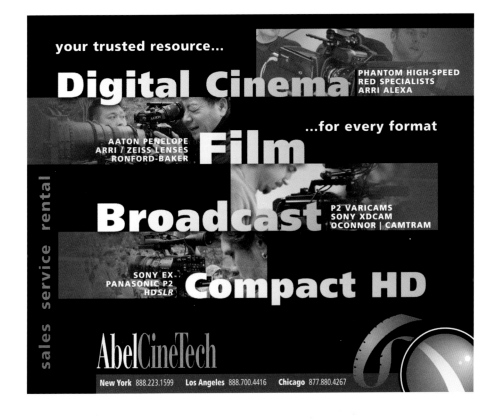

Aerial Action Productions/
Reel Orange   (949) 548-4524
316 La Jolla Dr.   www.reelorange.com
Newport Beach, CA 92663
Aircraft: Fixed Wing Aircraft & Ultralights
Camera Mounts: Fixed Wing Aerial Camera Platforms
Cameras: 16mm, 35mm, Digital & POV Helmet Cameras
Services: Aerial Coordination, Aerial Production & Pilots

Aerial Cinema Systems/   (661) 270-0565
Helicopters West, Inc.   (661) 810-9456
39120 Bouquet Canyon Rd.
Leona Valley, CA 93551
Aircraft: Fixed Wing Aircraft, Helicopters & Warbirds
Camera Mounts: Gyro-Stabilized, Nose, Outside, POV &
Side Mounts
Equipment: Police Searchlight & Safety and Cargo Equipment
Services: Aerial Coordination, Aerial Production & Pilots

Aerial Film Unit by   (800) 345-6737
Corporate Helicopters   (858) 505-5650
3753 John J. Montgomery Dr., Ste. 2 FAX (858) 505-5658
San Diego, CA 92123   www.corporatehelicopters.com
Aircraft: Helicopters
Camera Mounts: Camera Platforms, Gyro-Stabilized Mounts,
Helicopter Mounts, Nose Mounts, Side Mounts &
Wescam Mounts
Camera Mounts/Systems: Wescam
Cameras: Betacam, Digital Video, Gyro-Stabilized Camera
Systems & High Def
Equipment: Air to Ground Radios, Fuel Truck & Night
Sun Searchlights
Services: Aerial Coordination, Aerial Production, Helicopter
Refueling & Pilots

                                    (310) 998-7009
Aerial Filmworks   (808) 281-1921
                                    www.aerialfilmworks.com
Aerial Equipment: Gyro-Stabilized 5-Axis Camera Systems &
HDTV Helicopter and Lear Jet Camera Systems
Camera Mounts: Fixed Wing Camera Mount, Gyro-Stabilized
Mounts, Helicopter Mounts & Nose Mounts
Cameras: Gyro-Stabilized Camera Systems & High Def
Services: Aerial Production

                                    (661) 799-0154
Aerial Shot Productions   (661) 607-7266
24077 WhiteWater Dr. www.aerialshotproductions.com
Valencia, CA 91354
Aerial Equipment: Gyro-Stabilized 5-Axis Camera Systems
Aircraft: Fixed-Wing UAV RC Helicopters
Cameras: IMAX
Equipment: Aerial Camera Mounts and Systems
Services: Aerial Production & Second Unit Directors

Aerial Stunt Service/Joe Jennings   (310) 543-2222
3128 Via La Selva   www.skydive.tv
Palos Verdes Estates, CA 90274
Camera Mounts: Aircraft POV and Gyro-Stabilized Mounts
Cameras: 16mm, 35mm, Gyro-Stabilized and POV Helmet
Cameras & Skydiving
Equipment: BASE Jumping Equipment, Heavy Drop Cargo
Chutes, Parachutes & Skydiving Equipment
Services: Aerial Coordination & Pilots

Aerial Video Systems/AVS   (818) 954-8842
712 S. Main St.   FAX (818) 954-9122
Burbank, CA 91506   www.aerialvideo.com
Aerial Equipment: Gyro-Stabilized 5-Axis Camera Systems &
HDTV Helicopter and Lear Jet Camera Systems
Cameras: Aerial Cameras, Gyro-Stabilized Camera Systems,
HDTV, Helmet & High Def
Services: Aerial Production

McKERNAN
MOTION PICTURE AVIATION
AVIATION SPECIALISTS FOR THE MOTION PICTURE INDUSTRY

FILM · TELEVISION · COMMERCIALS

EXPERIENCE AND KNOWLEDGE:
- MOTION PICTURE PILOTS ASSOCIATION MEMBER
- COMMERCIAL HELICOPTER PILOTS
- COMMERCIAL FIXED WING PILOTS
- AERIAL COORDINATORS

LEADING SUPPLIER OF:
- HELICOPTER CAMERASHIPS
- TYLER CAMERA MOUNTS
- GYRO STABILIZED MOUNTS

PARTIAL LIST OF CREDITS:
RED DAWN-THE GREEN HORNET
VALENTINE'S DAY-PUBLIC ENEMIES
STATE OF PLAY-FLIGHT OF THE DRAGON
YOUNG AMERICANS-LAND OF THE LOST
TRAUMA-FLASH FORWARD-CSI
TOUR OF DUTY-AIRWOLF

DEMO REEL AVAILABLE UPON REQUEST

AVAILABLE SERVICES:
- DEPT. OF DEFENSE SUPPORT CONSULTANT
- STUNT COORDINATOR
- FAA MOTION PICTURE MANUAL
- STORYBOARD & SCRIPT CONSULTING
- FIXED WING / HELICOPTER
- PEEL PAINTING / MOCK UPS
- PICTURE AIRCRAFT
- PERMITS & INSURANCE

CONTACT INFORMATION:
OFFICE: 310.458.9176 · CELL: 310.993.4486 · SERVICE: 323.469.9980
WWW.HELICOPTERGUY.COM · EMAIL- PETER@HELICOPTERGUY.COM

Aerialdp.com   (310) 779-9935
www.aerialdp.com

Airborne Images, Inc.   (818) 783-1145
(310) 748-2795
www.airborneimages.com
Aircraft: Blimps, Fixed-Wing Aircraft & Helicopters
Camera Mounts: Belly Mounts, Camera Platforms, Fixed Wing
Camera Mount, Fixed Wing Camera Platforms, Gyro-Stabilized
Mounts, Skydive Helmet Mounts, Helicopter Mounts, Nose
Mounts, POV Mounts, Side Mounts, Tyler Camera Mounts,
Vibration Isolation Mounts & Wescam Mounts
Camera Mounts/Systems: Cineflex, Gyron, Pictorvision Eclipse,
Spacecam, Tyler & Wescam
Cameras: 16mm, 35mm, 65mm, Digital Video, Gyro-Stabilized
Camera Systems, HDTV, Helmet, High Def, IMAX,
Skydiving & Spacecam
Equipment: Aerial Camera Cable Systems, Air to Ground
Radios, BASE Jumping Equipment, Fuel Trucks, Night Sun
Searchlights, Overwater Safety Equipment, Parachutes, Police
Searchlights, Safety Equipment & Skydiving Equipment
Services: Aerial Coordination, Aerial Production, Consultation,
Ground Safety Consultation, Ground Safety Personnel, Ground
Safety Pilots, Helicopter Refueling, Pilots & Stabilized
Shooting Coordination

Airborne Imaging   (949) 583-9571
(714) 883-2334
FAX (949) 855-9186
www.airborneimaging.com
Aircraft: Remote-Controlled Airplanes, Blimps and Helicopters

Airpower Aviation Resources   (805) 402-0052
(805) 499-0307
702 Paseo Vista   FAX (805) 498-0357
Thousand Oaks, CA 91320 **www.airpower-aviation.com**
Aircraft: Civilian and Military Fixed Wing Aircraft & Helicopters
Services: Aerial Coordination, Aerial Production & Pilots

Altitude Aviation   (310) 379-4448
(310) 489-8938
200 Pier Ave., Ste. 128   FAX (310) 937-7112
Hermosa Beach, CA 90254 **www.altitudeaviation.com**
Aircraft: Fixed Wing Aircraft & Helicopters
Services: Aerial Coordination & Pilots

Angel City Air   (818) 896-9900
12653 Osborne St.   FAX (818) 686-1095
Pacoima, CA 91331   **www.aerialproduction.com**
Aircraft: Fixed-Wing Aircraft & HelicoptersCamera Mounts: Belly
Mounts, Camera Platforms, Gyro-Stabilized Mounts, Helicopter
Mounts & Nose Mounts
Camera Mounts/Systems: Cineflex, Eclipse,
Gyron & Spacecam
Equipment: Air to Ground Radios, Fuel Trucks, Night Sun
Searchlights & Police Searchlights
Services: Aerial Coordination, Aerial Production, Consultation,
Ground Safety Consultation, Ground Safety Personnel, Ground
Safety Pilots, Helicopter Refueling, Pilots & Stabilized
Shooting Coordination
Aerial Equipment: Gyro-Stabilized 5-Axis Camera Systems

ARIS Helicopters/Heli-Flite   (951) 359-5016
(800) 340-1969
6871 Airport Dr.   FAX (951) 359-5019
Riverside, CA 92504   **www.arishelicopters.com**
Aircraft: Gyrocopters, Gyroplanes & Helicopters
Camera Mounts: Aerial Platforms
Equipment: Safety Equipment
Services: Aerial Coordination, Aerial Production & Pilots

Beckman Rigging/BRS Rigging   (310) 532-3933
(661) 510-2518
13516 S. Mariposa Ave.   FAX (310) 532-3993
Gardena, CA 90247   **www.brsrigging.com**

Blackstar Helicopters Inc.   (661) 713-6671
10500 Airpark Way, Unit M2   FAX (877) 272-4764
Whiteman Airport   **www.blackstarhelicopters.com**
Pacoima , CA 91331
Aerial Equipment: Gyro-Stabilized Hi Def Camera Systems
Aircraft: Fixed-Wing Aircraft & Helicopters
Equipment: Air to Ground Radios, Camera Mounts/Systems,
Fuel Trucks & Night Sun Searchlights
Services: Aerial Coordination, Ground Safety Camera Pilots &
SAG Pilots

Branam Enterprises   (818) 885-6474
(877) 295-3390
9152 Independence Ave.   **www.branament.com**
Chatsworth, CA 91311
Equipment: Aerial Camera Cable Systems

Briles Wing & Helicopter, Inc.   (818) 994-1445
16303 Waterman Dr.   FAX (818) 994-1447
Van Nuys, CA 91406   **www.toflyla.com**
Aircraft: Helicopters

California Dreamin'   (800) 373-3359
33133 Vista del Monte Rd.   **www.californiadreamin.com**
Temecula, CA 92591
Aircraft: Bi-Planes & Hot Air Balloons

Ⓐ Camera Copters, Inc.   (888) 463-7953
(305) 793-7033
23421 Balmoral Ln.   **www.cameracopters.com**
West Hills, CA 91307
Aircraft: HelicoptersCamera Mounts: Gyro-Stabilized Camera
SystemsServices: Aerial Coordination & Pilots

Celebrity Helicopters   (877) 999-2099
961 W. Alondra Blvd.   FAX (877) 999-2099
Compton, CA 90220   **www.celebheli.com**
Aircraft: Fixed Wing Aircraft & Helicopters
Services: Aerial Coordination, Aerial Production,
Consultation & Pilots

Cinema Rentals, Inc.   (661) 222-7342
(818) 365-7999
25876 The Old Road, Ste. 174   FAX (661) 427-0881
Stevenson Ranch, CA 91381   **www.cinemarentals.com**
Camera Mounts: Remote-Controlled Helicopter Mounts

Aerial Equipment

Clay Lacy Aviation, Inc.
(818) 989-2900
(800) 423-2904
7435 Valjean Ave.
Van Nuys, CA 91406
FAX (818) 909-9537
www.claylacy.com
Aircraft: Fixed Wing Aircraft
Camera Mounts: Fixed Wing Aerial Camera Platforms
Services: Aerial Coordination, Aerial Production & Pilots

D & D Ballooning
(800) 510-9000
Aircraft: Hot Air Balloons
FAX (951) 303-8645
www.hotairadventures.com

Flying-Cam, Inc.
(310) 581-9276
3100 Donald Douglas Loop North
Ste. 203
Santa Monica, CA 90405
FAX (310) 581-9278
www.flying-cam.com
Cameras: Remote-Controlled Helicopter Cameras

Guardian Helicopters, Inc.
(818) 442-9904
16425 Hart St.
FAX (818) 442-9901
Van Nuys, CA 91406 www.guardianhelicoptersusa.com
Aircraft: Helicopters & Fixed Wing Aircraft
Camera Mounts: Nose, Spacecam, Tyler & Wescam
Equipment: Air to Ground Radios, Fuel Trucks, Mock-Ups,
Props & Search Lights
Services: Aerial Coordination, Ground Safety & Pilots

Gyron Aerial Systems
(626) 584-8722
39 E. Walnut St.
Pasadena, CA 91103
FAX (626) 584-4069
www.gyron.com
Camera Mounts: Gyron Gyro-Stabilized

Hang Gliding Aerobatics, Inc.
(760) 822-5667
www.johnheiney.com
Aircraft: Hang Gliders
Camera Mounts: Hang Glider Mounts & Ultralight
Services: Aerial Coordination

Hangar 1 Productions
(323) 810-7560
1910 W. Sunset Blvd., Ste. 900 www.hangar1project.com
Los Angeles, CA 90026
Aircraft: Fixed-Wing Aircraft & Helicopter
Camera Mounts/Systems: Gyron, Spacecam, Tyler & Wescam
Equipment: Air to Ground Radios, Fuel Trucks & Night
Sun Searchlights
Services: Aerial Coordination, Ground Safety, Pilots & Second
Unit Directors

Heli-USA
(818) 994-1445
(877) 863-5952
16303 Waterman Dr.
Van Nuys, CA 91406
FAX (818) 994-1447
www.toflyla.com
Aircraft: Helicopters

Ⓐ **Helifilms USA, Inc.**
(310) 487-0065
1299 Ocean Ave., Ste. 333
Santa Monica, CA 90401
FAX (310) 496-0405
www.helifilmsusa.com
Aircraft: Helicopters
Camera Mounts: Belly Mounts, Camera Platforms, Gyro-
Stabilized Mounts, Helicopter Mounts, Nose Mounts, Side
Mounts, Tyler Camera Mounts, Vibration Isolation Mounts &
Wescam Mounts
Camera Mounts/Systems: Gyron, Spacecam, Tyler & Wescam
Cameras: Gyro-Stabilized 5-Axis Camera Systems & High Def
Equipment: Air to Ground Radios, Fuel Trucks & Night
Sun Searchlights
Services: Aerial Coordination, Ground Safety Personnel,
Ground Safety Pilots, Helicopter Refueling & Pilots

Helinet Aviation Services
(818) 902-0229
(800) 221-8389
16644 Roscoe Blvd.
Van Nuys, CA 91406
FAX (818) 902-9278
www.helinet.com
Aircraft: Helicopters
Camera Mounts: Aerial Camera Mounts
Cameras: Cineflex HD Gyro-Stabilized Camera Systems

Horizon Helicopters, Inc.
(818) 621-5075
11271 Ventura Blvd., Ste. 430
Studio City, CA 91604
FAX (818) 701-4040
Aircraft: Helicopters

Hosking Aviation
(661) 251-5151
FAX (661) 414-8048
Aircraft: Bi-Wing, Fixed Wing Aircraft & Helicopters
Equipment: Fuel Trucks & Safety Equipment
Services: Aerial Coordination & Pilots

Indie Aerials
(818) 988-9382
(818) 994-9376
16425 Hart St.
Van Nuys, CA 91406
FAX (818) 994-9384
www.indieaerials.com

Largo Industries   **(310) 486-0415**
649 Palms Blvd.   FAX **(310) 305-9188**
Venice, CA 90291   **www.fred-north.com**
Equipment: Air to Ground Radios, Arri 435, Gyro-Stabilized
System & Nose and Side Mounts
Services: Aerial Coordination, Ground Safety & Pilots

     (562) 377-0396
Los Angeles Helicopters   **(800) 976-4354**
3501 Lakewood Blvd.   FAX **(562) 377-0449**
Long Beach, CA 90808   **www.lahelicopters.com**

     (310) 458-9176
Ⓐ McKernan Motion Picture Aviation   **(310) 993-4486**
     FAX **(310) 496-0744**
     www.helicopterguy.com
Aerial Equipment: Gyro-Stabilized 5-Axis Camera Systems &
Stab-C/Gyron
Aircraft: Fixed Wing Aircraft, Hang Gliders, Helicopters, Military
Fixed-Wing Aircraft, Ultralights & Warbirds
Camera Mounts/Systems: Gyron, Spacecam, Tyler & Wescam
Camera Mounts: Belly Mounts & Camera Platforms
Services: Aerial Coordination

Motion Picture Marine   **(310) 822-1100**
616 Venice Blvd.   FAX **(310) 822-2679**
Marina del Rey, CA 90291
     www.motionpicturemarine.com
Camera Mounts: Perfect Horizon Camera Stabilization Head

Nettmann Systems International   **(818) 365-4286**
1026 Griswold Ave.   FAX **(818) 361-6982**
San Fernando, CA 91340
     www.camerasystems.com/agents.htm
Aerial Equipment: Film Video-HDTV Helicopter and Lear Jet
Camera Systems, Gyro-Stabilized 5-Axis Camera Systems,
Stab-C/Gyron FS, Super-G & Vectorvision

Orbic Air, LLC   **(818) 988-6532**
16700 Roscoe Blvd.   **www.orbicair.com**
Van Nuys, CA 91406
Aerial Equipment: Gyro-Stabilized 5-Axis Camera Systems,
HDTV Helicopter and Lear Jet Camera Systems &
Stab-C/Gyron
Aircraft: Helicopters
Camera Mounts: Belly Mounts, Gyro-Stabilized Mounts, Heli-
copter Mounts, Nose Mounts, POV Mounts, Side Mounts, Tyler
Camera Mounts & Wescam Mounts
Camera Mounts/Systems: Gyron, Spacecam, Tyler & Wescam
Cameras: 16mm, 35mm, 65mm, Digital Video, Gyro-Stabilized
Camera Systems, HDTV, High Def & Spacecam
Equipment: Air to Ground Radios, Aircraft Intercom Systems,
Fuel Trucks, Night Sun Searchlights, Overwater Safety Equip-
ment, Police Searchlights & Safety Equipment
Services: Aerial Coordination, Aerial Production, Consultation,
Ground Production, Ground Safety Consultation, Ground Safety
Personnel, Ground Safety Pilots, Helicopter Refueling & Pilots

Orbic Helicopters, Inc.   **(805) 389-1070**
777 Aviation Dr.   FAX **(805) 389-1020**
Camarillo, CA 93010   **www.orbichelicopters.com**
Aircraft: Helicopters

Perris Valley Skydiving   **(951) 657-3904**
2091 Goetz Rd.   FAX **(951) 657-6178**
Perris, CA 92570   **www.skydiveperris.com**
Aircraft: Fixed Wing Aircraft
Camera Mounts: Wing Mounts
Cameras: POV Helmet Cameras
Equipment: Parachutes & Skydiving Equipment
Services: Aerial Coordination

     (818) 785-9282
Pictorvision Inc   **(800) 876-5583**
16238 Raymer St.   FAX **(818) 785-9787**
Van Nuys, CA 91406   **www.pictorvision.com**
Camera Mounts: 5-Axis Gyro-Stabilized Camera Systems,
Helicopter Mounts, Nose Mounts & Side Mounts
Cameras: 35mm, High Def, SD, Wescam & XR

     (818) 845-5970
Producers Air Force   **(818) 795-7463**
One Orange Grove Terrace   FAX **(818) 845-4033**
Burbank, CA 91501   **www.producersairforce.com**
Equipment: Air to Ground Radios
Services: Aerial Production, Aerial Coordination & Consultation

RF Film, Inc.   **(866) 985-3456**
     FAX **(866) 986-3456**
     www.rffilm.com

     (951) 245-9939
Skydive Elsinore, LLC   **(877) 843-5867**
20701 Cereal St.   FAX **(951) 245-3661**
Lake Elsinore, CA 92530   **www.skydiveelsinore.com**
Aircraft: Fixed Wing Aircraft
Camera Mounts: Fixed Wing Aerial Camera Platforms
Equipment: Parachutes & Skydiving Equipment
Services: Aerial Coordination & Pilots

South Coast Helicopters, Inc.   **(714) 562-0882**
3940 Artesia Ave.   FAX **(714) 562-0975**
Fullerton, CA 92833   **www.southcoasthelicopters.com**
Aircraft: Helicopters
Equipment: Air to Ground Radios, Fuel Trucks & Night Sun
Services: Aerial Coordination, Ground Safety Personnel & Pilots

SpaceCam Systems, Inc   **(818) 889-6060**
31111 Via Colinas, Ste. 201   FAX **(818) 889-6062**
Westlake Village, CA 91362   **www.spacecam.com**
Camera Mounts: Gyro-Stabilized Camera Mounts & Spacecam
Cameras: 35mm, 35mm VistaVision, 65mm,
HDTV & Spacecam
Services: Stabilized Shooting Coordination

Stearman Flight Center   **(909) 597-8511**
7000 Merrill Ave., Ste. 53   FAX **(909) 597-8511**
Chino, CA 91710   **www.silverwingswingwalking.com**
Aircraft: Vintage Airplanes

Studio Wings, Inc.   **(805) 320-9500**
855 Aviation Dr.   FAX **(805) 987-4720**
Camarillo, CA 93010   **www.studiowings.com**
Aircraft: Fixed Wing Aircraft, Helicopters & Jets
Camera Mounts: Gyro-Stabilized Mounts
Cameras: HDTV, High Def & Spacecam
Equipment: Air to Ground Radios, Night Sun Searchlights &
Police Helicopter Search Lights
Services: Aerial Coordination, Aerial Production, Consultation,
Ground Safety Consultation, Ground Safety Personnel, Pilots &
Second Unit Directors

     (818) 367-2430
Stunt Wings/Adventure Sports   **(818) 266-0874**
12623 Gridley St.   FAX **(818) 367-5363**
San Fernando, CA 91342   **www.stuntwings.com**
Aircraft: Hang Gliders, Hot Air Balloons, Parachutes, Paraglid-
ers & Ultralight Aircraft
Camera Mounts: Hang Gliding & Ultralight Camera Mounts
Cameras: Lightweight Gyro-Stabilized
Services: Aerial Coordination

     (818) 787-0205
Ⓐ Thornton Aircraft Company   **(626) 795-8604**
7520 Hayvenhurst Ave.   FAX **(818) 787-9334**
Van Nuys, CA 91406   **www.thorntonaircraft.com**
Aircraft: Fixed-Wing Aircraft, Jets, Military Fixed-Wing
Aircraft & Warbirds
Services: Aerial Coordination & Pilots

     (818) 989-4420
Tyler Camera Systems   **(800) 390-6070**
14218 Aetna St.   FAX **(818) 989-0423**
Van Nuys, CA 91401   **www.tylermount.com**
Camera Mounts: Gyro-Stabilized Helicopter Camera Mounts

Whirly Bird Films   **(310) 456-1123**
22848 Pacific Coast Hwy, Ste. 6
Malibu, CA 90265   **www.whirlybirdfilms.com**

Wolfe Air Aviation, Ltd.   **(626) 584-4060**
39 E. Walnut St.   FAX **(626) 584-4069**
Pasadena, CA 91103   **www.wolfeair.com**
Aircraft: Fixed Wing Aircraft & Helicopters
Camera Mounts: Vectorvision

Airborne Images, Inc.
(Helicopter Pilot)
(818) 783-1145
(310) 748-2795
www.airborneimages.com

Paul Barth
(888) 463-7953
(305) 793-7033
www.cameracopters.com

David Calvert-Jones
1299 Ocean Ave., Ste. 333
Santa Monica, CA 90401
(Helicopter Pilot)
(310) 487-0065
FAX (310) 496-0405
www.helifilmsusa.com

David Child
16700 Roscoe Blvd.
Van Nuys, CA 91406
(818) 988-6532
www.orbicair.com

Craig Dyer
(Helicopter Pilot)
(310) 383-0777

Cliff Fleming
(714) 751-3515
(714) 997-0469
FAX (714) 751-4705
www.moviepilots.com

Hartley Folstad
(Fixed Wing Pilot)
(909) 597-8511
FAX (909) 597-8511
www.silverwingswingwalking.com

David Gene Gibbs
(661) 254-6451
(818) 321-2689
FAX (661) 254-3940

Guardian Helicopters, Inc.
16425 Hart St.
Van Nuys, CA 91406 www.guardianhelicoptersusa.com
(Helicopter Pilot)
(818) 442-9904
FAX (818) 442-9901

Piergiorgio Gusso/TwinAir
7552 Hayvenhurst Pl.
Van Nuys, CA 91406
(818) 988-7573
FAX (818) 988-7578
www.twinair.net

Desiree Horton
(Helicopter Pilot)
(818) 621-5075
FAX (818) 701-4040

Craig Hosking
(661) 251-5151
FAX (661) 414-8048
www.hoskingaviation.com

Esteban Jimenez
10750 Sherman Way
Burbank, CA 91505
(Gyroplane Pilot & Helicopter Pilot)
(323) 500-8336
(323) 540-4354
www.copterpilot.com

Peter J. McKernan Jr.
(310) 458-9176
(310) 993-4486
FAX (310) 496-0744

Peter J. McKernan Sr.
(310) 993-4486
(310) 458-9176
FAX (310) 496-0744
www.helicopterguy.com

John Ward Nielsen
(Helicopter Pilot)
(323) 939-9540
(323) 939-7719
FAX (323) 939-7775

Fred North
649 Palms Blvd.
Venice, CA 90291
(310) 486-0415
FAX (310) 305-9188
www.fred-north.com

Robin Petgrave
(Helicopter Pilot)
(310) 938-2727
(877) 999-2099
FAX (877) 999-2099
www.celebheli.com

Alan D. Purwin
(818) 902-0229
(800) 221-8389
FAX (818) 902-9278
www.helinet.com

Dan Rudert (310) 993-2380
(661) 250-8150
(Helicopter Pilot) FAX (661) 250-8587
www.moviepilots.com

John D. Sarviss (661) 270-0565
(661) 810-9456
39120 Bouquet Canyon Rd.www.radicalcameracars.com
Leona Valley, CA 93551

Ivor Shier/Corporate Helicopters (858) 505-5650
(800) 345-6737
(Helicopter Pilot) FAX (858) 505-5658
www.corporatehelicopters.com

Rick Shuster (818) 947-5454
(805) 493-5044
(Aerial Coordinator & Helicopter Pilot) FAX (805) 493-0530
www.moviepilots.com

Glenn J. Smith (800) 210-7800
(562) 997-0224
(Helicopter Pilot) FAX (562) 997-0324
www.airliftconstruction.com

Steve Stafford/Studio Wings, Inc. (805) 320-9500
855 Aviation Dr. FAX (805) 987-4720
Camarillo, CA 93010 www.studiowings.com

Lance Strumpf (818) 402-1775
(818) 994-1445
16303 Waterman Dr. FAX (818) 994-1447
Van Nuys, CA 91406 www.toflyla.com

Chuck Tamburro (818) 881-6408
(818) 489-0256
(Helicopter Pilot) FAX (818) 881-6462

John Tamburro (661) 713-6671
10500 Airpark Way, Unit M2 FAX (877) 272-4764
Whiteman Airport www.blackstarhelicopters.com
Pacoima , CA 91331
(Aerial Coordinator & Pilot)

Greg Vernon/Hangar 1 Productions (323) 810-7560
1910 W. Sunset Blvd., Ste. 900
Los Angeles, CA 90026 www.hangar1project.com

Action Trax/Dan Wynands
(818) 903-3314
(818) 980-2123
2879 Irongate Pl.
FAX (805) 241-1137
Thousand Oaks, CA 91362   **www.camerabikes.tv**
(ATVs, High Speed Camera Motorcycles, Off-Road Camera
Vehicles, Side Platform Camera Bikes & Solo Camera Bikes)

Allan Padelford Camera Cars   (661) 268-1330
www.apcamcars.com
(360° Roof Mounted Motorized Crane Arm, Hi-Speed Camera
Cars with 3 Axis Remote Heads, Maverick Insert Bike, Process
Trailers & Technocranes)

Burbank Kawasaki
(818) 848-6627
(818) 749-5676
1329 N. Hollywood Way
FAX (818) 848-6630
Burbank, CA 91505   **www.burbankkawasaki.com**
(ATVs, Jet Skis & Motorcycles)

**Camera Car Industries/
Dean Goldsmith**   (818) 998-4798
12473 San Fernando Rd.   FAX (818) 833-5962
Sylmar, CA 91342   **www.cameracarindustries.com**
(3 Axis Remote Camera Car Cranes)

Camera Cars Unlimited, Inc.   (818) 889-9903
5331 Derry Ave., Ste. A   FAX (818) 889-4970
Agoura Hills, CA 91301   **www.cameracarsunlimited.com**
(Crane Ready Camera Car, Off-Road and Standard Camera
Cars, Process Trailers & Tow Dollies)

Camera Craft
(714) 330-9900
(714) 964-6920
(Camera Boats)   **www.cameracraftonline.com**

Carpenter Camera Cars   (818) 362-3261
13681 Fenton Ave.   FAX (818) 367-3241
Sylmar, CA 91342   **www.cameracars.com**
(2-Axle Insert Cars, 3-Axle Insert Cars, Air-Ride Process
Trailers, ATVs, Chase Cars, High Speed Camera Cars,
Mini High Speed Camera Cars, Process Trailers/Trucks &
Tow Dollies)

**Chapman/Leonard
Studio Equipment, Inc.**
(818) 764-6726
(888) 883-6559
12950 Raymer St.
FAX (888) 502-7263
North Hollywood, CA 91605   **www.chapman-leonard.com**
(Apollo Trailers, Camera Car Cranes & Tow Dollies)

Exotic Pursuits, Inc.
(818) 980-2123
(818) 903-3314
P.O. Box 46609   **www.exoticpursuits.com**
Los Angeles, CA 90046
(Chase Cars & High Speed Camera Cars)

Filmotechnic International Corp.   (310) 390-2500
www.filmotecnic.net
(Camera Car Cranes, High Speed Camera Cars & Off-Road
Gyro-Stabilized Equipment)

Ⓐ Filmotechnic USA
(310) 669-9888
(805) 453-1411
20432 S. Santa Fe, Ste. K
FAX (562) 684-0776
Carson, CA 90810   **www.filmo-usa.com**

Griptrix, Inc.   (818) 982-2510
12767 Saticoy St.   FAX (818) 982-8830
North Hollywood, CA 91605   **www.griptrix.com**
(ATVs, Camera Car Cranes, Crane Ready Camera Cars, Electric Camera Dolly, Off-Road Camera Cars & Tow Dollies)

Holladay Camera Bikes
(805) 740-6018
(323) 462-2301
FAX (805) 735-7205
www.camerabikes.com
(Bikes, High Speed Camera Motorcycles, Platforms & Sidecars)

L.A. Motorsports
(818) 222-6954
(877) 526-6867
(Hi-Speed)
FAX (866) 294-3266
www.lamsports.com

filmo-usa.com
310-669-9888

Performance Filmworks, Inc./   (805) 604-3399
Dean Bailey   (310) 721-4812
331 Hearst Dr.   FAX **(805) 604-3398**
Oxnard, CA 93030   **www.performancefilmworks.com**
(High-Speed Camera/Crane Cars, Off Road Vehicles &
Tracking Vehicles)

Pursuit Systems Inc.   **(818) 255-5850**
7255 Radford Ave.   **www.pursuitsystems.com**
North Hollywood, CA 91605

    (661) 270-0565
Radical Camera Cars   **(661) 810-9456**
39120 Bouquet Canyon Rd.**www.radicalcameracars.com**
Leona Valley, CA 93551
(Camera Racing Go Carts, High Speed Camera Cars,
Hovercrafts, Off-Road Camera Cars & Process Trucks)

    (866) 449-7447
Safari Technologies   **(818) 585-6653**
    FAX **(805) 830-1158**
   www.safaritechnologies.net

Shelly Ward Enterprises   **(818) 255-5850**
7255 Radford Ave.   FAX **(818) 255-5450**
North Hollywood, CA 91605   **www.shellywardent.com**

    (818) 623-1700
Shotmaker Camera Cars & Cranes   **(877) 708-7708**
10909 Vanowen St.   FAX **(818) 623-1710**
North Hollywood, CA 91605   **www.shotmaker.com**
(Air-Ride Process Trailers, Camera Car Cranes, Crane Ready
Camera Cars, Process Trailers/Trucks, Remote Cranes &
Tow Dollies)

Snowblind Snowmobiles   **(213) 247-4777**
11421 Hayvenhurst Ave.   **www.mtnx.com**
Granada Hills, CA 91344
(Camera Sleds & Snowmobiles)

    (818) 618-9988
Ultimate Arm/Adventure Equipment   **(805) 375-3200**
5506 Colodny Dr.   FAX **(805) 375-3211**
Agoura Hills, CA 91301   **www.ultimatearm.com**

US Camera Boats LLC   **(949) 230-9327**
    FAX **(949) 492-7783**
   www.uscameraboats.com
(Camera Boat & On-Water Filming Platform)

    (818) 355-2676
Vehicle Effects   **(818) 768-2343**
    FAX **(818) 846-7576**
   www.vehicleeffects.com
(High Performance and High Speed Off-Road Camera Cars &
Process Trailers)

    (818) 822-7549
Video Village Van   **(822) 822-7549**
10061 Riverside Dr., Ste. 566 **www.videovillagevan.com**
Toluca Lake, CA 91602

AbelCine
(818) 972-9078
(888) 700-4416
801 S. Main St., Ste. 104   FAX (818) 972-2673
Burbank, CA 91506   www.abelcine.com
16mm: Aaton, Super 16mm & Xtera
16mm Arri: Aaton
Heads: Cartoni, O'Connor & Sachtler
High Def: 1080i, 24P, 65mm, 720P, Mini DVs, Multi-Camera Systems, Panasonic, Phantom High-Speed and PS Technik Adaptors, Sony & Ultraprimes
Lenses: Angenieux, Animorphic, Canon, Century, Cooke, Elite, Fujinon, Telephoto, Variable, Zeiss & Zooms
Video: Digital, JVC, Panasonic & Sony
Other: Multi-Camera Systems, Splash Housing & Splashbags
Accessories: CamTram System, Digital Micro Force Zoom Control, Filters, Heads, Jibs, MovieTube Lens Adapter, Remote Heads, Underwater Housings & Visual FX Camera Systems

Alan Gordon Enterprises, Inc.
(323) 466-3561
5625 Melrose Ave.   FAX (323) 871-2193
Los Angeles, CA 90038   www.alangordon.com
16mm: Bell/Howell, Bolex, Canon Scoopic, Eclair & G.S.A.P.
16mm Arri: 16-M, 16-S, 16BL, SR2, SR2HS, SR3 & Super16
35mm Arri: 2C, 35-3 & BL4S
Heads: Bogen, Cartoni, O'Connor & Sachtler Fluid Head
Lenses: Primes & ZoomsVideo: Canon & Sony Digital Video Cameras and DV Steadicam
Other: Stop Motion & Video Assist Cameras

Alexa Rentals
(818) 562-1960
148 S. Victory Blvd.   FAX (818) 562-1270
Burbank, CA 91502   www.alexarentals.com
Heads: O'ConnorHigh Def: 1080I, 24P, 2K, 4K, 720P, Multi-Camera Systems & Ultra Primes
Lenses: Arri Ultra, Arri Alura, Telephoto, Zeiss & Zooms
Accessories: AJA KiPro, Follow Focus Package, OLED Monitor, SxS Card Reader, SxS Pro Card & Tiffen Filter

Angel City Air
(818) 896-9900
12653 Osborne St.   FAX (818) 686-1095
Pacoima, CA 91331   www.aerialproduction.com
Heads: 5 Axis Remote Heads & Wireless
High Def: 1080I/P, 24P, 720P, Multi-Camera Systems & Sony
Accessories: Hardware/Wireless Remote Control, Heads & Helicopter Mounts

Atlantic Cine Equipment, Inc.
(818) 794-9410
(212) 944-0003
FAX (443) 524-0210
www.aceeast.com
Heads: 5 Axis Remote Heads, MicroMote HD, MicroPlus HD, Mini-C & Stab-C Compact
High Def: Panasonic
Accessories: Remote Heads, SuperTower6 and SuperTower20 Telescopic Camera Towers & Track Runner and Track Runner Mini Tracking Systems

Atomic Studios
(323) 851-3825
(202) 438-9199
2556 E. Olympic Ave.   www.atomicstudios.com
Los Angeles, CA 90023
16mm: Arri SR3 & Nizo 801 MacroHeads:
Mini-Worrell & Sachtler
Lenses: ZeissVideo: Panasonic AJ-200, AJ-215 & DVX-100

Birns & Sawyer, Inc.
(323) 466-8211
5275 Craner Ave.   FAX (818) 358-4395
North Hollywood, CA 91601   www.birnsandsawyer.com
16mm: Aaton XTR-Prod & A-Minima
16mm Arri: SR2, SR2HS, SR3 & SR3HS
35mm: Aaton 35-3
35mm Arri: 35-3, 435, 535B, Arri 2C, BL-Evolution, BL4S & Moviecam Compact
Heads: Arri, Cartoni, Lambda Head, O'Connor, Ronford, Sachtler & Weaver-Steadman
High Def: Cooke S4s, Multi-Camera Systems, Panasonic and Sony Mini DVs, PS Technik Adaptors, SDX 900 & Ultra Primes

Camera Support
(818) 557-1400
(800) 995-5427
2827 N. San Fernando Blvd.   FAX (818) 557-1323
Burbank, CA 91504   www.camerasupport.com
16mm: Aaton XTR Prod and Accessories
Accessories: Camera Pedestals, Jibs & Steadicam Systems
Heads: 2 and 3 Axis Remote Heads
High Def: 720P and 1080I Cameras & Accessories
Video: Digital Video Cameras & Accessories
Other: Multi-Camera Systems

Camtec Motion Picture Cameras
(818) 841-8700
4221 W. Magnolia Blvd.   FAX (818) 841-8777
Burbank, CA 91505   www.camtec.tv
16mm: Aaton A-Minima & Arri SR2, SR2HS, SR3 and SR3HS
35mm: Arri 235, 35-III, 435 and 535b, Arricam & Reflex Eyemo
High Def: Panasonic Varicam
Lenses: Arri Ultra, Cooke S4, Hawk 150-450, Hawk V Anamorphics, Innovision Probe 2 Plus, Optimo Zoom, Revolution & Variable Primes
Accessories: Arri Wireless Lens Control, Cartoni Lambda, Digital Hard Drive Combo Units, Preston FIZ & Video Directors Finder

Cinema Camera Rentals
(310) 574-1524
(310) 923-3593
FAX (310) 574-1524
www.cinemacamerarentals.com
35mm: Stereoscopic Cameras & Underwater Cameras
Heads: O'ConnorHigh Def: 1080I, 24P, 4K, 65mm, 720P, DSLR, Housings, Iwerks 3-D, Panasonic, RED Cameras, Red Epic, Red MX & Scarlet
Lenses: Zeiss & ZoomsVideo: Digital & Panasonic
Accessories: 2' Video Format, Filters, Heads & Splash Housing

Cinema Rentals, Inc.　　　　　　(661) 222-7342
　　　　　　　　　　　　　　　　　(818) 365-7999
25876 The Old Road, Ste. 174　　FAX (661) 427-0881
Stevenson Ranch, CA 91381　　**www.cinemarentals.com**
35mm: Stunt, Crash and Underwater Cameras
Video: Digital Underwater Video & Lipstick Cameras

Clairmont Camera　　　　　　(818) 761-4440
4343 Lankershim Blvd.　　　　FAX (818) 761-0861
North Hollywood, CA 91602　　**www.clairmont.com**
16mm: Aaton A-Minima16mm Arri: SR3
35mm: Aaton 35-3, Moviecam Compact and SuperLight,
SuperAmerica & Wilcam VistaVision
35mm Arri: 35-3, 435, 535, BL3, BL4S, GT & STHigh Def:
Panasonic 24F & Sony F900
Other: Power Pods & Strobes

CrashCam Industries　　　　　(310) 990-3418
　　　　　　　　　　　　　　　www.edgutentag.com
35mm: Reflexed Eyemo Crash Systems
35mm Arri: 2C and 35-3 Crash Systems
Accessories: Arri 235/Preston FIZ Units

Division Camera　　　　　　(323) 465-7700
　　　　　　　　　　　　　　　(323) 571-9476
7022 W. Sunset Blvd.　　　　　FAX (323) 297-2773
Hollywood, CA 90028　　**www.divisioncamera.com**
Heads: Arri, Cartoni, O'Connor & Sachtler
High Def: 24P, RED Cameras, Sony & Ultra Primes
Lenses: Boroscope, Century, Close-Focus, Optimo Zoom,
Swing/Tilts, Variable, Zeiss & Zooms
Accessories: Digital Lens Control, Digital Micro Force Zoom
Control, Sliders & Steadicam Systems

Doggicam, Inc.　　　　　　　(818) 845-8470
1500 W. Verdugo Ave.　　　　FAX (818) 845-8477
Burbank, CA 91506　　　　　**www.doggicam.com**
16mm: Doggicam
35mm: Doggicam
Other: Body-Mount, Bulldog Wireless Remote Head, Doggimount, Lightweight Remote Sparrow Head, Power Slide,
Remote Follow Focus, Rhino Clamps & Super Slide

EVIDENCE Productions　　　　(323) 522-5298
　　　　　　　　　　　　　　　(310) 628-5400
1819 Winona Blvd.　　　　　FAX (323) 522-5298
Los Angeles, CA 90027　**www.evidenceproductions.com**
35mm: ARRI Alexa
Heads: O'Connor
Lenses: Angenieux, ARRI Alura Zooms & Zeiss
High Def: Red EPIC
Accessories: Sony F3 Super 35mm Sensor

Geo Film Group, Inc.　　　　(818) 376-6680
　　　　　　　　　　　　　　　(877) 436-3456
7625 Hayvenhurst Ave., Ste. 49　FAX (818) 376-6686
Van Nuys, CA 91406　　　　**www.geofilm.com**
35mm: Body Mount, Mini Vistavision & Pogo
35mm Arri: 235, 2C, 35-3 & 435-ES
Heads: 2 Axis Remote Heads, 3 Axis Remote Heads,
Lambda & O'Connor
Lenses: Angenieux & Zooms
Other: Arri 2C Crash Housing, Eyemo Crash Systems, Digital
Crash Housing & POV Camera

Geronimo Creek Film Company　(323) 997-0202
P.O. Box 6006　　　　　　　FAX (323) 417-4915
Burbank, CA 91510　　　**www.geronimocreek.com**
16mm: Arri SR2.9 Super 16mm
Heads: Ronford Support
Lenses: Zeiss MK2 Super Speed Primes & Canon 8-64 T2.4
Video: CEI 5 Flicker Free Color Video Assist & Sony 8" Portable
Monitor w/ Playback System
Accessories: ARRI AKS

Gyron Aerial Systems　　　　(626) 584-8722
39 E. Walnut St.　　　　　　FAX (626) 584-4069
Pasadena, CA 91103　　　　　**www.gyron.com**
Arri: Gyron Camera System
High Def: Gyron Camera System

HDPioneers.com LLC　　　　(310) 773-4823
11835 Olympic Blvd., Ste. 825　FAX (310) 479-2240
Los Angeles, CA 90064　　**www.hdpioneers.com**
16mm: Arri, Body Mount & Canon
35mm: Body Mount, Moviecam, Stereoscopic Cameras, Stunt
Cameras, Underwater Cameras & Vistavision
Heads: Arri, Bogen, Cartoni, Lambda, Lightweight, O'Connor,
Power Pod, Remote, Ronford & Sachtler
High Def: 1080I, 24P, 4K, 5k, 65mm, 720P, Cooke, Epic, Hous-
ings, Mini DVs, Multi-Camera Systems, Panasonic, Panavision,
PS Technik Adaptors, RED Epic Cameras, RED Scarlet, Sony,
Ultra Primes & Video-Capable DSLRs
Lenses: Angenieux, Anamorphic, Arri Ultra, Century, Close-
Focus, Cooke, Optimo Zoom, Portrait, RED Pro Anamorphics,
RED Pro Primes, Slant-Focus, Swing/Tilts, Telephoto, Variable,
Zeiss Compact Primes & Zooms
Video: Digital, JVC, Panasonic & Sony
Accessories: Beam Splitter Rigs, Body Mounts, Camera
Pedestals, Car Mounts, Color Video Doors/Taps, Digital Hard
Drive Combo Units, Digital Lens Control, Digital Micro
Force Zoom Control, Element Technica, Filters, Hardware/
Wireless Remote Control, Heads, Sliders, Steadicam Systems,
Stereoscopic Rigs, Video Tap/Assist Packages & Visual FX
Camera Systems

Hill Digital　　　　　　　(818) 445-9211
9714 La Canada Way　　　　**www.hilldigital.com**
Sunland, CA 91040
Digital Cameras: RED Epic, RED One &
Panasonic HD Cameras
Video: 24 Frame

Hollywood Camera, Inc.　　　(818) 972-5000
　　　　　　　　　　　　　　　(818) 720-8404
3100 N. Damon Way　　　　FAX (818) 972-5010
Burbank, CA 91505　　**www.hollywoodcamera.com**
16mm: Aaton XTR-Prod & A-Minima
16mm Arri: SR2, SR2HS, SR3 & SR3HS
35mm: Fries High Speed Reflex Visual Effects
Camera Packages
35mm Arri: 2C, 35-3, BL-4, BL4S, 435 Advanced, 535B &
Moviecam Compact
Heads: Arri, Cartoni, Lambda Head, O'Connor, Ronford,
Sachtler and Weaver-Steadman Remote Heads
High Def: Panasonic 720p VariCam, PS Technik Adaptors, SDX
900, Sony F900 & Mini DVs
Lenses: Cooke S4s, Zeiss Standard and Superspeeds & Zeiss
Ultra Primes

**HydroFlex Underwater Camera &
Lighting Systems**　　　　　(310) 301-8187
301 E. El Segundo Blvd.　　FAX (310) 821-9886
El Segundo, CA 90245　　　**www.hydroflex.com**
16mm: Aaton and Arri SR Underwater Housings
35mm Arri: 35-3, 435 Pan-Arri Surf & Shallow and Deep Water
Housings and Accessories
65mm: IMAX, Iwerks 3D & Panavision Underwater Housing-
sHigh Def: HD Housings & Splashbags
Heads: HydroHead 2 and 3 Axis Underwater Remote Heads
Video: Sony FX1 and Z1 & Mini DV Housings
Other: Light Meter Housing, Splashbags & Waterproof
Video Monitors

Infinite Siege　　　　　　(323) 578-4440

Innovision Optics　　　　　(310) 453-4866
1719 21st St.　　　　　　　FAX (310) 453-4677
Santa Monica, CA 90404　**www.innovisionoptics.com**
35mm: Underwater Cameras
Heads: 2 Axis Remote Heads & Weaver-Steadman
Lenses: Boroscope Lenses, Periscope & Probe Lens System
Video: RadCam Miniature Camera Car
Accessories: Body Mounts, Jibs & Kamtrax Slider
Other: 3-Axis Remote Head Cams, Portable Table Top Motion
Control Systems & Rollvision Wireless

Keslow Camera　　　　　　(310) 636-4600
11260 Playa Court　　　　FAX (310) 915-5335
Culver City, CA 90230　　**www.keslowcamera.com**
16mm Arri: SR3 & SR3HS
35mm Arri: 435ES, 535B, Arricam Studio and Lite & Moviecam
Compact and SL
High Def: RED Cameras
Lenses: Angenieux, Canon, Cooke, Leica Telephoto,
Revolution & Zeiss

Lexus Lighting, Inc.   (818) 768-4508
11225 Dora St.   FAX (805) 641-3273
Sun Valley, CA 91352   www.lexuslighting.com
35mm: ARRI 435/535B, ARRI Alexa HD, Canon 5D &
Phantom Gold
Other: Accessories, Lenses & Support

               (805) 640-6700
Libertypak   (323) 304-4404
407 Bryant Circle, Bldg. E   www.libertypak.com
Ojai, CA 93023
Accessories: Custom Packs, High Intensity Battery Belts,
Lithium Ion Battery Belts & Little Genny AC Packs

Motion Picture Marine/Perfect Horizon
Stabilization Head   (310) 822-1100
616 Venice Blvd.   FAX (310) 822-2679
Marina del Rey, CA 90291
          www.motionpicturemarine.com
Heads: Perfect Horizon Camera Stabilization Head

           (323) 467-1116
Moviola/Moviola Cameras   (800) 327-3724
1135 N. Mansfield Ave.   FAX (323) 464-1518
Los Angeles, CA 90038   www.moviola.com

Nebtek   (818) 768-8348
11152 Fleetwood St., Ste. 3   www.nebtek.com
Van Nuys, CA 91406
Heads: Power Pod

Nettmann Systems International   (818) 365-4286
1026 Griswold Ave.   FAX (818) 361-6982
San Fernando, CA 91340   www.camerasystems.com
Heads: Cam-Remote, Gyro-Stabilized, Gyron FS/Stab-C,
Kenworthy/Nettmann Snorkel, Mini-Mote, Stab-C Compact,
Super-G & Vectorvision

New Deal Studios, Inc.   (310) 578-9929
15392 Cobalt St.   FAX (310) 578-7370
Sylmar, CA 91342   www.newdealstudios.com
35mm: Fries/Mitchell
65mm: Fries/Mitchell
Other: Motion Control Systems & Video Assist

Old School Cameras   (818) 847-1555
2819 N. San Fernando Blvd.   FAX (818) 847-1556
Burbank, CA 91504   www.oldschoolcameras.com
16mm: Arri SR3 HS, Bolex, Éclair & Super16
35mm: Arri 35-2C, Arri 435, Eyemo Reflex Crash Cameras &
Moviecam
Heads: O'Connor & Sachtler
High Def: 4K & RED Cameras
Lenses: Slant-Focus, Zeiss & Zooms
Super 8mm: Beaulieu, Canon & Crystal Sync
Video: Panasonic
Accessories: Sliders, Steadicam Systems &
Underwater Housings

          (310) 286-2104
Ⓐ **Oppenheimer Cine Rental**   (877) 467-8666
16mm: Aaton XTR-Prod & XTR+   FAX (206) 467-9165
16mm Arri: SR2, SR2HS & SR3   www.oppcam.com
35mm: Aaton 35-3 & Moviecam Compact and SuperLight
35mm Arri: 2C, 35-3, 235, 435, BL3 & BL4
Heads: 3 Axis Remote Heads, Mako, Power Pod Remote Head,
Weaver-Steadman & Wireless
High Def: 1080i, 4K, 720P, Arri Alexa, HDX900, RED MX &
Varicam
Lenses: Cooke S4, Fujinon, Oppenheimer Camera, Optimo
Zoom & Zeiss
Accessories: Aerial Exposures Mounts, Boat Mounts, Splash
Housing, Steadicam Systems, Swiss Jib Crane, Tyler Helicopter
Mounts & Underwater Housings

Otto Nemenz International, Inc.   (323) 469-2774
870 Vine St.   FAX (323) 469-1217
Hollywood, CA 90038   www.ottonemenz.com
16mm Arri: SR3 & SR3HS
35mm: Arricam 235, LT and ST, Eyemo, Moviecam Compact
Mark2 & Moviecam Compact SL
35mm Arri: 2C, 35-3, 3C, 435, 535, 535B, BL3, BL4 & BL4S
Heads: 3 Axis Nodal Head, Arri Gearhead II & Power Pod
Remote Head
Lenses: 17-80 T2.3 Angenieux, 24-290mm T2.8, Angenieux
Optimo, Cooke S4 Primes & Zeiss Ultra and Variable Primes
Other: Color Video

Pace Technologies   (818) 561-3950
2020 N. Lincoln St.   FAX (818) 565-0006
Burbank, CA 91504   www.pacehd.com
Accessories: Underwater and Wet Environment
Camera Systems

          (818) 768-1573
Pacific Motion Control, Inc.   (661) 644-1516
9812 Glenoaks Blvd.   FAX (818) 768-1575
Sun Valley, CA 91352   www.pacificmotion.net
Heads: Motion Control Frame Accurate Sorensen Heads (2 or
3 Axis), Remote/Repeatable Aerohead (2 or 3 Axis), Remote/
Repeatable Talon & Sorensen Mini Head (2 or 3 Axis)
Accessories: Camera Sync Systems, Lynx C-50 Motion Control
Camera Motor, Motion Control Systems, Preston System
(Optional Kuper Interface) Remote Heads &
Time-Lapse Controller

Panavision   (818) 316-1000
Corporate Headquarters   FAX (818) 316-1111
6219 DeSoto Ave.   www.panavision.com
Woodland Hills, CA 91367
35mm: Millennium XL, Panaflex, Panaflex G, Panaflex G2 &
Panaflex Platinum
35mm Arri: 435ES and III, Arri 435 & Arri 235
High Def: Genesis Camera System, Sony F-23, Panavision/
Sony F-900 & F-900R
Lenses: Anamorphic and Spherical, Angenieux Zooms,
Close-Focus, Cooke Zooms, Frazier, High Def Primo Digital
Zooms and Primes, Hylen Lens System, Optimo Zooms, Primo
Series and Zooms, Slant-Focus & Zeiss
Other: 65mm Studio Handheld Lightweight Camera &
Panavision Remote Cranes and Heads

Panavision Hollywood   (323) 464-3800
6735 Selma Ave.   FAX (323) 469-5175
Hollywood, CA 90028   www.panavision.com
16mm: Aaton XTR-Prod & Panaflex 16
16mm Arri: SR2 Hi-Speed, SR3 & SR3 Hi-Speed
35mm: Aaton 35 III, Gold and Gold II, Millennium, Millennium
XL, Mitchell Mark II, Pan-Arri IIC, Pan-Arri III, Pan-Arri IIIC,
Pan-Arri 435ES, Panastar I, Panastar II, Panavision
Lightweight II & Platinum
High Def: Panavision & Sony
Lenses: Anamorphic and Spherical, Angenieux, Baltar,
Close-Focus, Frazier, Innovision Probe II, Kowa, Periscope,
Portrait, Primo Series, Slant-Focus, Swing and Tilts & Zeiss

Performance Filmworks, Inc./   (805) 604-3399
Dean Bailey   (310) 721-4815
331 Hearst Dr.   FAX (805) 604-3398
Oxnard, CA 93030   www.performancefilmworks.com
Heads: 3-Axis Gyrostabilized Remote Heads (with Horizon
Stabilization), 3D Compatible, Joystick, Wheels or
Panbar Controls

          (818) 766-6868
Photo-Plus   (800) 759-5722
4141 Elmer Ave.   www.ronvidor.com
Studio City, CA 91602
Other: GPI Steadicam Pro System

Photo-Sonics, Inc.   (818) 842-2141
820 S. Mariposa St.   FAX (818) 842-2610
Burbank, CA 91506   www.photosonics.com

          (818) 785-9282
Pictorvision Inc   (800) 876-5583
          FAX (818) 785-9787
16mm: Super 16   www.pictorvision.com
Accessories: 5 Axis Gyro-Stabilized Camera Systems, Cineflex,
Pictorvision Eclipse, Wescam & XRCameras: High Def & SD

Preston Cinema Systems (310) 453-1852
1659 11th St., Ste. 100 FAX (310) 453-5672
Santa Monica, CA 90404 www.prestoncinema.com
Accessories: Digital Lens Control, Digital Micro Force Zoom
Control & FI+Z and Light Ranger Auto Focus Systems

Pro8mm (818) 848-5522
2805 W. Magnolia Blvd. FAX (818) 848-5956
Burbank, CA 91505 www.pro8mm.com
Super 8mm: Beaulieu, Canon, Crystal Sync & Nizo

The Slider (805) 496-5289
(818) 344-5284
FAX (805) 496-4802
www.theslider.com
Accessories: 32" Video and Mitchell Mount Minisliders & 3', 4',
6', 8' Manual and Motorized Sliders

Slow Motion, Inc. (818) 982-4400
7211 Clybourn Ave. FAX (818) 982-8500
Sun Valley, CA 91352 www.slowmotioninc.com

SpaceCam Systems, Inc (818) 889-6060
31111 Via Colinas, Ste. 201 FAX (818) 889-6062
Westlake Village, CA 91362 www.spacecam.com
Accessories: Boat and Car Crane and Helicopter
Gyro-Stabilized Camera Mounts

Super 8 Film Cameras & 2nd Unit (213) 273-3661
(800) 470-4602
8630 Wilshire Blvd. www.super8guy.com
Beverly Hills, CA 90211
16mm: Bolex REX-4 & Canon Scoopic 16M
Heads: Bogen Camera Support & SteadyTracker
Lenses: Angenieux Zooms, Bolex Gel Filters, Kern Zooms &
Switar 6, 10, 16, 25, 26 Macro, 50 and 75mm
Super16: Bolex SBM & Eclair NPR
Super 8mm: Beaulieu 4008 Pro, Canon 1014XL-S
Crystal Sync & Nizo 801 Macro
Video: Live View Recording Monitor, Panasonic Lumix GH2 HD
1080 24P Camera, Prime Lenses & Zoom Lenses
Accessories: Super 8 Video Tap/Assist Packages

TCH/The Camera House (818) 997-3802
7351 Fulton Ave. FAX (818) 997-3885
North Hollywood, CA 91605 www.thecamerahouse.com
16mm: Arri SR3
35mm: Arri 35-2C, 35-3, 435 ES, 535 B, SR3, Arricam Studio
and Light & Moviecam SL and Compact
Heads: Arri, Cartoni, O'Connor, Ronford & Sachtler
Lenses: Cooke, Prime, Telephoto, Variable, Zeiss & Zoom

Tyler Camera Systems (818) 989-4420
(800) 390-6070
14218 Aetna St. FAX (818) 989-0423
Van Nuys, CA 91401 www.tylermount.com
Accessories: Gyro-Stabilized Helicopter Camera Mounts

Weekend Video & Company (323) 376-9191
High Def: Sony and Panasonic HD/1080i/23.98P

Wolfe Air Aviation, Ltd. (626) 584-4060
39 E. Walnut St. FAX (626) 584-4069
Pasadena, CA 91103 www.wolfeair.com
Camera Systems: Vectorvision

Wooden Nickel Lighting Inc. (818) 761-9662
6920 Tujunga Ave. FAX (818) 985-0717
North Hollywood, CA 91605
16mm Arri: SR2 www.woodennickellighting.com
35mm: Mitchell Fries High Speed
35mm Arri: 3 & BL3
Lenses: Angenieux, Cooke & Zeiss

5th & Sunset Los Angeles (310) 979-0212
12322 Exposition Blvd. FAX (310) 979-0214
Los Angeles, CA 90064 www.5thandsunsetla.com

A B Sea Photo (310) 645-8992
9136 S. Sepulveda Blvd. FAX (310) 645-3645
Los Angeles, CA 90045 www.absea.net/rentals
(Underwater Cameras and Equipment)

Ambient Digital, LLC (805) 415-4100
(626) 381-9397
8351 Leroy St. www.ambientdsr.com
San Gabriel, CA 91775
(Computer Controlled Multiple Still Camera Systems, Imaging
Supplies & Panoramic Photography)

Bel Air Camera Superstore (310) 208-5150
(800) 200-4999
10925 Kinross Ave. FAX (310) 208-7472
Los Angeles, CA 90024 www.belaircamera.com

Calumet Photographic, Inc. (323) 466-1238
1135 N. Highland Ave. FAX (323) 466-1906
Hollywood, CA 90038 www.calumetphoto.com

Deck Hand, Inc. (818) 557-8403
1905 Victory Blvd., Ste. 8 FAX (818) 557-8406
Glendale, CA 91201 www.deckhand.com
(HDSLR Cameras, Lenses, Monitors & Tripods)

Elephant Eye Media, Inc./EEM (310) 399-5560
212 Marine St., Ste. 209 FAX (310) 399-5553
Santa Monica, CA 90405 www.elephanteyemedia.com

Pasadena Camera Rental, Inc. (626) 796-3300
41 E. Walnut St. FAX (626) 432-6731
Pasadena, CA 91103 www.samyscamera.com

Pix (323) 936-8488
211 S. La Brea Ave. FAX (323) 936-5209
Los Angeles, CA 90036 www.pixcamera.com

Pro HD Rentals, Inc. (818) 450-1115
(310) 453-3301
FAX (310) 453-3310
www.prohdrentals.com

Reel EFX, Inc. (818) 762-1710
(213) 308-7289
5539 Riverton Ave. FAX (818) 762-1734
North Hollywood, CA 91601 www.reelefx.com
(Computer Controlled Multiple Still Camera System)

Samy's Camera (323) 938-2420
(800) 321-4726
431 S. Fairfax Ave. FAX (323) 937-2919
Los Angeles, CA 90036 www.samys.com

Samy's Camera (310) 450-4551
4411 Sepulveda Blvd. FAX (310) 450-8590
Culver City, CA 90230 www.samys.com

Smashbox Digital (323) 512-2046
1011 N. Fuller Ave., Ste. M FAX (323) 512-2035
Los Angeles, CA 90046 www.smashboxdigital.com

LA 411 — Motion Control — LA 411

Ⓐ Camera Control, Inc. (310) 581-8343
3317 Ocean Park Blvd. FAX (310) 581-8340
Santa Monica, CA 90405 www.cameracontrol.com

Fisher Technical Services Rentals (702) 997-1939
(866) 942-4098
www.ftsrentals.com

General Lift, LLC (310) 414-0717
111 Maryland St. FAX (310) 414-0705
El Segundo, CA 90245 www.general-lift.com

Image G (818) 761-6644
28490 Westinghouse Pl. www.imageg.com
Valencia, CA 91355

Innovision Optics (310) 453-4866
1719 21st St. FAX (310) 453-4677
Santa Monica, CA 90404 www.innovisionoptics.com
Mini Mover Motion Controller

New Deal Studios, Inc. (310) 578-9929
15392 Cobalt St. FAX (310) 578-7370
Sylmar, CA 91342 www.newdealstudios.com

Ⓐ Pacific Motion Control, Inc. (818) 768-1573
9812 Glenoaks Blvd. FAX (818) 768-1575
Sun Valley, CA 91352 www.pacificmotion.net
Cranes: Motion Control/Repeatable Cranes: Gazelle (Portable
6' Arm), Graphlite (Portable 10' or 13' Arm), Telescoping
Cranes: Super Scorpio Technocrane (30' or 37' Arm)
Dollies: Motion Control/Repeatable Zebra
(Portable 2' or 6' Arm) & The Bogie
Accessories: CGI Rig Interface Models, Frame Accurate Motion
Control Heads, Kuper Motion Control Systems, Model Movers,
Motion Control Lighting Cues, Motion Control Track (Straight
or 360° Curved), Motor Driver Systems, Preston System with
Kuper Interface, Remote/Repeatable Heads (Aerohead &
Talon) & Turn Tables

Absolute Sound	(818) 399-3419

Jack Bornoff (818) 905-0356

Cutting Edge Productions, Inc. (310) 326-4500
(818) 503-0400
22904 Lockness Ave. FAX (310) 326-4715
Torrance, CA 90501 www.cuttingedgeproductions.tv

Delicate Productions, Inc. (805) 388-1800
874 Verdulera St. FAX (805) 388-1037
Camarillo, CA 93010 www.delicate.com

Director's Choice HD (323) 658-7878
6062 Shadyglade Ave.
North Hollywood, CA 91606

Gary Raymond Sound Systems (805) 492-5858
P.O. Box 1722
Thousand Oaks, CA 91358

Impact AV (213) 494-9492
(800) 323-0490
FAX (323) 225-1389

Christopher Lennon (323) 459-6997

Planet 00:00:03 Sound Co./Tim Hays (818) 789-8799
(877) 737-6863
12400 Ventura Blvd. www.planet3soundco.com
Ste. 500
Studio City, CA 91604

Roll Sound, Inc./Robert Dreebin & (310) 629-2476
Alex Lamm (818) 540-5979
19712 Mayall St. FAX (818) 772-2614
Chatsworth, CA 91311 www.rollsound.biz

Skyland Sound, Inc. (310) 390-3520

Wilcox Sound and Communications (818) 504-0507
7680 Clybourn Ave., Ste. B FAX (818) 504-0921
Sun Valley, CA 91352 www.wilcoxsound.net

Ametron Audio Video
(323) 466-4321
(323) 464-1144
FAX (323) 871-0127
1546 N. Argyle Ave.
Hollywood, CA 90028
www.ametron.com

CET Universe
(818) 432-4330
801 S. Main St., Ste. 101
FAX (818) 755-7748
Burbank, CA 91506
www.cetuniverse.com
(Film Only, High Def Tape, New Video Stock & Tested Recans
and Short Ends)

Comtel Pro Media
(818) 450-1100
2201 N. Hollywood Way
FAX (818) 450-1144
Burbank, CA 91505
www.comtelpromedia.com

Eastman Kodak
(323) 962-9053
(800) 621-3456
1017 N. Las Palmas Ave., Ste. 100   FAX (800) 648-9805
Hollywood, CA 90038   www.kodak.com/go/motion
(Film Only)

Edgewise Media Services, Inc.
(323) 769-0900
(800) 824-3130
2201 N. Hollywood Way
FAX (323) 466-6815
Burbank, CA 91505
www.edgewise-media.com

Edgewise Media Services, Inc.
(714) 919-2020
(800) 444-9330
602 N. Cypress St.
FAX (714) 919-2010
Orange, CA 92867
www.edgewise-media.com

Empress Media, Inc.
(888) 683-6773
10777 Sherman Way
FAX (818) 255-3398
Sun Valley, CA 91352
www.empressdigital.com
(New Video Stock & Recycled Video Stock)

EVS
(818) 552-4590
(800) 238-8480
1819 Victory Bl.
FAX (818) 552-4591
Glendale, CA 91201
www.evsonline.com
(New and Recycled Video Stock)

Film Source LA
(818) 484-3236
(866) 537-1114
FAX (818) 688-0101
www.filmsourcela.com

Fujifilm USA, Inc.
Motion Picture Divison
(888) 424-3854
2220 W. Magnolia Blvd.
FAX (323) 465-8279
Burbank, CA 91506
www.fujifilmusa.com
(Film Only)

Media Distributors
(818) 980-9916
(888) 889-3130
4518 W. Vanowen St.
FAX (818) 980-9265
Burbank, CA 91505
www.mediadistributors.com

Moviola/Moviola Cameras
(323) 467-1116
(800) 468-3107
1135 N. Mansfield Ave.
FAX (323) 464-1518
Hollywood, CA 90038
www.moviola.com
(Video Only)

MSE Media Solutions
(323) 721-1656
(800) 626-1955
6013 Scott Way
FAX (323) 721-1506
Los Angeles, CA 90040
www.msemedia.com

Pro8mm
(818) 848-5522
2805 W. Magnolia Blvd.
FAX (818) 848-5956
Burbank, CA 91505
www.pro8mm.com
(Super 8 & Super 16)

Reel Good
(323) 876-5427
(213) 303-6886
7758 Sunset Blvd.
FAX (323) 876-5428
Los Angeles, CA 90046   www.reelgoodfilm.com
(16mm and 35mm Raw Stock & Hard Drives)

Revolt Pro Media
(818) 904-0001
7625 Hayvenhurst Ave., Ste. 27   FAX (818) 904-0005
Van Nuys, CA 91406   www.revoltpromedia.com
(High Def Tape, New Video Stock & Recycled Video Stock)

Shutterstock
(866) 663-3954
60 Broad St., 30th Fl.
FAX (347) 402-0710
New York, NY 10004
footage.shutterstock.com

Spectra Film & Video
(818) 762-4545
5626 Vineland Ave.
FAX (818) 762-5454
North Hollywood, CA 91601
www.spectrafilmandvideo.com

The Tape Company
(818) 847-0036
(800) 851-3113
4518 W. Vanowen St.   www.thetapecompany.com
Burbank, CA 91505

TapeOnline.com
(877) 893-8273
(615) 263-1838
FAX (615) 263-1411
www.tapeonline.com

TapeStockOnline.com
(888) 322-8273
(310) 352-4230
2034 E. Lincoln Ave., Box 426   FAX (310) 352-4233
Anaheim, CA 92806   www.tapestockonline.com
(Video Only)

Videotape Products, Inc.
(818) 566-9898
(800) 422-2444
2721 W. Magnolia Blvd.
FAX (818) 566-8989
Burbank, CA 91505
www.myvtp.com
(Video Only)

A West Coast Film Company, LLC   (818) 980-6131
4804 Laurel Canyon Blvd., Ste. 547   FAX (818) 980-6133
North Hollywood, CA 91607

Westside Media Group
(310) 979-3500
(818) 779-8600
12233 W. Olympic Blvd., Ste. 152   www.wmgmedia.com
West Los Angeles, CA 90064
(High Def Tape & New Video Stock)

Absolute Rentals   (818) 842-2828
2633 N. San Fernando Blvd.   FAX (818) 842-8815
Burbank, CA 91504   www.absoluterentals.com

Action Audio & Visual   (323) 461-4290
     (888) 406-8164
10834 Burbank Blvd., Ste. A-100   FAX (323) 461-4292
North Hollywood, CA 91601
www.actionaudioandvisual.com/products/
audio-rentals/
(Analog, Audio Props, DAT Recording Tape, Digital Multi-Track
Portable Recorders, Expendables, Microphones, Mixing
Boards, Playback Systems, Schoeps, Specialty Mics, Theatrical
Sound Systems, Underwater Communications &
Wireless Systems)

Advanced Audio Rental Inc.   (818) 955-7100
3096 N. Clyburn Ave.   FAX (818) 955-7176
Burbank, CA 91502   www.advancedaudiorentals.com

Alan Gordon Enterprises, Inc.   (323) 466-3561
5625 Melrose Ave.   FAX (323) 871-2193
Los Angeles, CA 90038   www.alangordon.com

All Electronics Corporation   (818) 904-0524
     (800) 826-5432
14928 Oxnard St.   FAX (818) 781-2653
Van Nuys, CA 91411   www.allelectronics.com

Alliant Event Services, Inc.   (909) 622-3306
     (800) 851-5415
196 University Pkwy   FAX (909) 622-3917
Pomona, CA 91768   www.alliantevents.com

Alternative Rentals   (310) 204-3388
5805 W. Jefferson Blvd.   FAX (310) 204-3384
Los Angeles, CA 90016   www.alternativerentals.com
(Schoeps, Specialty Mics, Wireless Systems & Zaxcom Digital
Multi-Track Portable Recorders)

Ametron Audio Video   (323) 466-4321
     (323) 464-1144
1546 N. Argyle Ave.   FAX (323) 871-0127
Hollywood, CA 90028   www.ametron.com

Angelcom Audio   (562) 948-3154
     FAX (562) 948-5324
www.angelcomaudio.com
(P.A. Systems, Playback Systems & Speakers)

Astro Audio Video Lighting, Inc.   (818) 549-9915
     (800) 427-8768
6615 San Fernando Rd.   FAX (818) 549-9921
Glendale, CA 91201   www.astroavl.com
(Analog, Audio Props, Expendables, Microphones, Speakers,
Specialty Microphones, Theatrical Sound Systems &
Wireless Systems)

ATK Audiotek   (661) 705-3700
28238 Avenue Crocker   FAX (661) 705-3707
Valencia, CA 91355   www.atkaudiotek.com

Audio Applications   (714) 508-1858
14791 Myford Rd.   FAX (714) 508-2362
Tustin, CA 92780   www.videoapps.com
(Analog, Digital Audio Workstations, Microphones, Playback
Systems, Players, Preamps, Speakers, Theatrical Sound
Systems, Wired and Wireless Intercom Systems & Wireless
IFB/PSM Systems)

Audio Rents, Inc.   (323) 874-1000
1541 N. Wilcox Ave.   FAX (323) 460-2676
Los Angeles, CA 90028   www.audiorents.com
(Analog, Audio Props, Digital Audio, Digital Multi-Track,
Microphones, Playback Systems, Players, Preamps, Speakers,
Specialty Microphones, Theatrical Sound Systems, Vintage
Gear & Wireless Systems)

Broadcast Store   (818) 998-9100
9420 Lurline Ave., Ste. C   FAX (818) 998-9106
Chatsworth, CA 91311   www.broadcaststore.com

CBS Studio Center   (818) 655-6311
4024 Radford Ave.   FAX (818) 655-5819
Studio City, CA 91604   www.cbssc.com

Ⓐ CineLUX Sound Services Inc.
(818) 566-3000
(888) 246-3589
www.cinelux.tv
4300 W. Victory Blvd.
Burbank, CA 91505
(Analog Mixers, Audio Props, Consignment, DAT Recording Tape, Digital Audio Workstations, Digital Multi-Track Portable Recorders, DPA, DV, Expendables, Lectrosonics, Microphones, Motorola Walkies, Playback Systems, Players, Plug and Play ENG Kits, Preamps, RF Antenna Systems, RF In-Ear, Sanken, Schopes, Sennheiser and Zaxcom Wireless, Sonotrim, Speakers, Specialty Microphones, Theatrical Sound Systems, Wendt, Wireless Ear Que Systems, Wireless PL, Wireless Systems & Yamaha Digital Consoles)

Coffey Sound & Communications, Inc.
(323) 876-7525
FAX (323) 876-4775
www.coffeysound.com
3325 Cahuenga Blvd. West
Hollywood, CA 90068

Cutting Edge Productions, Inc.
(310) 326-4500
(818) 503-0400
FAX (310) 326-4715
22904 Lockness Ave.
Torrance, CA 90501   www.cuttingedgeproductions.tv
(Analog, Audio Props, DAT Recording Tape, DV, Expendables, Microphones, Playback Systems, Players, Preamps, Speakers, Specialty Microphones, Theatrical Sound Systems, Vintage Gear & Wireless Systems)

Delicate Productions, Inc.
(805) 388-1800
FAX (805) 388-1037
www.delicate.com
874 Verdulera St.
Camarillo, CA 93010

Digital Sound Vision
(805) 630-0507
FAX (323) 488-9681

ELM, Ltd.
(818) 508-5995
www.elmlimited.com
13659 Victory Blvd., Ste. 583
Van Nuys, CA 91401

Farr Out Productions, LLC
(310) 902-5944
FAX (818) 830-3608
www.farroutpro.com
(Digital Multi-Track Portable Recorders, Microphones, Playback Systems, Speakers, Specialty Microphones & Wireless Systems)

Gary Raymond Sound Systems
(805) 492-5858
P.O. Box 1722
Thousand Oaks, CA 91358

HydroFlex Underwater Camera & Lighting Systems
(310) 301-8187
FAX (310) 821-9886
www.hydroflex.com
301 E. El Segundo Blvd.
El Segundo, CA 90245
(Underwater Communications and Speakers)

Imagecraft Productions
(818) 954-0187
FAX (818) 954-0189
www.imagecraft.tv
3318 Burton Ave.
Burbank, CA 91504

J.L. Fisher, Inc.
(818) 846-8366
FAX (818) 846-8699
www.jlfisher.com
1000 W. Isabel St.
Burbank, CA 91506

Lex Products Corp.
(818) 768-4474
FAX (818) 768-4040
www.lexproducts.com
11847 Sheldon St.
Sun Valley, CA 91352
(Power Distribution Systems and Cables for Sound Equipment)

Location Sound Corporation
(818) 980-9891
(800) 228-4429
FAX (818) 980-9911
www.locationsound.com
10639 Riverside Dr.
North Hollywood, CA 91602
(DAT Recording Tape, Digital Multi-Track Portable Recorders, Expendables, Microphones, Playback Systems, Players, Preamps, Speakers, Specialty Microphones, Walkies & Wireless Systems)

McNulty Nielsen, Inc.
(310) 704-1713
FAX (323) 372-3768
www.mcnultynielsen.com
6930 ½ Tujunga Ave.
North Hollywood, CA 91605
(Analog, Audio Props, Digital Multi-Track Portable Recorders, DV, Expendables, Microphones, Playback Systems, Players, Preamps, Speakers, Theatrical Sound Systems & Wireless Systems)

Nelson Sound, Inc.
(818) 545-8451
(800) 487-0787
FAX (818) 545-8467
www.nelsonsound.com
804 N. Grand Ave.
Covina, CA 91724

Pace Technologies
(818) 565-0005
FAX (818) 561-3950
www.pacehd.com
2020 N. Lincoln St.
Burbank, CA 91504
(Underwater Communications)

Planet 00:00:03 Sound Co./Tim Hays
(818) 789-8799
(877) 737-6863
www.planet3soundco.com
12400 Ventura Blvd.
Ste. 500
Studio City, CA 91604

Productionsound
(818) 842-8662
(818) 295-8662
FAX (818) 842-8662
(Vintage Gear)

Silver Pixel Productions
(818) 415-9572
www.silverpixelproductions.com

SSR Sound System Rentals
(323) 839-7705
www.ssrrentals.com
(Audio Props, Microphones, Speakers & Wireless Systems)

Studio On Wheels
(818) 419-0323
FAX (562) 698-3513
www.recordingtruck.com
(Mobile Recording Facilities)

Towards 2000, Inc.
(818) 557-0903
FAX (866) 836-5725
www.t2k.com
215 W. Palm Ave., Ste. 101
Burbank, CA 91502

Warner Bros. Studio Facilities - Production Sound & Video
(818) 954-2511
FAX (818) 954-2491
www.wbsoundandvideo.com
4000 Warner Blvd., Bldg. 43
Burbank, CA 91522

Wexler Video
(818) 846-9381
(800) 939-5371
FAX (818) 846-9399
www.wexlervideo.com
1111 S. Victory Blvd.
Burbank, CA 91502

Wilcox Sound and Communications
(818) 504-0507
FAX (818) 504-0921
www.wilcoxsound.net
7680 Clybourn Ave., Ste. B
Sun Valley, CA 91352

World of Video & Audio (WOVA)
(310) 659-5959
(866) 900-3827
FAX (310) 659-8247
www.wova.com
8717 Wilshire Blvd.
Beverly Hills, CA 90211
(DAT Recording Tape, DV, Microphones, Players, Playback Systems, Preamps, Speakers, Specialty Mics & Wireless Systems)

AcuPrompt Teleprompting Services (818) 576-1291
(866) 576-1291
19145 Parthenia St., Ste. A   FAX (818) 576-9981
Northridge, CA 91324   www.acuprompt.com

American Movie Company   (818) 855-1754
15353 Weddington St., Ste. B206
Sherman Oaks, CA 91411   www.americanmovieco.com

Christopher Augustine/
Teleprompters & Interrotron   (323) 572-0800
Tech/Ops   (323) 806-8070
christopheraugustine.com

Ⓐ **Bev Feldman's StarPrompt.TV**   (818) 445-7936
FAX (818) 790-6521
www.starprompt.tv

California Teleprompter   (858) 945-2076
P.O. Box 13024   FAX (858) 945-2076
La Jolla, CA 92039   www.calteleprompter.com

Crystal Pyramid Productions   (619) 644-3000
(800) 365-8433
7323 Rondel Court   FAX (619) 644-3001
San Diego, CA 92119   www.crystalpyramid.com

Ⓐ **Cue Tech Teleprompting**   (818) 487-2700
5527 Satsuma Ave.   FAX (818) 487-2750
North Hollywood, CA 91601   www.cue-tech.com

Greenberg Teleprompting   (818) 838-4437
(714) 288-8553
FAX (818) 838-0447
www.greenprompt.com

iPromptLA   (310) 837-0389
1220 24th St., Ste. 6   FAX (310) 837-0806
Santa Monica, CA 90404   www.ipromptla.com

Mary Stec's Channel Cue Cards   (818) 606-7895
(818) 991-8224
(Cue Cards)   FAX (818) 991-8839

McNulty Nielsen, Inc.   (310) 704-1713
(310) 704-1997
6930 ½ Tujunga Ave.   FAX (323) 372-3768
North Hollywood, CA 91601   www.mcnultynielsen.com

On Air Prompting   (818) 406-2582
3330 Barham Blvd.   www.onairprompting.com
Los Angeles, CA 90036

PC Prompting Systems   (818) 831-6554
18320 Ankara Court   FAX (818) 831-6574
Northridge, CA 91326   www.pcprompting.com

Prime Teleprompting   (818) 207-1520
18543 Devonshire St., Ste. 317
Northridge, CA 91324   www.primeteleprompting.com

Prompt Response   (888) 776-6787
1441 W. 132nd St.   FAX (949) 218-8105
Los Angeles, CA 90061   www.promptresponse.tv

Prompt Response   (949) 218-8103
(888) 776-6787
34812 Doheny Pl.   FAX (949) 218-8105
Capistrano Beach, CA 92624   www.promptresponse.tv

women with tools

Bev Feldman's
StarPrompt
Teleprompting
Services

818.790.7418 Office
818.445.7936 Cell
818.790.6521 Fax

StarPrompt.tv

Promptin' Circumstance West, LLC (323) 963-3542
www.promptinwest.com

ProPrompt, Inc./Compu=Prompt (323) 465-9441
5723 Melrose Ave., Ste. 204   FAX (323) 465-3587
Los Angeles, CA 90038   www.proprompt.com

(858) 538-9300
Q Systems Teleprompting (800) 538-9301
www.qsystemsteleprompting.com

(858) 272-7022
Tele-Cue (858) 735-7913
4458 Caminito Cuarzo   FAX (858) 272-7023
San Diego, CA 92117   www.telecueteleprompting.com

Vivi-Q Teleprompting Services, Inc. (818) 236-2177
2355 Honolulu Ave., Ste. 201   FAX (818) 236-2846
Montrose, CA 91020   www.vivi-q.com

3D Film Arts   (310) 577-3757 / (520) 907-2211
4121 Redwood Ave.   FAX (815) 642-4444
Los Angeles, CA 90066   www.3dfilmarts.com
(3D, Digital, S3D & Streoscopic)

Rob Abbey   (310) 991-0884 / (310) 456-3696

Leonardo Arterberry III   (323) 466-7232
(Digital)   www.videorama.com

AVS   (818) 954-8842
712 S. Main St.   FAX (818) 954-9122
Burbank, CA 91506   www.aerialvideo.com

Awesome Playback/Bob Lund   (310) 391-0550 / (310) 365-2305
(Digital & Tape-Based)

BlueScreen, LLC/Bob Kertesz   (323) 467-7572
(Digital)   www.bluescreen.com

Bobby Digital HD Video Assist   (323) 270-5568
4023 Tracy St.   FAX (323) 661-9543
Los Angeles, CA 90027   www.bobbydigitalhd.com
(Digital)

Kevin Boyd/Creative HD   (323) 350-3446
(Digital)   www.creativehd.com

Jeff Burrage/Digital Split   (310) 614-3920 / (310) 997-9011

Bob Chambers   (805) 777-1779 / (818) 486-7707
(Digital)

Steve Chambers/ Industry Assist Digital   (310) 398-3344 / (323) 547-0557
12743 Venice Blvd.   FAX (310) 398-3344
Los Angeles, CA 90066   www.industryassist.com

Mark Chapman   (323) 466-7232 / (213) 610-7746
www.videorama.com

ChillowVision HD   (323) 810-3456
11021 Wagner St.   FAX (310) 395-1920
Culver City, CA 90230   www.chillowvision.com
(Digital)

Cinelogic, Inc.   (818) 772-4777 / (818) 359-3589
(Digital)   www.videoassist.com

Cogswell Video Services, Inc.   (661) 257-9087
27636 Avenue Scott, Ste. B   FAX (661) 257-9478
Valencia, CA 91355   www.cogswellvideo.com
(Digital)

Crystal Pyramid Productions   (619) 644-3000 / (800) 365-8433
7323 Rondel Court   FAX (619) 644-3001
San Diego, CA 92119   www.crystalpyramid.com
(Digital & Tape Based)

Director's Choice Video/ Robert Morales   (323) 658-7878
(Digital)   FAX (818) 766-9250
www.directorschoicevideo.com

DVassist/Anthony DeSanto   (805) 279-1016 / (805) 499-6602
(Digital)

Scott M. Goldman/Video Systems   (310) 441-9836 / (310) 292-9284
(Digital)   FAX (310) 474-5282

Scott Hammar/Happy Jaq Video   (310) 770-0377
5158 Canoga Ave.   FAX (818) 346-5396
Woodland Hills, CA 91364

Kevin Hawks/ Circle Take Video Assist   (805) 490-3621

Hill Digital   (818) 445-9211
9714 La Canada Way   www.hilldigital.com
Sunland, CA 91040
(Digital & Tape Based)

Hoodman Corp.   (800) 818-3946 / (310) 222-8608
20445 Gramercy Pl., Ste. 201   FAX (310) 222-8623
Torrance, CA 90501   www.hoodmanusa.com

Impact AV   (213) 494-9492 / (800) 323-0490
635 Dimmick Dr.   FAX (323) 225-1389
Los Angeles, CA 90065
(Digital)

Inter Video	**(818) 843-3624**
2211 N. Hollywood Way	FAX **(818) 843-6884**
Burbank, CA 91505	**www.intervideo24.com**
(3D Record and Playback Packages)	

	(818) 262-7505
Rich Jackson/Lucky Jackson DV	**(818) 753-0533**

Brett Kelly/Kelly Video	**(818) 389-1583**

L.A. Video Assist	**(818) 402-6584**
(Digital)	

Man In The Box Video Assist/
Dempsey Tillman	**(818) 517-8865**
	FAX **(818) 887-0682**
	www.manintheboxvideo.com

Andy Minzes/Ready To Roll Video	**(818) 321-2117**
405 N. Sparks St.	FAX **(818) 842-5273**
Burbank, CA 91506	
(Digital)	

Michael Moretti/Lost Dog Video	**(310) 722-8351**
845 Second St.	**www.lostdogvideo.com**
Hermosa Beach, CA 90254	
(Digital)	

Nebtek	**(818) 768-8348**
11152 Fleetwood St., Ste. 3	**www.nebtek.com**
Sun Valley, CA 91352	
(Digital)	

	(310) 859-7573
Ocean Video/Jeb Johenning	**(213) 300-2000**
(Digital)	**www.oceanvideo.com**

	(310) 222-8614
On Tap Video Playback Systems	**(310) 488-8410**
(Digital)	FAX **(310) 222-8624**
	www.hoodmanusa.com

Palm Tree Video	**(619) 335-0421**
(Digital)	**www.palmtreevideo.com**

Anthony Perkins	**(323) 703-1184**
	www.chillowvision.com

	(661) 263-6070
Play It Again Sam/Sam Harrison	**(661) 803-9372**
(Digital)	

RF Film, Inc.	**(866) 985-3456**
	FAX **(866) 986-3456**
	www.rffilm.com

Erick H. Schultz/EZ Video	**(310) 430-2468**
(Digital)	

TV Productions, Inc./	
Thomas Vanasse	**(818) 763-4098**
3704 Mound View Ave.	
Studio City, CA 91604	
(Digital & HD)	

Videorama! Industries, LLC/	
Howard Van Emden	**(323) 466-7232**
1119 N. Hudson Ave.	FAX **(323) 466-7228**
Hollywood, CA 90038	**www.videorama.com**
(Digital)	

Video Assist Systems, Inc.	**(818) 606-8901**
(Digital)	FAX **(818) 222-5862**
	www.videoassistsystems.com

Video Hawks	**(818) 889-9655**
P.O. Box 7525	FAX **(818) 889-9755**
Westlake Village, CA 91359	**www.videohawks.com**
(Digital)	

	(310) 418-2963
Video Playback and Back and Back	**(310) 750-6477**
5508 Manitowac Dr.	
Palos Verdes, CA 90275	

	(310) 574-9385
Video Tech Services	**(310) 505-4015**
10866 Washington Blvd., Ste. 513	FAX **(310) 577-0850**
Culver City, CA 90232	**www.videotechservices.com**

	(818) 508-6214
Videodrone	**(323) 855-4278**
	FAX **(818) 508-6214**
	www.videodronehd.com
(High Def & Qtake-HD Editing and Compositing)	

	(818) 223-8884
Vision Prompt, Inc.	**(818) 642-5471**
23958 Craftsman Rd.	FAX **(818) 223-9559**
Calabasas, CA 91302	

Warner Bros. Studio Facilities -	
Production Sound Rentals	**(818) 954-2511**
4000 Warner Blvd., Bldg. 43	FAX **(818) 954-2901**
Burbank, CA 91522	**www.wbsoundandvideo.com**

Charlie Westfall/	**(818) 892-4100**
HD Video Assist, Inc.	**(818) 970-8962**
	FAX **(818) 892-4300**
	www.hdvideoassistla.com

Wolf Seeberg Video	**(310) 822-4973**
(Digital)	FAX **(310) 305-8918**
	www.wolfvid.com

A B Sea Photo   **(310) 645-8992**
9136 S. Sepulveda Blvd.   FAX **(310) 645-3645**
Los Angeles, CA 90045   **www.absea.net**
(24P, Broadcast Systems, Digital, HDV, High Def, Underwater
Housings & Underwater Systems)

Aaron & Le Duc   **(310) 452-2034**
     www.leducdesign.com

     (818) 972-9078
AbelCine   **(888) 700-4416**
801 S. Main St.   FAX **(818) 333-1899**
Burbank, CA 91506   **www.abelcine.com**
(24P, Broadcast Systems, Digital, High Def, Monitors, Phantom
High Speed Cameras, Projectors, Recorders, Specialty
Cameras & Underwater Housings)

Absolute Rentals   FAX **(818) 842-2828**
2633 N. San Fernando Blvd.   FAX **(818) 842-8815**
Burbank, CA 91504   **www.absoluterentals.com**
(3/4" SP Video Systems, Analog and Digital Video Systems,
Betacam and Betacam SP Systems, Broadcast and Digital
Betacam Systems, Broadcast Video Camera Systems, DV
Camera Systems, DVC Pro, DVCAM, Facilities, Flatscreens,
HD Camera Systems, HD-CAM HDV, Hi-8, High Def, Mini DV,
Mini DV 24P, Mini DV Video Camera Systems, Monitors, PAL,
Panasonic/Sony HD Cameras and VTR Systems, Portable Avid
Systems, Projectors, Recorders, Remote Heads, Sony DV,
Sony PD 150 VX2000 DCCam, Sony UVX 1800 BETACAM
SP VTR, Sound, Specialty Cameras, Video Camera Systems,
Video Equipment Repair & Video Recorders)

     (323) 461-4290
Action Audio & Visual   **(888) 406-8164**
10834 Burbank Blvd., Ste. A-100   FAX **(323) 461-4292**
North Hollywood, CA 91601
     www.actionaudioandvisual.com
(24P, Analog Systems, Betacam, Broadcast Systems,
Digiprimes, Digital, HDV, Hi-8, High Def, Magliner, Mini DV,
Monitors, Multi-Camera Systems, Playback Systems,
Recorders, Remote Heads, Sound Equipment, Specialty
Cameras, Steadicam Systems, Ultimatte, Video Assist
Systems & Wireless Monitoring)

Advanced Video, Inc.   **(323) 469-0707**
723 N. Cahuenga Blvd.
Hollywood, CA 90038

Aerial Video Systems/AVS   **(818) 954-8842**
712 S. Main St.   FAX **(818) 954-9122**
Burbank, CA 91506   **www.aerialvideo.com**
(High Def, Lipstick Cameras, RF/Microwave Wireless Video,
Specialty Cameras, Video Assist
Systems & Wireless Monitoring)

Alan Gordon Enterprises, Inc.   **(323) 466-3561**
5625 Melrose Ave.   FAX **(323) 871-2193**
Hollywood, CA 90038   **www.alangordon.com**
(Digital Beta and Video Cameras and Systems & Mini DV 24P)

Alternative Rentals   **(310) 204-3388**
5805 W. Jefferson Blvd.   FAX **(310) 204-3384**
Los Angeles, CA 90016   **www.alternativerentals.com**
(24P, DVC Pro, HD-CAM, HDV, Projectors, Wireless
Monitoring & Zeiss)

American Hi Definition, Inc.   **(818) 222-0022**
7635 Airport Business Pkwy   FAX **(818) 222-0818**
Van Nuys, CA 91406   **www.hi-def.com**
(Video Camera Projectors, Screens and Systems)

American Video Group   **(310) 477-1535**
2542 Aiken Ave.   **www.americanvideogroup.com**
Los Angeles, CA 90064
(Digital Betacam Camera Systems)

     (323) 466-4321
Ametron Audio Video   **(323) 464-1144**
1546 N. Argyle Ave.   FAX **(323) 871-0127**
Hollywood, CA 90028   **www.ametron.com**
(Video Camera Systems)

Artistic Resources Corporation   **(323) 965-5200**
535 N. Brand Blvd., Ste. 235   FAX **(323) 965-5209**
Glendale, CA 91203   **www.artisticresources.com**

     (818) 504-6026
Backstage Equipment, Inc.   **(800) 692-2787**
8052 Lankershim Blvd.   FAX **(818) 504-6180**
North Hollywood, CA 91605   **www.backstageweb.com**
(Cameras, Magliners, Remote Heads, Sound & Video Carts)

     (818) 841-9655
Band Pro Film & Digital, Inc.   **(888) 226-3776**
3403 W. Pacific Ave.   FAX **(818) 841-7649**
Burbank, CA 91505   **www.bandpro.com**
(¾", 24P, Accessories, Codex, Decks, Digiprimes, Digital,
DSLR, File-Based Recording, Financing, HDCAM, HDV, High
Def, Leica Summilux-C, Lipstick Cameras, Magliner, Monitors,
Multi-Camera Systems, Playback Systems, Recorders, Repair,
Sony F35, Stereoscopic Cameras, Video Camera Systems,
VTR & Wireless Monitoring)

Barber Tech   **(818) 982-7775**
2725 West Ave., Eighth Fl.   FAX **(661) 339-3235**
Lancaster, CA 93536   **www.barbertvp.com**
(Film Simulation Process Cameras & Projectors)

Barcon Video Productions   **(818) 248-9161**
3653 Mesa Lila Ln.   FAX **(818) 249-8884**
Glendale, CA 91208   **www.barryconrad.com**

     (818) 565-4399
Bexel   **(800) 225-6185**
2701 N. Ontario St.   FAX **(818) 847-1238**
Burbank, CA 91504   **www.bexel.com**
(Broadcast and Digital Betacam Systems)

Big Door   **(310) 546-6100**
2617 Manhattan Beach Blvd.   FAX **(424) 247-8382**
Redondo Beach, CA 90278   **www.bigdoor.tv**
(Betacam Systems)

Birns & Sawyer, Inc.   **(323) 466-8211**
5275 Craner Ave.   FAX **(818) 358-4395**
North Hollywood, CA 91601   **www.birnsandsawyer.com**

BlueScreen, LLC/Bob Kertesz   **(323) 467-7572**
     www.bluescreen.com
(Blue and Green Screen Facilities & Portable Ultimatte)

Broadcast Store   **(818) 998-9100**
9420 Lurline Ave., Ste. C   FAX **(818) 998-9106**
Chatsworth, CA 91311   **www.broadcaststore.com**
(Video Camera Systems)

C-Mount Industries, Inc.   **(310) 464-6888**
     FAX **(310) 464-6888**
     www.cmountindustries.com
(24P, Camera Crews, HDV, Lipstick Cameras, Mini DV,
Monitors, Production Trucks, Specialty Cameras, Underwater
Housings, Wireless Monitoring & Wireless Video)

     (661) 222-7342
Cinema Rentals, Inc.   **(818) 365-7999**
25876 The Old Road, Ste. 174   FAX **(661) 427-0881**
Stevenson Ranch, CA 91381   **www.cinemarentals.com**
(Digital and Hi-8 Underwater Video & Lipstick Cameras)

Claude Booth Company
Equipment Repairs   **(310) 980-3229**
12534 Valley View, Ste. 128   FAX **(714) 899-7837**
Los Angeles, CA 92845   **www.claudebooth.net**
(Video Camera and Equipment Repair)

Mobile Production Facilities

Designed for broadcast entertainment video production, the Background Images mobile production facilities and highly experienced Union Operators take the show on the road! Equipped with the latest in broadcast production technology and multiple expandos. These mobile production facilities are high-tech as well as spacious and comfortable environments to work in.

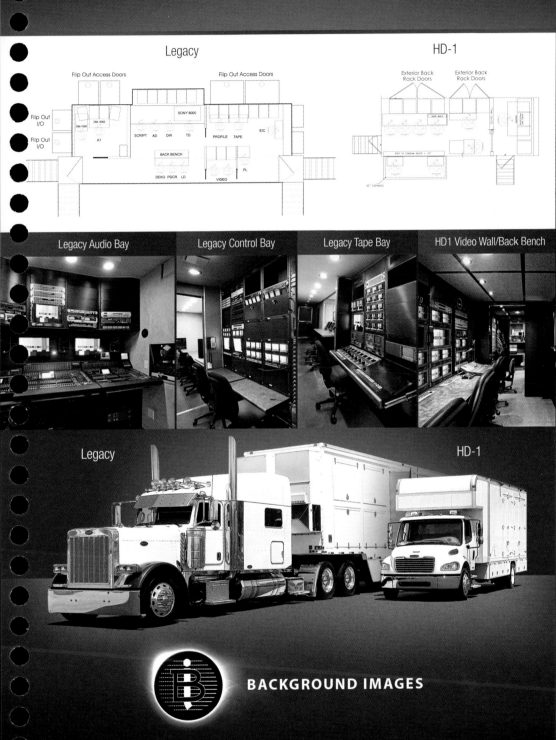

Legacy

HD-1

Legacy Audio Bay

Legacy Control Bay

Legacy Tape Bay

HD1 Video Wall/Back Bench

Legacy

HD-1

BACKGROUND IMAGES

Los Angeles
28908 N. Avenue Paine Unit B
Valencia, CA 91355
Ph. 661.257.5710 / 818.500.0454   Fax. 661.257.8510

Atlanta
1400 Veterans Memorial Hwy Suite 134-324
Mableton, GA 30126
Ph. 404.352.8848   Fax. 404.352.8858

Visit **www.bgimages.com/trucks/mobileunits.html**
to download specifications, monitor wall layout or take an interactive tour.

Broadcast ENG Package Available.

Crash Productions   (310) 489-6848
713 N. Mansfield Ave.   FAX (323) 939-9622
Los Angeles, CA 90038   www.crashproductions.com
(Betacam SP & Digital)

Creative Technology Los Angeles   (818) 779-2400
14000 Arminta St.   FAX (818) 779-2401
Panorama City, CA 91402   www.ctus.com
(Flatscreens, Flypacks, Multi-Camera Systems, Playback
Systems & Video Camera Systems)

   (619) 644-3000
Crystal Pyramid Productions   (800) 365-8433
7323 Rondel Court   FAX (619) 644-3001
San Diego, CA 92119   www.crystalpyramid.com
(Betacam SP and DV Camera Systems, Blue and Green
Screen, HDSR, HDV, High Def, Portable AVID Systems &
Underwater Camera Systems and Housings)

   (310) 326-4500
Cutting Edge Productions, Inc.   (818) 503-0400
22904 Lockness Ave.   FAX (310) 326-4715
Torrance, CA 90501   www.cuttingedgeproductions.tv
(¾", 24P, Analog Systems, Betacam, Blue Screen Facilities,
Broadcast Systems, Digital, Flatscreens, Green
Screen Facilities, HDV, Hi-8, High Def, Mini DV, Monitors,
Multi-Camera Systems, Playback Systems, Production Trucks,
Projectors, Recorders & Sound Equipment)

Deck Hand, Inc.   (818) 557-8403
1905 Victory Blvd., Ste. 8   FAX (818) 557-8406
Glendale, CA 91201   www.deckhand.com
(24P, D-5, Digi Beta, Digiprimes, Digital, DVCAM, DVCPro,
DVCPro HD, HD and SD Deck Rentals, HDCAM, HDCAM
SR, HDSLR Camera Packages and Lenses, HDV, High Def,
Monitors, Multi-Camera Systems, Recorders & Zeiss Compact
Prime Cine Lenses)

   (323) 465-7700
Division Camera   (323) 571-9476
7022 W. Sunset Blvd.   FAX (323) 297-2773
Hollywood, CA 90028   www.divisioncamera.com
(24P, 3D Systems, Digital Cinema Cameras, Equipment and
Workflow, Flatscreens, High Def, Mini DV, Monitors,
Multi-Camera Systems, Playback Systems, Projectors, Sound
Equipment, Specialty Cameras, Steadicam Systems, Video
Assist Systems & Wireless Monitoring)

Epiphany Media   (323) 819-1001
5300 Melrose Ave.   www.epiphanymedia.com
Hollywood, CA 90038
(Blue Screen Facilities, Broadcast Systems, Control Room
Packages, Flypacks, High Def, Multi-Camera Systems & Video
and Audio Equipment Rental)

   (818) 552-4590
EVS   (800) 238-8480
1819 Victory Bl.   FAX (818) 552-4591
Glendale, CA 91201   www.evsonline.com

   (818) 845-8066
Filmtools   (888) 807-1900
1400 W. Burbank Blvd.   FAX (818) 845-8138
Burbank, CA 91506   www.filmtools.com
(Camera Carts)

   (310) 514-3233
G. John Slagle Productions   (310) 871-6269
22 Golden Spur Ln.   www.slaglevideo.com
Rancho Palos Verdes, CA 90275
(Video Camera Systems)

   (714) 705-6088
Gear Monkey   (877) 411-4445
630 The City Dr., Ste. 175   FAX (714) 705-6080
Orange, CA 92868   www.gearmonkeyrentals.com
(Digital Betacam Systems, Monitors & Video Recorders)

   (310) 820-1113
George Meyer TV & Stereo   (310) 820-3480
12418 Santa Monica Blvd.   FAX (310) 826-9769
Los Angeles, CA 90025   www.georgemeyer-av.com
(Audio and Video Repair)

HDPioneers.com LLC   (310) 773-4823
11835 Olympic Blvd., Ste. 825   FAX (310) 479-2240
Los Angeles, CA 90064   www.hdpioneers.com
(24P, Camera Carts, Digital, Epic-X, HDV, High Def, Monitors,
Panasonic AF-100, Recorders, Red Epic-M, Red One,
Sony F3 & Sound Equipment)

Hermosa Pictures   (310) 909-8525
1850 Industrial St., Ste. 307   FAX (310) 349-3441
Los Angeles, CA 90021   www.hermosapictures.com
(24P, Analog Systems, Betacam, Broadcast Systems, Camera
Carts, Digiprimes, Digital, High Def, Mini DV, Monitors,
Multi-Camera Systems & Sound Equipment)

Illuminate –
Arts, Media & Entertainment   (323) 969-8822
3575 Cahuenga Blvd. West, Fourth Fl. FAX (323) 969-8840
Los Angeles, CA 90068   www.illuminatehollywood.com
(24P, Analog Systems, Betacam, Blue/Green Screen Facilities,
Broadcast Systems, Digiprimes, Digital Downconversions/
Dailies, Endoscopic Lenses, Flatscreens, HDV, Hi-8, High Def
Camera and Record Packages, Mini DV, Monitors,
Multi-Camera Systems, Playback Systems, Portable AVID
Systems, Production Trucks, Projectors, Recorders, Remote
Heads, Sound Equipment, Specialty Cameras, Steadicam
Systems, Ultimatte, Video Assist Systems &
Wireless Monitoring)

Imagecraft   (818) 954-0187
3318 Burton Ave.   FAX (818) 954-0189
Burbank, CA 91504   www.imagecraft.tv

Innovision Optics   (310) 453-4866
1719 21st St.   FAX (310) 453-4677
Santa Monica, CA 90404   www.innovisionoptics.com
(Endoscopic Lenses, HD Probe Lens System, Miniature
Cameras, Miniature Remote Camera Cars & Remote Heads)

Inter Video 3D   (818) 843-3624
2211 N. Hollywood Way   FAX (818) 843-6884
Burbank, CA 91505   www.intervideo24.com
(24 fps Playback Systems, 3D Record and Playback Packages,
Betacam SP, Flatscreens, Lipstick Cameras, PAL, Projectors,
Underwater Systems & Wireless Monitoring)

   (323) 953-5258
KCET Studios   (818) 692-5766
4401 Sunset Blvd.   FAX (323) 953-5496
Los Angeles, CA 90027   www.kcetstudios.com
(Broadcast Systems, Camera Carts, Digi Beta, Digital,
Endoscopic Lenses, Flatscreens, Flypacks, Green Screen
Facilities, HDV, High Def, Infrared Cameras, Lipstick Cameras,
Magliner, Mini DV, Monitors, Multi-Camera Systems, Playback
Systems, Portable AVID Systems, Production Trucks,
Projectors, Recorders, Remote Heads, Repair, Sound
Equipment, Specialty Cameras, Video Assist Systems &
Wireless Monitoring)

Mad Dog Video, Inc.   (818) 985-7766
5510 Satsuma Ave.   FAX (818) 508-6794
North Hollywood, CA 91601   www.maddogvideo.com
(Digi-Beta, DV-Cam SP-Beta, HDV & Hi-Def)

Mark Mardoyan   (818) 996-5566
(24P, Flypacks & Production Trucks)   FAX (818) 996-4082
markmardo.synthasite.com

   (323) 467-1116
Moviola/Moviola Cameras   (800) 468-3107
1135 N. Mansfield Ave.   FAX (323) 464-1518
Hollywood, CA 90038   www.moviola.com
(DVCAMs)

Old School Cameras   (818) 847-1555
2819 N. San Fernando Blvd.   FAX (818) 847-1556
Burbank, CA 91504   www.oldschoolcameras.com
(HDV, High Def, Mini DV, Monitors, Sound Equipment &
Wireless Monitoring)

   (818) 766-6868
Photo-Plus   (800) 759-5722
4141 Elmer Ave.   www.ronvidor.com
Studio City, CA 91602
(GPI Steadicam Pro System & Video Recorders)

Pictorvision Inc
(818) 785-9282
(800) 876-5583
FAX (818) 785-9787
www.pictorvision.com
16238 Raymer St.
Van Nuys, CA 91406
(High Def, Remote Heads & SD)

POV-HD
(310) 866-9300
(Specialized Mounts)

The Power Broker
(949) 375-0526
www.lomo235.com
101 N. Victory Blvd., Ste. L-95
Burbank, CA 91502
(24P, Digiprimes, Lens Test Projectors & Steadicam Systems)

Schulman Mobile Video
(323) 785-2528
FAX (323) 785-2529
www.schulmanmv.com
1320 N. Wilton Pl.
Hollywood, CA 90028
(Digital Satellite Production Trucks)

Silver Pixel Productions
(818) 415-9572
www.silverpixelproductions.com
(Betacam, Digital, HDV, High Def & Mini DV)

Sim Video Los Angeles
(323) 978-9000
FAX (323) 978-9018
www.simvideola.com
738 Cahuenga Blvd.
Hollywood, CA 90038
(Betacam SP Systems)

Sonnanstine Engineering
(310) 962-1429
www.soneng.com
5510 Satsuma Ave.
North Hollywood, CA 91601
(Video Camera and Equipment Repair)

Sony Electronics Inc.
(323) 352-5001
FAX (323) 352-5039
2706 Media Center Dr., Ste. 130
Los Angeles, CA 90065
(24P, Betacam, Broadcast Systems, HDV, High Def, Mini DV, Monitors, Playback Systems, Projectors, Recorders & Repair)

Sterling Productions
(626) 675-0994
600 N. Louise St., Ste. 8 www.sterlingproductionstv.com
Glendale, CA 91206
(Beta, DV and High Def Camera Systems)

Stone Electronics
(323) 931-2838
FAX (323) 931-7116
www.stoneelectronics.com
7928 Beverly Blvd.
Los Angeles, CA 90048
(Repair)

Sweetwater Digital Productions/ SVP, Inc.
(818) 902-9500
FAX (818) 902-0140
www.svptv.com
7635 Airport Business Park Way
Van Nuys, CA 91406
(24P, BetaSP, Digibeta and HD Video Camera Systems, Flypacks, High Def, Multi-Camera Systems, Production Trucks & Projectors)

Gary Taillon
(805) 443-3806

Touring Video, Inc.
(818) 504-3500
FAX (818) 504-3507
www.touringvideo.com
827 Hollywood Way, Ste. 424
Burbank, CA 91505
(Production Trucks)

Twelve Tone Productions
(323) 633-1000
(323) 633-3853
FAX (323) 934-3491
P.O. Box 36356
Los Angeles, CA 90036
www.twelvetoneproductions.com
(24P, Green Screen Facilities, HDV & Multi-Camera Systems)

Video Applications, Inc.
(714) 508-1858
(800) 835-5432
FAX (714) 508-2362
www.videoapps.com
14791 Myford Rd.
Tustin, CA 92780
(Broadcast Systems, Digital, Flatscreens, Flypacks, HDV, High Def, Lipstick Cameras, Mini DV, Monitors, Multi-Camera Systems, Playback Systems, Projectors, Recorders, Sound Equipment, Specialty Cameras & Video Projection Systems)

Video Assist Systems, Inc.
(818) 606-8901
(Monitors & Video Assist Systems)
FAX (818) 222-5862
www.videoassistsystems.com

Video Equipment Rentals
(818) 956-1444
(800) 794-1407
FAX (818) 241-4519
www.verrents.com
912 Ruberta Ave.
Glendale, CA 91201
(24P, Analog Systems, Betacam, Broadcast Systems, Digiprimes, Digital, Flatscreens, Flypacks, HDV, High Def, Lipstick Cameras, Mini DV, Monitors, Multi-Camera Systems, Playback Systems, Projectors, Recorders, Sound Equipment, Specialty Cameras, Steadicam Systems, Underwater Housings & Video Camera Systems)

Video Gear
(858) 356-0200
FAX (858) 356-0204
www.video-gear.com
11760 Sorento Valley Rd., Ste. M
San Diego, CA 92121
(Dolly Systems, HDV, Mini DV, Steadicam Systems & Sound Equipment)

Video Production Specialists (VPS) (866) 447-3877
FAX (310) 577-0850
www.videoproductionspecialists.com
(Beta SP & Digibeta Video Camera Systems)

Videowerks
(310) 393-8754
(310) 780-4156
FAX (310) 399-1829
www.videowerks.com
3435 Ocean Park Blvd., Ste. 107
Santa Monica, CA 90405
(24P, Betacam SP, DV Camera Systems, DVC Pro 50, DVC Pro 100, EX3, HDCAM, HDV, HDX900, High Def, HPX300, P2, Sony PDW 800 XDCAM & XDCAM)

Visionary Forces Broadcast Equipment Rentals
(818) 562-1960
FAX (818) 562-1270
www.visionaryforces.com
148 S. Victory Blvd.
Burbank, CA 91502
(¾", 24P, 3D Monitors, Arri Alexa, AJA KiPro, Apple ProRes, Betacam, Dolby Monitors, DVS Clipster, Encoding, Flatscreens, HDCAM-SR, HDV, High Def, Mini DV, Monitors, Recorders, Streaming & Transcoding)

VTR Interchange, Inc.
(818) 985-1467
FAX (909) 593-4327
www.vtrinterchange.com
1407 Foothill Blvd., Ste. 221
La Verne, CA 91750
(24P, Analog Systems, Betacam, Broadcast Systems, Digital, Flatscreens, Flypacks, Green Screen Facilities, HDV, High Def, Mini DV, Monitors, Multi-Camera Systems, Playback Systems, Production Trucks, Projectors, Recorders, Repair, Video Assist Systems & Wireless Monitoring)

Westcoast Video Productions, Inc.
(818) 785-8033
(800) 477-8417
FAX (818) 785-8035
www.wvpinc.com
14141 Covello St., Ste. 9A
Van Nuys, CA 91405
(Broadcast Systems, Flypacks, High Def & Multi-Camera Systems)

Wexler Video
(818) 846-9381
(800) 939-5371
FAX (818) 846-9399
www.wexlervideo.com
1111 S. Victory Blvd.
Burbank, CA 91502

Wintech Video
(818) 501-6565
FAX (818) 501-6566
www.wintechvideo.com
4455 Van Nuys Blvd.
Sherman Oaks, CA 91403
(Betacam Video Camera Systems)

World Wide Digital Services, Inc.
(818) 500-7559
FAX (818) 500-1227
www.worldwidela.com
1819 Dana St., Ste. E
Glendale, CA 91201
(24P, Analog and Digital Video Camera Systems, Broadcast Systems, Digiprimes, Flypacks, Green Screen Facilities, High Def, Lipstick Cameras, Multi-Camera Systems, Recorders, Sound Equipment & Wireless Monitoring)

Yada/Levine Video Productions
(323) 461-1616
FAX (323) 461-2288
www.yadalevine.com
1253 Vine St., Ste. 21A
Hollywood, CA 90038
(24P, Betacam, Betacam SP, Digital Betacam, HDV, High Def & Mini DV)

Action Audio & Visual
(323) 461-4290
(888) 406-8164
10834 Burbank Blvd.
FAX (323) 461-4292
North Hollywood, CA 91601 www.actionaudioandvisual.
com/products/visual-rentals/projectors

American Hi Definition, Inc.
(818) 222-0022
7635 Airport Business Pkwy
FAX (818) 222-0818
Van Nuys, CA 91406
www.hi-def.com
(Video Projection)

Astro Audio Video Lighting, Inc.
(818) 549-9915
(800) 427-8768
6615 San Fernando Rd.
FAX (818) 549-0681
Glendale, CA 91201
www.astroavl.com
(Flatscreens, Front Screen Projections, Large Screen Video
Projection, LCD Screens, LED Screens, Mobile LED Screens,
Plasma Screens, Rear Screen Projections, Video Playback,
Video Projection & Video Walls)

(A) Background Images, Inc.
(661) 257-5710
28908 N. Paine Ave., Ste. B
www.bgimages.com
Valencia, CA 91335

Cinematography Electronics, Inc.
(818) 706-3334
5321 Derry Ave., Ste. G
FAX (818) 706-3335
Agoura Hills, CA 91301
www.cinematographyelectronics.com
(Film/Video Synchronizing Control)

Cutting Edge Productions, Inc.
(310) 326-4500
(818) 503-0400
22904 Lockness Ave.
FAX (310) 326-4715
Torrance, CA 90501 www.cuttingedgeproductions.tv
(24 fps Computer Playback, 24 fps Video Playback, 24P
HD Process Projection, 30 fps Computer Playback, 30 fps
Video Playback, Cabling, Film/Video Synchronizing Control,
Flatscreens, Front Screen Projections, High-Output Large
Screen Video Projection, LCD Screens, Photography
Consultants, Plasma Screens, Rear Screen Projections, Video
Playback, Video Projection & Video Walls)

Cygnet Video
(661) 296-0374
(661) 713-9803
27355 Chesterfield Dr.
www.cygnetvideo.com
Valencia, CA 91354
(24/30 fps Computer and Video Playback & 24P HD
Process Projection)

ELM, Ltd.
(818) 508-5995
13659 Victory Blvd., Ste. 583
www.elmlimited.com
Van Nuys, CA 91401

Future Lighting
(310) 312-9772
(310) 346-1649
(Front/Rear Projection)
www.futurelighting.net

Courtney M. Goodin
(323) 937-4978
(323) 465-9441
FAX (323) 935-6698
(24 fps Computer Playback, 24 fps Video Playback, 24P HD
Process Projection, 30 fps Computer Playback, 30 fps Video
Playback, Film/Video Synchronizing Control, LCD Screens &
Video Playback)

Hill Digital
(818) 445-9211
9714 La Canada Way
www.hilldigital.com
Sunland, CA 91040
(24/30FPS Video/Computer Playback & Graphics)

Impact Video
(818) 972-1774
3088 Clybourn Ave.
FAX (818) 972-1329
Burbank, CA 91505
www.impactav.com
(LED Screens & Video Walls)

**Independent Studio
Services, Inc./ISS**
(818) 951-5600
9545 Wentworth St.
FAX (818) 951-2850
Sunland, CA 91040
www.issprops.com
(24/30 fps Video Playback)

Innovative Design Technologies
(800) 558-3080
(818) 376-1920
7635 Airport Business Park Way
FAX (818) 376-1915
Van Nuys, CA 91406
(Projection & Video Walls)

Inter Video
(818) 843-3624
2211 N. Hollywood Way
FAX (818) 843-6884
Burbank, CA 91505
www.intervideo24.com
(24 fps Computer Playback, 24 fps Video Playback, 24P HD
Process Projection, 3D Projection and Display, Flatscreens &
High-Output Large Screen Video Projection)

JumboScreen
(818) 540-4282
(866) 665-8626
3262 Futura Point
FAX (805) 492-3879
Thousand Oaks, CA 91362
www.jumboscreen.com
(Mobile LED Video Screen)

Khaos Digital
(323) 762-2260
6007 Waring Ave.
www.khaosdigital.com
Hollywood, CA 90038
(24 fps Computer Playback, 24 fps Video Playback, 24P
HD Process Projection, 30 fps Computer Playback, 30 fps
Video Playback, Cabling, Film/Video Synchronizing Control,
Flatscreens, Front Screen Projections, High-Output Large
Screen Video Projection, LCD Screens, LED Screens, Mobile
LED Screens, Photography Consultants, Plasma Screens,
Rear Screen Projections, Video Playback, Video Projection &
Video Walls)

Mann Consulting
(415) 546-6266
(888) 746-8227
FAX (415) 546-4099
www.mann.com
(24/30 fps Computer Graphics & Video Playback)

Todd A. Marks/Production Suppliers
(818) 340-0545
(818) 439-8066
FAX (818) 340-3355
www.prosuppliers.com
(24 fps Computer Playback, 24 fps Video Playback, 24P HD
Process Projection, 30 fps Computer Playback, 30 fps Video
Playback, Cabling, Computer Graphics, Custom Projection and
Playback System Designs, Film/Video Synchronizing Control,
Flatscreens, Front Screen Projections, High-Output Large
Screen Video Projection, LCD Screens, LED Screens, Mobile
LED Screens, Photography Consultants, Plasma Screens,
Playback Graphics, Rear Screen Projections, Video Playback,
Video Projection & Video Walls)

John Monsour
(323) 650-5706
(323) 632-2751
2062 Stanley Hills Dr.
Los Angeles, CA 90046
(24 fps Computer Screen Graphics, Photography Consultant &
Video Playback)

New Deal Studios, Inc.
(310) 578-9929
15392 Cobalt St.
FAX (310) 578-7370
Sylmar, CA 91342
www.newdealstudios.com
(Blue and Green Screen)

Playback Technologies
(818) 556-5030
135 N. Victory Blvd.
FAX (818) 556-5034
Burbank, CA 91502
www.playbacktech.com
(24/30 fps Computer and Video Playback)

Reaction Audio Visual
(949) 600-8235
(877) 273-6887
9951 Muirlands
FAX (949) 600-8238
Irvine, CA 92618
www.reactionav.com
(Flatscreens, Front and Rear Screen Projections, LCD Screens,
Plasma Screens & Video Projection)

Screenworks NEP
(951) 279-8877
1580 Magnolia Ave.
FAX (951) 279-1460
Corona, CA 92879
www.screenworksnep.com
(LED Screens, Mobile LED Screens & Video Projection)

Make Your Project Shine

Headquartered in Los Angeles, with a location in Atlanta, Background Images Inc. is your premier one stop service provider for all your Video Display, Audio and Lighting needs.

Our team consists of industry veterans from both sides of the globe, bringing world-class skills and ideas to your table. With our passion for new technology and our innovative thinking, we can ensure that all aspects of your event, no matter what the scale, will be of the highest quality.

Professional Presentation & Event Production Equipment | 24/7 Support

- Pre-Production & Budgeting
- Experienced Union Operators & Technicians
- Mobile Production Facilities
- Broadcast ENG Packages
- Multi-Display Show Control
- HD/SD Camera Packages

- Large & Multi-Screen Video Projection
- Lighting
- Plasma
- LCD Screens
- LED Screens
- Audio Systems

See our ad for Mobile Production Units under Video Cameras & Equipment.

LOS ANGELES
661.257.5710

ATLANTA
404.352.8848

www.bgimages.com

BACKGROUND IMAGES

Sweetwater Digital
Productions/SVP, Inc.   (818) 902-9500
7635 Airport Business Park Way   FAX (818) 902-0140
Van Nuys, CA 91406   www.svptv.com
(24 fps Computer Playback, 24 fps Video Playback, 24P HD
Process Projection, 30 fps Computer Playback, 30 fps Video
Playback, Flatscreens, Front Screen Projections, High-Output
Large Screen Video Projection, LCD Screens, LED Screens,
Mobile LED Screens, Photography Consultants, Plasma
Screens, Rear Screen, Projections, Video Playback, Video
Projection & Video Walls)

Gary Taillon   (805) 443-3806

                                   (310) 457-2830
Ira D. Toles   (310) 560-5555
(24/30 fps Video Playback)

Towards 2000, Inc.   (818) 557-0903
215 W. Palm Ave., Ste. 101   FAX (866) 836-5725
Burbank, CA 91502   www.t2k.com
(Projection & Video Walls)

                                   (661) 297-6697
Vidcom/Mark I. Scott   (818) 335-1354
21201 Georgetown Dr.   FAX (661) 297-6697
Saugus, CA 91350   www.markiscott.com
(24 fps Computer Playback, 24 fps Video Playback, 24P HD
Process Projection, 30 fps Computer Playback, 30 fps Video
Playback, Cabling, CRT, Film/Video Synchronizing Control,
Flatscreens, Front Screen Projections, High-Output Large
Screen Video Projection, LCD Screens, LED Screens, Mobile
LED Screens, Plasma Screens, Projection, Rear Screen
Projections, Video Playback, Video Projection & Video Walls)

                                   (714) 508-1858
Video Applications, Inc.   (800) 835-5432
14791 Myford Rd.   FAX (714) 508-2362
Tustin, CA 92780   www.videoapps.com
(30 fps Computer Playback, 30 fps Video Playback,
Flatscreens, Front Screen Projections, High-Output Large
Screen Video Projection, LCD Screens, LED Screens, Plasma
Screens, Rear Screen Projections, Video Playback &
Video Projection)

Video Production Specialists (VPS)   (866) 447-3877
                                   FAX (310) 577-0850
                     www.videoproductionspecialists.com
(24/30 fps Video Playback, Projection & Video Walls)

Warner Bros. Studio Facilities -
Production Sound & Video   (818) 954-2511
4000 Warner Blvd., Bldg. 43   FAX (818) 954-2491
Burbank, CA 91522   www.wbsoundandvideo.com

Video Playback, 24 FPS, Video Display & Projection

NOTES:

LA 411

LA 411 FEATURE

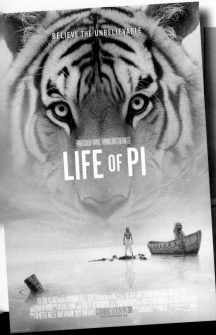

LIFE OF PI

BY MARJ GALAS

DP Claudio Miranda on "Life of Pi"

The prospect of working with director Ang Lee on "Life of Pi" excited DP Claudio Miranda, but he didn't expect he'd get the chance.

"I've done terrible at interviews over the years; I've never got a job from one," said Miranda. "But we had a fantastic meeting."

Prior to shooting Lee poured over 3D examples. He was keenly aware of poor choices that resulted in eye discomfort. Part of Miranda's pre-production process involved recreating 3D errors, then illustrating techniques they could employ to resolve them. Pre-production also required extensive camera tests. Most digital cameras read sun glistening off water as noise. Miranda found the Arri Alexa handled details of the water's surface well without presenting an image that felt electronic

Experimentation was necessary to capture comfortable 3D images of Pi adrift on a small lifeboat. Early tests where the camera was attached to the boat focusing on the horizon resulted in queasiness. Once the rigging was established, the next hurdle was capturing the characteristics of an untamed ocean on a soundstage. While construction was underway on a 30 x 90 meter tank, Miranda, Lee and members of the crew ventured out to sea to plot the course of the sun and discover how evening light interacts with the water.

"One magical moment occurred in the middle of the ocean at 11:00pm," said Miranda. "The water was filled with phosphorescent plankton. We all dived in to experience how it gave off light."

While most of the film takes place at sea, a number of scenes were set and shot in India. One scene in particular held a special appeal to Miranda as a cinematographer: a ceremony lit entirely by candle light.

"It is a real location and ceremony in India. I really wanted to push that feeling; we had over 100,000 candles," said Miranda. "Producers, crew, actors, anyone around was lighting candles. 99% of all the lighting in that scene is candles. It looks amazing, I'm really giddy about that scene."

ABRIDGED FROM AN LA 411 NEWSLETTER ARTICLE PUBLISHED NOVEMBER 2012

A ADVERTISER SYMBOL

**Refer to the General Index for
cross-referencing items in this section.**

Christie (714) 236-8610
10550 Camden Dr. FAX (714) 503-3375
Cypress, CA 90630 www.christiedigital.com

Cinedigm Digital Cinema Corp. (323) 463-2144
6255 Sunset Blvd., Ste. 1025 FAX (323) 463-1319
Hollywood, CA 90028 www.cinedigm.com

Deluxe Digital Cinema (818) 525-3445
300 S. Flower St. FAX (818) 525-3443
Burbank, CA 91502
www.bydeluxe.com/services_digital_initiatives.php

Dolby Laboratories, Inc. (818) 823-2800
3601 W. Alameda Ave. FAX (818) 557-0890
Burbank, CA 91505 www.dolby.com/consumer/
technology/dolby-digital-cinema.html
(3-D Glasses & Projectors)

Doremi Labs, Inc. (818) 562-1101
1020 Chestnut St. FAX (818) 562-1109
Burbank, CA 91506 www.doremilabs.com

Dvidea 33 1 55 43 79 01
Paris Innovation Masséna FAX 33 1 55 43 75 01
Hall B, Seventh Fl. www.dvidea.com
15 rue Jean-Baptiste Berlier
Paris 75013 France

EVS Broadcast Equipment (818) 846-9600
101 S. First St., Ste. 404 FAX (973) 575-7812
Burbank, CA 91504 www.evs.tv

Kodak (323) 464-6131
6700 Santa Monica Blvd. FAX (323) 468-1568
Los Angeles, CA 90038 www.kodak.com/go/motion
(TMS (Theatre Management System))

Real D (310) 385-4000
100 N. Crescent Dr., Ste. 120 FAX (310) 385-4001
Beverly Hills, CA 90210 www.reald.com
(Projectors)

Sony Corporation (201) 930-1000
One Sony Dr. pro.sony.com
Park Ridge, NJ 07656

Technicolor Digital Cinema (818) 260-4532
2233 N. Ontario St. www.technicolordigitalcinema.com
Burbank, CA 91504

Texas Instruments (972) 995-2011
P.O. Box 660199 www.dlp.com
Dallas, TX 75266
(Projectors)

Archion Technologies
(888) 655-8555
(818) 840-0777
700 S. Victory Blvd.
Burbank, CA 91502
FAX (818) 840-0877
www.archion.com

CET Universe
(818) 432-4330
801 S. Main St., Ste. 101
Burbank, CA 91506
FAX (818) 755-7748
www.cetuniverse.com
(Hard Drive Sales)

EditShare
(617) 782-0479
61 N. Beacon St.
Boston, MA 02134
FAX (617) 782-1071
www.editshare.com

Facilis Technology Inc.
(978) 562-7022
577 Main St.
Hudson, MA 01749
FAX (978) 562-9022
www.facilis2.com

G-Technology
(310) 449-4599
3528 Hayden Ave., Second Fl. South
Culver City, CA 90232
FAX (310) 449-4670
www.g-technology.com

Infortrend Corporation
(408) 988-5088
2200 Zanker Rd., Ste. 130
San Jose, CA 95131
FAX (408) 988-6288
www.infortrend.com

Isilon Systems, Inc.
(206) 315-7500
3101 Western Ave.
Seattle, WA 98121
FAX (206) 315-7501
www.isilon.com

JMR Electronics, Inc.
(818) 993-4801
8968 Fullbright Ave.
Chatsworth, CA 91311
www.jmr.com

New Hat
(310) 401-2220
1819 Colorado Ave.
Santa Monica, CA 90404
FAX (310) 401-2224
www.newhat.tv

Rorke Data, Inc. Information
(800) 328-8147
(952) 829-0300
7626 Golden Triangle Dr.
Eden Prairie, MN 55344
FAX (952) 829-0988
www.rorke.com

3ality Digital LLC   **(818) 333-3000**
55 E. Orange Grove Ave.   FAX **(818) 333-3001**
Burbank, CA 91502   **www.3alitydigital.com**

Deluxe Digital Cinema   **(818) 525-3445**
300 S. Flower St.   FAX **(818) 525-3443**
Burbank, CA 91502
  www.bydeluxe.com/services_digital_initiatives.php

Digital Jungle Post Production   **(323) 962-0867**
6363 Santa Monica Blvd.   FAX **(323) 962-9960**
Hollywood, CA 90038   **www.digijungle.com**
D.C.P. Digital Cinema Project

Dolby Laboratories, Inc.   **(818) 823-2800**
3601 W. Alameda Ave.   FAX **(818) 557-0890**
Burbank, CA 91505   **www.dolby.com/consumer/**
      technology/dolby-digital-cinema.html

Efilm   **(323) 463-7041**
1146 N. Las Palmas Ave.   FAX **(323) 465-7342**
Hollywood, CA 90038   **www.efilm.com**

GDC Digital Services   **(818) 972-4370**
1016 W. Magnolia Blvd.   FAX **(877) 643-2872**
Burbank, CA 91506   **www.gdc-digitalservices.com**

Hueman Interest   **(310) 765-4051**
531 Main St., Ste. 101   FAX **(310) 765-4052**
El Segundo, CA 90245   **www.huemaninterest.com**
Acquisitions & Workflows: Arri Alexa, HDCam-SR & SI-2K
Workflows: Cineform 2D and 3D, Codex, Red Post &
S.two OB-1
On-Set Dailies and Playback: 2K, 3D Stereographic, 4K, HD,
Red Rocket & Sync Sound
Other: CDL Generation Services, Data Wrangling, Digital Cin-
ema Workflow Design, Digital Negative LTO Archiving, On-Set
Data Backup & Transcoding

Indie DCP   **(818) 562-1258**
148 S. Victory Blvd.   FAX **(818) 562-1270**
Burbank, CA 91502   **www.indiedcp.com**

Laser Pacific Media Corporation   **(323) 462-6266**
809 N. Cahuenga Blvd.   FAX **(323) 464-3233**
Hollywood, CA 90038   **www.laserpacific.com**

Modern Videofilm, Inc.   **(818) 840-1700**
4411 W. Olive Ave.   **www.mvfinc.com**
Burbank, CA 91505

Qube Cinema, Inc.   **(818) 392-8155**
601 S. Glenoaks Blvd., Ste. 102   FAX **(818) 301-0401**
Burbank, CA 91502   **www.qubecinema.com**

Stereomedia   **(818) 442-7538**
12185 Laurel Terrace Dr.   FAX **(818) 761-3510**
Studio City, CA 91604   **www.3dstereomedia.com**

Stereoscope Studios   **(818) 729-0372**
727 N. Victory Blvd.   FAX **(818) 729-0374**
Burbank, CA 91502   **www.stereo3d.tv**

Technicolor Digital Cinema   **(818) 260-4532**
2233 N. Ontario St. **www.technicolordigitalcinema.com**
Burbank, CA 91504

Visionary Forces Broadcast
Equipment Rentals   **(818) 562-1960**
148 S. Victory Blvd.   FAX **(818) 562-1270**
Burbank, CA 91502   **www.visionaryforces.com**
(3D Mastering, D.C.I. Compliant, D.C.P. Digital Cinema Project,
Digital Rapids Encoder & DVS Clipster)

All In One Productions (323) 780-8880
1111 Corporate Center Dr., Ste. 303 FAX (323) 780-8887
Monterey Park, CA 91754 www.allinone-usa.com

Brown Bag Films and Hi Def (310) 617-5178
608 Fernwood Pacific Dr. www.films-and-hi-def.com
Topanga, CA 90290

CCI Digital, Inc. (818) 562-6300
2921 W. Alameda Ave. FAX (818) 562-8222
Burbank, CA 91505 www.ccidigital.com

Copy Right Video (818) 786-3000
14932 Delano St. FAX (818) 786-3007
Van Nuys, CA 91411 www.copyrightvideo.com

Custom Video (310) 543-4901
707 Torrance Blvd., Ste. 105 www.customvideo.tv
Redondo Beach, CA 90277

Deck Hand, Inc. (818) 557-8403
1905 Victory Blvd., Ste. 8 FAX (818) 557-8406
Glendale, CA 91201 www.deckhand.com

(323) 603-5220
DG FastChannel (800) 324-5672
3330 Cahuenga Blvd. West, Fourth Fl. FAX (323) 603-5300
Los Angeles, CA 90068 www.dgfastchannel.com

Digital Jungle Post Production (323) 962-0867
6363 Santa Monica Blvd. FAX (323) 962-9960
Hollywood, CA 90038 www.digijungle.com

Duplitech Corporation (310) 781-1101
2639 Manhattan Beach Blvd., Ste. A FAX (310) 781-1109
Redondo Beach, CA 90278 www.duplitech.com

(818) 985-9570
DVD-IT Media Consulting (888) 993-8248
11031 Tiara St. FAX (866) 467-3145
North Hollywood, CA 91601 www.dvd-replication.com

The Edit Bay (714) 978-7878
571 N. Poplar St., Ste. I FAX (714) 978-7858
Orange, CA 92868 www.theeditbay.com

HD Creative Services (323) 461-3715
723 N. Cahuenga Blvd. www.hdcreativeservices.com
Hollywood, CA 90038

(818) 840-7200
Level 3 Post (818) 840-7889
2901 W. Alameda, Third Fl. www.level3post.com
Burbank, CA 91505

Lightning Media (323) 957-9255
1415 N. Cahuenga Blvd. www.lightningmedia.com
Hollywood, CA 90028

(619) 644-3000
New & Unique Videos (800) 365-8433
7323 Rondel Court FAX (619) 644-3001
San Diego, CA 92119 www.newuniquevideos.com

Ⓐ The Studios at Paramount (323) 956-3991
The Studios at Paramount Post Production Services
5555 Melrose Ave. www.thestudiosatparamount.com
Los Angeles, CA 90038

(818) 556-5700
Point360 (866) 968-4336
1133 N. Hollywood Way FAX (818) 556-5753
Burbank, CA 91505 www.point360.com

(310) 481-7000
Point360 (866) 968-4336
12421 W. Olympic Blvd. FAX (323) 466-7406
Los Angeles, CA 90064 www.point360.com

Post Digital Services (323) 845-0812
1258 N. Highland Ave., Ste. 210 FAX (323) 845-0812
Hollywood, CA 90038 www.postdigitalservices.com

Post Media Group, Inc. (310) 289-5959
337 S. Robertson Blvd., Ste. 201www.postmediagroup.tv
Beverly Hills, CA 90211

(310) 451-0333
Santa Monica Video, Inc. (800) 843-3827
1505 11th St. FAX (310) 458-3350
Santa Monica, CA 90401 www.smvcompletemedia.com

Tylie Jones & Associates, Inc. (818) 955-7600
58 E. Santa Anita Ave. FAX (818) 955-8551
Burbank, CA 91502 www.tylie.com

Victory Studios LA (818) 769-1776
10911 Riverside Dr., Ste. 100 FAX (818) 760-1280
North Hollywood, CA 91602 www.victorystudiosla.com

(310) 979-3500
Westside Media Group (818) 779-8600
12233 W. Olympic Blvd., Ste. 152 www.wmgmedia.com
West Los Angeles, CA 90064

(310) 659-5959
World of Video & Audio (WOVA) (866) 900-3827
8717 Wilshire Blvd. FAX (310) 659-8247
Beverly Hills, CA 90211 www.wova.com

Aaron & Le Duc (310) 452-2034
www.leducdesign.com

Absolute Rentals (818) 842-2828
2633 N. San Fernando Blvd. FAX (818) 842-8815
Burbank, CA 91504 www.absoluterentals.com

AlphaDogs, Inc. (818) 729-9262
1612 W. Olive Ave., Ste. 200 FAX (818) 729-8537
Burbank, CA 91506 www.alphadogs.tv

Alternative Rentals (310) 204-3388
5805 W. Jefferson Blvd. FAX (310) 204-3384
Los Angeles, CA 90016 www.alternativerentals.com

Artistic Resources Corporation (323) 965-5200
535 N. Brand Blvd., Ste. 235 FAX (323) 965-5209
Glendale, CA 91203 www.artisticresources.com

Audio Video Systems International (818) 888-7625
5101 Tendilla Ave. FAX (818) 888-9862
Woodland Hills, CA 91364
www.provideoequipment.com

Avid (818) 557-2520
(800) 949-2843
101 S. First St., Ste. 200 FAX (818) 557-2558
Burbank, CA 91502 www.avid.com

B2 Services, Inc. (818) 566-8769
2312 W. Burbank Blvd. FAX (818) 566-1378
Burbank, CA 91506 www.b2services-inc.com

Big Time Picture Company, Inc. (310) 207-0921
1629 Stanford St. FAX (310) 826-0071
Santa Monica, CA 90404 www.bigtimepic.com

Broadcast Store (818) 998-9100
9420 Lurline Ave., Ste. C FAX (818) 998-9106
Chatsworth, CA 91311 www.broadcaststore.com

Brown Bag Films and Hi Def (310) 617-5178
608 Fernwood Pacific Dr. www.films-and-hi-def.com
Topanga, CA 90290

Catalyst Post Services (818) 841-4952
3029 W. Burbank Blvd. FAX (818) 566-4175
Burbank, CA 91505 www.catalystpost.com

Christy's Editorial (818) 845-1755
(800) 556-5706
3625 W. Pacific Ave. FAX (818) 845-1756
Burbank, CA 91505 www.christys.net

Crescent Hollywood, LLC (310) 745-0491
(213) 280-9690
6031 Acacia St. FAX (310) 694-8555
Los Angeles, CA 90056 www.crescenthollywood.com

Deck Hand, Inc. (818) 557-8403
1905 Victory Blvd., Ste. 8 FAX (818) 557-8406
Glendale, CA 91201 www.deckhand.com

The Digital Difference (310) 581-8800
1201 Olympic Blvd. FAX (310) 581-8808
Santa Monica, CA 90404 www.digdif.com

Digital Systems Media (949) 215-7151
(877) 629-7810
17702 Mitchell North, Ste. 110 FAX (949) 215-6399
Irvine, CA 92614 www.digitalsystemsmedia.com

editSource (310) 572-7230
12044 Washington Blvd. FAX (310) 572-7238
Los Angeles, CA 90066 www.theeditsource.com

EPS-Cineworks (818) 766-5000
3753 Cahuenga Blvd. West FAX (818) 623-7547
Studio City, CA 91604
www.electricpicturesolutions.com

Firestarter Rentals (310) 420-5146
880 W. First St., Ste. 513 FAX (866) 450-6716
Los Angeles, CA 90012

Fotokem Nonlinear Services (818) 846-3101
(800) 368-6536
2801 W. Alameda Ave. www.fotokem.com
Burbank, CA 91505

Global Entertainment Partners/GEP (818) 380-8133
3747 Cahuenga Blvd. West FAX (818) 979-8133
Studio City, CA 91604 www.gepartners.com

Go Edit, Inc. (818) 284-6260
5614 Cahuenga Blvd. FAX (818) 985-6260
North Hollywood, CA 91601 www.goedit.tv

HD Creative Services (323) 461-3715
723 N. Cahuenga Blvd. www.hdcreativeservices.com
Hollywood, CA 90038

Hollywood-DI (323) 850-3550
1041 N. Formosa Ave., Bldg. 10 FAX (323) 850-3551
Los Angeles, CA 90046 www.hollywooddi.com

Hula Post Production (818) 954-0200
1111 S. Victory Blvd. FAX (818) 954-0211
Studio City, CA 91502 www.hulapost.com

JuRifilm Entertainment, Inc. (310) 915-9559
4404 Westlawn Ave. FAX (310) 391-4217
Los Angeles, CA 90066 www.jurifilm.com

Kasdin Productions (310) 914-4847
www.kasdin.com

Key Code Media, Inc. (818) 303-3900
270 S. Flower St. FAX (818) 303-3901
Burbank, CA 91502 www.keycodemedia.com

LA Digital Post, Inc. (310) 954-8650
(818) 487-5000
2260 Centinela Ave. FAX (310) 954-8686
West Los Angeles, CA 90064 www.ladigital.com

LA Digital Post, Inc. (818) 487-5000
(310) 954-8650
11311 Camarillo St. FAX (818) 487-5015
Toluca Lake, CA 91602 www.ladigital.com

LJK Consult, LLC (323) 896-7541
FAX (323) 655-0549
www.ljkconsult.com

M.G. Digital, Inc. (310) 558-3907
(310) 558-3424
8549 Higuera St., Ste. 101 FAX (310) 559-7800
Culver City, CA 90232 www.mgdigital.us

Moviola/J & R Film Company (323) 467-1116
(800) 468-3107
1135 N. Mansfield Ave. FAX (323) 464-1518
Hollywood, CA 90038 www.moviola.com

Pivotal Post (818) 760-6000
(818) 760-6007
4142 Lankershim Blvd. FAX (818) 760-6012
North Hollywood, CA 91602 www.pivotalpost.com

Pixel Plantation (818) 566-7777
4111 W. Alameda Ave., Ste. 301
Burbank, CA 91505 www.pixelplantation.com

Planet Post	(619) 723-6690
	(619) 435-0888
	www.planetpost.net

Post Media Group, Inc. (310) 289-5959
337 S. Robertson Blvd., Ste. 201 www.postmediagroup.tv
Beverly Hills, CA 90211

Precision Productions + Post (310) 839-4600
10718 McCune Ave. FAX (310) 839-4601
Los Angeles, CA 90034 www.precisionpost.com

Promax Systems, Inc. (949) 727-3977
(800) 977-6629
18241 McDurmott West, Ste. A FAX (949) 727-3546
Irvine, CA 92614 www.promax.com

QSR Systems (323) 200-2155
(661) 294-3999
FAX (661) 257-6380
www.qsrsystems.com

Runway (310) 636-2000
1415 N. Cahuenga Blvd. FAX (310) 636-2034
Los Angeles, CA 90028 www.runway.com

Sim Video Los Angeles (323) 978-9000
738 Cahuenga Blvd. FAX (323) 978-9018
Hollywood, CA 90038 www.simvideola.com

Thumbwar (310) 910-9030
5700 Melrose Ave., Ste. 302 FAX (310) 910-9031
Los Angeles, CA 90038 thumbwar.tv

Touring Video, Inc. (818) 504-3500
827 Hollywood Way, Ste. 424 FAX (818) 504-3507
Burbank, CA 91505 www.touringvideo.com

TV Magic, Inc. (818) 841-6886
107 W. Valencia Ave. www.tvmagic.tv
Burbank, CA 91502

TV Pro Gear (818) 246-7100
(877) 887-7643
1630 Flower St. FAX (818) 246-1945
Glendale, CA 91201 www.tvprogear.com

Video Equipment Rentals (818) 956-1444
(800) 794-1407
912 Ruberta Ave. FAX (818) 241-4519
Glendale, CA 91201 www.verrents.com

Visionary Forces
Broadcast Equipment Rentals (818) 562-1960
148 S. Victory Blvd. FAX (818) 562-1270
Burbank, CA 91502 www.visionaryforces.com

Westside Media Group (310) 979-3500
(818) 779-8600
12233 W. Olympic Blvd., Ste. 152 www.wmgmedia.com
West Los Angeles, CA 90064

Wexler Video (818) 846-9381
(800) 939-5371
1111 S. Victory Blvd. FAX (818) 846-9399
Burbank, CA 91502 www.wexlervideo.com

Abekas/Accom
(650) 470-0900
1090 O'Brien Dr.   FAX (650) 470-0913
Menlo Park, CA 94025   www.abekas.com
(Video Editing Systems, Processing Tools and Storage)

AJA Video
(530) 274-2048
(800) 251-4224
180 Litton Dr.   FAX (530) 274-9442
Grass Valley, CA 95945   www.aja.com
(Interface Tools & Video Converters)

Amphibico
(514) 333-8666
459 Deslauriers   FAX (514) 333-1339
Montreal, QC H4N 1W2 Canada   www.amphibico.com
(Underwater Camera Housings and Accessories)

Angenieux
+33 477 90 78 00
(Lenses)   FAX +33 477 90 78 03
www.angenieux.com

Apple, Inc.
(408) 996-1010
One Infinite Loop   www.apple.com
Cupertino, CA 95014
(Video Editing Systems and Monitors)

Auto Desk
(415) 507-5000
111 McInnis Pkwy   FAX (415) 507-5100
San Rafael, CA 94903   www.autodesk.com
(Video Editing and FX Systems)

Avid
(818) 557-2520
(800) 949-2843
101 S. First St., Ste. 200   FAX (818) 557-2558
Burbank, CA 91502   www.avid.com
(Video Editing and FX Systems)

Band Pro Film & Digital, Inc.
(818) 841-9655
(888) 226-3776
3403 W. Pacific Ave.   FAX (818) 841-7649
Burbank, CA 91505   www.bandpro.com
(Accessories, Camera Mounts, Camera Test Systems,
Cameras, Codex, D-Cinema Cameras, Decks, Disk
Recorders, DSLR, File-Based Recording, Filters, Financing,
HD-CAM, Ice Cube Cameras, Leica Summilux-C, Lenses,
Lipstick Cameras, Monitors, Prime Lenses, Recorders, Sony
F35, Stereoscopic Cameras, Video Accessories,
Video Monitors & Viewfinders)

Blackmagic
(408) 954-0500
2875 Bayview Dr.   www.blackmagic-design.com
Fremont, CA 94538
(Converters, Noise Reducers & Post Processors)

BOXX Technologies, Inc.
(512) 835-0400
(877) 877-2699
10435 Burnet Rd., Ste. 120   FAX (512) 835-0434
Austin, TX 78758   www.boxxtech.com
(Video Editing and FX Systems)

Canon
(800) 321-4388
One Canon Plaza   www.canonbroadcast.com
Lake Success, NY 11042
(Lenses)

CELCO
(909) 481-4648
8660 Red Oak Ave.   FAX (909) 481-6899
Rancho Cucamonga, CA 91730   www.celco.com
(Film Recorders)

Chyron Corporation
(631) 845-2000
Five Hub Dr.   FAX (631) 845-3895
Melville, NY 11747   www.chyron.com
(Video Graphics Systems)

Cobalt Digital, Inc.
(217) 344-1243
(800) 669-1691
2406 E. University Ave.   FAX (217) 344-1245
Urbana, IL 61802   www.cobaltdigital.com
(Video Conversion Tools)

Compix Media
(949) 585-0055
26 Edelman   FAX (949) 585-0320
Irvine, CA 92618   www.compix.tv
(Character Generators)

Digital Projection, Inc.
(770) 420-1350
55 Chastain Rd., Ste. 115   FAX (770) 420-1360
Kennesaw, GA 30144   www.digitalprojection.com
(DLP-Based Projection Systems)

Doggicam, Inc.
(818) 845-8470
1500 W. Verdugo Ave.   FAX (818) 845-8477
Burbank, CA 91506   www.doggicam.com
(Remote Heads)

Dolby Laboratories, Inc.
(818) 823-2800
3601 W. Alameda Ave.   FAX (818) 557-0890
Burbank, CA 91505   www.dolby.com
(Audio Processing Systems)

Doremi Labs, Inc.
(818) 562-1101
1020 Chestnut St.   FAX (818) 562-1109
Burbank, CA 91506   www.doremilabs.com
(Disk Recorders & Video Servers)

Draper, Inc.
(800) 238-7999
411 S. Pearl St.   FAX (765) 987-7142
Spiceland, IN 47385   www.draperinc.com
(Front and Rear Projection Screens)

DSC Laboratories
(905) 673-3211
3565 Nashua Dr.   FAX (905) 673-0929
Mississauga, ON L4V 1R1 Canada   www.dsclabs.com
(Camera Test Systems)

DVS Digital Video, Inc.
(818) 846-3600
300 E. Magnolia Blvd., Ste. 102   FAX (818) 846-3648
Burbank, CA 91502   www.dvsus.com
(Video Processing Tools)

Electrosonic, Inc.
(818) 333-3600
(888) 343-3604
3320 N. San Fernando Blvd.   FAX (818) 566-4923
Burbank, CA 91504   www.electrosonic.com
(Display and Projection Systems)

Evertz
(905) 335-3700
212 N. Evergreen St.   FAX (905) 335-3573
Burbank, CA 91505   www.evertz.com
(Video Processing Tools)

eyeon Software, Inc.
(416) 686-8411
(Video Compositing and FX Systems)   FAX (416) 698-9315
www.eyeonline.com

Faraday Technology, Ltd.
+44 (0) 1782 661501
(Delay Lines & Filters)   FAX +44 (0) 1782 630101
www.faradaytech.com

FOR-A Corporation of America
(714) 894-3311
11125 Knott Ave., Ste. A   FAX (714) 894-5399
Cypress, CA 90630   www.for-a.com
(Video Processing Tools)

Fujinon, Inc.
(973) 633-5600
10 High Point Dr.   FAX (973) 633-5216
Wayne, NJ 07470   www.fujinon.com
(Lenses)

Gyron Systems International, A Division of
Wolfe Air Aviation, Ltd.
(626) 584-8722
39 E. Walnut St.   FAX (626) 584-4069
Pasadena, CA 91103   www.gyron.com
(Aerial Equipment)

Harris Corp.
(818) 717-6800
(800) 231-9673
(Video Graphics Systems)   FAX (818) 525-2587
broadcast.harris.com

Iconix
(800) 783-1080
418 Chapala St.
www.iconixvideo.com
Santa Barbara, CA 93101
(HD Video Camera Systems)

Ikegami Electronics (USA), Inc.
(310) 297-1900
2631 Manhattan Beach Blvd.
FAX (310) 536-9550
Redondo Beach, CA 90278
www.ikegami.com

Image Systems
(818) 769-8111
4605 Lankershim Blvd., Ste. 700
FAX (818) 769-1888
North Hollywood, CA 91602
www.imagesystems.se
(Video Processing Tools)

JVC Professional Products
(973) 317-5000
1700 Valley Rd.
FAX (973) 317-5030
Wayne, NJ 07470
www.jvc.com/pro
(HD Pro-Camcorders and Systems)

Key Digital Systems
(914) 667-9700
521 E. Third St.
FAX (914) 668-8666
Mount Vernon, NY 10553
www.keydigital.com
(Video Processing Tools)

Keywest Technology
(913) 492-4666
(800) 331-2019
14563 W. 96th Terrace
FAX (913) 322-1864
Lenexa, KS 66215
www.keywesttechnology.com
(Video Processing Tools)

KTech Telecommunications, Inc.
(818) 773-0333
21540 Prairie St., Ste. B
FAX (818) 773-8330
Chatsworth, CA 91311
www.ktechtelecom.com
(Video Processing Tools)

Leader Instruments Corporation
(714) 527-9300
(800) 645-5104
6484 Commerce Dr.
www.leaderamerica.com
Cypress, CA 90630
(Video Monitors and Accessories)

LSI Logic
(800) 372-2447
1621 Barber Ln.
www.lsi.com
Milpitas, CA 95035
(Communications Semiconductors)

Maxell Corporation of America
(973) 653-2400
Three Garret Mountain Plaza, Ste. 300 FAX (973) 653-2450
Woodland Park, NJ 07424
www.maxell.com
(Tape Stock)

Miller Camera Support, LLC
(973) 857-8300
218 Little Falls Rd.
FAX (973) 857-8188
Cedar Grove, NJ 07009
www.miller.com.au

Miranda
(514) 333-1772
(Video Processing Tools)
FAX (514) 333-9828
www.miranda.com

Multidyne
(516) 671-7278
(800) 488-8378
191 Forest Ave.
FAX (516) 671-3362
Locust Valley, NY 11560
www.multidyne.com
(Fiber Optic Transport Products)

NEC
(800) 338-9549
395 N. Service Rd., Ste. 407
www.necus.com
Melville, NY 11747
(Display Systems/Monitors)

Nettmann Systems International
(818) 365-4286
1026 Griswold Ave.
FAX (818) 361-6982
San Fernando, CA 91340
www.camerasystems.com
(Aerial Camera Systems & Remote Heads)

OpTex
+44 (0) 20 8236 1212
(Lenses)
FAX +44 (0) 20 8236 1414
www.optexint.com

Oracle/Sun Microsystems
(650) 506-7000
(800) 392-2999
500 Oracle Pkwy
www.oracle.com
Redwood Shores, CA 94065
(Video Servers and Systems)

P & S Technik
+49 89 45 09 82 30
FAX +49 89 45 09 82 40
www.pstechnik.de
(Digital Image Converters, Lenses & Optics)

**Panasonic Broadcast &
Television Systems Co.**
(323) 436-3500
3330 Cahuenga Blvd. West
Los Angeles, CA 90068 www.panasonic.com/broadcast

Panavision
(818) 316-1000
Corporate Headquarters
FAX (818) 316-1111
6219 DeSoto Ave.
www.panavision.com
Woodland Hills, CA 91367
(Camera Lenses and Systems)

Pinnacle Systems, Inc.
(650) 526-1600
280 N. Bernardo Ave.
FAX (650) 526-1601
Mountain View, CA 94043
www.pinnaclesys.com
(Video Editing and FX Systems)

Pixel Power, Inc.
(818) 276-4515
(954) 943-2026
400 S. Victory Blvd., Ste. 309
FAX (818) 450-0763
Burbank, CA 91502
www.pixelpower.com
(Video Graphics Systems)

PixelTools Corporation
(408) 374-5327
10721 Wunderlich Dr.
FAX (408) 374-8074
Cupertino, CA 95014
www.pixeltools.com
(Software Encoding and Repair Utilities)

Quantel, Inc.
(323) 436-7600
(Video Editing and FX Systems)
FAX (323) 878-2596
www.quantel.com

QuStream
(256) 726-9200
(800) 328-1008
103 Quality Circle, Ste. 210
FAX (256) 726-9271
Huntsville, AL 35805
www.pesa.com
(Routing Switcher Systems)

QuVIS Technologies Inc.
(785) 272-3656
(800) 554-8116
900 SW 39th St., Ste. N
FAX (785) 272-3657
Topeka, KS 66609
www.quvis.com
(Video Processing Tools and Storage)

R.C. Gear
(323) 465-3900
(800) 714-8099
6100 Melrose Ave.
FAX (323) 465-3600
Los Angeles, CA 90038
www.rc-gear.com
(Character Generators & Video Graphics Systems)

RED Digital Cinema
(949) 206-7900
20291 Valencia Circle
FAX (949) 206-7990
Lake Forest, CA 92630
www.red.com

Sachtler Corporation of America
(818) 847-8666
Camera Dynamics Inc.
FAX (818) 847-1205
2701 N. Ontario St.
www.sachtler.com
Burbank, CA 91504
(Camera Support Equipment)

Sencore
(605) 978-4600
(800) 736-2673
3200 Sencore Dr.
www.sencore.com
Sioux Falls, SD 57107
(Broadcast Facility Systems & Video Servers)

Sharp Electronics Corporation
(201) 529-8200
(866) 484-7825
Professional Display Division
FAX (201) 529-9636
Sharp Plaza, Mail Stop One
www.sharpusa.com
Mahwah, NJ 07495
(Display and Projection Tools, Projection Systems &
Video Monitors)

Sierra Video Systems
(530) 478-1000
P.O. Box 2462
FAX (530) 478-1105
Grass Valley, CA 95945
www.sierravideo.com
(Modular Terminal Equipment & Routing Switchers)

Snell & Wilcox, Inc. (818) 556-2616
3519 Pacific Ave. FAX (818) 556-2626
Burbank, CA 91505 www.snellwilcox.com
(Video Processing Tools)

(949) 587-3500
Sonnet Technologies, Inc. (949) 587-3526
Eight Autry FAX (949) 457-6350
Irvine, CA 92618 www.sonnettech.com

Sony Electronics Inc. Broadcast &
Production Solutions Division (201) 930-1000
www.sony.com/hdcamsr

Stradis (404) 320-0110
2200 Century Parkway NE, Ste. 900 FAX (404) 320-3132
Atlanta, GA 30345 www.stradis.com
(MPEG-2 Video Decoders)

Teleview +82 70 7018 8900
(Receivers) FAX +82 31 703 9223
www.teleview.co.kr

(818) 989-4420
Tyler Camera Systems (800) 390-6070
14218 Aetna St. FAX (818) 989-0423
Van Nuys, CA 91401 www.tylermount.com
(Gyro-Stabilized Helicopter Camera Mounts)

Utah Scientific (801) 575-8801
4750 Wiley Post Way, Ste. 150 FAX (801) 537-3099
Salt Lake City, UT 84116 www.utsci.com
(Switchers)

Visual Matrix Corporation (818) 843-4831
P.O. Box 11028 FAX (818) 843-6544
Burbank, CA 91504 www.visual-matrix.com
(Converters)

5th Wall
(323) 461-0600
6311 Romaine St., Ste. 7135   **www.5thwall.tv**
Hollywood, CA 90038
(Color Correction, Compositing & Online)

Aaron & Le Duc
(310) 452-2034
www.leducdesign.com
(Color Correction, Compositing, Computer Graphics, Down/Upconversions, File Transfers, Non-Linear Online & Titling/Character Generation)

Absolute Films
(626) 442-6454
(323) 692-1010
1441 Huntington Dr., Bldg. 301   FAX **(626) 448-1930**
South Pasadena, CA 91030   **www.absolutefilms.net**
(Color Correction, Computer Graphics, File Transfers, Film To HD/Datacine, Linear and Non-Linear Online, Titling/Character Generation & Upconversions)

Absolute Post
(818) 567-6190
(818) 842-7966
4119 W. Burbank Blvd.   FAX **(818) 567-6199**
Burbank, CA 91505   **www.absoluterentals.com**
(Color Correction, Compositing, Computer Graphics, Downconversions, File Transfers, Film to HD/Telecine, HD to Film Transfers, Linear and Non-Linear Online & Titling/Character Generation)

Aftershock Digital
(323) 658-5700
8222 Melrose Ave., Ste. 304   FAX **(323) 658-5200**
Los Angeles, CA 90046   **www.editkings.com**
(Color Correction, Compositing, Computer Graphics, Down/Upconversions, File Transfers & Non-Linear Online)

All In One Productions
(323) 780-8880
1111 Corporate Center Dr., Ste. 303   FAX **(323) 780-8887**
Monterey Park, CA 91754   **www.allinone-usa.com**
(Color Correction, Compositing, Down/Upconversions, File Transfers, Non-Linear Online & Titling/Character Generation)

AlphaDogs, Inc.
(818) 729-9262
1612 W. Olive Ave., Ste. 200   FAX **(818) 729-8537**
Burbank, CA 91506   **www.alphadogs.tv**
(Color Correction, Compositing, File Transfers, Non-Linear Offline & Non-Linear Online)

Arsenal FX
(310) 453-5400
1620 Euclid St.   **www.arsenalfx.tv**
Santa Monica, CA 90404
(Color Correction, Compositing, Computer Graphics, Non-Linear Offline, Non-Linear Online & Tape to Tape Correction)

Autonomy, Inc.
(213) 814-2919
www.autonomy.tv
(Color Correction, Compositing, Computer Graphics, File Transfers, Non-Linear Online, Titling/Character Generation & Upconversions)

Bobine Telecine Post
(310) 582-1240
1447 Cloverfield Blvd., Ste. 101   FAX **(310) 582-1245**
Santa Monica, CA 90404   **www.bobinetelecine.com**
(Color Correction, Compositing, Down/Upconversions, File Transfers, Film to HD/Telecine and Datacine & HD to Film Transfers)
Contact: Julie Airale

CCI Digital, Inc.
(818) 562-6300
2921 W. Alameda Ave.   FAX **(818) 562-8222**
Burbank, CA 91505   **www.ccidigital.com**
(Color Correction, Compositing, Computer Graphics, Down/Upconversions, File Transfers, Film to HD/Telecine and Datacine, Linear and Non-Linear Online & Titling/Character Generation)

Chemical Effects
(310) 587-9100
225 Santa Monica Blvd., Ninth Fl.   FAX **(310) 587-9299**
Santa Monica, CA 90401   **www.chemicaleffects.tv**
(Computer Graphics & Non-Linear Online)

Company 3 LA
(310) 255-6600
1661 Lincoln Blvd., Ste. 400   FAX **(310) 255-6602**
Santa Monica, CA 90404   **www.company3.com**
(Color Correction, Compositing, Down/Upconversions, File Transfers, Film to HD/Telecine and Datacine & Linear and Non-Linear Online)

Different by Design
(310) 689-2470
(310) 569-8038
12233 W. Olympic Blvd., Ste. 120   FAX **(310) 689-2471**
Los Angeles, CA 90064   **www.dxdproductions.com**
(Color Correction, Downconversions, File Transfers, Non-Linear Online & Titling/Character Generation)

DVS Intelestream
(818) 566-4151
(818) 841-6750
2625 W. Olive   FAX **(818) 566-4453**
Burbank, CA 91505   **www.dvs.tv**
(Color Correction, Down/Upconversions & HD to Film Transfers)

Encore Hollywood
(323) 466-7663
6344 Fountain Ave.   FAX **(323) 467-5539**
Hollywood, CA 90028   **www.encorehollywood.com**
(Color Correction, Compositing, Computer Graphics, Down/Upconversions, File Transfers, Film to HD/Telecine, Linear and Non-Linear Online & Titling/Character Generation)

Fancy Film
(323) 661-0391
4212 Santa Monica Blvd.   **www.fancyfilm.com**
Los Angeles, CA 90029
(Color Correction, Compositing, Down/Upconversions, File Transfers, Non-Linear Offline, Non-Linear Online & Titling/Character Generation)

FILMLOOK Media and Post/ FILMLOOK Inc.
(818) 845-9200
2917 W. Olive Ave.   FAX **(818) 845-9238**
Burbank, CA 91505   **www.filmlook.com**
(Captions, Color Correction, Computer Graphics, Downconversions, Duplication, File Transfers, Non-Linear Offline, Non-Linear Online, Subtitles, Tape to Tape Correction, Titling/Character Generation & Upconversions)
Contacts: Anna Cordova & Robert Faber

FotoKem
(818) 846-3101
(818) 846-3102
2801 W. Alameda Ave.   FAX **(818) 841-2130**
Burbank, CA 91505   **www.fotokem.com**
(Color Correction, Compositing, Down/Upconversions, File Transfers, Film to HD/Telecine and Datacine, HD to Film Transfers, Linear and Non-Linear Online & Titling/Character Generation)

FXF Productions, Inc.
(310) 577-5009
1024 Harding Ave., Ste. 201   FAX **(310) 577-1960**
Venice, CA 90291   **www.fxfproductions.com**

A Gosch Production
(818) 729-0000
www.goschproductions.com
(Color Correction, Compositing, Computer Graphics, File Transfers, Down/Upconversions, Linear and Non-Linear Online & Titling/Character Generation)

HD Cinema
(310) 434-9500
12233 Olympic Blvd., Ste. 134   FAX **(310) 434-9600**
Los Angeles, CA 90064   **www.hd-cinema.com**
(Color Correction, Compositing, Computer Graphics, Downconversions, File Transfers, Non-Linear Online & Titling/Character Generation)

HD Pictures & Post, Inc.
(310) 264-2575
12233 West Olympic Blvd., Ste.120   FAX **(310) 689-2471**
Los Angeles, CA 90064
(3D Conversion From All Formats, Captions & Foreign Language Subtitles)

HTV - High Technology Video
(323) 969-8822
(818) 760-7600
3575 Cahuenga Blvd. West, Ste. 490   FAX **(323) 969-8860**
Los Angeles, CA 90068   **www.htvinc.net**
(Color Correction, Compositing, Computer Graphics,
Downconversions, File Transfers, Film to HD/Telecine and
Datacine, HD to Film Transfers, Non-Linear Online &
Titling/Character Generation)

The Institution Post   **(818) 566-7801**
423 N. Fairview St.   **www.the-institution.com**
Burbank, CA 91505

Inter Video 3D   **(818) 843-3624**
2211 N. Hollywood Way   FAX **(818) 843-6884**
Burbank, CA 91505   **www.intervideo24.com**
(3D Editing and Viewing)

LA Digital Post, Inc.
(818) 487-5000
(310) 954-8650
11311 Camarillo St.   FAX **(818) 487-5015**
Toluca Lake, CA 91602   **www.ladigital.com**
(Avid Systems, Color Correction, Compositing, Duplication,
Final Cut Pro Systems, Graphics, HD Editing, HD Online,
HD/SD Finishing, Offline, Standards Conversions & Visual FX)

LA Digital Post, Inc.
(310) 954-8650
(818) 487-5000
2260 Centinela Ave.   FAX **(310) 954-8686**
West Los Angeles, CA 90064   **www.ladigital.com**
(Avid Systems, Color Correction, Compositing, Duplication,
Final Cut Pro Systems, Graphics, HD Editing, HD Online,
HD/SD Finishing, Offline, Standards Conversions & Visual FX)

Laser Pacific Media Corporation   **(323) 462-6266**
809 N. Cahuenga Blvd.   FAX **(323) 464-3233**
Hollywood, CA 90038   **www.laserpacific.com**
(Color Correction, Compositing, Down/Upconversions, File
Transfers, Film to HD/Telecine and Datacine, HD to Film
Transfers, Linear Online & Titling/Character Generation)

Level 3 Post
(818) 840-7200
(818) 840-7889
2901 W. Alameda, Third Fl.   **www.level3post.com**
Burbank, CA 91505
(Color Correction, Compositing, Computer Graphics, Down/
Upconversions, File Transfers, Film to HD/Telecine, Non-Linear
Online & Titling/Character Generation)

Light Iron   **(323) 472-8300**
6381 De Longpre Ave.   FAX **(323) 832-8432**
Los Angeles, CA 90028   **www.lightiron.com**
(Color Correction, File Transfers & Non-Linear Online)

Lightning Media   **(323) 957-9255**
1415 Cahuenga Blvd.   **www.lightningmedia.com**
Hollywood, CA 90028
(Color Correction, Compositing, Computer Graphics,
Down/Upconversions, File Transfers, Film to HD/Telecine and
Datacine, HD to Film Transfers, Linear and Non-Linear Online &
Titling/Character Generation)

Los Feliz Post   **(818) 859-3500**
905 East Mountain St.   **www.lfpost.com**
Glendale, CA 91207
(Color Correction, Down/Upconversions, Non-Linear Online &
Titling/Character Generation)

New Hat   **(310) 401-2220**
1819 Colorado Ave.
Santa Monica, CA 90404

Pixel Blues, Inc.   **(818) 766-4600**
411 W. Alameda Blvd., Ste. 401   FAX **(818) 953-9696**
North Hollywood, CA 91602   **www.pixelblues.com**
(Color Correction, Compositing, Computer Graphics,
Down/upconversions, File Transfers, Non-Linear Online &
Titling/Character Generation)

Pixel Plantation   **(818) 566-7777**
4111 W. Alameda Ave., Ste. 301
Burbank, CA 91505   **www.pixelplantation.com**
(Color Correction, Compositing, Computer Graphics,
Downconversions, Duplication, Non-Linear Offline, Non-Linear
Online & Upconversions)

Point360
(323) 957-5500
(866) 968-4336
1147 Vine St.   FAX **(323) 466-7406**
Hollywood, CA 90038   **www.point360.com**
(Color Correction, Computer Graphics, Down/Upconversions,
File Transfers, Film to HD/Telecine and Datacine, Linear and
Non-Linear Online & Titling/Character Generation)

Point360   **(310) 481-7000**
12421 W. Olympic Blvd.   FAX **(310) 207-8404**
Los Angeles, CA 90064   **www.point360.com**
(Compositing, File Transfers, Non-Linear Online & Titling/
Character Generation)

Point360
(818) 556-5700
(866) 968-4336
1133 N. Hollywood Way   FAX **(818) 556-5753**
Burbank, CA 91505   **www.point360.com**
(Captions, Color Correction, Compositing, Computer Graphics,
Downconversions, Duplication, File Transfers, Film to
HD/Datacine, Film to HD/Telecine, HD to Film Transfers, Linear
Online, Non-Linear Online, Standards Conversions, Subtitles,
Tape to Tape Correction, Titling/Character
Generation & Upconversions)

Post and Beam   **(310) 828-1128**
1623 Stanford St.   **www.postandbeam.tv**
Santa Monica, CA 90404
(Captions, Color Correction, Compositing, Computer
Graphics, Downconversions, File Transfers, Non-Linear
Online & Upconversions)

Post Digital Services   **(323) 845-0812**
1258 N. Highland Ave., Ste. 210   FAX **(323) 845-0812**
Hollywood, CA 90038   **www.postdigitalservices.com**
(Captions, Color Correction, Compositing, Computer Graphics,
Downconversions, Duplication, File Transfers, HD to Film
Transfers, Linear Offline, Non-Linear Offline, Non-Linear Online,
Standards Conversions, Subtitles, Tape to Tape Correction,
Titling/Character Generation & Upconversions)

Post Logic Studios   **(323) 461-7887**
1800 N. Vine St., Ste. 100   FAX **(323) 461-7790**
Los Angeles, CA 90028   **www.postlogic.com**
(Color Correction, Compositing, Computer Graphics,
Down/Upconversions, File Transfers, Film to HD/Telecine and
Datacine, HD to Film Transfers, Linear and Non-Linear Online &
Titling/Character Generation)

Post Media Group, Inc.   **(310) 289-5959**
337 S. Robertson Blvd., Ste. 201 **www.postmediagroup.tv**
Beverly Hills, CA 90211

Precision Productions + Post   **(310) 839-4600**
10718 McCune Ave.   FAX **(310) 839-4601**
Los Angeles, CA 90034   **www.precisionpost.com**
(Color Correction, Compositing, Computer Graphics,
Downconversions, File Transfers, HD to Film Transfers,
Non-Linear Online & Titling/Character Generation)

Prime Digital Media Services   **(661) 964-0220**
28111 Avenue Stanford   FAX **(661) 964-0550**
Valencia, CA 91355   **www.primedigital.com**
(Color Correction, Compositing, Computer Graphics,
Down/Upconversions, File Transfers, HD to Film Transfers,
Linear and Non-Linear Online & Titling/Character Generation)

Qube Cinema, Inc.   **(818) 392-8155**
601 S. Glenoaks Blvd., Ste. 102   FAX **(818) 301-0401**
Burbank, CA 91502   **www.qubecinema.com**
(Digital Cinema Servers and Software & Digital Film Mastering)

Raycom Media   **(818) 846-0101**
2901 W. Alameda Ave.   FAX **(818) 846-0277**
Burbank, CA 91505   **www.raycompost.com**
(Captions, Color Correction, Computer Graphics,
Down/Upconversions, Duplication, File Transfers &
Non-Linear Online)

Red Dog Post & Design   **(310) 237-6438**
www.reddogpost.com
(All Language Captioning and Subtitling)

Ring of Fire   (310) 966-5055
1538 20th St.   FAX **(310) 966-5056**
Santa Monica, CA 90404   **www.ringoffire.com**
(Compositing, Computer Graphics, Down/Upconversions, File
Transfers, Linear and Non-Linear Online &
Titling/Character Generation)

RIOT LA   (310) 434-6500
730 Arizona Ave.   FAX **(310) 434-6510**
Santa Monica, CA 90401   **www.rioting.com**
(Color Correction, Compositing, Computer Graphics,
Down/Upconversions, File Transfers, Film to HD/Telecine and
Datacine, HD to Film Transfers, Linear and Non-Linear Online &
Titling/Character Generation)

Shapeshifter   (323) 876-3444
3405 Cahuenga Blvd. West   FAX **(323) 876-3444**
Los Angeles, CA 90068   **www.shapeshifterpost.com**
(Color Correction, Compositing, Computer Graphics,
Downconversions, File Transfers, Non-Linear Online, Titling/
Character Generation & Upconversions)

Solventdreams   (323) 906-9700
227 N. Avenue 66   FAX **(323) 225-5235**
Los Angeles, CA 90042   **www.solventdreams.com**
(Color Correction, Compositing, Computer Graphics,
Down/Upconversions, Linear and Non-Linear Online &
Titling/Character Generation)

SSI/Advanced Post Services   (323) 969-9333
7165 Sunset Blvd.   FAX **(323) 969-8333**
Los Angeles, CA 90046   **www.ssipost.com**
(Color Correction, Compositing, Computer Graphics,
Down/Upconversions, File Transfers, Film to HD/Telecine and
Datacine, HD to Film Transfers, Linear and Non-Linear Online &
Titling/Character Generation)

Stargate Digital   (626) 403-8403
1001 El Centro St.   FAX **(626) 403-8444**
South Pasadena, CA 91030   **www.stargatestudios.net**
(Compositing, Computer Graphics, Down/Upconversions, File
Transfers, HD to Film Transfers, Linear and Non-Linear
Online & Titling/Character Generation)

STEELE Studios   (310) 656-7770
5737 Mesmer Ave.   FAX **(310) 391-9055**
Culver City, CA 90230   **www.steelevfx.com**
(3D Stereoscopic, Color Correction, Compositing, Computer
Graphics, Downconversions, Duplication, File Transfers,
HD Online, Linear Offline, Linear Online, Standards
Conversions, Tape to Tape Correction, Titling/Character
Generation & Upconversions)

Stewart Sound Factory   (714) 973-3030
204 N. Broadway, Ste. N   FAX **(714) 973-2530**
Santa Ana, CA 92701   **www.stewartsound.com**

Switch Studios   (310) 301-1800
316 S. Venice Blvd.   FAX **(310) 496-1964**
Venice, CA 90291   **www.switch-studios.com**
(Color Correction, Compositing, Computer Graphics, File
Transfers, Non-Linear Online & Titling/Character Generation)

Technicolor Creative Services -
Hollywood   (323) 817-6600
6040 Sunset Blvd.   **www.technicolor.com**
Hollywood, CA 90028
(Color Correction, Compositing, Computer Graphics,
Down/Upconversions, File Transfers, Film to HD/Telecine and
Datacine, HD to Film Transfers, Linear and Non-Linear Online &
Titling/Character Generation)

Universal Studios Digital Services   (818) 777-4728
100 Universal City Plaza, Bldg. 3153
Universal City, CA 91608
     www.filmmakersdestination.com
(Color Correction, Duplication, Editing, Encoding & Telecine)

Victory Studios LA   (818) 769-1776
10911 Riverside Dr., Ste. 100   FAX **(818) 760-1280**
North Hollywood, CA 91602   **www.victorystudiosla.com**
(Color Correction, Downconversions, Duplication, File
Transfers, Non-Linear Offline, Non-Linear Online,
Title/Character Generation & Upconversions)

View Studio, Inc.   (805) 745-8814
385 Toro Canyon Rd.   **www.viewstudio.com**
Carpinteria, CA 93013
(Color Correction & Compositing)

West Post Digital   (310) 857-5000
1703 Stewart St.   FAX **(310) 857-5060**
Santa Monica, CA 90404   **www.westpostdigital.com**
(Color Correction, Compositing, Computer Graphics,
Down/Upconversions, Non-Linear Online &
Titling/Character Generation)

     (310) 979-3500
Westside Media Group   (818) 779-8600
12233 W. Olympic Blvd., Ste. 152   **www.wmgmedia.com**
West Los Angeles, CA 90064
(Captions, Color Correction, Compositing, Computer Graphics,
Downconversions, Duplication, File Transfers, Film Transfers,
Non-Linear Offline, Non-Linear Online, Standards Conversions,
Subtitles, Titling/Character Generation & Upconversions)
Contacts: Dan Gitlin, Lewis Lipstone & Shirley Lipstone

     (310) 659-5959
World of Video & Audio (WOVA)   (866) 900-3827
8717 Wilshire Blvd.   FAX **(310) 659-8247**
Beverly Hills, CA 90211   **www.wova.com**
(DVCPro, HDCam and HDV
Downconversions & Upconversions)

Alternative Rentals (310) 204-3388
FAX (310) 204-3384
www.alternativerentals.com

American Film Institute (AFI) (323) 856-7600
2021 N. Western Ave. FAX (323) 467-4578
Los Angeles, CA 90027 www.afi.com

American Hi Definition, Inc. (818) 222-0022
7635 Airport Business Pkwy FAX (818) 222-0818
Van Nuys, CA 91406 www.hi-def.com

Arenas (323) 785-5535
3375 Barham Blvd. FAX (323) 785-5560
Los Angeles, CA 90068
www.arenasgroup.com/info-screen.html

The Cahuenga Theater (323) 822-7237
1415 N. Cahuenga Blvd. www.cahuengatheater.com
Hollywood, CA 90028

The Charles Aidikoff
Screening Room (310) 274-0866
150 S. Rodeo Dr., Ste. 140 FAX (310) 550-1794
Beverly Hills, CA 90212 www.aidikoff.tv

Cinespace (323) 817-3456
6356 Hollywood Blvd., Second Fl. FAX (323) 860-9794
Hollywood, CA 90028 www.cinespace.info

The Culver Studios (310) 202-1234
9336 W. Washington Blvd. FAX (310) 202-3536
Culver City, CA 90232 www.theculverstudios.com

Delicate Productions, Inc. (805) 388-1800
874 Verdulera St. FAX (805) 388-1037
Camarillo, CA 93010 www.delicate.com

Dick Clark Screening Room (310) 255-4699
2900 Olympic Blvd., First Fl.
Santa Monica, CA 90404
www.dickclarkproductionstheatre.com

(310) 369-2406
Fox Studios (310) 369-4636
10201 W. Pico Blvd. FAX (310) 369-0503
Los Angeles, CA 90035 www.foxpost.com

Goethe-Institut (323) 525-3388
5750 Wilshire Blvd., Ste. 100 FAX (323) 934-3597
Los Angeles, CA 90036 www.goethe.de/losangeles

Hollywood-DI (323) 850-3550
1041 N. Formosa Ave. FAX (323) 850-3551
Fairbanks Theater www.hollywooddi.com
West Hollywood, CA 90046

Indie DCP (818) 562-1258
148 S. Victory Blvd. FAX (818) 562-1270
Burbank, CA 91502 www.indiedcp.com

LACMA (The Los Angeles County (323) 857-6039
Museum Of Art) (323) 857-4768
5905 Wilshire Blvd. FAX (323) 857-6021
Los Angeles, CA 90036 www.lacma.org

Los Angeles Center Studios (213) 534-3000
1201 W. Fifth St., Ste. T-110 FAX (213) 534-3001
Los Angeles, CA 90017 www.lacenterstudios.com

Los Angeles Film School Theater (323) 860-0789
6363 Sunset Blvd. www.lafilm.edu
Los Angeles, CA 90028

Oasis Imagery (323) 469-9800
6500 Sunset Blvd. FAX (323) 462-4620
Los Angeles, CA 90028 www.oasisimagery.com

Pacific Design Center/
SilverScreen Theater (310) 657-0800
8687 Melrose Ave. FAX (310) 652-8576
West Hollywood, CA 90069
www.pacificdesigncenter.com

Ⓐ The Studios at Paramount (323) 956-5520
The Studios at Paramount Post Production Services
5555 Melrose Ave. www.thestudiosatparamount.com
Los Angeles, CA 90038

Raleigh Studios - Hollywood (323) 960-3456
5300 Melrose Ave. FAX (323) 960-4712
Hollywood, CA 90038 www.raleighstudios.com

Raleigh Studios - Manhattan Beach (323) 960-3456
1600 Rosecrans Ave. FAX (310) 727-2710
Manhattan Beach, CA 90266 www.raleighstudios.com

(310) 244-5721
Sony Pictures Studios (310) 244-2303
10202 W. Washington Blvd.
Culver City, CA 90232 www.sonypicturesstudios.com

Spartan Mobile Suites, Inc. (310) 587-3377
3727 W. Magnolia Blvd., Ste. 156 FAX (661) 702-0550
Burbank, CA 91505 www.spartanmobilesuites.com

(310) 701-8925
SSG - Screening Services Group (310) 659-3875
8670 Wilshire Blvd., Ste. 112 FAX (310) 861-9005
Beverly Hills, CA 90211 www.studioscreenings.com

Switch Studios (310) 301-1800
316 S. Venice Blvd. FAX (310) 496-1964
Venice, CA 90291 www.switch-studios.com

Theatrical Concepts, Inc. (818) 597-1100
3030 Triunfo Canyon Rd. FAX (818) 597-0202
Agoura Hills, CA 91301 www.theatrical.com

(310) 392-8508
Vidiots Annex (310) 392-8509
302 Pico Blvd. FAX (310) 392-0099
Santa Monica, CA 90405 www.vidiotsannex.com

Warner Bros. Studio Facilities -
Projection (818) 954-2144
4000 Warner Blvd. FAX (818) 954-7915
Burbank, CA 91522 www.wbpostproduction.com

Action Footage/
Warren Miller Entertainment (800) 729-3456
(Extreme/Adventure Sports) www.warrenmiller.com

(310) 459-2526
Action Sports/Scott Dittrich Films (212) 681-6565
P.O. Box 301 FAX (310) 456-1743
Malibu, CA 90265 www.actionsportsstockfootage.com
(Animals, Nature, People & Sports)

AeronauticPictures.com (805) 985-2320
(Aerial & Location) www.aeronauticpictures.com/
royalty-free-stock-footage/

(310) 317-9996
All-Stock (800) 323-0079
P.O. Box 1705 www.all-stock.com
Pacific Palisades, CA 90272
(Animals, Nature, People & Sports)

America by Air
Stock Footage Library (800) 488-6359
154 Euclid Blvd. FAX (413) 235-1462
Lantana, FL 33462 www.hdfootage.com
(Aerials, Contemporary & International)

Animation Trip (619) 825-8875
38030 La Mesa Blvd., Ste. 200
La Mesa, CA 91942 www.animationtrip.com/licensing
(Computer Animation)

Apex Stock (818) 890-0444
13240 Weidner St. FAX (818) 890-7041
Los Angeles, CA 91331 www.apexstock.com

(541) 863-4429
Artbeats (800) 444-9392
1405 N. Myrtle Rd. FAX (541) 863-4547
Myrtle Creek, OR 97457 www.artbeats.com
(Aerials, Backgrounds, Effects, Establishments, Lifestyles,
Nature & Reference)

Axiom Images, Inc. (661) 713-6671
10500 Airpark Way, Ste. M2 www.axiomimages.com
Pacoima, CA 91331
Aerial Stock Footage: 5K to 1080

(818) 299-9720
BBC Motion Gallery, Los Angeles (818) 432-4000
4144 Lankershim Blvd., Ste. 200 FAX (818) 299-9763
North Hollywood, CA 91602 www.bbcmotiongallery.com
(Arts, Bloopers, Communications, Current Events, Destinations,
Entertainment, Historical, Leisure, Lifestyles, Medicine, Music,
Natural History, News, Politics, Reality, Science, Stock,
Technology, Travel and Locations, Universal Newsreels &
Wildlife)

(212) 705-9399
BBC Motion Gallery, New York (917) 267-5460
747 Third Ave. FAX (212) 705-9342
New York, NY 10017 www.bbcmotiongallery.com
(Arts, Bloopers, Communications, Current Events, Destinations,
Entertainment, Historical, Leisure, Lifestyles, Medicine, Music,
Natural History, News, Politics, Reality, Science, Stock,
Technology, Travel and Locations, Universal Newsreels &
Wildlife)

(323) 436-7070
BlackLight Films (323) 436-2229
3371 Cahuenga Blvd. West FAX (323) 436-2230
Hollywood, CA 90068 www.blacklightfilms.com

(310) 305-8384
Blue Sky Stock Footage/Bill Mitchell (877) 992-5477
P.O. Box 177 FAX (310) 823-0924
Santa Fe, NM 87504 www.blueskyfootage.com
(All Subjects)

Budget Films, Inc. (323) 660-0187
4427 Santa Monica Blvd. FAX (323) 660-5571
Los Angeles, CA 90029 www.budgetfilms.com
(Beauty, Clouds, Deserts, Fireworks, Moon, National Parks,
Nature & Sunsets)

Camera One (206) 523-3456
8523 15th Ave. NE FAX (206) 523-3668
Seattle, WA 98115 www.cameraone.us
(Aerials, Archeology, Caribbean, Cities, Clouds, Eclipse,
Europe, Landscapes, Lightning, Moons, National Parks, Natural
and Traffic/Urban Time-Lapse, Nature, Northwest, Outdoor
Sports, Scenics, Southwest, Storms, Sunrises and Sunsets,
Underwater, Whitewater & Wildlife)

CelebrityFootage (310) 360-9600
320 South Almont Dr. FAX (310) 360-9696
Beverly Hills, CA 90211 www.celebrityfootage.com
(Award Ceremonies, Celebrities, Entertainment, Events,
Hollywood, Movie Premieres, People, Red Carpet
Arrivals & Stars)

(310) 277-0400
Classic Images (800) 949-2547
469 S. Bedford Dr. FAX (310) 277-0412
Beverly Hills, CA 90212 www.classicimg.com
(1890s–Present, Aerials, Americana, Archival, Cartoons,
Cityscapes, Commercials, Educational, Historical, Hollywood,
Industry, Music, Nature, Newsreel, Sports, Technology,
Time-Lapse, Travel, Underwater, Vintage TV and
Film & Wildlife)

The Communications Group, Inc. (919) 828-4086
P.O. Box 50157 FAX (919) 832-7797
Raleigh, NC 27650 www.cgfilm.com
(Aerials, Boston, North Carolina Cities, Farms and
Landscapes & The Big Dig)

Fish Films Footage World (818) 905-1071
4548 Van Noord Ave. www.footageworld.com
Studio City, CA 91604
(Aerials, Alaska, Animals, Cities, Extreme Sports, Implosions,
Nature, Time-Lapse, Travel, Underwater, Weather & Wildlife)

The Footage Store (818) 326-3344
www.footagestore.com
(Beauty, Nature, Scenics, Time Lapse & Wildlife)

(310) 822-1400
FootageBank HD (888) 653-1400
13470 Washington Blvd., Ste. 210 FAX (310) 822-4100
Marina del Rey, CA 90292 www.footagebank.com
(Aerials, Animals, Archival, CGI, Landscapes, Lifestyle,
Playback Content, Space, Sports, Technology, Time-Lapse,
Travel, Underwater, Wildlife & Worldwide Locations)

Framepool Inc. (800) 331-1314
150 Alhambra Circle, Ste. 800 FAX (866) 928-6637
Miami, FL 33134 www.framepool.com
(Aerials, Agriculture, Animals, Architecture, Cityscapes, Clouds,
Contemporary, Cultures, Deserts, Flowers, Forests,
International People and Scenery, Landscapes, Lightning,
Lifestyles, Mountains, Nature, Rivers, Skies, Space, Sports,
Suns and Moons, Technology, Time-Lapse & Wildlife)

(310) 402-4626
Framepool Inc. (800) 331-1314
1480 Vine St., Ste. 704 FAX (866) 928-6637
Los Angeles, CA 90028 www.framepool.com
(Aerials, Aerospace, Agriculture, Animals, Cityscapes, Clouds,
Commercials, Contemporary, Cultures, Deserts, Flowers,
International People and Scenery, Landscapes, Lightning,
Lifestyles, Mountains, Nature, Scenic, Seasons, Space,
Stars/Comets/Planets, Storms, Time-Lapse, Traffic,
Transportation, Underwater & Wildlife)

Global ImageWorks, LLC (201) 384-7715
65 Beacon St. FAX (201) 501-8971
Haworth, NJ 07641 www.globalimageworks.com
(All Subjects)

Greenscreen Animals (310) 622-4487
(877) 563-8023
1510 11th St., Ste. 101 FAX (310) 496-1237
Santa Monica, CA 90401 www.greenscreenanimals.com
(Animal, Entertainment, Feature Films, High Def, High
Resolution, Technology, Television & Wildlife)

GregHensley.com (970) 984-3158
www.greghensley.com

The Hollywood Film Registry (310) 456-8184
5473 Santa Monica Blvd., Ste. 408 FAX (323) 957-2159
Los Angeles, CA 90029
(All Subjects)

Home Planet Productions (805) 965-9848
(818) 422-4144
FAX (805) 965-2329
www.homeplanetproductions.com

Howard Hall Productions (858) 259-8989
2171 La Amatista Rd. FAX (858) 792-1467
Del Mar, CA 92014 www.howardhall.com
(Aerials, Animals, Clouds, Landscapes, Mountains, Nature,
Oceans, Skies, Suns and Moons, Time-Lapse,
Underwater & Wildlife)

Image Bank Films and
Archive Films by Getty Images (800) 462-4379
6300 Wilshire Blvd., 16th Fl. FAX (323) 202-4207
Los Angeles, CA 90048 www.gettyimages.com
(Archival & Contemporary)

National Geographic Digital Motion (866) 523-9097
(720) 212-0820
www.ngdigitalmotion.com
(Archeology, Architecture, Ceremonies, Cities, Landmarks,
Natural Disasters, Natural History, People, Wildlife &
World Scenes)

New & Unique Videos (619) 644-3000
(800) 365-8433
7323 Rondel Court FAX (619) 644-3001
San Diego, CA 92119 www.newuniquevideos.com
(Aerials, Animals, Archival Film, Beaches and Sunsets,
Bloopers, Cities, Islands, Contemporary, Corporate, Agricultural,
Current Events, Industrial, International, Lifestyles, Medical,
Military, People, San Diego, Scenics, Southern California,
Sports, Travel and Locations, Technological,
Underwater & Wildlife)

Oddball Film + Video (415) 558-8112
(415) 558-8122
275 Capp St. FAX (415) 558-8116
San Francisco, CA 94110 www.oddballfilm.com
(Americana, International, Nature, Timelapse & Wildlife)

Producers Library (818) 752-9097
(800) 944-2135
10832 Chandler Blvd. FAX (818) 752-9196
North Hollywood, CA 91601 www.producerslibrary.com
(Cities, Nature, News, Red Carpet & Scenics)

Reel Orange (949) 548-4524
316 La Jolla Dr. www.reelorange.com
Newport Beach, CA 92663
(Aerials, Environmental & Grand Canyon)

Shutterstock (866) 663-3954
60 Broad St., 30th Fl. FAX (347) 402-0710
New York, NY 10004 footage.shutterstock.com

Silverman Stock Footage (804) 338-2234
210 Douglass St. FAX (718) 764-4411
Brooklyn, NY 11217 www.silvermanstockfootage.com
(Aerials, Airplanes, Americana, Animals, Architecture, Archival,
Cityscapes, Clouds, Contemporary, Cultures, Deserts, Extreme
Sports, Flowers, International People, Landscapes, Lifestyles,
Nature, Oceans, Scenics, Space, Storms, Suns and Moons,
Time-Lapse, Traffic & Underwater)

Sports Cinematography Group (310) 785-9100
(212) 744-5333
73 Market St. FAX (310) 564-7500
Venice, CA 90291
(Sports) www.sportscinematographygroup.com

StormStock (817) 276-9500
P.O. Box 122020 FAX (817) 795-1132
Arlington, TX 76012 www.stormstock.com
(Blizzards, Beaches, Caribbean, Clouds, Disasters,
Environmental, Fires, Flash Floods, Hail, Hurricane Katrina,
Hurricanes, Landscapes, Lightning, Microbursts, Natural
Disasters, Natural History, Nature, Oceans, Radar, Science,
Seasons, Skies, Storm Clouds, Storms, Sunrises, Sunsets,
Time-Lapse, Tornadoes, Traffic & Waves)

T3Media (Thought Equity Motion) (818) 432-4000
4130 Cahuenga Blvd., Ste. 315 FAX (818) 760-0820
Universal City, CA 91602 www.t3licensing.com
(All Subjects)

Universal Studios
Stock Footage Library (818) 777-1695
100 Universal Plaza, Bldg. 2313A FAX (818) 866-0763
Lower Level www.filmmakersdestination.com
Universal City, CA 91608
(Selected Subjects)

US Air Force Motion Picture Office (310) 235-7522
(310) 235-7511
10880 Wilshire Blvd., Ste. 1240 FAX (310) 235-7500
Los Angeles, CA 90024 www.airforcehollywood.af.mil
(Air Force)

US Army Office of Public Affairs (310) 235-7621
(310) 235-7622
10880 Wilshire Blvd., Ste. 1250 FAX (310) 235-6075
Los Angeles, CA 90024
(US Army) www.defenselink.mil/faq/pis/PC12FILM.html

Wings Wildlife Production, Inc. (877) 542-1355
www.wingswildlife.com
(African and North American Wildlife)

WTTW Digital Archives (773) 509-5412
5400 N. St. Louis Ave. FAX (773) 509-5307
Chicago, IL 60625 www.wttwdigitalarchives.com
(Cityscapes, Flowers, Music Performance/Concerts, National
Parks, Rural, Scenics, Trains, Tsunami Disaster and Relief,
U.S. Landmarks & U.S. Troops/Iraq)

Ametron Audio Video
(323) 466-4321
(323) 464-1144
FAX (323) 871-0127
www.ametron.com

Broadcast Store
9420 Lurline Ave., Ste. C
Chatsworth, CA 91311
(818) 998-9100
FAX (818) 998-9106
www.broadcaststore.com

CET Universe
801 S. Main St., Ste. 101
Burbank, CA 91506
(818) 432-4330
FAX (818) 755-7748
www.cetuniverse.com

Edgewise Media Services, Inc.
2201 N. Hollywood Way
Burbank, CA 91505
(323) 769-0900
(800) 824-3130
FAX (323) 466-6815
www.edgewise-media.com

Edgewise Media Services, Inc.
602 N. Cypress St.
Orange, CA 92867
(714) 919-2020
(800) 444-9330
FAX (714) 919-2010
www.edgewise-media.com

Empress Media, Inc.
10777 Sherman Way
Sun Valley, CA 91352
(888) 683-6773
FAX (818) 255-3398
www.empressdigital.com

EVS
1819 Victory Bl.
Glendale, CA 91201
(818) 552-4590
(800) 238-8480
FAX (818) 552-4591
www.evsonline.com

Film Source LA
(818) 484-3236
(866) 537-1114
FAX (818) 688-0101
www.filmsourcela.com

Media Distributors
4518 W. Vanowen St.
Burbank, CA 91505
(818) 980-9916
(888) 889-3130
FAX (818) 980-9265
www.mediadistributors.com

Moviola/Moviola Cameras
1135 N. Mansfield Ave.
Los Angeles, CA 90038
(323) 467-1116
(800) 468-3107
FAX (323) 464-1518
www.moviola.com

MSE Media Solutions
6013 Scott Way
Los Angeles, CA 90040
(323) 721-1656
(800) 626-1955
FAX (323) 721-1506
www.msemedia.com

Reel Good
7758 Sunset Blvd.
Los Angeles, CA 90046
(323) 876-5427
(213) 303-6886
FAX (323) 876-5428
www.reelgoodfilm.com

Revolt Pro Media
7625 Hayvenhurst Ave., Ste. 32
Van Nuys, CA 91406
(818) 904-0001
FAX (818) 904-0005
www.revoltpromedia.com

The Tape Company
4518 W. Vanowen St.
Burbank, CA 91505
(818) 847-0036
(800) 851-3113
www.thetapecompany.com

TapeOnline.com
(877) 893-8273
(615) 263-1838
FAX (615) 263-1411
www.tapeonline.com

TapeStockOnline.com
2034 E. Lincoln Ave., Box 426
Anaheim, CA 92806
(888) 322-8273
(310) 352-4230
FAX (310) 352-4233
www.tapestockonline.com

Videotape Products, Inc.
2721 W. Magnolia Blvd.
Burbank, CA 91505
(818) 566-9898
(800) 422-2444
FAX (818) 566-8989
www.myvtp.com

Westside Media Group
12233 W. Olympic Blvd., Ste. 152
West Los Angeles, CA 90064
(310) 979-3500
(818) 779-8600
www.wmgmedia.com

3ality Digital LLC   (818) 333-3000
55 E. Orange Grove Ave.   FAX (818) 333-3001
Burbank, CA 91502   www.3alitydigital.com
(3-D Cameras)

A B Sea Photo   (310) 645-8992
9136 S. Sepulveda Blvd.   FAX (310) 645-3645
Los Angeles, CA 90045   www.absea.net
(Underwater Housings)

Aaron & Le Duc   (310) 452-2034
www.leducdesign.com
(1080i, 24P, 4K Cameras, Canon, HD-CAM, HDSR, HDV,
Panasonic & Sony)

AbelCine   (818) 972-9078
       (888) 700-4416
801 S. Main St., Ste. 104   FAX (818) 972-2673
Burbank, CA 91506   www.abelcine.com
(1080i, 24P, 720P, Accessories, D-5, Decks, HD-CAM, HDSR,
HDV, Monitors, Panasonic, Phantom HD High-Speed Camera,
Projectors, PS Technik Adaptors, SDX 900, Sony & VTR
Systems)

Absolute Rentals   (818) 842-2828
2633 N. San Fernando Blvd.   FAX (818) 842-8815
Burbank, CA 91504   www.absoluterentals.com
(1080i, 24P, 720P and 1080i HD Camera Systems, HD
Facilities, HD Online Final Cut Pro Editorial Facility, HD-CAM,
HDSR, HDV, Panasonic/Sony HD Cameras and TVR Systems,
Projectors, Screens and Video Camera Systems, SDX 900,
Sony and Panasonic Mini DVx & Video Projection Systems)

Action Audio & Visual   (323) 461-4290
       (888) 406-8164
10834 Burbank Blvd., Ste. A-100   FAX (323) 461-4292
North Hollywood, CA 91601
www.actionaudioandvisual.com
(1080i, 24P, 720P, Accessories, Converters, Cooke S4s, Decks,
HD-CAM, HDSR, HDV, Monitors, Multi-Camera Systems,
Panasonic, Portable Ultimatte, PS Technik Adaptors, SDX 900,
Sony, Sync Generators, Ultra Primes, Wireless Monitoring &
Zeiss Digiprimes)

Alan Gordon Enterprises, Inc.   (323) 466-3561
5625 Melrose Ave.   FAX (323) 871-2193
Los Angeles, CA 90038   www.alangordon.com

Alexa Rentals   (818) 562-1960
148 S. Victory Blvd.   FAX (818) 562-1270
Burbank, CA 91502   www.alexarentals.com
(1080i, 24P, 3-D Glasses, 4K Cameras, 720P, Accessories,
Converters, D-5, D.C.I. Compliant, Decks, DVC-Pro,
HD-CAM, HDSR, HDV, KiPro, Monitors, Multi-Camera Systems,
Panasonic, Scopes, Sony, Sync Generators, Ultra Primes, VTR
Systems & Zeiss Digiprimes)

All In One Productions   (323) 780-8880
1111 Corporate Center Dr., Ste. 303   FAX (323) 780-8887
Monterey Park, CA 91754   www.allinone-usa.com

Alliant Event Services, Inc.   (909) 622-3306
       (800) 851-5415
196 University Pkwy   FAX (909) 622-3917
Pomona, CA 91768   www.alliantevents.com
(Multi-Camera Packages)

Alternative Rentals   (310) 204-3388
5805 W. Jefferson Blvd.   FAX (310) 204-3384
Los Angeles, CA 90016   www.alternativerentals.com
(Angenieux Optimos Lenses, Arri Alexa Cameras, Arri Master
Primes, Cooke S5s, Panasonic, Red Epic Cameras & Sony)

American Hi Definition, Inc.   (818) 222-0022
7635 Airport Business Pkwy   FAX (818) 222-0818
Van Nuys, CA 91406   www.hi-def.com
(Screens, Projectors & Video Camera Systems)

American Video Group   (310) 477-1535
2542 Aiken Ave.   www.americanvideogroup.com
Los Angeles, CA 90064

Ametron Audio Video   (323) 466-4321
       (323) 464-1144
1546 N. Argyle Ave.   FAX (323) 871-0127
Hollywood, CA 90028   www.ametron.com

Artistic Resources Corporation   (323) 965-5200
535 N. Brand Blvd., Ste. 235   FAX (323) 965-5209
Glendale, CA 91203   www.artisticresources.com

Atlantic Cine Equipment, Inc.   (818) 794-9410
       (212) 944-0003
       FAX (443) 524-0210
       www.aceeast.com
(1080i, 24P, 720P, HD Heads, Multi-Camera Systems &
Panasonic)

B2 Services, Inc.   (818) 566-8769
2312 W. Burbank Blvd.   FAX (818) 566-1378
Burbank, CA 91506   www.b2services-inc.com
(1080i, 24P, 720P, D-5, Decks, DVC-Pro, HD-CAM, HDSR,
HDV & Monitors)

Band Pro Film & Digital, Inc.   (818) 841-9655
       (888) 226-3776
3403 W. Pacific Ave.   FAX (818) 841-7649
Burbank, CA 91505   www.bandpro.com
(24P, 4K Cameras, 720P, Accessories, Codex, Decks, DSLR,
File-Based Recording, Financing, HD-CAM, HDSR, HDV, Leica
Summilux-C, Monitors, Multi-Camera Systems, Sony F35,
Stereoscopic Cameras, Sync Generators, Ultra Primes, VTR
Systems, Wireless Monitoring & Zeiss Digiprimes)

Bexel   (818) 565-4399
       (800) 225-6185
2701 N. Ontario St.   FAX (818) 841-1572
Burbank, CA 91504   www.bexel.com

Big Door   (310) 546-6100
2617 Manhattan Beach Blvd.   FAX (424) 247-8382
Redondo Beach, CA 90278   www.bigdoor.tv

Birns & Sawyer, Inc.   (323) 466-8211
5275 Craner Ave.   FAX (818) 358-4395
North Hollywood, CA 91601   www.birnsandsawyer.com
(Cooke S4s, Mini DVs, Multi-Camera Systems, Panasonic,
PS Technik Adaptors, SDX 900, Sony & Ultra Primes)

BlueScreen, LLC/Bob Kertesz   (323) 467-7572
137 N. Larchmont Blvd., Ste. 508   www.bluescreen.com
Los Angeles, CA 90004
(Blue and Green Screen Facilities & Portable Ultimatte)

Broadcast Store   (818) 998-9100
9420 Lurline Ave., Ste. C   FAX (818) 998-9106
Chatsworth, CA 91311   www.broadcaststore.com

Brown Bag Films and Hi Def   (310) 617-5178
608 Fernwood Pacific Dr.   www.films-and-hi-def.com
Topanga, CA 90290

Cablecam Inc.   (818) 349-4955
21303 Itasca St.   FAX (818) 349-3879
Chatsworth, CA 91311   www.cablecam.com

Camera Support   (818) 557-1400
       (800) 995-5427
2827 N. San Fernando Blvd.   FAX (818) 557-1323
Burbank, CA 91504   www.camerasupport.com
(720P and 1080i HD Camera Systems, Accessories,
Multi-Camera Concert Packages & HD Online Final Cut Pro
Editorial Facility)

Cameron Pace Group   (818) 565-0005
2020 N. Lincoln St.   FAX (818) 861-3950
Burbank, CA 91504   www.cameronpace.com

Cimavision, Inc.   (310) 614-3644
www.cimavisioninc.com

Cinema Camera Rentals
(310) 574-1524
(310) 923-3593
FAX (310) 574-1524
www.cinemacamerarentals.com
(4K Cameras, Arri Acessories, DSLR, Element Technica Accessories, Monitors, Panasonic, RED Cameras, Red Epic, Red MX, Scarlet, Tripods & Zeiss Prime Superspeed Lenses)

Cinema Rentals, Inc.
(661) 222-7342
(818) 365-7999
25876 The Old Road, Ste. 174
FAX (661) 427-0881
Stevenson Ranch, CA 91381
www.cinemarentals.com

Clairmont Camera
(818) 761-4440
4343 Lankershim Blvd.
FAX (818) 761-0861
North Hollywood, CA 91602
www.clairmont.com

Coastal Media Group
(818) 880-9800
26660 Agoura Rd.
FAX (818) 579-9026
Calabasas, CA 91302
www.coastalmediagroup.com

Crescent Hollywood, LLC
(310) 745-0491
(213) 280-9690
6031 Acacia St.
FAX (310) 745-0691
Los Angeles, CA 90056
www.crescenthollywood.com
(1080i, 24P, 720P, Accessories, Converters, Decks, DVC-Pro, Editing Facilities, Monitors, Multi-Camera Concert Packages, Multi-Camera Systems & Panasonic)

Cutting Edge Productions, Inc.
(310) 326-4500
(310) 367-0416
22904 Lockness Ave.
FAX (310) 326-4715
Torrance, CA 90501
www.cuttingedgeproductions.tv
(1080i, 24P, 720P, Blue Screen Facilities, Decks, Green Screen Facilities, HDV, Monitors, Multi-Camera Concert Packages, Multi-Camera Systems, Production Trucks, Projectors, Sony & VTR Systems)

Deck Hand, Inc.
(818) 557-8403
1905 Victory Blvd., Ste. 8
FAX (818) 557-8406
Glendale, CA 91201
www.deckhand.com
(24P, D-5, Decks, DVC-Pro, HD-CAM, HDSLR Cameras and Lenses, HDSR, HDV, Lenses, Monitors, Multi-Camera Systems, Panasonic, Sony, VTR Systems & Zeiss Compact Prime Cine)

Division Camera
(323) 465-7700
(323) 571-9476
7022 W. Sunset Blvd.
FAX (323) 297-2773
Hollywood, CA 90028
www.divisioncamera.com
(1080i, 24P, 3D Glasses, 3D Systems, 4K Cameras, 720P, Accessories, Converters, Digital Cinemas Cameras, Equipment and Workflow, Editing Facilities, HDV, Monitors, Multi-Camera Systems, Panasonic, Projectors, PS Technik Adaptors, RED Cameras. Sony, Ultra Primes & Wireless Monitoring)

Doggicam, Inc.
(818) 845-8470
1500 W. Verdugo Ave.
FAX (818) 845-8477
Burbank, CA 91506
www.doggicam.com

editSource
(310) 572-7230
(310) 466-3624
12044 Washington Blvd.
FAX (310) 572-7238
Los Angeles, CA 90066
www.theeditsource.com

EVS
(818) 552-4590
(800) 238-8480
1819 Victory Bl.
FAX (818) 552-4591
Glendale, CA 91201
www.evsonline.com

Farr Out Productions, LLC
(310) 902-5944
FAX (818) 830-3608
www.farroutpro.com
(1080i, 24P, 720P, HDV, HDX900, Panasonic, Sony & Wireless Video Monitoring)

Fellpro
(310) 490-5185
(310) 318-3962
www.fellpro.com

Gemini 3D
(310) 395-4739
(Stereoscopic Cameras)
www.gemini3dcamera.com

Gyron Systems International, A Division of Wolfe Air Aviation, Ltd.
(626) 584-8722
39 E. Walnut St.
FAX (626) 584-4069
Pasadena, CA 91103
www.gyron.com

HD Camera Rentals
(323) 737-1314
4125 W. Jefferson Blvd.
FAX (310) 861-0163
Los Angeles, CA 90016
www.hdcamerarentals.com
(3D Glasses, 2K, 3.5K and 4K Cameras, Arri Alexa, Cooke S4s, Element Technica 3D Systems, High Def, Monitors, Panasonic, PS Technik Adaptors, RED Cameras, Sony, Stereoscopic Cameras & Ultra Primes)

HD Cinema
(310) 434-9500
12233 Olympic Blvd., Ste. 120
FAX (310) 499-5237
Los Angeles, CA 90064
www.hdcinema.com
(3D Cameras, 3D Stereo Mirror Rigs, Arri Alexa, DVC-Pro HD, Editing Facilities, HDCAM, HDCAM-SR, Panasonic, RED MX and Epic 4K Cameras & Sony)

HD Prod Video LA, LLC
(818) 400-2900
25626 Christie Court
www.hdprola.com
Stevenson Ranch, CA 91381

Helinet Aviation Services
(818) 902-0229
(866) 435-4638
16644 Roscoe Blvd.
FAX (818) 902-9278
Van Nuys, CA 91406
www.helinet.com

Hermosa Pictures
(310) 909-8525
1850 Industrial St., Ste. 307
FAX (310) 349-3441
Los Angeles, CA 90021
www.hermosapictures.com
(1080i, 24P, 720P, Accessories, Canon, Monitors, Multi-Camera Systems, Panasonic & Sony)

Hollywood Camera, Inc.
(818) 972-5000
(818) 720-8404
3100 N. Damon Way
FAX (818) 972-5010
Burbank, CA 91505
www.hollywoodcamera.com

Home Planet Productions
(805) 965-9848
(818) 422-4144
FAX (805) 965-2329
www.homeplanetproductions.com

HVS Productions
(858) 573-0987
8957 Complex Dr.
FAX (858) 569-0094
San Diego, CA 92123
www.hvsprod.com

Imagecraft Productions
(818) 954-0187
3318 Burton Ave.
FAX (818) 954-0189
Burbank, CA 91504
www.imagecraft.tv

Innovision Optics
(310) 453-4866
1719 21st St.
FAX (310) 453-4677
Santa Monica, CA 90404
www.innovisionoptics.com
(Accessories & Probe Lenses)

Inter Video 3D
(818) 843-3624
2211 N. Hollywood Way
FAX (818) 8436884
Burbank, CA 91505
www.intervideo24.com
(3D Monitors, 3D Projectors, 3D Support Gear, Aerial, Crew, HD Camera Packages, HD Lipstick Cameras, POV, Sterographers, Stereoscopic Cameras, Sync Generators & Underwater)

John Sharaf Photography
(310) 451-4048
(310) 650-6996
16132 Alcima Ave.
FAX (310) 454-6768
Pacific Palisades, CA 90272
www.sharaf.net
(Arri Alexas, G&E Truck Packages & PDW700 and 800 Cameras)

Kasdin Productions
(310) 914-4847
2117 Colby Ave.
www.kasdin.com
Los Angeles, CA 90025

kosmos innertainment group
(310) 490-5369
FAX (310) 641-8439
www.red31.com
(1080i, 24P, 4K Cameras, 720P, Converters, HDV, Monitors, Multi-Camera Concert Packages, Multi-Camera Systems, Projectors, RED Cameras & Sony)

Moviola/Moviola Cameras — (323) 467-1116 / (800) 468-3107
1135 N. Mansfield Ave.   FAX (323) 464-1518
Los Angeles, CA 90038   www.moviola.com

Nettmann Systems International   (818) 365-4286
1026 Griswold Ave.   FAX (818) 361-6982
San Fernando, CA 91340   www.camerasystems.com
(Gyro Stabilized Remote Heads & Track Systems)

Old School Cameras   (818) 847-1555
2819 N. San Fernando Blvd.   FAX (818) 847-1556
Burbank, CA 91504   www.oldschoolcameras.com
(1080i, 24P, 4K Cameras, 720P, Converters, Editing Facilities,
HD-CAM, HDV, Monitors, Panasonic, RED Cameras, Sony,
Wireless Monitoring & Zeiss Super Speed Primes)

Pace Technologies   (818) 565-0005
2020 N. Lincoln St.   FAX (818) 561-3950
Burbank, CA 91504   www.pacehd.com

Panavision   (818) 316-1000
Corporate Headquarters   FAX (818) 316-1111
6219 DeSoto Ave.   www.panavision.com
Woodland Hills, CA 91367

Panavision Hollywood   (323) 464-3800
6735 Selma Ave.   FAX (323) 469-5175
Hollywood, CA 90028   www.panavision.com

Performance Filmworks, Inc./   (805) 604-3399
Dean Bailey   (310) 721-4815
331 Hearst Dr.   FAX (805) 604-3398
Oxnard, CA 93030   www.performancefilmworks.com

Pictorvision Inc   (818) 785-9282 / (800) 876-5583
16238 Raymer St.   FAX (818) 785-9787
Van Nuys, CA 91406   www.pictorvision.com

Pivotal Post   (818) 760-6000
4142 Lankershim Blvd.   FAX (818) 760-6011
North Hollywood, CA 91602   www.pivotalpost.com
(1080i, 24P, HD Online Final Cut Pro Editorial Facility, HD-CAM,
HDSR, HDV, Projectors & Video Projection Systems)

POV-HD   (310) 866-9300
(Specialized Mounts)

The Power Broker   (949) 375-0526
101 N. Victory Blvd., Ste. L-95   www.lomo235.com
Burbank, CA 91502
(1080i, 24P, Angenieux 25-250 Anamorphic Zoom Lens, Cooke
S4s, Canon D-5 Chop-Chop HDSR in Russian Anamorphic
Lens Mount, Anamorphic Lenses, HD-CAM, HDSR, Monitors,
Lens Test Projectors, Kowa, Lomo, Not Hawks, Powerscope
MK II, PS Technik Adaptors, RED Cameras, Ultra Primes &
Zeiss Digiprimes)

Pro HD Rentals, Inc.   (818) 450-1115 / (310) 453-3301
2201 N. Hollywood Way   FAX (818) 450-1157
Burbank, CA 91505   www.prohdrentals.com
(1080i, 24P, 720P, Accessories, Canon DSLR 5D/7D,
Converters, D-5, DVC-Pro, Green Screen Facilities, HD-CAM,
HDSR, HDV, Monitors, Panasonic, RED Cameras & Sony)

Railroad Studios   (818) 396-4985
1500 Railroad St.   FAX (818) 396-4986
Glendale, CA 91204   www.railroadstudios.com

RED Digital Cinema   (949) 206-7900
20291 Valencia Circle   FAX (949) 206-7990
Lake Forest, CA 92630   www.red.com

RentHD.com/Lightpost Productions   (818) 955-7678
1701 W. Burbank Blvd., Ste. 201   FAX (818) 955-5181
Burbank, CA 91506   www.renthd.com
(24p, 720P and 1080i HD Camera Systems, HD Facilities, HD
Online Final Cut Pro Editorial Facility, HD-CAM, HDV,
Panasonic HD Cameras, Sony HDSR & VTR Systems)

Revolver Films   (310) 827-2441
4040 Del Rey Ave., Ste. 5   FAX (310) 827-2661
Marina del Rey, CA 90292   www.revolverfilmsla.com

Schulman Mobile Video   (323) 785-2528
1320 N. Wilton Pl.   FAX (323) 785-2529
Hollywood, CA 90028   www.schulmanmv.com
(1080i, HD-CAM & Production Trucks)

Sim Video Los Angeles   (323) 978-9000
738 Cahuenga Blvd.   FAX (323) 978-9018
Hollywood, CA 90038   www.simvideola.com

Sony Corporation   (201) 930-1000
One Sony Dr.   pro.sony.com
Park Ridge, NJ 07656

Stereomedia   (818) 442-7538
12185 Laurel Terrace Dr.   FAX (818) 761-3510
Studio City, CA 91604   www.3dstereomedia.com

T-stop, inc.   (323) 544-1000
957 Cole Ave.   FAX (323) 544-4970
Los Angeles, CA 90038   www.t-stopinc.com
(1080i, 24P, 4K Cameras, 720P, Accessories, Arri Alexa,
Converters, DVC-Pro, Monitors, Multi-Camera Concert
Packages, Panasonic, Production Trucks, Red Cameras, RED
MX, Stereoscopic Cameras & Ultra Primes)

Gary Taillon   (805) 443-3806

TCH/The Camera House   (818) 997-3802 / (818) 427-6219
7351 Fulton Ave.   FAX (818) 997-3885
North Hollywood, CA 91605   www.thecamerahouse.com

Touring Video, Inc.   (818) 504-3500
FAX (818) 504-3507
www.touringvideo.com

Twelve Tone Productions   (323) 633-1000 / (323) 633-3853
P.O. Box 36356   FAX (323) 934-3491
Los Angeles, CA 90036
www.twelvetoneproductions.com
(1080i, 24P, 720P, Accessories, Green Screen Facilities,
HD-CAM, HDV & Multi-Camera Systems)

Tyler Camera Systems   (818) 989-4420 / (800) 390-6070
14218 Aetna St.   FAX (818) 989-0423
Van Nuys, CA 91401   www.tylermount.com

Video Applications, Inc.   (714) 508-1858 / (800) 835-5432
14791 Myford Rd.   FAX (714) 508-2362
Tustin, CA 92780   www.videoapps.com
(1080i, 720P, Converters, D-5, Decks, DVC-Pro, HD-CAM,
Monitors, Multi-Camera Systems, Panasonic, Projectors,
Sony & Video Projection Systems)

Video Equipment Rentals   (818) 956-1444 / (800) 794-1407
912 Ruberta Ave.   FAX (818) 241-4519
Glendale, CA 91201   www.verrents.com
(1080i, 24P, 720P, Accessories, Converters, D-5, Decks, DVC-
Pro, HD-CAM, HDSR, HDV, Monitors, Multi-Camera Systems,
Panasonic, Projectors, RED Cameras, SDX 900, Sony, Sync
Generators, Ultra Primes, VTR Systems & Zeiss Digiprimes)

Video Production Specialists (VPS)   (866) 447-3877
FAX (310) 577-0850
www.videoproductionspecialists.com
(24P, HDV, Screens and Video Camera Systems & Video
Projection Systems)

Videowerks   (310) 393-8754 / (310) 780-4156
3435 Ocean Park Blvd., Ste. 107   FAX (310) 399-1829
Santa Monica, CA 90405   www.videowerks.com
(1080i, 24P, 720P, DVC-PRO 100 HDV, HDX900,
Panasonic P2 & Sony HD-CAM)

Visionary Forces Broadcast
Equipment Rentals   (818) 562-1960
148 S. Victory Blvd.   FAX **(818) 562-1270**
Burbank, CA 91502   **www.visionaryforces.com**
(1080i, 24P, 3D Monitors, 720P, ARRI Alexa, AJA KiPro,
Apple ProRes, Converters, D-5, Decks, Dolby PRM Monitors,
DVCPRO-HD, DVS Clipster, HD Monitors, HDCAM, HDCAM-
SR, HDV, Panasonic, Sony, Sync Generators, Ultra Primes,
VTR Systems & Zeiss Digiprimes)

                                       (818) 785-8033
Westcoast Video Productions, Inc. **(800) 477-8417**
14141 Covello St., Ste. 9A   FAX **(818) 785-8035**
Van Nuys, CA 91405   **www.wvpinc.com**

                                       (310) 979-3500
Westside Media Group   **(818) 779-8600**
12233 W. Olympic Blvd., Ste. 152   **www.wmgmedia.com**
West Los Angeles, CA 90064
(1080i, 24P, 4K Cameras, 720P, Converters, D-5, Decks,
DVC-Pro, Editing Facilities, HD-CAM, HDSR, HDV, Monitors,
Panasonic, Sony, Sync Generators & VTR Systems)

                                       (818) 846-9381
Wexler Video   **(800) 939-5371**
1111 S. Victory Blvd.   FAX **(818) 846-9399**
Burbank, CA 91502   **www.wexlervideo.com**

Wintech Video   **(818) 501-6565**
4455 Van Nuys Blvd.   FAX **(818) 501-6566**
Sherman Oaks, CA 91603   **www.wintechvideo.com**

World Wide Digital Services, Inc.   **(818) 500-7559**
1819 Dana St., Ste. E   FAX **(818) 500-1227**
Glendale, CA 91201   **www.worldwidela.com**
(1080i, 4K Cameras, 720P, Converters, Cooke S4s, D-5,
DVC-Pro, HD-CAM, HDSR, Monitors, Multi-Camera Systems,
Panasonic, PS Technik Adaptors, RED Cameras, Sony, S-Two
OB-1 Recorder, Ultra Primes & Zeiss Digiprimes)

NEW GIRL

BY MARJ GALAS

Production Designer Michael Whetstone on "New Girl"

Production designer Jeff Sage established the primary set on "New Girl." Once the series was picked up, production designer Michael Whetstone stepped in to take over where Sage left off. 411 spoke with Whetstone to learn what it takes to pick up the reigns.

411: Jeff Sage was telling me about the "dead areas." Did you go in and work out those areas?

MW: The first thing I did when I got the job was call him up. He had a lot of different ideas on things to change. For example, outside the front door they put a flat in the pilot. We really wanted to utilize that space. We built an elevator and a lobby so you get a sense of where they live.

411: I know casting was finalized after the building of the set. What are some of the ways you've been able to add the personality of the full cast?

MW: A lot of the furniture we brought in was from flea markets, thrift stores—trying to give it a rougher edge. These people live in this immense, beautiful loft that you aren't quite sure they can afford.

411: The lighting design in the apartment tends to be bright. Do you try to maintain that style with all environments?

MW: You can certainly consider color palettes when you are on location. I could give you a four page story on how much time and energy we put into the backdrops that are out the window.

411: You must have a team of location scouts looking for places?

MW: Our location manager is Jesse Cole and he and I have worked on "Curb Your Enthusiasm" which is 90% location work, so we have a short-hand when it comes to locations.

411: Would you say he's the first person you speak to after you read the script?

MW: We all sit down in a concept meeting. Liz Meriwether, the show's creator, is the one we will go to if we can't figure something out. A lot of the things in the script have come from her life.

ABRIDGED FROM AN 411 NEWSLETTER ARTICLE PUBLISHED DECEMBER 2011

Ⓐ ADVERTISER SYMBOL

**Refer to the General Index for
cross-referencing items in this section.**

8 Ball Manufacturing LLC   **(661) 252-3344**
16016 Baker Canyon Rd. **www.8ballcamerasupport.com**
Saugus, CA 91390
Accessories: Sliders 24" to 72"

Active Remote Systems, LLC   **(310) 235-1953**
    (800) 316-0067
11771 1/2 Pico Blvd.   FAX **(310) 235-1131**
Los Angeles, CA 90064   **www.activeremote.com**
Cranes: 15', 21', 30', 45' and 50' Technocranes and Aerocrane
& Super TechnoCranes
Arms: Modular Swiss Jib w/ 35' Reach
Dollies: Barby & Hot Dog
Accessories: 2 and 3 Axis Remote Heads, Hot Gears, Mo-Sys
Digital Lambda, Power Pod 2000, Power Pod Plus, Preston
FIZ, Scorpio Heads, Stabilized Scorpio, & Z Head

ADP Camera Cranes, Inc./   **(818) 972-2728**
David Rhea   **(714) 315-9495**
124 N. Naomi St.   FAX **(818) 972-2728**
Burbank, CA 91505
Arms: CamMate 5'-40'Cranes: Jib Arms

Ahern Entertainment   **(818) 834-7669**
10403 Glenoaks Blvd.   FAX **(818) 686-1982**
Pacoima, CA 91331   **www.ahernentertainment.com**

Alan Gordon Enterprises, Inc.   **(323) 466-3561**
5625 Melrose Ave.   FAX **(323) 871-2193**
Los Angeles, CA 90038   **www.alangordon.com**

Any Point of View, Inc.   **(818) 219-1667**
    (818) 504-6500
    FAX **(818) 394-6300**
    www.anypov.com
Accessories: 2 and 3 Axis Remote Heads, Digital Hot Gears
and Remote Follow Focus Systems, Steadicam Systems &
Vinten Quatro Studio Air Pedestals
Arms: 4'-40' Jimmy Jib Triangles

Ⓐ Atlantic Cine Equipment, Inc.   **(818) 794-9410**
    (212) 944-0003
    FAX **(443) 524-0210**
    www.aceeast.com
Dollies: Track Runner & Track Runner Mini
Heads: Mini-C & Stab-C Compact
Telescopic Camera Towers: SuperTower6 & SuperTower20
Accessories: 2 Axis Remote Heads, 5 Axis Remote Heads,
Aerial Camera Winch Systems, Cable-Suspended Systems,
CamRail Systems, Dolly Tracks, High Speed Camera Tracking
Systems, Remote Camera Systems & Remote Heads

Atomic Studios   **(323) 851-3825**
    (202) 438-9199
2556 E. Olympic Ave.   **www.atomicstudios.com**
Los Angeles, CA 90023
Cranes: Triangle Jimmy Jib
Dollies: PhantomAccessories: Dolly Track, Steadicam
Systems & Track Wheel Sets

Barber Tech Video Products   **(818) 982-7775**
    (877) 887-6388
2725 W Ave. L8   FAX **(661) 339-3235**
Lancaster, CA 93536   **www.barbertvp.com**
Arms: Jib Systems
Booms: 20' Barber Boom & Barber Baby Boom
Accessories: Camera Car Shock Mount & Remote Focus
and Zoom

Big Shot Camera Cranes/
Brian Gaetke   **(818) 729-9339**
    FAX **(818) 729-9331**
    www.bigshot.tv
Arms: 80' Akela Crane, 55' Akela Crane Jr. & 30' Jimmy Jib
Accessories: Remote Hot Head

Bikes..Camera..Action!   **(310) 995-2084**
1105 Bonilla
Topanga, CA 90290
Accessories: Super Light Camera Mounts for Bicycles, Hang
Gliders, Motorcycles and Ultralight Planes

Birns & Sawyer, Inc. (323) 466-8211
5275 Craner Ave. FAX (818) 358-4395
North Hollywood, CA 91601 www.birnsandsawyer.com
Arms: Porta-Jib & Porta-Jib Dual and Traveller
Dollies: Cameleon, Losmandy, Porta-Glide, Sierra & Studio

Cablecam Inc. (818) 349-4955
21303 Itasca St. FAX (818) 349-3879
Chatsworth, CA 91311 www.cablecam.com
Accessories: Cable-Suspended Camera Tracking
Systems & Mounts

Camera Car Industries/
Dean Goldsmith (818) 998-4798
12473 San Fernando Rd. FAX (818) 833-5962
Sylmar, CA 91342 www.cameracarindustries.com
Accessories: 3 Axis Remote Camera Systems

Camera Control, Inc. (310) 581-8343
3317 Ocean Park Blvd. FAX (310) 581-8340
Santa Monica, CA 90405 www.cameracontrol.com
Cranes: Live Action & Miniature Motion Control Cranes: Milo
and Milo Long Arm Motion Control Systems & Talos Motion
Control Rig
Dollies: Modular Motion Control Rig
Accessories: Motion Control Heads, Sleds and Turntables,
Ultihead Motion Control Systems, CGI Rig Models, Flair Motion
Control Systems, Motion Control Sliders, Model Movers &
Remote/Repeatable Heads

(818) 557-1400
Camera Support (800) 995-5427
2827 N. San Fernando Blvd. FAX (818) 557-1323
Burbank, CA 91504 www.camerasupport.com
Arms: 6'–40' Jib Systems
Accessories: 2 and 3 Axis Remote Heads, CamRail Systems,
Lencin and Vinten Fulmar Pedestals, Pan/Tilt Heads &
Steadicam Systems

(818) 781-3497
Champion Crane Rental, Inc. (323) 875-1248
12521 Branford St. FAX (818) 896-6202
Pacoima, CA 91331 www.championcrane.us
Cranes: 40'–265' ReachAccessories: Camera Baskets,
Light Bars & Rain Bars

❹ Chapman/Leonard (818) 764-6726
Studio Equipment, Inc. (888) 883-6559
12950 Raymer St. FAX (888) 502-7263
North Hollywood, CA 91605 www.chapman-leonard.com
Arms: Lenny Plus, Lenny II Plus, Lenny Mini, Plus III & Stinger
Jib Arm w/ Glider
Cranes: Nike, Super Apollo, Super Nova, Titan II & Zeus
Dollies: Hustler IV, Hybrid III, Olympian, Peewee, Sidewinder,
Super Peewee II, Super Peewee III & Super Peewee IV
Accessories: Bases: ATB, CS, Hy Hy Maverik,
Olympian III & Raptor

(310) 850-0710
Chris Rhodes Productions (888) 200-2383
P.O. Box 691901 FAX (323) 874-5076
Los Angeles, CA 90069 www.technocrane.net
Arms: 6'–40' CamMate Jib System 2000 & 17', 24', 30' and 50'
Telescopic Cranes
Dollies: Dolly w/ Track
Accessories: Remote Pan/Tilt Heads & Z-Axis/Dutch Head

Cinematic Experience, Inc./
Mark Sofil (323) 515-2967
FAX (866) 336-9840
www.marksofil.com
Arms: 6'-30' Jib, Jimmy Jib & Triangle Jimmy
Booms: Jib Arms
Accessories: 2 Axis Remote Heads, 3 Axis Remote Heads &
Wide Angle Lenses

(888) 802-7263
Cinemoves, Inc./Technocrane, Ltd. (941) 492-9175
FAX (818) 475-5406
www.cinemoves.com
Cranes: Super TechnoCranes & TechnoCranes
Dollies: Filou Rig Runner Trackable Remote Camera System

The Crane Company (818) 252-7700
13105 Saticoy St. www.thecranecompanyinfo.com
North Hollywood, CA 91605

(310) 577-1185
CraneShot LLC (310) 503-1122
12512 Gilmore Ave. FAX (310) 306-4027
Los Angeles, CA 90066 www.craneshot.com

(818) 903-4343
Cranium, Inc. (888) 272-6486
13770 Purple Ridge Ave. FAX (818) 890-6093
Kagel Canyon, CA 91342 www.cranium.tv
Telescoping Camera Cranes: 17', 24', 30' & 45' (Moviebird
Telescoping Cranes)
Sectional Cranes: Aerojib 8', CamMate 30', Felix 18', Foxy 23',
Galaxy 57', Giraffe 30' & GF-16(Phoenix) 55'
Rideable Cranes: Galaxy(36'), Giraffe (24'), GF-16(40')
Remote Heads: 2 & 3 Axis Mo-Sys Lambda, Stabilized 3-Axis
Mo-Sys Lambda, Stabilized Scorpio 4
Motion Control: 2 and 3 Axis Mo-sys Lambda, Moco Sled
Dolly & Moco Focus, Camera and Lens Control

Doggicam, Inc. (818) 845-8470
1500 W. Verdugo Ave. FAX (818) 845-8477
Burbank, CA 91506 www.doggicam.com
Accessories: Body-Mount, Bulldog Wireless Remote Head,
Doggimount, Lightweight Remote Sparrow Head, Power Slide,
Remote Follow Focus, Rhino Clamps & Super Slide

Phillip Ebeid/Summit Cranes (818) 909-7933
www.summitcranes.com
Cranes: Portable Jimmy Jib & Remote Head 6'–31' Reach

El Monte Filmworks (818) 209-5056
www.elmontefilmworks.com
Arms: CamMate & Jib Arms
Dollies: Cruiser Dolly
Accessories: Dolly Tracks, Preston, Remote Follow Focus,
Remote Heads & Remote Zooms

Filmotechnic International Corp. (310) 390-2500
www.filmotecnic.net
Cranes: Russian Arm
Accessories: 3 Axis Remote Heads, Camera Car Mounts,
Flight Head, High Speed Camera Tracking Systems & Shock
Absorber CAR Mount System

(310) 669-9888
❹ Filmotechnic USA (805) 453-1411
20432 S. Santa Fe Ave., Ste. K FAX (562) 684-0776
Carson, CA 90810 www.filmo-usa.com
Arms: Camera Car Gyro-Sabilized Remote Arm
Cranes: Russian Crane & Russian Arm
Accessories: 3 Gyro-Stabilized Heads, FH-5 Heads &
3D Heads

(702) 997-1939
Fisher Technical Services Rentals (866) 942-4098
www.ftsrentals.com

Fluid Pictures, Inc./ (818) 704-7873
Eastwood Productions (818) 355-5936
www.fluidpicturesinc.com
Arms: 7'-40' Jimmy Jib w/ 3rd Axis Head, Dolly and Track
Accessories: 5'-15' and 10'-33' Telescoping Column
Towercams, Remote Heads & Steadicams

(818) 679-4906
Flying Visual Art, Inc. (818) 630-5701
www.flyingvisualart.com

Focal Motion Inc. (818) 653-6287
www.focalmotion.com
Accessories: Pan/Tilt HeadsArms: Jimmy Jib

Focus on Cars (310) 762-1370
20434 S. Santa Fe Ave. FAX (310) 763-7110
Long Beach, CA 90810 www.southbaystudios.com
Accessories: ATV and Car Camera Mounts

G.I. 66 Productions, Inc. (818) 917-4664
5311 Captains Pl. FAX (818) 865-8924
Agoura Hills, CA 91301 www.gi66productions.com

(805) 578-2292
GCS/General Crane Services, Inc. (818) 571-0944
1606 River Wood Court www.craneservices.com
Simi Valley, CA 93063

416

J.L.Fisher

Motion Picture & Television Equipment

"J.L. Fisher products are proudly made in the U.S.A."

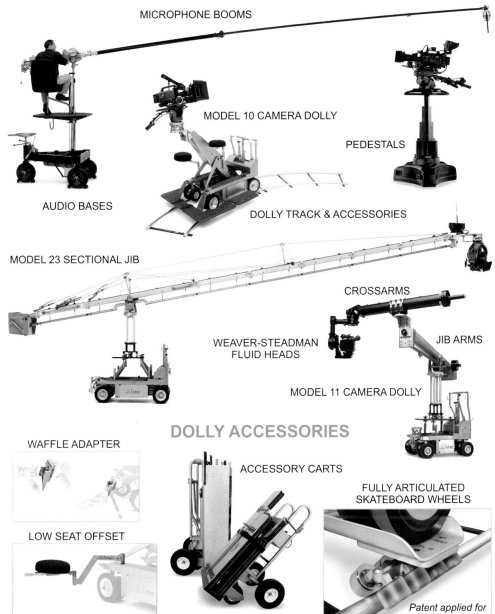

MICROPHONE BOOMS

MODEL 10 CAMERA DOLLY

PEDESTALS

AUDIO BASES

DOLLY TRACK & ACCESSORIES

MODEL 23 SECTIONAL JIB

CROSSARMS

WEAVER-STEADMAN FLUID HEADS

JIB ARMS

MODEL 11 CAMERA DOLLY

DOLLY ACCESSORIES

WAFFLE ADAPTER

ACCESSORY CARTS

FULLY ARTICULATED SKATEBOARD WHEELS

LOW SEAT OFFSET

Patent applied for

AVAILABLE FOR RENTAL WORLDWIDE

J.L. Fisher, Inc.
1000 Isabel Street, Burbank, CA 91506 U.S.A.
Tel: (818) 846-8366   Fax: (818) 846-8699
Web: www.jlfisher.com e-mail: info@jlfisher.com

J.L. Fisher, GmbH
Emil-Hoffmann-Str. 55-59 50996 Köln, Germany
Tel: +49 2236 3922 0   Fax: +49 2236 3922 12
Web: www.jlfisher.de e-mail: info@jlfisher.de

Geo Film Group, Inc.   (818) 376-6680
(877) 436-3456
7625 Hayvenhurst Ave., Ste. 49   FAX (818) 376-6686
Van Nuys, CA 91406   www.geofilm.com
Arms: Jan Jib Cranes: Extreme & Javelin
Accessories: 2 Axis Remote Heads, 3 Axis Remote Heads, Hot
Heads, Mini Shot, Pan/Tilt Heads, Power Pods,
Preston & SL Pods

Gold Coast Crane Service   (805) 230-1114
(818) 414-1980
FAX (805) 578-6020
Accessories: Box Spreader Bars, Camera Baskets, Light Bars,
Man Baskets & Rain Bars

Griptrix, Inc.   (818) 982-2510
12767 Saticoy St.   FAX (818) 982-8830
North Hollywood, CA 91605   www.griptrix.com
Accessories: Camera Car Mounts
Arms: Aerocrane Jib & Jib Systems
Cranes: Jib Arms
Dollies: Electric Camera Dolly, Panther, Western & Wheelchair

Holladay Camera Bikes   (805) 740-6018
(323) 462-2301
FAX (805) 735-7205
www.camerabikes.com
Accessories: Motorcycle Camera Mounts

Hot Gears   (818) 780-2708
16644 Roscoe Blvd., Ste. 34   FAX (818) 989-5408
Van Nuys, CA 91406   www.hotgears.com
Accessories: 2 and 3 Axis Remote Heads

Image G/Ikonographics   (818) 761-6644
28490 Westinghouse Pl., Ste. 160   www.imageg.com
Valencia, CA 91355
Cranes: Bulldog I 16' and 22' Motion Control Cranes, Bulldog
II 22' and 32' Motion Control Cranes, Gazelle Motion Control
Portable System (6' Arm), Graphlite & Hyena Motion Control
Portable System
Dollies: Greyhound Motion Control Portable System & Rocket
Sled Motion Control Portable System
Accessories: 3', 4', 6' Sliders and Silent Sliders, 360° Axis,
Dolly Track, Gazelle, Graphite, Kuper, Model Movers, Motion
Control, Motion Control Accessories, Pan/Tilt Heads Frame
Accurate Motion Control Heads, Sorensen Design Track and
Turn Table & Zebra

Innovision Optics   (310) 453-4866
1719 21st St.   FAX (310) 453-4677
Santa Monica, CA 90404   www.innovisionoptics.com
Arms: Z-Jib Zero Gravity Arm
Accessories: 2 Axis Remote Heads, 3-Axis Remote Head, Body
Mounts, CamRail Systems, Doggimounts, High Speed Camera
Tracking Systems, Model Movers, Pan/Tilt Heads, Rotation/
Linear Motion Control Tables, Sliders & Turn Tables

Ⓐ J.L. Fisher, Inc.   (818) 846-8366
1000 W. Isabel St.   FAX (818) 846-8699
Burbank, CA 91506   www.jlfisher.com
Arms: Fisher Jib 20, 21, 22 and 23
Booms: Fisher Microphone w/ 16'–29' Reach
Dollies: Fisher 9, 10 and 11 Heads: Vector 700
Accessories: Quattro Pedestal

JB Slider   (818) 345-3127
(818) 388-2898
19159 Rosita St.   FAX (818) 705-0753
Tarzana, CA 91356   www.jbslider.com
Accessories: 2' and 3' Sliders

Jib Solutions, Inc.   (818) 367-6337
(818) 321-2224
15021 Briarhill Dr.   FAX (818) 367-3081
Sylmar, CA 91342   www.video8film.com
Arms: 15' and 24' Technojib Telescoping Jib Arms, Jimmy
Jibs & Triangle Jimmy
Cranes: Jib Arms
Accessories: 2 Axis Remote Heads, Dutch Heads &
Remote Heads

Jibmasters, Inc.   (310) 993-5456
(805) 496-6999
1248 Willsbrook Court   FAX (805) 494-9999
Westlake Village, CA 91361
Arms: 30' Reach Accessories: Dutch Head & Wide
Angle Lenses

JibWorks/Mark Koonce   (818) 986-2535
www.jibworks.com
Accessories: 2 Axis Remote Heads, 3 Axis Remote Heads,
ATV Mounts, Dolly Tracks, Hot Heads, Pan/Tilt Heads, Remote
Camera Systems, Remote Follow Focus & Towercams
Arms: Jib Systems & Triangle JimmyCranes: GatorCams &
Jib Arms

KCW Studios (626) 698-0029
816 S. Date Ave. FAX (626) 872-2377
Alhambra, CA 91803 www.kcwstudios.com

Line 204 Inc. (323) 960-0113
837 N. Cahuenga Blvd. FAX (323) 960-0163
Hollywood, CA 90038 www.line204.com

Logan Cinema Equipment Rental (323) 702-8502
Arms: Jimmy Jib

(954) 605-7095
Moose Media Camera Cranes (323) 383-1054
1888 N Redding Way www.themoosemedia.com
Upland, CA 91784
Accessories: 2 Axis Remote Heads, 3 Axis Remote Heads &
ATV Mounts
Arms: Jimmy Jib & Triangle Jimmy

Motion Picture Marine (310) 822-1100
616 Venice Blvd. FAX (310) 822-2679
Marina del Rey, CA 90291
www.motionpicturemarine.com
Accessories: Perfect Horizon Camera Stabilization Head

Motor Reflex (818) 761-7749
P.O. Box 7153 www.motorreflex.com
Burbank, CA 91510
Accessories: Kuper Motion Control and Stepper-Driver
Packages, Motion Control Drive Units and Accessories, Preston
FIZ-to-Moco Blackboxes & TruePos Track Encoder/Display

(541) 840-3366
Willy Nemeth/Good Medicine Hat (541) 476-0598
Accessories: ATV and Car Camera Mounts

Nettmann Systems International (818) 365-4286
1026 Griswold Ave. FAX (818) 361-6982
San Fernando, CA 91340 www.camerasystems.com
Accessories: Cam-Remote/Mini-Mote, Gyro-Stabilized 5-Axis
Remote Heads: Gyron FS/Stab-C and Stab-C Compact &
Kenworthy/Nettman Snorkel

(310) 286-2104
Oppenheimer Cine Rental (877) 467-8666
FAX (206) 467-9165
www.oppcam.com
Cranes: 42' Braced Super Swiss Jib Crane
Accessories: Power Pod Remote Head

(818) 768-1573
Pacific Motion Control, Inc. (661) 644-1516
9812 Glenoaks Blvd. FAX (818) 768-1575
Sun Valley, CA 91352 www.pacificmotion.net
Cranes: Motion Control/Repeatable Cranes: Gazelle (Portable
6' Arm), Graphlite (Portable 14' Arm) & Technodolly
Telescoping Cranes: Super Scorpio Technocrane (30' or 37'
Arm) & Technocrane
Dollies: Bogey & Motion Control/Repeatable Zebra
(Portable 2' or 5' Arm)
Accessories: 2 Axis Cinema Pro Head, 2 Axis Remote Heads,
2 Axis Talon Head, 3 Axis Aerohead, CGI Rig Interface Models,
Frame Accurate Motion Control Heads, Kuper Motion Control,
Model Movers, Motion Control Lighting Cues, Motion Control
Track (Straight or 360 degree Curved), Motor Driver Systems,
Preston, Remote Camera Systems, Remote/Repeatable
Heads, Stepper-Driver Packages & Turn Tables

Panavision Remote Systems (818) 316-1080
6219 DeSoto Ave. FAX (818) 316-1081
Woodland Hills, CA 91367 www.panavision.com
Cranes: 32' Louma 2, 35' & 45' Moviebirds, Supertechno 50, 30
and 22 & Techno 15'
Crane Bases: Motorized Multi-Terrain Base
Remote Heads: 2 and 3 Axis Remote Heads, Hot Heads, Key
Head, Libra, Mo-Sys, Power Pod & Scorpio
Accessories: 2', 3', 3.5', 4' and 6' Sliders, Air Floater, Digital
HME Intercoms, Matrix Mount, Out Front Mount, Panamount &
Preston Focus Systems

Performance Filmworks, Inc./ (805) 604-3399
Dean Bailey (310) 721-4815
331 Hearst Dr. FAX (805) 604-3398
Oxnard, CA 93030 www.performancefilmworks.com
Accessories: 3-Axis Gyrostabilized Remote Heads (with
Horizon Stabilization), 3D Compatible, Joystick, Wheel or
Panbar Controls, Preston Systems, Rain Deflectors, 2D and 3D
Leveling Heads, Suspension Mounts & Wireless Systems
Cranes: Gyrostabilized Remote Cranes, High-Speed Camera/
Crane Cars, Off Road Vehicles & Tracking Vehicles

(818) 785-9282
Pictorvision Inc (800) 876-5583
16238 Raymer St. FAX (818) 785-9787
Van Nuys, CA 91406 www.pictorvision.com
Accessories: 5 Axis Gyro-Stabilized Camera Systems, Cineflex,
Pictorvision Eclipse, Wescam & XR

Pursuit Systems Inc. (818) 255-5850
7255 Radford Ave. www.pursuitsystems.com
North Hollywood, CA 91605

Quixote Studios (323) 461-1408
1000 N. Cahuenga Blvd. FAX (323) 461-5517
Los Angeles, CA 90038 www.quixote.com

(866) 449-7447
Safari Technologies (818) 585-6653
P.O. Box 5417 FAX (805) 830-1158
Palm Springs, CA 92263 www.safaritechnologies.net
Arms: SR4 Car Mount
Accessories: Remote Pan/Tilt Heads

Service Vision USA (818) 623-1970
12035 Sherman Way FAX (818) 759-6911
North Hollywood, CA 91605 www.servicevisionusa.com
Cranes: 30' SuperScorpio Crane with 8' Extention & 9'–50'
Carbon Fibre
Accessories: 2 and 3 Axis Remote Heads, 3 Axis Remote
Camera Systems, 360° Axis, Gyro Stabilized Remote Heads,
Remote Follow Focus, Remote Heads, Remote Pan/Tilt Heads,
Scorpio III, Scorpio Mini Head & Scorpio Stabilized Head

(805) 496-5289
The Slider (818) 344-5284
FAX (805) 496-4802
www.theslider.com
Accessories: 32" Video and Mitchell Mount Minisliders & 3', 4',
6', 8' Manual and Motorized Sliders

(877) 933-7226
Spydercam (303) 941-1900
28130 Avenue Crocker, Ste. 322 www.spydercam.com
Valencia, CA 91355
Accessories: 2-D and 3-D Suspended Camera Systems, Cable-
Suspended Systems, Rigging Systems & High Speed Camera
Tracking Systems

Straight Shoot'r Cranes, Inc. (818) 609-8310
18434 Oxnard St., Ste H FAX (818) 609-8311
Tarzana, CA 91356 www.straightshootr.com
Accessories: Pan/Tilt HeadsCranes: Jib Arms

(818) 917-5677
Techno-Jib Rentals (888) 520-2090
Arms: Techno-Jib T24 and T15 www.technojibrentals.com

(818) 582-3022
Telescopic Camera Cranes, Inc. (310) 947-5126
www.telescopiccameracranes.com

Terra-Flite (323) 223-2709
3811 San Rafael Ave.
Los Angeles, CA 90065
Arms: 16' Gyro-Stabilized Arm w/ 8' Reach & 9' Vertical Range
and 14" Min. Height

(818) 618-9988
Ultimate Arm/Adventure Equipment (805) 375-3200
5506 Colodny Dr. FAX (805) 375-3211
Agoura Hills, CA 91301 www.ultimatearm.com

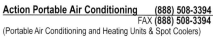

Action Portable Air Conditioning (888) 508-3394
FAX (888) 508-3394
(Portable Air Conditioning and Heating Units & Spot Coolers)

Aggreko Event Services (818) 767-7288
(888) 918-4874
11180 Penrose St. FAX (818) 767-7782
Sun Valley, CA 91352 www.aggreko.com
(Air Conditioning Units & Heaters)

Air on Location, Inc. (818) 307-4558
(Portable Air Conditioning Units) FAX (818) 712-6933
www.aironlocation.net

Atlas Sales & Rentals, Inc. (800) 972-6600
(310) 320-9800
20410 Gramercy Pl. FAX (310) 320-9870
Torrance, CA 90501 www.atlassales.com
(Portable Air Conditioning Units, Fans and Heaters & Spot Coolers)

Cinema Air, Inc. (805) 732-6517
FAX (805) 526-6905
www.cinemaair.com
(Portable Air Conditioning Units and Heating Units & Spot Coolers)

DJ Safety, Inc. (323) 221-0000
2623 N. San Fernando Rd. FAX (323) 221-0001
Los Angeles, CA 90065 www.djsafety.com
(Pool Heating)

Elegant Mist, LLC (310) 428-5180
(310) 857-6644
www.elegantmist.com

Kohler Rental (310) 518-5118
(310) 600-3063
766 Gifford Ave. FAX (920) 459-1846
San Bernardino, CA 92408
www.kohlereventservices.com

A **La Brea Air, Inc.**
(800) 452-2732
(310) 258-9100
5601 W. Slauson Ave., Ste. 262   FAX (310) 258-9110
Culver City, CA 90230   www.labrearentals.com
(Air Conditioning and Heating Equipment and Systems)

Line 204 Inc.   (323) 960-0113
837 N. Cahuenga Blvd.   FAX (323) 960-0163
Hollywood, CA 90038   www.line204.com

Location Air   (855) 444-4757
17600 Crusader Ave.   FAX (855) 444-4329
Cerritos, CA 90703   www.locationair.tv

Malibu Mobile Air   (818) 590-2455
5737 Kanan Rd., Ste. 531   FAX (818) 706-2945
Agoura Hills, CA 91301
(Air Conditioning Units, Heating Units & Portable Units)

Quixote Studios   (323) 461-1408
1000 N. Cahuenga Blvd.   FAX (323) 461-5517
Los Angeles, CA 90038   www.quixote.com

Sony Pictures Studios   **(310) 244-6926**
10202 W. Washington Blvd.   FAX **(310) 244-8090**
Culver City, CA 90232   **www.sonypicturesstudios.com**
(Blowers, Pool Heaters, Portable Air Conditioning Units &
Ventilation Fans)

Ⓐ Studio Air Conditioning, Inc.   **(818) 222-4143**
5171 N. Douglas Fir Rd., Ste. 6   FAX **(818) 222-2092**
Calabasas, CA 91302   **www.studioair.com**
(24 Hour Service, Air Conditioning Units, Generators, Heaters,
Portable Units & Trailer Mounted Units)

Sunbelt Rentals   **(818) 996-7100**
18251 Napa St.   FAX **(818) 701-9113**
Northridge, CA 91325   **www.sunbeltrentals.com**

Sunbelt Rentals   **(714) 994-6360**
1170 N. Main St.   FAX **(714) 994-7512**
Orange, CA 92867   **www.sunbeltrentals.com**

A-1 Coast Rental
(310) 326-1910
(800) 932-6278
24000 Crenshaw Blvd.
FAX (310) 326-1547
Torrance, CA 90505
www.a1coastrentals.com

A-Line Crane Rental Services, Inc.
(714) 261-3536
(800) 524-7972
18032-C Lemon Dr., Ste. 212
FAX (714) 744-5802
Yorba Linda, CA 92886
www.alinecranes.com

A.O. Richardson
(818) 242-3129
(818) 242-0888
4311 San Fernando Rd.
FAX (818) 548-0349
Glendale, CA 91204
www.aorichardson.com

B & G Industrial Rentals
(310) 327-0804
(800) 536-3019
1627 W. 130th St.
FAX (310) 327-9174
Gardena, CA 90249
www.bgrentalsinc.com
(24-Hour Service)

Hertz Entertainment Services
(818) 840-8247
(818) 391-4104
3111 N. Kenwood St.
FAX (818) 847-0941
Burbank, CA 91505
www.hertzentertainment.com

Kohler Rental
(310) 518-5118
(310) 600-3063
766 Gifford Ave.
FAX (920) 459-1846
San Bernardino, CA 92408
www.kohlereventservices.com

Power Trip Rentals
(310) 667-4433
(310) 292-0974
2950 E. Harcourt St.
FAX (310) 604-3233
Rancho Dominguez, CA 90221
www.powertriprentals.net

RMR Equipment Rental Inc.
(661) 510-8516
(661) 257-3303
32016 N. Castaic Rd.
FAX (661) 294-8522
Castaic, CA 91384
www.rmrwatertrucks.com

Sunbelt Rentals
(323) 255-0916
(800) 667-9328
3311 San Fernando Rd.
FAX (323) 255-2187
Los Angeles, CA 90065
www.sunbeltrentals.com

Sunstate Equipment Company
(888) 456-4560
(800) 870-9110
17310 S. Main St.
FAX (714) 779-9767
Carson, CA 90248
www.sunstateequip.com

Sunstate Equipment Company
(888) 456-4560
(800) 870-9110
4460 E. La Palma Ave.
FAX (714) 779-9767
Anaheim, CA 92807
www.sunstateequip.com

Sunstate Equipment Company
(888) 456-4560
(800) 870-9110
205 W. Magnolia Blvd.
FAX (714) 779-9767
Burbank, CA 91502
www.sunstateequip.com

Sunstate Equipment Company
(888) 456-4560
(800) 870-9110
32311 Dunlap Blvd.
FAX (714) 779-9767
Yucaipa, CA 92399
www.sunstateequip.com

Sunstate Equipment Company
(888) 456-4560
(800) 870-9110
5590 Eastgate Mall
FAX (714) 779-9767
San Diego, CA 92121
www.sunstateequip.com

United Rentals
(818) 842-5288
203 W. Olive Ave.
FAX (818) 842-9970
Burbank, CA 91502
www.unitedrentals.com

Acey Decy Lighting — (818) 408-4444
200 Parkside Dr. — FAX (818) 408-2777
San Fernando, CA 91340 — www.aceydecy.com

Anytime Production Equipment Rentals, Inc. — (323) 461-8483
755 N. Lillian Way — FAX (323) 461-2338
Hollywood, CA 90038 — www.anytimerentals.com

Apache Rental Group — (818) 842-9944 / (818) 842-9875
3910 W. Magnolia Blvd. — FAX (818) 842-9269
Burbank, CA 91505 — www.apacherentalgroup.com

Birns & Sawyer, Inc. — (323) 466-8211
5275 Craner Ave. — FAX (818) 358-4395
North Hollywood, CA 91601 — www.birnsandsawyer.com

Board Brothers — (323) 600-3969
820 Thompson Ave., Ste. 3 — www.boardbrothers.net
Glendale, CA 91201
(Layout Boards & Mats)

Board Patrol — (818) 508-4633 / (323) 965-1478
(Layout Boards) — FAX (818) 508-4638
www.theboardpatrol.com

Board Sily — (818) 590-5878
(Layout Boards)

Board Stiff, Inc. — (310) 516-7881 / (323) 855-4640
1847 W. 144th St. — FAX (310) 516-7882
Gardena, CA 90249 — www.boardstiff.com
(Layout Board)

Ⓐ Bulbtronics — (323) 461-6262 / (800) 245-2852
2210 N. Screenland Dr. — FAX (323) 461-7307
Burbank, CA 91505 — www.bulbtronics.com

Castex Rentals — (323) 462-1468
1044 Cole Ave. — FAX (323) 462-3719
Hollywood, CA 90038 — www.castexrentals.com

Concept Lighting, Inc. — (818) 767-1122
11274 Goss St. — FAX (818) 768-9900
Sun Valley, CA 91352 — www.conceptlight.com

The Culver Studios — (310) 202-3363
9336 W. Washington Blvd. — FAX (310) 202-3516
Culver City, CA 90232 — www.theculverstudios.com

Direct Tools & Fasteners — (818) 500-8843
1710 Standard Ave. — FAX (818) 500-7358
Glendale, CA 91201 — www.directtools.com

Entertainment Lighting Services (ELS) — (818) 769-9800 / (800) 622-6628
11440 Sheldon St. — FAX (818) 769-2100
Sun Valley, CA 91352 — www.elslights.com
(Lighting Expendables & Production Expendables)

Expendable Supply Store — (818) 407-7800 / (800) 233-7830
12800 Foothill Blvd. — FAX (818) 407-7875
Sylmar, CA 91342 — www.hollywoodrentals.com

Expendables Plus — (818) 841-8282
5375 W. San Fernando Rd. — FAX (818) 841-3345
Los Angeles, CA 90039 — www.cinelease.com

The Expendables Recycler — (818) 901-9796
5812 Columbus Ave. — FAX (818) 901-6010
Van Nuys, CA 91411 — www.expendablesrecycler.com
(Camera and Lighting Expendables)

Express Layout Boards, Inc. — (661) 255-0602 / (661) 857-1715
24504 Apple St. — FAX (661) 255-0602
Santa Clarita, CA 91321

Filmtools — (818) 845-8066 / (888) 807-1900
1400 W. Burbank Blvd. — FAX (818) 845-8138
Burbank, CA 91506 — www.filmtools.com
(Camera Expendables)

Fox Studios — (310) 369-2528 / (310) 369-4636
Studio Supply, 10201 W. Pico Blvd. — FAX (310) 369-4078
Los Angeles, CA 90035 — www.foxstudiosupply.com
(Camera Expendables, Construction and Paint Supplies & Production Office Expendables)

GAM Products, Inc. — (323) 935-4975 / (888) 426-2656
4975 W. Pico Blvd. — FAX (323) 935-2002
Los Angeles, CA 90019 — www.gamonline.com
(Lighting Expendables & Special Effects Projection Equipment)

Hollywood Center Studios — (323) 860-0000
1040 N. Las Palmas Ave. — FAX (323) 860-8105
Hollywood, CA 90038 — www.hollywoodcenter.com

Hollywood Rentals/ESS/Olesen — (818) 407-7800
12800 Foothill Blvd. — FAX (818) 407-7875
Sylmar, CA 91342 — www.hollywoodrentals.com

Imagecraft Productions — (818) 954-0187
3318 Burton Ave. — FAX (818) 954-0189
Burbank, CA 91504 — www.imagecraft.tv

Jack Rubin & Sons, Inc. — (818) 562-5100
520 S. Varney St. — FAX (818) 562-5101
Burbank, CA 91502 — www.wirerope.net

Kinetic Lighting — (310) 837-3204 / (800) 908-3842
722 Thompson Ave. — FAX (310) 837-8695
Glendale, CA 91201 — www.kineticlighting.com

Lay'd Out — (310) 455-4384 / (310) 963-2203
P.O. Box 252 — FAX (310) 455-1393
Topanga, CA 90290 — www.laydout.org
(Layout Boards)

Layout Lou — (310) 980-0430 / (424) 245-6336
www.layoutboard.net
(Installation Services, Layout Boards & Production Expendables)

Lexus Lighting, Inc. — (818) 768-4508
11225 Dora St. — FAX (805) 641-3273
Sun Valley, CA 91352 — www.lexuslighting.com
(2-Lamp and 4-Lamp Dimmable Flourescent Ballasts, Camera Expendables, Lighting Expendables & T8, T12, 32K and 56K Flourescent Lamps)

Line 204 Inc. — (323) 960-0113
837 N. Cahuenga Blvd. — FAX (323) 960-0163
Hollywood, CA 90038 — www.line204.com

Location Sound Corporation — (818) 980-9891 / (800) 228-4429
10639 Riverside Dr. — FAX (818) 980-9911
North Hollywood, CA 91602 — www.locationsound.com
(Production Expendables)

LocoMats — (818) 376-8386
7064 Gerald Ave. — FAX (818) 376-8648
Van Nuys, CA 91406 — www.locomats.com
(Layout Boards)

The Lot
(323) 850-3180
(323) 850-2832
1041 N. Formosa Ave.   www.thelotstudios.com
West Hollywood, CA 90046

Maggie's Layout Board   (818) 344-6601
18653 Ventura Blvd., Ste. 450   FAX **(818) 344-3566**
Tarzana, CA 91356   **www.maggieslayoutboard.com**

Mat Men
(323) 632-4368
(310) 704-5939
2160 E. Woodlyn Rd.   FAX **(310) 943-1852**
Pasadena, CA 91104   **www.matmen.net**
(Layout Boards & Mats)

MPR Photographic Rentals   (310) 762-1360
South Bay Studios   FAX **(310) 639-2055**
20434 S. Santa Fe Ave.   **www.southbaystudios.com**
Long Beach, CA 90810

Out of Frame Production Rentals   (323) 462-1898
1124 N. Citrus Ave.   FAX **(323) 462-1897**
Hollywood, CA 90038   **www.outofframela.com**
(Camera Expendables, Layout Boards, Lighting Expendables &
Production Expendables)

Paladin Group, Inc.
(323) 874-7758
(323) 851-8222
7351 Santa Monica Blvd.   FAX **(323) 851-7328**
Los Angeles, CA 90046

Panavision Panastore   (818) 316-1000
Corporate Headquarters   FAX **(818) 316-1111**
6219 DeSoto Ave.   **www.panastore.com**
Woodland Hills, CA 91367
(Camera Expendables)

Ⓐ The Studios at Paramount   (323) 956-5114
The Studios at Paramount Grip & Lighting Expendables
5555 Melrose Ave.   **www.thestudiosatparamount.com**
Hollywood, CA 90038

Pasadena Camera Rental, Inc.   (626) 796-3300
41 E. Walnut St.   FAX **(626) 432-6731**
Pasadena, CA 91103   **www.samyscamera.com**

Paskal Lighting   (818) 896-5233
12685 Van Nuys Blvd.   FAX **(818) 485-0157**
Pacoima, CA 91331   **www.paskal.com**

(818) 762-0884
Premier Lighting & Production Co.   (800) 770-0884
12023 Victory Blvd.   FAX **(818) 762-0896**
North Hollywood, CA 91606   **www.premier-lighting.com**

(323) 957-9933
Quixote Studios - Griffith Park   (818) 553-2960
4585 Electronics Pl.   FAX **(323) 957-9944**
Griffith Park, CA 90039   **www.quixote.com**

Quixote Studios Expendables Store   (323) 960-9191
Quixote Studios   FAX **(323) 960-3366**
1000 N. Cahuenga Blvd.   **www.quixote.com**
Los Angeles, CA 90038

The Rag Place, Inc.   (818) 765-3338
13160 Raymer St.   FAX **(818) 765-3860**
North Hollywood, CA 91605   **www.theragplace.com**

Ragtime Rentals, Inc.   (818) 837-7077
11970 Borden Ave.   FAX **(818) 837-5096**
San Fernando, CA 91340   **www.ragtimerentals.com**

Raleigh Studios - Hollywood   (323) 960-3456
5300 Melrose Ave.   FAX **(323) 960-4712**
Hollywood, CA 90038   **www.raleighstudios.com**

Raleigh Studios - Manhattan Beach   (323) 960-3456
1600 Rosecrans Ave.   FAX **(310) 727-2710**
Manhattan Beach, CA 90266   **www.raleighstudios.com**

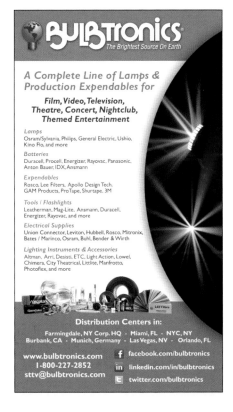
Grip & Lighting Expendables

Raleigh Studios - Playa Vista (323) 960-3456
5600 S. Campus Center Dr. www.raleighstudios.com
Playa Vista, CA 90094

Rose Brand (818) 505-6290
(800) 360-5056
10616 Lanark St. FAX (818) 505-6293
Sun Valley, CA 91352 www.rosebrand.com

Sequoia Illumination (818) 563-1000
(888) 647-2777
2428 N. Ontario St. FAX (818) 563-1001
Burbank, CA 91504 www.sequoiaillumination.com

Set Stuff, Inc. (323) 993-9500
1105 N. Sycamore Ave. FAX (323) 993-9506
Hollywood, CA 90038 www.setstuffrentals.com

ShowBiz Enterprises, Inc. (818) 989-7007
15541 Lanark St. FAX (818) 989-8272
Van Nuys, CA 91406 www.showbizenterprises.com

Siren Studios (323) 467-3559
(323) 960-9045
6063 W. Sunset Blvd. FAX (323) 461-6744
Hollywood, CA 90028 www.sirenstudios.com
(Lighting & Production Expendables)

SirReel - LA & San Diego (888) 477-7335
(818) 859-7766
(Production Expendables) FAX (888) 477-7313
www.sirreel.us

Skye Rentals (323) 462-5934
1016 Mansfield Ave. FAX (323) 462-5935
Hollywood, CA 90038 www.skyerentals.com
(Camera Expendables, Layout Boards, Lighting Expendables &
Production Expendables)

Studio Depot/Mole-Richardson Co. (323) 851-0111
900 N. La Brea Ave. FAX (323) 851-7854
Hollywood, CA 90038 www.studiodepot.com

Superior Studio Specialties (323) 278-0100
(800) 354-3049
2239 S. Yates Ave. FAX (323) 278-0111
Commerce, CA 90040 www.superiorstudio.com

TCH/The Camera House (818) 997-3802
7351 Fulton Ave. FAX (818) 997-3885
North Hollywood, CA 91605 www.thecamerahouse.com

TM Motion Picture
Equipment Rentals, Inc. (818) 846-3100
101 E. Linden Ave. FAX (818) 846-3459
Burbank, CA 91502 www.tmequipmentrentals.com

Visions In Color, Inc. (818) 566-1114
2101 W. Burbank Blvd. FAX (818) 566-6817
Burbank, CA 91506
(Bulbs & Lighting Expendables)

Warner Bros. Studio Facilities -
Mill Store (818) 954-4444
4000 Warner Blvd., Bldg. 44 FAX (818) 954-5753
Burbank, CA 91522 www.wbmillstore.com

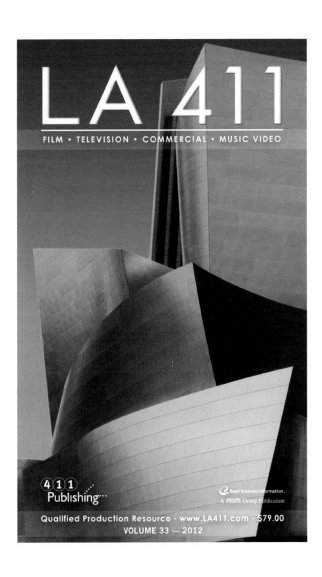

Acey Decy Lighting (818) 408-4444
200 Parkside Dr. FAX (818) 408-2777
San Fernando, CA 91340 www.aceydecy.com

Action Grip, LLC (818) 389-7618
33483 Domino Hill Rd. FAX (818) 450-0447
Agua Dulce, CA 91390 www.actiongripllc.com

Albuquerque Studios (505) 227-2000
5650 University Blvd. SE FAX (505) 227-2001
Albuquerque, NM 87106 www.abqstudios.com

Alliance Grip Trucks (213) 819-1777
2617 Corralitas Dr. FAX (323) 666-0828
Los Angeles, CA 90039 www.alliancegrip.com

American Grip (818) 768-8922
8468 Kewen Ave. FAX (818) 768-0564
Sun Valley, CA 91352 www.americangrip.com

Anytime Production
Equipment Rentals, Inc. (323) 461-8483
755 N. Lillian Way FAX (323) 461-2338
Hollywood, CA 90038 www.anytimerentals.com

(818) 968-1517
ATB Studios (818) 531-2918
157 W. Providencia Ave. FAX (818) 846-1007
Burbank, CA 91502 www.atb-studios.com

(323) 851-3825
Atomic Studios (202) 438-9199
2556 E. Olympic Ave. www.atomicstudios.com
Los Angeles, CA 90023

(818) 504-6026
Backstage Equipment, Inc. (800) 692-2787
8052 Lankershim Blvd. FAX (818) 504-6180
North Hollywood, CA 91605 www.backstageweb.com

(310) 532-3933
Beckman Rigging/BRS Rigging (661) 510-2518
13516 S. Mariposa Ave. FAX (310) 532-3993
Gardena, CA 90247 www.brsrigging.com

(310) 579-2277
Berkeley Avenue Productions (512) 296-7804
155 W. Washington Blvd., Ste. 650
Los Angeles, CA 90015 www.berkeleyavenue.com

Bill Ferrell Co. (818) 767-1900
10556 Keswick St. FAX (818) 767-2901
Sun Valley, CA 91352 www.billferrell.com

Birns & Sawyer, Inc. (323) 466-8211
5275 Craner Ave. FAX (818) 358-4395
North Hollywood, CA 91601 www.birnsandsawyer.com

(818) 846-7171
Borrmann Metal Center (800) 801-2677
110 W. Olive Ave. FAX (818) 846-9347
Burbank, CA 91502 www.borrmannmetalcenter.com

(818) 885-6474
Branam Enterprises (877) 295-3390
9152 Independence Ave. www.branament.com
Chatsworth, CA 91311

Bullet Grip, Inc. (818) 832-8707
FAX (818) 832-8807
www.bulletgrip.com

Cam Film Services (818) 957-6180
5201 Castle Rd.
La Cañada Flintridge, CA 91011

Castex Rentals (323) 462-1468
1044 Cole Ave. FAX (323) 462-3719
Hollywood, CA 90038 www.castexrentals.com

CBS Studio Center (818) 655-5711
4024 Radford Ave. FAX (818) 655-5443
Studio City, CA 91604 www.cbssc.com

(310) 287-3600
Century Studio Corporation (888) 878-2437
8660 Hayden Pl., Ste. 100 FAX (310) 287-3608
Culver City, CA 90232 www.centurystudio.com

Chapman/Leonard (818) 764-6726
Studio Equipment, Inc. (888) 883-6559
12950 Raymer St. FAX (888) 502-7263
North Hollywood, CA 91605 www.chapman-leonard.com

Cine Power & Light, Inc. (818) 846-0123
10845 Vanowen St., Ste. G www.cinepowerlight.com
North Hollywood, CA 91605

Cinelease, Inc. (818) 841-8282
5375 W. San Fernando Rd. FAX (818) 954-9641
Los Angeles, CA 90039 www.cinelease.com

Cineworks, Inc. (818) 252-0001
8125 Lankershim Blvd. FAX (818) 252-0003
North Hollywood, CA 91605 www.cineworksinc.com

Concept Lighting, Inc. (818) 767-1122
11274 Goss St. FAX (818) 768-9900
Sun Valley, CA 91352 www.conceptlight.com

(323) 965-7676
Crosslight Grip & Lighting (310) 721-0356
5429 Washington Blvd. FAX (323) 965-7675
Los Angeles, CA 90016 www.crosslight.tv

The Culver Studios (310) 202-1234
9336 W. Washington Blvd. FAX (310) 202-3516
Culver City, CA 90232 www.theculverstudios.com

(661) 702-8971
Dan Reilly Grip Rentals (661) 803-3132
30956 N. Stone Creek Rd. FAX (661) 702-8972
Castaic, CA 91384

Digital Film Studios (818) 771-0019
11800 Sheldon St., Ste. C FAX (818) 351-1155
Sun Valley, CA 91352 www.digitalfilmstudios.com

(323) 465-7700
Division Camera (323) 571-9476
7022 W. Sunset Blvd. FAX (323) 297-2773
Hollywood, CA 90028 www.divisioncamera.com

Entertainment Lighting (818) 769-9800
Services (ELS) (800) 622-6628
11440 Sheldon St. FAX (818) 769-2100
Sun Valley, CA 91352 www.elslights.com

(818) 848-5801
First Call Grip Equipment (818) 381-3137
1317 N. San Fernando Blvd., Ste. 503 FAX (818) 848-5801
Burbank, CA 91504

(818) 383-6376
FM Grip & Lighting, Inc. (818) 897-9111
10312 Norris Ave., Ste. D FAX (818) 897-9113
Pacoima, CA 91331 www.fmgnl.com

(310) 369-4747
Fox Studios (310) 369-4636
Grip Department, 10201 W. Pico Blvd. FAX (310) 969-1456
Los Angeles, CA 90035 www.foxstudiosgrip.com

Geronimo Creek Film Company (323) 529-3638
FAX (323) 417-4915
www.geronimocreek.com

Greg Mustin Rentals (805) 559-7612
FAX (805) 374-6060

Grip Brothers, Inc. (661) 259-5602	**The Lot** (323) 850-2832
25538 Via Ventana FAX (661) 259-5053	(310) 901-7352
Valencia, CA 91381	1041 N. Formosa Ave. FAX (323) 850-2909
	West Hollywood, CA 90046 www.thelotstudios.com

Grip Brothers, Inc.   (661) 259-5602
25538 Via Ventana   FAX (661) 259-5053
Valencia, CA 91381

The Lot   (323) 850-2832 / (310) 901-7352
1041 N. Formosa Ave.   FAX (323) 850-2909
West Hollywood, CA 90046   www.thelotstudios.com

The Grip Company   (818) 421-6695 / (818) 474-7261
595 Fresh Meadows Rd.   FAX (818) 886-5039
Simi Valley, CA 93065   www.thegripco.com

Matthews Studio Equipment   (818) 843-6715 / (800) 237-8263
2405 Empire Ave.   FAX (323) 849-1525
Burbank, CA 91504   www.msegrip.com

Grip Jet   (818) 424-4747 / (800) 474-7538
Box 47, 12653 Osborne St.   www.gripjet.com
Pacoima, CA 91331

McNulty Nielsen, Inc.   (310) 704-1713
6930 1/2 Tujunga Ave.   FAX (323) 372-3768
North Hollywood, CA 91605   www.mcnultynielsen.com

HALA Lighting & Grip   (818) 883-4771 / (818) 288-6004
23919 Newhall Rd., Ste. X   FAX (818) 883-4871
Santa Clarita, CA 91321   www.halastudios.com

Mobile Movie Studio   (818) 429-4085 / (806) 773-4243
FAX (818) 845-3485
www.mobilemoviestudio.com

Hollywood Rentals/ESS/Olesen   (818) 407-7800
12800 Foothill Blvd.   FAX (818) 407-7875
Sylmar, CA 91342   www.hollywoodrentals.com

Modern Studio Equipment, Inc.   (818) 764-8574
7414 Bellaire Ave.   FAX (818) 764-2958
North Hollywood, CA 91605   www.modernstudio.com

Icarus Rigging   (323) 660-4112
3531 Casitas Ave.   FAX (323) 660-6135
Los Angeles, CA 90039   www.icarusrigging.com

Monster Lighting   (818) 261-5108 / (310) 614-5385
5117 Strohm Ave.   FAX (818) 301-2008
North Hollywood, CA 91601   www.monsterlighting.com

Imagecraft Productions   (818) 954-0187
3318 Burton Ave.   FAX (818) 954-0189
Burbank, CA 91504   www.imagecraft.tv

MPR Photographic Rentals   (310) 762-1360
South Bay Studios   FAX (310) 639-2055
20434 S. Santa Fe Ave.   www.southbaystudios.com
Long Beach, CA 90810

Industrial Metal Supply Co.   (818) 729-3333 / (800) 339-6033
8300 San Fernando Rd.   FAX (818) 729-3334
Sun Valley, CA 91352   www.industrialmetalsupply.com

Occidental Studios, Inc.   (213) 384-3331
201 N. Occidental Blvd.   FAX (213) 384-2684
Los Angeles, CA 90026   www.occidentalstudios.com

J.L. Fisher, Inc.   (818) 846-8366
1000 W. Isabel St.   FAX (818) 846-8699
Burbank, CA 91506   www.jlfisher.com

Out of Frame Production Rentals   (323) 462-1898
1124 N. Citrus Ave.   FAX (323) 462-1897
Hollywood, CA 90038   www.outofframela.com

Jack Rubin & Sons, Inc.   (818) 562-5100
520 S. Varney St.   FAX (818) 562-5101
Burbank, CA 91502   www.wirerope.net

Pacific LightSmith, LLC   (310) 261-4751 / (310) 677-8458
P.O. Box 9189   FAX (310) 677-8458
Marina del Rey, CA 90295   www.pacificlightsmithllc.com

Kevin Coon Grip Truck Rental   (661) 645-7168
16969 Forrest St.
Canyon Country, CA 91351

Paladin Group, Inc.   (323) 874-7758 / (323) 851-8222
7351 Santa Monica Blvd.   FAX (323) 851-7328
Los Angeles, CA 90046

LA Grip & Electric   (910) 616-3801 / (417) 718-3906
10989 Bluffside Dr., Ste. 3312   www.lagrip.com
Studio City, CA 91604

Ⓐ The Studios at Paramount   (323) 956-5114
The Studios at Paramount Grip Services
5555 Melrose Ave.   www.thestudiosatparamount.com
Los Angeles, CA 90038

LA Grip & Lighting   (818) 703-5956
23469 Justice St.   FAX (818) 703-5956
West Hills, CA 91304

Pasadena Camera Rental, Inc.   (626) 796-3300
41 E. Walnut St.   FAX (626) 432-6731
Pasadena, CA 91103   www.samyscamera.com

lapinegrip Co.   (818) 765-6335 / (310) 365-9534
13105 Saticoy St.   FAX (818) 919-3155
North Hollywood, CA 91605   www.lapinegrip.com

Paskal Lighting   (818) 896-5233
12685 Van Nuys Blvd.   FAX (818) 485-0157
Pacoima, CA 91331   www.paskal.com

Leonetti Company   (818) 890-6000
10601 Glenoaks Blvd.   FAX (818) 890-6116
Pacoima, CA 91331   www.leonetticompany.com

Pollution Studios   (323) 380-8033
3239 Union Pacific Ave.   www.pollutionstudios.com
Los Angeles, CA 90023

Lexus Lighting, Inc.   (818) 768-4508
11225 Dora St.   FAX (805) 641-3273
Sun Valley, CA 91352   www.lexuslighting.com

Premier Lighting & Production Co.   (818) 762-0884 / (800) 770-0884
12023 Victory Blvd.   FAX (818) 762-0896
North Hollywood, CA 91606   www.premier-lighting.com

Lightshapes   (818) 753-4883 / (818) 516-4606
4547 Biloxi Ave.   FAX (818) 753-0181
Toluca Lake, CA 91602   www.light-shapes.com

PRG   (818) 252-2600
9111 Sunland Blvd.   FAX (818) 252-2620
Sun Valley, CA 91352   www.prg.com

Line 204/Angstrom Lighting   (323) 960-0113
837 N. Cahuenga Blvd.   FAX (323) 960-0163
Hollywood, CA 90038   www.line204.com

Quixote Studios - Griffith Park   (323) 957-9933
4585 Electronics Pl.   FAX (323) 957-9944
Griffith Park, CA 90039   www.quixote.com

Los Angeles Rag House   (818) 276-1130
100 E. Santa Anita Ave.   FAX (818) 842-2150
Burbank, CA 91502   www.laraghouse.com

The Rag Place, Inc.   (818) 765-3338
13160 Raymer St.   FAX (818) 765-3860
North Hollywood, CA 91605   www.theragplace.com

Ragtime Rentals, Inc. (818) 837-7077	**Sony Pictures Studios** (310) 244-5827
11970 Borden Ave. FAX (818) 837-5096	10202 W. Washington Blvd. FAX (310) 244-1316
San Fernando, CA 91340 www.ragtimerentals.com	Culver City, CA 90232 www.sonypicturesstudios.com

Railroad Studios (818) 396-4985
1500 Railroad St. FAX (818) 396-4986
Glendale, CA 91204 www.railroadstudios.com

Raleigh Studios - Hollywood (323) 960-3456
5300 Melrose Ave. FAX (323) 960-4712
Hollywood, CA 90038 www.raleighstudios.com

Raleigh Studios - Manhattan Beach (323) 960-3456
1600 Rosecrans Ave. FAX (310) 727-2710
Manhattan Beach, CA 90266 www.raleighstudios.com

Raleigh Studios - Playa Vista (323) 960-3456
5600 S. Campus Center Dr. www.raleighstudios.com
Playa Vista, CA 90094

The Rosenthal Group (818) 252-1010
10625 Cohasset St. FAX (818) 252-1070
Sun Valley, CA 91352 www.therosenthalgroup.com

Sage Lighting & Grip (818) 384-5529
2219 W. Olive Ave., Ste. 335 FAX (818) 831-7788
Burbank, CA 91506 www.sagelightingusa.com

(323) 938-2420
Samy's Camera (800) 321-4726
431 S. Fairfax Ave. FAX (323) 937-2919
Los Angeles, CA 90036 www.samys.com

Samy's Camera (310) 450-4551
4411 Sepulveda Blvd. FAX (310) 450-8590
Culver City, CA 90230 www.samys.com

(818) 563-1000
Sequoia Illumination (888) 647-2777
2428 N. Ontario St. FAX (818) 563-1001
Burbank, CA 91504 www.sequoiaillumination.com

Skye Lighting (323) 462-5934
1016 Mansfield Ave. FAX (323) 462-5935
Hollywood, CA 90038 www.skyerentals.com

Smashbox Studios (323) 851-5030
1011 N. Fuller Ave. FAX (323) 851-5029
West Hollywood, CA 90046 www.smashboxstudios.com

Smashbox Studios (323) 851-5030
8549 Higuera St. FAX (323) 851-5029
Los Angeles, CA 90323 www.smashboxstudios.com

Stage 1901 (310) 919-0950
1901 S. Bundy Dr. www.stage1901.com
Los Angeles, CA 90025

Studio Depot/Mole-Richardson Co. (323) 851-0111
900 N. La Brea Ave. FAX (323) 851-7854
Hollywood, CA 90038 www.studiodepot.com

Sun Valley Cabinets (818) 767-2228
7554 Clybourn Ave. FAX (818) 767-4427
Sun Valley, CA 91352 www.sunvalleycabinets.com

(818) 402-2009
TDS Grip & Canvas, LLC (818) 876-0060
4838 Heaven Ave.
Woodland Hills, CA 91364

**TM Motion Picture
Equipment Rentals, Inc.** (818) 846-3100
101 E. Linden Ave. FAX (818) 846-3459
Burbank, CA 91502 www.tmequipmentrentals.com

United Rentals (562) 695-0748
3455 San Gabriel River Pkwy FAX (562) 615-2191
Pico Rivera, CA 90660 www.unitedrentals.com

(818) 777-1590
Universal Studios Grip Department (800) 892-1979
100 Universal City Plaza, Bldg. 4250-1
Universal City, CA 91608
www.filmmakersdestination.com

(818) 567-3000
🅐 **VER Sales, Inc.** (800) 229-0518
2509 N. Naomi St. FAX (818) 567-3018
Burbank, CA 91504 www.versales.com

**Warner Bros. Studio Facilities -
Grip Department** (818) 954-1590
4000 Warner Blvd. FAX (818) 954-4806
Burbank, CA 91522 www.wbgripdept.com

Wooden Nickel Lighting Inc. (818) 761-9662
6920 Tujunga Ave. FAX (818) 985-0717
North Hollywood, CA 91605
www.woodennickellighting.com

Workhorse Productions, Inc. (323) 791-7757
6368 Santa Monica Blvd. FAX (323) 395-5647
Los Angeles, CA 90038 www.workhorseproductions.us

A-Line Crane Rental Services, Inc.
(714) 261-3536
(800) 524-7972
18032-C Lemon Dr., Ste. 212   FAX (714) 744-5802
Yorba Linda, CA 92886   www.alinecranes.com

B & G Industrial Rentals
(310) 327-0804
(800) 536-3019
1627 W. 130th St.   FAX (310) 327-9174
Gardena, CA 90249   www.bgrentalsinc.com
(Air Winches, Chain Hoists, Forklifts & Scaffolding)

Beckman Rigging/BRS Rigging
(310) 532-3933
(661) 510-2518
13516 S. Mariposa Ave.   FAX (310) 532-3993
Gardena, CA 90247   www.brsrigging.com
(Chain Hoists & Truss Systems)

California Crane Rental
(562) 244-1547
(800) 772-7263
8509 Chetle Ave.   FAX (562) 907-4495
Santa Fe Springs, CA 90670
www.californiacraneandrigging.com
(Cranes, Man Baskets, Non-Reflective Flat Black Booms &
Offset Jibs)

Champion Crane Rental, Inc.
(818) 781-3497
(323) 875-1248
12521 Branford St.   FAX (818) 896-6202
Pacoima, CA 91331   www.championcrane.us
(Truck Cranes)

Contractors Crane Service
(818) 785-5758
(818) 898-1019
7023 Valjean Ave.   FAX (818) 785-6952
Van Nuys, CA 91406   www.contractorscrane.com

Entertainment Lighting
(818) 769-9800
Services (ELS)
(800) 622-6628
11440 Sheldon St.   FAX (818) 769-2100
Sun Valley, CA 91352   www.elslights.com
(Chain Hoists, Light Bars, Rigging & Truss Systems)

Gold Coast Crane Service
(805) 230-1114
(818) 414-1980
FAX (805) 578-6020
(Box Spreader Bars, Camera Baskets, Light Bars,
Man Baskets & Rain Bars)

Hertz Entertainment Services
(818) 840-8247
(818) 391-4104
3111 N. Kenwood St.   FAX (818) 847-0941
Burbank, CA 91505   www.hertzentertainment.com
(Booms, Camera Baskets, Forklifts, Man Baskets, Non-
Reflective Booms, Offset Jibs, Rigging & Scissorlifts)

Kish Rigging, Inc.
(805) 532-1300
5400 Commerce Ave.   FAX (805) 532-1332
Moorpark, CA 93021   www.kishrigging.com
(Chain Hoists & Truss Systems)

L.A. Propoint, Inc.
(818) 767-6800
10870 La Tuna Canyon   FAX (818) 767-3900
Sun Valley, CA 91352   www.lapropoint.com
(Box Spreader Bars, Chain Hoists, Light Bars, Rigging &
Truss Systems)

Mike Brown Grandstands, Inc.
(800) 266-2659
(Scaffolding)   FAX (626) 303-5115
www.mbgs.com

ShowRig
(310) 538-4175
15823 S. Main St.   FAX (310) 538-4180
Los Angeles, CA 90248   www.sgps.net
(Chain Hoists & Truss Systems)

Skjonberg Controls, Inc.
(805) 650-0877
1363 Donlon St., Ste. 6   FAX (805) 650-0360
Ventura, CA 93003   www.skjonberg.com

Studio City Rentals
(818) 543-0300
100 E. Cedar Ave.   FAX (818) 955-9683
Burbank, CA 91502   www.studiocityrental.com

United Rentals
(818) 340-5881
7755 Canoga Ave.   FAX (818) 340-0035
Canoga Park, CA 91304   www.unitedrentals.com

United Rentals
(562) 695-0748
3455 San Gabriel River Pkwy   FAX (562) 615-2191
Pico Rivera, CA 90660   www.unitedrentals.com
(Booms, Forklifts, Scaffolding & Scissorlifts)

United Rentals
(818) 842-5288
203 W. Olive Ave.   FAX (818) 842-9970
Burbank, CA 91502   www.unitedrentals.com
(Booms, Forklifts, Scaffolding & Scissorlifts)

United Rentals
(805) 644-7319
3665 Market St.   FAX (805) 644-2409
Ventura, CA 93003   www.unitedrentals.com

United Rentals
(858) 565-7122
5580 Kearny Villa   FAX (858) 565-6279
San Diego, CA 92123   www.unitedrentals.com

United Rentals
(661) 948-2654
43631 Sierra Hwy   FAX (661) 951-0685
Lancaster, CA 93543   www.unitedrentals.com

Van Nuys Scaffold
(818) 988-9750
(800) 773-7328
17960 Tulson St.   FAX (661) 252-7873
Granada Hills, CA 91344

4Wall Entertainment (818) 252-7481
5375 W. San Fernando Rd. FAX **(818) 252-7642**
Los Angeles, CA 90039 **www.4wall.com**
(24-Hour Service, Blacklight, Bulbs, Chimeras, DMX
Programmable Automated Lighting, HMIs, Soft Box Lighting,
Strobe Lighting, Studio Lighting, Theatrical Expendables,
Theatrical Lighting & Xenon Lighting)

A & M Production Services (818) 562-9678
816 N. Victory Blvd. (818) 404-3777
Burbank, CA 91502 FAX **(818) 562-9674**
(Lighting) **www.amlighting.com**

Ace Rentals Inc (818) 255-5995
11950 Sherman Rd. FAX **(818) 255-5355**
North Hollywood, CA 91605 **www.acegenerators.com**
(24-Hour Service, Fueling Service, Generators &
Small Generators)

Acey Decy Lighting (818) 408-4444
200 Parkside Dr. FAX **(818) 408-2777**
San Fernando, CA 91340 **www.aceydecy.com**

Adept Lighting (805) 701-2344
3505 N. Quarzo Circle FAX **(805) 523-8660**
Thousand Oaks, CA 91362 **www.adeptlighting.com**
(24-Hour Service, Fluorescent Lighting & Generators)

Aerolight, Inc. Balloon Lighting (818) 606-4240
(866) 785-2376
11328 Goss St. FAX **(818) 698-0371**
Sun Valley, CA 91352 **www.aerolightballoons.com**
(24-Hour Service, HMIs, Lighting Balloons & Tube Balloons)

Aggreko Event Services (818) 767-7288
(888) 918-4874
11180 Penrose St. FAX **(818) 767-7782**
Sun Valley, CA 91352 **www.aggreko.com**
(Generators)

Airstar Space Lighting (818) 753-0066
(800) 217-9001
15206 Keswick St. FAX **(818) 753-0067**
Van Nuys, CA 91405 **www.airstar-light.us**
(Tungsten/HMI Lighting Balloons)

Albuquerque Studios (505) 227-2000
5650 University Blvd. SE FAX **(505) 227-2001**
Albuquerque, NM 87106 **www.abqstudios.com**

Alliant Event Services, Inc. (909) 622-3306
(800) 851-5415
196 University Pkwy FAX **(909) 622-3917**
Pomona, CA 91768 **www.alliantevents.com**

American Mobile Power Co. (818) 845-5474
3300 W. Burbank Blvd.
Burbank, CA 91505
(Generators)

Ample Power (877) 224-9030
3840 Brittany Ln. FAX **(818) 276-8421**
La Crescenta, CA 91214
www.amplepowergenerators.com

ArcLight Efx, Inc. (818) 394-6330
9338 San Fernando Rd. FAX **(818) 252-3486**
Sun Valley, CA 91352 **www.arclightefx.com**
(Lighting)

ASAP Generators (818) 968-9227
(24-Hour Service; Generators) FAX **(818) 487-0300**
www.asapgenerators.com

Astro Audio Video Lighting, Inc. (818) 549-9915
(800) 427-8768
6615 San Fernando Rd. FAX **(818) 549-0681**
Glendale, CA 91201 **www.astroavl.com**
(24-Hour Service, Blacklight, Small Generators, Strobe
Lighting & Theatrical Lighting)

At Power, LLC (877) 576-1099
(818) 424-1396
5722 Telephone Rd., Ste. C12-104 FAX **(877) 576-1099**
Ventura, CA 93003 **www.atpower.biz**
(24-Hour Service, Fueling Service, Generators, Light Towers,
Small Generators & Transformers)

Atomic Studios (323) 851-3825
(202) 438-9199
2556 E. Olympic Ave. **www.atomicstudios.com**
Los Angeles, CA 90023

Available Light/JT Services (760) 505-1605
(800) 439-1605
5251 Dixon Rd. **www.jtservices.com**
Oceanside, CA 92056
(24-Hour Service, Chimeras, Fluorescent Lighting, Green
Screen & HMIs)

BEBEE Generators (310) 605-5001
2301 E. Gladwick St. FAX **(310) 605-5002**
Rancho Dominguez, CA 90220

Bender ET, Inc. (800) 382-2953
4555 W. Chermak FAX **(818) 565-3552**
Burbank, CA 91505 **www.bender.org**
(Electrical Safety Equipment/GFCI)

Berkeley Avenue Productions (310) 579-2277
(512) 296-7804
155 W. Washington Blvd., Ste. 650
Los Angeles, CA 90015 **www.berkeleyavenue.com**

Birns & Sawyer, Inc. (323) 466-8211
5275 Craner Ave. FAX **(818) 358-4395**
North Hollywood, CA 91601 **www.birnsandsawyer.com**

BST Power, LLC (818) 253-7349
(310) 753-2043
FAX **(310) 246-2332**
www.bstpwr.com
(24-Hour Service, Electric Cable Packages, Fueling Service,
Generators, Light Towers, Line Frequency Meters, Small
Generators, Transformers & Truck Mounted Generators)

Burbank Kawasaki (818) 848-6627
1329 N. Hollywood Way FAX **(818) 848-6630**
Burbank, CA 91505 **www.burbankkawasaki.com**
(Small Generators)

Cam Film Services (818) 957-6180
5201 Castle Rd.
La Cañada Flintridge, CA 91011
(Lighting)

Castex Rentals (323) 462-1468
1044 Cole Ave. FAX **(323) 462-3719**
Hollywood, CA 90038 **www.castexrentals.com**
(Generators, HMIs & Kino Flos)

CBS Studio Center (818) 655-5231
4024 Radford Ave. FAX **(818) 655-8331**
Studio City, CA 91604 **www.cbssc.com**

Century Studio Corporation (310) 287-3600
(888) 878-2437
8660 Hayden Pl., Ste. 100 FAX **(310) 287-3608**
Culver City, CA 90232 **www.centurystudio.com**
(Lighting)

Checkers Industrial Products, LLC (800) 438-9336
(Cable Protectors & Cable Ramps) FAX **(720) 890-4858**
www.cableprotector.com

Cine Power & Light, Inc. (818) 846-0123
10845 Vanowen St., Ste. G **www.cinepowerlight.com**
North Hollywood, CA 91605

Cinelease, Inc. (818) 841-8282
5375 W. San Fernando Rd. FAX **(818) 954-9641**
Los Angeles, CA 90039 **www.cinelease.com**

Cinematography Electronics, Inc.   **(818) 706-3334**
5321 Derry Ave., Ste. G   FAX **(818) 706-3335**
Agoura Hills, CA 91301
     www.cinematographyelectronics.com
(Line Frequency Meters)

       (818) 843-4560
Cinemills Corporation   **(877) 262-4647**
2021 Lincoln St.   FAX **(818) 843-7834**
Burbank, CA 91504   **www.cinemills.com**
(Lighting)

Cinerep/Amps   **(818) 882-2677**
20420 Corisco St.   FAX **(818) 882-2447**
Chatsworth, CA 91311   **www.cinerepamps.com**
(Generators & Small Generators)

Cineworks, Inc.   **(818) 252-0001**
8125 Lankershim Blvd.   FAX **(818) 252-0003**
North Hollywood, CA 91605   **www.cineworksinc.com**
(Lighting)

       (888) 502-8639
City Lights Motion Picture Lighting   **(213) 952-8243**

Concept Lighting, Inc.   **(818) 767-1122**
11274 Goss St.   FAX **(818) 768-9900**
Sun Valley, CA 91352   **www.conceptlight.com**

Copy That Lighting   **(818) 522-1620**
25852 McBean Pkwy., Ste. 535   FAX **(818) 812-9183**
Santa Clarita, CA 91355
(Blue and Green Screen & Fluorescent Lighting)

The Culver Studios   **(310) 202-1234**
9336 W. Washington Blvd.   FAX **(310) 202-3516**
Culver City, CA 90232   **www.theculverstudios.com**
(Lighting)

D-Zyn Elements   **(818) 332-0819**
7324 Reseda Blvd., Ste. 254   FAX **(818) 332-1479**
Reseda, CA 91335   **www.d-zyns.com**
(Lighting Design, Strobe Lighting & Theatrical Lighting)

       (818) 768-8886
DADCO   **(818) 982-9764**
11273 Goss St.   FAX **(818) 765-0914**
Sun Valley, CA 91352   **www.dadcopowerandlights.com**
(24-Hour Service, Generators & Small Generators)

       (310) 836-4860
Davis Fluorescent Lighting   **(800) 300-2852**
8530 Venice Blvd.   FAX **(310) 836-0289**
Los Angeles, CA 90034
(Lighting)

Delicate Productions, Inc.   **(805) 388-1800**
874 Verdulera St.   FAX **(805) 388-1037**
Camarillo, CA 93010   **www.delicate.com**

Digital Film Studios   **(818) 771-0019**
11800 Sheldon St., Ste. C   FAX **(818) 351-1155**
Sun Valley, CA 91352   **www.digitalfilmstudios.com**

Direct Lighting, Inc.   **(818) 908-1937**
7842 Burnet Ave.   FAX **(818) 908-3312**
Van Nuys, CA 91405   **www.directlighting.net**
(Lighting)

       (323) 465-7700
Division Camera   **(323) 571-9476**
7022 W. Sunset Blvd.   FAX **(323) 297-2773**
Hollywood, CA 90028   **www.divisioncamera.com**
(Fluorescent Lighting, Lighting, Small Generators &
Soft Box Lighting)

Entertainment Lighting   **(818) 769-9800**
Services (ELS)   **(800) 622-6628**
11440 Sheldon St.   FAX **(818) 769-2100**
Sun Valley, CA 91352   **www.elslights.com**
(Blacklight, Bulbs, Electrical Safety Equipment, Fiber Optics,
Fluorescent Lighting, HMIs, LED Lighting, Light Towers, Soft
Box Lighting, Strobe Lighting, Theatrical Lighting &
Xenon Lighting)

Feldman Production Services   **(818) 790-7069**
4648 El Camino Corto   **www.combotruck.com**
La Cañada Flintridge, CA 91011
(Chimeras, Dimmers, Fluorescent Lighting, Fours, Green
Screen, HMIs, Kino Flo, Lighting & Tungsten)

       (310) 456-9464
Finnlight   **(310) 968-1986**
     www.finnlight.com
(Lighting, Lighting Equipment & Softbox Lighting)

       (818) 752-2626
Fisher Light   **(800) 888-0187**
16555 Gault St.   FAX **(818) 345-3111**
Van Nuys, CA 91406   **www.fisherlight.com**
(Balloon Lights)

       (818) 383-6376
FM Grip & Lighting, Inc.   **(818) 897-9111**
10312 Norris Ave., Ste. D   FAX **(818) 897-9113**
Pacoima, CA 91331   **www.fmgrip.com**
(Lighting)

       (310) 369-1133
Fox Studios   **(310) 369-4636**
Set Lighting Department   FAX **(310) 969-8850**
10201 W. Pico Blvd.   **www.foxstudiossetlighting.com**
Los Angeles, CA 90035

Geronimo Creek Film Company   **(323) 997-0202**
P.O. Box 6006   FAX **(323) 417-4915**
Burbank, CA 91510   **www.geronimocreek.com**
(Lighting)

Goodwin Production and   **(805) 499-7040**
Design Services   **(818) 414-6699**
(5-Ton Grip and Lighting Truck & Crews) FAX **(805) 499-7078**
     www.goodwinfilmlighting.biz

Henderson Lighting   **(858) 775-0040**

Hero Productions   **(323) 257-0454**
P.O. Box 91725   FAX **(323) 256-8969**
Los Angeles, CA 90041   **www.heroproductions.net**
(24-Hour Service, Blacklight, Blue Screen, Chimeras, Dedo
Lighting, Fiber Optics, Fluorescent Lighting, Generators, Green
Screen, HMIs, Light Towers, Lithium Ion Battery Belts, Small
Generators, Soft Box Lighting, Strobe Lighting &
Theatrical Lighting)

Hollywood Center Studios   **(323) 860-0000**
1040 N. Las Palmas Ave.   FAX **(323) 860-8105**
Hollywood, CA 90038   **www.hollywoodcenter.com**
(Lighting)

Hollywood Rentals/ESS/Olesen   **(818) 407-7800**
12800 Foothill Blvd.   FAX **(818) 407-7875**
Sylmar, CA 91342   **www.hollywoodrentals.com**
(Blue Screen, Bulbs, Chimeras, Fluorescent Lighting,
Generators, Green Screen, HMIs, Lighting, Lithium Ion Battery
Belts, Small Generators & Theatrical Lighting)

HydroFlex Underwater Camera & Lighting
Systems   **(310) 301-8187**
301 E. El Segundo Blvd.   FAX **(310) 821-9886**
El Segundo, CA 90245   **www.hydroflex.com**
(Fluorescent, HMI & Incandescent Underwater
Lighting Systems)

       (818) 686-6400
Illumination Dynamics   **(866) 544-4843**
13571 Vaughn St.   FAX **(818) 686-6776**
San Fernando, CA 91340
     www.illuminationdynamics.com

Innovision Optics   **(310) 453-4866**
1719 21st St.   FAX **(310) 453-4677**
Santa Monica, CA 90404   **www.innovisionoptics.com**
(Dedo Lighting & Fiber Optics)

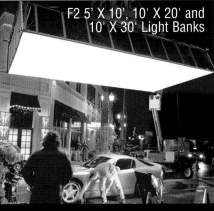
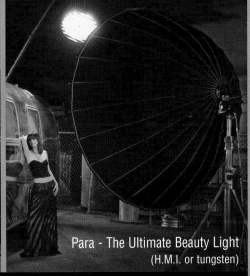

JCR Lighting (310) 376-4223 (310) 993-5768
125 34th St.
Hermosa Beach, CA 90254
(Lighting)

Kinetic Lighting (310) 837-3204 (800) 908-3842
722 Thompson Ave. FAX (310) 837-8695
Glendale, CA 91201 www.kineticlighting.com
(Blacklight, Bulbs & Theatrical Lighting)

Kino Flo, Inc. (818) 767-6528
2840 N. Hollywood Way FAX (818) 767-7517
Burbank, CA 91505 www.kinoflo.com
(Lighting)

Kohler Rental (310) 518-5118 (310) 600-3063
766 Gifford Ave. FAX (920) 459-1846
San Bernardino, CA 92408 www.kohlerrental.com
(Generators)

LA City Biodiesel (818) 701-6845
9009 Independence Ave. FAX (818) 701-6808
Canoga Park, CA 91304 www.lacitybiodiesel.com
(Biodiesel)

LA Grip & Electric (910) 616-3801 (417) 718-3906
10989 Bluffside Dr., Ste. 3312 www.lagrip.com
Studio City, CA 91604

Leonetti Company (818) 890-6000
10601 Glenoaks Blvd. FAX (818) 890-6116
Pacoima, CA 91331 www.leonetticompany.com
(24-Hour Service, Blue Screen, Bulbs, Chimeras, Fluorescent Lighting, Green Screen, HMIs & Lighting Balloons)

Lex Products Corp. (818) 768-4474
11847 Sheldon St. FAX (818) 768-4040
Sun Valley, CA 91352 www.lexproducts.com
(Cables, Dimming and Control Systems, Electrical Safety Equipment, Electrical Switches and Panels & Power Distribution Systems)

Lexus Lighting, Inc./ Xenons by Lexus (818) 768-4508
11225 Dora St. FAX (805) 641-3273
Sun Valley, CA 91352 www.lexuslighting.com
(Dimmable Fluorescent Lighting Systems, HMIs, T8 and T12 Fluorescent Lamps & Xenon Lighting)

Libertypak (805) 640-6700 (323) 304-4404
407 Bryant Circle, Bldg. E www.libertypak.com
Ojai, CA 93023
(AC Packs, Custom Packs, High Intensity Battery Belts & Lithium Ion Battery Belts)

Light It! LLC (866) 871-2102
FAX (866) 871-2152
(Bulbs, Chimeras, Dedo Lighting, Electrical Safety Equipment, Fluorescent Lighting, HMIs, Lithium Ion Battery Belts, Small Generators & Soft Box Lighting)

Lights/Camera/Action, Inc. (323) 525-1976
217 S. Lorraine Blvd. FAX (323) 525-1905
Los Angeles, CA 90004
(Lighting)

Line 204/Angstrom Lighting (323) 960-0113
837 N. Cahuenga Blvd. FAX (323) 960-0163
Hollywood, CA 90038 www.line204.com
(Theatrical Lighting)

Litepanels, Inc. (818) 782-5100
7322 Valjean Ave. FAX (818) 782-5102
Van Nuys, CA 91406 www.litepanels.com
(Lighting)

Litewerks of California (818) 767-2233
11271 Ventura Blvd., Ste. 700 FAX (818) 767-2234
Studio City, CA 91604 www.litewerks.net
(Generators & Theatrical Lighting)

The Lot (323) 850-3180 (323) 850-2832
1041 N. Formosa Ave. www.thelotstudios.com
West Hollywood, CA 90046
(Lighting)

LumaPanel/T8 Technology Co. (877) 586-2726
www.lumapanel.com

McNulty Nielsen, Inc. (310) 704-1713
6930 ½ Tujunga Ave. FAX (323) 372-3768
North Hollywood, CA 91601 www.mcnultynielsen.com
(24-Hour Service, Blue Screen, Bulbs, Chimeras, Fluorescent
Lighting, Green Screen, HMIs, Line Frequency Meters, Small
Generators, Soft Box Lighting & Theatrical Lighting)

(619) 417-4943
Mobile Lighting, Inc. (760) 431-7198
6912 Goldfinch Pl.
Carlsbad, CA 92011
(Lighting)

(818) 261-5108
Monster Lighting (310) 614-5385
5117 Strohm Ave. FAX (818) 301-2008
North Hollywood, CA 91601 www.monsterlighting.com
(Briese Lighting, Fluorescents, Generators, HMIs, Small
Generators & Soft Box Lighting)

(641) 673-0411
Musco Lighting (800) 825-6020
15320 Valencia Ave. FAX (888) 397-8736
Fontana, CA 92335 www.musco.com

Ⓐ **New Mexico Lighting & Grip Co.** (505) 227-2500
FAX (505) 227-2510
www.nmlgc.com

Ⓐ **Night Lights by Bebee, Ltd.** (310) 605-5001
2301 E. Gladwick St. FAX (310) 605-5002
Rancho Dominguez, CA 90220
www.nightlightsbybebee.com
(24-Hour Service, Generators, HMIs, Lighting & Lighting
Crane Trucks)

Occidental Studios, Inc. (213) 384-3331
201 N. Occidental Blvd. FAX (213) 384-2684
Los Angeles, CA 90026 www.occidentalstudios.com
(Lighting)

(818) 368-8143
On the Spot Lighting Rentals, Inc. (818) 414-2367
FAX (818) 368-8143
www.onthespotlightingandpower.com

Out of Frame Production Rentals (323) 462-1898
1124 N. Citrus Ave. FAX (323) 462-1897
Hollywood, CA 90038 www.outofframela.com
(Blue Screen, Generators, Green Screen & Small Generators)

Pace Technologies (818) 565-0005
2020 N. Lincoln St. FAX (818) 561-3950
Burbank, CA 91504 www.pacehd.com
(HMI and Incandescent Underwater Lighting Systems)

(310) 261-4751
Pacific LightSmith, LLC (310) 677-8458
P.O. Box 9189 FAX (310) 677-8458
Marina del Rey, CA 90295 www.pacificlightsmithllc.com

(323) 874-7758
Paladin Group, Inc. (323) 851-8222
7351 Santa Monica Blvd. FAX (323) 851-7328
Los Angeles, CA 90046

Ⓐ **The Studios at Paramount**
Set Lighting (323) 956-5391
5555 Melrose Ave. www.thestudiosatparamount.com
Hollywood, CA 90038
(Lighting)

Pasadena Camera Rental, Inc. (626) 796-3300
41 E. Walnut St. FAX (626) 432-6731
Pasadena, CA 91103 www.samyscamera.com

Paskal Lighting (818) 896-5233
12685 Van Nuys Blvd. FAX (818) 485-0157
Pacoima, CA 91331 www.paskal.com

Photo-Sonics, Inc. (818) 842-2141
820 S. Mariposa St. FAX (818) 842-2610
Burbank, CA 91506 www.photosonics.com
(High Intensity Soft Box Lighting)

Portable Power, Inc. (818) 365-3366
628 Celis St. FAX (818) 365-3399
San Fernando, CA 91340 www.portablepowerinc.com
(Generators)

(310) 667-4433
Power Trip Rentals (310) 292-0974
2950 E. Harcourt St. FAX (310) 604-3233
Rancho Dominguez, CA 90221
www.powertriprentals.net
(24-Hour Service, Fueling Service, Generators, Light Towers &
Small Generators)

(818) 762-0884
Premier Lighting & Production Co. (800) 770-0884
12023 Victory Blvd. FAX (818) 762-0896
North Hollywood, CA 91606 www.premier-lighting.com

PRG (818) 252-2600
9111 Sunland Blvd. FAX (818) 252-2620
Sun Valley, CA 91352 www.prg.com
(HMIs, Lighting Balloons & Theatrical Lighting)

Prima Equipment Co. (818) 984-2024
5275 Craner Ave.
North Hollywood, CA 91615
(Fluorescent Lighting, Repairs & Soft Box Lighting)

Production Equipment Services, Inc.(818) 779-2114
15021 Keswick St. FAX (818) 779-2119
Van Nuys, CA 91405 www.pe-services.net
(Generator Repairs)

(562) 463-6040
Quinn Power Systems (562) 463-6000
3500 Shepherd St. FAX (562) 463-7156
City of Industry, CA 90601 www.quinnpower.com
(Generators)

Quixote Studios (323) 461-1408
1000 N. Cahuenga Blvd. FAX (323) 461-5517
Los Angeles, CA 90038 www.quixote.com

Quixote Studios - Griffith Park (323) 957-9933
4585 Electronics Pl. FAX (323) 957-9944
Griffith Park, CA 90039 www.quixote.com

Railroad Studios (818) 396-4985
1500 Railroad St. FAX (818) 396-4986
Glendale, CA 91204 www.railroadstudios.com
(24-Hour Service, Blue Screen, Bulbs, Generators, Green
Screen, HMIs, Small Generators, Soft Box Lighting &
Strobe Lighting)

(805) 525-3306
Rain For Rent (805) 331-0175
333 S. 12th St. FAX (805) 525-7663
Santa Paula, CA 93061 www.rainforrent.com
(Generators)

Raleigh Studios - Hollywood (323) 960-3456
5300 Melrose Ave. FAX (323) 960-4712
Hollywood, CA 90038 www.raleighstudios.com
(Lighting)

Raleigh Studios - Manhattan Beach (323) 960-3456
1600 Rosecrans Ave. FAX (310) 727-2710
Manhattan Beach, CA 90266 www.raleighstudios.com

Raleigh Studios - Playa Vista (323) 960-3456
5600 S. Campus Center Dr. www.raleighstudios.com
Playa Vista, CA 90094

Ⓐ **The Rosenthal Group** (818) 252-1010
10625 Cohasset St. FAX (818) 252-1070
Sun Valley, CA 91352 www.therosenthalgroup.com
(Chimeras, Dedo Lighting, Fiber Optics, Green Screen, HMIs,
Lithium Ion Battery Belts, Small Generators & Soft Box Lighting)

Sage Lighting & Grip	(818) 384-5529
2219 W. Olive Ave., Ste. 335	FAX **(818) 831-7788**
Burbank, CA 91506	**www.sagelightingusa.com**

	(323) 938-2420
Samy's Camera	**(800) 321-4726**
431 S. Fairfax Ave.	FAX **(323) 937-2919**
Los Angeles, CA 90036	**www.samys.com**

Samy's Camera	(310) 450-4551
4411 Sepulveda Blvd.	FAX **(310) 450-8590**
Culver City, CA 90230	**www.samys.com**

	(818) 563-1000
Sequoia Illumination	**(888) 647-2777**
2428 N. Ontario St.	FAX **(818) 563-1001**
Burbank, CA 91504	**www.sequoiaillumination.com**

SGPS, Inc.	(310) 538-4175
15823 S. Main St.	FAX **(310) 538-4180**
Los Angeles, CA 90248	**www.sgps.net**
(Lighting)	

Sky Productions	(818) 442-1527
	www.skyproduction.net
(24-Hour Service, Blacklight, Dedo Lighting, Electrical Safety Equipment, Fluorescent Lighting, Generators, Light Towers, Lighting Balloons & Theatrical Lighting)	

Skylight Balloon Lighting	(866) 765-4448
	www.skylightballoon.com

Smashbox Studios	(323) 851-5030
1011 N. Fuller Ave.	FAX **(323) 851-5029**
West Hollywood, CA 90046	**www.smashboxstudios.com**

Smashbox Studios	(323) 851-5030
8549 Higuera St.	FAX **(323) 851-5029**
Los Angeles, CA 90323	**www.smashboxstudios.com**

Sony Pictures Studios	(310) 244-5810
10202 W. Washington Blvd.	FAX **(310) 244-2365**
Culver City, CA 90232	**www.sonypicturesstudios.com**
(Lighting)	

Source Lighting & Grip Rentals, Inc.	(323) 463-5555
1111 N. Beachwood Dr.	**www.sourcefilmstudio.com**
Los Angeles, CA 90038	
(Blue Screen, Chimeras, Dedo Lighting, Fluorescent Lighting, Generators, Green Screen, HMIs, Incandescent Underwater Lighting Systems, Line Frequency Meters & Small Generators)	

	(800) 930-3944
Sourcemaker Balloon Lighting	**(818) 565-3550**
(Lighting Balloons)	**www.lightingballoons.com**

Stage 1901	(310) 919-0950
1901 S. Bundy Dr.	**www.stage1901.com**
Los Angeles, CA 90025	
(Lighting)	

Stage Tech	(562) 407-1133
14523 Marquardt Ave.	FAX **(562) 407-1306**
Santa Fe Springs, CA 90630	**www.stage-tech.com**
(Lighting)	

Star Power Generators	(818) 982-2200
7416 Varna Ave., Ste. F	FAX **(818) 982-2229**
North Hollywood, CA 91605	
	www.starpowergenerators.com
(24-Hour Service & Generators)	

Studio Air Conditioning, Inc.	(818) 222-4143
5171 N. Douglas Fir Rd., Ste. 6	FAX **(818) 222-2092**
Calabasas, CA 91302	**www.studioair.com**
(24 Hour Service & Generators)	

Studio Depot/Mole-Richardson Co.	(323) 851-0111
900 N. La Brea Ave.	FAX **(323) 851-7854**
Hollywood, CA 90038	**www.studiodepot.com**

Sun Lighting Services, Inc.	(818) 898-1550
11970 Borden Ave.	FAX **(818) 898-1552**
San Fernando, CA 91340	**www.sunlightingservices.net**

Sunbelt Rentals	(818) 996-7100
18251 Napa St.	FAX **(818) 701-9113**
Northridge, CA 91325	**www.sunbeltrentals.com**

Sunbelt Rentals	(714) 994-6360
1170 N. Main St.	FAX **(714) 994-7512**
Orange, CA 92867	**www.sunbeltrentals.com**

Team Imagination, Inc.	(310) 541-7790
916 Silver Spur Rd., Ste. 110	FAX **(310) 541-8797**
Rolling Hills Estates, CA 90274	
(Lighting)	**www.teamimagination.com**

TM Motion Picture	
Equipment Rentals, Inc.	(818) 846-3100
101 E. Linden Ave.	FAX **(818) 846-3439**
Burbank, CA 91502	**www.tmequipmentrentals.com**

Towards 2000, Inc.	(818) 557-0903
215 W. Palm Ave., Ste. 101	FAX **(866) 836-5725**
Burbank, CA 91502	**www.t2k.com**
(Lighting)	

	(818) 389-9565
Unilux/Blue Feather Lighting	**(800) 635-2743**
19630 Lanark St.	FAX **(818) 701-5404**
Reseda, CA 91335	**www.unilux.com**
(Strobe Lighting)	

United Rentals	(818) 842-5288
203 W. Olive Ave.	FAX **(818) 842-9970**
Burbank, CA 91502	**www.unitedrentals.com**
(Generators with Light Towers)	

Universal Studios	(818) 777-1590
Set Lighting Department	(800) 892-1979
100 Universal City Plaza, Bldg. 4250-1	
Universal City, CA 91608	
	www.filmmakersdestination.com
(Bulbs, Electrical Safety Equipment, Fluorescent Lighting, Generators, HMIs, Lighting Balloons, Strobe Lighting & Theatrical Lighting)	

Visual Terrain, Inc.	(661) 775-7758
25217 Avenue Tibbitts	FAX **(661) 775-7708**
Santa Clarita, CA 91355	**www.visualterrain.net**
(Lighting)	

Warner Bros. Studio Facilities -	(818) 954-1874
Set Lighting	(818) 954-2322
4000 Warner Blvd.	FAX **(818) 954-4806**
Burbank, CA 91522	**www.wbsetlighting.com**
(Lighting)	

	(949) 588-7822
Waywest Lighting & Camera, Inc.	(714) 381-0100
22432 Lombardi	FAX **(949) 588-7922**
Laguna Hills, CA 92653	**www.waywest.tv**
(Lighting)	

Wooden Nickel Lighting Inc.	(818) 761-9662
6920 Tujunga Ave.	FAX **(818) 985-0717**
North Hollywood, CA 91605	
(Lighting)	**www.woodennickellighting.com**

Workhorse Productions, Inc.	(323) 791-7757
6368 Santa Monica Blvd.	FAX **(323) 395-5647**
Los Angeles, CA 90038	**www.workhorseproductions.us**
(Chimeras, Generators, HMIs, Small Generators, Soft Box Lighting & Strobe Lighting)	

	(818) 841-6400
Zilla Lighting For Film (Tomzilla)	(800) 424-7477
157 W. Providencia Ave.	FAX **(818) 841-9948**
Burbank, CA 91502	**www.zillalighting.com**

A & S Case Company
(818) 509-5920
(800) 394-6181
FAX (818) 509-1397
5260 Vineland Ave.
North Hollywood, CA 91601   www.ascase.com
(Camera and Equipment Cases)

Absolute Rentals
(818) 842-2828
FAX (818) 842-8815
2633 N. San Fernando Blvd.
Burbank, CA 91504   www.absoluterentals.com
(Camera and Equipment Cases & Camera Expendables)

Accelerated Rentals and Location Services Corp.
(661) 251-3135
FAX (661) 251-3125
www.acceleratedrentals.com

ACME Production Rentals
(310) 817-9617
3615 Keystone Ave., Ste. 5
Los Angeles, CA 90034
(Walkies)

Alliant Event Services, Inc.
(909) 622-3306
(800) 851-5415
FAX (909) 622-3917
196 University Pkwy
Pomona, CA 91768   www.alliantevents.com

Antelope Valley Locations and Production Services
(661) 946-1515
FAX (661) 946-0454
42848 150th St. East
Lancaster, CA 93535   www.avlocations.com

Anvil Cases/Calzone Case Co.
(626) 968-4100
(800) 359-2684
FAX (626) 968-1703
15730 Salt Lake Ave.
City of Industry, CA 91745   www.anvilcases.com

Anytime Production Equipment Rentals, Inc.
(323) 461-8483
FAX (323) 461-2338
755 N. Lillian Way
Hollywood, CA 90038   www.anytime-rentals.com
(AC Units, Canopies, Dumpsters, Expendables, Heaters, MistFans, Stanchions, Stunt Pads, Trailers & Walkies)

Apache Rental Group
(818) 842-9944
(818) 842-9875
FAX (818) 842-9269
3910 W. Magnolia Blvd.
Burbank, CA 91505   www.apacherentalgroup.com
(Canopies, Chairs, Coolers, Heaters & Tables)

Atomic Production Supplies
(818) 566-8811
FAX (818) 566-8311
2621 N. Ontario St.
Burbank, CA 91504 www.atomicproductionsupplies.com
(Canopies, Chairs, Coolers & Tables)

Backstage Equipment, Inc.
(818) 504-6026
(800) 692-2787
FAX (818) 504-6180
8052 Lankershim Blvd.
North Hollywood, CA 91605   www.backstageweb.com
(Camera, Magliner, Remote Head, Sound & Video Carts)

BST Power, LLC
(818) 253-7349
(310) 753-2043
FAX (310) 246-2332
(Golf Cars)
www.bstpwr.com

Camera Essentials
(626) 844-3722
FAX (323) 686-5230
91 N. Daisy Ave.
Pasadena, CA 91107   www.cameraessentials.com
(Camera and Equipment Raincovers, Ditty Bags & Film Changing Tents)

Cases by Masco
(800) 772-1960
41187 Sandalwood Circle   www.casesbymasco.com
Murrieta, CA 92565
(Camera and Equipment Cases)

Castex Rentals
(323) 462-1468
FAX (323) 462-3719
1044 Cole Ave.
Hollywood, CA 90038   www.castexrentals.com
(Canopies, Directors Chairs, Tables, Traffic Safety Equipment & Wardrobe Racks)

Checkers Industrial Products, LLC   (800) 438-9336
FAX (720) 890-4858
www.cableprotector.com

Choura Event Rentals
(310) 320-6200
FAX (310) 781-8227
www.choura.us
(Canopies, Chairs, Coolers, Heaters, Helium Tanks, Portable Stages, Stanchions, Tables, Tents & Wardrobe Racks)

CineBags
(818) 662-0605
(Bags & Pouches)
FAX (818) 662-0613
www.cinebags.com

Cineworks, Inc.
(818) 252-0001
FAX (818) 252-0003
8125 Lankershim Blvd.
North Hollywood, CA 91605   www.cineworksinc.com

Clean Strike Rental & Cleaning
(562) 803-3701
(562) 879-2207
FAX (562) 803-3702
12214 Lakewood Blvd., Bldg. 9
Downey, CA 90242   www.cleanstrikerentals.com
(Dumpsters & Portable Restrooms)

DeWayne Events
(661) 251-4342
FAX (661) 251-2488
16520 Diver St.
Canyon Country, CA 91387
(Canopies & Tents)

Dortons, Inc.
(951) 685-6014
(323) 751-3486
(Tents)

Earl Hays Press
(818) 765-0700
FAX (818) 765-5245
10707 Sherman Way
Sun Valley, CA 91352   www.theearlhayspress.com

Environmental Noise Control/ Behrens & Associates
(800) 679-8633
(310) 679-8623
FAX (310) 331-1538
13806 Inglewood Ave.
Hawthorne, CA 90250
www.environmental-noise-control.com
(Acoustical Blankets & Panels)

Golf Cars - LA, Inc.
(661) 251-2201
16439 Sierra Hwy   www.golfcars-la.com
Canyon Country, CA 91351

Golf Cars and Industrial Vehicles, Inc.
(818) 349-4102
FAX (818) 349-4112
9550 Owensmouth Ave.
Chatsworth, CA 91311   www.yamaha-golf-carts.com
(Golf Cars)

Heavy Artillery Production Rentals   (310) 295-1202
FAX (310) 295-1202
3200 S. La Cienega Blvd.
Los Angeles, CA 90016 www.heavyartilleryrentals.com
(Bullhorns, Chairs, Cones, Coolers, Director Chairs, Heaters, Misters, Mobile Services, Tables, Tents, Traffic Safety Equipment, Walkies & Wardrobe Racks)

Hollywood Tentworks
(877) 883-3131
(818) 890-0214
FAX (877) 883-3132
10244 Norris Ave.
Pacoima, CA 91331   www.tentworks.com
(A/C, Canopies, Chairs, Heaters, Portable Stages, Tables & Tents)

Innerspace Cases
(818) 767-3030
(800) 806-7689
FAX (818) 767-6118
11555 Cantara St., Ste. I
North Hollywood, CA 91605 www.innerspacecases.com

International E-Z UP, Inc.
(951) 781-0843
(800) 457-4233
FAX (951) 781-0586
1601 Iowa Ave.
Riverside, CA 92507   www.ezup.com
(Tents)

ITC Barricades, Inc. (714) 892-5858 / (661) 816-6270
P.O. Box 858 FAX (714) 892-5887
Westminster, CA 92684 **mysite.verizon.net/itcbarricades/**
(Traffic Safety Equipment)

JCL Barricade Company (213) 622-9775
2334 E. Eighth St. FAX (213) 622-9790
Los Angeles, CA 90021 **www.jclbarricade.com**
(Barricades & Posting Signs)

Kayam Theatre and Concert Tent Company (213) 484-5010
17141 Covello St. **www.kayam.co.uk**
Lake Balboa, CA 91406
(Tents)

LARedCarpets.com (910) 431-9004
(Red Carpets, Ropes & Stanchions) **www.laredcarpets.com**

Lex Products Corp. (818) 768-4474
11847 Sheldon St. FAX (818) 768-4040
Sun Valley, CA 91352 **www.lexproducts.com**
(Audio, Data and Power Cables, Dimming and Control Systems, Electrical Switches and Panels & Power Distribution Systems)

Line 204 Inc. (323) 960-0113
837 N. Cahuenga Blvd. FAX (323) 960-0163
Hollywood, CA 90038 **www.line204.com**
(Canopies, Chairs, Coolers & Tables)

Melmat, Inc. (714) 379-4555 / (800) 635-6289
5333 Industrial Dr. FAX (714) 379-4554
Huntington Beach, CA 92649 **www.melmat.com**

Mike Brown Grandstands, Inc. (800) 266-2659
FAX (626) 303-5115
www.mbgs.com
(Bleachers, Crowd Control Barricades, Disabled Persons Lifts and Ramps, Grandstands, Portable Stages, Stanchions & Turnstiles)

Out of Frame Production Rentals (323) 462-1898
1124 N. Citrus Ave. FAX (323) 462-1897
Hollywood, CA 90038 **www.outofframela.com**
(Barricades, Bullhorns, Camera Expendables, Canopies, Chairs, Cones, Coolers, Crowd Control Equipment, Directors Chairs, Heaters, Misters, Stanchions, Street Closures, Tables, Tents, Traffic Control, Traffic Safety Equipment, Walkies & Wardrobe Racks)

Pacific Production Services, Inc. (323) 260-4777 / (213) 360-7844
1481 E. Fourth St. FAX (323) 415-6180
Los Angeles, CA 90033 **www.lafilmpermits.com**
(Safety and Traffic Equipment)

Panavision Panastore (818) 316-1000
Corporate Headquarters FAX (818) 316-1111
6219 DeSoto Ave. **www.panavision.com**
Woodland Hills, CA 91367
(Accessories & Camera Expendables)

Power Trip Rentals (310) 667-4433 / (310) 292-0974
2950 E. Harcourt St. FAX (310) 604-3233
Rancho Dominguez, CA 90221
www.powertriprentals.net

Print Technology (310) 273-9450 / (877) 613-9450
8899 Beverly Blvd., Ste. 803 FAX (310) 273-8450
Los Angeles, CA 90048 **www.print-technology.com**
(Business Forms & Stationery Systems)

The Production Truck, Inc. (818) 459-0425
711 Ruberta Ave. FAX (818) 459-0427
Glendale, CA 91201 **www.theproductiontruck.com**
(Chairs, Coolers, Directors Chairs, Heaters, Tents & Wardrobe Racks)

Quixote Studios (323) 461-1408
1000 N. Cahuenga Blvd. FAX (323) 461-5517
Los Angeles, CA 90038 **www.quixote.com**
(Canopies, Chairs, Coolers, Misters & Tables)

RC Production Rentals (626) 483-7679
13105 Saticoy St. FAX (310) 943-0480
North Hollywood, CA 91605
www.rcproductionrentals.com
(Bags, Barricades, Bullhorns, Camera Carts, Camera Expendables, Canopies, Chairs, Cones, Coolers, Directors Chairs, Heaters, Street Closures, Tables, Tents, Traffic Control, Traffic Safety Equipment, Walkies & Wardrobe Racks)

Rock Bottom Rentals (310) 315-2600 / (800) 794-5444
1310 Westwood Blvd. FAX (310) 582-1178
Los Angeles, CA 90024 **www.rockbottomrentals.com**
(Cell Phones, Junxion Box, Mifi Data Card, Satellite Phones, USB Data Cards, Walkies & Wirelss Fax Machines)

Set Stuff, Inc. (323) 993-9500
1105 N. Sycamore Ave. FAX (323) 993-9506
Hollywood, CA 90038 **www.setstuffrentals.com**
(Air Conditioners, Canopies, Coolers, Directors Chairs, Heaters, Tables, Tents & Traffic Safety Equipment)

SirReel - LA & San Diego (888) 477-7335 / (818) 859-7766
FAX (888) 477-7313
www.sirreel.us

Skye Rentals (323) 462-5934
1016 Mansfield Ave. FAX (323) 462-5935
Hollywood, CA 90038 **www.skyerentals.com**
(Barricades, Bullhorns, Camera Carts, Camera Cases, Camera Expendables, Canopies, Chairs, Cones, Coolers, Directors Chairs, Equipment Cases, Heaters, Misters, Tables, Tents, Traffic Control, Traffic Safety Equipment, Walkies & Wardrobe Racks)

Sun Aired Bag Company (310) 372-7225 / (424) 269-1649
3645 Inglewood Ave., Ste. 3 FAX (310) 372-5825
Redondo Beach, CA 90278 **www.sunaired.com**
(Mesh Clothing Bags)

T.Z. Case (909) 392-8806 / (888) 892-2737
1786 Curtiss Court FAX (909) 392-8406
La Verne, CA 91750 **www.tzcase.com**
(Camera and Equipment Cases)

Tent Kings of Los Angeles (818) 720-5126 / (310) 880-5128
3238 N. San Fernando Blvd. FAX (818) 557-8320
Burbank, CA 91504 **www.tentkings.com**

Traffic Management, Inc. (800) 763-3999
2435 Lemon Ave. FAX (562) 424-0266
Signal Hill, CA 90755 **www.trafficmanagement.com**
(Barricades, Cones, Crowd Control Equipment, Street Closures, Traffic Control, Traffic Plans & Traffic Safety Equipment)

Workhorse Productions, Inc. (323) 791-7757
6368 Santa Monica Blvd. FAX (323) 395-5647
Los Angeles, CA 90038 **www.workhorseproductions.us**
(Camera Expendables, Canopies, Chairs, Cones, Coolers, Crowd Control Equipment, Directors Chairs, Film Changing Tents, Heaters, Tables, Tents, Traffic Control, Traffic Safety Equipment, Walkies & Wardrobe Racks)

A Wynning Event (310) 481-9300 / (310) 729-2590
433 N. Camden Dr., Ste. 400 FAX (310) 571-0976
Beverly Hills, CA 90210 **www.awynningevent.com**
(Chairs, Heaters, Tables & Tents)

Xpendable Rentals (323) 656-0905
5925 Santa Monica Blvd. FAX (323) 375-1711
Hollywood, CA 90038 **www.xpendablerentals.com**
(Barricades, Bullhorns, Camera Carts, Canopies, Chairs, Cones, Coolers, Directors Chairs, Heaters, Helium Tanks, Misters, Road Signs, Tables, Tents, Traffic Safety Equipment, Walkies & Wardrobe Racks)

**Accelerated Rentals and
Location Services Corp.** (661) 251-3135
(Gators & Utility Vehicles) FAX (661) 251-3125
www.acceleratedrentals.com

Affordable West, Inc. (323) 467-7182
1040 N. La Brea Ave. FAX (323) 467-6520
Hollywood, CA 90038

 (323) 850-0826
Avon Studio Transportation (800) 432-2866
7080 Santa Monica Blvd. FAX (323) 467-4239
Los Angeles, CA 90038 www.avonrents.com

 (310) 274-6969
Beverly Hills Rent-A-Car (855) 818-6969
9732 S. Santa Monica Blvd. FAX (310) 550-1700
Beverly Hills, CA 90210 www.bhrentacar.com

 (818) 253-7349
BST Power, LLC (310) 753-2043
 FAX (310) 246-2332
 www.bstpwr.com
(Camera Vans, Crew Cabs, Flatbeds, Liftgate Trucks, Lighting
Vans, Office Trailers, Refuelers, Single Genrator Vans, Sound/
Video Trailers, Stake Beds, Stake Beds with Generator,
Tractors, Trailers, Twin Generator Vans & Utility Vehicles)

Budget Truck Rental (213) 749-9104
 www.budgettruck.com

California Rent-A-Car (310) 477-2727
1033 N. Fuller Ave. FAX (310) 477-9176
Los Angeles, CA 90046 www.productioncarrental.com
(Pickups)

California Truck Rental (562) 699-3434
2555 Pellissier Pl. FAX (562) 699-3493
Whittier, CA 90601
(Camera Vans, High Cubes, Liftgate Trucks, Stake Beds &
Tractors)

cameratruck.com (818) 540-6189
 www.digitalimagingtechnician.com

Cine Power & Light, Inc. (818) 846-0123
10845 Vanowen St., Ste. G www.cinepowerlight.com
North Hollywood, CA 91605

Fox Studios (310) 369-2533
Transportation, 10201 W. Pico Blvd. FAX (310) 369-4078
Los Angeles, CA 90035
 www.foxstudiostransportation.com

 (323) 957-3333
Galpin Studio Rentals (800) 256-6219
1763 N. Ivar Ave. FAX (323) 856-6790
Hollywood, CA 90028 www.galpinstudiorentals.com
(3 Ton, 4 Ton, 4 Wheel Drive, 5 Ton, Camera Vans, Cargo Vans,
Crew Cabs, Flatbeds, High Cubes, Liftgate Trucks, Pickups,
Picture Vehicles, Production Cubes, Refuelers, Stake Beds &
Wardrobe Cubes)

 (323) 857-0111
Galpin Studio Rentals (800) 256-6219
3200 La Cienega Blvd. FAX (323) 964-6234
Los Angeles, CA 90016 www.galpinstudiorentals.com
(3 Tons, 4 Tons, 4 Wheel Drive Trucks/SUVs, 5 Tons, Camera
Cubes, Cargo Vans, Crew Cabs, Flatbeds, High Cubes, Liftgate
Trucks, Pickups, Picture Cars, Picture Vehicles, Production
Cubes, Refuelers, Stake Beds & Wardrobe Cubes)

Heavy Artillery Production Rentals (310) 295-1202
3200 S. La Cienega Blvd. FAX (310) 295-1202
Los Angeles, CA 90016 www.heavyartilleryrentals.com
(Production Cubes)

 (818) 762-9282
Hertz Equipment Rental Corporation (888) 777-2700
5556 Vineland Ave. FAX (818) 762-9440
North Hollywood, CA 91601 www.hertzequip.com

Hollywood Rentals/ESS/Olesen (818) 407-7800
12800 Foothill Blvd. FAX (818) 407-7875
Sylmar, CA 91342 www.hollywoodrentals.com
(Production Vans with Twin Generators)

Jeffrey Markowitz Productions/ (323) 461-8887
Grip Truck LA (877) 297-8887
760 N. Cahuenga Blvd. FAX (323) 784-7040
Hollywood, CA 90038 www.griptruckla.com

Lexus Lighting, Inc. (818) 768-4508
11225 Dora St. FAX (805) 641-3273
Sun Valley, CA 91352 www.lexuslighting.com
(Camera and Lighting Trucks)

 (888) 878-2531
N Motion Studio Rentals (818) 837-4595
13101 Foothill Blvd. FAX (818) 837-4590
Sylmar, CA 91342 www.unitedtruckcenters.com

**Ⓐ The Studios at Paramount
Transportation** (323) 956-5151
5555 Melrose Ave. www.thestudiosatparamount.com
Los Angeles, CA 90038

 (213) 628-1255
Penske Truck Leasing Co. (800) 222-0277
2300 E. Olympic Blvd. FAX (213) 891-1686
Los Angeles, CA 90021
 www.olympiclosangelestruckrental.com

Quixote Studios (323) 960-9070
1000 N. Cahuenga Blvd. FAX (323) 467-1318
Los Angeles, CA 90038 www.quixote.com

Ⓐ Ryder Studio Rentals (818) 566-1208
6901 San Fernando Rd. FAX (818) 566-1858
Glendale, CA 91201 www.ryder.com

Ryder Studio Rentals (213) 748-8601
1508 S. Alameda St. FAX (213) 744-0551
Los Angeles, CA 90021 www.ryder.com

Ryder Studio Rentals (818) 701-9332
19133 Parthenia St. FAX (818) 701-6551
Northridge, CA 91324 www.ryder.com

 (818) 563-1000
 (888) 647-2777
Sequoia Illumination FAX (818) 563-1001
2428 N. Ontario St.
Burbank, CA 91504 www.sequoiaillumination.com

Skye Rentals (323) 462-5934
1016 Mansfield Ave. FAX (323) 462-5935
Hollywood, CA 90038 www.skyerentals.com
(Production Cubes & Stake Beds)

Sony Pictures Studios (310) 244-7016
10202 W. Washington Blvd. FAX (310) 244-7995
Culver City, CA 90232 www.sonypicturesstudios.com
(Cargo Vans, Cars, Cranes, Forklifts, Golf Cart Rental, Storage
Containers, Trailers, Transportation & Trucks)

 (818) 554-5062
Specialty Car Locators (661) 451-2100
(Crew Cab Stakebeds) FAX (661) 554-7063
www.specialtycarlocators.com/equipmentforrent.htm

Studio Equipment Rentals, Inc. (661) 714-0858
45259 23rd St. FAX (661) 942-7125
Lancaster, CA 93536
(Utility Vehicles)

 (213) 273-3661
Super 8 Film Cameras & 2nd Unit (800) 470-4602
8630 Wilshire Blvd. www.justneeds2.com
Beverly Hills, CA 90211
(Camera and Lighting Van)

Suppose U Drive　　　　　　　**(818) 243-3151**
Truck Rental Service　　　　　**(800) 404-8800**
3809 San Fernando Rd.　　　FAX **(818) 243-7968**
Glendale, CA 91204　　　**www.supposeudrive.com**

TCH/The Camera House　　　　**(818) 997-3802**
7351 Fulton Ave.　　　　　　FAX **(818) 997-3885**
North Hollywood, CA 91605　**www.thecamerahouse.com**

　　　　　　　　　　　　　(800) 528-4285
U-Haul　　　　　　　　　　**(800) 468-4285**
　　　　　　　　　　　　　www.uhaul.com

Universal Studios Transportation　　**(818) 777-2966**
100 Universal City Plaza　　　FAX **(818) 866-1521**
Bldg. 8166, First Fl.　　**www.filmmakersdestination.com**
Universal City, CA 91608
(Cargo Vans, Crew Cabs, Flatbeds, High Cubes, Liftgate
Trucks, Pickups, Production Cubes, Stake Beds, Tractors,
Trailers, Twin Generator Vans & Utility Vehicles)

　　　　　　　　　　　　　(818) 822-7549
Video Village Van　　　　　　**(822) 822-7549**
10061 Riverside Dr., Ste. 566 **www.videovillagevan.com**
Toluca Lake, CA 91602

The Walt Disney Studios -
Transportation Department　　　**(818) 560-2254**
500 S. Buena Vista St.
Burbank, CA 91521

Warner Bros. Studio Facilities -
Transportation Department　　　**(818) 954-4106**
4000 Warner Blvd.　　　　　FAX **(818) 954-4471**
Burbank, CA 91522　　　**www.wbsftransportation.com**

　　　　　　　　　　　　　(760) 257-3734
Willie's On & Off Road Center　　**(760) 953-3303**
48301 National Trails Hwy　　FAX **(760) 257-3335**
Newberry Springs, CA 92365　**www.williesoffroad.com**
(Off-Road Vehicles)

Workhorse Productions, Inc.　　**(323) 791-7757**
6368 Santa Monica Blvd.　　FAX **(323) 395-5647**
Los Angeles, CA 90038　**www.workhorseproductions.us**
(Cargo Vans, High Cubes & Production Cubes)

NOTES:

LA 411

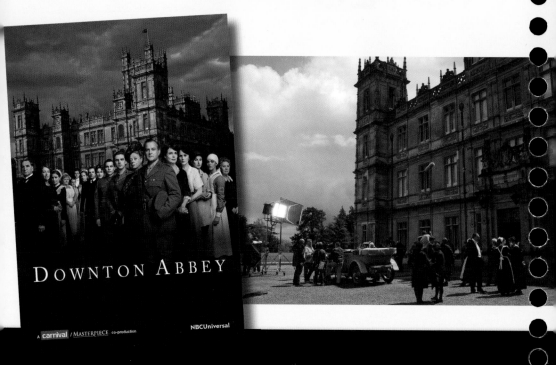

A carnival / MASTERPIECE co-production   NBCUniversal

DOWNTON ABBEY

BY MARJ GALAS

Composer John Lunn on "Downton Abbey"

Composer John Lunn didn't turn to the music of the early 1900s when scoring "Downton Abbey." He decided to focus on pop.

"The music of the 1920s wouldn't work with the storylines of 'Downton Abbey,'" said Lunn. "The harmony is simple, almost like pop music, but crunched into the 1920s opulence." Lunn has been composing TV music for over twenty years. While many of the series have been period pieces, he's mindful of being pigeonholed. Although "Downton Abbey" is set in the early 1900s, Lunn saw some exciting opportunities with the series.

"Most other period dramas are based on a book," said Lunn. "Downton is original, so things can change."

Lunn found inspiration from season one's opening sequence of a train to create the score. He saw a correlation between the mechanics of the train and the livelihood of the servants who are crucial to the ongoing saga of Downton. Lunn's application of this inspiration began with notes from a piano, then a grand, sweeping melody.

Typically, Lunn has six month's lead time with the overall story. This knowledge of the direction plot points will take allows him to develop themes for specific characters and situations. One example is the theme that accompanies Lady Mary and Matthew's screen time.

"You get the feeling they belong together. The same music, when she said goodbye when he went to war, worked for his proposal when used with a variation," said Lunn.

There are some themes that are maintained through a series, such as the music used for Lady Mary and Matthew, however not all music is appropriate to carry from season to season. Much of the music Lunn crafted for season two related to specific occasions and story threads such as the continuation of World War One, and these melodies were no longer relevant. As the third season begins the characters will be moving into the roaring twenties, and Lunn is contemplating introducing some jazz into the score. Until he determines its effect on the tone and the feel of the episodes, he won't commit to its use.

ABRIDGED FROM AN LA 411 NEWSLETTER ARTICLE PUBLISHED SEPTEMBER 2012

**Refer to the General Index for
cross-referencing items in this section.**

Aerial Film Unit by   (800) 345-6737
Corporate Helicopters   (858) 505-5650
3753 John J. Montgomery Dr., Ste. 2   FAX (858) 505-5658
San Diego, CA 92123   **www.corporatehelicopters.com**
(Helicopters)

    (818) 783-1145
Airborne Images, Inc.   (310) 748-2795
www.airborneimages.com
(Fixed-Wing Aircraft & Helicopters)

    (805) 402-0052
Airpower Aviation Resources   (805) 499-0307
FAX (805) 498-0357
www.airpower-aviation.com

    (310) 379-4448
Altitude Aviation   (310) 489-8938
200 Pier Ave., Ste. 128   FAX (310) 937-7112
Hermosa Beach, CA 90254   **www.altitudeaviation.com**

Angel City Air   (818) 896-9900
12653 Osborne St.   FAX (818) 686-1095
Pacoima, CA 91331   **www.aerialproduction.com**
(Fixed-Wing Aircraft & Helicopters)

    (951) 359-5016
ARIS Helicopters/Heli-Flite   (800) 340-1969
6871 Airport Dr.   FAX (951) 359-5019
Riverside, CA 92504   **www.arishelicopters.com**

Blackstar Helicopters Inc.   (661) 713-6671
10500 Airpark Way   FAX (877) 272-4764
Unit M2, Whiteman Airport
Pacoima, CA 91331   **www.blackstarhelicopters.com**

    (888) 463-7953
Camera Copters, Inc.   (305) 793-7033
23421 Balmoral Ln.   **www.cameracopters.com**
West Hills, CA 91307

Hangar 1 Productions   (323) 810-7560
1910 W. Sunset Blvd., Ste. 900 **www.hangar1project.com**
Los Angeles, CA 90026

Helifilms USA, Inc.   (310) 487-0065
1299 Ocean Ave., Ste. 333   FAX (310) 496-0405
Santa Monica, CA 90401   **www.helifilmsusa.com**
(Helicopters)

    (818) 902-0229
Helinet Aviation Services   (800) 221-8389
FAX (818) 902-9278
www.helinet.com

    (818) 781-4742
Jet Productions   (877) 895-1790
FAX (818) 781-4743
www.jetproductions.net

    (310) 458-9176
McKernan Motion Picture Aviation   (310) 993-4486
FAX (310) 496-0744
www.helicopterguy.com

Stearman Flight Center   (909) 597-8511
7000 Merrill Ave., Ste. 53   FAX (909) 597-8511
Chino, CA 91710   **www.silverwingswingwalking.com**
(Bi-Planes, Fixed-Wing Aircraft & Vintage)

Studio Wings, Inc.   (805) 320-9500
855 Aviation Dr.   FAX (805) 987-4720
Camarillo, CA 93010   **www.studiowings.com**
(Bi-Planes, Helicopters & Jets)

    (818) 367-2430
Stunt Wings/Adventure Sports   (818) 266-0874
12623 Gridley St.   FAX (818) 367-5363
San Fernando, CA 91342   **www.stuntwings.com**

Thornton Aircraft Company   (818) 787-0205
7520 Hayvenhurst Ave.   FAX (818) 787-9334
Van Nuys, CA 91406   **www.thorntonaircraft.com**
(Fixed-Wing Aircraft, Jets & Military)

Aardzark (818) 556-3500
707 S. Main St. FAX (818) 450-0777
Burbank, CA 91506
(Animatronics, Characters and Creatures,
Makeup FX & Puppets)

(818) 943-5264
Alex In Wonderland, Inc. (818) 943-5263
FAX (818) 558-4397
www.alexinwonderland.com

All Effects Company, Inc. (818) 298-3730
5440 Tujunga Ave., Ste. 1217 www.allfx.com
North Hollywood, CA 91601

**Almost Human Special
Make Up EFX** (310) 838-6993
3650 Eagle Rock Blvd. FAX (310) 838-6999
Los Angeles, CA 90065 www.almosthuman.net
(Makeup FX & Prosthetics)

Alterian, Inc. (626) 856-1499
P.O. Box 2166 FAX (626) 856-1495
Irwindale, CA 91706 www.alterianinc.com
(Animatronics, Articulated Dummies, Body Suits, Cadavers,
Castings, Characters, Creatures, Foam Sculpting, Hand
Puppets, Life-Like Replicas, Makeup FX, Marionettes, Masks,
Mechanical Puppets, Miniatures, Models, Molds, Oversized
Props, Prosthetics, Puppets, Radio-Controlled Puppets,
Remote-Controlled FX, Robotics, Sculpting, Special FX Props,
Statues & Vacuum-Forming)

Amalgamated Dynamics, Inc. (818) 882-8638
20100 Plummer St. FAX (818) 882-7327
Chatsworth, CA 91311 www.studioadi.com
(Animatronics, Creatures, Makeup FX & Puppets)

(818) 584-4115
American Makeup and FX (336) 264-2302
3827 Saticoy St. www.amefx.com
Van Nuys, CA 91402
(Articulated Urethane Dummies, Body Suits, Body Parts,
Cadavers, Castings, Character/Creature Body Suits,
Characters, Creatures, Custom Animal FX, Full Body Suits,
Hand Puppets, Life-Like Replicas, Makeup FX and Prosthetics,
Masks, Sculpting, Sculpture, Slip Rubber Masks, Special FX
Props & Statues)

**Anatomorphex/
The Sculpture Studio** (818) 768-2880
8210 Lankershim Blvd., Ste. 14 www.anatomorphex.com
North Hollywood, CA 91605
(Animatronics, Creatures, Makeup FX & Puppets)

Animal Makers, Inc. (805) 523-1900
11991 Discovery Court, Ste. 411 FAX (805) 523-1903
Moorpark, CA 93021 www.animalmakers.com/store
(Animatronics, Articulated Dummies, Body Suits, Characters,
Computer Enhanced Puppetry, Creatures, Foam Sculpting,
Life-Like Replicas, Masks, Mechanical Puppets, Models,
Prosthetics, Puppets, Radio-Controlled Puppets, Remote-
Controlled FX, Robotics, Sculpting & Special FX Props)

**Animated FX, Inc./
Dave Nelson & Norman Tempia** (818) 879-9440
FAX (818) 879-9441
www.animatedfx.net
(Animatronics, Characters, Marionettes, Mechanical Puppets,
Puppets & Radio-Controlled Puppets)

Arteffex/Dann O'Quinn (818) 506-5358
911 Mayo St. FAX (323) 255-4599
Los Angeles, CA 90042 www.acfxo.com
(Animatronics, Casting, Characters, Creatures, Foam Sculpting,
Hand Puppets, Makeup FX, Masks, Mechanical Puppets,
Miniatures, Models, Molds, Oversized Props, Prosthetics,
Puppets, Radio-Controlled Puppets, Remote-Controlled FX,
Robotics, Sculpting, Special FX Props & Statues)

Autonomous F/X, Inc. (818) 901-6005
6115 Tyrone Ave. FAX (818) 901-6089
Van Nuys, CA 91401 www.autonomousfx.com
(Animatronics, Articulated Dummies, Body Suits, Cadavers,
Creatures, Hand Puppets, Life-Like Replicas, Masks,
Miniatures, Oversized Props, Prosthetics, Puppets,
Radio-Controlled Puppets & Remote-Controlled FX)

Bellfx, LLC (818) 590-4992
1908 First St. www.bellfx.com
San Fernando, CA 91340
(Animatronics, Puppetry & Robotics)

Bischoff's Taxidermy & Animal EFX (818) 843-7561
54 E. Magnolia Blvd. FAX (818) 567-2443
Burbank, CA 91502 www.bischoffs.net
(Custom Animal EFX)

Bob Baker Marionettes (213) 250-9995
1345 W. First St. FAX (213) 250-1120
Los Angeles, CA 90026 www.bobbakermarionettes.com
(Puppet Makers)

The Character Shop (805) 306-9441
4735 Industrial St., Ste. 4-B FAX (805) 306-9444
Simi Valley, CA 93063 www.character-shop.com
(Aliens, Animals, Animatronics, Body Suits, Castings,
Characters and Creatures, Hand Puppets, Life-Like Replicas,
Makeup FX, Marionettes, Mechanical Puppets, Prosthetics,
Puppets, Radio-Controlled Puppets, Remote-Controlled
Articulation, Robotics & Special FX Props)

Chiodo Bros. Productions, Inc. (818) 842-5656
110 W. Providencia Ave. FAX (818) 848-0891
Burbank, CA 91502 www.chiodobros.com
(Prosthetics & Puppets)

Creative Character Engineering (818) 901-0507
16110 Hart St. FAX (818) 901-8417
Van Nuys, CA 91406 www.creativecharacter.com
(Animatronics, Creatures, Makeup FX, Prosthetics & Ultra-
Realistic Rental Babies)

(323) 319-6501
The Creature Company (661) 433-5283
www.creaturecompany.com
(3D Printing, 3D Scanning, Animatronics, Articulated Dummies,
Body Scanning, Body Suits, Cadavers, Castings, Characters,
Creatures, Foam Sculpting, Hand Puppets, Life-Like Replicas,
Makeup FX, Marionettes, Masks, Mechanical Puppets,
Miniatures, Models, Molds, Oversized Props, Prosthetics,
Puppets, Radio-Controlled Puppets, Remote-Controlled FX,
Robotics, Sculpting, Special FX Props, Statues &
Vacuum-Forming)

Creature Effects, Inc. (323) 850-3228
3325 Cahuenga Blvd. FAX (323) 850-3280
Los Angeles, CA 90068 www.creaturefxinc.com
(Animatronics, Body Suits, Creatures, Makeup FX, Prosthetics
Puppets & Special FX Props)

CWS (818) 568-5361
(Animatronics, Articulated Dummies, Body Suits, Cadavers,
Castings, Characters, Creatures, Hand Puppets, Life-Like
Replicas, Makeup FX, Masks, Mechanical Puppets, Molds,
Prosthetics, Puppets, Radio-Controlled Puppets, Robotics,
Sculpting, Special FX Props & Statues)

Douglas White Effects (818) 785-4148
6859 Valjean Ave., Ste. 5 www.dweffects.com
Van Nuys, CA 91406
(Makeup FX, Oversized Props, Radio-Controlled Puppets &
Sculpting)

**Dynamic Design International,
LLC/Darren Perks** (818) 439-8447
FAX (623) 386-6826
www.dynamicdesignintl.com

Festival Artists, Inc.
(626) 334-9388
(626) 303-6042
FAX (626) 969-8595
120 N. Aspan Ave.
Azusa, CA 91702
www.festivalartists.org
(Oversized Props & Welding)

Film Illusions, Inc.
(626) 974-5896
FAX (626) 974-5806
1735 S. Grand Ave.
Glendora, CA 91740
www.filmillusions.com
(Animatronics & Puppets)

Flix FX, Inc.
(818) 765-3549
(877) 326-8433
FAX (818) 765-0135
7327 Lankershim Blvd., Ste. 4
North Hollywood, CA 91605
www.flixfx.com
(Animatronics & Puppets)

**Gary J. Tunnicliffe's
Two Hours in the Dark, Inc.**
(818) 837-1045
12473 Gladstone Ave., Ste. Q
Sylmar, CA 91342
www.twohoursinthedark.net

Global Effects, Inc.
(818) 503-9273
FAX (818) 503-9459
7115 Laurel Canyon Blvd.
North Hollywood, CA 91605
www.globaleffects.com
(Body Suits, Characters, Creature Suits, Makeup FX, Masks,
Oversized Props, Robotics, Special FX Props, Statues,
Vacuum-Forming & Welding)

Ric Heitzman
(323) 308-8013
(Puppetry)
www.richeitzman.com

Hello Boss Effects
(818) 317-1190
www.helloboss.net
(Body Suits, Characters, Creatures, Human Replicas, Life-Like
Replicas, Mechanical Puppets, Prosthetics, Special Effects
Makeup & Special Makeup)

Image Creators
(310) 710-7128
www.creators2000.com
(Animal Puppets, Animatronics, Body Suits, Creatures,
Marionettes, Mechanical Puppets, Prosthetics, Puppets,
Remote-Controlled FX & Robotics)

Imagivations
(818) 767-6767
FAX (818) 767-3637
11314 Sheldon St.
Sun Valley, CA 91352
www.imagivations.com
(Foam Sculpting, Miniatures, Models &
Remote-Controlled Props)

**Independent Studio
Services, Inc./ISS**
(818) 951-5600
9545 Wentworth St.
www.issprops.com
Sunland, CA 91040

Jim Henson's Creature Shop
(323) 802-1525
(877) 677-5427
FAX (323) 802-1891
1416 N. La Brea Ave.
Los Angeles, CA 90028
www.creatureshop.com
(Animatronics & Puppets)

Kent Allen Jones
(310) 429-9422
(Sculpture)

KNB EFX Group, Inc.
(818) 901-6562
FAX (818) 576-9965
9300 Eton Ave.
Chatsworth, CA 91311
www.knbefxgroup.com

Scott Land
(310) 975-5865
FAX (626) 599-9993
839 E. Citrus Ave.
Redlands, CA 92374
www.thepuppetman.com
(Marionettes & Puppets)

Legacy Effects
(818) 782-0870
FAX (818) 792-4322
340 Parkside Dr.
San Fernando, CA 91340
www.legacyefx.com
(Animatronics, Casting, Characters and Creatures, Creature
Suits, Makeup FX, Mechanical Puppets, Molds, Remote-
Controlled FX and Robotics, Prosthetics & Puppets)

**Makeup & Effects
Laboratories, Inc./MEL**
(818) 982-1483
FAX (818) 982-5712
7110 Laurel Canyon Blvd., Bldg. E
North Hollywood, CA 91605
www.melefx.com
(Animatronics, Miniatures, Oversized and Soft Props, Radio-
Controlled Puppets & Vacuum-Forming)

The Mannequin Gallery
(818) 834-5555
FAX (818) 834-5558
12350 Montague St., Ste. E
Pacoima, CA 91331
www.mannequingallery.com
(Mannequins & Sculpting)

Marc's Creature Company Inc.
(818) 442-9283
(661) 645-6023
14732 Lull St.
www.marcscreaturecompany.com
Van Nuys, CA 91405
(Animal Suits, Animatronics, Characters, Creature Suits,
Creatures, Mechanical Puppets, Molds, Radio-Controlled
Puppets, Remote-Controlled FX, Robotics, Sculpting,
Special FX Props & Welding)

Masters FX, Inc./Todd Masters
(818) 834-3000
(604) 683-5311
FAX (818) 834-9755
www.mastersfx.com
(Animatronic Puppets, Articulated Urethane Dummies, Body
Suits, Castings, Characters, Computer Enhanced Puppetry,
Creatures, Life-Like Replicas, Makeup FX, Masks, Mechanical
Puppets, Molds, Prosthetics & Radio-Controlled Puppets)

Michael Burnett Productions, Inc.
(818) 768-6103
P.O. Box 16627
FAX (815) 550-1247
North Hollywood, CA 91615
www.mbpfx.com
(Animatronics, Creatures, Full Body Suits, Makeup FX,
Mechanical Puppets & Slip Rubber Masks)

Mike Tristano & Co.
(818) 522-0969
FAX (818) 888-6447
www.moviegunguy.com
(Body Parts, Cadavers, Makeup FX & Prosthetics)

Multivision FX
(818) 288-6839
(818) 288-6839
www.multivisionfx.com
(Animatronics, Articulated Dummies, Body Suits, Cadavers,
Castings, Characters, Computer Enhanced Puppetry,
Creatures, Creature Suits, Foam Sculpting, Hand Puppets,
Life-Like Replicas, Makeup FX, Marionettes, Masks,
Mechanical Puppets, Miniatures, Models, Molds, Oversized
Props, Prosthetics, Puppets, Radio-Controlled Puppets,
Remote-Controlled FX, Robotics, Sculpting, Special FX Props,
Statues, Vacuum-Forming & Welding)

NAC Co.
(805) 376-0206
(805) 405-7337
1772-J E. Avenida de Los Arboles
FAX (805) 376-8407
Thousand Oaks, CA 91362
www.naceffects.com
(Animatronics, Remote-Controlled FX, Robotics &
Special FX Props)

NBC New York Prosthetics Shop
(212) 664-4093
30 Rockefeller Plaza
www.filmmakersdestination.com
New York, NY 10112

Optic Nerve Studios, Inc.
(818) 771-1007
FAX (818) 771-1009
9818 Glenoaks Blvd.
Sun Valley, CA 91352
www.opticnervefx.com
(Animatronics, Characters and Creatures, Creature Suits, Full
Body Suits, Miniatures, Prosthetics & Special FX Makeup)

Pacific Vision Productions, Inc.
(626) 441-4869
210 Pasadena Ave.
www.pacificvision.com
South Pasadena, CA 91030
(Animatronics, Electronics & Rigging)

Christine Papalexis
(323) 665-8062
FAX (323) 665-1214
(Body Suits, Creatures, Foam Sculpting, Hand and Remote-
Controlled Puppets, Marionettes & Puppet Fabrication)

Pat Brymer Creations
(323) 259-0400
136 N. Avenue 61, Ste. 102
FAX (323) 259-0358
Los Angeles, CA 90042
www.pbcreations.com
(Foam Sculpting, Hand Puppets, Oversized Props, Puppets,
Radio-Controlled Puppets & Rigging)

Animatronics, Puppets & Makeup FX

Puppet Studio   **(818) 506-7374**
10903 Chandler Blvd.   FAX **(818) 506-7374**
North Hollywood, CA 91601   **www.puppetstudio.com**
(Computer Enhanced Puppetry, Hand Puppets, Marionettes &
Puppet FX)

                        (818) 846-6740
Quantum Creation FX, Inc.   **(818) 268-5128**
3210 W. Valhalla Dr.   FAX **(818) 846-0047**
Burbank, CA 91505   **www.quantumcreationfx.com**
(Animatronics, Articulated Dummies, Body Suits, Cadavers,
Castings, Characters, Creatures, Foam Sculpting, Hand
Puppets, Life-Like Replicas, Makeup FX, Marionettes, Masks,
Mechanical Puppets, Miniatures, Models, Molds, Oversized
Props, Prosthetics, Puppets, Radio-Controlled Puppets,
Remote-Controlled FX, Robotics, Sculpting, Special FX Props,
Statues, Vacuum-Forming & Welding)

                        (818) 209-8046
Ralis Special Makeup Effects   **(213) 622-3936**
3727 W. Magnolia Blvd., Ste. 407   **www.ralisfx.com**
Burbank, CA 91505
(Animatronics, Articulated Dummies, Body Suits, Cadavers,
Castings, Characters, Creatures, Foam Sculpting, Hand
Puppets, Life-Like Replicas, Makeup FX, Marionettes, Masks,
Mechanical Puppets, Miniatures, Models, Molds, Prosthetics,
Puppets, Radio-Controlled Puppets, Sculpting, Special FX
Props, Vacuum-Forming & Welding)

René and His Artists Productions   **(818) 848-6809**
707-A Main St.   FAX **(818) 848-3112**
Burbank, CA 91506
(Body Suits, Marionettes, Radio-Controlled Puppets &
Ventriloquist Figures)

                        (909) 923-5671
Rubens Display World   **(909) 923-5672**
1482 E. Francis St.   FAX **(909) 923-5670**
Ontario, CA 91761   **www.rubensdisplay.com**
(Mannequins)

Sheep's Clothing Productions   **(818) 812-6599**
                      FAX **(888) 780-5895**
     www.sheepsclothingproductions.com
(Animatronics, Articulated Dummies, Body Suits,
Cadavers, Castings, Characters, Computer Enhanced
Puppetry, Creatures, Foam Sculpting, Hand Puppets, Life-Like
Replicas, Makeup FX, Marionettes, Masks, Mechanical
Puppets, Miniatures, Models, Molds, Oversized Props,
Prosthetics, Puppets, Radio-Controlled Puppets,
Remote-Controlled FX, Robotics, Sculpting, Special FX Props,
Statues, Vacuum-Forming & Welding)

Smith FX, Inc.   **(818) 601-8800**
             www.shaunsmithfx.com

Spectral Motion, Inc.   **(818) 956-6080**
1849 Dana St.   FAX **(818) 956-6083**
Glendale, CA 91201   **www.spectralmotion.com**
(Animatronics, Body Suits, Characters and Creatures, Makeup
FX, Miniatures, Models, Prosthetics, Puppets &
Vacuum-Forming)

Stevie FX   **(818) 915-3615**
(Creatures, Makeup FX & Prosthetics)   FAX **(818) 206-0169**
              www.steviefx.com

Sticks & Stones   **(818) 352-9538**
                  FAX **(818) 352-9538**
      www.sticksandstonesfx.com
(Animatronics, Makeup FX, Prosthetics & Puppets)

Sunset Optometric Center Inc.   **(323) 668-2702**
4445 Sunset Blvd.   FAX **(323) 668-1210**
Los Angeles, CA 90027   **www.sunsetoptometric.com**

Techworks FX Studios, Inc.   **(661) 298-1094**
                    FAX **(661) 298-0929**
       www.techworksstudios.com
(Animatronics, Creatures, Makeup FX, Prosthetics, Puppets,
Robots & Sculpting)

Tony Urbano & Tim Blaney Puppetry **(310) 572-1917**
11664 National Blvd., Ste. 148   FAX **(310) 572-1917**
Los Angeles, CA 90064
(Marionettes, Puppeteered FX & Puppets)

Acrylic Airlines Inc. (310) 664-7036
46 Thornton Ave. www.michelecastagnetti.com
Venice, CA 90291
(Art Rentals, Cleared Artwork Rentals, Cleared Artwork Sales,
Custom Artwork, Digital Fabrication, Fabrication, Fine Art
Rentals, Fine Art Reproduction, Poster Art & Sculptures)

Art Pic (818) 503-5999
6826 Troost Ave. FAX (818) 503-5995
North Hollywood, CA 91605 www.artpic2000.com
(Art Rentals)

Artagogo (310) 753-9991
(Fine Art Rentals) www.artagogo.net

Munish Asnani (323) 383-5663
www.munishasani.com

The Canvas Peddler (818) 985-8830
5543 Satsuma Ave. FAX (818) 985-5554
North Hollywood, CA 91601
(Custom Framing)

(323) 669-1604
Chris' Art Resource/C.A.R. (323) 363-8723
1035 N. Myra Ave. www.chrisrentsart.com
Los Angeles, CA 90029
(Art Rentals)

D.R.G. Enterprises, Inc. (818) 908-0100
5900 Kester Ave. FAX (818) 908-0505
Van Nuys, CA 91411
(Custom Framing)

(323) 469-4073
Dina Art Ltd. (310) 508-5563
6433 W. Sunset Blvd. FAX (323) 469-4072
Los Angeles, CA 90028 www.dinaart.com
(Cleared Artwork Rentals and Sales, Custom Framing,
Fabrication & Poster Art)

(310) 675-2715
Bridget Duffy (310) 422-2910
5016 W. 118th St. www.duffyart.com
Hawthorne, CA 90250

(323) 461-4900
Film Art LA (888) 858-7107
5722 W. Jefferson Blvd., Dock 1 FAX (323) 461-4959
Los Angeles, CA 90016 www.filmartla.com
(Cleared Art Rentals & Digital Fine Art Reproductions)

Galerie Lakaye (323) 460-7333
(Art Rentals) FAX (323) 460-7330
www.galerielakaye.com

Gallery of Functional Art (310) 829-6990
Bergamot Station FAX (310) 829-5707
2525 Michigan Ave., Ste. E3
Santa Monica, CA 90404 www.galleryoffuctionalart.com
(Contemporary & Eclectic)

Ghettogloss Gallery (323) 871-8100
1646 N. Spring St. www.ghettogloss.com
Los Angeles, CA 90012

(818) 767-8448
H. Studio (800) 242-8992
8640 Tamarack Ave. FAX (818) 767-5334
Sun Valley, CA 91352 www.hstudio.com
(Acrylic Sculptures)

Hollywood Studio Gallery (323) 462-1116
1035 N. Cahuenga Blvd. FAX (323) 462-5113
Hollywood, CA 90038
(Fabrication)

(818) 691-3389
Jules Custom Artwork & Portraits (213) 448-6145
picasaweb.google.com/108527287304019140070
(Cleared Artwork Sales, Custom Artwork, Fabrication, Plush Toy
Fabrication, Portrait Art & Sculptures)

Kevin Barry Fine Art Associates (323) 951-1860
8210 Melrose Ave. FAX (323) 951-1866
Los Angeles, CA 90046 www.kevinbarryfineart.com
(Art Rentals & Framing)

Lacy Primitive & Fine Art (310) 271-0807
1240 Sierra Alta Way FAX (310) 271-0806
Los Angeles, CA 90069 www.lacygallery.com
(Abstract, Contemporary and Minimalist Painting Art Rentals)

Mardine Davis Art Consulting (323) 369-8058
www.mardinedavisart.com
(Cleared Artwork Rentals, Cleared Artwork Sales, Custom
Framing, Digital Fabrication, Fine Art Rentals, Fine Art
Reproduction, Poster Art & Sculptures)

Modern Props (323) 934-3000
5500 W. Jefferson Blvd. FAX (323) 934-3155
Los Angeles, CA 90016 www.modernprops.com
(Cleared Contemporary Art Rentals & Sculptures)

(323) 578-5083
Nicole Elias Art (323) 461-6717
(Fine Art Rentals)

Ⓐ The Studios at Paramount (323) 956-3729
The Studios at Paramount Sign Shop & Graphic Services,
5555 Melrose Ave. www.thestudiosatparamount.com
Hollywood, CA 90038

Perrell Fine Art (323) 933-8630
145 N. La Brea, Ste. E FAX (323) 933-8629
Los Angeles, CA 90036 www.perrellfineart.com
(Art Framing and Rentals)

Pinacoteca Picture Props (323) 965-2722
5735 W. Adams Blvd. FAX (323) 965-2730
Los Angeles, CA 90016 www.pinaprops.com
(Art Rentals)

Santa Monica Fine Art Studios (310) 383-0687
2900 Airport Ave., Ste. E www.spotorangedesign.com
Santa Monica, CA 90405
(Art Rentals)

Sculpture and Paintings by
Bruce Gray (323) 223-4059
688 S. Avenue 21 www.brucegray.com
Los Angeles, CA 90031
(Art Rentals, Cleared Artwork Rentals, Cleared Artwork Sales,
Custom Artwork, Fabrication, Fine Art Rentals & Sculptures)

Singh Imports: Fine Art
Objects of India (310) 559-3826
3816 W. Jefferson Blvd. FAX (310) 559-3829
Los Angeles, CA 90016 www.singhimports.com
(1850s-1950s Indian, Buddhist and Hindu Art Rentals, Cleared
Artwork Rentals, Cleared Artwork Sales, Fine Art Rentals,
Paintings, Prints & Sculptures)

Sports and the Arts (818) 400-9390
(Art Rentals) www.sportart.net

Stone Art (310) 395-6303
419 Wilshire Blvd. FAX (310) 395-8871
Santa Monica, CA 90401 www.stoneartframeshop.com
(Framing)

Sunny Meyer Fine Art Restoration (818) 989-3721
www.oldart.com
(Art Restoration, Custom Artwork & Custom Framing)

U-Frame It Gallery (818) 781-4500
(818) 402-8579
13630 Sherman Way FAX (818) 781-7479
Van Nuys, CA 91405 www.uframeitgallery.com
(Cleared Artwork Rentals, Cleared Artwork Sales, Custom
Framing, Poster Art & Restoration)

Doug Wright/Prop Art (323) 461-5842
(323) 868-5831
www.douglaswrightfineart.com
(Custom Artwork, Fabrication & Sculptures)

Aaron Bros. (818) 243-7661
www.aaronbrothers.com

Baller Hardware (323) 665-4149
(Art Supplies) www.ballerhardware.com

Blick Art Materials (323) 933-9284
7301 W. Beverly Blvd. FAX (323) 933-9794
Los Angeles, CA 90036 www.dickblick.com

Blick Art Materials (626) 795-4985
44 S. Raymond Ave. www.dickblick.com
Pasadena, CA 91105

Blick Art Materials (310) 479-1416
11531 Santa Monica Blvd. www.dickblick.com
West Los Angeles, CA 90025

The Button Store (323) 658-5473
8344 W. Third St. FAX (323) 782-0940
Los Angeles, CA 90048

Buy-Lines Co., Inc. (323) 463-4855
5444 Melrose Ave.
Hollywood, CA 90038
(Czech Glass Beads)

(818) 762-1059
Cameraflauge (213) 304-9323
11635 Sheldon St. FAX (818) 762-0207
Sun Valley, CA 91352 www.cameraflauge.com
(Paints)

Cane & Basket Supply Co. (323) 939-9644
1283 S. Cochran Ave. FAX (323) 939-7237
Los Angeles, CA 90019 www.caneandbasket.com
(Bamboo, Raffia & Sea Grass)

Carter Sexton Artists' Materials (818) 763-5050
www.cartersexton.com

Continental Art Supplies (818) 345-1044
www.continentalart.com

(310) 204-1212
Graphaids, Inc. (800) 866-6601
3030 S. La Cienega Blvd. FAX (310) 204-5730
Culver City, CA 90232 www.graphaids.com

Graphaids, Inc. (310) 820-0445
12400 Santa Monica Blvd. FAX (310) 820-5506
West Los Angeles, CA 90025 www.graphaids.com

Kit Kraft, Inc. (818) 509-9739
12109 Ventura Pl. www.kitkraft.biz
Studio City, CA 91604
(Beads, Jewels, Paints & Trims)

McManus & Morgan, Inc. (213) 387-4433
2506 W. Seventh St. www.mcmanusmorgan.com
Los Angeles, CA 90057
(Fine Art Papers & Stationery)

(310) 393-9634
Michael's Arts & Crafts (800) 642-4235
1427 Fourth St. FAX (310) 395-2096
Santa Monica, CA 90401 www.michaels.com

Mittel's Art Center (310) 399-9500
2499 Lincoln Blvd. www.mittels.net
Venice, CA 90291
(Framing, Paints & Papers)

Mittel's Art Center (818) 710-0517
22100 Ventura Blvd. www.mittels.net
Woodland Hills, CA 91364
(Framing, Paints & Papers)

Moskatels (213) 689-4830
(Craft Supplies) FAX (213) 622-3803

Pearl Art & Craft Supplies, Inc. (310) 854-4900
1250 S. La Cienega Blvd. FAX (310) 854-4908
Los Angeles, CA 90035 www.pearlpaint.com

Swain's (818) 243-3129
537 N. Glendale Ave. www.swainsart.com
Glendale, CA 91206

(310) 478-5775
Utrecht Art Supply Center (800) 223-9132
11677 Santa Monica Blvd. FAX (310) 478-5675
West Los Angeles, CA 90025 www.utrechtart.com

Alpha Wolf Special Effects (213) 700-2054
(818) 429-9382
www.specialeffects9.blogspot.com
(Atmospheric FX, Confetti Special FX and Cannon Systems,
Fog FX/Machines, Mechanical FX, Powderman, Public Display
Fireworks, Pyrotechnics, Rain FX/Machines,
Smoke FX/Machines, Snow FX/Machines, Special FX
Coordinator, Weather FX/Machines & Wind FX/Machines)

ANA Special Effects, Inc. (818) 909-6999
7021 Hayvenhurst Ave.   FAX (818) 782-0635
Van Nuys, CA 91406   www.anaspecialeffects.com

Artistry In Motion Confetti, Inc. (818) 994-7388
15101 Keswick St.   FAX (818) 994-7688
Van Nuys, CA 91405   www.artistryinmotion.com
(Confetti Special FX and Cannon Systems)

Astro Audio Video Lighting, Inc. (818) 549-9915
6615 San Fernando Rd.   FAX (818) 549-0681
Glendale, CA 91201   www.astroavl.com
(Atmospheric FX, Blacklights, Confetti Special FX and Cannon
Systems, Fog FX/Machines, Laser FX, Lightning FX,
Projections, Smoke FX/Machines & Snow FX/Machines)

Automatrix Effects/David Waine (323) 469-0088
137 N. San Fernando Rd., Ste. 134   FAX (323) 395-0570
Burbank, CA 91504   www.automatrixfx.com

Bill Ferrell Co. (818) 767-1900
10556 Keswick St.   FAX (818) 767-2901
Sun Valley, CA 91352   www.billferrell.com
(Confetti Special FX and Cannon Systems)

Boom Boom Effects (818) 772-6699
11100-8 Sepulveda Blvd., Ste. 339   FAX (818) 772-6689
Mission Hills, CA 91345

Calbor Enterprises Two, Inc. (818) 760-3222
(818) 262-5329
FAX (818) 760-2238
www.pyro-fx.net
(Confetti Special FX and Cannon Systems, Fog FX/Machines,
Powderman, Public Display Fireworks, Pyrotechnics, Rain FX/
Machines, Smoke FX/Machines, Snow FX/Machines, Special
FX Coordinator, Weather FX/Machines & Wind FX/Machines)

Jerry Chavez (818) 400-4625
(Pyrotechnics)

Cinefx/Josh Hakian (818) 835-9338
3737 Patrick Henry Pl.
Agoura Hills, CA 91301
(Atmospheric FX, Fog FX/Machines, Mechanical FX,
Powderman, Pyrotechnics, Rain FX/Machines, Snow FX/
Machines, Special FX Coordinator, Weather FX/Machines &
Wind FX/Machines)

Dan Murphy Special Effects (661) 269-5181
www.murphy-special-effects.com
(Atmospheric FX, Mechanical FX, Pyrotechnics &
Special FX Coordinator)

Dan Donley (213) 200-2810
(Public Display Fireworks)

Eddie Surkin Special FX/
Etan Enterprises (818) 203-5466
6127 Melvin Ave.   FAX (818) 342-1952
Tarzana, CA 91356
(Pyrotechnic Special FX)

The Effects Group (323) 876-0992
(Atmospheric FX & Pyrotechnics)   FAX (323) 876-0288
www.theeffectsgroup.net

F/X Concepts, Inc./Lou Carlucci (818) 508-1094
P.O. Box 1008   FAX (818) 508-1094
Santa Clarita, CA 91386
(Fog, Smoke and Wind Machines)

Flix FX, Inc. (818) 765-3549
(877) 326-8433
7327 Lankershim Blvd., Ste. 4   FAX (818) 765-0135
North Hollywood, CA 91605   www.flixfx.com
(Fog, Rain, Snow and Wind Effects)

Flutter Fetti (877) 321-1999
(504) 522-0300
FAX (504) 522-0304
www.flutterfetti.com

Full Scale Effects (818) 760-0875
(818) 760-0042
6875 Tujunga Ave.   FAX (818) 760-0876
North Hollywood, CA 91605   www.fullscaleeffects.com

Future Lighting (310) 312-9772
(310) 346-1649
(Cloud and Fire Wall Projections)   www.futurelighting.net

Gary F. Bentley Special
Effects Systems
(Atmospheric and Mechanical FX)
(323) 664-1509
(323) 365-2914
FAX (323) 661-7320

Jet Effects
6910 Farmdale Ave.
North Hollywood, CA 91605
(818) 764-5644
FAX (818) 764-6655
www.jeteffects.net

Laser Magic Productions
18220 Margate St.
Tarzana, CA 91356
(Laser FX)
(818) 345-1900
www.laser-magic.com

Lazarus Lighting Design
14701C Arminta St.
Van Nuys, CA 91402
(Fiber Optic Special FX Lighting)
(818) 956-3211
(800) 553-5554
FAX (818) 956-3233
www.lldco.com

Line 204/Angstrom Lighting
837 N. Cahuenga Blvd.
Hollywood, CA 90038
(Fog Machines)
(323) 960-0113
FAX (323) 960-0163
www.line204.com

Long Beach Ice
16526 S. Normandie Ave.
Gardena, CA 90247
(Atmospheric FX & Snow FX/Machines)
(888) 438-1956
(562) 438-8129
FAX (562) 856-1356
www.longbeachice.com

Long Beach Ice
1600 Cherry Ave.
Long Beach, CA 90813
(Atmospheric FX & Snow FX/Machines)
(888) 438-1956
(562) 438-8129
FAX (562) 856-1356
www.longbeachice.com

Luminys Systems Corp.
11961 Sherman Rd.
North Hollywood, CA 91605
(Lightning FX)
(323) 461-6361
(800) 321-3644
FAX (818) 827-3921
www.luminyscorp.com

MagicSnow Systems
8581 Santa Monica Blvd., Ste. 219 www.magicsnow.com
Los Angeles, CA 90069
(Artificial Snow FX, Snow FX/Machines &
Weather FX/Machines)
(310) 289-9852

Neil Marquis
(818) 780-0118
(213) 280-4552

Mini-Fog/Prop Services Unlimited
(Atmospheric FX, Compact Fog Generators,
Fog FX/Machines & Smoke FX/Machines)
(323) 462-2272
(213) 968-1068
FAX (323) 469-9204

Newhall Ice Co.
22502 Fifth St.
Newhall, CA 91321
(Snow Machines)
(661) 259-0893
(818) 362-9742
FAX (661) 259-0691
newhallicecompany.com

North Hollywood Ice Co.
5257 Craner Ave.
North Hollywood, CA 91601 www.northhollywoodice.com
(Snow Machines)
(818) 762-2237
(818) 984-3770
FAX (818) 762-6750

Nu-Salt Laser Light
Shows International
(Laser FX)
(619) 742-8981
nusaltlaser.com

Ⓐ The Studios at Paramount
The Studios at Paramount
Manufacturing and Special Effects
5555 Melrose Ave.   www.thestudiosatparamount.com
Hollywood, CA 90038
(Environmental Effects & Steam Effects)
(323) 956-5140
FAX (323) 862-2325

Rain For Rent
333 S. 12th St.
Santa Paula, CA 93061
(Rain Machines, Pumps & Tanks)
(805) 525-3306
(805) 331-0175
FAX (805) 525-7663
www.rainforrent.com

Reel EFX, Inc.
5539 Riverton Ave.
North Hollywood, CA 91601
(Atmospheric FX)
(818) 762-1710
(213) 308-7289
FAX (818) 762-1734
www.reelefx.com

Reelistic FX, Inc./John Gray
21318 Hart St.
Canoga Park, CA 91303
(818) 346-2484
(818) 621-2484
FAX (818) 346-2710
www.r-fx.com

Reliable Snow Service
(Atmospheric FX & Snow FX/Machines)
(661) 269-2093
FAX (661) 269-2237
www.reliablesnowservice.com

Renegade Effects Group
11312 Hartland St.
North Hollywood, CA 91605   www.renegadeeffects.com
(818) 362-8061
FAX (818) 980-8849

Roger George Rentals
14525 Bessemer St.
Van Nuys, CA 91411
(Weather FX Machines)
(818) 994-3049
FAX (818) 994-9432
www.rogergeorge.com

RPI Entertainment & Media Group
3527 Isabel Dr.
Los Angeles, CA 90065
(Atmospheric FX, Blacklights, Confetti Special FX and Cannon
Systems, Fiber Optics, Fog FX/Machines, Laser FX, Lightning
FX, Projections, Public Display Fireworks, Pyrotechnics, Smoke
FX/Machines, Snow FX/Machines & Special FX Lighting)
(323) 960-9014
(323) 656-9014
FAX (775) 252-6627
www.rpime.com

Schwartz Oil Company, Inc.
27241 Henry Mayo Dr.
Valencia, CA 91355
(Pyrotechnics)
(661) 259-4000
(818) 365-9214
FAX (661) 257-0137
www.socifuel.com

Jeff Scott
(Atmospheric FX & Pyrotechnics)
(213) 709-9190
(323) 469-9980

Set Stuff, Inc.
1105 N. Sycamore Ave.
Hollywood, CA 90038
(Diffusion Smokers & Fog, Pyrotechnic, Snow and Wind FX)
(323) 993-9500
FAX (323) 993-9506
www.setstuffrentals.com

Shannon Luminous Materials, Inc.
304 N. Townsend St., Ste. A
Santa Ana, CA 92703
(Blacklight Paint, Blacklights & Coatings)
(714) 550-9931
(800) 543-4485
FAX (714) 550-9938
www.blacklite.com

Sky-Tracker Moving Xenon/
Searchlights
(Special FX Lighting)
(949) 350-7101
(800) 472-2353
FAX (949) 305-0918
www.skytrackerusa.com

Snow Business Hollywood, Inc.
21318 Hart St.
Canoga Park, CA 91303
(818) 884-3009
FAX (818) 884-3110
www.snowbusinesshollywood.com

Ⓐ Special Effects Unlimited, Inc.
1005 Lillian Way
Hollywood, CA 90038 www.specialeffectsunlimited.com
(Atmospheric FX, Confetti Special FX and Cannon Systems,
Fog FX/Machines, Mechanical FX, Pyrotechnics, Rain FX/
Machines, Smoke FX/Machines, Snow FX/Machines, Special
FX Lighting, Turntables, Weather FX/Machines &
Wind FX/Machines)
(323) 466-3361
FAX (323) 466-5712

Atomspheric/Lighting FX & Pyrotechnics

Spectrum Effects Enterprises, Inc. (323) 871-4445
(661) 510-5633
Raleigh Studios FAX (661) 244-4469
5300 Melrose Ave., Ste. 101D **www.spectrumeffects.com**
Hollywood, CA 90038
(Pyrotechnics)

State Fire Marshal - Motion Picture/
Entertainment Unit (626) 305-1908
602 E. Huntington Dr., Ste. A FAX **(626) 305-5173**
Monrovia, CA 91016 **www.fire.ca.gov**
(Pyrotechnics Only)

Stutsman Effects, Inc. (310) 457-6661
(310) 922-4705
FAX (310) 457-4061
www.stutsfx.com
(Atmospheric and Mechanical FX, Design, Fabrication, Fog
FX/Machines, Operation, Powderman, Pyrotechnics, Rain FX/
Machines, Smoke FX/Machines, Snow FX/Machines, Special
FX Coordinator, Weather FX/Machines & Wind FX/Machines)

Surefire Special Effects, Inc. (310) 345-7288
FAX (714) 693-0382
www.surefirefx.com

TLC-Creative Special Effects (310) 822-6790
(800) 447-3585
13428 Maxella Ave., Ste. 261 FAX (310) 821-4010
Los Angeles, CA 90292 **www.tlciscreative.com**
(Laser Special FX)

Ultimate Effects (661) 298-3033
(818) 253-5947
16805 Sierra Hwy FAX (661) 298-3029
Canyon Country, CA 91351 **www.ultimateeffects.com**

Unilux/Blue Feather Lighting (818) 389-9565
(800) 635-2743
19630 Lanark St. FAX (818) 701-5404
Reseda, CA 91335 **www.unilux.com**
(Strobe Lighting FX)

Universal Studios Property (818) 777-2784
100 Universal City Plaza FAX (818) 866-1543
Universal City, CA 91608 **www.filmmakersdestination.com**

Joseph Viskocil (310) 823-9600
(310) 625-3107
(Pyrotechnics)

Warner Bros. Studio Facilities -
Special Effects (818) 954-1365
4000 Warner Blvd. FAX (818) 954-1424
Burbank, CA 91522 **www.wbspecialeffects.com**

West EFX, Inc. (818) 762-1059
(213) 304-9323
11635 Sheldon St. FAX (818) 762-0207
Sun Valley, CA 91352 **www.westefx.com**

YLS Entertainment (714) 995-4588
10853 Portal Dr. FAX (562) 598-4123
Los Alamitos, CA 90720 **www.ylsentertainment.com**
(Laser Display FX and Systems)

A and C Harbour Lites, Ltd. (310) 926-9552
P.O. Box 9279 FAX (310) 356-3579
Marina Del Rey, CA 90295
(Barges, Camera/Picture Boats, Canoes, Charters, Charts,
Inflatables, Jet Skis, Kayaks, KiteBoards, Maps, Marine Props,
Nautical Equipment/Supplies, Nautical Props, Powerboats,
Sailboats, Submarines, Support Boats, Surfboards,
Tugboats & Yachts)

Action Watersports (310) 827-2233
4144 Lincoln Blvd. www.actionwatersports.com
Marina del Rey, CA 90292
(Kayaks, Kite Boards, Skate Boards, Snow Boards &
Surf Boards)

**Aerial Action Productions/
Reel Orange** (949) 548-4524
316 La Jolla Dr. www.reelorange.com
Newport Beach, CA 92663
(Canoes, Kayaks & White Water Camera and Picture Rafts)

Antiques of the Sea (562) 592-1752
P.O. Box 23, 16811 Pacific Coast Hwy
Sunset Beach, CA 90742 www.antiquesofthesea.com
(Nautical Props)

(323) 707-3411
Aqua Rescue (323) 707-3415
(Inflatables, Jet Skis & Nautical Props) FAX (818) 293-0049
www.aquarescue.com

(562) 433-2863
Aquavision (562) 688-3038
3708 E. Fourth St. FAX (562) 433-2863
Long Beach, CA 90814 www.aquavision.net
(Camera and Picture Boats & Marine Props)

Burbank Kawasaki (818) 848-6627
1329 N. Hollywood Way FAX (818) 848-6630
Burbank, CA 91505 www.burbankkawasaki.com
(Jet Skis)

(562) 983-3600
Cal-Western Boat Company (562) 984-2000
(Yachts) FAX (562) 983-3603
www.marinefilmyachtservices.com

(310) 821-3433
California Sailing Academy (310) 821-3434
14025 Panay Way FAX (310) 821-4141
Marina del Rey, CA 90292
www.californiasailingacademy.com
(Camera and Picture Boats & Nautical Antiques)

(562) 533-1043
Captain Dave's Marine Services, Inc. (877) 345-9009
1951 Golden West St., PMB 223 FAX (714) 375-7276
Huntington Beach, CA 92648
www.captaindavesmarineservice.com
(Barges, Camera/Picture Boats, Canoes, Inflatables, Kayaks,
Marine Coordination, Marine Props, Nautical
Equipment/Supplies, Nautical Props, Powerboats, Sailboats,
Submarines, Support Boats, Tugboats & Yachts)

(562) 596-7105
CAT Marine Production Services (714) 235-7578
FAX (714)-771-3356
www.extremesportsfilming.com
(Barges, Camera/Picture Boats, Canoes, Charters, Charts,
Hovercrafts, Inflatables, Jet Skis, Kayaks, KiteBoards, Maps,
Marine Props, Nautical Equipment/Supplies, Nautical Props,
Powerboats, Sailboats, Submarines, Support Boats,
Surfboards, Tugboats, White Water Rafts & Yachts)

Catalina Island Channel Express (800) 481-3470
95 Berth www.catalinaexpress.com
San Pedro, CA 90731

(818) 764-3015
The Catamaran Store (818) 764-8334
11629 Vanowen St.
North Hollywood, CA 91605

(818) 365-7999
Cinema Aquatics (805) 207-5797
www.cinemaaquatics.com

Cinema Safety & (310) 614-0206
Marine Services, Inc. (805) 207-5797
1534 N. Moorpark Rd., Ste. 108 FAX (805) 241-3954
Thousand Oaks, CA 91360 www.cinemasafety.com
(Barges, Camera/Picture Boats, Canoes, Inflatables, Jet Skis,
Kayaks, Marine Props, Nautical Equipment/Supplies, Support
Boats, Surfboards & White Water Rafts)

(949) 675-8888
Cinemafloat (714) 801-5553
1624 W. Oceanfront Walk FAX (949) 644-3073
Newport Beach, CA 92663
(Barges, Camera and Picture Boats, Marine Props & Tugboats)

CineMarine Team - (661) 222-7342
Cinema Rentals, Inc. (818) 365-7999
25876 The Old Road, Ste. 174 FAX (661) 427-0881
Stevenson Ranch, CA 91381 www.cinemarineteam.com
(Camera and Picture Boats)

Elite Yacht Charters (310) 552-7968
468 N. Camden Dr., Ste. 200 FAX (310) 553-2551
Beverly Hills, CA 90210 www.eliteyacht.com

Executive Yacht Management, Inc. (310) 306-2555
644 Venice Blvd. FAX (310) 306-1147
Marina del Rey, CA 90291 www.yacht-management.com
(Camera Boats, Canoes, Marine Props, Picture Boats,
Powerboats, Sailboats, Support Boats & Yachts)

Hornblower Cruises & Events (310) 301-6000
Fisherman's Village www.hornblower.com
13755 Fiji Way
Marina del Rey, CA 90292

Instinct Charters (949) 470-3800
24182 Okeechobee Ln. FAX (949) 470-3800
Lake Forest, CA 92630
(Camera/Picture Boats, Charters, Marine Props, Powerboats,
Support Boats & Yachts)

(310) 645-0196
M. G. Marine (310) 650-8913
8324 Altavan Ave.
Los Angeles, CA 90045

Motion Picture Marine (310) 822-1100
616 Venice Blvd. FAX (310) 822-2679
Marina del Rey, CA 90291
www.motionpicturemarine.com
(Camera and Picture Boats & Nautical Props)

(949) 723-9696
Nautical Decor Newport Trading Co. (949) 673-7353
2810 Newport Blvd.
Newport Beach, CA 92663
(Nautical Props)

(562) 594-9276
Nautical Film Services (310) 729-6920
P.O. Box 50066 FAX (562) 594-9242
Long Beach, CA 90815 www.nauticalfilmservices.com

**Naval Historical
Education Foundation** (949) 500-9966
1670 Sunflower Ave. FAX (714) 434-9001
Costa Mesa, CA 92626 www.jollyboats.org
(Jolly Boats, Long Boats & Naval Equipment/Supplies)

Next Level Sailing
(858) 922-3522
(800) 644-3454
Embarcadero at Harbor Dr. **www.stars-stripes.com**
San Diego, CA 92101
(America's Cup Sailboats & Camera Boats)

Jimmy O'Connell
(310) 968-0549
(310) 452-5774
306 Market St., Ste. A FAX (310) 452-5774
Venice, CA 90291

Offshore Grip Marine, Inc.
(310) 547-3515
23852 Pacific Coast Hwy, Ste. 764 FAX (310) 943-3328
Malibu, CA 90265 **www.offshoregripmarine.com**
(Barges, Camera and Picture Boats, Inflatables, Jet Skis,
Kayaks, Marine Props, Nautical Equipment/Supplies, Nautical
Props, Powerboats, Sailboats, Submarines, Support Boats,
Tugboats & Yachts)

Picture Vehicles Unlimited
(661) 295-7711
25111 Rye Canyon Loop FAX (661) 295-7721
Santa Clarita, CA 91355 **www.picturevehicles.com**

Premiere Yacht Charters
(619) 410-5222
(619) 808-2822
1380 Harbor Island Dr. FAX (800) 530-7668
San Diego, CA 92101 **www.premiereyachtcharters.com**
(Barges, Camera/Picture Boats, Canoes, Charters, Charts,
Inflatables, Jet Skis, Kayaks, KiteBoards, Maps, Marine Props,
Nautical Equipment/Supplies, Nautical Props, Powerboats,
Sailboats, Submarines, Support Boats, Surfboards, Tugboats,
White Water Rafts & Yachts)

Privateer Lynx
(866) 446-5969
(949) 723-7814
(Early 19th Century Tallship) FAX (949) 723-1958
www.privateerlynx.org

Ship's Trader
(818) 884-9088
21235 San Miguel St. **www.antiquesofadventure.com**
Woodland Hills, CA 91364
(Charters & Nautical Props)

Studio Sea Management, Inc.
(818) 519-4399
(Camera and Picture Boats) FAX (888) 297-5947

Capt. Troy Waters
(310) 713-9193
FAX (310) 943-3328
(Barges, Camera/Picture Boats, Inflatables, Jet Skis, Marine
Props, Nautical Props, Powerboats, Sailboats, Submarines,
Support Boats, Tugboats & Yachts)

West Coast Water Tenders
(661) 250-2585
(661) 510-8128
FAX (661) 250-2584
www.westcoasth20.com

All Powder Coating/Waag (818) 989-5008
16000 Strathern FAX (818) 989-5226
Van Nuys, CA 91406 www.waag.com

Alpine Carpet One (310) 773-3422
3961 S. Sepulveda Blvd. www.alpinecarpetone.com
Culver City, CA 90230

ALSA Corporation (323) 581-5200
2640 E. 37th St. FAX (323) 589-4400
Vernon, CA 90058 www.alsacorp.com
(Chrome Finishing)

Anawalt Lumber Co. (323) 464-1600
1001 N. Highland Ave. FAX (323) 464-3997
Hollywood, CA 90038 www.anawaltlumber.com

Anawalt Lumber Co. (310) 652-6202
641 N. Robertson Blvd. FAX (310) 652-3010
West Hollywood, CA 90069 www.anawaltlumber.com

Anawalt Lumber Co. (310) 478-0324
11060 W. Pico Blvd. FAX (310) 478-1916
West Los Angeles, CA 90064 www.anawaltlumber.com

Andrews Powder Coating, Inc. (818) 700-1030
9801 Independence Ave. FAX (818) 700-0904
Chatsworth, CA 91311 www.powdercoater.com
(Metal Finishing)

(818) 901-9876
Astek Wallcovering, Inc. (800) 432-7930
15924 Arminta St. FAX (818) 901-9891
Van Nuys, CA 91406 www.astekwallcovering.com
(Color Matching, Custom and Period Wall Coverings, Vintage
Recreations, Window Films & Wood Veneers)

(818) 982-0514
ATC Distributing Corporation (800) 445-6759
12110 Sherman Way FAX (818) 982-8932
North Hollywood, CA 91605
(Formica, Laminating, Metals & Wood Veneers)

Aul Pipe Tubing and Steel (323) 267-1200
2701 Bonnie Beach Pl. FAX (323) 267-1258
Los Angeles, CA 90023 www.aulsteel.com

B & B Hardware (310) 390-9413
12450 W. Washington Blvd. FAX (310) 390-1625
Los Angeles, CA 90066

B & T Industrial Supply, Inc. (818) 982-3475
13008 Sherman Way FAX (818) 982-3624
North Hollywood, CA 91605 www.btindustrial.com

Baller Hardware (323) 665-4149
www.ballerhardware.com

Bobco Metals Company (877) 952-6226
2000 S. Alameda St. FAX (888) 572-2662
Los Angeles, CA 90058 www.bobcometal.com

(818) 846-7171
Borrmann Metal Center (800) 801-2677
110 W. Olive Ave. FAX (818) 846-9347
Burbank, CA 91502 www.borrmannmetalcenter.com

Bourget Flagstone Co. (310) 829-4010
1810 Colorado Ave. FAX (310) 829-6261
Santa Monica, CA 90404 www.bourgetbros.com
(Stone)

(818) 845-8301
California Do It Center (818) 407-3888
3221 W. Magnolia Blvd. FAX (818) 846-9214
Burbank, CA 91505 www.doitcenter.com

California Do It Center (805) 497-2753
3775 Thousand Oaks Blvd. FAX (805) 497-9289
Thousand Oaks, CA 91360 www.doitcenter.com

California Panel & Veneer (562) 926-5834
14055 Artesia Blvd. FAX (562) 926-3139
Cerritos, CA 90703 www.calpanel.com
(Formica & Plywood)

California Quarry Products (661) 942-3992
www.californiaquarryproducts.com
(Bulk Landscape Materials)

Catalina Paint (818) 347-7775
6941 Topanga Canyon Blvd. FAX (818) 347-7632
Canoga Park, CA 91303 www.catalinapaint.com

Catalina Paint (818) 772-8888
8814 Reseda Blvd. www.catalinapaint.com
Northridge, CA 91324

Catalina Paint (818) 765-2629
7107 Radford Ave. FAX (818) 764-7065
North Hollywood, CA 91605 www.catalinapaint.com

Culver City Industrial Hardware (310) 398-1251
5429 S. Sepulveda Blvd. www.culverhardware.com
Culver City, CA 90230

Decorator's Laminating Service (323) 933-5877
(Coating & Laminating) FAX (323) 934-8476

Design Hardware (323) 930-1330
6053 W. Third St. FAX (323) 930-0459
Los Angeles, CA 90036 www.designhardware.com
(Bathroom Fixtures & Door Hardware)

(323) 464-4157
Dunn-Edwards (323) 469-1743
FAX (323) 464-1607
www.dunnedwards.com

(323) 650-2000
Emser Tile (323) 650-2010
8431 Santa Monica Blvd. FAX (323) 650-1589
Los Angeles, CA 90069 www.emsertile.com
(Granite, Marble, Slate & Tile)

(310) 369-2528
Fox Studios (310) 369-4636
Studio Supply, 10201 W. Pico Blvd. FAX (310) 369-4078
Los Angeles, CA 90035 www.foxstudiosupply.com
(Custom Doors and Windows & Wood Moulding)

(323) 467-2468
Frazee Paint Co. (800) 477-9991
(Color Matching) FAX (323) 467-7834
www.frazeepaint.com

Harters Distributors (818) 899-9917
(Formica) www.hartersurfaces.com

Holo-Walls, LLC (818) 735-3565
FAX (818) 530-7852
www.holowalls.com
(Flooring, Laminating, Metals, Wall Coverings & Windows)

The Home Depot (805) 983-0653
401 W. Esplanade Dr. www.homedepot.com
Oxnard, CA 93030

The Home Depot (818) 716-9141
6345 Variel Ave. www.homedepot.com
Woodland Hills, CA 91367

The Home Depot	(858) 277-8910
4255 Genesee	www.homedepot.com
San Diego, CA 92117	

The Home Depot	(619) 280-0230
5920 Fairmount Ave.	www.homedepot.com
San Diego, CA 92120	

	(818) 246-9600
The Home Depot	(800) 553-3199
5040 San Fernando Rd.	www.homedepot.com
Glendale, CA 91204	

The Home Depot	(310) 822-3330
12975 W. Jefferson Blvd.	www.homedepot.com
Los Angeles, CA 90066	

The Home Depot	(323) 461-3303
5600 Sunset Blvd.	FAX (213) 860-3147
Los Angeles, CA 90028	www.homedepot.com

The Home Depot	(818) 764-9600
11600 Sherman Way	www.homedepot.com
North Hollywood, CA 91605	

	(818) 729-3333
Industrial Metal Supply Co.	(800) 339-6033
8300 San Fernando Rd.	FAX (818) 729-3334
Sun Valley, CA 91352 www.industrialmetalsupply.com	
(Metals & Metal Finishing)	

Koontz Hardware	(310) 652-0123
8914 Santa Monica Blvd.	FAX (310) 652-7123
West Hollywood, CA 90069	www.koontz.com

	(323) 469-0063
Linoleum City	(800) 559-2489
4849 Santa Monica Blvd.	FAX (323) 912-1932
Hollywood, CA 90029	www.linoleumcity.com
(Carpeting, Linoleum & Tile)	

Mann Brothers Paint	(323) 936-5168
758 N. La Brea Ave.	FAX (323) 936-1980
Hollywood, CA 90038	www.mannbrothers.com

Mark's Paints	(818) 766-3949
4830 Vineland Ave.	FAX (818) 766-0068
North Hollywood, CA 91601	www.markspaint.com

	(805) 376-0206
NAC Co.	(805) 405-7337
1772-J E. Avenida de Los Arboles	FAX (805) 376-8407
Thousand Oaks, CA 91362	www.naceffects.com

Newhall Paint Store	(661) 259-3454
	FAX (661) 259-5864
www.newhallpaintstore.com	

Nova Color Artists Acrylic Paint	(310) 204-6900
5894 Blackwelder St.	www.novacolorpaint.com
Culver City, CA 90232	

Orchard Supply Hardware/OSH	(818) 557-2755
641 N. Victory Blvd.	FAX (818) 557-2753
Burbank, CA 91502	www.osh.com

Orchard Supply Hardware/OSH	(323) 871-1707
5525 Sunset Blvd.	FAX (323) 871-5985
Hollywood, CA 90028	www.osh.com

	(310) 571-3838
Orchard Supply Hardware/OSH	(310) 571-3839
2020 S. Bundy Dr.	FAX (310) 571-3841
West Los Angeles, CA 90025	www.osh.com

Panelite	(323) 297-0115
	FAX (323) 297-0122
	www.panelite.us
(Color Matching, Custom, Flooring, Landscape Materials, Wall Coverings & Windows)	

	(323) 957-3060
PPG/Pittsburgh Paint	(818) 269-8158
1036 N. Highland Ave.	FAX (323) 957-3061
Hollywood, CA 90038	www.ppg.com
(Coating, Color Matching, Custom, Flameproofing, Metal Finishing, Paints/Painting Equipment, Period & Wall Coverings)	

Reliable Hardware Company	(818) 753-8558
11319 Vanowen St.	FAX (818) 753-4778
North Hollywood, CA 91605 www.reliablehardware.com	

Rompage Hardware	(323) 467-2129
	FAX (323) 467-1639
	www.truevalue.com

	(818) 505-6290
Rose Brand	(800) 360-5056
10616 Lanark St.	FAX (818) 505-6293
Sun Valley, CA 91352	www.rosebrand.com

Sepulveda Building Materials	(310) 217-0134
359 E. Gardena Blvd.	FAX (310) 436-1400
Gardena, CA 90248	www.sepulveda.com
(Landscape Materials & Masonry)	

SOS Metals	(310) 217-8848
	FAX (310) 217-8088
	www.sosmetals.com

Southland Lumber &	(323) 776-3530
Supply Co., Inc.	(310) 641-8150
	FAX (310) 641-5243

Sprayco, Inc.	(323) 934-5669
1198 S. La Brea Ave.	FAX (323) 934-3025
Los Angeles, CA 90019	
(Paint & Painting Equipment)	

	(310) 559-2335
Spraylat Corporation	(800) 867-7729
	FAX (310) 836-6094
	www.spraylat.com

Stock Building Supply	(818) 842-2177
640 N. Victory Blvd.	FAX (818) 842-2679
Burbank, CA 91502	www.stocksupply.com

Stock Building Supply	(323) 469-1951
6641 Santa Monica Blvd.	FAX (323) 469-5027
Hollywood, CA 90038	www.stocksupply.com

Stock Building Supply	(323) 478-2200
3250 San Fernando Rd.	FAX (323) 478-2201
Los Angeles, CA 90065	www.stocksupply.com

Stock Building Supply	(310) 881-2000
3860 Grandview Blvd.	FAX (310) 881-2019
Los Angeles, CA 90066	www.stocksupply.com

	(818) 982-6046
Stock Building Supply	(800) 478-3779
7151 Lankershim Blvd.	FAX (818) 982-9564
North Hollywood, CA 91605	www.stocksupply.com

Tashman Screens & Hardware	(323) 656-7028
	FAX (323) 656-0213
	www.tashmans.com

	(562) 435-4826
Tell Steel	(800) 734-8355
	FAX (562) 437-6894
	www.tellsteel.com

TTS Products	(323) 268-1347
2822 E. Olympic Blvd.	FAX (323) 268-8093
Los Angeles, CA 90023	

Universal Studios Property	(818) 777-2784
100 Universal City Plaza	FAX (818) 866-1543
Universal City, CA 91608 www.filmmakersdestination.com	

The Wallpaper Bin	(818) 407-1831
9250 Reseda Blvd.	FAX (818) 407-1832
Northridge, CA 91324	www.wallpaperbinla.com

Warner Bros. Studio Facilities -
Mill Store	(818) 954-4444
4000 Warner Blvd., Bldg. 44	FAX (818) 954-5753
Burbank, CA 91522	www.wbmillstore.com

West Coast Sign Supply	(323) 732-6666
2240 W. Washington Blvd.	FAX (323) 732-6660
Los Angeles, CA 90018 www.westcoastsignsupply.com

Wildfire, Inc. - Lighting &	(310) 755-6780
Visual Effects	(800) 937-8065
2908 Oregon Court, Ste. G1	FAX (310) 755-6781
Torrance, CA 90503	www.wildfirefx.com
(Fixtures & Paints/Painting Equipment)

Zal Industrial	(323) 262-0259
4905 Telegraph Rd.	FAX (323) 262-6050
Los Angeles, CA 90022	www.zalindustrial.com

Building/Surface Materials & Hardware

Action Portable Air Conditioning (888) 508-3394
(Tents) FAX (888) 508-3394

Anytime Production Equipment
Rentals, Inc. (323) 461-8483
755 N. Lillian Way FAX (323) 461-2338
Hollywood, CA 90038 www.anytime-rentals.com
(Canopies)

(818) 842-9944
Apache Rental Group (818) 842-9875
3910 W. Magnolia Blvd. FAX (818) 842-9269
Burbank, CA 91505 www.apacherentalgroup.com
(Canopies)

Atomic Production Supplies (818) 566-8811
2621 N. Ontario St. FAX (818) 566-8311
Burbank, CA 91504 www.atomicproductionsupplies.com
(Canopies)

Camera Essentials (626) 844-3722
91 N. Daisy Ave. FAX (323) 686-5230
Pasadena, CA 91107 www.cameraessentials.com
(Tents)

Castex Rentals (323) 462-1468
1044 Cole Ave. FAX (323) 462-3719
Hollywood, CA 90038 www.castexrentals.com
(Canopies)

Chester's Circus & (323) 751-3486
Carnival Equipment (951) 233-6014
(Canvas Tenting) FAX (323) 778-2025

Choura Event Rentals (310) 320-6200
(Canopies & Tents) FAX (310) 781-8227
www.choura.us

Classic Tents (310) 328-5060
540 Hawaii Ave. www.classictentrentals.com
Torrance, CA 90503
(Tents)

(626) 579-4454
Creative Inflatables (800) 446 3528
9872 Rush St. FAX (626) 579-5561
South El Monte, CA 91733 www.creativeinflatables.com
(Tents)

DeWayne Events (661) 251-4342
16520 Diver St. FAX (661) 251-2488
Canyon Country, CA 91387

(951) 685-6014
Dortons, Inc. (323) 751-3486
(Tents)

(562) 402-8335
Eide Industries, Inc. (800) 422-6827
16215 Piuma Ave. FAX (562) 924-2233
Cerritos, CA 90703 www.eideindustries.com
(Canopies)

(909) 355-7400
Exclusive Tent Rentals (323) 377-0650
(Tents) www.exclusivetentrentals.com

Hollywood Tentworks (877) 883-3131
10244 Norris Ave. FAX (877) 883-3132
Pacoima, CA 91331 www.tentworks.com

(951) 781-0843
International E-Z UP, Inc. (800) 457-4233
1601 Iowa Ave. FAX (951) 781-0586
Riverside, CA 92507 www.ezup.com
(Tents)

Kayam Theatre and
Concert Tent Company (213) 484-5010
17141 Covello St. www.kayam.co.uk
Lake Balboa, CA 91406
(Tents)

(323) 751-3486
L.A. Circus (323) 547-5960
7531 La Salle Ave. www.lacircus.com
Los Angeles, CA 90047
(Tents)

Line 204 Inc. (323) 960-0113
837 N. Cahuenga Blvd. FAX (323) 960-0163
Hollywood, CA 90038 www.line204.com
(Canopies)

Out of Frame Production Rentals (323) 462-1898
1124 N. Citrus Ave. FAX (323) 462-1897
Hollywood, CA 90038 www.outofframela.com
(Canopies & Tents)

The Production Truck, Inc. (818) 459-0425
711 Ruberta Ave. FAX (818) 459-0427
Glendale, CA 91201 www.theproductiontruck.com
(Tents)

Quixote Studios (323) 461-1408
1000 N. Cahuenga Blvd. FAX (323) 461-5517
Los Angeles, CA 90038 www.quixote.com
(Canopies)

Set Stuff, Inc. (323) 993-9500
1105 N. Sycamore Ave. FAX (323) 993-9506
Hollywood, CA 90038 www.setstuffrentals.com
(Tents)

Skye Rentals (323) 462-5934
1016 Mansfield Ave. FAX (323) 462-5935
Hollywood, CA 90038 www.skyerentals.com

(818) 720-5126
Tent Kings of Los Angeles (310) 880-5128
3238 N. San Fernando Blvd. FAX (866) 736-0570
Burbank, CA 91504 www.tentkings.com
(Tents)

(310) 481-9300
A Wynning Event (310) 729-2590
433 N. Camden Dr., Ste. 400 FAX (310) 571-0976
Beverly Hills, CA 90210 www.awynningevent.com

Xpendable Rentals (323) 656-0905
5925 Santa Monica Blvd. FAX (323) 375-1711
Hollywood, CA 90038 www.xpendablerentals.com
(Canopies)

All Powder Coating/Waag   **(818) 989-5008**
16000 Strathern   FAX **(818) 989-5226**
Van Nuys, CA 91406   **www.waag.com**

Automatrix Effects/David Waine   **(323) 469-0088**
137 N. San Fernando Rd., Ste. 134   FAX **(323) 395-0570**
Burbank, CA 91504   **www.automatrixfx.com**

B.A.D. Company   **(818) 504-2404**
11174 Fleetwood St.   FAX **(818) 504-2458**
Sun Valley, CA 91352   **www.thebadcompany.net**
(Custom Fabrication, Paint & Rigging)

   (818) 506-5598
Tony Berardinelli   **(818) 391-0267**
   FAX **(818) 506-5598**

Best-Log Intercontinental   **(818) 435-2159**
8801 Whitaker Ave.   FAX **(818) 936-0194**
Northridge, CA 91343 **www.bestlog-intercontinental.com**

Camera Ready Cars   **(714) 444-1700**
11161 Slater Ave.   FAX **(714) 444-0700**
Fountain Valley, CA 92708   **www.metalcrafters.com**
(Automotive Display Stands)

Customs by Eddie Paul   **(310) 322-8035**
A Division of EP Industries, Inc.   **(310) 259-0542**
1330 E. Franklin Ave.   FAX **(310) 322-8044**
El Segundo, CA 90245   **www.deadlinetv.net**
(Automotive Display Stands, Car Manipulation & Car Mounts)

DH Automotive   **(323) 842-8393**
   dhautomotive.biz

Executive Productions   **(310) 456-8833**
3957 Ridgemont Dr.   FAX **(310) 456-5692**
Malibu, CA 90265

Focus on Cars   **(310) 762-1370**
20434 S. Santa Fe Ave.   FAX **(310) 763-7110**
Long Beach, CA 90810   **www.southbaystudios.com**

Ghostlight Industries Inc.   **(818) 898-1938**
956 Griswold Ave.   FAX **(818) 898-1948**
San Fernando, CA 91340   **www.ghostlightla.com**
(Buses, Car Manipulation, Car Mounts & Lifts)

Hollywood Picture Cars   **(323) 466-2277**
3957 Ridgemont Dr., Ste. 101   FAX **(310) 456-5692**
Malibu, CA 90265   **www.hollywoodpicturecars.com**

Industrial Artists   **(626) 355-1913**
803 Woodland Dr.
Sierra Madre, CA 91024

   (323) 851-5678
Jeffries Automotive Styling   **(818) 980-5367**
3077 Cahuenga Blvd.
Los Angeles, CA 90068

   (818) 404-7936
Kit Car/Kit Riedel   **(818) 404-7937**

   (818) 222-6954
L.A. Motorsports   **(877) 526-6867**
   FAX **(866) 294-3266**
   www.lamsports.com

L.A. Prep, Inc.   **(562) 595-8886**
2700 Signal Pkwy   **www.laprepinc.com**
Signal Hill, CA 90806
(Automotive Display Stands, Car Manipulation, Car Mounts,
Lifts & Turntables)

   (661) 943-6151
Mobile Tinting   **(661) 810-3839**
41021 Walrus Way   **www.tintthis.com**
Palmdale, CA 93551
(Window Tinting)

Mr. Vintage Machine   **(213) 369-0281**
   www.mistervintagemachine.com

   (805) 376-0206
NAC Co.   **(805) 405-7337**
1772-J E. Avenida de Los Arboles   FAX **(805) 376-8407**
Thousand Oaks, CA 91362   **www.naceffects.com**

   (541) 840-3366
Willy Nemeth/Good Medicine Hat   **(541) 476-0598**
(Car Mounts)

Ⓐ The Studios at Paramount   **(323) 956-5140**
The Studios at Paramount   FAX **(323) 862-2325**
Manufacturing and Special Effects
5555 Melrose Ave.   **www.thestudiosatparamount.com**
Hollywood, CA 90038

Performance Filmworks, Inc./   **(805) 604-3399**
Dean Bailey   **(310) 721-4812**
331 Hearst Dr.   FAX **(805) 604-3398**
Oxnard, CA 93030   **www.performancefilmworks.com**

Picture Car Warehouse   **(818) 341-8975**
8400 Reseda Blvd.   FAX **(818) 341-8926**
Northridge, CA 91324   **www.picturecarwarehouse.net**

Picture Vehicles Unlimited   **(661) 295-7711**
25111 Rye Canyon Loop   FAX **(661) 295-7721**
Santa Clarita, CA 91355   **www.picturevehicles.com**

Precision Prep   **(818) 834-2222**
9388 Remick Ave.   FAX **(818) 834-2225**
Arleta, CA 91331

   (619) 258-9010
Promotional Products   **(800) 258-9010**
10062 Vista Parque   FAX **(619) 328-9293**
Lakeside, CA 92040   **www.vehicledisplays.com**
(Automotive Display Stands)

Pursuit Systems Inc.   **(818) 255-5850**
7255 Radford Ave.   **www.pursuitsystems.com**
North Hollywood, CA 91605

Rainbow Industries   **(818) 786-9030**
   FAX **(818) 786-9034**
   www.rainbowindustries.ws

Rick's Stunt Car Service/   **(818) 341-9526**
Motion Picture Driving Clinic   **(818) 796-1497**
8560 Variel Ave.
Canoga Park, CA 91304
   www.rickseamanstuntdrivingschool.com

   (661) 259-4000
Schwartz Oil Company, Inc.   **(818) 365-9214**
27241 Henry Mayo Dr.   FAX **(661) 257-0137**
Valencia, CA 91355   **www.socifuel.com**
(Mobile Refueling Systems & Studio Fueling Trucks)

Shelly Ward Enterprises   **(818) 255-5850**
   FAX **(818) 255-5450**
   www.shellywardent.com

   (818) 376-0661
Sierra Mobile Window Tinting   **(661) 251-9536**
7837 Sepulveda Blvd., Ste. 14   FAX **(818) 376-0655**
Van Nuys, CA 91405   **www.sierratint.com**

Sunset Glass Tinting
(310) 391-3400
(323) 735-7713
4859 Slauson Ave., Ste. 288   www.sunsettinting.com
Los Angeles, CA 90056

Swift Car Mounts/Bruce Swift
(818) 341-4537
(818) 808-9500
8800 Winnetka Ave. www.home.earthlink.net/~bswift52
Northridge, CA 91324
(Car Mounts)

Trans FX, Inc.
(805) 485-6110
2361 Eastman Ave.   FAX (805) 751-0149
Oxnard, CA 93030   www.transfx.com

Unique Movie Cars, Inc.
(888) 345-6227
FAX (702) 566-6194
www.uniquemoviecarslasvegas.com

Vehicle Effects
(818) 355-2676
(818) 768-2343
7606 Clybourn Rd.   FAX (818) 846-7576
Sun Valley, CA 91352   www.vehicleeffects.com

Jack Weimer
(818) 504-4131
(818) 448-2000
10949 Tuxford St.
Sun Valley, CA 91352

Color-Correct Props

Color Correct, USA   (310) 904-0500
3615 Hayden Ave.
Culver City, CA 90232

Comp 24
(818) 562-6676
(818) 621-4632
1919 Empire Ave.   FAX (818) 842-4623
Burbank, CA 91504   www.comp24.com

Dennis Curtin Studio, Inc.   (310) 827-8850
1919 Empire Ave.   FAX (818) 842-4623
Burbank, CA 91504   www.denniscurtin.com

So Cal Production Source   (310) 699-2787
FAX (310) 618-0129
www.scpsunlimited.com

Ⓐ ABC Studios - Costume Department (818) 553-4800
545 Circle Seven Dr.   FAX (818) 545-0468
Glendale, CA 91201   www.abcstudioscostumes.com

Action Sets and Props/
WonderWorks **(818) 992-8811**
7231 Remmet Ave.   FAX (818) 347-4330
Canoga Park, CA 91303   www.wonderworksweb.com
(Spacesuits)

Alterian, Inc. **(626) 856-1499**
P.O. Box 2166   FAX (626) 856-1495
Irwindale, CA 91706   www.alterianinc.com
(Animal/Character Costumes, Armor, Beading, Construction,
Contemporary, Custom, Design, Embroidery, Full Costume
Construction, Full Costume Design, Futuristic Costuming,
Mascots, Masks, Spacesuits & Special FX Costumes)

Alva's Dance and Theatrical Supply (310) 519-1314
1417 W. Eighth St.   FAX (310) 831-6110
San Pedro, CA 90732   www.alvas.com
(Dance Costume Rentals)

Anatomorphex/
The Sculpture Studio **(818) 768-2880**
8210 Lankershim Blvd., Ste. 14 www.anatomorphex.com
North Hollywood, CA 91605
(Full Costume Construction)

Arteffex/Dann O'Quinn **(818) 506-5358**
911 Mayo St.   FAX (323) 255-4599
Los Angeles, CA 90042   www.acfxo.com
(Animal/Character Costumes, Custom Costume Construction,
Mascots, Masks & Special FX Costumes)

Baron California Hats **(818) 563-3025**
1619 W. Burbank Blvd.   FAX (818) 563-4025
Burbank, CA 91506   www.baronhats.com
(Rentals)

Bittersweet Butterfly
Fancy Lingerie and Flowers **(323) 660-4303**
1406 Micheltorena   FAX (323) 665-9114
Los Angeles, CA 90026   www.bittersweetbutterfly.com
(Contemporary, Evening Gowns, Rentals, Undergarments,
Vintage & Wedding Gowns)

Bon Choix Couture, Inc. **(818) 729-9994**
1223 S. Flower St.   FAX (818) 729-9995
Burbank, CA 91502   www.bonchoixcouture.com
(Beading, Construction, Contemporary, Custom, Dancewear,
Embroidery, Full Costume Construction, Full Costume Design,
Furs, Futuristic Costuming, Gloves, Horseback Riding Apparel,
Knitwear, Leather, Military, Period–Present, Police, Special FX
Costumes, Undergarments, Uniforms & Western Wear)

Broken Horn **(626) 337-4266**
1022 Leorita St.   FAX (626) 337-4283
Baldwin Park, CA 91706   www.brokenhornsaddlery.com
(English and Western Riding Apparel and Tack)

Lynda Burdick **(323) 662-7612**
(Hats)   FAX (323) 662-7612
      www.lyndahats.com

Caravan West Productions **(661) 268-8300**
35660 Jayhawker Rd.   FAX (661) 268-8301
Agua Dulce, CA 91390   www.caravanwest.com
(1860-1910 Vintage Western Wear)

Chic Little Devil Style House **(310) 403-6929**
1206 Maple Ave., 11th Fl.
Los Angeles, CA 90015 www.chiclittledevilstylehouse.com

Cinnabar **(818) 842-8190**
4571 Electronics Pl.   FAX (818) 842-0563
Los Angeles, CA 90039   www.cinnabar.com
(Full Costume Construction and Design)

Nina Correa **(310) 390-6761**
(Full Costume Construction)   FAX (310) 398-3889

Costume Rentals Corporation **(818) 753-3700**
11149 Vanowen St.   FAX (818) 753-3737
North Hollywood, CA 91605
      www.costumerentalscorp.com

Douglas White Effects **(818) 785-4148**
6859 Valjean Ave., Ste. 5   FAX (818) 785-2567
Van Nuys, CA 91406   www.dweffects.com

Eastern Costume Company **(818) 982-3611**
7243 Coldwater Canyon Ave.   FAX (818) 982-1905
North Hollywood, CA 91605   www.easterncostume.com
(Beading, Construction, Contemporary, Costume Makers,
Custom, Dancewear, Design, Embroidery, Ethnic Apparel,
Evening Gowns, Flight Gear, Full Costume Construction, Full
Costume Design, Furs, Futuristic Costuming, Gloves, Hats,
Horseback Riding Apparel, Knitwear, Leathers, Mascots,
Masks, Military Uniforms, Period-Present, Police, Props,
Religious Garments, Rentals, Screenprinting, Shoes/Boots,
Spacesuits, Undergarments, Uniforms, Vintage, Wardrobe
Supplies, Wedding Gowns & Western Wear)

      (310) 369-1897
Fox Studios   **(310) 369-4636**
Costume Department   FAX (310) 369-2487
10201 W. Pico Blvd.   www.foxstudioscostumes.com
Los Angeles, CA 90035
(Contemporary, Custom & Rentals)

Francine Lecoultre Design Studio **(310) 666-9970**
(Period, Sculptural and Special FX Costume Construction)

      (323) 441-1986
Gaspar Gloves   **(323) 702-7620**
      FAX (323) 227-6993
      www.gaspargloves.com

      (323) 874-6630
Dana Gillette   **(323) 533-5078**
      FAX (323) 874-6630
(Construction and Design, Elvis Jumpsuits &
On-Set Seamstress)

Global Effects, Inc. **(818) 503-9273**
7115 Laurel Canyon Blvd.   FAX (818) 503-9459
North Hollywood, CA 91605   www.globaleffects.com
(Actor Climate Systems, Animal/Character Costumes, Armor,
Construction, Flight Gear, Full Costume Construction, Full
Costume Design, Futuristic Costuming, Horseback Riding
Apparel, Leathers, Mascots, Masks, Medieval Armor, Military,
Period, Rentals, Shoes/Boots, Spacesuits, Special FX
Costumes & Uniforms)

Golyester Antiques **(323) 931-1339**
136 S. La Brea Ave.   www.golyester.com
Los Angeles, CA 90036
(Vintage Costumes and Textile Rentals)

Gregory's Tux Shop **(818) 980-5480**
12051 Magnolia Blvd.   FAX (818) 980-5084
North Hollywood, CA 91607   www.tuxedosonline.com

      (323) 660-9892
James Hayes   **(213) 503-0710**
1832 Maltman Ave.   www.jameshayesstudio.com
Los Angeles, CA 90026
(Animal/Character Costume Construction and Design, Full
Costume Construction and Design, Futuristic Costuming, Hats,
Leathers, Mascots, Little People Costume Construction and
Design, Period–Present, Puppet Costume Construction and
Design, Special FX Costumes & Undergarments)

      (323) 464-4444
Hollywood Toys & Costumes   **(800) 554-3444**
6600 Hollywood Blvd.   FAX (323) 464-4644
Hollywood, CA 90028 www.yourhollywoodcostumes.com
(Animal Walkaround Costume Rentals)

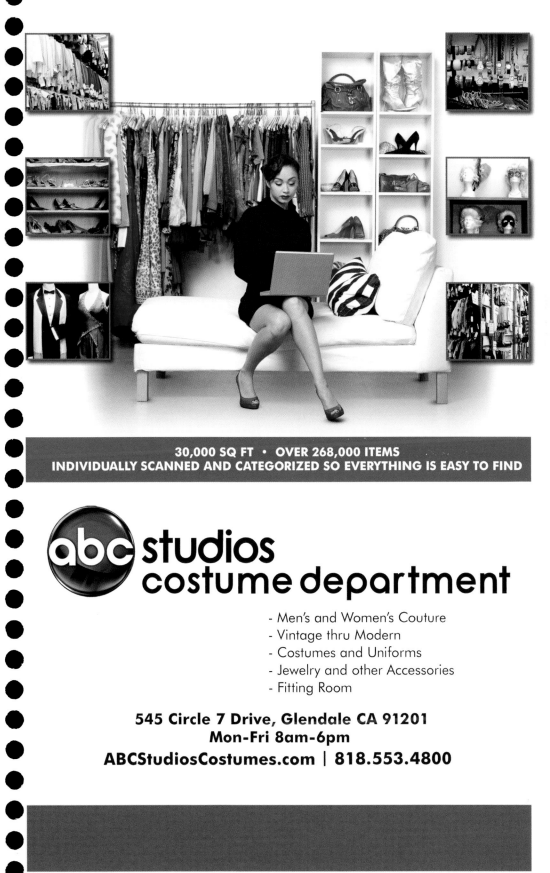

Image Creators (310) 710-7128
www.imagecreators.net
(Animal, Character, Creature and Special FX Costume
Construction)

J & M Costumers, Inc. (818) 760-1991
5708 Gentry Ave. www.jmcostumers.com
North Hollywood, CA 91607

(310) 990-1478
KCL Productions (310) 739-2534
21337 Rambla Vista www.kclproductions.com
Malibu, CA 90265
(Animal Costumes, Character Costumes, Construction,
Custom, Design, Full Costume Construction, Full Costume
Design, Mascots, Masks, Special FX Costumes & Walkarounds)

Kowboyz (505) 984-1256
FAX (505) 984-7620
www.kowboyz.com
(Cowboy Boots, Clothing, Hats, Leathers & Vintage)

(323) 751-3486
L.A. Circus (323) 547-5960
7531 La Salle Ave. www.lacircus.com
Los Angeles, CA 90047

Leahpatra Knitwear (310) 951-9095
(Knitwear) www.leahpatra.com

Louise Green Millinery Co. (310) 479-1881
1616 Cotner Ave. FAX (310) 479-2838
Los Angeles, CA 90025 www.louisegreen.com
(Custom & Period Hats)

**Makeup & Effects
Laboratories,Inc./MEL** (818) 982-1483
7110 Laurel Canyon Blvd., Bldg. E FAX (818) 982-5712
North Hollywood, CA 91605 www.melefx.com
(Hard and Soft Walkarounds)

**Margaretrose Custom
Clothing Design** (323) 852-4787
306 S. Edinburgh Ave. FAX (323) 852-4789
Los Angeles, CA 90048 www.margaretrosedesign.net
(Contemporary, Custom, Dancewear, Design, Evening Gowns,
Full Costume Construction, Full Costume Design, Uniforms &
Wedding Gowns)

Mia Gyzander Costumes, Inc. (818) 308-6729
(Construction & Design) www.miagyzander.com

**Motion Picture Costumes &
Supplies, Inc.** (818) 557-1247
3811 Valhalla Dr. FAX (818) 557-1695
Burbank, CA 91505
(1776–Present Costumes and Uniforms)

(818) 239-4849
Musotica Wear, Inc. (800) 240-0221
3727 W. Magnolia Blvd., Ste. 452 FAX (818) 239-4842
Burbank, CA 91505 www.musotica.com
(Animal/Character Costumes, Contemporary, Custom,
Dancewear, Evening Gowns, Full Costume Design, Faux Furs,
Gloves, Hats, Knitwear, Leathers, Military, Police, Shoes/Boots,
Special FX Costumes & Undergarments)

Muto-Little (323) 469-1618
519 N. Larchmont Blvd. FAX (323) 469-0298
Los Angeles, CA 90004 www.mutolittlecostumes.com
(Costume Construction)

One Night Affair (310) 474-7808
1726 S. Sepulveda Blvd. www.onenightaffair.com
West Los Angeles, CA 90025
(Designer Evening and Wedding Gown Rentals)

Palace Costume and Prop Co. (323) 651-5458
835 N. Fairfax Ave. FAX (323) 658-7133
Los Angeles, CA 90046 www.palacecostume.com
(1850s–Present Costume Rentals)

Pat Brymer Creations (323) 259-0400
136 N. Avenue 61, Ste. 102 FAX (323) 259-0358
Los Angeles, CA 90042 www.pbcreations.com
(Animal/Character Costumes, Custom & Mascots)

(818) 845-5970
Producers Air Force (818) 795-7463
One Orange Grove Terrace FAX (818) 845-4033
Burbank, CA 91501 www.producersairforce.com
(Flight Gear & Jet Fighter Mock-ups)

Prop Masters, Inc. (818) 846-3915
2721 W. Empire Ave. FAX (818) 846-1278
Burbank, CA 91504 www.propmastersinc.com
(Armor, Character Walkarounds, Space Suits &
Special FX Costumes)

reVamp (213) 488-3387
834 S. Broadway, Ste. 1200 FAX (775) 366-0036
Los Angeles, CA 90014 www.revampvintage.com

(323) 666-0680
Silvia's Costumes (323) 666-0702
4964 Hollywood Blvd. FAX (323) 666-6397
Los Angeles, CA 90027 www.silviascostumes.com
(Hand Embroidery & Period–Present Costume
Construction and Design)

Somper Furs (310) 273-5262
2270 W. Washington Blvd. FAX (310) 285-0842
Los Angeles, CA 90018 www.somperfurs.com
(Cashmere Capes, Furs & Leathers)

(310) 244-7260
Sony Pictures Studios (310) 244-5995
5933 W. Slauson Ave. FAX (310) 244-3378
Culver City, CA 90230 www.sonypicturesstudios.com

Denyse Specktor/The Big Yarn (805) 205-5869
www.thebigyarn.com

Sticks & Stones (818) 352-9538
FAX (818) 352-9538
www.sticksandstonesfx.com
(Full Costume Construction and Design; No Rentals)

Super Suit Factory (213) 700-1827
245 E. Glenarm St. www.supersuitfactory.com
Pasadena, CA 91106
(Animal/Character and Special FX Constumes)

(323) 222-6217
Susan Nininger Studio (213) 819-0640
www.susannininger.com
(Contemporary, Period and Sculptural Costume Construction)

Suss Design (323) 954-9637
7352 Beverly Blvd. FAX (323) 954-9674
Los Angeles, CA 90036 www.sussdesign.com
(Knitwear)

Sword & The Stone (818) 562-6548
723 N. Victory Blvd. FAX (818) 562-6549
Burbank, CA 91502 www.swordandstone.com
(Armor, Chain Mail and Leather Costumes)

(818) 375-1022
Total Fabrication, Inc. (877) 362-6322
FAX (818) 375-1023
www.totalfab.com
(Armor, Animal and Character Costume Construction and
Design, Full Costume Construction, Full Costume Design,
Futuristic Costuming, Mascots, Masks & Special FX Costumes)

**United American Costume/
American Costume** (818) 764-2239
12980 Raymer St. FAX (818) 765-7614
North Hollywood, CA 91605
(1700s–Present Costumes and Uniforms)

United Pacific Studios (213) 489-2001
729 E. Temple St. FAX (213) 489-2098
Los Angeles, CA 90012 www.unitedpacificstudios.com

Universal Studios
Costume Department   **(818) 777-2722**
100 Universal City Plaza   FAX **(818) 866-1544**
Bldg. 4250/3054   **www.filmmakersdestination.com**
Universal City, CA 91608
(Vintage and Contemporary Clothing and Accessories)

                                              (310) 582-8230
Ursula's Costumes, Inc.   **(310) 582-8231**
2516 Wilshire Blvd.   FAX **(310) 582-8233**
Santa Monica, CA 90403   **www.ursulascostumes.com**
(Costumes, Makeup, Masks & Wigs)

Warner Bros. Studio Facilities -   **(818) 954-1297**
Costume Department   **(800) 375-3085**
4000 Warner Blvd., Bldg. 153   FAX **(818) 954-3685**
Burbank, CA 91522   **www.wbcostumedept.com**

Ellene Warren   **(310) 559-5363**
(Beading, Custom Knit and Crochet, Embroidery, Full Costume
Design, Gloves, Hats & Knitwear; No Rentals)

Western Costume Co.   **(818) 760-0900**
11041 Vanowen St.   FAX **(818) 508-2190**
North Hollywood, CA 91605
                           www.lawardrobesupplies.com
(Character, Contemporary, Military & Period)

Aero Shade   (323) 655-2411
FAX **(323) 655-3180**
www.aeroshadeco.com

American Screen &
Window Coverings, Inc.   **(626) 453-0888**
1903 Central Ave.   FAX **(626) 453-0768**
South El Monte, CA 91733

Black Sheep Enterprises   **(818) 909-2299**
15745 Stagg St.   FAX **(818) 909-2288**
Van Nuys, CA 91406   **www.blacksheepent.net**
(Theatrical Drapery Fabrication and Rigging)

Blindsgalore.com   **(877) 702-5463**
6555 Nancy Ridge Dr., Ste. 100   FAX **(858) 643-9282**
San Diego, CA 92121   **www.blindsgalore.com**

    (818) 287-3800
Dazian Rentals   **(877) 232-9426**
7120 Case Ave.   FAX **(818) 287-3812**
North Hollywood, CA 91605   **www.dazian.com**

    (562) 402-8335
Eide Industries, Inc.   **(800) 422-6827**
16215 Piuma Ave.   FAX **(562) 924-2233**
Cerritos, CA 90703   **www.eideindustries.com**
(Awnings)

Fox Studios   **(310) 369-2290**
Drapery Department   FAX **(310) 369-4785**
10201 W. Pico Blvd.   **www.foxstudiosdrapery.com**
Los Angeles, CA 90035
(Custom Drapery Fabrication, Rentals & Upholstery)

    (323) 662-1134
Grosh Scenic Rentals   **(877) 363-7998**
4114 Sunset Blvd.   FAX **(323) 664-7526**
Los Angeles, CA 90029   **www.grosh.com**

Melrose Drapery   **(323) 464-8404**
6053 ½ Melrose Ave.   **www.melrosedrapery.com**
Los Angeles, CA 90038

Mod Plus, LLC   **(818) 982-0900**
6846 N. Lankershim Blvd.   **www.modplus.net**
North Hollywood, CA 91605
(20x20 Black Drape Rental)

Omega/Cinema Props   **(323) 466-8201**
5857 Santa Monica Blvd.   FAX **(323) 467-7473**
Hollywood, CA 90038   **www.omegacinemaprops.com**

    (323) 666-2502
Patmar Company   **(800) 341-5757**
4715 Melrose Ave.   FAX **(323) 666-5445**
Los Angeles, CA 90029   **www.patmarcompany.com**
(Window Treatments Only)

    (714) 921-9800
Quest Drape   **(877) 783-7888**
480 W. Meats Ave.   FAX **(866) 929-2488**
Orange, CA 92865   **www.questdrape.com**
(Curtains, Custom, Rentals & Theatrical Drapery)

Rent What? Inc.   **(310) 639-7000**
1978 Gladwick St.   FAX **(310) 639-7015**
Rancho Dominguez, CA 90220   **www.rentwhatinc.com**
(Curtains, Custom, Fabrication, Rentals & Theatrical Drapery)

    (818) 505-6290
Rose Brand   **(800) 360-5056**
10616 Lanark St.   FAX **(818) 505-6293**
Sun Valley, CA 91352   **www.rosebrand.com**
(Theatrical Draperies)

    (818) 503-0596
S & K Theatrical Draperies, Inc.   **(800) 341-3165**
7313 Varna Ave.   FAX **(818) 503-0599**
North Hollywood, CA 91605
    www.sktheatricaldraperies.com

Sew What? Inc.   **(310) 639-6000**
1978 E. Gladwick St.   FAX **(310) 639-6036**
Rancho Dominguez, CA 90220   **www.sewwhatinc.com**
(Curtains, Custom, Rentals & Theatrical Drapery)

ShowBiz Enterprises, Inc.   **(818) 989-7007**
15541 Lanark St.   FAX **(818) 989-8272**
Van Nuys, CA 91406   **www.showbizenterprises.com**
(Theatrical Draperies)

Stern's Draperies, Inc.   **(818) 789-3838**
FAX **(818) 789-0222**

Triangle Scenery   **(323) 662-8129**
1215 Bates Ave.   FAX **(323) 662-8120**
Los Angeles, CA 90029   **www.tridrape.com**

Universal Studios Property   **(818) 777-2784**
100 Universal City Plaza   FAX **(818) 866-1543**
Universal City, CA 91608
    www.filmmakersdestination.com

Valley Drapery/Linen Trees   **(818) 892-7744**
16616 Schoenborn St.   FAX **(818) 892-7884**
North Hills, CA 91343   **www.valleydrapery.com**

Warner Bros. Studio Facilities -
Drapery Department   **(818) 954-4426**
4000 Warner Blvd.   FAX **(818) 954-3428**
Burbank, CA 91522   **www.wbdrapery.com**

Aaron Cleaners   (310) 392-1843
(Same Day Service Before 9am) **www.aaroncleaners.com**

Apple Cleaners   (310) 208-1985
(Same Day Service Before 9:30am)

Brown's Cleaners   (310) 451-8531

     (310) 318-8047
Door to Door Valet Cleaners   (310) 871-1141
901 Manhattan Ave.   **www.doortodoorcleaners.com**
Manhattan Beach, CA 90266

Effrey's   (310) 858-7400

Four Seasons Cleaners   (323) 848-9158
8042 Santa Monica Blvd.
Los Angeles, CA 90046
(Same Day Service Before Noon)

George's Cleaning   (310) 826-6380
12120 Santa Monica Blvd.
Los Angeles, CA 90025

Highland Express   (323) 938-2884
(One Hour Service Available)

Hill Top Cleaners   (818) 761-6668
(Same Day Service Before 10am)   FAX **(818) 761-7780**
www.hilltopcleaners.com

Hollyway Cleaners   (323) 654-1271
(Same Day Service Before Noon)

La Cienega One Hour   (310) 659-7474
(Same Day Service Before 11am)   FAX **(310) 659-2612**
www.lacienegacleaners.com

Leonard's   (310) 274-9073
(Same Day Service Before 10:30am)

Merry Go Round Cleaners   (310) 277-5165
9038 Burton Way   **www.merrygoroundcleaners.com**
Beverly Hills, CA 90211
(Same Day Service Before 10am)

Milt & Edie's Dry Cleaners   (818) 846-4734
4021 W. Alameda Ave.   FAX **(818) 972-2739**
Burbank, CA 91506 **www.miltandediesdrycleaners.com**
(Four-Hour Service Available)

     (323) 654-1383
Peter's Magnolia Cleaners   (323) 653-0060
(Same Day Service Before 10am)   FAX **(323) 654-3096**
www.petersmagnoliacleaners.com

Premier Suede/   (949) 244-0943
Leather & Specialty Cleaners   (800) 245-2378
3419 Via Lido, Ste. 167
Newport Beach, CA 92663
     www.leather-suedefurniturecleaning.com
(Same Day Service Before 9:30am)

Antique Mall-Sherman Oaks (818) 906-0338
14034 Ventura Blvd. www.soantiquemall.com
Sherman Oaks, CA 91423
(Antique–Present, Costume Jewelry Design, Estate Jewelry, Eyeglasses, Fine Jewelry, Period, Rentals, Reproductions, Vintage, Watches & Wedding Rings)

(818) 506-4478
Avi Traditional Silversmithing (818) 355-0490
11131 Vanowen St., Ste. C FAX (818) 506-8766
North Hollywood, CA 91605 www.silversmith.com

Dr. Elise Brisco/
Hollywood Vision Center (323) 954-5800
955 S. Carrillo Dr., Ste. 105 FAX (323) 954-5807
Los Angeles, CA 90048 www.hollywoodvision.com
(Special FX Contact Lenses)

(760) 568-5111
Buckin' Ham Palace (760) 408-2055
(Antique, Costume Jewelry Design, Period, Rentals, Reproductions, Vintage & Watches)

(310) 729-1978
ByLaShan Jewelry (310) 314-3365
www.bylashan.com
(Belt Buckles, Costume Jewelry Design, Cuff Links, Gemstones & Semi-Precious Stones and Crystals)

Chic Little Devil Style House (310) 403-6929
1206 Maple Ave., 11th Fl.
Los Angeles, CA 90015
www.chiclittledevilstylehouse.com

Claude Morady (310) 275-3104
9615 Brighton Way, Ste. 338 FAX (310) 275-3754
Beverly Hills, CA 90210 www.claudemorady.com
(Antique–Contemporary Estate Jewelry)

Crystalarium (310) 652-8006
8500 Melrose Ave., Ste. 105 FAX (310) 652-8007
West Hollywood, CA 90069 www.crystalarium.com
(Crystal, Custom Gold and Silver Jewelry, Gems & Minerals)

(818) 888-8055
Face Value Props (818) 348-1320
5305 Tendilla Ave. www.facevalueprops.com
Woodland Hills, CA 91364
(Vintage and Contemporary Eyeglasses and Watches)

Femme Metale Inc. (951) 279-9737
2556 Avenida Del Vista, Ste. 201 FAX (951) 279-9747
Corona, CA 92882 www.femmemetale.com

Gail Freeman Antique &
Estate Jewelry (818) 632-0044
6433 Topanga Canyon Blvd., Ste. 211
Woodland Hills, CA 91303
(Antique and Estate Jewelry)

Dr. Jonathan Gording, Optometry (310) 470-4289
2035 Westwood Blvd. FAX (310) 474-3423
West Los Angeles, CA 90025 www.drgording.com
(Special FX Contact Lenses)

The Hand Prop Room, L.P. (323) 931-1534
5700 Venice Blvd. FAX (323) 931-2145
Los Angeles, CA 90019 www.hpr.com
(Antique–Present, Costume Jewelry, Eyeglasses, Fine Jewelry, Period, Reproductions, Sunglasses, Vintage, Watches & Wedding Rings)

Harry Winston Jewelers (310) 271-8554
310 N. Rodeo Dr. FAX (310) 271-8526
Beverly Hills, CA 90210 www.harrywinston.com

History for Hire (818) 765-7767
7149 Fair Ave. FAX (818) 765-1304
North Hollywood, CA 91605 www.historyforhire.com
(Antique–Contemporary Watches)

Image Optics (818) 981-3343
16745 Saticoy St., Ste. 102 FAX (818) 780-5498
Sherman Oaks, CA 91403
(Antique–Present Eyeglasses, Rentals, Purchase & Product Placement)

Jewelry Prop Shop/
Skinny Dog Design Group, Inc. (562) 436-7237
1750 E. Florida St. www.jewelrypropshop.com
Long Beach, CA 90802
(Costume Jewelry Design, Fine Jewelry, Gemstones, Period, Rentals, Reproductions & Wedding Rings)

Junk for Joy Vintage, Etc. (818) 569-4903
3314 W. Magnolia Blvd. www.junkforjoy.com
Burbank, CA 91505
(Period and Vintage Jewelry and Eyewear)

L. Wilmington & Co. (213) 624-8314
611 Wilshire Blvd., Ste. 1116 FAX (213) 624-7438
Los Angeles, CA 90017 www.lwilmington.com
(Custom Jewelry)

l.a. Eyeworks (323) 931-7795
7386 Beverly Blvd. FAX (323) 931-7712
Los Angeles, CA 90036 www.laeyeworks.com
(Eyeglasses & Sunglasses)

l.a. Eyeworks (323) 653-8255
7407 Melrose Ave. FAX (323) 653-8176
Los Angeles, CA 90046 www.laeyeworks.com

Liza Shtromberg Jewelry (323) 913-1444
2120 N. Hillhurst Ave. FAX (323) 913-1427
Los Angeles, CA 90027 www.lizashtromberg.com
(Handmade Silver and Gold Designer Jewelry)

Oliver Peoples (310) 657-2553
8642 Sunset Blvd. FAX (310) 657-7308
West Hollywood, CA 90069 www.oliverpeoples.com
(Eyeglasses & Sunglasses)

Optical Outlook (310) 447-8630
11677 San Vicente Blvd.
Los Angeles, CA 90049
www.dandeutschopticaloutlook.com
(Eyeglasses & Sunglasses)

Optical Outlook (818) 752-8606
12050 Ventura Blvd. FAX (818) 752-3043
Studio City, CA 91604
www.dandeutschopticaloutlook.com

Optical Outlook (310) 652-9144
8555 Sunset Blvd. FAX (310) 652-9108
West Hollywood, CA 90069
www.dandeutschopticaloutlook.com

Palace Costume and Prop Co. (323) 651-5458
835 N. Fairfax Ave. FAX (323) 658-7133
Los Angeles, CA 90046 www.palacecostume.com
(Ethnic and Period Jewelry)

The Pasadena Antique (626) 449-7706
Center & Annex (626) 449-9445
444 & 480 S. Fair Oaks Ave. FAX (626) 449-3386
Pasadena, CA 91105 www.pasadenaantiquecenter.com
(Antique–Present, Costume Jewelry Design & Vintage)

Prop Specs (323) 935-7776
FAX (323) 935-7778
www.propspecs.com
(Antique–Present Eyeglasses and Sunglasses)

Specs Appeal (323) 650-0988
7976 Santa Monica Blvd. FAX (323) 650-1579
Los Angeles, CA 90046 www.specsappealonline.com
(Contact Lenses, Eyeglasses & Sunglasses)

Spirited Bead & Klews Gallery, Inc. (661) 823-1930
(661) 823-1395
FAX (661) 823-1930
www.klewexpressions.com
(Ethnic and Modern Polymer Clay Jewelry)

Thanks for the Memories/TFTM (323) 852-9407
8319 Melrose Ave. FAX (323) 852-9407
Los Angeles, CA 90069
(Antique–Present, Costume Jewelry Design, Estate Jewelry,
Period, Rentals, Vintage & Watches)

Van Cleef & Arpels of California, Inc. (310) 276-1161
(877) 826-2533
332 N. Rodeo Dr. FAX (310) 276-8835
Beverly Hills, CA 90210 www.vancleef-arpels.com

Wanna Buy a Watch?, Inc. (323) 653-0467
8465 Melrose Ave. FAX (323) 653-9101
West Hollywood, CA 90069 www.wannabuyawatch.com
(Antique–Contemporary Watches and Wedding Rings)

Zirconmania (800) 858-6541
110 E. Ninth St., Ste. A1090 www.zirconmania.com
Los Angeles, CA 90079
(Costume Jewelry Design, Fine Jewelry, Period, Rentals,
Vintage & Wedding Rings)

Adam Basma Bazaar, Inc.   (323) 934-9493
   (213) 400-2525
1551 S. La Cienga Blvd.   www.adambasma.com
Los Angeles, CA 90035
(African, Antique, Ethnic, Indian, Middle Eastern, Theatrical
Fabrics, Treating, Trims, Upholstery & Vintage Textiles)

Archive Edition Textiles/
Textile Artifacts   (310) 676-2424
12575 Crenshaw Blvd.   FAX (310) 676-2242
Hawthorne, CA 90250   www.archiveedition.com
(Antique and Vintage Fabrics and Trim, Linens, Reproduction
Antique Fabrics, Upholstery & Vintage Textiles)

B. Black & Sons/King's Road   (213) 624-9451
548 S. Los Angeles St.   FAX (213) 624-9457
Los Angeles, CA 90013   www.bblackandsons.com

Caldelle Leather   (310) 314-8800
915 S. Mateo St., Ste. 106   www.caldelle.com
Los Angeles, CA 90021

Calico Corners   (818) 766-1120
   FAX (818) 766-8725
   www.calicocorners.com

California Flameproofing &
Processing Co., Inc.   (626) 792-6981
170 N. Halstead St.   FAX (626) 792-1071
Pasadena, CA 91107   www.californiaflameproof.com

Cameraflauge   (818) 762-1059
   (213) 304-9323
11635 Sheldon St.   FAX (818) 762-0207
Sun Valley, CA 91352   www.cameraflauge.com
(Blue/Green Screen Suits)

Cinergy Textiles, Inc.   (213) 748-4400
1422 Griffith Ave.   FAX (213) 748-3400
Los Angeles, CA 90021   www.cinergytextiles.com
(Furs, Knitting Supplies, Linens, Theatrical Fabrics & Trims)

Dazian Fabrics   (818) 287-3800
   (877) 432-9426
7120 Case Ave.   FAX (818) 287-3810
North Hollywood, CA 91605   www.dazian.com

Diamond Foam Company   (323) 931-8148
611 S. La Brea Ave.   FAX (323) 931-2086
Los Angeles, CA 90036
   www.diamondandfoamfabrics.com

A Dyeing Art   (818) 246-5440
325 Mira Loma Ave.   FAX (818) 246-5448
Glendale, CA 91204   www.adyeingart.com
(Fabric Dyeing)

F & S Fabrics   (310) 441-2477
10654 W. Pico Blvd.   FAX (310) 470-0228
Los Angeles, CA 90064   www.fandsfabrics.com
(Upholstery)

F & S Fabrics   (310) 475-1637
10629 W. Pico Blvd.   FAX (310) 470-0228
Los Angeles, CA 90064   www.fandsfabrics.com

Firetect   (661) 298-8801
   (800) 380-8801
26951 Ruether Ave., Ste. D   FAX (661) 298-8851
Canyon Country, CA 91351   www.firetect.com
(Flameproofing)

Foam Mart   (818) 848-3626
   (800) 943-8362
628 N. Victory Blvd.   FAX (323) 849-4245
Burbank, CA 91502   www.foammart.com
(Back Drop Material, Duyvetyne, Flameproofing, Furs, Outdoor
Canvas and Vinyls, Specialty Fabrics, Upholstery & Vinyls)

Francine Lecoultre Design Studio   (310) 666-9970
(Fabrics & Dyeing)

Golyester Antiques   (323) 931-1339
136 S. La Brea Ave.   www.golyester.com
Los Angeles, CA 90036
(Vintage Textiles)

J. Robert Scott, Inc.   (310) 680-4226
8737 Melrose Ave.   FAX (310) 659-4994
West Hollywood, CA 90069   www.jrobertscott.com

Lee's Decorative Showcase   (661) 702-9000
   (800) 347-5337
27333 West Muirfield Ln.   FAX (661) 702-9002
Valencia, CA 91355   www.leesdec.com
(Decorative Trimming, Fabrics & Tassels)

Michael Levine, Inc.   (213) 622-6259
920 S. Maple Ave.   FAX (213) 683-0504
Los Angeles, CA 90015

Norm's   (310) 559-4323
   FAX (310) 836-0387
   www.normsfoam.com

Oriental Silk Import & Export   (323) 651-2323
8377 Beverly Blvd.   FAX (323) 651-2323
Los Angeles, CA 90048   www.orientalsilk.com

Robbins Fabrics, Inc.   (323) 724-6180
2524 W. Beverly Blvd.   FAX (323) 724-6985
Montebello, CA 90640   www.robbinsfabrics.com

Rose Brand   (818) 505-6290
   (800) 360-5056
10616 Lanark St.   FAX (818) 505-6293
Sun Valley, CA 91352   www.rosebrand.com
(Theatrical Fabrics and Fabric Treating)

Sew What? Inc.   (310) 639-6000
1978 Gladwick St.   FAX (310) 639-6036
Rancho Dominguez, CA 90220   www.sewwhatinc.com

Denyse Specktor/The Big Yarn   (805) 205-5869
(Knitting Supplies)   www.thebigyarn.com

The Way We Wore   (323) 937-0878
334 S. La Brea Ave.   FAX (323) 936-6578
Los Angeles, CA 90036   www.thewaywewore.com
(Vintage Textiles)

Caravan West Productions   **(661) 268-8300**
35660 Jayhawker Rd.   FAX **(661) 268-8301**
Agua Dulce, CA 91390   **www.caravanwest.com**

    (310) 821-1434
Howard Coleman   **(310) 466-1650**
13131 Mindanao Way, Ste. 6   **www.gunwrangler.com**
Marina del Rey, CA 90292
(Armorer; Modern & Period)

FX House Associates   **(650) 855-9461**
P.O. Box 1536   **www.fxha.com**
Palo Alto, CA 94302

Global Effects, Inc.   **(818) 503-9273**
7115 Laurel Canyon Blvd.   FAX **(818) 503-9459**
North Hollywood, CA 91605   **www.globaleffects.com**
(Armor, Edged Weapons, Guns & Period)

The Hand Prop Room, L.P.   **(323) 931-1534**
5700 Venice Blvd.   FAX **(323) 931-2145**
Los Angeles, CA 90019   **www.hpr.com**
(Armor, Edged Weapons, Explosives, Guns & Period)

**Independent Studio
Services, Inc./ISS**   **(818) 951-5600**
9545 Wentworth St.   **www.issprops.com**
Sunland, CA 91040

LCW Props   **(818) 243-0707**
6439 San Fernando Rd.   FAX **(818) 243-1830**
Glendale, CA 91201   **www.lcwprops.com**

**Mike Tristano & Co., Weapons &
Historical Military Props**   **(818) 522-0969**
(Armor, Edged Weapons, Guns & Period) FAX **(818) 888-6447**
    www.moviegunguy.com

Omega/Cinema Props   **(323) 466-8201**
5857 Santa Monica Blvd.   FAX **(323) 461-3643**
Hollywood, CA 90038   **www.omegacinemaprops.com**

Sword & The Stone   **(818) 562-6548**
723 N. Victory Blvd.   FAX **(818) 562-6549**
Burbank, CA 91502   **www.swordandstone.com**

Tactical Edge Group   **(818) 361-5569**
    www.propguys.com/weapons/

Tactical Media Group   **(310) 880-6018**
578 Washington Blvd., Ste. 346
Marina del Rey, CA 90292   **www.tacticalmediagroup.net**
(Military Weapons & Military Uniforms)

AAA Flag & Banner Mfg. Co.   **(800) 266-4222**
8966 National Blvd.   FAX **(310) 836-7253**
Los Angeles, CA 90034   **www.aaaflag.com**
(Backdrops, Banners, Billboards, Day/Night Backdrops, Digital
Prints, Display Stands, Displays, Flags, Floor Graphics,
Graphics, Hanging Display, Hardware, Installation, Large
Format, Pennants, Pole Banners, Pop Displays, Posters,
Signage, Trade Show & Vehicle Wraps)

                                        (310) 213-6292
Aalco Signs & Graphics   **(562) 927-2500**
6424 Clara St.   FAX **(562) 927-7400**
Bell Gardens, CA 90201
(Signage)

Alex Pitt Photography   **(323) 665-4492**
                  www.alexpittphotography.com
(Banners, Digital Prints, Displays & Graphics)

Alley Kat Graphic   **(818) 480-8610**
1800 Victory Blvd.   FAX **(818) 242-7371**
Glendale, CA 91201   **www.alleykatgraphic.com**

Alpha Sign Company   **(818) 788-9401**
13831 Ventura Blvd.   FAX **(818) 788-0478**
Sherman Oaks, CA 91423   **www.alphasign.com**
(Sign Fabrication)

American Signs & Graphics   **(323) 938-7446**
311 N. Robertson Blvd., Ste. 161   FAX **(323) 938-7447**
Beverly Hills, CA 90211   **www.americansignsinc.com**
(Banners, Custom Signs, Graphics, Repair & Waterjet Lettering)

Art, Signs & Graphics   **(818) 503-7997**
6939 Farmdale Ave.   FAX **(818) 503-7999**
North Hollywood, CA 91605
                  www.artsignsandgraphics.com

Banners and Flags Unlimited/
Banner Marketing Group   **(805) 528-5018**
1147 E. Grand Ave.   FAX **(805) 528-5018**
Arroyo Grande, CA 93420
                  www.bannermarketinggroup.com
(Banners, Flags, Graphics, Labels, Point of Purchase Displays,
Posters & Signage)

                                        (213) 749-1262
Beagle Easel   **(562) 276-5483**
2201 Compton Ave.
Los Angeles, CA 90011
(Canvases, Crates, Easels, Panels, Shapes & Tables)

Ⓐ **Beyond Image Graphics, Inc.**   **(818) 547-0899**
1853 Dana St.   FAX **(818) 547-1470**
Glendale, CA 91201   **www.beyondimagegraphics.com**

Burbank Sign Co.   **(818) 846-1298**
454 N. Moss St.   FAX **(818) 846-0005**
Burbank, CA 91502   **www.burbanksign.com**
(Hand Lettering and Painting & Vintage Aircraft Nose Art)

Carwraps, Inc.   **(866) 972-7227**
7222 Valjean Ave.   **www.carwraps.net**
Van Nuys, CA 91406
(Banners, Billboards, Custom Lettering, Digital Prints, Displays,
Graphics, Hand Lettering, Letters, Logos, Posters, Point of
Purchase Displays, Signage, Vehicle Graphics &
Vehicle Wraps)

                                        (818) 252-6611
Charisma Design Studio, Inc.   **(800) 891-8617**
8414 San Fernando Rd.   FAX **(818) 252-6610**
Sun Valley, CA 91352   **www.charismadesign.com**
(Custom Lettering, Displays, Full-Service Shop, Letters, Logos,
Signage, Waterjet Cutting & Waterjet Lettering)

Cinnabar   **(818) 842-8190**
4571 Electronics Pl.   FAX **(818) 842-0563**
Los Angeles, CA 90039   **www.cinnabar.com**
(Billboards)

Colby Poster Printing Company   **(213) 747-5108**
1332 W. 12th Pl.   FAX **(213) 747-3209**
Los Angeles, CA 90015   **www.colbyposter.com**
(Billboards, Posters & Signage)

Collins Visual Media   **(818) 686-6581**
10518 Johanna Ave.   FAX **(818) 806-3229**
Shadow Hills, CA 91040   **www.collinsvisualmedia.com**
(Banners, Billboards, Custom Lettering, Digital Prints, Displays,
Electric Sign Fabrication, Flags, Full-Service Shop, Graphics,
Hand Lettering, Hand Painting, Labels, Letters, License Plates,
Logos, Newspapers, Point of Purchase Displays, Posters,
Printed Inserts, Repair, Sign Painting, Signage &
Vacuum-Formed Signs)

                                        (626) 932-0082
Concept Design   **(800) 846-0717**
718 Primrose Ave.   FAX **(626) 932-0072**
Monrovia, CA 91016   **www.conceptdesigninc.com**

Continental Scenery, Inc.   **(818) 768-8075**
7802 Clybourn Ave.   FAX **(818) 768-6939**
Sun Valley, CA 91352   **www.continentalscenery.com**

                                        (323) 467-4467
D'ziner Sign Co.   **(877) 397-6736**
1536 N. Highland Ave.   FAX **(323) 467-4494**
Hollywood, CA 90028   **www.showbizsigns.com**

Dangling Carrot Creative   **(661) 295-6610**
27520 Avenue Mentry   FAX **(661) 295-6699**
Valencia, CA 91355   **www.danglingcarrotcreative.com**

                                        (818) 287-3800
Dazian Fabrics   **(877) 432-9426**
7120 Case Ave.   FAX **(818) 287-3810**
North Hollywood, CA 91605   **www.dazian.com**
(Custom Banners and Displays)

Dennis Curtin Studio, Inc.   **(310) 827-8850**
1919 Empire Ave.   FAX **(818) 842-4623**
Burbank, CA 91504   **www.denniscurtin.com**

Designer Diner   **(818) 621-4751**
(Signs & Graphics)

Designing Letters   **(310) 702-4042**
4032 Marcasel Ave.   FAX **(310) 398-6002**
Los Angeles, CA 90066   **www.designingletters.com**
(Calligraphy, Custom Lettering, Graphics, Hand Lettering, Hand
Painting, Historical Writing, Illuminated Manuscripts,
Letters & Logos)

DesignTown, USA   **(310) 840-2940**
3615 Hayden Ave.   FAX **(310) 840-2935**
Culver City, CA 90232   **www.designtownusa.com**
(Banners, Billboards, Custom Lettering, Digital Prints, Displays,
Electric Sign Fabrication, Flags, Full-Service Shop, Graphics,
Hand Lettering, Hand Painting, Labels, Letters, License Plates,
Logos, Newspapers, Point of Purchase Displays, Posters,
Printed Inserts, Repair, Sign Painting, Signage,
Vacuum-Formed Signs, Vehicle Wraps, Waterjet Cutting &
Waterjet Lettering)

Earl Hays Press   **(818) 765-0700**
10707 Sherman Way   FAX **(818) 765-5245**
Sun Valley, CA 91352   **www.theearlhayspress.com**
(Generic Labels, License Plates, Newspapers & Printed Inserts)

                                        (818) 765-3549
Flix FX, Inc.   **(877) 326-8433**
7327 Lankershim Blvd., Ste. 4   FAX **(818) 765-0135**
North Hollywood, CA 91605   **www.flixfx.com**
(Vinyl Graphics & Vacuum-Formed Signs)

                                        (310) 369-2762
Fox Studios   **(310) 369-4636**
Sign Shop, 10201 W. Pico Blvd.   FAX **(310) 286-9462**
Los Angeles, CA 90035   **www.foxstudiossignshop.com**
(Full-Service Sign Shop)

The Hand Prop Room, L.P. (323) 931-1534
5700 Venice Blvd. FAX (323) 931-2145
Los Angeles, CA 90019 www.hpr.com
(Banners, Custom Lettering, Displays, Full-Service Shop,
Graphics, Labels, Letters, License Plates, Logos, Newspapers,
Posters, Printed Inserts, Signage & Waterjet Cutting)

Heaven or Las Vegas Neon (310) 636-0081
11814 W. Jefferson Blvd. FAX (310) 636-1959
Culver City, CA 90230 www.rentneon.com
(Signage)

i Communications, Inc. (818) 252-1300
7648 San Fernando Rd. FAX (818) 252-1385
Sun Valley, CA 91352 www.icommnetwork.net
(Signage)

JCL Graphics (213) 622-9775
2334 E. Eighth St. FAX (213) 622-9790
Los Angeles, CA 90021 www.bannersuperstore.com

Liquid Language,
The Art of Lettering (949) 458-3770
www.liquidlanguage.com

(323) 468-9931
Living Color Events (323) 468-9037
FAX (323) 468-9037
www.livingcolorgraphics.com

Mandex Led Motion Displays (805) 497-8006
2350 Young Ave. FAX (818) 889-4569
Thousand Oaks, CA 91360 www.ledsignage.com

(818) 552-6584
MetroMedia Technologies, Inc./MMT (800) 999-4668
1225 Los Angeles St. FAX (818) 552-6601
Glendale, CA 91204 www.mmt.com
(Banners, Billboards, Building Wraps, Custom Lettering,
Graphic Props, Point of Purchase Displays, Posters & Signage)

New Image Graphics & Printing (323) 876-1102
7109 Sunset Blvd. FAX (323) 874-8838
Los Angeles, CA 90046 www.newimagegraphic.com

Omega/Cinema Props (323) 466-8201
5857 Santa Monica Blvd. FAX (323) 461-3643
Hollywood, CA 90038 www.omegacinemaprops.com

Ⓐ **The Studios at Paramount** (323) 956-3729
The Studios at Paramount Sign Shop & Graphic Services
5555 Melrose Ave. www.thestudiosatparamount.com
Hollywood, CA 90038

Perlman Creative Group (310) 709-2091
P.O. Box 4016 www.perlmancreative.com
Newport Beach, CA 92661
(Banners, Billboards, Digital Prints, Displays, Full-Service Shop,
Graphics, Labels, Logos, Newspapers, Point of Purchase
Displays, Posters, Printed Inserts & Signage)

Production Graphics (818) 255-3000
6945 Farmdale Ave. FAX (818) 255-3399
North Hollywood, CA 91605
www.production-graphics.com

Prolab Digital Imaging (310) 625-4411
5441 W. 104th St. FAX (310) 846-4496
Los Angeles, CA 90045 www.prolabdigital.com

Really Fake Digital (800) 761-6995
518 N. Lake Ave. FAX (626) 666-3338
Pasadena, CA 91101 www.reallyfake.com
(Custom, Digital Imaging, Graphics & Signage)

Scenic Express, Inc. (323) 254-4351
3019 Andrita St. FAX (323) 254-4411
Los Angeles, CA 90065 www.scenicexpress.net

Sew What? Inc. (310) 639-6000
1978 Gladwick St. FAX (310) 639-6036
Rancho Dominguez, CA 90220 www.sewwhatinc.com

Sign Comm (213) 383-2111
3224 Beverly Blvd. FAX (213) 383-2128
Los Angeles, CA 90057 www.signcomminc.com

(323) 932-9231
Sign Makers (888) 744-6625
5772 W. Venice Blvd. FAX (323) 932-8605
Los Angeles, CA 90019 www.signmakers.com
(Banners & Signs)

Sign Zone (323) 465-8200
4873 Melrose Ave. FAX (323) 465-8202
Los Angeles, CA 90029 www.signzonela.com

Signtist, LLC (323) 658-5222
353 S. Fairfax Ave. FAX (323) 658-5226
West Hollywood, CA 90291 www.signtist.com

Signtist, LLC (310) 577-0300
4200 S. Lincoln Blvd. FAX (310) 581-5639
Marina Del Rey, CA 90292 www.signtist.com

Solbrook Display Corporation (818) 761-3297
8700 De Soto Ave., Ste. 210
Canoga Park, CA 91304

Studio Graphics (818) 951-5600
9545 Wentworth St. FAX (818) 951-2850
Sunland, CA 91040 www.issprops.com
(Generic Labels, License Plates, Newspapers & Signage)

(323) 962-0009
Total Look Studios Hollywood (323) 854-6775
1617 N. El Centro, Ste. 9
Hollywood, CA 90028
www.christopherxavierlozano.com
(Banners, Billboards, Custom Lettering, Digital Prints, Displays,
Graphics, Logos, Posters, Printed Inserts & Signage)

Universal Studios Graphic
Design & Sign Shops (818) 777-2350
100 Universal City Plaza FAX (818) 866-0209
Bldg. 4250/3054 www.filmmakersdestination.com
Universal City, CA 91608

The Unknown Artist (714) 662-0662
1565 Scenic Ave., Ste. C FAX (714) 662-0428
Costa Mesa, CA 92626 www.unknownartist.com

Enrico Ramon Venegas (323) 867-8414
www.enrico101.com
(Banners, Billboards, Graphics, Digital Prints, Hand Lettering,
Hand Painting, Logos, Scenic Artist & Sign Painting)

The Walt Disney Studios -
Sign Graphics Department (818) 560-5488
500 S. Buena Vista St. FAX (818) 563-3987
Burbank, CA 91521 studioservices.go.com

Warner Bros. Studio Facilities -
Design Studio/Sign & Scenic Art (818) 954-1815
4000 Warner Blvd. FAX (818) 954-2806
Burbank, CA 91522 www.wbsignshop.com

we-designstudio (323) 284-5130
P.O. Box 411223 FAX (561) 455-9644
Los Angeles, CA 90041 www.designstudio.com

WestOn Letters (818) 503-9472
7259 N. Atoll Ave. FAX (818) 503-9475
North Hollywood, CA 91605 www.westonletters.com
(Letters, Logos & Sign Systems)

Flags, Graphics & Signage

Almost Christmas Prop Shoppe/   (310) 286-0921
Cathy Christmas   (310) 748-4521
5057 Lankershim Blvd.   FAX (818) 285-9630
North Hollywood, CA 91601   www.christmasprops.com

California Nursery Specialties/
Cactus Ranch   (818) 894-5694
(Cactus & Succulent Plants)   FAX (818) 894-7794
www.california-cactus-succulents.com

Flower Art   (323) 935-6800
5859 W. Third St.   FAX (323) 935-6801
Los Angeles, CA 90036   www.flowerartla.com
(Artificial/Silk Plants and Flowers, Cacti, Christmas
Arrangements, Floral Designs, Trees & Wedding Arrangements)

Great Greens, Inc./Randy Martens   (805) 643-3486
2960 N. Ventura Ave.   FAX (805) 643-1954
Ventura, CA 93001

Green Set, Inc.   (818) 764-1231
11617 Dehougne St.   FAX (818) 764-1423
North Hollywood, CA 91605   www.greenset.com

   (714) 850-9227
Instant Jungle International   (800) 447-4007
2560 S. Birch St.   FAX (714) 850-9228
Santa Ana, CA 92707   www.instantjungle.com

Jackson Shrub Supply, Inc.   (818) 982-0100
11505 Vanowen St.   FAX (818) 982-1310
North Hollywood, CA 91605   www.jacksonshrub.com

Kimura Bonsai & Landscape   (818) 343-4090
17230 Roscoe Blvd.   FAX (818) 343-6101
Northridge, CA 91325
(Greensman, Landscaping & Trees)

   (818) 597-7790
Make Be-Leaves   (800) 634-1402
5311 Derry Ave., Ste. C   FAX (818) 597-7799
Agoura Hills, CA 91301   www.makebe-leaves.com
(Silk Flowers, Plants and Trees)

Omega/Cinema Props   (323) 466-8201
5857 Santa Monica Blvd.   FAX (323) 461-3643
Hollywood, CA 90038   www.omegacinemaprops.com

   (805) 986-8277
Pacific Sod   (800) 942-5296
305 W. Hueneme Rd.   FAX (805) 986-5210
Camarillo, CA 93012   www.pacificsod.com
(Grass, Sod & Wildflower Sod)

   (818) 787-9171
The Plant Connection   (323) 874-9102
   FAX (818) 787-8619
www.theplantconnection.org

Sandy Rose Floral, Inc.   (818) 980-4371
6850 Vineland Ave., Ste. C   FAX (818) 980-4598
North Hollywood, CA 91605   www.sandyrose.com

   (323) 278-0100
Superior Studio Specialties   (800) 354-3049
2239 S. Yates Ave.   FAX (323) 278-0111
Commerce, CA 90040   www.superiorstudio.com
(Artificial Plants and Flowers)

   (800) 893-6688
Tic-Tock   (323) 874-3034
1603 N. La Brea Ave.   FAX (323) 874-6134
Hollywood, CA 90028   www.tictock.com
(Floral Set Design)

Advanced Foam
1745 W. 134th St.
Gardena, CA 90249

(310) 515-0466
FAX (310) 515-3548
www.advancedfoam.com

A Atlas Foam Products
12836 Arroyo St.
Sylmar, CA 91342

(818) 837-3626
FAX (818) 837-1114
www.atlasfoam.com

Burman Industries
13536 Saticoy St.
Van Nuys, CA 91402

(818) 782-9833
FAX (818) 782-2863
www.burmanfoam.com

Daniels Engraving Co., Inc.
571 Fifth St.
San Fernando, CA 91340

(818) 837-3222
FAX (818) 837-1002
www.danielsdse.com

DeRouchey Urethane Creations Inc.
24771 Anchor Lantern St.
Dana Point, CA 92629
www.deroucheyurethanefoam.com
(24-Hour Service, Mobile Units & Spray Urethane Foam)

(949) 240-1960
(949) 289-0211
FAX (949) 361-4810

Diamond Foam Company
801 S. La Brea Ave.
Los Angeles, CA 90036
www.diamondandfoamfabrics.com

(323) 931-8148
FAX (323) 931-2086

Festival Artists, Inc.
120 N. Aspan Ave.
Azusa, CA 91702
www.festivalartists.org
(Mobile Units & Spray Urethane Foam)

(626) 334-9388
(626) 303-6042
FAX (626) 969-8595

Foam Mart
628 N. Victory Blvd.
Burbank, CA 91502
www.foammart.com
(Closed Cell Foam, Ensolite, L200-L600, Pillow Forms, Polyurethan Foam, Sound Proofing Foam & Stuffing)

(818) 848-3626
(800) 943-8362
FAX (323) 849-4245

Foam Sales and Marketing
1005 W. Isabel St.
Burbank, CA 91506   www.foamsalesandmarketing.com

(818) 558-5717
FAX (818) 558-5724

Foamway.com
(3D Foam Backgrounds, Chrome Mannequins, Chrome Props & Mobile Units)

(323) 908-3493
(514) 998-6935
FAX (450) 687-2326
www.foamway.com

Lee's Decorative Showcase
27333 West Muirfield Ln.
Valencia, CA 91355

(661) 702-9000
(800) 347-5337
FAX (661) 702-9002
www.leesdec.com

Storyland Studios/Foam Works
590 Crane St.
Lake Elsinore, CA 92530

(951) 674-0998
(800) 218-1932
FAX (951) 674-0245
www.foamworks.com

Trans FX, Inc.
2361 Eastman Ave.
Oxnard, CA 93030

(805) 485-6110
FAX (805) 751-0149
www.transfx.com

West Coast Sign Supply
2240 W. Washington Blvd.
Los Angeles, CA 90018 www.westcoastsignsupply.com

(323) 732-6666
FAX (323) 732-6660

Accessory Preview, Inc.   (323) 931-2050
353 N. La Brea Ave.   FAX (323) 931-2090
Los Angeles, CA 90036   www.accessorypreview.com
(Accessories, Antique–Contemporary, Asian and African
Artifacts, Bathroom Accessories, Cleared Art, Eclectic, Fossils,
Lighting, Minerals, Organic Artifacts & Shells and Corals)

Acme Design Group   (818) 767-8888
www.acme-designgroup.com

Antique Mall-Sherman Oaks   (818) 906-0338
14034 Ventura Blvd.   www.soantiquemall.com
Sherman Oaks, CA 91423
(Accessories, Antique–Contemporary, Deco, Eclectic,
Glassware, Hand Props, Lighting, Period & Vintage)

Aquatic Design   (310) 822-7484
          (310) 420-8379
4943 McConnell Ave., Ste. K   FAX (310) 822-8644
Los Angeles, CA 90066   www.aquatic2000.com
(Aquariums)

Arte de Mexico   (818) 753-4510
          (818) 769-5090
5356 Riverton Ave.   FAX (818) 769-9425
North Hollywood, CA 91601   www.artedemexico.com
(Antique, Eclectic & Mexican)

Avi Traditional Silversmithing   (818) 506-4478
          (818) 355-0490
11131 Vanowen St., Ste. C   FAX (818) 506-8766
North Hollywood, CA 91605   www.silversmith.com

Bits, Pieces & Leaves   (818) 505-6550
14006 Riverside Dr.   FAX (818) 505-1036
Sherman Oaks, CA 91423
(Garden & Patio)

Bleu Moon   (323) 939-9919
5374 W. Pico Blvd.   www.bleumoon.us
Los Angeles, CA 90019
(Indian and Asian Accessories, Antiques, Custom, Art, Eclectic,
Garden and Patio, Lighting, Office, Reproductions, Rugs,
Tapestries, Upholstery & Vintage)

Brainworks, Inc.   (323) 782-1425
          (323) 376-3113
5364 West Pico Blvd.   www.brainworksart.com
Los Angeles, CA 90019

Brook Furniture Rental   (818) 386-2158
15125 Ventura Blvd.   FAX (818) 386-0351
Sherman Oaks, CA 91403   www.bfr.com

Chestnuts & Papaya   (323) 937-8450
5042 Wilshire Blvd., Ste. 610   FAX (323) 937-7940
Los Angeles, CA 90036   www.chestnutsandpapaya.com

Connoisseur Antiques   (323) 658-8432
8468 Melrose Pl.   FAX (323) 658-7285
Los Angeles, CA 90069   www.connoisseurantiques.com
(European Antique Furniture and Accessories)

Contents Ltd.   (323) 655-2700
P.O. Box 691339   FAX (323) 655-2706
Los Angeles, CA 90069   www.contentsltd.com
(Accessories, Acrylic, Antique–Contemporary, Custom, Deco,
Eclectic, Garden and Patio, Glassware, Modern, Office, Period,
Reproductions, Rugs, Tapestries, Upholstery & Vintage)

Cort Furniture Rental   (310) 652-2678
8484 Wilshire Blvd.   FAX (310) 657-5615
Beverly Hills, CA 90211   www.cort.com
(Home & Office)

Cort Furniture Rental   (818) 907-5496
14140 Ventura Blvd.   FAX (818) 907-6415
Sherman Oaks, CA 91423   www.cort.com
(Home & Office)

Crest Office Furniture   (800) 833-4848
2840 N. Lima St., Ste. 110   www.crestoffice.com
Burbank, CA 91504
(Office)

Denmark 50   (323) 650-5222
          (323) 852-1939
7974 Melrose Ave.
Los Angeles, CA 90046
(Mid-Century, Modern, Upholstery & Vintage)

Design Direct   (818) 761-4488
Pacific Design Center, P.O. Box 1295
Studio City, CA 91614
(Contemporary and Period Fabric and Furniture)

Designer 8* Studio Rental   (323) 962-2062
          (800) 709-7007
6525 Sunset Blvd., Ste. G-2   FAX (310) 764-0394
Hollywood, CA 90028   www.designer8studiorental.com
(Custom & Modern Chic)

Designer's Furniture Resource   (818) 244-3061
300 S. Brand Blvd.   FAX (818) 244-1740
Glendale, CA 91204   www.dfglendale.com
(Accessories, Custom, Eclectic, Modern, Reproductions, Rugs,
Upholstery & Vintage)

Diva   (310) 278-3191
8801 Beverly Blvd.   www.divafurniture.com
Los Angeles, CA 90048
(Contemporary)

Dozar Office Furnishings   (310) 559-9292
9937 Jefferson Blvd., Ste. 100   FAX (310) 559-9009
Culver City, CA 90232   www.dozarrents.com
(Accessories, Contemporary, Custom, Eclectic & Office)

Emmerson Troop   (323) 653-9763
8111 Beverly Blvd.   FAX (323) 653-5445
Los Angeles, CA 90046   www.emmersontroop.com
(Antique–Modern & Asian)

Fine Custom Upholstery   (310) 837-5541
c/o Club Chair Inc, 8929 National Blvd.
Los Angeles, CA 90034 www.finecustomupholstery.com
(Art Deco Club Chairs, Reproductions & Upholstery)

FormDecor, Inc.   (310) 558-2582
14371 Industry Circle   www.formdecor.com
La Mirada, CA 90638
(Accessories, Acrylic, Custom, Eclectic, Garden and Patio,
Glassware, Hand Props, Lighting, Office, Prop House,
Reproductions, Rugs & Upholstery)

Galerie Lakaye   (323) 460-7333
          FAX (323) 460-7330
          www.galerielakaye.com

H. Studio   (818) 767-8448
          (800) 242-8992
8640 Tamarack Ave.   FAX (818) 767-5334
Sun Valley, CA 91352   www.hstudio.com
(Acrylic & Modern)

Hollywood Parts   (818) 255-0617
12580 Saticoy St., Bldg. C   FAX (818) 255-0613
North Hollywood, CA 91605   www.hollywoodparts.com
(Asset Management Storage and Sales,
Antique–Contemporary, Bondage Themed Equipment and
Furniture, Custom, Deco, Garden and Patio, Glassware, Hand
Props, Lighting, Modern, Office, Period, Prop House,
Reproductions, Rugs, Tapestries & Vintage)

Hopper's Office & Drafting Furniture   (323) 254-7362
          (800) 762-7717
2901 Fletcher Dr.   FAX (323) 254-8226
Los Angeles, CA 90065   www.draftingfurniture.com
(Drafting & Office)

House of Brienza, Inc.   (310) 839-9254
2358 S. Robertson Blvd.   FAX (310) 839-3254
Los Angeles, CA 90034
(Antique, Custom & Pine)

House of Props, Inc.   (323) 463-3166
1117 N. Gower St.   FAX (323) 463-8302
Hollywood, CA 90038   www.houseofpropsinc.com
(Antiques, China, Desktop Accessories, Fine Art, Hand
Props & Lamps)

J. Green, Inc.   (310) 428-0635
917 Lake St.   www.jgreenfurniture.com
Venice, CA 90291
(Custom, Fine Wood & Upholstery)

                              (323) 735-6455
Jan's & Co., French Antiques, Inc.   (323) 735-6392
1904 W. Adams Blvd.   FAX (323) 735-6240
Los Angeles, CA 90018   www.jansantiques.com
(Accessories, Antique, Eclectic, French Antiques, Lighting,
Office, Period, Prop House, Sculptures, Tapestries & Vintage)

Jefferson West, Inc.   (310) 558-3031
9310 Jefferson Blvd.   FAX (310) 558-4296
Culver City, CA 90232   www.jeffersonwest.com
(Antiques)

Jonathan Adler   (323) 658-8390
8125 Melrose Ave.   FAX (323) 658-8930
Los Angeles, CA 90046   www.jonathanadler.com
(Modern)

Kids Only Furniture & Accessories (818) 841-5544
1801 W. Verdugo Ave.   FAX (818) 841-5522
Burbank, CA 91506   www.kidsonlyfurniture.com
(Accessories, Baby Furniture, Childrens Furniture,
Contemporary, Custom, Kids Furniture, Modern, Office & Rugs)

Lawrence of La Brea   (323) 935-1100
671 S. La Brea Ave.   FAX (323) 935-1199
Los Angeles, CA 90036   www.lawrenceoflabrea.com
(Antique–Present Rugs)

Lennie Marvin Enterprises, Inc.   (818) 841-5882
3110 Winona Ave.   FAX (818) 841-2896
Burbank, CA 91504   www.propheaven.com
(Antique–Present Prop House)

                              (323) 665-5070
Living Room   (213) 448-0511
3531 Sunset Blvd.   FAX (323) 665-7056
Los Angeles, CA 90026   www.livingroomhome.com

**Los Feliz Rattan &
Wicker Showroom**   (818) 848-8462

Pat McGann   (310) 657-8708
746 N. La Cienega Blvd.   FAX (310) 358-0977
West Hollywood, CA 90069 www.patmcganngallery.com
(20th Century Design, Antiques & Art)

Modern Chair Rental   (562) 943-2500
1301 South Beach Blvd., Ste. C   FAX (562) 943-2511
La Habra, CA 90631   www.modernchairrental.com
(Accessories, Acrylic, Antique, Antique–Contemporary,
Contemporary, Custom, Deco, Modern, Office, Prop House,
Reproductions & Vintage)

                              (323) 651-5082
Modern One   (323) 651-0946
7956 Beverly Blvd.   FAX (323) 651-1130
Los Angeles, CA 90048   www.modern1.com
(Contemporary)

Modern Props   (323) 934-3000
5500 W. Jefferson Blvd.   FAX (323) 934-3155
Los Angeles, CA 90016   www.modernprops.com
(Art Deco, Contemporary and Modern Home, Garden and
Patio, Lighting & Office Accessories and Furniture)

Modernica   (213) 683-1963
2118 E. Seventh Pl.   FAX (213) 623-7565
Los Angeles, CA 90021   www.modernicaprops.net
(Accessories, Acrylic, Antique, Antique–Contemporary,
Contemporary, Custom, Deco, Eclectic, Garden and Patio,
Glassware, Hand Props, Lighting, Modern, Office, Period, Prop
House, Reproductions, Rugs, Tapestries, Upholstery & Vintage)

Mosaik   (323) 525-0337
7378 Beverly Blvd.   FAX (323) 525-0341
Los Angeles, CA 90036   www.e-mosaik.com
(Antique, Eclectic, Garden and Patio, Lighting,
Moroccan & Rugs)

Noble Forge   (818) 765-5004
7416 Varna Ave., Ste. D   FAX (661) 286-1166
North Hollywood, CA 91355   www.nobleforge.com
(Blacksmiths, Custom Metalwork & Fireplace Screens)

Off the Wall   (323) 930-1185
7325 Melrose Ave.   FAX (323) 930-1595
Los Angeles, CA 90046   www.offthewallantiques.com
(1920s–50s Art Deco and Eclectic Accessories & Lighting)

Office Connection   (949) 756-8882
1392 McGaw Ave.   FAX (949) 756-8883
Irvine, CA 92614   www.office-connection.net
(Office Furniture)

Office Furniture LA   (323) 750-6206
7625 Crenshaw Blvd.   FAX (323) 750-6208
Los Angeles, CA 90043   www.laofficefurniture.com

Old Pine Furnishings   (818) 507-7077
1830 Dana St.   FAX (818) 507-8799
Glendale, CA 91201   www.oldpinefurnishings.com
(Antique, Country, Garden & Patio)

Omega/Cinema Props   (323) 466-8201
5857 Santa Monica Blvd.   FAX (323) 461-3643
Hollywood, CA 90038   www.omegacinemaprops.com
(Antique–Present Prop House)

Omega/Cinema Props   (323) 466-8201
CP Four, 706 N. Cahuenga Blvd.   FAX (323) 467-2749
Hollywood, CA 90038   www.omegacinemaprops.com
(Antique–Present Prop House)

Omega/Cinema Props   (323) 466-8201
CP Three, 1107 N. Bronson Ave.   FAX (323) 467-7473
Hollywood, CA 90038   www.omegacinemaprops.com
(Antique–Present Prop House)

Omega/Cinema Props   (323) 466-8201
CP Two, 5755 Santa Monica Blvd.   FAX (323) 962-0345
Hollywood, CA 90038   www.omegacinemaprops.com
(Antique–Present Prop House)

The Pasadena Antique   (626) 449-7706
Center & Annex   (626) 449-9445
444 & 480 S. Fair Oaks Ave.   FAX (626) 449-3386
Pasadena, CA 91105 www.pasadenaantiquecenter.com
(Accessories, Antique–Contemporary, Deco, Eclectic, Garden
and Patio, Glassware, Hand Props, Lighting, Modern, Mission,
Rugs & Vintage)

Period Props   (818) 807-6677
1536 N. Evergreen St.
Burbank, CA 91505
(Prop House)

Pinacoteca   (323) 965-2722
5735 W. Adams Blvd.   FAX (323) 965-2730
Los Angeles, CA 90016   www.pinacotecaprops.com

Prop Services West - Hollywood   (818) 503-2790
7040 Laurel Canyon Blvd.   FAX (818) 503-2712
North Hollywood, CA 91605 www.propserviceswest.com
(Accessories, Antique–Contemporary, Eclectic, Mission, Prop
House & Rugs)

The Public Store Inc.   (888) 947-8673   (818) 553-1700
4536 Cutter St.   FAX (818) 937-9213
Los Angeles, CA 90039   www.thepublicstore.com

RC Vintage   (818) 765-7107   (323) 462-4510
7100 Tujunga Ave.   FAX (818) 765-7197
North Hollywood, CA 91605   www.rcvintage.com
(Vintage–Contemporary Prop House)

Retro Gallery   (323) 936-5261
1100 S. La Brea Ave.   FAX (323) 936-5262
Los Angeles, CA 90019   www.retroglass.com
(20th Century Glassware)

The Rug Warehouse   (310) 838-0450
3270 Helms Ave.   FAX (310) 204-0855
Los Angeles, CA 90034   www.therugwarehouse.com
(Antique–Modern Rugs)

Sculpture and Paintings by Bruce Gray   (323) 223-4059
688 S. Avenue 21   www.brucegray.com
Los Angeles, CA 90031
(Aluminum and Steel Sculpture, Art Furniture, Contemporary,
Custom, Eclectic, Garden and Patio, Mobiles & Modern)

Silk Roads Design Gallery   (323) 857-5588
145 N. La Brea Ave.   FAX (323) 933-9364
Los Angeles, CA 90036   www.silkroadsgallery.com
(Antiques, Asian Art & Furnishings)

Singh Imports:
Fine Art Objects of India   (310) 559-3826
3816 W. Jefferson Blvd.   FAX (310) 559-3829
Los Angeles, CA 90016   www.singhimports.com
(17th Century–Contemporary Indian, Architectural Fragments,
Islamic and Arabic Accessories, Antique, Garden and Patio,
Office, Oil Lamps, Reproductions, Rugs, Tapestries & Vintage)

Sleep Exquisite   (310) 478-3800
11727 Gateway Blvd.   www.sleepexquisite.com
Los Angeles, CA 90064
(Futons, Japanese Antiques and Bedding, Tansu &
Tatami Mats and Platforms)

Sony Pictures Studios   (310) 244-5999
5933 W. Slauson Ave.   FAX (310) 244-0999
Culver City, CA 90230   www.sonypicturesstudios.com

Sunny Meyer Fine Art   (818) 989-3721
(Art Rentals)   www.oldart.com

Sweet Smiling Home, Inc.   (213) 687-9630
2449 Hunter St.   FAX (213) 687-9638
Los Angeles, CA 90021   www.sweetsmilinghome.com
(Antique and Contemporary Chinese and Indonesian Furniture)

Thanks for the Memories/TFTM   (323) 852-9407
8319 Melrose Ave.   FAX (323) 852-9407
Los Angeles, CA 90069
(Accessories, Antique–Contemporary, Deco, Garden and Patio,
Glassware, Hand Props, Lighting, Modern, Office, Period,
Rugs, Tapestries, Upholstery & Vintage)

Universal Patio Furniture   (818) 762-9088
11055 Ventura Blvd.   FAX (818) 762-8249
Studio City, CA 91604   www.unifurn.com
(Patio Furniture)

Universal Studios Property   (818) 777-2784
100 Universal City Plaza   FAX (818) 866-1543
Universal City, CA 91608
(Custom)   www.filmmakersdestination.com

Warisan   (323) 938-3960
5619 W. Fourth St., Ste. 4   FAX (323) 938-3959
Los Angeles, CA 90036   www.warisan.com
(Asian Antiques)

Warner Bros. Studio Facilities - Property   (818) 954-2181
4000 Warner Blvd.   FAX (818) 954-4965
Burbank, CA 91522   www.wbpropertydept.com

Wertz Bros. Antique Mart   (310) 452-1800   (310) 477-4251
1607 Lincoln Blvd.   FAX (310) 452-1521
Santa Monica, CA 90404   www.wertzbrothers.com

Wertz Brothers Furniture, Inc.   (310) 477-4251
11879 Santa Monica Blvd.   FAX (310) 477-5136
West Los Angeles, CA 90025   www.wertzbrothers.com
(Used Home Furnishings)

Woven Accents   (310) 652-6520   (800) 222-7847
525 N. La Cienega Blvd.   FAX (310) 652-6594
Los Angeles, CA 90048   www.wovenonline.com
(Antique and Modern Rugs & Tapestries)

California Attractions, Ltd.   (818) 999-6255
8023 Van Nuys Blvd.
Van Nuys, CA 91409
(Carnival Equipment)

Candyland Amusements   (818) 266-4056
18653 Ventura Blvd., Ste. 235   FAX (818) 345-7988
Tarzana, CA 91356   www.candylandamusements.com

Chester's Circus &   (323) 751-3486
Carnival Equipment   (951) 233-6014
(Carnival and Circus Equipment)   FAX (323) 778-2025

   (800) 300-6114
Christiansen Amusements, Inc.   (760) 735-8542
P.O. Box 997   FAX (760) 735-8543
Escondido, CA 92033   www.amusements.com
(Carnival Equipment, Carnival Rides, Food Concessions,
Games & Slides)

   (626) 579-4454
Creative Inflatables   (800) 446 3528
9872 Rush St.   FAX (626) 579-5561
South El Monte, CA 91733   www.creativeinflatables.com
(Custom Inflatable Props, Jumpers, Misting Stations,
Slides & Tents)

DeWayne Events   (661) 251-4342
16520 Diver St.   FAX (661) 251-2488
Canyon Country, CA 91387
(Carnival and Circus Equipment)

   (951) 685-6014
Dortons, Inc.   (323) 751-3486
(Carnival and Circus Props)

   (323) 660-8180
Family Amusement Corporation   (800) 262-6467
876 N. Vermont Ave.   FAX (323) 660-8976
Los Angeles, CA 90029   www.familyamusement.com
(Antique Slot Machines, Arcade and Video Games, Billiard
Tables, Jukeboxes, Pinball Machines & Simulators)

   (310) 821-4490
Family Entertainment   (800) 379-4626
333 Washington Blvd., Ste. 360   FAX (310) 821-0522
Marina del Rey, CA 90292   www.familyentertainment.biz
(Carnival Rides & Gaming Equipment)

   (323) 871-1796
Franz Harary Productions   (323) 855-9886
(Magical Illusions)   www.harary.com

Grissom BIT Services   (760) 801-8283
(Carnival Rides & Games)   FAX (760) 737-8144

Hollywood Picture Cars   (323) 466-2277
3957 Ridgemont Dr., Ste. 101   FAX (310) 456-5692
Malibu, CA 90265   www.hollywoodpicturecars.com
(Jukeboxes, Penny Arcade Games & Pinball Machines)

   (323) 464-4444
Hollywood Toys & Costumes   (800) 554-3444
6600 Hollywood Blvd.   FAX (323) 464-4644
Hollywood, CA 90028
   www.yourhollywoodcostumes.com
(Toys & Magic Supplies)

   (323) 751-3486
Ⓐ L.A. Circus   (323) 547-5960
   www.lacircus.com
(Vintage–Modern Carnival and Circus Props & Canvas Tents)

Lucky Entertainment   (310) 277-9666
10271 Almayo Ave., Ste. 101   FAX (310) 284-8151
West Los Angeles, CA 90064
   www.luckyentertainment.com
(Artificial Cake, Carnival and Gambling Equipment, Jukeboxes,
Refreshment Carts & Video Games)

North American Amusements, Inc.   (909) 357-7130
11101 Calabash Ave.   FAX (909) 357-7136
Fontana, CA 92337   www.shamrockshows.com
(Carnival Rides, Food Concessions & Gaming Equipment)

Ⓐ Play-Well   (626) 793-0603
686 S. Fair Oaks Ave.   FAX (626) 793-2552
Pasadena, CA 91105   www.play-well.com
(Backyard Swing Sets, Play Houses & Playground Equipment)

   (818) 765-7107
RC Vintage   (323) 462-4510
7100 Tujunga Ave.   FAX (818) 765-7197
North Hollywood, CA 90028   www.rcvintage.com

   (323) 663-0122
Soap Plant/Wacko/La Luz de Jesus   (323) 666-7667
4633 Hollywood Blvd.   FAX (323) 663-0243
Los Angeles, CA 90027   www.laluzdejesus.com

   (818) 889-3336
Team Play Events   (818) 889-2224
2854 Triunfo Canyon Rd.   FAX (818) 889-2416
Agoura Hills, CA 91301   www.teamplayevents.com
(Billiard Tables, Carnival Equipment, Carnival Rides, Casino
Equipment, Circus Equipment, Classic Video Arcade Games,
Food Concessions, Games, Gaming Equipment, Inflatables,
Jumpers, Misting Stations, Novelties, Pinball Machines,
Refreshment Carts, Simulators, Slides, Tents & Video Games)

   (818) 842-3330
The Train Shack   (800) 572-9929
1030 N. Hollywood Way   FAX (818) 842-4562
Burbank, CA 91505   www.trainshack.com
(Toy Trains & Accessories)

A to Z Glass   (323) 723-3449
(800) 734-4933
(Breakaway, Glazed, Mirror & Tempered) FAX (323) 728-5506

Adamm's Stained Glass   (310) 451-9390
1426 Fourth St.   FAX (310) 451-9386
Santa Monica, CA 90401   www.adammsgallery.com
(Beveled, Carved, Custom, Etched, Fabrication, Leaded,
Restoration, Sculpted, Stained & Translucent)

Alfonso's Breakaway Glass, Inc.   (818) 768-7402
(866) 768-7402
8070 San Fernando Rd.   FAX (818) 767-6969
Sun Valley, CA 91352
www.alfonsosbreakawayglass.com

All New Glass & Mirror Co.   (323) 936-5245
FAX (323) 936-0280

Alva's Dance and Theatrical Supply   (310) 519-1314
1417 W. Eighth St.   FAX (310) 831-6110
San Pedro, CA 90732   www.alvas.com

ANA Special Effects, Inc.   (818) 909-6999
7021 Hayvenhurst Ave.   FAX (818) 782-0635
Van Nuys, CA 91406   www.anaspecialeffects.com
(Breakaway)

Charisma Design Studio, Inc.   (818) 252-6611
(800) 891-8617
8414 San Fernando Rd.   FAX (818) 252-6610
Sun Valley, CA 91352   www.charismadesign.com
(Carved, Custom, Decorative, Etched, Fabrication, Mirror,
Sculpted, Tempered & Waterjet Cutting)

Classic Glass Co.   (818) 519-0344
FAX (805) 375-3017
(Carved, Etched, Leaded, Mirror, Stained & Tempered)

Continental Glazing   (661) 295-8100
25050 Avenue Kearny, Ste. 115
Valencia, CA 91355

Giroux Glass, Inc.   (213) 747-7406
850 W. Washington Blvd.   FAX (213) 747-8778
Los Angeles, CA 90015   www.girouxglass.com
(Breakaway, Etched, Glazed & Mirror)

Hollywood Glass Company   (323) 661-7774
(323) 665-8829
5119 Hollywood Blvd.   FAX (323) 661-7261
Los Angeles, CA 90027   www.hollywood-glass.com

I.M.G. Glass & Mirror   (818) 968-0987
FAX (805) 579-0743
(Beveled, Breakaway, Carved, Custom, Decorative, Etched,
Fabrication, Glazed, Leaded, Mirror, Motion Effects,
Restoration, Tempered, Translucent & Waterjet Cutting)

International Glass Block   (323) 585-6368
1316 E. Slauson Ave.   FAX (323) 587-4421
Los Angeles, CA 90011   www.vetromosaico.com
(Glass Blocks)

**James Thomas Stained &
Leaded Glass**   (818) 763-5693
4375 Tujunga Ave.   FAX (818) 763-5692
Studio City, CA 91604   www.jtstainedglass.com
(Beveled, Etched, Leaded & Stained)

Motion Picture Glass   (818) 885-8700
9607 Canoga Ave.   FAX (818) 885-8701
Chatsworth, CA 91311

Pacific GlassWorks, Inc.   (310) 444-9191
FAX (310) 444-9161
www.pacificglassworks.com

Rohan Glass Co., Inc.   (818) 984-1000
(323) 877-6000
12442 Oxnard St.   FAX (323) 877-7447
North Hollywood, CA 91606   www.rohanglass.com
(Beveled, Breakaway, Custom, Mirror & Tempered)

Ruben's Glass & Mirrors   (323) 937-4774
616 S. La Brea Ave.   FAX (323) 937-0215
Los Angeles, CA 90036   www.rubens-glass.com

Shower Door Doctor   (818) 781-4957
(800) 540-0555
(Mirror & Tempered)   FAX (818) 762-2524

Special Effects Technologies, Inc.   (310) 490-6406
(310) 294-1161
7606 W. 91st St.   FAX (213) 947-1327
Los Angeles, CA 90045   acryliciceshop.com
(Custom Glass, Etched & Motion Effects)

Superior Glass Service   (323) 663-1167
(800) 237-3366
FAX (323) 663-1168
www.framelessdepot.com

UltraGlas, Inc.   (818) 772-7744
(800) 777-2332
9200 Gazette Ave.   FAX (818) 772-8231
Chatsworth, CA 91311   www.ultraglas.com
(Decorative, Embossed & Translucent)

A & S Case Company
(818) 509-5920
(800) 394-6181
5260 Vineland Ave.
FAX (818) 509-1397
North Hollywood, CA 91601   www.ascase.com
(Wardrobe Cases)

**Anytime Production
Equipment Rentals, Inc.**   (323) 461-8483
755 N. Lillian Way   FAX (323) 461-2338
Hollywood, CA 90038   www.anytimerentals.com
(Hangers, Makeup Tables, Portable Makeup Stations,
Steamers, Wardrobe Mirrors & Wardrobe Racks)

Apache Rental Group
(818) 842-9944
(818) 842-9875
3910 W. Magnolia Blvd.   FAX (818) 842-9269
Burbank, CA 91505   www.apacherentalgroup.com
(Wardrobe Supplies)

Atomic Production Supplies   (818) 566-8811
2621 N. Ontario St.   FAX (818) 566-8311
Burbank, CA 91504
www.atomicproductionsupplies.com
(Wardrobe Supplies)

Ball Beauty Supplies
(323) 655-2330
(800) 588-0244
416 N. Fairfax Ave.   www.ballbeauty.com
Los Angeles, CA 90036

Beauty Company   (310) 475-3531
10863 W. Pico Blvd.
West Los Angeles, CA 90064

Cal-East Imports   (310) 278-2520
232 S. Beverly Dr., Ste. 211   FAX (310) 278-4761
Beverly Hills, CA 90212
(Hairpieces & Wigs)

Cases for Visual Arts, Inc.
(818) 981-4238
(818) 693-6304
(Portable Makeup Stations)   FAX (818) 501-4215
www.casesforvisualarts.com

Castex Rentals   (323) 462-1468
1044 Cole Ave.   FAX (323) 462-3719
Hollywood, CA 90038   www.castexrentals.com
(Hangers, Makeup Cases, Makeup Supplies, Makeup Tables,
Portable Makeup Stations, Wardrobe Mirrors &
Wardrobe Racks)

Charlie Wright, Ltd.   (818) 347-4566
18645 Hatteras St., Ste. 121   FAX (818) 346-1043
Woodland Hills, CA 91364   www.wrighthair.com
(Wigs)

Chic Little Devil Style House   (310) 403-6929
1206 Maple Ave., 11th Fl.
Los Angeles, CA 90015
www.chiclittledevilstylehouse.com

Cinema Secrets   (818) 846-0579
4400 Riverside Dr.   FAX (818) 846-0431
Burbank, CA 91505   www.cinemasecrets.com
(Hair and Makeup Supplies)

Dinair   (818) 780-4777
5315 Laurel Canyon Blvd., Ste. 201   FAX (818) 780-4748
North Hollywood, CA 91607   www.dinair.com
(Hair and Makeup Supplies)

Extensions Plus   (818) 881-5611
17738 Sherman Way   FAX (818) 881-5220
Reseda, CA 91335   www.extensions-plus.com
(Hair and Wig Extensions)

Favian Wigs by Natascha   (818) 346-1104
23547 Hatteras St.   FAX (818) 346-1338
Woodland Hills, CA 91367
(Wigs)

Fred Segal Apothia   (323) 651-1935
8118 Melrose Ave.   FAX (323) 653-2178
Los Angeles, CA 90046   www.apothia.com

Frend's Beauty Supply
(818) 769-3834
(323) 877-4828
5270 Laurel Canyon Blvd.   FAX (818) 769-8124
North Hollywood, CA 91607
www.frendsbeautysupply.com

Galaxy Manufacturing Co.
(323) 728-3980
(800) 876-4599
5411 Sheila St.   FAX (323) 728-5971
Los Angeles, CA 90040   www.galaxymfg.com
(Barber and Beauty Salon Equipment)

Hair and Compounds   (818) 997-8810
FAX (818) 997-8860
www.haircompounds.com
(Hair and Wig Extensions, Hair Care Products & Wigs)

Hair Extensions By Sara Sierra   (626) 826-7313
1124 S. Cajon Ave.
West Covina, CA 91791

Industry Hair   (818) 562-1858
(By Appointment Only)

Innerspace Cases
(818) 767-3030
(800) 806-7689
11555 Cantara St., Ste. I   FAX (818) 767-6118
North Hollywood, CA 91605   www.innerspacecases.com
(Makeup and Wardrobe Cases)

The Joe Blasco Makeup Center
(323) 467-4949
(800) 553-1580
1670 Hillhurst Ave., Ste. 202   FAX (323) 664-7142
Los Angeles, CA 90027   www.joeblasco.com

Larchmont Beauty Center   (323) 461-0162
208 N. Larchmont Blvd.   FAX (323) 461-0164
Los Angeles, CA 90004   www.larchmontbeauty.com

Line 204 Inc.   (323) 960-0113
837 N. Cahuenga Blvd.   FAX (323) 960-0163
Hollywood, CA 90038   www.line204.com
(Wardrobe Supplies)

Lorac Cosmetics, Inc.
(818) 678-3939
(800) 845-0705
FAX (818) 678-3930
www.loraccosmetics.com

M.A.C.
(310) 659-6201
(800) 588-0070
(Makeup)   www.maccosmetics.com

Make Believe, Inc.   (310) 396-6785
3240 Pico Blvd.   FAX (310) 396-1936
Santa Monica, CA 90405
www.makebelieveinccostumes.com
(Hair and Makeup Supplies)

Naimie's Beauty Supply
(818) 655-9922
(818) 655-9933
12640 Riverside Dr.   FAX (818) 655-9999
Valley Village, CA 91607   www.naimies.com

Ole Henriksen Face/Body   (310) 854-7700
8622-A W. Sunset Blvd.   FAX (310) 854-1869
Los Angeles, CA 90069   www.olehenriksen.com
(Skin Care Products)

Origins   (626) 564-1790
(Makeup)   www.origins.com

Out of Frame Production Rentals   (323) 462-1898
1124 N. Citrus Ave.   FAX (323) 462-1897
Hollywood, CA 90038   www.outofframela.com
(Hangers, Makeup Tables, Portable Makeup Stations,
Steamers, Wardrobe Mirrors, Wardrobe Racks &
Wardrobe Supplies)

                                       (323) 469-9421
Outfitters Wig Co.   (323) 461-7822
6626 Hollywood Blvd.   FAX (323) 462-4730
Hollywood, CA 90028
(Custom Design Wigs & Human and Synthetic Eyelashes,
Facial Hair, Hair, Hairpieces, Wigs and Wig Extensions)

Quixote Studios   (323) 461-1408
1000 N. Cahuenga Blvd.   FAX (323) 461-5517
Los Angeles, CA 90038   www.quixote.com
(Wardrobe Supplies)

Riquette International   (310) 551-5253
269 S. Beverly Dr., Ste. 200   FAX (310) 551-5254
Beverly Hills, CA 90212
(Hair and Makeup Supplies)

                                       (877) 895-8215
Salon Equipment International   (877) 461-2972
16640 Bellflower Blvd.   FAX (562) 925-2461
Bellflower, CA 90706   www.salonequipment.com
(Barber and Beauty Equipment)

Set Stuff, Inc.   (323) 993-9500
1105 N. Sycamore Ave.   FAX (323) 993-9506
Hollywood, CA 90038   www.setstuffrentals.com
(Makeup Tables, Racks & Wardrobe Mirrors)

Studio Makeup Academy   (323) 465-4002
1438 N. Gower St., Studio 308
Hollywood, CA 90028 www.studiomakeupacademy.com

                                       (310) 372-7225
Sun Aired Bag Company   (424) 269-1649
3645 Inglewood Ave., Ste. 3   FAX (310) 372-5825
Redondo Beach, CA 90278   www.sunaired.com
(Wardrobe Bags, Racks and Supplies)

                                       (909) 392-8806
T.Z. Case   (888) 892-2737
1786 Curtiss Court   www.tzcase.com
La Verne, CA 91750
(Makeup Cases)

Temptu Pro   (310) 857-6778
2381 Rosecrans Ave., Ste. 100   www.temptu.com
El Segundo, CA 90245
(Airbrush Equipment and Accessories, Portable Makeup
Stations, Skin Care Products & Theatrical Makeup)

Travel Auto Bag Co. Inc.   (800) 361-6142
                                   FAX (201) 837-9427
                                 www.travelautobag.com
(Hangers, Makeup Cases, Steamers, Wardrobe Bags,
Wardrobe Cases, Wardrobe Racks & Wardrobe Supplies)

                                       (323) 651-4540
UVASUN   (323) 646-2004
8242 W. Third St., Ste. 100   FAX (323) 651-4150
Los Angeles, CA 90048   www.uvasun.com
(Air Brush Tanning & Tanning Beds)

West Hollywood Beauty
Supply & Salon   (323) 656-2237
                              www.westhollywoodbeauty.com

Wigged Out/Carol F. Doran   (818) 353-9650
                           www.caroldoranwiggedout.com
(Facial Hair, Hairpieces & Wigs)

Wilshire Beauty   (323) 937-2001
5401 Wilshire Blvd.   www.wilshirebeauty.com
Los Angeles, CA 90036

Wilshire Wigs & Accessories   (818) 761-9447
5241 Craner Ave.   FAX (818) 761-9779
North Hollywood, CA 91601   www.wilshirewigs.com
(Facial Hair, Hair and Wig Extensions, Hair Supplies,
Hairpieces & Wigs)

Cal Ice Company   (310) 590-1260
229 Glasgow Ave.
Engelwood, CA 90301
(Block, Crushed, Cubed, Dry & Snow)

Ice FX   (818) 785-1143
                             (888) 830-8383
14243 Bessemer St.   www.unionice.com/icefx.htm
Van Nuys, CA 91401
(Custom Cut, Dry, Photo & Snow)

LA Ice Art   (310) 670-1444
                             (323) 578-4244
(Block & Sculpted)   www.laiceart.com

Long Beach Ice   (888) 438-1956
                             (562) 438-8129
1600 Cherry Ave.   FAX (562) 856-1356
Long Beach, CA 90813   www.longbeachice.com
(Beverage, Block, Crushed, Cubed, Custom Cut, Dry,
Fabrication, Photo, Sculpted, Shards & Snow)

Long Beach Ice   (888) 438-1956
                             (562) 438-8129
16526 S. Normandie Ave. FAX (562) 856-1356
Gardena, CA 90247   www.longbeachice.com
(Beverage, Block, Crushed, Cubed, Custom Cut, Dry,
Fabrication, Photo, Sculpted, Shards & Snow)

Robin McCarthy   (818) 883-6223
4918 Escobedo Dr.
Woodland Hills, CA 91364
(Portable Plastic Ice Skating Surfaces)

Michael Plesh and Company   (818) 768-4444
(Fabrication & Fake Ice Cubes)   www.propmakers.com

                             (661) 259-0893
Newhall Ice Co.   (818) 362-9742
22502 Fifth St.   FAX (661) 259-0691
Newhall, CA 91321   newhallicecompany.com
(24-Hour Service; Block, Crushed, Cubed & Dry)

                             (818) 762-2237
North Hollywood Ice Co. (818) 984-3770
5257 Craner Blvd.   FAX (818) 762-6750
North Hollywood, CA 91601
(Dry & Photo)   www.northhollywoodice.com

Reliable Snow Service   (661) 269-2093
(Beverage, Clear Block, Dry Ice & Snow) FAX (661) 269-2237
                          www.reliablesnowservice.com

                             (310) 490-6406
Special Effects Technologies, Inc.   (310) 294-1161
7606 W. 91st St.   FAX (213) 947-1327
Los Angeles, CA 90045   acryliciceshop.com
(Beverage Ice, Fabrication & Fake Ice Cubes and Shards)

Willy Bietak Productions, Inc.   (310) 576-2400
1404 Third St. Promenade, Ste. 200   FAX (310) 576-2405
Santa Monica, CA 90401   www.bietakproductions.com
(Portable Ice Skating Surfaces)

Alpha Medical Resources, Inc. (818) 504-9090
7990 San Fernando Rd. www.alphaprops.com
Sun Valley, CA 91352

Angelus Medical & Optical Co., Inc. (310) 769-6060
13007 S. Western Ave. FAX (310) 769-1999
Gardena, CA 90249 www.angelusmedical.com
(Dental, Medical & Optical Props)

(310) 227-8200
Carrie Becks/A-1 Medical Advisor (310) 678-7601
345 Richmond St. FAX (310) 227-8205
El Segundo, CA 90245 www.redm33.com
(Ultrasound Equipment)

C.P. Two (323) 466-8201
5755 Santa Monica Blvd. FAX (323) 962-0345
Hollywood, CA 90038 www.omegacinemaprops.com

Dapper Cadaver (818) 771-0818
www.dappercadaver.com

E.C. Prop Rentals, Inc. (818) 764-2008
11846 Sherman Way FAX (818) 764-2374
North Hollywood, CA 91605 www.ecprops.com

(323) 728-3980
Galaxy Manufacturing Co. (800) 876-4599
5411 Sheila St. FAX (323) 728-5971
Los Angeles, CA 90040 www.galaxymfg.com
(Chiropractic and Massage Tables & Dental and
Medical Equipment)

History for Hire (818) 765-7767
7149 Fair Ave. FAX (818) 765-1304
North Hollywood, CA 91605 www.historyforhire.com

**Independent Studio
Services, Inc./ISS** (818) 951-5600
9545 Wentworth St. FAX (818) 951-2850
Sunland, CA 91040 www.issprops.com

Kingpin/MyMedSource (888) 755-9370
FAX (888) 755-9371
www.mymedsource.com

LCW Props (818) 243-0707
6439 San Fernando Rd. FAX (818) 243-1830
Glendale, CA 91201 www.lcwprops.com

Lennie Marvin Enterprises, Inc. (818) 841-5882
3110 Winona Ave. FAX (818) 841-2896
Burbank, CA 91504 www.propheaven.com

**Lynn Harding Antique Instruments of the
Professions and Sciences** (805) 646-0204
103 W. Aliso St. FAX (805) 646-0204
Ojai, CA 93023
(Antique Scientific Instruments)

Modern Props (323) 934-3000
5500 W. Jefferson Blvd. FAX (323) 934-3155
Los Angeles, CA 90016 www.modernprops.com
(Hospital, Medical, Optical & Scientific Instruments)

Morgue Prop Rentals (818) 957-2178
www.morgueproprentals.com

(323) 936-4104
Pico Medical Rents & Sells (800) 676-0400
6035 W. Pico Blvd. FAX (323) 936-3454
Los Angeles, CA 90035 www.shoppicomedical.com

Premiere Props (818) 768-3800
11500 Sheldon St. FAX (818) 768-3808
Sun Valley, CA 91352
(Contemporary and Period Props)

The Rational Past (310) 903-3663
FAX (310) 476-6278
www.therationalpast.com

Technical Props, Inc. (818) 761-4993
FAX (818) 761-5059

A & D Music Incorporated (949) 768-7110
22322 Colonna Dr. FAX (949) 716-7667
Laguna Hills, CA 92653 **www.admusic.net**
(Amplifiers, Antique, D.J. Gear, Drums, Guitars, Harps, Horns,
Keyboard Instruments, Microphones, Percussion, Rare
Instruments, Speakers & Strings)

Adam's Music (310) 839-3575
10612 W. Pico Blvd. FAX (310) 839-0167
Los Angeles, CA 90064 **www.adamsmusic.com**
(Amplifiers, Antique, Drums, Guitars, Horns, Keyboard
Instruments, Microphones, Percussion, Pianos, Rare
Instruments, Speakers & Strings)

CenterStaging LLC (818) 559-4333
3407 Winona Ave. FAX (818) 848-4016
Burbank, CA 91504 **www.centerstaging.com**
(Amplifiers, D.J. Gear, Drums, Guitars, Keyboard Instruments,
Microphones, Percussion, Pianos, Playback Systems, Rare
Instruments, Speakers, Strings, Wireless In-Ear Monitor
Systems, Wireless Guitar Systems & Wireless Mircophones)

Drum Doctors (818) 244-8123
520 Commercial St. FAX (818) 244-8120
Glendale, CA 91203 **www.drumdoctors.com**

(213) 359-0328
Drum Fetish (323) 397-4320
(Drums) **www.drumfetish.com**

Enchanted Melodies/CNS (818) 894-5694
8925 Densmore Ave. FAX (818) 894-7794
North Hills, CA 91343
(Antique Circus Organ with Operator)

Harps Unlimited (818) 986-3262
14122 Dickens St.
Sherman Oaks, CA 91423
(Harps & Rare Instruments)

Harpworld Music Company (818) 377-4085
P.O. Box 28-0189 **www.harpworld.com**
Northridge, CA 91328
(Antique–Present Harps, Harp Cases & Music Stands)

(818) 954-8500
Hollywood Piano Company (888) 697-4266
1033 Hollywood Way **www.hollywoodpiano.com**
Burbank, CA 91505

Kasimoff-Blüthner Piano Co. (323) 466-7707
337 N. Larchmont Blvd. FAX (323) 466-7708
Los Angeles, CA 90004
www.kasimoffpianoslosangeles.com
(Antique, Celesta, Harpsichords, Keyboard Instruments,
Pianos & Rare Instruments)

L.A. Percussion Rentals (310) 666-8152
26450 Ruether Ave., Ste. 208 FAX (661) 424-1986
Santa Clarita, CA 91350 **www.lapercussionrentals.com**
(Amplifiers, Antique, Drums, Guitars, Keyboard Instruments,
Microphones, Orchestral, Percussion, Rare Instruments,
Speakers & World/Ethnic Instruments)

Music Prop Services (818) 982-4100
7309 Clybourn Ave., Ste. 6 **www.musicprops.com**
Sun Valley, CA 91352
(Amplifiers, D.J. Gear, Drums, Guitars, Horns, Large Speakers,
Microphones, Pianos, Strings, Set Dressing & Prop House)

Norman's Rare Guitars (818) 344-8300
18969 Ventura Blvd. FAX (818) 344-1260
Tarzana, CA 91356 **www.normansrareguitars.com**
(Amps, Fretted String Instruments & Guitars)

Peter Rotter Music Services (818) 876-7500
4766 Park Granada, Ste. 106 FAX (818) 876-7503
Calabasas, CA 91302 **www.prmusicservices.com**

Studio Instrument Rentals/SIR (323) 957-5460
6465 Sunset Blvd. FAX (323) 957-5472
Hollywood, CA 90028 **www.sirla.com**

(818) 753-0148
Third Encore (800) 339-8850
10917 Vanowen St. FAX (818) 753-0151
North Hollywood, CA 91605 **www.3rdencore.com**
(Musical Instruments)

American Signs & Graphics　　　(323) 938-7446
311 N. Robertson Blvd., Ste. 161　　FAX (323) 938-7447
Beverly Hills, CA 90211　　**www.americansignsinc.com**

　　　　　　　　　　　　　　　　　　(626) 932-0082
Concept Design　　　　　　　　(800) 846-0717
718 Primrose Ave.　　　　　　FAX (626) 932-0072
Monrovia, CA 91016　　**www.conceptdesigninc.com**
(Fabrication)

The Hand Prop Room, L.P.　　　(323) 931-1534
5700 Venice Blvd.　　　　　　FAX (323) 931-2145
Los Angeles, CA 90019　　　　　　**www.hpr.com**
(Hand Props Only, Period–Present, Sales and
Rentals & Vintage)

Heaven or Las Vegas Neon　　　(310) 636-0081
11814 W. Jefferson Blvd.　　　FAX (310) 636-1959
Culver City, CA 90230　　　　**www.rentneon.com**

Hollywood Neon, Inc.　　　　　(323) 852-9611
　　　　　　　　　　　www.hollywoodneon.com

Neon by Ohashi　　　　　　　(323) 258-8701
6267 Saylin Ln.　　　　　　FAX (323) 258-4917
Los Angeles, CA 90042　　　**www.ohashineon.com**
(Fabrication)

Nights of Neon, Inc.　　　　　(818) 756-4791
13815 Saticoy St.　　　　　FAX (818) 756-4744
Van Nuys, CA 91402　　**www.nightsofneon.com**
(Fabrication & Props)

　　　　　　　　　　　　　　　　　　(818) 765-7107
RC Vintage　　　　　　　　　(323) 462-4510
7100 Tujunga Ave.　　　　　FAX (818) 765-7197
North Hollywood, CA 90028　　**www.rcvintage.com**
(Period–Present Signage)

Ahead Stereo   **(323) 931-8873**
7428 Beverly Blvd.   FAX **(323) 937-7285**
Los Angeles, CA 90036   **www.aheadstereo.com**
(Sound Equipment Rentals)

Alan Gordon Enterprises, Inc.   **(323) 466-3561**
5625 Melrose Ave.   FAX **(323) 871-2193**
Hollywood, CA 90038   **www.alangordon.com**
(Antique, Cameras, Microphones, Projectors, Prop Cameras,
Rentals & Sound Equipment)

                     (818) 767-7202
Apex Electronics   **(323) 875-1308**
8909 San Fernando Rd.   FAX **(818) 767-1341**
Sun Valley, CA 91352   **www.apexelectronic.com**
(Aircraft and Military Electronics)

Apex Jr.   **(818) 248-0416**
1450 W. 228th St., Ste. 4   FAX **(424) 263-4614**
Torrance, CA 90501   **www.apexjr.com**
(Electronic Props and Supplies)

                     (818) 549-9915
Astro Audio Video Lighting, Inc.   **(800) 427-8768**
6615 San Fernando Rd.   FAX **(818) 549-0681**
Glendale, CA 91201   **www.astroavl.com**
(Microphones, Rentals, Sound Equipment, Televisions & Video)

Coast Recording Props   **(818) 755-4692**
10715 Magnolia Blvd.   FAX **(818) 755-4694**
North Hollywood, CA 91601   **www.coastrecording.com**
(Prop Cameras & Radio Station and Recording Studio Props)

                     (800) 427-2382
CRE - Computer & A/V Solutions   **(888) 444-1059**
5732 Buckingham Pkwy   FAX **(877) 440-5252**
Culver City, CA 90230   **www.computerrentals.com/**
         products/Mac/Mac_rentals_Specialist.php
(Computer and Video Props, Graphic Displays, LED Electronic
Displays, Projectors & Rentals)

                     (818) 888-8055
Face Value Props   **(818) 348-1320**
5305 Tendilla Ave.   **www.facevalueprops.com**
Woodland Hills, CA 91364
(Prop Cameras & Vintage Cameras, Microphones and Radios)

The Hand Prop Room, L.P.   **(323) 931-1534**
5700 Venice Blvd.   FAX **(323) 931-2145**
Los Angeles, CA 90019   **www.hpr.com**
(Antique, Cameras, Dummy Equipment, Electronic, Electronic
Surveillance Equipment, LED Electronic Displays, Microphones,
Military, News Beta Cameras, Projectors, Prop Cameras,
Radios, Sound Equipment, Still Cameras, Video & Vintage)

Inter Video   **(818) 843-3624**
2211 N. Hollywood Way   FAX **(818) 843-6884**
Burbank, CA 91505   **www.intervideo24.com**
(Computer and Video Props, Electronic Surveillance
Equipment, News Beta Cameras, Prop Cameras,
Televisions & Video)

                     (800) 948-6902
MacEnthusiasts Inc.   **(800) 615-0492**
10600 W. Pico Blvd.   FAX **(310) 626-8472**
Los Angeles, CA 90064   **www.macenthusiasts.com**
(Mac Computers, Projectors & Rentals)

                     (805) 497-8006
Mandex Led Motion Displays   **(818) 825-9664**
2350 Young Ave.   **www.ledsignage.com**
Thousand Oaks, CA 91360
(Graphic Displays, LED Clocks, LED Counters, LED Electronic
Displays, LED Timers & Rentals)

Practical Props   **(818) 982-3198**
11754 Vose St.   FAX **(818) 980-7894**
North Hollywood, CA 91605   **www.practicalprops.com**

Prolab Digital Imaging   **(310) 625-4411**
5441 W. 104th St   FAX **(310) 846-4496**
Los Angeles, CA 90045   **www.prolabdigital.com**

Satellite America, Inc.   **(818) 710-9348**
22030 Ventura Blvd., Ste. E   FAX **(818) 710-1423**
Woodland Hills, CA 91364
(Satellite Dishes)

So Cal Production Source   **(310) 699-2787**
                   FAX **(310) 618-0129**
             www.scpsunlimited.com
(Aircraft, Antique, Cameras, Computer, Dummy Equipment,
Electronic, Electronic Surveillance Equipment, Graphic
Displays, LED Electronic Displays, Microphones, Military, News
Beta Cameras, Projectors, Prop Cameras, Radio Station and
Recording Studio, Radios, RED Cameras, Rentals, Satellite
Dishes, Sound Equipment, Still Cameras, Supplies, Televisions,
Video & Vintage)

                     (661) 775-1655
Studio Prop Rentals, Inc.   **(818) 679-4000**
21170 Centre Pointe Pkwy, Ste. 200
Santa Clarita, CA 91350   **www.studioproprentals.com**
(Cameras, Computers, Contemporary News Beta Cameras
and Accessories, Electronics, Props, Radios, Rentals, Sound
Equipment & Telephones)

This Town Productions   **(213) 926-7000**
1155 N. La Cienega Blvd.   **www.thistown.tv**
PH 7, P.O. Box 69179
West Hollywood, CA 90069
(Prop Cameras & Vintage Audio and Video Props)

1 A Aardvark, Inc.
(818) 609-0777
(310) 463-4489
17757 Victory Blvd.   FAX (818) 609-0666
Reseda, CA 91335   www.aardvarkprops.com
(Ambulances, Antique, ATVs, Buses, Cabin Cruisers, Camera Cars Classics, Carriages, Cigarette Boats, Classic, Contemporary, Convertibles, Cutaways, Damaged, Domestics, Emergency Vehicles, European, Exotics, Farm Vehicles, Fire Trucks, Fishing Boats, Futuristic, Hearses, Helicopters, High Performance, Horse and Buggy, Hot Rods, HumVees, Jeeps, Limousines, Lowriders, Luxury, Military Vehicles, Motorboats, Motorcycles, Muscle Cars, Police Vehicles, Rescue Vehicles, RVs, Salvage, Scooters, Semi Trucks, Sleighs, Sports Cars, Storage, Stunt Cars, Tanks, Taxis, Tractor Trailers, Trains, Troop Carriers, Trucks, Vehicle Coordination, Vehicle Transportation, Vintage, Wagons, Water Trucks, Woodies & Yachts)

1 A Action Picture Cars
(818) 767-2355
(818) 767-2121
11040 Olinda St.   FAX (818) 767-2311
Sun Valley, CA 91352   www.actionpicturecars.com
(Antique, ATVs, Buses, Classic, Contemporary, Convertibles, Cutaways, Damaged, Domestics, European, Exotics, Farm Vehicles, Hearses, High Performance, Hot Rods, Jeeps, Limousines, Lowriders, Luxury, Motorboats, Motorcycles, Muscle Cars, Police Vehicles, RVs, Salvage, Scooters, Sports Cars, Stunt Cars, Taxis, Trucks & Vintage)

1 A Constant Change Picture Vehicles
(818) 355-8824
15500 Erwin St., Ste. 328   www.seemyrentals.com
Van Nuys, CA 91411
(Ambulances, ATVs, Buses, Cabin Cruisers, Camera Cars, Classic–Contemporary, Convertibles, Domestics, European, Exotics, Farm Vehicles, Fire Trucks, Helicopters, Jeeps, Limousines, Military Vehicles, Motorcycles, Muscle Cars, Police Cars, RVs, Salvage, Scooters, Sports Cars, Storage, Taxis, Trailers, Trucks & Vehicle Coordination and Transportation)

310 Picture Cars
(310) 678-8007
6709 La Tijera Blvd., Ste. 247   FAX (310) 878-0338
Los Angeles, CA 90045
facebook.com/picturecardivision
(Ambulances, Buses, Cigarette Boats, Classics, Damaged, Emergency, Exotics, Fire Trucks, Limousines, Lowriders, Military Vehicles, Motorcycles, Muscle Cars, Taxis, Vehicle Coordination & Vehicle Transportation)

A-Z Bus Sales, Inc.
(951) 781-7188
(800) 437-5522
1900 S. Riverside Ave.   FAX (951) 778-2950
Colton, CA 92324   www.a-zbus.com

ABA Antique Autos, Inc./ ABA Picture Vehicles
(310) 323-9028
8306 Wilshire Blvd., PMB 900   www.abaaa.com
Beverly Hills, CA 90211
(Contemporary and Vintage Buses, Cars, Horse and Buggy & Trucks)

Action Antique Period Picture Cars   (562) 693-5641
2684 Turnbull Canyon Rd.
City of Industry, CA 91745
(Antiques, Antique Mechanic's Tools & Classic Cars and Trucks)

Advanced Fire & Rescue Services
(818) 837-7336
(661) 299-4801
16205 Lost Canyon Rd.   FAX (661) 298-3069
Canyon Country, CA 91387   www.advancedfire.com
(Fire Engines & Rescue Vehicles)

All Major Productions
(818) 344-5454
21221 Pacific Coast Hwy   FAX (310) 456-5692
Malibu, CA 90265
(Classic–Contemporary Cars, Motorcycles & Vehicle Transportation)

Arista Picture Vehicles
(562) 889-1999
8132 Firestone Blvd., Ste. 41   FAX (562) 928-1112
Downey, CA 90241
(Antique–Present, Buses, Classics, Convertibles, Exotics, Fire Trucks, Motorcycles Custom Built and Classic, Police Cars, Sports Cars & Taxis)

Armytrucks, Inc.
(661) 252-8511
(818) 523-6013
FAX (661) 252-8561
www.armytrucksinc.com
(Damaged, HumVees, Military Vehicles, Tanks, Vehicle Coordination & Vehicle Transportation)

Autotopia Collection & Picture Cars (512) 439-9416
3400 W. Olive Ave., Ste. 350   www.autotopiala.com
Burbank, CA 91505
(Classic, Contemporary, Convertibles, Domestics, European, Exotics, High Performance, Hot Rods, Jeeps, Limousines, Lowriders, Luxury, Muscle Cars, RVs, Sports Cars, Storage, Trailers, Vehicle Coordination & Vintage)

Avon Studio Transportation
(323) 850-0826
(800) 432-2866
7080 Santa Monica Blvd.   FAX (323) 467-4239
Los Angeles, CA 90038   www.avonrents.com
(Contemporary)

Avon Studio Transportation
(310) 277-4455
(800) 432-2866
9224 Olympic Dr.   FAX (310) 277-0675
Beverly Hills, CA 90212   www.avonrents.com

Avon Studio Transportation
(310) 392-8618
(800) 432-2866
2411 Lincoln Blvd.   FAX (310) 399-0901
Santa Monica, CA 90405   www.avonrents.com

B & R Police Motorcycle Studio Rentals
(818) 994-6673
P.O. Box 5669   FAX (818) 994-5513
Santa Monica, CA 90409   www.pmsrentals.com
(Classic–Contemporary)

Barry's Reel Vehicles
(661) 254-8114
FAX (661) 254-8115

Beverly Hills Rent-A-Car
(310) 274-6969
(855) 818-6969
9732 S. Santa Monica Blvd.   FAX (310) 550-1700
Beverly Hills, CA 90210   www.bhrentacar.com
(Camera Cars, Classics, Exotics, Sports Cars, Trucks & Vehicle Transportation)

Bircheff's Army Trucks
(909) 214-8413
(909) 985-6862
(Jeeps, Military Vehicles & Vintage)   FAX (909) 989-2030
www.armytruckrental.com

Bongorama
(310) 569-0354
www.blackhorsemedia.com
(Classic, High Performance, Hot Rods, Lowriders, Muscle Cars, Salvage, Sports Cars, Stunt Cars, Vehicle Coordination & Vehicle Transportation)

Bothwell Ranch
(818) 347-9000
5300 Oakdale Ave.   FAX (818) 587-9215
Woodland Hills, CA 91364
(Antiques & Classics)

Burbank Kawasaki
(818) 848-6627
(818) 749-5676
1329 N. Hollywood Way   FAX (818) 848-6630
Burbank, CA 91505   www.burbankkawasaki.com
(ATVs, Jet Skis & Motorcycles)

Cat Production Services/
Extreme Sports Filming (562) 596-7105
www.extremesportsfilming.com
(Ambulances, Antique, ATVs, Buses, Cabin Cruisers, Camera
Cars, Carriages, Cigarette Boats, Classic, Contemporary,
Convertibles, Cutaways, Damaged, Domestics, Emergency
Vehicles, European, Exotics, Farm Vehicles, Fire Trucks,
Fishing Boats, Futuristic, Hearses, Helicopter, High
Performance, Horse and Buggy, Hot Rods, HumVees, Jeeps,
Limousines, Lowriders, Luxury, Military Vehicles, Motorboats,
Motorcycles, Muscle Cars, Police Vehicles, Rescue Vehicles,
RVs, Salvage, Scooters, Semi Trucks, Sleighs, Sports Cars,
Storage, Stunt Cars, Tanks, Taxis, Tractor Trailers, Trailers,
Trains, Troop Carriers, Trucks, Vehicle Coordination, Vehicle
Transportation, Vintage, Wagons, Water Trucks,
Woodies & Yachts)

Cinema Vehicle Services (818) 780-6272
12580 Saticoy St. FAX (818) 780-1340
North Hollywood, CA 91605 www.cinemavehicles.com
(Classic–Contemporary)

(818) 905-6267
Classic Auto Rental Services (888) 647-6557
15445 Ventura Blvd., Ste. 60 FAX (818) 906-1249
Sherman Oaks, CA 91403 www.classicautorental.com
(1920's-Present Day Cars, Ambulances, Antique, Appraisals,
Arbitration, Bentleys, Buick, Buses, Cadillac, Car Rental, Chevy,
Classics, Contemporary, Convertibles, Damaged, Domestics,
European, Exotics, Farm Vehicles, Ford, Hero Cars, High
Performance, Hot Rods, Jeeps, Limousines, Lincoln, Luxury,
Motorhomes, Muscle Cars, Oldsmobile, Packard, Rolls-Royces,
Sports Cars, Taxis, Trailers, Trucks, Vehicle Coordination,
Vehicle Transportation, Vintage, Wagons & Woodies)

(818) 728-0607
Classic Car Rental Connection (800) 494-8092
17514 Ventura Blvd. FAX (818) 728-0684
Encino, CA 91316 www.101classiccarrental.com
(Antiques & Classics)

Classic Car Suppliers (310) 659-1711
1484 Sunset Plaza Dr. www.classiccarsuppliers.com
West Hollywood, CA 90069
(Antiques, Classics, Convertibles, Exotics & High
Performance Cars)

(800) 550-3125
Classic Limos (949) 495-3125
30251 Golden Lantern, E-510 FAX (949) 495-1652
Laguna Niguel, CA 92677 www.classiclimousines.com
(Classics, Limousines & Vintage)

Classy Chassis Rentals (818) 321-9022
18375 Ventura Blvd., Ste. 260 FAX (818) 881-0130
Tarzana, CA 91356 www.classychassisrentals.com
(1950s-1960s, Antique, Bentley, Classic, European,
Limousines, Luxury, Rolls Royce, Vintage & Wedding Cars)

Cornwell & Sheridan Motors, (310) 217-9060
Classic Auto Rentals (310) 995-8973
15700 S. Broadway FAX (310) 516-9427
Gardena, CA 90248 www.old-cars.net
(Antiques, Army Jeeps, Classics, Convertibles, Exotics, High
Performance, Limousines, Motorcycles & Vintage Cars)

(714) 630-0700
Corvette Mike (714) 342-2570
1133 N. Tustin Ave. FAX (714) 630-1810
Anaheim, CA 92807 www.corvettemike.com
(Classic Corvettes)

Customs by Eddie Paul, A Division (310) 322-8035
of EP Industries, Inc. (310) 259-0542
1330 E. Franklin Ave. FAX (310) 322-8044
El Segundo, CA 90245 www.deadlinetv.net
(Futuristic, High Performance, Hot Rods, Motorcycles &
Stunt Cars)

DH Automotive (323) 842-8393
dhautomotive.biz

Dougs Vintage Trailers (760) 949-3115
12567 Empire Pl. www.dougsvintagetrailers.com
Victorville, CA 92392
(Camera Cars & Trailers)

Dream Machines of America (323) 936-6141
105 S. Fairfax Ave. FAX (323) 936-2305
Los Angeles, CA 90036
(Antiques & Classics)

(800) 538-8799
Dream One (310) 670-5466
(Limousines) FAX (323) 933-1677
www.dreamonesedans.com

EagleRider Motorcycle Rentals (310) 536-6777
11860 S. La Cienega Blvd. FAX (310) 536-6776
Los Angeles, CA 90250 www.eaglerider.com

Executive Productions (310) 456-8833
3957 Ridgemont Dr. FAX (310) 456-5692
Malibu, CA 90265
(Antique, Contemporary, Exotics & Rare Cars)

EZ 1 Movie Cars (310) 717-3099
1450 W. 228th St., Ste. 27
Torrance, CA 90501

Five-Star Military Vehicles (310) 740-6931
FAX (714) 841-0317
www.militaryvehicles.com
(HumVees, Jeeps, Land Rovers, Tanks & Troop Carriers)

(323) 957-3333
Galpin Studio Rentals (800) 256-6219
1763 N. Ivar Ave. FAX (323) 856-6790
Hollywood, CA 90028 www.galpinstudiorentals.com
(Classic–Contemporary Cars, Motorcycles and Tractor Trailers)

(818) 891-1751
Galpin Studio Rentals (800) 256-6219
8353 Sepulveda Blvd. FAX (818) 778-3027
North Hills, CA 91343 www.galpinstudiorentals.com

Ghostlight Industries Inc. (818) 898-1938
956 Griswold Ave. FAX (818) 898-1948
San Fernando, CA 91340 www.ghostlightla.com
(Classic, Contemporary, Domestics, Emergency Vehicles,
Exotics, Farm Vehicles, Hearses, Hot Rods, Limousines,
Military Vehicles, Police Vehicles, Rescue Vehicles, Sports
Cars, Tanks, Taxis, Trucks, Vehicle Coordination and
Transportation & Vintage)

(805) 581-4700
Hardline Products Marine Group (805) 732-5341
677 Cochran St. FAX (805) 581-0022
Simi Valley, CA 93065
www.hardlineproducts.com/marinegroup
(Cabin Cruisers, Cigarette Boats, Fishing Boats, Jet Boats,
PWC & Yachts)

Harley-Davidson/Buell of Glendale (818) 246-5618
3717 San Fernando Rd. FAX (818) 246-5785
Glendale, CA 91204 www.glendaleharley.com

Michael Harper-Smith (818) 705-8655
5375 Tampa Ave. FAX (818) 996-3741
Tarzana, CA 91356 www.eurofilmcars.com
(European Vehicles Only: Cars, Double-Decker Buses,
Limousines, London Taxis, Motorcycles, Scooters,
Trucks & Vans)

(909) 593-3964
Hollywood Fire Authority (909) 227-1794
www.hollywoodfire.biz
(Fire Truck, Fire Trucks, Hook Ladder, Ambulances, Emergency
Vehicles, Fire Engines & Rescue Vehicles)

Hollywood Fires (661) 252-7629
FAX (661) 251-5165
www.hollywoodfires.com

Picture Vehicles

Hollywood Picture Cars (323) 466-2277
3957 Ridgemont Dr., Ste. 101   FAX (310) 456-5692
Malibu, CA 90265   www.hollywoodpicturecars.com
(Antique–Contemporary)

(818) 988-8860
Hypercycle (818) 261-7104
15941 Arminta St.   FAX (818) 988-8834
Van Nuys, CA 91406   www.hypercycle.com

(323) 851-5678
Jeffries Automotive Styling (818) 980-5367
3077 Cahuenga Blvd.
Los Angeles, CA 90068
(Antiques, Classics, Exotics, Futuristic and Stunt Cars &
Hot Rods)

(323) 345-4366
Jimmy's 411 Classics (310) 739-5795
2220 S. Beverly Glen, Ste. 305   FAX (323) 345-4366
Los Angeles, CA 90064   www.411classics.com

(818) 768-1678
Joe Ortiz Fire Trucks (818) 974-2218
11340 Allegheny St.   FAX (818) 768-1907
Sun Valley, CA 91352
(Ambulances & Fire Trucks)

(661) 270-0565
John Sarviss Stunt Equipment (661) 810-9456
39120 Bouquet Canyon Rd. www.radicalcameracars.com
Leona Valley, CA 93551
(Stunt Camera Cars)

(818) 713-0552
K4 Motorsports, Inc. (323) 462-2301
24907 Anza Dr.   FAX (818) 422-3763
Valencia, CA 91355   www.k4motorsports.com
(Race Cars & Semi Trucks)

Kick Ass Cars and Bikes (310) 278-9309
FAX (310) 278-9322
www.kickasscarsandbikes.com

(818) 222-6954
L.A. Motorsports (877) 526-6867
FAX (866) 294-3266
www.lamsports.com
(Classic–Contemporary Racing Vehicles &
Vehicle Transportation)

Lane Ranch & Company (661) 942-0435
42220 10th St. West, Ste. 101   FAX (661) 942-7485
Lancaster, CA 93534   www.laneranch.net
(Antique Cars, Farm Vehicles and Trucks)

(818) 361-9176
Mel Underwood Water Trucks, Inc. (800) 675-4855
13201 Foothill Blvd.   FAX (818) 361-9617
Sylmar, CA 91342
(Water Trucks)

Mr. Vintage Machine (213) 369-0281
www.mistervintagemachine.com
(Antique, Buses, Classic, Convertibles, Customs, European,
Exotics, Fire Trucks, Hearses, High Performance, Hot Rods,
Imports, Jeeps, Lowriders, Luxury, Micro Cars, Mopeds,
Motorboats, Motorcycles, Muscle Cars, Off Road Vehicles, RVs,
Scooters, Semi Trucks, Sidecars, Specialty Vehicles, Sports
Cars, Stock Cars, Trailers, Trucks, Vans, Vehicle Coordination,
Vintage, Wagons & Woodies)

NationwidePictureCars.Com (310) 659-1711
www.nationwidepicturecars.com
(Classic–Contemporary Cars, Motorcycles and Trucks)

OC Film Cars (714) 369-3122
1801 E. Katella Ave., Ste. 3001   www.ocfilmcars.com
Anaheim, CA 92805

Olympic Rent A Car (310) 751-6501
9230 W. Olympic Blvd., Ste. 204
Beverly Hills, CA 90212   www.olympicrentacar.com

Picture Car Warehouse (818) 341-8975
8400 Reseda Blvd.   FAX (818) 341-8926
Northridge, CA 91324   www.picturecarwarehouse.net
(Antiques–Present, Classics, Convertibles, Exotics, High
Performance, Military, Motorcycles, Police,
Sports Cars & Trucks)

(818) 769-0999
Picture Cars (818) 419-4405
5518 Vineland Ave.
North Hollywood, CA 91601
(Antique–Present, Classics, Convertibles, Exotics, Motorcycles,
Police and Sports Cars & Taxis)

Picture Vehicles Unlimited (661) 295-7711
25111 Rye Canyon Loop   FAX (661) 295-7721
Santa Clarita, CA 91355   www.picturevehicles.com
(Classics, Exotics, Race Cars & Semi Trucks)

(951) 684-5926
Regional Transit Service (951) 233-7732
2805 Cadet St.   FAX (951) 352-4596
Riverside, CA 92504
www.rts-regionaltransitservice.com
(Buses, City Transit Buses & Vintage)

Rent-A-Wreck (310) 826-7555
12333 W. Pico Blvd.   FAX (310) 207-0681
Los Angeles, CA 90064   www.rentawreck.com

San Bernardino Railroad
Historical Society (562) 438-9613
(1927 Steam Locomotive)   www.sbrhs.org

Scooters Bellissimo/Go, Scoot Go! (626) 523-7224
1730 La Senda Pl.   www.scootersbellissimo.com
South Pasadena, CA 91030
(Scooters)

(562) 941-0107
Secure Transportation (800) 856-9994
13111 Meyer Rd.   FAX (562) 906-2947
Whittier, CA 90605   www.securetransportation.com
(Hearses & Limousines)

(818) 762-0700
Showmobiles, Inc. (818) 822-4049
www.showmobilesinc.com
(Ambulances, Antique, ATVs, Buses, Carriages, Cigarette
Boats, Classic, Convertibles, Customs, European, Exotics,
Farm Vehicles, Fire Trucks, Fishing Boats, Hearses,
Helicopters, High Performance, Hot Rods, Imports, Jeeps,
Lowriders, Luxury, Micro Cars, Military Vehicles, Mopeds,
Motorboats, Motorcycles, Muscle Cars, Off Road Vehicles,
Police Vehicles, Rescue Vehicles, RVs, Scooters, Semi Trucks,
Sidecars, Specialty Vehicles, Sports Cars, Stock Cars, Tanks,
Tractor Trailers, Trailers, Trucks, Vans, Vehicle Coordination,
Vintage, Wagons, Water Trucks, Woodies & Yachts)

(818) 251-9700
Silverado Coach Company, Inc. (800) 544-7999
(Antiques, Classics & Rare Cars)   FAX (818) 884-4997
www.silveradocoach.com

(818) 554-5062
Specialty Car Locators (661) 451-2100
FAX (661) 554-7063
www.specialtycarlocators.com/equipmentforrent.htm
(Classic–Contemporary Military Vehicles, Police
Cars and Taxis)

(818) 882-2927
Specialty Vehicle Association (818) 523-3532
4121 Paredo Way, Ste. E
Simi Valley, CA 93063
(Classic–Contemporary Cars, Motorcycles and Trucks)

(818) 765-1201
Studio Picture Vehicles (818) 781-4223
7502 Wheatland Ave.   FAX (818) 506-4789
Sun Valley, CA 91352 www.studiopicturevehicles.com
(Ambulances, Detective Cars, Police Cars & Street Vehicles)

Sweet Sidecar Dude! (310) 560-8758
(Sidecar Motorcycle)

Terence of London   **(818) 364-7474**
13175 San Fernando Rd.
Sylmar, CA 91342
(British Taxis & Double-Decker Buses)

Transformedia   **(310) 210-9272**
2107 Curtis Ave., Ste. B
Redondo Beach, CA 90278
(Picture Vehicle Coordination)

Ann G. Troy   **(805) 729-1923**
P.O. Box 5883
Santa Barbara, CA 93108
(Picture Vehicle Coordination)

Unique Movie Cars, Inc.   **(888) 345-6227**
FAX **(702) 566-6194**
www.uniquemoviecarslasvegas.com
(Antiques, Contemporary and Futuristic Cars & Stunt Vehicles)

Vehicle Center   **(626) 288-1541**
(Four-Door Jeeps)   FAX **(626) 288-9559**

        (818) 355-2676
Vehicle Effects   **(818) 768-2343**
FAX **(818) 846-7576**
www.vehicleeffects.com
(Classic–Contemporary Muscle Cars and Trucks & Picture
Vehicle Coordination)

        (661) 259-7788
Veluzat Motion Picture Rentals   **(661) 259-9669**
P.O. Box 220597   FAX **(661) 259-3788**
Newhall, CA 91322   **www.melodyranchstudio.com**
(US/Foreign Military Vehicles)

VintageTrailerCrazy.com   **(949) 689-3964**
www.VintageTrailerCrazy.com
(Restored 1940's, 1950's Vintage Trailers, Airstreams, Canned
Hams, Hot Rods, RVs & Woodies)

Warner Bros. Studio Facilities -
Fire Department   **(818) 954-3269**
4000 Warner Blvd.   FAX **(818) 954-6957**
Burbank, CA 91522   **www.wbsf.com**
(Fire Engines & Rescue Vehicles)

The Wood N' Carr   **(562) 498-8730**
2345 Walnut Ave.   FAX **(562) 985-3360**
Signal Hill, CA 90755   **www.woodncarr.net**
(Camera Cars, Exotics & Woodies)

WW2 Military Vehicle Rentals, Ltd.   **(949) 632-4345**
www.ww2militaryvehiclerentals.com
(Jeeps, Military Vehicles, Tanks, Troop Carriers, Vehicle
Coordination and Transportation & World War II Vehicles)

Aquatic Design
(310) 822-7484
(310) 320-8379
4943 McConnell Ave., Ste. K   FAX (310) 822-8655
Los Angeles, CA 90066   www.aquatic2000.com
(Customized Aquariums)

California Quality Plastics   (909) 930-5535
2226 Castle Harbor Pl. South   FAX (909) 930-5540
Ontario, CA 91761   www.calplastics.com

Calsak Plastics
(310) 928-4100
(877) 777-0405
19801 S. Rancho Way, Ste. B   FAX (310) 928-4111
Rancho Dominguez, CA 90220   www.calsakplastics.com

Circle K Products   (951) 695-1955
P.O. Box 909   FAX (951) 695-0605
Temecula, CA 92593
(Liquid Plastics, Mold-Making & Silicones)

Fiberlay
(760) 520-1020
(800) 297-4541
5304 Custer St.   FAX (760) 520-1025
San Diego, CA 92110   www.walcomaterials.com
(Adhesives, Epoxies, Mold-Making, Silicones & Urethanes)

Flix FX, Inc.
(818) 765-3549
(877) 326-8433
7327 Lankershim Blvd., Ste. 4   FAX (818) 765-0135
North Hollywood, CA 91605   www.flixfx.com
(Vacuum-Forming)

Fox Studios
(310) 369-2712
(310) 369-4636
Staff Shop, 10201 W. Pico Blvd.   FAX (310) 969-1006
Los Angeles, CA 90035   www.foxstudiosstaff.com
(Acrylics, Fiberglass, Resin & Vacuum-Forming)

Graphic Spider/Custom Acrylic   (310) 844-7640
13004 S. Figueroa   FAX (310) 844-7641
Los Angeles, CA 90061   www.graphicspider.com
(3-D Cnc Milling, Acrylics, Aquariums, Custom, Fabrication, Cut
Letters, Fiberglass, Liquid Plastics, Plastics, Plexiglas, Resins,
Signage & Wood Cutting)

**Makeup & Effects
Laboratories, Inc./MEL**   (818) 982-1483
7110 Laurel Canyon Blvd., Bldg. E   FAX (818) 982-5712
North Hollywood, CA 91605   www.melefx.com
(Mold-Making & Vacuum-Forming)

Ⓐ **The Studios at Paramount**   (323) 956-5140
The Studios at Paramount   FAX (323) 862-2325
Manufacturing and Special Effects
5555 Melrose Ave.   www.thestudiosatparamount.com
Los Angeles, CA 90038

Planet Plastics   (909) 393-8222
14954 La Palma Dr.   FAX (909) 393-2552
Chino, CA 91710   www.planetplastics.com
(Acrylics & Plastics)

Plastic Depot   (818) 843-3030
2907 San Fernando Blvd.   FAX (818) 843-5451
Burbank, CA 91504   www.plasticdepotofburbank.com
(Acrylics, Fiberglass & Plastics)

Plastic Fabricators, Inc.
(310) 577-5342
(310) 577-5341
4943 McConnell Ave., Ste. M   FAX (310) 577-5342
Los Angeles, CA 90066   www.plasticfabricatorsinc.com
(Aquariums, Custom, Fabrication, Plastics, Plexiglas, Thermo
Forming & Vacuum-Forming)

Plastic Mart   (310) 268-1404
11665 Santa Monica Blvd.   FAX (310) 268-1411
Los Angeles, CA 90025   www.plasticmart.net
(Plastics & Plexiglas)

Projex International
(661) 268-0999
(877) 251-9095
9555 Hierba Rd.   FAX (661) 268-1885
Agua Dulce, CA 91390   www.projexinternational.com
(Fiberglass Fabrication and Props & Mold-Making)

Prop Masters, Inc.   (818) 846-3915
2721 W. Empire Ave.   FAX (818) 846-1278
Burbank, CA 91504   www.propmastersinc.com
(Fabrication, Mold-Making & Vacuum-Forming)

Regal Piedmont Plastics
(562) 404-4014
(800) 400-7342
17000 Valley View   FAX (562) 404-2855
La Mirada, CA 90638   www.regalpiedmontplastics.com
(Plastics & Plexiglas)

Rose Brand
(818) 505-6290
(800) 360-5056
10616 Lanark St.   FAX (818) 505-6293
Sun Valley, CA 91352   www.rosebrand.com

Sabic Polymershapes
(562) 942-9381
(866) 437-7427
9905 Pioneer Blvd.   FAX (562) 801-6267
Santa Fe Springs, CA 90670
www.sabicpolymershapes.com
(Acrylics, Adhesives, Custom, Epoxies, Fabrication,
Mold-Making Materials, Mylars, Plastics, Plexiglas, Silicones,
Thermo Forming, Urethanes, Vacuum-Forming & Vinyls)

Specialty Resources Company   (213) 819-6477
11651 Hart St.   FAX (213) 819-6477
North Hollywood, CA 91605   www.aliendecor.com
(Acrylics, Fiberglass, Hoses & Plastics)

Universal Studios Staff Shop   (818) 777-2337
100 Universal City Plaza, Bldg. 4250-1 FAX (818) 723-5952
Universal City, CA 91608
www.filmmakersdestination.com
(Acrylics, Custom, Fabrication, Fiberglass, Mold-Making,
Plexiglas, Resins, Thermo Forming & Vacuum-Forming)

Vinyl Technology, Inc.   (626) 443-5257
200 Railroad Ave.   FAX (626) 443-0531
Monrovia, CA 91016   www.vinyltechnology.com
(Fabrication)

**Warner Bros. Studio Facilities -
Staff Shop**   (818) 954-2269
4000 Warner Blvd., Bldg. 44   FAX (818) 954-2016
Burbank, CA 91522   www.wbstaffshop.com

West Coast Sign Supply   (323) 732-6666
2240 W. Washington Blvd.   FAX (323) 732-6660
Los Angeles, CA 90018 www.westcoastsignsupply.com

Clearance Domain LLC
(800) 562-1231
(310) 898-1233
FAX (888) 562-5120
www.clearancedomain.com

Creative Entertainment Services (818) 748-4800
2550 N. Hollywood Way, Ste. 100   FAX (818) 847-8625
Burbank, CA 91505   www.acreativegroup.com

Davie-Brown Entertainment (310) 754-4300
4721 Alla Rd.   www.daviebrown.com
Marina del Rey, CA 90292

Hadler Public Relations, Inc. (818) 552-7300
801 N. Brand Blvd., Ste. 620   www.hadlerpr.com
Glendale, CA 91203

HERO Entertainment Marketing, Inc. (805) 527-2000
4590 Ish Dr., Ste. 140   FAX (805) 527-2022
Simi Valley, CA 93063   www.heropp.com

I.S.M. Entertainment, Inc. (831) 824-8001
343 Soquel Ave., Ste. 523   FAX (831) 824-8002
Santa Cruz, CA 95062   www.ismentertainment.com

Keppler Entertainment, Inc. (310) 910-1885
137 Arena St.   www.keppler.com
El Segundo, CA 90266

Motion Picture Magic (818) 953-7494
3605 W. Pacific Ave.   FAX (818) 953-7113
Burbank, CA 91505   www.motionpicturemagic.com

Norm Marshall & Associates (818) 982-3505
11059 Sherman Way   FAX (818) 503-1936
Sun Valley, CA 91352   www.normmarshall.com

Pier 3 Entertainment (310) 376-5115
811 N. Catalina Ave., Ste. 1308   FAX (310) 318-5858
Redondo Beach, CA 90277
www.pier3entertainment.com

1 On 1 Computing Technologies   (818) 992-0584
(818) 254-5448
5824 Kentland Ave.   www.1on1comp.com
Woodland Hills, CA 91367
(Motion Control Rigs, Robotics, Robotic Props & Turntables)

360 Designworks/
360 Propworks Inc.   (310) 863-5984
www.360designworks.com
(Action Props, Custom, Foam Sculpting, FX Props, Mechanical
FX, Miniatures, Models, Oversized Props, Product Pours, Prop
Fabrication, Prototyping, Rigging, Sculpted Props & Welding)

Ⓐ Action Sets and Props   (818) 992-8811
7231 Remmet Ave.   FAX (818) 347-4330
Canoga Park, CA 91303   www.wonderworksweb.com
(Foreground Miniatures, FX Props & Space Suits)

Alex In Wonderland, Inc.   (818) 943-5264
(818) 943-5263
FAX (818) 558-4397
www.alexinwonderland.com

Alfonso's Breakaway Glass, Inc.   (818) 768-7402
(866) 768-7402
8070 San Fernando Rd.   FAX (818) 767-6969
Sun Valley, CA 91352

www.alfonsosbreakawayglass.com

All Access Staging & Productions   (310) 784-2464
1320 Storm Pkwy   FAX (310) 517-0899
Torrance, CA 90501   www.allaccessinc.com
(Turntables)

All Effects Company, Inc.   (818) 298-3730
5440 Tujunga Ave., Ste. 1217   www.allfx.com
North Hollywood, CA 91601

All Sets   (310) 430-0971
(310) 430-0970
2529 N. San Fernando Rd.   FAX (323) 221-9600
Los Angeles, CA 90065   www.allsets.com
(Action Props, Artificial Foods, Breakaways,
Computer-Controlled, Custom, Electronics, Foam Sculpting,
FX Props, Gadgetry, Hydraulics, Mechanical FX, Miniatures,
Models, Oversized Props, Prop Fabrication, Prototyping,
Radio-Controlled, Remote-Controlled, Rigging, Robotics,
Rubber Props, Sculpted Props, Skeleton Replication, Toy
Fabrication, Weapon Fabrication & Welding)

ANA Special Effects, Inc.   (818) 909-6999
7021 Hayvenhurst Ave.   FAX (818) 782-0635
Van Nuys, CA 91406   www.anaspecialeffects.com
(Action Props & Breakaways)

Anatomorphex/
The Sculpture Studio   (818) 768-2880
8210 Lankershim Blvd., Ste. 14   www.anatomorphex.com
North Hollywood, CA 91605
(Mechanical FX, Miniatures, Models & Statues)

Animal Makers, Inc.   (805) 523-1900
11991 Discovery Court, Ste. 411   FAX (805) 523-1903
Moorpark, CA 93021   www.animalmakers.com/store
(Action Props, Computer-Controlled, Custom, FX Props,
Mechanical FX, Models, Prop Fabrication, Radio-Controlled,
Robotics, Sculpted Props & Skeleton Replication)

Arteffex/Dann O'Quinn   (818) 506-5358
911 Mayo St.   FAX (323) 255-4599
Los Angeles, CA 90042   www.acfxo.com
(Action Props, Artificial Foods, Custom, Foam Sculpting, FX
Props, Gadgetry, Mechanical FX, Miniatures, Models, Motion
Control Systems, Oversized Props, Prop Fabrication,
Prototyping, Radio-Controlled, Remote-Controlled, Robotics,
Rubber Props, Sculpted Props & Toy Fabrication)

Artistic Entertainment Services   (626) 334-9388
120 N. Aspan   FAX (626) 969-8595
Azusa, CA 91702   www.aescreative.com

Automatrix Effects/David Waine   (323) 469-0088
137 N. San Fernando Rd., Ste. 134
Burbank, CA 91504   www.automatrixfx.com

Beckman Rigging/BRS Rigging   (310) 532-3933
(661) 510-2518
13516 S. Mariposa Ave.   FAX (310) 532-3993
Gardena, CA 90247   www.brsrigging.com
(Flying & Rigging)

Behold 3D   (323) 319-6501
(433) 433-5283
www.behold3d.com

Bellfx, LLC   (818) 590-4992
1908 First St.   www.bellfx.com
San Fernando, CA 91340
(Action Props, Mechanical FX, Prototypes & Robotics)

Benchmark Scenery, Inc.   (818) 507-1351
1757 Standard Ave.   FAX (818) 507-1354
Glendale, CA 91201   www.benchmarkscenery.com
(Turntables)

Bill Ferrell Co.   (818) 767-1900
10556 Keswick St.   FAX (818) 767-2901
Sun Valley, CA 91352   www.billferrell.com
(Motion Control Systems, Revolving Stages & Turntables)

Bone Clones, Inc.   (818) 709-7991
21416 Chase St., Ste. 1   FAX (818) 709-7993
Canoga Park, CA 91304   www.boneclones.com
(Human and Animal Bone, Skeleton and Skull Replications)

Greg Bonura   (818) 292-7663
(818) 386-8203
(Gadgetry & Hand and Specialty Props)

29 YEARS OF SERVICE

SPACE SHUTTLE
SPACE STATION
SETS & SUITS
MINIATURES OF
ALL TYPES

WONDERWORKS
818.992.8811

WWW.WONDERWORKSWEB.COM

Boom Boom Effects   (818) 772-6699
11100-8 Sepulveda Blvd., Ste. 339   FAX (818) 772-6689
Mission Hills, CA 91345
(Action Props)

                 (818) 885-6474
Branam Enterprises   (877) 295-3390
9152 Independence Ave.   www.branament.com
Chatsworth, CA 91311
(Flying & Rigging)

Bravo! Productions   (562) 435-0065
110 W. Ocean Blvd., Ste. 537   FAX (562) 435-4421
Long Beach, CA 90802   www.bravoevents-online.com
(Fabricated, Miniature, Oversized and Sculpted Props)

                 (818) 252-6611
Charisma Design Studio, Inc.   (800) 891-8617
8414 San Fernando Rd.   FAX (818) 252-6610
Sun Valley, CA 91352   www.charismadesign.com
(Custom, Foam Sculpting, FX Props, Mechanical FX, Oversized
Props, Sculpted Props & Waterjet Cutting)

Cinefx/Josh Hakian   (818) 835-9338
3737 Patrick Henry Pl.
Agoura Hills, CA 91301
(Mechanical FX)

Cinema Production Services, Inc.   (818) 989-2164
8743 Shirley Ave.   www.cpsfx.com
Northridge, CA 91324
(Action Props, Breakaways, FX Props, Mechanical FX,
Miniatures, Models, Oversized Props, Prop Fabrication,
Prototyping, Radio-Controlled, Toy Fabrication,
Vacuum-Forming & Welding)

Cinnabar   (818) 842-8190
4571 Electronics Pl.   FAX (818) 842-0563
Los Angeles, CA 90039   www.cinnabar.com
(Foam Sculpting, Miniatures, Models, Props, Prop Fabrication,
Prototyping & Welding)

Circle K Products   (951) 695-1955
P.O. Box 909   FAX (951) 695-0605
Temecula, CA 92593
(Action Props, Miniatures, Models, Prop Fabrication, Rubber
Props & Skeleton Replication)

Custom Movie Props   (310) 466-2910
     www.custommovieprops.com
(Action Props, Breakaways, Electronics, Fiberglass, Foam
Sculpting, FX Props, Gadgetry, Mechanical FX, Metal
Fabrication, Miniatures, Models, Oversized Props, Prop
Fabrication, Prototyping, Radio-Controlled, Rubber Props,
Sculpted Props, Toy Fabrication, Vacuum-Forming, Weapon
Fabrication & Welding)

Customs by Eddie Paul, A Division   (310) 322-8035
of EP Industries, Inc.   (310) 259-0542
1330 E. Franklin Ave.   FAX (310) 322-8044
El Segundo, CA 90245   www.deadlinetv.net
(Action Props, Custom, Foam Sculpting, FX Props, Gadgetry,
Hydraulics, Marine Equipment, Mechanical FX, Miniatures,
Models, Oversized Props, Prop Fabrication, Prototyping,
Radio-Controlled, Remote-Controlled, Rigging, Robotics,
Sculpted Props, Skeleton Replication, Toy Fabrication,
Turntables, Vacuum-Forming, Weapon Fabrication & Welding)

Dennis Curtin Studio, Inc.   (310) 827-8850
1919 Empire Ave.   FAX (818) 842-4623
Burbank, CA 91504   www.denniscurtin.com

DesignTown, USA   (310) 840-2940
3615 Hayden Ave.   FAX (310) 840-2935
Culver City, CA 90232   www.designtownusa.com
(Action Props, Breakaways, Custom, Electronics, Foam
Sculpting, FX Props, Gadgetry, Mechanical FX, Miniatures,
Models, Oversized Props, Pottery, Prop Fabrication,
Prototyping, Rubber Props, Sculpted Props, Vacuum-Forming,
Waterjet Cutting & Welding)

Don Wayne Magic, Inc.   (818) 763-3192
10907 Magnolia Blvd., Ste. 467
North Hollywood, CA 91601   www.donwaynemagic.com
(FX and Magic Props)

Douglas White Effects   (818) 785-4148
6859 Valjean Ave., Ste. 7   FAX (818) 785-2567
Van Nuys, CA 91406   www.dweffects.com
(Molds & Remote-Controlled Props)

DowDesign   (949) 650-3000
(Miniatures)   www.dowdesign.com

The Effects Group   (323) 876-0992
(Mechanical FX)   FAX (323) 876-0288
     www.theeffectsgroup.net

Elden Design/Elden Sets,
Props and Backdrops   (323) 550-8922
2767 W. Broadway   www.eldenworks.com/rickelden
Eagle Rock, CA 90041
(Custom, Flying, Gadgetry, Oversized Props, Prop Fabrication,
Prototyping, Rigging & Sculpted Props)

Electronic Design & Development   (818) 298-0827
27735 Rainier Rd.
Castaic, CA 91384

F/X Concepts, Inc./Lou Carlucci   (818) 508-1094
P.O. Box 1008   FAX (818) 508-1094
Santa Clarita, CA 91386
(Mechanical Special FX Props)

Fantasy II Film Effects   (818) 252-5781
     FAX (818) 252-5995
     www.fantasy2filmeffects.com
(Custom, Flying, Forced Perspective, FX Props, Marine
Equipment, Miniature Special Effects, Mechanical FX, Models,
Motion Control Systems, Prop Fabrication, Radio-Controlled,
Remote-Controlled Vehicles, Rigging, Rubber Props, Scale
Models, Sculpted Props, Underwater & Welding)

              (626) 334-9388
Festival Artists, Inc.   (626) 303-6042
120 N. Aspan Ave.   FAX (626) 969-8595
Azusa, CA 91702   www.festivalartists.org
(Foam Sculpting, Oversized Props & Welding)

Flanders Control Cables   (626) 792-7384
340 S. Fair Oaks Ave.   FAX (626) 792-5341
Pasadena, CA 91105   www.flandersco.com
(Mechanical FX and Rigging)

              (818) 765-3549
Flix FX, Inc.   (877) 326-8433
7327 Lankershim Blvd., Ste. 4   FAX (818) 765-0135
North Hollywood, CA 91605   www.flixfx.com
(Action Props, Artificial Foods, Custom, Electronics, Foam
Sculpting, FX Props, Gadgetry, Hydraulics, Mechanical FX,
Miniatures, Models, Oversized Props, Prop Fabrication,
Prototyping, Radio-Controlled, Remote-Controlled, Robotics,
Rubber Props, Toy Fabrication, Turntables,
Vacuum-Forming & Welding)

              (310) 369-2712
Fox Studios   (310) 369-2713
Staff Shop, 10201 W. Pico Blvd.   FAX (310) 969-1006
Los Angeles, CA 90035   www.foxstudiosstaff.com
(Acrylic, Custom Fabrication, Fiberglass, Plaster, Resin &
Vacuum-Forming)

              (818) 760-0875
Full Scale Effects   (818) 760-0042
6875 Tujunga Ave.   FAX (818) 760-0876
North Hollywood, CA 91605   www.fullscaleeffects.com

              (818) 840-9484
Gilderfluke & Co., Inc.   (800) 776-5972
205 S. Flower St.   FAX (818) 840-9485
Burbank, CA 91502   www.gilderfluke.com
(Motion Control Systems)

Global Effects, Inc. (818) 503-9273
7115 Laurel Canyon Blvd. FAX (818) 503-9459
North Hollywood, CA 91605 www.globaleffects.com
(Action Props, Custom, FX Props, Gadgetry, Mechanical FX, Miniatures, Oversized Props, Pottery, Prop Fabrication, Robotics, Rubber Props, Sculpted Props, Skeleton Replication & Weapon Fabrication)

Grant McCune Design, Inc. (818) 779-1920
6836 Valjean Ave. FAX (818) 781-9108
Van Nuys, CA 91406 www.gmdfx.com
(Mechanical FX, Miniatures, Models & Prototypes)

The Hand Prop Room, L.P. (323) 931-1534
5700 Venice Blvd. FAX (323) 931-2145
Los Angeles, CA 90019 www.hpr.com
(Action Props, Artificial Foods, Computer-Controlled, Custom, Electronics, Fabrication, Foam Sculpting, FX Props, Gadgetry, Mechanical FX, Models, Oversized Props, Prop Fabrication, Radio-Controlled, Remote-Controlled, Rubber Props, Sculpted Props, Vacuum-Forming & Waterjet Cutting)

(805) 496-0249
Rufus Herrick (206) 232-7100

HM Design (818) 985-8636
6353 Teesdale Ave. FAX (818) 985-8636
North Hollywood, CA 91606

HMS Creative Productions (818) 764-6151
1317 N. San Fernando Blvd., Ste. 144 FAX (818) 764-0620
Burbank, CA 91504 www.hms-studios.com
(Custom, Electronics, Foam Sculpting, Metal Fabrication, Miniatures, Models, Product Pours, Prop Fabrication, Prototyping, Rubber Props, Sculpted Props, Toy Fabrication, Welding & Vacuum-Forming)

(323) 465-3137
Hollywood Welding (323) 816-0440
1045 N. Hudson Ave. FAX (323) 465-5941
Hollywood, CA 90038 www.hollywoodwelding.com
(Fabrication & Welding)

I.D.F. Studio Scenery (818) 982-7433
6844 Lankershim Blvd. FAX (818) 982-7435
North Hollywood, CA 91605 www.idfstudioscenery.com

Icarus Rigging (323) 660-4112
3531 Casitas Ave. FAX (323) 660-6135
Los Angeles, CA 90039 www.icarusrigging.com
(Mechanical FX and Rigging)

Imagivations (818) 767-6767
11314 Sheldon St. FAX (818) 767-3637
Sun Valley, CA 91352 www.imagivations.com

**Independent Studio
Services, Inc./ISS** (818) 951-5600
9545 Wentworth St. www.issprops.com
Sunland, CA 91040

Industrial Artists (626) 355-1913
803 Woodland Dr.
Sierra Madre, CA 91024
(Action Props, Custom Turntables & Mechanical FX)

Innovision Optics (310) 453-4866
1719 21st St. FAX (310) 453-4677
Santa Monica, CA 90404 www.innovisionoptics.com
(Portable Tabletop Motion Control Systems)

Ironwood (818) 265-2055
1514 Flower St. FAX (818) 265-1680
Glendale, CA 91201 www.ironwoodscenic.com
(Rigging)

Jet Effects (818) 764-5644
6910 Farmdale Ave. FAX (818) 764-6655
North Hollywood, CA 91605 www.jeteffects.net
(Fabrication, Miniatures & Prop FX)

L.A. Propoint, Inc. (818) 767-6800
10870 La Tuna Canyon FAX (818) 767-3900
Sun Valley, CA 91352 www.lapropoint.com
(Action Props, FX Props, Gadgetry, Hydraulics, Mechanical FX, Motion Control Systems, Prototyping, Rigging, Turntables & Welding)

Peter McKinney (310) 863-5984
FAX (310) 356-3815
www.360designworks.com
(Action Props, Custom, FX Props, Mechanical FX, Miniatures, Models, Oversized Props, Product Pours, Prop Fabrication, Prototyping, Rigging & Welding)

Merritt Productions, Inc. (818) 760-0612
10845 Vanowen St. www.merrittproductions.com
North Hollywood, CA 91605
(Action Props, Mechanical FX & Miniatures)

Michael Plesh and Company (818) 768-4444
www.propmakers.com
(Ceramics, Custom, Oversized Props & Prototypes)

(818) 314-8211
Modelwerkes/Gene Rizzardi (661) 298-0627
www.modelwerkes.com
(Action Props, Breakaways, Custom, Foam Sculpting, FX Props, Gadgetry, Mechanical FX, Miniatures, Models, Prop Fabrication, Prototyping. Remote-Controlled, Rubber Props, Sculpted Props & Vacuum-Forming)

Modern Props (323) 934-3000
5500 W. Jefferson Blvd. FAX (323) 934-3155
Los Angeles, CA 90016 www.modernprops.com
(Contemporary, Electronic and Futuristic Props)

(805) 376-0206
NAC Co. (805) 405-7337
1772-J E. Avenida de Los Arboles FAX (818) 376-8407
Thousand Oaks, CA 91362 www.naceffects.com
(Action Props, Flying and Rigging, Mechanical FX, Motion Control Systems, Prototypes & Robotics)

New Deal Studios, Inc. (310) 578-9929
15392 Cobalt St. FAX (310) 578-7370
Sylmar, CA 91342 www.newdealstudios.com
(Mechanical FX, Miniatures & Models)

Optic Nerve Studios, Inc. (818) 771-1007
9818 Glenoaks Blvd. FAX (818) 771-1009
Sun Valley, CA 91352 www.opticnervefx.com
(Action Props, Breakaways, Futuristic, Mechanical FX, Miniatures, Models, Prop-Fabrication, Robotics & Vacuum-Forming)

Pacific Vision Productions, Inc. (626) 441-4869
210 Pasadena Ave. www.pacificvision.com
South Pasadena, CA 91030

🅐 **The Studios at Paramount Manufacturing
and Special Effects** (323) 956-5140
5555 Melrose Ave. www.thestudiosatparamount.com
Los Angeles, CA 90038

Peter Geyer Action Props, Inc. (818) 768-0070
8235 Lankershim Blvd., Ste. G www.actionprops.com
North Hollywood, CA 91605

**Pottery Manufacturing &
Distributing, Inc.** (310) 323-7772
18881 S. Hoover St. FAX (310) 323-6613
Gardena, CA 90248 www.potterymfg.com
(Concrete, Glazed & Terra Cotta Pottery)

Precision Turntable Services (661) 252-8444
28155 La Veda Ave. www.precisionturntables.com
Santa Clarita, CA 91387
(Turntables)

Prop Masters, Inc. (818) 846-3915
2721 W. Empire Ave. FAX **(818) 846-1278**
Burbank, CA 91504 **www.propmastersinc.com**
(Action and Oversized Props, Miniatures, Molds, Sculpting &
Vacuum-Forming)

Prop Services Unlimited/Jim Fox **(323) 462-2272**
FAX **(323) 469-9204**
(Gadgetry, Mechanical FX, Product Pours & Rigging)

Pure Imagination Co. **(818) 609-9629**
7940 Yolanda Ave. FAX **(866) 238-7703**
Reseda, CA **www.pureimaginationco.com**
(Action Props, Foam Sculpting, Gadgetry, Miniatures, Models,
Prop Fabrication, Radio-Controlled, Remote-Controlled, Rubber
Props Sculpted Props & Toy Fabrication)

(818) 846-6740
Quantum Creation FX, Inc. **(818) 268-5128**
3210 W. Valhalla Dr. FAX **(818) 846-0047**
Burbank, CA 91505 **www.quantumcreationfx.com**
(Action Props, Artificial Foods, Breakaways, Ceramics,
Computer-Controlled, Custom, Electronics, Extreme Sports,
Flying, Foam Sculpting, FX Props, Gadgetry, Hydraulics,
Mechanical FX, Miniatures, Models, Motion Control Systems,
Oversized Props, Pottery, Product Pours, Prop Fabrication,
Prototyping, Robotics, Rubber Props, Sculpted Props, Skeleton
Replication, Toy Fabrication, Vacuum-Forming, Weapon
Fabrication & Welding)

Rando Productions, Inc. **(818) 982-4300**
11939 Sherman Rd. FAX **(818) 982-4320**
North Hollywood, CA 91605 **www.randoproductions.com**
(Hydraulics & Mechanical and Motion Control
Rigging and Turntables)

(818) 762-1710
Reel EFX, Inc. **(213) 308-7289**
5539 Riverton Ave. FAX **(818) 762-1734**
North Hollywood, CA 91601 **www.reelefx.com**
(Mechanical FX)

(818) 346-2484
Reelistic FX, Inc./John Gray **(818) 621-2484**
(Action Props & Mechanical FX) FAX **(818) 346-2710**
www.r-fx.com

Renegade Effects Group **(818) 362-8061**
11312 Hartland St. FAX **(818) 980-8849**
North Hollywood, CA 91605 **www.renegadeeffects.com**
(Miniatures, Models & Vacuum-Forming)

Sculptors Pride Design Studios **(626) 256-4779**
902 S. Primrose Ave.
Monrovia, CA 91016
(Architectual, Miniatures & Oversized and Sculpted Props)

The Shape Shop **(310) 532-4391**
16709 Gramercy Pl., Ste. B **www.theshapeshop.net**
Torrance, CA 90247
(Custom, Miniatures, Models, Molds, Oversized Props, Prop
Fabrication, Prototyping, Rubber Props & Vacuum-Forming)

Shelly Ward Enterprises **(818) 255-5850**
(Turntables) FAX **(818) 255-5450**
www.shellywardent.com

Snow Business Hollywood, Inc. **(818) 884-3009**
21318 Hart St. FAX **(818) 884-3110**
Canoga Park, CA 91303
www.snowbusinesshollywood.com
(Ice Cubes, Icicles, Igloos & Snowmen)

So Cal Production Source **(310) 699-2787**
FAX **(310) 618-0129**
www.scpsunlimited.com
(Action Props, Artificial Foods, Breakaways, Ceramics,
Computer-Controlled, Custom, Electronics, Extreme Sports,
Flying, Foam Sculpting, FX Props, Gadgetry, Hydraulics,
Lasercutting, Marine Equipment, Mechanical FX, Miniatures,
Models, Motion Control Systems, Oversized Props, Pottery,
Product Pours, Prop Fabrication, Prototyping, Radio-Controlled,
Remote-Controlled, Rigging, Robotics, Rubber Props, Sculpted
Props, Skeleton Replication, Toy Fabrication, Turntables,
Vacuum-Forming, Waterjet Cutting, Weapon
Fabrication & Welding)

(310) 490-6406
Special Effects Technologies, Inc. **(310) 294-1161**
7606 W. 91st St. FAX **(213) 947-1327**
Los Angeles, CA 90045 **acryliciceshop.com**
(Motion Rigging, Prop Making, Tabletop Rigs & Turntables)

Special Effects Unlimited, Inc. **(323) 466-3361**
1005 Lillian Way FAX **(323) 466-5712**
Hollywood, CA 90038 **www.specialeffectsunlimited.com**
(Mechanical FX)

Specialty International **(818) 349-0810**
20730 Dearborn St. FAX **(818) 349-0910**
Chatsworth, CA 91311 **www.specialtyinternational.com**
(Laser Cutting, Metal Fabrication & Welding)

Spectral Motion, Inc. **(818) 956-6080**
1849 Dana St. FAX **(818) 956-6083**
Glendale, CA 91201 **www.spectralmotion.com**
(Action Props, Mechanical FX, Miniatures, Models, Molds,
Robotics & Space Suits)

(323) 871-4445
Spectrum Effects Enterprises, Inc. **(661) 510-5633**
Raleigh Studios FAX **(661) 244-4469**
5300 Melrose Ave., Ste. 101D
Hollywood, CA 90038 **www.spectrumeffects.com**
(Mechanical FX)

(818) 999-0339
F. Lee Stone/Stonefx **(818) 642-2850**
9201 Grundy Ln.
Chatsworth, CA 91311
(Mechanical FX)

Studio Art & Technology **(818) 951-5620**
9545 Wentworth St. FAX **(818) 951-2850**
Sunland, CA 91040
www.issprops.com/manufacturing.aspx
(Electronics, Hydraulics, Miniatures, Rigging & Welding)

(818) 367-2430
Stunt Wings/Adventure Sports **(818) 266-0874**
12623 Gridley St. FAX **(818) 367-5363**
San Fernando, CA 91342 **www.stuntwings.com**
(Action Props, Extreme Sports, Flying & Specialized Rigging)

(310) 457-6661
Stutsman Effects, Inc. **(310) 922-4705**
FAX **(310) 457-4061**
(Action Props, Hydraulics, Mechanical FX, Miniatures,
Rigging & Welding)

Sword & The Stone **(818) 562-6548**
723 N. Victory Blvd. FAX **(818) 562-6549**
Burbank, CA 91502 **www.swordandstone.com**
(Edged Weapons Fabrication, Jewelry, Metal Armor & Silver
and Bronze Casting)

Techworks FX Studios, Inc. **(661) 298-1094**
FAX **(661) 298-0929**
www.techworksstudios.com
(Action Props, Bone Replications, FX Props, Gadgetry,
Mechanical FX, Prop Fabrication, Remote-Controlled, Robotic
Props, Robotics, Sculpted Props, Silicone Rubber Props, Space
Suits & Weapon Fabrication)

Prop Fabrication & Mechanical FX

Trans FX, Inc.   (805) 485-6110
2361 Eastman Ave.   FAX (805) 751-0149
Oxnard, CA 93030   www.transfx.com
(Mock-Ups & Model Makers)

Tribal Scenery   (818) 558-4045
3216 Vanowen St.   FAX (818) 558-4356
Burbank, CA 91505   www.tribalscenery.com

         (818) 985-9357
The Village Art Project   (310) 210-9300
11602 Ventura Blvd.   FAX (818) 985-8211
Studio City, CA 91604   www.thevillageartproject.com
(Ceramics & Pottery)

Vision Scenery Corporation   (818) 567-2818
26 E. Providencia Ave.   FAX (818) 567-2839
Burbank, CA 91502   www.visionscenery.com
(Action Props, Artificial Foods, Breakaways, Custom,
Electronics, Foam Sculpting, FX Props, Gadgetry, Hydraulics,
Mechanical FX, Miniatures, Models, Oversized Props, Product
Pours, Prop Fabrication, Prototyping, Radio-Controlled,
Remote-Controlled, Rigging, Robotics, Rubber Props, Sculpted
Props, Skeleton Replication, Toy Fabrication, Turntables,
Vacuum-Forming, Waterjet Cutting, Weapon
Fabrication & Welding)

The Walt Disney Studios   (818) 560-5488
Property Department, 500 S. Buena Vista St.
Burbank, CA 91521   studioservices.go.com

Warner Bros. Studio Facilities -
Special Effects   (818) 954-1365
4000 Warner Blvd.   FAX (818) 954-1424
Burbank, CA 91522   www.wbspecialeffects.com
(Prop Manufacturing & Special FX Rentals)

         (818) 762-1059
West EFX, Inc.   (213) 304-9323
11635 Sheldon St.   FAX (818) 762-0207
Sun Valley, CA 91352   www.westefx.com

Ⓐ WonderWorks   (818) 992-8811
7231 Remmet Ave.   FAX (818) 347-4330
Canoga Park, CA 91303   www.wonderworksweb.com
(Foreground Miniatures, FX Props & Space Suits)

         (818) 888-8055
Face Value Props   (818) 348-1320
5305 Tendilla Ave.   www.facevalueprops.com
Woodland Hills, CA 91364

The Hand Prop Room, L.P.   (323) 931-1534
5700 Venice Blvd.   FAX (323) 931-2145
Los Angeles, CA 90019   www.hpr.com

History for Hire   (818) 765-7767
7149 Fair Ave.   FAX (818) 765-1304
North Hollywood, CA 91605   www.historyforhire.com

LCW Props   (818) 243-0707
6439 San Fernando Rd.   FAX (818) 243-1830
Glendale, CA 91201   www.lcwprops.com

Modern Props   (323) 934-3000
5500 W. Jefferson Blvd.   FAX (323) 934-3155
Los Angeles, CA 90016   www.modernprops.com

Omega/Cinema Props   (323) 466-8201
5857 Santa Monica Blvd.   FAX (323) 461-3643
Hollywood, CA 90038   www.omegacinemaprops.com

Prop Services West - Hollywood   (818) 503-2790
7040 Laurel Canyon Blvd.   FAX (818) 503-2712
North Hollywood, CA 91605   www.propserviceswest.com

         (818) 765-7107
RC Vintage   (323) 462-4510
7100 Tujunga Ave.   FAX (818) 765-7197
North Hollywood, CA 90028   www.rcvintage.com

Sony Pictures Studios   (310) 244-5999
5300 Alla Rd.   FAX (310) 244-0999
Los Angeles, CA 90066   www.sonypicturesstudios.com

         (661) 775-1655
Studio Prop Rentals, Inc.   (818) 679-4000
21170 Centre Pointe Pkwy, Ste. 200
Santa Clarita, CA 91350   www.studioproprentals.com

Universal Studios Property   (818) 777-2784
100 Universal City Plaza   FAX (818) 866-1543
Universal City, CA 91608
         www.filmmakersdestination.com

Warner Bros. Studio Facilities -
Property   (818) 954-2181
4000 Warner Blvd.   FAX (818) 954-4965
Burbank, CA 91522   www.wbpropertydept.com

Prop Fabrication & Mechanical FX/Prop Houses

Alpine Fixtures & Sheet Metal, Inc. (323) 734-7200
(323) 766-6040
FAX (323) 734-0058

Angel Appliances (818) 892-7227
(877) 835-6030
8545 Sepulveda Blvd. FAX (818) 892-3524
Sepulveda, CA 91343 www.angelappliances.com

Antique Stove Heaven (323) 298-5581
5414 S. Western Ave. FAX (323) 298-0029
Los Angeles, CA 90062 www.antiquestoveheaven.com
(1800s–1950s)

Bleau-Bush Co., Inc. (323) 735-1561
3225 W. Washington Blvd. FAX (323) 735-0874
Los Angeles, CA 90018 www.kitchenavatar.com

C.P. Two (323) 466-8201
5755 Santa Monica Blvd. www.omegacinemaprops.com
Hollywood, CA 90038

Choura Event Rentals (310) 320-6200
FAX (310) 781-8227
www.choura.us
(Cookware, Dishes, Glassware, Griddles, Grills,
Ovens & Silverware)

The Dish Factory (213) 687-9500
(213) 687-9501
FAX (213) 617-0074
www.dishfactory.com

Gourmet Depot (800) 543-7549
(415) 777-5144
(Kitchen Appliance Replacement Parts) FAX (415) 495-5141
www.thegourmetdepotco.com

History for Hire (818) 765-7767
7149 Fair Ave. FAX (818) 765-1304
North Hollywood, CA 91605 www.historyforhire.com
(Period Equipment)

LA Party Rents (818) 989-4300
(310) 785-0000
13520 Saticoy St. FAX (818) 989-3593
Van Nuys, CA 91402 www.lapartyrents.com

Lennie Marvin Enterprises, Inc. (818) 841-5882
3110 Winona Ave. FAX (818) 841-2896
Burbank, CA 91504 www.propheaven.com

Objects (310) 839-6363
3650 Holdrege Ave. FAX (310) 839-6262
Los Angeles, CA 90016 www.ob-jects.com
(Contemporary Kitchen Dressing)

Ⓐ Rick Enterprises (818) 847-1144
4320 W. Vanowen St. FAX (818) 847-1119
Burbank, CA 91505

Star Restaurant Equipment &
Supply Co. (818) 782-4460
6178 Sepulveda Blvd. FAX (818) 782-8179
Van Nuys, CA 91411 www.starkitchen.com

Surfas (310) 558-1458
FAX (310) 558-1459
www.cafesurfas.com

Tavern Soda Service (818) 349-1414
FAX (818) 349-9819
(Antique–Present Bar Setups, Beer Taps and Soda Equipment)

Williams-Sonoma (310) 274-9127
339 N. Beverly Dr. www.williams-sonoma.com
Beverly Hills, CA 90210

Williams-Sonoma (626) 795-5045
142 S. Lake Ave. www.williams-sonoma.com
Pasadena, CA 91101

Williams-Sonoma (818) 906-2787
Fashion Square, 14006 Riverside Dr.
Sherman Oaks, CA 91423 www.williams-sonoma.com

1st Phil's Animal Rentals (805) 521-1100
P.O. Box 309   FAX (805) 521-0956
Piru, CA 93040   www.philsanimalrentals.com
(Carriages & Wagons)

A1-Stuntworld, Inc./Gianni Biasetti (310) 666-3004
(909) 797-7621
www.stuntworldinc.com
(Basejumping Gear, Parachutes, Rigging & Skydiving Gear)

ABC Caskets Factory (323) 268-1783
1705 N. Indiana St.   FAX (323) 268-5215
Los Angeles, CA 90063   www.abettercasket.com
(Casket Fabrication and Rental & Cemetery Lowering Device)

Action Sets and Props/
WonderWorks (818) 992-8811
7231 Remmet Ave.   FAX (818) 347-4330
Canoga Park, CA 91303   www.wonderworksweb.com
(Outer Space Props)

Adam Basma Bazaar, Inc. (323) 934-9493
(310) 854-3500
1551 S. La Cienega Blvd.   www.adambasma.com
Los Angeles, CA 90035
(Middle Eastern)

Ⓐ **Aero Mock-Ups, Inc.** (818) 982-7327
(888) 662-5877
13126 Saticoy St.   FAX (818) 982-0122
North Hollywood, CA 91605   www.aeromockups.com
(Aircraft, Aircaft Interiors & Airline Props)

Air Designs (818) 768-6639
11900 Wicks St.   FAX (818) 768-6675
Sun Valley, CA 91352   www.airdesigns.net
(Automotive Props & Diner and Restaurant Equipment)

Air Hollywood (818) 890-0444
13240 Weidner St.   FAX (818) 890-7041
Los Angeles, CA 91331   www.airhollywood.com
(Airline Mock Ups, Airplane Mock Ups, Airplane Props, Airport
Props, Cockpit, Jet Interior, Props, Security Props,
Signage & X-Ray Machines)

Airpower Aviation Resources (805) 402-0052
(805) 499-0307
702 Paseo Vista   FAX (805) 498-0357
Thousand Oaks, CA 91320   www.airpower-aviation.com

Almost Christmas Prop Shoppe/ (310) 286-0921
Cathy Christmas (310) 748-4521
5057 Lankershim Blvd.   FAX (818) 285-9630
North Hollywood, CA 91601   www.christmasprops.com
(Christmas Decorations and Lights)

Alva's Ballet Barres (310) 519-1314
(800) 403-3447
1417 W. Eighth St.   FAX (310) 831-6110
San Pedro, CA 90732   www.alvas.com
(Ballet Bars & Dancers Props)

American Softtub Co. (818) 957-8827
2520-B Foothill Blvd.   www.americansoftub.com
La Crescenta, CA 91214
(Portable Hot Tubs & Spas)

Apex Electronics (818) 767-7202
(323) 875-1308
8909 San Fernando Rd.   FAX (818) 767-1341
Sun Valley, CA 91352   www.apexelectronic.com
(Aircraft, Electronics & Military Props)

Aquatic Design (310) 822-7484
4943 McConnell Ave., Ste. K   FAX (310) 822-8644
Los Angeles, CA 90066   www.aquatic2000.com
(Aquarium Rentals & Water Tanks)

Armstrong's Antique (714) 761-1320
Plumbing & Lighting (714) 488-7300
2820 W. Orange Ave.   FAX (714) 761-1320
Anaheim, CA 92804
(1890s–1940s)

Aviation Warehouse (760) 388-4215
20020 El Mirage Airport Rd.   FAX (760) 388-4236
El Mirage, CA 92301   www.aviationwarehouse.net

Award Winners (818) 349-3932
(818) 943-1634
8939 Reseda Blvd.   www.awardwinners.net
Northridge, CA 91324
(Awards, Gold Records & Trophies)

Ben Gordon: Balloon Artist (323) 454-3166
www.bengordonballoons.com

Big Events, Inc. (760) 477-2655
1613 Ord Way   FAX (760) 477-2656
Oceanside, CA 92056   www.bigeventsonline.com

Bindery (323) 962-2109
(323) 428-7222
5720 Melrose Ave.   www.charlenematthews.com
Los Angeles, CA 90038
(Bookbinding & Book Props)

Bischoff's Taxidermy & Animal EFX (818) 843-7561
54 E. Magnolia Blvd.   FAX (818) 567-2443
Burbank, CA 91502   www.bischoffs.net
(Furs, Hides & Lifesized Mounted Animals)

Bob Gail Special Events (310) 202-5200
3321 La Cienega Pl. FAX (310) 839-4558
Los Angeles, CA 90016 www.bobgail.com
(Prop House)

Bugs Are My Business/
Steve Kutcher (626) 836-0322
1801 Oakview Ln. www.bugsaremybusiness.com
Arcadia, CA 91006
(Preserved Butterflies and Insects & Rubber Bugs)

(818) 983-1959
C & C Fence Co., Inc. (800) 660-3382
12822 Sherman Way FAX (818) 765-2729
North Hollywood, CA 91605 www.candcfence.com
(Chain Link, Iron and Metal Fences)

C.P. Four (323) 466-8201
706 N. Cahuenga Blvd. FAX (323) 467-2749
Hollywood, CA 90038 www.omegacinemaprops.com

California Casket Company (323) 660-1236
3153 Glendale Blvd. FAX (323) 660-1198
Glendale, CA 90039 www.calcasket.com
(Caskets, Gravemarkers & Urns)

(310) 390-9969
California Casket Company (800) 787-1400
12553 W. Venice Blvd. FAX (310) 390-2272
Los Angeles, CA 90066 www.calcasket.com
(Caskets, Gravemarkers & Urns)

Cannon's Great Escapes (818) 385-7092
35358 Rancho Rd. FAX (818) 581-4130
Yucaipa, CA 92399 www.cannonsgreatescapes.com
(Handcuffs, Manacles & Restraints)

Caravan West Productions (661) 268-8300
35660 Jayhawker Rd. FAX (661) 268-8301
Agua Dulce, CA 91390 www.caravanwest.com
(1860-1910 Firearms, Cannons and Western Props)

Central City Studio (310) 295-7751
737 Terminal St., Bldg. C FAX (213) 622-6292
Los Angeles, CA 90021 www.centralcitystudiola.com
(Hospital & Medical)

Cinema Crates/
Hallenbeck's General Store & Cafe (818) 985-5916
5510 Cahuenga Blvd. FAX (818) 985-0113
North Hollywood, CA 91601
(Barrels, Crates, Gym Lights & Period General Store Props)

Complete Props (818) 445-1480
(Silent Paper and Plastic Bags) www.completeprops.net

(626) 932-0082
Concept Design (800) 846-0717
718 Primrose Ave. FAX (626) 932-0072
Monrovia, CA 91016 www.conceptdesigninc.com
(Exhibit and Theatrical Props & Podiums)

(626) 579-4454
Creative Inflatables (800) 446 3528
9872 Rush St. FAX (626) 579-5561
South El Monte, CA 91733 www.creativeinflatables.com
(Custom Inflatable Props)

(877) 927-6939
Crowd In A Box (416) 275-0422
(Inflatable Extras) FAX (888) 601-2910
www.crowdinabox.com

Crystalarium (310) 652-8006
8500 Melrose Ave., Ste. 105 FAX (310) 652-8007
West Hollywood, CA 90069 www.crystalarium.com
(Crystals, Gold, Jewelry, Mineral Specimens, Rare Gems,
Sculpture & Silver)

Damian Canvas Works (310) 822-2343
4230 Del Rey Ave., Ste. 405
Marina del Rey, CA 90292
www.damiancanvasworks.com

(714) 436-0705
Dekra-Lite (800) 436-3627
3102 W. Alton Ave. FAX (714) 436-0612
Santa Ana, CA 92704 www.dekra-lite.com
(Banners, Christmas Decorations and Lighting, Display Signs,
Graphic and Large Format Printing, Holiday Trees, LED
Lighting & Tree Lighting)

Design Models, Inc. (818) 642-9987
www.designmodels.com

E.C. Prop Rentals, Inc. (818) 764-2008
11846 Sherman Way FAX (818) 764-2374
North Hollywood, CA 91605 www.ecprops.com
(Commercial & Industrial)

Engineered Storage Systems, Inc. (626) 961-0961
1038 W. Kirkwall Rd. FAX (626) 330-2235
Azusa, CA 91702 www.engineeredstorage.com
(Industrial Equipment, Lockers, Pallet Racks & Shelving)

(818) 845-9039
Film Flies (818) 398-6409
145 S. Glenoaks Blvd., PMB 435 www.filmflies.com
Burbank, CA 91502
(LIfe-Size Replicas of Bees, Bugs, Butterflies, Houseflies,
Insects and Wasps)

(818) 765-3549
Flix FX, Inc. (877) 326-8433
7327 Lankershim Blvd., Ste. 4 FAX (818) 765-0135
North Hollywood, CA 91605 www.flixfx.com
(Large Aquariums & Shimmer Tanks)

(626) 795-8733
The Folk Tree (626) 793-4828
217 S. Fair Oaks Ave. FAX (626) 793-4841
Pasadena, CA 91105 www.folktree.com
(Latin American and World Crafts)

Freshpark LLC (714) 369-2495
7412 Count Circle FAX (714) 369-2185
Huntington Beach, CA 92647 www.freshpark.com
(Skateboards & Ramps)

Specialty Props

G & F Carriages (909) 820-4600 / (866) 590-0054
2175 S. Willow Ave.
FAX (909) 820-4903
Bloomington, CA 92316 www.gandfcarriages.com
(Horse Drawn Carriages & Wagons)

Galerie Lakaye (323) 460-7333
FAX (323) 460-7330
www.galerielakaye.com

Gonzo Bros. (310) 828-4989
www.gonzobrothers.com
(Cardboard Crowds & Inflatable Figures)

Goodies Props, Inc. (818) 252-1892
9990 Glenoaks Blvd. FAX (818) 504-2927
Sun Valley, CA 91352
(Prop House)

Gustintaero (818) 890-5983
(Aircraft Mock-Ups) www.gustintaero.com

(A) The Hand Prop Room, L.P. (323) 931-1534
5700 Venice Blvd. FAX (323) 931-2145
Los Angeles, CA 90019 www.hpr.com
(Antique, Hi-Tech and Oversized Props)

Hart Brothers Livestock (951) 312-9009 / (951) 677-6810
P.O. Box 514 FAX (951) 600-3805
Temecula, CA 92593
(Chuck Wagon, Cowboy Gear, Stagecoach & Wagons)

HEF Studio Pool Service, LLC (818) 439-6234
FAX (818) 758-8440
www.hefpool.com
(Pool and Water Tank Filtration and Maintenance)

History for Hire (818) 765-7767
7149 Fair Ave. FAX (818) 765-1304
North Hollywood, CA 91605 www.historyforhire.com
(Prop House)

Hollywood Cinema Production Resources (310) 258-0123
P.O. Box 88459 FAX (310) 258-0124
Los Angeles, CA 90009 www.hollywoodcpr.org
(Prop House)

Hollywood Parts (818) 255-0617 / (818) 445-6676
12580 Saticoy St., Bldg. C FAX (818) 255-0613
North Hollywood, CA 91605 www.hollywoodparts.com
(Asset Management Storage and Sales & Props/Wardrobe from Productions)

The Home Beer, Wine & Cheesemaking Shop (818) 884-8586 / (800) 559-9922
22836-2 Ventura Blvd. FAX (818) 224-3812
Woodland Hills, CA 91364
(Barrels, Bottles, Caps & Corks)
www.homebeerwinecheese.com

Independent Studio Services, Inc./ISS (818) 951-5600
9545 Wentworth St. www.issprops.com
Sunland, CA 91040
(Period–Present Prop House)

The Inflatable Crowd Company (310) 488-9631
Los Angeles, CA 90066 www.inflatablecrowd.com
(Inflatable Mannequins)

Ingalls Conveyors, Inc. (323) 837-9900 / (800) 826-4554
140 E. Whittier Blvd. FAX (323) 837-9990
Montebello, CA 90640 www.ingallsconveyors.com
(Adjustable and Roller Speed Belt Conveyors)

Jets & Props (818) 505-0199 / (818) 324-0884
(Aviation Props) FAX (818) 505-0199
www.jetsandprops.com

Lane Ranch & Company (661) 942-0435
42220 10th St. West, Ste. 101 FAX (661) 942-7485
Lancaster, CA 93534 www.laneranch.net
(Farm Props, Mechanical Bulls, Wagons & Windmills)

Lennie Marvin Enterprises, Inc. (818) 841-5882
3110 Winona Ave. FAX (818) 841-2896
Burbank, CA 91504 www.propheaven.com
(Prop House)

Lifestyle Pool & Spa (818) 997-3255
5830 Sepulveda Blvd. FAX (818) 997-3026
Van Nuys, CA 91411 www.lifestyleoutdoor.com
(Pools & Spas)

Liz's Antique Hardware (323) 939-4403
453 S. La Brea Ave. FAX (323) 939-4387
Los Angeles, CA 90036 www.lahardware.com
(Antique and Contemporary Hardware and Lighting & Reproductions)

Lundin Farm (661) 252-6140 / (818) 618-9959
(Farm Props) www.rrstar.net

Lynn Harding Antique Instruments of the Professions and Sciences (805) 646-0204
103 W. Aliso St. FAX (805) 646-0204
Ojai, CA 93023
(Antique Scientific Instruments)

Medical Purchasing Corp. (323) 753-5575
5419 S. Vermont
Los Angeles, CA 90037

Mike Tristano & Co., Weapons & Historical Military Props (818) 522-0969
FAX (818) 888-6447
www.moviegunguy.com
(Guns and Accessories, Military Props and Equipment, Modern and Period Firearms & Weapons)

Mod Plus, LLC (818) 982-0900
(12' Light Columns) www.modplus.net

Model Trains by René (818) 848-6809
707-A Main St. FAX (818) 848-3112
Burbank, CA 91506

Modern Props (323) 934-3000
5500 W. Jefferson Blvd. FAX (323) 934-3155
Los Angeles, CA 90016 www.modernprops.com
(Contemporary, Electronic and Futuristic Props)

Mosaik (323) 525-0337
7378 Beverly Blvd. FAX (323) 525-0341
Los Angeles, CA 90036 www.e-mosaik.com
(Moroccan Props)

(A) Mr. Pool/P.M. Sales (818) 345-1528 / (818) 903-9682
18441 Vanowen St. FAX (818) 345-0292
Reseda, CA 91335 www.mr-pool.com
(Galvanized Steel, Glass Tanks, Vinyl Lined & Wood Pools)

N.S. Aerospace Props (818) 765-1087
7429 Laurel Canyon Blvd. FAX (818) 765-8969
North Hollywood, CA 91605 www.nortonsalesinc.com
(Rocket Components, Engines, Fittings, Gauges & Valves)

NAC Co. (805) 376-0206 / (805) 405-7337
1772-J E. Avenida de Los Arboles FAX (805) 376-8407
Thousand Oaks, CA 91362 www.naceffects.com

NatureMaker (760) 438-4244 / (800) 872-1889
6225 El Camino Real FAX (760) 438-4344
Carlsbad, CA 92009 www.naturemaker.com
(Foam, Metal, Preserved, Silk and Wood Faux Trees)

Eleanor Nieuwenhuis/Food for Film (323) 240-8482
(323) 342-0064
FAX (323) 441-8425
eleanorfoodstyles.com
(Background and Edible Props & Hero and Beauty Foods)

Oceanic Arts (562) 698-6960
12414 E. Whittier Blvd. FAX (562) 945-0868
Whittier, CA 90602 www.oceanicarts.net
(Tropical Polynesian Building and Decorating Materials)

Omega/Cinema Props (323) 466-8201
5857 Santa Monica Blvd. FAX (323) 461-3643
Hollywood, CA 90038 www.omegacinemaprops.com
(Prop House)

Pacific Miniatures (714) 447-4478
2021 Raymer Ave. FAX (714) 447-4465
Fullerton, CA 92833 www.pacmin.com
(Aircraft Miniatures)

Ⓐ **The Studios at Paramount** (323) 956-5140
The Studios at Paramount FAX (323) 862-2325
Manufacturing and Special Effects
5555 Melrose Ave. www.thestudiosatparamount.com
Hollywood, CA 90038

The Pasadena Antique (626) 449-7706
Center & Annex (626) 449-9445
444 & 480 S. Fair Oaks Ave. FAX (626) 449-3386
Pasadena, CA 91105 www.pasadenaantiquecenter.com
(Vintage African-American, Asian and Latin Books, Electronics,
Ephemera, Fountains, Medical Props, Memorabilia, Records,
Statues, Toys and Tribal Art)

Period Props (818) 807-6677
1536 N. Evergreen St.
Burbank, CA 91505
(Prop House)

Plastica (323) 655-1051
8405 W. Third St. www.plasticashop.com
Los Angeles, CA 90048
(Collectible and Vintage Plastic Items)

Political Campaign Buttons (323) 655-4968
8391 Beverly Blvd., PMB 321 www.hfarchive.com
Los Angeles, CA 90048

Practical Props (818) 982-3198
11754 Vose St. FAX (818) 980-7894
North Hollywood, CA 91605 www.practicalprops.com
(Lamps, Lighting Fixtures & Radios)

Prop Services West - Hollywood (818) 503-2790
7040 Laurel Canyon Blvd. FAX (818) 503-2712
North Hollywood, CA 91605 www.propserviceswest.com
(Home Furnishings & Prop House)

(818) 846-6740
Quantum Creation FX, Inc. (818) 268-5128
3210 W. Valhalla Dr. FAX (818) 846-0047
Burbank, CA 91505 www.quantumcreationfx.com

(818) 765-7107
RC Vintage (323) 462-4510
7100 Tujunga Ave. FAX (818) 765-7197
North Hollywood, CA 91605 www.rcvintage.com
(1940s–60s Diner Equipment, Casino Equipment, Gas Station
Props, Jukeboxes, Lighting Fixtures and Street Dressing)

Rent a Center (818) 505-1903
6522 Laurel Canyon Blvd. FAX (818) 505-8413
North Hollywood, CA 91606 www.rentacenter.com

Reseda Discount
Pottery & Fountains (818) 345-1832
7313 Reseda Blvd. FAX (818) 705-4582
Reseda, CA 91335 www.resedadiscountpottery.com
(Fountains, Pottery & Statues)

Safari Ethiopian Store (323) 935-5749
1049 S. Fairfax Ave. www.ethiopiandesign.com
Los Angeles, CA 90019
(African Artifacts, Cloth and Jewelry)

San Bernardino Railroad
Historical Society (562) 438-9613
(1927 Steam Locomotive) www.sbrhs.org

Scroggins Aviation (702) 348-7731
FAX (702) 953-7307
www.scrogginsaviation.com
(Mock-ups and Props of Commercial Aircraft, Cockpits, Crash
Wreckage & Passenger Cabins)

Singh Imports: Fine Art
Objects of India (310) 559-3826
3816 W. Jefferson Blvd. FAX (310) 559-3829
Los Angeles, CA 90016 www.singhimports.com
(Architectural Remains, Asian Antiques, Buddhist Statuary,
Decorative Accessories, Folk Art, Gypsy Art, Hindu Statuary,
Indian Antiques, Indian Furniture, Islamic Antiques & Tribal Art)

Skinny Dog Design Group, Inc. (562) 436-7237
1750 E. Florida St. www.jewelrypropshop.com
Long Beach, CA 90802
(Jewelry)

So Cal Production Source (310) 699-2787
FAX (310) 618-0129
www.scpsunlimited.com
(Motion Capture Props & Rapid Prototyping)

(323) 663-0122
Soap Plant/Wacko/La Luz de Jesus (323) 666-7667
4633 Hollywood Blvd. FAX (323) 663-0243
Los Angeles, CA 90027 www.laluzdejesus.com
(Rare Artwork, Books, Props & Toys)

(661) 775-1655
Studio Prop Rentals, Inc. (818) 679-4000
21170 Centre Pointe Pkwy, Ste. 200
Santa Clarita, CA 91350 www.studioproprentals.com
(Prop House & Rentals)

Sweet Smiling Home, Inc. (213) 687-9630
2449 Hunter St. FAX (213) 687-9638
Los Angeles, CA 90021 www.sweetsmilinghome.com
(Architectural Elements, Objets D'Art, Religious Icons, Stone
Statues & Tribal and Vintage Textiles)

Tail Man Mermaids & More (310) 530-0616
(Aquatic Props & Mermaid/Merman Tails) FAX (310) 530-0616
www.mermaidrentals.com

Towards 2000, Inc. (818) 557-0903
215 W. Palm Ave., Ste. 101 FAX (866) 836-5725
Burbank, CA 91502 www.t2k.com
(Discotheque, Laser & Robotic Lighting Equipment)

Universal Studios Graphic
Design & Sign Shops (818) 777-2350
100 Universal City Plaza FAX (818) 866-0209
Bldg. 4250/3054 www.filmmakersdestination.com
Universal City, CA 91608
(Generic Product Props, Grave Markers, Signs and Banners &
Vehicle Graphics)

Universal Studios Property (818) 777-2784
100 Universal City Plaza FAX (818) 866-1543
Universal City, CA 91608
www.filmmakersdestination.com

(818) 769-0436
Valley Martial Arts Supply (800) 508-0825
5638 Lankershim Blvd. FAX (818) 769-3257
North Hollywood, CA 91601 www.valleymartialarts.com
(Swords)

Vedanta Bookshop (800) 816-2242
1946 Vedanta Pl. www.vedanta.com
Hollywood, CA 90068

Vinyl Technology, Inc. (626) 443-5257
200 Railroad Ave. FAX (626) 443-0531
Monrovia, CA 91016 www.vinyltechnology.com
(Fabrication)

Vision Scenery Corporation (818) 567-2818
26 E. Providencia Ave. FAX (818) 567-2839
Burbank, CA 91502 www.visionscenery.com

Action Watersports   **(310) 827-2233**
4144 Lincoln Blvd.   **www.actionwatersports.com**
Marina del Rey, CA 90292
(Jet Skis, Sailboards, Snowboards & Surfboards)

Burbank Kawasaki   **(818) 848-6627**
1329 N. Hollywood Way   FAX **(818) 848-6630**
Burbank, CA 91505   **www.burbankkawasaki.com**
(Jet Skis, Motorcycles, Off-Road Sport Vehicles & Scooters)

Cat Production Services/
Extreme Sports Filming   **(562) 596-7105**
www.extremesportsfilming.com
(Cabin Cruisers, Cigarette Boats, Classic, Dune Buggies,
Fishing Boats, Jet Skis, Motorcycles, Off-Road, Sailboards,
Scooters, Sea-Doos, Watercraft & Yachts)

EagleRider Motorcycle Rentals   **(310) 536-6777**
11860 S. La Cienega Blvd.   FAX **(310) 536-6776**
Los Angeles, CA 90250   **www.eaglerider.com**
(Harley-Davidsons)

Golf Cars - LA, Inc.   **(661) 251-2201**
16439 Sierra Hwy   **www.golfcars-la.com**
Canyon Country, CA 91351

    (805) 581-4700
Hardline Products Marine Group   **(805) 732-5341**
677 Cochran St.   FAX **(805) 581-0022**
Simi Valley, CA 93065
www.hardlineproducts.com/marinegroup
(Cabin Cruisers, Cigarette Boats, Fishing Boats, Jet Boats,
PWC & Yachts)

Harley-Davidson/Buell of Glendale   **(818) 246-5618**
3717 San Fernando Rd.   FAX **(818) 246-5785**
Glendale, CA 91204   **www.glendaleharley.com**

    (323) 466-7191
Honda of Hollywood   **(800) 371-3718**
6525 Santa Monica Blvd.   FAX **(323) 372-3200**
Hollywood, CA 90038   **www.honda4u.com**
(BMW, Honda, Kawasaki and Suzuki Motorcycles, Jet Skis &
Sea-Doos)

    (818) 766-6134
Honda of North Hollywood   **(800) 800-6134**
5626 Tujunga Ave.   **www.hondaofnorthhollywood.com**
North Hollywood, CA 91601
(Motorcycles & Sea-Doos)

    (818) 988-8860
Hypercycle   **(818) 261-7104**
15941 Arminta St.   FAX **(818) 988-8834**
Van Nuys, CA 91406   **www.hypercycle.com**

LA's Jet-Skier Fun Team   **(310) 569-1099**
(Jet Skis & Watercraft)   **www.jetskifun.com**

Scooters Bellissimo/Go, Scoot Go!   **(626) 523-7224**
1730 La Senda Pl.   **www.scootersbellissimo.com**
South Pasadena, CA 91030
(Scooters)

Snowblind Snowmobiles   **(213) 247-4777**
11421 Hayvenhurst Ave.
Granada Hills, CA 91344
    www.snowblindsnowmobiles.com
(Snowmobiles & Snow Vehicles)

    (818) 355-2676
Vehicle Effects   **(818) 768-2343**
7606 Clybourn Rd.   FAX **(818) 846-7576**
Sun Valley, CA 91352   **www.vehicleeffects.com**

    (760) 257-3734
Willie's On & Off Road Center   **(760) 953-3303**
48301 National Trails Hwy   FAX **(760) 257-3335**
Newberry Springs, CA 92365   **www.williesoffroad.com**
(Dune Buggies & Off-Road Sport Vehicles)

Adventure 16 Wilderness Outfitters (310) 473-4574
11161 W. Pico   www.adventure16.com
Los Angeles, CA 90064

Archery House, LLC   (858) 254-4058
(Archery)   www.archeryhouse.com

Beverly Hills Bike Shop   (310) 275-2453
854 S. Robertson Blvd.   FAX (310) 657-9611
Los Angeles, CA 90035   www.bhbikeshop.com

Big Five Sporting Goods   (818) 842-5479
510 N. Victory Blvd.   www.big5sportinggoods.com
Burbank, CA 91502

Big Five Sporting Goods   (818) 246-1100
144 N. Central Ave.   www.big5sportinggoods.com
Glendale, CA 91203

Big Five Sporting Goods   (323) 651-2909
6601 Wilshire Blvd.   www.big5sportinggoods.com
Los Angeles, CA 90048

Big Five Sporting Goods   (818) 769-5526
12033 Ventura Pl.   www.big5sportinggoods.com
Studio City, CA 91604

Bikes..Camera..Action!   (310) 995-2084
1105 Bonilla
Topanga, CA 90290
(Bicycles & Racing Equipment)

Bob Marriott's Flyfishing Store   (714) 525-1827
2700 W. Orangethorpe Ave.   FAX (714) 525-5783
Fullerton, CA 92833   www.bobmarriotts.com

Captain Nemo U/W Operations   (310) 626-7083
904 Silver Spur Rd., Ste. 386   FAX (310) 534-4185
Rolling Hills Estates, CA 90274
(Scuba Equipment)

Champs   (818) 547-4808
                            www.champssports.com

Curtis Gym Equipment   (818) 897-2804
10275 Glenoaks Blvd., Ste. 7   FAX (818) 838-1149
Pacoima, CA 91331
(Barbells, Boxing Equipment, Dumbells, Exercise Equipment
Rental, Gymnasium Equipment, Racks, Weight Machines/
Benches & Wrestling Equipment)

Dive N' Surf   (310) 372-8423
504 N. Broadway   FAX (310) 372-0937
Redondo Beach, CA 90277   www.divensurf.com

                                    (310) 828-3492
                                    (888) 832-6122
Doc's Ski Haus
2929 Santa Monica Blvd.   FAX (310) 828-1472
Santa Monica, CA 90404   www.docsskihaus.com
(Skiing & Snowboarding)

                                    (818) 888-2935
DT Trampolines Inc.   (800) 649-4945
P.O. Box 6214   FAX (818) 888-2951
Woodland Hills, CA 91365   www.dttrampolines.com
(Trampolines)

                                    (323) 734-2507
Fold-A-Goal   (800) 542-4625
4856 W. Jefferson Blvd.   FAX (323) 734-0731
Los Angeles, CA 90016   www.fold-a-goal.com
(Soccer Equipment)

Freshpark LLC   (714) 369-2495
7412 Count Circle   FAX (714) 369-2185
Huntington Beach, CA 92647 www.freshpark.com
(Bicycles, Exercise Equipment, Martial Arts, Period, Racing
Equipment & Rental)

                                    (818) 955-2645
Hollywood Fitness Trainers   (877) 702-2348
22647 Ventura Blvd., Ste. 262 www.wizardofyouth.com
Woodland Hills, CA 91364
(Exercise and Gymnasium Equipment)

                                    (323) 969-9875
Hollywoodivers.com   (877) 657-2822
(Scuba Gear)   FAX (323) 969-9734
                            www.hollywoodivers.com

I. Martin Imports/Bicycles   (323) 653-6900
8330 Beverly Blvd.   FAX (323) 653-5670
Los Angeles, CA 90048   www.imartin.com

                                    (310) 855-1946
Merchant of Tennis   (310) 202-7800
1118 S. La Cienega Blvd.   FAX (310) 652-9905
Los Angeles, CA 90035

On Track   (800) 697-2999
2901 Winona Ave.   FAX (818) 563-9705
Burbank, CA 91504   www.ontrackandfield.com
(Track and Field Equipment)

                                    (800) 376-3339
Out-Fit   (805) 584-1500
25 W. Easy St., Ste. 306   FAX (805) 426-8120
Simi Valley, CA 93065   www.out-fit.net

Pro Fight Shop   (323) 460-4600
1062 Vine St.   www.rentaboxingring.com
Los Angeles, CA 90038
(Boxing, Boxing Rings, Display Clocks, Exercise Equipment,
Gymnasium Equipment, Heavy Bags, Martial Arts, MMA Cages,
Punching Bags, UFC Cages, Wrestling Equipment, Wrestling
Ring Rentals & Wrestling Rings)

Quantum Rock Extreme Sports   (310) 378-2171
P.O. Box 4032   FAX (310) 378-9383
Rolling Hills Estates, CA 90274   www.quantumrock.com
(Rock Climbing Walls)

R.E.I. Co-Op   (310) 727-0728
1800 Rosecrans Ave., Ste. E   FAX (310) 727-0735
Manhattan Beach, CA 90266   www.rei.com

R.E.I. Co-Op   (818) 831-5555
18605 Devonshire St.   FAX (818) 831-3235
Northridge, CA 91324   www.rei.com

R.E.I. Co-Op   (714) 505-0205
2962 El Camino Real   www.rei.com
Tustin, CA 92782

The Racket Doctor   (323) 663-6601
3214 Glendale Blvd.   FAX (323) 663-4329
Los Angeles, CA 90039   www.racketdoctor.com

Reel Bikes   (714) 287-8989
8464 Indianapolis Ave.   FAX (714) 969-1173
Huntington Beach, CA 92646 www.reelbikes.net
(Bicycles, Exercise Equipment, Period & Rentals)

Rent Fitness Equipment.com   (877) 736-8348
2640 E. Del Amo Blvd.   FAX (310) 943-2761
Carson, CA 90221   www.rentfitnessequipment.com
(Exercise Equipment)

Roger Dunn Golf Shop   (818) 763-3622
5445 Lankershim Blvd.   FAX (818) 763-4101
North Hollywood, CA 91602
                            www.worldwidegolfshops.com

Safety Cycle Shop   (323) 464-5765
1014 N. Western Ave.   www.safetycycle.com
Los Angeles, CA 90029

Santa Monica Surf Shop (310) 451-7977
1335 Fourth St. FAX (310) 453-8405
Santa Monica, CA 90403
www.santamonicasurfshop.com

(310) 830-6161
Score, American Soccer Co., Inc. (800) 626-7774
726 E. Anaheim St. FAX (800) 426-1222
Wilmington, CA 90744 www.scoresports.com
(Soccer Equipment)

Scuba Haus (310) 828-2916
2501 Wilshire Blvd. FAX (310) 829-5083
Santa Monica, CA 90403 www.scubahaus.com

(800) 347-2822
Scuba.com (949) 459-9900
1752 Langley Ave. FAX (949) 221-9323
Irvine, CA 92614 www.diversdiscount.com

Sport Chalet (818) 558-3500
201 E. Magnolia Blvd., Ste. 145 FAX (818) 567-2020
Burbank, CA 91501 www.sportchalet.com

Sport Chalet (310) 657-3210
Beverly Connection FAX (310) 657-2201
100 N. La Cienega Blvd. www.sportchalet.com
Los Angeles, CA 90048

Sport Chalet (818) 790-9800
Two Sport Chalet Dr. FAX (818) 790-1051
La Cañada Flintridge, CA 91011 www.sportchalet.com

Sport Chalet (310) 821-9400
13455 Maxella Ave. FAX (310) 823-0485
Marina del Rey, CA 90292 www.sportchalet.com

Sports Authority (818) 727-2200
8700 Tampa Ave. FAX (818) 727-9836
Northridge, CA 91324 www.sportsauthority.com

Sportsrobe/Sports Studio (310) 559-3999
Ventures, LLC (800) 666-2787
8654 Hayden Pl. FAX (310) 559-4767
Culver City, CA 90232 www.sportsstudio.net
(Contemporary and Period Athletic Uniforms, Equipment,
On-Field Wardrobe Support, Silk Screening and Embroidery &
Sports Coordination)

(818) 769-6977
Val Surf & Sports (888) 825-7883
4810 Whitsett Ave. FAX (818) 769-4318
Valley Village, CA 91617 www.valsurf.com

(818) 769-0436
Valley Martial Arts Supply (800) 508-0825
5638 Lankershim Blvd. FAX (818) 769-3257
North Hollywood, CA 91601 www.valleymartialarts.com
(Boxing, Martial Arts & Wrestling)

(310) 534-0305
VS Athletics (800) 676-7463
4035 S. Higuera St. FAX (888) 415-5212
San Luis Obispo, CA 93401 www.vsathletics.com
(Display Clocks & Track and Field Equipment)

Sporting Goods

Sony Pictures Studios   **(310) 244-5999**
5933 W. Slauson Ave.   FAX **(310) 244-0999**
Culver City, CA 90230   **www.sonypicturesstudios.com**

United Pacific Studios   **(213) 489-2001**
729 E. Temple St.   FAX **(213) 489-2098**
Los Angeles, CA 90012   **www.unitedpacificstudios.com**

Universal Studios Property   **(818) 777-2784**
100 Universal City Plaza   FAX **(818) 866-1543**
Universal City, CA 91608
     www.filmmakersdestination.com

Universal Studios Stock Units   **(818) 777-1126**
100 Universal City Plaza, Bldg. 3156
Universal City, CA 91608
     www.filmmakersdestination.com

Warner Bros. Studio Facilities -
Property   **(818) 954-2181**
4000 Warner Blvd.   FAX **(818) 954-4965**
Burbank, CA 91522   **www.wbpropertydept.com**

Barneys New York   **(310) 276-4400**
     FAX **(310) 777-5842**
     www.barneys.com

Bloomingdale's   **(310) 360-2714**
8500 Beverly Blvd., Beverly Center   FAX **(310) 360-2752**
Los Angeles, CA 90048   **www.bloomingdales.com**
Contact: Jennifer Stoelt

Bloomingdale's   **(818) 325-2301**
14060 Riverside Dr., Fashion Square   FAX **(818) 325-2240**
Sherman Oaks, CA 91423   **www.bloomingdales.com**
Contact: Bobbe Aiona

Fred Segal/Ron Herman   **(323) 651-4129**
8100 Melrose Ave.   FAX **(323) 651-5238**
Los Angeles, CA 90046   **www.ronherman.com**
Contact: Sandy Melvin

Giorgio Armani   **(310) 271-5555**
436 N. Rodeo Dr.   **www.giorgioarmani.com**
Beverly Hills, CA 90210

     (213) 765-3100
Guess?, Inc.   **(212) 730-7200**
1444 S. Alameda St.   FAX **(213) 765-5915**
Los Angeles, CA 90021   **www.guess.com**
Contacts: Leilani Augustine & Nina Flood

     (310) 659-9660
Macy's   **(310) 659-4752**
Beverly Center, 8500 Beverly Blvd.   FAX **(310) 657-2798**
Los Angeles, CA 90048
Contact: Staci Davis

Macy's   **(818) 379-7855**
Fashion Square   FAX **(818) 905-6948**
14000 Riverside Dr., Third Fl.
Sherman Oaks, CA 91423
Contact: Elvira Lutz

Monopoly   **(323) 655-0704**
8421 W. Third St.   FAX **(213) 625-8169**
Los Angeles, CA 90048
Contact: Mikhail Vortman

Nordstrom   **(818) 592-4622**
Topanga Plaza, 6602 Topanga Canyon Blvd.
Canoga Park, CA 91303
Contacts: Wendy Laurence-Williams &
Michelle Traysoote-Morales

Nordstrom   **(818) 502-1683**
Glendale Galleria, 200 W. Broadway   FAX **(818) 502-2142**
Glendale, CA 91210   **www.nordstrom.com**
Contact: Gretchen Hengel

Nordstrom   **(310) 254-1670**
Westside Pavillion   FAX **(310) 254-2778**
10830 W. Pico Blvd.   **www.nordstrom.com**
Los Angeles, CA 90064
Contact: Debra Hastain

     (310) 271-6726
Saks Fifth Ave.   **(310) 887-5546**
Contacts: Pui Ko & Fernando Meneses

Sy Devore   **(818) 783-2700**
12930 Ventura Blvd., Store 124   FAX **(818) 501-4302**
Studio City, CA 91604   **www.sydevore.com**
Contact: Danny Marsh

Antoine's Tailoring (310) 275-8045

Nina Correa (310) 390-6761
FAX (310) 398-3889

Costume Rentals Corporation (818) 753-3700
11149 Vanowen St. FAX (818) 753-3737
North Hollywood, CA 91605
www.costumerentalscorp.com

Eastern Costume Company (818) 982-3611
7243 Coldwater Canyon Ave. FAX (818) 982-1905
North Hollywood, CA 91605 **www.easterncostume.com**

(310) 369-1897
Fox Studios (310) 369-4636
Costume Department FAX (310) 369-2487
10201 W. Pico Blvd. **www.foxstudioscostumes.com**
Los Angeles, CA 90035

Hans the Tailor (323) 653-2957

J & M Costumers, Inc. (818) 760-1991
5708 Gentry Ave. **www.jmcostumers.com**
North Hollywood, CA 91607

(323) 666-0680
Silvia's Costumes (323) 666-0702
4964 Hollywood Blvd. FAX (323) 666-6397
Los Angeles, CA 90027 **www.silviascostumes.com**

Universal Studios
Costume Department (818) 777-2722
100 Universal City Plaza FAX (818) 866-1544
Bldg. 4250/3054 **www.filmmakersdestination.com**
Universal City, CA 91608

Warner Bros. Studio Facilities - (818) 954-1297
Costume Department (800) 375-3085
4000 Warner Blvd., Bldg. 153 FAX (818) 954-3685
Burbank, CA 91522 **www.wbcostumedept.com**

(310) 659-0210
Wild Lotus (323) 356-6284
8539 W. Sunset Blvd., Ste. 18 **www.wildlotususa.com**
West Hollywood, CA 90069

AA Surplus Sales — (323) 526-3622 / (800) 273-7062
2940 E. Olympic Blvd.   FAX (323) 526-3617
Los Angeles, CA 90023   www.aasurplus.com
(Military)

Armies of the World — (818) 243-7265
507 E. Colorado St.   FAX (818) 243-3625
Glendale, CA 91205
(WWI–Present Military)

California Surplus Mart — (323) 465-5525
6263 Santa Monica Blvd.   FAX (323) 465-2418
Hollywood, CA 90038
(Badges, Boots, Camping Equipment, Firefighting, Military,
Period, Police, Restaurant, Russian Military, Vietnam &
World War II)

Costume Rentals Corporation — (818) 753-3700
11149 Vanowen St.   FAX (818) 753-3737
North Hollywood, CA 91605
www.costumerentalscorp.com

CSi — (909) 629-6869 / (714) 313-8908
395 E. Commercial St.   FAX (909) 629-6651
Pomona, CA 91767

Eastern Costume Company — (818) 982-3611
7243 Coldwater Canyon Ave.   FAX (818) 982-1905
North Hollywood, CA 91605   www.easterncostume.com
(Beading, Construction, Contemporary, Costume Makers,
Custom, Dancewear, Design, Embroidery, Ethnic Apparel,
Evening Gowns, Flight Gear, Full Costume Construction, Full
Costume Design, Furs, Futuristic Costuming, Gloves, Hats,
Horseback Riding Apparel, Knitwear, Leathers, Mascots,
Masks, Military Uniforms, Period-Present, Police, Props,
Religious Garments, Rentals, Screenprinting, Shoes/Boots,
Spacesuits, Undergarments, Uniforms, Vintage, Wardrobe
Supplies, Wedding Gowns & Western Wear)

Glamour — (323) 666-2122
4951 W. Sunset Blvd.   FAX (323) 666-2123
Los Angeles, CA 90027
(Beautician, Domestic, Medical & Restaurant)

Hollywood Fire Authority — (909) 593-3964 / (909) 227-1794
(Fire Fighter)   www.hollywoodfire.biz

Motion Picture Costumes & Supplies, Inc. — (818) 557-1247
3811 Valhalla Dr.   FAX (818) 557-1695
Burbank, CA 91505
(1776–Present Military & Police)

R.D.D. USA — (213) 742-0666
3200 South Grand Ave.   FAX (213) 726-2321
Los Angeles, CA 90007   www.rddusa.com
(Camping, Military & Security)

The Russian Store/G & J Imports — (818) 999-1257
7657 Winnetka Ave., Ste. 203   FAX (818) 700-0999
Canoga Park, CA 91306   www.russianstore.net
(Russian Military)

Score, American Soccer Co., Inc. — (310) 830-6161 / (800) 626-7774
726 E. Anaheim St.   FAX (800) 426-1222
Wilmington, CA 90744   www.scoresports.com

Sidney's — (310) 837-1291
4334 Sepulveda Blvd.   FAX (310) 313-1225
Culver City, CA 90230   www.sidneysuniforms.com
(Industrial, Medical, Postal & Security)

Sportsrobe — (310) 559-3999 / (800) 666-2787
8654 Hayden Pl.   FAX (310) 559-4767
Culver City, CA 90232   www.sportsstudio.net
(Contemporary and Period Athletic Uniforms, Equipment & Silk
Screening and Embroidery)

Supply Sergeant — (818) 845-9433 / (800) 336-5225
503 N. Victory Blvd.   FAX (818) 845-2017
Burbank, CA 91502   www.supplysergeant.com
(Camping, Military & Sports)

Supply Sergeant — (323) 463-4730 / (800) 336-5225
6664 Hollywood Blvd.   FAX (323) 465-1073
Hollywood, CA 90028   www.supplysergeant.com

Supply Sergeant — (310) 458-4166 / (800) 336-5225
1431 Lincoln Blvd.   www.supplysergeant.com
Santa Monica, CA 90401

Uniwear — (213) 746-6040
uniwearuniforms.com
(Medical, Military, Police, Postal & Security)

Archive Edition Textiles/
Textile Artifacts   **(310) 676-2424**
12575 Crenshaw Blvd.   FAX **(310) 676-2242**
Hawthorne, CA 90250   **www.archiveedition.com**
(Antique and Vintage Lace and Trim & Reproduction
Antique Fabrics)

                                         (323) 938-8604
Buffalo Exchange   **(323) 938-9204**
131 N. La Brea Ave.   FAX **(520) 622-7015**
Los Angeles, CA 90036   **www.buffaloexchange.com**
(Contemporary–Vintage)

The Button Store   **(323) 658-5473**
8344 W. Third St.   FAX **(323) 782-0940**
Los Angeles, CA 90048
(Antique & Vintage)

                                         (323) 951-9255
Catwalk Designer Vintage   **(213) 400-7159**
459 N. Fairfax Ave.   FAX **(323) 951-9258**
Los Angeles, CA 90036   **www.catwalkla.com**
(Antique, Contemporary, Designer, Hats, Purses, Rentals,
Undergarments, Victorian & Vintage)

Chuck's Vintage   **(323) 653-5386**
7515 Melrose Ave.   **www.chucksvintage.com**
Los Angeles, CA 90046

Daddyo's   **(818) 760-6750**
10361 Margate St.
North Hollywood, CA 91601
(Vintage 1900s–80s)

Decades, Inc.   **(323) 655-0223**
8214 ½ Melrose Ave.   **www.decadesinc.com**
Los Angeles, CA 90046
(1960s–70s Vintage Couture)

Mister Freedom   **(323) 653-2014**
7161 Beverly Blvd.   FAX **(323) 932-9590**
Los Angeles, CA 90036   **www.misterfreedom.com**
(Antique, Original, Rentals, Used, Victorian, Vintage & Western)

Hubba Hubba   **(818) 845-0636**
3220 W. Magnolia Blvd.
Burbank, CA 91505

Iguana Vintage Clothing   **(818) 907-6716**
14422 Ventura Blvd.   **www.iguanaclothing.com**
Sherman Oaks, CA 91403

It's a Wrap! Production
Wardrobe Sales   **(818) 567-7366**
3315 W. Magnolia Blvd.   **www.itsawraphollywood.com**
Burbank, CA 91505
(Period–Present)

Jet Rag   **(323) 939-0528**

Junk for Joy Vintage, Etc.   **(818) 569-4903**
3314 W. Magnolia Blvd.   **www.junkforjoy.com**
Burbank, CA 91505
(Original 1950s–80s)

Lily   **(310) 724-5757**
9044 Burton Way
Beverly Hills, CA 90211

Meow   **(562) 438-8990**
2210 E. Fourth St.   **www.meowvintage.com**
Long Beach, CA 90814
(1940s–80s)

Out of the Closet   **(323) 934-1956**
360 N. Fairfax Ave.   FAX **(323) 934-1750**
Los Angeles, CA 90028   **www.outofthecloset.org**
(Antique, Contemporary, Designer, Jewelry, Original, Shoes,
Used & Vintage)

Out of the Closet   **(323) 664-4394**
6210 Sunset Blvd.   FAX **(323) 467-6258**
Los Angeles, CA 90028   **www.outofthecloset.org**

Out of the Closet   **(323) 664-4394**
3160 Glendale Blvd.   FAX **(323) 662-0988**
Los Angeles, CA 90039   **www.outofthecloset.org**

Ozzie Dots - Costume &
Vintage Clothing   **(323) 663-2867**
4637 Hollywood Blvd.   FAX **(323) 663-0501**
Los Angeles, CA 90027   **www.ozziedots.com**
(Hats, Purses, Undergarments, Victorian, Vintage & Western)

                                         (310) 385-9036
The Paper Bag Princess   **(416) 925-2603**
8818 W. Olympic Blvd.   FAX **(310) 385-9052**
Beverly Hills, CA 90211 **www.thepaperbagprincess.com**
(1920s–Present Designer Apparel)

The Pasadena Antique   **(626) 449-7706**
Center & Annex   **(626) 449-9445**
444 & 480 S. Fair Oaks Ave.   FAX **(626) 449-3386**
Pasadena, CA 91105 **www.pasadenaantiquecenter.com**
(Victorian–1970s Clothing, Hats and Purses & Western)

Playclothes   **(818) 557-8447**
3100 W. Magnolia Blvd.   **www.vintageplayclothes.com**
Burbank, CA 91505
(1920s–80s Vintage Costumes)

Polkadots and Moonbeams   **(323) 651-1746**
8367 W. Third St. **www.polkadotsandmoonbeams.com**
Los Angeles, CA 90048

Ragg Mopp   **(323) 666-0550**
3816 W. Sunset Blvd.   **www.raggmoppvintage.net**
Los Angeles, CA 90026

Ravishing Resale   **(323) 655-8480**
8127 W. Third St.
Los Angeles, CA 90048
(Vintage–Contemporary)

                                         (323) 936-6210
Re-Mix Vintage Shoes   **(888) 254-1813**
7605 ½ Beverly Blvd.   FAX **(323) 930-0650**
Los Angeles, CA 90036   **www.remixvintageshoes.com**
(Never Worn)

Resurrection Vintage Clothing   **(323) 651-5516**
8006 Melrose Ave.   **www.ressurectionvintage.com**
Los Angeles, CA 90046

reVamp   **(213) 488-3387**
834 S. Broadway, Ste. 1200   FAX **(775) 366-0036**
Los Angeles, CA 90014   **www.revampvintage.com**

Slow Clothing   **(323) 655-3725**
7474 Melrose Ave.   **www.slow7474.com**
Los Angeles, CA 90046

Squaresville   **(323) 669-8464**
1800 N. Vermont Ave.
Los Angeles, CA 90027

Unique Vintage
(818) 848-1764
(800) 721-6589
2013 W. Magnolia Blvd.   www.unique-vintage.com
Burbank, CA 91506
(Contemporary, Original & Vintage)

Vintage American Clothing   (310) 490-4173
12818 S. Normandie Ave.   FAX (310) 538-5459
Gardena, CA 90249 www.vintageamericanclothing.com

Wasteland, Inc.   (323) 653-3028
7428 Melrose Ave.   FAX (323) 653-4185
Los Angeles, CA 90046   www.wastelandclothing.com

The Way We Wore   (323) 937-0878
334 S. La Brea Ave.   FAX (323) 936-6578
Los Angeles, CA 90036   www.thewaywewore.com
(20th Century, Antique, Designer, Hats, Lace, Original, Purses,
Trim, Undergarments, Used, Victorian & Vintage)

Water Trucks

A-1 Water Trucks
(805) 680-0372
(805) 685-5000
P.O. Box 1552   FAX (805) 683-2361
Santa Barbara, CA 93116   www.a1water.net
(Water Trucks: 2000–4000 Gallons)

Agua Dulce Water Trucks   (818) 216-3680
14854 Lassen St.   FAX (818) 892-7710
Mission Hills, CA 91345
(Water Trucks: 2500 & 4000 Gallons)

Alotta H20 Water Truck Services   (714) 692-0692
23300 Azela Circle   FAX (714) 692-1162
Yorba Linda, CA 92887   www.alottah2o.com
(Water Trucks: 2000–2800 Gallons)

Antelope Valley Locations and
Production Services   (661) 946-1515
42848 150th St. East   FAX (661) 946-0454
Lancaster, CA 93535   www.avlocations.com

Bertrand Enterprises   (760) 446-6600
1210 Graaf Ave.   FAX (760) 446-2669
Ridgecrest, CA 93555
(Water Trucks: 4000 Gallons)

Blast Off Enterprises
(760) 519-9012
(760) 519-9012
P.O. Box 2550   FAX (760) 751-8421
Valley Center, CA 92082
(Water Trucks: 2500–4000 Gallons)

Four C's Equipment   (661) 619-3542
7751 Citation Ln.   FAX (661) 845-0719
Bakersfield, CA 93307
(Water Trucks: 4000 Gallons)

Hollywood Fires   (661) 252-7629
12059 Davenport Rd.   FAX (661) 251-5165
Agua Dulce, CA 91390   www.hollywoodfires.com

Jensen Water Trucks   (310) 455-2463
1137 Fernwood Pacific Dr.   FAX (310) 455-0168
Topanga, CA 90290
(Fire Trucks: 1000 Gallons & Water Trucks: 2500 &
4000 Gallons)

Mel Underwood Water Trucks, Inc.
(818) 361-9176
(800) 675-4855
13201 Foothill Blvd.   FAX (818) 361-9617
Sylmar, CA 91342
(Water Trucks: 2000–4500 Gallons)

RMR Equipment Rental Inc.
(661) 510-8516
(661) 257-3303
(Water Trucks: 2500 & 4000 Gallons)   FAX (661) 294-8522
www.rmrwatertrucks.com

Sid's Watertrucks   (818) 606-6008
P.O. Box 1282   FAX (805) 579-3714
Reseda, CA 91337
(Water Trucks: 2500–4000 Gallons)

Silver Bullet Water Trucks   (951) 681-3537
P.O. Box 324   FAX (951) 737-7445
Norco, CA 92860
(Water Trucks: 2500 Gallons)

Water in Motion Co.
(818) 266-4907
(818) 266-4919
805 San Fernando Ave.   FAX (909) 624-9031
Burbank, CA 91502   www.nationwidemovietrucks.com
(Fire Trucks & Water Trucks)

Weber Water Truck Rentals
(760) 325-4894
(760) 272-9134
28404 Taos Court   FAX (760) 327-3549
Palm Springs, CA 92234
(Water Trucks: 4000 Gallons)

West Coast Water Tenders
(661) 250-2585
(661) 510-8128
(Fire Trucks & Water Trucks)   FAX (661) 250-2584
www.westcoasth20.com

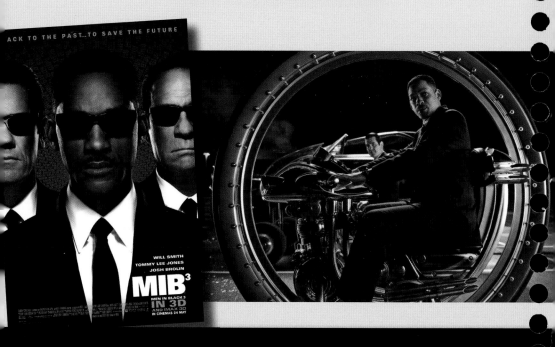

MEN IN BLACK III

BY MARJ GALAS

Ken Ralston and Jay Redd, VFX Supervisors, Ken Hahn, Digital Effects Supervisor, and Spencer Cook, Animation Supervisor, on "Men In Black III"

For VFX Supervisors Jay Redd and Ken Ralston, working on "Men in Black III" was a labor of love. Effects such as Agent J's (Will Smith) fall from the Chrysler Building took two years to complete, and the recreation of Shea Stadium required a supervised team of nearly 200 people. Redd and Ralston also had to ensure all the effects were 3D ready. Employing software such as Maya and proprietary systems used by Sony Pictures Imageworks that involved tracing and cutting out shapes then layering the depth of field, the VFX supervisors felt creating 3D ready effects was a cake walk.

"There was no real impact on us," said Redd. "We used a system we were comfortable and familiar with, and that didn't cause any hold ups."

Digital effects supervisor Ken Hahn and his team had to recreate both events and structures from specific moments in time, such as the 1969 NY Mets World Series winning game and the Apollo 11 lift off.

"Jay Redd went down to Cape Canaveral and got onto one of the launch pads and shot a lot of photographs we referenced for the background," said Hahn. 'The rocket, the concrete base, lift off, the flames and smoke, all that we created in a computer." Hahn wanted to be certain to integrate the director's visual style into the handling of the 3D, as it had been done with great success in "Alice in Wonderland" and "G-Force," 3D features he'd previously worked on.

"Barry Sonnenfeld has a unique style; he shoots everything with a 22 millimeter prime lens," said Hahn. "For comedy he prefers that it's more compressed, everything is closer to the audience.

As animation supervisor, Spencer Cook collaborated closely with special effects makeup artist Rick Baker and his team to create digital prosthetics, particularly noticeable in villain Boris.

"There is a symbiotic part of Boris that lives inside of his hand," said Cook. "Rick Baker's studio designed the sculpted creation and we used that to build the digital version. There was never an animatronic version; it was animated digitally."

ABRIDGED FROM AN LA 411 NEWSLETTER ARTICLE PUBLISHED JUNE 2012

A ADVERTISER SYMBOL

**Refer to the General Index for
cross-referencing items in this section.**

310 Artists Agency   **(310) 278-4787**
3500 W. Olive Ave., Ste. 300   **www.310artists.com**
Burbank, CA 91505
(Reps for Storyboard Artists)

9 Agency   **(310) 430-9902**
   FAX **(310) 469-7899**
   www.9-agency.com
(Reps for Wardrobe Stylists/Costume Designers, Directors of
Photography, Editors and Production Designers)

A.S.A. Medical Services Division   **(323) 662-9787**
P.O. Box 727   FAX **(323) 662-1569**
Montrose, CA 91021   **www.asafilmcrew.com**
(EMTs, Lifeguards, Nurses, Paramedics, Rescue Technicians,
Safety Consultants, Set Security, Set Medics & Studio
Teachers/Welfare Workers)

Action Artists Agency   **(323) 337-4666**
   www.action-artists.com
(Reps for Set Sketchers and Storyboard Artists)

   (310) 775-5723
Agency Celebrity Artists   **(214) 930-9875**
   www.agencycelebrityartists.com
(Reps for Hair and Makeup Artists)

Aim Artists Agency   **(323) 931-2745**
509 N. Sycamore Ave.   FAX **(323) 931-2747**
Los Angeles, CA 90036   **www.aimartist.com**
(Reps for Hair and Makeup Artists and Wardrobe Stylists)

All Crew Agency   **(818) 206-0144**
2920 W. Olive Ave., Ste. 201   FAX **(818) 206-0169**
Burbank, CA 91505   **www.allcrewagency.com**
(Reps for Costume Designers, Directors of Photography, First
Assistant Directors, Hair and Makeup Artists, Producers,
Production Designers, Production Managers, Prosthetics
Artists, Script Supervisors and Sound Mixers)

Ambitious Entertainment   **(818) 990-8993**
   www.ambitiousent.com
(Reps for Art Directors/Production Designers, Commercial
Directors and Directors of Photography)

   (323) 933-0200
Artist Untied   **(415) 957-0500**
   FAX **(415) 957-0555**
   www.artistuntied.com
(Reps For Hair and Makeup Artists, Prop Stylists and
Wardrobe Stylists)

Artists by Timothy Priano   **(310) 274-0032**
120 El Camino Dr., Ste. 100   FAX **(310) 278-7520**
Los Angeles, CA 90212
   www.artistsbytimothypriano.com
(Reps for Hair and Makeup Artists and Wardrobe Stylists)

   (323) 445-4910
artists' services   **(415) 824-4423**
   www.artists-services.com
(Reps for Hair and Makeup Artists, Prop Masters &
Wardrobe Stylists)

ArtMix Beauty   **(310) 943-8102**
2332 S. Centinela Ave., Ste. C   FAX **(310) 943-8101**
Los Angeles, CA 90064   **www.artmixbeauty.com**
(Reps for Hair and Makeup Artists and Wardrobe Stylists)

   (310) 943-8100
ArtMix Photography   **(718) 596-2400**
2332 S. Centinela Ave., Ste. C   FAX **(310) 943-8101**
Los Angeles, CA 90064   **www.artmixphotography.com**
(Reps for Stills Photographers)

   (818) 905-0790
@baby! baby!/Lynn Raines   **(818) 216-8666**
2830 S. Robertson Blvd.   FAX **(818) 501-0768**
Los Angeles, CA 90034   **www.atbabybaby.com**
(Referral for Baby Wranglers, Nurses and Studio Teachers/
Welfare Workers)

Beauty & Photo   **(323) 549-3100**
3737 Greenwood Ave.   FAX **(323) 549-9881**
Los Angeles, CA 90066   **www.beautyandphoto.com**
(Reps for Hair and Makeup Artists)

Casala, Ltd.   **(818) 432-7404**
11600 Ventura Blvd.   FAX **(818) 432-7405**
Studio City, CA 91604   **www.childreninfilm.com**
(Referral for Medics, Nurses and Studio Teachers/Welfare
Workers)

Celestine Agency   **(310) 998-1977**
1548 16th St.   FAX **(310) 998-1978**
Santa Monica, CA 90404   **www.celestineagency.com**
(Reps for Hair and Makeup Artists, Set Decorators and
Wardrobe Stylists)

Cloutier Remix   **(310) 839-8722**
2632 La Cienega Ave.   FAX **(310) 839-8730**
Los Angeles, CA 90034   **www.cloutieragency.com**
(Reps for Hair and Makeup Artists and Wardrobe Stylists)

   (800) 352-7397
Crew Connection   **(303) 526-4900**
   FAX **(303) 526-4901**
   www.crewconnection.com
(Nationwide and International Crew Booking)

Dattner Dispoto & Associates   **(310) 474-4585**
10635 Santa Monica Blvd., Ste. 165   FAX **(310) 474-6411**
Los Angeles, CA 90025   **www.ddatalent.com**
(Reps for Directors of Photography & Production Designers)

Dawn to Dusk Agency (323) 850-6783
(212) 431-8631
8306 Wilshire Blvd., Ste. 412
Beverly Hills, CA 90211
(Reps for Hair and Makeup Artists and Wardrobe Stylists)

Digital Artists Agency/DAA (310) 788-3918
13323 Washington Blvd., Ste. 304 FAX (310) 788-3415
Los Angeles, CA 90066 www.d-a-a.com
(Reps for Visual FX Artists)

Dion Peronneau Agency (323) 299-4043
5482 Wilshire Blvd., Ste. 1512 FAX (323) 299-4269
Los Angeles, CA 90036 www.dionperonneau.com
(Reps for Hair and Makeup Artists and Wardrobe Stylists)

The Directors Network (818) 906-0006
(Reps for Commercial Directors) FAX (818) 301-2224
www.thedirectorsnetwork.com

Eastern Talent Agency (323) 856-3000
849 S. Broadway, Ste. 811 FAX (323) 856-3009
Los Angeles, CA 90014 www.easterntalent.net
(Reps for Costume Designers, Directors of Photography,
Editors, First Assistant Directors, Production Designers and
Stunt Coordinators)

Ennis, Inc. (310) 587-3512
(Reps for Hair and Makeup Artists and www.ennisinc.com
Wardrobe Stylists/Costume Designers)

Epiphany Artist Group, Inc. (323) 660-6353
FAX (323) 660-0094
(Reps for Hair and Makeup Artists and Wardrobe Stylists)

Exclusive Artists Management (323) 436-7766
7700 Sunset Blvd., Ste. 205 FAX (323) 436-7799
Los Angeles, CA 90046 www.eamgmt.com
(Reps for Hair and Makeup Artists and Wardrobe Stylists)

Famous Frames, Inc. (310) 642-2721
(800) 530-3375
5839 Green Valley Circle, Ste. 104 FAX (310) 642-2728
Culver City, CA 90230 www.famousframes.com
(Reps for Storyboard Artists)

FIRE House Management (888) 839-0101
FAX (888) 839-2943
www.firehousemanagement.com
(Reps for Hair and Makeup Artists and Wardrobe Stylists)

Frameworks Artists (323) 665-7736
983 Manzanita St. FAX (323) 662-4381
Los Angeles, CA 90029 www.frameworks-la.com
(Reps for Storyboard Artists)

The Gersh Agency (310) 274-6611
(212) 997-1818
9465 Wilshire Blvd., Sixth Fl. www.gershagency.com
Beverly Hills, CA 90212
(Reps for Costume Designers, Directors of Photography,
Editors, Producers and Production Designers)

GSK & Associates (323) 782-1854
6399 Wilshire Blvd., Ste. 415 FAX (323) 345-5690
Los Angeles, CA 90048 www.gsktalent.com
(Reps for Costume Designers, Directors of Photography,
Editors, Line Producers, Production Designers, Sound Mixers,
UPMs & VFX Supervisors)

Innovative Artists (310) 656-5151
1617 Broadway, Third Fl. FAX (310) 656-5156
Santa Monica, CA 90404 www.innovativeartists.com
(Reps for Art Directors/Production Designers, Directors of
Photography, Producers and Wardrobe Stylists/Costume
Designers)

**International Creative
Management - ICM** (310) 550-4000
10250 Constellation Blvd. www.icmtalent.com
Los Angeles, CA 90067
(Reps for Costume Designers, Directors of Photography,
Editors, Producers and Production Designers)

iTalent Company (818) 284-6423
FAX (866) 755-0708
www.italentco.com
(Reps for Directors of Photography, Editors, Hair and Makeup
Artists and Wardrobe Stylists/Costume Designers)

LA Rep (213) 446-1720
FAX (323) 656-1756
www.larep.net
(Reps for Hair and Makeup Artists, Photographers & Wardrobe,
Prop and Product Stylists)

Leslie Alyson Inc. (310) 601-2355
350 S. Beverly Dr., Ste. 200 www.lesliealyson.com
Beverly Hills, CA 90212
(Reps for Hair and Makeup Artists)

**MacGowan Spencer
Creative Agency** (310) 489-0502
www.macgowanspencer.com
(Reps for Hair and Makeup Artists)

The Mack Agency (818) 753-6300
4804 Laurel Canyon Blvd., Ste. 825
Valley Village, CA 91607 www.themackagency.net
(Reps for Conceptual Artists, Directors of Photography &
Production Designers)

Magnet LA (323) 297-0250
6363 Wilshire Blvd., Ste. 650 FAX (323) 297-0249
Los Angeles, CA 90048 www.magnetla.com
(Reps for Art Directors, Hair and Makeup Artists and
Wardrobe Stylists)

Martone MGMT (213) 908-6754
3324 ½ Bellevue Ave. FAX (213) 375-7882
Los Angeles , CA 90026 www.martonemgmt.com
(Reps for Art Directors, Directors of Photography &
Production Designers)

Ⓐ Media Services Camera (888) 746-6871
Crews Worldwide (508) 481-2212
www.media-services.com/crews

The Mirisch Agency (310) 282-9940
8840 Wilshire Blvd., Ste. 100 FAX (310) 282-0702
Los Angeles, CA 90211 www.mirisch.com
(Reps for Camera Operators, Costume Designers, Directors
of Photography, Editors, Producers, Production Designers &
Visual Effects Supervisors)

Montana Artists Agency (310) 623-5500
9150 Wilshire Blvd., Ste. 100 FAX (310) 623-5515
Beverly Hills, CA 90212 www.montanartists.com
(Reps for Directors of Photography, Editors, First Assistant
Directors, Producers, Production Designers, Stunt
Coordinators, UPMs and Visual FX Supervisors)

MS Management (323) 935-8455
(Reps for Hair Stylists, Make-up FAX (323) 935-3143
Artists and Wardrobe Stylists) www.ms-management.com

The Murtha Agency (310) 395-4600
1025 Colorado Ave., Ste. B FAX (310) 395-4622
Santa Monica, CA 90401 www.murthaagency.com
(Reps for Costume Designers, Directors of Photography,
Editors & Producers)

New York Office (323) 468-2240
(212) 545-7895
6605 Hollywood Blvd., Ste. 200 FAX (323) 468-2244
Los Angeles, CA 90028 www.nyoffice.net
(Reps for Costume Designers, Directors of Photography,
Editors, Hair and Makeup Artists and Production Designers)

On Location Education (818) 541-9077
(800) 800-3378
400 Columbus Ave., Ste. 7S FAX (914) 747-2750
Los Angeles, CA 90046 www.onlocationeducation.com
(Referral for Studio Teachers/Welfare Workers)

Opus Beauty (323) 856-8540
6442 Santa Monica Blvd., Ste. 200B FAX (323) 871-8311
Los Angeles, CA 90038 www.opusbeauty.com
(Reps for Hair and Makeup Artists and Wardrobe Stylists)

Paradigm, A Talent &
Literary Agency   (310) 288-8000
360 N. Crescent Dr.   FAX (310) 288-2000
Beverly Hills, CA 90210   **www.paradigmagency.com**
(Reps for Costume Designers, Directors of Photography,
Editors, Makeup Artists, Producers & Production Designers)

Partos Company   (310) 458-7800
227 Broadway, Ste. 204   FAX (310) 587-2250
Santa Monica, CA 90401   **www.partos.com**
(Reps for Directors of Photography, Production Designers and
Wardrobe Stylists)

Photogenics   (310) 733-2550
8549 Higuera St.   FAX (310) 815-8632
Culver City, CA 90232   **www.photogenicsmedia.com**
(Reps for Hair and Makeup Artists and Wardrobe Stylists)

Radiant Artists   (323) 463-0022
2701 N. Sixth St.   FAX (323) 375-0231
Burbank, CA 91504   **www.radiantartists.com**
(Reps for Directors of Photography and Production Designers)

The Rappaport Agency   (323) 464-4481
6311 Romaine St., Ste. 7204   FAX (323) 464-5030
Hollywood, CA 90038   **www.rappagency.com**
(Reps for Stills Photographers)

Rescues Unlimited, Inc.   (800) 966-0883
P.O. Box 3086   FAX (909) 592-7656
Covina, CA 91722
(Reps for Rescue Technicians)

The Rex Agency   (323) 446-2007
6311 Romaine St., Ste. 7235   FAX (323) 466-1966
Los Angeles, CA 90038   **www.therexagency.com**
(Reps for Art Directors, Hair and Makeup Artists and
Wardrobe Stylists)

Rocket Science Talent   (818) 876-9618
5023 N. Parkway Calabasas   FAX (818) 876-8501
Calabasas, CA 91302   **rocketsciencetalent.com**
(Reps for Visual FX Supervisors & Producers)

                                (310) 822-2898
Rouge Artists, Inc.   (310) 570-1150
2433 Boone Ave.   FAX (310) 827-7367
Venice, CA 90291   **www.rougeartists.com**
(Reps for Hair and Makeup Artists and Wardrobe Stylists)

Russell Todd Agency   (818) 985-1130
5238 Goodland Ave.   FAX (818) 985-1134
Valley Village, CA 91607 **www.russelltoddagency.com**
(Reps for Steadicam Operators)

Sandra Marsh & Associates   (310) 285-0303
9150 Wilshire Blvd., Ste. 220   FAX (310) 285-0218
Beverly Hills, CA 90212   **www.sandramarsh.com**
(Reps for Costume Designers, Directors of Photography,
Editors, Production Designers and Sound Production Mixers)

The Schneider
Entertainment Agency   (818) 222-5200
22287 Mulholland Hwy, Ste. 210 FAX (818) 222-5284
Calabasas, CA 91302 **www.schneiderentertainment.com**
(Reps for Directors of Photography, Hair and Makeup Artists
and Steadicam Operators)

                                (310) 966-4005
Sesler & Company   (416) 504-1223
6524 W. Olympic Blvd.   FAX (323) 988-0930
Los Angeles, CA 90048   **www.seslercompany.com**
(Reps for Directors of Photography)

Sheldon Prosnit Agency   (310) 652-8778
800 S. Robertson Blvd., Ste. 6 FAX (310) 652-8772
Los Angeles, CA 90035   **www.lspagency.net**
(Reps for Directors of Photography and Production Designers)

The Skouras Agency   (310) 395-9550
1149 Third St., Third Fl.   FAX (310) 395-4295
Santa Monica, CA 90403   **www.skouras.com**
(Reps for Directors of Photography and Production Designers)

Sternworld Creative Management   (310) 439-1903
923 Marco Pl.   FAX (310) 439-1904
Venice, CA 90291   **www.sternworld.net**
(Reps for Design, Marketing, Music and Promotion Companies)

Streetlights Production
Assistant Program   (323) 960-4540
(Production Assistant Training and Crews)   FAX (323) 960-4546
                          www.streetlights.org

                                (818) 559-9797
The Studio Teachers (IA Local 884)   (818) 559-9600
(Referral for Studio Teachers) **www.thestudioteachers.com**

TAMU Artist Agency   (310) 721-0735
137 S. Robertson Blvd., Ste. 111   FAX (323) 571-3498
Beverly Hills, CA 90211   **www.tamuartistagency.com**
(Reps for Hair and Makeup Artists and Wardrobe Stylists)

TDN Artists   (818) 906-0006
(Reps for Directors of Photography)   FAX (818) 301-2224
                          www.tdnartists.com

@Teacher! Teacher!   (310) 559-1918
(Referral for Baby Wranglers,   FAX (818) 501-0768
Nurses and Studio Teachers/Welfare Workers)

TellAVision   (310) 230-5303
1060 20th St., Ste. 8   FAX (310) 388-5550
Santa Monica, CA 90403   **www.tellavisionagency.com**
(Reps for 3-D FX Artists, Storyboard Artists & Visual Research/
Treatment Design)

Tracey Mattingly, LLC   (323) 462-5000
(Reps for Hair and Makeup Artists   FAX (323) 462-5001
and Wardrobe Stylists)w   **www.traceymattingly.com**

United Talent Agency   (310) 273-6700
9560 Wilshire Blvd., Ste. 500   FAX (310) 247-1111
Beverly Hills, CA 90212   **www.utaproduction.com**
(Reps for Costume Designers, Directors of Photography and
Production Designers)

                                (310) 574-9385
Video Tech Services   (310) 505-4015
10866 Washington Blvd., Ste. 513   FAX (310) 577-0850
Culver City, CA 90232   **www.videotechservices.com**
(Reps for Camera Operators, Gaffers and Lighting Directors,
Sound Production Mixers and Video Assist and VTR Operators)

The Wall Group LA   (310) 276-0777
518 N. La Cienega Blvd.   FAX (310) 276-0107
Los Angeles, CA 90048   **www.thewallgroup.com**
(Reps for Hair and Makeup Artists)

WatchReels.com   (818) 953-4930
84 E. Santa Anita   FAX (818) 392-8707
Burbank, CA 91502   **www.watchreels.com**

William Morris Endeavor   (310) 285-9000
9601 Wilshire Blvd.   FAX (310) 285-9010
Beverly Hills, CA 90210   **www.wmeentertainment.com**

                                (310) 246-0446
Workgroup, Ltd.   (415) 567-7023
(Reps for Hair and Makeup Artists)   FAX (415) 674-1950
                          www.workgroup-ltd.com

WPA - Worldwide
Production Agency   (323) 703-1333
5358 Melrose Ave.   FAX (323) 703-1334
West Office Bldg., Ste. 209W   **wp-a.com**
Hollywood, CA 90038
(Reps for Art Directors/Production Designers, Directors of
Photography & Line Producers)

                                (323) 937-1010
Zenobia Agency, Inc.   (888) 639-6917
130 S. Highland Ave.   FAX (323) 937-1133
Los Angeles, CA 90036   **www.zenobia.com**
(Reps for Food Stylists, Hair and Makeup Artists, Location
Scouts, Prop Stylists & Wardrobe Stylists)

A A A Amphibious Medics
(818) 219-5522
(877) 878-9185
FAX (818) 301-2665
www.amphibiousmedics.com
(Ambulances, EMTs, Lifeguards, Medics, Nurses, Rescue
Technicians, Safety Consultants, Safety Divers &
Travel Medicine)

A.S.A. Medical Services Division   (323) 662-9787
P.O. Box 727   FAX (323) 662-1569
Montrose, CA 91021   www.asafilmcrew.com
(Ambulances, EMTs, Lifeguards, Nurses, Paramedics, Safety
Consultants and Divers & Set Medics)

Martin L. Alpert, M.D.   (310) 393-0739
(On Set, Travel and Tropical Physician) FAX (310) 395-2063

Alpha Ambulance, Inc.
(323) 937-0308
(323) 370-3073
425 S. Fairfax Ave., Ste. 205   FAX (323) 937-4893
Los Angeles, CA 90036   www.aambulance.com
(Ambulances, EMTs, Lifeguards, Medics & Rescue Technicians)

American Rescue Services, Inc.
(323) 664-5816
(323) 377-4062
1582 Altivo Way
Los Angeles, CA 90026
(EMTs, Lifeguards, Medics, Nurses,
Safety Divers & Paramedics)

Aqua Rescue
(323) 707-3411
(323) 707-3415
FAX (818) 293-0049
www.aquarescue.com
(Lifeguards, Medics, Safety Divers & Underwater Safety)

Aquavision
(562) 433-2863
(562) 688-3038
3708 E. Fourth St.   FAX (562) 433-2863
Long Beach, CA 90814   www.aquavision.net
(Referral for EMTs, Lifeguards, Medics, Rescue Technicians,
Safety Consultants, Safety Divers, Swiftwater Rescue
Technicians & Technical Advisors)

@baby! baby!/Lynn Raines
(818) 905-0790
(818) 216-8666
2830 S. Robertson Blvd.   FAX (818) 501-0768
Los Angeles, CA 90034   www.atbabybaby.com
(Referral for Nurses)

Ben Baker, RN   (818) 468-5385
www.imdb.com/name/nm1629353/
(Baby Nurse, EMTs, Lifeguards, Medics & Nurses)

Steve Baruch   (661) 373-8270
FAX (661) 554-1785
www.moviemedx.com
(EMTs, Lifeguards, Medics, Production Safety Coordination,
Rescue Technicians, Safety Divers & Technical Advisors)

Cory L. Berg
(323) 644-1289
(323) 497-9774
(Paramedic)   FAX (323) 644-1289

Sandra Leigh Bolish   (661) 645-7347

Kasi Brown   (310) 962-8682
(EMT)

Casala, Ltd.   (818) 432-7404
11600 Ventura Blvd.   FAX (818) 432-7405
Studio City, CA 91604   www.childreninfilm.com
(Referral for Lifeguards, Nurses and Paramedics)

Tom Case
(661) 273-8649
(661) 755-6073

Cinema Safety &   (310) 614-0206
Marine Services, Inc.   (805) 207-5797
1534 N. Moorpark Rd., Ste. 108   FAX (805) 241-3954
Thousand Oaks, CA 91360   www.cinemasafety.com
(Lifeguards, Medics, Nurses, Rescue Technicians, Safety
Consultants, Safety Divers, Technical Advisors & Underwater)

Code Blue Medics   (661) 644-3422
24307 Magic Mountain Pkwy, Ste. 361 FAX (661) 253-0135
Santa Clarita, CA 91355   www.codebluemedics.com
(Ambulances, EMTs, Lifeguards, MDs, Military Combat Medics,
Nurses, Paramedics, Rescue Divers, Safety Consultants, Set
Medics, Technical Advisors & Travel Medicine)

Sean Cussen   (562) 618-4357

Robert Cymbal
(818) 219-0520
(818) 360-0120
FAX (818) 360-2408
(Lifeguards, Marine Coordination, Medics, Rescue Technicians,
Safety Divers & Technical Advisors)

Don DeBaun   (310) 408-7629

Entertainment Industry Physicians   (323) 464-2151
7080 Hollywood Blvd., Ste. 1101   FAX (323) 464-2903
Hollywood, CA 90028

First Aid Services of San Diego, Inc.
(619) 708-5555
(888) 457-5273
5907 Erlanger St.   FAX (858) 457-1641
San Diego, CA 92122   www.firstaidservices.com
(Ambulances, EMTs, Lifeguards, Medics, Nurses &
Technical Advisors)

Tammy Yazgulian Frost
(818) 655-5341
(661) 904-1520
FAX (818) 655-8570

Gerber Ambulance Service (310) 466-8476
19801 Mariner Ave. FAX (310) 542-1152
Torrance, CA 90503 www.gerberambulance.com
(Ambulances, EMT's, Nurses & Paramedics)

(661) 755-7855
Timothy Hall (661) 259-1389
(EMT & Medic)

Healthy Traveler Clinic (626) 584-1200
1250 E. Green St., Ste. 100 FAX (626) 584-2900
Pasadena, CA 91106 www.healthytraveler.com
(Travel Medicine)

(310) 773-5678
Hollywood Set Medics (310) 564-6542
P.O. Box 292318 www.hollywoodsetmedics.net
Hollywood, CA 90029
(EMTs, Lifeguards, Paramedics, Set Medics, Stand By
Ambulance & Studio Teachers)

Jon P. Ko (818) 355-2506
(EMT, Medic, Safety Consultant & Travel Medicine)

(562) 741-6230
Liberty Ambulance (310) 846-4012
9441 Washburn Rd. FAX (562) 741-6230
Downey, CA 90242 www.libertyambulance.com

Joel Markman (310) 488-3724
FAX (310) 399-2592
(EMT, Lifeguard, Medic & Technical Advisor)

(818) 632-8072
Michael Matus (818) 505-8072
FAX (707) 516-3573

(818) 660-5150
McCormick Ambulance (888) 349-8944
13933 Crenshaw Blvd. www.mccormickambulance.com
Hawthorne, CA 90250
(Ambulances, EMTs, Medics, Paramedics & Technical Advisors)

**Motion Picture First Aid
Employees (IA Local 767)** (818) 641-5765
2520 W. Olive Ave., Ste. 320 FAX (818) 474-1570
Burbank, CA 91505 www.iatse767.org

My Concierge Doctor (310) 400-0362
2080 Century Park East, Ste. 1405 FAX (310) 788-8477
Los Angeles, CA 90067 www.myconciergemd.com
(Cast Exams, EMTs, Medics, Nurses, On Call Doctor, Rescue
Technicians, Safety Consultants, Technical Advisors &
Travel Medicine)

(661) 433-8255
Paul Nolan (661) 252-6134

David O'Leary (805) 558-6754
(Paramedic)

---

(323) 297-0700
Ⓐ **Passport Health** (888) 499-7277
333 South Hope St., Ste. C145 FAX (323) 549-9423
Los Angeles, CA 90071 www.passporthealthusa.com
(Travel Medicine)

Stephen Patt, M.D. (310) 582-1114
(Cast Exams, Safety Consultant, Technical Advisor &
Travel Medicine)

Rescues Unlimited, Inc. (800) 966-0883
P.O. Box 3086 FAX (909) 592-7656
Covina, CA 91722
(Rescue Technicians)

Terri L. Rock, M.D. (310) 829-7625
FAX (310) 319-2468
www.tripmedicine.com
(Cast Exams, On Set Family Physician, Travel Immunizations &
Travel Medicine)

Schaefer Ambulance (323) 209-7243
4627 Beverly Blvd. FAX (323) 465-1892
Los Angeles, CA 90004 www.schaeferamb.com
(Ambulances, EMTs, Medics & Nurses)

(909) 880-2979
Symons Event Safety (866) 728-3548
P.O. Box 10333 FAX (909) 880-9279
San Bernardino, CA 92423
www.symonsambulence.com
(Ambulances, EMTs, Medics, Nurses, Paramedics, Rescue
Technicians, Safety Consultants, Technical Advisors &
Travel Medicine)

@Teacher! Teacher! (310) 559-1918
(Referral for Nurses) FAX (818) 501-0768

Claudio Tepper (310) 926-4051
www.imdb.com/name/nm4461864/
(Ambulances, EMT, Lifegaurd, Medic, Nurse, Paramedic,
Rescue Technician, Safety Consultant, Safety Diver, Set Medic,
Technical Advisor & Travel Medicine)

Kim Thio (805) 732-3488
(Paramedic) www.studiomedical.com

Tower I.D. Medical Associates, Inc. (310) 358-2300
8635 W. Third St., Ste. 1180W FAX (310) 358-2308
Los Angeles, CA 90048
(Travel Medicine)

(818) 929-3203
Lynn Wyett (818) 348-4441
(EMTs)

9 Agency	(310) 430-9902
(Reps for Production Designers)	FAX (310) 469-7899
	www.9-agency.com

Fanae Aaron	(323) 463-0022
	www.radiantartists.com

Gabriel Abraham	(323) 578-2112
	www.gabrielabraham.com

Ken Adam	(310) 282-9940
	www.mirisch.com

Heidi Adams	(213) 880-1229
	www.heidiadams.com

Jeb Adams	(818) 338-9296
	(818) 681-4179
(Art Director & Production Designer)	

Maher Ahmad	(310) 288-8000
	www.paradigmagency.com

All Crew Agency	(818) 206-0144
2920 W. Olive Ave., Ste. 201	FAX (818) 206-0169
Burbank, CA 91505	www.allcrewagency.com
(Reps for Production Designers)	

James Allen	(818) 762-2747
	(310) 282-9940
	FAX (818) 762-2747

Jade Altman	(323) 855-5515
	(323) 222-1001
(Art Director & Production Designer)	FAX (866) 521-3573
	www.depict33.com

Patricia Altman	(323) 855-6710
	(323) 222-1001
	www.depict33.com

Stephen Altman	(310) 274-6611
	www.gershagency.com

Miranda Amador	(310) 557-8458
	FAX (310) 557-8458

Ambitious Entertainment	(818) 990-8993
	www.ambitiousent.com
(Reps for Art Directors/Production Designers)	

Ruth Ammon	(310) 656-5151
	www.innovativeartists.com

Nathan Amondson	(310) 656-5151
	www.innovativeartists.com

Amy Ancona	(310) 274-6611
	www.gershagency.com

Susan Anderson	(323) 466-2007
	www.therexagency.com

Fred Andrews	(310) 288-8000
	(323) 605-3099
	www.paradigmagency.com

Conrad E. Angone	(323) 664-9756
(Art Director & Production Designer)	

Atli Arason	(818) 753-6300
	www.themackagency.net

Steve Arnold	(818) 326-1440
(Production Designer)	www.steve-arnold.com

Michelle Ashley	(323) 449-1538
(Set Decorator)	FAX (323) 851-2249

Jamin Assa	(310) 474-4585
	www.ddatalent.com

Alan Au	(310) 428-1951

Paul Austerberry	(310) 458-7800
	www.partos.com

Ken E. Averill	(323) 697-6057
	(310) 474-4585
	www.kenaverill.com

Paul Avery	(323) 468-2240
	www.nyoffice.net

Ramsey Avery	(310) 623-5500
	www.montanartists.com

Michael Alex Bain	(323) 856-8540
	www.opusbeauty.com

Laura Ballinger	(310) 623-5500
	www.montanartists.com

Benjamin Bamps	(323) 468-2240
	www.nyoffice.net

Carlos Barbosa	(310) 623-5500
	www.montanartists.com

Phillip Barker	(310) 474-4585
	www.ddatalent.com

Guy Barnes	(310) 395-4600
	www.murthaagency.com

Russell Barnes	(310) 274-6611
	www.gershagency.com

Walter Barnett	(310) 458-7800
	www.partos.com

K.K. Barrett	(310) 273-6700
	www.utaproduction.com

Poppy Bartlett	(323) 297-0250
	www.magnetla.com

Francesca Bartoccini	(323) 712-0650
(Art Director & Production Designer)	

Edward Bash	(818) 249-6979
	(323) 376-4047
	FAX (818) 249-8179

Larry Basso/Basso Design	(323) 401-8801
	www.bassodesign.com

Amelia Battaglio	(310) 703-7251
	(917) 405-8758
	www.detaglia.com

Hannah Beachler	(310) 474-4585
	www.ddatalent.com

Stephen Beatrice	(310) 274-6611
	www.gershagency.com

Eric Beauchamp	(323) 251-5113
	(310) 246-3133
	www.ericbeauchamp.com

Sophie Becher | (310) 285-0303
www.sandramarsh.com

Judy Becker | (310) 273-6700
www.utaproduction.com

Michael Bednark | (323) 297-0250
www.magnetla.com

Jeffrey Beecroft | (626) 398-3337
(626) 786-2310
(Production Designer) | www.jeffreybeecroft.com

Max Bellhouse | (323) 297-0250
www.magnetla.com

Christy Belt | (310) 822-4730
(310) 991-4730
FAX (310) 822-4730

Laurence Bennett | (310) 656-5151
www.innovativeartists.com

Jesse Benson | (323) 703-1333
wp-a.com

Mark Benson | (310) 422-4400
(Production Designer) | www.prototypestudio.com

Peter K. Benson | (323) 703-1333
wp-a.com

Richard Berg | (818) 206-0144
www.allcrewagency.com

Ryan Berg | (310) 623-5500
www.montanartists.com

Kate Bergh | (213) 706-9254

Julie Berghoff | (310) 274-6611
www.gershagency.com

Roshelle Berliner | (310) 652-8778
www.lspagency.net

Andrew Bernard | (323) 468-2240
www.nyoffice.net

Greg Berry | (310) 282-9940
www.mirisch.com

Jon Billington | (310) 274-6611
www.gershagency.com

Kevin Bird | (310) 395-4600
www.murthaagency.com

Max Biscoe | (310) 288-8000
www.paradigmagency.com

Dan Bishop | (310) 395-9550
www.skouras.com

Jim Bissell | (310) 395-9550
www.skouras.com

Perry Andelin Blake | (310) 392-8422
(310) 710-6663
www.gershagency.com

David Blass | (310) 623-5500
www.montanartists.com

Stuart Blatt | (310) 656-5151
www.innovativeartists.com

Susan Block | (310) 623-5500
www.montanartists.com

Jerry Blohm | (310) 770-3366
(305) 299-7364
www.jerryblohm.com
(Art Director, Production Designer, Prop Master & Set Decorator)

Gavin Bocquet | (310) 395-9550
www.skouras.com

Bill Boes | (310) 285-9000
www.wmeentertainment.com

Oana Bogdan | (310) 779-3134
(Art Director) | www.oanab.com

Frank Bollinger | (323) 856-3000
www.easterntalent.net

Michael Bolton | (310) 395-9550
www.skouras.com

David Bomba | (310) 395-9550
www.skouras.com

John Lord Booth | (310) 395-9550
www.skouras.com

Merideth Boswell | (310) 395-4600
www.murthaagency.com

Bob Bottieri | (818) 206-0144
www.allcrewagency.com

Simon Bowles | (310) 285-0303
www.sandramarsh.com

Ruth Bracken | (707) 495-7667
(707) 823-7957
(Set Decorator) | FAX (707) 581-2046
www.ruthbdesigns.com

Brian Branstetter | (310) 474-4585
www.ddatalent.com

Charles Breen | (310) 288-8000
www.paradigmagency.com

Albert Brenner | (310) 282-9940
www.mirisch.com

Richard Bridgland | (310) 274-6611
www.gershagency.com

David Brisbin | (310) 274-6611
www.gershagency.com

Brigitte Broch | (310) 285-0303
www.sandramarsh.com

Cara Brower | (323) 463-0022
www.radiantartists.com

Christopher Brown | (323) 856-3000
www.easterntalent.net

Tom Brown | (310) 474-4585
www.dattnerdispoto.com

Bill Brzeski | (310) 274-6611
www.gershagency.com

Gae Buckley | (310) 395-4600
www.murthaagency.com

Martina Buckley | (818) 206-0144
www.allcrewagency.com

Michael Budge | (818) 612-7764
(323) 845-4144
www.michaelbudge.com
(Art Director & Production Designer)

William Budge	(818) 753-6300	Stefania Cella	(310) 656-5151
	www.themackagency.net		www.innovativeartists.com
Katherine Bulovic	(818) 206-0144	Scott Chambliss	(310) 656-5151
	www.allcrewagency.com		www.innovativeartists.com
Robb Buono	(310) 285-9000	Sue Chan	(310) 282-9940
	www.wmeentertainment.com		www.mirisch.com
Elizabeth Burhop/	(312) 961-3132	David Chapman	(310) 656-5151
ART department TV	(323) 646-0426		www.innovativeartists.com
(Production Designer)	www.artdept.tv	Todd Cherniawsky	(310) 458-7800
	(310) 562-9478		www.partos.com
Keith Brian Burns	(310) 285-0303	James Chinlund	(323) 297-0250
	www.keithbrianburns.com		www.magnetla.com
Don Burt	(310) 395-9550	Barry Chusid	(310) 656-5151
	www.skouras.com		www.innovativeartists.com
	(310) 458-7800	Ged Clarke	(310) 285-9000
Jenny Burton	(201) 750-9404		www.lspagency.net
	www.partos.com	Michael Paul Clausen	(310) 282-9940
Linda Burton	(310) 288-8000		www.mirisch.com
	www.paradigmagency.com	Jim Clay	(310) 285-0303
Sharon Busse	(310) 288-8000		www.sandramarsh.com
(Production Designer)	www.paradigmagency.com	Nelson Coates	(310) 288-8000
Danny Butch	(323) 821-2999		www.paradigmagency.com
(Set Decorator)		Michael Scott Cobb	(310) 652-8778
	(310) 274-6611		www.lspagency.net
Rick Butler	(914) 473-5173	Sandy Cochrane	(310) 623-5500
	www.gershagency.com		www.montanartists.com
Damien Byrne	(323) 468-2240	Bill Coggon	(818) 400-4747
	www.nyoffice.net	(Prop Master)	www.billcoggon.com
Eugenio Caballero	(310) 652-8778		(323) 703-1333
	www.lspagency.net	Lester Cohen	(845) 687-4503
Joe Cabrera	(310) 288-8000		wp-a.com
	www.paradigmagency.com	John Collins	(310) 656-5151
Andrea Callerino	(323) 297-0250		www.innovativeartists.com
	www.magnetla.com	Roger Collins	(323) 876-4020
Allan Cameron	(310) 395-9550	Mike Conte	(323) 463-0022
	www.skouras.com		www.radiantartists.com
Charlie Campbell	(818) 284-6423	Claudio (Pache) Contreras	(310) 395-9550
	www.italentco.com		www.skouras.com
Franco Carbone	(310) 288-8000	Toby Corbett	(310) 285-9000
	www.paradigmagency.com		www.wmeentertainment.com
Charisse Cardenas	(310) 395-4600	Michael Corenblith	(310) 395-9550
	www.murthaagency.com		www.skouras.com
Jonathan Carlson	(310) 288-8000	Peter Cosco	(310) 623-5500
	www.paradigmagency.com		www.montanartists.com
Jean-Philippe Carp	(323) 468-2240	David Courtemarche	(310) 345-0160
	www.nyoffice.net		www.davidcourtemarche.com
Stephanie Carroll	(310) 395-4600	Stuart Craig	(310) 395-9550
	www.murthaagency.com		www.skouras.com
Richard Carter	(310) 344-4750	David Crank	(310) 395-9550
	FAX (310) 393-4266		www.skouras.com
Kent Casey	(323) 466-2007	Lauren Crasco	(310) 656-5151
	www.therexagency.com		www.innovativeartists.com
Jeremy Cassells	(310) 656-5151	Paul Cross	(323) 703-1333
	www.innovativeartists.com		wp-a.com
Eve Cauley	(323) 251-5331		

William Cruse (323) 463-4022 www.allcrewagency.com	John Doliner (818) 206-0144 www.allcrewagency.com
Howard Cummings (310) 273-6700 www.utaproduction.com	David Donley (213) 706-1969 (Art Director & Production Designer) FAX (213) 384-5354 homepage.mac.com/ddonley213/
Keith Cunningham (310) 395-9550 www.skouras.com	Kitty Doris-Bates (310) 288-8000 www.paradigmagency.com
Bruce Curtis (310) 274-6611 www.gershagency.com	Daniel T. Dorrance (310) 656-5151 www.innovativeartists.com
Charlie Daboub (310) 285-0303 www.sandramarsh.com	Carl Dove (310) 998-1977 www.celestineagency.com
Dattner Dispoto & Associates (310) 474-4585 10635 Santa Monica Blvd., Ste. 165 FAX (310) 474-6411 Los Angeles, CA 90025 www.ddatalent.com (Reps for Production Designers)	(323) 829-3005 Paul Dove (626) 345-9594 (Art Director & Production Designer) www.pixesky.net
Matthew Davies (310) 288-8000 www.paradigmagency.com	Justin Dragonas (310) 474-4585 www.justindragonas.com
Jennifer A. Davis (310) 395-9550 www.skouras.com	Thomas Drotar (310) 399-5700 www.thomasdrotar.com
Cece de Stefano (310) 656-5151 www.innovativeartists.com	Tom Duffield (310) 282-9940 www.mirisch.com
Robert De Vico (323) 468-2240 www.nyoffice.net	Philip Duffin (213) 300-9020
Jackson DeGovia (310) 395-9550 www.skouras.com	Henry Dunn (310) 623-5500 www.montanartists.com
Jennifer Dehghan (310) 288-8000 www.paradigmagency.com	Jerry Dunn (818) 206-0144 www.allcrewagency.com
John De Meo (310) 285-0303 www.sandramarsh.com	Guy Dyas (310) 273-6700 www.utaproduction.com
Therese DePrez (310) 274-6611 www.gershagency.com	Chad Dziewior (323) 297-0250 www.magnetla.com
Russell De Rozario (310) 273-6700 www.unitedtalent.com	Eastern Talent Agency (323) 856-3000 849 S. Broadway, Ste. 811 FAX (323) 856-3009 Los Angeles, CA 90014 www.easterntalent.net (Reps for Production Designers)
Linda DeScenna (310) 395-9550 www.skouras.com	Debra Echard (310) 458-7800 www.partos.com
Beth De Sort (310) 625-4282 (Set Decorator)	Garvin Eddy (310) 288-8000 www.paradigmagency.com
Chad Detweiller (310) 288-8000 www.paradigmagency.com	Jason Edmonds (310) 458-7800 www.partos.com
Franckie Diago (310) 623-5500 www.montanartists.com	Bill Eigenbrodt (310) 656-5151 www.innovativeartists.com
Ermanno Di Febo-Orsini (818) 284-6423 www.italentco.com	Bob Einfrank (310) 893-4241 (Art Director & Production Designer) www.bobeinfrank.com
Mark Digby (310) 274-6611 www.gershagency.com	William A. Elliott (310) 395-4600 www.murthaagency.com
Alex DiGerlando (310) 652-8778 www.lspagency.net	Suzette Ervin (310) 282-9940 www.mirisch.com
Chris Dileo (213) 908-6754 www.martonemgmt.com	Deborah Evans (310) 474-4585 www.ddatalent.com
Leslie Dilley (310) 274-6611 www.gershagency.com	Jeffrey Everett (310) 285-9000 www.wmeentertainment.com
Marco Belli DiMaccio (310) 285-9000 www.wmeentertainment.com	Ricky Eyres (310) 623-5500 www.montanartists.com
Francesca Di Mottola (310) 285-9000 www.wmeentertainment.com	David Faithfull (323) 463-0022 www.radiantartists.com
Maria Djurkovic (310) 273-6700 www.utaproduction.com	

Art Directors/Production Designers

Leila Fakouri	(415) 407-8440
	FAX (213) 747-2412
	www.maderadesign.org
	(310) 717-9034
Sean Falkner	(562) 799-1514
	mysite.verizon.net/resv3n82/
(Art Director, Lead Man, Production Designer, Prop Master, Set Buyer, Set Decorator, Set Dresser & Sign Design)	
Chris Farmer	(818) 753-6300
	www.themackagency.net
Dante Ferretti	(310) 285-0303
	www.sandramarsh.com
Thomas Fichter	(310) 623-5500
	www.montanartists.com
Jason Fijel	(310) 474-4585
	www.ddatalent.com
Marc Fisichella	(310) 652-8778
	www.lspagency.net
Jack Fisk	(310) 395-9550
	www.skouras.com
Michael Fitzgerald	(310) 623-5500
	www.montanartists.com
David Fitzpatrick	(310) 652-8778
	www.lspagency.net
Todd Fjelsted	(323) 466-2007
	www.therexagency.com
Jan-Peter Flack	(323) 703-1333
	wp-a.com
Jack Flanagan	(323) 297-0250
	www.magnetla.com
Molly Flanegin	(323) 855-4225
Rick Floyd	(213) 908-6754
	www.martonemgmt.com
Tom Foden	(310) 395-9550
	www.skouras.com
Beauchamp Fontaine	(818) 550-7855
(Set Decorator)	www.beauchamp-fontaine.com
Amanda Ford	(310) 623-5500
	www.montanartists.com
Roger Ford	(310) 395-9550
	www.skouras.com
Christina Forestieri	(310) 274-0032
	www.artistsbytimothypriano.com
Laura Fox	(310) 285-9000
	www.wmeentertainment.com
Robert Fox	(310) 652-8778
	www.lspagency.net
Sarah Frank	(310) 395-4600
	www.murthaagency.com
Shepherd Frankel	(310) 273-6700
	www.utaproduction.com
Eric Fraser	(310) 623-5500
	www.montanartists.com
Mark Freeborn	(818) 284-6423
	FAX (866) 755-0708
	www.italentco.com

Robbie Freed	(310) 474-4585
	www.dattnerdispoto.com
Doug Freeman	(310) 633-1448
(Art Director & Production Designer)	www.jetsets.net
Mark Friedberg	(310) 395-4600
	www.murthaagency.com
Alexandre Fymat	(323) 468-2240
	www.nyoffice.net
Michael Gallenberg	(818) 284-6423
	www.italentco.com
Lolly Gallup	(818) 550-0300
	FAX (818) 550-9952
Bradley Garlock	(323) 703-1333
	wp-a.com
Joseph Garrity	(310) 285-0303
	www.sandramarsh.com
Norman Garwood	(310) 285-0303
	www.sandramarsh.com
Dennis Gassner	(310) 274-6611
	www.gershagency.com
Michael Gaw	(818) 764-5644
(Art Director & Production Designer)	FAX (818) 764-6655
	www.michaelgaw.com
Stephen Geaghan	(310) 288-8000
	www.paradigmagency.com
Barry Gelber	(310) 801-1728
Cecil Gentry	(310) 474-4585
	www.ddatalent.com
James (jimmyg) Georgopoulos	(310) 699-6935
(Art Director)	www.jamesgeorgopoulos.org
	(310) 274-6611
The Gersh Agency	(212) 997-1818
9465 Wilshire Blvd., Sixth Fl.	www.gershagency.com
Beverly Hills, CA 90212	
(Reps for Production Designers)	
	(917) 969-8443
Chris Giammalvo	(323) 468-2240
(Production Designer)	www.chrisg.tv
Suzanne Gibson	(626) 791-0068
	FAX (626) 791-0068
Darren Gilford	(310) 273-6700
	www.unitedtalent.com
Chris Gimmalvo	(323) 468-2240
	www.nyoffice.net
Jodi Ginnever	(818) 206-0144
	www.allcrewagency.com
Christopher Glass	(310) 273-6700
	www.unitedtalent.com
	(323) 997-7999
Aaron A. Goffman	(800) 655-3305
(Property Master)	FAX (323) 997-7999
	www.goffman.tv
Dina Goldman	(310) 395-9550
	www.skouras.com
Jess Gonchor	(310) 395-4600
	www.murthaagency.com

Nick Goodman	(818) 985-0210	Sean Hargreaves	(310) 395-9550
	FAX (818) 985-0240		www.skouras.com
	www.nickgoodman.com		
		Chase Harlan	(310) 656-5151
	(310) 474-4585		www.innovativeartists.com
Chris Goodmanson	(562) 900-8265		
dda.wiredrive.com/l/eb/?bundleProfile=f8b4288f0f915		Donald Lee Harris	(310) 623-5500
	bcb1578d82ffc46e260		www.montanartists.com
Beth Goodnight	(818) 679-2401	Stan Harris	(646) 246-3722
(Production Designer)	FAX (818) 988-8440		www.swharris.com
	www.companyincsets.com		
		Brentan Harron	(310) 288-8000
Max Gottlieb	(310) 458-7800		www.paradigmagency.com
	www.partos.com		
		Tom Hartman	(310) 458-7800
Michael Grasley	(310) 652-8778		www.partos.com
	www.lspagency.net		
		Helen Harwell	(310) 428-3940
Sarah Greenwood	(310) 395-9550	(Art Director & Production Designer)	
	www.skouras.com		
		Donna Hattin	(310) 623-5500
Arv Grewal	(310) 395-9550		www.montanartists.com
	www.skouras.com		
		Sean Haworth	(310) 282-9940
Joaquin Grey	(323) 703-1333	(Production Designer)	www.mirisch.com
	wp-a.com		
		James Hegedus	(818) 284-6423
Clay Griffith	(310) 656-5151		www.italentco.com
	www.innovativeartists.com		
		Rick Heinrichs	(310) 285-0303
Tim Grimes	(310) 395-9550		www.sandramarsh.com
	www.skouras.com		
		Ric Heitzman	(323) 308-8013
Zack Grobler	(310) 656-5151		www.richeitzman.com
	www.innovativeartists.com		
		Mark Helf	(323) 466-2007
Bill Groom	(310) 274-6611		www.therexagency.com
	www.gershagency.com		
		Ron Hellman	(323) 297-0250
David Gropman	(310) 395-9550		www.magnetla.com
	www.skouras.com		
		Stephen Hendrickson	(310) 282-9940
Theresa Guleserian	(310) 458-7800		www.mirisch.com
	www.partos.com		
		Devorah Herbert	(310) 273-6700
Bruno Hadjadj	(323) 468-2240		www.utaproduction.com
	www.nyoffice.net		
		Jennifer Herwitt	(213) 220-8698
Alex Hajdu	(818) 762-0635	(Set Decorator)	www.herwitt.com
	www.watchreels.com/alexhajdu		
		Jeffrey Higinbotham	(310) 458-7800
Jeff Hall	(818) 990-8993		www.partos.com
	www.ambitiousent.com		
		Derek Hill	(310) 285-9000
Vita Hall	(323) 376-4895		www.wmeentertainment.com
	FAX (323) 876-9807		
		Jeremy Hindle	(310) 273-6700
Jason Hamilton	(323) 297-0250		www.utaproduction.com
	www.magnetla.com		
		Marcia Hinds	(310) 395-4600
Alexander Hammond	(310) 623-5500		www.murthaagency.com
	www.montanartists.com		
		Jaymes Hinkle	(310) 285-9000
	(310) 282-9940		www.wmeentertainment.com
Peter J. Hampton	(310) 822-9113		
	www.peterjhampton.com	Mark Hofeling	(310) 623-5500
			www.montanartists.com
Caroline Hanania	(310) 395-9550		
	www.skouras.com	Richard Holland	(310) 656-5151
			www.innovativeartists.com
Tom Hannam	(310) 623-5500		
	www.montanartists.com	Aaron Hom	(323) 937-1010
			www.zenobia.com
	(917) 855-1188		
John Hansen	(310) 288-8000	Eliott Hostetter	(310) 652-8778
	www.hansendesigninc.com		www.lspagency.net
Kenneth Hardy	(310) 623-5500	Brock Houghton	(323) 449-6924
	www.montanartists.com		

Jan Houllevigue	(323) 468-2240
	www.nyoffice.net
Angela Howard	(917) 363-7707
Richard Hudolin	(310) 282-9940
	www.mirisch.com
Denise Hudson	(310) 288-8000
	www.paradigmagency.com
Molly Hughes	(310) 285-0303
	www.sandramarsh.com
Will Hughes-Jones	(310) 288-8000
	www.paradigmagency.com
Clark Hunter	(310) 285-9000
	www.wmeentertainment.com
Jon Hutman	(310) 274-6611
	www.gershagency.com
Mark Hutman	(310) 274-6611
	www.gershagency.com
Anthony Ianni	(310) 458-7800
	www.partos.com
Eddie Inda	(323) 937-1010
	www.zenobia.com
Suzuki Ingerslev	(310) 285-9000
	www.wmeentertainment.com

Innovative Artists (310) 656-5151
1617 Broadway, Third Fl.   FAX (310) 656-5156
Santa Monica, CA 90404   www.innovativeartists.com
(Reps for Art Directors/Production Designers)

**International Creative
Management - ICM** (310) 550-4000
10250 Constellation Blvd.   www.icmtalent.com
Los Angeles, CA 90067
(Reps for Production Designers)

Colin D. Irwin	(323) 856-3000
	www.easterntalent.net
Andrew Jackness	(310) 395-4600
	www.andrewjackness.com
Craig Jackson	(310) 623-5500
	www.montanartists.com
Gemma Jackson	(310) 395-9550
	www.skouras.com
Regan Jackson	(310) 285-9000
	www.wmeentertainment.com
Matthew C. Jacobs	(310) 623-5500
	www.montanartists.com
Maia Javan	(310) 285-9000
	www.wmeentertainment.com
Joey Jenkins	(310) 458-7800
	www.partos.com
Kells Jesse	(310) 458-7800
	www.partos.com
Bruton Jones	(310) 288-8000
	www.paradigmagency.com
Melanie Jones	(213) 908-6754
	www.martonemgmt.com
Steven Jones-Evans	(310) 274-6611
	www.gershagency.com

Francois Jordaan	(310) 458-7800
	www.partos.com
Steven Jordan	(310) 285-9000
	www.wmeentertainment.com
Johnny Josselyn	(213) 810-4003
	FAX (323) 446-8484
	www.johnnyjos.com
Karl Juliusson	(310) 273-6700
	www.unitedtalent.com
Chester Kaczenski	(310) 652-8778
	www.lspagency.net
Rachel Kamerman	(310) 656-5151
	www.innovativeartists.com
Brian Kane	(310) 623-5500
	www.montanartists.com
Corey Kaplan	(310) 656-5151
	www.innovativeartists.com
John Kasadra	(310) 282-9940
	www.mirisch.com
Jesse Kaufmann	(323) 297-0250
	www.magnetla.com
Kevin Kavanaugh	(310) 395-9550
	www.skouras.com
Jaeson Kay	(818) 206-0144
	www.allcrewagency.com
Liz Kay	(310) 285-9000
	www.wmeentertainment.com
Michael Keeling	(310) 458-7800
	www.partos.com
Chad Keith	(310) 652-8778
	www.lspagency.net
Victor Kempster	(310) 395-9550
	www.skouras.com
Jessica Kender	(310) 282-9940
	www.mirisch.com
Morgan Kennedy	(310) 474-4585
	www.dattnerdispoto.com
	(323) 935-1127
K.J.B. Kiely	(213) 706-8162
	FAX (323) 930-5611
Lilly Kilvert	(310) 274-6611
	www.gershagency.com
Steve Kimmel	(310) 652-8778
(Production Designer)	FAX (323) 669-0343
	www.lspagency.net
Robb Wilson King	(310) 623-5500
	www.montanartists.com
Trae King	(310) 285-9000
	www.wmeentertainment.com
Holli Kingsbury	(310) 274-0032
	www.artistsbytimothypriano.com
Paul Kirby	(310) 395-9550
	www.skouras.com
Sonja Klaus	(310) 288-8000
	www.paradigmagency.com

Miljen Kljakovic	(310) 285-0303	Richard B. Lewis	(310) 282-9940
	www.sandramarsh.com		www.richardblewisdesign.com
Ray Kluga	(310) 656-5151	George Liddle	(310) 395-4600
	www.innovativeartists.com		www.murthaagency.com
Jeff Knipp	(310) 623-5500	Kara Lindstrom	(310) 623-5500
	www.montanartists.com		www.montanartists.com
Christian Svanes Kolding	(310) 848-7310	Barbara Ling	(310) 395-9550
	www.christiansvaneskolding.com		www.skouras.com
Gary Kordan	(323) 856-3000	Nicole Lobart	(818) 753-6300
	www.easterntalent.net		www.themackagency.net
Doug Kraner	(310) 656-5151	Sharon Lomofsky	(310) 274-6611
	www.innovativeartists.com		www.sharonlomofsky.com
Michael Krantz	(323) 703-1333	Santo Loquasto	(310) 288-8000
	wp-a.com		www.paradigmagency.com
John Kretschmer	(310) 623-5500	Taylor Lorentz	(310) 276-0777
	www.montanartists.com		www.thewallgroup.com
Lena Kuffner	(310) 276-0777	Cory Lorenzen	(310) 274-6611
	www.thewallgroup.com		www.gershagency.com

Sara Kugelmass — (310) 458-7800 — www.partos.com

Richard C. Lowe — (213) 610-0878
(Prop Master) — FAX (310) 664-1001
www.lowejinx.com

Charlie Lagola — (310) 288-8000 — www.paradigmagency.com

Joseph Lucky — (310) 288-8000 — www.paradigmagency.com

Bill Lakoff — (818) 261-9448
FAX (818) 994-1526
www.wtldesignsinc.com

Hugo Luczyc-Wyhowski — (310) 395-9550 — www.skouras.com

Guy Lalande — (310) 623-5500 — www.montanartists.com

Patrick Lumb — (310) 623-5500
(Production Designer) — www.montanartists.com

Neil Lamont — (310) 285-0303 — www.sandramarsh.com

Nicholas Lundy — (310) 656-5151 — www.innovativeartists.com

Peter Lamont — (310) 652-8778 — www.lspagency.net

Jeffrey Luther — (661) 722-9251 / (661) 400-5829
(Art Director & Production Designer)

Richard Lassalle — (323) 703-1333 — wp-a.com

Marcos Lutyens — (310) 282-9940 — www.mirisch.com

Abraham Latham — (310) 943-8102 — www.artmixbeauty.com

The Mack Agency — (818) 753-6300
4804 Laurel Canyon Blvd., Ste. 825
Valley Village, CA 91607 — www.themackagency.net
(Reps for Production Designers)

Julian LaVerdiere — (310) 395-9550 — www.skouras.com

Steve Lawrence — (310) 395-9550 — www.skouras.com

Laura Maffeo — (323) 937-1010 — www.zenobia.com

David Lazan — (310) 656-5151 — www.innovativeartists.com

Magnet LA — (323) 297-0250
6363 Wilshire Blvd., Ste. 650 — FAX (323) 297-0249
Los Angeles, CA 90048 — www.magnetla.com
(Reps for Art Directors)

Lauryn LeClere — (818) 760-7746 / (818) 681-2114
FAX (818) 760-7748
www.lecleredesign.com

Grant Major — (310) 273-6700 — www.utaproduction.com

Charles Lee — (310) 652-8778 — www.lspagency.net

Aran Mann — (310) 274-6611 — www.gershagency.com

Jonathan Lee — (310) 285-0303 — www.sandramarsh.com

Jeff Mann — (310) 285-9000 — www.wmeentertainment.com

Steven Legler — (310) 962-4952
(Art Director & Production Designer) — www.leglerart.com

Michael Manson — (213) 300-6010
(Art Director & Production Designer)

Dan Leigh — (310) 285-0303 — www.sandramarsh.com

Stephen Marsh — (310) 623-5500 — www.montanartists.com

Douglas C. Lewis — (213) 700-7424
(Set Decorator)

Paul Martin — (310) 652-8778 / (323) 578-1946
www.lspagency.net

Art Directors/Production Designers

Kate Martindale	(310) 998-1977
	www.celestineagency.com

Martone MGMT (213) 908-6754
3324 1/2 Bellevue Ave. FAX (213) 375-7882
Los Angeles, CA 90026 www.martonemgmt.com
(Reps for Art Directors/Production Designers)

Anastasia Masaro	(310) 395-4600
	www.murthaagency.com

Happy Massee	(310) 288-8000
	www.paradigmagency.com

Teresa Mastropierro	(310) 652-8778
	www.lspagency.net

Zach Mathews	(310) 285-9000
	www.wmeentertainment.com

Gary Matteson	(323) 573-7753
	www.garymattesondesign.com

Arthur Max	(310) 395-4600
	www.murthaagency.com

Caty Maxey	(818) 206-0144
	www.allcrewagency.com

Andrew McAlpine	(310) 285-0303
	www.sandramarsh.com

Stephen McCabe	(310) 623-5500
	www.montanartists.com

Alex McDowell	(818) 753-6300
	www.themackagency.net

Stephen J. McHale	(805) 405-4123
	FAX (818) 475-1453

Peter McKinney (310) 863-5984
FAX (310) 356-3815
www.mckinneyprodesign.com
(Art Director, Production Designer & Set Decorator)

Deborah McLean	(323) 937-1010
	www.zenobia.com

Cabot McMullen	(310) 600-3693
	www.cmi-nyc.com

Anthony Medina	(310) 656-5151
	www.innovativeartists.com

Doug J. Meerdink	(310) 623-5500
	www.montanartists.com

Irwin Mehlman	(310) 350-9683

Greg Melton	(310) 288-8000
	www.paradigmagency.com

Carlos Menendez	(310) 474-4585
	www.dattnerdispoto.com

Andrew Menzies	(310) 656-5151
	www.innovativeartists.com

James Merifield	(310) 285-0303
	www.sandramarsh.com

Philip Messina	(310) 395-9550
	www.skouras.com

Carey Meyer	(310) 623-5500
	www.montanartists.com

Tom Meyer	(310) 273-6700
	www.utaproduction.com

Elizabeth Mickle	(310) 285-9000
	www.wmeentertainment.com

Bruce Miller	(310) 652-8778
	www.lspagency.net

Chris Anthony Miller	(818) 206-0144
	www.allcrewagency.com

Gille Mills	(310) 276-0777
	www.thewallgroup.com

	(626) 441-8975
Michelle Minch	(626) 695-1227
	FAX (626) 441-8118
	www.michelleminch.com

The Mirisch Agency (310) 282-9940
8840 Wilshire Blvd., Ste. 100 FAX (310) 282-0702
Los Angeles, CA 90211 www.mirisch.com
(Reps for Production Designers)

Nigel Mitchell	(818) 206-0144
	www.allcrewagency.com

Montana Artists Agency (310) 623-5500
9150 Wilshire Blvd., Ste. 100 FAX (310) 623-5515
Beverly Hills, CA 90212 www.montanartists.com
(Reps for Production Designers)

Cecilia Montiel	(310) 652-8778
	www.lspagency.net

	(818) 990-8993
Elizabeth Moore	(323) 459-8160
	www.eamoore.com

	(323) 497-7502
Dan Morski	(818) 881-4358
	FAX (818) 881-3208
	www.giantfin.com/dan_morski

John Mott	(323) 856-3000
	www.easterntalent.net

Alan E. Muraoka	(323) 856-3000
	www.easterntalent.net

Scott P. Murphy	(310) 623-5500
	www.montanartists.com

The Murtha Agency (310) 395-4600
1025 Colorado Ave., Ste. B FAX (310) 395-4622
Santa Monica, CA 90401 www.murthaagency.com
(Reps for Production Designers)

Jane Musky	(310) 395-9550
	www.skouras.com

John Myhre	(310) 285-0303
	www.sandramarsh.com

Rika Nakanishi	(818) 753-6300
	www.themackagency.net

Ariana Nakata	(310) 458-7800
	www.partos.com

Ondrej Nekvasil	(310) 623-5500
	www.montanartists.com

	(310) 395-9550
Janet Nelson	(323) 851-1512
	www.skouras.com

Joseph Nemec	(310) 458-7800
	www.partos.com

Jesse Nemeth	(310) 276-0777
	www.thewallgroup.com

New York Office
6605 Hollywood Blvd., Ste. 200
Los Angeles, CA 90028
(Reps for Production Designers)

(323) 468-2240
(212) 545-7895
FAX (323) 468-2244
www.nyoffice.net

Jill Nicholls
(323) 297-0250
www.magnetla.com

Andy Nicholson
(818) 753-6300
www.themackagency.net

Marco Niro
(310) 285-0303
www.sandramarsh.com

Tony Noble
(310) 285-9000
www.wmeentertainment.com

Eric Norlin
(310) 623-5500
www.montanartists.com

Patricia Norris
(310) 395-4600
www.murthaagency.com

Daniel Novotny
(310) 288-8000
www.paradigmagency.com

Michael Novotny
(310) 652-8778
www.lspagency.net

Christopher Nowak
(310) 623-5500
www.montanartists.com

Paul Oberman
(310) 652-8778
www.lspagency.net

Michael Okowita
(323) 856-3000
www.easterntalent.net

Gary A. Olson
(Prop Master)
(818) 761-8426
(818) 749-6577

Maxwell Orgell
(323) 703-1333
wp-a.com

Stefano Maria Ortolani
(310) 395-4600
www.murthaagency.com

Aaron Osborne
(310) 273-6700
www.utaproduction.com

Rachel O'Toole
(310) 623-5500
www.montanartists.com

Laurent Ott
(310) 652-8778
www.lspagency.net

Neville Page
(323) 703-1333
wp-a.com

Claude Pare
(310) 274-6611
www.gershagency.com

Salvador Parra
(310) 652-8778
www.lspagency.net

Partos Company
227 Broadway, Ste. 204
Santa Monica, CA 90401
(Reps for Production Designers)

(310) 458-7800
FAX (310) 587-2250
www.partos.com

Owen Paterson
(310) 273-6700
www.utaproduction.com

Janet Patterson
(310) 285-0303
www.sandramarsh.com

Victoria Paul
(310) 656-5151
www.innovativeartists.com

Randall Peacock
(323) 297-0250
www.magnetla.com

Tule Peak
(310) 458-7800
www.partos.com

Robert Pearson
(323) 703-1333
wp-a.com

Vincent Peranio
(310) 623-5500
www.montanartists.com

Paul Peters
(310) 288-8000
www.paradigmagency.com

Kirk Petruccelli
(310) 285-9000
www.wmeentertainment.com

Nigel Phelps
(310) 273-6700
www.utaproduction.com

Ian Phillips
(310) 395-9550
www.skouras.com

Kevin Phipps
(310) 285-0303
www.sandramarsh.com

Herbert Pinter
(310) 395-4600
www.murthaagency.com

Dave Pirinelli
(213) 434-7523
web.mac.com/dpart2/

Denise Pizzini
(310) 623-5500
www.montanartists.com

Agustin Plotquin
(310) 430-0971
(310) 430-0970
FAX (323) 221-9600
www.allsets.com

Patti Podesta
(310) 288-8000
www.paradigmagency.com

Peter Politanoff
(310) 288-8000
www.paradigmagency.com

Gideon Ponte
(323) 297-0250
www.magnetla.com

Katterina Powers
(310) 288-8000
www.paradigmagency.com

Anthony Pratt
(310) 285-0303
www.sandramarsh.com

Kim Healy Pretti
(818) 325-5086
www.kimpretti.com

Clement Price-Thomas
(310) 395-9550
www.skouras.com

Ben Procter
(310) 285-0303
www.sandramarsh.com

Robert J. Quinn
(818) 517-6155

Radiant Artists
2701 N. Sixth St.
Burbank, CA 91504
(Reps for Production Designers)

(323) 463-0022
FAX (323) 375-0231
www.radiantartists.com

Steve Ralph
(213) 400-9340
(262) 567-9813
www.steveralphdesign.com

Gary Randall
(818) 504-9211
(323) 376-3046
www.garyrandalldesigns.com

Art Directors/Production Designers

Ida Random	(310) 395-9550 www.skouras.com	Anne Ross	(310) 968-0007 www.anneross.com
Bjorn Reddington	(213) 280-6460 FAX (805) 684-8717	David Ross	(310) 943-8102 www.artmixbeauty.com
Jeremy Reed	(310) 273-6700 www.utaproduction.com	Edward L. Rubin	(310) 656-5151 www.innovativeartists.com
Seth Reed	(310) 288-8000 www.paradigmagency.com	Antonello Rubino	(310) 623-5500 www.montanartists.com
Kim Rees	(951) 377-6570 (323) 463-0022 www.radiantartists.com	Beth Rubino	(310) 395-4600 www.murthaagency.com
Chuck Renaud (Art Director & Production Designer) www.chuckrenaud.com	(323) 254-4420 (917) 204-6034	Duane Russell	(805) 512-8989 (818) 687-2310 FAX (818) 763-4428 www.strongarmscenery.com

Ida Random — (310) 395-9550 — www.skouras.com
Anne Ross — (310) 968-0007 — www.anneross.com
Bjorn Reddington — (213) 280-6460 — FAX (805) 684-8717
David Ross — (310) 943-8102 — www.artmixbeauty.com
Jeremy Reed — (310) 273-6700 — www.utaproduction.com
Edward L. Rubin — (310) 656-5151 — www.innovativeartists.com
Seth Reed — (310) 288-8000 — www.paradigmagency.com
Antonello Rubino — (310) 623-5500 — www.montanartists.com
Kim Rees — (951) 377-6570 / (323) 463-0022 — www.radiantartists.com
Beth Rubino — (310) 395-4600 — www.murthaagency.com
Chuck Renaud (Art Director & Production Designer) — (323) 254-4420 / (917) 204-6034 — www.chuckrenaud.com
Duane Russell — (805) 512-8989 / (818) 687-2310 — FAX (818) 763-4428 — www.strongarmscenery.com

The Rex Agency — (323) 466-2007 — FAX (323) 466-1966 — www.therexagency.com
6311 Romaine St., Ste. 7235
Los Angeles, CA 90038
(Reps for Art Directors)

Chris Ryan — (818) 416-7912
(Prop Master)

Vincent Reynaud — (310) 652-8778 — www.lspagency.net

Wendy Samuels — (310) 503-9255
(Art Director & Production Designer) — FAX (310) 202-6466 — www.wendysamuels.com

Michael Reynolds — (323) 297-0250 — www.magnetla.com

David Sandefur — (310) 623-5500 — www.montanartists.com

Norman Reynolds — (310) 395-9550 — www.skouras.com

William Sandell — (310) 274-6611 — www.gershagency.com

Andy Reznik — (310) 285-9000 — www.wmeentertainment.com

John Sanders — (818) 284-6423 — www.italentco.com

Andy Rhodes — (310) 395-9550 — www.skouras.com

Sandra Marsh & Associates — (310) 285-0303 — FAX (310) 285-0218 — www.sandramarsh.com
9150 Wilshire Blvd., Ste. 220
Beverly Hills, CA 90212
(Reps for Production Designers)

Steve Rick/The Prop Connection — (323) 788-8468
(Art Director & Prop Master) — FAX (757) 257-5140

Gerard Santos — (323) 297-0250 — www.magnetla.com

Mark Ricker — (310) 395-9550 — www.skouras.com

Tom Sayer — (310) 623-5500 — www.montanartists.com

Marc Rizzo/Rizzo Design Inc. — (818) 437-6520
466 Foothill Blvd., Ste. 392 — www.rizzodesign.com
La Canada, CA 91206
(Art Director, Production Designer & Set Designer)

Darcy Scanlin — (323) 468-2240 — www.nyoffice.net

Tino M. Schaedler — (310) 273-6700 — www.utaproduction.com

Nanci B. Roberts — (818) 951-3226 / (818) 395-5419 — FAX (818) 951-3316 — www.art4reel.com

Curtis Schnell — (310) 652-8778 — www.lspagency.net

Mary Margaret Robinson — (323) 656-6131
(Production Designer, Set Buyer & Set Decorator)

Jeff Schoen — (310) 623-5500 — www.montanartists.com

Barry Robison — (310) 273-6700 — www.utaproduction.com

Oliver Scholl — (310) 274-6611 — www.gershagency.com

Alan Roderick-Jones — (310) 457-3029 / (310) 985-4265 — www.alanrjstudios.com

Kyle Schuneman — (323) 466-2007 — www.therexagency.com

Jan Roelfs — (310) 395-9550 — www.skouras.com

Jason Schuster — (310) 918-4266

Meghan Rogers — (310) 623-5500 — www.montanartists.com

Stephen Scott — (310) 652-8778 — www.lspagency.net

Evan Rohde — (310) 652-8778 — www.lspagency.net

Miriam Seger — (213) 705-8003

Philip Rosenberg — (310) 274-6611 / (772) 708-1700

Francois Seguin — (310) 285-0303 — www.sandramarsh.com

Roland Rosenkranz — (310) 623-5500 — www.montanartists.com

Anne Seibel — (310) 652-8778 — www.lspagency.net

Niels Sejer — (310) 652-8778 — www.lspagency.net

Linda Sena — (323) 856-3000 www.easterntalent.net	Tom Southwell — (310) 288-8000 www.paradigmagency.com
Chime Serra — (323) 297-0250 www.magnetla.com	Johannes Spalt — (323) 463-0022 www.radiantartists.com
Bella Serrell — (323) 463-0022 www.radiantartists.com	Chris Spellman — (310) 285-9000 www.wmeentertainment.com
Sharon Seymour — (310) 395-9550 www.skouras.com	Jennifer Spence — (310) 458-7800 www.partos.com
Bob Shaw — (310) 395-4600 www.murthaagency.com	James Spencer — (310) 288-8000 www.paradigmagency.com
Phil Shearer — (818) 990-8993 www.ambitiousent.com	Annie Sperling — (310) 652-8778 www.lspagency.net

Sheldon Prosnit Agency — (310) 652-8778
800 S. Robertson Blvd., Ste. 6 — FAX (310) 652-8772
Los Angeles, CA 90035 — www.lspagency.net
(Reps for Production Designers)

Carol Spier — (310) 285-0303
www.sandramarsh.com

Maxine Shepard — (310) 623-5500
www.montanartists.com

Ricardo Spinace — (310) 623-5500
www.montanartists.com

Richard Sherman — (310) 458-7800
www.partos.com

Neil Spisak — (310) 395-9550
www.skouras.com

Bruce Shibley — (310) 663-9163
FAX (866) 312-9846
www.bruceshibley.com

Carl Sprague — (323) 468-2240
www.nyoffice.net

Naomi Shohan — (310) 395-4600
www.murthaagency.com

Anthony Rivero Stabley — (323) 440-1455

Craig Siebels — (310) 288-8000
www.paradigmagency.com

Eloise Stammerjohn — (310) 623-5500
www.montanartists.com

Maya Sigel — (323) 468-2240
www.nyoffice.net

Allan Starski — (310) 282-9940
www.mirisch.com

Ross Silverman — (323) 683-5263
www.rosssilverman.com

Craig Stearns — (310) 656-5151
www.innovativeartists.com

David Skinner — (310) 285-9000
www.wmeentertainment.com

Jon Gary Steele — (310) 273-6700
www.utaproduction.com

The Skouras Agency — (310) 395-9550
1149 Third St., Third Fl. — FAX (310) 395-4295
Santa Monica, CA 90403 — www.skouras.com
(Reps for Production Designers)

James Steuart — (323) 703-1333
wp-a.com

Bjarne Sletteland — (310) 770-8223
(505) 466-1436
FAX (505) 466-1436

Eve Stewart — (310) 474-4585
www.dattnerdispoto.com

Jane Stewart — (310) 285-9000
www.wmeentertainment.com

Naomi Slodki — (323) 663-8616
(323) 972-6480
FAX (323) 667-1452

Missy Stewart — (310) 273-6700
www.unitedtalent.com

Penn Smith — (818) 259-0967
www.pennsmithdesign.com

Adam Stockhausen — (310) 395-4600
www.murthaagency.com

Arnd Stockhausen — (213) 595-4755
(Production Designer) — FAX (818) 246-2080
www.filmdesign.biz

Rusty Smith — (310) 285-9000
www.wmeentertainment.com

John Stoddart — (310) 395-9550
www.skouras.com

Wayne T. Smith — (818) 780-0118
(011) 642 7 472 3787
(Art Director & Production Designer)

David Stone — (310) 471-5568
(310) 880-1539
FAX (310) 471-1638
www.davidstonedesign.net
(Art Director, Production Designer & Prop Master)

Mark Snelgrove — (310) 285-9000
www.wmeentertainment.com

David L. Snyder — (310) 656-5151
www.innovativeartists.com

Carol Strober — (323) 661-4881
(Production Designer) — FAX (310) 661-5223
www.carolstrober.com

Dawn Snyder — (310) 623-5500
www.montanartists.com

Robert Stromberg — (310) 273-6700
www.unitedtalent.com

Alfred Sole — (310) 623-5500
www.montanartists.com

Chris Stull — (323) 703-1333
wp-a.com

Patrick Sullivan	(310) 458-7800
	www.partos.com
Christopher Tandon	(310) 288-8000
	www.paradigmagency.com
Yohei Taneda	(310) 285-0303
	www.sandramarsh.com
Mark Tanner	(310) 474-4585
	www.dattnerdispoto.com
Sue Tebbutt	(310) 285-9000
	www.wmeentertainment.com
Dale Thaw	(310) 869-3516
	FAX (866) 807-6895
	www.dalethaw.com
Brent Thomas	(310) 623-5500
	www.montanartists.com
Wynn Thomas	(310) 285-0303
	www.sandramarsh.com
Kevin Thompson	(310) 273-6700
	www.utaproduction.com
	(213) 200-8308
Bradley Thordarson	(310) 656-5151
(Production Designer)	www.bradleythordarson.com
Thomas Thurnauer	(323) 297-0250
	www.magnetla.com
Jodie Tillen	(310) 656-5151
	www.innovativeartists.com
Hughes Tissandier	(310) 652-8778
	www.lspagency.net
Ethan Tobman	(310) 285-9000
	www.wmeentertainment.com
Matt Tognacci	(818) 990-8993
	www.ambitiousent.net
Philip Toolin	(310) 656-5151
	www.innovativeartists.com
	(310) 822-2898
Nick Tortorici	(310) 721-6462
	www.set-design.com
Ginger Tougas	(323) 703-1333
	wp-a.com
Richard Toyon	(310) 288-8000
	www.paradigmagency.com
Luca Tranchino	(310) 395-9550
	www.skouras.com
Bernardo Trujillo	(310) 623-5500
	www.montanartists.com
United Talent Agency	(310) 273-6700
9560 Wilshire Blvd., Ste. 500	FAX (310) 247-1111
Beverly Hills, CA 90212	www.utaproduction.com
(Reps for Production Designers)	
Shane Valentino	(323) 297-0250
	www.magnetla.com
Katherine Vallin	(323) 493-5533
(Production Designer)	
Kristen Vallow	(310) 458-7800
	www.partos.com
Gregory Van Horn	(310) 656-5151
	www.innovativeartists.com

Rene Vas	(310) 458-7800
	www.partos.com
Sandy Veneziano	(310) 395-4600
	www.murthaagency.com
Edward Verreaux	(310) 656-5151
	www.innovativeartists.com
Jay Vetter	(310) 282-9940
	www.mirisch.com
Jamie Vickers	(310) 505-2445
Ron Volz	(310) 720-2002
	FAX (323) 937-3939
	www.ronvolz.com
Patrizia Von Brandenstein	(310) 282-9940
	www.mirisch.com
Frank Walsh	(310) 623-5500
	www.montanartists.com
Tom Walsh	(310) 395-4600
	www.murthaagency.com
Jerry Wanek	(310) 623-5500
	www.montanartists.com
Ryan Warren	(323) 703-1333
	wp-a.com
David Wasco	(310) 273-6700
	www.utaproduction.com
Dennis Washington	(310) 395-4600
	www.murthaagency.com
Dominic Watkins	(310) 273-6700
	www.utaproduction.com
Robert Webb	(310) 458-7800
	www.partos.com
Loren Weeks	(310) 656-5151
	www.innovativeartists.com
Dan Weil	(310) 273-6700
	www.utaproduction.com
Eric Weiler	(310) 288-8000
	www.paradigmagency.com
Marla Weinhoff	(310) 474-4585
	www.marlaweinhoffstudio.com
John Francis Welbanks	(818) 206-0144
	www.allcrewagency.com
Bo Welch	(310) 273-6700
	www.unitedtalent.com
David Weller/David Weller Design	(818) 506-7817
(Production Designer)	FAX (818) 506-8875
	www.wellerdesign.com
	(626) 524-6900
Martin Whist	(310) 273-6700
	www.whistdesign.com
Cary White	(310) 282-9940
	www.mirisch.com
David White	(323) 297-0250
	www.magnetla.com
Ise White	(310) 274-0032
	www.artistsbytimothypriano.com
Francis Whitebloom	(310) 458-7800
	www.partos.com

| Teri Whittaker | (310) 285-9000 |
| | www.teriwhittakerdesigns.com |

	(818) 340-7576
Adele Wilson	(818) 219-9650
(Set Decorator)	

| Steven Wolff | (310) 623-5500 |
| | www.montanartists.com |

| Charles Wood | (310) 285-0303 |
| | www.sandramarsh.com |

| Mark Worthington | (310) 288-8000 |
| | www.paradigmagency.com |

WPA - Worldwide	
Production Agency	(323) 703-1333
5358 Melrose Ave.	FAX (323) 703-1334
West Office Bldg., Ste. 209W	wp-a.com
Hollywood, CA 90038	
(Reps for Production Designers)	

	(323) 868-7490
Jack Wright III	(415) 868-9023
(Art Director & Production Designer)	

| Stuart Wurtzel | (310) 282-9940 |
| | www.mirisch.com |

| Michael Wylie | (323) 314-5468 |
| (Production Designer) | |

| Eugenio Zanetti | (310) 285-0303 |
| | www.sandramarsh.com |

| Bob Ziembicki | (310) 623-5500 |
| | www.montanartists.com |

| Frank Zito | (818) 206-0144 |
| | www.allcrewagency.com |

Baby Wranglers

	(818) 905-0790
@baby! baby!/Lynn Raines	(818) 216-8666
	FAX (818) 501-0768
	www.atbabybaby.com

A.S.A. Studio Teachers Association	(323) 662-9787
	FAX (323) 662-1569
	www.asafilmcrew.com

Maxine Abarbara	(818) 518-7115
	FAX (818) 347-9347
	www.castudioteacher.info

| A. Kathleen Chambers-Schelhorse | (415) 680-0809 |

	(323) 663-3512
Carol Hart	(323) 841-9192
	FAX (323) 661-2124

	(310) 820-4522
Janie Teller	(646) 331-9456
	www.thestudyshack.com

	(310) 980-0290
Alicia Kalvin	(310) 459-6875
	www.studioteacher.org

| | (310) 836-8877 |
| Jill McKay | (310) 617-8245 |

	(818) 385-0000
Stacey Parzik	(818) 648-1667
	www.partiesbystacey.com

Cyndi Raymond	(323) 428-2906
	FAX (323) 938-7714
	www.cyndiraymond.com

| Mark Ruegg | (818) 590-9994 |
| | FAX (818) 232-9115 |

| Linda Stone Shure | (310) 488-1826 |
| | FAX (310) 204-5683 |

| | (602) 740-5598 |
| Linda Stanley | (310) 372-1449 |

| Jack Stern | (818) 970-7540 |

	(818) 559-9797
The Studio Teachers (IA Local 884)	(818) 559-9600
	www.thestudioteachers.com

| Saena Yi | (310) 801-7921 |

John Abbene	(310) 457-3290

	(818) 782-8635
Jack Arnet	(818) 203-2026
(Aerial & Tyler Equipment)	

	(323) 656-2246
Chuck Bemis	(323) 397-8454
(First AC & Motion Control)	

Paul Brady	(818) 540-6189
(Second AC) www.digitalimagingtechnician.com	

	(661) 254-6900
Bob Brown	(805) 341-6673
	FAX (661) 254-6900
	us.imdb.com/name/nm0113141/

Donald Burghardt	(661) 803-4577
(First AC)	

Michael Caparelli	(323) 447-3637
(First AC)	

	(818) 888-9117
Richard Carlson	(818) 298-8624
	FAX (818) 888-7723

	(323) 270-5259
Stephen Craker	(503) 588-2071
(Second AC)	

Ronnie Dennis	(818) 519-8167

	(818) 706-1095
Vito DePalma	(818) 606-3011
(First AC)	

Del DePierro	(213) 300-7771
(Motion Control) www.deldepierro.com	

Robert Eber	(310) 913-1707
	FAX (310) 450-8264

David Eubank	(818) 766-7500
	www.davideubank.com
(First AC, High Def, Remote Heads & Steadicam)	

Stephen Franklin	(310) 739-6614

Alan M. Gitlin	(818) 266-6321
(High Def)	

Chuck Gomez	(347) 834-2835
(First AC)	

	(818) 887-0823
Bob Hall	(818) 618-0823
(Steadicam)	FAX (801) 365-9617

George Hesse	(310) 801-8967
(First AC & High Def)	

Jay Anthony (Tony) Jones	(310) 918-7407
(First AC, High Def & Second Unit)	

	(323) 965-1062
John Malvino	(323) 828-7932

Lee Morris	(323) 251-3839

	(805) 405-7197
Ryne A. Niner	(805) 241-9565
	FAX (805) 241-9584
	www.nineraks.com

David Ortiz	(714) 745-5149

Leslie Otis	(310) 395-5539

	(626) 794-8361
Clint Palmer	(818) 261-6463
(Aerial & Special FX)	

	(805) 798-1545
Ronald Henry Raschke	(805) 649-3544

	(805) 920-9006
Michael Riba	(818) 430-8612
(Remote Heads, Second Unit & Steadicam)	

David Riley	(323) 664-1630

	(818) 706-3203
Rob Rubin	(818) 216-2162
(Aerial, Remote Heads, Second AC & Underwater)	

	(818) 346-4604
Jon Sharpe	(818) 419-2064

	(818) 231-3359
Andy Sydney	(818) 783-2341
	FAX (818) 830-0444
(High Def, Remote Heads, Steadicam & Underwater)	

	(818) 974-2672
Adan Torres	(818) 974-2672
(First AC, High Def, Second AC & Second Unit)	

Greg Ulrich	(661) 904-2219
(First AC, Motion Control, Remote Heads, Second Unit & Special FX)	

Jon Zarkos	(310) 365-7856

	(818) 753-6300
Eric Zimmerman	(310) 849-1948
(Aerial, Steadicam & Underwater)	

Dan Adams
(310) 828-2628
(310) 828-7745

Steven A. Adelson
(604) 506-6552
(818) 985-1130
(Steadicam)

Dan Ayers
(818) 425-7252
(Steadicam)
www.steadidan.com

Wayne Baker
(818) 991-9676
(818) 472-1780
(Aerial & Underwater)
FAX (818) 991-9677
www.waynebaker.com

Eddie Barber
(818) 982-7775
(Barber Booms)
FAX (661) 339-3235
www.barbertvp.com

Tim Bellen
(818) 985-1130
(Steadicam)
www.russelltoddagency.com

George Bianchini
(310) 399-6300
(Steadicam)
www.steadygeorge.com

Maceo Bishop
(818) 985-1130
www.russelltoddagency.com

Tom Boyd
(818) 974-1937
(Underwater)
www.taboyd.com

Kurt Braun
(818) 752-0100
(High Def, Second Unit & Steadicam)

Joe Broderick
(818) 968-2805
(Steadicam)

Art Brown
(310) 576-4992
(Action Sports, High Def, Second Unit, Small Format
Cameras & Underwater)

Scott Browner
(805) 370-1014
(818) 298-5440
resumereels.com/browner
(High Def, Remote Heads, Second Unit & Underwater)

Bill Brummond
(310) 780-7911
(Steadicam)
FAX (310) 364-0014

Greg Bubb
(310) 663-9665
(Steadicam)

Jose Bugarin
(626) 482-3479
www.buddysystems.tv

Joseph W. Calloway
(626) 798-8222
(626) 827-7331
FAX (626) 798-4577
www.callowayfilms.com
(Action Sports, Aerial, High Def, Remote Heads,
 Second Unit & Underwater)

Peter Cavaciuti
(818) 222-5200
www.schneiderentertainment.com

Dave Chameides
(323) 377-3324
(Steadicam)

Jeff L. Clark
(661) 312-6131
(Steadicam)
www.jeffclarksteadicam.com

Jeffrey R. Clark
(661) 295-1325
(805) 506-1959
(Aerial, Skiing & Steadicam)
www.jefclark.com

Barry Conrad
(818) 248-9161
www.barryconrad.com

Richard Crow
(310) 944-4367
(Steadicam)
www.gotsteadicam.com

Britt Cyrus
(818) 667-9654
(818) 757-1430

Rick Davidson
(323) 913-3402
(323) 327-2705
(Steadicam)
www.russelltoddagency.com

Collin Davis
(310) 729-9803

Richard W. Davis
(661) 424-9288
(818) 681-8742
(Steadicam)

Dan R. Dayton
(661) 547-8604
(760) 249-6889
(Aerial)

John Pierre Dechene
(818) 889-6749
(Aerial, High Def, Remote Heads, Second Unit,
Special FX & Underwater)

Rick Denman
(310) 995-2084
(310) 455-2084

Joel Deutsch
(310) 628-5400
(Second Unit & Underwater)
www.evidencecameras.com

Glenn Di Vincenzo
(818) 366-7525
(818) 437-5551
(Steadicam)

David Dougherty
(818) 782-3503
(213) 718-5132
(Barber Boom)

Rick Drapkin
(818) 261-6977
(Aerial, Remote Heads, Steadicam & Underwater)

Phillip Ebeid
(818) 909-7933
(818) 458-4495
(Aerial & Remote Heads)
www.summitcranes.com

Jason Ellson
(323) 363-4074
(Steadicam)
www.schneiderentertainment.com

David Emmerichs
(323) 962-7800
(Remote Heads & Steadicam)
FAX (323) 962-7878
www.schneiderentertainment.com

Farr Out Productions, LLC
(310) 902-5944
(Reps for Camera Operators)
FAX (818) 830-3608
www.farroutpro.com

Jerome Fauci
(843) 795-5402
(310) 809-4345
(Steadicam)
FAX (818) 808-0042
www.gocamerasupport.com

Kenn Ferro
(818) 985-1130
(Steadicam)
www.russelltoddagency.com

Lance Fisher
(323) 868-5108
(323) 935-4803
www.lancesfisher.com
(Action Sports, Aerial, High Def, Remote Heads & Second Unit)

Eric Fletcher
(818) 566-9875
(Steadicam)
www.russelltoddagency.com

Candide Franklyn
(818) 222-5200
www.schneiderentertainment.com

Tom (Frisby) Fraser
(818) 216-5306
3086 Anderson Dr.   www.greenstreetproductions.net
Simi Valley, CA 93065
(High Def, Remote Heads, Second Unit & Special FX)

David J. Frederick   (310) 261-3541
(310) 474-6299
www.imdb.com/name/nm0292774/
(3D, Action Sports, Aerial, High Def, Remote Heads, Second
Unit, Special FX, Steadicam & Underwater)

Buddy Fries   (310) 670-9663

Brian Gaetke   (818) 219-2043
FAX (818) 729-9331

Kirk Gardner   (818) 222-5200
www.schneiderentertainment.com

Christopher George   (818) 974-0434
(Steadicam)

Kristin Glover   (310) 365-6305
FAX (310) 398-3042

Bob Gorelick   (310) 915-0627
(310) 869-9959
(Steadicam)   FAX (310) 915-0157
www.schneiderentertainment.com

Bruce Alan Greene   (818) 985-1130
(High Def & Steadicam)   www.brucealangreene.com

Mark Hardin   (818) 761-7749
(Motion Control & Special FX)   www.markhardin.com

Joshua Harrison   (818) 985-1130
www.russelltoddagency.com

Kent Harvey   (310) 699-3674
(Aerial, High Def & Second Unit)   www.kentharvey.com

Chris Hayes   (917) 626-9050
(323) 876-0160
(Action Sports, Aerial, High Def, Motion Control, Remote
Heads, Second Unit & Special FX)

Sandy Hays   (818) 985-1130
(Steadicam)   www.russelltoddagency.com

M. Todd Henry   (310) 545-5545
(310) 224-0148
FAX (310) 545-7305

Jerry Hill   (818) 772-9256
(Steadicam)   FAX (818) 772-9251
www.steadimoves.com

Keith Holland   (323) 856-4728
www.keithholland.com
(Action Sports, Aerial, High Def, Motion Control, Second Unit,
Special FX & Underwater)

Colin Hudson   (818) 222-5200
www.schneiderentertainment.com

Jeffrey Hunt   (818) 317-2140
(Steadicam)

Erik Ippel   (310) 746-8353
(808) 375-7468
(Underwater)   www.h2ocine.com

Gene Jackson   (323) 935-5342
(High Def)

Alec Jarnagin   (917) 804-6606
(818) 985-1130
www.floatingcamera.com

Simon Jayes   (818) 402-2389
www.imdb.com/name/nm0419735/
(Remote Heads & Steadicam)

Joe Jennings   (310) 543-2222
(Aerial, Helicopter, Skydiving & Stunts)   www.skydive.tv

Peter Jensen   (310) 791-7010
(Steadicam)   FAX (310) 791-0780

Andrew (AJ) Johnson   (818) 222-5200
www.schneiderentertainment.com

Peter Jordan   (310) 866-9300
(POV)

Jacques Jouffret   (310) 459-0700
(818) 985-1130
(Steadicam)   FAX (310) 459-7885
www.russelltoddagency.com

John Joyce   (818) 985-1130
(Steadicam)   www.russelltoddagency.com

Ross Judd   (818) 469-2028
members.dslextreme.com/users/rossteadijudd
(Steadicam)

Mark Karavite   (818) 985-1130
www.russelltoddagency.com

Lawrence Karman   (310) 450-4728
(310) 351-7016
(Steadicam)

Michael Kelem   (310) 486-2008
(Aerial, High Def & Second Unit)

Dan Kneece   (310) 877-2661
(310) 822-5751
www.imdb.com/name/nm0460638/
(High Def & Second Unit)

Bud Kremp   (818) 985-1130
www.russelltoddagency.com

Mark LaBonge   (818) 222-5200
(Steadicam)   www.schneiderentertainment.com

Aaron Land   (424) 835-1080
(High Def)   www.happypixelstudios.com

Michael Levine   (310) 489-6848
FAX (323) 939-9622
www.crashproductions.com

Michael Lloyd   (859) 583-6036
www.michaelaldenlloyd.com

David Luckenbach   (213) 369-7077
(805) 646-9745
www.davidluckenbach.com
(Remote Heads, Steadicam & Underwater)

Cedric Martin   (310) 998-7154
(Steadicam)   www.cedricmartin.com

Michael May   (661) 917-0259
(Steadicam)

Peter McCaffrey   (818) 222-5200
www.schneiderentertainment.com

Mike McGowan   (818) 985-1130
(Steadicam)   www.russelltoddagency.com

Scott Meyer   (818) 730-4900
www.scottfilms.com

Jody Miller   (310) 251-0057
(818) 985-1130
(Steadicam)   FAX (310) 399-3419
www.russelltoddagency.com

Mark E. Moore   (818) 222-5200
(Steadicam)   www.schneiderentertainment.com

Mark Nelson (858) 598-6494	**Mark Sofil** (323) 515-2967
(Action Sports & High Def) FAX (858) 694-0546	(Action Sports & High Def) FAX (866) 336-9840
www.visualconcepts.tv	www.marksofil.com

Mark Nelson (858) 598-6494
(Action Sports & High Def)   FAX **(858) 694-0546**
www.visualconcepts.tv

(818) 876-0041
Randy Nolen (818) 807-2398
(Steadicam)   FAX **(818) 876-0041**

Neal Norton (818) 985-1130
(Steadicam)   www.russelltoddagency.com

Mark O'Kane (818) 883-0075
(Steadicam)

Brad Olander (760) 944-4475
(Steadicam)   www.olandercamera.com

Gerry O'Malley (626) 484-0150
(Steadicam)

Andrew Parke (310) 367-1140
(Stereographer)   dimensionwerks3d.com

David Parrish (818) 765-6037
FAX **(928) 441-8243**
www.wide-screen.com/david.html

(818) 999-9796
Bruce Pasternack (818) 943-9796
(Remote Heads)   FAX **(818) 999-9796**

Chris Patterson (310) 962-3498
FAX **(310) 962-3498**
www.chrispattersonfilms.com

Serge T. Poupis (818) 972-5000
FAX **(818) 972-5010**
www.hollywoodcamera.com
(High Def, Motion Control & Second Unit)

Cynthia Pusheck (323) 497-8489
(Underwater)

(661) 287-1555
Brooks Robinson (661) 904-4788
(Steadicam)   FAX **(661) 287-3353**
www.brooksrobinsoncamera.com

Peter Rosenfeld (818) 222-5200
www.schneiderentertainment.com

Russell Todd Agency (818) 985-1130
5238 Goodland Ave.   FAX **(818) 985-1134**
Valley Village, CA 91607   www.russelltoddagency.com
(Reps for Steadicam Operators)

Michael Santy (415) 309-2365

**The Schneider
Entertainment Agency** (818) 222-5200
22287 Mulholland Hwy, Ste. 210   FAX **(818) 222-5284**
Calabasas, CA 91302
www.schneiderentertainment.com
(Reps for Steadicam Operators)

Andy Shuttleworth (323) 573-2032
(Steadicam)   FAX **(323) 850-1276**

John Skotchdopole (310) 994-7114

Michael Stumpf (323) 697-6090
(Steadicam)   www.steadicamstumpf.com

Robert Sullivan (818) 714-1080

Paul Taylor (818) 985-1130
(Steadicam)   www.russelltoddagency.com

Taj Teffaha (714) 612-7691
(Steadicam)

Henry Tirl (818) 222-5200
(Steadicam)   www.schneiderentertainmentagency.com

Eric Tramp (909) 214-7202
(Steadicam)

Bela Trutz (310) 901-5411
(Steadicam)

(310) 399-8000
Joseph Valentine (310) 245-0345

(818) 344-5284
Ron G. Veto (818) 372-5585
(Steadicam)   www.ronveto.com

(310) 574-9385
Video Tech Services (310) 505-4015
10866 Washington Blvd., Ste. 513   FAX **(310) 577-0850**
Culver City, CA 90232   www.videotechservices.com
(Reps for Camera Operators)

(818) 766-6868
Ron Vidor (800) 759-5722
www.ronvidor.com

(323) 478-1500
Stefan von Bjorn (323) 363-7711
(Steadicam)   FAX **(323) 478-1554**
www.stefanvonbjorn.com

Richard S. Walden (818) 244-3159
(Aerial, Action Sports, High Def, Motion Control, Remote
Heads, Second Unit & Special FX)

David Waldman (323) 841-9253
www.david-waldman.com

Michael Walker (818) 621-4492

(323) 369-9461
Andreas Wood (818) 703-9372
(Steadicam)   FAX **(818) 703-9372**
www.andreaswood.com

(203) 470-3885
Ian Woolston-Smith (310) 402-5130
(Steadicam)   www.iancam.com

(818) 989-4420
Elizabeth Ziegler (818) 469-6732
(Steadicam)   FAX **(818) 989-0423**

Steven A. Adelson	(604) 506-6552 (310) 745-3339
William S. Arnot	(917) 417-4701
Dan Ayers	(818) 425-7252 www.steadidan.com
Tim Bellen	(818) 985-1130 www.russelltoddagency.com
George Bianchini	(310) 399-6300 www.steadygeorge.com
Maceo Bishop	(818) 985-1130 www.russelltoddagency.com
Kurt Braun	(818) 752-0100
Joe Broderick	(818) 968-2805
Bill Brummond	(310) 780-7911 FAX (310) 364-0014
Greg Bubb	(310) 663-9665
Dave Chameides	(323) 377-3324 www.davechameides.com
Jeff L. Clark	(661) 312-6131 www.jeffclarksteadicam.com
Jeffrey R. Clark	(661) 295-1325 (805) 506-1959 www.jefclark.com
Richard Crow	(310) 944-4367 www.gotsteadicam.com
Rick Davidson	(323) 913-3402 (323) 327-2705 www.russelltoddagency.com
Richard W. Davis	(661) 424-9288 (818) 681-8742
Glenn Di Vincenzo	(818) 366-7525 (818) 437-5551
Alfeo Dixon	(323) 639-3367 (404) 456-6957 www.alfeo.com
Rick Drapkin	(818) 261-6977
William Eichler	(818) 985-1130 www.russelltoddagency.com
Jason Ellson	(323) 363-4074 www.schneiderentertainment.com
David Emmerichs	(323) 962-7800 FAX (323) 962-7878 www.schneiderentertainment.com
Jerome Fauci	(843) 795-5402 (310) 809-4345 FAX (818) 808-0042 www.gocamerasupport.com
Kenn Ferro	(818) 985-1130 www.russelltoddagency.com
Eric Fletcher	(818) 566-9875 www.russelltoddagency.com

David J. Frederick	(310) 261-3541 (310) 474-6299 www.soc.org
Christopher George	(818) 974-0434
Mark Goellnicht	(818) 985-1130 www.russelltoddagency.com
Beatriz Gomez	(818) 917-4664 FAX (818) 865-8924 www.gi66productions.com
Bob Gorelick	(310) 915-0627 (310) 869-9959 FAX (310) 915-0157 www.schneiderentertainment.com
Bruce Alan Greene	(818) 985-1130 (818) 802-9252 www.brucealangreene.com
David Allen Grove	(323) 385-3456 www.steadicamoperator.com
Joshua Harrison	(818) 985-1130 www.russelltoddagency.com
Sandy Hays	(818) 985-1130 www.russelltoddagency.com
Jerry Hill	(818) 772-9256 FAX (818) 772-9251 www.steadimoves.com
Jeffrey Hunt	(818) 317-2140 www.russelltoddagency.com
Alec Jarnagin	(917) 804-6606 (818) 985-1130 www.floatingcamera.com
Simon Jayes	(818) 402-2389 www.imdb.com/name/nm0419735/
Peter Jensen	(310) 791-7010 FAX (310) 791-0780
Christopher Jones	(818) 985-1130 www.russelltoddagency.com
Jacques Jouffret	(310) 459-0700 (818) 985-1130 FAX (310) 459-7885 www.russelltoddagency.com
John Joyce	(818) 985-1130 www.russelltoddagency.com
Ross Judd	(818) 469-2028 members.dslextreme.com/users/rossteadijudd
Mark Karavite	(818) 985-1130 www.russelltoddagency.com
Lawrence Karman	(310) 450-4728 (310) 351-7016
David Knight	(818) 985-1130 www.russelltoddagency.com
Bud Kremp	(818) 985-1130 www.russelltoddagency.com
Mark LaBonge	(818) 222-5200 www.schneiderentertainment.com

Tommy Lohmann **(818) 222-5200** www.schneiderentertainment.com	Manolo Rojas **(818) 985-1130** www.russelltoddagency.com

Tommy Lohmann   **(818) 222-5200**
www.schneiderentertainment.com

(213) 369-7077
David Luckenbach   **(805) 646-9745**
www.davidluckenbach.com

Cedric Martin   **(310) 998-7154**
www.cedricmartin.com

Michael May   **(661) 917-0259**

Bill McClelland   **(858) 883-4078**
www.sunsetproductionstudios.com

BJ McDonnell   **(818) 985-1130**
www.russelltoddagency.com

Mike McGowan   **(818) 985-1130**
www.russelltoddagency.com

Christopher TJ McGuire   **(661) 839-7432**
www.ar-mcguire.com

Mark Meyers   **(818) 985-1130**
www.russelltoddagency.com

(310) 251-0057
Jody Miller   **(818) 985-1130**
FAX **(310) 399-3419**
www.russelltoddagency.com

Mark E. Moore   **(818) 222-5200**
www.schneiderentertainment.com

(818) 807-2398
Randy Nolen   **(818) 876-0041**
FAX **(818) 876-0041**

Brian Nordheim   **(818) 985-1130**
www.russelltoddagency.com

Neal Norton   **(818) 985-1130**
www.russelltoddagency.com

Mark O'Kane   **(818) 883-0075**

Brad Olander   **(760) 944-4475**
www.olandercamera.com

Gerry O'Malley   **(626) 484-0150**

Christopher Paul   **(323) 468-2240**
www.nyoffice.net

Matt Petrosky   **(818) 985-1130**
www.russelltoddagency.com

(661) 287-1555
Brooks Robinson   **(661) 904-4788**
FAX **(661) 287-3353**
www.brooksrobinsoncamera.com

Manolo Rojas   **(818) 985-1130**
www.russelltoddagency.com

Russell Todd Agency   **(818) 985-1130**
5238 Goodland Ave.   FAX **(818) 985-1134**
Valley Village, CA 91607   www.russelltoddagency.com
(Reps for Steadicam Operators)

Thomas Schnaidt   **(818) 985-1130**
www.russelltoddagency.com

The Schneider
Entertainment Agency   **(818) 222-5200**
22287 Mulholland Hwy, Ste. 210   FAX **(818) 222-5284**
Calabasas, CA 91302

    www.schneiderentertainment.com
(Reps for Steadicam Operators)

Andy Shuttleworth   **(323) 573-2032**
FAX **(323) 850-1276**

Daniel Stilling   **(213) 840-4525**
www.camerapilot.com

Michael Stumpf   **(323) 697-6090**
www.steadicamstumpf.com

Paul Taylor   **(818) 985-1130**
www.russelltoddagency.com

Taj Teffaha   **(714) 612-7691**

Henry Tirl   **(818) 222-5200**
www.schneiderentertainmentagency.com

Eric Tramp   **(909) 214-7202**

Bela Trutz   **(310) 901-5411**

(818) 344-5284
Ron G. Veto   **(818) 372-5585**
www.ronveto.com

(818) 766-6868
Ron Vidor   **(800) 759-5722**
www.ronvidor.com

(323) 478-1500
Stefan von Bjorn   **(323) 363-7711**
FAX **(323) 478-1554**
www.stefanvonbjorn.com

(323) 369-9461
Andreas Wood   **(818) 703-9372**
FAX **(818) 703-9372**
www.andreaswood.com

(203) 470-3885
Ian Woolston-Smith   **(310) 402-5130**
www.iancam.com

(818) 989-4420
Elizabeth Ziegler   **(818) 469-6732**
FAX **(818) 989-0423**

All Set Certified Craft Services	(323) 350-3269

Aloha Craft Service/
Janice Fernandez   (714) 396-2168

Ambrosia Craft Service   (310) 649-0564
FAX (310) 649-0264

Ate 1 Ate   (818) 915-2850
47 Seaview Terrace, Ste. A
Santa Monica, CA 90401

Big Bites Craft Service   (818) 769-6188
FAX (818) 769-6188
(Breakfasts, Beverages, Coffee, Juices & Snacks)

Craftabilities   (323) 874-4550
(323) 243-1803
(Catering For Non-Union/Crowd Extras) FAX (323) 874-3831

The Crafty Canuck   (310) 717-1219
7800 Midfield Ave.   www.craftycanuck.net
Los Angeles, CA 90045
(24-Hour Service, Breakfast, Coffee Services,
Juices & Smoothies)

Custom Breakfast Catering   (661) 254-8119
(661) 904-5188
(Breakfast)

A Cut Above Craft Service   (213) 590-7487

Fatty's Craft Service   (818) 298-3073

First Resort Craft Service/   (818) 849-6703
Drew Marks   (310) 490-8508

Getting Fresh Craft Service   (818) 416-9813
www.gettingfreshcrafty.com

Girls Gone Crafty   (626) 675-3694

A Good Craft   (323) 559-1144
www.agoodcraft.net
(24-Hour Service, Coffee Service, Continental (Cold) Breakfast,
Juices & Smoothies)

Heydorff & Associates   (818) 243-4686
(818) 422-8869

Hollywood Hottie Dogs   (323) 841-1686
1309 1/2 Preston Way   www.hollywoodhottiedogs.com
Venice, CA 90291
(24-Hour Service,Catering For Non-Union/Crowd Extras, Coffee
Service, Lunch, Mobile Kitchen Facilities, Second Meals &
Hot Dogs)

The Hungry Eye   (213) 361-3051
(818) 841-3665

Jimmy Campbell Craft Services/
Breakfast   (310) 621-4352
www.jimmycampbellcrafty.com

Kit & Kaboodle   (310) 270-7836
(310) 770-2294
2633 Lincoln Blvd., Ste. 430 www.knkcraftservices.com
Santa Monica, CA 90405

Krafty World/Daniel Poole   (818) 845-7388
(818) 298-3073

Laura Bagano, Inc.   (818) 701-0857
(818) 472-2864
FAX (818) 701-0888

Main Street Munchies   (323) 650-5947
www.mainstreetmunchies.com
(Breakfasts, Cappuccinos & Smoothies)

Beverly McIntyre/Heart & Soul   (818) 505-9240
(818) 624-7856

MGMCrafty   (818) 381-3632
(818) 823-6739
17415 Mayflower Dr.   mgmcrafty.webs.com
Granada Hills, CA 91344

Mojave Film Services   (760) 799-4414
P.O. Box 88   www.mojavefilmservices.com
Joshua Tree, CA 92252
(24-Hour Service, Breakfasts, Catering For Non-Union/Crowd
Extras, Coffee Service, Juices, Lunch, Mobile Kitchen Facilities,
Second Meals & Smoothies)

Nelly's Craft Service   (818) 288-0755
8442 Forsythe St.   FAX (818) 352-4808
Sunland, CA 91040

Off The Shelf Craft Division LLC   (310) 990-4973
9854 National Blvd., Ste. 234   FAX (310) 440-0794
Los Angeles, CA 90034

Patrick's Location Catering   (805) 388-5544
FAX (805) 388-5544
(24-Hour Service & Mobile Kitchen Facilities)

Perkside Coffee   (818) 231-5281
7300 Oak Park Ave.   www.perkside.com
Van Nuys, CA 91406
(24-Hour Service, Coffee Service & Smoothies)

Pit Stop Coffee   (310) 882-8181
www.pitstopcoffee.net
(24-Hour Service, Breakfasts, Catering For Non-Union/Crowd
Extras, Coffee Service, Lunch & Second Meals)

She's Crafty   (818) 974-9566
(818) 376-0836
FAX (818) 376-0836

Smoothies Craft Service   (818) 535-2654
(818) 535-0866

Taste Catering, Inc.   (949) 215-7373
FAX (949) 215-7494
www.tastecateringcafe.com
(24-Hour Service, Breakfasts, Catering For Non-Union/Crowd
Extras, Coffee Service, Juices, Lunch, Mobile Kitchen Facilities,
Second Meals & Smoothies)

Team Banzai Craft Service   (626) 664-4760
(24-Hour Service, Breakfasts, Catering For Non-Union/Crowd
Extras, Coffee Service, Juices, Lunch, Second Meals &
Smoothies)

White Linen Crafty   (213) 447-4799
FAX (213) 250-2313
(24-Hour Service, Breakfasts, Coffee Service, Gourmet, Juices,
Organic, Smoothies & Vegan)

Patrick Blewett	(805) 415-4100 (626) 381-9397 www.ambientdsr.com
Paul Brady	(818) 540-6189 www.digitalimagingtechnician.com
Mark Cameron	(310) 574-1524 (310) 923-3593 FAX (310) 574-1524 www.cinemacamerarentals.com
Susan A. Campbell	(818) 203-9190
Jeffrey R. Clark	(661) 295-1325 (805) 506-1959 www.jefclark.com
Keith Collea	(310) 577-3757 (520) 907-2211 FAX (815) 642-4444 www.3dfilmarts.com
Dan Coplan	(323) 627-0773 (818) 762-3373 www.dancoplan.com
Lyndel Crosley	(818) 424-6186 www.lcrosley.com
Britt Cyrus	(818) 667-9654
Doug DeGrazzio	(626) 797-1528 (818) 404-4265 FAX (626) 398-6413
David DeMore	(818) 764-8918
Benjamin Hopkins	(310) 765-4051 (310) 717-9493 FAX (310) 765-4052 www.huemaninterest.com
Cliff Hsui	(818) 623-8818 www.powerhousefilms.us
Dale Hunter	(818) 516-0303
Jay Anthony (Tony) Jones	(310) 918-7407
Scott Meyer	(818) 730-4900 www.scottfilms.com
Evan Nesbitt	(323) 463-0476 (323) 314-5928 www.evannesbitt.com
Ryne A. Niner	(805) 405-7197 (805) 241-9565 FAX (805) 241-9584 www.nineraks.com
Ethan Phillips	(213) 819-2449
Ryan M. Sheridan	(818) 635-8071 FAX (818) 345-7663 www.sheridandesign.com
Bill Sturcke	(805) 501-3289
Steve Tacon	(310) 283-0953 (310) 306-7893
Gary Taillon	(805) 443-3806
Tom Tcimpidis	(818) 366-4837
Derek Wan	(323) 788-3883 FAX (323) 780-8887 www.allinone-usa.com
Robert D. Zeigler	(818) 893-7545 (818) 816-0363 FAX (818) 894-8807

9 Agency   (310) 430-9902
(Reps for Directors of Photography)   FAX (310) 469-7899
www.9-agency.com

Hisham Abed   (323) 703-1333
wp-a.com

Ivan Abel   (310) 474-4585
www.ddatalent.com

Damian Acevedo   (323) 468-2240
(Film & High Def)   www.nyoffice.net

Steve Ackerman   (818) 832-7919
(Film & High Def)   FAX (818) 832-9458

Tom Ackerman   (310) 274-6611
www.gershagency.com

Barry Ackroyd   (310) 273-6700
www.unitedtalent.com

Lance Acord   (310) 474-4585
www.dattnerdispoto.com

Marshall Adams   (310) 623-5500
www.montanartists.com

Eric Adkins   (213) 276-0287
(Film, High Def & Special FX)   www.adkinsdop.com

Brian Agnew   (310) 652-8778
www.lspagency.net

Magni Agustsson   (310) 474-4585
www.ddatalent.com

Lloyd Ahern   (310) 623-5500
www.montanartists.com

Martin Ahlgren   (310) 285-9000
(Film & High Def)   www.wmeentertainment.com

Maryse Alberti   (310) 474-4585
(Film & High Def)   www.ddatalent.com

Maxime Alexandre   (310) 458-7800
www.partos.com

All Crew Agency   (818) 206-0144
2920 W. Olive Ave., Ste. 201   FAX (818) 206-0169
Burbank, CA 91505   www.allcrewagency.com
(Reps for Directors of Photography)

Russ T. Alsobrook   (626) 755 4191

Gonzalo Amat   (310) 288-8000
www.paradigmagency.com

Michel Amathieu   (310) 652-8778
www.lspagency.net

Ambitious Entertainment   (818) 990-8993
(Reps for Directors of Photography)   www.ambitiousent.com

Mitch Amundsen   (323) 703-1333
wp-a.com

Eric Roy Anderson   (661) 245-5929
(310) 740-7678
www.ericroyanderson.com
(Film, High Def, Remote Heads & Second Unit)

Daniel Andreas   (310) 986-3370
(Film & High Def)   www.24pcine.com

Tim Angulo   (818) 206-0144
(805) 680-8108
www.allcrewagency.com

Steve Annis   (310) 652-8778
www.lspagency.net

Javier Aquirresarobe   (310) 474-4585
www.ddatalent.com

Daniel Aranyo   (310) 623-5500
www.montanartists.com

Thierry Arbogast   (310) 550-4000
www.icmtalent.com

Anthony Arendt   (310) 458-7800
www.partos.com

Fernando Arguelles   (310) 474-4585
www.ddatalent.com

Adam Arkapaw   (310) 285-9000
www.wmeentertainment.com

David A. Armstrong   (310) 656-5151
www.innovativeartists.com

John Aronson   (310) 395-4600
www.murthaagency.com

Howard Atherton   (310) 395-4600
www.murthaagency.com

Bernard Auroux   (310) 573 5034
(Film & High Def)   www.bernardauroux.com

Chris Austin   (213) 999-7060
(Film & High Def)   www.chrisaustin.tv

Tsuneo Azuma   (310) 717-6442
(Film & High Def)   www.zumamoon.us

Kirk Bachman   (310) 457-9366
(310) 579-5357
FAX (310) 457-1829
www.kirkbachman.com
(Film, High Def, Remote Heads & Second Unit)

Fredrik Backar   (310) 273-6700
www.unitedtalent.com

Rebecca Baehler   (323) 703-1333
(Film & High Def)   wp-a.com

Christopher Baffa   (323) 703-1333
wp-a.com

James Bagdonas   (310) 288-8000
www.paradigmagency.com

John Bailey   (310) 273-6700
(Film & High Def)   www.utaproduction.com

Thimios Bakatakis   (310) 652-8778
www.lspagency.net

Ted L. Baker   (310) 373-0274
(310) 266-7274
(High Def)   FAX (310) 373-0274
www.tedbakerdp.com

Jamie Barber   (310) 623-5500
www.montanartists.com

Laurent Bares   (310) 282-9940
www.mirisch.com

Jeff Barklage (818) 906-0006
(Film & High Def) www.tdnartists.com

(818) 222-5200
Michael Walker Barnard (310) 828-8239
(Second Unit) www.schneiderentertainment.com

John Barr (323) 703-1333
wp-a.com

Will Barratt (323) 703-1333
wp-a.com

Frank Barrera (818) 284-6423
www.italentco.com

Dave Barrett (310) 285-9000
(Second Unit) www.wmeentertainment.com

(310) 569-6594
Michael Barrett (310) 273-6700
www.utaproduction.com

John S. Bartley (310) 395-4600
(Film & High Def) www.murthaagency.com

Bojan Bazelli (310) 474-4585
www.dattnerdispoto.com

(323) 703-1333
Rhet Bear (626) 893-2375
(Film & High Def) www.rhetbear.com

Christophe Beaucarne (310) 652-8778
www.lspagency.net

Adam Beckman (310) 474-4585
(Film & High Def) www.ddatalent.com

Dion Beebe (310) 550-4000
www.icmtalent.com

(661) 298-8868
John Behring (818) 416-4868
(Film & High Def)

(949) 837-5311
Bruce Benedict (949) 929-1178
FAX (949) 837-9668
www.brucebenedictphoto.com
(Action Sports, Film, High Def & Second Unit)

Peter Benison (323) 345-1811
www.peterbenison.com

(310) 458-7800
Bill Bennett (323) 223-2709
FAX (310) 733-5482
www.wfb4.com
(65mm, Action Sports, Aerial, Film , High Def, Large Format,
Remote Heads, Second Unit, Special FX & VistaVision)

Jeremy Benning (310) 966-4005
www.seslercompany.com

Ulrik Boel Bentzen (310) 285-9000
www.wmeentertainment.com

Andreas Berger (310) 656-5151
www.innovativeartists.com

Christian Berger (310) 474-4585
www.ddatalent.com

Gabriel Beristain (310) 273-6700
www.utaproduction.com

Craig Berkos (310) 940-1329

Michael D. Bernard (213) 353-9900
(Film & High Def) www.michaelbernard.us

Steven Bernstein (310) 623-5500
(Film & High Def) www.montanartists.com

Leslie Bernstien (626) 354-6200
(High Def, Second Unit & Special FX) www.xlntpictures.com

(323) 791-3676
Barry Berona (212) 564-7892
www.barryberona.com
(Film, High Def, Second Unit & Special FX)

Pablo Berron (818) 906-0006
www.thedirectorsnetwork.com

Alain Betrancourt (310) 395-9550
(Film & High Def) www.skouras.com

Will Bex (310) 458-7800
www.partos.com

Adam Biddle (818) 753-6300
(Film & High Def) www.themackagency.net

Luca Bigazzi (310) 652-8778
www.lspagency.net

Scott Billups (818) 990-8993
(Film & High Def) www.ambitiousent.com

Nixon Binney (310) 285-9000
(Film & High Def) www.wmeentertainment.com

Hans Bjerno (909) 393-1704

Stephen Blackman (323) 463-0022
www.radiantartists.com

Marc Blandori (818) 206-0144
www.allcrewagency.com

Robert Blatman (949) 246-7480
(Action Sports, Aerial, Film, High Def & Second Unit)

Philipp Blaubach (310) 274-6611
www.gershagency.com

Christopher Blauvelt (310) 652-8778
www.lspagency.net

Hagen Bodganski (310) 550-4000
www.icmtalent.com

Kip Bogdahn (323) 463-0022
(Film & High Def) www.radiantartists.com

Oliver Bokelberg (310) 274-6611
www.gershagency.com

Cira Felina Bolla (310) 282-9940
www.cirafelinabolla.com

Peter Bonilla (323) 819-2348
(Digital & Film) www.peterbonilla.com

Roger Bonnici (310) 623-5500
www.montanartists.com

Michael Bonvillain (310) 285-9000
www.wmeentertainment.com

Eli Born (323) 703-1333
wp-a.com

Vinit Borrison (310) 458-7800
www.partos.com

Harlan Bosmajian (310) 656-5151
www.innovativeartists.com

(310) 880-4715
Richard Bowen (510) 898-1891

John Boyd	(818) 990-8993
	www.ambitiousent.com
Russell Boyd	(310) 395-4600
	www.murthaagency.com
Geoff Boyle	(323) 703-1333
	wp-a.com
Kurt Brabbee	(818) 284-6423
	www.italentco.com
Natasha Braier	(310) 652-8778
	www.lspagency.net
Uta Briesewitz	(310) 285-9000
	www.wmeentertainment.com
Collin Brink	(323) 468-2240
	www.nyoffice.net
Robert Brinkmann	(310) 395-4600
	www.murthaagency.com
Mark Brinster	(818) 990-8993
(Film & High Def)	www.ambitiousent.com
Eric Broms	(310) 550-4000
	www.icmtalent.com
Alice Brooks	(310) 458-7800
(Film & High Def)	www.partos.com
Gordon Brown	(818) 206-0144
	www.allcrewagency.com
Jonathan Brown	(310) 285-9000
	www.wmeentertainment.com
Justin Brown	(310) 395-9550
	www.skouras.com
Nicolaj Bruel	(310) 285-9000
	www.wmeentertainment.com
Jesse Brunt	(818) 206-0144
	www.allcrewagency.com
Eigil Bryld	(310) 395-9550
	www.skouras.com
Bobby Bukowski	(310) 474-4585
(Film & High Def)	www.dattnerdispoto.com
Vance Burberry	(310) 458-7800
(Film & High Def)	www.partos.com
Don Burgess	(310) 274-6611
	www.gershagency.com
Tony Burns	(818) 206-0144
(Film & High Def)	www.burnsdp.com
David Burr	(310) 395-4600
	www.murthaagency.com
Stephen H. Burum	(310) 395-4600
	www.murthaagency.com
Frank Byers	(310) 623-5500
	www.montanartists.com
Patrick Cady	(310) 274-6611
	www.gershagency.com
Brian Callahan	(323) 876-7302
(Film & High Def)	FAX (323) 876-7303
Jerry G. Callaway	(818) 222-5200
(Second Unit)	www.schneiderentertainment.com

	(626) 798-8222
Joseph W. Calloway	(626) 827-7331
	FAX (626) 798-4577
	www.callowayfilms.com
(Action Sports, Aerial, Film, High Def, Remote Heads, Second Unit, Special FX & Underwater)	
Antonio Calvache	(323) 703-1333
(High Def)	wp-a.com
	(323) 573-4166
Tom Camarda	(310) 656-5151
(Film & High Def)	FAX (323) 221-5086
	www.tomcamarda.net
Paul Cameron	(310) 474-4585
(Film & High Def)	www.dattnerdispoto.com
Tom Campbell	(805) 965-4951
(Film & High Def)	FAX (805) 965-7449
	www.tomcampbell.com
	(661) 245-3581
Matt Cantrell	(661) 619-2601
	FAX (661) 245-3581
Yves Cape	(310) 652-8778
	www.lspagency.net
	(818) 896-0977
Marco Cappetta	(818) 648-3609
(Film & High Def)	www.cinemarco.com
	(323) 856-3000
Bob Carmichael	(310) 739-0650
(Second Unit)	www.bobcarmichael.com
Russell Carpenter	(323) 703-1333
	wp-a.com
James Carter	(310) 656-5151
(Film & High Def)	www.innovativeartists.com
Ron Carter	(213) 610-9954
(Film & High Def)	www.roncarterdp.com
Lula Carvalho	(310) 274-6611
	www.gershagency.com
Paolo Cascio	(818) 974-3800
	www.pchollywood.com
(Film, High Def, Remote Heads & Second Unit)	
Alan Caso	(310) 288-8000
	www.paradigmagency.com
Pedro Castro	(310) 652-8778
(Film & High Def)	www.pedrocastro.net
Sarah Cawley	(310) 288-8000
	www.paradigmagency.com
Doug Chamberlain	(310) 656-5151
	www.innovativeartists.com
Caroline Champetier	(310) 285-9000
	www.wmeentertainment.com
Robert Chappell	(323) 703-1333
	wp-a.com
Cesar Charlone	(310) 550-4000
	www.icmtalent.com
Chuy Chavez	(310) 274-6611
	www.gershagency.com
Claudio Chea	(310) 623-5500
	www.montanartists.com
Enrique Chediak	(310) 273-6700
(Film & High Def)	www.unitedtalent.com

Andre Chemetoff (310) 285-9000 www.wmeentertainment.com	Stephen C. Confer (310) 664-8989 (310) 849-1934 (Film, High Def & Remote Heads)
Steve Chivers (310) 395-9550 www.wmeentertainment.com	Barry Conrad (818) 248-9161 FAX (818) 249-8884 www.barryconrad.com (Aerial, High Def, Second Unit & Steadicam)
Christopher Chomyn (213) 300-2126 (213) 290-2126 (Film & High Def) www.chrischomyn.com	Robert Copeland (310) 399-0440 FAX (310) 399-2550
Shu Chou (310) 458-7800 www.partos.com	Martin Coppen (310) 285-9000 (Film) www.wmeentertainment.com
James Chressanthis (310) 652-8778 (323) 493-8505 (Film & High Def) www.lspagency.net	Ericson Core (310) 274-6611 www.gershagency.com
Andrew Grant Christensen (310) 656-5151 www.innovativeartists.com	Simon Coull (323) 468-2240 (Film & High Def) www.nyoffice.net
Dana Christiaansen (818) 906-0006 (310) 422-5044 www.thedirectorsnetwork.com	Brandon Cox (310) 623-5500 www.montanartists.com
Simon Christidis (323) 703-1333 wp-a.com	Tom Cox (661) 803-0091 (Aerial, Film & High Def) www.tomcoxdp.com
Ted Chu (310) 254-5396 (516) 306-4988 (Aerial, Film, High Def, Remote Heads & Second Unit)	Nelson Cragg (310) 652-8778 www.lspagency.net
Chunghoon Chung (310) 285-9000 www.wmeentertainment.com	Crash (310) 285-9000 www.wmeentertainment.com
Michael J. Ciancio (213) 908-6754 www.martonemgmt.com	Crew Connection (800) 352-7397 (303) 526-4900 (Referral for Directors of Photography) FAX (303) 526-4901 www.crewconnection.com
C.P. Cima (310) 614-3644 (Film & High Def) www.cimavisioninc.com	Jeff Cronenweth (310) 474-4585 (Film & High Def) www.dattnerdispoto.com
Claire Best & Associates (323) 601-5001 736 Seward St. www.clairebest.net Los Angeles, CA 90038 (Reps for Directors of Photography)	Attila Csoboth (310) 474-4585 www.ddatalent.com
	Dean Cundey (310) 274-6611 www.gershagency.com
Bob Clark (818) 822-1254 (Film & High Def)	Erik S. Curtis (818) 206-0144 www.allcrewagency.com
Curtis Clark (323) 703-1333 (Film & High Def) wp-a.com	Oliver Curtis (310) 285-9000 www.wmeentertainment.com
Manuel Alberto Claro (310) 652-8778 www.lspagency.net	Jeff Cutter (323) 703-1333 wp-a.com
Jonathon Cliff (310) 458-7800 www.partos.com	Svetlana Cvetko (323) 703-1333 wp-a.com
Olivier Cocaul (310) 656-5151 (Film & High Def) www.innovativeartists.com	Stefan Czapsky (310) 474-4585 (Film & High Def) www.dattnerdispoto.com
Patrice Lucien Cochet (310) 274-6611 www.gershagency.com	Edward G. Dadulak (818) 400-2900 (Film, High Def & Second Unit) www.hdprola.com
Chuck Cohen (323) 856-3000 www.easterntalent.net	Shane Daly (323) 703-1333 wp-a.com
Joseph Colangelo (818) 753-6300 www.themackagency.net	Lee Daniel (310) 497-6884
Christophe Collette (310) 966-4005 www.seslercompany.com	Greg Daniels (310) 386-4112 (310) 937-1905 www.gregdanielsdp.com (Action Sports, Greenscreen & High Def)
Flor Collins (310) 652-8778 www.lspagency.net	Steve Danyluk (310) 458-7800 www.partos.com
Joe Collins (310) 623-5500 www.montanartists.com	David Darby (310) 395-4600 (909) 626-7785 www.daviddarby.com (Film, High Def, Remote Heads & Second Unit)
Peter L. Collister (310) 274-6611 www.gershagency.com	

Directors of Photography

Dattner Dispoto & Associates (310) 474-4585	**P.J. Dillon** (310) 285-0303
10635 Santa Monica Blvd., Ste. 165 FAX (310) 474-6411	(Film & High Def) www.sandramarsh.com
Los Angeles, CA 90025 www.ddatalent.com	
(Reps for Directors of Photography)	**Phil Dillon** (818) 906-0006
	www.tdnartists.com
Didier Daubeach (310) 656-5151	
www.innovativeartists.com	**Andrew Dintenfass** (818) 753-6300
	(Film & High Def) www.themackagency.net
Allen Daviau (310) 395-9550	
(Film & High Def) www.skouras.com	**Alex Disenhof** (310) 623-5500
	www.montanartists.com
Ben Davis (310) 550-4000	
www.icmtalent.com	**Scott Dittrich** (310) 459-2526
	(Action Sports) www.sdfilms.com
Collin Davis (310) 729-9803	
(Film & High Def)	(818) 259-0112
	Mark Doering-Powell (818) 932-9329
Don Davis (310) 474-4585	FAX (818) 932-9090
(Film & High Def) www.dattnerdispoto.com	(Film, High Def, Second Unit, Special FX & Underwater)
(714) 536-6868	**Patrick Michael Dolan** (310) 480-0507
Doug Davis (714) 376-5738	(Film & High Def) FAX (800) 479-6106
(Film, High Def & Second Unit) FAX (714) 536-6868	www.elmontefilmworks.com
web.mac.com/d2films	
	Lawrence Dolkart (323) 463-0022
Elliot Davis (310) 395-9550	(Film & High Def) www.radiantartists.com
www.skouras.com	
	Peter Donahue (310) 474-4585
Roger Deakins (310) 550-4000	(Film & High Def) www.dattnerdispoto.com
www.icmtalent.com	
	(310) 395-9550
John de Borman (310) 274-6611	**Dicran (Deke) Donelian** (212) 387-7955
www.gershagency.com	(Film & High Def) www.dekedonelian.com
Anghel Decca (310) 623-5500	**Barry Donlevy** (310) 623-5500
www.angheldecca.com	www.montanartists.com
(Action Sports, Aerial, Film, High Def & Remote Heads)	
	(323) 703-1333
Thomas Del Ruth (818) 284-6423	**Jack Donnelly** (914) 764-0917
www.italentco.com	(Film & High Def) wp-a.com
Bruno Delbonnel (310) 273-6700	**Rob Doumitt** (213) 952-8243
(Film & High Def) www.utaproduction.com	
	Dermott Downs (310) 285-9000
Benoit Delhomme (310) 395-9550	(Film & High Def) www.wmeentertainment.com
www.skouras.com	
	Christopher Doyle (310) 550-4000
Ricardo Della Rosa (310) 652-8778	www.icmtalent.com
www.lspagency.net	
	Stuart Dryburgh (310) 274-0032
Paul De Lumen (310) 623-5500	www.gershagency.com
www.montanartists.com	
	Simon Duggan (323) 703-1333
Frankie DeMarco (310) 652-8778	wp-a.com
www.lspagency.net	
	Ray Dumas (310) 966-4005
(917) 224-1810	(Film & High Def) www.seslercompany.com
Jim Denault (310) 274-6611	
(Film & High Def)	**Cameron Duncan** (310) 623-5500
	www.montanartists.com
Maurice DePas (818) 292-6531	
(Film)	**Keith Dunkerley** (310) 656-5151
	www.innovativeartists.com
Joe DeSalvo (323) 703-1333	
wp-a.com	**Andrew Dunn** (310) 395-9550
	www.skouras.com
Caleb Deschanel (310) 274-6611	
www.gershagency.com	**Giles Dunning** (310) 285-9000
	(Film & High Def) www.wmeentertainment.com
Joel Deutsch (310) 628-5400	
www.evidencecameras.com	**Lex DuPont** (310) 288-8000
(Film, High Def, Second Unit & Underwater)	www.paradigmagency.com
Craig DiBona (323) 856-3000	**Autumn Durald** (310) 474-4585
(Film & High Def) www.easterntalent.net	www.ddatalent.com
Ketil Dietrichson (310) 652-8778	**Marcos Durian** (818) 753-6300
(Film & High Def) www.lspagency.net	www.themackagency.net
Joe di Gennaro (818) 749-4957	**Patrick Duroux** (310) 652-8778
(Film & High Def)	www.lspagency.net

Marcelo Durst	(310) 458-7800
	www.partos.com
Chris Duskin	(310) 282-9940
	www.mirisch.com
Todd M. Duym	(310) 966-4005
	www.seslercompany.com
John Ealer	(323) 468-2240
(Film)	www.nyoffice.net
Eastern Talent Agency	(323) 856-3000
849 S. Broadway, Ste. 811	FAX (323) 856-3009
Los Angeles, CA 90014	www.easterntalent.net
(Reps for Directors of Photography)	
Timothy Eaton	(866) 535-1972
(Film & High Def)	www.veritestudios.com
Robert Eberlein	(310) 277-0070
(Film, High Def & Special FX)	
Pawel Edelman	(310) 550-4000
	www.icmtalent.com
Eric Edwards	(310) 656-5151
(Film)	www.innovativeartists.com
David Eggby	(310) 395-4600
(Film & High Def)	www.murthaagency.com
Eagle Egilsson	(310) 285-9000
(Film & High Def)	www.wmeentertainment.com
Par Ekberg	(310) 285-9000
	www.wmeentertainment.com
Erwan Elies	(310) 458-7800
	www.partos.com
Mark Ellensohn	(310) 503-0133
(Film & High Def)	
Paul Elliott	(310) 285-0303
	www.sandramarsh.com
Frederick Elmes	(310) 395-4600
	www.murthaagency.com
Robert Elswit	(310) 273-6700
(Film & High Def)	www.utaproduction.com
Ross Emery	(323) 703-1333
	wp-a.com
Kevin Emmons	(719) 330-0201
(Film & High Def)	FAX (719) 488-9111
	www.emmonsdp.com
	(818) 753-6300
Eric Engler	(323) 937-7877
(Film & High Def)	www.themackagency.net
Matyas Erdely	(310) 652-8778
	www.lspagency.net
Evan Estern	(323) 468-2240
	www.nyoffice.net
Lukas Ettlin	(310) 273-6700
(Film & High Def)	www.utaproduction.com
Jallo Faber	(310) 273-6700
	www.utaproduction.com
B. Sean Fairburn	(818) 621-3912
(Film & High Def)	www.seanfairburn.com

Stefano Falivene	(818) 222-5200
	www.schneiderentertainment.com
Christopher Faloona	(310) 288-8000
	www.paradigmagency.com
Marco Fargnoli	(818) 284-6423
	www.italentco.com
Farr Out Productions, LLC	(310) 902-5944
(Reps for Directors of Photography)	FAX (818) 830-3608
	www.farroutpro.com
Jim Fealy	(310) 474-4585
(Film)	www.dattnerdispoto.com
	(818) 415-1869
Gary Feblowitz	(612) 281-1869
(Film & High Def)	FAX (952) 912-0519
	www.hdwave.com
Buzz Feitshans IV	(310) 288-8000
	www.paradigmagency.com
Ruurd M. Fenenga	(323) 782-1854
(High Def)	www.highdef.nl
	(310) 456-1530
Michael Ferris	(310) 749-5850
(High Def & Underwater)	FAX (310) 456-1433
Cort Fey	(310) 656-5151
	www.innovativeartists.com
James Fideler	(323) 468-2240
	www.nyoffice.net
Michael Fimognari	(310) 285-9000
	www.wmeentertainment.com
	(310) 474-4585
Russell Fine	(917) 940-0765
(Film & High Def)	www.dattnerdispoto.com
	(310) 838-5698
Steven Finestone	(310) 713-9994
(Film & High Def)	www.stevenfinestone.com
Bobby Finley	(818) 222-5200
	www.schneiderentertainment.com
Bruce L. Finn	(310) 623-5500
(Film & High Def)	www.montanartists.com
Cale Finot	(310) 288-8000
	www.paradigmagency.com
Mauro Fiore	(310) 550-4000
	www.icmtalent.com
Jac Fitzgerald	(310) 395-9550
	www.skouras.com
Michael Fitzmaurice	(310) 458-7800
(Film)	www.partos.com
Tim Fleming	(310) 274-6611
	www.gershagency.com
John C. Flinn III	(310) 656-5151
	www.innovativeartists.com
Eduardo Flores Torres	(310) 282-9940
	www.mirisch.com
E.J. Foerster	(310) 273-6700
(Second Unit)	www.utaproduction.com
Larry Fong	(323) 703-1333
(Film & High Def)	wp-a.com

554

Directors of Photography

Stephane Fontaine (310) 273-6700 www.utaproduction.com	**Anthony Gaudioz** (310) 623-5500 www.montanartists.com
Trevor Forrest (310) 474-4585 www.ddatalent.com	**Eric Gautier** (310) 652-8778 www.lspagency.net
Crille Forsberg (310) 273-6700 (Film & High Def) www.utaproduction.com	**David Geddes** (310) 656-5151 www.innovativeartists.com
Ian Forsyth (404) 580-1798 (Film & High Def) www.forsythimages.com	**Darren Genet** (310) 415-3919 (310) 656-5151 www.innovativeartists.com
Eric Foster (310) 656-5151 (Film & High Def) www.innovativeartists.com	**Dejan Georgevich** (310) 656-5151 www.innovativeartists.com
Robert Fraisse (323) 703-1333 wp-a.com	**The Gersh Agency** (310) 274-6611 (212) 997-1818 9465 Wilshire Blvd., Sixth Fl. www.gershagency.com Beverly Hills, CA 90212 (Reps for Directors of Photography)
David Franco (310) 458-7800 www.partos.com	
Lasse Frank (310) 273-6700 www.unitedtalent.com	**Helge Gerull** (310) 395-9550 (Film & High Def) www.skouras.com
Greig Fraser (310) 273-6700 www.utaproduction.com	**Mike Gerzevitz** (310) 439-0101 (310) 967-4878 (Film & High Def) www.mikegerz.com
Patrick Fraser (323) 363-6125 (818) 753-6300 (Film & High Def) www.themackagency.net	**Pierre Gill** (310) 285-9000 www.wmeentertainment.com
Jonathan Freeman (310) 274-6611 www.gershagency.com	**Xavi Gimenez** (310) 652-8778 www.lspagency.net
Adam Frisch (310) 652-8778 www.lspagency.net	**Michael Givens** (310) 579-2572 (Film & High Def) www.michaelgivens.com
Josh Fritts (818) 206-0144 www.allcrewagency.com	**Michael Goi** (310) 288-8000 www.paradigmagency.com
Tak Fujimoto (310) 395-9550 www.skouras.com	**Stephen Goldblatt** (310) 395-9550 www.skouras.com
Guy Furner (310) 475-8767 (212) 924-8505 (Film & High Def) FAX (212) 924-8544	**Max Goldman** (323) 703-1333 (Film & High Def) www.wmeentertainment.com
Steve Gainer (310) 285-9000 www.wmeentertainment.com	**Paul Goldsmith** (310) 474-4585 www.dattnerdispoto.com
Scott Galinsky (310) 288-8000 www.paradigmagency.com	**Alfonso Gomez-Rejon** (310) 285-9000 (Second Unit) www.wmeentertainment.com
Joe Gallagher (323) 856-3000 www.easterntalent.net	**Dana Gonzales** (310) 652-8778 (Film & High Def) www.lspagency.net
Brendan Galvin (310) 285-9000 www.wmeentertainment.com	**Frederic Goodich** (310) 430-6793 (3D Stereo, Film & High Def) www.fredericgoodich.com
Omer Ganai (310) 273-6700 (Film & High Def) www.utaproduction.com	**Nathaniel Goodman** (310) 288-8000 www.paradigmagency.com
Robert Gantz (310) 474-4585 www.ddatalent.com	**Ronald C. Goodman** (818) 889-6060 (Aerial) FAX (818) 889-6062 www.spacecam.com
Damian Garcia (323) 703-1333 wp-a.com	**Magdalena Gorka** (310) 282-9940 www.mirisch.com
Ron Garcia (310) 288-8000 (Film & High Def) www.rongarciadp.com	**Dylan Goss** (310) 989-3131
William Garcia (818) 206-0144 (Film & High Def) www.allcrewagency.com	**Trish Govoni** (310) 623-5500 (Film & High Def) www.montanartists.com
Greg Gardiner (310) 285-9000 www.wmeentertainment.com	**Michael Grady** (310) 550-4000 www.icmtalent.com
James Gardner (310) 966-4005 (Film & High Def) www.seslercompany.com	**Stuart Graham** (310) 652-8778 www.lspagency.net
Wyatt Garfield (323) 703-1333 wp-a.com	**Joe Grasso** (818) 906-0006 www.tdnartists.com

Eduard Grau	(310) 550-4000
	www.icmtalent.com
Kevin Graves	(323) 856-3000
(Film & High Def)	www.easterntalent.net
Jack Green	(310) 274-6611
	www.gershagency.com
Jesse Green	(310) 395-9550
(Film & High Def)	www.skouras.com
Michael Green	(310) 474-4585
	www.ddatalent.com
Adam Greenberg	(310) 274-6611
	www.gershagency.com
Bryan Greenberg	(323) 656-7818
(Film & High Def)	FAX (323) 656-3202
Robbie Greenberg	(310) 458-7800
(Film)	www.partos.com
David Gribble	(310) 652-8778
	www.lspagency.net
Frank Griebe	(310) 285-9000
	www.wmeentertainment.com
Mel Griffith	(310) 458-7800
	www.partos.com
Xavier Perez Grobet	(310) 474-4585
	www.dattnerdispoto.com
Derek Grover	(310) 291-1372
(Film & High Def)	
Tom Grubbs	(310) 457-5539
(Film & High Def)	
Keith Gruchala	(818) 633-3577
(Action Sports, Aerial, Film, High Def, Second Unit, Special FX & Steadicam)	
Alexander Gruszynski	(310) 285-9000
	www.wmeentertainment.com
Ottar Gudnason	(310) 474-4585
	www.dattnerdispoto.com
John Gulesrian	(310) 458-7800
	www.partos.com
Max Gutierrez	(310) 809-1778
	www.maxgutierrez.net
Craig Haagensen	(310) 285-9000
	www.wmeentertainment.com
Eric J. Haase	(310) 656-5151
(Film & High Def)	www.innovativeartists.com
Welles Hackett	(310) 285-9000
(Film & High Def)	www.wmeentertainment.com
Gregor Hagey	(310) 623-5500
	www.montanartists.com
Karl Hahn	(323) 703-1333
	wp-a.com
Conrad W. Hall	(310) 395-4600
	www.murthaagency.com
Geoffrey Hall	(323) 703-1333
	wp-a.com
Jess Hall	(310) 550-4000
	www.icmtalent.com

	(323) 703-1333
Warren Hansen	(323) 365-4427
(Film & High Def)	www.warrenhansen.com
	(310) 463-9894
Anthony Hardwick	(310) 288-8000
(Film & High Def)	www.paradigmagency.com
David Harp	(323) 703-1333
	wp-a.com
Russell Harper	(213) 944-0200
	www.russellharper.net
Greg Harrington	(323) 856-3000
	www.easterntalent.net
Randy Hart	(818) 768-4508
(Film & High Def)	FAX (818) 768-4270
Jason Harvey	(818) 753-6300
	www.themackagency.net
Kent Harvey	(310) 699-3674
(Film, High Def & Second Unit)	www.kentharvey.com
Kim Haun	(818) 501-4898
(Film & High Def)	FAX (818) 788-5633
	www.kimhaun.com
Peter Hawkins	(213) 604-5999
James Hawkinson	(310) 458-7800
	www.partos.com
	(310) 390-9190
Bob Hayes	(310) 717-6625
	www.floatinglantern.net
(Film, High Def, Remote Heads, Second Unit & Special FX)	
Bill Heath	(818) 206-0144
	www.allcrewagency.com
Matthew Heckerling	(310) 282-9940
	www.mirisch.com
Bernd Heinl	(818) 284-6423
	www.italentco.com
Wolfgang Held	(323) 468-2240
(Film & High Def)	www.nyoffice.net
Richard Henkels	(310) 285-9000
	www.wmeentertainment.com
David Hennings	(310) 656-5151
	www.innovativeartists.com
Scott Henriksen	(310) 246-3175
(Film & High Def)	www.scotthenriksen.com
James Henry	(323) 703-1333
	wp-a.com
Jean-Francois Hensgens	(310) 285-0303
	www.sandramarsh.com
Mathias Herndl	(310) 623-5500
	www.montanartists.com
Karl Herrmann	(310) 282-9940
	www.mirisch.com
Ron Hersey	(323) 856-3000
	www.easterntalent.net
Gregg Heschong	(818) 547-9697
(Film & High Def)	FAX (818) 547-9698
Joshua Hess	(310) 395-9550
	www.skouras.com

Directors of Photography

Danny Hiele	(310) 550-4000
	www.icmtalent.com
David Higgs	(310) 273-6700
	www.unitedtalent.com
Henner Hofmann	(310) 282-9940
(Film & High Def)	www.mirisch.com
Julian Hohndorf	(310) 395-9550
	www.skouras.com
Philip Holahan	(818) 206-0144
	www.allcrewagency.com
Adam Holender	(310) 288-8000
	www.paradigmagency.com
	(949) 631-4311
Doug Holgate	(949) 375-4997
(Aerial)	FAX (949) 631-4835
Ernest Holzman	(310) 273-6700
	www.utaproduction.com
Zoltan Honti	(310) 274-6611
	www.gershagency.com
Nathan Hope	(310) 395-4600
(Film & High Def)	www.murthaagency.com
Doug Hostetter	(818) 753-6300
	www.themackagency.net
	(323) 821-3351
Tom Houghton	(212) 690-1007
(Film & High Def)	FAX (212) 690-1026
	www.tomhoughton.com
John Houtman	(310) 966-4005
	www.seslercompany.com
Robert Howard	(310) 413-6683
	(661) 799-0154
Steve Howell	(661) 607-7266
(Aerial)	www.stevehowelldp.com
Ray Huang	(213) 249-3656
	www.tenbuckcut.com/Ray
	(310) 623-5500
Brian Rigney Hubbard	(212) 997-1818
(Film & High Def)	www.vermillionsyndicate.com
Angus Hudson	(323) 703-1333
	wp-a.com
Tim Hudson	(310) 550-4428
David Huey	(818) 679-2994
(Film & High Def)	www.purepictures.com
Paul Hughen	(310) 623-5500
	www.montanartists.com
Kent Hughes	(818) 468-6068
(Aerial, Film, High Def & Remote Heads)	
Rob Humphreys	(310) 550-4000
	www.icmtalent.com
Jackson Hunt	(310) 458-7800
	www.partos.com
Jay Hunter	(310) 458-7800
	www.partos.com
Jim Hunter	(323) 252-0909
(Film & High Def)	www.jim-hunter.com
Mott Hupfel	(310) 273-6700
(Film & High Def)	www.utaproduction.com

Shane Hurlbut	(323) 703-1333
	wp-a.com
Philip Hurn	(818) 206-0144
(Film & High Def)	www.allcrewagency.com
Slawomir Idziak	(310) 395-9550
	www.skouras.com
Samy Inayeh	(310) 966-4005
	www.seslercompany.com
Innovative Artists	(310) 656-5151
1617 Broadway, Third Fl.	FAX (310) 656-5156
Santa Monica, CA 90404	www.innovativeartists.com
(Reps for Directors of Photography)	
Dave Insley	(310) 623-5500
	www.montanartists.com
International Creative	
Management - ICM	(310) 550-4000
10250 Constellation Blvd.	www.icmtalent.com
Los Angeles, CA 90067	
(Reps for Directors of Photography)	
	(310) 248-4022
John Inwood	(917) 690-4313
(Film & High Def)	FAX (310) 276-3207
	www.watchreels.com/johninwood
Judy Irola	(323) 856-3000
(Film & High Def)	www.easterntalent.net
Matthew Irving	(310) 656-5151
	www.innovativeartists.com
Mark Irwin	(310) 288-8000
	www.paradigmagency.com
Toby Irwin	(310) 273-6700
	www.utaproduction.com
Levie Isaacks	(310) 656-5151
	www.innovativeartists.com
	(646) 515-5995
Mai Iskander	(310) 458-7800
(Film & High Def)	www.partos.com
iTalent Company	(818) 284-6423
522 Wilshire Blvd., Ste. K	FAX (866) 755-0708
Santa Monica, CA 90401	www.italentco.com
(Reps for Directors of Photography)	
Tim Ives	(310) 285-9000
(Film & High Def)	www.wmeentertainment.com
Dale Iwamasa	(310) 768-2920
(Film & High Def)	
Frederik Jacobi	(310) 474-4585
	www.ddatalent.com
David Jacobson	(310) 458-7800
	www.partos.com
Alan Jacoby	(310) 801-9297
	www.vortexfilms.com
Igor Jadue-Lillo	(323) 703-1333
(Film & High Def)	wp-a.com
Roman Jakobi	(323) 703-1333
(Film & High Def)	wp-a.com
Peter James	(310) 395-9550
	www.skouras.com
	(917) 804-6606
Alec Jarnagin	(818) 985-1130
(Film & High Def)	www.floatingcamera.com

Johnny E. Jensen (310) 457-1393
www.johnnyjensenasc.com
(Film, High Def & Second Unit)

Matthew Jensen (310) 623-5500
www.montanartists.com

Jon Joffin (310) 474-4585
www.dattnerdispoto.com

Christopher W. Johnson (424) 456-0090
www.christopherwindsorjohnson.com
(Action Sports, Aerial, Film, High Def, Second Unit, Special FX,
Steadicam & Underwater)

David Johnson (310) 274-6611
www.gershagency.com

Hugh Johnson (310) 395-4600
www.murthaagency.com

Shelly Johnson (310) 274-6611
www.gershagency.com

David R. Jones (310) 623-5500
www.montanartists.com

Ian Jones (818) 222-5200
www.schneiderentertainment.com

J. Wesley Jones (310) 282-9940
www.mirisch.com

Bengt Jan Jonsson (310) 656-5151
www.innovativeartists.com

Nemanja Jovanov (310) 458-7800
www.partos.com

Imre Juhasz (323) 788-4132
+36 30 372 4894
www.imrejuhasz.com
(Film & High Def)

Pergrin Jung (310) 849-1771
(310) 454-9036
FAX (310) 454-9084
www.pergrinjung.com

Kristian Kachikis (310) 474-4585
www.dattnerdispoto.com
(Film & High Def)

Emmanuel Kadosh (323) 703-1333
wp-a.com

Janusz Kaminski (310) 550-4000
www.icmtalent.com

Michael Karasick (323) 856-3000
www.easterntalent.net

Daniel Karp (818) 990-8993
www.ambitiousent.com
(Film & High Def)

Ben Kasulke (310) 273-6700
www.utaproduction.com

Stephen M. Katz (323) 468-2240
www.nyoffice.net

Stephen Kazmierski (310) 623-5500
www.montanartists.com

Glen Keenan (310) 966-4005
www.seslercompany.com

Daron Keet (818) 206-0144
www.allcrewagency.com

Steve Keith-Roach (310) 273-6700
www.utaproduction.com

Gavin Kelly (310) 288-8000
www.paradigmagency.com

Kira Kelly (323) 463-0022
www.radiantartists.com

Ken Kelsch (818) 206-0144
www.allcrewagency.com
(Film & High Def)

Victor J. Kemper (310) 282-9940
www.mirisch.com

Wayne Kennan (818) 889-1023
(Film & High Def)

Francis Kenny (310) 274-6611
www.gershagency.com

Martin Kenzie (310) 550-4000
www.icmtalent.com

Ian Kerr (818) 753-6300
www.themackagency.net

Joe Kessler (310) 433-1901

Rolf Kestermann (310) 656-5151
www.innovativeartists.com

Scott Kevan (310) 274-6611
www.gershagency.com

Darius Khondji (310) 550-4000
www.icmtalent.com

Kyle Kibbe (310) 474-4585
www.dattnerdispoto.com
(Film)

Jan Kiesser (310) 656-5152
www.jankiesser.com
(Film & High Def)

Ji-Yong Kim (310) 656-5151
www.innovativeartists.com

Shawn Kim (310) 652-8778
www.lspagency.net

Jeffrey L. Kimball (310) 458-7800
www.partos.com

Jim Kimura (323) 559-1110
FAX (626) 398-1387
www.tdnartists.com
(Aerial, Film, High Def, High Spped, Motion Control, Remote
Heads, Second Unit, Special FX, Tabletop
Photography & Underwater)

Sean Kirby (310) 652-8778
www.lspagency.net

Rainer Klausmann (310) 285-0303
www.sandramarsh.com

William Klayer (310) 623-5500
www.montanartists.com

David Klein (310) 288-8000
www.paradigmagency.com

Thomas Kloss (310) 652-8778
www.lspagency.net
(Film & High Def)

Dan Kneece (310) 877-2661
(310) 822-5751
www.dankneece.com

James Kniest (323) 463-0022
www.radiantartists.com

Douglas Koch (310) 966-4005
www.seslercompany.com

Directors of Photography

Matthias Koenigswieser	(310) 652-8778
	www.lspagency.net
Lajos Koltai	(310) 395-9550
	www.skouras.com
Pete Konczal	(310) 285-9000
	www.wmeentertainment.com
Tanja Koop	(310) 285-0303
	www.sandramarsh.com
Eric Koretz	(310) 458-7800
	www.partos.com
Petra Korner	(310) 458-7800
	www.partos.com
Peter Kowalski	(310) 623-5500
	www.montanartists.com
Jon Kranhouse	(310) 459-8844
(Aerial & Special FX)	www.hydrooptix.com
Eric Kress	(310) 623-5500
	www.montanartists.com
Tom Krueger	(323) 703-1333
(Film & High Def)	wp-a.com
Alwin Kuchler	(310) 274-6611
	www.gershagency.com
Ben Kufrin	(310) 623-5500
	www.montanartists.com
Ellen Kuras	(310) 273-6700
(Film & High Def)	www.utaproduction.com
Toyomichi Kurita	(310) 285-0303
	www.sandramarsh.com
Roy Kurtluyan	(818) 378-0033
	www.newcircuit.com
(Action Sports, Film, High Def, Second Unit, Special FX & Underwater)	
Ben Kutchins	(310) 656-5151
	www.innovativeartists.com
Flavio Labiano	(310) 474-4585
	www.dattnerdispoto.com
Joseph Labisi	(310) 962-6394
	(310) 246-3190
(Film & High Def)	www.josephlabisi.com
Robert La Bonge	(310) 623-5500
	www.montanartists.com
Ed Lachman	(310) 273-6700
(Film)	www.utaproduction.com
Romain Lacourbas	(323) 703-1333
	wp-a.com
Marc Laliberte Else	(310) 966-4005
	www.seslercompany.com
Alejandro Lalinde	(310) 652-8778
	www.lspagency.net
Rod Lamborn	(323) 703-1333
(Film & High Def)	wp-a.com
Giovanni Lampassi	(310) 288-8000
	www.paradigmagency.com
Dan Landin	(310) 550-4000
	www.icmtalent.com

Stöps Langensteiner	(310) 652-8778
(Film & High Def)	www.lspagency.net
Christophe Lanzenberg	(323) 703-1333
(Film & High Def)	wp-a.com
David Lanzenberg	(310) 395-9550
	www.skouras.com
Jacek Laskus	(323) 703-1333
	wp-a.com
Paul Laufer	(310) 652-8778
	www.lspagency.net
Dan Laustsen	(310) 285-0303
	www.sandramarsh.com
Steve Lawes	(310) 285-0303
	www.sandramarsh.com
Michael Paul Lawler	(323) 663-8716
(Miniatures & Visual FX)	
Tal Lazar	(310) 282-9940
	www.mirisch.com
	(310) 285-9000
Tom Lazarevich	(312) 613-9226
(Film & High Def)	www.lazfilms.com
Pascal Lebegue	(310) 285-9000
	www.wmeentertainment.com
	(619) 778-4433
Jim LeBlanc	(360) 370-5718
(Film & High Def)	www.jimleblancdp.com
Patti Lee	(310) 288-8000
	www.paradigmagency.com
	(323) 574-5617
Philip Lee	(818) 284-6423
(Film & High Def)	FAX (818) 753-0571
	www.italentco.com
Jason Lehel	(310) 285-0303
	www.sandramarsh.com
Alexandre Lehmann	(310) 288-8000
	www.paradigmagency.com
David Lena	(310) 480-7007
	FAX (310) 399-2425
	www.davidlena.com
(Action Sports, Aerial, Film, High Def & Second Unit)	
Denis Lenoir	(310) 652-8778
(Film & High Def)	
John R. Leonetti	(310) 623-5500
(Film & High Def)	www.montanartists.com
Matthew F. Leonetti	(310) 458-7800
	www.partos.com
Yorick LeSaux	(310) 273-6700
	www.utaproduction.com
Andrew Lesnie	(310) 273-6700
(Film & High Def)	www.utaproduction.com
Philippe Le Sourd	(310) 395-9550
	www.skouras.com
Michael Levine	(310) 489-6848
	FAX (323) 939-9622
	www.crashproductions.com
Jordan Levy	(310) 623-5506
(Film & High Def)	www.jordanlevy.com

Peter Levy	(310) 395-4600
	www.murthaagency.com
Sam Levy	(310) 474-4585
	www.dattnerdispoto.com
Yaron Levy	(310) 656-5151
	www.innovativeartists.com
Darren Lew	(310) 273-6700
(Film & High Def)	www.utaproduction.com
Matthew Libatique	(310) 273-6700
(Film & High Def)	www.utaproduction.com
Charles Libin	(323) 703-1333
	www.luminaria.net/reels/reelindex.html
(Film & High Def)	
John Lichtwardt	(818) 206-0144
	www.allcrewagency.com
Charlie Lieberman	(818) 284-6423
(Film & High Def)	www.italentco.com
Karl Walter Lindenlaub	(310) 285-9000
	www.wmeentertainment.com
John Lindley	(310) 474-4585
(Film & High Def)	www.ddatalent.com
	(310) 274-6611
Jimmy Lindsey	(212) 634-8157
	www.jimmylindsey.com
Ralph Linhardt	(818) 206-0144
	www.allcrewagency.com
Philip Linzey	(310) 288-8000
(Film & High Def)	www.paradigmagency.com
J.P. Lipa	(818) 206-0144
	www.allcrewagency.com
Jody Lee Lipes	(310) 652-8778
	www.lspagency.net
Jeanne Lipsey	(310) 395-9550
(Film & High Def)	www.skouras.com
Rainer Lipski	(818) 906-0006
	www.tdnartists.com
Matthew Lloyd	(323) 703-1333
	wp-a.com
Michael Lloyd	(859) 583-6036
	www.michaelaldenlloyd.com
Ginny Loane	(310) 458-7800
	www.partos.com
Mateo Londono	(310) 474-4585
(Film)	www.dattnerdispoto.com
Gordon Lonsdale	(310) 656-5151
(Film & High Def)	www.innovativeartists.com
Rick Lopez	(323) 468-2240
	www.nyoffice.net
Emmanuel Lubezki	(323) 703-1333
(Film & High Def)	wp-a.com
Pedro Luque	(310) 458-7800
	www.partos.com
Franz Lustig	(310) 652-8778
	www.lspagency.net
John Lynch	(310) 395-9550
	www.skouras.com

Jens Maasboel	(310) 656-5151
	www.innovativeartists.com
Chris Mably	(310) 458-7800
	www.partos.com
Julio Macat	(310) 288-8000
	www.paradigmagency.com
William MacCollum	(323) 363-4140
	www.watchreels.com/williammaccollum
(Film & High Def)	
Rob Macey	(818) 281-3925
(High Def)	FAX (818) 240-8715
	www.nothingfilms.com
The Mack Agency	(818) 753-6300
4804 Laurel Canyon Blvd., Ste. 825	
Valley Village, CA 91607	www.themackagency.net
(Reps for Directors of Photography)	
Peter Mackay	(818) 341-5101
	www.petermackay.net
Dylan Macleod	(310) 966-4005
	www.seslercompany.com
Glen MacPherson	(310) 395-4600
	www.murthaagency.com
Chris Magee	(310) 928-3453
(Aerial, Film & High Def)	www.chrismagee.com
Rick MaGuire	(310) 623-5500
	www.montanartists.com
Paul Maibaum	(310) 288-8000
	www.paradigmagency.com
Maz Makhani	(310) 248-2000
(Film & High Def)	www.mazmakhani.com
Mihai Malaimare	(310) 274-6611
	www.gershagency.com
Maher Maleh	(310) 656-5151
	www.innovativeartists.com
Max Malkin	(310) 395-9550
(Film & High Def)	www.skouras.com
Denis Maloney	(310) 656-5151
	www.innovativeartists.com
Matt Mania	(818) 206-0144
(Film & High Def)	www.allcrewagency.com
Teodoro Maniaci	(310) 274-6611
	www.gershagency.com
Chris Manley	(310) 652-8778
	www.lspagency.net
	(619) 843-9005
Gary C. Manske	(619) 523-5000
(Special FX)	FAX (619) 225-2244
	ckmanske.googlepages.com/home
Anthony Dod Mantle	(310) 550-4000
	www.icmtalent.com
Billy D. Marchese	(310) 422-7971
(Film & High Def)	
Barry Markowitz	(323) 703-1333
(Film & High Def)	wp-a.com
Pedro Marquez	(310) 458-7800
	www.partos.com

Directors of Photography

Horacio Marquinez	(310) 623-5500	Stephen McGehee	(310) 285-9000
	www.montanartists.com		www.wmeentertainment.com
Adam Marsden	(310) 966-4005	Tom McGrath	(310) 474-4585
	www.seslercompany.com	(Film & High Def)	www.dattnerdispoto.com
Nicola Marsh	(310) 656-5151	Bruce McGregor	(415) 383-1121
	www.innovativeartists.com		www.highdefvisions.com
Pascal Marti	(323) 468-2240	Kieran McGuigan	(310) 273-6700
(Film)	www.nyoffice.net		www.unitedtalent.com
Stephanie Martin	(310) 395-9550	Christopher TJ McGuire	(661) 839-7432
	www.skouras.com		www.ar-mcguire.com
Alejandro Martinez	(310) 623-5500	Derek McKane	(310) 395-9550
	www.montanartists.com	(Film & High Def)	www.skouras.com

Martone MGMT (213) 908-6754
3324 1/2 Bellevue Ave. FAX (213) 375-7882
Los Angeles, CA 90026 www.martonemgmt.com
(Reps for Directors of Photography)

		Robert McLachlan	(310) 273-6700
		(Film & High Def)	www.utaproduction.com
		Ross McLennan	(310) 652-8778
			www.lspagency.net
Steve Mason	(310) 395-4600	Geary McLeod	(310) 288-8000
	www.murthaagency.com		www.paradigmagency.com
Harry Mathias	(805) 379-9003	Stephen McMahon	(310) 393-5065
(Film & High Def)		(Film & High Def)	
John Mathieson	(310) 273-6700	Todd McMullen	(310) 273-6700
	www.unitedtalent.com		www.utaproduction.com
James Matlosz	(310) 474-4585	Michael McMurray	(310) 623-5500
(Film & High Def)	www.ddatalent.com		www.montanartists.com
Shawn Maurer	(310) 656-5151	Stephen McNutt	(310) 656-5151
(Film & High Def)	www.innovativeartists.com	(Film & High Def)	www.innovativeartists.com
Tim Maurice-Jones	(310) 273-6700	Joe Meade	(310) 395-9550
(Film & High Def)	www.utaproduction.com		(310) 578-9383
Joe Maxwell	(310) 652-8778	(Film & High Def)	www.skouras.com
(Film & High Def)	www.lspagency.net	Igor Meglic	(310) 413-7908
Michael Mayers	(310) 623-5500	(Film & High Def)	
	www.montanartists.com	Phil Meheux	(310) 395-9550
Marco Mazzei	(310) 847-9105		www.skouras.com
	www.marcomazzei.net	Sharone Meir	(310) 274-6611
(3D, Film, High Def, RED Camera & Special FX)			www.gershagency.com
Don McAlpine	(310) 274-6611	Ernesto Melara	(818) 206-0144
	www.gershagency.com		www.allcrewagency.com
Bruce McCleery	(323) 703-1333	Alex Melman	(310) 274-6611
	wp-a.com		www.gershagency.com
Jason McCormick	(310) 474-4585	Adam Meltzer	(323) 864-9130
	www.ddatalent.com	(Film & High Def)	www.meltzerdp.com
Craig McCourry	(310) 928-3470		(818) 848-1269
	www.mccourry.com	Nick Mendoza Jr.	(818) 288-8921
Sam McCurdy	(310) 458-7800	(Film & High Def)	www.nickmendoza.biz
	www.partos.com	Peter Menzies Jr.	(310) 285-9000
Adam McDaid	(310) 458-7800		www.wmeentertainment.com
	www.partos.com	Simon Mestel	(310) 966-4005
Michael McDonough	(310) 652-8778		www.seslercompany.com
	www.lspagency.net		(562) 692-2286
Russ McElhatton	(323) 856-3000	Rexford Metz	(310) 480-9172
	www.easterntalent.net	(Aerial, Underwater & Visual FX)	FAX (562) 692-2286
David McFarland	(310) 285-9000		www.rexfordmetz.com
	www.wmeentertainment.com	Scott Meyer	(818) 730-4900
		(Film & High Def)	www.scottfilms.com
Seamus McGarvey	(310) 550-4000	Sion Michel	(323) 428-7751
	www.icmtalent.com	(Film & High Def)	www.sionmichel.com

Anastas Michos (310) 550-4000
www.icmtalent.com

Michael Mieke (310) 285-9000
(Film) www.wmeentertainment.com

Tristan Milani (310) 656-5151
www.innovativeartists.com

C. Kim Miles (310) 623-5500
www.montanartists.com

David Miller (310) 623-5500
www.montanartists.com

Michael Millikan (818) 206-0144
www.allcrewagency.com

Dan Mindel (310) 395-9550
www.skouras.com

Charles Minsky (805) 450-2604
(310) 623-5500
www.montanartists.com

Claudio Miranda (310) 474-4585
(Film & High Def) www.dattnerdispoto.com

The Mirisch Agency (310) 282-9940
8840 Wilshire Blvd., Ste. 100 FAX (310) 282-0702
Los Angeles, CA 90211 www.mirisch.com
(Reps for Directors of Photography)

Zubin Mistry (310) 550-4000
www.icmtalent.com

Amir Mokri (310) 274-6611
(Film & High Def) www.gershagency.com

William H. Molina (210) 379-0961
(Film & High Def) homepage.mac.com/molinadp/WHM

Jo Molitoris (310) 474-4585
www.dattnerdispoto.com

Montana Artists Agency (310) 623-5500
9150 Wilshire Blvd., Ste. 100 FAX (310) 623-5515
Beverly Hills, CA 90212 www.montanartists.com
(Reps for Directors of Photography)

Joseph Montgomery (805) 773-6550
(213) 500-3304
(Film & High Def) FAX (805) 773-6136

Felix Monti (310) 623-5500
www.montanartists.com

Luc Montpellier (310) 285-9000
www.wmeentertainment.com

George Mooradian (818) 505-0050
(310) 623-5500
(Film & High Def) FAX (818) 505-0050
www.georgemooradian.com

Donald M. Morgan (818) 830-0513
(Film & High Def)

Polly Morgan (310) 458-7800
www.partos.com

Kramer Morgenthau (310) 273-6700
(Film & High Def) www.utaproduction.com

Damien Morisot (323) 468-2240
(Film) www.nyoffice.net

Laust Trier Mork (310) 652-8778
www.lspagency.net

Michael R. Morris (323) 496-0191
(818) 951-5359
(Film & Second Unit) www.michaelrobinsonmorris.com

David Morrison (323) 463-0022
(Film & High Def) www.radiantartists.com

Aaron Morton (310) 395-9550
www.skouras.com

Steven Moses (323) 703-1333
wp-a.com

Peter Moss (310) 395-4600
(Film & High Def) www.murthaagency.com

David Moxness (310) 474-4585
www.dattnerdispoto.com

M. David Mullen (323) 468-2240
(Film & High Def) www.nyoffice.net

Robby Muller (310) 395-4600
www.murthaagency.com

Zak Mulligan (310) 395-4600
www.murthaagency.com

J. Michael Muro (310) 274-6611
www.gershagency.com

Fred Murphy (310) 274-6611
www.gershagency.com

Fletcher Murray (818) 841-9660
(Film & High Def) FAX (818) 841-8370
www.theassociation.tv

The Murtha Agency (310) 395-4600
1025 Colorado Ave., Ste. B FAX (310) 395-4622
Santa Monica, CA 90401 www.murthaagency.com
(Reps for Directors of Photography)

Jean-Noel Mustonen (310) 458-7800
www.partos.com

Jeffrey Mygatt (323) 856-3000
www.easterntalent.net

David Myrick (310) 285-9000
www.wmeentertainment.com

Tetsuo Nagata (310) 273-6700
www.utaproduction.com

Hiro Narita (310) 282-9940
(Film, High Def & Second Unit) www.mirisch.com

Guillermo Navarro (310) 458-7800
(Film) www.partos.com

Michael Negrin (310) 656-5151
(Film & High Def) www.innovativeartists.com

David Negron Jr. (323) 856-3000
www.easterntalent.net

Mikel Neiers (310) 623-5500
www.montanartists.com

Arlene Donnelly Nelson (310) 474-4585
www.ddatalent.com

Mark Nelson (858) 598-6494
(Action Sports & High Def) FAX (858) 694-0546
www.visualconcepts.tv

Alex Nepomniaschy (310) 656-5151
www.innovativeartists.com

Evan Nesbitt	(323) 463-0476
	(323) 314-5928
(Film, High Def & Second Unit)	www.evannesbitt.com

	(323) 468-2240
New York Office	(212) 545-7895
6605 Hollywood Blvd., Ste. 200	FAX (323) 468-2244
Los Angeles, CA 90028	www.nyoffice.net
(Reps for Directors of Photography)	

Robert New	(323) 856-3000
	www.easterntalent.net

John C. Newby	(310) 656-5151
	www.innovativeartists.com

	(818) 486-4916
Yuri Neyman	(323) 436-7593
(Film & High Def)	

Christopher S. Nibley	(818) 850-0096
(Film, High Def, Second Unit & Special FX)	www.nibley.com

Ramsey Nickell	(310) 285-9000
(Film)	www.wmeentertainment.com

Bridger Nielson	(323) 703-1333
(Film & High Def)	wp-a.com

Carl Nilsson	(310) 474-4585
(Film & High Def)	www.dattnerdispoto.com

Vern Nobles	(310) 395-4600
	www.murthaagency.com

Austin Nordell	(818) 753-6300
	www.themackagency.net

Chris Norr	(310) 623-5500
(Film & High Def)	www.montanartists.com

David Norton	(310) 395-9550
(Film & High Def)	www.skouras.com

	(213) 300-3901
Crescenzo G.P. Notarile	(323) 464-3901
(Film & High Def)	FAX (323) 464-3909
	www.crescenzo.la

Ben Nott	(310) 550-4000
	www.icmtalent.com

David B. Nowell	(661) 251-3456
(Aerial & Second Unit)	FAX (661) 251-3864

Vasco Nunes	(323) 468-2240
(Film)	www.nyoffice.net

Giles Nuttgens	(310) 474-4585
	www.dattnerdispoto.com

Richard Ocean	(626) 922-5777
(3D, Film, & High Def)	www.richardocean.com

Brian O'Connell	(310) 384-6185
(Film & High Def)	

	(310) 474-4585
Sean O'Dea	(310) 880-0537
(Film & High Def)	www.dattnerdispoto.com

Rene Ohashi	(310) 966-4005
(Film & High Def)	www.seslercompany.com

Daryn Okada	(310) 395-4600
	www.murthaagency.com

	(323) 882-6391
Thomas Olgeirsson	(703) 577-6195
(Film & High Def)	www.olgeirsson.com

Jules O'Loughlin	(310) 273-6700
	www.unitedtalent.com

Patrick D. O'Mara	(310) 901-5514
(Film & High Def)	FAX (310) 545-0136

Trent Opaloch	(310) 395-9550
	www.skouras.com

Yaron Orbach	(310) 652-8778
	www.lspagency.net

Oktay Ortabasi	(818) 845-3230
(Film, High Def & Second Unit)	FAX (818) 333-0795
	www.dreamingtreeproductions.com

Michael D. O'Shea	(310) 395-4600
	www.murthaagency.com

Roman Osin	(310) 550-4000
	www.icmtalent.com

	(917) 796-3997
Hernan Michael Otaño	(310) 288-8000

Toshiaki Ozawa	(310) 474-4585
(Film & High Def)	www.ddatalent.com

Chuck Ozeas	(323) 703-1333
(Film & High Def)	wp-a.com

Michael Ozier	(310) 285-9000
(Film & High Def)	www.michaelozier.com

Vince Pace	(818) 759-7322
(Film & High Def)	FAX (818) 759-7323
	www.pacehd.com

	(310) 313-3762
Angelo Pacifici	(818) 990-8993
(Film & High Def)	FAX (310) 745-1949
	www.ambitiousent.com

Gyula Pados	(310) 395-9550
	www.skouras.com

Sam Painter	(213) 999-1985
(High Def)	

Antonio Paladino	(310) 395-9550
	www.skouras.com

Gary Palmer	(310) 720-7009
	www.thesuninmotion.com

Anthony Palmieri	(310) 282-9940
	www.mirisch.com

Robert Papais	(310) 458-7800
	www.partos.com

Phedon Papamichael	(310) 656-5151
(Film & High Def)	www.innovativeartists.com

	(323) 350-8822
Charles Papert	(310) 282-9940
	FAX (323) 843-9357
	www.charlespapert.com

Paradigm, A Talent &	
Literary Agency	(310) 288-8000
360 N. Crescent Dr.	FAX (310) 288-2000
Beverly Hills, CA 90210	www.paradigmagency.com
(Reps for Directors of Photography)	

Andrij Parekh	(310) 395-9550
(Film & High Def)	www.andrijparekh.com

Lee Ford Parker	(310) 928-3165
(Second Unit & Special FX)	www.mocoman.com

Phil Parmet (310) 288-8000 www.paradigmagency.com	**Wally Pfister** (310) 550-4000 www.icmtalent.com
Feliks Parnell (310) 623-5500 www.montanartists.com	**Aaron Phillips** (310) 395-9550 (Film) www.skouras.com
Barry Parrell (310) 458-7800 (Film & High Def) www.partos.com	**Jeffrey Phillips** (818) 206-0144 www.allcrewagency.com
Partos Company (310) 458-7800 227 Broadway, Ste. 204 FAX (310) 587-2250 Santa Monica, CA 90401 www.partos.com (Reps for Directors of Photography)	**Sean MacLeod Phillips** (310) 395-4739
	André Pienaar (310) 458-7800 (Film & High Def) www.partos.com
Heloisa Passos (310) 395-9550 www.skouras.com	**Tony Pierce-Roberts** (310) 395-9550 (Film & High Def) www.skouras.com
(805) 320-3304 **Philip Pastuhov** (415) 389-9019 (Action Sports, Aerial, Film, High Def & Second Unit)	**Timothy Pike** (323) 463-0022 (Film & High Def) www.radiantartists.com
Mark Patten (310) 395-9550 www.skouras.com	**Michael Pinkey** (818) 781-9233 (Film & High Def) www.watchreels.com/pinkey
Chris Patterson (310) 962-3498 FAX (310) 962-3498 www.chrispattersonfilms.com (Action Sports, Aerial, Film, High Def & Second Unit)	(805) 965-9848 **Tom Piozet** (818) 422-4144 (High Def) FAX (805) 965-2329 www.homeplanetproductions.com
Peter Pau (310) 274-6611 www.gershagency.com	**Aaron Platt** (310) 395-9550 www.skouras.com
Brett Pawlak (310) 623-5500 www.montanartists.com	**Mark Plummer** (310) 550-4000 www.icmtalent.com
Daniel C. Pearl (323) 525-1976 FAX (323) 525-1905 www.danielpearldp.com (Film, High Def, Remote Heads, Special FX & Underwater)	**Ekkehart Pollack** (310) 656-5151 www.innovativeartists.com
	Jake Polonsky (310) 474-4585 www.dattnerdispoto.com
Brian Pearson (310) 395-4600 www.murthaagency.com	**Marco Pontecorvo** (310) 288-8000 www.paradigmagency.com
Christopher Pearson (310) 288-8000 www.paradigmagency.com	**Bill Pope** (310) 550-4000 www.icmtalent.com
Nicola Pecorini (310) 395-4600 www.murthaagency.com	**Dick Pope** (310) 273-6700 www.unitedtalent.com
(310) 628-8158 **Lonnie Peralta** (310) 577-5009 (Film, High Def & Second Unit) FAX (310) 577-1960 www.lonnieperalta.com	**Zoran Popovic** (310) 656-5151 www.innovativeartists.com
	Christopher Popp (323) 856-3000 (Film, High Def & Second Unit) www.easterntalent.net
John Perez (323) 463-0022 www.radiantartists.com	(213) 819-0000 **Steven Poster** (310) 246-3190 www.stevenposter.com
Dave Perkal (310) 625-6541 (Film & High Def) www.daveperkal.com	**Arnaud Potier** (310) 652-8778 www.lspagency.net
Frank Perl (310) 474-4585 www.ddatalent.com	**Thierry Pouget** (323) 468-2240 www.nyoffice.net
Ray Peschke (818) 206-0144 (Film & High Def) www.allcrewagency.com	**Tico Poulakakis** (310) 966-4005 www.seslercompany.com
Jon Peter (323) 463-0022 www.radiantartists.com	**Munn Powell** (310) 273-6700 www.utaproduction.com
Barry Peterson (310) 273-6700 www.utaproduction.com	**Jaron Presant** (310) 458-7800 www.jaronpresant.com
Lowell Peterson (310) 288-8000 www.paradigmagency.com	**Darrin Prescott** (310) 273-6700 (Second Unit) www.utaproduction.com
Steeven Petitteville (323) 703-1333 wp-a.com	**Tom Priestley** (310) 288-8000 (Film & High Def) www.paradigmagency.com
Sebastian Pfaffenbichler (310) 395-9550 (Film & High Def) www.skouras.com	**Rodrigo Prieto** (310) 550-4000 www.icmtalent.com

Directors of Photography

Christopher Probst	(310) 652-8778	**Adam Richards**	(310) 652-8778
	www.lspagency.net		www.lspagency.net

Fortunato Procopio (917) 209-3427
(Film & High Def) www.fortunatoprocopio.com

Evan Prosofsky (310) 458-7800
www.partos.com

Wei K. Pun (818) 753-6300
www.themackagency.net

Cynthia Pusheck (323) 497-8489
homepage.mac.com/cpush/Menu13.html
(Film, High Def, Second Unit & Underwater)

Roger Quillin (310) 801-1731
(Aerial, Film & High Def) www.lostsquadron.com/q

Declan Quinn (310) 474-4585
(Film & High Def) www.ddatalent.com

Atanas Radev (323) 230-0701
(Film & High Def)

Radiant Artists (323) 463-0022
2701 N. Sixth St. FAX (323) 375-0231
Burbank, CA 91504 www.radiantartists.com
(Reps for Directors of Photography)

Michael Ragen (310) 458-7800
www.partos.com

(310) 429-2541
Stephen Ramsey (323) 650-4974
(Film & High Def)

Krishna Rao (310) 288-8000
www.paradigmagency.com

(818) 681-1495
Jeff Ravitz (818) 934-0789
(High Def) www.intensityadvisors.com

Ossi Rawi (310) 285-0303
www.sandramarsh.com

Andrew Rawson (310) 623-5500
www.montanartists.com

Kiran Reddy (323) 856-3000
www.easterntalent.net

(310) 251-2956
Larry Reibman (310) 288-8000
(Film & High Def)

(818) 342-3664
Neil Reichline (818) 400-1014
(Action Sports, Film & High Def) neilreichline.zenfolio.com

Manfred Reiff (310) 401-3211
(Film & High Def) www.manfredreiff.com

Tami Reiker (310) 474-4585
www.dattnerdispoto.com

Gosta Reiland (310) 395-9550
www.skouras.com

Arthur Reinhart (310) 474-4585
www.ddatalent.com

Joshua Reis (310) 623-5500
www.montanartists.com

William Rexer II (310) 395-9550
(Film & High Def) www.skouras.com

Brian J. Reynolds (310) 623-5500
www.montanartists.com

Robert Richardson (310) 395-9550
www.skouras.com

Ross Richardson (310) 395-9550
(Film & High Def) www.skouras.com

Kevin Richey (323) 463-0022
www.radiantartists.com

Bob Richman (323) 703-1333
(Film & High Def) wp-a.com

Anthony Richmond (310) 273-6700
(Film & High Def) www.utaproduction.com

Tom Richmond (310) 458-7800
(Film & High Def) www.partos.com

Jan Richter-Friis (310) 285-9000
(Film) www.wmeentertainment.com

Ross Riege (310) 623-5500
www.montanartists.com

Antonio Riestra (310) 285-0303
www.sandramarsh.com

Lisa Rinzler (310) 274-6611
www.gershagency.com

Heimo Ritzinger (818) 906-0006
www.tdnartists.com

Eric Robbins (310) 458-7800
www.partos.com

Jim Roberson (323) 856-3000
(Film & High Def) www.easterntalent.net

Philip Robertson (310) 623-5500
www.montanartists.com

Randall Robinson (310) 463-0531
(Action Sports, Aerial, Film & Second Unit)

Eliot Rockett (323) 856-3000
(Film & High Def) www.easterntalent.net

Bill Roe (310) 395-4600
www.murthaagency.com

Glenn Roland (310) 475-0937
(Aerial, Film, High Def & Special FX) FAX (310) 475-0939
www.glennrolandfilms.com

David Rom (323) 703-1333
wp-a.com

Serge Roman (310) 458-7800
www.partos.com

(310) 301-8187
Pete Romano (310) 282-9940
(Underwater) FAX (310) 301-3065

(310) 251-9931
Charles Rose (310) 657-6840
(Film & High Def) FAX (310) 657-6840

Jamie Rosenberg (917) 566-7705
www.jamierosenbergdp.com

Jim Rosenthal (818) 252-1010
(Film & High Def) FAX (818) 252-1070
www.therosenthalgroup.com

Noah M. Rosenthal (310) 623-5500
www.montanartists.com

Chuck Rosher (Film & High Def)	(310) 888-4077
Pierre Rouger	(310) 285-9000 www.wmeentertainment.com
Philippe Rousselot	(310) 274-6611 www.gershagency.com
Ashley Rowe	(310) 550-4000 www.icmtalent.com
Mauricio Rubinstein	(310) 288-8000 www.paradigmagency.com
David Rudd (Film, High Def, Remote Heads & Second Unit)	(310) 623-5500 (310) 573-9080 FAX (310) 573-1511 www.directorofphoto.com
Mattias Rudh	(310) 458-7800 www.partos.com
Martin Ruhe	(310) 474-4585 www.dattnerdispoto.com
Danny Ruhlmann	(310) 474-4585 www.dattnerdispoto.com
Manel Ruiz	(310) 474-4585 www.dattnerdispoto.com
Juan Ruiz-Anchia	(310) 274-6611 www.gershagency.com
Brad Rushing (Film & High Def)	(310) 623-5500 www.bradrushingdp.com
Richard Rutkowski (Film & High Def)	(212) 732-9331 www.360d.com/rr
John W. Rutland	(310) 623-5500 www.montanartists.com
Mark Rutledge	(323) 856-3000 www.easterntalent.net
Robbie Ryan	(310) 274-6611 www.gershagency.com
Steven L. Rychetnik	(310) 623-5500 www.montanartists.com
Nic Sadler (Film & High Def)	(323) 703-1333 www.nicsadler.com
Mehran Salamati (Film & High Def)	(818) 780-2708 (310) 455-7201 FAX (818) 989-5408 www.hotgears.com
Gilbert Salas	(310) 623-5500 www.montanartists.com
Josh Salzman (Film & High Def)	(323) 703-1333 wp-a.com
Andres Sanchez (Aerial, Film, High Def, Remote Heads & Second Unit)	(310) 683-0709 www.andresdp.com
Tony Sanders (Film & High Def)	(714) 444-3000 FAX (714) 444-3001 www.sandersstudio.tv
Linus Sandgren	(310) 273-6700 www.unitedtalent.com

Sandra Marsh & Associates 9150 Wilshire Blvd., Ste. 220 Beverly Hills, CA 90212 (Reps for Directors of Photography)	(310) 285-0303 FAX (310) 285-0218 www.sandramarsh.com
Luis Sansans	(310) 273-6700 www.utaproduction.com
Adam Santelli (Film & High Def)	(323) 703-1333 wp-a.com
Germano Saracco (Action Sports, Aerial, Film, High Def, Remote Heads, Second Unit & Special FX)	(310) 463-8538 www.germanosaracco.com
Isi Sarfati	(310) 282-9940 www.mirisch.com
Chris Sargent	(310) 395-9550 www.skouras.com
Kevin Sarnoff	(310) 413-9293 www.kevinsarnoff.com
Harris Savides (Film & High Def)	(310) 395-9550 www.skouras.com
Nick Sawyer	(310) 458-7800 www.partos.com
Malik H. Sayeed	(310) 474-4585 www.dattnerdispoto.com
Giorgio Scali (Film & High Def)	(310) 285-9000 www.wmeentertainment.com
Richard Schaefer (Film, High Def, Second Unit & Underwater)	(714) 508-9700 www.highimpactpictures.com
Roberto Schaefer (Film & High Def)	(310) 285-9000 www.wmeentertainment.com
Alessandre Scherilla	(310) 458-7800 www.partos.com
Tobias Schliessler	(310) 395-9550 www.skouras.com
Martial Schmeltz	(310) 458-7800 www.partos.com
Eric Schmidt (Film & High Def)	(323) 703-1333 wp-a.com
Rohn Schmidt	(310) 288-8000 www.paradigmagency.com
Dan Schmit (Film & High Def)	(323) 860-5100 FAX (310) 860-9111
Greg Schmitt	(323) 463-0022 www.radiantartists.com
The Schneider Entertainment Agency 22287 Mulholland Hwy, Ste. 210 Calabasas, CA 91302 (Reps for Directors of Photography)	(818) 222-5200 FAX (818) 222-5284 www.schneiderentertainment.com
Aaron Schneider	(310) 656-5151 www.innovativeartists.com
Michael Schreitel	(310) 656-5151 www.innovativeartists.com
Frederick Schroeder	(310) 288-8000 www.paradigmagency.com

Directors of Photography

Kristina M. Schulte-Eversum (818) 206-0144	**Sheldon Prosnit Agency** (310) 652-8778
www.allcrewagency.com	800 S. Robertson Blvd., Ste. 6 FAX (310) 652-8772
	Los Angeles, CA 90035 www.lspagency.net
(619) 644-3000	(Reps for Directors of Photography)
Mark (Wiz) Schulze (800) 365-8433	
(Action Sports, High Def & Underwater) FAX (619) 644-3001	**Stephen Sheridan** (310) 282-9940
www.crystalpyramid.com	(Film & High Def) www.mirisch.com
(310) 260-6424	**Therese Sherman** (818) 402-0706
Philip D. Schwartz (310) 699-2980	www.explodedviewla.com
www.watchreels.com/philipschwartz	(Action Sports, Film & Second Unit)
(Film, High Def, Remote Heads & Second Unit)	
	Bobby Shore (310) 623-5500
John Schwartzman (310) 395-4600	www.montanartists.com
www.murthaagency.com	
	(818) 516-3883
(909) 399-0200	**Yuval Shousterman** (818) 453-1269
Carlo Scialla (212) 564-7892	www.yuvaldp.com
FAX (212) 564-7849	
(Film, High Def, Special FX & Underwater) www.sradp.com	**Andrew Shulkind** (310) 282-9940
	www.andrewshulkind.com
Gary Scott (323) 856-3000	(Film, High Def, Remote Heads, Second Unit, Special FX,
www.easterntalent.net	Steadicam & Underwater)
Richard Scudder (323) 373-6483	(310) 652-8778
(Film & High Def)	**Sidney Sidell** (661) 799-8560
	(Film & High Def) FAX (661) 799-8570
John Seale (310) 395-4600	wp-a.com
www.murthaagency.com	
	Matthew J. Siegel (310) 722-8872
Robert Seaman (818) 206-0144	www.siegeldp.com
www.allcrewagency.com	(3D, Film, High Def, Second Unit & Special FX)
Christian Sebaldt (818) 599-9646	**Newton Thomas Sigel** (310) 474-4585
(Film & Special FX) www.shortstackfilmworks.com	(Film & High Def) www.ddatalent.com
Larkin Seiple (323) 703-1333	**Josh Silfen** (323) 468-2240
wp-a.com	www.nyoffice.net
Andrzej Sekula (310) 550-4000	**John Simmons** (310) 623-5500
www.icmtalent.com	(Film & High Def) www.montanartists.com
Jonathan Sela (323) 703-1333	(213) 986-6827
wp-a.com	**Peter Simonite** (512) 633-2928
Lorenzo Senatore (310) 623-5500	**Geoffrey Simpson** (310) 395-4600
www.montanartists.com	www.murthaagency.com
(310) 274-6611	**Harold Skinner** (818) 516-1766
Ken Seng (718) 755-7100	(Film & High Def) www.haroldskinner.com
(Film, High Def & Underwater) www.kenseng.com	
	The Skouras Agency (310) 395-9550
Ben Seresin (310) 395-9550	1149 Third St., Third Fl. FAX (310) 395-4295
www.skouras.com	Santa Monica, CA 90403 www.skouras.com
	(Reps for Directors of Photography)
Michael Seresin (323) 703-1333	
wp-a.com	(310) 514-3233
	G. John Slagle (310) 892-6447
Edwardo Serra (310) 273-6700	(Film & High Def) www.slaglevideo.com
(Film & High Def) www.utaproduction.com	
	Adam Sliwinski (818) 206-0144
(310) 966-4005	www.allcrewagency.com
Sesler & Company (416) 504-1223	
6524 W. Olympic Blvd. FAX (323) 988-0930	**Michael Slovis** (323) 856-3000
Los Angeles, CA 90048 www.seslercompany.com	(Film & High Def) www.easterntalent.net
(Reps for Directors of Photography)	
	(510) 658-1604
Afshin Shahidi (323) 703-1333	**Don Matthew Smith** (818) 206-0144
(Film & High Def) wp-a.com	(Film & High Def) www.allcrewagency.com
Garrett Shannon (323) 856-3000	**John Smith** (323) 856-3000
www.easterntalent.net	www.easterntalent.net
Neil Shapiro (310) 395-9550	(917) 882-9127
www.skouras.com	**Noah David Smith** (818) 906-0006
	www.noahdavidsmith.com
(310) 451-4048	
John Sharaf (310) 650-6996	**Steven Douglas Smith** (888) 345-6464
(Film & High Def) FAX (310) 454-6768	(Film & High Def) www.directorofphotography.org
www.sharaf.net	

Troy Smith (818) 222-5200 www.schneiderentertainment.com	**John Stokes** (323) 856-3000 www.easterntalent.net
Ben Smithard (310) 474-4585 www.dattnerdispoto.com	**Vittorio Storano** (310) 550-4000 www.icmtalent.com
Peter Smokler (310) 230-4325 (310) 962-2506 (Film & High Def) FAX (310) 459-4625 www.chimponachain.com/Smokler12-271.mov	**Lukas Strebel** (310) 285-0303 www.sandramarsh.com
	Daryl Studebaker (323) 363-5491 (Film & High Def)
Bing Sokolsky (818) 769-9154 (310) 623-5500 (Film & High Def) www.sokolsky.tv	**David G. Stump** (323) 650-5662 (Film, High Def & Visual FX) FAX (323) 650-5663
Paul Sommers (818) 542-3016 (213) 400-8693 www.paulsommers.com	**Vladimir Subotic** (323) 468-2240 www.nyoffice.net
Christopher Soos (323) 463-0022 (Film & High Def) www.radiantartists.com	**Tim Suhrstedt** (310) 656-5151 www.innovativeartists.com
Peter Sova (310) 656-5151 (Film & High Def) www.innovativeartists.com	**Shawn Sundby** (818) 206-0144 www.allcrewagency.com
Glynn Speeckaert (310) 285-9000 www.wmeentertainment.com	**Bruce Surtees** (310) 274-6611 www.gershagency.com
Tyler Spindel (310) 285-9000 (Second Unit) www.wmeentertainment.com	**Peter Suschitzky** (310) 395-9550 www.skouras.com
Dante Spinotti (310) 395-4600 www.murthaagency.com	**Morgan Susser** (310) 288-8000 www.paradigmagency.com
Christian Sprenger (310) 288-8000 www.paradigmagency.com	**Darko Suvak** (310) 273-6700 (Film & High Def) www.utaproduction.com
Stephen St. John (310) 474-4585 www.dattnerdispoto.com	**Russell Swanson** (310) 285-9000 (Film & High Def) www.wmeentertainment.com
Johnny St. Ours (323) 468-2240 www.nyoffice.net	**Brian Sweeney** (661) 713-4371 (Film & High Def)
Terry Stacey (310) 273-6700 (Film & High Def) www.utaproduction.com	**Rob Sweeney** (310) 288-8000 www.paradigmagency.com
Florian Stadler (323) 377-2242 (310) 474-4585 (Film & High Def) www.florianstadler.com	**Eric Swenson** (888) 965-4321 FAX (888) 965-4321 (Film, High Def, Second Unit & Special FX) www.ericvfx.com
John Stanier (818) 206-0144 (Film & High Def) www.allcrewagency.com	**Jeremy Sykes** (619) 435-0888 (Film & High Def) www.sykesfilm-tv.com
Oliver Stapleton (310) 550-4000 www.icmtalent.com	**Attila Szalay** (310) 623-5500 www.montanartists.com
Brendan Steacy (310) 966-4005 www.seslercompany.com	**Masanobu Takayanagi** (310) 550-4000 www.icmtalent.com
Eric Steelberg (310) 550-4000 www.icmtalent.com	**Yasu Tanida** (310) 395-4600 www.murthaagency.com
Arnaud Stefani (310) 458-7800 www.partos.com	**Nick Taylor** (626) 201-9901 (Aerial, Film, High Def, Remote Heads & Second Unit)
Ueli Steiger (310) 458-7800 (Film) www.partos.com	**Rodney Taylor** (310) 474-4585 (Film & High Def) www.dattnerdispoto.com
Henrik Stenberg (310) 474-4585 www.dattnerdispoto.com	**TDN Artists** (818) 906-0006 (Reps for Directors of Photography) FAX (818) 301-2224 www.tdnartists.com
Edward Stephenson (310) 285-9000 (Film & High Def) www.wmeentertainment.com	**Marten Tedin** (310) 395-9550 (Film & High Def) www.skouras.com
David P. Stern (818) 788-7876 (818) 907-7012	**Manuel Teran** (310) 285-0303 www.sandramarsh.com
Tom Stern (310) 550-4000 www.icmtalent.com	**Gary Thieltges** (323) 668-2331 (818) 845-8470 (Film & High Def) FAX (818) 845-8477 www.doggicam.com
David Stockton (310) 474-4585 www.dattnerdispoto.com	

Directors of Photography

John Thomas	(310) 656-5151
	www.innovativeartists.com
Mike Thomas	(714) 761-4163
Yon Thomas	(310) 656-5151
	www.innovativeartists.com
Donald Thorin Jr.	(310) 623-5500
	www.montanartists.com
Donald Thorin	(310) 288-8000
	www.paradigmagency.com
Rich Thorne	(323) 856-3000
	www.easterntalent.net
Darran Tiernan	(310) 285-9000
	www.wmeentertainment.com
Romeo Tirone	(310) 285-9000
(Film & High Def)	www.wmeentertainment.com
John Toll	(310) 395-4600
	www.murthaagency.com
Paul Tolton	(310) 966-4005
(Film & High Def)	www.seslercompany.com
John Toon	(310) 550-4000
	www.icmtalent.com
Salvatore Totino	(310) 395-9550
	www.skouras.com
Luciano Tovoli	(310) 288-8000
	www.paradigmagency.com
Eric Treml	(310) 474-4585
(Film & High Def)	www.dattnerdispoto.com
Massimiliano Trevis	(310) 285-0303
	www.sandramarsh.com
Mattias Troelstrup	(310) 623-5500
	www.montanartists.com
Sergey Trofimov	(323) 703-1333
	wp-a.com
Wyatt Troll	(310) 474-4585
	www.dattnerdispoto.com
Brandon Trost	(310) 623-5500
	www.montanartists.com
	(805) 705-2050
Tracy Trotter	(805) 705-2151
(Film & High Def)	
	(323) 222-3302
Chris Tufty	(213) 713-4534
	FAX (323) 222-3306
	www.christufty.com
(Film, High Def, Remote Heads & Second Unit)	
	(310) 395-9550
Andrew Turman	(310) 962-6287
(Action Sports, Film, High Def, Remote Heads,	
Special FX & Underwater)	
Franck Tymezuk	(323) 703-1333
	wp-a.com
Matt Uhry	(310) 623-5500
(Film & High Def)	www.montanartists.com
United Talent Agency	(310) 273-6700
9560 Wilshire Blvd., Ste. 500	FAX (310) 247-1111
Beverly Hills, CA 90212	www.utaproduction.com
(Reps for Directors of Photography)	

Sean Valentini	(310) 966-4005
	www.seslercompany.com
Stephane Vallee	(323) 703-1333
	wp-a.com
Theo Van de Sande	(310) 656-5151
(Film & High Def)	www.innovativeartists.com
Brett Van Dyke	(310) 966-4005
	www.seslercompany.com
Joost Van Gelder	(310) 273-6700
	www.unitedtalent.com
Hoyte Van Hoytema	(310) 273-6700
	www.unitedtalent.com
Joost Van Starrenburg	(310) 703-1333
(Film & High Def)	wp-a.com
Riego Van Wersch	(310) 656-5151
	www.innovativeartists.com
	(917) 559-4276
Checco Varese	(310) 458-7800
(Film & High Def)	www.checcovarese.com
Mark Vargo	(310) 395-4600
(2nd Unit Director)	www.murthaagency.com
Roman Vas'yanov	(310) 273-6700
	www.unitedtalent.com
Jan Velicky	(310) 273-6700
	www.utaproduction.com
Billy Velten	(818) 906-0006
(Film & High Def)	www.tdnartists.com
Jeffrey Venditti	(310) 663-7677
(Film & High Def)	FAX (310) 656-5156
	www.jeffvenditti.com
Alex Vendler	(310) 623-5500
	www.montanartists.com
Pieter Vermeer	(310) 285-9000
(Film & High Def)	www.wmeentertainment.com
	(310) 617-6813
Steven Vernon	(818) 753-6300
(Film & High Def)	FAX (310) 338-9725
	www.themackagency.net
Carlos Veron	(310) 395-9550
	www.skouras.com
	(818) 766-6868
Ron Vidor	(800) 759-5722
	www.ronvidor.com
Amy Vincent	(310) 395-4600
(Film & High Def)	www.murthaagency.com
Lyle Vincent	(310) 395-4600
	www.murthaagency.com
Tuomo Virtanen	(310) 458-7800
	www.partos.com
	(323) 478-1500
Stefan von Bjorn	(323) 363-7711
(Film & High Def)	FAX (323) 478-1554
	www.stefanvonbjorn.com
Stefan von Borbely	(310) 395-9550
	www.skouras.com
Wedigo Von Schultzendorff	(310) 395-9550
	www.skouras.com

Christos Voudouris	(323) 468-2240
(Film)	www.nyoffice.net
Steven Wacks	(323) 633-3853
	www.twelvetoneproductions.com
Thaddeus Wadleigh	(310) 455-0633
(Film & High Def)	www.films-and-hi-def.com
William Wages	(310) 656-5151
	www.innovativeartists.com
David Wagreich	(310) 656-5151
(Film & High Def)	www.innovativeartists.com
David Waldman	(323) 841-9253
(Film & High Def)	www.david-waldman.com
Michael Wale	(310) 474-4585
	www.ddatalent.com
Mandy Walker	(310) 550-4000
	www.icmtalent.com
Rick Walker	(818) 993-1099
(Film & High Def)	FAX (818) 993-0062
James Wall	(310) 474-4585
	www.ddatalent.com
Garry Waller	(805) 217-7141
(Film & High Def)	www.murthaagency.com
Derek Wan	(323) 788-3883
(Film & High Def)	FAX (323) 780-8887
	www.allinone-usa.com
Kevin Ward	(818) 590-0606
(Film & High Def)	www.shoottothrill.net
Vincent Warin	(310) 656-5151
	www.innovativeartists.com
Pete Warrilow	(818) 225-8520
(Film & High Def)	www.petewarrilow.com
Michael Watson	(310) 288-8000
	www.paradigmagency.com
William Webb	(323) 703-1333
	wp-a.com
Curtis Wehr	(310) 395-4600
(Film & High Def)	www.murthaagency.com
Mark Weingartner	(818) 222-5200
	www.schneiderentertainment.com
Byron Werner	(310) 623-5500
	www.montanartists.com
Jonathan West	(310) 623-5500
	www.montanartists.com
Tom Weston	(310) 623-5500
	www.montanartists.com
Haskell Wexler	(310) 395-9550
	(310) 395-0090
	FAX (310) 458-6768
Howard Wexler	(310) 396-3416
	(310) 880-2219
(Film & High Def)	www.howardwexler.com
Julian Whatley	(310) 474-4585
(Film & High Def)	www.dattnerdispoto.com
James Whitaker	(310) 395-9550
	www.skouras.com

Nicole Hirsch Whitaker	(323) 463-0022
(Film & High Def)	www.radiantartists.com
Joseph White	(310) 656-5151
	www.innovativeartists.com
	(818) 985-1582
Kenneth Wiatrak	(818) 425-8310
(Film, High Def & Visual FX)	FAX (818) 766-4584
	www.wiatrak.us
	(424) 240-5042
Matthew Williams	(818) 590-4528
(Film & High Def)	www.williamsdp.com
Scott Williams	(310) 623-5500
	www.montanartists.com
David Wilson	(323) 463-0022
	www.radiantartists.com
Erik Wilson	(310) 285-9000
	www.wmeentertainment.com
Steve Windon	(323) 703-1333
	wp-a.com
Nicholas Wise	(323) 468-2240
	www.nyoffice.net
Alexander Witt	(310) 395-4600
	www.murthaagency.com
Rob Witt	(323) 703-1333
	wp-a.com
	(310) 395-9550
Anthony Wolberg	(718) 643-0017
(Film & High Def)	www.skouras.com
Oliver Wood	(310) 395-4600
	www.murthaagency.com
Matthew Woolf	(310) 656-5151
(Film)	www.innovativeartists.com
	(203) 470-3885
Ian Woolston-Smith	(310) 402-5130
	www.iancam.com
(Aerial, Film, High Def, Remote Heads, Second Unit & Steadicam)	
WPA - Worldwide	
Production Agency	(323) 703-1333
5358 Melrose Ave.	FAX (323) 703-1334
West Office Bldg., Ste. 209W	wp-a.com
Hollywood, CA 90038	
(Reps for Directors of Photography)	
Peter Wunstorf	(310) 285-9000
	www.wmeentertainment.com
Joseph Yacoe	(310) 246-3175
(Film & High Def)	www.wmeentertainment.com
Yoshikatsu Yasaki	(310) 458-7800
	www.partos.com
Steve Yedlin	(310) 656-5151
(Film & High Def)	www.innovativeartists.com
Robert D. Yeoman	(310) 395-4600
	www.murthaagency.com
Gary Young	(818) 206-0144
	www.allcrewagency.com
Jim Zabilla	(323) 856-3000
(Film & High Def)	www.easterntalent.net

Haris Zambarloukos	(310) 273-6700
	www.unitedtalent.com
Peter Zeitlinger	(310) 274-6611
	www.gershagency.com
	(310) 827-4305
Massimo Zeri	(310) 869-0831
(Aerial, Film & High Def)	www.massimozeri.com
Jerzy Zielinski	(310) 623-5500
	www.montanartists.com
John Zilles	(310) 458-7800
(Film & High Def)	www.partos.com
	(818) 753-6300
Eric Zimmerman	(310) 849-1948
	www.themackagency.net

Joe Zizzo	(310) 395-9550
(Film & High Def)	www.skouras.com
Jake Zortman	(310) 779-8655
(Film & High Def)	www.jakezortman.com
Vilmos Zsigmond	(818) 753-6300
(Film & High Def)	www.themackagency.net
Pete Zuccarini	(310) 274-6611
	www.gershagency.com
Pietro Zuercher	(310) 623-5500
	www.montanartists.com
Kenneth Zunder	(310) 623-5500
	www.montanartists.com
Marcel Zyskind	(310) 273-6700
	www.utaproduction.com

All Crew Agency   (818) 206-0144
2920 W. Olive Ave., Ste. 201   FAX (818) 206-0169
Burbank, CA 91505   www.allcrewagency.com
(Reps for First Assistant Directors)

Benita Allen   (310) 652-8778
www.lspagency.net

Bryan Altham   (818) 391-3678
www.quitbotheringme.com

Todd Amateau   (310) 652-8778
www.lspagency.net

Emie H. Amemiya   (323) 463-3033

Steve Andrews   (310) 285-0303
www.sandramarsh.com

Roger Barth   (310) 877-3063

Mike Bell   (818) 929-0475

Brian Bender   (415) 699-6200 / (415) 504-6601 / FAX (415) 504-6603

Anne Berger (Spanish)   (562) 597-7157 / (310) 430-4591 / FAX (562) 597-7157

Christopher A. Berger   (310) 502-2446 / (310) 394-8041

Lee Blaine   (626) 808-9760 / (310) 428-4420 / FAX (626) 798-8074 / www.leeblaine.com

Jason Blumenfeld   (310) 435-3547

Craig Borden   (323) 856-3000
www.easterntalent.net

Kevin Brady   (310) 937-8955 / (310) 502-9099 / FAX (310) 937-8955

J. Stephen Buck   (760) 402-5199 / (760) 944-8596

Thomas McAuley Burke   (310) 623-5500
www.montanartists.com

Jim Burnett   (505) 897-4126 / (310) 418-3020 / FAX (505) 897-4776

Patrick Burns   (818) 908-3361

Todd Burrows   (818) 437-0015

Nelson Cabrera   (310) 699-3133
www.nelsoncabrera.com

John Callas   (310) 393-4519 / (310) 344-5334 / FAX (310) 395-4412

Cole Campbell   (626) 893-6242

Lisa Campbell-Demaine   (323) 650-4817 / (818) 404-1914

Steve Carmendy   (310) 463-4874

Randy Carter   (818) 242-4088 / (818) 206-0144
www.allcrewagency.com/home/talent.php5?id=2

John Castor   (323) 225-3392 / (323) 646-7953

Jonathan Chambers   (904) 982-7711 / (310) 736-6597
www.jonathanchambers.net

Jamie Christopher   (310) 623-5500
www.montanartists.com

Claire Best & Associates   (323) 601-5001
736 Seward St.   www.clairebest.net
Los Angeles, CA 90038
(Reps for First Assistant Directors)

Brent Clark   (805) 512-6601 / FAX (805) 652-1941

William P. Clark   (310) 623-5500
www.montanartists.com

Audrey S. Cohen   (310) 993-3375 / (305) 385-2204 / FAX (310) 208-6776

Tom Cooney   (818) 705-2619 / (818) 929-1234 / FAX (818) 343-6746

Richard Cowan   (310) 623-5500
www.montanartists.com

Dennis Crow   (818) 206-0144
www.allcrewagency.com

Lynn D'Angona   (310) 623-5500
www.montanartists.com

Dave Darmour   (310) 393-9004 / (323) 363-3930

Max Day   (310) 623-5500
www.montanartists.com

Trent De Haan   (310) 822-8989 / (310) 729-7979

Joel DeLoach   (323) 436-7433

Richard Denault   (310) 623-5500
www.montanartists.com

Theodore de Rose   (310) 980-3854 / +44 (0) 7901 675 201
www.imdb.com/name/nm1282830/

Steve Dietrich   (818) 760-2915 / (818) 422-3470 / FAX (818) 980-2028

Michael J. Dill-Cruz   (310) 707-6659

Paul DiStefano   (818) 753-9753 / (818) 257-1252

Greg Dobbin   (818) 206-0144
www.allcrewagency.com

Brian Donnelly   (310) 880-9400

Gary Dorf   (310) 476-8380 / (310) 740-0995 / FAX (818) 789-6435

Dale Dreher	(310) 600-5020
www.mavericklocations.com	
Larry Droguett	(206) 979-7724
FAX (818) 755-4504	
Eastern Talent Agency	(323) 856-3000
849 S. Broadway, Ste. 811	FAX (323) 856-3009
Los Angeles, CA 90014	www.easterntalent.net
(Reps for First Assistant Directors)	
Alan Edmisten	(310) 379-4015
Jodi Ehrlich	(323) 462-3456
(French)	
Brian J. Ellis	(818) 206-0144
FAX (818) 206-0169	
www.allcrewagency.com	
Shadie Elnashai	(323) 856-3000
www.easterntalent.net	
Sergio Ercolessi	(310) 652-8778
www.lspagency.net	
Luc Etienne	(310) 273-6700
www.unitedtalent.com	
Leslie M. Evers	(310) 600-7373
	(805) 570-8320
Tom Fauntleroy	(805) 898-1035
Edoardo Ferretti	(310) 623-5500
www.montanartists.com	
Jim Feyereisen	(310) 877-1112
FAX (310) 999-6535	
	(323) 344-1348
Jack Fitch	(323) 481-1828
FAX (323) 344-9678	
James J. Fitzpatrick	(818) 506-8051
	(818) 848-9129
Ruth Frazier	(818) 288-0815
FAX (818) 558-5772	
Franny Freiberger	(818) 415-5554
	(818) 231-2260
Bruce Fritzberg	(972) 735-9878
Walter Gasparovic	(310) 273-6700
www.utaproduction.com	
Kent Gates	(818) 667-5368
www.freewebtown.com/callsheet/	
Cara Giallaza	(310) 623-5500
www.montanartists.com	
	(805) 374-6090
Ken Gilbert	(805) 208-1753
	(310) 382-0303
Cellin Gluck	(310) 399-9898
FAX (310) 496-3046	
	(818) 781-7025
Stephen Goepel	(818) 404-7570
Marty Gold	(818) 892-3665
Travis A. Gold	(818) 968-3653
	(310) 877-1081

Tim Goldberg	(310) 450-1220
FAX (310) 319-1392	
www.oceanparkpix.com	
Alan Goluboff	(310) 623-5500
www.montanartists.com	
	(323) 610-0501
Rosser Goodman	(818) 206-0144
Tommy Gormley	(310) 273-6700
www.utaproduction.com	
	(415) 990-4470
Janice K. Goto	(415) 383-1225
James Grasso	(310) 455-7169
Michael Gray	(805) 558-6671
Louis J. Guerra	(310) 623-5500
www.montanartists.com	
Dave Halls	(323) 856-3000
www.easterntalent.net	
	(323) 665-7718
Mark Hansson	(323) 646-0402
FAX (323) 665-3080	
	(818) 763-3041
Jonathan Haze	(818) 314-7997
FAX (818) 763-3042	
Rafael C. Herrera	(310) 221-3456
FAX (818) 785-2663	
	(661) 255-0953
Glen A. Hettinger	(661) 400-4577
www.glenhettinger.com	
Todd Hilyard	(323) 856-3000
www.easterntalent.net	
	(818) 389-8341
Bill Hoyt	(818) 308-6834
Wickham Irwin	(818) 489-5212
C. Hardy James	(503) 702-3544
FAX (503) 824-2751	
Scott Javine	(818) 645-2808
Michael A. Kahler	(310) 938-2938
	(818) 253-1626
Doron Kauper	(818) 907-6028
FAX (818) 804-5121	
	(818) 754-1357
Thomas A. Keith	(213) 300-9451
	(310) 375-7423
Jack Kelly	(310) 683-8585
FAX (310) 347-4028	
	(310) 390-4747
Jay Kelman	(310) 386-0098
	(310) 204-2986
Michael Klick	(310) 720-2986
FAX (310) 204-5155	
	(310) 652-8966
Ned Kopp	(415) 467-1817
Anthony Kountz	(323) 856-3000
www.easterntalent.net	

Erwin Kramer	(310) 446-1866 (310) 266-8146 FAX (310) 446-1856 www.erwinkramer.com
Coni Lancaster	(310) 749-8962 (310) 823-3115
Christopher Landry	(818) 206-0144 www.allcrewagency.com
Rock Lane	(310) 393-1997 (310) 480-3245 FAX (310) 393-8527
Rick Lange	(310) 489-0033 (323) 851-8012 FAX (323) 851-6317
Roger La Page	(818) 368-3243 (818) 468-7191 FAX (818) 368-3243
Vincent Lascoumes	(310) 623-5500 www.montanartists.com
Bill Latka	(310) 990-1938
Dan Lazarovits	(310) 623-5500 www.montanartists.com
Richard Levin	(818) 206-0144 www.allcrewagency.com
Jeff Lewis	(310) 717-1752
Tim Lovekin	(310) 344-6918
Sonny Lowe (French)	(310) 994-8097
Scott Luhrsen	(323) 871-0201 (323) 791-1909 FAX (323) 871-0315
Earl Mann	(818) 371-1135
Jason Manz	(917) 817-0718 FAX (646) 558-0458
Gary Marcus	(310) 273-6700 www.unitedtalent.com
Sandy Martin	(323) 851-3755 (213) 509-7722 FAX (323) 851-4359
Richard Marvin	(818) 563-2073 (213) 760-9204
Steve Marvin	(505) 820-3334 (818) 563-2073 FAX (505) 820-3334
Nicholas Mastandrea	(310) 273-6700 www.utaproduction.com
Bonnie Matchinga	(323) 851-7623 (323) 851-5151 FAX (323) 851-9598
Eugene Mazzola	(206) 499-8984 (626) 296-6943 www.eugenemazzola.com
Kevin P. McCarthy	(323) 782-3969 (323) 253-5319
Gregory McCollum	(818) 952-5374 (818) 535-7794 FAX (818) 952-5379

John McKeown	(310) 623-5500 www.montanartists.com
Josh McLaglen	(310) 273-6700 www.utaproduction.com
Peter Merwin	(818) 618-6101 (818) 953-8920
Liz T. Miles	(310) 993-0022 www.liztmiles.com
Milos Milicevic	(310) 273-6700 www.unitedtalent.com
Bobby Miller	(949) 494-3263 FAX (949) 494-7945
Leslie Miretti	(310) 399-2000
Montana Artists Agency 9150 Wilshire Blvd., Ste. 100 Beverly Hills, CA 90212 (Reps for First Assistant Directors)	(310) 623-5500 FAX (310) 623-5515 www.montanartists.com
Linda Montanti	(310) 274-8898
Richard Muessel	(310) 245-1990 FAX (323) 512-5374
Kieran Mullaney	(818) 508-5979 (818) 903-9305
Justin Muller	(310) 273-6700 www.utaproduction.com
Rip Murray	(310) 288-8000 www.paradigmagency.com
Steve Nemiroff	(310) 473-4100 FAX (310) 473-4100
M. Margaret O'Brien-Sparks	(818) 388-9726 (818) 997-1993 FAX (818) 997-1993
Robin Randal Oliver	(323) 856-3000 www.easterntalent.net
Pamela O'Mara	(310) 901-5515 (310) 545-0136
Mark Oppenheimer	(310) 391-6907 (310) 740-0134 FAX (310) 391-6007
Nilo Otero	(310) 623-5500 www.montanartists.com
Paul Papanek	(323) 732-0776
Philip A. Patterson	(310) 623-5500 www.montanartists.com
Randy Pearl	(310) 989-7656
Julian Petrillo	(323) 856-3000 www.easterntalent.net
Thomas D. Phillips	(818) 469-5322 FAX (888) 504-4339 www.phillipsnewmedia.com
Michael Pitt	(310) 623-5500 www.montanartists.com
Korey Pollard	(310) 623-5500 www.montanartists.com

First Assistant Directors

Cynthia A. Potthast	(323) 653-9801 (818) 359-1100
Bruce Pratt	(310) 990-4286 (818) 222-4052 FAX (818) 222-4062
Jack Provost	(818) 988-8150 (818) 422-0998 FAX (818) 988-8152 www.jackprovost.com
Kari Rantala	(805) 984-3468 (805) 469-6536 FAX (805) 984-3468
Ron Rapiel	(310) 390-5454 (310) 890-1100
Rhonda L. Raulston	(626) 695-8921
Jolyon Reese	(818) 206-0144 www.allcrewagency.com
Craig Respol	(818) 346-4641 (310) 776-1229
Darin Rivetti	(310) 273-6700 www.utaproduction.com
Jason Roberts	(310) 623-5500 www.montanartists.com
Chad Rosen	(310) 623-5500 www.montanartists.com
Drew Ann Rosenberg	(323) 856-3000 www.easterntalent.net
Jody Rosenthal	(310) 317-0489 (310) 804-2684 FAX (310) 317-0420
Ethan Ross	(310) 990-1655
David Sardi	(310) 623-5500 www.montanartists.com
Lisa Satriano	(310) 273-6700 www.unitedtalent.com
Nick Satriano	(310) 273-6700 www.unitedtalent.com
James Sbardellati	(818) 631-8459 FAX (818) 248-8459
Elizabeth Scherberger	(818) 206-0144 www.allcrewagency.com
Larry Schreiner	(310) 874-2164
Robert Schultz	(213) 500-7787
Jan Scott	(310) 833-1770
Jeffrey J. Scruton	(310) 454-8290 FAX (310) 459-4051
Larry Serraino	(661) 607-6528 FAX (661) 254-6402
Jerry Shanks	(818) 506-0502 FAX (818) 506-0502
Jim Shippee	(310) 480-5988
Thom Sidoti	(323) 957-1454 FAX (323) 871-0610 www.agavefilms.com

Scott Siegal	(213) 713-0154
Sebastian Silva	(310) 623-5500 www.montanartists.com
Tim Silver (French)	(310) 739-7356 (310) 399-5122
Eric Siss	(310) 628-7226
Al Smith	(310) 452-3751 (310) 864-8550
Matthew D. Smith	(310) 293-8747
Chris Soldo	(310) 968-6877 (805) 969-7920
Peter Soldo	(310) 623-5500 www.montanartists.com
Bruce Speyer	(310) 623-5500 www.montanartists.com
Marlon Staggs	(213) 479-9384
Tony Steinberg	(323) 856-3000 www.easterntalent.net
Dan Steinbrocker	(310) 410-1000 FAX (310) 410-0008
Brad Stevenson	(213) 716-7893 (818) 222-8251
Kennedy Taylor (Japanese)	(323) 253-4649
Mark Taylor	(310) 623-5500 www.montanartists.com
Debby Timmons	(818) 203-5655
Jay Tobias	(310) 623-5500 www.montanartists.com
Jeff Tuttle	(626) 824-1222 011 (61) 4 5722 2464
Franklin A. Vallette	(310) 623-5500 www.montanartists.com
Marc Vance	(310) 890-2414
Christian Van Fleet	(818) 762-3810 (562) 577-7526
Pete Vanlaw	(818) 642-3810 FAX (818) 769-2847 www.western-branch.com
P.J. Voeten	(310) 273-6700 www.utaproduction.com
Jey Wada	(323) 855-9595 www.imdb.com/name/nm0905261/resume
John Warran	(818) 621-6662 www.johnwarran.com
David Webb	(310) 273-6700 www.utaproduction.com
Bobby Weinstein	(310) 306-1960 FAX (310) 306-1820
Ree Whitford	(818) 424-9988 www.reewhitford.com

Pete Whyte	(310) 623-5500 www.montanartists.com	Stewart Young	(818) 206-0144 www.allcrewagency.com
Kevin Williams	(310) 623-5500 www.montanartists.com	Joseph A. Zaki	(310) 623-5500 www.montanartists.com
Kim Winther	(310) 273-6700 www.utaproduction.com	Raymond Zarro	(310) 460-2424 FAX (310) 399-7614
Katarina Wittich	(323) 221-1023	Jack Ziga	(323) 664-9862 (323) 465-9862
Ian Woolf	(818) 704-4237 (818) 970-4237 FAX (818) 704-6706	Joel R. Zimmerman	(310) 993-5703 www.joelzimmerman.com
Cyrus Yavneh	(310) 951-3470	Eddie H. Ziv	(310) 623-5500 www.montanartists.com
Don Yorkshire	(818) 632-7475 (818) 760-7474 FAX (818) 760-7016	Leslie Zurla	(818) 762-4346 (818) 207-1743 FAX (818) 506-8483

Nir Adar	(323) 937-1010
	www.zenobia.com
	(323) 463-9990
Valerie Aikman-Smith	(323) 365-1994
	FAX (323) 463-9991
	www.valerieaikman-smith.com
Alphonse Culinary Engineer	(562) 733-8954
(Food Stylist)	
Shellie Anderson	(818) 427-6168
(Food Stylist)	www.shellieanderson.com
Alise Arato	(323) 937-1010
	www.zenobia.com
Associates James & Julia/	
Julia Weinberg	(310) 274-2383
1015 Gayley Ave., Ste. 210	FAX (310) 821-0232
Los Angeles, CA 90024	
(Home Economist)	
	(213) 718-6262
Oona Austin	(253) 549-2475
(Food Stylist)	
	(714) 532-6852
Carolyn L. Avelino	(714) 323-0173
	FAX (714) 532-6853
Lisa Barnet	(626) 376-5932
	www.lisabarnet.com
	(626) 202-5214
Camille's	(626) 791-4081
(Food Stylist)	FAX (866) 222-7760
	www.camilleskitchen.com
	(310) 503-7107
Debbie Castaldi	(310) 398-2375
	FAX (310) 398-2375
	www.flickr.com/photos/castaldifoodimages/
Sienna DeGovia	(323) 376-3762
(Food Stylist & Home Economist)	www.siennacake.com
	(951) 536-3374
Paris DeJesus	(951) 780-1341
(Food Stylist & Home Economist)	
Marti DeLucia-Brown	(714) 425-7492
Cheryl Dent	(310) 251-2149
(Food Stylist & Home Economist)	www.cheryldent.biz
B.J. Doerfling	(818) 991-0581
(Food Stylist & Home Economist)	FAX (818) 991-0581
Suzy Eaton	(323) 937-1010
	www.zenobia.com
Edible Style/Wendy Loring Blasdel	(818) 903-4483
	FAX (818) 548-2557
	www.ediblestyle.com
	(323) 240-8482
Eleanor	(323) 342-0064
	FAX (323) 441-8425
	eleanorfoodstyles.com
Elizabeth James & Associates, Inc.	(949) 632-5410
	FAX (562) 592-9412
Food Savvy Incorporated/	
Andy Sheen-Turner	(323) 333-0070
(Food Stylist)	www.foodsavvywebsite.com

Kris Foreman	(310) 871-2642
Beth Fortune	(310) 948-0631
	www.bethfortune.com
	(310) 552-7921
Tobi Frank-Martin	(818) 667-7565
(Home Economist)	FAX (818) 222-4385
Saba Gaziyani	(323) 937-1010
	www.zenobia.com
Gourmet Proppers, Ltd./	
Bonnie Belknap	(818) 566-4140
(Food Stylist)	FAX (818) 563-2218
	www.gourmetproppers.com
Marsha Harris	(323) 937-1010
	www.zenobia.com
Alice M. Hart/Food for Film Stylists	(323) 363-2531
	www.foodforfilm.com
Jean Hodges/Showgrits	(818) 567-2405
(Food Stylist)	www.showgrits.com
Mark Holcomb	(949) 215-7373
(Food Stylist)	FAX (949) 215-7494
	www.tastecateringcafe.com
	(310) 739-6664
Kimberly Huson	(310) 396-2403
(Food Stylist)	www.stylefood.com
Acirema Landa	(323) 937-1010
	www.zenobia.com
Maelle	(323) 697-9763
(Food Stylist)	www.maelle.com
Sylvia Marmolejo	(323) 936-9893
(Food Stylist)	FAX (323) 936-1503
	www.smstyling.com
Deborah McLean	(323) 937-1010
	www.zenobia.com
Janet Miller	(323) 937-1010
(Home Economist)	www.zenobia.com
	(213) 713-5832
Esther Nieuwenhuis	(323) 654-9840
	(323) 658-6144
Marjorie Ohrnstein	(323) 573-9622
(Food Stylist)	www.funfoodcatering.com
David Pogul	(619) 283-8030
(Food Stylist)	
Judy Peck Prindle	(323) 939-7009
	FAX (323) 939-4219
Carrie Ann Purcell	(323) 937-1010
	www.zenobia.com
	(310) 948-0951
Marina Rodríguez	(310) 478-4738
Carolyn Sato	(310) 502-1391
	(415) 775-8552
David Shalleck/VOLOCHEF	(415) 713-1967
1125 Broadway, Ste. 203	FAX (415) 775-1140
San Francisco, CA 94109	www.volochef.com
(Culinary Producer & Food Stylist)	

Lorraine Shapiro	(323) 653-8899
(Home Economist)	FAX (323) 653-8899
	(310) 390-0383
Susan Southcott	(310) 621-2232
(Food Stylist)	
	(310) 285-8361
Norman W. Stewart	(323) 251-7674
	www.zenobia.com/normanstewart
Denise Stillman	(949) 496-4841
	www.stylistforfood.com
	(310) 890-0527
Debi Halpert Storosh	(310) 397-3300
(Home Economist)	

Jen Tauritz Gotch	(323) 937-1010
	www.zenobia.com
	(310) 477-7997
Helene Tsukasa	(310) 251-3180
(Food Stylist)	
Yona Tulk	(323) 559-2774
	(323) 937-1010
Zenobia Agency, Inc.	(888) 639-6917
130 S. Highland Ave.	FAX (323) 937-1133
Los Angeles, CA 90036	www.zenobia.com
(Reps For Food Stylists)	

Victor Abbene	(818) 700-1398
	(310) 505-4212
	FAX (818) 700-1319
David Adams	(818) 691-6477
(Electrician & Gaffer)	davidmccabeadams.com
Steve Adams	(310) 962-0935
Richard Alarian	(805) 207-9100
Karl Alexander	(818) 307-9404
	(818) 889-7206
	FAX (818) 889-7668
	www.karlalexanderbooks.com
Michael Ambrose	(213) 598-8179
	www.imdb.com/name/nm0003307/
Ronald Anderson	(520) 419-1490
	(800) 577-9635
	FAX (520) 623-3144
	www.mistyproductionservice.com
Daniele R. Benoit	(818) 389-9565
	FAX (818) 701-5404
	www.unilux.com
Bjorn Boisen	(310) 261-4751
Randall Burak	(818) 363-3305
	(818) 599-5121
	FAX (818) 363-3305
Russell Caldwell	(310) 463-7431
	FAX (818) 474-7016
Joseph W. Calloway	(626) 798-8222
	(626) 827-7331
(Lighting Designer & Lighting Director)	FAX (626) 798-4577
	www.callowayfilms.com
Dwight D. Campbell	(818) 957-6180
	(818) 419-6532
Brett Carleton	(323) 997-0202
	FAX (323) 417-4915
	www.brettcarleton.com
Doug Dale	(805) 584-1240
	(805) 377-6042
	FAX (805) 584-1240
David Devlin	(212) 439-1106
	(213) 368-4660
	FAX (310) 496-2789
	www.daviddevlin.com
Rob Doumitt	(213) 952-8243
Jack English	(818) 645-6046
(Gaffer)	
Christian Epps	(323) 632-5632
	www.christianepps.com
(Lighting Designer & Lighting Director)	
Jerry Feldman	(818) 219-1806
(Lighting Director)	www.jerryfeldmandp.com
Tom Feldman	(818) 790-7069
(Gaffer & Lighting Director)	www.tomfeldman.com
John Gilmour	(805) 485-7067
	(805) 901-9817
(Gaffer & Lighting Director)	

Randy Glass	(949) 498-4956
	(949) 697-1484
	FAX (949) 492-6256
William R. Glasscock	(818) 903-7788
(Rigging Gaffer)	FAX (818) 655-8390
Mark Goodwin	(805) 499-7040
	(818) 414-6699
(3-D Format & Gaffer)	FAX (805) 499-7078
	www.goodwinfilmlighting.biz
Barry Gross	(323) 770-6111
Ted Hayash	(818) 653-5786
	www.tedhayash.com
Rick Heebner	(818) 606-4322
Myron Hyman	(661) 510-8457
Joe Jorden	(818) 789-1499
	(818) 517-0990
Irv Katz	(310) 399-5985
Michael Wm. Katz	(310) 396-9387
	www.imdb.com/name/nm0441797/
Kevin Kelley	(818) 535-7169
Greg Kendrick	(949) 588-7822
	(714) 381-0100
	FAX (949) 588-7922
	www.waywest.tv
Len Levine	(310) 663-1359
Chris Lewis	(818) 897-4392
	(818) 517-4162
	FAX (818) 897-3554
(Gaffer, Lighting Designer & Lighting Director)	
Brad Lipson	(818) 355-7157
Geordie MacDonald	(818) 784-2871
	(818) 425-3551
Mel Maxwell	(818) 762-3032
Tim McArdle	(818) 368-8143
	(818) 414-2367
(Lighting Director)	FAX (818) 368-8143
Rob McCarthy	(661) 254-7470
	(661) 609-2034
(Gaffer & Lighting Director)	FAX (661) 254-1454
Jim McEachen	(805) 640-7200
	(310) 709-4705
Jeff McGrath	(310) 567-1023
	FAX (310) 374-1639
Alan McKay	(818) 848-5470
(Electrician)	
Charles A. McNamara	(917) 830-5839
	(973) 204-7002
	charliemcnamara.com
Patrick Melly	(310) 398-7082
	(310) 488-1299
	FAX (310) 398-7182

Tim Morton (818) 941-5053 / (818) 661-0750	**Roger Sassen** (818) 348-5909 / (818) 429-2413 FAX (818) 702-0689
(Gaffer, Lighting Designer & Lighting Director)	

Tim Morton (818) 941-5053
(818) 661-0750
(Gaffer, Lighting Designer & Lighting Director)

Kevin Mulvey (818) 516-4606
FAX (818) 753-0181
www.light-shapes.com
(Gaffer, Lighting Designer & Lighting Director)

Patrick M. Murray (818) 632-6320
(Gaffer)

Michael Off (818) 679-9332
(800) 508-8020
(Gaffer, Lighting Designer & Lighting Director)

Gustavo Oliva (310) 717-3790
www.gustavooliva.com

Michael Palmer (310) 489-6453

Michael Parsons (310) 753-7040
FAX (310) 837-1211

Tim Phelps (619) 250-7829
(619) 691-0556
FAX (619) 691-0444
(Gaffer, Lighting Designer & Lighting Director)

Rudy Pohlert (818) 222-7462
FAX (818) 225-0499

Raman N. Rao (310) 365-6955
(Gaffer & Lighting Director)

Jeff Ravitz (818) 934-0789
(818) 681-1495
(Lighting Designer) www.intensityadvisors.com

Gerald A. Rhodes (661) 252-6358
(661) 803-0869
www.jeryrig.com

John C. Rogers (310) 376-4223
(310) 993-5768

Karen Roseme (323) 697-8382

Jim Rosenthal (818) 252-1010
FAX (818) 252-1070
www.therosenthalgroup.com

Andrea Sachs (818) 497-5777

Brad Sargent (818) 398-0864
(Electrician, Gaffer & Lighting Director)

Roger Sassen (818) 348-5909
(818) 429-2413
FAX (818) 702-0689

A. Iggy Scarpitti (323) 653-0802
(323) 810-7878
FAX (323) 651-9383

Bill Silic (818) 898-1550
(805) 559-4525
FAX (818) 898-1552

Harold Skinner (818) 516-1766
www.haroldskinner.com

Alex Skvorzov (661) 254-9043
(818) 359-0900
FAX (661) 254-8395

Scott A. Spencer (818) 674-2132
FAX (805) 578-6074

Stuart Spohn (626) 254-0570

JT Teiper (760) 505-1605
(760) 643-1600
www.jtservices.com

Jon Tower (310) 573-1777
(310) 650-8560
FAX (310) 230-1222

Joel Unangst (213) 481-2520

Video Tech Services (310) 574-9385
(310) 505-4015
10866 Washington Blvd., Ste. 513 FAX (310) 577-0850
Culver City, CA 90232 www.videotechservices.com
(Reps for Gaffers and Lighting Directors)

Tom Voelpel (818) 359-2880
(661) 255-3342
FAX (661) 255-3342

Mark Vuille (310) 798-1062
(310) 629-0176
(Gaffer & Lighting Designer) www.light-works.net

Larry Wallace (310) 822-1263
(Gaffer)

Joseph Warren (805) 501-1439

Kenneth Wheeland (310) 455-1401
(310) 663-9411

Elan Yaari (310) 392-2446
(310) 210-2741

Michel Barrère (323) 654-3445 / (323) 821-4310

Jeff Beebe (661) 645-1305
(Key Grip)

Pat Campea Jr. (818) 885-5161 / (818) 970-0248
(Underwater) FAX (818) 885-5161

Brett Carleton (323) 997-0202
FAX (323) 417-4915
www.brettcarleton.com

Kevin Coon (661) 645-7168

Rick Davis (818) 599-4749
www.grip411.com
(Best Boy, Dolly Grip, Jib Operator, Key Grip, Motion Control & Rigging Grip)

Jerry Deats (818) 366-2043

Marty Eichmann (661) 251-7532

R. Shawn Ensign (310) 546-4860

Jerry Giacalone (805) 341-2692 / (805) 496-0249
(Key Grip) FAX (805) 496-4802

John Gilmour (805) 485-7067 / (805) 901-9817
(Key Grip)

Gregg Guellow (818) 985-2038 / (818) 482-4309
FAX (818) 763-7451

Jorge Guzman (310) 612-0445
(Key Grip & Underwater) FAX (310) 836-4307

Billy Haas (818) 886-9027 / (818) 207-4803

Jack P. Johnson (818) 378-9609

Casey Jones (818) 782-3723

Greg Karamov (818) 434-8661

Irv Katz (310) 399-5985

Michael Kenner (818) 424-4747 / (800) 474-7538
www.gripjet.com

Kevin Kernohan (818) 943-9055
FAX (818) 366-0852

Thomas Levy (415) 515-5547 / (415) 669-7777
(Underwater) FAX (415) 669-7777

Gregory Lorick (310) 600-3522 / (310) 440-3414
(Key Grip) FAX (310) 440-3454

Bill Manning (818) 703-5956
(Best Boy, Dolly Grip & Key Grip) FAX (818) 703-5956

Michael E. Matteson (818) 640-3117 / (818) 893-9192
(Key Grip & Rigging Grip) FAX (818) 895-2562

Tom D. May (818) 879-9845 / (818) 846-3100
FAX (818) 846-3511

Rob Meckler (310) 600-7539

Michael Milella (818) 891-0101 / (818) 606-5030
(Best Boy, Dolly Grip, Jib Operator & Key Grip)

Bob Miyamoto (310) 645-3885
(Key Grip)

Greg Mustin (805) 559-7612

Willy Nemeth (541) 840-3366 / (541) 476-0598

David Novak (310) 663-9147

George Peters (805) 375-1414 / (818) 618-9988
FAX (805) 375-1153
www.ultimatearm.com

Tim Pogoler (818) 281-1616
www.timcoworks.com
(Best Boy, Dolly Grip, Jib Operator, Key Grip, Motion Control, Rigging Grip & Underwater)

Dan Reilly (661) 702-8971 / (661) 803-3132
FAX (661) 702-8972

Josh Rich (310) 450-1927 / (310) 251-9317
(Key Grip & Underwater) FAX (310) 450-1927

Terry Ruffner (661) 312-3645 / (661) 259-8881

Jimmie Salazar (310) 375-4008

Mark Sannes (310) 316-4034 / (310) 415-0056

T.D. Scaringi (818) 402-2009 / (818) 876-0060
(Underwater)

Pat Sheetz (818) 894-2060

James Shelton (818) 957-1577 / (818) 370-7715
FAX (818) 957-1599

Michael Shore (310) 420-1443

Craig Shumard (818) 768-1573 / (661) 644-1516
(Motion Control) FAX (818) 768-1575
www.pacificmotion.net

Chett Spinney (805) 469-7176
FAX (828) 254-6769

John Stabile (818) 886-0869 / (818) 421-6695
FAX (818) 886-5039

Mark Stanley (818) 489-4700
(Key Grip)

Bruce J. Swift (818) 341-4537 / (818) 808-9500
www.home.earthlink.net/~bswift52/
(Best Boy, Dolly Grip, Key Grip, Rigging Grip & Underwater)

Michael G. Uva   (310) 901-3287
     (310) 366-5822
     www.kastandkrew.com
(Best Boy, Dolly Grip, Jib Operator, Key Grip, Motion Control, Rigging Grip & Underwater)

Jean-Pierre Visier   (310) 670-2265
(Underwater)

Donald Vos   (818) 848-5801
     (818) 381-3137
(Key Grip)   FAX (818) 848-5801

Stewart White   (818) 904-9114
     (818) 400-3456

Amanda Abizaid　(323) 937-1010
www.zenobia.com

Heidi Aburas　(323) 767-3373
(Body Painting, Grooming, Makeup, Special FX
Makeup & Wigs)

Matt Adams　(310) 733-2550
(Hair)　www.photogenicsmedia.com

Agency Celebrity Artists　(310) 775-5723
(214) 930-9875
www.agencycelebrityartists.com
(Reps for Hair and Makeup Artists)

Agostina　(323) 436-7766
(Makeup)　www.eamgmt.com

Diane Aiello　(310) 998-1977
www.celestineagency.com

Misa Aikawa　(310) 709-8596
www.misamakeup.com
(Body Painting, Hair, Makeup, Special FX Makeup & Wigs)

Aim Artists Agency　(323) 931-2745
509 N. Sycamore Ave.　FAX (323) 931-2747
Los Angeles, CA 90036　www.aimartist.com
(Reps for Hair and Makeup Artists)

Taylor Alderson　(310) 210-9510
www.tayloralderson.com
(Grooming, Hair, Makeup, Manicurist & Wigs)

Alejandra　(310) 274-0032
(Grooming & Hair)　www.artistsbytimothypriano.com

Alicia　(562) 787-2426
www.makeupandhairbyalicia.com
(Body Painting, Hair, Makeup, Special FX Makeup & Wigs)

All Crew Agency　(818) 206-0144
2920 W. Olive Ave., Ste. 201　FAX (818) 206-0169
Burbank, CA 91505　www.allcrewagency.com
(Reps for Hair and Makeup Artists)

Jo Allen　(323) 937-1010
(Makeup)　www.zenobia.com

Shirlena Allen　(323) 850-6783
(Hair)

Keith Alston　(323) 937-1010
(Special FX Makeup)　www.zenobia.com

Ana-Maria　(310) 274-0032
(Manicurist)　www.artistsbytimothypriano.com

Lauren Anderson　(310) 276-0777
(Makeup)　www.thewallgroup.com

Enzo Angileri　(310) 839-8722
(Hair)　www.cloutieragency.com

Livio Angileri　(323) 931-2745
(Hair)　www.aimartist.com

Alma Anguiano　(310) 485-0404
www.mkartists.com

Jonathan Antin　(310) 733-2550
(Hair)　www.photogenicsmedia.com

Raina Antle　(323) 385-3163
(Colorist, Grooming, Hair & Makeup)　www.rainaantle.com

Jenna Anton　(310) 998-1977
(Makeup)　www.celestineagency.com

Terri Apanasewicz　(310) 839-8722
(Makeup)　www.cloutieragency.com

Alan Apone　(310) 601-2355
www.lesliealyson.com

Kathy Aragon　(310) 274-0032
www.artistsbytimothypriano.com

Gregory Arlt　(323) 436-7766
(Makeup)　www.eamgmt.com

Elena Arroy　(818) 887-9535
(818) 825-0706
FAX (818) 887-9535
www.elenaarroy.com

Artist Untied　(323) 933-0200
(415) 957-0500
(Reps for Hair and Makeup Artists)　FAX (415) 957-0555
www.artistuntied.com

Artists by Timothy Priano　(310) 274-0032
120 El Camino Dr., Ste. 100　FAX (310) 278-7520
Los Angeles, CA 90212
www.artistsbytimothypriano.com
(Reps for Hair and Makeup Artists)

artists' services　(323) 445-4910
(415) 824-4423
8581 Santa Monica Blvd., Ste. 437
West Hollywood, CA 90069　www.artists-services.com
(Reps for Hair & Makeup Artists)

ArtMix Beauty　(310) 943-8102
2332 S. Centinela Ave., Ste. C　FAX (310) 943-8101
Los Angeles, CA 90064　www.artmixbeauty.com
(Reps for Hair and Makeup Artists)

Jen Atkin　(310) 276-0777
(Hair)　www.thewallgroup.com

Barbara Augustus-Johnson　(323) 856-8928

Tena Austin　(323) 876-4692
(Grooming & Makeup)　FAX (323) 876-0292

Alan Avendano　(323) 856-8540
(Makeup)　www.opusbeauty.com

Riad Azar　(323) 856-8540
(Hair)　www.opusbeauty.com

Amanda B.　(323) 497-7648

Valerie B　(323) 856-8540
www.opusbeauty.com

Taylor Babaian　(310) 839-8722
(Hair & Makeup)　www.cloutieragency.com

David Babaii　(323) 462-5000
(Hair)　www.traceymattingly.com

Nancy Baca　(818) 358-3112
(213) 359-3235

Tom Bachik　(310) 839-8722
(Manicurist)　www.cloutieragency.com

Elaina Badro　(323) 935-8455
(Makeup)　www.ms-management.com

Jake Bailey　(310) 276-0777
(Makeup)　www.thewallgroup.com

Vivian Baker　(310) 601-2355
www.lesliealyson.com

Jenna Baltes	(310) 274-0032	**Luca Blandi**	(310) 274-0032
	www.artistsbytimothypriano.com	(Hair)	www.artistsbytimothypriano.com

Jenna Baltes (310) 274-0032
www.artistsbytimothypriano.com

Meredith Baraf (310) 274-0032
(Makeup) www.artistsbytimothypriano.com

Lynn Barber (818) 222-5200
(Makeup) www.schneiderentertainment.com

Donna Bard (805) 490-3151
(Makeup) www.donnabard.com

Cori Bardo (323) 297-0250
(Hair) www.magnetla.com

Kimberlee Barlow (213) 446-1720
www.larep.net

Eric Barnard (323) 931-2745
www.aimartist.com

Melissa Barone (323) 935-8455
(Hair) www.ms-management.com

Frederique Barrera (213) 359-5899
www.frederiqueb.com
(Grooming, Makeup & Special FX Makeup)

Joshua Barrett (310) 274-0032
(Grooming & Hair) www.artistsbytimothypriano.com

Traci Barrett (323) 466-2007
www.therexagency.com

Gina Barrington (323) 436-7766
www.eamgmt.com

Pauline Barry (415) 290-9532
www.paulinebarry.com

Mary Jean Beach (909) 590-1688
(Makeup) www.makeupbymaryjean.com

Beauty & Photo (323) 549-3100
3737 Greenwood Ave. FAX (323) 549-9881
Los Angeles, CA 90066 www.beautyandphoto.com
(Reps for Hair and Makeup Artists)

Hether Beckrest (310) 246-0446
www.workgroup-ltd.com

Sabrina Bedrani (323) 462-5000
(Makeup) www.traceymattingly.com

Saisha Beecham (310) 839-8722
www.cloutieragency.com

Marco Berardini (310) 839-8722
(Grooming & Makeup) www.cloutieragency.com

Miles Berdache (323) 445-4910
www.artists-services.com

Bridget Bergman (310) 493-0113

Marsha Bialo (310) 447-8300
(Manicurist) www.bpolished.com

Lucia Bianca (818) 845-8899
(818) 415-4458
(Makeup) FAX (818) 845-8899

Christian Bier (323) 931-2745
www.aimartist.com

Candice Birns (323) 466-2007
(Hair) www.therexagency.com

Kate Biscoe (323) 839-0550
(212) 741-0202
(Makeup) FAX (323) 666-5277

Luca Blandi (310) 274-0032
(Hair) www.artistsbytimothypriano.com

Oscar Blandi (310) 274-0032
(Hair) www.artistsbytimothypriano.com

Monika Blunder (310) 276-0777
(Makeup) www.thewallgroup.com

Elan Bongiorno (310) 998-1977
(Makeup) www.celestineagency.com

Kasha Bonnell (323) 436-7766
www.eamgmt.com

Jenn Bouley-Gemmell (323) 854-2220
FAX (310) 372-1782

Marissa Bourbonnais (323) 850-6783
(Makeup)

Kareen Boursier (323) 937-1010
www.zenobia.com

Halle Bowman (310) 276-0777
(Hair) www.thewallgroup.com

Felicity Bowring (310) 601-2355
(Makeup) www.lesliealyson.com

Annemarie M. Bradley (818) 222-5200
(Hair) www.schneiderentertainment.com

Anna Branson (323) 446-2007
(Makeup) www.therexagency.com

Alexis Brazel (323) 466-2007
(Makeup) www.therexagency.com

June Brickman (818) 917-2792

Sunnie Brook (310) 998-1977
www.celestineagency.com

Jenni Brown (310) 291-5117

Tasha Reiko Brown (323) 931-2745
www.aimartist.com

Natalia Bruschi (310) 276-0777
(Hair) www.thewallgroup.com

Belinda Bryant (213) 620-8505
(213) 393-3600
(Body Painting, Grooming, Makeup & Special FX Makeup)

Kara Yoshimoto Bua (323) 462-5000
(Makeup) www.traceymattingly.com

Jennifer Budner (310) 266-2155
(Makeup) FAX (760) 544-9009

Michelle Buhler (818) 284-6423
(Makeup) www.italentco.com

Michele Burke (818) 748-8841
(Body Painting, Makeup & Special FX Makeup)

Michael Burnett (818) 768-6103
(Makeup) FAX (818) 768-6136
www.mbpfx.com

Gina Burrus (714) 717-8736
FAX (714) 846-6130
www.ginaburrus.com
(Body Painting, Grooming, Makeup & Special FX Makeup)

Mary Burton (310) 278-8086
(Makeup)

Lorna Butler (310) 274-0032
www.artistsbytimothypriano.com

Hair & Makeup Artists

Peter Butler (Hair)	(323) 462-5000 www.traceymattingly.com	

Peter Butler (323) 462-5000
(Hair) www.traceymattingly.com

Christina Buzas (310) 274-0032
(Hair) www.artistsbytimothypriano.com

Jeremy Byrne (323) 935-8455
(Hair) www.ms-management.com

Christi Cagle (323) 466-2007
(Hair) www.therexagency.com

John Caglione (310) 601-2355
(Makeup) www.lesliealyson.com

Martha Callender (818) 489-3429
(Makeup; French & Spanish)

Cheryl Calo (310) 839-8722
(Hair & Makeup) www.cloutieragency.com

Rudy Calvo (323) 299-4043
(Makeup) www.dionperonneau.com

Coleen Campbell-Olwell (323) 436-7766
(Makeup) www.eamgmt.com

Gio Campora (310) 276-0777
(Hair) www.thewallgroup.com

Riawna Capri (310) 276-0777
(Grooming) www.thewallgroup.com

Laverne Caracuzzi (805) 494-6484
(Makeup)

(212) 582-8052
Jamie Cardillo-Lee (202) 701-9641
www.elevationtalent.com
(Body Painting, Grooming, Hair & Makeup)

Kim Carillo (310) 998-1977
(Makeup) www.celestineagency.com

Siobhan Carmody (818) 206-0144
(Makeup) www.allcrewagency.com

Damien Carney (323) 466-2007
(Hair) www.therexagency.com

Philip Carreon (310) 276-0777
www.thewallgroup.com

Will Carrillo (310) 998-1977
(Hair) www.celestineagency.com

Terri Carter (323) 299-4043
(Makeup) www.dionperonneau.com

Luis Casco (310) 839-8722
www.cloutieragency.com

Gloria Casney (310) 601-2355
(Hair) www.lesliealyson.com

Leo Corey Castellano (818) 222-5200
(Makeup) www.schneiderentertainment.com

Paul Anthony Castro (323) 931-2745
www.aimartist.com

Cat (310) 775-5723
www.agencycelebrityartists.com

Gianpaolo Ceciliato (323) 462-5000
www.traceymattingly.com

Celestine Agency (310) 998-1977
1548 16th St. FAX (310) 998-1978
Santa Monica, CA 90404 www.celestineagency.com
(Reps for Hair and Makeup Artists)

Sherri Celis (310) 274-0032
www.artistsbytimothypriano.com

Joanne Cervelli-Smith (310) 395-7770

Amy Chance (310) 998-1977
(Makeup)

Cassie Chapman (323) 445-4910
www.artists-services.com

Jenny Cho (310) 276-0777
(Hair) www.thewallgroup.com

Lori Cincotta (310) 463-3579
(Body Painting, Colorist, Grooming, Hair, Makeup, Manicurist, Special FX Makeup & Wigs)

Luann Claps (818) 222-5200
(Makeup) www.schneiderentertainment.com

Camille Clark (323) 931-2745
www.aimartist.com

Chris Clark (818) 284-6423
(Hair) www.italentco.com

Jenni Clark (818) 516-8929
www.jenniclark.com

Jeremy Clark (323) 931-2745
(Hair) www.aimartist.com

Nicola Clarke (818) 222-5200
(Hair) www.schneiderentertainment.com

Terry Clotiaux (310) 285-9000
(Special FX Makeup) www.wmeentertainment.com

Cloutier Remix (310) 839-8722
2632 La Cienega Ave. FAX (310) 839-8730
Los Angeles, CA 90403 www.cloutieragency.com
(Reps for Hair and Makeup Artists)

(323) 856-0551
Dian Bethune Coble (323) 646-1071
(Body Painting, Grooming, Hair, Makeup & Wigs)

Liza Coggins (323) 931-2745
(Makeup) www.aimartist.com

Lauren Kaye Cohen (323) 462-5000
(Makeup) www.traceymattingly.com

(310) 395-1073
Connie Cole (310) 502-2434
(Grooming, Hair & Makeup) FAX (310) 395-1073

Christy Coleman (310) 276-0777
(Makeup) www.thewallgroup.com

Claire Coleman (323) 937-1010
www.zenobia.com

(310) 823-0508
Kim Collea (520) 906-9076
FAX (815) 642-4444

Tyler Colton (310) 998-1977
www.celestineagency.com

Jerry Constantine (310) 288-8000
(Special FX Makeup) www.paradigmagency.com

Colleen Conway (323) 931-2745
(Hair) www.aimartist.com

Mary Cook (818) 206-0144
www.allcrewagency.com

Fran Cooper (Makeup)	(310) 943-8102 www.artmixbeauty.com
Sergio Corvacho (Makeup)	(323) 297-0250 www.magnetla.com
David Cox (Hair)	(310) 998-1977 www.celestineagency.com
Anthony Cristiano (Hair)	(310) 274-0032 www.artistsbytimothypriano.com
Jill Crosby	(310) 839-8722 www.cloutieragency.com
Christina Culinski	(323) 931-2745 www.aimartist.com
Heather Curie (Makeup)	(310) 839-8722 www.cloutieragency.com
Syd Curry (Hair)	(323) 856-8540 www.opusbeauty.com
Donna D. (Manicurist)	(310) 274-0032 www.artistsbytimothypriano.com
Elizabeth Dahl (Grooming & Makeup)	(323) 469-9035 (310) 562-6370 www.makeupbyelizabeth.com
Christophe Danchaud (Makeup)	(323) 297-0250 www.magnetla.com
Danilo (Hair)	(310) 276-0777 www.thewallgroup.com
Jennifer Daranyi	(323) 935-8455 www.ms-management.com
Daven (Hair)	(310) 998-1977 www.celestineagency.com
Erica Davidson	(323) 931-2745 www.aimartist.com
Nettie Davis (Grooming & Manicurist)	(323) 578-9039 www.nettiedavis.com
Dawn to Dusk Agency 8306 Wilshire Blvd., Ste. 412 Beverly Hills, CA 90211 (Reps for Hair and Makeup Artists)	(323) 850-6783 (212) 431-8631
Tarra Day (Makeup)	(818) 284-6423 www.italentco.com
Beatrice De Alba	(323) 937-1010 www.zenobia.com
Jerry DeCarlo (Hair)	(310) 601-2355 www.lesliealyson.com
Danielle Decker	(310) 943-8102 www.artmixbeauty.com
Kelsey Deenihan	(323) 436-7766 www.eamgmt.com
Anabel DeHaven	(310) 274-0032 www.artistsbytimothypriano.com/make-up/ anabel-dehaven
Patrice Delaroche (Hair)	(310) 998-1977 www.celestineagency.com
Athena Demetrios (Makeup)	(310) 435-9029 (530) 334-5213
Sterfon Demings (Hair)	(818) 206-0144 www.allcrewagency.com
Jillian Dempsey (Makeup)	(310) 276-0777 www.thewallgroup.com
Debra Denson	(818) 284-6423 www.italentco.com
Sue Devitt (Makeup)	(310) 839-8722 www.cloutieragency.com
Ken Diaz (Makeup)	(310) 601-2355 www.lesliealyson.com
Angela DiCarlo	(323) 468-2240 www.nyoffice.net
Debra Dietrich (Hair)	(818) 206-0144 www.allcrewagency.com
Denise M. Dillaway (Grooming, Hair & Makeup)	(310) 600-8654
Jay Diola (Hair)	(323) 935-8455 www.ms-management.com
Dion Peronneau Agency 5482 Wilshire Blvd., Ste. 1512 Los Angeles, CA 90036 (Reps for Hair and Makeup Artists)	(323) 299-4043 FAX (323) 299-4269 www.dionperonneau.com
Monica DiVenti	(310) 450-4160
Tihomira Dobranova (Makeup)	(323) 304-2996 www.tihomira.com
Kyra Dorman	(310) 274-0032 www.artistsbytimothypriano.com
Lucie Doughty (Colorist & Hair)	(310) 739-3375 FAX (310) 391-9149 www.luciedoughty.com
Linda Dowds (Makeup)	(818) 284-6423 www.italentco.com
Wendy Doyle	(323) 937-1010 www.zenobia.com
Bari Dreiband-Burman (Makeup)	(818) 980-6587 www.burmanstudio.com
Pati Dubroff (Makeup)	(310) 276-0777 www.thewallgroup.com
Debi Dumas (Colorist)	(310) 274-0032 www.artistsbytimothypriano.com
Rosie Duprat-Fort (Special FX Makeup)	(818) 206-0144 www.allcrewagency.com
Stephan Dupuis (Special FX Makeup)	(323) 445-4910 www.artists-services.com
Georgie Eisdell (Grooming, Hair & Makeup)	(310) 276-0777 www.thewallgroup.com
Gloria Elias-Foeillet (Makeup)	(310) 998-1977 www.celestineagency.com
Alexis Ellen (Makeup)	(323) 446-2007 www.therexagency.com
Dave Elsey (Special FX Makeup)	(818) 206-0144 www.allcrewagency.com
Ennis, Inc. (Reps for Hair and Makeup Artists)	(310) 587-3512 www.ennisinc.com

Hair & Makeup Artists

Epiphany Artist Group, Inc. (323) 660-6353	**Marcus Francis** (310) 276-0777
(Reps for Hair and Makeup Artists) FAX (323) 660-0094	www.thewallgroup.com
Mary Erickson (877) 242-6878	**Robin Fredriksz** (323) 297-0250
www.lamakeup.com	www.magnetla.com
Ronaldo Escobar (323) 937-1010	**Brett Freedman** (310) 998-1977
www.zenobia.com	www.celestineagency.com
(213) 999-5212	(818) 340-4852
Gunn Espegard (323) 512-7180	**Edward French** (818) 317-9997
www.gunnespegard.com	(Makeup) FAX (818) 340-4837
	www.edwardfrench.com
Exclusive Artists Management (323) 436-7766	
7700 Sunset Blvd., Ste. 205 FAX (323) 436-7799	(310) 274-0032
Los Angeles, CA 90046 www.eamgmt.com	**Beth Fricke** (323) 243-0583
(Reps for Hair and Makeup Artists)	www.artistsbytimothypriano.com/artists/bethfricke
	(Manicurist)
Fabiola (310) 927-7080	
(Makeup; Spanish) www.fabiolamakeup.com	**Alan Friedman** (818) 881-1473
Stefen Fangmeier (310) 285-9000	**Mary-Jane Frost** (310) 276-0777
(Special FX Makeup) www.wmeentertainment.com	(Makeup) www.thewallgroup.com
Barbara Farman (310) 839-8722	**Elisabeth Fry** (818) 206-0144
(Grooming, Hair & Makeup) www.cloutieragency.com	(Makeup) www.allcrewagency.com
Joe Farulla (818) 206-0144	**Kelcey Fry** (818) 469-0026
(Makeup) www.allcrewagency.com	www.lipspink.com
Karen Faye (213) 509-7208	**Catherine Furniss** (310) 998-1977
www.karen-faye.com	(Grooming) www.celestineagency.com
Kathryn Miles Fenton (818) 988-7038	**Toni G.** (818) 284-6423
(Makeup)	www.italentco.com
Nancy Ferguson (818) 883-8808	**Eric Gabriel** (323) 466-2007
(Makeup)	(Hair) www.therexagency.com
Eric Ferrell (323) 299-4043	**Mary E. Gaffney** (213) 407-5392
(Makeup) www.dionperonneau.com	(Makeup)
Debra Ferullo (323) 462-5000	**Jane Galli** (310) 601-2355
(Makeup) www.traceymattingly.com	www.lesliealyson.com
Jeffrey Fetzer (323) 937-1010	**Craig Gangi** (323) 462-5000
www.zenobia.com	(Hair) www.traceymattingly.com
Jen Fiamengo (310) 998-1977	**Michelle Garbin** (310) 283-5118
www.celestineagency.com	(Makeup)
Ray Filipowicz (888) 839-0101	**Lisa Garner** (310) 274-0032
(Makeup) www.firehousemanagement.com	(Grooming & Makeup) www.artistsbytimothypriano.com
FIRE House Management (888) 839-0101	**Cheryl Gates** (310) 775-5723
(Reps for Hair and Makeup Artists) FAX (888) 839-2943	www.agencycelebrityartists.com
www.firehousemanagement.com	
	Sharon Gault (323) 856-8540
Andrew Fitzsimons (310) 274-0032	(Makeup) www.opusbeauty.com
(Hair) www.artistsbytimothypriano.com	
	Asia Geiger (310) 998-1977
Sean Flanigan (310) 601-2355	www.celestineagency.com
www.lesliealyson.com	
	Kay Georgiou (818) 222-5200
Stephanie Flor (310) 274-0032	(Hair) www.schneiderentertainment.com
www.artistsbytimothypriano.com	
	Casey Geren (310) 274-0032
Linda Flowers (310) 601-2355	(Hair) www.artistsbytimothypriano.com
www.lesliealyson.com	
	Garret Gervais (323) 856-8540
Vincent Ford (310) 274-0032	(Makeup) www.opusbeauty.com
(Makeup) www.artistsbytimothypriano.com	
	Giannandrea (310) 276-0777
April Foreman (310) 276-0777	(Hair) www.thewallgroup.com
(Manicurist) www.thewallgroup.com	
	Pam Gillespie (323) 937-1010
Mary Jo Fortin (310) 457-6446	www.zenobia.com
(805) 649-9064	**Giovanni Giuliano** (310) 998-1977
Karen Fraker (805) 455-0563	(Hair) www.celestineagency.com
www.karenfraker.com	

Robin Glaser (323) 466-2007	**Loni Hale** (310) 274-0032
(Makeup) www.therexagency.com	www.artistsbytimothypriano.com
Tamara Gold (310) 801-1342	(323) 466-4441
www.theredlipstickreporter.com	**Mindy Hall** (310) 415-2294
(Body Painting, Grooming & Makeup)	FAX (323) 460-4442
	www.miltonagency.com
Jan Golden (818) 458-2569	
www.goldenjan.com	**Lucy Halperin** (323) 856-8540
	www.opusbeauty.com
John Goodwin (818) 206-0144	
(Special FX Makeup) www.allcrewagency.com	**Keiko Hamaguchi** (310) 998-1977
	(Hair) www.celestineagency.com
Kim Goodwin (310) 839-8722	
(Hair & Makeup) www.cloutieragency.com	**Paula Jane Hamilton** (213) 705-0202
	(Body Painting & Makeup) www.paulajanehamilton.com
Rachel Goodwin (310) 276-0777	
(Makeup) www.thewallgroup.com	**Su Han** (818) 489-6125
	(Makeup & Grooming) www.suhanmakeup.com
Leon Gorman (323) 297-0250	
(Hair) www.magnetla.com	**Jonathan Hanousek** (323) 436-7766
	(Hair) www.eamgmt.com
Lauren Gott (310) 943-8102	
(Makeup) www.artmixbeauty.com	**Lina Hanson** (323) 462-5000
	(Makeup) www.traceymattingly.com
Casey Gouveia (310) 998-1977	
www.celestineagency.com	**Pat Harris** (310) 594-6568
	(Body Painting, Makeup & Special FX Makeup)
Patricia Grande (818) 284-6423	
(Hair) www.italentco.com	**Clifford Hashimoto** (323) 445-4910
	www.artists-services.com
Marina Gravani (310) 274-0032	
(Makeup) www.artistsbytimothypriano.com	**Heather Hawkins** (323) 937-1010
	www.zenobia.com
Bruce Grayson (310) 274-0032	
(Makeup) www.artistsbytimothypriano.com	**Dawn Haynes** (323) 850-6783
	(Men's Grooming)
April Greaves (310) 998-1977	
(Makeup) www.celestineagency.com	**Kristin Heitkotter** (310) 998-1977
	(Hair) www.celestineagency.com
Caprice Green (323) 549-3100	
www.beautyandphoto.com	**Andrea Helgadottir** (323) 297-0250
	(Makeup) www.magnetla.com
Kimberly Greene (818) 291-1884	
(Makeup)	(818) 780-7766
	Sharin Helgestad (213) 792-6677
Dina Gregg (323) 931-2745	
(Makeup) www.aimartist.com	**Adrienne Herbert** (310) 998-1977
	(Grooming & Makeup) www.celestineagency.com
Gudrun (310) 839-8722	
www.cloutieragency.com	**Valerie Hernandez** (323) 856-8540
	www.opusbeauty.com
Luis Guillermo (310) 274-0032	
(Grooming & Hair) www.artistsbytimothypriano.com	**Kerry Herta** (310) 822-2898
	www.rougeartists.com
Barbara Guilliaume (323) 436-7766	
(Grooming) www.eamgmt.com	**Cathy Highland** (323) 931-2745
	(Makeup) www.aimartist.com
Mary Guthrie (310) 274-0032	
www.artistsbytimothypriano.com	**Stephanie Hobgood** (323) 436-7766
	(Hair) www.eamgmt.com
Myles Haddad (323) 931-2745	
(Hair) www.aimartist.com	**Steven Hoeppner** (310) 274-0032
	www.artistsbytimothypriano.com
Susan Haddon (310) 998-1977	(Grooming, Hair & Makeup)
www.celestineagency.com	
	Byrd Holland (818) 558-1954
Sharon Hagen (310) 480-8489	(Makeup) FAX (818) 558-1954
www.sharonhagen7.com	
	Bryan Hollingshead (323) 252-5830
(818) 225-1080	(Grooming & Makeup)
Gail Hagopian (818) 645-6135	
(Makeup)	**Adrienne Houle** (323) 937-1010
	(Makeup) www.zenobia.com
Monique Hahn (626) 676-1389	
(Grooming, Hair & Makeup) www.moniquemakeup.com	**Maryellen Howe** (323) 937-1010
	www.zenobia.com
(818) 919-6017	
Nedra Hainey (818) 813-7018	**Daniel Howell** (323) 462-5000
FAX (323) 850-7165	(Hair) www.traceymattingly.com

Claudia Humburg (310) 733-2550 www.photogenicsmedia.com (Body Painting, Hair & Makeup)	**Allyson Joyner** (213) 216-1328 www.allysonjoyner.com (Body Painting, Colorist, Grooming, Hair, Makeup, Special FX Makeup & Wigs)
Paul Hyett (818) 206-0144 (Makeup & Special FX Makeup) www.allcrewagency.com	**Stella Kae** (310) 839-8722 www.cloutieragency.com
Mahfud Ibrahim (323) 436-7766 www.eamgmt.com	**Kali** (310) 998-1977 (Hair) www.celestineagency.com
Munemi Imai (323) 297-0250 (Makeup) www.magnetla.com	**Karoliina Kangas** (323) 856-8540 www.opusbeauty.com
Annie Ing (310) 998-1977 (Makeup) www.celestineagency.com	**Michael Kanyon** (310) 998-1977 (Hair) www.celestineagency.com
Melanie Inglessis (323) 297-0250 (Makeup) www.magnetla.com	**Bethany Karlyn** (323) 856-8540 (Makeup) www.opusbeauty.com
Jarrett Iovinella (323) 297-0250 (Hair) www.magnetla.com	(310) 489-9908 **Katinka** (310) 306-8484 (Grooming, Hair & Makeup) www.katinkamakeup.com
Bradley Irion (310) 274-0032 (Hair) www.artistsbytimothypriano.com	(310) 288-0818 **Janice Kavanagh** (310) 486-6266 FAX (310) 288-0812
Thea Istenes (310) 733-2550 (Makeup) www.photogenicsmedia.com	**Karen Kawahara** (310) 839-8722 (Makeup) www.cloutieragency.com
iTalent Company (818) 284-6423 522 Wilshire Blvd., Ste. K FAX (866) 755-0708 Santa Monica, CA 90401 www.italentco.com (Reps for Hair and Makeup Artists)	**Carla Kay** (310) 839-8722 (Manicurist) www.cloutieragency.com
Jennifer J. (310) 839-8722 (Colorist) www.cloutieragency.com	**Julianne Kay** (310) 839-8722 www.cloutieragency.com
Lisa Jachno (323) 931-2745 (Manicurist) www.aimartist.com	**Kazumi** (888) 839-0101 www.firehousemanagement.com
Glen Jackson (310) 274-0032 www.artistsbytimothypriano.com	**Cheri Keating** (310) 276-0777 www.thewallgroup.com
Amanda Jacobellis (310) 858-1970 www.makeupmandy.com	(818) 508-1533 **Trisha Kelley** (818) 809-9980
Ian James (310) 276-0777 (Hair) www.thewallgroup.com	**David Keough** (310) 998-1977 (Hair) www.celestineagency.com
Sean James (323) 856-8540 (Grooming & Hair) www.opusbeauty.com	**Richard Keough** (310) 839-8722 (Hair) www.cloutieragency.com
Tara Jean (310) 943-8102 (Hair) www.artmixbeauty.com	**Noriko Kerns** (323) 466-2007 www.therexagency.com
Helen Jeffers (323) 931-2745 www.aimartist.com	**Hyunsoo Kim** (323) 935-8455 (Hair) www.ms-management.com
Troy Jensen (310) 998-1977 (Makeup) www.celestineagency.com	**Connie King** (310) 775-5723 www.agencycelebrityartists.com
Kathy Jeung (323) 297-0250 (Makeup) www.magnetla.com	**Peter King** (818) 222-5200 (Hair) www.schneiderentertainment.com
Ashlie Johnson (310) 276-0777 (Manicurist) www.thewallgroup.com	**Yukiko Kinkel** (310) 489-0502 (Hair & Makeup) www.macgowanspencer.com
Rosie Johnston (323) 436-7766 (Makeup) www.eamgmt.com	**Todd Kleitsch** (818) 284-6423 www.italentco.com
(818) 584-4115 **Dean Jones** (336) 264-2302	**Martina Kohl** (310) 614-8353 www.martinakohl.com
Jacqui Jordan (323) 937-1010 www.zenobia.com	**Vassilis Kokkinidis** (310) 822-2898 (Hair) www.rougeartists.com
Kevin Josephson (213) 446-1720 (Hair) www.larep.net	**Lena Koro** (323) 462-5000 (Makeup) www.traceymattingly.com
(310) 459-8917 **Valerie Joslin** (310) 801-7289	**Nina Kraft** (310) 486-6236 (Makeup)

Peter Kukla   (310) 200-4164

Kimmi Kyees   (310) 998-1977
(Manicurist)   www.celestineagency.com

LA Rep   (213) 446-1720
3219 Laurel Canyon Blvd.   FAX (323) 656-1756
Studio City, CA 91604   www.larep.net
(Reps for Hair and Makeup Artists)

Rebecca Lafford   (818) 222-5200
(Makeup)   www.schneiderentertainment.com

Julia Lallas   (818) 284-6423
(Makeup)   www.italentco.com

Alex LaMarsh   (310) 274-0032
www.artistsbytimothypriano.com

Marci Landgraf   (323) 937-1010
www.zenobia.com

Marie Larkin   (323) 842-3580
(Hair)

Brithney Lashaun   (323) 935-8455
www.ms-management.com

Didier Lavergne   (310) 282-9940
(Makeup)   www.mirisch.com

Johnny Lavoy   (310) 943-8102
(Hair)   www.artmixbeauty.com

Rosemary Lawrence   (626) 797-0104
FAX (323) 761-6418

Debbie Leavitt   (310) 839-8722
(Manicurist)   www.cloutieragency.com

Nicki Ledermann   (310) 601-2355
www.lesliealyson.com

Marie-Josee LeDuc   (323) 931-2745
(Makeup)   www.aimartist.com

Adruitha Lee   (818) 284-6423
(Hair)   www.italentco.com

Billie Lee   (323) 937-1010
www.zenobia.com

Norma Lee   (323) 654-5790
     (818) 384-0013
(Hair)

Sonia Lee   (323) 436-7766
www.eamgmt.com

Susan Reilly Lehane   (818) 222-5200
(Makeup)   www.schneiderentertainment.com

Lisa Leming   (714) 914-6397
www.lisaleming.com

Mauricio Lemus   (707) 334-9008
www.mauriciolemus.com
(Grooming, Hair, Makeup & Wigs)

Sam Leonardi   (323) 462-5000
(Hair)   FAX (323) 462-5001
www.traceymattingly.com

Leslie Alyson Inc.   (310) 601-2355
350 S. Beverly Dr., Ste. 200   www.lesliealyson.com
Beverly Hills, CA 90212
(Reps for Hair and Makeup Artists)

Hilda Levierge   (323) 466-2007
(Makeup)   www.therexagency.com

Angela Levin   (323) 462-5000
(Makeup)   www.traceymattingly.com

Tracey Levy   (818) 284-6423
(Makeup)   www.italentco.com

Joycelyne Lew   (323) 466-3100
     (213) 999-5514
FAX (323) 469-7138

Stephen Lewis   (323) 436-7766
(Grooming, Hair & Makeup)   www.eamgmt.com

Aaron Light   (310) 998-1977
(Hair)   www.celestineagency.com

Virginia Linzee   (310) 839-8722
www.cloutieragency.com

Melanie Littlewood   (760) 409-5110
www.hairandmakeupartistrybymelanie.com
(Airbrush Makeup, Body Painting, Eye Lash Extensions, Hair,
Special FX Makeup & Wigs)

Jeanine Lobell   (323) 297-0250
(Makeup)   www.magnetla.com

Lolita   (323) 299-4043
www.dionperonneau.com

Sherrie Long   (213) 302-0313
     (415) 608-9220
www.sherrielong.com
(Grooming, Hair, Makeup, Manicurist, Special FX
Makeup & Wigs)

Sergio Lopez-Rivera   (310) 839-8722
(Makeup)   www.cloutieragency.com

Lottie   (310) 276-0777
(Makeup)   www.thewallgroup.com

Ashleigh Louer   (323) 935-8455
(Makeup)   www.ms-management.com

Billy Lowe   (310) 430-4045
(Hair)   www.billylowe.com

Christopher Xavier Lozano   (323) 962-0009
     (323) 854-6775
www.tlshollywood.com

Gina Luca   (323) 935-8455
(Makeup)   www.ms-management.com

Tammy Ly   (323) 937-1010
(Manicurist)   www.zenobia.com

Juanita Lyon   (310) 998-1977
www.celestineagency.com

Helene Macaulay   (310) 274-0032
(Makeup)   www.artistsbytimothypriano.com

Sheryl Macauley   (323) 937-1010
(Manicurist)   www.zenobia.com

**MacGowan Spencer
Creative Agency**   (310) 489-0502
www.macgowanspencer.com
(Reps for Grooming, Hair and Makeup Artists)

Natalie MacGowan Spencer   (310) 489-0502
www.macgowanspencer.com

Brian Magallones   (323) 436-7766
(Hair)   www.eamgmt.com

Magnet LA   (323) 297-0250
6363 Wilshire Blvd., Ste. 650   FAX (323) 297-0249
Los Angeles, CA 90048   www.magnetla.com
(Reps for Hair and Makeup Artists)

Mai-Li (310) 395-8286	**Hazuki Matsushita** (310) 709-0400
(Makeup)	www.hazukimakeup.com
Sage Maitri (310) 276-0777	**Dawn Mattocks** (323) 251-3305
(Makeup) www.thewallgroup.com	FAX (866) 760-9105
	www.dawnmattocks.com
Tré Major (323) 850-6783	(Body Painting, Colorist, Grooming, Hair, Makeup, Manicurist,
(Hair)	Special FX Makeup & Wigs)
Renee Majour (310) 998-1977	**Randi Måvestrand** (310) 951-3966
www.celestineagency.com	(Makeup) www.randimavestrand.com
Donna Malatino (310) 804-7391	(818) 509-9707
www.donnamalatino.com	**Francesca Maxwell** (818) 259-9223
(Colorist, Grooming, Hair, Makeup & Wigs)	FAX (818) 509-9707
Cervando Maldonado (310) 276-0777	**Diane Mazur** (818) 222-5200
www.thewallgroup.com	www.schneiderentertainment.com
(818) 763-3300	**Suzy Mazzarese-Allison** (310) 601-2355
Annie Maniscalco (818) 468-4527	www.lesliealyson.com
FAX (818) 763-3300	
	Kayleen McAdams (310) 276-0777
Monet Mansano (323) 937-1010	(Makeup) www.thewallgroup.com
(Makeup) www.zenobia.com	
	Lori McCoy Bell (818) 222-5200
Melanie Manson (310) 880-2825	(Hair) www.schneiderentertainment.com
www.melaniemanson.com	
(Body Painting, Grooming, Makeup & Special FX Makeup)	**Christian McCulloch** (323) 462-5000
	(Makeup) www.traceymattingly.com
Manuella (310) 274-0032	
(Grooming & Hair) www.artistsbytimothypriano.com	**Thomas McKiver** (310) 274-0032
	(Hair) www.artistsbytimothypriano.com
Maranda (310) 276-0777	
www.thewallgroup.com	**Patrick Melville** (310) 274-0032
	(Hair) www.artistsbytimothypriano.com
Christian Marc (310) 998-1977	
www.celestineagency.com	**Melvone** (310) 733-2550
	(Makeup) www.photogenicsmedia.com
(213) 712-5935	
Cassi Mari (310) 287-8082	**Ivan Mendoza** (310) 246-0446
	www.workgroup-ltd.com
Jeanette Marie (213) 446-1720	
(Hair & Makeup) www.larep.net	**Liz Mendoza** (310) 489-0502
	(Special FX Makeup) www.macgowanspencer.com
Richard Marin (310) 839-8722	
(Hair) www.cloutieragency.com	**Anthony Merante** (323) 931-2745
	(Makeup) www.aimartist.com
Denise Markey (310) 274-0032	
(Makeup) www.artistsbytimothypriano.com	(818) 219-7662
	Myke Michaels (818) 905-9059
Anne Marso (310) 570-7027	www.wolfpackfilmworks.com
(Grooming, Hair & Makeup) www.annemarso.com	(Hair, Makeup & Special FX Makeup)
Lorenzo Martin (310) 839-8722	**Michelle** (310) 775-5723
(Hair) www.cloutieragency.com	www.agencycelebrityartists.com
Glenn Marziali (310) 274-0032	(818) 843-5208
(Makeup) www.artistsbytimothypriano.com	**Patty Miller** (213) 217-0914
	(Hair)
Jonathan Mason (310) 274-0032	
(Hair) www.artistsbytimothypriano.com	**Terry Millet** (323) 297-0250
	(Hair) www.magnetla.com
Steven Mason (323) 436-7766	
(Hair) www.eamgmt.com	**Judd Minter** (323) 931-2745
	(Hair) www.aimartist.com
(818) 834-3000	
Todd Masters (604) 683-5311	**Karan Mitchell** (323) 462-5000
(Special FX Makeup) FAX (818) 834-9755	(Makeup) www.traceymattingly.com
www.mastersfx.com	
	Benjamin Mohapi (323) 856-8540
Mary Mastro (310) 601-2355	(Hair) www.opusbeauty.com
www.lesliealyson.com	
	Laura Mohberg (323) 462-5000
Robin Mathews (818) 284-6423	(Makeup) www.traceymattingly.com
(Makeup & Special FX Makeup) www.italentco.com	
	Julie A. Mollo (323) 459-2789
Matin (310) 274-0032	FAX (323) 665-2339
(Makeup) www.artistsbytimothypriano.com	www.juliemakeup.com
	Tatyana Molot (310) 274-0032
	(Manicurist) www.artistsbytimothypriano.com

Erin Ayanian Monroe (310) 839-8722	**Nenci Nevarez** (310) 398-7014
(Makeup) www.cloutieragency.com	www.nencinevarez.com
	(Colorist, Grooming, Hair, Makeup & Wigs)
Damian Monzillo (323) 854-2887	
(Hair) (323) 931-2745	**New York Office** (323) 468-2240
www.scissorandcomb.com	(212) 545-7895
	6605 Hollywood Blvd., Ste. 200 FAX (323) 468-2244
Matthew Monzon (323) 462-5000	Los Angeles, CA 90028 www.nyoffice.net
(Hair) www.traceymattingly.com	(Reps for Hair and Makeup Artists)
Louise Moon (323) 436-7766	**Davy Newkirk** (323) 462-5000
www.eamgmt.com	(Hair) www.traceymattingly.com
Chantal Moore (310) 839-8722	**Noel Nichols** (323) 446-2007
(Grooming) www.cloutieragency.com	(Makeup) www.therexagency.com
Elizabeth Morache (310) 246-0446	**Douglas Noe** (818) 284-6423
(Hair) www.workgroup-ltd.com	www.italentco.com
Mylah Morales (310) 998-1977	**Paul Norton** (323) 462-5000
(Makeup) www.celestineagency.com	(Hair) www.traceymattingly.com
Alyssa Morgan (323) 935-8455	**Jennifer Nudelman** (310) 489-0502
(Makeup) www.ms-management.com	(Makeup) www.macgowanspencer.com
Anne Morgan (310) 601-2355	**Glenn Nutley** (310) 998-1977
www.lesliealyson.com	(Grooming, Hair & Makeup) www.celestineagency.com
Emily Moses (323) 856-8540	**Heidi Nymark** (310) 998-1977
(Makeup) www.opusbeauty.com	www.celestineagency.com
Gil Mosko (818) 219-3109	**Nyrie** (310) 943-8102
(719) 676-2270	www.artmixbeauty.com
(Makeup & Special FX Makeup) www.gmfoam.com	
	Lydia O'Carroll (310) 839-8722
Autumn Moultrie (323) 436-7766	www.cloutieragency.com
(Makeup) www.eamgmt.com	
	Elaine Offers (323) 436-7766
Donald Mowat (310) 467-4152	(Makeup) www.eamgmt.com
(323) 957-4602	
(Makeup)	**Olive** (323) 466-2007
	(Makeup) www.therexagency.com
Tracy Moyer (310) 998-1977	
www.celestineagency.com	**Barbara Olvera** (818) 222-5200
	(Hair) www.schneiderentertainment.com
MS Management (323) 935-8455	
(Reps for Hair and Makeup Artists) FAX (323) 935-3143	**Bridget O'Neill** (323) 874-5796
www.ms-management.com	(Grooming & Makeup) FAX (323) 874-5797
Nellie Muganda (323) 937-1010	**Opus Beauty** (323) 856-8540
www.zenobia.com	6442 Santa Monica Blvd., Ste. 200B FAX (323) 871-8311
	Los Angeles, CA 90038 www.opusbeauty.com
Kelly Muldoon (818) 222-5200	(Reps for Hair and Makeup Artists)
(Hair) www.schneiderentertainment.com	
	Vincent Oquendo (323) 462-5000
Roz Music (323) 297-0250	(Makeup) www.traceymattingly.com
www.magnetla.com	
	Valli O'Reilly (323) 937-1010
Naja (310) 998-1977	www.zenobia.com
(Manicurist) www.celestineagency.com	
	Paola Orlando (310) 274-0032
Sue Nam (310) 274-0032	www.artistsbytimothypriano.com
(Manicurist) www.artistsbytimothypriano.com	
	Carlos Ortiz (310) 839-8722
Candace Neal (310) 601-2355	(Hair) www.cloutieragency.com
(Hair) www.lesliealyson.com	
	Ermahn Ospina (818) 284-6423
Pamela Neal (323) 436-7766	(Makeup) www.italentco.com
www.eamgmt.com	
	Charlotte Ostergren (310) 822-2898
Ve Neill (310) 601-2355	(Makeup) www.rougeartists.com
(Makeup) www.lesliealyson.com	
	Simone Otis (323) 937-1010
Thomas Nellen (818) 222-5200	www.zenobia.com
(Makeup) www.schneiderentertainment.com	
	Yvonne Ouellette (949) 218-3948
Glenn Neufeld (310) 288-8000	(714) 293-0223
(Special FX Makeup) www.paradigmagency.com	FAX (949) 218-3958
	www.yvonneouellette.com

Hair & Makeup Artists

Dina Ousley	(818) 308-8500
	FAX (818) 308-8501
	www.dinair.com
Shane Paish	(310) 998-1977
(Makeup)	www.celestineagency.com
Yiotis Panayiotou	(310) 998-1977
(Hair)	www.celestineagency.com
Tena Parker Baker	(661) 714-4665
(Hair)	FAX (310) 390-9154
Angie Parker	(310) 822-2898
	www.rougeartists.com
Sarah Pascoe	(702) 372-8601
Claudia Pascual	(305) 793-8255
(Makeup)	
Shayna Passaretti	(401) 338-5602
(Hair)	
Deborah Patino Rutherford	(818) 371-9719
(Makeup, Character Makeup & Special FX Makeup)	
Jeffrey Paul	(323) 436-7766
(Grooming, Hair & Makeup)	www.eamgmt.com
	(818) 553-6756
Denise Pauly-Hovey	(818) 416-8549
	FAX (818) 553-6654
	www.denisepauly.com
Frankie Payne	(323) 856-8540
(Hair)	www.opusbeauty.com
	(917) 834-4444
Kristen Paynter	(323) 468-2240
	www.kpaynter.com
Colin Penman	(818) 222-5200
(Makeup)	www.schneiderentertainment.com
Troy Peppin	(323) 856-8540
	www.opusbeauty.com
Vicki Peters	(323) 937-1010
	www.zenobia.com
Randi Petersen	(310) 274-0032
(Hair)	www.artistsbytimothypriano.com
Shannon Pezatta	(323) 299-4043
(Makeup)	www.dionperonneau.com
Daniel Phillips	(818) 206-0144
	www.allcrewagency.com
Marilyn Patricia Phillips	(818) 482-0588
(Hair)	FAX (818) 848-1915
Mary Phillips	(323) 297-0250
(Makeup)	www.magnetla.com
Photogenics	(310) 733-2550
8549 Higuera St.	FAX (310) 815-8632
Culver City, CA 90232	www.photogenicsmedia.com
(Reps for Hair and Makeup Artists)	
Carol Pierce	(310) 629-9729
Daniele Piersons	(323) 931-2745
	www.aimartist.com
Kim Pineda	(407) 716-0569
(Makeup)	
Jennifer Pitt	(323) 462-5000
(Makeup)	www.traceymattingly.com

Cheryl Platt	(323) 446-2007
(Makeup)	www.therexagency.com
Stephanie Pohl	(310) 839-8722
(Hair)	www.cloutieragency.com
Lisa Postma	(310) 998-1977
(Manicurist)	www.celestineagency.com
Marilyn Poucher	(818) 257-8002
(Makeup)	
Isaac Prado	(323) 931-2745
(Body Painting, Hair & Makeup)	www.aimartist.com
Toany Preusse	(310) 775-5723
	www.agencycelebrityartists.com
Vanessa Price	(323) 466-2007
(Hair)	www.therexagency.com
Q Hardy	(323) 299-4043
(Hair)	www.dionperonneau.com
Tim Quinn	(310) 274-0032
(Makeup)	www.artistsbytimothypriano.com
Serena Radaelli	(310) 839-8722
(Hair)	www.cloutieragency.com
Renee Rael	(323) 933-0200
	www.artistuntied.com
Robert Ramos	(310) 998-1977
(Hair)	www.celestineagency.com
K.G. Ramsey	(818) 206-0144
	www.allcrewagency.com
Shannon Rasheed	(310) 998-1977
	www.celestineagency.com
Carol Raskin	(818) 206-0144
	www.allcrewagency.com
Nelly Recchia	(323) 931-2745
(Body Painting)	www.aimartist.com
Darrell Redleaf	(818) 769-9021
	FAX (818) 769-0323
	www.darrellredleaf.com
(Colorist, Grooming, Hair, Makeup & Wigs)	
Ryan Reed	(818) 222-5200
	www.schneiderentertainment.com
Laini Reeves	(323) 462-5000
(Hair)	www.traceymattingly.com
Patricia Regan	(310) 601-2355
(Makeup)	www.lesliealyson.com
The Rex Agency	(323) 466-2007
6311 Romaine St., Ste. 7235	FAX (323) 466-1966
Los Angeles, CA 90038	www.therexagency.com
(Reps for Hair and Makeup Artists)	
	(323) 882-6822
Leah Rial	(323) 702-2356
(Makeup)	FAX (323) 882-6767
Tania Ribalow	(818) 222-5200
(Makeup)	www.schneiderentertainment.com
	(916) 925-7434
Julia Richardson	(415) 515-9840
(Makeup)	www.californiamakeup.com
Andrea Richter	(323) 299-4043
(Makeup)	www.dionperonneau.com

Danny Rishoff (Hair)	(323) 462-5000 www.traceymattingly.com	**Stephan Salyers** (Makeup)	(323) 848-6952 web.mac.com/stephensalyers
Carlos Rittner (Makeup)	(323) 937-1010 www.zenobia.com	**Samelia**	(310) 822-2898 www.rougeartists.com
Helen Robertson (Makeup)	(310) 998-1977 www.celestineagency.com	**Dominique Samuel** (Makeup)	(310) 274-0032 www.artistsbytimothypriano.com
Ben Robin	(818) 206-0144 www.allcrewagency.com	**Adrienne Sanchez** (Makeup)	(323) 935-8455 www.ms-management.com

Lia Robin
(818) 515-9840
FAX (661) 255-5505
www.liarobin.com
(Grooming, Hair, Makeup & Special FX Makeup)

Gina Sandler
(213) 509-0785
www.ginasandler.com
(Body Painting, Grooming, Makeup & Special FX Makeup)

Wendy Robin
(702) 503-4888
FAX (702) 577-0777
www.studiowoflasvegas.com
(Body Painting, Grooming, Makeup & Special FX Makeup)

Kathleen Sandoval
(Makeup)
(323) 937-1010
www.zenobia.com

Maria Sandoval
(Hair)
(818) 822-7453
FAX (866) 350-7389

Jeannia Robinette
(Makeup)
(323) 462-5000
www.traceymattingly.com

Erica Sauer
(Grooming)
(323) 436-7766
www.eamgmt.com

Melissa Rogers
(Makeup)
(310) 998-1977
www.celestineagency.com

Michelle Saunders
(Manicurist)
(310) 998-1977
www.celestineagency.com

Bob Romero
(Makeup)
(818) 981-3338
(818) 953-6625
FAX (818) 981-3339
www.bobromero.com

Vanessa Scali
(Makeup)
(323) 462-5000
www.traceymattingly.com

Alexandra Schafer
(323) 856-8540
www.opusbeauty.com

Roque
(Hair)
(323) 462-5000
www.traceymattingly.com

Mara Schiaveti
(Hair)
(310) 839-8722
www.cloutieragency.com

Ashlee Rose
(Hair)
(310) 943-8102
www.artmixbeauty.com

Joanna Schlipp
(Makeup)
(310) 839-8722
www.cloutieragency.com

Fleury Rose
(Manicurist)
(310) 274-0032
www.artistsbytimothypriano.com

Diana Schmidtke
(310) 276-0777
www.thewallgroup.com

Roshar
(Makeup)
(888) 839-0101
www.firehousemanagement.com

The Schneider Entertainment Agency
(818) 222-5200
22287 Mulholland Hwy, Ste. 210   FAX (818) 222-5284
Calabasas, CA 91302
www.schneiderentertainment.com
(Reps for Hair and Makeup Artists)

Charles Gregory Ross
(818) 206-0144
www.allcrewagency.com

Christine Ross
(818) 207-5535
(Hair & Makeup)   www.christinerossmakeupartist.com

Ulli Schober
(Makeup)
(310) 998-1977
www.celestineagency.com

Rouge Artists, Inc.
(310) 822-2898
(310) 570-1150
2433 Boone Ave.   FAX (310) 827-7367
Venice, CA 90291   www.rougeartists.com
(Reps for Hair and Makeup Artists)

Janeen Schreyer
(Makeup)
(818) 222-5200
www.schneiderentertainment.com

Nicola Schuller
(818) 284-6423
www.italentco.com

Wendy Rowe
(Makeup)
(323) 297-0250
www.magnetla.com

Peter Serraino
(661) 755-6849

Celena Rubin
(310) 502-3223
www.artofmakeup.com
(Grooming, Hair, Makeup & Special FX Makeup)

Nichole Servin
(310) 943-8102
www.artmixbeauty.com

Lisa Ruckh
(213) 716-1723
www.beautybylisa.com
(Body Painter, Grooming, Hair, Makeup, Special FX
Makeup & Wigs)

Tara Shakespeare
(323) 937-1010
www.zenobia.com

Ronit Shapow
(Makeup)
(323) 466-2007
www.therexagency.com

Tania D. Russell
(323) 317-0344
www.makeupwerks.com

Sheenon
(Hair)
(323) 462-5000
www.traceymattingly.com

Patrice Ryan
(213) 700-2765

Yvette Shelton
(Hair)
(323) 850-6783

Robert Ryan
(Makeup)
(310) 864-6936
www.bobryandesign.com

Kate Shorter
(323) 661-2605
(323) 646-9816

Maital Sabban
(Makeup)
(323) 935-8455
www.ms-management.com

Mari Shten
(Makeup)
(310) 274-0032
www.artistsbytimothypriano.com

Christophe Saluzzo
(Hair)
(310) 839-8722
www.cloutieragency.com

Hair & Makeup Artists

Sienree	(310) 998-1977	Charles Baker Strahan	(310) 274-0032
	www.celestineagency.com	(Hair)	www.artistsbytimothypriano.com
Rea Ann Silva	(323) 856-8540	Jo Strettell	(323) 297-0250
(Makeup)	www.opusbeauty.com	(Makeup)	www.magnetla.com
Arlene Silver	(310) 210-7935	Collier Strong	(310) 839-8722
		(Makeup)	www.cloutieragency.com
Joe J. Simon	(310) 274-0032	Jetty Stutzman	(323) 931-2745
(Makeup)	www.artistsbytimothypriano.com		www.aimartist.com

Sharon Simon (661) 296-5996 / (818) 389-7303 / FAX (661) 296-5996
(Body Painting, Makeup & Special FX Makeup)

Anouck Sullivan (310) 246-0446
www.workgroup-ltd.com

Larry Sims (323) 436-7766
(Hair) www.eamgmt.com

Sarah Sullivan (323) 556-3455 / (310) 408-0861
(Makeup) FAX (323) 556-3456
www.margaretmaldonado.com

Veronica Sjoen (323) 933-0200
www.artistuntied.com

Tracey Sutter (310) 839-8722
(Manicurist) www.cloutieragency.com

Ben Skervin (323) 297-0250
(Hair) www.magnetla.com

Michelle Tabor Ramos (323) 931-2745
www.aimartist.com

Mikal Sky (310) 694-7933 / (310) 663-1914 / FAX (213) 748-3654
www.skyboxmakeup.com
(Body Painting, Colorist, Grooming, Hair, Makeup, Manicurist, Special FX Makeup & Wigs)

Solina Tabrizi (818) 284-6423
(Hair) www.italentco.com

Sparkle Tafao (323) 935-8455
(Makeup) www.ms-management.com

Robin Slater (310) 345-7095
www.imakeup.com
(Beauty Makeup, Body Painting, High Def Air Brush Makeup & Special FX Makeup)

Rob Talty (323) 297-0250
www.magnetla.com

Tamami (323) 466-2007
(Makeup) www.therexagency.com

Dina Sliwiak (323) 468-2240
www.nyoffice.net

Bernhard Tamme (310) 839-8722
(Hair) www.cloutieragency.com

Elizabeth Sloan (213) 706-3562
www.elizabethsloan.com/make-up
(Body Painting, Grooming, Hair & Makeup)

TAMU Artist Agency (310) 721-0735
137 S. Robertson Blvd., Ste. 111   FAX (323) 571-3498
Beverly Hills, CA 90211   www.tamuartistagency.com
(Reps for Hair and Makeup Artists)

Erin Lee Smith (323) 462-5000
(Makeup) www.traceymattingly.com

Ryan Taniguchi (323) 931-2745
www.aimartist.com

Patti Song (310) 839-8722
c/o Cloutier Remix Agency   FAX (310) 839-8730
2632 La Cienega Avenue
Los Angeles, CA 90034
(Colorist)   www.cloutierremix.com/pattisong

Deborah Taylor (818) 222-5200
(Makeup) www.schneiderentertainment.com

Jamie Taylor (310) 276-0777
www.thewallgroup.com

Hee Soo (323) 466-2007
(Makeup) www.therexagency.com

Peggy Teague (818) 704-1410 / (818) 929-8814
(Makeup) FAX (818) 704-1410

Kimberley Spiteri (818) 222-5200
www.schneiderentertainment.com

Sheri Darlyn Terry (310) 998-1977
(Makeup) www.celestineagency.com

John Stapleton (323) 931-2745
(Makeup) www.aimartist.com

Peg Thielen (818) 506-6161
(Grooming & Makeup) www.pegthielen.com

Robert Steinken (310) 839-8722
(Hair) www.cloutieragency.com

Benjamin Thigpen (310) 274-0032
(Hair) www.artistsbytimothypriano.com

Molly Stern (310) 276-0777
(Makeup) www.thewallgroup.com

Dominie Till (818) 206-0144
www.allcrewagency.com

Fiona Stiles (310) 276-0777
(Makeup) www.thewallgroup.com

Kim Todd (323) 299-4043
www.dionperonneau.com

Tanya Stine (323) 299-4043
(Hair) www.dionperonneau.com

D. Garen Tolkin (323) 436-7766
(Grooming, Hair & Makeup) www.eamgmt.com

Randy Stodghill (323) 856-8540
(Hair) www.opusbeauty.com

David Tolls (310) 246-0446
www.workgroup-ltd.com

Mitch Stone (310) 839-8722
(Grooming & Hair) www.cloutieragency.com

Francesca Tolot (310) 839-8722
(Makeup) www.cloutieragency.com

Lisa Storey (310) 276-0777
(Makeup) www.thewallgroup.com

Peter Tothpal   (310) 601-2355
www.lesliealyson.com

Tracey Mattingly, LLC   (323) 462-5000
(Reps for Hair and Makeup Artists)   FAX (323) 462-5001
www.traceymattingly.com

Anh-Co Tran   (323) 446-2007
(Hair)   www.therexagency.com

Travisean   (323) 931-2745
www.aimartist.com

Patrick Tumey   (310) 998-1977
(Makeup)   www.celestineagency.com

Mary Ann Valdes   (818) 284-6423
www.italentco.com

Matthew VanLeeuwen   (323) 297-0250
(Makeup)   www.magnetla.com

Leah Vautrot   (818) 284-6423
(Makeup)   www.italentco.com

Terrie Velazquez-Owen   (818) 284-6423
(Hair)   www.italentco.com

Kim Verbeck   (310) 276-0777
(Grooming)   www.thewallgroup.com

Melanie Verkins   (818) 388-2204

Robert Vetica   (323) 297-0250
(Hair)   www.magnetla.com

Sylvia Viau   (310) 839-8722
(Grooming, Hair & Makeup)   www.cloutieragency.com

Lona Vigi   (323) 297-0250
(Hair)   www.magnetla.com

Johnny Villanueva   (323) 462-5000
(Hair)   www.traceymattingly.com

Anne Visconti   (323) 934-9810
(Hair & Wigs)

Gina Viviano   (310) 274-0032
(Manicurist)   www.artistsbytimothypriano.com

Bertrand W.   (323) 462-5000
(Hair)   www.traceymattingly.com

Vickie Waite   (805) 427-2310
FAX (805) 492-3680
www.bridalbeauty.info

Ewan Walker   (323) 299-4043
(Makeup)   www.dionperonneau.com

The Wall Group LA   (310) 276-0777
518 N. La Cienega Blvd.   FAX (310) 276-0107
Los Angeles, CA 90048   www.thewallgroup.com
(Reps for Hair and Makeup Artists)

Melissa Walsh   (323) 549-3100
www.beautyandphoto.com

Emily Kate Warren   (323) 445-4910
www.artists-services.com

Greta Weatherby   (323) 445-4910
www.artists-services.com

Charlene Wee   (818) 625-5985
(Makeup)

Rick Wellman   (310) 274-0032
(Colorist)   www.artistsbytimothypriano.com

                   (818) 415-7212
Angie Wells   (800) 372-7994
(Makeup & Special FX Makeup)   www.angiewells.com

Kyle White   (310) 274-0032
www.artistsbytimothypriano.com

Prisca Wille   (323) 868-5760
FAX (323) 257-0696
www.prisca.com

Cindy Williams   (310) 601-2355
www.lesliealyson.com

Kurt Williams   (310) 285-9000
(Special FX Makeup)   www.wmeentertainment.com

Lindsey Williams   (310) 274-0032
www.artistsbytimothypriano.com

Shannon Grey Williams   (310) 822-2898
www.rougeartists.com

William Williams   (323) 466-2007
(Hair)   www.therexagency.com

Michelle Wilson   (323) 578-2133
www.michelledoesmakeup.com
(Grooming, Hair & Makeup)

                   (805) 984-7298
Ellen Wong   (310) 570-7242
(Body Painting, Grooming & Makeup)   www.ellenwong.net

Natalie Wood   (818) 206-0144
(Makeup)   www.allcrewagency.com

Rachel Wood   (310) 274-0032
(Makeup)   www.artistsbytimothypriano.com

                   (310) 246-0446
Workgroup, Ltd.   (415) 567-7023
(Reps for Hair and Makeup Artists)   FAX (415) 674-1950
www.workgroup-ltd.com

Mitsy Yamaguchi   (310) 822-2898
(Makeup)   www.rougeartists.com

Negin Zand   (310) 276-0777
(Colorist)   www.thewallgroup.com

                   (323) 937-1010
Zenobia Agency, Inc.   (888) 639-6917
130 S. Highland Ave.   FAX (323) 937-1133
Los Angeles, CA 90036   www.zenobia.com
(Reps for Hair and Makeup Artists)

Mitch Ackerman (310) 623-5500	**Bonnie Benwick** (310) 623-5500
www.montanartists.com	www.montanartists.com
Penny Adams (310) 288-8000	**Linda Berenstein Mason** (323) 650-4449
(Line Producer) www.paradigmagency.com	(Line Producer)
Brian Ades (310) 503-8080	**Lester Berman** (310) 288-8000
	www.paradigmagency.com
Gilbert Adler (310) 623-5500	**Yvonne M. Bernard** (310) 382-4535
www.montanartists.com	FAX (310) 798-3001
Neal Ahern (310) 288-8000	**Tim Berry** (818) 206-0144
(Line Producer) www.paradigmagency.com	www.allcrewagency.com
All Crew Agency (818) 206-0144	**Stuart Besser** (310) 288-8000
2920 W. Olive Ave., Ste. 201 FAX (818) 206-0169	www.paradigmagency.com
Burbank, CA 91505 www.allcrewagency.com	
(Reps for Producers)	**Michael Beugg** (310) 273-6700
	www.utaproduction.com
Donald V. Allen (310) 390-5522	
FAX (310) 390-6520	(818) 506-5829
	Dolly Tarazon Billinger (818) 645-6115
(310) 374-2786	(Line Producer)
Kelly Amato (310) 600-8224	
	(310) 821-2221
Emie H. Amemiya (323) 463-3033	**Stuart Black** (310) 804-1479
Gideon Amir (310) 656-5151	**Doug Blake** (310) 656-5151
www.innovativeartists.com	www.innovativeartists.com
Ray Angelic (310) 273-6700	**Laurie Boccaccio** (213) 706-3484
www.utaproduction.com	(Line Producer)
Todd Arnow (310) 288-8000	**Adam Bohling** (310) 623-5500
www.paradigmagency.com	www.montanartists.com
(213) 741-9301	**Hope Grossman Bolois** (818) 905-7972
William Artope (310) 466-1040	FAX (818) 784-3050
FAX (213) 741-6301	
www.wildeyedent.com	**Ron Bozman** (310) 273-6700
	www.unitedtalent.com
Ken Ashe (310) 896-8681	
	Drew Bracken (818) 606-5478
Bill Bannerman (310) 285-9000	
(Line Producer) www.wmeentertainment.com	**Blair Breard** (310) 273-6700
	www.utaproduction.com
Moe Bardach (310) 623-5500	
www.montanartists.com	**Richard Brick** (310) 282-9940
	www.mirisch.com
Louise Barlow (310) 993-8172	
www.louisebarlow.com	**Adam Brightman** (310) 288-8000
	www.paradigmagency.com
Tally Barr (310) 285-9000	
(Line Producer) www.wmeentertainment.com	**Harry Bring** (310) 623-5500
	www.montanartists.com
LuAnn Barry-Goldman (310) 474-2439	
FAX (310) 474-5282	(818) 559-8656
www.1stwaveproductions.com	**Terri Lee Brook** (310) 720-3477
	FAX (818) 559-1569
Bill Beasley (310) 288-8000	
www.paradigmagency.com	**G. Mac Brown** (310) 205-5812
Steve Beers (310) 288-8000	**Pola Brown** (323) 528-2755
(Line Producer) www.paradigmagency.com	www.workhorsemediatv.com
Dana Belcastro (310) 273-6700	**Rick Brown** (310) 922-1946
www.utaproduction.com	(Line Producer)
Bernard Bellew (310) 273-6700	**Steven Brown** (310) 656-5151
www.unitedtalent.com	www.innovativeartists.com
Marc Benardout (323) 697-8154	**Pieter Jan Brugge** (310) 656-5151
FAX (413) 691-8154	www.innovativeartists.com
www.birthmarc.com	
	Gary Bryman (310) 612-6767
Robert Bennett (310) 956-0346	www.gbryman.com
www.hdrepublic.com	

Shirley Bukrey-Lloyd (Spanish)	(310) 306-1502
Patrick Burns	(818) 908-3361
Tommy Burns	(310) 623-5500 www.montanartists.com
Thomas Busch (Line Producer)	(323) 703-1333 wp-a.com
Marol Butcher	(323) 906-9088 (323) 497-0097
John Callas	(310) 393-4519 (310) 344-5334 FAX (310) 395-4412
Marie Cantin (Line Producer)	(310) 285-9000 www.wmeentertainment.com
Katie Carlson	(310) 625-6244
Don Carmody	(310) 282-9940 www.mirisch.com
Wayne Carmona	(310) 288-8000 www.paradigmagency.com
Randy Carter	(818) 242-4088 (818) 206-0144 www.allcrewagency.com/home/talent.php5?id=2
Debbie Cass	(310) 623-5500 www.montanartists.com
Mark Castro	(213) 309-7680 FAX (626) 628-3959
Bruce Catania	(818) 990-8993 www.ambitiousent.com
Ronnie Chong	(310) 288-8000 www.paradigmagency.com
Claire Best & Associates 736 Seward St. Los Angeles, CA 90038 (Reps for Producers)	(323) 601-5001 www.clairebest.net
David Coatsworth	(310) 273-6700 www.unitedtalent.com
Lisa Cochran (Line Producer)	(310) 288-8000 www.paradigmagency.com
Tim Coddington	(310) 623-5500 www.montanartists.com
Audrey S. Cohen	(310) 993-3375 (305) 385-2204 FAX (310) 208-6776
Ron Colby	(310) 623-5500 www.montanartists.com
Frank Conway	(310) 623-5500 www.montanartists.com
Mark Cooper	(323) 703-1333 wp-a.com
Lena Cordina (Line Producer)	(310) 623-5500 www.montanartists.com
John Corser	(213) 200-1477 (323) 843-2203 FAX (323) 843-9486 www.corser.com
Brian Cowan (Line Producer)	(310) 288-8000 www.paradigmagency.com

Rob Cowan (Line Producer)	(310) 288-8000 www.paradigmagency.com
Clint Cowen	(323) 497-8117
Kristen Cox	(818) 749-6608 FAX (323) 851-1659 www.16x9productions.com
Scott Craig	(323) 665-2069 (213) 364-4894
Adam Cramer	(323) 703-1333 wp-a.com
Chris Crawford (Line Producer)	(323) 912-9175 (323) 646-1375
Ruthie Crossley	(310) 918-5352
Terry Crotzer	(818) 990-8993 www.ambitiousent.com
Bill Curran	(310) 392-1035 (310) 729-4701
Michelle Currinder	(213) 703-6424
Douglas Curtis	(310) 282-9940 www.mirisch.com
Madelyn Curtis	(310) 459-8976
Russell Curtis	(818) 994-1802
Dave Darmour	(310) 393-9004 (323) 363-3930
Rick Days	(323) 221-9003
Joe Dea	(818) 990-8993 www.ambitiousent.com
Kate Dean (Line Producer)	(310) 656-5151 www.innovativeartists.com
Heather Dear (Line Producer)	(805) 699-5327
Darren Demetre	(310) 623-5500 www.montanartists.com
Maurice DePas	(818) 292-6531
Beth DePatie	(310) 288-8000 www.paradigmagency.com
Diana De Vries (Line Producer)	(323) 864-7975 FAX (310) 358-3174
Kimberly Dickens	(323) 703-1333 wp-a.com
Steve Dietrich	(818) 760-2915 (818) 422-3470 FAX (818) 980-2028
Kat Dillon	(310) 399-7839
Joe Dishner (Line Producer)	(818) 284-6423 www.italentco.com
Karen Dixon	(310) 386-8082 www.karendandcompany.com
Robert Doherty	(310) 656-5151 www.innovativeartists.com
Anita Zommers Dollens	(310) 912-1798

Producers

Connie Dolphin (310) 656-5151 www.innovativeartists.com	Barry Fink (310) 880-0311 (Line Producer)
Carr Donald (818) 419-7400 FAX (818) 508-1193	Preston Fischer (310) 623-5500 www.montanartists.com
Brian Donnelly (310) 880-9400	Debbie A. Fisher (310) 475-8767
Sarah J. Donohue (818) 206-0144 www.allcrewagency.com	Karin Fittante (323) 937-1010 www.zenobia.com
Gary Dorf (310) 476-8380 (310) 740-0995 FAX (818) 789-6435	Aimee Flaherty (818) 206-0144 www.allcrewagency.com
Janice Doskey (914) 261-2267 (866) 545-8878 (French)	Michael Flynn (310) 273-6700 www.utaproduction.com
Lori Douglas (310) 288-8000 (Line Producer) www.paradigmagency.com	D.J. Ford (323) 731-4214 (818) 621-5184
Ned Doyle (310) 480-4190 (973) 763-6679	Jan Foster (310) 623-5500 (Line Producer) www.montanartists.com
Henri Dragonas (323) 896-5889 (Line Producer)	Michael Fottrell (323) 703-1333 wp-a.com
Peggy Dunn (310) 200-3979 (310) 398-4867	JP Fox (310) 351-2549
James R. Dyer (310) 273-6700 www.unitedtalent.com	Billy Frank (818) 981-2327 FAX (818) 981-2440 www.mihp.tv
Elaine Dysinger (310) 656-5151 www.innovativeartists.com	Katterli Frauenfelder (310) 395-9550 www.skouras.com
Bob Engelman (310) 288-8000 www.paradigmagency.com	Ruth Frazier (818) 848-9129 (818) 288-0815 FAX (818) 558-5772
Buddy Enright (310) 623-5500 (Line Producer) www.montanartists.com	Franny Freiberger (818) 415-5554 (Line Producer)
Edy H. Enriquez (310) 836-9011 (323) 252-0904 FAX (310) 836-9010 www.x1fx.com	Jeff Freilich (310) 288-8000 (Line Producer) www.paradigmagency.com
	Ron French (310) 288-8000 (Line Producer) www.paradigmagency.com
Jose Luis Escolar (310) 623-5500 www.montanartists.com	Louis G. Friedman (310) 656-5151 www.innovativeartists.com
Leslie M. Evers (310) 600-7373 (Line Producer)	Nona Sue Friedman (323) 468-9975 (310) 562-2161
Marty Ewing (323) 703-1333 (Line Producer) wp-a.com	Bruce Fritzberg (818) 231-2260 (972) 735-9878
Ross T. Fanger (323) 703-1333 wp-a.com	Ursula Gabel Baird (310) 489-6352
Dawn Fanning Moore (626) 695-1112 (626) 791-5811 FAX (626) 791-9611 (Line Producer)	Karen Gainer (818) 395-6131
	Michael Gallant (310) 623-5500 www.montanartists.com
Denise Daniels Fanning (213) 399-9831	Debbie Galloway (818) 424-2353 (Line Producer)
Franny Faull (310) 614-0992	Pat Garvin (310) 453-2597
Tom Fauntleroy (805) 570-8320 (805) 898-1035	Kent Gates (818) 667-5368 www.freewebtown.com/callsheet/
Thom Fennessey (323) 650-2500 www.collaborationfactory.com	Loucas George (310) 288-8000 www.paradigmagency.com
Greg Ferguson (818) 519-8764	The Gersh Agency (310) 274-6611 (212) 997-1818 9465 Wilshire Blvd., Sixth Fl. www.gershagency.com Beverly Hills, CA 90212 (Reps for Producers)
Scott Ferguson (310) 623-5500 www.montanartists.com	
Caique Martins Ferreira (310) 623-5500 www.montanartists.com	

Ted Gidlow (Line Producer)	(310) 288-8000 www.paradigmagency.com
Jason Gilbert	(310) 804-0436
Ken Gilbert	(805) 374-6090 (805) 208-1753
Bruce Wayne Gillies	(310) 656-5151 www.innovativeartists.com
Grace Gilroy	(310) 623-5500 www.montanartists.com
Kathy Gilroy	(310) 623-5500 www.montanartists.com
Peter Giuliano	(310) 273-6700 www.unitedtalent.com
Hilary Glaholt (Line Producer)	(310) 710-2717
Cellin Gluck	(310) 382-0303 (310) 399-9898 FAX (310) 496-3046
Nanette Gobel	(310) 801-2164
Marty Gold	(818) 892-3665
Jon Goldberg	(310) 401-1122 (310) 936-2077 jongoldberg.virb.com
Phillip M. Goldfarb (Line Producer)	(310) 288-8000 www.paradigmagency.com
Jared Goldman (Line Producer)	(310) 288-8000 www.paradigmagency.com
Nigel Goldsack	(310) 285-0303 www.sandramarsh.com
Charlie Goldstein	(310) 288-8000 www.paradigmagency.com
Craig Golin	(818) 990-8993 www.ambitiousent.com
John N. Gomez	(805) 587-2982 www.johngomez.tv
Gregory E. Goodman	(310) 273-6700 www.unitedtalent.com
Arthur Gorson (Line Producer)	(323) 876-3331 www.wildindigo.tv
Janice K. Goto	(415) 990-4470 (415) 383-1225
David Grace	(310) 656-5151 www.innovativeartists.com
Robert Graf	(310) 273-6700 www.unitedtalent.com
Jeff Granbery (Segment Producer)	(213) 373-1099 (949) 515-0100 www.gstudios.net
Mark Greenberg	(310) 623-5500 www.montanartists.com
Callum Greene	(310) 273-6700 www.unitedtalent.com
Justis Greene (Line Producer)	(323) 703-1333 wp-a.com

Katy Greene	(310) 406-8800
Susan Gross	(310) 829-6202
Megan Gutman	(310) 574-9591 FAX (310) 564-7766 www.megagproductions.com
Jacqueline Hakim	(310) 871-7181
Naia Hall	(323) 650-4893 (530) 362-2201
Ken Halsband (Line Producer)	(310) 288-8000 www.paradigmagency.com
Greg A. Hampson (Line Producer)	(310) 288-8000 www.paradigmagency.com
Shari Hanson	(415) 370-9600
John Hardy (Line Producer)	(310) 395-9550 www.skouras.com
Jim Hart	(310) 288-8000 www.paradigmagency.com
Joel Hatch (Line Producer)	(323) 703-1333 wp-a.com
Tracy Hauser	(310) 293-2752
Jamie Haynes	(310) 570-1150 FAX (310) 827-7367
Jonathan Haze	(818) 763-3041 (818) 314-7997 FAX (818) 763-3042
Allison Heath	(310) 729-3302
Bob Heath (Line Producer)	(310) 288-8000 www.paradigmagency.com
Laura Brown Heflin	(310) 322-0007 (310) 779-7955
Youree Henley	(323) 497-9600
Kendall Henry (Line Producer)	(323) 462-5934 (626) 688-0409
Peter Heslop (Line Producer)	(310) 288-8000 www.paradigmagency.com
Paul Hettler	(415) 608-6758 (415) 381-1606
Cynthia Hill	(310) 753-9991 www.artagogo.net
Michael Hissrich (Line Producer)	(310) 285-9000 www.wmeentertainment.com
Alex Ho (Line Producer)	(310) 285-9000 www.wmeentertainment.com
Victor Ho	(310) 285-0303 www.sandramarsh.com
Ulla Hoeller (French & German)	(323) 394-1248
Sam Hoffman (Line Producer)	(310) 288-8000 www.paradigmagency.com
Lisa Hollingshead (Line Producer)	(310) 880-7556 (310) 454-0861

Antonia Holt	(323) 871-0201
(French)	(213) 810-5059
John Hopgood	(818) 760-6923
(Line Producer)	
Craig Houchin	(818) 951-5959
	www.craighouchin.com
Chantal Houle	(310) 953-9166
(French)	www.chantalhoule.com
Scott Howard	(818) 789-5032
Michael Huens	(323) 365-5797
	www.wolvesatthedoor.com
Holly D. Hughes	(818) 951-6889
Tim Iacofano	(310) 656-5151
	www.innovativeartists.com
Joseph Iberti	(310) 282-9940
	www.mirisch.com

International Creative Management - ICM
(310) 550-4000
www.icmtalent.com
10250 Constellation Blvd.
Los Angeles, CA 90067
(Reps for Producers)

Caroline Jaczko	(310) 288-8000
	www.paradigmagency.com
Tracey Jeffrey	(310) 623-5500
	www.montanartists.com
Bill Johnson	(310) 623-5500
	www.montanartists.com
Polly Johnson	(310) 721-1276
(Line Producer)	
Bronston Jones	(310) 849-4994
	www.attackads.tv
Stephen Jones	(310) 273-6700
	www.unitedtalent.com
Anna Joseph	(310) 628-9233
John Joseph	(818) 990-8993
	www.ambitiousent.com
Georgia Kacandes	(310) 273-6700
	www.unitedtalent.com
Elena Kakoullis	(213) 446-6262
	FAX (213) 626-5330
Mark Kalbfeld	(310) 497-1645
	(818) 879-9955
Avram Butch Kaplan	(310) 656-5151
	www.innovativeartists.com
Dan Kaplow	(310) 285-9000
(Line Producer)	www.wmeentertainment.com
Tom Karnowski	(310) 623-5500
	www.montanartists.com
Jan Katz Black	(310) 821-2221
	(310) 804-0913
Amy Kaufman	(310) 285-9000
(Line Producer)	www.wmeentertainment.com
Doron Kauper	(818) 253-1626
	(818) 907-6028
	FAX (818) 804-5121

Dessa Kaye	(818) 766-7318
Richard Kaylor	(310) 463-3845
	www.richkaylor.com
Barbara Kelly	(310) 288-8000
	www.paradigmagency.com
Nate Kelly	(310) 623-5500
	www.montanartists.com
Jay Kelman	(310) 390-4747
	(310) 386-0098
	FAX (310) 915-6650
Kristy Kessler	(310) 968-7713
Ric Kidney	(310) 273-6700
	www.unitedtalent.com
Todd King	(310) 285-9000
(Line Producer)	www.wmeentertainment.com
Nancy Kissock	(310) 475-5615
	FAX (310) 475-5615
Michael Klick	(310) 204-2986
	(310) 720-2986
	FAX (310) 204-5155
Rob Knox	(323) 876-6435
	FAX (323) 446-8339
Buzz Koenig	(310) 282-9940
	www.mirisch.com
Dan Kolsrud	(310) 273-6700
	www.utaproduction.com
David Koplan	(310) 285-9000
(Line Producer)	www.wmeentertainment.com
Chris Kraft	(323) 791-5135
	FAX (323) 372-3614
Erwin Kramer	(310) 446-1866
	(310) 266-8146
(Line Producer)	FAX (310) 446-1856
	www.erwinkramer.com
Don Kurt	(310) 623-5500
	www.montanartists.com
Roger La Page	(818) 368-3243
	(818) 468-7191
	FAX (818) 368-3243
Coni Lancaster	(310) 749-8962
	(310) 823-3115
Patti Lancaster	(310) 479-1424
	FAX (310) 445-3301
Christopher Landry	(818) 206-0144
	www.allcrewagency.com
Cleve Landsberg	(323) 703-1333
(Line Producer)	wp-a.com
Kathy Landsberg	(310) 288-8000
(Line Producer)	www.paradigmagency.com
Henry Lange	(310) 288-8000
(Line Producer)	www.paradigmagency.com
Christine Larson-Nitzsche	(310) 288-8000
	www.paradigmagency.com
Marc Lasko	(310) 451-0301
Bill Latka	(310) 990-1938

David Leaf	(818) 990-8993
	www.ambitiousent.com
Julien Lemaitre	(310) 395-9550
	www.skouras.com
Mary Leonard	(626) 791-9790
	www.maryleonard.net
Darcy Leslie-Parsons	(310) 963-6629
	(310) 736-1663
	www.brewsterparsons.com
Deven LeTendre	(818) 414-2020
	FAX (626) 577-6814
Diane Leuci	(631) 827-2784
(Line Producer)	
Peter Lhotka	(310) 623-5500
	www.montanartists.com
Herb Linsey	(323) 874-9487
Patty Long	(310) 474-4585
(Line Producer)	www.ddatalent.com
Louise Lovegrove	(310) 623-5500
	www.montanartists.com
Sonny Lowe	(310) 994-8097
(French)	
Lindy Lucas	(310) 877-1066
	www.lindylucas.com
Martha Lucas	(323) 376-9699
Jose Ludlow	(310) 623-5500
	www.montanartists.com
Scott Luhrsen	(323) 871-0201
	(323) 791-1909
	FAX (323) 871-0315
Margot Lulick	(310) 288-8000
(Line Producer)	www.paradigmagency.com
Scott Lumpkin	(310) 288-8000
	www.paradigmagency.com
Tom Luse	(310) 623-5500
	www.montanartists.com
Don MacBain	(310) 910-1220
Peter MacGregor-Scott	(310) 282-9940
	www.mirisch.com
Neil Machlis	(310) 282-9940
	www.mirisch.com
Paul Manix	(818) 414-2229
Earl Mann	(818) 906-3309
	(818) 371-1135
John Marias	(310) 394-4214
	(310) 245-4204
Anthony Mark	(310) 623-5500
	www.montanartists.com
Patrick Markey	(310) 623-5500
	www.montanartists.com
Paul Marks	(310) 623-5500
	www.montanartists.com
Gina Marsh	(310) 285-0303
	www.sandramarsh.com

Theresa Marth	(818) 760-7174
	(818) 404-9314
Cherylanne Martin	(310) 623-5500
	www.montanartists.com
Keegan Martin	(818) 990-8993
	www.ambitiousent.com
Sandy Martin	(323) 851-3755
	(213) 509-7722
	FAX (323) 851-4359
Fatima Martins	(310) 899-0923
(Portuguese & Spanish)	
Karyn McCarthy	(310) 273-6700
	www.utaproduction.com
Lisa McClelland	(310) 457-3290
	(310) 924-2022
Maura McCoy	(310) 266-7511
	(310) 857-6672
	FAX (310) 301-3575
Michael McDonnell	(323) 703-1333
	wp-a.com
Christopher McKinnon	(310) 572-7929
	(213) 494-7404
	www.afewgoodideas.com
Josh McLaglen	(310) 273-6700
	www.utaproduction.com
Mark McNair	(310) 273-6700
	www.utaproduction.com
Craig McNeil	(310) 288-8000
	www.paradigmagency.com
Jerry McNutt	(818) 990-8993
	www.ambitiousent.com
Adam Merims	(310) 273-6700
	www.unitedtalent.com
Anita Miller	(805) 927-3566
Bobby Miller	(949) 494-3263
	FAX (949) 494-7945
Jeff Miller	(323) 851-2001
	(310) 344-9404
	FAX (323) 851-2061
Terry Miller	(310) 288-8000
(Line Producer)	www.paradigmagency.com
Leslie Miretti	(310) 399-2000
The Mirisch Agency	(310) 282-9940
8840 Wilshire Blvd., Ste. 100	FAX (310) 282-0702
Los Angeles, CA 90211	www.mirisch.com
(Reps for Producers)	
Scott Mislan	(310) 880-9043
	www.imdb.com/name/nm0006502/
Kim Monaco	(310) 994-1529
Philip A. Mondello	(213) 399-7624
Montana Artists Agency	(310) 623-5500
9150 Wilshire Blvd., Ste. 100	FAX (310) 623-5515
Beverly Hills, CA 90212	www.montanartists.com
(Reps for Producers)	
Alexander J. Moon	(323) 428-8641

Leanne Moore (Line Producer)	(310) 288-8000 www.paradigmagency.com	**Kerry Orent**	(310) 273-6700 www.unitedtalent.com
Mark Moran (Line Producer)	(310) 285-9000 www.wmeentertainment.com	**Ben Ormand** (Line Producer)	(310) 285-9000 www.wmeentertainment.com
Justin Moritt	(818) 206-0144 www.allcrewagency.com	**Ken Ornstein** (Line Producer)	(310) 288-8000 www.paradigmagency.com
Sharon Morov	(310) 383-6572	**Wayne Nelson Page**	(818) 990-8993 www.ambitiousent.com
Caylyn Eastin Morris	(310) 963-1522	**Paul Papanek**	(323) 732-0776
JJ Morris	(323) 868-8806	**Brian Parker**	(310) 656-5151 www.innovativeartists.com
Robyn L. Moskow (Line Producer)	(562) 434-6918 (213) 910-8855	**George Parra**	(310) 623-5500 www.montanartists.com
Samson Mucke	(310) 656-5151 www.innovativeartists.com	**Beth Pearson**	(310) 567-5725
Jack Murray	(310) 285-9000 www.wmeentertainment.com	**Emily Perez**	(310) 804-7479 FAX (818) 352-2667 www.emilyperez.net
The Murtha Agency 1025 Colorado Ave., Ste. B Santa Monica, CA 90401 (Reps for Producers)	(310) 395-4600 FAX (310) 395-4622 www.murthaagency.com	**David Persoff** (Line Producer)	(323) 791-3840
Matt Myers (Line Producer)	(310) 288-8000 www.paradigmagency.com	**Lou Phillips** (Line Producer)	(310) 288-8000 www.paradigmagency.com
Tina Nakane	(213) 500-4700	**Denise Pouchet**	(818) 415-5044 (818) 566-1381 FAX (818) 566-1381
Todd Nelson	(213) 384-0810 (213) 220-1028 www.braska.com	**Rick Powers**	(310) 710-9397
Merilee Newman	(310) 384-6184	**Greg Prange**	(310) 288-8000 www.paradigmagency.com
David Nicksay	(310) 273-6700 www.unitedtalent.com	**Erik Press**	(213) 324-2366
Elizabeth Nicole	(323) 937-1010 www.zenobia.com	**Patricia Priest**	(727) 612-6277 (323) 466-3288
Beryt Nisenson (Line Producer)	(713) 256-8044 (323) 638-5870 FAX (713) 400-9151 www.berytn.com	**Jack Provost**	(818) 988-8150 (818) 422-0998 FAX (818) 988-8152 www.jackprovost.com
Kevin Noonan	(310) 251-6880	**Michael Rachmil**	(310) 288-8000 www.paradigmagency.com
Vanessa Norris-Nalle	(818) 437-0470 (714) 849-6491	**Nakiya Ramsey**	(310) 500-0223
Nellie Nugiel (Line Producer)	(310) 285-9000 www.wmeentertainment.com	**Ron Rapiel**	(310) 390-5454 (310) 890-1100
M. Margaret O'Brien-Sparks	(818) 388-9726 (818) 997-1993 FAX (818) 997-1993	**David Reid**	(310) 623-5500 www.montanartists.com
Gary Odom	(818) 990-8993 www.ambitiousent.com	**Joseph Reidy**	(310) 395-9550 www.skouras.com
Colleen O'Donnell	(818) 591-1953 (818) 437-1133	**Kevin Reidy**	(310) 656-5151 www.innovativeartists.com
Jennifer Ogden	(310) 282-9940 www.mirisch.com	**Craig Repass**	(310) 420-1955
Erin O'Malley (Line Producer)	(310) 285-9000 www.wmeentertainment.com	**Craig Respol**	(818) 346-4641 (310) 776-1229
Pamela O'Mara	(310) 901-5515 (310) 545-0136	**Kathryn L. Rhodes**	(310) 475-0709
Karri O'Reilly	(323) 691-5539 www.karrioco.com	**Guy Riedel**	(310) 288-8000 www.paradigmagency.com
		Christina Ritzmann	(310) 454-4805 (310) 613-4854 FAX (310) 454-4818

Gary Robinson	(310) 247-0818
	FAX (310) 858-2254
	www.sharpcut.com
	(818) 519-4660
Denise Rocchietti	(818) 783-3214
Vicki Dee Rock	(310) 288-8000
	www.paradigmagency.com
David Roessell	(310) 288-8000
(Line Producer)	www.paradigmagency.com
	(310) 488-1959
Karen Rohrbacher	(310) 459-4708
(Line Producer)	
Jake Rose	(310) 288-8000
(Line Producer)	www.paradigmagency.com
Louise Rosner	(310) 273-6700
	www.unitedtalent.com
Jennifer Roth	(310) 273-6700
	www.utaproduction.com
Richard Rothschild	(310) 288-8000
(Line Producer)	www.paradigmagency.com
Edward Royce	(949) 752-7761
	FAX (949) 752-2034
	www.royceentertainmentgroup.com
Ann Ruark	(310) 273-6700
	www.unitedtalent.com
Kelly Andrea Rubin	(310) 498-1805
	www.signature-ent.com
	(310) 392-2302
Danny Rubio	(310) 435-9260
	FAX (310) 392-2302
	(310) 503-6911
Steve Ruggieri	(818) 368-0666
	FAX (818) 360-0237
Joel Sadilek	(310) 282-9940
	www.mirisch.com
Steven Saeta	(310) 285-9000
(Line Producer)	www.wmeentertainment.com
Richard Sampson	(323) 703-1333
	wp-a.com
Jeremiah Samuels	(310) 273-6700
	www.unitedtalent.com
Amy M. Samuelson	(310) 463-1238
	www.amysamuelson.com
	(323) 939-9309
Rayna Saslove	(323) 440-5827
Malcolm Scerri-Ferrante	(310) 623-5500
	www.montanartists.com
Richard Schlesinger	(310) 285-0303
	www.sandramarsh.com
Robert Schmidt	(818) 842-1929
Sascha Schneider	(310) 288-8000
(Line Producer)	www.paradigmagency.com
	(310) 577-0877
Sarah Schoessler Faura	(310) 259-0600
	FAX (310) 919-1877
John D. Schofield	(310) 273-6700
	www.unitedtalent.com

Larry Schreiner	(310) 874-2164
Ellen Schwartz	(323) 703-1333
	wp-a.com
Ron Schwary	(310) 285-9000
(Line Producer)	www.wmeentertainment.com
Jan Scott	(310) 833-1770
Don Scotti	(310) 990-0646
Jeffrey J. Scruton	(310) 454-8290
	FAX (310) 459-4051
Paige Seidel	(213) 810-6526
	(310) 452-9644
Hani Selim	(310) 480-8738
	FAX (310) 452-9655
	www.concreteimages.com
Larry Serraino	(661) 607-6528
	FAX (661) 254-6402
Kim Shapiro	(818) 389-6888
Robert Shapiro	(310) 282-9940
	www.mirisch.com
Richard Sharkey	(310) 623-5500
	www.montanartists.com
Roee Sharon	(323) 447-4618
Kyra Shelgren	(818) 207-4330
(Line Producer)	
Dona Shine	(818) 519-7972
(Line Producer)	
Jim Shippee	(310) 480-5988
Michael Shores	(323) 791-9433
(Line Producer)	www.heavenanimage.com
Jason Shubb	(310) 288-8000
(Line Producer)	www.paradigmagency.com
Ira Shuman	(310) 273-6700
	www.utaproduction.com
Thom Sidoti	(323) 957-1454
	FAX (323) 871-0610
	www.agavefilms.com
Scott Siegal	(213) 713-0154
	(213) 760-4322
Marc Siegel	(323) 653-3550
	FAX (323) 653-3553
Jeffrey Silver	(310) 273-6700
	www.unitedtalent.com
	(310) 739-7356
Tim Silver	(310) 399-5122
Robert D. Simon	(310) 656-5151
	www.innovativeartists.com
Jimmy Simons	(310) 288-8000
	www.paradigmagency.com
Eric Siss	(310) 628-7226
Jay Sisson	(213) 820-3075
(Spanish)	
Enzo Sisti	(310) 395-4600
	www.murthaagency.com

Producers

Lindsay Skutch	(805) 341-3554 (805) 687-9852
Al Smith	(310) 452-3751 (310) 864-8550
Iain Smith	(310) 285-0303 www.sandramarsh.com
Jeanne Stack (Line Producer)	(310) 456-3272 (310) 600-1599
Marlon Staggs	(213) 479-9384
Suzanne Stanford	(310) 989-5787
Patrick Stapleton	(310) 623-5500 www.montanartists.com
Sharon Starr	(818) 994-7017
Peter Steen	(818) 990-8993 www.ambitiousent.com
Gregg Stern	(310) 292-0915 FAX (505) 982-0163
Nicolas Stern	(310) 273-6700 www.utaproduction.com
Philip Steuer	(310) 273-6700 www.unitedtalent.com
Brad Stevenson	(213) 716-7893 (818) 222-8251
Michael Stricks	(310) 288-8000 www.paradigmagency.com
Cristen Car Strubbe	(310) 273-6700 www.utaproduction.com
Andrew Sugerman	(310) 288-8000 www.paradigmagency.com
Bergen Swanson (Line Producer)	(310) 623-5500 www.montanartists.com
Joel Tabbush	(818) 481-9396
Michele Tamme	(818) 804-8797
Maryann Tanedo	(310) 288-7868
Sal Tassone (French, Italian & Spanish)	(310) 455-7822 (310) 403-0007 FAX (310) 455-1245
Lisa Tauscher	(310) 422-7981
Eileen Terry (Line Producer)	(310) 663-9370 (808) 780-8707
Sheridan Thayer	(310) 623-5500 www.montanartists.com
Joshua Throne	(310) 623-5500 www.montanartists.com
Debbie Tietjen	(310) 418-3632
Michael Tillman	(323) 938-1756 (323) 788-3383
Debby Timmons	(818) 203-5655
Lisa Timmons	(818) 708-8589

Steven Tobenkin	(310) 621-1122 FAX (310) 388-1403
Peter Tobyansen	(310) 273-6700 www.utaproduction.com
Joanne Toll	(310) 285-9000 www.wmeentertainment.com
Ken Topolsky	(310) 288-8000 www.paradigmagency.com
Marvin G. Towns	(818) 206-0144 www.allcrewagency.com
Clayton Townsend	(310) 395-9550 www.skouras.com
Lee Trask	(310) 396-5023
Judy Trotter	(805) 705-2150
Maureen Tunney (Line Producer)	(818) 907-9456 (818) 645-7149
Randy Turrow	(818) 206-0144 www.allcrewagency.com
Jeff Tuttle	(626) 824-1222 011 (61) 4 5722 2464
Richard Vane	(310) 273-6700 www.unitedtalent.com
Kelly Van Horn	(818) 762-3810 (310) 282-9940 www.mirisch.com
Pete Vanlaw	(818) 642-3810 FAX (818) 769-2847 www.western-branch.com
Kevan Van Thompson (Line Producer)	(323) 703-1333 wp-a.com
Jim Van Wyck	(310) 282-9940 www.mirisch.com
Chrisann Verges	(310) 273-6700 www.unitedtalent.com
Susan Vogelfang (Line Producer)	(310) 306-2648
John Vohlers	(310) 623-5500 www.montanartists.com
Chip Vucelich (Line Producer)	(310) 623-5500 www.montanartists.com
Allan Wachs	(310) 589-4841 (310) 467-5131
Steve Wakefield	(310) 623-5500 www.montanartists.com
Mark Walejko	(310) 344-8949
E. Bennett Walsh	(310) 285-0303 www.sandramarsh.com
Peter Ware	(310) 288-8000 www.paradigmagency.com
Jeff Waxman	(310) 273-6700 www.unitedtalent.com
Francine Weiner (Line Producer)	(818) 419-4800

Bobby Weinstein   (310) 306-1960
FAX (310) 306-1820

Danielle Weinstock   (310) 288-8000
(Line Producer)   www.paradigmagency.com

Dara Weintraub   (310) 273-6700
www.unitedtalent.com

Bonnie Weis   (310) 623-5500
(Line Producer)   www.montanartists.com

Phyllis Weisband-Fibus   (818) 726-2611
(818) 760-8111
FAX (818) 760-8112

Alice West   (310) 288-8000
(Line Producer)   www.paradigmagency.com

Jaki West   (310) 374-2082
(Line Producer)

Jon Douglas West   (818) 761-4488
(818) 915-4746
FAX (818) 761-2112

Kathy Wheelock   (818) 901-0987

Sara E. White   (310) 623-5500
www.montanartists.com

Ree Whitford   (818) 424-9988
(Line Producer)   www.reewhitford.com

Shannon Wickliffe   (323) 422-8834
(619) 961-5669
(Line Producer)   www.shannonwickliffe.com

Jan Wieringa   (323) 363-1110

William C. Wiles   (949) 702-3313
(949) 640-6246

Bob Williams   (310) 623-5500
(Line Producer)   www.montanartists.com

Michael Williams   (818) 206-0144
www.allcrewagency.com

Shawn Williamson   (310) 273-6700
www.utaproduction.com

Bill Wilson   (310) 623-5500
(Line Producer)   www.montanartists.com

Tom Wilson   (323) 662-7976
www.nobodyproductions.com

William W. Wilson   (310) 623-5500
www.montanartists.com

Ken Winber   (310) 463-5576
(515) 720-3985

Tony Winley   (310) 623-5500
www.montanartists.com

Ralph Winter   (323) 703-1333
(Line Producer)   wp-a.com

Stan Wlodkowski   (310) 273-6700
www.unitedtalent.com

David Wolfson   (818) 371-5678
(512) 345-5197
FAX (512) 345-5668
www.spoonfilms.com

Jason Wolk   (213) 804-4743
(Spanish)   www.jasonwolk.net

Johanna Woollcott   (323) 856-0352
(310) 592-6120

Steve Woroniecki   (310) 344-1442

WPA - Worldwide
Production Agency   (323) 703-1333
5358 Melrose Ave.   FAX (323) 703-1334
West Office Bldg., Ste. 209W   wp-a.com
Hollywood, CA 90038
(Reps for Line Producers)

Craig Wyrick-Solari   (310) 288-8000
(Line Producer)   www.paradigmagency.com

Diana Young   (310) 862-4201
(310) 990-9503
www.bajalaprod.com

Gabrielle Yuro   (310) 500-8153

Meredith Zamsky   (310) 623-5500
www.montanartists.com

Raymond Zarro   (310) 460-2424
FAX (310) 399-7614

Don Zepfel   (310) 282-9940
www.mirisch.com

Jack Ziga   (323) 664-9862
(323) 465-9862

Joel R. Zimmerman   (310) 993-5703
www.joelzimmerman.com

Ray Zimmerman   (310) 285-0303
www.sandramarsh.com

Leslie Zurla   (818) 762-4346
(818) 207-1743
(Line Producer)   FAX (818) 506-8483

Beth Alonso	(310) 228-8268
	FAX (866) 291-0439
Lisa Azuma	(310) 430-3143
(Japanese)	
	(310) 600-9625
Lisa Bemel	(212) 452-2314
Pepper Carlson	(310) 261-4099
	FAX (310) 681-0238
	www.peppercarlson.com
	(818) 766-3974
Julie Clark	(818) 692-5631
Danielle Flores	(323) 953-6408
Tambre Leighn	(310) 994-4043
	www.coachingbytambre.com

Katie Mustard	(310) 285-9000
	www.wmeentertainment.com
Michyl-Shannon Quilty	(818) 415-7359
	www.imdb.com/name/nm1025085/
Patricia M. Soto	(310) 641-1300
Shawn Tolleson	(310) 880-0144
Ann G. Troy	(805) 729-1923
Lois Walker	(323) 467-1067
Lisa Yesko	(818) 551-0132
Julie Zafiratos	(323) 497-9796
	www.imdb.com/name/nm1270657/

Brian Ades (310) 503-8080 (UPM)	**Laurie Devine** (818) 968-2806 (UPM)
Gonul Aldogan (310) 600-3957	**Cathy Diaz** (818) 310-6519
Linda Aliber-Karson (323) 936-7938 (UPM)	**Kevan Dirinpour** (310) 293-2371 (French) FAX (310) 388-3184

All Crew Agency (818) 206-0144
2920 W. Olive Ave., Ste. 201 FAX (818) 206-0169
Burbank, CA 91505 www.allcrewagency.com
(Reps for Production Managers)

Janice Doskey (914) 261-2267
(French; UPM) (866) 545-8878

Bridget Allen (323) 999-1749
Sketch Pictures www.sketchpictures.com
Los Angeles, CA
(Broadcast, Film, Multimedia, SFX & VFX)

Dale Dreher (323) 777-3410
(310) 600-5020
www.mavericklocations.com

Patti Allen (310) 656-5151
www.innovativeartists.com

Don Dunn (818) 259-1589
(UPM) www.dunnfilms.com

Jodi Ehrlich (323) 462-3456
(UPM)

Laura Anderson (323) 936-4247
(UPM) (323) 646-6569

Dana Eudaily (310) 985-4532
(UPM) (310) 985-4532

Donnalee Austen (323) 333-1010
(UPM)

Stephanie E. Evans (818) 257-3220
(UPM)

Mark A. Baker (310) 623-5500
www.montanartists.com

Denise Daniels Fanning (213) 399-9831
(UPM)

Yvette Bergeron (310) 398-0199
(UPM) FAX (310) 313-4875

Andrea Fein-Primack (818) 998-4957
(310) 386-3386

Sarah Brunie (818) 243-1514

Lauri Fetch (805) 495-4021

Shirley Bukrey-Lloyd (310) 306-1502
(Spanish; UPM)

Debbie A. Fisher (310) 475-8767
(UPM)

Paul Cajero (310) 623-5500
www.montanartists.com

Angela Frisbie (818) 209-9342

Brian Campbell (310) 656-5151
www.innovativeartists.com

Cathy Gibson (310) 623-5500
www.montanartists.com

Warren Carr (310) 623-5500
www.montanartists.com

Maureen Gibson (818) 381-7810
(UPM) www.mospace.net

D.J. Carson (310) 623-5500
www.montanartists.com

Nanette Gobel (310) 801-2164

Randy Carter (818) 242-4088
(818) 206-0144
www.allcrewagency.com/home/talent.php5?id=2
(UPM)

Rosser Goodman (323) 610-0501
(UPM) (818) 206-0144

Susan Gross (310) 829-6202

Lori Berk Chapman (213) 700-7180
(UPM) (818) 980-9040
FAX (323) 345-5866

Ari Hakim (310) 489-7739

Allison Heath (310) 729-3302
(UPM)

Devon Clark (310) 795-0237
(UPM)

Lori Hoffman (310) 621-2516
(UPM)

Chris Crawford (323) 912-9175
(UPM) (323) 646-1375

Victor Hsu (310) 273-6700
www.utaproduction.com

Crew Connection (800) 352-7397
(303) 526-4900
(Referral for Production Managers) FAX (303) 526-4901
www.crewconnection.com

Denyse Hurley (213) 623-2884
(323) 791-5399
(Production Supervisor)

Stacey Daarstad (951) 764-9225

Candes Kehn (818) 203-0313
(UPM)

Lisa Dabao (310) 283-3924

Nikolas Korda (310) 273-6700
www.utaproduction.com

Gina D'Agostino (909) 744-2618
(UPM)

Mirjam Kositchek (UPM)	(310) 702-9520
Andre Kusmierz (UPM)	(310) 415-8025
Brooke Lawrence (UPM)	(310) 560-9787
Bonnie Lena (German; UPM)	(310) 990-8223 (310) 399-2007 FAX (310) 399-2425
Josie Leonard-Straub (UPM)	(310) 552-3414 (213) 503-6123 FAX (310) 286-7850
Lindy Lucas (UPM)	(310) 877-1066 www.lindylucas.com
Byron A. Martin	(818) 206-0144 www.allcrewagency.com
Fatima Martins (Portuguese & Spanish)	(310) 899-0923
Terry Maxfield	(213) 399-0047
Jonathan McCoy	(310) 623-5500 www.montanartists.com
Stephen McDaniel (UPM)	(310) 699-1912
Susan McGonigle	(310) 770-7715
Ron McLeod	(310) 656-5151 www.innovativeartists.com
Jibralta Merrill (French; UPM)	(818) 980-2091
Moira Michiels (UPM)	(310) 963-1750
Montana Artists Agency 9150 Wilshire Blvd., Ste. 100 Beverly Hills, CA 90212 (Reps for UPMs)	(310) 623-5500 FAX (310) 623-5515 www.montanartists.com
Justin Moritt	(818) 206-0144 www.allcrewagency.com
Doreen Murphy	(818) 956-1279 (323) 573-3231 FAX (818) 956-1280
Steve Nemiroff (UPM)	(310) 473-4100 FAX (310) 473-4100
Nancy Noever (UPM)	(310) 480-8685
John O'Rourke	(323) 856-3000 www.easterntalent.net
Robert Ortiz	(310) 623-5500 www.montanartists.com
Kathy Palmer	(310) 339-0987
Hoon Park (UPM)	(310) 503-0974 FAX (310) 507-0194
Joann Perritano	(310) 623-5500 www.montanartists.com
Patrick Porter	(310) 455-0294
Nakiya Ramsey	(310) 500-0223

Craig Repass	(310) 420-1955
Scott H. Rice (UPM)	(323) 656-5006 (213) 804-4080 FAX (323) 656-0736
Pablo Richards (UPM)	(323) 868-5039
Gilbert Riley (UPM)	(310) 804-7513
Rebecca Rivo	(310) 623-5500 www.montanartists.com
Ted Robbins	(323) 816-3474
Rob Rolsky	(310) 623-5500 www.montanartists.com
Steven Rood	(310) 980-1700
Adam Roodman (UPM)	(310) 570-7775
Cecilia Roque	(310) 623-5500 www.montanartists.com
Jessica Roulston	(310) 754-9447 www.imdb.com/name/nm0745730/
Jeremy Rubin (UPM)	(818) 332-4005 www.jeremyrubin.com/resume.htm
Steve Ruggieri (UPM)	(310) 503-6911 (818) 368-0666 FAX (818) 360-0237
Michael Schlenker (UPM)	(310) 560-0274
Robert Schmidt (UPM)	(818) 842-1929
Rob Sexton	(310) 793-1097 (310) 903-6800
Kathleen E. Simons (UPM)	(818) 497-8889 (423) 239-4949
Susan Smith	(310) 821-9428 (310) 383-7357 FAX (310) 821-9428
Suzanne Stanford (UPM)	(310) 989-5787
Dawn Stennes (UPM)	(323) 394-4331
Keith Stephenson (UPM)	(323) 819-1001 (323) 654-8413 www.epiphanymedia.com
Mike Sterner (UPM)	(619) 644-3000 FAX (619) 644-3001 www.crystalpyramid.com
Jeffrey Stott (UPM)	(310) 273-6700 www.utaproduction.com
Robin Sweet (UPM)	(310) 623-5500 www.montanartists.com
Scott Thaler	(818) 206-0144 www.allcrewagency.com
Valerie Thomas (UPM)	(310) 877-3058

Joel Todaro (310) 990-7386 (UPM)	**Leslie D. Waldman** (818) 985-8976 (UPM)
Marvin G. Towns (818) 206-0144 www.allcrewagency.com	**Karen Waters** (310) 821-5636 (310) 463-5922
Randy Turrow (818) 206-0144 www.allcrewagency.com	(323) 422-8834 **Shannon Wickliffe** (619) 961-5669 (UPM) www.shannonwickliffe.com
(310) 994-2454 **James S. Unger** (323) 656-3667	**Wendy Williams** (310) 623-5500 www.montanartists.com
Gary M. Van Fleet (818) 645-3841 (UPM)	**David Witz** (310) 623-5500 (UPM) www.montanartists.com
(818) 585-3571 **Sandra Vaughan** (530) 235-1922 (UPM)	**Julie Zafiratos** (323) 497-9796 (UPM) www.imdb.com/name/nm1270657/
Andjelka Vlaisavljevic (310) 623-5500 (UPM) www.montanartists.com	

Advanced Images/Tony Haig   (310) 399-0269
                               FAX (310) 399-0269

Alex Pitt Photography   (323) 665-4492
         www.alexpittphotography.com

Charles Allen   (626) 795-1053
131 N. San Gabriel Blvd., Ste. 108 www.charlesallen.com
Pasadena, CA 91107

Anna Englert Photography   (858) 344-1771
P.O. Box 202   www.annaenglert.com
La Jolla, CA 92038

                                   (818) 201-7671
Betsy Annas   (818) 509-8400
                               FAX (818) 509-0098

                                   (310) 943-8100
ArtMix Photography   (718) 596-2400
2332 S. Centinela Ave., Ste. C FAX (310) 943-8101
Los Angeles, CA 90064   www.artmixphotography.com
(Reps for Stills Photographers)

Sherry Rayn Barnett   (818) 766-8787
                               FAX (818) 766-4587
         www.sherrybarnettphotography.com

Carl Schneider Photography   (310) 923-6565
              www.carlschneider.com

Lionel Cassini   (818) 687-3437
              www.lionelcassini.com

                                   (323) 828-1882
Saint Clic/WeeGee   (818) 606-9002
                    www.saintclic.com

                                   (818) 782-1155
Byron J. Cohen   (818) 416-9989
                 www.byronjcohen.com

David Fairchild Photography   (310) 316-5547
267 Palos Verdes Dr. West, Ste. 12
Palos Verdes Estates, CA 90274
              web.me.com/davidfairchildstudio/
David_Fairchild_Studio_Portfolio/Portfolio_1.html

Dennis Davis Photography   (213) 434-3344
110 W. Ocean Blvd., Ste. 351
Long Beach, CA 90802
              www.dennisdavisphotography.com

Jerry De Wilde   (323) 662-6491
              www.dewildephotography.com

Fernando Escovar   (818) 726-7269
                    www.fotographer.com

Kevin Estrada   (818) 381-1025
                               FAX (267) 375-2475
                    www.moviestills.net

                                   (213) 373-1099
Granbery Studios   (949) 515-0100
200 Fairway Pl.   www.gstudios.net
Costa Mesa, CA 92627

                                   (818) 508-9155
🅐 Dean Hendler   (818) 601-1177
                    www.deanhendler.com

David Henriksen   (818) 599-9823

                                   (310) 930-6335
Pierre J. Hörmann   (310) 930-2426
                               FAX (310) 568-9045
                    www.isa-worldwide.com

Jim Cox Photography   (310) 657-3600
                    www.jimcox.net

John P. Johnson   (818) 438-1035
                    www.johnjohnsonphoto.com

Kelvin Jones   (310) 390-5161
                    www.kelvinjonesphoto.com

Karl Larsen Photography   (310) 663-1206
                               FAX (617) 812-0273
                    www.karllarsen.com

Kenneth Dolin Photography   (213) 415-1838
                    www.kennethdolin.com

                                   (818) 885-1545
Kubeisy Photography   (888) 478-4557
                    www.digital-ops.com

Kyla Photography   (310) 922-1881
                    www.kylaphoto.com

LA Rep   (213) 446-1720
3219 Laurel Canyon Blvd.   FAX (323) 656-1756
Studio City, CA 91604   www.larep.net
(Reps for Production Stills Photographers)

                                   (323) 654-8352
R. Dean Larson   (323) 654-8368

David Lena	**(310) 480-7007**
	FAX **(310) 399-2425**
	www.davidlena.com

	(818) 352-3747
Lisa Dare Photography	**(818) 370-2480**
	FAX **(818) 352-3747**

Christine Loss	**(818) 366-2043**

	(323) 962-0009
Christopher Xavier Lozano	**(323) 854-6775**
	www.tlshollywood.com

Michael Rueter Photography	**(818) 268-3630**
	www.michaelrueter.com

Keith Nakata	**(323) 653-0455**

	(323) 258-9629
Robert Anthony Nese	**(818) 247-2149**

	(310) 202-8547
Stanley D. Newton	**(310) 710-2541**
	www.stanleynewtonphoto.com

Guy Noffsinger	**(310) 386-0972**
	www.yourphotoguy.com

Yoshi Ohara	**(310) 327-0056**
	FAX **(310) 327-0808**
	www.marznet.com

	(805) 528-8585
Abe Perlstein	**(805) 234-1253**
	www.abes3dworld.blogspot.com

The Rappaport Agency	**(323) 464-4481**
6311 Romaine St., Ste. 7204	FAX **(323) 464-5030**
Hollywood, CA 90038	**www.rappagency.com**
(Reps for Stills Photographers)	

robert/robert	**(310) 344-5111**
419 S. Cochran Ave.	**www.robertrobert.com**
Los Angeles, CA 90036	

Sam Urdank Photographer	**(310) 877-8319**
	www.samurdank.com

Richard Scudder	**(323) 373-6483**
P.O. Box 691344	
West Hollywood, CA 90069	

Sherburne Photography	**(310) 570-9094**
	www.sherburnephotography.com

	(818) 563-2511
SheShooter/Carey Hendricks	**(323) 440-8823**
	www.sheshooter.com

Daniel Shudo	**(310) 806-0355**
	www.danielshudo.com

Erik Thureson	**(818) 404-3600**
	www.lightbox57.com

	(323) 743-8161
Derek Van Oss/(dvo) photo	**(917) 922-0742**
	www.dvophoto.com

	(818) 565-8003
Joseph Viles	**(818) 556-1557**
	www.josephviles.com

Gregg E. Amodei	(805) 493-1409 (805) 844-1409
Christopher Amy (French & Spanish)	(310) 836-1650 (310) 678-8202
artists' services 8581 Santa Monica Blvd., Ste. 437 West Hollywood, CA 90069 www.artists-services.com (Reps for Prop Masters)	(323) 445-4910 (415) 824-4423
David Baker (Set Decorator)	(310) 850-1911
Jeff Barber (Prop Stylist)	(213) 507-0809
Jeffrey Bellamy (Set Decorator)	(626) 403-0394 (626) 824-0094
Greg Bonura	(818) 292-7663 (818) 386-8203
Edwin Brewer	(323) 422-0064
John Brunot	(818) 262-9305
R. Spencer Burt (Set Decorator)	(310) 489-4743 (310) 478-4738
Jerry Chavez	(818) 400-4615 (818) 985-0494
Barry Conner (Product Stylist & Prop Stylist)	(818) 314-0523 (818) 991-0904
Kirk DeMusiak (Set Decorator & Underwater) www.kirkdemusiak.com	(310) 827-1978 (310) 963-6994 FAX (310) 827-3298
Jeff Dombro www.jeffdombro.com	(818) 426-7888 (661) 253-3512
Dan Donley (Underwater)	(213) 200-2810
Jonathan Drake	(818) 825-0705 (818) 887-9535 FAX (818) 887-9535
Steven P. Duchscherer	(818) 708-3647
Steven Eaton (Set Decorator)	(661) 297-3504 (818) 422-5004
Robert Feffer (Prop Stylist & Set Decorator)	(818) 886-1154 (818) 681-7239
Stephen Flynn	(213) 248-9530
Jim Fox (Prop Rigs)	(323) 462-2272 FAX (323) 469-9204
Marc Gannes	(818) 348-6107 (213) 712-7360 FAX (818) 348-4507
David L. Glazer FAX (818) 713-1741 www.davidglazer.net	(818) 521-8037
Aaron A. Goffman FAX (323) 997-7999 www.goffman.tv	(323) 997-7999 (800) 655-3305
Jon Gold (Art Director)	(818) 625-4408
Peter N. Griffith	(818) 692-0900
Mikel Hands FAX (818) 842-3501 www.mikelhandsreel.com	(818) 802-1196
Rufus Herrick	(805) 496-0249 (206) 232-7100
Glen Houghton	(310) 779-8100 (760) 436-0287
Jim Johnson	(213) 760-5491
Jonathan Lee (Set Decorator)	(818) 731-7724 (818) 907-7231 FAX (818) 986-4856
Priscilla Levy (Set Decorator & Underwater)	(415) 669-7777 (916) 296-5037 FAX (415) 669-7777
Douglas C. Lewis	(213) 700-7424
Ronnie Lombard	(818) 613-8705
Tony Maccario	(661) 513-8749
David Marais	(213) 712-6011
Tom Margules	(818) 225-7767 (818) 519-7767
Neil Marquis	(818) 780-0118 (213) 280-4552
Daniele Maxwell www.artistuntied.com	(323) 933-0200
Robin L. Miller	(213) 400-6045
Craig Osler www.propertymaster.biz	(818) 702-0075
Tim Perovich (Prop Stylist & Set Decorator)	(805) 526-2780
John Puhara (Set Decorator)	(323) 663-7320 FAX (323) 663-7320
Steven Renick	(310) 422-5177
Jacqueline Sartino (Set Decorator)	(760) 320-0724 FAX (323) 653-2979
Gary Shartsis (Set Decorator)	(818) 957-0620 (818) 398-1728
Bjarne Sletteland (Set Decorator)	(310) 770-8223 (505) 466-1436 FAX (505) 466-1436

Dan Spaulding	(310) 993-2850
	FAX (818) 845-9259
	www.spaulding.tv
Michael Storosh	(310) 753-3110
(Prop Stylist)	FAX (310) 305-9994
Josh Paul Thomas	(213) 908-6754
(Prop Stylist)	www.martonemgmt.com

	(323) 462-7854
John Vonk	(323) 632-8931
(Set Decorator)	
	(818) 761-4488
Jon Douglas West	(818) 915-4746
(Set Decorator)	FAX (818) 761-2112
	(213) 500-1119
Jeff White	(310) 398-4172
	(310) 864-4075
Randy Young	(310) 323-3326

All Crew Agency   (818) 206-0144
2920 W. Olive Ave., Ste. 201   FAX **(818) 206-0169**
Burbank, CA 91505   **www.allcrewagency.com**
(Reps for Prosthetics Artists)

Almost Human, Inc.   (310) 838-6993
3650 Eagle Rock Blvd.   FAX **(310) 838-6999**
Los Angeles, CA 90065   **www.almosthuman.net**

Alterian, Inc.   (626) 856-1499
P.O. Box 2166   FAX **(626) 856-1495**
Irwindale, CA 91706   **www.alterianinc.com**

    (818) 584-4115
American Makeup and FX   (336) 264-2302
3827 Saticoy St.   **www.amefx.com**
Van Nuys, CA 91402

Anatomorphex/
The Sculpture Studio   (818) 768-2880
8210 Lankershim Blvd., Ste. 14   **www.anatomorphex.com**
North Hollywood, CA 91605

Michele Burke   (818) 748-8841

Michael Burnett   (818) 768-6103
    FAX **(818) 768-6136**
    www.mbpfx.com

The Character Shop   (805) 306-9441
4735 Industrial St., Ste. 4-B   FAX **(805) 306-9444**
Simi Valley, CA 93063   **www.character-shop.com**

Bari Dreiband-Burman   (818) 980-6587
    www.burmanstudio.com

Dynamic Design International, LLC/   (818) 923-8798
Darren Perks   (818) 439-8447
    FAX **(623) 386-6826**
    www.dynamicdesignintl.com

    (818) 317-9997
Edward French   (818) 340-4852
    www.edfrenchmakeupfx.com

Alan Friedman   (818) 881-1473

Gary J. Tunnicliffe's
Two Hours in the Dark, Inc.   (818) 837-1045
12473 Gladstone Ave., Ste. Q   FAX **(818) 837-1842**
Sylmar, CA 91342   **www.2hoursinthedark.com**

GM Foam, Inc.   (818) 782-9833
13536 Saticoy St.   FAX **(818) 782-2863**
Van Nuys, CA 91402   **www.gmfoam.com**

Byrd Holland   (818) 558-1954
    FAX **(818) 558-1954**

    (818) 508-1533
Trisha Kelley   (818) 809-9980

Kevin Marks   (818) 613-2746

    (818) 834-3000
Masters FX, Inc./Todd Masters   (604) 683-5311
    FAX **(818) 834-9755**
    www.mastersfx.com

Multivision FX   (818) 288-6839
    www.multivisionfx.com

Deborah Patino   (818) 371-9719

    (818) 209-8046
Ralis Special Makeup Effects   (213) 622-3936
3727 W. Magnolia Blvd., Ste. 407   **www.ralisfx.com**
Burbank, CA 91505

Rick Stratton's (Strat-Tatts)
Temporary Tattoos   (818) 951-1051
6942 St. Estaban St.   FAX **(818) 951-8051**
Tujunga, CA 91042
    home.roadrunner.com/~bludney/index.html

    (818) 981-3338
Bob Romero   (818) 953-6625
    FAX **(818) 981-3339**
    www.bobromero.com

Smith FX, Inc.   (818) 601-8800
    www.shaunsmithfx.com

Stevie FX   (818) 915-3615
    FAX **(818) 206-0169**
    www.steviefx.com

Yvette Alcala	(310) 927-2404

All Crew Agency (818) 206-0144
2920 W. Olive Ave., Ste. 201 FAX (818) 206-0169
Burbank, CA 91505 www.allcrewagency.com
(Reps for Script Supervisors)

(310) 210-0823
Robin Anderson (310) 396-5063
(Spanish & Visual FX) FAX (310) 399-8473

(818) 569-0210
Sheryl Appleton (818) 422-0612
(Spanish) FAX (818) 569-3713
www.sherylappleton.com

(310) 745-4444
Suzanne Armstrong (310) 766-2738
FAX (310) 745-4600

(323) 952-4067
Karolyn Austen (323) 770-6418

(310) 927-3055
Barbara Babchick (818) 908-2466
(Computer Frame Capturing, Motion Control & Visual FX)

Patricia Baker (818) 886-7503

Cassandra Barrère (323) 654-3445
(Spanish)

(310) 301-6021
Elizabeth Barton (808) 823-6156
(Motion Control & Visual FX) FAX (808) 823-6840

(310) 600-9625
Lisa Bemel (212) 452-2314

Ana Birch (310) 864-5131
FAX (509) 562-8781
(Computer Frame Capturing, Motion Control, Visual FX;
Portuguese & Spanish)

Towie Bixby (818) 206-0144
www.allcrewagency.com

(310) 657-1900
Joanie Blum (503) 392-3437
(Italian)

Lisa Bobonis (323) 377-9866

Mellanie Bradfield (323) 459-7260

(310) 398-8150
Georgia Bragg (310) 345-8817
FAX (310) 398-4340

Janine M. Brauns (818) 326-7707
(Computer Notes)

(310) 822-2961
Jeanne Byrd-Hall (213) 220-9247

Jennifer Carriere (818) 206-0144
www.allcrewagency.com

(818) 416-4972
Maggie Causey (310) 457-2384

(818) 429-7980
Ulyssa Childs (818) 865-8765

Diane Collins (818) 206-0144
www.allcrewagency.com

(818) 761-3800
Patti Dalzell (818) 523-0403
(Computer Frame Capturing)

Sarah Dart (213) 247-8811
(Digital Excel Notes, Frame Capturing, Motion Control &
Visual FX; French)

(510) 339-6352
Carol De Pasquale (510) 543-6864
(French)

(310) 398-2711
Susan Dear (310) 922-2822
FAX (310) 398-5521
(Computer Frame Capturing, Digital Script Notes, Motion
Control & Visual FX)

(323) 658-7704
Dawn 'DeDe' Dreiling (323) 547-4484
FAX (323) 658-7704

(310) 641-1302
Diane Durant (310) 989-5082

(310) 562-7358
Denise Eldridge (310) 305-1922

(310) 251-1415
Monica Fernandez (310) 656-0366
(Spanish; Computer Frame Capturing, Digital Editorial Notes,
Motion Control & Visual FX)

(310) 390-6311
Veronica Flynn (310) 367-7653
(French & Spanish)

Jane Forbes (818) 206-0144
www.allcrewagency.com

(805) 497-1797
Jennifer Jurwich Freudenberg (818) 512-2990
(Computer Frame Capturing, Motion Control & Visual FX)

Sandra Gainsforth (818) 957-3446
FAX (360) 361-7664

Sherry Gallarneau (213) 247-2113

(626) 357-4820
Dawn Gilliam (626) 298-2119
(Computer Frame Capturing, Motion Control & Visual FX)

(310) 962-2404
Cori Glazer (310) 455-3343
(Computer Frame Capturing, Motion Control & Visual FX)

(323) 467-4439
Jane Goldsmith (323) 697-3795
(Computer Frame Capturing, Motion Control & Visual FX)

Pauline Gray (626) 831-2290
(Computer Frame Capturing, Director's Treatments, Motion
Control & Visual FX)

Jill Gurr (323) 467-9039
(Italian, French & Spanish; Visual FX) FAX (323) 467-9642

(310) 392-8058
Sharon Hagen (310) 396-1210
FAX (310) 392-8058

Jane Hampton (310) 569-1769

Heather Harris (818) 383-6265

Dora Hopkins	(310) 488-5003

Ira Hurvitz — (626) 300-8123

Catherine Jelski — (310) 386-8624 / (310) 398-7504
www.catherinejelski.com
(Computer Frame Capturing, Motion Control &
Visual FX; German)

Jessica Jordan — (310) 979-8889
home.sprintmail.com/~jessjordan/index.html
(Computer Frame Capturing, Motion Control & Visual FX)

Veda Kaplan — (310) 849-9598

Bridgette Kelley — (323) 934-2034 / (323) 369-4228

Kelly Kelley — (323) 861-0913 / (818) 206-0144
www.allcrewagency.com

Kristy Kelly — (310) 922-6537

Sandra King — (323) 893-3866 / (909) 866-0992
FAX (909) 866-0992

Marie Lamotte — (310) 396-3737
(French)

Louann Lightfoot — (818) 599-3288
(Computer Frame Capturing, Digital Scripts & Visual FX)

Christine Loss — (818) 366-2043
(Spanish)

Cara Lowe — (310) 562-4021

Kathy Lubinsky — (323) 650-6875

Cheryl Malat — (310) 663-8336 / (212) 799-9160

Lauren Malkasian — (323) 953-6633 / (323) 229-0333

Mary Manix — (818) 216-2228

Tina Marrie — (818) 753-2089 / (818) 590-0996
(Computer Frame Capturing, Motion Control & Visual FX)

Britta Martinez — (213) 503-5777
(German, Motion Control & Visual FX)

J. Kelly Mayes — (310) 418-7228 / (818) 249-5899

Agnes Mazzola — (310) 569-1506
(Computer Frame Capturing, Motion Control & Visual FX)

Lyn McKissick — (323) 363-1953

Vanessa Meier — (323) 309-7936
(E-Notes & Visual FX)

Tracey Merkle — (310) 393-5712 / (310) 849-3837
FAX (310) 393-0097

Morgan — (323) 466-5500 / (323) 466-7426
FAX (323) 466-4282

Jennifer Morris — (310) 961-0077

Kathleen Mulligan — (310) 968-1370 / (310) 312-6578
FAX (310) 312-6578

Jennifer J. Mullins — (213) 716-0409 / (626) 794-4603

Beth Multer — (818) 206-0144
www.allcrewagency.com

Jora Nelstein — (323) 933-5272 / (323) 363-9956
(Dutch; Motion Control & Visual FX) FAX (323) 933-5272

Nila Neukum — (310) 351-2777 / (310) 839-7488

Mary Ann Newfield — (323) 463-9570 / (213) 819-9570
(Motion Control & Visual FX)

Kathleen Newport — (818) 426-3804 / (949) 276-8462
(Motion Control & Visual FX) FAX (949) 276-8462

Monica Ochoa — (714) 892-5480 / (714) 815-0097
(Spanish) FAX (714) 892-5480

Donna Parish — (626) 798-2329 / (323) 829-6557
FAX (626) 798-3666

Paulette Pasternack — (818) 999-9796 / (818) 943-9736
FAX (818) 999-9796

Mary M. Patton — (310) 455-1519
(Spanish)

Victoria Peters — (310) 545-8118 / (310) 545-0303

Daria Price — (917) 579-7259 / (323) 962-7536

Ana Maria Quintana — (818) 548-5296 / (213) 712-1909
(Computer Frame Capture, Motion Capture, Motion Control,
Spanish & Visual FX)

Trudy Ramirez — (310) 292-1233 / (505) 268-2401

Bruce Resnik — (818) 206-0144
www.allcrewagency.com

Tricia Ronten — (310) 829-0434 / (310) 990-8346

Linda Salazar — (310) 375-4008

Melisa Sanchez — (310) 569-3345
FAX (310) 356-3615
(Italian, Russian & Spanish; Computer Frame Capturing, Motion
Control & Visual FX)

Debbie Sannes — (310) 316-4034 / (310) 415-4454

Shatsy — (323) 464-8081 / (323) 646-4730
FAX (323) 464-5575
(Motion Control & Visual FX; French & Spanish)

Susan Shparago-VanDernoot — (310) 213-7708
(All Digital) www.hollywoodscripty.com

Laura Shrewsbury — (310) 301-8385 / (310) 591-9551
(French) FAX (310) 301-8385

Beth A. Smith	(818) 206-0144
	www.allcrewagency.com
	(310) 455-7169
Catherine Smythe-Grasso	(310) 710-7673
Nancy Solomon	(818) 321-3719
Gretchen Somerfeld	(213) 706-1550
(French)	
Lisa Soulé	(310) 849-5472
Leslie Steadman	(310) 413-7285
Rooh Steif	(213) 200-7700
(Computer Frame Capturing, Motion Control & Visual FX)	
Scott Stephens	(818) 281-7852
	FAX (818) 776-8546
Michele Tedlis	(818) 398-4291
(Computer Frame Capturing)	www.micheletedlis.com

Mark Thomas	(310) 453-1700
Caroline Tolley	(818) 206-0144
	www.allcrewagency.com
Marion Tumen	(310) 459-1146
	(310) 702-6141
Ingrid Urich-Sass	(310) 205-0659
(French & Spanish)	FAX (310) 284-8160
Judith Vogt	(626) 798-7470
Marvel Wakefield	(310) 876-2303
	(916) 201-6989
Tracey Weddle	(916) 359-4759
	FAX (916) 359-4759
	(310) 710-5275
Denise (Nisey) Woods	(310) 316-2342
(Computer Frame Capturing, Motion Control & Visual FX)	

Linda Aliber-Karson	(323) 936-7938
C.C. Barnes	(310) 344-4327
Roger Barth	(310) 877-3063
David Berke	(310) 305-2428 (310) 344-2676 FAX (310) 305-2428
Mike Bocek	(213) 344-6050 www.mikebocek.com
Rick Brown	(310) 922-1946
Lori Berk Chapman	(213) 700-7180 (818) 980-9040 FAX (323) 345-5866
Debbie Collura	(818) 955-7730
Eugene Davis	(818) 209-5486
Seth Edelstein	(310) 595-4198
John Elmore	(323) 855-4420 (310) 839-0708
Brad Ewing	(213) 220-0175
Maureen Gibson	(818) 381-7810 www.mospace.net
Niles Goodsite	(818) 998-6455
Steve Griffin	(310) 656-5151 www.innovativeartists.com

Chris Hayden (Underwater)	(818) 889-0828 (310) 963-2461
Jamie Haynes	(310) 570-1150 FAX (310) 827-7367
Glen A. Hettinger	(661) 255-0953 (661) 400-4577 www.glenhettinger.com
John R. Hunstable	(626) 797-1774 (818) 371-1566
Sharon Lorick	(310) 440-3404 FAX (310) 440-3454
Anita Miller	(805) 927-3566 FAX (805) 927-3566
Jennifer Miller	(310) 739-1322
Lucille OuYang	(310) 837-7776 (310) 721-4554 FAX (310) 837-7780
Steve Ruggieri	(310) 503-6911 (818) 368-0666 FAX (818) 360-0237
Chad Saxton	(310) 659-1947 (310) 739-1935
Patricia M. Soto	(310) 641-1300
Melissa Stubbs	(310) 285-0303 www.sandramarsh.com
Judy Trotter	(805) 705-2150

Stacey Anne	(323) 937-1010 www.zenobia.com	**Elizabeth Nicole**	(323) 937-1010 www.zenobia.com
Michelle Ashley	(323) 449-1538 FAX (323) 851-2249	**Stephen Pappas**	(310) 998-1977 www.celestineagency.com
Antonio Ballatore	(310) 998-1977 www.celestineagency.com	**Marjolijn Reuter**	(323) 937-1010 www.zenobia.com
Sharon Bonney	(310) 804-7097 (310) 823-9191	**Rachel Roderick-Jones**	(310) 457-3029 (310) 430-0494
Ruth Bracken	(707) 495-7667 (707) 823-7957 FAX (707) 581-2046 www.ruthbdesigns.com	**Carla Roley**	(323) 937-1010 www.zenobia.com
Celestine Agency 1548 16th St. Santa Monica, CA 90404 (Reps for Set Decorators)	(310) 998-1977 FAX (310) 998-1978 www.celestineagency.com	**Rob Scruggs**	(805) 529-3989 (805) 231-7532
		Lauren Shields	(323) 937-1010 www.zenobia.com
Becket Cook	(310) 276-0777 www.thewallgroup.com	**Jane Shirkes**	(323) 344-0487
Robin del Pino	(323) 937-1010 www.zenobia.com	**Jean Simone**	(818) 242-1790 (818) 434-1881
Caryl Eagle	(323) 937-1010 www.zenobia.com	**Joyce Artman Smith**	(661) 254-5445 (818) 434-3224 www.joyceartmansmith.com
Suzy Eaton	(323) 937-1010 www.zenobia.com	**Gary Spain**	(415) 722-3510 www.garyspaindesign.com
Diane Ewing	(323) 937-1010 www.zenobia.com	**Christine Staggs**	(213) 709-3902
John Geary	(310) 998-1977 www.celestineagency.com	**Kris Starr-Davila**	(818) 884-6068 (818) 968-7212 FAX (818) 884-6085
Stefanie Girard	(818) 558-6878 (818) 618-6878	**Liz Stewart**	(310) 258-0234 www.lizstewartdesign.com
Jennifer Herwitt	(213) 220-8698 www.herwitt.com	**Jen Tauritz Gotch**	(323) 937-1010 www.zenobia.com
Derek Hughes	(310) 733-2550 www.photogenicsmedia.com	**Ann G. Troy**	(805) 729-1923
Kathleen Devlin Hughes	(818) 767-8686 (213) 400-7223 FAX (818) 767-8646	**Erinn Valencich**	(310) 274-0032 www.artistsbytimothypriano.com
		Katherine Vallin	(323) 493-5533
John M. Kelly (Prop Master)	(818) 769-4950 (213) 999-1303 FAX (818) 769-4950	**Julia Weinberg**	(310) 274-2383 FAX (310) 821-0232
Melody LaVigna	(818) 996-2855 FAX (818) 996-4181	**Donna Willinsky**	(323) 828-2280 picasaweb.google.com/DonnaWillinsky/ ExamplesOfMyWork#
Deborah McLean	(323) 937-1010 www.zenobia.com	**Kira Wolman**	(323) 937-1010 www.zenobia.com
Jules Moore	(323) 937-1010 www.zenobia.com		

Jon Ailetcher	(818) 516-5186
	(818) 830-1647
	www.jamixer.com

Lee Alexander	(831) 428-2794
(Sound Mixer)	

All Crew Agency	(818) 206-0144
2920 W. Olive Ave., Ste. 201	FAX (818) 206-0169
Burbank, CA 91505	www.allcrewagency.com
(Reps for Sound Production Mixers)	

Beau Baker	(818) 398-4119
	(818) 505-8908
	FAX (866) 583-1545
	www.imdb.me/beau

David Barr-Yaffe	(818) 206-0144
	www.allcrewagency.com

Steve Bedaux	(818) 566-3000
	(888) 246-3589
	www.cinelux.tv
(Audio Supervisor, RF Audio Specialist, Sound Mixer & Sound Recordist)	

Gerald Beg	(805) 407-4945
(Boom Operator, French & Sound Utility)	

Izak Ben-Meir	(310) 829-7037
	(213) 999-5959
	FAX (310) 829-6237

Glenn E. Berkovitz	(310) 902-1148
	(310) 313-2776
	FAX (310) 398-2776

Jack Bornoff	(818) 905-0356

Steve Bowerman	(805) 496-1716
	(818) 522-9943

Forrest Brakeman	(818) 952-2589
	(818) 384-1491

Mark D. Burton	(818) 419-7571
(Production Sound Mixer)	

Crew Chamberlain	(714) 447-8090
	FAX (714) 525-6028

Moe Chamberlain	(323) 871-0413
	(213) 281-0537
	FAX (323) 871-0623

Cinematicks, Inc.	(310) 396-8229
	(310) 420-8078
254 San Juan Ave.	FAX (310) 396-4123
Venice, CA 90291	www.cinematicks.com

Juan Cisneros	(818) 206-0144
	www.allcrewagency.com

John S. Coffey	(323) 876-7525
	FAX (323) 876-4775
	www.coffeysound.com

Ron Cogswell	(818) 368-6450

Peter Commans	(714) 323-0438

Thomas Curley	(323) 304-4962
	(518) 253-1879
	www.curleysound.com

James Dehr	(310) 455-2308
	(818) 424-2290

Dave Diamond	(310) 430-9376
(Production Sound Recording)	FAX (323) 913-9141

Bob Dreebin	(310) 629-2476
	(623) 561-9204
	FAX (623) 561-5813
	www.rollsound.biz

Robert Eber	(310) 450-8164
	(310) 913-1707
	FAX (310) 450-8264

Andrew Edelman	(310) 499-6199
	www.imdb.com/name/nm0248973/

Joseph Ekins	(818) 720-7436

Farr Out Productions, LLC	(310) 902-5944
(Reps for Sound Mixers)	FAX (818) 830-3608
	www.farroutpro.com

Chuck Fitzpatrick	(818) 249-6667
	(818) 731-5030

Joe Foglia	(818) 633-4449
	(954) 974-1500
	FAX (818) 276-8480
	www.southeastaudio.com

Kirk Francis	(310) 285-0303
	www.sandramarsh.com

Devin Golub	(323) 365-7480
(Boom Operator)	

Courtney M. Goodin	(323) 937-4978
	(323) 465-9441
	FAX (323) 935-6698
	www.bwfwidget.com

Richard Bryce Goodman	(310) 474-1100
	(310) 600-0222
(French)	FAX (310) 474-1003
	www.imdb.com/name/nm0329208/

Albee Gordon	(323) 666-1331
	(323) 363-2773
	FAX (323) 666-1331

Gary Gossett	(805) 732-7946
	FAX (805) 522-5231

Brett Grant-Grierson	(818) 606-5700
	www.ears4hire.com

Steven Grothe	(310) 528-2887
(Japanese & Spanish)	

Dennis Grzesik	(818) 388-7358
	FAX (503) 214-7521
	www.moviebizsound.com

Kip Gynn	(310) 397-7758
	(216) 496-1555
	www.imdb.com/name/nm0350484
(Boom Operator, Mixer, Playback & Utility)	

John Halaby	(310) 312-8810
	(310) 963-8810
	FAX (310) 312-9910

Don Hale	(619) 710-6858
	(323) 205-6857
	www.imdb.com/name/nm0354891/

Cameron Hamza	(310) 390-3520
	(310) 430-9046
	www.imdb.com/name/nm0359118/

Mark Hanes	(323) 466-4803 (949) 494-7870
Patrick Hanson	(310) 406-6511
Scott Harber	(323) 662-0912 (323) 459-6691
Steve Hawk	(213) 448-9322 (818) 260-9013 FAX (818) 260-9013
Michael Emeric Hayes	(818) 681-6879 www.emeric.com
Tim Hays	(818) 789-8799 (877) 737-6863 www.planet3soundco.com
Jim Hilton	(818) 988-4969
Ken Isley	(818) 782-3072
Bob Israel	(714) 843-1990 (888) 799-2202
Randy Johnson	(818) 508-0374 (818) 281-5573
Fred Johnston	(818) 752-0813 (520) 907-1155
Charles Kelly	(323) 664-1658 (323) 528-9479 FAX (323) 664-1658
David M. Kelson	(310) 560-2430 www.imdb.com/name/nm0447093/
Daniel G. Kent	(310) 502-6116 (310) 375-5952
Joe Kenworthy	(818) 606-6800 FAX (818) 782-8447
Theodore Kerhulas	(818) 784-9025
David Kirschner	(818) 314-8225 (818) 906-3534 FAX (818) 906-8806
C. Darin Knight	(818) 700-0633 (818) 389-4851
Alex Lamm (Spanish)	(818) 540-5979
B.J. Lehn	(310) 600-1445
Christopher Lennon	(323) 459-6997
William Macpherson	(213) 200-9401 www.soundspeed.com
Itzhak Ike Magal (Hebrew)	(323) 314-0948 (928) 554-4448 www.ikemagal.com
Erik Magnus	(310) 902-3735 web.mac.com/emagnus
Jim Mansen	(818) 599-2974 (480) 816-1380
William Martel Jr.	(323) 375-4428 www.impactaudioinc.com
David McJunkin	(310) 874-3355 (562) 598-0301 www.locationdigital.com

Richard Mercado	(323) 253-2066 (323) 461-4290 FAX (323) 461-4292 www.actionaudioandvisual.com
Sunny Meyer (Spanish)	(818) 989-3721
Senator Mike Michaels (Japanese)	(213) 389-7372 (888) 389-7372 FAX (213) 389-3299 www.mandy.com/stu001.html
Michael C. Moore	(310) 729-1920
Oliver Moss (Sound Recordist)	(310) 412-2399
Steve Nelson www.imdb.com/name/nm0625753/ (Production Sound Mixer)	(818) 612-1383
Rob Newell	(310) 963-3201 (310) 828-2017
Jacques Nosco	(805) 794-0476
Paul Oppenheim	(310) 659-6744
Phillip W. Palmer	(818) 206-0144 www.allcrewagency.com
Bruce Perlman	(213) 359-9187 (323) 933-4489 FAX (323) 933-0249
Doc Pierce	(310) 629-9437
Roger Pietschmann	(323) 668-0203 (323) 810-4910
Lisa Pinero (Spanish)	(310) 422-5735
Michael Reilly	(310) 600-0298 (310) 473-7142
Morteza Rezvani (Farsi)	(310) 471-6667 (310) 497-0790
Lewis Rosen	(818) 763-2882
Sean P. Rush	(818) 206-0144 www.allcrewagency.com
Sandra Marsh & Associates 9150 Wilshire Blvd., Ste. 220 Beverly Hills, CA 90212 (Reps for Sound Production Mixers)	(310) 285-0303 FAX (310) 285-0218 www.sandramarsh.com
Jamie Scarpuzza www.soundwavesurfer.com (Boom Operator, Production Sound Mixer & Sound Recordist)	(323) 774-9368
David Schneiderman	(805) 963-8240 (805) 637-3758
Jan Schulte (Dutch)	(310) 374-2629 (310) 850-9077
Wolf Seeberg (French & German)	(310) 822-4973 FAX (310) 305-8918 www.wolfvid.com
Mark Sheret	(818) 516-2797 FAX (360) 824-7362
David Silver	(818) 415-9572 www.silverpixelproductions.com

Sound Mixers

Cabell Smith	(310) 776-0550
	(310) 573-9295
(French & Spanish)	FAX (310) 230-1222
Tom Stasinis	(805) 630-0507
	FAX (323) 488-9681
Roger V. Stevenson	(310) 770-4630
Scott D. Stolz	(310) 993-3303
Lee Strosnider	(323) 851-5456
	FAX (323) 851-5456
	(323) 595-8191
J. Woody Stubblefield	(323) 595-8191
Jim Stuebe	(310) 994-2090
	(323) 654-2076
Jim Tanenbaum	(323) 497-7949
Joe Thompson	(619) 995-1552
	(818) 842-8662
Pat Toma	(818) 295-8662
(Hebrew & Spanish)	FAX (818) 842-8662

Paul Trautman	(818) 438-8698
Janet Urban	(805) 300-2039
(French & Spanish)	
	(310) 574-9385
Video Tech Services	(310) 505-4015
10866 Washington Blvd., Ste. 513	FAX (310) 577-0850
Culver City, CA 90232	www.videotechservices.com
(Reps for Sound Production Mixers)	
Stephan Von Hase	(818) 206-0144
	www.allcrewagency.com
Ed White	(818) 370-5126
Marc Wielage	(818) 486-7747
	www.cinesound.tv
Jerry Wolfe	(818) 624-7116
(Spanish)	www.imdb.com/Name?Wolfe,+Gerald+B.
David Wyman	(310) 435-4915
	www.thesounddept.com

A.S.A. Medical Services Division (323) 662-9787	**Celeste Armstrong** (818) 502-9008 / (323) 868-4440
P.O. Box 727 FAX (323) 662-1569	(Baby Wrangler, Studio Teacher & Welfare Worker)
Montrose, CA 91021 www.asafilmcrew.com	
(Reps for Studio Teachers/Welfare Workers)	**Adria August** (310) 471-5000 / (818) 378-6882

A.S.A. Studio Teachers Association (323) 662-9787
P.O. Box 727 FAX (323) 662-1569
Montrose, CA 91021 www.asafilmcrew.com
(Baby Nurses, Baby Wranglers, Studio Teachers & Welfare Workers)

Ⓐ **@baby! baby!/Lynn Raines** (818) 905-0790 / (818) 216-8666
2830 S. Robertson Blvd. FAX (818) 501-0768
Los Angeles, CA 90034 www.atbabybaby.com
(Referral for Baby Wranglers and Studio Teachers/Welfare Workers)

Maxine Abarbara (818) 518-7115
FAX (818) 347-9347
www.castudioteacher.info
(Baby Wrangler, Studio Teacher & Welfare Worker)

Barbara L. Bass (818) 905-0766
FAX (818) 906-2242

Kathy Abbott (818) 464-5390 / (818) 464-5425

Josie Batorski (310) 458-7941 / (310) 428-1704

Franci Agajanian (310) 379-9989 / (310) 480-9898
FAX (310) 379-4098

Kathy Berk (818) 399-3206 / (336) 294-0228

Juel Anderson (818) 249-2920 / (818) 559-9600

Book Her for Studio Teacher (818) 400-5916 / (916) 212-9222
(Baby Wrangler, Child Wrangler, Spanish, Studio Teacher & Welfare Worker)

Apple Entertainment/Lucas Moore (310) 526-7328 / (818) 288-4259

Charmaine A. Boos (818) 222-2090 / (818) 372-3762
FAX (818) 222-2095

Helen Bricker	(310) 473-3302
Maxine Brooks	(213) 618-0816
www.studioteachers.com	
(Studio Teacher & Welfare Worker)	
	(310) 836-1366
Judith M. Brown	(310) 487-1772
Mike Bujko	(323) 662-9787
	FAX (323) 662-1569
	www.asafilmcrew.com
(Baby Wrangler, Studio Teacher & Welfare Worker)	
	(310) 652-5330
Polly Businger	(818) 559-9600
	(310) 714-3101
Cecilia Cardwell	(310) 398-6454
	FAX (310) 398-6454
	www.stuioteachers.com
Michael Carter	(323) 717-5545
	www.miketeaches.com
Casala, Ltd.	(818) 432-7404
11600 Ventura Blvd.	FAX (818) 432-7405
Studio City, CA 91604	www.childreninfilm.com
(Referral for Studio Teachers/Welfare Workers)	
A. Kathleen Chambers-Schelhorse	(415) 680-0809
(Baby Wrangler & Studio Teacher)	

John Chisholm	(213) 392-1564
(Baby Wrangler)	FAX (626) 403-3320
www.sharesomeknowledge.com	
Bill Clark	(818) 371-6722
	(818) 404-1237
Kathy Cornell	(818) 789-1114
	FAX (818) 789-1112
	(760) 214-7475
Marsha Craig	(760) 436-8874
	(323) 296-3422
Ruth Ann Crudup-Brown	(818) 389-3905
	FAX (626) 568-9909
	(310) 452-8271
Cheryl Diamond	(310) 804-3381
	(310) 829-5869
Phil Eisenhower	(310) 428-7287
Dr. Caren M. Elin, D.C.	(805) 448-1424
	FAX (805) 344-4255
	(925) 324-2159
Steve Elster	(310) 837-7542
	(310) 454-9643
Karen Erlich	(310) 286-5785

Rhoda C. Fine	(818) 363-6736 (800) 936-8130 FAX (818) 360-8139 www.studioteacher.com
Nancy A. Flint	(818) 505-1993 (818) 415-2461
Terry Foley	(626) 824-2963
Mandy Friedrich	(818) 486-6958 (818) 981-8388
Elise Ganz 117 Oak Dr. San Rafael, CA 94901 (Baby Wrangler, Studio Teacher & Welfare Worker)	(310) 275-8524 (415) 517-5456 FAX (415) 459-5352 www.thestudioteachers.com
Frank Gieb (Studio Teacher & Welfare Worker)	(818) 439-3994
Rhona Gordon	(818) 501-6468 (818) 486-4542
Marcy Gossett	(213) 819-4669 (323) 293-3632 FAX (323) 291-1219 www.studioteacher2.com
Claudette Grand (Studio Teacher & Welfare Worker)	(310) 392-0772 (310) 990-0026
Leslie Hall (Studio Teacher)	(310) 839-4222
Carol Hart (Baby Wrangler)	(323) 663-3512 (323) 841-9192 FAX (323) 661-2124
Monique Hernandez-Fisher (Studio Teacher)	(661) 718-2274 (661) 917-0336
Allison Hindin (Baby Wrangler, Studio Teacher & Welfare Worker)	(310) 418-8446 (310) 474-6500 FAX (310) 943-2774 www.studioteacherbabywrangler.com
Cliff M. Hirsch	(310) 457-7935 (805) 573-9442 FAX (310) 457-7935
Millie Lucas Hirsch	(562) 243-0612 (562) 372-4196
Gloria Hoffman	(626) 446-3592
Judy Jennings	(805) 544-4474 (818) 648-6500 www.studioteachers.com
Eva Jensen	(714) 525-5005 (714) 746-7241 FAX (714) 525-5005
Rob Johnston (Studio Teacher)	(310) 741-0925
Alicia Kalvin (Baby Wrangler, Studio Teacher & Welfare Worker)	(310) 980-0290 (310) 459-6875 www.studioteacher.org
Helen Karagozian	(310) 454-3426 (310) 922-1496 FAX (310) 454-3426
Jill Kimmel	(818) 429-9399 (818) 865-9065 FAX (818) 865-8260

Nancy Klein	(818) 981-8479 (818) 497-8880 FAX (818) 981-1601
Hermine Kosta	(310) 820-8152 (818) 559-9600
Carole Levine (Studio Teacher)	(323) 650-5821 (323) 810-2310 FAX (323) 650-1640
Abby Logan	(818) 516-5972
Chavonne Long	(626) 665-9149 (626) 296-9006
Bonnie Mackie	(626) 622-3006 (619) 435-8710
Jill McKay (Baby Wrangler, Studio Teacher & Welfare Worker)	(310) 836-8877 (310) 617-8245
Beth McManigill (Studio Teacher & Welfare Worker)	(818) 807-3163 www.setteacher.com
Kevin Moll (Japanese; Studio Teacher & Welfare Worker)	(323) 385-1313 FAX (419) 715-9741 www.kevinmoll.com
Cynthia R. Nakane (Baby Wrangler, Studio Teacher & Welfare Worker)	(805) 924-0678 (323) 573-1970
Geraldine Needle (Studio Teacher & Welfare Worker)	(714) 609-2450
Ⓐ On Location Education 400 Columbus Ave., Ste. 7S Los Angeles, CA 90046 www.onlocationeducation.com (Referral for Studio Teachers/Welfare Workers)	(818) 541-9077 (800) 800-3378 FAX (914) 747-2750
Stella Pacific/Terrific Teachers	(818) 464-5425 (562) 867-0700 www.stellapacificmanagement.com
James Panger	(310) 488-9840
Stacey Parzik (Baby Wrangler)	(818) 385-0000 (818) 648-1667 www.partiesbystacey.com
Caryl Pine-Crasnick	(310) 306-0685 (310) 780-5528
Heather Poundstone	(310) 699-8323
Nancy Pyne-Hapke (Baby Wrangler, Studio Teacher & Welfare Worker)	(818) 782-2311 (818) 497-2441 FAX (818) 782-2322
Jana Raines	(909) 989-3111 (801) 505-2514
Jeffrey Raines (Baby Wrangler, Studio Teacher & Welfare Worker)	(818) 203-2674 (818) 906-3315
Lynn Raines	(818) 905-0790 (310) 216-8666 FAX (818) 501-0768 www.atbabybaby.com
Cyndi Raymond (Baby Wrangler, Studio Teacher & Welfare Worker)	(323) 428-2906 FAX (323) 938-7714 www.cyndiraymond.com

Studio Teachers/Welfare Workers

Linda Resnick	(310) 476-6355
	(310) 749-6700
	FAX (310) 476-2620

Myra Rosenthal	(818) 886-1108
	FAX (818) 407-8985

	(323) 650-7422
Bobbie Ross	(323) 229-5129
	FAX (323) 650-6321

	(323) 933-4226
Sharon Sacks	(213) 713-7256
	FAX (323) 935-7384

	(310) 858-7853
Suzy Salerno	(310) 387-7458
	FAX (310) 858-7853

	(805) 492-6574
Margaret L. Schlaifer	(818) 984-1696
	FAX (805) 492-6584

	(818) 907-8703
Craig Schoenfeld	(818) 422-9097
(Studio Teacher & Welfare Worker)	FAX (818) 907-8703

Linda Stone Shure	(310) 488-1826
(Baby Wrangler)	FAX (310) 204-5683

Mike Simon	(818) 357-3154
(Studio Teacher & Welfare Worker)	FAX (419) 735-8829

www.teachingthestars.com

	(818) 506-5591
Arlene Singer-Gross	(818) 424-5513
	FAX (818) 506-1709

	(818) 414-3121
Jo Ann M. Smith	(818) 892-0845

www.thestudioteachers.com

	(602) 740-5598
Linda Stanley	(310) 372-1449
(Baby Wrangler & Studio Teacher)	

Jack Stern	(818) 970-7540
(Baby Wrangler)	

Julie Stevens	(323) 960-5222

www.educatingyoungstars.com
(Baby Wrangler, Studio Teacher & Welfare Worker)

	(310) 219-0191
Lorraine Hendricks Stewart	(661) 805-3999

	(818) 559-9797
A The Studio Teachers (IA Local 884)	(818) 559-9600

www.thestudioteachers.com
(Referral for Baby Wranglers, Studio Teachers and Welfare Workers)

	(310) 820-4522
A @Teacher! Teacher!	(310) 559-1918
	FAX (818) 501-0768

(Baby Wranglers, Studio Teachers/Welfare Workers & Tutors)

Janie Teller	(646) 331-9456

www.thestudyshack.com
(Baby Wrangler, Studio Teacher & Welfare Worker)

	(818) 363-5573
Jack Tice	(818) 363-3247
	FAX (818) 363-5573

	(310) 822-9496
Marsha Whittaker	(310) 963-0644

	(323) 681-9394
Richard Wicklund	(213) 841-3666
	FAX (323) 681-9394

Wendy Wilhite	(818) 522-8674

	(323) 394-1233
Lois Yaroshefsky	(323) 650-6956
(Studio Teacher & Welfare Worker)	

Saena Yi	(310) 801-7921
(Baby Wrangler, Studio Teacher & Welfare Worker)	

Academy of Interactive Arts &
Sciences (AIAS) (818) 876-0826
23622 Calabassas Rd., Ste. 300 FAX **(818) 876-0850**
Calabassas, CA 91302 **www.interactive.org**

Academy of Motion Picture
Arts & Sciences (AMPAS) (310) 247-3000
8949 Wilshire Blvd. FAX **(310) 859-9619**
Beverly Hills, CA 90211 **www.oscars.org**

Academy of Television Arts &
Sciences (ATAS) (818) 754-2800
5220 Lankershim Blvd., Second Fl. FAX **(818) 761-2827**
North Hollywood, CA 91601 **www.emmys.org**

Advertising Age (323) 522-6256
4611 La Mirada Ave. **www.adage.com**
Los Angeles, CA 90048

Affiliated Property
Craftspersons (IA Local 44) (818) 769-2500
12021 Riverside Dr. FAX **(818) 769-1739**
North Hollywood, CA 91607 **www.local44.com**

American Federation of Musicians/
West Coast (323) 461-5401
817 Vine St. FAX **(323) 461-5409**
Hollywood, CA 90038 **www.afm.org**

(323) 969-4333
American Society of
Cinematographers (ASC) (800) 448-0145
1782 N. Orange Dr. FAX **(323) 882-6391**
Hollywood, CA 90028 **www.theasc.com**

American Society of Composers,
Authors & Publishers (ASCAP) (323) 883-1000
7920 Sunset Blvd., Ste. 300 FAX **(323) 883-1049**
Los Angeles, CA 90046 **www.ascap.com**

The Animation Guild (818) 845-7500
1105 N. Hollywood Way FAX **(818) 843-0300**
Burbank, CA 91505 **www.animationguild.org**

Art Directors Guild/Scenic, Title &
Graphic Artists (IA Local 800) (818) 762-9995
11969 Ventura Blvd., Second Fl. FAX **(818) 762-9997**
Studio City, CA 91604 **www.artdirectors.org**

Association of Film Commissioners
International (323) 461-2324
8530 Wilshire Blvd., Ste. 210 FAX **(413) 375-2903**
Beverly Hills, CA 90211 **www.afci.org**

Association of Independent Commercial
Producers (AICP) (323) 960-4763
650 N. Bronson Ave., Ste. 223B FAX **(323) 960-4766**
Los Angeles, CA 90004 **www.aicp.com**

Association of Independent (310) 586-9799
Creative Editors (AICE) (212) 665-2679
www.aice.org

Casting Society of America (CSA) (323) 463-1925
606 N. Larchmont Blvd., Ste. 4B **www.castingsociety.com**
Los Angeles, CA 90004

Commercial Casting
Directors Association (CCDA) (818) 782-9900
13425 Ventura Blvd., Ste. 200 FAX **(818) 782-0030**
Sherman Oaks, CA 91423 **www.ccdala.com**

Costume Designers
Guild (IA Local 892) (818) 752-2400
11969 Ventura Blvd., First Fl. FAX **(818) 752-2402**
Studio City, CA 91604
www.costumedesignersguild.com

Directors Guild of America (DGA) (310) 289-2000
7920 Sunset Blvd. FAX **(310) 289-2029**
Los Angeles, CA 90046 **www.dga.org**

Directors Guild of America, Inc./ (323) 866-2200
Producers Pension & Health (310) 289-2000
8436 W. Third St., Ste. 900 FAX **(323) 653-2375**
Los Angeles, CA 90048 **www.dga.org**

Film Independent (310) 432-1200
9911 W. Pico Blvd., 11th Fl. FAX **(310) 432-1203**
Los Angeles, CA 90035 **www.filmindependent.org**

Hollywood Post Alliance (213) 614-0860
846 S. Broadway, Ste. 601 FAX **(213) 614-0890**
Los Angeles, CA 90014 **www.hpaonline.com**

IATSE & MPTAAC/
West Coast (AFL-CIO) (818) 980-3499
10045 Riverside Dr., Second Fl. FAX **(818) 980-3496**
Toluca Lake, CA 91602 **www.iatse-intl.org**

IATSE (IA Local 122) (619) 640-0042
3737 Camino Del Rio South, Ste. 307 FAX **(619) 640-0045**
San Diego, CA 92108 **www.iatse122.com**

IATSE (IA Local 442) (805) 878-0013
www.iatse442.org

IATSE (IA Local 504) (714) 774-5004
FAX **(714) 774-7683**
www.iatse504.com

International Cinematographers
Guild (IA Local 600) (323) 876-0160
7755 Sunset Blvd. FAX **(323) 876-6383**
Los Angeles, CA 90046 **www.cameraguild.com**

International Sound (818) 985-9204
Technicians (IA Local 695) (323) 877-1052
5439 Cahuenga Blvd. FAX **(818) 760-4681**
North Hollywood, CA 91601 **www.695.com**

International Stunt Association (ISA) (818) 501-5225
4454 Van Nuys Blvd., Ste. 214 FAX **(818) 501-5656**
Sherman Oaks, CA 91403 **www.isastunts.com**

Makeup Artists &
Hair Stylists (IA Local 706) (818) 295-3933
828 N. Hollywood Way FAX **(818) 295-3930**
Burbank, CA 91505 **www.local706.org**

A Minor Consideration (310) 523-3691
14530 Denker Ave. **www.minorcon.org**
Gardena, CA 90247

Motion Picture
Association of America (MPAA) (818) 995-6600
15301 Ventura Blvd. FAX **(818) 382-1790**
Sherman Oaks, CA 91403 **www.mpaa.org**

Motion Picture
Costumers (IA Local 705) (818) 487-5656
4731 Laurel Canyon Blvd., Ste. 201 FAX **(818) 487-5663**
Valley Village, CA 91607
www.motionpicturecostumers.org

Motion Picture
Editors Guild (IA Local 700) (800) 705-8700
7715 Sunset Blvd., Ste. 200 FAX **(323) 876-0861**
Los Angeles, CA 90046 **www.editorsguild.com**

Motion Picture First Aid
Employees (IA Local 767) (818) 641-5765
2520 W. Olive Ave., Ste. 320 FAX **(818) 474-1570**
Burbank, CA 91505 **www.iatse767.org**

Motion Picture Industry   (818) 769-0007
Pension & Health Plan   (888) 369-2007
11365 Ventura Blvd., First Fl.   FAX **(818) 508-4714**
Studio City, CA 91604   **www.mpiphp.org**

Motion Picture
Set Painters (IA Local 729)   (818) 842-7729
1811 W. Burbank Blvd.   FAX **(818) 846-3729**
Burbank, CA 91506   **www.ialocal729.com**

Motion Picture Studio Grips &
Crafts Service (IA Local 80)   (818) 526-0700
2520 W. Olive Ave., Ste. 200   **www.iatselocal80.org**
Burbank, CA 91505

Motion Picture Studio   (619) 275-0125
Mechanics (IATSE Local 495)   (619) 518-7442
1717 Morena Blvd.   FAX **(619) 275-2578**
San Diego, CA 92110   **www.ia495.org**

Ornamental Plasterers, Sculptors &
Modelers (AFL-CIO Local 755)   (818) 379-9711
13245 Riverside Dr., Ste. 350   FAX **(818) 379-9985**
Sherman Oaks, CA 91423   **www.local755.com**

Producers Guild of America (PGA)   (310) 358-9020
8530 Wilshire Blvd., Ste. 450   FAX **(310) 358-9520**
Beverly Hills, CA 90211   **www.producersguild.org**

Professional Musicians
Local 47 (AFM)   (323) 462-2161
817 Vine St.   FAX **(323) 461-3090**
Hollywood, CA 90038   **www.promusic47.org**

SAG-AFTRA   (323) 954-1600
5757 Wilshire Blvd.   **www.sagaftra.org**
Los Angeles, CA 90036

Script Supervisors/Continuity, Coordinators,
Accountants & Allied Production
Specialists (IA Local 871)   (818) 509-7871
11519 Chandler Blvd.   FAX **(818) 506-1555**
North Hollywood, CA 91601   **www.ialocal871.org**

Set Decorators Society of America   (818) 255-2425
7100 Tujunga Ave., Ste. A   FAX **(818) 982-8597**
North Hollywood, CA 91605   **www.setdecorators.org**

Society of Camera Operators (SOC)   (818) 382-7070
P.O. Box 2006   **www.soc.org**
Toluca Lake, CA 91610

Southern California
Broadcasters Association   (310) 930-5595
5670 Wilshire Blvd., Ste. 200   FAX **(310) 932-1425**
Los Angeles, CA 90036   **www.scba.com**

Stagehands for Theater &
TV (IA Local 33)   (818) 841-9233
1720 W. Magnolia Blvd.   FAX **(818) 567-1138**
Burbank, CA 91506   **www.ia33.org**

Studio Electrical Lighting
Technicians (IA Local 728)   (818) 985-0728
1001 W. Magnolia Blvd.   FAX **(818) 954-0732**
Burbank, CA 91506   **www.iatse728.org**

Studio Transportation
Drivers (Teamsters Local 399)   (818) 985-7374
P.O. Box 6017   FAX **(818) 985-0097**
North Hollywood, CA 91603   **www.ht399.org**

Stuntmen's Association of
Motion Pictures   (818) 766-4334
5200 Lankershim Blvd., Ste. 190   FAX **(818) 766-5943**
North Hollywood, CA 91601   **www.stuntmen.com**

Stuntwomen's Association of
Motion Pictures   (818) 762-0907
12457 Ventura Blvd., Ste. 208   FAX **(818) 762-9534**
Studio City, CA 91604   **www.stuntwomen.com**

   (214) 451-0023
TAF/TP   (877) 256-9298
4819 Woodall St.   FAX **(214) 561-7332**
Dallas, TX 75247   **www.shoottexas.org**

United Stuntwomen's
Association, Inc. (USA)   (818) 508-4651
   FAX **(818) 508-7074**
   www.usastunts.com

Visual Effects Society   (818) 981-7861
5335 Balboa Blvd., Ste. 205   FAX **(819) 981-0179**
Encino, CA 91316   **www.visualeffectssociety.com**

Women in Animation (WIA)   (818) 759-9596
P.O. Box 17706   **www.womeninanimation.org**
Encino, CA 91416

Women in Film (WIF)   (323) 935-2211
6100 Wilshire Blvd., Ste. 710   FAX **(323) 935-2212**
Los Angeles, CA 90048   **www.wif.org**

Women's Image Network   (310) 229-5365
2118 Wilshire Blvd., Ste. 144   **www.winfemme.com**
Santa Monica, CA 90403

Writers Guild of
America West (WGAw)   (323) 951-4000
7000 W. Third St.   FAX **(323) 782-4800**
Los Angeles, CA 90048   **www.wga.org**

Mark Bailey   (760) 672-3626
(Gangboss)

Bruce Comtois   (818) 262-5353

Chris Cordola   (310) 339-3394
FAX (310) 313-0298

Louis Dargenzio   (818) 504-2809
www.ziorentals.com

Noah Vincent Ford   (818) 421-1361

Joe Gonzalez   (661) 510-7650
FAX (661) 513.9776
www.buboosky.com

J. Bud Graves   (818) 335-2130
(415) 336-6257
FAX (818) 761-8383

Philip Henderson   (818) 266-4907
(818) 266-4919
(Car Coordinator, Driver & Gang Boss)   FAX (909) 624-9031
nationwidemovietrucks.com

Mark D. Hysen   (818) 261-9288

Michael Ingold   (661) 993-5393
(Commercial Gang Boss)   FAX (661) 414-8090
www.alohastudiorentals.com

Brian Jelloe   (213) 792-9052

Mel Langford   (661) 857-3177

Kevin McBride   (805) 701-7249
(805) 498-0624

Dale McDowell   (323) 459-1278

Tom Oberlin   (818) 266-9911

Moses Paskowitz II   (818) 424-1312
FAX (818) 343-5432

Blake Steelgrave   (818) 652-7377
(661) 298-8912
FAX (661) 298-8912
www.pmfarms.biz
(Car Coordinator, Driver & Picture Car Coordinator)

John Yarbrough   (310) 210-9272

Lance Acquasanta (310) 863-4626
www.videotechservices.com
(Camera Operator, Director of Photography & Safety Diver)

Bob Anderson (562) 433-2863
(562) 688-3038
FAX (562) 433-2863
www.aquavision.net
(Director of Photography, Grip, Marine Coordinator,
Producer & Safety)

Ronald Anderson (520) 419-1490
(800) 577-9635
FAX (520) 623-3144
www.mistyproductionservice.com
(Gaffer)

Wayne Baker (818) 991-9676
(818) 472-1780
FAX (818) 991-9677
www.waynebaker.com
(Camera Operator)

Tom Boyd (818) 974-1937
www.taboyd.com
(Camera Operator)

Devon Clark (310) 453-5250
(310) 795-0237
(Production Manager)

Customs by Eddie Paul, (310) 322-8035
A Division of EP Industries, Inc. (310) 259-0542
1330 E. Franklin Ave. FAX (310) 322-8044
El Segundo, CA 90245 www.deadlinetv.net
(Marine Coordinator & Producer)

John Pierre Dechene (818) 889-6749
(818) 889-6749
(Camera Operator)

Dan Donley (213) 200-2810
(Prop Master)

Gary Dorf (310) 476-8380
(310) 740-0995
FAX (818) 789-6435
(First AD & Producer)

Michael Ferris (310) 456-1530
(310) 749-5850
FAX (310) 456-1433
(Director of Photography)

Steven Guerrero (310) 864-2000
www.aquaticcinema.com

Jorge Guzman (310) 612-0445
FAX (310) 836-4307
(Marine Coordinator & Safety)

H2O Cine (310) 746-8353
(808) 375-7468
www.h2ocine.com
(Camera Operator)

Chris Hayden (818) 889-0828
(310) 963-2461
(Second AD)

Bob Hayes (310) 390-9190
(310) 717-6625
www.floatinglantern.net
(Director of Photography)

Rene Herrera (323) 707-3411
(323) 707-3415
FAX (818) 293-0049
www.aquarescue.com
(Grip)

C. Hardy James (503) 702-3544
FAX (503) 824-2751
(First AD)

Capt. Lance Julian (808) 224-0801
(323) 856-3000
FAX (323) 856-3009
www.easterntalent.net
(Marine Coordinator)

Michael Kari (805) 647-0650
(805) 861-3038
www.adlertanks.com
(Marine Coordinator)

Jim Kimura (323) 559-1110
FAX (626) 398-1387
www.tdnartists.com
(Camera Operator & Director of Photography)

Priscilla Levy (916) 296-5035
(415) 669-7777
FAX (415) 669 7777
(Prop Master)

Thomas Levy (415) 515-5547
(415) 669-7777
FAX (415) 669 7777
(Key Grip)

Tim McArdle (818) 368-8143
(818) 414-2367
FAX (818) 368-8143
(Gaffer)

Patrick M. Murray (818) 632-6320
FAX (818) 301-2591
(Gaffer)

Michael Neipris (562) 594-9276
FAX (562) 594-9242
www.nauticalfilmservices.com

Jimmy O'Connell (310) 968-0549
(310) 452-5774
FAX (310) 452-5774

Tim Pogoler (818) 281-1616
www.timcoworks.com
(Grip)

Cynthia Pusheck (323) 497-8489
(Camera Operator)

Pete Romano (310) 301-8187
(310) 282-9940
FAX (310) 301-3065
(Director of Photography)

Karen Roseme (323) 697-8382
(Gaffer)

Roger Sassen (818) 348-5909
(818) 429-2413
FAX (818) 702-0689
(Gaffer)

Capt. Chris Shearman (818) 610-1103
(310) 650-4455
FAX (818) 610-1128
www.on-screenmarine.com
(Marine Coordinator)

Mike Thomas (714) 761-4163
(Director of Photography)

Michael G. Uva (310) 901-3287
(310) 366-5822
www.kastandkrew.com
(Key Grip)

Ron Vidor (818) 766-6868
(800) 759-5722
www.ronvidor.com
(Camera Operator)

Jean-Pierre Visier (310) 670-2265
(Key Grip)

Mark Vollmen (310) 567-8218

Jon Douglas West (818) 761-4488
(818) 915-4746
FAX (818) 761-2112
(Producer & Prop Master)

Jon Zarkos (310) 365-7856
(Camera Assistant)

Rob Abbey	(310) 991-0884
	(310) 456-3696

Leonardo Arterberry III — (323) 466-7232
www.videorama.com

Steve Beach — (323) 578-6133

Jeff Benard/Videodrone
(Digital)
(323) 855-4278
(818) 508-6214
FAX (818) 508-6214
www.videodronehd.com

Kevin Boyd/Creative HD
(Digital)
(323) 350-3446
www.creativehd.com

Tim Bruns
(Digital)
(818) 889-9655
www.videohawks.com

Jeff Burrage/Digital Split
(310) 614-3920
(310) 997-9011

Mike Carlson — (310) 947-1673

Bob Chambers
(Digital)
(805) 777-1779
(818) 486-7707

**Steve Chambers/
Industry Assist Digital**
(Digital & Tape Based)
(310) 398-3344
(323) 547-0557
FAX (310) 398-3344
www.industryassist.com

Mark Chapman
(323) 466-7232
(213) 610-7746
www.videorama.com

Sam Cherroff
(Digital)
(818) 772-4777
(818) 359-3589
www.videoassist.com

Sam Clemans
(Digital)
(619) 335-0421
www.palmtreevideo.com

Keith Collea
(310) 823-0508
(520) 907-2211
FAX (815) 642-4444
www.imdb.com/name/nm0007205/

Leo Coltrane
(323) 466-7232
www.videorama.com

Glenn Derry
(Digital)
(818) 889-9655
www.videohawks.com

Anthony DeSanto/DVassist
(Digital)
(805) 279-1016
(805) 499-6602

Michael Dorfman/Dorfman Digital — (818) 404-5179
FAX (323) 843-9730
www.dorfmandigital.com

Bobby Espinosa/HD Video Assist — (323) 270-5568
(Digital)
FAX (323) 661-9543
www.bobbydigitalhd.com

Tim Flugum
(Digital)
(818) 212-8660

Scott M. Goldman/Video Systems
(310) 441-9836
(310) 292-9284
FAX (310) 474-5282

Tom L. Greger
(310) 418-2963
(310) 750-6477
FAX (208) 445-0926

Scott Hammar
(310) 770-0377
(818) 346-5362

Jim Harling
(Digital)
(818) 889-9655
www.videohawks.com

Sam Harrison/Play It Again Sam
(Digital)
(661) 263-6070
(661) 803-9372

**Kevin Hawks/
Circle Take Video Assist** — (805) 490-3621

Dean Hendler
(Digital)
(818) 508-9155
(818) 601-1177
www.deanhendler.com

Kurt Herbal
(Digital)
(818) 889-9655
www.videohawks.com

Chris B. Hill
(Digital & Tape Based)
(818) 445-9211
(818) 353-9211
www.hilldigital.com

John Hill
(Digital)
(818) 606-8901
(818) 222-5852
FAX (818) 222-5862
www.videoassistsystems.com

Brad Huffman — (805) 750-0401

Rich Jackson/Lucky Jackson DV
(818) 262-7505
(818) 753-0533
www.luckyjackson.com

Tom Janetzke
(626) 255-7523
www.videorama.com

Willow Jenkins
(Digital)
(323) 810-3456
FAX (310) 395-1920
www.chillowvision.com

Jeb Johenning/Ocean Video
(310) 859-7573
(213) 300-2000
FAX (310) 275-8676
www.oceanvideo.com

Brett Junod/Full HD Video Assist — (310) 592-0997
(Digital)

Brett Kelly/Kelly Video — (818) 389-1583

Robert Kenworthy — (818) 825-0077

Tom Loewy/Video Hawks
(Digital)
(818) 889-9655
FAX (818) 889-9755
www.videohawks.com

Chris Lum
(Digital)
(818) 889-9655
www.videohawks.com

Bob Lund/Awesome Playback
(Digital & Tape Based)
(310) 391-0550
(310) 365-2305

Brian Maris
(Digital)
(562) 708-6429
(562) 866-5178

William Martel Jr. — (323) 375-4428

Andy Minzes/Ready To Roll Video — (818) 321-2117

Dan Moore
(818) 957-8040
(818) 517-2022
FAX (818) 957-7457
www.videohawks.com

Robert Morales/	
Director's Choice Video (323) 658-7878	**Bryce Shields** (818) 425-7960
	(Digital)
Michael Moretti/Lost Dog Video (310) 722-8351	**Brad Smulson** (818) 402-6584
845 Second St. www.lostdogvideo.com	(Digital & Tape-Based)
Hermosa Beach, CA 90254	
	Robert Sullivan (818) 714-1080
(310) 378-3103	
Tom Myrick (310) 387-2858	**Gary Taillon** (805) 443-3806
(Digital) FAX (310) 378-3154	
	Terrence Tally (818) 378-8073
(801) 550-1648	(Digital) FAX (818) 951-1744
Gaylen Nebeker (818) 768-8348	
(Digital) FAX (801) 467-0307	**Brian Thesing** (310) 704-1080
www.nebtek.com	
	Thomas Thonson (323) 466-7232
(310) 890-7480	www.videorama.com
Sean Newhouse (323) 790-1732	
(Digital) FAX (323) 460-6063	(310) 457-2830
www.maneaterproductions.com	**Ira D. Toles** (310) 560-5555
(310) 589-2211	**Howard Van Emden/** (323) 697-6221
Richard Northcutt (310) 293-7661	**Videorama! Industries, LLC** (323) 466-7232
(Digital) FAX (310) 589-2211	FAX (323) 466-7232
	www.videorama.com
Robert Panza (310) 729-0108	
(Digital) www.videorama.com	**Thomas Vanasse/** (818) 763-4098
	TV Productions, Inc. (323) 646-8136
(818) 621-2594	(3D, Digital, HD, Qtake & VFX)
Mike Pickel (818) 343-6808	
(Digital) www.videohawks.com	(818) 298-3666
	Lance Jay Velazco (323) 272-6655
(213) 598-1056	(Digital) www.imdb.com/name/nm1100854/
Andrew Rozendal (818) 366-3784	
(Digital) www.nebtek.com	(310) 574-9385
	Video Tech Services (310) 505-4015
(323) 225-5091	10866 Washington Blvd., Ste. 513 FAX (310) 577-0850
Dave Schmalz (213) 308-0702	Culver City, CA 90232 www.videotechservices.com
	(Reps for VTR Operators)
(310) 222-8614	
Bob Schmidt (310) 488-8410	(310) 770-7915
(Digital) FAX (310) 222-8624	**Bill Weiss** (310) 479-3496
www.hoodmanusa.com	(Digital & Tape Based)
(310) 222-8614	(818) 892-4100
Mike Schmidt (310) 488-8410	**Charlie Wesfall/HD Video Assist, Inc.** (818) 970-8962
(Digital) FAX (310) 222-8624	FAX (818) 892-4300
www.hoodmanusa.com	www.hdvideoassistla.com
Erick H. Schultz/EZ Video (310) 430-2468	**Eric Williams** (323) 466-7232
	www.videorama.com
Wolf Seeberg (310) 822-4973	
FAX (310) 305-8918	**Adam Yoblon** (310) 738-7548
www.wolfvid.com	(Digital)
(310) 678-7269	
Jeffery Shafer (310) 836-7892	
(Digital)	

9 Agency (310) 430-9902
FAX (310) 469-7899
www.9-agency.com
(Reps for Wardrobe Stylists/Costume Designers)

Angela Aaron (323) 466-2007
www.therexagency.com

Marie Abma (323) 856-3000
www.easterntalent.net

Gemina Aboitiz (310) 839-8722
www.cloutieragency.com

Catherine Adair (310) 656-5151
www.innovativeartists.com

Julie Hayes Adams (310) 995-1111

Deborah Afshani (310) 839-8722
www.cloutieragency.com

Aim Artists Agency (323) 931-2745
509 N. Sycamore Ave. FAX (323) 931-2747
Los Angeles, CA 90036 www.aimartist.com
(Reps for Wardrobe Stylists/Costume Designers)

Lindsay Albanese (310) 274-0032
www.artistsbytimothypriano.com

Wess Albrecht (310) 403-8986
www.wessalbrecht.com

Mary Beth Alessandri (323) 937-1010
www.zenobia.com

All Crew Agency (818) 206-0144
2920 W. Olive Ave., Ste. 201 FAX (818) 206-0169
Burbank, CA 91505 www.allcrewagency.com
(Reps for Costume Designers)

Jason Alper (310) 285-9000
www.wmeentertainment.com

Charlie Altuna (310) 822-2898
www.rougeartists.com

Dorothy Amos (310) 285-0303
www.sandramarsh.com

Soyon An (323) 856-3000
www.easterntalent.net

Michael Angel (310) 998-1977
www.celestineagency.com

Stacey Anne (323) 937-1010
www.zenobia.com

Arielle Antoine (323) 297-0250
www.magnetla.com

Deena Appel (310) 656-5151
www.innovativeartists.com

Johanna Argan (310) 288-8000
www.paradigmagency.com

Arnelle (323) 299-4043
www.dionperonneau.com

(323) 933-0200
Artist Untied (415) 957-0500
(Reps For Wardrobe Stylists) FAX (415) 957-0555
www.artistuntied.com

Artists by Timothy Priano (310) 274-0032
120 El Camino Dr., Ste. 100 FAX (310) 278-7520
Los Angeles, CA 90212
www.artistsbytimothypriano.com
(Reps for Wardrobe Stylists)

(323) 445-4910
artists' services (415) 824-4423
8581 Santa Monica Blvd., Ste. 437
West Hollywood, CA 90069 www.artists-services.com
(Reps for Wardrobe Stylists)

ArtMix Beauty (310) 943-8102
2332 S. Centinela Ave., Ste. C FAX (310) 943-8101
Los Angeles, CA 90064 www.artmixbeauty.com
(Reps for Wardrobe Stylists)

Catherine Ashton (818) 206-0144
www.allcrewagency.com

Hayley Atkin (310) 276-0777
www.thewallgroup.com

Isabelle Aubin (323) 931-2745
www.aimartist.com

Victoria Auth (310) 656-5151
www.innovativeartists.com

Varya Avdyushko (310) 652-8778
www.lspagency.net

Agnes Baddoo (213) 505-3478
www.agnesbaddoo.com

Hala Bahmet (310) 623-5500
www.montanartists.com

Janis Bakken (323) 933-0200
www.artistuntied.com

Inanna Bantu (917) 740-7694
house-of-inanna.com

Britt Bardo (323) 297-0250
www.magnetla.com

Kirk Bardole (323) 937-1010
www.zenobia.com

Pauline Barry (415) 290-9532
www.paulinebarry.com

Linda Bass (310) 656-5151
www.innovativeartists.com

Stacy Battat (310) 274-6611
www.gershagency.com

Zoe Battles Moore (213) 446-1720
www.larep.net

Carol Beadle (310) 652-8778
www.lspagency.net

Paul Beahan (323) 297-0250
www.magnetla.com

Jenny Beavan (310) 273-6700
www.utaproduction.com

Alexis Beck (323) 297-0250
www.magnetla.com

Angee Beckett	(323) 650-8187 (213) 484-9307 FAX (323) 650-8187
Nicole Beckett	(323) 804-4550 www.nicolebeckett.com
Sarah Beers	(310) 623-5500 www.montanartists.com
Robert Behar	(323) 913-1566 (323) 251-4046 FAX (323) 660-3909 www.rowbinc.com
Fifi Bell	(323) 299-4043 www.dionperonneau.com
Erin Benach	(310) 652-8778 www.lspagency.net
Marlene Jaye Benson	(310) 306-1084 (310) 998-5400 FAX (310) 578-8204
Eric Berg	(323) 446-2007 www.therexagency.com
Kate Bergh	(213) 706-9254
Cynthia Bergstrom	(818) 284-6423 www.italentco.com
Nancy Bernal	(310) 458-7800 www.partos.com
Arjun Bhasin	(310) 395-4600 www.murthaagency.com
Hannah Bhuiya	(310) 458-7800 www.partos.com
Christine Bieselin Clark	(323) 578-0895 (310) 623-5500 FAX (323) 660-2356
Aubry Binzer	(323) 466-2007 www.therexagency.com
Heidi Bivens	(310) 652-8778 www.lspagency.net
Christina Blackaller	(323) 297-0250 www.magnetla.com
Robert Blackman	(310) 288-8000 www.paradigmagency.com
Marlene Blackwell	(310) 435-2814 (310) 454-9440 www.mmblackwell.com
Yvonne Blake	(310) 285-0303 www.sandramarsh.com
Phillip Bloch	(310) 839-8722 www.cloutieragency.com
Kasey Blue	(323) 933-0200 www.artistuntied.com
Bénédicte Bodard-Willis	(818) 783-6215
Johnetta Boone	(818) 284-6423 www.italentco.com
Marissa Borsetto	(310) 656-5151 www.innovativeartists.com

Liz Botes	(310) 822-2898 www.rougeartists.com
Gwen Bouzon	(415) 695-1254 FAX (415) 695-1254
Kim Bowen	(323) 297-0250 www.magnetla.com
Lisa Michelle Boyd	(323) 856-8540 www.opusbeauty.com
Michael T. Boyd	(310) 656-5151 www.innovativeartists.com
Paula Bradley	(323) 297-0250 www.magnetla.com
Claire Breaux	(310) 458-7800 www.partos.com
Mark Bridges	(310) 273-6700 www.utaproduction.com
Ana Brillembourg	(310) 274-0032 www.artistsbytimothypriano.com
Tom Broecker	(310) 274-6611 www.gershagency.com
Margo Brumme	(323) 445-4910 www.artists-services.com
Melissa Bruning	(310) 288-8000 www.melissabruning.com
Jennifer Bryan	(310) 623-5500 www.montanartists.com
Katherine Jane Bryant	(323) 856-3000 (323) 463-0022 www.easterntalent.net
Marie H. Burk	(323) 663-8509 (323) 481-2931 FAX (323) 667-0135
Kristin M. Burke	(310) 285-0303 www.sandramarsh.com
Lorraine Calvert	(323) 856-3000 www.easterntalent.net
Dana Campbell	(310) 652-8778 www.lspagency.net
Susie Carlson	(818) 888-9117 (818) 212-9117 FAX (818) 888-7723
Lorraine Carson	(310) 623-5500 www.montanartists.com
Ruth Carter	(310) 656-5151 www.innovativeartists.com
Debbie Castaldi	(310) 503-7107 (310) 398-2375 FAX (310) 398-2375
Celestine Agency 1548 16th St. Santa Monica, CA 90404 (Reps for Wardrobe Stylists)	(310) 998-1977 FAX (310) 998-1978 www.celestineagency.com
Mari-An Ceo	(310) 458-7800 www.partos.com

Lisa Cera	(786) 586-8794 (415) 777-9099 www.fordartists.com
Kishu Chand	(323) 931-2745
Christann C. Chanell	(888) 242-6355 FAX (888) 242-6313 www.christannchanell.com
Tim Chappel	(310) 274-6611 www.gershagency.com
Arturo Chavez	(323) 462-5000 www.traceymattingly.com
Michelene Cherie	(323) 937-9095 FAX (323) 937-9095 www.cheriecreative.com
Susan Chevalier	(310) 614-5130 susanchevalier.com
Pamela Withers Chilton	(310) 623-5500 www.montanartists.com
Randall Christensen	(323) 856-3000 www.easterntalent.net
Wendy Chuck	(310) 458-7800 www.partos.com
Michael Cioffoletti	(310) 998-1977 www.celestineagency.com
Michael Clancy	(323) 468-2240 www.nyoffice.net
Michele Clapton	(310) 285-0303 www.sandramarsh.com
Kecia Clark	(310) 998-1977 www.celestineagency.com
Christian Classen	(310) 274-0032 www.artistsbytimothypriano.com
Cloutier Remix 2632 La Cienega Ave. Los Angeles, CA 90034 (Reps for Wardrobe Stylists)	(310) 839-8722 FAX (310) 839-8730 www.cloutieragency.com
Sarah Cobb	(323) 297-0250 www.magnetla.com
Garth Condit	(310) 274-0032 www.artistsbytimothypriano.com
Shawn-Holly Cookson	(323) 856-3000 www.easterntalent.net
Kate Corrigan-Lee	(310) 702-2884
Carole Cotten	(323) 937-1010 www.zenobia.com
Jamie Coulter	(323) 937-1010 www.zenobia.com
Betsy Cox	(310) 656-5151 www.innovativeartists.com
Ane Crabtree	(310) 652-8778 www.lspagency.net
Marcy Craig	(310) 600-5211
Shay Cunliffe	(310) 285-0303 www.sandramarsh.com

Carol Cutshall	(310) 652-8778 www.lspagency.net
Bina Daigeler	(310) 623-5500 www.montanartists.com
Eric Daman	(310) 285-9000 www.wmeentertainment.com
Courtney Daniel	(310) 623-5500 www.montanartists.com
Elvis Davis	(818) 206-0144 www.allcrewagency.com
Sharen Davis	(310) 285-0303 www.sandramarsh.com
Dawn to Dusk Agency 8306 Wilshire Blvd., Ste. 412 Beverly Hills, CA 90211 (Reps for Wardrobe Stylists)	(323) 850-6783 (212) 431-8631
Kate DeBlasio	(323) 297-0250 www.magnetla.com
Tracie Delaney	(310) 458-7800 www.partos.com
Sophie de Rakoff	(323) 297-0250 www.magnetla.com
Jessica de Ruiter	(310) 276-0777 www.thewallgroup.com
Sarah de Sa Rego	(310) 274-6611 www.gershagency.com
Louise de Teliga	(310) 770-8558 www.louisedeteliga.com
Kathleen Detoro	(310) 623-5500 www.montanartists.com
Marie-Sylvie Deveau	(310) 274-6611 www.gershagency.com
Roman Diaz	(323) 309-1738 www.romandiaz.com
Dion Peronneau Agency 5482 Wilshire Blvd., Ste. 1512 Los Angeles, CA 90036 (Reps for Wardrobe Stylists)	(323) 299-4043 FAX (323) 299-4269 www.dionperonneau.com
Maria Divaris	(310) 839-8722 www.cloutieragency.com
Marina Draghici	(310) 285-0303 www.sandramarsh.com
Mynka Draper	(310) 274-6611 www.gershagency.com
Jenna Drobnick	(323) 445-4910 www.artists-services.com
Candice Dubkousky	(323) 463-0022 www.radiantartists.com
Justin Ducoty	(310) 822-2898 www.rougeartists.com
Tere Duncan	(310) 652-8778 www.lspagency.net
John Dunn	(310) 274-6611 www.gershagency.com

Wardrobe Stylists/Costume Designers

Jenny Eagan	(310) 395-4600
	www.murthaagency.com
Patti Early	(818) 762-9908
Eastern Talent Agency	(323) 856-3000
849 S. Broadway, Ste. 811	FAX (323) 856-3009
Los Angeles, CA 90014	www.easterntalent.net
(Reps for Costume Designers)	
Lauren Ehrenfeld	(310) 998-1977
	www.celestineagency.com
Matthew Englebert	(310) 839-8722
	www.cloutieragency.com
Ennis, Inc.	(310) 587-3512
	www.ennisinc.com
(Reps for Wardrobe Stylists/Costume Designers)	
Epiphany Artist Group, Inc.	(323) 660-6353
9903 Santa Monica Blvd., Ste. 480	FAX (323) 660-0094
Beverly Hills, CA 90212	
(Reps for Wardrobe Stylists)	
Joseph Episcopo	(323) 856-8540
	www.opusbeauty.com
Nicoletta Ercole	(310) 395-4600
	www.murthaagency.com
Mary Erickson	(877) 242-6878
	www.lamakeup.com
Caroline Eselin	(310) 273-6700
	www.unitedtalent.com
Leesa Evans	(323) 297-0250
	www.magnetla.com
Jennifer Eve	(310) 623-5500
	www.montanartists.com
Timothy Everest	(323) 464-4481
	www.rappagency.com
Exclusive Artists Management	(323) 436-7766
7700 Sunset Blvd., Ste. 205	FAX (323) 436-7799
Los Angeles, CA 90046	www.eamgmt.com
(Reps for Wardrobe Stylists)	
Lynn Falconer	(310) 623-5500
	www.lynnfalconer.com
	(310) 393-3597
Ellen Falguiere	(310) 403-3831
Andrea Federman	(323) 856-3000
	www.easterntalent.net
Kathleen Felix-Hager	(310) 656-5151
	www.innovativeartists.com
Deborah Ferguson	(310) 998-1977
	www.celestineagency.com
Mariestela Fernandez	(310) 285-0303
	www.sandramarsh.com
April Ferry	(310) 273-6700
	www.utaproduction.com
Valentine Fillol-Cordier	(323) 297-0250
	www.magnetla.com
FIRE House Management	(888) 839-0101
(Reps for Wardrobe Stylists)	FAX (888) 839-2943
	www.firehousemanagement.com

	(818) 985-0086
Maureen Fletcher	(818) 681-1324
Danny Flynn	(323) 931-2745
	www.aimartist.com
Amanda Ford	(310) 623-5500
	www.montanartists.com
	(213) 482-5057
Hank Ford	(323) 633-6817
	www.hankford.net
Leah Forester	(310) 733-2550
	www.photogenicsmedia.com
Sharman Forman-Hyde	(323) 876-6317
	www.sharmanformanhyde.com
Mary Jane Fort	(310) 274-6611
	www.gershagency.com
Marie France	(310) 282-9940
	www.mirisch.com
Scott Free	(323) 466-2007
	www.rexagency.com
Meg Freeman	(310) 503-2116
Louise Frogley	(310) 273-6700
	www.utaproduction.com
Michele Gampel	(818) 515-7890
	www.mgampel.com
Sue Gandy	(323) 856-3000
	www.easterntalent.net
Camille Garmendia	(310) 458-7800
	www.partos.com
Pierre-Yves Gayraud	(310) 652-8778
	www.lspagency.net
Vanessa Geldbach	(323) 436-7766
	www.eamgmt.com
Judith R. Gellman	(310) 623-5500
	www.montanartists.com
Catherine George	(310) 285-9000
	www.wmeentertainment.com
Jenny Gering	(310) 288-8000
	www.paradigmagency.com
	(310) 274-6611
The Gersh Agency	(212) 997-1818
9465 Wilshire Blvd., Sixth Fl.	FAX (310) 274-4035
Beverly Hills, CA 90212	www.gershagency.com
(Reps for Costume Designers)	
Jean Lee Getson	(323) 466-2007
	www.therexagency.com
Melanie Ghisays	(818) 206-0144
	www.allcrewagency.com
Zoe Glassner	(310) 998-1977
	www.celestineagency.com
Danny Glicker	(323) 297-0250
	www.magnetla.com
Beth Goodman	(323) 972-5655
	www.bethgoodmanstylist.com

Louisa Gravelle	(310) 779-8977
	(310) 798-8841
	FAX (310) 798-3801
	www.louisagravell.com
Wendy Greiner	(310) 623-5500
	www.montanartists.com
Lee Grenrock-Viles	(818) 556-1557
	(818) 355-1433
Madison Guest	(323) 937-1010
	www.zenobia.com
Jenni Gullett	(310) 623-5500
	www.montanartists.com
Mia Gyzander	(818) 308-6729
	www.miagyzander.com
Jonas Hallberg	(323) 462-5000
	www.traceymattingly.com
Hope Hanafin	(310) 285-0303
	www.sandramarsh.com
Alicia Hankes	(323) 937-1010
	www.zenobia.com
Mary Claire Hannan	(310) 474-4585
	www.ddatalent.com
Suzie Hardy	(323) 935-8455
	www.ms-management.com
LuEllyn Harper	(323) 856-3000
	www.easterntalent.net
Lee Harris	(310) 276-0777
	www.thewallgroup.com
Roemehl Hawkins	(310) 656-5151
	www.innovativeartists.com
Dawn Haynes	(323) 850-6783
Sanja Hays	(310) 656-5151
	www.innovativeartists.com
Roberta Haze	(310) 623-5500
	www.montanartists.com
Kate Healey	(310) 656-5151
	www.innovativeartists.com
Cathleen Healy	(310) 274-0032
	www.artistsbytimothypriano.com
Betsy Heimann	(310) 623-5500
	www.montanartists.com
Frank Helmer	(310) 273-6700
	www.utaproduction.com
Lindy Hemming	(310) 273-6700
	www.utaproduction.com
Sandra Hernandez	(310) 656-5151
	www.innovativeartists.com
Alix Hester	(310) 274-6611
	www.gershagency.com
Sid Hicks	(323) 447-1701
	www.sidhicks.com
Erin Hirsh	(310) 822-2898
	www.rougeartists.com

Rebecca Hofherr	(310) 652-8778
	www.lspagency.net
Michael Holdaway	(323) 385-6113
	www.michaelholdaway.com
Laura Anne Hollabaugh	(323) 445-4910
	www.artists-services.com
Eric Hollis	(310) 733-2550
	www.photogenicsmedia.com
Shakira Holmes	(323) 445-4910
	www.artists-services.com
Judy Ruskin Howell	(310) 652-8778
	www.lspagency.net
Lawren Howell	(310) 276-0777
	www.thewallgroup.com
Innovative Artists	(310) 656-5151
1617 Broadway, Third Fl.	FAX (310) 656-5156
Santa Monica, CA 90404	www.innovativeartists.com
(Reps for Wardrobe Stylists/Costume Designers)	
International Creative	
Management - ICM	(310) 550-4000
10250 Constellation Blvd.	www.icmtalent.com
Los Angeles, CA 90067	
(Reps for Costume Designers)	
Janine Israel	(310) 998-1977
	www.celestineagency.com
iTalent Company	(818) 284-6423
522 Wilshire Blvd., Ste. K	FAX (866) 755-0708
Santa Monica, CA 90401	www.italentco.com
(Reps for Wardrobe Stylists/Costume Designers)	
Sasa Jalali	(323) 931-2745
	www.aimartist.com
Francine Jamison-Tanchuck	(310) 273-6700
	www.utaproduction.com
Dillon Jay	(310) 274-0032
	www.artistsbytimothypriano.com
Lisa Jensen	(818) 284-6423
	(818) 395-7911
	www.italentco.com
Aldene Johnson	(323) 297-0250
	www.magnetla.com
Darryle Johnson	(310) 288-8000
	www.paradigmagency.com
Jane Johnston	(323) 468-2240
	www.nyoffice.net
Betsy Jones	(805) 969-5501
Carlton Jones	(323) 850-6783
Gary Jones	(310) 273-6700
	www.utaproduction.com
Jeanette Jones	(213) 446-1720
	www.larep.net
Kelli Jones	(310) 623-5500
	www.montanartists.com
Shiffy Kagan	(323) 931-2745
	www.aimartist.com
Michael Kaplan	(310) 273-6700
	www.utaproduction.com

Wardrobe Stylists/Costume Designers

Chrisi Karvonides-Dushenko (310) 623-5500 www.montanartists.com	Stefanie Lain (818) 284-6423 www.italentco.com
Katie & Lindsey (310) 274-0032 www.artistsbytimothypriano.com	Jennifer Laine (310) 274-0032 www.artistsbytimothypriano.com
Jo Katsaras (310) 285-0303 www.sandramarsh.com	Wallace G. (Woody) Lane Jr. (323) 856-3000 www.easterntalent.net
Leah Katznelson (310) 623-5500 www.montanartists.com	(323) 851-9444 Erin Lareau/Topaz (323) 708-8005 www.topazwardrobe.com
Jayne Marie Kehoe (818) 216-1154 FAX (818) 715-9970	Suttirat Larlarb (310) 623-5500 www.montanartists.com
Kool Keita (310) 733-2550 www.photogenicsmedia.com	Stacy Lauwers (323) 896-2845 www.stacylauwers.com
Angelina Kekich (310) 623-5500 www.montanartists.com	(310) 457-1796 Valerie Laven-Cooper (310) 251-2172 FAX (310) 457-1796
Angela Kelley (310) 274-0032 www.artistsbytimothypriano.com	Christopher Lawrence (310) 656-5151 www.innovativeartists.com
Kemal & Karla (310) 276-0777 www.thewallgroup.com	(310) 288-3411 Jennifer Lax (510) 848-4748
Adeel Khan (310) 274-0032 www.artistsbytimothypriano.com	(Wardrobe Supervisor)
Mary Kate Killilea (323) 856-3000 www.easterntalent.net	Debra LeClair (310) 458-7800 www.partos.com
Perri Kimono (310) 701 0448	Francine Lecoultre (310) 666-9970
Holli Kingsbury (310) 274-0032 www.artistsbytimothypriano.com	Derek Lee (323) 299-4043 www.dionperonneau.com
Shane Klein (310) 246-0446 www.workgroup-ltd.com	Sara Leete (646) 298-9045 www.saraleete.com
(323) 556-3455 George Kotsiopoulos (212) 404-4527	Melanie Leftick (213) 908-6754 www.martonemgmt.com
(323) 937-1010 Paula Kowalczyk (917) 744-6120 www.paulakowalczyk.com	Pauline Leonard (310) 839-8722 www.cloutieragency.com
Susan Kowarsh Hall (310) 200-4138	Shauna Leone (323) 856-3000 www.easterntalent.net
Gini Kramer-Goldman (310) 403-0409 FAX (310) 398-1221	Henny Letailleur (323) 937-1010 www.zenobia.com
Christina Kretschmer (917) 553-7622 www.ckretschmer.com	Leigh Leverett (323) 856-3000 www.easterntalent.net
Azan Kung (310) 804-2469 www.electricacid.com	Jennifer Levy (323) 297-0250 www.magnetla.com
Rachel Sage Kunin (310) 656-5151 www.innovativeartists.com	Thea Lewis (323) 937-1010 www.zenobia.com
Anne Kunisaki (323) 445-4910 www.artists-services.com	George Liddle (310) 395-4600 www.murthaagency.com
Shirley Kurata (323) 297-0250 www.magnetla.com	Maya Lieberman (310) 458-7800 www.partos.com
Jeffrey Kurland (310) 458-7800 www.partos.com	Marylou Lim (213) 944-3021
Kurt & Bart (323) 549-3100 www.beautyandphoto.com	Kate Lindsay (626) 437-2817 www.katelindsay.com
Kelle Kutsugeras (310) 285-9000 www.wmeentertainment.com	Mandi Line (310) 282-9940 www.mirisch.com
LA Rep (213) 446-1720 (Reps for Wardrobe Stylists) FAX (323) 656-1756 www.larep.net	George Little (310) 656-5151 www.innovativeartists.com

Marc Littlejohn	(888) 839-0101
www.firehousemanagement.com	
Elin Litzinger	(323) 646-9581
	(818) 769-9006
Pie Lombardi	(818) 642-3601
Betty Pecha Madden	(323) 681-9394
	FAX (323) 681-9394
Molly Maginnis	(310) 656-5151
www.innovativeartists.com	

Magnet LA (323) 297-0250
6363 Wilshire Blvd., Ste. 650   FAX (323) 297-0249
Los Angeles, CA 90048   www.magnetla.com
(Reps for Wardrobe Stylists)

Kasia Walicka Maimone	(310) 395-4600
www.murthaagency.com	
Ann Somers Major	(310) 288-8000
www.paradigmagency.com	
Maryam Malakpour	(323) 556-3455
	FAX (323) 556-3456
www.maryammalakpour.com	
Karen Malecki	(310) 623-5500
www.montanartists.com	
Karen Mann	(310) 822-2898
www.rougeartists.com	
Bobbie Mannix	(310) 995-0803
	FAX (661) 251-9321
www.bobbiemannix.com	
Dana Marasca	(310) 998-1977
www.celestineagency.com	
Jessica Margolis	(323) 297-0250
www.magnetla.com	
Simonetta Mariano	(310) 623-5500
www.montanartists.com	
Meredith Markworth-Pollack	(310) 623-5500
www.montanartists.com	
Nancy Martin	(323) 856-3000
www.easterntalent.net	
Bernard Martinez	(323) 935-8455
www.ms-management.com	
	(323) 842-4373
Ramona Martinez	(323) 934-4375
	FAX (323) 934-4375
www.ramonamartinez.com	
Michelle Martini	(323) 297-0250
www.magnetla.com	

Martone MGMT (213) 908-6754
3324 1/2 Bellevue Ave.   FAX (213) 375-7882
Los Angeles, CA 90026   www.martonemgmt.com
(Reps for Wardrobe Stylists/Costume Designers)

Caroline Marx	(310) 285-9000
www.wmeentertainment.com	
Agata Maskiewicz	(323) 856-3000
www.easterntalent.net	
Stephane Maslansky	(310) 623-5500
www.montanartists.com	

Michelle Matland	(310) 288-8000
www.paradigmagency.com	
Julie Matos	(310) 839-8722
www.cloutieragency.com	
Mona May	(310) 458-7800
www.partos.com	
Graciela Mazon	(310) 285-0303
www.sandramarsh.com	
Liz McClean	(323) 297-0250
www.magnetla.com	
Debra McGuire	(310) 274-6611
www.gershagency.com	
Billy Ray McKenna	(310) 656-5151
www.innovativeartists.com	
Nonja McKenzie	(323) 856-8540
www.opusbeauty.com	
Samantha McMillen	(310) 276-0777
www.thewallgroup.com	
Gail McMullen	(310) 282-9940
www.mirisch.com	
Heidi Meek	(323) 856-8540
www.opusbeauty.com	
Mimi Melgaard	(310) 656-5151
www.innovativeartists.com	
Giovanna Melton	(310) 623-5500
www.montanartists.com	
Ilene Meltzer	(323) 856-3000
www.easterntalent.net	
Albert Mendonca	(310) 998-1977
www.celestineagency.com	
Antoinette Messam	(310) 623-5500
www.montanartists.com	
Lynette Meyer	(310) 623-5500
www.montanartists.com	
Michele Michel	(310) 652-8778
www.lspagency.net	
Patrik Milani	(323) 297-0250
www.magnetla.com	
Louise Mingenbach	(310) 273-6700
www.utaproduction.com	

The Mirisch Agency (310) 282-9940
8840 Wilshire Blvd., Ste. 100   FAX (310) 282-0702
Los Angeles, CA 90211   www.mirisch.com
(Reps for Costume Designers)

Sonu Mishra	(310) 623-5500
www.montanartists.com	
Hope Misterek	(323) 931-2745
www.aimartist.com	
Jessica Moazami	(310) 274-0032
www.artistsbytimothypriano.com	
Christie Moeller	(323) 937-1010
www.zenobia.com	
Lisa Moir	(323) 933-0200
www.artistuntied.com	

Tish Monaghan	(310) 656-5151	Kathryn Nixon	(323) 468-2240
	www.innovativeartists.com		www.nyoffice.net
Susan Monaster	(310) 306-8936	Patricia Norris	(310) 395-4600
			www.murthaagency.com
Elaine Montalvo	(323) 856-3000	Ray Oliveira	(323) 466-2007
	www.easterntalent.net		www.therexagency.com
Fredo Montes	(310) 274-0032	Danny O'Neill	(323) 933-0200
	www.artistsbytimothypriano.com		www.artistuntied.com
John Moore	(310) 822-2898		
	www.rougeartists.com		

Opus Beauty (323) 856-8540
6442 Santa Monica Blvd., Ste. 200B   FAX (323) 871-8311
Los Angeles, CA 90038   www.opusbeauty.com
(Reps for Wardrobe Stylists)

Shelli Moore	(323) 935-8455	Kathy O'Rear	(310) 395-4600
	www.ms-management.com		www.murthaagency.com
Jacquelyn Moran	(323) 468-2240	Daniel Orlandi	(310) 273-6700
	www.nyoffice.net		www.utaproduction.com
Beth Morgan	(323) 856-3000	Orlee	(323) 297-0250
	www.easterntalent.net		www.magnetla.com
Mia Morgan	(310) 839-8722	Bic Owen	(310) 623-5500
	www.cloutieragency.com		www.montanartists.com
Kathryn Morrison	(310) 656-5151	Richard Owings	(310) 282-9940
	www.innovativeartists.com		www.mirisch.com
Chrissy Morton	(310) 458-7800	Lydia Paddon	(310) 458-7800
	www.partos.com		www.partos.com

MS Management (323) 935-8455
(Reps for Wardrobe Stylists)   FAX (323) 935-3143
www.ms-management.com

Nina Padovano (818) 881-4358
(323) 497-7128
FAX (818) 881-3208

Abigail Murray	(310) 285-9000
	www.wmeentertainment.com

Partos Company (310) 458-7800
227 Broadway, Ste. 204   FAX (310) 587-2250
Santa Monica, CA 90401   www.partos.com
(Reps for Wardrobe Stylists)

Jeanne Murray	(310) 998-1977	Jessica Paster	(310) 998-1977
	www.celestineagency.com		www.celestineagency.com

The Murtha Agency (310) 395-4600
1025 Colorado Ave., Ste. B   FAX (310) 395-4622
Los Angeles, CA 90401   www.murthaagency.com
(Reps for Costume Designers)

		Beth Pasternak	(310) 274-6611
			www.gershagency.com
Isis Mussenden	(310) 285-0303	Beatrix Aruna Pasztor	(310) 274-6611
	www.sandramarsh.com		www.gershagency.com
April Napier	(323) 297-0250	Gretchen Patch	(213) 709-1797
	www.magnetla.com		www.gretchenpatch.com
Michael Nash	(310) 998-1977	Karen Patch	(310) 273-6700
	www.celestineagency.com		www.utaproduction.com

New York Office (323) 468-2240
(212) 545-7895
6605 Hollywood Blvd., Ste. 200   FAX (323) 468-2244
Los Angeles, CA 90028   www.nyoffice.net
(Reps for Costume Designers)

		Janet Patterson	(310) 285-0303
			www.sandramarsh.com
Jill Newell	(310) 285-9000	Paul & Isabelle	(323) 931-2745
	www.wmeentertainment.com		www.aimartist.com
Ha Nguyen	(310) 274-6611	Gaelle Paul	(310) 998-1977
	www.gershagency.com		www.celestineagency.com
Eric Niemand	(323) 297-0250	Oliva Miles Payne	(310) 285-9000
	www.magnetla.com		www.wmeentertainment.com
Bojana Nikitovic	(310) 623-5500	Gabriella Pescucci	(310) 285-0303
	www.montanartists.com		www.sandramarsh.com
Martina Nilsson	(323) 856-8540	Christine Peters	(310) 285-0303
	www.opusbeauty.com		www.sandramarsh.com
Susan Nininger	(323) 222-6217	Christopher Peterson	(310) 274-6611
			www.gershagency.com

Arianne Phillips	(310) 273-6700
	www.unitedtalent.com
Gersha Phillips	(310) 285-9000
	www.wmeentertainment.com
Photogenics	(310) 733-2550
8549 Higuera St.	FAX (310) 815-8632
Culver City, CA 90232	www.photogenicsmedia.com
(Reps for Wardrobe Stylists)	
Dayna Pink	(310) 273-6700
	www.unitedtalent.com
Jen Pinkston	(323) 931-2745
	www.aimartist.com
Carlo Poggioli	(310) 285-0303
	www.sandramarsh.com
Juliet Polcsa	(323) 468-2240
	www.nyoffice.net
Priscilla Polley	(323) 297-0250
	www.magnetla.com
Romeo Pompa	(323) 654-8065
	(323) 620-8554
	FAX (323) 654-8065
Joseph Porro	(310) 274-6611
	www.gershagency.com
Candy Poskin	(323) 466-2007
	www.therexagency.com
Milka Prica	(310) 998-1977
	www.celestineagency.com
Patia Prouty	(310) 652-8778
	www.lspagency.net
Monique Prudhomme	(310) 656-5151
	www.innovativeartists.com
Annie Psaltiras	(310) 276-0777
	www.thewallgroup.com
Tiffany Puhy	(310) 430-9902
	www.9-agency.com
Nissa Quanstrom	(310) 492-5930
	www.aubribalk.com/losangeles.htm
Beau Quillian	(310) 998-1977
	www.celestineagency.com
LeeAnn Radeka	(310) 288-8000
	www.paradigmagency.com
Rita Rago	(310) 822-2898
	www.rougeartists.com
Marina Ray	(323) 377-0933
	www.marinaray.com
Alysia Raycraft	(917) 685-2236
	(310) 656-5151
	www.alysiaraycraft.com
Luke Reichle	(310) 656-5151
	www.innovativeartists.com
Maude Retchin-Feil	(310) 738-1318
	(805) 845-1916

Marjolijn Reuter	(323) 937-1010
	www.zenobia.com
Edgar Revilla	(323) 289-5988
	www.edgarrevilla.com
The Rex Agency	(323) 466-2007
6311 Romaine St., Ste. 7235	FAX (323) 466-1966
Los Angeles, CA 90038	www.therexagency.com
(Reps for Wardrobe Stylists)	
Sally Rice	(310) 729-8861
	(949) 581-0583
	FAX (949) 581-0583
	www.sallyricefotos.com
Basia Richard	(310) 274-0032
	www.artistsbytimothypriano.com
Jacki Roach	(323) 468-2240
	www.nyoffice.net
David Robinson	(310) 273-6700
	www.unitedtalent.com
Marcell Rocha	(310) 246-0446
	www.workgroup-ltd.com
Neil Rodgers	(323) 462-5000
	www.traceymattingly.com
Nola Roller	(323) 459-4447
	www.nolaroller.com
Melina Root	(310) 623-5500
	www.montanartists.com
Penny Rose	(310) 285-9000
	www.wmeentertainment.com
Jo Rosen	(818) 206-0144
	www.allcrewagency.com
Sabrina Rosen	(310) 623-5500
	www.montanartists.com
Anne Ross	(310) 968-0007
	www.anneross.com
Rouge Artists, Inc.	(310) 822-2898
	(310) 570-1150
2433 Boone Ave.	FAX (310) 827-7367
Venice, CA 90291	www.rougeartists.com
(Reps for Wardrobe Stylists)	
Shoshana Rubin	(310) 656-5151
	www.innovativeartists.com
Bon Russell	(323) 309-1615
	FAX (323) 654-4772
Alexa Ryan	(310) 274-0032
	www.artistsbytimothypriano.com
Mindy Saad	(310) 998-1977
	www.celestineagency.com
Sam Saboura	(310) 822-2898
	www.rougeartists.com
Robert Saduski	(818) 206-0144
	www.allcrewagency.com
Angelique Salzmann	(323) 436-7766
	www.eamgmt.com
Sharon Taylor Sampson	(818) 206-0144
	www.allcrewagency.com

Evet Sanchez	(310) 276-0777
	www.thewallgroup.com
Roland Sanchez	(310) 288-8000
	www.paradigmagency.com
Vicki Sanchez	(310) 282-9940
	www.mirisch.com
Sandra Marsh & Associates	(310) 285-0303
9150 Wilshire Blvd., Ste. 220	FAX (310) 285-0218
Beverly Hills, CA 90212	www.sandramarsh.com
(Reps for Costume Designers)	
Cory Savage	(323) 445-1560
	www.corysavage.com
Eddie Schachrow	(310) 998-1977
	www.celestineagency.com
Peggy Schnitzer	(310) 274-6611
	www.gershagency.com
Nicole Christine Schott	(818) 693-9618
	www.nicolechristinedesign.com
Alexis Scott	(310) 623-5500
	www.montanartists.com
Deborah Scott	(310) 656-5151
	www.innovativeartists.com
Zeca Seabra	(323) 656-6117
Kelvin Seah	(323) 931-2745
	www.aimartist.com
Justine Seymour	(323) 856-3000
	www.justine-seymour.com
Mychael Shandra	(310) 994-3154
	www.mychaelshandra.com
	(212) 634-8114
Laura Jean Shannon	(310) 458-7800
	www.partos.com
Sammy Sheldon	(310) 273-6700
	www.utaproduction.com
Elizabeth Shelton	(818) 284-6423
	www.italentco.com
Shinko	(323) 466-2007
	www.therexagency.com
Gena Sigala	(310) 246-0446
	www.workgroup-ltd.com
Charmaine Simmons	(323) 465-7289
Sarah Jane Slotnick	(323) 856-3000
	www.easterntalent.net
	(818) 662-7057
Jules Smith	(213) 999-5110
	www.clothesmith.com
Laury Smith	(323) 856-8540
	www.opusbeauty.com
Rhonda Spies	(323) 436-7766
	www.eamgmt.com
Annie Spong	(323) 931-2745
	www.aimartist.com
Peggy Stamper	(310) 623-5500
	www.montanartists.com

Estee Stanley	(310) 276-0777
	www.thewallgroup.com
Katia Stano	(310) 656-5151
	www.innovativeartists.com
April Steiner	(323) 436-7766
	www.eamgmt.com
Nancy Steiner	(323) 297-0250
	www.magnetla.com
	(818) 761-4488
Jodie Stern	(818) 807-6707
Elizabeth Stewart	(310) 276-0777
	www.thewallgroup.com
Alvin Stillwell	(310) 998-1977
	www.celestineagency.com
Amy Stofsky	(323) 856-3000
	www.easterntalent.net
Callan Stokes	(323) 937-1010
	www.zenobia.com
Jennifer Stone	(818) 571-6114
	www.jenstonestyling.com
	(310) 476-6890
Neysa Stone	(310) 962-9260
	FAX (310) 471-1638
Casey Storm	(323) 297-0250
	www.magnetla.com
Sonja Streater	(818) 434-3113
Cynthia Summers	(310) 288-8000
	www.paradigmagency.com
Tara Swennen	(310) 276-0777
	www.thewallgroup.com
David Tabbert	(323) 446-2007
	www.therexagency.com
TAMU Artist Agency	(310) 721-0735
137 S. Robertson Blvd., Ste. 111	FAX (323) 571-3498
Beverly Hills, CA 90211	www.tamuartistagency.com
(Reps for Wardrobe Stylists)	
Machiko Tanaka	(323) 664-5948
	(323) 632-0532
Julieta Tapia	(323) 468-9222
	www.rootbeercostumer.com
Jill Taylor	(310) 285-9000
	www.wmeentertainment.com
Sheree Thiel	(818) 679-3756
David Thomas	(323) 856-8540
	www.opusbeauty.com
Kimberly Tillman	(310) 656-5151
	www.innovativeartists.com
	(323) 258-2664
Lisa Tilney	(323) 314-7474
Michelle Tomaszewski	(323) 297-0250
	www.magnetla.com
Tracey Mattingly, LLC	(323) 462-5000
(Reps for Wardrobe Stylists)	FAX (323) 462-5001
	www.traceymattingly.com

Samantha Traina	(310) 276-0777 www.thewallgroup.com	Paula Vila	(310) 403-7330
Sue Tsai	(310) 998-1977 www.celestineagency.com	Julie Vogel	(917) 520-7490 www.julievogel.com
Joan Tucker	(323) 731-7088 (323) 365-2001 FAX (323) 732-1808 www.joantucker.com	Mary Vogt	(310) 274-6611 www.gershagency.com
		Christine Wada	(310) 623-5500 www.montanartists.com
Simon Tuke	(310) 656-5151 www.innovativeartists.com	Keith Wager	(323) 356-2682 www.keithwager.com
Arianne Tunney	(323) 462-5000 www.traceymattingly.com	Cathryn Wagner	(323) 856-3000 www.easterntalent.net
Tracy Tynan	(310) 282-9940 www.mirisch.com	Karyn Wagner	(310) 285-0303 www.sandramarsh.com
Genevieve Tyrrell	(310) 656-5151 www.innovativeartists.com	Barcie Waite	(818) 206-0144 www.allcrewagency.com
United Talent Agency 9560 Wilshire Blvd., Ste. 500 Beverly Hills, CA 90212 (Reps for Costume Designers)	(310) 273-6700 FAX (310) 247-1111 www.utaproduction.com	Deborah Waknin	(310) 276-0777 www.thewallgroup.com
		Ariyela Wald-Cohain	(818) 371-7568 www.ariyela.com
Ilaria Urbinati	(310) 276-0777 www.thewallgroup.com	Sarah Wallner	(818) 252-7800 (213) 618-3636 FAX (818) 527-7803 www.sarahwallner.com
Valade (Wardrobe Stylist)	(818) 929-4313 (626) 298-6081 FAX (626) 298-6081		
		Gregory Wein	(310) 274-0032 www.artistsbytimothypriano.com
Terri Valazza	(818) 997-6050 (818) 808-6770 FAX (818) 997-3328 www.tvalazza.com	Becks Welch	(310) 276-0777 www.thewallgroup.com
Marilyn Vance	(310) 282-9940 www.mirisch.com	Alexandra Welker	(310) 623-5500 www.montanartists.com
Douglas VanLaningham	(323) 856-8540 www.opusbeauty.com	Michelle Wendell	(310) 403-6929 www.chiclittledevilstylehouse.com
Antonio Vega	(310) 405-5649 www.antoniovegastyling.com	Wendi & Nicole	(310) 276-0777 www.thewallgroup.com

Jacqueline West	(310) 274-6611	Jenna Wright	(310) 458-7800
	www.gershagency.com		www.partos.com
Ise White	(310) 274-0032	Johnny Wujek	(323) 297-0250
	www.artistsbytimothypriano.com		www.magnetla.com
Cindy Whitehead	(310) 379-2112	Jeanne Yang	(310) 276-0777
	www.cindywhitehead.com		www.thewallgroup.com
Naomi Wilding	(310) 839-8722	Hiroshi Yoshida	(323) 933-0200
	www.cloutieragency.com		www.artistuntied.com
Michael Wilkinson	(310) 273-6700	Kate Young	(323) 297-0250
	www.utaproduction.com		www.magnetla.com
Sharon Williams	(310) 998-1977	Camille Yvette	(323) 935-8455
	www.celestineagency.com		www.ms-management.com
Daren Willis	(818) 601-0489	Marie Zelenka-Hootsmans	(310) 237-6438
	FAX (818) 980-2248		www.baesjou.net

Jacqueline West — (310) 274-6611 — www.gershagency.com

Ise White — (310) 274-0032 — www.artistsbytimothypriano.com

Cindy Whitehead — (310) 379-2112 — www.cindywhitehead.com

Naomi Wilding — (310) 839-8722 — www.cloutieragency.com

Michael Wilkinson — (310) 273-6700 — www.utaproduction.com

Sharon Williams — (310) 998-1977 — www.celestineagency.com

Daren Willis — (818) 601-0489 — FAX (818) 980-2248

Christie Wittenborn — (310) 623-5500 — www.montanartists.com

Lizz Wolf — (310) 623-5500 — www.montanartists.com

Leila Wolford — (310) 274-0032 — www.artistsbytimothypriano.com

Albert Wolsky — (310) 458-7800 — www.partos.com

Durinda Wood — (310) 623-5500 — www.montanartists.com

Jenna Wright — (310) 458-7800 — www.partos.com

Johnny Wujek — (323) 297-0250 — www.magnetla.com

Jeanne Yang — (310) 276-0777 — www.thewallgroup.com

Hiroshi Yoshida — (323) 933-0200 — www.artistuntied.com

Kate Young — (323) 297-0250 — www.magnetla.com

Camille Yvette — (323) 935-8455 — www.ms-management.com

Marie Zelenka-Hootsmans — (310) 237-6438 — www.baesjou.net

Zenobia Agency, Inc.
(323) 937-1010
(888) 639-6917
130 S. Highland Ave.
Los Angeles, CA 90036
FAX (323) 937-1133
www.zenobia.com
(Reps for Wardrobe Stylists)

Rachel Zoe — (310) 276-0777 — www.thewallgroup.com

Mary Zophres — (310) 273-6700 — www.utaproduction.com

Alison Zukovsky — (310) 717-4810 — www.alisonzukovsky.com

The following has been kindly provided by Paul Petersen, president of A Minor Consideration, www.minorcon.org, (310) 532-1345. The editors would like to thank Paul for his help with this section. The contact info for the State Labor Commission (DLSE) is: San Francisco (415) 703-5300, Los Angeles (213) 620-6330 and San Diego (619) 220-5451.

There have been a number of changes in the world of working children, some major, most just technical in nature. The Young Performer's Data Base, compiled by the American Humane Association and funded by a grant from SAG and the IACF no longer appears on the Screen Actors Guild website and is being up-dated. For the latest "State-by-State" information we suggest you contact On Location Education (www.onlocationeducation.com) or Children In Film, (www.childreninfilm.com).

On union productions be aware that the theatrical unions' contracts travel with union children no matter where they work, and employers must remember this important contractual language: "Wherever there is a conflict in law or regulation pertaining to minors, the strictest interpretation shall apply."

Mandatory education and mandatory Coogan Accounts are now in place in New York State, Louisiana and, of course, California. Coogan set-asides are pending in New Jersey and Connecticut. Make sure your payroll company knows the requirements of the 15% Coogan set-aside and the parental obligation to supply this account information.

Safety and education are important elements whenever a minor is employed. You have two IATSE locals willing and able to help your production company. Don't be shy about calling the Studio Teachers, Local 884, IATSE, or Studio First Aid, Local 767, IATSE. Tell them how you plan to employ the minor, especially if you're using infants, and they will supply the information you need.

In California, the Department of Labor Standards and Enforcement has oversight and issues both the Permit to Employ and the child's Work Permit. The Department of Industrial Relation's Web site provides a complete listing under this heading:
California Code of Regulations, Title 8
Chapter 6. Division of Labor Standards Enforcement
Subchapter 2. Employment of Minors in the Entertainment Industry

8 CCR Section 11755.3—Studio Teacher's Authority.
The studio teacher, in addition to teaching, shall also have the responsibility for caring and attending to the health, safety and morals of minors under 16 years of age for whom they have been provided by the employer, while such minors are engaged or employed in any activity pertaining to the entertainment industry and subject to these regulations. In the discharge of these responsibilities, the studio teacher shall take cognizance of such factors as working conditions, physical surroundings, signs of the minor's mental and physical fatigue, and the demands placed upon the minor in relation to the minor's age, agility, strength and stamina. The studio teacher may refuse to allow the engagement of a minor on a set or location and may remove the minor there from, if in the judgment of the studio teacher, conditions are such as to present a danger to the health, safety or morals of the minor. Any such action by the studio teacher may be immediately appealed to the Labor Commissioner who may affirm or countermand such action.

8 CCR Section 11755.4—Studio Teacher's Remuneration.
The remuneration of the studio teacher shall be paid by the employer.

Paul Peterson
A Minor Consideration
(310) 532-1345
www.minorcon.org

ENTERTAINMENT INDUSTRY—SUMMARY CHART

AGE	WORK TIME SCHOOL IN SESSION	WORK TIME SCHOOL NOT IN SESSION	CONCURRENT REQUIREMENTS
15 days to 6 months	May only be employed between 9:30 a.m. and 11:30 a.m. or between 2:30 p.m. and 4:30 p.m. [8 CCR 11764]	20 minutes work activity 2 hrs. max at employment site	Permits to work and employ required. [8 CCR 11751] Parent or guardian must be present. [8 CCR 11757] 1 studio teacher and 1 nurse must be present for each 3 or fewer infants 15 days to 6 weeks old. [8 CCR 11760, 11755.2] 1 studio teacher and 1 nurse must be present for each 10 or fewer infants 6 weeks to 6 months old. [8 CCR 11760, 11755.2] May not be exposed to light exceeding 100 footcandles for more than 30 seconds. [8 CCR 11760]
6 months to 2 years	May only be employed between 5 a.m. and 12:30 a.m. [LC 1308.7]	2 hours work activity 4 hours max at employment site Balance for rest and recreation	Permits to work and employ required unless the minor is a high school graduate or equivalent. [8 CCR 11751] High School graduates may be employed as adults. Parent or guardian must be present. [8 CCR 11757] Studio teacher must be present. [8 CCR 11751.1]
2 years to 6 years	May only be employed between 5 a.m. and 12:30 a.m. [LC 1308.7]	3 hours work activity 6 hours max at employment site Balance for rest and recreation	1 studio teacher required per 10 minors. [8 CCR 11755.1] 1 studio teacher per 20 minors on weekends, holidays, and school breaks and vacations. [8 CCR 11755.1]
6 years to 9 years	4 hours work activity 3 hours school 1 hour rest and recreation 8 hrs. max at employment site May only be employed between 5 a.m. and 12:30 a.m. (to 10 p.m. preceding schooldays ≥ 4 hours).[LC 1308.7]	6 hours work activity 1 hour rest and recreation	Studio teachers are responsible for the health, safety, and morals of the minor. [8CCR 11755.2] Minors in grades one through six must be tutored between the hours of 7 a.m. and 4 p.m. Minors in grades seven through twelve must be tutored between the hours of 7 a.m. and 7 p.m. [EC 48225.5]
9 years to 16 years	5 hours work activity 3 hours school 1 hour rest and recreation 9 hrs. max at employment site May only be employed between 5 a.m. and 12:30 a.m. (to 10 p.m. preceding schooldays ≥ 4 hours).[LC 1308.7]	7 hours work activity 1 hour rest and recreation	Permits to work and employ required unless a high school graduate or equivalent. High school graduates may be employed as adults.
16 years to 18 years	6 hours work activity 3 hours school 1 hour rest and recreation 10 hrs. max at employment site May only be employed between 5 a.m. and 12:30 a.m. (to 10 p.m. preceding schooldays ≥ 4 hours).[LC 1308.7]	8 hours work activity 1 hour rest and recreation	Studio teacher need only be present for minors' schooling if minor still required to attend school.
Regular School Attendance and Work Hours	Compute work hours for each age group by subtracting 6 hours from the max time at employment site for tutored minors when school in session. The difference is the maximum work hours for these minors. Thus, 9 to16 year-olds who attend regular school may only work up to 3 hours on a schoolday. The 1-hour of rest and recreation is not required, but the workday may be extended one-half hour by a meal period. No work permitted during regular school hours. **Exception:** Minors 14 and over may work up to 8 hours during regular school hours for each of 2 consecutive days if excused with the school's written permission. [8 CCR 11760]		
Max Day/Week	No minor may be employed over 8 hours in a day. [LC 1308.7, 1392] or over 48 hours in a week. [LC 1308.7] **No exceptions.**		
Meal Periods	Meal periods are not work time. Workdays extended up to one-half hour for a meal period. [8 CCR 11761] Meals must be within 6 hours of call time and/or previous meal period. Teachers may require an earlier meal period.		
Travel Time	Travel between studio and location is work time. Up to 45 minutes travel from on-location, overnight lodging to work site is not generally considered work time. Travel between school or home and studio is not work time. [8 CCR 11759]		
Day's End	12 hours must elapse between dismissal and next day's call time. **No exceptions.** [8 CCR 11760]		
Make-up Off Set	Make-up in minor's home by persons employed on the same project is work time, and may not begin before 8:30 a.m. 12 hours must elapse between dismissal and the beginning of the next day's make-up/hairdressing. [8 CCR 11763]		
Out of State	California employers who employ resident minors outside of California under contractual arrangements made within California, must comply with all California child labor laws and regulations. [8 CCR 11756]		

Note: Daily work and school hour schedules for tutored minors of all age groups are provided in 8 CCR 11760.

Signatory Requirements

Who is the Signatory to a union contract?

A production company producing a bona fide commercial project that wishes to hire union labor should be a signatory to the union. Legally a company is not required to sign a union contract. However, union employees are barred by their union from accepting work offered by a production company that has not signed the union agreement. Some unions have separate agreements for AICP and non-AICP companies.

A production company may become a union signatory in three ways:

Production Company Signs Directly

Commits the production company to observe all aspects of the union contract. DGA, SAG, Local 600 East and the IATSE Commercial Production Agreement require direct signatory. The advertising agency or client is usually the SAG signatory; rarely is the production company a SAG signatory. (SAG signatory issues are covered in greater depth in the introduction to the SAG Contracts.) In certain circumstances, a union might offer the production company a Letter of Adherence (LOA) that covers a single project rather than a Term Agreement, which covers all projects, but this is becoming less common.

The following unions require production companies to sign agreements directly with them:

> DGA (if Non-AICP)
> IATSE Commercial Production Agreement (Covers L.A. County and rest of U.S. except New York and San
>   Francisco; covers Local 600 Nationwide)
> IATSE Local 16 - San Francisco
> IATSE Local 52 Studio Mechanics (Non-AICP Independent version)
> IATSE Local 600 Cinematographers - Single Production Agreements when available
> IATSE Local 829 Set Designers, Scenic Artists & Stylists
> Teamsters Local 399 - Separate Driver and Location Scout Agreements (Non-AICP Independent version)

Production Company Signs Via AICP

Association of Independent Commercial Producers member companies are not automatically signatories to any contract. To become a signatory, a company must sign an agreement through the AICP:

> DGA (AICP member companies)
> IATSE Commercial Production Agreement (Covers L.A. County and rest of U.S. except New York and San
>   Francisco; covers Local 600 Nationwide)
> IATSE Local 52 - Studio Mechanics (Must sign Trust Acceptance)
> IATSE Local 476 - Chicago (Agreement for locally based companies only)
> Teamsters Local 399 - Separate Driver and Location Scout Agreements (AICP version)

Payroll Service Acts as Signatory

In the past, some unions have allowed the payroll service to function as the signatory. This means that the production company need not sign a union contract before hiring union personnel. This is a rare exception.

Union Responsibilities of Production Company

Whichever form of signatory is used, producers are required to follow all terms and conditions of the applicable union contract(s). In general these provisions include, but are not limited to:

Staffing requirements
Wage rates
Overtime
Meal penalties
Turnaround

In general, all employees working in classifications covered by a collective bargaining agreement are entitled to receive

the wages, benefits and other terms specified in the collective bargaining agreement regardless of whether they are members of a union.

Right to work laws do not permit an employer to avoid union terms and conditions; they only give the employee the right not to join the union (not withstanding any union security provisions contained in the collective bargaining agreement; see Right to Work Laws information contained later in this guide).

As a practical matter, most union agreements do not permit the mixing of crews. It should be noted that in many situations IATSE is allowing the hiring of qualified non-union workers as long as the producer covers them under the full provisions of the contract. You should check with your payroll service in the event that it becomes necessary to utilize a mixed crew.

Premium Day Guidance - Commercial Union Agreements

Many union contracts allow for a flexible workweek, usually referred to as "Any 5 of 7". This means that the workweek can start on any day of the week and that Saturday and Sunday are not necessarily Premium days. As a result of these flexible workweek provisions, questions arise in regard to defining 6th or 7th Premium days and what constitutes the start of a new week.

While all the agreements discussed here provide for the "Any 5 of 7" flexible workweek (except DGA, which provides for 5 consecutive days only), they fall into two categories in the interpretation of the determination of the 6th and 7th Premium days.

1. Per the AICP, for the following agreements, accepted practice is that 6th and 7th Premium rates are assigned when a $\underline{6^{th}}$ or 7th day is worked within a 7 day week as established by the first day of work. Thus if there is a day off within the workweek, there is no possibility of a 7th day Premium within that week.

    Commercial Production Agreement - Except NE Corridor
    Local 399 Teamsters
    Local 16 San Francisco
    Local 399 Location Scouts/Managers
        Note: Exempt category – 12 hr Flat rate. No OT except 1.5x for 7th day on same project.
    Local 817 Location Scouts/Managers (AICP Only)

2. Per the AICP, for the following agreements, accepted practice is that 6th and 7th Premium rates are assigned when work is performed on the 6th or 7th consecutive day of a week as established by the first day of work. Thus a day off within the workweek does not change the assignment of 6th or 7th day Premiums to the 6th or 7th consecutive day of that week.
    Local 817* Teamsters / Location Managers (Non-AICP)
    Local 829 Scenic Artists
    DGA
    Local 52** Studio Mechanics - NY
    NE Corridor - Commercial Production Agreement
    - Local 600 East
    - Local 161 - Script
    - Local 798 - Hair & Makeup

    * Local 817 - Only if there are four or more shoot days within jurisdiction. Otherwise, no flexible workweek.

    ** Local 52 Notes
        54 hours off ends a 5-day workweek.
        34 hours off ends a 6-day workweek.
        Tracking by department starts at the Pre-light and includes replacement hires.
        New function hires are tracked individually.
        Sunday work "other than photography" requires 5-hour call at double time.
        In a week where Sunday is not worked (34 hours turnaround), 7th day is paid at 1.5x.
            In both situations, two consecutive days off with no work and no travel start a new workweek.

    Only SAG has no flexible workweek. Saturday and Sunday are premium days.

New York		Los Angeles
Steve Bizenov		Tina Bassir
(646) 829-0702	**MEDIA SERVICES**	(310) 471-9369
steve@media-services.com	ENTERTAINMENT ACCOUNTING, PAYROLL & SOFTWARE	tina@media-services.com

IATSE COMMERCIAL PRODUCTION AGREEMENT

Working Rules & Conditions

Term of Contract		10/1/10 - 9/30/2013
Contracted Day		8 consecutive hours
Contracted Workweek		Any 5 or 6 consecutive days of 7
Calls	Day/Night	Anytime Time begins at Set Call Time
	Partial Day	No Except Travel Days - Min. 4 hours/ Max. 8 hrs @ 1x
Overtime	1.5x	9-12 hrs, 6th day up to 12 hours
	2x	After 12 hrs, 7th day, Holidays
	3x	6th day after 12 hrs worked
	4x	7th day after 12 hrs worked
	Increments	¼ hr increments
Turnaround	Daily	10 hours (9 hrs overnight location, portal-to-portal. DP/Camera Operator: 10 hrs.)
Penalty	If rest at least 6 hrs	Base or OT rate when released plus 1x for invaded hours
	If rest less than 6 hrs	Base or OT rate when released plus 1x for day until 10 hr rest period provided
Meals	Intervals	6 hr intervals, 1st meal no earlier than 3 hrs
	Lengths	½ hr to 1 hr
	Penalties	1st ½ hr or fraction - $7.50, 2nd ½ hr or fraction - $10, Each additional - $15
	Second Meal	May be deducted if it is outside min call
	Extensions	1st may be extended 15 min to complete setup. 2nd may be extended 30 min to complete setup or wrap
	Walking Meal	Any second meal, excluding NDB, may be a non-deductible walking meal, provided crew is dismissed within 1 hr from time meal was due
Production Zone		Within a circular 30 mile zone from intersection of City Hall for designated production centers
Location Rules		Per Diem allowance and housing or housing allowance to be provided
		Air Transportation: Coach or better
Work Time/ Travel Time Provisions		Overnight locations: Work: Set call to set dismissal. 1 hr allowable travel time. Excess paid as work time.
		Travel Days: Min 4 hrs, Max 8 hrs Straight Time. Mileage at current IRS rate.
Cancellation of Call		By 3pm of prior non-work day; By end of prior work day
		Penalty: Work Day - 8 hrs pay Travel Day - 4 hrs pay
Minimum Staffing		No requirements. Staffing must be consistent with past practices. There is practical interchangeability within the production crafts.
		Covers classifications traditionally covered by IATSE. Excludes office clerical, PA's and guards.
		Commercial stylists are not included in the agreement, but Costume Designers and Costumers are.
Payment of Wages		No special provisions. Most states require payment within 2 weeks. CA has severe late payment penalties
Hazardous Work		No special provisions, except in NE Corridor. See NE Corridor Notes page.
Jurisdiction		Throughout U.S., Puerto Rico and U.S. Virgin Islands. See Jurisdiction: Within LA rates page for exceptions.
Pension Health & Welfare		Rates vary geographically. See AICP - IATSE Commercial Production Agreements - PH & W rates page.
		Travel and Idle Days on location: 8 hrs PH & W contribution
Holidays		New Year's Day Martin Luther King Day President's Day Memorial Day
		Independence Day Labor Day Thanksgiving Day Christmas Day
Union Security TV Commercial Roster		Preference of employment: First consideration to those referred by local unions.
		Workers who are not current members of the union may be hired based on advertiser or agency requirements or documented industry experience. All are covered by all of agreement's provisions.
		Marine coordinators, boat handlers & operators covered, if not covered by another union.
Notes		>Outside LA County, NY & Phila Zones, producers must notify LA or NY IA office prior to shoot.
		>Producers must be direct signatory to full agreement. No letters of adherence.
		>Excludes PSAs and spec commercials. P&W contributions optional on PSAs.
		>Excludes traditional low budget commercials w/ single day cost of $75K or less and total cost of $300K or less.
		>Excludes Non-Trad low budget commercials with single day cost of $50K or less and total cost of $750K or less.
		>For ALL low budget, wage rates subject to individual negotiation. P&W normal.
		>IATSE or crew may appoint a Job Steward for each production.
		>Scope of Agreement - Where Employer has no effective control portions of pre and post production not covered. Employers not prevented from subcontracting for services consistent with industry practice.
		>Higher Classification - Two or more hours work in higher classification requires higher rate for day.
		>Recognize jurisdiction over commercials made by traditional means for any medium including Internet.
		>Internet commercials by non-traditional means to be negotiated, all but wages & work rules apply.
Phone numbers		LA IATSE: 818-980-3499, NY: 212-730-1770 LA AICP: 323-960-4763, NY: 212-929-3000

New York		Los Angeles
Steve Bizenov	**MEDIA**	Tina Bassir
(646) 829-0702	**SERVICES**	(310) 471-9369
steve@media-services.com	ENTERTAINMENT ACCOUNTING, PAYROLL & SOFTWARE	tina@media-services.com

IATSE COMMERCIAL PRODUCTION AGREEMENT

L.A. County Minimum Rates 10/1/12 - 9/30/13

Classification	Hourly	8-hour Day	Daily On Call	Weekly On Call
LOCAL 600				
Director of Photography	101.02	808.17		
Camera Operator	61.85	494.82		
First Assistant Cameraman	44.74	357.90		
Second Assistant Camera	41.10	328.77		
Camera Loader/Utility	35.17	281.36		
Digital Imaging Technician	58.94	471.48		
LOCAL 695				
Sound Mixer	69.01	552.11		
Boom Operator	46.59	372.75		
Sound Utility	46.59	372.75		
VTR/Video Playback	46.59	372.75		
LOCAL 80				
Key Grip	43.31	346.47		
2nd Grip	38.78	310.24		
Dolly Grip	40.17	321.34		
Grip	37.03	296.21		
Entry Level Grip	32.40	259.16		
Craft Service	31.39	251.08		
LOCAL 728				
Lighting Gaffer	43.31	346.47		
2nd Electrician	38.78	310.24		
Dimmer Operator	37.87	302.98		
Electrician	37.03	296.21		
Entry Level Electrician	32.40	259.16		
LOCAL 44				
Property Master	43.31	346.47		
2nd Prop	37.87	302.98		
3rd Prop	35.49	283.89		
Propmaker Foreman	43.50	348.02		
Propmaker	37.87	302.98		
Set Decorator (On Call)			623.38	2,631.75
Special Effects Foreperson	43.50	348.02		
Lead Effects	40.17	321.34		
Effects	37.87	302.98		
Lead Set Dresser	37.87	302.98		
Set Dresser	35.49	283.89		
Construction Coordinator (On Call)			605.75	2,560.50
LOCAL 892				
Costume Designer (On Call)			585.95	2,441.99
LOCAL 705				
Key Costumer	41.16	329.26		
2nd Costumer	38.30	306.41		
3rd Costumer	35.79	286.33		
Entry Level Costumer	27.94	223.50		
LOCAL 706				
Key Makeup Artist	49.30	394.37		
2nd Makeup Artist	41.96	335.70		
3rd Makeup Artist	38.03	304.20		
Key Hair Stylist	48.90	391.19		
2nd Hair Stylist	42.89	343.13		
3rd Hair Stylist	36.56	292.45		
LOCAL 871				
Script Supervisor	36.17	289.35		

New York		Los Angeles
Steve Bizenov		Tina Bassir
(646) 829-0702	**MEDIA SERVICES**	(310) 471-9369
steve@media-services.com	ENTERTAINMENT ACCOUNTING, PAYROLL & SOFTWARE	tina@media-services.com

Classification	Hourly	8-hour Day	Daily On Call	Weekly On Call
LOCAL 767				
First Aid	33.79	270.34		
LOCAL 800				
Art Director (On Call)				3,445.97
Assistant Art Director (On Call)				2,578.98
LOCAL 729				
Paint Foreperson	63.78	510.24		
Painter	37.87	302.98		
LOCAL 800				
Lead Scenic Artist	56.14	449.13		
Scenic Artist	50.77	406.12		
LOCAL 884				
Studio Teacher/Welfare Worker	47.03	376.26		

Five Day Studio "On Call" Rate	
CLASSIFICATION	10/1/12 - 9/30/13
Production Accountant	2,576.42
Production Office Coordinator	1,546.63
Assistant Production Accountant	1,460.69
Assistant Production Office Coordinator	916.56
Art Department Coordinator	916.56

New York
Steve Bizenov
(646) 829-0702
steve@media-services.com

MEDIA
SERVICES
ENTERTAINMENT ACCOUNTING, PAYROLL & SOFTWARE

Los Angeles
Tina Bassir
(310) 471-9369
tina@media-services.com

LOCAL 399 TEAMSTERS - AICP & INDEPENDENT

Working Rules & Conditions

Term of Contract		2/1/11 - 1/31/14
Contracted Day		8 consecutive hours
Contracted Workweek		Any 5 or 6 consecutive days of 7
Calls	Day/Night	Not mentioned
	Partial Day	No Except Travel Days - Min. 4 hours/ Max. 8 hrs @ 1x
Overtime	1.5x	9-12 hrs, 6th day up to 12 hours
	2x	After 12 hrs, 7th day, Holidays
	3x	6th day after 12 hrs worked
	4x	7th day after 12 hrs worked
	Increments	¼ hr increments Overtime premiums not compounded
Turnaround	Daily	9 hours (8 hrs overnight location)
Penalty	If rest at least 8 hrs	1x for invaded hours
	If rest at least 6 hrs	Premium rate for invaded hours
	If rest less than 6 hrs	Premium rate for day until 9 hr rest period is provided
Meals	Intervals	6 hr intervals, 1st meal no earlier than 3 hrs, except for early call crew provided w/ Non-Deductible Breakfast
	Lengths	½ hr - 1 hr
	Penalties (follow IA)	1st ½ hr or fraction - $7.50, 2nd ½ hr or fraction - $10, Each additional - $15
	Second Meal	
	Extensions	1st may be extended 15 min to complete setup. 2nd may be extended 30 min to complete setup or wrap
	Walking Meal	Any second meal, excluding NDB, may be a non-deductible walking meal, provided crew is dismissed within 1 hr from time meal was due
Studio Zone		> Within a circular 30 mile zone from intersection of Beverly Blvd. and La Cienega Blvd. in Los Angeles
Location Rules		> Per Diem allowance and housing or housing allowance to be provided.
		> Air Transportation - Domestic: Coach or better, International: Business Class
		> Local Hires: Fair consideration shall be given to those referred by affiliated local unions.
		> Not required to transport teamster drivers to distant locations to drive motorhomes/ housecars
Work Time/ Travel Time Provisions		Travel Days: Min 4 hrs, Max 8 hrs Straight Time. Mileage at current IRS rate.
Cancellation of Call		By 3pm of prior non-work day; By end of prior work day
		Penalty: Work Day - 8 hrs pay Travel/Wrap Day - 4 hrs pay
Minimum Staffing		> If there is covered equipment, One Gang Boss for each production hired from Group 1 or 2 of Industry Experience Roster. Gang Boss may not be a Driver/Grip or Driver/Electrician or drive any Exempt Equipment (Such as Production Vans, Motorhomes, Chapman Cranes Camera Cars, etc.-See App. B)
		> No Gang Boss needed if four or less production vehicles. (Teamster or Non Teamster) (See list Art. 5)
		> Gang Boss may not work on more than one production at a time.
		> Gang Boss: 1. Must call/clear members within 2 hours of call or hire; 2.Must supervise parking of all vehicles; 3. Must travel on every job w/covered vehicle taken from LA; 4. May be released after 10hrs on STAGE day when no work to perform.
		> Operators of regulated vehicles requiring Class A or B comm'l license are subject to agrmt.
		> Preference of Employment (Roster) does not apply to drivers of Motorhomes, Exempt Vehicles and hyphenate drivers.
		> One driver to be assigned to each piece of covered equipment; will help with load, unload and fueling.
		> On Shoot Day only Teamster must shuttle cast and crew (not agency) to and from parking lot and set.
		> 15 passenger vans driven by Teamsters only on shoot days.
Payment of Wages		No special provisions, but CA requires payment on same schedule as staff. Penalties are high.
Hazardous Work		No special provisions
Jurisdiction		CA. AZ, HI, NV. Production Co has option of adding CO, NM, OR, UT and WA through an Area Standards Supplement (otherwise negotiated on case by case basis).
Pension Health & Welfare		Follows IATSE Commercial Production Agreement. Rates vary geographically. See AICP - IATSE Commercial Production Agreements - PH & W rates page. Effective 2/1/12 and 2/1/13
		Travel and Idle Days on location: 8 hrs PH & W contribution
Holidays		New Year's Day Martin Luther King Day President's Day Memorial Day
		Independence Day Labor Day Thanksgiving Day Christmas Day

New York

Steve Bizenov

(646) 829-0702

steve@media-services.com

MEDIA
SERVICES

ENTERTAINMENT ACCOUNTING, PAYROLL & SOFTWARE

Los Angeles

Tina Bassir

(310) 471-9369

tina@media-services.com

Covered Vehicles	Non-Exempt Vehicles - Subject to Seniority Grouping
	10 Ton Trucks Driveable Generators (Class B) 200 Amps bolted to truck
	Fuel Trucks Passenger Vans
	Vehicles towing three axled trailers, generator, trailers w/three or more rooms or any trailer exceeding 10,000 lbs
	All cast and hair/makeup trailers that contain plumbing are to be operated by Teamsters.
	When a single cube truck is required for Grip/Electric, that vehicle does not require a Teamster driver. All vehicles containing grip/electric equipment, on any production requiring a gang boss, must be operated by Teamsters.
	On shoot days only, if there is at least one vehicle working in the Art/Prop department, it must be operated by a Teamster unless it is a cube truck and that cube is the only art/prop vehicle. When 4 or more art/prop vehicles are required, at least 2 of them must be operated by Teamsters.
	> Stake bed trucks not requiring A or B License are covered by Independent agreement
	Specialized Equipment - Exempt from Seniority Grouping Only
	Production Vans - (400 Amp Gen Min.) Camera Cars
	Chapman Cranes Catering Trucks
	Car Carriers (4 vehicles or more) Water Trucks
	Highway Buses (38+ Pass. Incl. Driver) Hydro-cranes (5 Ton or more)
	Honeywagons Motorhomes/Housecars
	Mobile Kitchens - Driver/Cooks (Class A), but NOT assistants
	5 Ton trucks w/covered box not requiring a Class A or B license
Notes	> Producers must be direct signatory to full agreement.
	> Location Scouts and Managers - Paid under separate agreement.
	> Higher Classification - 2 or more hours work in higher classification requires higher rate for day.
	> Non-rostered drivers may be hired when designated by advertiser or agency due to special conditions.
	> Overnight locations - Teamsters paid for idle days on overnight locations only if they or any IA crew are working on production.
	> Where Employer has no effective control portions of pre and post production, they not covered.
	> Employers not prevented from subcontracting for services consistent with industry practice.
	> No use of non-covered equipment to deliberately avoid terms of agreement.
	> See Agreement for new No-Hire, Hyphenate and Safety Passport provisions.
	> AICP Members are not required to sign the Wrangler Sideletter. Terms are same as this agreement.
	> Excludes public service announcements, spec commercials and low budget commercials whose aggregate shooting schedule is two days or more. Single day not more than $75K and. total costs do not exceed $300K
	> On low budget commercials, wage rates subject to individual negotiation. P&W normal.
	> Employees must sign Confidentiality or Non-Disclosure Agreements if provided by employer.
Phone numbers	Local 399: 818-980-3499 LA AICP: 323-960-4763

New York
Steve Bizenov
(646) 829-0702
steve@media-services.com

MEDIA SERVICES
ENTERTAINMENT ACCOUNTING, PAYROLL & SOFTWARE

Los Angeles
Tina Bassir
(310) 471-9369
tina@media-services.com

LOCAL 399 LOCATION SCOUTS/ MANAGERS - AICP ONLY

Working Rules & Scale Rates

Term of Contract		2/1/11 - 1/31/14			
Contracted Day		12 hours "On call" consecutive hours			
Contracted Workweek		Not specified, but state law requires premium pay for 6th and 7th days			
Calls	Day/Night	Not mentioned			
	Partial Day	No			
Overtime	1.5x	N/A - Considered exempt under wage & hour law			
(Shoot days only)	2x	N/A			
	3x	N/A			
	4x	N/A			
	Increments	On shoot days only: 1/10th of daily rate for work in excess of 14 hours			
Turnaround	Daily	9 hrs			
	Weekly				
Penalty		1.5x for invaded hours			
Meals	Intervals	CA law: No more than 6 hour intervals			
	Lengths	CA law: ½ hr - 1 hr			
	Penalties	Not covered			
	Extensions	Not covered			
	Walking Meal	Not covered			
Studio Zone		Not covered			
Location Rules		Not covered			
Work Time/ Travel Time Provisions		Not covered			
Cancellation of Call		Anytime before 8pm on the prior day			
Minimum Staffing		Any Location Scouts or Location Managers needed			
Payment of Wages		CA law requires payment on same schedule as staff. Penalties are high.			
Hazardous Work		No special provisions			
Jurisdiction		Los Angeles County and when transported out of L.A. County. Not required to transport out of L.A. Production Co has option of adding AZ, CO, HI, NV, NM, OR, UT, WA and CA outside L.A. County through an Area Standards Supplement (otherwise negotiated on case by case basis).			
Pension Health & Welfare		Follows IATSE Commercial Production Agreement. Rates vary geographically. See AICP - IATSE Commercial Production Agreements - PH & W rates page. Travel and Idle Days on location: 8 hrs PH & W contribution			
Holidays		2x for work on recognized SAG Agreement holidays			
Scale Rates		Daily	2/27/11	2/1/12	2/1/13
		Loc. Scout/Manager:	$591.00	$603.06	$615.12
Notes		> Industry Roster: All employees must be listed on Roster unless less than 16 are available on 1st day of job > Location Mgr. MUST be employed on any non-self contained location Self Contained Locations include: studio Lots, warehouses, stages, filming ranches and any private property with off-street parking sufficient that no equipment is parked on public property > Min. Kit rental $50 per day for entire kit including cell. Mileage at IRS allowable rates > Replacing a scout with a manager is not a violation of the agreement > Excludes public service announcements, spec commercials. Also excludes low budget commercials whose aggregate shooting schedule is two days or more and single day cost does not exceed $75K nor aggregate production costs do not exceed $225K > On low budget commercials, wage rates subject to individual negotiation. P&W normal > Employees must sign Confidentiality or Non-Disclosure Agreements if provided by employer.			
Phone numbers		Local 399: 818-985-7374	AICP LA: 323-960-4763, NY: 212-929-3000		

New York
Steve Bizenov
(646) 829-0702
steve@media-services.com

MEDIA
SERVICES
ENTERTAINMENT ACCOUNTING, PAYROLL & SOFTWARE

Los Angeles
Tina Bassir
(310) 471-9369
tina@media-services.com

LOCAL 399 LOCATION SCOUTS/ MANAGERS - INDEPENDENT

Working Rules & Scale Rates

Term of Contract		2/27/11 - 1/31/14			
Contracted Day		12 hours "On call" consecutive hours			
Contracted Workweek		Any 7 consecutive day commencing with the first day			
Calls	Day/Night	Not mentioned			
	Partial Day	No			
Overtime	1.5x	Over 12 hrs or 6th day (12.5% of 12 hr rate = 1.5x based on 12 hr rate)			
(Calculated on 10	2x	7th Day - Considered exempt under wage & hour law			
hr day rate)	3x	N/A			
	4x	N/A			
	Increments	"…major portion" of hour			
Turnaround	Daily	9 hrs			
	Weekly				
Penalty		1.5x for invaded hours			
Meals	Intervals	CA law: No more than 6 hour intervals			
	Lengths	CA law: ½ hr - 1 hr			
	Penalties	Not covered			
	Extensions	Not covered			
	Walking Meal	Not covered			
Studio Zone		30 mile zone from Beverly Blvd. and La Cienega Blvd.			
Location Rules		Per Diem and housing or allowance to be provided			
Work Time/ Travel Time Provisions		Travel days are at minimum rate			
Cancellation of Call		Not covered			
Minimum Staffing		Any Location Scouts or Location Managers needed			
		Location Manager MUST be employed on any non-self-contained location. Self-contained locations include: studio lots, warehouses, stages, filming ranches and any private property with off-street parking sufficient that no equipment is parked on public property.			
Payment of Wages		CA law requires payment on same schedule as staff. Penalties are high.			
Hazardous Work		No special provisions			
Jurisdiction		AZ, CA, CO, HI, NV, NM, OR, UT, WA			
Pension Health & Welfare		Follows IATSE Commercial Production Agreement. Rates vary geographically. See AICP - IATSE Commercial Production Agreements - PH & W rates page.			
		Travel and Idle Days on location: 8 hrs PH & W contribution			
Holidays		2x for work on recognized SAG Agreement holidays			
Scale Rates		Daily	2/27/11	2/1/12	2/1/13
		Location Scout/ Manager:	$679.91	$693.51	$707.38
		Asst. Loc. Manager	$325.05	$331.55	$338.18
Notes		> Definition of Work: Locating sites, Contacting property owners, Negotiating property rentals, Obtaining permission & permits, Maintaining conditions of rental agmt., Liaison with film councils & driving others if does not interfere with their duties.			
		> Industry Roster: For LA work or hired in LA to work anywhere else. All employees must be listed on Roster unless less than 16 are available on 1st day of job or are requested by advertiser or agency due to special abilities or training. L399 to be notified.			
		> Min. Kit rental $50 per day. Mileage at IRS allowable rates. Reimbursment of other expenses.			
		> Excludes public service announcements, spec commercials. Also excludes low budget commercials whose aggregate shooting schedule is two days or more and single day cost does not exceed $75K nor aggregate production costs do not exceed $225K.			
		> On low budget commercials, wage rates subject to individual negotiation. P&W normal.			
Phone numbers		Local 399: 818-985-7374	AICP LA: 323-960-4763, NY: 212-929-3000		

New York
Steve Bizenov
(646) 829-0702
steve@media-services.com

MEDIA SERVICES
ENTERTAINMENT ACCOUNTING, PAYROLL & SOFTWARE

Los Angeles
Tina Bassir
(310) 471-9369
tina@media-services.com

DGA NATIONAL COMMERCIALS AGREEMENT

Working Rules & Conditions

Term of Contract		12/1/11 - 11/30/14
Contracted Day		12 consecutive hours
Contracted Workweek		Any 5 consecutive days, commencing with the first of such 5 days.
Calls	Day/Night	Anytime 1st & 2nd AD Calls must begin at earliest of cast and crew calls
	Partial Day	No
Overtime (Based on Contracted Day)	**9th – 12th hours**	1.5x
	13th & 14th hour	1.75x
	15th hour	2.3333x
	16th hour	8.168x
	17th hour	0x (no pay for 17th hour, Double Day already reached in hour 16)
	18th hour	14x (Triple Day)
	6th day	150% of day rate + overtime as above
	7th day & holidays	200% of day rate + overtime as above
	Increments	Whole hours
	Additional	Work on 5th day which extends into 6th day before completion of 12 hrs is paid at 2x 1st AD cannot be dismissed prior to crew 2nd AD cannot be dismissed until AD duties are completed Over 18 hrs - Producer must offer 1st class hotel or car service to employee's home or hotel
Turnaround	Daily	8 hrs
Penalty	If short	1 day's pay for each 5 hr period until 8 hr rest is achieved
Meals	Intervals	
	Lengths	Reasonable time provided - Meal time is work time
	Penalties	If no dinner provided by 7:30pm and day started 9am or earlier - $30.00
Location Rules		Lodging - 1st Class Air Transportation - Coach for all domestic travel, but 1st or Business Class for international travel over 5 hrs. - AD/UPM normally same class as Director, except where int'l travel is 5+ hours, in which case AD/UPM may travel Business Class even if Director is traveling 1st Class. Layovers - Non-worked days on location are paid at straight time. Members shall not be required to drive transportation vehicles. Producer must provide minimum $100K travel insurance for travel to or from location. Proof must be provided. Idle Day & Travel Home at End of Shoot (if no work performed): May be paid at different rate of pay from work day, but must be at least scale.
Work Time/ Travel Time Provisions		Travel time is work time. Travel to distant loc. on 6th, 7th or holidays is 1x time, if no work performed. Except Report to studios: East - Within 5 Boroughs of NYC ---- West - LA County
Cancellation Fee		One day's pay if Agency cancels or postpones less than 48 hrs prior to call and 1st and 2nd ADs make best effort to replace work. See contract for additional rules. Does not apply to work reduced by accelerated schedule or after prod. has started. No PH&W on Fee. Cancellation or termination of job being worked on by 2 PM or owe for the next day.

Minimum Staffing
 	
See AICP Provisions below
		> Director
		> 1st AD: Whenever a Director is employed, including screen tests
		> 2nd AD: Not less than one shooting day of each commercial
		                       When need to control background or crowds
		                       When 12 or more persons are photographed.
		> Must include Dir. & 1st AD on all location shoot days when shoot is 4 days or more and cast and crew is 10 or more
		> When Director sent out of U.S., 1st AD must be sent, unless destination country refuses work permit or production subsidy would be lost. (See special AICP Provisions below)
		> UPM shall be hired if UPM duties are being performed, but there is no min. staffing.
		> Southern CA and Third Area qualification lists to be established in addition to current NY list.

New York
Steve Bizenov
(646) 829-0702
steve@media-services.com

MEDIA SERVICES
ENTERTAINMENT ACCOUNTING, PAYROLL & SOFTWARE

Los Angeles
Tina Bassir
(310) 471-9369
tina@media-services.com

	> If 2nd AD member works as Location Scout, must be treated as DGA member. Does not apply in LA County, NY or where other unions have jurisdiction.
Payment of Wages	Per state and federal timely payment requirements
Hazardous Work Insurance	$500K death and/or dismemberment. $500 per week total disability coverage
Pay	Pay $150 per incident - Max $300 per day
Jurisdiction	U.S. based companies: Wherever they work.
Pension Health & Welfare	See rates page
Holidays	New Year's Day Martin Luther King Day President's Day Memorial Day Independence Day Labor Day Thanksgiving Day Christmas Day
Notes	> Staffing violations subject to triple damages > 1st AD may not be dismissed prior to his/her crew. > Commercial Project Listing Form must be submitted prior to 1st day of production, incl. foreign productions > Minimum 1st AD Prep: 1 day for 1-2 day shoot, 2 days for 3+ day shoot or two or more significantly different or distant locations. > Special provisions for Spec Spots, Internet and Public Service Announcements. - See Contract. > Excludes low budget commercials with single day production of $75K or less and aggregate cost of $300K or less. Wage rates subject to individual negotiation. PH&W based on scale rates for UPMs and ADs. PH&W based on Presumed Salary for non-Principal Directors. > Signatory Producers may not subcontract to non-signatory producers. > Signatory Producers may be contracted by non-signatory producers, but must notify DGA within 10 days or project will be considered signatory. > DGA will consider requests for signatory employers to provide production services to non-signatory foreign prod. co's producing commercials for non-US/Canada markets. 1st & 2nd ADs must be hired. > Signators are bound to Basic Agmt. and other DGA agreements including production of scripted and reality TV shows, feature films, documentaries, industrials and internet projects. Does not cover music videos.
AICP Special Work Rules	> No 1st AD needed unless crew is more than 6 and cast no more than 1. (Dir. not incl.) > No 1st AD prep day needed if shoot is less than 5 hours. If goes over 5 hrs - 1 AD owed for prep day > No 1st on prep day for 1 day shoot if: Limbo product shots w/no talent or Minor reshoots or > Stop Motion photography or Pick-up shots > No 2nd AD needed for "table top" production, if not required by needs of the production. > UPM shall be hired if UPM duties being handled substantially by one employee, but there is no min. staffing. > No need to travel US 1st AD to foreign countries outside No. America if shoot is 3 or fewer shoot days and is awarded less than 10 bus. days prior to first Shoot day or when job costs are no more than $300K. Local 1st AD to be given preference of employment > On a job shot entirely outside North America where the employer DOES travel a U.S. based 1st AD from the U.S. and the job costs are not >$450K, the terms and conditions of employment are negotiable (P&W to be based on scale) > Projects in Canada and Mexico require sending of US 1st AD unless destination country refuses work permit or production subsidy would be lost. > Special provisions apply AICP to companies located in the Midwest. Contact DGA for info. > DGA members employed as Location Scouts within 75 miles of Chicago paid as DGA 2nd Ads.
AICP Pension Health & Welfare	Presumed Salaries for P&W Calculation: See Rates Page
AICP Director-Deferred Membership	Directors may defer membership not later than 10 shoot days or one year from Director's first shoot day. Applies to director regardless of number of companies worked for. Producers must notify Guild. All other provisions, including PH&W apply.
DGA Office Phone numbers	Los Angeles: 310-289-2000, New York: 212-581-0370, Chicago: 312-644-5050

New York

Steve Bizenov

(646) 829-0702

steve@media-services.com

MEDIA
SERVICES
ENTERTAINMENT ACCOUNTING, PAYROLL & SOFTWARE

Los Angeles

Tina Bassir

(310) 471-9369

tina@media-services.com

SCREEN ACTORS GUILD
COMMERCIALS CONTRACT DEPARTMENT
5757 Wilshire Blvd., Los Angeles, CA 90036
(323) 549-6858 for commercial queries only.
All other questions, call (323) 954-1600.
www.sag.org

The following is a brief interpretation of the Screen Actors Guild 2009 Commercials Contract relating to Principal Performers. This digest is possible due to the generous assistance of the Screen Actors Guild. For more complete information, LA 411 recommends that the reader contact the Screen Actors Guild's Commercials Department.

Auditions
The first 2 auditions are allowed without compensation if one hour or less. Additional time is paid in 30 minute units @ $37.00 per unit. 3rd callbacks are $148.10 for the first 2 hours and $37.00 per half hour thereafter. 4th callbacks are $296.10 for the first 4 hours and $37.00 per half hour thereafter. No payment is due for the first 2 hours of a 3rd or 4th audition if 3 or fewer performers are called back and no performers are on a 1st audition.

Bookings & Cancellations

A Performer is booked when:

1. Given written notice of acceptance.
2. A form contract signed by the producer is delivered to the performer or when a form contract unsigned by the producer is delivered to a performer and is executed by performer and returned to producer within 48 hours.
3. A script is delivered to the performer (does not include delivery for auditions or for the performer to review for possible employment).
4. Fitted (does not include wardrobe tests).
5. Given a verbal call which he/she accepts.
6. Told he/she will be used but no date is set.
7. Told not to accept an engagement for a spot advertising a competitive product or service.

The Producer shall have the right to cancel any call without payment because of impossibility of production due to "Force Majeure." Postponement of a call to a mutually acceptable date may be made by the Producer upon 24 hours notification (except on Saturdays, Sundays and holidays), as long as the new booking date is made within 15 working days of original date and payment of one half day of the session fee is paid. If production does not take place within 15 days, another half session payment is due and the Performer is thereupon released. None of these payments are creditable toward any session fees payable to the Performer if production should take place at a later date.

Employment
1. Session fees must be paid and postmarked within 12 working days.
2. On-camera principals/stunt performers' session fee is $592.20 for an 8-hour day. The voice-over session fee is $445.30 for a 2-hour session.
3. Performer is paid for each commercial shot on the same day. Performer is paid for each day whether or not the commercial is completed. In other words, the Performer is paid a session fee for the number of days or the number of commercials, whichever is greater.
4. If Performer is called in to re-shoot, session fees are due and payable depending on quantity of commercials and number of days.
5. For each tag or dealer identification made beyond one, The voice over rate shall be paid $132.45 . This fee is paid for each tag numbered two through 25. $73.50 is paid for each tag 26 through 50. $40.05 is paid for each tag 51+. If called in for the sole purpose of making tags, a session fee and a specified rate applies for each tag beyond one. (Contact SAG for the specific tier-step rate and whether any other session fee rate is applicable.)
6. Commercials made initially for use on the Internet or in New Media: Producer may bargain freely with Performer and shall pay Performer compensation in such amount as shall be agreed by direct bargaining with the Performer or the Performer's agent. Effective April 1, 2011, Performers shall be compensated at not less than the minimum session rates.

Work Time

1. All on-camera Principals' sessions are based on an eight-hour day. That does not include their meal periods. Off-camera (voice over) Performers' sessions are based on two-hour engagements.
2. Performer's rate for the ninth and tenth hours of work is time-and-one-half, and the 11th hour of work is paid at double the Performer's hourly rate.
3. Overtime for Principals earning more than 2x the session fee per commercial per day shall be paid 1 1/2 x (instead of double time) after 10 hours.
4. Principal Performers making more than double scale for the session (over $1,184.40 per commercial) shall receive 1 1/2 x their session rate for Saturdays and Sundays. Performers making $1,184.40 or less shall receive double their session rate.
5. Rest periods from time of dismissal to first call thereafter must be 12 hours. Exceptions to this are made when the last shot of the day is an exterior shot on a nearby location and the next day's shooting begins with exterior photography. Then the rest period may be reduced to 10 hours. The reduced rest period pertains only to those performers who are in the respective scenes.

(Contact SAG for other exceptions.)

Night Work

Night work is defined as work between 8 p.m. and 6 a.m., except that a first call for the day at 5 a.m. or thereafter shall not constitute night work.

Except as above provided, the Performer shall receive premium pay for each hour of night work equal to 10% of his/her hourly rate for such hours. In the computation of such premium pay, the hourly rate of the Performer for such hours is first determined, and 10% thereof is added as the night work premium.

Travel Time

1. The Los Angeles Studio Zone is defined as that area within a radius of 30 miles of the intersection of Beverly and La Cienega Boulevards.
2. Travel to and from location when no services are rendered requires a full session fee. There are no half day or hourly rates.
3. Travel time shall be paid as work time if Performer is working. Overtime caused by travel to and from location is paid at straight time in quarterly units.
4. All travel past midnight shall be paid at 1 1/2 x Performer's rate, in quarterly units.
5. If traveling to and from LAX and JFK, add one hour. If traveling to and from La Guardia, add 1/2 hour.

Meals & Meal Penalties

1. Meal periods must be within six hours of first call in-studio or on location. Second meal period must be within six hours following completion of first meal period.
2. Meal penalty is $25.00 for first 1/2 hour violation, second 1/2 hour is $25.00, third 1/2 hour and each 1/2 hour thereafter is paid at $50.00.
3. If makeup, wardrobe or hairdress preparation time will disrupt the Performer's normal meal period, the Producer may provide that Performer with a working meal (e.g., coffee, sandwiches) before the Performer's set call if no deduction is made from work time for meal periods.

Mileage & Parking

Mileage based on rate which IRS provides may be paid as a travel expense allowance not reported as income. The Producer shall provide supervised or secured parking.

Travel, Transportation & Accommodations

1. All travel expenses and lodging accommodations shall be furnished by the Producer including first class transportation to and from location for air travel of 1,000 or more air miles. For air travel of less than 1,000 miles, coach service may be provided. Producer shall provide a reasonable single room accommodation.
2. Necessary traveling expenses and meal per diem at breakfast ($10.95), lunch ($16.40), and dinner ($30.25).

Holidays

New Year's Day, Martin Luther King Jr.'s Birthday, Washington's Birthday (Presidents' Day), Memorial Day, July 4, Labor Day, Thanksgiving, Christmas. Holidays that fall on a Sunday will be attributed to the following Monday.

Principals working on a holiday are entitled to double time for all hours worked.

Pension and health contribution is 15.5%.

Visit www.sag.org for more information.